HANDBOOK
of
PSYCHOLOGY

HANDBOOK
of
PSYCHOLOGY

VOLUME 3
BIOLOGICAL PSYCHOLOGY

Michela Gallagher
Randy J. Nelson

Volume Editors

Irving B. Weiner

Editor-in-Chief

John Wiley & Sons, Inc.

Copyright © 2003 by John Wiley & Sons, Inc., Hoboken, New Jersey. All rights reserved.

Published simultaneously in Canada.

No part of this publication may be reproduced, stored in a retrieval system, or transmitted in any form or by any means, electronic, mechanical, photocopying, recording, scanning, or otherwise, except as permitted under Section 107 or 108 of the 1976 United States Copyright Act, without either the prior written permission of the Publisher, or authorization through payment of the appropriate per-copy fee to the Copyright Clearance Center, Inc., 222 Rosewood Drive, Danvers, MA 01923, (978) 750-8400, fax (978) 750-4470, or on the web at www.copyright.com. Requests to the Publisher for permission should be addressed to the Permissions Department, John Wiley & Sons, Inc., 111 River Street, Hoboken, NJ 07030, (201) 748-6011, fax (201) 748-6008, e-mail: permcoordinator@wiley.com.

Limit of Liability/Disclaimer of Warranty: While the publisher and author have used their best efforts in preparing this book, they make no representations or warranties with respect to the accuracy or completeness of the contents of this book and specifically disclaim any implied warranties of merchantability or fitness for a particular purpose. No warranty may be created or extended by sales representatives or written sales materials. The advice and strategies contained herein may not be suitable for your situation. You should consult with a professional where appropriate. Neither the publisher nor author shall be liable for any loss of profit or any other commercial damages, including but not limited to special, incidental, consequential, or other damages.

This publication is designed to provide accurate and authoritative information in regard to the subject matter covered. It is sold with the understanding that the publisher is not engaged in rendering professional services. If legal, accounting, medical, psychological or any other expert assistance is required, the services of a competent professional person should be sought.

Designations used by companies to distinguish their products are often claimed as trademarks. In all instances where John Wiley & Sons, Inc. is aware of a claim, the product names appear in initial capital or all capital letters. Readers, however, should contact the appropriate companies for more complete information regarding trademarks and registration.

For general information on our other products and services please contact our Customer Care Department within the U.S. at (800) 762-2974, outside the United States at (317) 572-3993 or fax (317) 572-4002.

Wiley also publishes its books in a variety of electronic formats. Some content that appears in print may not be available in electronic books.

Library of Congress Cataloging-in-Publication Data:

Handbook of psychology / Irving B. Weiner, editor-in-chief.
     p.   cm.
    Includes bibliographical references and indexes.
    Contents: v. 1. History of psychology / edited by Donald K. Freedheim — v. 2. Research
methods in psychology / edited by John A. Schinka, Wayne F. Velicer — v. 3. Biological
psychology / edited by Michela Gallagher, Randy J. Nelson — v. 4. Experimental
psychology / edited by Alice F. Healy, Robert W. Proctor — v. 5. Personality and social
psychology / edited by Theodore Millon, Melvin J. Lerner — v. 6. Developmental
psychology / edited by Richard M. Lerner, M. Ann Easterbrooks, Jayanthi Mistry — v. 7.
Educational psychology / edited by William M. Reynolds, Gloria E. Miller — v. 8.
Clinical psychology / edited by George Stricker, Thomas A. Widiger — v. 9. Health psychology /
edited by Arthur M. Nezu, Christine Maguth Nezu, Pamela A. Geller — v. 10. Assessment
psychology / edited by John R. Graham, Jack A. Naglieri — v. 11. Forensic psychology /
edited by Alan M. Goldstein — v. 12. Industrial and organizational psychology / edited
by Walter C. Borman, Daniel R. Ilgen, Richard J. Klimoski.
    ISBN 0-471-17669-9 (set) — ISBN 0-471-38320-1 (cloth : alk. paper : v. 1)
— ISBN 0-471-38513-1 (cloth : alk. paper : v. 2) — ISBN 0-471-38403-8 (cloth : alk. paper : v. 3)
— ISBN 0-471-39262-6 (cloth : alk. paper : v. 4) — ISBN 0-471-38404-6 (cloth : alk. paper : v. 5)
— ISBN 0-471-38405-4 (cloth : alk. paper : v. 6) — ISBN 0-471-38406-2 (cloth : alk. paper : v. 7)
— ISBN 0-471-39263-4 (cloth : alk. paper : v. 8) — ISBN 0-471-38514-X (cloth : alk. paper : v. 9)
— ISBN 0-471-38407-0 (cloth : alk. paper : v. 10) — ISBN 0-471-38321-X (cloth : alk. paper : v. 11)
— ISBN 0-471-38408-9 (cloth : alk. paper : v. 12)
    1. Psychology. I. Weiner, Irving B.

BF121.H1955 2003
150—dc21

              2002066380

Handbook of Psychology **Preface**

Psychology at the beginning of the twenty-first century has become a highly diverse field of scientific study and applied technology. Psychologists commonly regard their discipline as the science of behavior, and the American Psychological Association has formally designated 2000 to 2010 as the "Decade of Behavior." The pursuits of behavioral scientists range from the natural sciences to the social sciences and embrace a wide variety of objects of investigation. Some psychologists have more in common with biologists than with most other psychologists, and some have more in common with sociologists than with most of their psychological colleagues. Some psychologists are interested primarily in the behavior of animals, some in the behavior of people, and others in the behavior of organizations. These and other dimensions of difference among psychological scientists are matched by equal if not greater heterogeneity among psychological practitioners, who currently apply a vast array of methods in many different settings to achieve highly varied purposes.

Psychology has been rich in comprehensive encyclopedias and in handbooks devoted to specific topics in the field. However, there has not previously been any single handbook designed to cover the broad scope of psychological science and practice. The present 12-volume *Handbook of Psychology* was conceived to occupy this place in the literature. Leading national and international scholars and practitioners have collaborated to produce 297 authoritative and detailed chapters covering all fundamental facets of the discipline, and the *Handbook* has been organized to capture the breadth and diversity of psychology and to encompass interests and concerns shared by psychologists in all branches of the field.

Two unifying threads run through the science of behavior. The first is a common history rooted in conceptual and empirical approaches to understanding the nature of behavior. The specific histories of all specialty areas in psychology trace their origins to the formulations of the classical philosophers and the methodology of the early experimentalists, and appreciation for the historical evolution of psychology in all of its variations transcends individual identities as being one kind of psychologist or another. Accordingly, Volume 1 in the *Handbook* is devoted to the history of psychology as it emerged in many areas of scientific study and applied technology.

A second unifying thread in psychology is a commitment to the development and utilization of research methods suitable for collecting and analyzing behavioral data. With attention both to specific procedures and their application in particular settings, Volume 2 addresses research methods in psychology.

Volumes 3 through 7 of the *Handbook* present the substantive content of psychological knowledge in five broad areas of study: biological psychology (Volume 3), experimental psychology (Volume 4), personality and social psychology (Volume 5), developmental psychology (Volume 6), and educational psychology (Volume 7). Volumes 8 through 12 address the application of psychological knowledge in five broad areas of professional practice: clinical psychology (Volume 8), health psychology (Volume 9), assessment psychology (Volume 10), forensic psychology (Volume 11), and industrial and organizational psychology (Volume 12). Each of these volumes reviews what is currently known in these areas of study and application and identifies pertinent sources of information in the literature. Each discusses unresolved issues and unanswered questions and proposes future directions in conceptualization, research, and practice. Each of the volumes also reflects the investment of scientific psychologists in practical applications of their findings and the attention of applied psychologists to the scientific basis of their methods.

The *Handbook of Psychology* was prepared for the purpose of educating and informing readers about the present state of psychological knowledge and about anticipated advances in behavioral science research and practice. With this purpose in mind, the individual *Handbook* volumes address the needs and interests of three groups. First, for graduate students in behavioral science, the volumes provide advanced instruction in the basic concepts and methods that define the fields they cover, together with a review of current knowledge, core literature, and likely future developments. Second, in addition to serving as graduate textbooks, the volumes offer professional psychologists an opportunity to read and contemplate the views of distinguished colleagues concerning the central thrusts of research and leading edges of practice in their respective fields. Third, for psychologists seeking to become conversant with fields outside their own specialty and for persons outside of psychology seeking information about psychological matters, the *Handbook* volumes serve as a reference source for expanding their knowledge and directing them to additional sources in the literature.

The preparation of this *Handbook* was made possible by the diligence and scholarly sophistication of the 25 volume editors and co-editors who constituted the Editorial Board. As Editor-in-Chief, I want to thank each of them for the pleasure of their collaboration in this project. I compliment them for having recruited an outstanding cast of contributors to their volumes and then working closely with these authors to achieve chapters that will stand each in their own right as

valuable contributions to the literature. I would like finally to express my appreciation to the editorial staff of John Wiley and Sons for the opportunity to share in the development of this project and its pursuit to fruition, most particularly to Jennifer Simon, Senior Editor, and her two assistants, Mary Porterfield and Isabel Pratt. Without Jennifer's vision of the *Handbook* and her keen judgment and unflagging support in producing it, the occasion to write this preface would not have arrived.

IRVING B. WEINER
Tampa, Florida

Volume Preface

The topic of this volume represents a perspective that can be traced to the founding of psychology as a scientific discipline. Since the late 19th century, biological psychologists have used the methods of the natural sciences to study relationships between biological and psychological processes. Today, a natural science perspective and the investigation of biological processes have increasingly penetrated all areas of psychology. For instance, social and personality psychologists have become conversant with evolutionary concepts in their studies of traits, prejudice, and even physical attraction. Many cognitive psychologists have forsaken black boxes in favor of functional magnetic resonance imaging brain scans, and clinical psychologists, as participants in the mental health care of their clients, have become more familiar with the basis for the action of pharmacological therapeutics on the brain. The scientific revolution in molecular biology and genetics will continue to fuel the biological psychology perspective. Indeed, it can be anticipated that some of the most significant scientific discoveries of the 21st century will come from understanding the biological basis of psychological functions.

The contributors to this volume provide the reader with an accessible view of the contemporary field of biological psychology. The chapters span content areas from basic sensory systems to memory and language and include a perspective on different levels of scientific analysis from molecules to computational models of biological systems. We have assembled this material with a view toward engaging the field and our readership in an appreciation of the accomplishments and special role of biological psychology in the discipline. Notwithstanding the trend for a greater influence of biological studies in the field of psychology in general, biological psychology represents a distinctive fusion of biology and psychology in its theory and methods. For example, evolution as a fundamental tenet in the field of biology has long permeated the work of biological psychologists. The rapid growth in publications in the area of evolutionary psychology over the past two decades suggests a growing acceptance of the importance of evolutionary ideas in the behavioral sciences.

In addition to this influence, the contribution of biology, rooted in evolutionary and ethological traditions, has sustained a broad base of comparative studies by biological psychologists, as reflected in the contents of this volume. Research in the field of psychology using different species serves a dual purpose. Many studies using nonhuman species are motivated by the utility of information that can be gained that is relevant to humans, using a range of preparations and techniques in research that are not otherwise possible. Of equal importance, comparative research provides insights into variation in biological organisms. Studies of a variety of species can show how different solutions have been achieved for both processing input from the environment and elaborating adaptive behavioral strategies. The organization and content of this volume focus squarely on the need to recognize these dual objectives in studies of biological and psychological processes.

The question of how translation is made across species is ever more central to the undertaking of biological psychology. In the not-distant past, most psychologists viewed research using nonhuman animals as irrelevant to a broad range of psychological functions in humans, including affective and cognitive processes that were considered exclusive capacities of the human mind and social lives of humans in relationships. Today, animal models are increasingly recognized as possessing at least some elements of cognitive and affective processes that are potentially informative for understanding normal functions and disorders in humans. This progress has contributed to a number of research areas described in the ensuing chapters, many of which include insights that have come from using new gene targeting technology. Because human studies do not provide the opportunity for rigorous experimental control and manipulation of genetic, molecular, cellular, and brain and behavioral system processes, the use of genetically manipulated mice has become a powerful tool in research. At the same time, the limitations and pitfalls of wholesale acceptance of such animal models are clear to biological psychologists. In addition to the fact that mouse species have faced different evolutionary pressures and adapted to different ecological niches, the use of genetically altered systems presents new challenges because these novel mice are likely to express new constraints and influences beyond their target characters. The tradition of comparative studies of different animal species makes the role of biological psychology central to the effort to use these new and powerful approaches to advance scientific understanding.

A related overriding theme in biological psychology is the significance of translating across levels of analysis. Biological descriptions of psychological processes are viewed by many, particularly outside the field, as a reductionist endeavor. As such, reductionism might represent merely a descent to a level of description in which psychological functions are translated into the physical and chemical lexicon of molecular events. It is increasingly evident that research directed across levels of analysis serves yet another purpose. In addition to determining biological substrates, such investigations can work in the other direction, to test between competing hypotheses and models of psychological functions. It is also the case that molecular biologists who study the brain are increasingly seeking contact with investigators who work at the level of systems. More genes are expressed in the brain than in all other organs of the body combined. Gene expression is controlled by intricate information-processing networks within a neuron and is inextricably tied to the activity of neurons as elements in larger information-processing systems. Psychological functions (e.g., the conditions that are sufficient to produce long-term memory or the environmental inputs that are necessary to elicit maternal behavior) will aid in understanding the functional significance of complex molecular systems at the cellular level. Scientific advances are rapidly shifting the biological psychology paradigm from one of reductionism to an appreciation that vertical integration across levels of analysis is essential to understand the properties of biological organisms.

In chapter 1 Russil Durrant and Bruce J. Ellis introduce some of the core ideas and assumptions that comprise the field of evolutionary psychology. Although they focus on reproductive behaviors, Durrant and Ellis also illustrate how the ideas of evolutionary psychology can be employed in the development of specific, testable hypotheses, about human mind and behavior. Their ideas go far past the usual mating behaviors, and they even provide an adaptive scenario for self-esteem studies. Durrant and Ellis note that one of the most crucial tasks for evolutionary psychologists in the coming decades will be the identification and elucidation of psychological adaptations. Although most of the obvious and plausible psychological adaptations have already been cataloged, many more remain undiscovered or inadequately characterized. Because adaptations are the product of natural selection operating in ancestral environments, and because psychological traits such as jealousy, language, and self-esteem are not easily reconstructed from material evidence such as fossils and artifacts, direct evidence for behavioral adaptations may be difficult to obtain. One of the challenges for evolutionary psychology, according to Durrant and Ellis, is to develop increasingly more rigorous and systematic

methods for inferring the evolutionary history of psychological characteristics, as well as to determine how best to characterize psychological adaptations.

As mentioned, within the past 10 years a novel intellectual bridge has been formed between psychology and molecular biology. Molecular biologists have mapped large segments of the mouse genome as part of the ambitious Human Genome Project. As genes have been identified and sequenced, molecular biologists have begun the difficult task of identifying the functions of these genes. An increasingly common genetic engineering technique used to discover the function of genes is targeted disruption (*knockout*) of a single gene. By selectively disrupting the expression of a single gene, molecular biologists reason that the function of that targeted gene can be determined. In other cases, a specific gene is added (*knockin*). In many cases, the phenotypic description of knockout and knockin mice includes alterations in behavior. In chapter 2 Stephen C. Maxson explores behavior genetics, generally, and describes the implications of molecular genetics for psychology, specifically. He describes classic studies on the heritability of behavior (viz., selective breeding) as well as twin and adoption studies. Maxson adroitly documents gene mapping and genome projects in relation to behavioral studies. After presenting an introduction to molecular and developmental genetics, he emphasizes the importance of population genetics in studies of the evolution of behavior. Finally, Maxson explores the ethical and legal manifestations of behavioral genetics in the context of academics and society as a whole.

Using the comparative method has been particularly successful for understanding the sensory and perceptual machinery in animals. In chapter 3 Gerald H. Jacobs describes the great success that he and others have had using the comparative approach to elucidate the mechanisms and processes underlying vision. Most studies of nonhuman vision are likely motivated to understand human vision. The remaining studies of vision in nonhuman animals are aimed at understanding comparative features of vision in their own right, often from an evolutionary perspective with the intent to discover common and different solutions for seeing. Jacobs considers both approaches in his review of comparative vision. After a description of the fundamental features of photic environments, he provides basic design features and describes the evolution of eyes. Jacobs then focuses on photosensitivity as a model of the comparative approach. He details photopigments, ocular filtering, and the role of the nervous system in photosensitivity. Three important issues in comparative vision—detection of change, resolution of spatial structure, and use of chromatic cues—are also addressed. Finally, Jacobs includes a section on the difficulty of measuring animal vision, as well as his perspective of where this field is likely to evolve.

In chapter 4 Cynthia F. Moss and Catherine E. Carr review some of the benefits and problems associated with a comparative approach to studies of hearing. Comparative audition also has a primary goal of understanding human audition, but a larger proportion of this field is dedicated to understanding the relationship between the sensory system of the animal and its biologically relevant stimuli as compared to comparative vision. The ability to detect and process acoustic signals evolved many times throughout the animal kingdom, from insects and fish to birds and mammals (homoplasies). Even within some animal groups, there is evidence that hearing evolved independently several times. Ears appear not only on opposite sides of the head, but also on a variety of body parts. Out of this diversity, many fascinating, specific auditory adaptations have been discovered. A surprising number of general principles of organization and function have emerged from studies of diverse solutions to a common problem. Comparative studies of audition attempt to bring order to the variation and to deepen our understanding of sound processing and perception.

Moss and Carr review many common measures of auditory function, anatomy, and physiology in selective species in order to emphasize general principles and noteworthy specializations. They cover much phylogenetic ground, reviewing insects, fishes, frogs, reptiles, birds, and mammals. The chapter begins with a brief introduction to acoustic stimuli, followed by a review of ears and auditory systems in a large sample of species, and concludes with a comparative presentation of auditory function in behavioral tasks.

Behavioral studies of auditory systems reveal several common patterns across species. For example, hearing occurs over a restricted frequency range, often spanning several octaves. Absolute hearing sensitivity is best over a limited frequency band, typically of high biological importance to the animal, and this low-threshold region is commonly flanked by regions of reduced sensitivity at adjacent frequencies. Absolute frequency discrimination and frequency selectivity generally decrease with an increase in sound frequency. Some animals, however, display specializations in hearing sensitivity and frequency selectivity for biologically relevant sounds, with two regions of high sensitivity or frequency selectivity corresponding with information, for example, about mates *and* predators. One important goal of comparative audition is to trace adaptations in the auditory periphery and merge those adaptations with central adaptations and behavior.

The history and state of the art of, as well as future studies in, comparative motor systems are presented by Karim Fouad, Hanno Fischer, and Ansgar Büschges in chapter 5. The authors carefully construct an argument for a concept of central control of locomotion and the principles of pattern-generating networks for locomotion. In common with sensory systems to understand locomotor activity, the authors argue that a multilevel approach is needed and present data ranging from the molecular and cellular level (i.e., identification of the neurons involved, their intrinsic properties, the properties of their synaptic connections, and the role of specific transmitters and neuromodulators) to the system level (i.e., functional integration of these networks in complete motor programs). They emphasize that both invertebrate and vertebrate locomotor systems have been studied on multiple levels, ranging from the interactions between identifiable neurons in identified circuits to the analysis of gait. The review focuses on (a) the principles of cellular and synaptic construction of central pattern-generating networks for locomotion, (b) their location and coordination, (c) the role of sensory signals in generating a functional network output, (d) the main mechanisms underlying their ability to adapt through modifications, and (e) basic features in modulating the network function.

Each human sensory system provides an internal neural representation of the world, transforming energy in the environment into the cellular coding machinery of vast networks of neurons. In studies of sensory information processing in nonhuman primates, particularly in the Old World monkeys, we encounter research that brings us close to understanding functions of the human brain. Chapters 6 through 8 provide a current guide to sensory modalities in the primate brain that occupy extensive cortical systems.

Research on the visual system in primates has outpaced all other modalities. In chapter 6 Tatiana Pasternak, James W. Bisley, and David Calkins provide the reader with an extensive background of knowledge on the neuroanatomical organization of visual pathways and functional properties of visually responsive neurons. Their chapter follows the stream of the visual system from eye through multiple parallel processing and hierarchically organized systems in cortex. It also covers one of the most significant topics in vision research in recent years, *viz.,* the extent to which the properties of visually responsive neurons are psychologically tuned at virtually all levels of cortical processing. Rather than passive processing of input from the retina, neurons in the visual system are strongly influenced by the behavioral significance of the stimulus, manifesting effects of current attention and past experience.

It can be anticipated that the current pace of research will rapidly expand our understanding of other sensory modalities with extensive cortical processing systems in the primate brain. In chapter 7 Troy A. Hackett and Jon H. Kaas present an up-to-date account of the anatomy and physiology of information processing in the auditory system. Relative to the visual and somatosensory systems, the organization of subcortical auditory pathways in the primate brain is exceedingly complex. At the same time, many findings on the subcortical processing of auditory information in primates complement findings in other mammalian species. By comparison with other species, the auditory representation in cortex is greatly expanded in the primate brain. Research using nonhuman primates supports a model of parallel and hierarchical organization in the auditory cortex that may broadly share features with the visual system. The orderly topography and pattern of cortico-cortical connections define two streams of auditory processing. The responsiveness of neurons in auditory belt and parabelt regions further indicates a specialization for information about *what* and *where,* a distinction made in parallel streams in the visual system. The chapter provides an interesting discussion of research using complex stimuli, such as species-typical calls, to characterize the auditory objects or events for which the *what* pathway may be specialized in nonhuman primates.

In dynamic and complex environments, all mammals rely on visual and auditory systems to obtain information. In the basic tasks of survival—whether evasion of predators, navigation of territory, or location of food and water—these modalities make it possible to identify and localize objects at a distance. Tactile perception becomes a key modality in primates' ability to identify and manipulate objects within arm's reach. In chapter 8 Steven Hsiao, Ken Johnson, and Takashi Yoshioka focus on tactile perception, a system that begins with the transduction of information by four types of cutaneous mechanoreceptors. The authors review evidence that information from each of these receptor types serves a distinctive role in tactile perception. Among these, the rapidly adapting class has exquisite sensitivity to minute movement of the skin, as little as 4 μm to 5 μm. By contrast, the slowly adapting Type 1 class operates over a greater dynamic range of stimulation but has extraordinary spatial resolution. These and other mechanoreceptors share virtually identical properties in humans and in nonhuman primates. As the pathways for tactile perception are followed into cortical networks, a theme from previous chapters recurs. Tactile responsive neurons, similar to neurons in the visual and auditory cortical systems, are strongly influenced by psychological variables of attention and experience.

We all learned and accepted that there are five primary senses—that is, until we stubbed our toes and recalled our "sixth sense." A critical sensory system that alerts us to real or potential tissue damage is pain. In chapter 9 Terence

Coderre, Catherine Bushnell, and Jeffrey Mogil explore the mechanisms of pain. They note that pain has recently come to be thought of as two separate sensory entities: (a) physiological pain and (b) pathological pain. Physiological pain reflects a typical reaction of the somatosensory system to noxious stimulation. Physiological pain is adaptive. Rare individuals who cannot process physiological pain information frequently injure themselves and are unaware of internal damage that is normally signaled by pain. Predictably, such individuals often become disfigured and have a significantly shortened life span. Pathological pain reflects the development of abnormal sensitivity in the somatosensory system, usually precipitated by inflammatory injury or nerve damage. The most common features of pathological pain are pain in the absence of a noxious stimulus, increased duration of response to brief-stimulation stimuli, or perception of pain in response to normally nonpainful stimulation. The neurological abnormalities that account for pathological pain remain unspecified and may reside in any of the numerous sites along the neuronal pathways that both relay and modulate somatosensory inputs.

Chapter 9 provides a comprehensive review of the current knowledge concerning the anatomical, physiological, and neurochemical substrates that underlie both physiological and pathological pain. Thus, Coderre and colleagues have described in detail the pathways that underlie the transmission of inputs from the periphery to the central nervous system (CNS), the physiological properties of the neurons activated by painful stimuli, and the neurochemicals that mediate or modulate synaptic transmission in somatosensory pathways. The review is organized by neuroanatomy into separate sections: (a) the peripheral nervous system and (b) the CNS, which is further divided into (a) the spinal cord dorsal horn and (b) the brain. The authors made a special effort to identify critical advances in the field of pain research, especially the processes by which pathological pain develops following tissue or nerve injury, as well as how pain is modulated by various brain mechanisms. The multidimensional nature of pain processing in the brain emphasizes the multidimensional nature of pain, using anatomical connectivity, physiological function, and brain imaging techniques. Finally, the authors provide some insights into future pain sensitivity and expression research, with a focus on molecular biology and behavioral genetics.

The ability to detect chemicals in the environment likely represents the most primitive sensory faculty and remains critical for survival and reproductive success in modern prokaryotes, protists, and animals. Chemicals in solution are detected by the taste sensory system; chemical sensation has a central role in the detection of what is edible and where it is found. It is well known, for example, that the flavor of food (i.e., the combination of its taste and smell) is a major determinant of ingestion. Humans are able to detect volatile chemicals in air with our olfactory sensory system. Individuals may use chemical senses to protect themselves from ingesting or inhaling toxins that can cause harm. The chemical senses, olfaction and taste, are reviewed in chapter 10 by Patricia M. Di Lorenzo and Steven L. Youngentob.

Until recently, the study of taste and olfaction has progressed at a relatively slow pace when compared to the study of the other sensory modalities such as vision or audition. This reflects, in part, the difficulty in defining the physical dimensions of chemosensory stimuli. We can use human devices to deliver exactly 0.5-m candles of 484 μm of light energy to the eye and then conduct appropriate psychophysics studies consistently across laboratories and across participants. Until recently, however, it has been impossible to present, for example, 3 units of rose smells to an experimental participant. In the absence of confidence that any given array of stimuli would span the limits of chemical sensibility, investigators have been slow to agree on schemes with which taste and olfactory stimuli are encoded by the nervous system. As Di Lorenzo and Youngentob reveal, technological advances, particularly in the realm of molecular neuroscience, are providing the tools for unraveling some of the longstanding mysteries of the chemical senses. Some of the surprising findings that have resulted from this increasingly molecular approach to chemosensation are the discovery of a fifth basic taste quality (i.e., umami) and the discovery that the differential activation of different subsets of sensory neurons, to various degrees, forms the basis for neural coding and further processing by higher centers in the olfactory pathway. For both olfaction and taste, the careful combination of molecular approaches with precise psychophysics promise to yield insights into the processing of chemical signals. Next, we move from input to output.

To fuel the brain and locomotor activities, we need energy. Because most bacteria and all animals are heterotrophs, they must eat to obtain energy. What and how much we eat depends on many factors, including factors related to palatability or taste, learning, social and cultural influences, environmental factors, and physiological controls. The relative contribution of these many factors to the regulation of feeding varies across species and testing situations. In chapter 11 Timothy H. Moran and Randall R. Sakai detail the psychobiology of food and fluid intake. They focus on three interacting systems important in the regulation of feeding: (a) signals related to metabolic state, especially to the degree adiposity; (b) affective signals related to taste and nutritional consequences that serve to reinforce aspects of ingestive behavior;

and (c) signals that arise within an individual meal that produce satiety. Moran and Sakai also identify the important interactions among these systems that permit the overall regulation of energy balance.

Individuals are motivated to maintain an optimal level of water, sodium, and other nutrients in the body. Claude Bernard, the 19th-century French physiologist, was the first to describe animals' ability to maintain a relatively constant internal environment, or *milieu intérieur*. Animals are watery creatures. By weight, mammals are approximately two-thirds water. The cells of animals require water for virtually all metabolic processes. Additionally, water serves as a solvent for sodium, chloride, and potassium ions, as well as sugars, amino acids, proteins, vitamins, and many other solutes, and is therefore essential for the smooth functioning of the nervous system and for other physiological processes. Because water participates in so many processes, and because it is continuously lost during perspiration, respiration, urination, and defecation, it must be replaced periodically. Unlike minerals or energy, very little extra water is stored in the body. When water use exceeds water intake, the body conserves water, mainly by reducing the amount of water excreted from the kidneys. Eventually, physiological conservation can no longer compensate for water use and incidental water loss, and the individual searches for water and drinks.

Regulation of sodium intake and regulation of water intake are closely linked to one another. According to Moran and Sakai, the body relies primarily on osmotic and volumetric signals to inform the brain of body fluid status and to engage specific neurohormonal systems (e.g., the renin-angiotensin system) to restore fluid balance. As with food intake, signals that stimulate drinking, as well as those that terminate drinking, interact to ensure that the organism consumes adequate amounts of both water and electrolytes. The signals for satiety, and how satiety changes the taste and motivation for seeking food and water, remain to be specified.

We continue with a review of motivated behavior in chapter 12. Elaine M. Hull and Juan M. Dominguez review the recent progress made in understanding sexual differentiation, as well as the hormonal and neural mechanisms that drive and direct male and female sexual behavior. They begin their chapter by considering the adaptive function of sexual behavior by asking why sexual reproduction is by far the most common means of propagating multicellular species, even though asexual reproduction is theoretically much faster and easier. The prevailing hypothesis is that sexual behavior evolved to help elude pathogens that might become so precisely adaptive to a set of genetically identical clones that future generations of the host species would never rid themselves of the pathogens. By mixing up the genomic character of their offspring, sexually reproducing creatures could prevent the pathogens—even with their faster generational time and hence faster evolution—from too much specialization. Pathogens that preyed on one specific genome would be extinct after the single generation of gene swapping that occurs with each sexual union. Thus, sexual reproduction has selected pathogens to be generalists among individuals, although sufficiently specific to be limited to a few host species.

Hull and Dominguez next provide a description of the copulatory patterns that are common across mammalian species and summarize various laboratory tests of sexual behavior. After a thorough description of sexual behavior, the mechanisms underlying sexual behavior are presented. Because hormones are important for sex differentiation in all mammalian and avian species and because hormones also activate sexual behavior in adulthood, the chapter focuses on the endocrine mechanisms underlying sexual behavior and explores the mechanisms by which hormones modulate brain and behavior. The authors next describe the hormonal and neural control of female sexual behavior, followed by a similar treatment of the regulation of male sexual behavior. In each case, they first summarize the effects of pharmacological and endocrine treatments on sexual behavior. The pharmacological data indicate which neurotransmitter systems are involved in the various components of sexual behavior (e.g., sexual motivation vs. performance). A variety of techniques has been used to determine where in the brain sexual behavior is mediated, including lesions and stimulation, local application of drugs and hormones, and measures of neural activity. Finally, Hull and Dominguez observe that the hormonal and neural mechanisms that control sexual behavior are similar to the mechanisms that regulate other social behaviors.

The authors close with a series of questions and issues that remain largely unanswered. For example, they suggest that more neuroanatomical work is necessary to track the neural circuits underlying sexual behavior in both females and males. Neurotransmitter signatures of those neurons are important pieces of the puzzle, as well as neurotransmitter receptor interactions and intracellular signal transduction activation in response to various neurotransmitter and hormonal effects. What changes in gene transcription are induced by specific hormones? How do rapid membrane effects of steroids influence sexual behavior? What changes in gene transcription mediate the effects of previous sexual experience? They close with broader questions that include the interrelationships among sexual and other social behaviors, and how species-specific differences in behavior are related to their ecological niches. All of these issues are critical for a full understanding of sexual behavior.

Life on Earth evolves in the presence of pronounced temporal fluctuations. The planet rotates daily on its axis. Light availability and temperature vary predictably throughout each day and across the seasons. The tides rise and subside in predictable ways. These fluctuations in environmental factors exert dramatic effects on living creatures. For example, daily biological adjustments occur in both plants and animals, which perform some processes only at night and others only during the day. Similarly, daily peaks in the metabolic activity of warm-blooded animals tend to coincide with the daily onset of their physical activity. Increased activity alone does not drive metabolic rates; rather, the general pattern of metabolic needs is anticipated by reference to an internal biological clock. The ability to anticipate the onset of the daily light and dark periods confers sufficient advantages that endogenous, self-sustained circadian clocks are virtually ubiquitous among extant organisms In chapter 13 Federica Latta and Eve Van Cauter discuss the importance of biological clocks and sleep on cognition and behavior.

In addition to synchronizing biochemical, physiological, and behavioral activities to the external environment, biological clocks are important to multicellular organisms for synchronizing the internal environment. For instance, if a specific biochemical process is most efficiently conducted in the dark, then individuals that mobilize metabolic precursors, enzymes, and energy sources just prior to the onset of dark would presumably have a selective advantage over individuals that organized their internal processes at random times. Thus, there is a daily temporal pattern, or phase relationship, to which all biochemical, physiological, and behavioral processes are linked.

Latta and Van Cauter provide an overview of the circadian system, as well as its development. Then, they discuss the regulation of sleep in the context of biological rhythms and show how sleep-wake homeostasis interacts with alertness and cognitive function, mood, cardiovascular, metabolic, and endocrine regulation. Their chapter closes with a description of sleep disorders in the context of circadian dysregulation.

Preceding chapters in the volume considered specific motivated behaviors, such as feeding and mating. In chapter 14 Krista McFarland and Peter W. Kalivas deal with neural circuitry in the brain that is relevant to many different goal-directed behaviors. Whether the goal is food or a sexual partner, common circuitry is now believed to be required for activating and guiding behavior to obtain desired outcomes. This brain system, referred to here as the *motive circuit,* involves a network of structures and their interconnections in the forebrain that control motor output systems. The authors present a scheme, based on much evidence, that the motive circuit is comprised of two separate but interactive subsystems. One of these provides control over goal-directed behavior under routine circumstances, where prior experience has established efficient direct control over response systems. The other subcortical-limbic circuit serves a complementary function to allow new learning about motivationally relevant stimuli.

The motive circuit described by McFarland and Kalivas includes not only anatomically defined pathways but also definition of the neurochemical identity of neurons in the system. This information has proven vital because the motive circuit is an important target for drugs of interest for their psychological effects. Indeed, the field of psychopharmacology has converged to a remarkable degree on the brain regions described in this chapter. Substances of abuse, across many different classes of agents such as cocaine and heroin, depend on this neural system for their addictive properties. Consequently, the role of subsystems within the motive circuit in drug addiction is a topic of great current interest. Within the scheme described in the chapter, drug-seeking behavior, including the strong tendency to relapse into addiction, may reflect an inherent property of circuit function that controls routine responses or habits. Behavioral and neural plasticity underlying addiction is becoming an increasingly important topic of study in this area of biological psychology for providing an inroad to effective treatment for drug abuse.

Emotion encompasses a wide range of experience and can be studied through many variables, ranging from verbal descriptions to the measurement of covert physiological responses, such as heart rate. In chapter 15 Michael Davis and Peter J. Lang consider this topic, broadly spanning research in humans and other species. From this comparative perspective, there is no doubt that emotions are fundamentally adaptive, capturing attention and strongly engaging a disposition to action. Succinctly put, emotions move us.

Davis and Lang elaborate on a useful framework for organizing the diverse phenomena of emotion, in which emotions are considered along two dimensions. On one dimension of valence, emotional states range from positive (happy, confident) to negative (fear, anger). These different emotional states, in turn, are associated with different behavioral tendencies, strongly engaging output systems based on the integration of current information and past experience. In addition, both positive and negative emotional states can range from relative calm to high degrees of arousal, providing a second dimension. Finally, the topic of emotion not only encompasses the regulation of internal emotional states that motivate behavior expressive of those states, but also may be important for the cognitive evaluation of the emotional content of complex perceptual cues. Davis and Lang are adept guides in covering a range of psychological studies, as

well as research on neural systems involved in emotional processes.

The authors give detailed treatment to one model of emotion that has become well studied across species. Perhaps it is not surprising that the emotion of fear, which is basic to survival, possesses many common features across mammalian species. Research over the past decade or so has also revealed that neural systems engaged in settings that evoke fear show strong homology in humans and other mammals, including laboratory rodents. The study of fear has in turn become one of best defined models in which to study the neural basis of learning. Circumstances associated with aversive events provide cues that become potent activators of fear, preparing organisms to deal with threat and danger. Because the circuitry in the brain for this form of learning is delineated, scientists are making progress in understanding the exact sites and mechanisms where communication between neurons is altered to produce this form of emotional learning. In this chapter the reader encounters a field where vertical integration from behavior to synaptic plasticity is advancing at a rapid pace.

Life is challenging. The pressure of survival and reproduction takes its toll on every individual living on the planet; eventually and inevitably the wear and tear of life leads to death. Mechanisms have evolved to delay death presumably because, all other things being equal, conspecific animals that live the longest tend to leave the most successful offspring. In the Darwinian game of life, individuals who leave the most successful offspring win. Although some of the variation in longevity reflects merely good fortune, a significant part of the variation in longevity among individuals of the same species reflects differences in the ability to cope with the demands of living. All living creatures are dynamic vessels of equilibria, or homeostasis. Any perturbation to homeostasis requires energy to restore the original steady-state. An individual's total energy availability is partitioned among many competing needs, such as growth, cellular maintenance, thermogenesis, reproduction, and immune function. During environmental energy shortages, nonessential processes such as growth and reproduction are suppressed. If homoeostatic perturbations require more energy than is readily available after nonessential systems have been inhibited, then survival may be compromised. All living organisms currently exist because of evolved adaptations that allow individuals to cope with energetically demanding conditions. Surprisingly, the same neuroendocrine coping mechanisms are engaged in all of these cases, as well as in many other situations.

The goal of chapter 16, written by Angela Liegey Dougall and Andrew Baum, is to present the effects of stress and coping on immune function. Because description should always precede formal analyses in science, it is important to agree on what is meant by *stress*. This first descriptive step has proved to be difficult in this field; however, it remains critical in order to make clear predictions about mechanisms. To evaluate the brain regions involved in mediating stress, there must be some consensus about what the components of the stress response are. The term *stress* has often been conflated to include the stressor, the stress response, and the physiological intermediates between the stressor and stress responses. The concept of stress was borrowed from an engineering-physics term that had a very specific meaning (i.e., the forces outside the system that act against a resisting system). The engineering-physics term for the intrinsic adjustment is *strain*. For example, gravity and wind apply stress to a bridge; the bending of the metal under the pavement in response to the stress is the strain. Had we retained both terms, we would not be in the current terminological predicament. It is probably too late to return to the original engineering-physics definition of these terms in biological psychology because despite the confusing array of indefinite uses of the term *stress,* an impressive scientific literature integrating endocrinology, immunology, psychology, and neuroscience has developed around the concept of stress. What, then, does it mean to say that an individual is under stress? For the purposes of this chapter, Dougall and Baum use some of the prevailing homeostatic notions of stress to arrive at a flexible working definition.

The authors next describe coping, which is a way to counteract the forces of stress. Next, Dougall and Baum describe the psychological and behavioral responses to stress and emphasize the effects of stress on immune function. Although stress causes many health problems for individuals, all the news is not bleak. Dougall and Baum review the various stress management interventions. In some areas researchers are making remarkable progress at identifying the genetic and molecular mechanisms of stress with little regard for the integrative systems to which these molecular mechanisms contribute. In other areas scientists are still struggling to parse out the interactive effects of behavioral or emotional factors such as fear and anxiety on stress responsiveness. Obviously, a holistic approach is necessary to understand the brain stress system—perhaps more importantly than for other neural systems. Acute stress can actually bolster immune function, whereas chronic stress is always immunosuppressant. One important goal of future stress research, according to Dougall and Baum, is to determine how and when acute stress becomes chronic and how to intervene to prevent this transition.

As indicated throughout this volume, biological psychology represents a distinctive fusion of biology and psychology. In chapter 17 Peter C. Holland and Gregory F. Ball provide a synthesis of perspectives on learning from these different disciplines. The study of animal learning, firmly rooted in the origins of psychology, has traditionally emphasized the role of experience in shaping behavior and sought to identify general principles that encompass the phenomena of learning. Given their perspective, experimental psychologists have long studied laboratory animals as grist for developing a general process theory of learning. Their studies have traditionally used tasks in which exposure to environmental events is tightly controlled and discrete responses are monitored. In contrast, the ethological approach based in the field of biology has historically emphasized constraints on learning and viewed experience-dependent adaptations in relatively specialized domains, often studied in naturalistic settings. Holland and Ball show how each of these approaches has contributed to our understanding of the adaptive capacities of organisms. Studies of animal learning have revealed a rich complexity of well-defined associative processes, which have come to include representational functions in the cognitive domain. At the same time, biological psychology has become more eclectic in its approach with an integration of the ethological perspective into the field. The synthesis provided in this chapter is a particularly good example of fertilization across disciplines.

The topic of learning is continued in chapter 18 by Joseph Steinmetz, Jeansok Kim, and Richard F. Thompson. Here the focus is on the use of specific models of learning to investigate biological substrates. The authors present a variety of preparations in which a neural systems analysis has shed light on the neural circuits and mechanisms of learning. Those preparations range from research in relatively simple organisms, such as invertebrates, to several forms of learning in mammals that have closely tied research in laboratory animals to an understanding of the neural basis of learning in humans.

Among the models of learning, the authors discuss in particular depth research on eye-blink conditioning, a simple form of Pavlovian conditioning that was first demonstrated in humans about 70 years ago. Since that time, behavioral and neuroscientific research has transformed eye-blink conditioning into a powerful paradigm for the interdisciplinary study of brain and behavior. The operational simplicity and minimal sensory, motor, and motivational demands of the procedure make it applicable with little or no modification across a range of animal species—rodents, rabbits, cats, monkeys, humans—and across the life span, from early infancy to old age. As detailed in the chapter, we now have extensive knowledge of the neurobiological mechanisms of eye-blink conditioning. Studies in both animals and humans implicate the cerebellum and hippocampus in eye-blink conditioning. Simple associative learning is mediated by well-characterized brainstem-cerebellar circuitry, whereas more complex, higher order conditioning phenomena appear to depend on interactions of this circuitry with forebrain structures such as the hippocampus. This research arguably provides one of the best-characterized models of neural systems analysis and vertical integration in behavioral neuroscience.

The study of memory is now firmly grounded in the recognition that multiple memory systems exist. In chapter 19 Howard Eichenbaum traces the historical antecedents of this understanding. As a record of experience, habits and skills develop with practice and are enduring forms of memory. Habits and skills control routine simple activities as well as the exquisitely refined performance of the virtuoso. Historically, memory in the form of habits and skills can be seen as the focus of behaviorism in which effects of experience were studied in terms of stimulus and response topographies. Such forms of procedural memory that are exhibited in performance have been distinguished from declarative memory. Declarative memory refers to deficits encountered in amnesic syndromes where habit and skill memory (among other procedural types of memory) are entirely preserved but patients have a profound inability either to recollect episodes of experience consciously from the past or to acquire new knowledge.

The distinction between forms of declarative and procedural memory has become well established in studies of human memory. Eichenbaum shows how these distinctions are addressed in research on neurobiological systems. In particular, the chapter deals with the challenge of translating declarative memory into studies with laboratory animals. The neural circuitry critical for this form of memory is similarly organized in the human brain and in the brains of other species including laboratory rodents. Neural structures in the medial temporal lobe, including the hippocampus, are linked to information-processing systems in cortex. The chapter deals with research that shows how the organization and function of this system allows for distinctive features of cognitive memory, involving representational networks that can be flexibly accessed and used in novel situations. These properties of memory can be tested across human and nonhuman subjects alike. The animal models, in particular, are an important setting for research on the neural mechanisms of memory, including the cellular machinery that alters and maintains changes in synaptic connections.

A central problem in comparative biology and psychology is to determine the evolutionary mechanisms underlying similarity between species. As Marc Hauser points out in his chapter on comparative cognition (chapter 20), there are two categories of similarity. One category is characterized by *homologies,* traits shared by two or more species that arose from a common ancestor that expressed the same trait. The second category is characterized by *homoplasies,* similar traits that evolved independently in different taxonomic groups usually via convergence. These distinctions are always important in comparative approaches, but they are particularly critical when considering primate cognition, where the bias is to assume that homology underlies similar cognitive functions. Few investigators can make this distinction, primarily because of a lack of good comparative data. Hauser argues that (comparative) primate cognition should make deeper connections with studies of brain function, generally, and human infant cognitive development, specifically. He uses two examples: (a) the construction of a number sense and (b) the ability to process speech, to make the case that the apolygynous marriage between Darwin's theory of evolution and the representational-computational theory of mind that tends to dominate much of current cognitive science is a productive endeavor. In the case of number, many animals, primates included, can discriminate small numbers precisely and large numbers approximately. Hauser argues that over the course of human evolution we acquired a mechanism that allowed only our species to discriminate large numbers precisely, and this capacity ultimately led to our unique gift for complex mathematics. With respect to speech-processing mechanisms, Hauser argues that humans share with other animals all of the core perceptual tools for extracting the salient features of human speech, but that more comparative neuroanatomical work, tracing circuitry and establishing functional connectivity, is necessary to determine the evolutionary history of speech processing among primates.

Interest in systems specialized for language in the human brain has a long history, dating from the earliest descriptions of aphasia by neurologists in the 19th century. In chapter 21 Eleanor M. Saffran and Myrna F. Schwartz guide the reader through this field of study from its historical roots to the contemporary era, in which new tools and approaches are advancing knowledge in unprecedented ways. The chapter deals in detail with the kinds of inferences about the fundamental properties of language that have been gleaned from the patterns of language breakdown after brain damage. This area of cognitive neuropsychology has a long tradition in the field. The authors then describe how recent studies of brain activation in normal subjects using functional neuroimaging technology have confirmed many functions assigned to specific brain regions and circuits based on cases of brain damage. They also consider the discrepancies that have emerged from comparison of these different approaches. Finally, the chapter includes a discussion of another powerful approach in research in which computational modeling has become an important adjunct to empirical investigations in the biological study of language.

A broad perspective on the use of computational models in biological psychology is the subject of chapter 22. Randall C. O'Reilly and Yuko Munakata discuss a variety of biologically based models, ranging from those focused on the properties of single neurons as information-processing units to more extensive models used to study the properties of neurons in networks that serve a range of psychological functions.

To provide a background to computational modeling of both single neurons and networks, the authors first discuss the biological properties that are central for defining and constraining models of simulated neurons. Activation functions for such models can vary with respect to the real properties of neurons that they incorporate, yielding an increasing complexity in how a neuron is simulated. For example, they describe how variables, such as single-point integration versus multiple compartments or biological constraints on weighting of inputs, can affect the properties of a simulated neuron.

A fundamental question in the study of neuron function is the nature of the code for information. Firing rate, which refers to the frequency of action potentials, has long been studied as a coding mechanism. O'Reilly and Munakata address the debate between models based on rate codes and those that consider other coding possibilities such as the precise timing of spikes.

For psychological functions, ranging from perception and attention to learning and memory, processing systems involve networks of large numbers of neurons. O'Reilly and Munakata describe the basic organization and properties of network models for the study of these functions. They then go on to describe specific implementations. For example, they provide an extensive discussion of learning. In particular, they discuss two influential learning devices incorporated into computational models: a Hebbian mechanism, which rapidly inculcates change in a network based on correlated activity, and error-driven mechanisms that can acquire many input-output mappings for which Hebbian mechanisms are inadequate.

Much of the material in the chapter on computational modeling is relevant to empirical research discussed in other chapters on sensory information processing and learning. O'Reilly and Munakata's discussion of modeling relevant to memory mechanisms especially complements material discussed by Eichenbaum in chapter 19. Computational models of the properties of hippocampus and cortex as a system for declarative memory reveal a distinctive information storage process that can integrate information over many different experiences. The interleaving process modeled in this system allows the formation of overlapping representations that encode shared structure across different experiences, while at the same time minimizing interference between neural representations of different events. In this and other examples discussed in the chapter, computational modeling provides an important adjunct to the empirical base of research in the field.

A well-worn debate on nature versus nurture has long occupied the field of psychology. This question is at the heart of research on development. To what extent is development prearranged by our genetic endowment, and to what extent does experience play a role? In chapter 22, on experience and development, James E. Black shows how biological psychology has contributed to our understanding of these variables of nature and nurture, and of their interactions.

Black first emphasizes the degree to which brain structure is predetermined such that early development protects against variations in constructing complex neural systems. He next describes how many neural systems have evolved to capture and orchestrate carefully the role of experience in brain development. In such cases neural systems respond to experience only in a relatively narrow developmental window, referred to as a sensitive or critical period. It is interesting that this experience-expectant development is biologically controlled in many different systems by a sequence in which neural connections are overproduced and experience is then allowed to eliminate a large proportion of connections. The process of overproduction and selective elimination of synapses at a specific developmental stage allows the brain to be shaped by experience in a specialized domain. Black illustrates this process by drawing on studies of the effects of early experience on the visual system. The process, however, can be extended to other domains involving social behavior and higher cognitive functions. Indeed, the scaffolding of experience-expectant development may be such that sensitive periods are designed to build progressively on one another.

Experience-expectant development is distinguished from experience-dependent development. In the former case, biology sets the stage for a modeling of brain development based on experiences that can be anticipated to occur for all members of a species within a limited time frame. Experience-dependent development involves the brain's susceptibility to experiences that can be unique to the individual member of a species. The brain plasticity in this case is not limited to a defined critical period but is available throughout life.

Although much of our current understanding of experience and development is based on basic research in laboratory animals, Black discusses in depth the evidence that these principles also apply to humans. He carefully considers the limitations of currently available data and the gaps that need to be filled.

In closing this preface, we wish to express our gratitude to the contributing authors. This volume of the Handbook represents the field of biological psychology with its deep roots in the history of our discipline and its vital and exciting opportunities for new discovery in the 21st century.

MICHELA GALLAGHER
RANDY J. NELSON

Contents

Contributors

Gregory F. Ball, PhD
Department of Psychology
Johns Hopkins University
Baltimore, Maryland

Andrew Baum, PhD
Department of Psychiatry
University of Pittsburgh Medical Center
Pittsburgh, Pennsylvania

James W. Bisley, PhD
Laboratory 1 Sensorimotor Research
National Eye Institute
Bethesda, Maryland

James E. Black, MD, PhD
University of Illinois
Beckman Institute, NPA
Urbana, Illinois

Ansgar Büschges
Zoologisches Institut
Universität zu Köln
Köln, Germany

M. Catherine Bushnell, PhD
Pain Mechanisms Laboratory
Clinical Research Institute of Montreal
Montreal, Quebec, Canada

David Calkins, PhD
Department of Opthamology and Center for Visual Science
University of Rochester Medical Center
Rochester, New York

Catherine E. Carr, PhD
Zoology Department
University of Maryland
College Park, Maryland

Terence J. Coderre, PhD
Pain Mechanisms Laboratory
Clinical Research Institute of Montreal
Montreal, Quebec, Canada

Michael Davis, PhD
Emory University School of Medicine
Department of Psychiatry
Atlanta, Georgia

Patricia M. Di Lorenzo, PhD
State University of New York
Psychology Department
Binghamton, New York

Juan M. Dominguez, MA
Department of Psychology
SUNY Buffalo
Buffalo, New York

Angela Liegey Dougall, PhD
Department of Psychiatry
University of Pittsburgh Medical Center
Pittsburgh, Pennsylvania

Russil Durrant, PhD
Department of Psychology
University of Canterbury
Christchurch, New Zealand

Howard Eichenbaum, PhD
Department of Psychology
Boston University
Boston, Massachusetts

Bruce J. Ellis, PhD
Department of Psychology
University of Canterbury
Christchurch, New Zealand

Hanno Fischer
School of Biology
University of St. Andrews
St. Andrews, Scotland

Karim Fouad
Brain Research Institute
University of Zurich
Zurich, Switzerland

Troy A. Hackett, PhD
Department of Hearing and
    Speech Sciences
Vanderbilt University
Nashville, Tennessee

Marc D. Hauser, PhD
Department of Psychology
Harvard University
Cambridge, Massachusetts

Peter C. Holland, PhD
Department of Psychology
Johns Hopkins University
Baltimore, Maryland

Steven Hsiao, PhD
Krieger Mind/Brain Institute
Department of Neuroscience
Johns Hopkins University
Baltimore, Maryland

Elaine M. Hull, PhD
Department of Psychology
SUNY Buffalo
Buffalo, New York

Gerald H. Jacobs, PhD
Department of Psychology and Neuroscience
    Research Institute
University of California, Santa Barbara
Santa Barbara, California

Ken Johnson, PhD
Krieger Mind/Brain Institute
Department of Neuroscience
Johns Hopkins University
Baltimore, Maryland

Jon H. Kaas, PhD
Department of Psychology
Vanderbilt University
Nashville, Tennessee

Peter W. Kalivas, PhD
Department of Physiology
University of South Carolina
Charleston, South Carolina

Jeansok Kim
Department of Psychology
Yale University
New Haven, Connecticut

Peter J. Lang, PhD
National Institute of Mental Health CSEA
University of Florida
Gainesville, Florida

Federica Latta, PhD
Department of Medicine
University of Chicago
Chicago, Illinois

Stephen C. Maxson, PhD
Department of Psychology
University of Connecticut
Storrs, Connecticut

Krista McFarland, PhD
Physiology and Neuroscience
Medical University of South Carolina
Charleston, South Carolina

Jeffrey S. Mogil, PhD
Department of Psychology
McGill University
Montreal, Quebec, Canada

Timothy H. Moran, PhD
Department of Psychiatry
Johns Hopkins University
Baltimore, Maryland

Cynthia F. Moss, PhD
Department of Psychology
College of Behavioral and Social Sciences
University of Maryland
College Park, Maryland

Yuko Munakata
Department of Psychology
University of Colorado, Boulder
Boulder, Colorado

Randall C. O'Reilly
Department of Psychology
University of Colorado at Boulder
Boulder, Colorado

Tatiana Pasternak, PhD
Department of Neurobiology and Anatomy
University of Rochester Medical Center
Rochester, New York

Eleanor M. Saffran
Department of Communication Sciences
Department of Neurology
University of California, Berkeley
Berkeley, California

Randall R. Sakai, PhD
Department of Psychiatry
University of Cincinnati
Cincinnati, Ohio

Myrna F. Schwartz
Moss Rehabilitation Center
Philadelphia, Pennsylvania

Joseph E. Steinmetz, PhD
Department of Psychology
Indiana University
Bloomington, Indiana

Richard F. Thompson, PhD
Neuroscience Program
University of Southern California
Los Angeles, California

Eve Van Cauter, PhD
Department of Medicine
University of Chicago
Chicago, Illinois

Takashi Yoshioka
Johns Hopkins University
Krieger Mind Brain Institute
Baltimore, Maryland

Steven L. Youngentob, PhD
Physiology Department
SUNY Health Sciences Center
Syracuse, New York

CHAPTER 1

Evolutionary Psychology

RUSSIL DURRANT AND BRUCE J. ELLIS

Evolutionary psychology is the application of the principles and knowledge of evolutionary biology to psychological theory and research. Its central assumption is that the human brain is comprised of a large number of specialized mechanisms that were shaped by natural selection over vast periods of time to solve the recurrent information-processing problems faced by our ancestors (Symons, 1995). These problems include such things as choosing which foods to eat, negotiating social hierarchies, dividing investment among offspring, and selecting mates. The field of evolutionary psychology focuses on identifying these information-processing problems, developing models of the brain-mind mechanisms that may have evolved to solve them, and testing these models in research (Buss, 1995; Tooby & Cosmides, 1992).

The field of evolutionary psychology has emerged dramatically over the last 15 years, as indicated by exponential growth in the number of empirical and theoretical articles in the area (Table 1.1). These articles extend into all branches of psychology—from cognitive psychology (e.g., Cosmides, 1989; Shepard, 1992) to developmental psychology (e.g., Ellis, McFadyen-Ketchum, Dodge, Pettit, & Bates, 1999; Weisfeld, 1999), abnormal psychology (e.g., Mealey, 1995;

Price, Sloman, Gardner, Gilbert, & Rhode, 1994), social psychology (e.g., Daly & Wilson, 1988; Simpson & Kenrick, 1997), personality psychology (e.g., Buss, 1991; Sulloway, 1996), motivation-emotion (e.g., Nesse & Berridge, 1997; Johnston, 1999), and industrial-organizational psychology (e.g., Colarelli, 1998; Studd, 1996). The first undergraduate textbook on evolutionary psychology was published in 1999 (Buss, 1999), and since then at least three other undergraduate textbooks have been published in the area (Barrett, Dunbar, & Lycett, 2002; Cartwright, 2000; Gaulin & McBurney, 2000).

In this chapter we provide an introduction to the field of evolutionary psychology. We describe the methodology that evolutionary psychologists use to explain human cognition and behavior. This description begins at the broadest level with a review of the basic, guiding assumptions that are employed by evolutionary psychologists. We then show how evolutionary psychologists apply these assumptions to develop more specific theoretical models that are tested in research. We use examples of sex and mating to demonstrate how evolutionary psychological theories are developed and tested.

TABLE 1.1 Growth of Publications in the Area of Evolutionary Psychology, as Indexed by the PsycINFO Database

Years of Publication	Number of Publications[a]
1985–1988	4
1989–1992	25
1993–1996	100
1997–2000	231

[a]Number of articles, books, and dissertations in the PsycINFO database that include either the phrase *evolutionary psychology* or *evolutionary psychological* in the title, in the abstract, or as a keyword. All articles from the *Journal of Evolutionary Psychology*, which is a psychoanalytic journal, were excluded.

LEVELS OF EXPLANATION IN EVOLUTIONARY PSYCHOLOGY

Why do siblings fight with each other for parental attention? Why are men more likely than women to kill sexual rivals? Why are women most likely to have extramarital sex when they are ovulating? To address such questions, evolutionary psychologists employ multiple levels of explanation ranging from broad metatheoretical assumptions, to more specific middle-level theories, to actual hypotheses and predictions that are tested in research (Buss, 1995; Ketelaar & Ellis, 2000). These levels of explanation are ordered in a hierarchy (see Figure 1.1) and constitute the methodology that evolutionary psychologists use to address questions about human nature.

At the top of the hierarchy are the basic metatheoretical assumptions of modern evolutionary theory. This set of guiding assumptions, which together are referred to as evolutionary metatheory, provide the foundation that evolutionary scientists use to build more specific theoretical models. We begin by describing (a) the primary set of metatheoretical assumptions that are consensually held by evolutionary scientists and (b) the special set of metatheoretical assumptions that distinguish evolutionary psychology. We use the term *evolutionary psychological metatheory* to refer inclusively to this primary and special set of assumptions together.

As shown in Figure 1.1, at the next level down in the hierarchy, just below evolutionary psychological metatheory, are *middle-level evolutionary theories*. These theories elaborate the basic metatheoretical assumptions into a particular psychological domain such as mating or cooperation. In this chapter we consider two related middle-level evolutionary theories—parental investment theory and good genes sexual

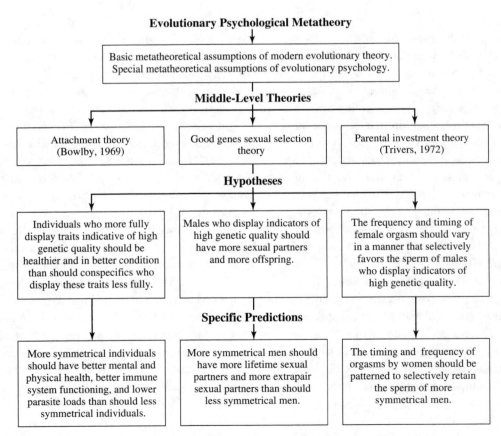

Figure 1.1 The hierarchical structure of evolutionary psychological explanations (adapted from Buss, 1995).

selection theory—each of which applies the assumptions of evolutionary psychological metatheory to the question of reproductive strategies. In different ways these middle-level theories attempt to explain differences between the sexes as well as variation within each sex in physical and psychological adaptations for mating and parenting.

At the next level down are the actual hypotheses and predictions that are drawn from middle-level evolutionary theories (Figure 1.1). A *hypothesis* is a general statement about the state of the world that one would expect to observe if the theory from which it was generated were in fact true. *Predictions* are explicit, testable instantiations of hypotheses. We conclude this chapter with an evaluation of hypotheses and specific predictions about sexual behavior that have been derived from good genes sexual selection theory. Special attention is paid to comparison of human and nonhuman animal literatures.

THE METATHEORY LEVEL OF ANALYSIS

Scientists typically rely on basic (although usually implicit) metatheoretical assumptions when they construct and evaluate theories. Evolutionary psychologists have often called on behavioral scientists to make explicit their basic assumptions about the origins and structure of the mind (see Gigerenzer, 1998). Metatheoretical assumptions shape how scientists generate, develop, and test middle-level theories and their derivative hypotheses and predictions (Ketelaar & Ellis, 2000). These basic assumptions are often not directly tested after they have been empirically established. Instead they are used as a starting point for further theory and research. Newton's laws of motion form the metatheory for classical mechanics, the principles of gradualism and plate tectonics provide a metatheory for geology, and the principles of adaptation through natural selection provide a metatheory for biology. Several scholars (e.g., Bjorklund, 1997; Richters, 1997) have argued that the greatest impediment to psychology's development as a science is the absence of a coherent, agreed-upon metatheory.

A metatheory operates like a map of a challenging conceptual terrain. It specifies both the landmarks and the boundaries of that terrain, suggesting which features are consistent and which are inconsistent with the core logic of the metatheory. In this way a metatheory provides a set of powerful methodological heuristics: "Some tell us what paths to avoid (negative heuristic), and others what paths to pursue (positive heuristic)" (Lakatos, 1970, p. 47). In the hands of a skilled researcher, a metatheory "provides a guide and prevents certain kinds of errors, raises suspicions of certain explanations or

observations, suggests lines of research to be followed, and provides a sound criterion for recognizing significant observations on natural phenomena" (Lloyd, 1979, p. 18). The ultimate contribution of a metatheory is that it synthesizes middle-level theories, allowing the empirical results of a variety of different theory-driven research programs to be explicated within a broader metatheoretical framework. This facilitates systematic cumulation of knowledge and progression toward a coherent big picture, so to speak, of the subject matter (Ketelaar & Ellis, 2000).

METATHEORETICAL ASSUMPTIONS THAT ARE CONSENSUALLY HELD BY EVOLUTIONARY SCIENTISTS

When asked what his study of the natural world had revealed about the nature of God, biologist J. B. S. Haldane is reported to have made this reply: "That he has an inordinate fondness for beetles." Haldane's retort refers to the extraordinary diversity of beetle species found throughout the world—some 290,000 species have so far been discovered (E. O. Wilson, 1992). Beetles, moreover, come in a bewildering variety of shapes and sizes, from tiny glittering scarab beetles barely visible to the naked eye to ponderous stag beetles with massive mandibles half the size of their bodies. Some beetles make a living foraging on lichen and fungi; others subsist on a diet of beetles themselves.

The richness and diversity of beetle species are mirrored throughout the biological world. Biologists estimate that anywhere from 10 to 100 million different species currently inhabit the Earth (E. O. Wilson, 1992), each one in some respect different from all others. How are we to explain this extraordinary richness of life? Why are there so many species and why do they have the particular characteristics that they do? The general principles of genetical evolution drawn from modern evolutionary theory, as outlined by W. D. Hamilton (1964) and instantiated in more contemporary so-called selfish gene theories of genetic evolution via natural and sexual selection, provide a set of core metatheoretical assumptions for answering these questions. Inclusive fitness theory conceptualizes genes or individuals as the units of selection (see Dawkins, 1976; Hamilton, 1964; Williams, 1966). In contrast, "multilevel selection theory" is based on the premise that natural selection is a hierarchical process that can operate at many levels, including genes, individuals, groups within species, or even multi-species ecosystems. Thus, multilevel selection theory is conceptualized as an elaboration of inclusive fitness theory (adding the concept of group-level adaptation) rather than an alternative to it (D. S. Wilson &

Sober, 1994). Whereas inclusive fitness theory is consensually accepted among evolutionary scientists, multilevel selection theory is not. Thus, this review of basic metatheoretical assumptions only focuses on inclusive fitness theory.

Natural Selection

During his journey around the coastline of South America aboard the HMS *Beagle,* Charles Darwin was intrigued by the sheer diversity of animal and plant species found in the tropics, by the way that similar species were grouped together geographically, and by their apparent fit to local ecological conditions. Although the idea of biological evolution had been around for some time, what had been missing was an explanation of *how* evolution occurred—that is, what had been missing was an account of the *mechanisms* responsible for evolutionary change. Darwin's mechanism, which he labeled *natural selection,* served to explain many of the puzzling facts about the biological world: Why were there so many species? Why are current species so apparently similar in many respects both to each other and to extinct species? Why do organisms have the specific characteristics that they do?

The idea of natural selection is both elegant and simple, and can be neatly encapsulated as the result of the operation of three general principles: (a) phenotypic variation, (b) differential fitness, and (c) heritability.

As is readily apparent when we look around the biological world, organisms of the same species vary in the characteristics that they possess; that is, they have slightly different *phenotypes*. A whole branch of psychology—personality and individual differences—is devoted to documenting and understanding the nature of these kinds of differences in our own species. Some of these differences found among members of a given species will result in differences in *fitness*— that is, some members of the species will be more likely to survive and reproduce than will others as a result of the specific characteristics that they possess. For evolution to occur, however, these individual differences must be *heritable*— that is, they must be reliably passed on (via shared genes) from parents to their offspring. Over time, the characteristics of a population of organisms will change as heritable traits that enhance fitness will become more prevalent at the expense of less favorable variations.

For example, consider the evolution of bipedalism in humans. Paleoanthropological evidence suggests that upright walking (at least some of the time) was a feature of early hominids from about 3.5 million years ago (Lovejoy, 1988). Presume that there was considerable variation in the propensity to walk upright in the ancestors of this early hominid species as the result of differences in skeletal structures, relevant neural programs, and behavioral proclivities. Some hominids did and some did not. Also presume that walking on two feet much of the time conferred some advantage in terms of survival and reproductive success. Perhaps, by freeing the hands, bipedalism allowed objects such as meat to be carried long distances (e.g., Lovejoy, 1981). Perhaps it also served to cool the body by reducing the amount of surface area exposed to the harsh tropical sun, enabling foraging throughout the hottest parts of the day (e.g., Wheeler, 1991). Finally, presume that these differences in the propensity for upright walking were heritable in nature—they were the result of specific genes that were reliably passed on from parents to offspring. The individuals who tended to walk upright would be, on average, more likely to survive (and hence, to reproduce) than would those who did not. Over time the genes responsible for bipedalism would become more prevalent in the population as the individuals who possessed them were more reproductively successful than were those who did not, and bipedalism itself would become pervasive in the population.

Several points are important to note here. First, natural selection shapes not only the physical characteristics of organisms, but also their behavioral and cognitive traits. The shift to bipedalism was not simply a matter of changes in the anatomy of early hominids; it was also the result of changes in behavioral proclivities and in the complex neural programs dedicated to the balance and coordination required for upright walking. Second, although the idea of natural selection is sometimes encapsulated in the slogan *the survival of the fittest,* ultimately it is *reproductive* fitness that counts. It doesn't matter how well an organism is able to survive. If it fails to pass on its genes, then it is an evolutionary dead end, and the traits responsible for its enhanced survival abilities will not be represented in subsequent generations. This point is somewhat gruesomely illustrated by many spider species in which the male serves as both meal and mate to the female—often at the same time. Ultimately, although one must survive to reproduce, reproductive goals take precedence.

Adaptation

Natural selection is the primary process which is responsible for evolutionary change over times as more favorable variants are retained and less favorable ones are rejected (Darwin, 1859). Through this filtering process, natural selection produces small incremental modifications in existing phenotypes, leading to an accumulation of characteristics that are organized to enhance survival and reproductive success. These characteristics that are produced by natural selection are termed *adaptations*. Adaptations are inherited and reliably developing characteristics of species that have been selected for because of their causal role in enhancing the survival and reproductive success of the individuals that possess them (see Buss, Haselton, Shackelford, Bleske, & Wakefield, 1998; Dawkins, 1986; Sterelny & Griffiths, 1999; Williams, 1966, 1992, for definitions of adaptation).

Adaptations have biological *functions.* The immune system functions to protect organisms from microbial invasion, the heart functions as a blood pump, and the cryptic coloring of many insects has the function of preventing their detection by predators. The core idea of evolutionary psychology is that many psychological characteristics are adaptations—just as many physical characteristics are—and that the principles of evolutionary biology that are used to explain our bodies are equally applicable to our minds. Thus, various evolutionary psychological research programs have investigated psychological mechanisms—for mate selection, fear of snakes, face recognition, natural language, sexual jealousy, and so on—as biological adaptations that were selected for because of the role they played in promoting reproductive success in ancestral environments.

It is worth noting, however, that natural selection is not the only causal process responsible for evolutionary change (e.g., Gould & Lewontin, 1979). Traits may also become fixated in a population by the process of genetic drift, whereby neutral or even deleterious characteristics become more prevalent due to *chance* factors. This may occur in small populations because the fittest individuals may turn out—due to random events—not to be the ones with the greatest reproductive success. It does not matter how fit you are if you drown in a flood before you get a chance to reproduce. Moreover, some traits may become fixated in a population not because they enhance reproductive success, but because they are genetically or developmentally yoked to adaptations that do. For example, the modified wrist bone of the panda (its "thumb") seems to be an adaptation for manipulating bamboo, but the genes responsible for this adaptation also direct the enlarged growth of the corresponding bone in the panda's foot, a feature that serves no function at all (Gould, 1980).

There is much debate among evolutionary biologists and philosophers of biology regarding the relative importance of different evolutionary processes (see Sterelny & Griffiths, 1999, for a good introduction to these and other issues in the philosophy of biology). The details of these disputes, however, need not concern us here. What is important to note is that not all of the products of evolution will be biological adaptations with evolved functions. The evolutionary process also results in *by-products* of adaptations, as well as a residue of *noise* (Buss et al., 1998; Tooby & Cosmides,

1992). Examples of by-products are legion. The sound that hearts make when they beat, the white color of bones, and the human chin are all nonfunctional by-products of natural selection. In addition, random variation in traits—as long as this variation is selectively neutral (neither enhancing nor reducing biological fitness)—can also be maintained as residual noise in organisms.

Demarcating the different products of evolution is an especially important task for evolutionary psychologists. It has often been suggested that many of the important phenomena that psychologists study—for example, reading, writing, religion—are by-products of adaptations rather than adaptations themselves (e.g., Gould, 1991a). Of course, even by-products can be furnished with evolutionary explanations in terms of the adaptations to which they are connected (Tooby & Cosmides, 1992). Thus, for example, the whiteness of bones is a by-product of the color of calcium salts, which give bones their hardness and rigidity; the chin is a by-product of two growth fields; and reading and writing are by-products (in part) of the evolved mechanisms underlying human language (Pinker, 1994).

The important question is *how* to distinguish adaptations from nonadaptations in the biological world. Because we cannot reverse time and observe natural selection shaping adaptations, we must make inferences about evolutionary history based on the nature of the traits we see today. A variety of methods can (and should) be employed to identify adaptations (see M. R. Rose & Lauder, 1996). Evolutionary psychologists, drawing on the work of George Williams (1966), typically emphasize the importance of *special design* features such as economy, efficiency, complexity, precision, specialization, reliability, and functionality for identifying adaptations (e.g., Buss et al., 1998; Pinker, 1997; Tooby & Cosmides, 1990). One hallmark that a trait is the product of natural selection is that it demonstrates *adaptive complexity*—that is, the trait is composed of a number of interrelated parts or systems that operate in concert to generate effects that serve specific functions (Dawkins, 1986; Pinker, 1997).

Echolocation in bats is a good example of such a trait. A collection of interrelated mechanisms allows foraging bats to maneuver around obstacles in complete darkness and to pick out small rapidly moving prey on the wing. Echolocating bats have a number of *specialized* mechanisms that precisely, reliably, and efficiently enable them to achieve the *function* of nocturnal locomotion and foraging. Bats have mechanisms that allow them to produce rapid, high-frequency, short-wavelength cries that are reflected by small objects. Moreover, the frequency and rapidity of these cries are modified depending on the distance of the object being detected (low-frequency waves penetrate further but can only be used to detect large objects). Bats also have specialized mechanisms that protect their ears while they are emitting loud sounds, and their faces are shaped to enhance the detection of their returning echoes. It is extraordinary unlikely that such a complex array of intertwining processes could have arisen by chance or as a *by-product* of evolutionary processes. Thus, one has clear warrant in this case to assert that echolocation in bats is a biological adaptation.

Many traits, however, may not be so clearly identifiable as adaptations. Furthermore, there are often disputes about just what *function* some trait has evolved to serve, even if one can be reasonably sure that it is the product of natural selection. In adjudicating between alternative evolutionary hypotheses, one can follow the same sort of strategies that are employed when comparing alternative explanations in any domain in science—that is, one should favor the theory or hypothesis that best explains the evidence at hand (Haig & Durrant, 2000; Holcomb, 1998) and that generates novel hypotheses that lead to new knowledge (Ketelaar & Ellis, 2000).

Consider, for example, the alternative explanations that have been offered for the origin of orgasm in human females.

- Female orgasm serves no evolved function and is a by-product of selection on male orgasm, which is necessary for fertilization to occur (Gould, 1991b, pp. 124–129; Symons, 1979).
- Orgasm is an adaptation that promotes pair-bonding in the human species (Eibl-Eibesfeldt, 1989).
- Female orgasm is an adaptation that motivates females to seek multiple sexual partners, confusing males about paternity and thus reducing the probability of subsequent male infanticide (Hrdy, 1981).
- Female orgasm is an adaptation that serves to enhance sperm retention, therefore allowing females to exert some control over the paternity of their offspring via differential patterns of orgasm with specific male partners, especially those of high genetic quality (Baker & Bellis, 1993; Smith, 1984).

Although all of these models have some plausibility, it is the last suggestion that is beginning to be accepted as the best current explanation. Baker and Bellis (1993) have demonstrated that females retain more sperm if they experience copulatory orgasms up to 45 min after—or at the same time as—their male partners. Thus, depending on their timing, orgasms appear to enhance the retention of sperm via the "up-suck" from the vagina into the cervix. The selective sperm retention model predicts that women will experience more orgasms—and specifically, more high-sperm-retention orgasms—with men who have specific indicators of genetic

quality. This prediction has been supported in research on dating and married couples (Thornhill, Gangestad, & Comer, 1995). Moreover, the occurrence of high sperm retention orgasms are a significant predictor of a desire for pregnancy in women, suggesting that female orgasms are one mechanism for increasing the likelihood of conception (Singh, Meyer, Zambarano, & Hurlbert, 1998).

Although there are a number of theories of extrapair mating in human females (mating that occurs outside of a current, ongoing relationship), one prominent suggestion is that extrapair mating has evolved to enhance reproductive success by increasing selective mating with males who demonstrate high genetic quality (e.g., Gangestad, 1993; Greiling & Buss, 2000). In support of this idea, men who possess indicators of high genetic quality (as assessed by degree of symmetry of bilateral physical traits) are more likely to be chosen by women specifically as extrapair sex partners but not as partners in long-term relationships (Gangestad & Simpson, 2000). Further, Bellis and Baker (1990) found that women were most likely to copulate with extrapair partners but not with in-pair partners during the fertile phase of their menstrual cycles. Finally, as a result of the type and frequency of orgasms experienced by women, it appears that levels of sperm retention are significantly higher during extrapair copulations than during copulations with in-pair partners (Baker & Bellis, 1995).

In summary, although more research needs to be done, our best current explanation for the human female orgasm is that it is an adaptation specifically, precisely, and efficiently designed to manipulate the paternity of offspring by favoring the sperm of males of high genetic quality. This model (a) concurs with what is known about female orgasm; (b) generated specific, testable predictions about patterns of variation in female orgasm that were as yet unobserved and were not forecast by competing models; (c) generated interesting new lines of research on female orgasm that provided support for the predictions; and (d) led to acquisition of new knowledge about the timing and probability of female orgasm with different partners.

Sexual Selection

Not all adaptations can be conceptualized as adaptations for survival per se. Although the bat's complex system of echolocation enables it to navigate and forage in darkness, the human female orgasm has no such obvious utilitarian function. As Darwin (1871) clearly recognized, many of the interesting features that plants and animals possess, such as the gaudy plumage and elaborate songs of many male birds, serve no obvious survival functions. In fact, if anything, such traits are likely to reduce survival prospects by attracting predators, impeding movement, and so on. Darwin's explanation for such characteristics was that they were the product of a process that he labeled *sexual selection*. This kind of selection arises not from a struggle to survive, but rather from the competition that arises over mates and mating (Andersson, 1994; Andersson & Iwasa, 1996). If—for whatever reason—having elongated tail feathers or neon blue breast plumage enables one to attract more mates, then such traits will increase reproductive success. Moreover, to the extent that such traits are also heritable, they will be likely to spread in the population, even if they might diminish survival prospects.

Although there is some debate about how best to conceptualize the relationship between natural and sexual selection, sexual selection is most commonly considered a component or special case of natural selection associated with mate choice and mating. This reflects the fact that differential fitness concerns differences in both survival and reproduction. Miller (1999) notes that "both natural selection and sexual selection boil down to one principle: Some genes replicate themselves better than others. Some do it by helping their bodies survive better, and some by helping themselves reproduce better" (p. 334). Whereas the general processes underlying natural and sexual selection are the same (variation, fitness, heritability), the products of natural and sexual selection can look quite different. The later parts of this chapter review sexual selection theory and some of the exciting research it has generated on human mating behavior.

To summarize, we have introduced the ideas of natural and sexual selection and shown how these processes generate adaptations, by-products, and noise. We have also discussed ways in which adaptations can be distinguished from non-adaptations and have offered some examples drawn from recent research in evolutionary psychology. It is now time to consider an important theoretical advance in evolutionary theorizing that occurred in the 1960s—inclusive fitness theory—that changed the way biologists (and psychologists) think about the nature of evolution and natural selection. Inclusive fitness theory is the modern instantiation of Darwin's theory of adaptation through natural and sexual selection.

Inclusive Fitness Theory

Who are adaptations good for? Although the answer may seem obvious—that they are good for the organisms possessing the adaptations—this answer is only partially correct; it fails to account for the perplexing problem of altruism. As Darwin puzzled, how could behaviors evolve that conferred advantage to other organisms at the expense of the principle organism that performed the behaviors? Surely such acts of generosity would be eliminated by natural selection because they decreased rather than increased the individual's chances of survival and reproduction.

The solution to this thorny evolutionary problem was hinted at by J. B. S. Haldane, who, when he was asked if he would lay down his life for his brother, replied, "No, but I would for two brothers or eight cousins" (cited in Pinker, 1997, p. 400). Haldane's quip reflects the fact that we each share (on average) 50% of our genes with our full siblings and 12.5% of our genes with our first cousins. Thus, from the gene's-eye point of view, it is just as advantageous to help two of our siblings to survive and reproduce as it is to help ourselves. This insight was formalized by W. D. Hamilton (1964) and has come to be known variously as *Hamilton's rule, selfish-gene theory* (popularized by Dawkins, 1976), *kin-selection theory,* or *inclusive fitness theory.*

The core idea of inclusive fitness theory is that evolution works by increasing copies of genes, not copies of the individuals carrying the genes. Thus, the genetic code for a trait that reduces personal reproductive success can be selected for if the trait, on average, leads to more copies of the genetic code in the population. A genetic code for altruism, therefore, can spread through kin selection if (a) it causes an organism to help close relatives to reproduce and (b) the cost to the organism's own reproduction is offset by the reproductive benefit to those relatives (discounted by the probability that the relatives who receive the benefit have inherited the same genetic code from a common ancestor). For example, a squirrel who acts as a sentinel and emits loud alarm calls in the presence of a predator may reduce its own survival chances by directing the predator's attention to itself; however, the genes that are implicated in the development of alarm-calling behavior can spread if they are present in the group of close relatives who are benefited by the alarm calling.

SPECIAL METATHEORETICAL ASSUMPTIONS OF EVOLUTIONARY PSYCHOLOGY

In addition to employing inclusive fitness theory, evolutionary psychologists endorse a number of special metatheoretical assumptions concerning how to apply inclusive fitness theory to human psychological processes. In particular, evolutionary psychologists argue that we should primarily be concerned with how natural and sexual selection have shaped *psychological mechanisms* in our species; that a *multiplicity* of such mechanisms will exist in the human mind; and that they will have evolved to solve *specific* adaptive problems encountered in *ancestral environments*. Although these general points also apply to other species, they are perhaps especially pertinent in a human context and they have received much attention from evolutionary psychologists. We consider these special metatheoretical assumptions, in turn, in the following discussion.

Psychological Mechanisms as the Main Unit of Analysis

Psychological adaptations, which govern mental and behavioral processes, are referred to by evolutionary psychologists as *psychological mechanisms*. Evolutionary psychologists emphasize that genes do not cause behavior and cognition directly. Rather, genes provide blueprints for the construction of psychological mechanisms, which then interact with environmental factors to produce a range of behavioral and cognitive outputs. Most research in evolutionary psychology focuses on identifying evolved psychological mechanisms because it is at this level where invariances occur. Indeed, evolutionary psychologists assert that there is a core set of universal psychological mechanisms that comprise our shared human nature (Tooby & Cosmides, 1992).

To demonstrate the universal nature of our psychological mechanisms, a common rhetorical device used by evolutionary psychologists (e.g., Brown, 1991; Ellis, 1992; Symons, 1987) is to imagine that a heretofore unknown tribal people is suddenly discovered. Evolutionary psychologists are willing to make a array of specific predictions—in advance—about the behavior and cognition of this newly discovered people. These predictions concern criteria that determine sexual attractiveness, circumstances that lead to sexual arousal, taste preferences for sugar and fat, use of cheater detection procedures in social exchange, nepotistic bias in parental investment and child abuse, stages and timing of language development, sex differences in violence, different behavioral strategies for people high and low in dominance hierarchies, perceptual adaptations for entraining, tracking, and predicting animate motion, and so on. The only way that the behavior and cognition of an unknown people can be known in advance is if we share with those people a universal set of specific psychological mechanisms.

Buss (1999, pp. 47–49) defines an evolved psychological mechanism as a set of structures inside our heads that (a) exist in the form they do because they recurrently solved specific problems of survival and reproduction over evolutionary history; (b) are designed to take only certain kinds of information from the world as input; (c) process that information according to a specific set of rules and procedures; (d) generate output in terms of information to other psychological mechanisms and physiological activity or manifest behavior that is directed at solving specific adaptive problems

(as specified by the input that brought the psychological mechanism on-line).

Consider, for example, the psychological mechanisms underlying disgust and food aversions in humans. These psychological mechanisms, which are designed to find certain smells and tastes more aversive than others, can be said to have several features:

- They exist in the form they do because they recurrently solved specific problems of survival over evolutionary history. As an omnivorous species, humans consume a wide variety of plant and animal substances. Not all such substances, however, are safe to eat. Many plants contain natural toxins, and many animal products are loaded with parasites that can cause sickness and death. The psychological mechanisms underlying disgust and food aversions function to reduce the probability of ingesting and digesting dangerous plant and animal substances.

- These mechanisms are designed to take a specific and limited class of stimuli as input: the sight, touch, and especially taste and smell of plant and animal substances that were regularly harmful to our ancestors. Feces and animal products are especially likely to harbor lethal microorganisms and, cross-culturally, are most likely to elicit disgust (Rozin & Fallon, 1987).

- Inputs to the psychological mechanisms underlying disgust and food aversions are then processed according to a set of decision rules and procedures, such as (a) avoid plant substances that taste or smell bitter or especially pungent (indicating high concentrations of plant toxins; Profet, 1992); (b) avoid animal substances that emit smells suggestive of spoilage (indicating high levels of toxin-producing bacteria; Profet, 1992); (c) avoid foods that one has become sick after consuming in the past (Seligman & Hager, 1972); (d) and avoid foods that were not part of one's diet in the first few years of life (especially if it is an animal product; Cashdan, 1994).

- When relevant decision rules are met, behavioral output is then generated, manifested by specific facial expressions, physical withdrawal from the offending stimuli, nausea, gagging, spitting, and vomiting.

- This output is specifically directed at solving the adaptive problem of avoiding consumption of harmful substances and of expelling these substances from the body as rapidly as possible if they have been consumed.

Evolutionary psychologists assume that humans possess a large number of specific psychological mechanisms (e.g., the ones underlying food aversions and disgust) that are directed at solving specific adaptive problems. This assumption is commonly referred to as the *domain specificity* or *modularity* of mind.

Domain Specificity of Psychological Mechanisms

Evolutionary psychologists posit that the mind comprises a large number of content-saturated (*domain-specific*) psychological mechanisms (e.g., Buss, 1995; Cosmides & Tooby, 1994; Pinker, 1997). Although evolutionary psychologists assert that the mind is *not* comprised primarily of content-free (*domain-general*) psychological mechanisms, it is likely that different mechanisms differ in their levels of specificity and that there are some higher-level executive mechanisms that function to integrate information across more specific lower-level mechanisms.

The rationale behind the domain-specificity argument is fairly straightforward: What counts as adaptive behavior differs markedly from domain to domain. The sort of adaptive problems posed by food choice, mate choice, incest avoidance, and social exchange require different kinds of solutions. As Don Symons (1992) has pointed out, there is no such thing as a general solution because there is no such thing as a general problem. The psychological mechanisms underlying disgust and food aversions, for example, are useful in solving problems of food choice but not those of mate choice. If we used the same decision rules in both domains, we would end up with some very strange mates and very strange meals indeed. Given the large array of adaptive problems faced by our ancestors, we should expect a commensurate number of domain-specific solutions to these problems.

A clear analogy can be drawn with the functional division of labor in human physiology. Different organs have evolved to serve different functions and possess properties that allow them to fulfill those functions efficiently, reliably, and economically: The heart pumps blood, the liver detoxifies poisons, the kidneys excrete urine, and so on. A super, all-purpose, domain-general internal organ—heart, liver, kidney, spleen, and pancreas rolled into one—faces the impossible task of serving multiple, incompatible functions. Analogously, a super, all-purpose, domain-general brain-mind mechanism faces the impossible task of efficiently and reliably solving the plethora of behavioral problems encountered by humans in ancestral environments. Thus, neither an all-purpose physiological organ nor an all-purpose brain-mind mechanism is likely to evolve. Evolutionary psychologists argue that the human brain-mind instead contains domain-specific information processing rules and biases.

These evolved domain-specific mechanisms are often referred to as psychological *modules*. The best way to conceptualize such modules, however, is a matter of some contention. Jerry Fodor (1983), in his classic book *The Modularity of Mind,* suggests that modules have the properties of being domain-specific, innately specified, localized in the brain, and able to operate relatively independently from other such systems. Potentially good examples of such psychological modules in humans include language (Pinker, 1994), face recognition (Bruce, 1988), and theory of mind (Baron-Cohen, 1995). For example, the systems underlying language ability are specially designed to deal with linguistic information, emerge in development with no formal tuition, and appear to be located in specific brain regions independent from other systems, as indicated by specific language disorders (aphasias), which can arise from localized brain damage.

Not all of the evolved psychological mechanisms proposed by evolutionary psychologists, however, can be so readily characterized. Many mechanisms—such as landscape preferences, sexual jealousy, and reasoning processes—may be domain-specific in the sense of addressing specific adaptive problems, but they are neither clearly localized (neurally speaking) nor especially autonomous from other systems. It seems most plausible to suggest that there is a considerable degree of integration and interaction between different psychological mechanisms (Karmiloff-Smith, 1992). It is this feature of human cognitive organization that allows for the tremendous flexibility and creativity of human thought processes (Browne, 1996). It is also not clear whether domain specificity is best characterized by way of specific computational mechanisms or in terms of domain-specific bodies of mental representations (Samuels, 2000).

We should also expect—in addition to whatever taxonomy of specialized mechanisms that is proposed for the human mind—that there are some domain-general processes as well. The mechanisms involved in classical and operant conditioning may be good candidates for such domain-general processes. However, even these domain-general processes appear to operate in different ways, depending on the context in question. As illustrated in a series of classic studies by Garcia and colleagues (e.g., Garcia & Koelling, 1966), rats are more likely to develop some (adaptively relevant) associations than they are others, such as that between food and nausea but not between buzzers and nausea. Similar prepared learning biases have been demonstrated in monkeys (Mineka, 1992) and also in humans (Seligman & Hagar, 1972). For example, humans are overwhelmingly more likely to associate anxiety and fear with evolutionarily relevant threats such as snakes, spiders, social exclusion, and heights than with more dangerous but evolutionarily novel threats such as cars, guns, and power lines (Marks & Nesse, 1994).

In sum, although some doubt remains over the nature and number of domain-specific psychological mechanisms that humans (and other animals) possess, the core idea of specialized adaptive processes instantiated in psychological mechanisms remains central to evolutionary psychology. An approach to the human mind that highlights the importance of evolved domain-specific mechanisms can advance our understanding of human cognition by offering a theoretically guided taxonomy of mental processes—one that promises to better carve the mind at its natural joints.

The Environment of Evolutionary Adaptedness

The concept of biological adaptation is necessarily an historical one. When we claim that the thick insulating coat of the polar bear is as an adaptation, we are claiming that possession of that trait advanced reproductive success in *ancestral* environments. All claims about adaptation are claims about the past because natural selection is a gradual, cumulative process. The polar bear's thick coat arose through natural selection because it served to ward off the bitter-cold arctic weather during the polar bear's evolutionary history. However, traits that served adaptive functions and thus were selected for in past environments may not still be adaptive in present or future environments. In a globally warmed near-future, for example, the polar bear's lustrous pelt may become a handicap that reduces the fitness of its owner due to stress from overheating. In sum, when environments change, the conditions that proved advantageous to the evolution of a given trait may no longer exist; yet the trait often remains in place for some time because evolutionary change occurs slowly. Such vestigial traits are eventually weeded out by natural selection (if they consistently detract from fitness).

The environment in which a given trait evolved is termed its *environment of evolutionary adaptedness* (EEA). The EEA for our species is sometimes loosely characterized as the Pleistocene—the 2-million-year period that our ancestors spent as hunter-gatherers in the African savanna, prior to the emergence of agriculture some 10,000 years ago. The emphasis on the Pleistocene is perhaps reasonable given that many of the evolved human characteristics of interest to psychologists, such as language, theory of mind, sophisticated tool use, and culture, probably arose during this period. However, a number of qualifications are in order. First, the Pleistocene itself captures a large span of time, in which many changes in habitat, climate and species composition took place. Second, there were a number of different hominid species in existence during this time period, each inhabiting its own specific ecological niche. Third, many of the adaptations that humans possess have their origins in time periods that substantially predate the Pleistocene era. For example, the mechanisms underlying human attachment and

sociality have a long evolutionary history as part of our more general primate and mammalian heritage (Foley, 1996). Finally, some evolution (although of a relatively minor character) has also probably occurred in the last 10,000 years, as is reflected in population differences in disease susceptibility, skin color, and so forth (Irons, 1998).

Most important is that different adaptations will have different EEAs. Some, like language, are firmly anchored in approximately the last 2 million years; others, such as infant attachment, reflect a much lengthier evolutionary history (Hrdy, 1999). It is important, therefore, that we distinguish between the EEA of a *species* and the EEA of an *adaptation*. Although these two may overlap, they need not necessarily do so (Crawford, 1998). Tooby and Cosmides (1990) summarize these points clearly when they state that "the 'environment of evolutionary adaptedness' (EEA) is not a place or a habitat, or even a time period. Rather, it is a statistical composite of the adaptation-relevant properties of the ancestral environments encountered by members of ancestral populations, weighted by their frequency and fitness-consequences" (pp. 386–387). Delineating the specific features of the EEA for any given adaptation, then, requires an understanding of the evolutionary history of that trait (e.g., is it shared by other species, or is it unique?) and a detailed reconstruction of the relevant environmental features that were instrumental in its construction (Foley, 1996).

It is not uncommon to hear the idea that changes wrought by "civilization" over the last 10,000 years have radically changed our adaptive landscape as a species. After all, back on the Pleistocene savanna there were no fast food outlets, plastic surgery, antibiotics, dating advertisements, jet airliners, and the like. Given such manifest changes in our environment and ways of living, one would expect much of human behavior to prove odd and maladaptive as psychological mechanisms that evolved in ancestral conditions struggle with the many new contingencies of the modern world. An assumption of evolutionary psychology, therefore, is that mismatches between modern environments and the EEA often result in dysfunctional behavior (such as overconsumption of chocolate ice cream, television soap operas, video games, and pornography). Real-life examples of this phenomenon are easy to find. Our color constancy mechanisms, for instance, evolved under conditions of natural sunlight. These mechanisms fail, however, under some artificial lighting conditions (Shepard, 1992). Similarly, the dopamine-mediated reward mechanisms found in the mesolimbic system in the brain evolved to provide a pleasurable reward in the presence of adaptively relevant stimuli like food or sex. In contemporary environments, however, these same mechanisms are subverted by the use of psychoactive drugs such as cocaine and amphetamines, which deliver huge dollops of pleasurable reward in the absence of the adaptively relevant stimuli—often to the users' detriment (Nesse & Berridge, 1997).

Although we can detail many ways in which contemporary and ancestral environments differ, much probably also remains the same. Humans everywhere, for example, still find and attract mates, have sex, raise families, make friends, have extramarital affairs, compete for status, consume certain kinds of food, spend time with kin, gossip, and so forth (Crawford, 1998). Indeed, Crawford (1998) argues that we should accept as our null hypothesis that current and ancestral environments do *not* differ in important and relevant respects for any given adaptation. Most important is that current and ancestral environments do not have to be identical in every respect for them to be the same in terms of the relevant details required for the normal development and expression of evolved psychological mechanisms. For example, the languages that people speak today are undoubtedly different from the ones our ancestors uttered some 100,000 years ago. However, what is necessary for the development of language is not the input of some specific language, but rather any kind of structured linguistic input. Adaptations have *reaction norms,* which are the range of environmental parameters in which they develop and function normally. For most adaptations, these norms may well encompass both current and ancestral environments (Crawford, 1998).

To summarize, in this section we have outlined three special metatheoretical assumptions that evolutionary psychologists use in applying inclusive fitness theory to human cognition and behavior. First, the appropriate unit of analysis is typically considered to be at the level of evolved psychological mechanisms, which underlie behavioral output. Second, evolutionary psychologists posit that these mechanisms are both large in number and constitute specialized information processing rules that were designed by natural selection to solve specific adaptive problems encountered during human evolutionary history. Finally, these mechanisms have evolved in ancestral conditions and are characterized by specific EEAs, which may or may not differ in important respects from contemporary environments.

THE MIDDLE-LEVEL THEORY LEVEL OF ANALYSIS

The metatheoretical assumptions employed by evolutionary psychologists are surrounded by a protective belt, so to speak, of auxiliary theories, hypotheses, and predictions (see Buss, 1995; Ketelaar & Ellis, 2000). A primary function of the protective belt is to provide an empirically verifiable means of linking metatheoretical assumptions to observable data. In essence, the protective belt serves as the problem-solving machinery of the metatheoretical research program because it is used to provide indirect evidence in support of the metatheory's basic assumptions (Lakatos, 1970). The protective belt does more, however, than just protect the meta-theoretical assumptions: It uses these assumptions to extend our knowledge of particular domains. For example, a group of physicists who adopt a Newtonian metatheory may construct several competing middle-level theories concerning a particular physical system, but none of these theories would violate Newton's laws of mechanics. Each physicist designs his or her middle-level theory to be consistent with the basic assumptions of the metatheory, even if the middle-level theories are inconsistent with each other. Competing middle-level theories attempt to achieve the best operationalization of the core logic of the metatheory as it applies to a particular domain. The competing wave and particle theories of light (generated from quantum physics metatheory) are excellent contemporary exemplars of this process.

After a core set of metatheoretical assumptions become established among a community of scientists, the day-to-day workings of these scientists are generally characterized by the *use of*—not the *testing of*—these assumptions. Metatheoretical assumptions are used to construct plausible alternative middle-level theories. After empirical evidence has been gathered, one of the alternatives may emerge as the best available explanation of phenomena in that domain. It is this process of constructing and evaluating middle-level theories that characterizes the typical activities of scientists attempting to use a metatheory to integrate, unify, and connect their varying lines of research (Ketelaar & Ellis, 2000).

Middle-level evolutionary theories are specific theoretical models that provide a link between the broad metatheoretical assumptions used by evolutionary psychologists and the specific hypotheses and predictions that are tested in research. Middle-level evolutionary theories are consistent with and guided by evolutionary metatheory but in most cases cannot be directly deduced from it (Buss, 1995). Middle-level theories elaborate the basic assumptions of the metatheory into a particular psychological domain. For example, parental investment theory (Trivers, 1972) applies evolutionary metatheory to the question of why, when, for what traits, and to what degree selection favors *differences between the sexes* in reproductive strategies. Conversely, attachment theory (Bowlby, 1969; Simpson, 1999), life history theory (e.g., Chisholm, 1999), and good genes sexual selection theory (e.g., Gangestad & Simpson, 2000) each in different ways applies evolutionary metatheory to the question of why, when, for what traits, and to what degree selection favors *differences within each sex* in reproductive strategies. In this section we review parental investment theory and good genes sexual selection theory as exemplars of middle-level evolutionary theories.

Parental Investment Theory

Imagine that a man and a woman each had sexual intercourse with 100 different partners over the course of a year. The man could potentially sire 100 children, whereas the woman could potentially give birth to one or two. This huge discrepancy in the number of offspring that men and women can potentially produce reflects fundamental differences between the sexes in the costs of reproduction. Sperm, the sex cells that men produce, are small, cheap, and plentiful. Millions of sperm are produced in each ejaculate, and one act of sexual intercourse (in principle) is the minimum reproductive effort needed by a man to sire a child. By contrast, eggs, the sex cells that women produce, are large, expensive, and limited in number. Most critical is that one act of sexual intercourse *plus* 9 months gestation, potentially dangerous childbirth, and (in traditional societies) years of nursing and carrying a child are the minimum amount of reproductive effort required by a woman to successfully reproduce. These differences in what Trivers (1972) has termed *parental investment* have wide-ranging ramifications for the evolution of sex differences in body, mind, and behavior. Moreover, these differences hold true not only for humans but also for all mammalian species.

Trivers (1972) defined parental investment as "any investment by the parent in an individual offspring's chance of surviving (and hence reproductive success) at the cost of the parent's ability to invest in other offspring" (p. 139). Usually, but not always, the sex with the greater parental investment is the female. These differences in investment are manifest in various ways, from basic asymmetries in the size of male and female sex cells (a phenomenon known as *anisogamy*) through to differences in the propensity to rear offspring. For most viviparous species (who bear live offspring), females also shoulder the burden of gestation—and in mammals, lactation and suckling. In terms of parental investment, the sex that invests the most becomes a *limiting resource* for the other, less investing sex (Trivers, 1972). Members of the sex that invests less, therefore, should compete among themselves for breeding access to the other, more investing sex. Because males of many species contribute little more than sperm to subsequent offspring, their reproductive success is primarily constrained by the number of fertile females that they can inseminate. Females, by contrast, are constrained by

the number of eggs that they can produce and (in species with parental care) the number of viable offspring that can be raised. Selection favors males in these species who compete successfully with other males or who have qualities preferred by females that increase their mating opportunities. Conversely, selection favors females who choose mates who have good genes and (in paternally investing species) are likely to provide external resources such as food or protection to the female and her offspring (Trivers, 1972).

Parental investment theory, in combination with the metatheoretical assumptions of natural and sexual selection, generates an array of hypotheses and specific predictions about sex differences in mating and parental behavior. According to parental investment theory, the sex that invests more in offspring should be more careful and discriminating in mate selection, should be less willing to engage in opportune mating, and should be less inclined to seek multiple sexual partners. By contrast, the sex investing less in offspring should be less choosy about whom they mate with, compete more strongly among themselves for mating opportunities (i.e., take more risks and be more aggressive in pursuing sexual contacts), and be more inclined to seek multiple mating opportunities. The magnitude of these sex differences should depend on the magnitude of differences between males and females in parental investment during a species' evolutionary history. In species in which males only contribute their sperm to offspring, males should be much more aggressive than should females in pursuing sexual contacts with multiple partners, and females should be much choosier than should males in accepting or rejecting mating opportunities. In contrast, in species such as humans in which both males and females typically make high levels of investment in offspring, sex differences in mating competition and behavior should be more muted. Nonetheless, the sex differences predicted by parental investment theory are well documented in humans as well as in many other animals. In humans, for example, men are more likely than are women to pursue casual mating opportunities and multiple sex partners, men tend to have less rigid standards than women do for selecting mates, and men tend to engage in more extreme intrasexual competition than women do (Buss, 1994; Daly & Wilson, 1988; Ellis & Symons, 1990; Symons, 1979).

Among mammalian species, human males are unusual insofar as they contribute nonnegligible amounts of investment to offspring. Geary (2000), in a review of the evolution and proximate expression of human paternal investment, has proposed that (a) over human evolutionary history fathers' investment in families tended to improve but was not essential to the survival and reproductive success of children and (b) selection consequently favored a mixed paternal strategy, with different men varying in the extent to which they allocated resources to care and provisioning of children. Under these conditions, selection should favor psychological mechanisms in females that are especially attuned to variation in potential for paternal investment. This hypothesis has been supported by much experimental and cross-cultural data showing that when they select mates, women tend to place relatively strong emphasis on indicators of a man's willingness and ability to provide parental investment (e.g., Buss, 1989; Ellis, 1992; Symons, 1979). These studies have typically investigated such indicators as high status, resource-accruing potential, and dispositions toward commitment and cooperation.

The other side of the coin is that men who invest substantially in offspring at the expense of future mating opportunities should also be choosy about selecting mates. Men who provide high-quality parental investment (i.e., who provide valuable economic and nutritional resources; who offer physical protection; who engage in direct parenting activities such as teaching, nurturing, and providing social support and opportunities) are themselves a scarce resource for which women compete. Consequently, high-investing men should be as careful and discriminating as women are about entering long-term reproductive relationships. Along these lines, Kenrick, Sadalla, Groth, and Trost (1990) investigated men's and women's minimum standards for selecting both short-term and long-term mates. Consistent with many other studies (e.g., Buss & Schmitt, 1993; Symons & Ellis, 1989), men were found to have minimum standards lower than those of women for short-term sexual relationships (e.g., one-night stands); however, men elevated their standards to levels comparable to those of women when choosing long-term mates (Kenrick et al., 1990).

Mate Retention Strategies

In species with internal fertilization (all mammals, birds, reptiles, and many fish and insects), males cannot identify their offspring with certainty. In such species, males who invest paternally run the risk of devoting time and energy to offspring who are not their own. Thus, male parental investment should only evolve as a reproductive strategy when fathers have reasonably high confidence of paternity—that is, males should be selected to be high-investing fathers only to offspring who share their genes. When male parental investment does evolve, selection should concomitantly favor the evolution of male strategies designed to reduce the chance of diverting parental effort toward unrelated young (Daly, Wilson, & Weghorst, 1982; Symons, 1979). Mate retention strategies (including anatomical and behavioral adaptations) are favored

by sexual selection in paternally investing species because they increase the probability that subsequent investment made by fathers in offspring contributes to their own fitness and not to that of other males.

A fascinating array of mate retention strategies has been documented in many animal species. Male damselflies, for example, possess a dual-function penis that has special barbs that enables them to remove any sperm from prior matings before inseminating the female themselves. Furthermore, male damselflies remain physically attached to the female after mating until she has laid her eggs, thus ensuring that other males cannot fertilize them. In many species of birds with biparental care, males adjust their subsequent paternal investment (e.g., feeding of nestlings) depending on their degree of paternity certainty as determined by such factors as time spent with the mate and degree of extrapair matings in which she has engaged. The greater the likelihood that the offspring he is raising is *not* his own, the less investment is offered (e.g., Moller, 1994; Moller & Thornhill, 1998; but see Kempenaers, Lanctot, & Robertson, 1998). Sexual jealousy in humans has also been proposed as an evolved motivational system that underlies mate retention behaviors and functions to reduce the probability of relationship defection and to increase certainty of paternity in males (Buss, 2000; Daly et al., 1982). Daly et al. (1982) suggest that in men, pervasive mate retention strategies include "the emotion of sexual jealousy, the dogged inclination of men to possess and control women, and the use or threat of violence to achieve sexual exclusivity and control" (p. 11).

Females, of course, are not passive spectators to these male manipulations, but have evolved a host of strategies themselves to advance their own inclusive fitness. In many species females may try to extract investment from males through various means such as withholding sex until resources are provided, obscuring the time that they are fertile to encourage prolonged male attention, and preventing males from investing resources in multiple females. Furthermore, in some circumstances it may benefit females to extract material resources from one male while pursuing extrapair matings with other males who may be of superior genetic quality (see early discussion of the function of female orgasm; see also Buss, 1994; Greiling & Buss, 2000; for birds, see Moller & Thornhill, 1998; Petrie & Kempenaers, 1998).

Although the general pattern of greater female parental investment and less male parental investment is most common, a variety of species exhibit the opposite arrangement. For example, in a bird species called the red-necked phalarope, it is the male who takes on the burden of parental investment, both incubating and feeding subsequent offspring. As predicted by parental investment theory, it is the female in this species who is physically larger, who competes with other females for reproductive opportunities, and who more readily pursues and engages in multiple matings. In addition, levels of parental investment may vary *within* a species over time, with corresponding changes in mating behavior. For example, in katydids or bush crickets, males contribute to offspring by offering mating females highly nutritious sperm packages called spermatophores. When food resources are abundant, males can readily produce these spermatophores. Under these conditions, males compete with each other for mating access to females and readily pursue multiple mating opportunities. When food resources are scarce, however, spermatophores are costly to produce. Under these conditions, it is the females who compete with each other for mating access to males with the valued spermatophores, and it is females who more readily engage in multiple matings (see Andersson, 1994, pp. 100–103). These examples of so-called *sex-role reversed species* illustrate that sex differences do not arise from biological sex per se; rather, they arise from differences between the sexes in parental investment.

Parental investment theory is one of the most important middle-level theories that guides research into many aspects of human and animal behavior. Both the nature and the magnitude of sex differences in mating and parental behaviors can be explained by considering differences between the sexes in parental investment over a species' evolutionary history. A host of general hypotheses and specific predictions have been derived from considering the dynamics of parental investment and sexual selection, and much empirical evidence in both humans and other animals has been garnered in support of these hypotheses and predictions. Parental investment theory is one of the real triumphs of evolutionary biology and psychology and gives support to a host of important metatheoretical assumptions.

Good Genes Sexual Selection Theory

In order to adequately characterize the evolution of reproductive strategies, one must consider parental investment theory in conjunction with other middle-level theories of sexual selection. In this section we provide a detailed overview of good genes sexual selection theory, as well as briefly summarize the three other main theories of sexual selection (via direct phenotypic benefits, runaway processes, and sensory bias).

The male long-tailed widowbird, as its name suggests, has an extraordinarily elongated tail. Although the body of this East African bird is comparable in size to that of a sparrow, the male's tail feathers stretch to a length of up to 1.5 meters during the mating season. These lengthy tail feathers do little to enhance the male widowbird's survival prospects: They do not aid in flight, foraging, or defense from predators. Indeed, having to haul around such a tail is likely to reduce survival prospects through increased metabolic expenditure, attraction of predators, and the like. The question that has to be asked of the male widowbird's tail is how it could possibly have evolved. The short answer is that female widow birds *prefer* males with such exaggerated traits—that is, the male widowbird's extraordinary tail has evolved by the process of *sexual selection*. That such a female preference for long tails exists was confirmed in an ingenious manipulation experiment carried out by Malte Andersson (1982). In this study, some males had their tail feathers experimentally reduced while others had their tails enhanced. The number of nests in the territories of the males with the supernormal tails significantly exceeded the number of nests in the territories of those males whose tails had been shortened. Clearly female widowbirds preferred to mate with males who possess the superlong tails.

To explain *why* the female widowbird's preference for long tails has evolved, we need to consider the various mechanisms and theories of sexual selection. The two main mechanisms of sexual selection that have been identified are mate choice (usually, but not always, by females) and contests (usually, but not always, between males). The male widowbird's elongated tail is an example of a trait that has apparently evolved via female choice. The 2.5-m tusk of the male narwhal, by contrast, is a trait that appears to have evolved in the context of male-male competition. Other, less studied mechanisms of sexual selection include scrambles for mates, sexual coercion, endurance rivalry, and sperm competition (Andersson, 1994; Andersson & Iwasa, 1996). In his exhaustive review of sexual selection in over 180 species, Andersson (1994) documents evidence of female choice in 167 studies, male choice in 30 studies, male competition in 58 studies, and other mechanisms in 15 studies. Sexual selection, as illustrated in a recent book by Geoffrey Miller (2000), has also been proposed as an important mechanism for fashioning many traits in our own species, including such characteristics as music, art, language, and humor.

Four main theories about how sexual selection operates have been advanced: via good genes, direct phenotypic benefits, runaway processes, and sensory bias. These different theories, however, are not necessarily mutually exclusive and may be used together to explain the evolution of sexually selected traits. The core idea of *good genes sexual selection* is that the outcome of mate choice and intrasexual competition will be determined by traits that indicate high genetic viability (Andersson, 1994; Williams, 1966). Males (and, to a lesser extent, females) of many bird species, for example, possess a bewildering variety of ornaments in the form of wattles, plumes, tufts, combs, inflatable pouches, elongated tail feathers, and the like. Moreover, many male birds are often splendidly attired in a dazzling array of colors: iridescent blues, greens, reds, and yellows. Keeping such elaborate visual ornamentation in good condition is no easy task. It requires time, effort, and—critically—good health to maintain. Females who consistently choose the brightest, most ornamented males are likely to be choosing mates who are in the best condition, which reflects the males' underlying genetic quality. Even if females receive nothing more than sperm from their mates, they are likely to have healthier, more viable, and more attractive offspring if they mate with the best quality males. According to Hamilton and Zuk (1982), bright plumage and elaborate secondary sexual characteristics, such as the male peacock's resplendent tail, are accurate indicators of the relative parasite loads of different males. A heavy parasite load signals a less viable immune system and is reflected in the condition of such traits as long tail feathers and bright plumage.

Many secondary sexual characteristics therefore act as *indicators* of genetic quality. Moreover, according to the *handicap principle* developed by Amotz Zahavi (1975; Zahavi & Zahavi, 1997), such traits must be costly to produce if they are to act as reliable indicators of genetic worth. If a trait is not expensive to produce, then it cannot serve as the basis for good genes sexual selection because it will not accurately reflect the condition of its owner. However, if the trait relies on substantial investment of metabolic resources to develop—as does the male widowbird's tail—then only those individuals in the best condition will be able to produce the largest or brightest ornament. In this case, expression of the trait will accurately reflect underlying condition.

In a slightly different take on the handicap principle, Folstad and Karter (1992) have suggested that in males, high levels of testosterone, which are necessary for the expression of secondary sexual characteristics (those sex-linked traits that are the product of sexual selection), also have harmful effects on the immune system. According to this *immunocompetence handicap* model, only the fittest males will be able to develop robust secondary sexual characteristics, which accurately indicate both high levels of testosterone and a competent immune system—and therefore high genetic quality. These general hypotheses were supported in a recent meta-analysis of studies on parasite-mediated sexual selection. This meta-analysis demonstrated a strong negative relationship between parasite load and the expression of male secondary sexual characteristics. In total, the most extravagantly ornamented individuals are also the healthiest ones—and thus the most preferred as mates (Moller, Christie, & Lux, 1999). Of course in species in which there is substantial paternal investment (including humans), males will also be choosy about whom they mate with and will also select mates with indicators of high genetic fitness. In many bird species, for example, both males *and* females are brightly colored or engage in complex courtship dances. Thus, relative levels of parental investment by males and females substantially influence the dynamics of good genes sexual selection.

Genes, of course, are not the only resources that are transferred from one mate to another in sexually reproducing species. Although the male long-tailed widowbird contributes nothing but his sperm to future offspring, in many species parental investment by both sexes can be substantial. It benefits each sex, therefore, to attend to the various resources that mates contribute to subsequent offspring; thus, one of the driving forces behind sexual selection is the *direct phenotypic benefits* that can be obtained from mates and mating. These benefits encompass many levels and types of investment—from the small nuptial gifts offered by many male insect species to the long-term care and provisioning of offspring.

Homo sapiens is a species commonly characterized by long-term pair-bonding and biparental care of offspring. Therefore, in addition to traits that indicate the presence of good genes, both males and females should be attentive to characteristics that signal the ability and willingness of potential mates to devote time and external resources to future offspring. As has been demonstrated in many studies of human mate preferences (see Buss, 1994), both males and females rate kindness and warmth as the most important attributes in long-term mates. A partner with the personality traits of kindness, honesty, and warmth is someone who is both more likely to remain in a long-term relationship and who will invest time and resources in future offspring. Women (more so than men) also rate the presence of status and resource-accruing potential as important attributes in potential mates (Buss, 1989), suggesting that males with the ability to contribute external resources to future offspring are favored.

It is important to note that some characteristics may be indicative of both good genes *and* the ability to offer direct phenotypic benefits; thus, these two different theories of sexual selection are not necessarily incompatible. For example, a male bird with bright, glossy plumage may be preferred as a mate not only because of his high genetic quality, but also because he is less likely to transmit parasites to prospective sexual partners. However, compatibility between good genes and direct benefits is often not apparent, and it is expected that the relative importance of these two mate selection criteria will vary on a species-by-species basis. We also expect variation to occur *within* species in the relative weighting of good genes versus direct phenotypic benefits in mate selection (Gangestad & Simpson, 2000; Gross, 1996). For example, Gangestad and Simpson (2000) have argued that human females make trade-offs between males with traits indicating good genes and males with traits signaling high likelihood of paternal investment. Some women at some times pursue a relatively unrestricted strategy of engaging in short-term sexual relationships with partners who may be high in genetic quality, whereas other women may adopt a more restricted strategy of selecting long-term partners who are likely to offer substantial paternal investment. The prevalence of extrapair mating in humans suggests that both strategies may be pursued simultaneously: Resources may be extracted from one high-investing male while extrapair matings are pursued with other males who display indicators of high genetic quality (see earlier discussion of the function of female orgasm). Men also must make trade-offs between seeking multiple sexual partners and investing substantially in only one or a few mates. Which strategies are chosen is determined in part by such factors as father absence, individual differences in mate value, and availability of mates (e.g., Draper & Harpending, 1982; Gangestad & Simpson, 2000; Kirkpatrick & Ellis, 2001).

So far we have discussed good genes and direct phenotypic benefits as ways of understanding the dynamics of sexual selection. Two other processes have also been suggested that can account for the evolution of sexually selected traits. The first of these theories—*runaway sexual selection* (Fisher, 1958)—states that preferences and traits coevolve through a feedback process that can lead to the rapid evolution of specific traits for essentially arbitrary reasons. For example, consider that females of given lizard species have a preference for males with an enlarged and elaborate head crest. This preference may have evolved initially because such males may have greater genetic viability (i.e., good genes) or because of some innate sensory bias (discussed further later in this chapter). Males with the enlarged crests will become more prevalent in the population and the female preference for the trait will also become more widespread. Males with large crests increase their inclusive fitness by enhanced mating opportunities and females advance their inclusive fitness because they are more likely to have male offspring with the enlarged crest, who will in turn be more likely to succeed in mating contexts. After the preference is in place, however, the elaborate crest may become decoupled from any indicator of health or fitness and simply spread because of the preference per se. The male crest will increase in size as the trait and the preference for the trait coevolve until the crest becomes so large and elaborate that it undermines survival.

Unlike good genes sexual selection, empirical evidence for the runaway process (in its pure form) is fairly sparse. However, Eberhard (1985, 1993) has suggested that the evolution of male genitalia may prove an instructive example of

runaway sexual selection in action. As documented in Eberhard's fascinating book, *Sexual Selection and Animal Genitalia,* male genitalia come in a bewildering variety of shapes and sizes—they are often decorated with knobs, spines, hooks, and flanges that are seemingly unrelated to the utilitarian task of sperm transfer. Eberhard (1993) argues that it is *un*likely that variations in penis morphology are useful indicators of the ability to resist parasites or of general male vigor (i.e., they are probably not reliable markers of good genes). It seems plausible instead to suggest that female preferences, due initially to biases towards certain kinds of tactile stimulation, have coevolved with genitalia morphology in classic runaway fashion, leading to the seemingly arbitrary array of genitalia structures found in the animal world.

A key aspect of the runaway process is that traits that are preferred are arbitrarily related to fitness in the sense that such traits do not indicate genetic viability (as is the case with good genes models). However, the runaway process has to begin with a preference that is usually based on actual viability or is the result of sensory bias. The *sensory bias* model of sexual selection involves the evolution of traits via sexual selection due to preferences resulting from sensory orientations that are the product of other selective processes (Ryan & Keddy-Hector, 1992). Whereas in good genes and runaway sexual selection, preferences and traits coevolve, the sensory bias theory requires the *prior* origin of preferences and the *latter* evolution of traits that exploit those preferences. The evolution of male calls of the Tungara frog appears to be explained by this sensory-bias model of sexual selection. Females prefer male frogs with low-frequency calls. Neurophysiological evidence indicates that the auditory system of female frogs is tuned in a way that is biased toward the low-frequency component of these calls. Because bigger male frogs produce lower-frequency calls, a good genes model of sexual selection may seem indicated. However, Ryan and Rand (1990) argue that because closely related frog species also demonstrate this female bias in the *absence* of male calling, the male trait arose to exploit the preexisting sensory bias of the females, which itself has arisen as the result of other selective forces.

Good genes sexual selection is another important middle-level theory that has proven valuable in generating a number of interesting and testable hypotheses about both human and nonhuman animal behavior. As we have discussed, good genes sexual selection theory is one of a number of alternative (although often compatible) middle-level theories of sexual selection. Making predictions that distinguish between these different middle-level applications of sexual selection metatheory can sometimes be difficult. However, as reviewed in the next section, good genes sexual selection theory (often in conjunction with parental investment theory) enables us to derive a number of general hypotheses and specific predictions that can be empirically tested.

THE HYPOTHESES LEVEL OF ANALYSIS

At the next level down in the hierarchy of explanation are the actual hypotheses drawn from middle-level evolutionary theories (see Figure 1.1). As noted earlier, a hypothesis is a general statement about the state of the world that one would expect to observe if the theory from which it was generated were in fact true. An array of hypotheses can often be derived from a single middle-level theory. These hypotheses can be considered to vary along a continuum of confidence (Ellis & Symons, 1990). At the top of the continuum are so-called firm hypotheses (such as the relation between relative parental investment and intrasexual competition for mating opportunities) that are clear and unambiguous derivations from an established middle-level evolutionary theory. As one moves down the continuum, however, firm hypotheses give way to more typical formulations—hypotheses that are inferred from a middle-level theory but not directly derived from it. This distinction can be illustrated by considering the issue of paternity uncertainty. The supposition that in species characterized by both internal female fertilization and substantial male parental investment, selection will favor the evolution of male mechanisms for reducing the probability of expending that investment on unrelated young is a firm hypothesis that can be directly derived from the theory. What form these mechanisms will take, however, cannot be directly derived from the theory because natural and sexual selection underdetermine specific evolutionary paths. Selection could favor the evolution of sexual jealousy, or it could favor the evolution of sperm plugs to block the cervix of female sexual partners following copulation (see earlier discussion of mate retention strategies). Given the universal occurrence of jealousy in humans (Daly et al., 1982), evolutionary psychologists have hypothesized that men's jealousy should be centrally triggered by cues to sexual infidelity, whereas women's jealousy should be centrally triggered by cues to loss of commitment and investment. This hypothesis is reasonably inferred from the theory but cannot be directly deduced from it. We refer to this type of hypothesis as an *expectation*. This hypothesis was originally proposed by Daly et al. (1982) and has since received considerable empirical support (Buss, Larsen, Westen, & Semmelroth, 1992; Buunk, Angleitner, Oubaid, & Buss, 1996; DeSteno & Salovey, 1996; Wiederman & Allgeier, 1993).

As one moves farther down the continuum of confidence into the area where inferences from middle-level theories are drawn farther from their core, expectations grade insensibly into interesting questions or hunches. At this level, different interpretations of the theory can and do generate different hypotheses. For example, Buss and Shackelford (1997) have proposed two competing evolutionary hypotheses concerning the effects of unequal attractiveness between romantic partners on women's mate retention behavior. The first hypothesis suggests that individuals (both women and men) married to others who are perceived as more attractive than the self will devote *more* effort to mate retention than will individuals married to others who are perceived as equally or less attractive than the self. The logic behind this hypothesis is that individuals who are married to relatively attractive partners are at greater risk of losing them. The second hypothesis suggests the opposite, but only for females: Women married to men who are perceived as more attractive than the self will relax their mate retention efforts. The logic behind this hypothesis focuses on the greater ability of men to fractionate their reproductive investment among multiple partners. For example, a man can simultaneously beget and raise children with three different women (a phenomenon that is quite common in polygynous societies), whereas it would take a woman several years to bear and raise children with three different men. Because of the male ability to partition investment, women may face the trade-off of obtaining a fraction of the attention and resources of a highly attractive male or the full attention and resources of a less attractive male. Buss and Shackelford (1997) suggest that women in unevenly matched marriages might devote *less* effort to mate retention, an implicit acknowledgment of the potential costs involved in trying to prevent the more attractive partner from devoting some of his resources to outside relationships.

Although this type of theorizing is admittedly speculative, it is inevitable at the lower end of the continuum of confidence—in domains where there is not strong middle-level theoretical development and about which relatively little is known. Studies designed to test these hypotheses often have an exploratory quality. The data obtained from testing such hypotheses, however, can work their way back up the explanatory hierarchy to enable the development of more rigorous theoretical models (Ketelaar & Ellis, 2000). In the following section, we review hypotheses derived from good genes sexual selection theory. We number these hypotheses and note whether (in our opinion) they are firm hypotheses, expectations, or hunches.

Good Genes Sexual Selection Theory: Hypotheses

The principles of good genes sexual selection theory in combination with parental investment theory have been used to generate a number of interesting hypotheses in a variety of species, including humans. In the following discussion we use the term *females* to refer to the sex that invests more in offspring and *males* to refer to the sex that invests less in offspring. We recognize, of course, that these sex roles are sometimes reversed.

For a given trait to be a *reliable* indicator of genetic value, it must be costly to produce. According to the handicap principle (Zahavi & Zahavi, 1997), traits that indicate good genes can only be maintained by individuals who are the fittest in the population, as indicated by their ability to maintain steady growth rates, resist parasites, compete successfully in intrasexual contests, and so forth. Consequently, good genes indicators that are preferred by members of the opposite sex should require substantial metabolic resources to develop and maintain. It follows, therefore, that individuals who more fully display traits indicative of high genetic quality should be healthier and in better condition than should conspecifics who display these traits less fully (H1; firm hypothesis). An implication of this hypothesis is that individuals with elaborate secondary sexual characteristics should have lower levels of parasitic infection. Further, traits indicative of good genes can only be developed to their fullest potential in individuals with robust immune systems that are able to overcome the immunosuppressant effects of sex hormones such as testosterone (see earlier discussion of immunocompetence handicap theory; Folstad & Karter, 1992). Expression of traits indicative of good genes, therefore, should be positively related to effective immune system functioning.

Evidence that sexually selected traits can increase reproductive success while reducing survival prospects (i.e., handicap traits) has accumulated in a number of species, including the European barn swallow. The male barn swallow is adorned with elongated tail feathers. Males with longer tail feathers are preferred by females and sire more offspring (Moller, 1994). However, males with such long tails are less efficient at foraging and are more likely to suffer predation by birds of prey (Moller et al., 1998). Thus, female preference for males with elongated tail feathers appears to reflect good genes sexual selection in action. A recent meta-analysis of studies assessing parasite load, immune function, and the expression of secondary sexual characteristics in a diverse array of species has found that the fullest expression of sexually selected traits is positively related to immune system functioning and negatively related to parasite load (Moller et al., 1999)—that is, the brightest, largest, most ornamented individuals are also the ones with the smaller number of parasites and the most robust immune systems.

An important factor influencing the intensity of good genes sexual selection is variance in reproductive success. Two principles are relevant here. First, there tends to be greater *variance* in male than in female reproductive success;

this is because males are more able to distribute their sex cells across multiple partners. Indeed, the ability of males to inseminate a large number of females often results in a sexual lottery in which some males win big while others lose out entirely. For example, in one study of elephant seals, a total of only eight males were found to be responsible for inseminating 348 females (Le Boeuf & Reiter, 1988). Second, because of this disparity, sexual selection tends to act more strongly on males than on females in shaping intrasexual competitive abilities and producing specialized fitness signals for attracting the opposite sex (Trivers, 1972; see also Cronin, 1991).

A core premise of good genes sexual selection is that certain traits have evolved because they are reliable indicators of genetic quality—that is, these traits reliably signal viability and good condition that can be passed on to offspring through genetic inheritance. All else being equal, individuals that possess such traits should be preferred as mates (H2; firm hypothesis), be more successful in intrasexual contests (H3; firm hypothesis), or both. Parental investment theory further suggests that males will be more likely than females to possess and display indicators of genetic quality (H4; expectation), whereas females will be more likely than males to select mates on the basis of these indicators (H5; expectation). In total, then, males that possess and display indicators of genetic quality should have more sexual partners and more offspring (H6; firm hypothesis). For example, among mandrills, a primate that inhabits the rainforests of West Africa, males who possess the brightest red and blue pigmentation on the face, rump, and genitals (which presumably are indicators of good genes) are more often preferred as mates by females. Further, DNA analysis has shown that they are also more likely than their less chromatically exuberant counterparts to sire offspring (Dixson, Bossi, & Wickings, 1993).

In species in which females engage in nonreproductive, situation-dependent sexual activity (rather than strictly cyclical sexual activity), females' preferences for males who display indicators of high genetic quality should vary as a function of their phase of the reproductive cycle. Around the time of ovulation, when females are most fertile, they should express the strongest preference for males with good genes. At other times in the reproductive cycle, when females are not ovulating, this preference should be more muted (H7; expectation). Humans are the clearest example of a primate that engages in sexual activity throughout the reproductive cycle. Other primates tend to be more seasonal and cyclical in their breeding activities than humans are, although not exclusively so (see Hrdy, 1981).

We earlier discussed the selective sperm retention hypothesis for female orgasm, which suggests that females exert some control over the paternity of their offspring by differential patterns of orgasm with specific male partners. In species characterized by female orgasm, the frequency and timing of female orgasm should vary in a manner that selectively favors the sperm of males who display indicators of high genetic quality (H8; hunch).

Good genes sexual selection theory has been used to generate hypotheses about mating effort, parental effort, and trade-offs between them. There are essentially three strategies that individuals can use to increase their reproductive success: (a) Increase the fitness of their offspring by mating with individuals of high genetic quality, (b) increase the fitness of their offspring by enhancing parental investment (by one or both parents), or (c) increase the number of offspring produced. No one strategy is inherently better than any other, and the pursuit of one strategy usually involves trade-offs with the others (see Gangestad & Simpson, 2000). For example, individuals who produce a greater number of offspring (c) tend to have lower fitness of offspring.

Consistent with (a), females can increase their reproductive success by preferentially investing in offspring that are sired by males of high genetic quality. Thus, among females there should be a positive correlation between levels of parental investment in offspring and the genetic quality of the offspring's father (H9; expectation). Peahens, for example, have been found to lay more eggs for peacocks with larger trains and more elaborate tails (Petrie & Williams, 1993).

In species characterized by long-term pair-bonding and biparental care of offspring, but in which individuals sometimes engage in short-term and extrapair mating, there should be a negative correlation between the genetic quality of males and levels of parental investment by males in offspring (H10; expectation). There are two bases for this hypothesis. First, males who possess reliable indicators of high genetic quality can afford to put less direct effort into offspring; this is because they make more valuable genetic contributions to offspring, and thus their female partners may be willing to tolerate less parental investment—devaluing (b)—in return for their good genes—enhancing (a). Second, diverting effort away from parental investment toward extrapair matings should yield greater payoffs for males of high genetic quality (because they are more popular on the mating market). Thus, males with good genes can be expected to devote proportionally more reproductive effort to mating (c) and less to parenting (b). A corollary of this hypothesis is that males who possess reliable indicators of good genes will engage in more short-term and extrapair mating (H11; expectation) and be more preferred by females as short-term and extrapair mates (H12; expectation).

Hypotheses 10–12 have been supported in an extensive series of studies on the European barn swallow. The barn swallow is small, migratory, insect-eating bird, which is characterized by pair-bonds that last the length of the breeding season and biparental care of offspring. Male and female birds are similar in many respects except that males have much longer tails than do females, which suggests that tail length is a sexually selected characteristic (Moller, 1994). Males with longer tail feathers not only tend to spend less time incubating and feeding offspring (Moller, 1994), but also are more preferred by females as primary mates, engage in more extrapair mating, and sire more extrapair offspring than do males with shorter tails (Moller & Tegelstrom, 1997). These data suggest that (a) females are willing to trade off parental investment for good genes in their primary pair-bonds and (b) females pursue extrapair copulations with males who possess indicators of good genes. We find it interesting that the probability of females' pursuing extrapair copulations decreases as a function of the length of the tail feathers of their primary mate (Moller, 1994), suggesting females who are already receiving high-quality genetic benefits have less motivation for extrapair mating.

In sum, hypotheses derived from good genes sexual selection theory can explain the origins of a wide variety of physical and behavioral traits across a diversity of animal species, from humans to scorpion flies. The specific ways in which these hypotheses are played out, however, depends on the nature of the species being studied. Humans and barn swallows, for example, both engage in medium- to long-term pair-bonding, both have greater female parental investment, and both are characterized by relatively frequent extrapair mating. We would expect, therefore, that females in both species will preferentially seek extrapair sex partners who possess indicators of good genes. However, specific markers of good genes vary across species. Human males do not possess elongated tail feathers, bright spots on their rump, or bright red faces. Thus, although the general hypotheses derived from good genes sexual selection theory have wide applicability, the detailed predictions derived from these hypotheses depend on the species under consideration. In the next section we describe specific predictions as they apply to human mating.

THE PREDICTION LEVEL OF ANALYSIS

Because hypotheses are often too general to be tested directly, it is at the next level of explanation—the level of specific predictions—where the battles between competing theoretical models are often played out. *Predictions* correspond to specific statements about the state of the world that one would expect to observe if the hypothesis were in fact true. They represent explicit, testable instantiations of hypotheses. One might argue that predictions form the substance of any theory, for here is where most of the action takes place as specific predictions are either supported or refuted.

The performance of evolution-based predictions provides the basis for evaluating the more general hypotheses from which they are drawn. For example, a number of specific predictions have been derived from the evolutionary hypothesis that men (more than women) will be intensely concerned about the sexual fidelity of reproductive-aged partners. Some of these predictions include (a) sexual infidelity by wives will be a more frequent cause of divorce than will sexual infidelity by husbands (Betzig, 1989); (b) the use or threat of violence by husbands to achieve sexual exclusivity and control of wives will vary as a function of wives' reproductive value, which peaks in the late teens and declines monotonically thereafter (M. Wilson & Daly, 1996); and (c) in the context of competing for romantic partners, the tactic of spreading rumors that a same-sex rival is sexually promiscuous will be more effective when performed by women than by men (because it raises the specter of cuckoldry; see Buss & Dedden, 1990). The fact that the first two predictions have been supported by extensive cross-cultural data whereas the third prediction has not been supported factors into one's evaluation of the more general hypothesis from which these predictions were generated. That two of the three predictions garnered strong support provides indirect support for the hypothesis. That the third prediction was rejected raises questions about the hypothesis. Ultimately, the value of the more general hypothesis and theoretical model is judged by the cumulative weight of the evidence (Ketelaar & Ellis, 2000).

Good Genes Sexual Selection Theory: Predictions

A number of specific, testable predictions can be derived from the hypotheses generated by good genes sexual selection theory. Although predictions can be made about the characteristics of a wide array of animal species, we focus in this section on a discussion of predictions pertaining specifically to humans. We consider the hypotheses outlined in the preceding section ("The Hypothesis Level of Analysis") and derive predictions relating specifically to human health and reproductive behavior. For each prediction we also review studies, where relevant, that have been carried out to test these specific predictions.

Before we examine these predictions in detail, it is worth considering just what traits in humans—like elongated tail feathers in male barn swallows—might be reliable indicators of good genes. One important marker of genetic quality that has emerged in research on a diverse array of species is a phenomenon known as *fluctuating asymmetry* (Moller &

Swaddle, 1997). Fluctuating asymmetry refers to small random deviations from perfect bilateral symmetry in different parts of the body. Higher levels of fluctuating asymmetry (i.e., more asymmetry) are believed to reflect developmental instability. This developmental imprecision can arise because of a range of factors, such as food deficiency, parasites, inbreeding, and exposure to toxic chemicals. Biologists have hypothesized that individuals with good genes are better able to buffer themselves against these genetic and environmental insults and thus tend to be more symmetrical. Because fluctuating asymmetry has a heritable component, mate preference for symmetrical, developmentally stable individuals can be expected to result in more viable offspring (see Moller & Swaddle, 1997). The specific predictions reviewed in this section focus on the relations between fluctuating asymmetry and both health and reproductive behavior.

1. More symmetrical individuals should have better mental and physical health, better immune system functioning, and lower parasite loads than should less symmetrical individuals (from H1). Although these predictions have only been tested in a small number of studies using human participants, initial results have been largely supportive. In studies of American undergraduates, levels of symmetry in both men and women have been found to positively correlate with psychometric intelligence (Furlow, Armijo-Prewitt, Gangestad, & Thornhill, 1997) and negatively correlate with measures of psychological, emotional, and physiological distress (Shackelford & Larsen, 1997). In addition, more symmetrical men have been found to have greater ejaculate size and better sperm quality (Manning, Scutt, & Lewis-Jones, 1998) and lower resting metabolic rates (Manning, Koukourakis, & Brodie, 1997) than have less symmetrical men. Perceived health has also been shown to be positively correlated with symmetry and averageness of male faces (Rhodes et al., 2001). Finally, in a study of men in rural Belize, the occurrence of life-threatening illnesses was found to be significantly higher in men who were less symmetrical (Waynforth, 1998). Taken together, these findings suggest that more symmetrical individuals, as predicted, tend to be healthier and in better physical and psychological condition than do their less symmetrical counterparts.

The remaining hypotheses (H2–H12) focus on the relations between markers of genetic fitness and reproductive behavior. Because of sex differences in parental investment, these hypotheses primarily concern *female preferences* for males who possess indicators of good genes and individual differences in *male mating behavior* as a function of genetic quality. An array of specific predictions have been derived from Hypotheses 2–12. As reviewed in the following discussion, empirical tests of these predictions have generated new lines of research that have substantially advanced our understanding of behavior in sexual and romantic relationships.

2. More symmetrical men should have more lifetime sexual partners (from H2–H6) and more extrapair sexual partners (from H10) than should less symmetrical men. These predictions have been tested in an initial series of studies on American undergraduates (reviewed in Gangestad & Simpson, 2000; Gangestad & Thornhill, 1997a). Symmetry was assessed by totaling right-left differences in seven bilateral traits (e.g., ankle girth, wrist girth). Consistent with the predictions, men who were more symmetrical were found to have more lifetime sexual partners (even after controlling for age and physical attractiveness) and more extrapair sexual encounters during ongoing relationships (even after controlling for relationship length, partners' extrapair sex, and both partners' physical attractiveness). In contrast, no consistent relation was found between women's symmetry and number of lifetime sexual partners or extrapair sexual relationships.

In ancestral environments, before the advent of reliable contraceptive methods, number of sexual partners can be expected to have been positively related to number of offspring. The finding that more symmetrical men in rural Belize both had more sexual partners and fathered more children lends support to this suggestion (Waynforth, 1998).

3. More symmetrical men should be more successful in intrasexual contests than should less symmetrical men (from H2, H4). This prediction has been tested both indirectly (by looking at the traits associated with fluctuating asymmetry) and directly (by examining behavior in experimental studies on mate competition). Men who are more symmetrical have been found to display higher levels of traits that are associated with success in intrasexual competition. Specifically, more symmetrical men tend to be bigger, to be more muscular and vigorous, to initiate more fights with other men, and to be more socially dominant than do less symmetrical men (reviewed in Gangestad & Simpson, 2000). Consistent with these correlational data, Simpson, Gangestad, Christensen, and Leck (1999) found that more symmetrical men competed more aggressively with other men for a lunch date with an attractive woman in a laboratory experiment. Each male participant was interviewed by the woman and then at the end of the interview was asked by the woman why she should choose him for the lunch date rather than the competitor (who was ostensibly in the next room). Compared with men who were less symmetrical, more symmetrical men tended to engage in competition with the rival, such as by directly comparing themselves with and belittling him. In total, the correlational and experimental data reviewed here suggest that more symmetrical men tend to display more costly traits,

such as large size and social and physical dominance, which facilitate success in direct intrasexual contests.

4. More symmetrical men should be preferred by women as short-term and extrapair sexual partners (from H11). Gangestad, Simpson, Cousins, and Christensen (1998) had women view videotapes of men being interviewed by an attractive woman (as described previously). The female participants then rated the male interviewee's attractiveness both as a potential long-term mate and as a short-term mate. A short-term mate was defined as either as a one-time sex partner or an extrapair sex partner. Women also completed a questionnaire that assessed their general *willingness* to have sex without commitment and emotional closeness. Women who reported more willingness to have sex without intimacy and commitment were categorized as being *inclined* toward short-term mating, whereas women who reported less willingness were categorized as being *disinclined* toward short-term mating. Among women who were inclined toward short-term mating, there was a significant positive correlation between the male interviewee's symmetry and the women's ratings of how attractive he was as a short-term mate (but not as a long-term mate). In contrast, among women who were disinclined toward short-term mating, male symmetry was uncorrelated with women's ratings of how attractive he was as either a short-term or a long-term mate. These data suggest that men who are more symmetrical are preferred as short-term mates specifically by women who are most inclined to engage in short-term mating. Moreover, Gangestad and Thornhill (1997b) found that male symmetry predicted the number of times that men were chosen by women as extrapair mates. Taken together, these data support the prediction that more symmetrical men should be more preferred by women as short-term and extrapair sexual partners.

5. Women's preferences for symmetrical men should be heightened around the time of ovulation when women are most fertile (from H7). This prediction has been supported in provocative new research on women's preference for the scent of symmetrical men as a function of variation in the menstrual cycle. This research employed what has been called a stinky T-shirt design, in which women sniffed shirts that had been slept in by different men and rated them on the pleasantness, sexiness, and intensity of their odors. The men who slept in these shirts were also measured on fluctuating asymmetry. The extraordinary finding was that the shirts worn by more symmetrical men were rated as smelling better than the shirts worn by less symmetrical men, but *only* by women who were likely to be in the fertile stage of their menstrual cycle (especially days 6–14). This finding was originally reported by Gangestad and Thornhill (1998a) and has since been replicated in their own lab in the United States (Thornhill & Gangestad, 1999) and in an independent lab in Germany (Rikowski & Grammar, 1999). These data suggest that the smell of men who are more symmetrical is preferred by women specifically when women are most likely to conceive.

6. Women's preferences for men with masculine facial characteristics should be heightened around the time of ovulation when women are most fertile (from H7). As discussed earlier, the immunocompetence handicap model suggests that only the fittest males will be able to develop robust secondary sexual characteristics, which accurately indicate both high levels of testosterone and a competent immune system (i.e., good genes). Exaggerated masculine facial characteristics, such as high cheekbones and a strong jaw and chin, are associated with high levels of testosterone and have been hypothesized to be reliable indicators of immunocompetence in men (see Folstad & Karter, 1992). Recent research in the United Kingdom and Japan has examined variation in women's preferences for male faces as a function of women's stage in the menstrual cycle (Penton-Voak et al., 1999; Penton-Voak & Perrett, 2000). Consistent with good genes sexual selection theory, more masculine-looking faces were preferred by women around the time of ovulation (when risk of conception is highest), especially in the context of short-term mating. In contrast, more feminine male faces, which may indicate dispositions toward increased paternal investment, were slightly preferred by women during other phases of the menstrual cycle (when risk of conception is lower). These data provide further evidence that men who display indicators of good genes are most preferred by women when they are most likely to get pregnant.

7. The timing and frequency of orgasms by women should be patterned to selectively retain the sperm of more symmetrical males (from H8). Thornhill et al. (1995) have conducted an initial test of this prediction on a sample of American undergraduates. The partners of more symmetrical men reported having more orgasms during sexual intercourse than did the partners of less symmetrical men (even after controlling for men's physical attractiveness). More important, levels of symmetry in male partners positively correlated with the frequency of high-sperm-retention orgasms in female partners (i.e., female orgasms occurring just prior to or after male orgasm). This effect has now been replicated in a second larger sample (Moller, Gangestad, & Thornhill, 1999). These data suggest that women increase their probability of conception when having sex with men of high genetic quality.

8. More symmetrical men should allocate less investment to ongoing relationships (from H10). Using the Partner-Specific Investment Inventory (Ellis, 1998), Gangestad and Thornhill (1998b) examined levels and types of investment in long-term dating relationships. More symmetrical men, who tended to allocate less investment to their dating relationships overall, were particularly likely to be less honest with their partners, to sexualize other women more, and to spend less time with their partners. The exception to this rule was that more symmetrical men tended to provide more physical protection to their partners. Although symmetrical men apparently devote less time and energy to their relationships overall, they may compensate (reproductively speaking) for this lack of investment by providing good genes and perhaps through their greater ability to physically protect their partners.

In conclusion, specific predictions drawn from hypotheses generated by good genes sexual selection theory have been tested across a range of studies. Although research derived from good genes sexual selection theory on humans is still in its early stages, an accumulating body of evidence now supports the supposition that a collection of male traits (reflected in levels of fluctuating asymmetry) have been selected for because of their role in advertising genetic quality to prospective mates. Good genes sexual selection theory has proven valuable in guiding research in a number of ways and has led to the detection of new phenomena. It is difficult imagine, for example, how other approaches to human mating could have predicted (let alone explained) the finding that men's symmetry is positively related to judgments of odor attractiveness by women who are most likely to be in the fertile stage of their menstrual cycle. Of course, there is much more to the dynamics of sexual and romantic relationships than can be explained by good genes sexual selection theory. This middle-level evolutionary theory has proved valuable, however, in both explaining and predicting a host of interesting phenomena relating to behavior in sexual and romantic relationships—not only in humans, but also in a wide range of animal species.

THE FUTURE OF EVOLUTIONARY PSYCHOLOGY

Evolutionary explanations have had a long—at times acrimonious—history in the behavioral sciences. Darwin's revolutionary theory of adaptation through natural selection, which explained the origins of human mental and behavioral characteristics in terms of evolution, transformed a long-standing worldview. Before Darwin, the prevailing belief was that "man" was created in God's divine image and held a special place at the center of the cosmos. Ever since Darwin, however, Homo sapiens has been viewed as firmly anchored in the natural world, as one species among millions in the great tree of life.

Darwin himself saw no problem in extrapolating his evolutionary ideas beyond the realm of bees, barnacles, and baboons to embrace the human species as well (e.g., Darwin, 1871, 1872). Others too, such as Darwin's protégé George Romanes (1882), appreciated the great explanatory power of evolutionary theory. Romanes used it to launch a comparative program of research aimed at illuminating the evolutionary origins of human intelligence. In America, the great nineteenth-century psychologist and philosopher William James (1890) also characterized human consciousness in a Darwinian fashion as a mechanism that enables humans to adapt to changing environments. James's evolution-inspired ideas were to spark the short-lived but influential functionalist movement in psychology in the early part of the twentieth century. The core idea of functionalism was that mind and behavior have *functions*—they serve to adapt organisms to their environment (e.g., Angell, 1907). Functionalist thinking in psychology, however, fell out of favor with the rise of behaviorism in the early part of the twentieth century. The behaviorist paradigm, which specified that a small number of domain-general learning mechanisms accounted for the rich repertoire of human (and animal) behavior, precluded an explanatory role for the kinds of species-specific, domain-specific psychological mechanisms that are central to functionalist, evolutionary analyses.

The return of evolutionary explanations in psychology can be traced to a number of important developments. First, behaviorism declined as psychology's dominant paradigm. Animal behavior research in the 1950s and 1960s demonstrated that the content-free learning processes specified by behaviorists simply could not account for the kinds of behaviors in which animals actually engaged (e.g., Breland & Breland, 1961; Garcia & Koelling, 1966). Behaviorism in its pure form also seemed unable to satisfactorily explain the origin of complex human traits such as language, which linguists such as Chomsky (1959) argued were built on a foundation of innate cognitive processes. Second, the development of a number of important middle-level evolutionary theories in the 1960s and 1970s, such as kin selection theory (Hamilton, 1964), parental investment theory (Trivers, 1972), and reciprocal altruism (Trivers, 1971) provided the basis for important new programs of research in evolutionary biology and psychology. These middle-level theories enabled evolutionary scientists to generate myriad testable hypotheses and predictions that spanned a diversity of animal species.

The formulation of these middle-level theories was important in the emergence in the late 1970s of sociobiology, which was defined by one of its principle architects, E. O. Wilson (1975), as "the systematic study of the biological basis of all social behavior" (p. 3). However, sociobiology proved to be a highly controversial discipline, especially when its adherents extended their ideas to explanations of human mental and behavioral characteristics. Sociobiological explanations were variously criticized as being untestable, unfalsifiable, deterministic, and ideologically unsound (e.g., S. Rose, Kamin, & Lewontin, 1984). Evolutionary psychology, as we have introduced it in this chapter, can be viewed historically as part of a long tradition of attempts to explain human psychological characteristics in evolutionary terms. The use of a coherent and powerful set of middle-level theories, the focus on evolved domain-specific psychological mechanisms, and a commitment to rigorous empirical testing, however, sets evolutionary psychology (in some respects) apart from its predecessors.

Controversy nonetheless remains over evolutionary explanations in psychology. Some critics continue to view evolutionary psychology as supporting a view of human nature that is based on genetic determinism—the idea that specific traits are caused by specific genes with a limited role for environmental factors. A glance at almost any publication by evolutionary psychologists, however, should be enough to see that this criticism is unfounded. It is almost universally agreed that *all* human traits are the result of the complex and dynamic interplay between genetic and environmental factors. Indeed, no evolutionary psychologist would argue that human behavior is rigidly fixed by virtue of our genetic inheritance; instead, much recent work in evolutionary psychology has emphasized the highly flexible and contingent nature of human psychological adaptations (e.g., Dekay & Buss, 1992; Gangestad & Simpson, 2000).

The criticism that evolutionary explanations are somehow untestable and lacking appropriate empirical rigor is still asserted by some critics of evolutionary psychology. This criticism is also unfounded (see Ketelaar & Ellis, 2000, and Ellis & Ketelaar, 2000, for detailed treatment of the issue of testability of evolutionary explanations). As demonstrated in this chapter, evolutionary psychologists employ a series of well-formulated middle-level theories that generate hypotheses and specific predictions that are testable and open to potential falsification. These empirical tests enable one to evaluate the middle-level evolutionary theories and metatheoretical assumptions from which the hypotheses and predictions are drawn. Despite the fact that human psychological characteristics are the product of evolutionary forces operating in ancestral environments, time machines are not essential methodological tools because modern humans carry around the legacy of ancestral adaptations that can be assessed using standard psychological methods.

The Impact of Evolutionary Psychology

Perhaps one of the most interesting questions regarding the future of evolutionary psychology concerns its scope of influence in the behavioral sciences. There is no question that evolutionary psychology has a broad range of applications. Indeed, evolutionary theory has been used to generate explanations of social behavior in all species, even those that are as yet undiscovered. Although the present chapter has focused primarily on reproductive strategies, evolutionary psychological theory and research extends into all major branches of psychology (e.g., Buss, 1999; Gaulin & McBurney, 2000). Will the endeavors of evolutionary psychologists thus serve to unify the currently fragmented discipline of psychology under the umbrella of a single metatheory? Does evolutionary psychology, as some suggest (e.g., Buss, 1995; Tooby & Cosmides, 1992), offer a radical new paradigm for psychological science?

To address this question, it is important to explicate the difference between evolutionary (*ultimate*) and nonevolutionary (*proximate*) explanations. Evolutionary psychological explanations focus on ultimate accounts of human psychological characteristics—that is, they explain *why* traits such as language or sexual jealousy exist in terms of the functions those traits served in ancestral environments. Nonevolutionary psychological explanations, by contrast, generally focus on *how* traits work in terms of proximate social, developmental, cognitive, or neural processes. Consider the phenomenon of morning sickness in pregnant women. An ultimate explanation for morning sickness is that it is an adaptation that has evolved because it helps to protect the pregnant woman and the developing fetus from the ingestion of toxic substances (Flaxman & Sherman, 2000; Profet, 1992). Proximate explanations of morning sickness focus on current physiological and psychological processes involved in food aversions during pregnancy. Proximate explanations address such questions as *What are the conditions under which morning sickness occurs, What neural circuits are involved,* and *What are the chemical changes that underpin increased olfactory sensitivity during the first trimester of pregnancy?* Neither type of explanation is inherently better than the other, nor does one preclude the other. Rather, ultimate and proximate explanations are complementary and mutually enriching.

Ultimate and proximate explanations, however, are not independent: They inform and influence each other. Discerning the evolved function of a psychological mechanism, for example, should aid in discovering how the mechanism works—that is, understanding evolved function can generate hypotheses about proximate mechanisms and causation. There are various ways to conceptualize the relation between different theories in science. Using the terminology employed by Thagard (1992), we suggest that it is unlikely that the explanations offered by evolutionary psychologists will entirely replace or supplant nonevolutionary explanations. This is because the two types of explanations target different levels of analysis (ultimate vs. proximate causation). Rather, we suggest that the theories offered by evolutionary psychologists tend to *sublate* extant proximal theories—that is, evolutionary psychological theories partly incorporate and partly reject such theories. Along these lines, we suggest that there are at least three ways in which evolutionary psychological theory and research influences the larger field of psychology.

1. Evolutionary Psychology Opens New Lines of Inquiry in Psychology

The use of evolutionary psychological models sometimes generates novel hypotheses and lines of research that had not—and in many cases could not—be derived from other theoretical models. One example of this point is the research on fluctuating asymmetry and reproductive behavior that was reviewed in this chapter. Another example is theory and research on father involvement and timing of daughters' reproductive development. Draper and Harpending (1982, 1988) have proposed a middle-level evolutionary theory of the role of father involvement in the development of female reproductive strategies. This theory posits that individuals have evolved to be sensitive to specific features of their early childhood environments, and that exposure to different early environments biases individuals toward acquisition of different reproductive strategies. Specifically, Draper and Harpending proposed that an important function of early experience is to induce in girls an understanding of the quality of male-female relationships and male parental investment that they are likely to encounter later in life. According to the theory, this understanding has the effect of canalizing a developmental track that has predictable outcomes for girl's reproductive behavior at maturity. Girls whose early family experiences are characterized by father absence (where women rear their children without consistent help from a man who is father to the children) perceive that male parental investment is not crucial to reproduction; these girls are hypothesized to develop in a manner that accelerates onset of sexual activity and reproduction, reduces reticence in forming sexual relationships, and orients the individual toward relatively unstable pair-bonds

(Draper & Harpending, 1982, 1988). Belsky, Steinberg, and Draper (1991; see also Surbey, 1990) added to this theory the hypothesis that girls from paternally deprived homes should also experience earlier pubertal maturation. From an evolutionary perspective, early pubertal maturation, precocious sexuality, and unstable pair-bonds are integrated components of an accelerated reproductive strategy. During human evolution, this accelerated strategy may have promoted female reproductive success in ecological contexts in which male parental investment was not crucial to reproduction.

Although variation in the timing of pubertal maturation in girls is a socially relevant topic (i.e., early-maturing girls experience relatively high rates of breast cancer, teenage pregnancy, depression, and alcohol consumption; e.g., Vikho & Apter, 1986; Udry & Cliquet, 1982; Caspi & Moffitt, 1991; Graber, Lewinsohn, Seeley, & Brooks-Gunn, 1997), there was almost no research on the psychosocial antecedents of this variation prior to publication of the evolutionary model. This gulf occurred because no other theory of socialization and child development provided a framework for studying timing of puberty. Indeed, researchers operating outside of the evolutionary umbrella had never thought to look at the relation between fathers' role in the family and daughters' maturational tempo. With the introduction of the evolutionary model of pubertal timing (see especially Belsky et al., 1991), this topic developed into a fruitful new area of research. Most studies suggest that girls reared in father-absent homes reach menarche several months earlier than do their peers reared in father-present homes (Moffitt, Caspi, Belsky, & Silva, 1992; Surbey, 1990; Wierson, Long, & Forehand, 1993). Moreover, some of these studies have found that the longer the period of father absence, the earlier the onset of daughters' menstruation (Moffitt et al., 1992; Surbey, 1990). However, not all studies (see Campbell & Udry, 1995) have found an accelerating effect for years of father absence on menarcheal age. Ellis and Garber (2000) found that years of stepfather presence, rather than years of biological father absence, best accounted for girls' pubertal timing (suggesting a possible pheromonal effect). Finally, Ellis et al. (1999) present longitudinal data showing that father-effects on daughters' pubertal timing involve more than just father-absent effects: Within father-present families, girls who had more distant relationships with their fathers during the first 5 years of life experienced earlier pubertal development in adolescence. Consistent with the original theorizing of Draper and Harpending (1982), the quality of fathers' investment in the family emerged as the most important feature of the proximal family environment in relation to daughters' reproductive development (Ellis et al., 1999).

2. Evolutionary Psychology Enriches Existing Bodies of Knowledge in Psychology

The use of an evolutionary psychological perspective may enrich existing bodies of theory and data in psychology. Evolutionary psychological metatheory, together with middle-level evolutionary theories, provide a powerful set of methodological heuristics that can provide guidance on what paths to follow (e.g., suggesting new hypotheses and providing criteria for recognizing significant observations) and what paths to avoid (e.g., raising suspicion of certain explanations or observations).

Consider, for example, theory and research on sexual jealousy in humans. Psychologists working outside of an explicitly evolutionary framework have contributed to our understanding of jealousy in numerous ways. A large body of empirical research has documented an array of cultural, developmental, and personality correlates of jealousy; detailed models of the causes of jealousy have been constructed; and the clinical management of pathological jealousy has been investigated (see Salovey, 1991; White & Mullen, 1989). Psychologists working inside an evolutionary psychological framework have also addressed the topic of jealousy, and this research has enriched the extant literature on jealousy in at least three ways.

First, the use of an evolutionary psychological framework has led to a variety of novel hypotheses about sexual and romantic jealousy that have generated fruitful new lines of research on the topic (see Buss, 2000). For example, evolutionary psychologists have hypothesized that levels of jealousy experienced by men (but not women) and amounts of time and energy expended on mate retention by men (but not women) will be negatively correlated with partner's age, regardless of one's own age. This gender-specific, age-specific hypothesis is based on the supposition that men with young, reproductive-aged partners are most at risk of being cuckolded and thus investing in offspring who are not their own. Consistent with this hypothesis, Flinn (1988) found that the amount of mate guarding engaged in by men in a Caribbean village decreased significantly when partners were pregnant or postmenopausal. Furthermore, Buss and Shackelford (1997) found that the amount of mate retention behavior engaged in by men (but not by women) was inversely related to the female partner's age, even after controlling for the male partner's age.

Second, evolutionary psychological approaches have been instrumental in correcting certain errors regarding the nature of jealousy. For example, the contention that jealousy is entirely a socially constructed emotion—essentially determined by cultural factors such as social roles and political institutions (e.g., Hupka, 1991; Bhugra, 1993)—has been questioned by evolutionary psychologists. Evolutionary psychologists conceptualize sexual jealousy as a biological adaptation designed by sexual selection to reduce paternity uncertainty and the threat of relationship loss (e.g., Daly et al., 1982). Sexual jealousy should be a universal emotion that is experienced in all cultures when a valued sexual relationship is threatened by a rival. Although some writers have claimed that sexual jealousy does not exist in some cultural groups such as Samoans and the Inuit, not to mention the swinging couples of the 1970s, subsequent analyses have shown that jealousy truly is a cross-cultural universal (Buss, 2000; Daly et al., 1982) and a major motive for homicide throughout the world (Daly & Wilson, 1988).

Third, an evolutionary perspective may prove valuable in integrating various middle-level theories of sexual and romantic jealousy. An extensive psychological literature has documented that feelings of jealousy are related to such factors as relationship quality, rival characteristics, partner similarity, gender, and attachment style (see White & Mullen, 1989). Various social and cognitive models, such as appraisal theory (White & Mullen, 1989) and self-evaluation maintenance theory (DeSteno & Salovey, 1996), have been suggested to account for these relations. An evolutionary psychological approach to jealousy may help integrate such models by providing overarching explanations for *why* certain patterns of appraisal occur in the specific contexts they do, and *why* jealousy is modified by such factors as relative mate value and the characteristics of rivals (Buss, 2000).

3. Evolutionary Psychology Radically Changes Certain Domains of Psychological Inquiry

In some domains, evolutionary psychology has offered more substantive changes to the kinds of explanations employed by nonevolutionary psychologists. For example, the metatheoretical assumptions of sexual selection theory, as instantiated in parental investment theory and good genes sexual selection theory, have radically changed theory and research on mate selection and intrasexual competition. Before the systematic application of evolutionary theory to human mate selection, most work in the area emphasized *proximity* (the tendency to date and marry people with whom one has regular social contact) and *matching* (the tendency to date and marry people whose value on the mating market is similar to one's own) as causal agents in mate selection (e.g., Myers, 1993). The proximity effect was explained as a function of the frequency of social interaction together with the principle that familiarity breeds fondness. The matching effect was conceptualized as an outcome of basic principles of social exchange.

Although proximity and matching are relevant to mate selection, the social models that were used to explain these phenomena have largely been supplanted by current evolutionary models of mating preferences and behavior. General principles of social exchange, familiarity, and interaction frequency simply proved inadequate to explain the facts about human mating. These principles could not account for universal differences between men and women in mate selection criteria (e.g., Buss, 1989), for systematic variation within each sex in orientation toward long-term versus short-term mating (e.g., Gangestad & Simpson, 2000), of for lawful variation across species in mating preferences and behavior (e.g., Trivers, 1985). It is just these types of questions that are addressed by parental investment theory and good genes sexual selection theory. Although some attempts have been made to integrate evolutionary and social exchange perspectives (e.g., Fletcher, in press; Kenrick, Groth, Trost, & Sadalla, 1993), the bottom line is that evolutionary psychological models have dramatically changed the nature of research on mating preferences and behavior (as reviewed in this chapter).

Future Directions

In this chapter we have introduced some of the core ideas and assumptions that comprise the field of evolutionary psychology. We have also illustrated how these ideas can be employed in the development of specific, testable hypotheses about human mind and behavior. The rapid growth in publications in the area of evolutionary psychology over the past decade suggests a growing acceptance of the importance of evolutionary ideas in the behavioral sciences. What can we expect, however, from evolutionary psychology in the twenty-first century? What are the crucial issues that need to be addressed by evolutionary psychologists, and how are evolutionary psychological ideas likely to influence the various subdisciplines of psychology?

Perhaps the most crucial task for evolutionary psychologists in the coming decades will be the identification and elucidation of psychological adaptations. As Buss (1999) notes, evolutionary psychologists have catalogued most of the obvious and plausible psychological adaptations (especially those relating to human mating), but many more remain undiscovered or inadequately characterized. The concept of biological adaptation, as George Williams (1966) has noted, is an onerous one and should only be deployed if the appropriate sorts of evidence to make such a claim are available. Because adaptations are the product of natural selection operating in ancestral environments, and because psychological traits such as jealousy, language, and self-esteem are not easily reconstructed from fossils and artifacts, direct evidence for biological adaptations may be difficult to come by (Lewontin, 1998; Richardson, 1996). One of the challenges for evolutionary psychology, therefore, will be to develop increasingly more rigorous and systematic methods for inferring the evolutionary history of psychological characteristics (see Durrant & Haig, 2001).

How best to characterize psychological adaptations also remains an important issue for evolutionary psychology. As we have seen, evolutionary psychologists assume that the human mind comprises a large number of domain-specific psychological mechanisms that have evolved to solve specific adaptive problems in our evolutionary past. However, many important questions remain regarding the relative specificity of such mechanisms, the way that they might develop over time in response to different environmental contexts, and how these mechanisms operate in terms of proximate cognitive and neurobiological processes.

Consider, for example, the theory that self-esteem acts as an interpersonal monitor—or sociometer—that tracks the membership status of individuals in social groups (Leary & Downs, 1995; Leary, Tambor, Terdal, & Downs, 1995). Leary and colleagues approached this well-studied psychological phenomenon by asking the important question: What is the (evolutionary) function of self-esteem? Their answer is that people do not strive for self-esteem as some kind of end point or ultimate goal. Rather, self-esteem reflects one's level of relative social inclusion or acceptance in social groups. Self-esteem, therefore, functions to motivate individuals to pursue courses of action that can restore or improve their acceptance by relevant others. In short, the self-esteem system is characterized as a psychological adaptation that has evolved to solve the recurrent adaptive problem of social exclusion and the fitness costs that such rejection would have entailed in ancestral environments.

However, many important questions remain regarding the nature of the self-esteem system, even if it can be plausibly considered a psychological adaptation. For example, Kirkpatrick and Ellis (2001) have suggested that one should expect self-esteem to be carved in to multiple domains to reflect the different types of interpersonal relationships that were important during human evolutionary history. Thus, they argue that there will be a number of different sociometers that gauge relative social inclusion in such domains as mating relationships, family relationships, and instrumental coalitions. Just how many different sociometers humans possess, however, remains an open question. Furthermore, we are only beginning to understand how the mechanisms underlying self-esteem develop over time in response to different environmental contexts and how they operate at a proximate cognitive and physiological level. One of the

important challenges for evolutionary psychology, therefore, lies in fleshing out the details of putative psychological adaptations such as self-esteem.

Over the next couple of decades, we expect that the coherent body of theory developed by evolutionary psychologists will be applied more regularly to many new fields in the behavioral sciences, especially such applied domains as organizational, environmental, and clinical psychology. For example, within clinical psychology, evolutionary explanations have been recently advanced for a variety of specific disorders, such as depression (Price et al., 1994), phobias (Marks & Nesse, 1994), substance abuse (Nesse & Berridge, 1997), and autism (Baron-Cohen, 1995). Even the very basis of the classification of mental disorders has been reconceptualized from an evolutionary perspective (Murphy & Stich, 2000). Specifically, Murphy and Stich urge that we should draw a fundamental distinction between mental disorders that arise from the *malfunction* of specific evolved psychological mechanisms, on the one hand, and those that occur due to a *mismatch* between our evolved psychological architecture and contemporary environments, on the other. Thus, autism can be plausibly conceptualized as the result of a malfunctioning of the theory of mind module, which has evolved to make inferences about others' behavior on the basis of imputed mental states such as beliefs and desires (Baron-Cohen, 1995). Depression, by contrast, as conceptualized by the social-competition model (Price et al., 1994), may result from increased likelihood of drawing unfavorable comparisons with other individuals due to the enlarged size of our potential social groups, brought about by population growth and advances in information technology.

In suggesting that evolutionary psychology will expand into new domains, we do not mean to imply that extant psychological theories will be overthrown or replaced. Rather, as more is known about the evolutionary origins of the human mind, more integrated theories can be developed—ones that recognize the important role of multiple explanations drawn across different levels of analysis.

In conclusion, Homo sapiens, like all other species, is the product of a history of evolution. Our opposable thumb, bipedal stance, and color visual system are all testimony to the gradual process of natural selection operating over vast spans of time. Just as the anatomical and physiological features of our bodies are explicable in evolutionary terms, so too are the complex array of psychological processes that make up the human brain-mind. The rapidly growing field of evolutionary psychology—from its broad metatheoretical assumptions to the specific predictions that are tested in research—offers a coherent and progressive paradigm aimed at uncovering the origins and functions of human mental and behavioral characteristics. In this chapter we have offered an introduction to some of the key ideas, issues, and methods that guide applications of evolutionary theory to human cognition and behavior. Although evolutionary psychology still meets resistance on some fronts, we believe that its value and potential for investigating questions of human nature is great.

REFERENCES

Andersson, M. (1982). Female choice selects for extreme tail length in a widowbird. *Nature, 299,* 818–820.

Andersson, M. (1994). *Sexual selection.* Princeton, NJ: Princeton University Press.

Andersson, M., & Iwasa, Y. (1996). Sexual selection. *Trends in Ecology and Evolution, 11,* 53–58.

Angell, J. R. (1907). The province of functional psychology. *Psychological Review, 14,* 61–91.

Baker, R. R., & Bellis, M. A. (1993). Human sperm competition: Ejaculate manipulation by females and a function for the female orgasm. *Animal Behavior, 46,* 887–909.

Baker, R. R., & Bellis, M. A. (1995). *Human sperm competition: Copulation, masturbation, and infidelity.* London: Chapman and Hall.

Baron-Cohen, S. (1995). *Mindblindness: An essay on autism and theory of mind.* Cambridge, MA: MIT Press.

Barrett, L., Dunbar, R., & Lycett, J. (2002). *Human evolutionary psychology.* Princeton, NJ: Princeton University Press.

Bellis, M. A., & Baker, R. R. (1990). Do females promote sperm competition?: Data for humans. *Animal Behaviour, 40,* 997–999.

Belsky, J., Steinberg, L., & Draper, P. (1991). Childhood experience, interpersonal development, and reproductive strategy: An evolutionary theory of socialization. *Child Development, 62,* 647–670.

Betzig, L. L. (1989). Causes of conjugal dissolution. *Current Anthropology, 30,* 654–676.

Bhugra, D. (1993). Cross-cultural aspects of jealousy. *International Review of Psychiatry, 5,* 271–280.

Bjorklund, D. F. (1997). In search of a metatheory for cognitive development (or Piaget is dead and I don't feel so good myself). *Child Development, 68,* 144–148.

Bowlby, J. (1969). *Attachment and loss* (Vol. 1). London: Penguin Books.

Breland, K., & Breland, M. (1961). The misbehavior of organisms. *American Psychologist, 15,* 1–18.

Brown, D. E. (1991). *Human universals.* New York: McGraw-Hill.

Browne, D. (1996). Cognitive versatility. *Minds and Machines, 6,* 507–523.

Bruce, V. (1988). *Recognizing faces.* Hillsdale, NJ: Erlbaum.

Buss, D. M. (1989). Sex differences in human mate preferences: Evolutionary hypotheses tested in 37 cultures. *Behavioral and Brain Sciences, 12,* 1–49.

Buss, D. M. (1991). Evolutionary personality psychology. *Annual Review of Psychology, 45,* 459–491.

Buss, D. M. (1994). *The evolution of desire: Strategies of human mating.* New York: Basic Books.

Buss, D. M. (1995). Evolutionary psychology: A new paradigm for psychological science. *Psychological Inquiry, 6,* 1–49.

Buss, D. M. (1999). *Evolutionary psychology: The new science of the mind.* Boston: Allyn and Bacon.

Buss, D. M. (2000). *The dangerous passion: Why jealousy is as necessary as love and sex.* New York: Free Press.

Buss, D. M., & Dedden, L. A. (1990). Derogation of competitors. *Journal of Social and Personal Relationships, 7,* 395–422.

Buss, D. M., Haselton, M. G., Shackelford, T. K., Bleske, A. L., & Wakefield, J. C. (1998). Adaptation, exaptations, and spandrels. *American Psychologist, 53,* 533–548.

Buss, D. M., Larsen, R., Westen, D., & Semmelroth, J. (1992). Sex differences in jealousy: Evolution, physiology, and psychology. *Psychological Science, 3,* 251–255.

Buss, D. M., & Schmitt, D. P. (1993). Sexual strategies theory: An evolutionary perspective on human mating. *Psychological Review, 100,* 204–232.

Buss, D. M., & Shackelford, T. K. (1997). From vigilance to violence: Mate retention tactics in married couples. *Journal of Personality and Social Psychology, 72,* 346–361.

Buunk, A. P., Angleitner, A., Oubaid, V., & Buss, D. M. (1996). Sex differences in jealousy in evolutionary and cultural perspective: Tests from the Netherlands, Germany, and the United States. *Psychological Science, 7,* 359–363.

Campbell, B. C., & Udry, J. R. (1995). Stress and age at menarche of mothers and daughters. *Journal of Biosocial Science, 27,* 127–134.

Cartwright, J. (2000). *Evolution and human behavior.* Cambridge, MA: MIT Press.

Cashdan, E. (1994). A sensitive period for learning about food. *Human Nature, 5,* 279–291.

Caspi, A., & Moffitt, T. E. (1991). Individual differences are accentuated during periods of social change: The sample case of girls at puberty. *Journal of Personality and Social Psychology, 61,* 157–168.

Chisholm, J. S. (1999). Attachment and time preference: Relations between early stress and sexual behavior in a sample of American University women. *Human Nature, 10,* 51–83.

Chomsky, N. (1959). Review of B. F. Skinner's *Verbal Behavior. Language, 35,* 26–58.

Colarelli, S. M. (1998). Psychological interventions in organizations: An evolutionary perspective. *American Psychologist, 53,* 1044–1056.

Cosmides, L. (1989). The logic of social exchange: Has natural selection shaped how humans reason? *Cognition, 31,* 187–276.

Cosmides, L., & Tooby, J. (1994). Origins of domain specificity: The evolution of functional organization. In L. A. Hirschfeld & S. A. Gelman (Eds.), *Mapping the mind: Domain specificity in cognition and culture* (pp. 85–117). Cambridge, UK: Cambridge University Press.

Crawford, D. (1998). Environments and adaptations: Then and now. In C. C. Crawford & D. L. Krebs (Eds.), *Handbook of evolutionary psychology: Ideas, issues, and applications* (pp. 275–302). Mahwah, NJ: Erlbaum.

Cronin, H. (1991). *The ant and the peacock: Altruism and sexual selection for Darwin to today.* New York: Cambridge University Press.

Daly, M., & Wilson, M. (1988). *Homicide.* Hawthorne, NY: Aldine

Daly, M., Wilson, M., & Weghorst, S. J. (1982). Male sexual jealousy. *Ethology and Sociobiology, 3,* 11–27.

Darwin, C. (1859). *On the origin of species by means of natural selection or the preservation of favoured races in the struggle for life.* London: John Murray.

Darwin, C. (1871). *The descent of man and selection in relation to sex.* London: John Murray.

Darwin, C. (1872). *The expression of the emotions in man and animals.* London: John Murray.

Dawkins, R. (1976). *The selfish gene.* Oxford, UK: Oxford University Press.

Dawkins, R. (1986). *The blind watchmaker.* New York: W. W. Norton.

DeKay, W. T., & Buss, D. M. (1992). Human nature, individual differences, and the importance of context: Perspectives from evolutionary psychology. *Current Directions in Psychological Science, 1,* 184–189.

DeSteno, D. A., & Salovey, P. (1996). Jealousy and the characteristics of one's rival: A self-evaluation maintenance perspective. *Personality and Social Psychology Bulletin, 22,* 920–932.

Dixson, A. F., Bossi, T., & Wickings, E. J. (1993). Male dominance and genetically determined reproductive success in the Mandrill (*Mandrillus sphinx*). *Primates, 34,* 525–532.

Draper, P., & Harpending, H. (1982). Father absence and reproductive strategy: An evolutionary perspective. *Journal of Anthropological Research, 38,* 255–273.

Draper, P., & Harpending, H. (1988). A sociobiological perspective on the development of human reproductive strategies. In K. B. MacDonald (Ed.), *Sociobiological perspectives on human development* (pp. 340–372). New York: Springer-Verlag.

Durrant, R., & Haig, B. D. (2001). How to pursue the adaptationist program in psychology. *Philosophical Psychology, 14,* 357–380.

Eberhard, W. G. (1985). *Sexual selection and animal genitalia.* Cambridge, MA: Harvard University Press.

Eberhard, W. G. (1993). Evaluating models of sexual selection: Genitalia as a test case. *The American Naturalist, 142,* 564–571.

Eibl-Eibesfeldt, I. (1989). *Human ethology.* Hawthorne, NY: Aldine de Gruyter.

Ellis, B. J. (1992). The evolution of sexual attraction: Evaluative mechanisms in women. In J. H. Barkow, L. Cosmides, & J. Tooby (Eds.), *The adapted mind: Evolutionary psychology and the generation of culture* (pp. 267–288). New York: Oxford University Press.

Ellis, B. J. (1998). The Partner-Specific Investment Inventory: An evolutionary approach to individual differences in investment. *Journal of Personality, 66,* 383–442.

Ellis, B. J., & Garber, J. (2000). Psychosocial antecedents of pubertal maturation in girls: Parental psychopathology, stepfather presence, and family and martial stress. *Child Development, 71,* 485–501.

Ellis, B. J., & Ketelaar, T. (2000). On the natural selection of alternative models: Evaluation of explanations in evolutionary psychology. *Psychological Inquiry, 11,* 56–68.

Ellis, B. J., McFayden-Ketchum, S., Dodge, K. A., Pettit, G. S., & Bates, J. E. (1999). Quality of early family relationships and individual differences in the timing of pubertal maturation in girls: A longitudinal test of an evolutionary model. *Journal of Personality and Social Psychology, 77,* 387–401.

Ellis, B. J., & Symons, D. (1990). Sex differences in fantasy: An evolutionary psychological perspective. *Journal of Sex Research, 27,* 527–556.

Fisher, R. A. (1958). *The genetical theory of natural selection.* New York: Dover.

Flaxman, S. M., & Sherman, P. W. (2000). Morning sickness: A mechanism for protecting mother and embryo. *Quarterly Review of Biology, 75,* 113–149.

Fletcher, G. J. O. (in press). *Exploring the relationship mind: The new science of intimate relationships.* London: Blackwell.

Flinn, M. V. (1988). Mate guarding in a Caribbean village. *Ethology and Sociobiology, 9,* 1–28.

Fodor, J. A. (1983). *The modularity of mind.* Cambridge, MA: MIT Press.

Foley, R. A. (1996). The adaptive legacy of human evolution: A search for the environment of evolutionary adaptedness. *Evolutionary Anthropology, 4,* 194–203.

Folstad, I., & Karter, A. J. (1992). Parasites, bright males, and the immunocompetence handicap. *The American Naturalist, 139,* 603–622.

Furlow, F. B., Armijo-Prewitt, T., Gangestad, S. W., & Thornhill, R. (1997). Fluctuating asymmetry and psychometric intelligence. *Proceedings of the Royal Society of London, 264B,* 823–829.

Gangestad, S. W. (1993). Sexual selection and physical attractiveness: Implications for mating dynamics. *Human Nature, 4,* 205–236.

Gangestad, S. W., & Simpson, J. A. (2000). The evolution of human mating: Trade-offs and strategic pluralism. *Behavioral and Brain Sciences, 23,* 573–644.

Gangestad, S. W., Simpson, J. A., Cousins, A. J., & Christensen, N. P. (1998). *Fluctuating asymmetry, women's sociosexuality, and context-specific mate preferences.* Manuscript submitted for publication.

Gangestad, S. W., & Thornhill, R. (1997a). Human sexual selection and developmental stability. In J. A. Simpson & D. T. Kenrick (Eds.), *Evolutionary social psychology* (pp. 169–195). Mahwah, NJ: Erlbaum.

Gangestad, S. W., & Thornhill, R. (1997b). The evolutionary psychology of extra-pair sex: The role of fluctuating asymmetry. *Evolution and Human Behavior, 18,* 69–88.

Gangestad, S. W., & Thornhill, R. (1998a). Menstrual cycle variation in women's preferences for the scent of symmetrical men. *Proceedings of the Royal Society of London, 265B,* 927–933.

Gangestad, S. W., & Thornhill, R. (1998b). *Sexual selection and relationship dynamics: Trade-offs between partner investment and fluctuating asymmetry.* Manuscript submitted for publication.

Garcia, J., & Koelling, R. A. (1966). Relation of cue to consequence in avoidance learning. *Psychonomic Science, 4,* 123–124.

Gaulin, S. J. C., & McBurney, D. H. (2000). *Psychology: An evolutionary approach.* Upper Saddle River, NJ: Prentice Hall.

Geary, D. C. (2000). Evolution and proximate expression of human paternal investment. *Psychological Bulletin, 126,* 55–77.

Gigerenzer, G. (1998). Surrogates for theories. *Theory and Psychology, 8,* 195–204.

Gould, S. J. (1980). *The panda's thumb: More reflections in natural history* (pp. 19–26). London: Penguin.

Gould, S. J. (1991a). Exaptation: A crucial tool for evolutionary psychology. *Journal of Social Issues, 47,* 43–65.

Gould, S. J. (1991b). *Bully for brontosaurus.* London: Penguin.

Gould, S. J., & Lewontin, R. C. (1979). The spandrels of San Marco and the Panglossian paradigm: A critique of the adaptationist programme. *Proceedings of the Royal Society of London, 205B,* 581–598.

Graber, J. A., Lewinsohn, P. M., Seeley, J. R., & Brooks-Gunn, J. (1997). Is psychopathology associated with the timing of pubertal development? *Journal of the American Academy of Child and Adolescent Psychiatry, 36,* 1768–1776.

Greiling, H., & Buss, D. M. (2000). Women's sexual strategies: The hidden dimension of extra-pair mating. *Personality and Individual Differences, 28,* 929–963.

Gross, M. R. (1996). Alternative reproductive strategies and tactics: Diversity within sexes. *Trends in Ecology and Evolution, 11,* 92–98.

Haig, B. D., & Durrant, R. (2000). Theory evaluation in evolutionary psychology. *Psychological Inquiry, 11,* 34–38.

Hamilton, W. D. (1964). The genetical evolution of social behavior: I. *Journal of Theoretical Biology, 7,* 1–16.

Hamilton, W. D., & Zuk, M. (1982). Heritable true fitness and bright birds: A role for parasites? *Science, 218,* 384–387.

Holcomb, H. R. (1998). Testing evolutionary hypotheses. In C. Crawford & D. L. Krebs (Eds.), *Handbook of evolutionary psychology: Ideas, issues, and applications* (pp. 303–334). Mahwah, NJ: Erlbaum.

Hrdy, S. B. (1981). *The women that never evolved.* Cambridge, MA: Harvard University Press.

Hrdy, S. B. (1999). *Mother nature: A history of mothers, infants, and natural selection.* New York: Pantheon Books.

Hupka, R. B. (1991). The motive for arousal of romantic jealousy: Its cultural origin. In P. Salovey (Ed.), *The psychology of jealousy and envy* (pp. 252–270). New York: Guilford Press.

Irons, W. (1998). Adaptively relevant environments versus the environment of evolutionary adaptedness. *Evolutionary Anthropology, 6,* 194–204.

James, W. (1890). *The principles of psychology.* New York: Henry Holt.

Johnston, V. S. (1999). *Why we feel: The science of human emotion.* Cambridge, MA: Perseus Books.

Karmiloff-Smith, A. (1992). *Beyond modularity: A developmental perspective on cognitive science.* Cambridge, MA: MIT Press.

Kempenaers, B., Lanctot, R. B., & Robertson, R. J. (1998). Certainty of paternity and paternal investment in eastern bluebirds and tree swallows. *Animal Behavior, 55,* 845–860.

Kenrick, D. T., Groth, G. E., Trost, M. R., & Sadalla, E. K. (1993). Integrating evolutionary and social exchange perspective on relationships: Effects of gender, self-appraisal, and involvement level on mate selection criteria. *Journal of Personality and Social Psychology, 64,* 951–969.

Kenrick, D. T., Sadalla, E. K., Groth, G., & Trost, M. R. (1990). Evolution, traits, and the stages of human courtship: Qualifying the parental investment model. *Journal of Personality, 58,* 97–116.

Ketelaar, T., & Ellis, B. J. (2000). Are evolutionary explanations unfalsifiable? Evolutionary psychology and the Lakatosian philosophy of science. *Psychological Inquiry, 11,* 1–22.

Kirkpatrick, L., & Ellis, B. J. (2001). An evolutionary psychological approach to self-esteem: Multiple domains and multiple functions. In G. J. O. Fletcher & M. S. Clark (Eds.), *The Blackwell handbook of social psychology: Vol. 2. Interpersonal processes* (pp. 411–436). Oxford, UK: Blackwell.

Lakatos, I. (1970). Falsificationism and the methodology of scientific research programmes. In I. Lakatos & A. Musgrave (Eds.), *Criticism and the growth of knowledge* (pp. 91–196). Cambridge, UK: Cambridge University Press.

Leary, M. R., & Downs, D. L. (1995). Interpersonal functions of the self-esteem motive: The self-esteem system as a sociometer. In M. H. Kernis (Ed.), *Efficacy, agency, and self-esteem* (pp. 123–144). New York: Plenum.

Leary, M. R., Tambor, E. S., Terdal, S. K., & Downs, D. L. (1995). Self-esteem as an interpersonal monitor: The sociometer hypothesis. *Journal of Personality and Social Psychology, 68,* 518–530.

Le Boeuf, B. J., & Reiter, J. (1988). Lifetime reproductive success in northern elephant seals. In T. H. Clutton-Brock (Ed.),

Reproductive success (pp. 344–362). Chicago: University of Chicago Press.

Lewontin, R. C. (1998). The evolution of cognition. In D. Scarborough & S. Sternberg (Eds.), *An invitation to cognitive science: Methods, models, and conceptual issues* (pp. 107–132). Cambridge, MA: MIT Press.

Lloyd, J. E. (1979). Mating behavior and natural selection. *The Florida Entomologist, 62,* 17–34.

Lovejoy, O. C. (1981). The origins of man. *Science, 211,* 341–349.

Lovejoy, O. C. (1988). The evolution of human walking. *Scientific American, 259,* 118–125.

Manning, J. T., Koukourakis, K., & Brodie, D. A. (1997). Fluctuating asymmetry, metabolic rate and sexual selection in human males. *Evolution and Human Behavior, 18,* 15–21.

Manning, J. T., Scutt, D., & Lewis-Jones, D. I. (1998). Developmental stability, ejaculate size, and sperm quality in men. *Evolution and Human Behavior, 19,* 273–282.

Marks, I. M., & Nesse, R. M. (1994). Fear and fitness: An evolutionary analysis of anxiety disorders. *Ethology and Sociobiology, 15,* 247–261.

Mealey, L. (1995). The sociobiology of sociopathy. *Behavioral and Brain Sciences, 18,* 523–599.

Miller, G. F. (1999). Evolution of music through sexual selection. In N. L. Wallin, M. Bjoern, & S. Brown (Eds.), *The origins of music.* Cambridge, MA: MIT Press.

Miller, G. F. (2000). *The mating mind: How sexual choice shaped the evolution of human nature.* New York: Doubleday.

Mineka, S. (1992). Evolutionary memories, emotional processing, and the emotional disorders. *The Psychology of Learning and Motivation, 28,* 161–206.

Moffitt, T. E., Caspi, A., Belsky, J., & Silva, P. A. (1992). Childhood experience and onset of menarche: A test of a sociobiological model. *Child Development, 63,* 47–58.

Moller, A. P. (1994). *Sexual selection and the barn swallow.* Oxford, UK: Oxford University Press.

Moller, A. P., Barbosa, A., Cuervo, J. J., de Lope, F., Merino, S., & Saino, N. (1998). Sexual selection and tail streamers in the barn swallow. *Proceedings of the Royal Society of London, 265B,* 409–414.

Moller, A. P., Christie, P., & Lux, E. (1999). Parasitism, host immune function, and sexual selection. *Quarterly Review of Biology, 74,* 3–20.

Moller, A. P., Gangestad, S. W., & Thornhill, R. (1999). Nonlinearity and the importance of fluctuating asymmetry as a predictor of fitness. *Oikos, 86,* 366–368.

Moller, A. P., & Swaddle, J. P. (1997). *Asymmetry, developmental stability, and evolution.* Oxford, UK: Oxford University Press.

Moller, A. P., & Tegelstrom, H. (1997). Extra-pair paternity and tail ornamentation in the barn swallow *Hirundo rustica. Behavioral Ecology and Sociobiology, 41,* 353–360.

Moller, A. P., & Thornhill, R. (1998). Male parental care, differential parental investment by females and sexual selection. *Animal Behavior, 55,* 1507–1515.

Murphy, D., & Stich, S. (2000). Darwin in the madhouse: evolutionary psychology and the classification of mental disorders. In P. Carruthers & A. Chamberlain (Eds.), *Evolution and the human mind: Modularity, language and meta-cognition* (pp. 62–92). Cambridge, UK: Cambridge University Press.

Myers, D. G. (1993). *Social psychology* (4th ed.). New York: McGraw-Hill.

Nesse, R. M., & Berridge, K. C. (1997). Psychoactive drug use in evolutionary perspective. *Science, 278,* 63–66.

Penton-Voak, I. S., & Perrett, D. I. (2000). Female preference for male faces changes cyclically: Further evidence. *Evolution and Human Behavior, 21,* 39–48.

Penton-Voak, I. S., Perrett, D., Castles, D., Burt, M., Koyabashi, T., & Murray, L. K. (1999). Female preferences for male faces changes cyclically. *Nature, 399,* 741–742.

Petrie, M., & Kempenaers, B. (1998). Extra-pair paternity in birds: Explaining variation between species and populations. *Trends in Ecology and Evolution, 13,* 52–58.

Petrie, M., & Williams, A. (1993). Peahens lay more eggs for peacocks with larger trains. *Proceedings of the Royal Society of London, 251B,* 127–131.

Pinker, S. (1994). *The language instinct.* London: Penguin.

Pinker, S. (1997). *How the mind works.* London: Penguin.

Price, J. S., Sloman, R., Gardner, R., Gilbert, P., & Rhode, P. (1994). The social competition hypothesis of depression. *British Journal of Psychiatry, 164,* 309–315.

Profet, M. (1992). Pregnancy sickness as adaptation: A deterrent to maternal ingestion of teratogens. In J. H. Barkow, L. Cosmides, & J. Tooby (Eds.), *The adapted mind: Evolutionary psychology and the generation of culture* (pp. 327–365). New York: Oxford University Press.

Rhodes, G., Zebrowitz, L. A., Clark, A., Kalick, M., Hightower, A., & McKay, R. (2001). Do facial averageness and symmetry signal health? *Evolution and Human Behavior, 22,* 31–47.

Richardson, R. C. (1996). The prospects for an evolutionary psychology: Human language and human reasoning. *Minds and Machines, 6,* 541–557.

Richters, J. E. (1997). The Hubble hypothesis and the developmentalist's dilemma. *Development and Psychopathology, 9,* 193–229.

Rikowski, A., & Grammar, K. (1999). Human body odour, symmetry and attractiveness. *Proceedings of the Royal Society of London, 266B,* 869–874.

Romanes, G. J. (1882). *Animal intelligence.* London: Kegan Paul.

Rose, M. R., & Lauder, G. V. (Eds.). (1996). *Adaptation.* San Diego, CA: Academic Press.

Rose, S., Kamin, L. J., & Lewontin, R. C. (1984). *Not in our genes: Biology, ideology and human nature.* London: Penguin Books.

Rozin, P., & Fallon, A. E. (1987). A perspective on disgust. *Psychological Review, 94,* 23–41.

Ryan, M. J., & Keddy-Hector, A. (1992). Directional patterns of female mate choice and the role of sensory bias. *The American Naturalist, 139,* S4–S35.

Ryan, M. J., & Rand, A. S. (1990). The sensory basis of sexual selection for complex calls in the tungara frog, *Physalaemus pustulosus* (sexual selection for sensory exploitation). *Evolution, 44,* 305–314.

Salovey, P. (Ed.). (1991). *The psychology of jealousy and envy.* New York: Guilford Press.

Samuels, R. (2000). Massively modular minds: Evolutionary psychology and cognitive architecture. In P. Carruthers & A. Chamberlain (Eds.), *Evolution and the human mind: Modularity, language and meta-cognition* (pp. 13–46). Cambridge, UK: Cambridge University Press.

Seligman, M., & Hagar, J. (1972). *Biological boundaries of learning.* New York: Appleton-Century-Crofts.

Shackelford, T. K., & Larsen, R. J. (1997). Facial asymmetry as an indicator of psychological, emotional, and physiological distress. *Journal of Personality and Social Psychology, 72,* 456–466.

Shepard, R. N. (1992). The perceptual organization of colors: An adaptation to regularities of the terrestrial world? In J. Barkow, L. Cosmides, & J. Tooby (Eds.), *The adapted mind: Evolutionary psychology and the generation of culture* (pp. 495–532). New York: Oxford University Press.

Simpson, J. A. (1999). Attachment theory in modern evolutionary perspective. In J. Cassidy & P. R. Shaver (Eds.), *Handbook of attachment theory and research* (pp. 115–140). New York: Guilford Press.

Simpson, J. A., Gangestad, S. W., Christensen, P. N., & Leck, K. (1999). Fluctuating asymmetry, sociosexuality, and intrasexual competitive tactics. *Journal of Personality and Social Psychology, 76,* 159–172.

Simpson, J. A., & Kenrick, D. T. (Eds.). (1997). *Evolutionary social psychology.* Mahwah, NJ: Erlbaum.

Singh, D., Meyer, W., Zambarano, R. J., & Hurlbert, D. F. (1998). Frequency and timing of coital orgasm in women desirous of becoming pregnant. *Archives of Sexual Behavior, 27,* 15–29.

Smith, R. L. (1984). Human sperm competition. In R. L. Smith (Ed.), *Sperm competition and the evolution of animal mating systems* (pp. 601–660). London: Academic Press.

Sterelny, K., & Griffiths, P. E. (1999). *Sex and death: An introduction to the philosophy of biology.* Chicago: University of Chicago Press.

Studd, M. V. (1996). Sexual harassment. In D. M. Buss & N. M. Malamuth (Eds.), *Sex, power, and conflict: Evolutionary and feminist perspectives* (pp. 54–89). New York: Oxford University Press.

Sulloway, F. J. (1996). *Born to rebel: Birth order, family dynamics, and creative lives.* London: Abacus.

Surbey, M. (1990). Family composition, stress, and human menarche. In F. Bercovitch & T. Zeigler (Eds.), *The socioendocrinology of primate reproduction* (pp. 71–97). New York: Liss.

Symons, D. (1979). *The evolution of human sexuality.* Oxford, UK: Oxford University Press.

Symons, D. (1987). If we're all Darwinians, what's the fuss about? In C. Crawford, M. Smith, & D. Krebs (Eds.), *Sociobiology and psychology: Ideas, issues, and applications* (pp. 91–125). Hillsdale, NJ: Erlbaum.

Symons, D. (1992). On the use and misuse of Darwinism in the study of behavior. In J. H. Barkow, L. Cosmides, & J. Tooby (Eds.), *The adapted mind: Evolutionary psychology and the generation of culture* (pp. 137–159). New York: Oxford University Press.

Symons, D. (1995). Beauty is in the adaptations of the beholder: The evolutionary psychology of human female sexual attractiveness. In P. R. Abramson & S. D. Pinkerton (Eds.), *Sexual nature, sexual culture* (pp. 80–118). Chicago: University of Chicago Press.

Symons, D., & Ellis, B. J. (1989). Human male-female differences in sexual desire. In A. Rasa, C. Vogel, & E. Voland (Eds.), *Sociobiology of sexual and reproductive strategies.* London: Chapman and Hall.

Thagard, P. (1992). *Conceptual revolutions.* Princeton, NJ: Princeton University Press.

Thornhill, R., & Gangestad, S. W. (1999). The scent of symmetry: A human sex phremone that signals fitness? *Evolution and human behavior, 20,* 175–201.

Thornhill, R., Gangestad, S. W., & Comer, R. (1995). Human female orgasm and mate fluctuating asymmetry. *Animal Behavior, 50,* 1601–1615.

Tooby, J., & Cosmides, L. (1990). The past explains the present: Emotional adaptations and the structure of ancestral environments. *Ethology and Sociobiology, 11,* 375–424.

Tooby, J., & Cosmides, L. (1992). The psychological foundation of culture. In J. H. Barkow, L. Cosmides, & J. Tooby (Eds.), *The adapted mind: Evolutionary psychology and the generation of culture* (pp. 19–137). New York: Oxford University Press.

Trivers, R. L. (1971). The evolution of reciprocal altruism. *Quarterly Review of Biology, 46,* 35–57.

Trivers, R. L. (1972). Parental investment and sexual selection. In B. Campbell (Ed.), *Sexual selection and the descent of man: 1871–1971* (pp. 136–179). Chicago: Aldine.

Trivers, R. L. (1985). *Social evolution.* Menlo Park, CA: Benjamin/Cummings.

Udry, J. R., & Cliquet, R. L. (1982). A cross-cultural examination of the relationship between ages at menarche, marriage, and first birth. *Demography, 19,* 53–63.

Waynforth, D. (1998). Fluctuating asymmetry and human male life-history traits in rural Belize. *Proceedings of the Royal Society of London, 265B,* 1497–1501.

Weisfeld, G. (1999). *Evolutionary principles of human adolescence.* New York: Basic Books.

Wheeler, P. E. (1991). The influence of bipedalism on the energy and water budgets of early hominids. *Journal of Human Evolution, 21,* 101–136.

White, G. L., & Mullen, P. E. (1989). *Jealousy: Theory, research, and clinical strategies.* New York: Guilford Press.

Whitten, A. (1987). Infants and adult males. In B. B. Smuts, D. L. Cheney, R. M. Seyfarth, R. W. Wrangham, & T. T. Struhsaker (Eds.), *Primate societies* (pp. 343–357). Chicago: University of Chicago Press.

Wiederman, M. W., & Allgeier, E. R. (1993). Gender differences in sexual jealousy: Adaptationist or social learning explanation? *Ethology and Sociobiology, 14,* 115–140.

Wierson, M., Long, P. J., & Forehand, R. L. (1993). Toward a new understanding of early menarche: The role of environmental stress in pubertal timing. *Adolescence, 28,* 913–924.

Williams, G. C. (1966). *Adaptation and natural selection.* Princeton, NJ: Princeton University Press.

Williams, G. C. (1992). *Natural selection: Domains, levels, and challenges.* New York: Oxford University Press.

Wilson, D. S., & Sober, E. (1994). Reintroducing group selection to the human behavioral sciences. *Behavioral and Brain Sciences, 17,* 585–654.

Wilson, E. O. (1975). *Sociobiology: The new synthesis.* Cambridge, MA: Harvard University Press.

Wilson, E. O. (1992). *The diversity of life.* London: Penguin Books.

Wilson, M., & Daly, M. (1996). Male sexual proprietariness and violence against wives. *Current Directions in Psychological Science, 5,* 2–7.

Zahavi, A. (1975). Mate selection: a selection for a handicap. *Journal of Theoretical Biology, 53,* 205–214.

Zahavi, A., & Zahavi, A. (1997). *The handicap principle: A missing piece of Darwin's puzzle.* New York: Oxford University Press.

CHAPTER 2

Behavioral Genetics

STEPHEN C. MAXSON

The field of behavior genetics is concerned with four issues in any animal species, including humans. These issues are (a) whether individual differences in a behavior are due to the effects of genes, (b) what the genes are that do or can effect individual differences in a behavior, (c) how genes and their interactions with the environment affect the development of a behavior, and (d) what genetic changes are involved in the evolution of a behavior. Although some aspects of the genetics of behavior have been investigated in a variety of organisms (see Ehrman & Parsons, 1981), most studies have been with four species. These are nematodes (*Caenorhabditis elegans*), fruit flies (*Drosophila melanogaster*), mice (*Mus musculus*) and humans (*Homo sapiens*).

The writings of two Victorians, Charles Darwin and his cousin Francis Galton, influenced different paths in the field of behavior genetics. One is concerned with the causes of variation in human behaviors, especially cognition, personality, psychopathology, and addictions; this path is derived largely from the works of Galton. The other is concerned with

the genetics of adaptive behaviors in animals and humans; this path is derived largely from the writings of Darwin; it is the main focus of this review. In each section of this chapter, the relevant genetics are considered first and then their application to some exemplar behaviors is described.

The structure of the genetic material called DNA (deoxyribonucleic acid) was first proposed by Watson and Crick (1953a). Implicit in the structure of DNA are the mechanisms for how genes are replicated, how they mutate, and what they do (Watson & Crick, 1953b). This discovery has had a profound effect on the biological sciences and is beginning to have one on psychology and the other behavioral sciences. The potential impact on the behavioral sciences was described in a seminal paper by Ginsburg (1958) that was published just 5 years after those by Watson and Crick on the structure and function of DNA. Ginsburg proposed that genetics was a tool for the study of behavior in four ways. First, it is a tool to dissect behavior into its natural units. Second, it is a tool to study the neural and other mechanisms of behavior. Third, it is a tool to study the effects of the environment on behavior. Fourth, it is a tool to study the evolution of behavior.

THE HERITABILITY OF BEHAVIOR

Background

The methods of quantitative genetics (see Falconer & McKay, 1997) are used to assess the relative roles of genes and environment in individual differences in behavior. In animals, inbreeding, selective breeding, and crossbreeding are used, and in animals and humans, the resemblance among relatives and nonrelatives is assessed. Basically, these methods allow the phenotypic variance to be partitioned into genetic and environmental components. This can be expressed as the ratio of genotypic to phenotypic variance; this ratio is known as the *heritability* of the trait. This ratio can vary from zero to one. The value is specific to the population in which it is measured, and its estimate always has an error term dependent on sample size. The following are considered in this section as examples: mating speed in fruit flies, aggression in stickleback fish, nest building in mice, and body weight in humans.

Mating Speed in Fruit Flies

Manning (1961) selectively bred for fast and slow mating speeds based on the time from being introduced to the mating chamber to the start of copulation. From 50 pairs of flies, the 10 fastest and 10 slowest pairs were selected. From these pairs, two fast-mating and two slow-mating lines were established, and a randomly bred control line was also maintained. After 25 generations of selective breeding, the mean mating speed was about 3 min in the *fast* line and 80 min in the *slow* line. The heritability computed from the response to selective breeding was .30, which demonstrates low to moderate genetic variability for this behavior. This study also demonstrated that the genes for variability in mating speed and general activity are not the same.

Aggression in Three-Spine Stickleback Fish

In stickleback fish, juveniles and adults of both sexes attack other species members, and attacks by adults of both sexes are usually territorial. Bakker (1994) selected for territorial attacks in males and females from a population of stickleback fish living in a fresh water stream in the Netherlands. High,

low, and control lines were developed. For adult male attacks, there was no change in the *high* line across the three generations of selective breeding, but there was a decrease in the *low* line over the three generations. For adult female attacks, there was an increase in the *high* and a decrease in the *low* lines over the three generations. Where heritability could be calculated, it ranged from .29 to .64 (moderate to high genetic contribution to variation). It may be concluded from these results that (a) there is genetic variability for these behaviors in the natural population, (b) there may have been more intense selection on male than female attacks, and (c) some of the genes for variability in male and female attacks may not be the same.

Nest Building in Mice

Mice build nests as adaptations to the cold. In one study, mice were selectively bred for the size of their nests as measured by grams of cotton used to build a nest (Lynch, 1994). The foundation population was a randomly bred heterogeneous stock, and there were two high, two low, and two control lines. After 15 generations of selection, the heritability computed from the response to selection was .28, which is moderate. There have been more than 48 generations of selection. Thus, there is genetic variability for this trait in the foundation population. Studies with natural populations of mice show that there is less genetic variability in mice from Maine than from Florida; this finding is consistent with there being more selection in Maine for thermoregulatory nest size than in Florida.

Body Weight in Humans

The regulation of body weight is an adaptive trait; this regulation has behavioral components, such as eating and exercise. The correlation for body weight of identical twins raised together is .80 for identical twins reared together and .72 for those raised apart, whereas it is .43 for fraternal twins (Grilo & Pogue-Geille 1981). The correlation for biological parents and adopted siblings is .23, similar to that for nonadoptive parents and offspring (.26). Also, the correlations for adoptive parent and child or adoptive siblings are essentially zero. These findings are consistent with a heritability of .70 for body weight and with nonshared rather than shared environmental effects on individual differences in body weight. The *shared environment* is that which differs from one family to another; the *nonshared environment* is conceived of as the portion of trait variance not explained by genetics or shared environment. For many individual differences in behavioral or mental traits of humans, most of the variance is due to genetic and nonshared environmental effects (Plomin, DeFries, McClearn, & McGuffin, 2000).

Summary

It is now firmly established that individual differences in every studied behavioral trait in any animal species, including humans, is a function of both genetic and environmental variability. That is to say, for no trait studied is the heritability either zero or one in outbred populations. The interesting issues now are (a) what are the genes that do or can affect a trait's variability, (b) how they interact with each other and the environment in the trait's development, and (c) what the genetic mechanisms are of species diversity in and evolution of behavioral adaptations. These issues are beginning to be understood with the aid of molecular genetics.

THE GENOME PROJECTS

An individual's nuclear genome consists of the DNA found on all the chromosomes in the nucleus of its cells; there is one molecule of DNA for each chromosome. The goal of the genome projects is to determine the sequence of the nucleotide bases—adenine, cytosine, guanine, or thymine (A, C, G, or T)—of the nuclear genome of one or more individuals in a species. This has been done for *C. elegans* with a genome size of 100 Mb (megabases), *D. melanogaster* with a genome size of 165 Mb, and *Homo sapiens* with a genome size of 3,300 Mb; it is nearing completion for *M. musculus* with a genome size 3,300 Mb. After the entire sequence is known for a species, it is possible to estimate the number of protein-coding genes in the genome; this now appears to be about 35,000 for humans. Also, the amino acid sequence in each protein can be deduced from the coding nucleotide triplets in the gene's structural region. Other sequences of a protein-coding gene bind proteins known as *transcription factors*. These factors and sequences together are involved in controlling when and where a gene is transcribed as RNA (ribonucleic acid). The transcribed RNA is processed into a messenger RNA (mRNA), and the mRNA is then translated into the sequences of amino acids in its protein. Many DNA sequences, however, appear not to be transcribed nor to regulate transcription; in mice and humans, these make up about 98% of the nuclear genome.

There is also DNA in the mitochondria; this DNA codes for the amino acid sequence of some of the proteins involved in energy metabolism. This DNA has been sequenced for many organisms. There are neurological effects of variants of these mitochondrial genes (Wallace, 1999), and these genes may also have behavioral effects.

IDENTIFYING THE GENES

Background

Genes with effects on behavior in mice can be detected by mutagenizing one allele of a gene (Takahashi, Pinto, & Vitaterna, 1994). There are then two copies (variants or alleles) of the gene, and the homozygotes for the two variants can be compared for differences in one or more behaviors. One mutagenesis approach targets a specific gene creating an allele that does not produce a functional protein. These are the so-called *knockout mutants*. To delete a specific gene, the DNA sequence of the gene must be already known, and the chromosomal location of the gene may or may not be known. Knockouts with effects on mouse behavior are reviewed in Nelson and Young (1998) and Crawley (2000). This approach is illustrated in the following section for genes with effects on mouse aggression. Another approach exposes male mice of an inbred strain to a chemical mutagen, such as N-ethyl-N-nitrosourea (ENU), with the goal of finding most—if not all—the genes that can cause variation in a trait such as a behavior. Dominant mutants would be detected in the first generation of progeny, and recessive mutants would be detected in subsequent generations of progeny. The chromosomal location and the DNA sequence of each mutant gene with a behavioral effect are then determined. There are large-scale behavioral mutagenesis projects at the Jackson Laboratory, Northwestern University, and The University of Tennessee Health Sciences Center. This approach is illustrated later in this chapter with the circadian rhythm gene known as Clock. Also, both mutagenesis approaches have also been used with nematodes (Segalat, 1999) and fruit flies (Jallon, 1999).

Genes with effects on behavior can also be detected by chromosomally mapping genes with existing allelic variants (see Segalat, 1999, for nematodes; see Sokolowski, 1999, for fruit flies; see Belknap, Dubay, Crabbe, & Buck, 1997, for mice; and see Plomin & Crabbe, 2000, for humans). Single gene variants with large effect can be mapped as illustrated for the foraging gene in *Drosophila*. Polygenic variants can also be mapped; later in the chapter, this is illustrated in mice for quantitative trait loci (QTLs) with effects on emotionality. A goal in mapping these is to eventually identify the actual protein coding genes with effects on a trait's variation. The markers that are used for gene mapping to a region of a chromosome are usually DNA variants (Plomin et al., 2000; Plomin & Crabbe, 2000). These include restriction fragment length polymorphisms (RFLPs), simple sequence length polymorphisms (SSLPs), and single nucleotide polymorphisms (SNPs). These markers have two advantages in mapping: Many of them are closely spaced on the linkage map of each chromosome, and they have no effect on the measured traits. Another approach is to associate DNA variants of candidate genes with behavior, as is illustrated for a human personality trait later in this chapter. The selection of candidate genes often depends on hypotheses about the neural and other mechanisms involved in a behavior.

Another approach to identifying genes with potential effects on behavior is to look for quantitative differences in gene expression in brains of genotypically or phenotypically different individuals. Genes that differ across these individuals in level of brain mRNA are candidates for ones with behavioral effects. DNA microchips can be used to determine what genes are being expressed in a tissue (e.g., as a region of brain) and how the level of expression differs between individuals of different genotype or phenotype (Nisenbaum, 2002). A single microchip can be used to assay for thousands of genes simultaneously. The assay is based on specific hybridization between some of the DNA of a gene and of that gene's mirror image or complimentary DNA (cDNA), which is synthesized from the gene's messenger RNA.

Knockout Mutants and Aggression in Mice

There is more than one type of aggression in mice and other animals (Maxson, 1992, 1999). The research with knockout mutants has focused on aggressive behavior known as *offense,* which has the adaptive function of obtaining and retaining resources such as space, food, and mates. It is also characterized by specific motor patterns and attack targets. About 25 genes with effects on offense in males have been identified (Maxson, Roubetoux, Guillot, & Goldman, 2001; Miczek, Maxson, Fish, & Faccidomo, 2001); most of these have been identified with knockouts. Many of the genes act on either hormone or neurotransmitter systems, and it has recently been suggested that many such genes ultimately act on offense by affecting one or more of the serotonergic neurotransmitter systems (Nelson & Chiavegatto, 2001).

The effect of a knockout on a trait is determined by comparing mice homozygous for the knockout allele with those homozygous for the normal or functional allele. In evaluating results with knockouts, there are several methodological concerns (Nelson, 1997):

- To avoid maternal effects, the mother of the two genotypes must be the same, and the offspring should be the result of the mating of a heterozygous female to a heterozygous male.

- Some knockout strain pairs are *coisogenic,* differing only in the normal and mutant alleles of a single gene, but others are only *congenic*—they differ not only in the mutant and normal alleles of gene of interest, but also in alleles of genes linked to it. For congenic strains, any differences may be due to the genes linked to the knockout rather than due to the knockout itself, as discussed by Gerlai (1996).

- Often the knockout is made in one inbred strain, such as one of the 129 inbred strains and then transferred to another strain. Sometimes the effect of a knockout seen in one strain background is not detected in another. For example, the knockout for the NOS-1 (nitric oxide synthase-1) gene increases attacks is lost after many generations of backcrossing to C57BL6 inbred strain mice (LeRoy et al., 2000).

- For many knockouts, the mutant gene is present from the time of conception. Thus, it was not possible to tell when or where in the mouse the gene was expressed with consequent behavioral effect. Recently, techniques have been developed that permit tissue- and temporal-specific knockouts in mice (Tsien, 1999). Similar techniques are available for *C. elegans* (Seglant, 1999) and *Drosophila* (Jallon, 1999).

Saturation Mutagenesis and Circadian Rhythms in Mice

Knockouts mutagenize a specific gene. Exposure to a chemical mutagen, such as ENU, in theory can mutagenize all the genes that can cause a trait to vary (Takahashi et al., 1994). This approach was first used in *Drosophila* (see review by Benzer, 1971); mutants on the X chromosome were detected for circadian rhythms, courtship, and learning-memory. Saturation mutagenesis has also been used with nematodes (Seglant, 1999). This approach was first used in mice to screen for mutants with effects on circadian rhythms.

Circadian rhythms in mice can be measured by observing their running in a wheel. Mice normally run at night in a 12 light, 12 dark schedule, with precise onset of locomotor activity. Even when maintained in constant darkness, mice (and all other animals examined) display this cycle of activity that deviates only slightly from the 24-hour pattern observed during a light-dark cycle. Because these rhythms persist in constant conditions as well as other evidence, it is well accepted that these rhythms are generated from within the organism. Male mice were treated with ENU and their progeny were screened for dominant mutations affecting circadian rhythms (Vitaterna et al., 1994). One mouse out of 300 had a circadian period that was 1 hour longer than normal. This mouse had a semidominant mutation that was named *Clock*. When initially placed in constant darkness, homozygous *Clock* mice have long circadian periods of 27 to 28 hours. After about 2 weeks in constant darkness, the homozygous *Clock* mice have a complete loss of circadian rhythms. Intraspecic mapping crosses were used to show that the *Clock* gene is located on Chromosome 5 of the mouse. It was then possible to positionally clone the DNA and thereby to identify the protein of this gene (King et al., 1997). *Clock* encodes a member of the basic-helix-loop-helix (bHLH) PAS family of transcription factors, and it has a key role in the regulating the genetics mechanism of the biological clock (Allada, White, So, Hall, & Rosbash, 2001; King & Takahashi, 2000). The role of *Clock* in circadian rhythms was confirmed with transgenic rescue (Antoch et al., 1997); for this, the normal allele of *Clock* was inserted into the *Clock* mutants. These mice have normal circadian rhythms.

Natural Variants and Foraging in Fruit Flies

There is a polymorphism in the foraging behavior of larval *Drosophila* (Sokolowski & Riedl, 1999). Rovers have longer foraging trails on food than do sitters. This difference is not seen in the absence of food. These variants occur in natural populations of flies; in these, there are about 70% rovers and 30% sitters. Breeding experiments showed that this polymorphism is due primarily to allelic differences in a single gene with a large effect, but that this trait is also influenced by other genes that each contribute small effects. Chromosomal analyses localized the gene, which was called *for,* to the second chromosome. Because minor genes and the environment affect the distribution of rover and sitter phenotypes, a lethal tagging technique was used to map *for* to Region 24 of the polytene chromosome map. Chromosome rearrangements were used to further map *for* to region 24A3-5 of the polytene chromosome map containing about 150 to 125 kb (kilobases) of DNA. It is now known that the *for* gene is the same as the gene *dg2*, which encodes a *Drosophila* cGMP/cGMP-dependent protein kinase (PKG). Insertion of transposon elements into *dg2* caused a change from rover to sitter phenotypes; removal of the transposon elements caused the behavior to revert back to rover.

Genome-Wide Scan to Map QTLs for Emotionality in Mice

When confronted with a novel and unexpected situation, such as an open field, mice may freeze, defecate and urinate, or simply explore the new environment (Broadhurst, 1960). These behaviors, singly or in combination, are often used as measures of emotionality. In mice, negative correlations between defecation and ambulation are fairly general, although the association is affected somewhat by environmental variables such as light or noise (Archer, 1973). To some extent, the relation also depends on the strain, sex, and early experience of the subjects.

In open-field tests, C57BL6 inbred strain of mice are much more active than BALB/c inbred strain of mice. These strains were crossed to obtain an F3 generation, which was the base population for selective breeding for open-field activity. Replicate high and low lines were selectively bred over 30 generations for open-field ambulation (DeFries, Gervais, & Thomas, 1978). Two unselected control lines were also bred for the 30 generations. After 30 generations of selection, there was a threefold difference between the high and low lines in ambulation, and there was no overlap in distribution of ambulation scores between the high and low lines. The defecation scores of the low lines were seven times higher than those of the high lines. Based on the response to selection, the heritability was .26 for ambulation and .11 for defecation, and the genetic correlation for ambulation and defecation scores was −.86.

An F3 of one of these high and low lines was bred to map QTLs for the strain differences (Flint et al., 1995). The most active and least active mice were screened for 84 DNA markers for which there were two alleles, and these 84 markers were spread across the 20 chromosomes of mice; this is known as a *genome-wide scan*. These were used to determine the chromosomal region (QTLs) associated with the open-field activity. Significant QTLs were found on Chromosomes 1, 4, 12, 15, 17, and 18. These six QTLs accounted for 26% of the phenotypic variance. There are several issues in evaluating such genome-wide scans to localize QTLs associated with a behavior. These are

- Because the association of the behavior with many DNA markers is tested, there is a risk of false positives (for mice, see Belknap et al., 1997; for humans, see Plomin & Crabbe, 2000). For this reason, QTLs should be confirmed by additional studies.
- The QTL is often a large region on a chromosome consisting of millions of base pairs of DNA and hundreds of genes. In order to positionally clone or identify positional candidates for the gene or genes underlying the QTL, the map distance between the QTL to the markers needs to be greatly reduced. The following illustrates one approach to resolving these issues (Talbot et al., 1999). For open-field behavior, the most active 20% and least active 20% of 751 mice of an heterogenous stock derived from an eight-way cross were screened for SSLPs closely spaced together in a 20 cM (centiMorgan) region of Chromosome 1. This not only confirmed that there is a QTL on Chromosome 1 with

an effect on ambulation, but it also mapped the QTL more precisely.

Candidate Genes: Association of D4 Receptor Gene and Novelty Seeking in Humans

Novelty seeking is one of four personality traits in Cloninger's theory of temperament development (Cloninger, Svrakic, & Przybeck, 1993). His theory predicts that genes acting on dopaminergic transmission would affect individual differences in novelty seeking. Associations between allelic variants of the dopamine D4 receptor (DRD4) were assessed in unselected samples (Benjamin et al., 1996; Ebstein et al., 1995). The seven alleles for the DRD4 receptor gene vary in the number of a 48-bp (base pair) repeat. In both studies, individuals with the longer alleles (6–8 repeats) had higher novelty seeking scores than did those with the shorter alleles (2–5 repeats). It may be that those with the longer alleles are dopamine deficient and seek novelty in order to increase dopamine release. Regardless, these variations in the D4DR gene account for about 4% of the phenotypic variation in novelty seeking.

The aforementioned study is a *candidate gene* rather than *whole genome scan* approach for finding genes with effects on individual differences in behavior; this type of approach presents the following methodological concerns:

- For association studies using population samples of humans, there may be artificial correlations between a candidate gene and a trait that are due to ethnic differences in frequency of the alleles of a candidate gene. This does not occur with within-family designs for association between a candidate gene and a trait. The association between length of repeat of the D4DR receptor and novelty seeking was also obtained in a within-family design.
- It is possible that an association may be a false positive. Hence, there should be independent confirmations of each reported association between a genetic variant and individual differences in behavior. There have been many replications of the association between length of repeat of the D4DR receptor and novelty (Plomin & Caspi, 1998). But there also have been a few failures to replicate this finding. This is likely to occur when the genetic variant has small effects on individual differences in the trait, as is the case for the effect of D4DR variants on novelty seeking.

Differences in Expression of Genes in the Brain

The technique of using DNA microchips is illustrated here for genes expressed in brain areas of two strains of mice. The inbred strains of mice are C57BL6 and 129SVEv, and the brain regions are midbrain, cerebellum, hippocampus, amygdala, entorhinal cortex, and cerebral cortex (Sandberg et al., 2000). Expression of 7,000 mouse genes were detected with the DNA microchip. Twenty-four of these were differentially expressed in all brain regions of the two strains, and 73 were differentially expressed in at least one of the brain regions of the two strains. These genes may be candidates for known behavioral differences between these strains. There are two methodological issues with regard to this approach.

- The microchip DNA arrays will not detect genes with low levels of mRNA. It is currently limited to detecting genes expressed at a relative abundance of 1/100000 mRNAs.
- There may be false positives with this technique. For this reason, findings on gene expression should be conformed with other techniques for detecting mRNAs such as Northern blots, RT-PCR (reverse transcriptase polymerase chain reaction), or *instu* hybridization.

This technique can also be used to study gene expression from human postmortem tissue. For example, it has been used to suggest that there may be differences between individuals with schizophrenia and normally functioning individuals in brain expression of two genes involved in synaptic function (Mirnics, Middleton, Lewis, & Levitt, 2001). But because premortem and postmortem factors can influence the findings with these tissues, these and similar results should be interpreted with caution, and genes implicated with this approach in phenotypic differences should be confirmed with other approaches. For example, one of the genes detected by microchip hybridization to be differentially expressed in the brains of normal and schizophrenic individuals are in a region on Chromosome 1 associated with the risk for schizophrenia.

Summary

Eventually, most (if not all) the genes that do or can cause variation in behaviors of nematodes, flies, and mice will be known, as will those that cause variation in human behavior. Because every gene does not affect every behavior in a species, behaviors can be grouped by the genes that cause them to vary. This would be the basis for a behavioral taxonomy based on gene effects as proposed by Ginsburg in 1958. Also, as genes with behavioral effects are identified in one species, they may be useful in two ways in the search for genes with behavioral effects in other species. First, DNA hybridization techniques can be used to search for *homologous genes*—ones similar in base pair sequence—in two species. For example, the period gene, which affects circadian rhythms, was first identified and sequenced in flies. The

DNA sequence of the period gene of flies was then used to see whether there were homologous genes in mice. This approach identified three period genes in mice. Second, the sequences of genes on chromosome segments are conserved in mammals. These homology maps can be used to suggest the chromosomal location in humans of a gene or QTL mapped in mice. For example, the QTL on Chromosome 1 with effects on emotionality of mice would be located in a specific region of human Chromosome 1.

DEVELOPMENTAL GENETICS OF BEHAVIOR

Background

Protein coding genes of eukaryotes essentially have two parts, the *structural regions* and the *regulatory regions*. The sequence of base pairs in the structural region codes for the sequence of amino acids in its protein. It serves as a template for synthesis of RNA; this is transcription. This RNA is first processed and the resulting mRNA is translated into the sequences of amino acids in the protein. The amino acid sequence of the protein is a determinant of its function. The base pair sequences in the regulatory region of a gene bind proteins known as *transcription factors*. Together, these determine when and where in the individual a gene is transcribed or expressed. In mice and humans, about 2% of the nuclear genome codes for proteins, and in mice about half of these genes are transcribed in adult brain. Further information on molecular genetics can be found in Lewin (1997) and on developmental genetics in Gilbert (2000).

In this context, three issues in developmental genetics of behavior are considered. These issues concern identifying (a) the pathway from DNA to a behavior, (b) the interaction of genes or epistasis and behavior, and (c) the effects of the interaction between genes and environments on behavior.

Pathways From the Gene to the Behavior

The initial step is to know the DNA sequences of a gene, thereby identifying the amino acid sequence of its protein. These sequences aid in identifying the cellular function of the gene. After this is known, the question becomes how varying that protein has behavioral effects.

For example, the gene for the enzyme nitric oxide synthase-1 (NOS-1) was knocked out. The homozygotes missing the enzyme in neurons are more aggressive than are those having the enzyme; these mice lack the gaseous neurotransmitter nitric oxide (NO; Nelson et al., 1995). The next steps would be to determine how the lack of NO increases aggression and how the presence of NO decreases aggression. It

has recently been shown that the knockout mice have reduced serotonin (5-HT) turnover and are deficient in $5HT_{1A}$ and $5HT_{1B}$ receptor function (Chiavegatto et al., 2001). It remains to be determined just how the presence and absence of NO affects the serotonin system and just how it in turn effects aggression. However, there is much evidence that the serotonin system is a major player in regulating aggressive behavior.

Gene Interactions and Behavior

Although it is possible to trace the effect of some individual genes from DNA to behavior, it is becoming increasingly clear that the effects of alleles of one gene on behavior depend on alleles of other genes. The interaction of the alleles of different genes is known as *epistasis*. The following is an example: The Y chromosomes of DBA1 and C57BL10 inbred mouse strains mice can differ in their effects on mouse aggression (Maxson, Trattner, & Ginsburg, 1979). This difference only occurs, however, if all or half the autosomal genes are from DBA1; it does not occur if all the autosomal genes are from C57BL10. Also, these types of interactions are often detected when knockout mutants in mice are transferred from one genetic background to another. For example, the knockout for the NOS-1 gene that increases attacks in one genetic background is lost after generations of backcrossing to C57BL6 mice (LeRoy et al., 2000).

In these examples with mice, the interacting genes are not known; however, interactions of pairs of genes are now being investigated in fruit flies. Epistatic interactions have been shown for recessive mutants with effects on olfaction (Fedorowicz, Fry, Arholt, & McKay, 1998). Others are looking at how allelic substitutions in a gene affect patterns of expression of many genes as a way to identify systems of interacting genes (Wahlsten, 1999). DNA microchips are used in this research. Greenspan (2001) has suggested that these systems of interactions may be very complex—networks of different genes can have the same behavioral effects and networks of the same genes can have different behavioral effects.

Genes, Environment, and Behavior

Effects of genes on behavior are dependent on the environment, just as effects of the environment on behavior are dependent on genes. For example, experience has effects on gene expression. Some of these are due to effects of experiences on levels of steroid hormones and thereby on gene expression in neurons. Others are due to effects of experience on synaptic transmission, which thereby affect gene expression in neurons. In this section, the effects of experience on gene expression are described for the circadian clock in mice; maternal care and pup development in rats; learning of birdsong; and long-term memory in mollusks, in fruit flies, and in mice.

If mice are kept in constant darkness, their circadian rhythm for wheel-running activity shows a cycle of about 24 hours, but the onset of activity drifts with each day in total darkness. The active period is known as *subjective day,* and the inactive period is known as *subjective night.* When mice and other rodents are exposed to light during the subjective night, the onset time for activity is shifted and the transcription of *c-fos* and several other immediate early genes in the suprachiasmatic nucleus (SCN) is induced (Kronhauser, Mayo, & Takahashi, 1996). Immediate early genes such as *c-fos* code for transcription factors that regulate the expression of other genes. It is believed that the expression of these genes resets the circadian clock in the SCN.

When crouching over their pups in arched-back nursing (ABN), mother rats lick and groom (LG) their pups (Meaney, 2001). This licking subsequently affects gene expression in the brains and the behavioral responses to stress of adult rats. There is variation in how much a mother rat licks and grooms her pups. As adults, pups with more LG have higher levels of corticotropin-releasing factor (CRF) mRNA in the hypothalamus and of glucocorticoid receptor mRNA in the hippocampus than do those with less LG. As adults, those with high-LG mothers are less fearful than are those with low-LG mothers. Also, females that had high-LG mothers lick their own pups more than do those that have low-LG mothers. This may represent one type of mechanism for nongenomic transfer of behavior across generations.

In some birds, there is a sensitive period for song learning. If at that time canaries or zebra finches are exposed to the song of taped tutors of their own species, the immediate early genes, Zenk and *c-fos* are induced in the forebrain structures NCM (caudal part of the neostriatum) and cHV (hyperstriatum ventral; Mello, Vicario, & Clayton, 1992). These regions appear to be involved in song learning and not in song production. This increase does not occur when each species is exposed to the song of another species or to simple bursts of sound.

Long-term memory for sensitization and classical conditioning in the mollusk *Aplysia,* classical conditioning in fruit flies, and spatial learning in mice involve changes in gene expression in the brain (Squire & Kandel, 2000). In each of these, the neural events of learning activate the transcription factor CREB (cyclic adenosine monophosphate response element binding protein); this then turns on other genes that cause changes in structure and function of nerve cells involved in long-term memory. For example, fruit flies are trained to associate an odor with an electric shock and another odor with the absence of an electric shock (Dubnau & Tully, 1998). The memory for these associations is tested by allowing them to choose between chambers with the two different odors. Flies have short-term memory lasting less than an hour and long-term memory lasting 24 hours or more. Flies were engineered to make CREB in response to heat shock. In non-heat-shocked flies, a single odor and electric shock pairing produces short-term but not long-term memory, whereas in heat-shocked flies, a single odor and electric shock pairing also produces long-term memory. Conversely, flies were engineered to make a protein that blocks transcription by CREB. Induction of this protein by heat shock blocked long-term but not short-term memory.

Summary

Genes are being used as Ginsburg (1958) proposed as tools to study the brain mechanisms of behavior and the effects of the environment on the development of behavior. It is of interest not only that the protein products of genes are involved in both, but also that the expression of genes are involved in both; this implies that although we can experimentally separate and manipulate genes and environment, they are in fact two sides of the same coin. For this reason, we should look beyond the old and tired nature-nurture controversy.

THE GENETICS OF BEHAVIORAL EVOLUTION

The evolution of behavioral adaptations is due to effects of natural selection on gene frequency. Details on population genetics may be found in Falconer and McKay (1997) and on molecular evolution in Page and Holmes (1998). In behavior genetics, the goal is to identify the genes and the changes in them that are the basis of the evolution of species differences in behavioral adaptations. Three examples are discussed in this section: the evolution of courtship song in fruit flies, the evolution of mating systems in voles, and the evolution of color vision in mammals. Respectively, these examples illustrate behavioral evolution due to change in the structural part of a gene, change in the regulatory part of the gene, and gene duplication with changes in both parts of the gene.

Evolution of the Courtship Song in Fruit Flies

Courtship by male fruit flies consists of several motor patterns. In one of these patterns, the male vibrates a wing; the sound produced is known as the *courtship song.* In *D. melanogaster,* variants of the period (per) gene affect this song. One of these abolishes the song; it is known as *per*[01]. Others change the timing of the wing vibrations and thereby the quality of the song. The song also varies among fruit fly species; furthermore, females of a species may prefer to mate with males singing their species song. This species variation is in part due to variation in the per gene (Colot, Hall, & Robash, 1998). When a cloned copy of the *D. similans* per gene was inserted into the genome of *D. melanaogaster* per[01], the male courtship song is restored but it resembles that of *D. similans* rather than that of *D. melanogaster* (Wheeler et al., 1991). Further analysis suggested that four or fewer amino acid substitution in a nonconserved region of the per protein may control the species difference in courtship song.

Evolution of Mating Systems in Voles

Prairie voles are monogamous and montane voles are polygamous. These two species also differ in partner preference, parenting, social contact, and aggression (DeVries, Taymans, & Carter, 1997). These species differences are due—at least in part—to species variants of an arginine vasopressin receptor (V1aR) gene (Young, Winslow, Nilsen, & Insel, 1997). The structural part of the gene is the same in the two species, but the regulatory regions differ between the two species. As a consequence, there is species variation in the expression of mRNA in regions of the forebrain and therefore in the forebrain distribution of the V1aR. Several lines of evidence suggest that this between-species neural variation may be involved in the between-species behavioral variation:

- Injection of arginine vasopressin (AVP) into the brain facilitates aggression in prairie voles and not in montane voles, whereas it facilitates auto-grooming in montane but not in prairie voles. Also, partner preference in prairie voles is blocked by brain injection of an AVP antagonist and facilitated by brain injection of AVP (Winslow et al., 1993).

- There are mice with a transgene for the prairie vole V1aR gene (Young, Nilsen, Waymire, MacGregor, & Insel, 1999). These mice have the same brain distribution of this receptor as prairie voles, and these mice exhibit increased affiliative behavior after brain injection of arginine vasopressin.

- A viral vector was used to insert another copy of the V1aR into neurons of a region of the basal ganglia in prairie voles (Pitkow et al., 2001). This increased V1aR binding in this region of the basal ganglia, and these males exhibited increased anxiety, affiliative behavior, and partner preference.

Evolution of Color Vision in Mammals

Most old world monkeys, great apes, and humans can discriminate between red and green, whereas all other mammals cannot (Bowmaker, 1991); this is—at least in part—due to the former's having three types of cones in the retina and the latter's having two types of cones. Each cone has its own opsin. *Opsins* are the proteins that confer spectral sensitivity on the visual receptors. Old world monkeys, great apes, and humans—but not other mammals—have cones with an opsin that is sensitive to the red end of the spectrum (Nathans, Thomas, & Hogness, 1986; Nathans, Merbs, Sung, Weitz, & Wang, 1992). The gene for the opsin sensitive to the red end of the spectrum is on the X chromosome of old world monkeys, great apes, and humans, and the gene for the opsin sensitive to the green region of the spectrum is on the X chromosome of all mammals. About 30 million years ago, the gene for the red opsin arose by gene duplication from the gene for the green opsin. At first, there were two green opsin genes. Then mutations accumulated in the structural region of one of these genes, changing its spectral sensitivity from green to red. There are seven amino acid differences between the red and the green opsins that appear to be critical for the difference in their spectral sensitivity. Changes in the DNA sequence of regulatory elements are likely; for example, the red opsin is synthesized in one cone and the green in another. Thus, after gene duplication, there are accumulated mutations in both the structural and regulatory regions of the second copy of the gene such that it came to code for a new protein with new expression patterns. This evolution by gene duplication has occurred many other times for other genes. For example, all the ion channel genes arose by gene duplications in common with the evolution of most of the serotonin receptor genes (Smith, 1991). Such genes are in families with similar DNA sequences. It is very likely that there were also behavioral consequences of these gene duplications.

Summary

It has been suggested that many genes are usually involved in the evolution of adaptations and speciation. But sometimes, as described previously, a single gene contributes most to the evolution of a trait. Also, it is possible for these genes to identify the DNA variant with effect on the behavior that has been subject to natural selection. In time, the molecular basis of many species differences in behavior and their evolution will be understood. For example, we will know just what are the sequence and functions of the 2% of DNA that differs between chimpanzees and humans and how this difference contributes to the species differences in behaviors.

FUTURE DIRECTIONS

The completion of the respective genome projects in nematodes, flies, mice, and humans will make it possible to identify all of the protein coding genes of these species as well as where and when the genes are transcribed, and the new protein initiative will eventually identify the structural conformation as well as metabolic or cellular function of each protein. This will greatly ease the task of identifying all the genes that can and do cause a behavior to vary in these four species, as well as that of tracing the pathways from gene to behavior. The great challenge will then be to understand how genes interact with each other, how they interact with the environment in the development and expression of behaviors, and how they relate to behavioral evolution.

The study of the genetics of behaviors in animals can and should be for more than just the development of models relevant to human behaviors. The genetics of animal behaviors should also be researched in order to discover general principles relating genes to behavior across animal species and to have a comparative genetics of adaptive behaviors within related species. For this, there will need to be genome projects in other taxonomic groups; such work is already taking place on bees and other insects, many farm animals, domestic dogs, domestic cats, other rodents, and many primates; I believe that this process represents the future of behavior genetics.

REFERENCES

Archer, J. (1973). Tests of emotionality on rats and mice: A review. *Animal Behavior, 21,* 205–235.

Allada, R., White, N. E., So, W. V., Hall, J. C., & Rosbash, M. (1998). A mutant *Drosophila* homolog of mammalian Clock disrupts circadian rhythms and transcription of period and timeless. *Cell, 93,* 781–804.

Antoch, M. P., Song, E. J., Chang, A. M., Vitaterna, M. H., Zhao, Y., Wilsbacher, L. D., Sangoram, A. M., King, D. P., Pinto, L. H., & Takahashi, J. S. (1997). Functional identification of the mouse circadian Clock gene by transgenic BAC rescue. *Cell, 89,* 655–667.

Bakker, Th. C. M. (1994). Evolution of aggressive behavior in the threespine stickleback. In M. A. Bell & S. A. Foster (Eds.), *The evolutionary biology of the threespine stickleback* (pp. 345–380). Oxford, UK: Oxford University Press.

Belknap, J. K., Dubay, C., Crabbe, J. C., & Buck, K. J. (1997). Mapping quantitative trait loci for behavioral traits in the mouse. In K. Blum & E. P. Npbel (Eds.), *Handbook of psychiatric genetics* (pp. 435–453). Boca Raton, FL: CRC Press.

Benjamin, J., Li, L., Patterson, C., Greenburg, B. D., Murphy, D. L., & Hamer, D. H. (1996). Population and familial association between the D4 dopamine receptor gene and measures of novelty seeking. *Nature Genetics, 12,* 81–84.

Benzer, S. (1971). From genes to behavior. *Journal of the American Medical Association, 218,* 1015–1022.

Bowmaker, J. K. (1991). The evolution of vertebrate visual pigments and photoreceptors. In J. R. Cronly-Dilllon & R. L. Gregory (Eds.), *Vision and visual dysfunction: Vol. 2. Evolution of the eye and visual systems* (pp. 63–81). Boca Raton, FL: CRC Press.

Broadhurst, P. L. (1960). Experiments in psychogenetics: Application of biometrical genetics to the inheritance of behavior. In H. J. Eysenck (Ed.), *Experiments in personality: Vol. 1. Psychogenetics and psychopharmacology* (pp. 1–102). London: Routledge.

Chiavegatto, S., Dawson, V. L., Mamounas, L. A., Koliatsos, V. E., Dawson, T. M., & Nelson, R. J. (2001). Brain serotonin dysfunction accounts for aggression in male mice lacking neuronal nitric oxide synthase. *Proceedings of the National Academy of Sciences, USA, 98,* 1277–1281.

Cloninger, C. R., Svrakic, D. M., & Przybeck, T. R. (1993). A psychobiological model of temperament and character. *Archives of General Psychiatry, 50,* 975–990.

Colot, H. V., Hall, J. C., & Robash, M. (1988). Interspecific comparison of the *period* gene of *Drosophila* reveals large blocks of non-conserved coding DNA. *European Molecular Biology Organization Journal, 7,* 3929–3937.

Crawley, J. N. (2000). *What's wrong with my mouse?* New York: Wiley-Liss.

DeFries, J. C., Gervais, M. C., & Thomas, E. A. (1978). Response to 30 generations of selection for open-field activity in laboratory mice. *Behavior Genetics, 8,* 3–13.

DeVries, A. C., Taymans, S. E., & Carter, C. S. (1997). Social modulation of corticosteroid responses in male prairie voles. *Annals of the New York Academy of Sciences, USA, 807,* 494–497.

Dubnau, J., & Tully, T. (1998). Gene discovery in *Drosophila:* New insights for learning and memory. *Annual Review of Neuroscience, 21,* 407–444.

Ehrman, L., & Parsons, P. A. (1981). *Behavior genetics and evolution.* New York: McGraw-Hill.

Ebstien, R. B., Novick, O., Umansky, R., Priel, B., Osher, Y., Blaine, D., Benett, E. R., Nemanov, R., Katz, M., & Belmaker, R. H. (1995). Dopamine D4 receptor (D4DR) exon III repeat polymorphism associated with the human personality trait of novelty seeking. *Nature Genetics, 12,* 78–80.

Falconer, D. S., & McKay, T. F. C. (1997). *Introduction to quantitative genetics* (4th ed.). Harlow, UK: Longman.

Fedorowicz, G. M., Fry, J. D., Arholt, R., & McKay, T. F. (1998). Epistatic interaction between smell-impaired loci in *Drosophila melanogaster. Genetics, 148,* 1885–1891.

Flint, J., Corely, R., DeFries, J. C., Fulker, D. W., Gray, J. A., Miller, S., & Collins, A. C. (1995). A simple genetic basis for a complex psychological trait in laboratory mice. *Science, 269,* 1432–1435.

Gerlai, R. (1996). Gene-targeting studies of mammalian behavior: Is it the mutation or the background genotype? *Trends in Neuroscience, 19,* 177–181.

Gilbert, S. F. (2000). *Developmental biology* (6th ed.). Sunderland, USA: Sinauer.

Ginsburg, B. E. (1958). Genetics as a tool in the study of behavior. *Perspectives in Biology and Medicine, 1,* 397–424.

Greenspan, R. J. (2001). The flexible genome. *Nature Reviews Genetics, 2,* 383–387.

Grilo, C. M., & Pogue-Geille, M. F. (1991). The nature of environmental influences on weight and obesity: A behavior genetic analysis. *Psychological Bulletin, 10,* 520–537.

Jallon, J.-M. (1999). Genetic analysis of *Drosophila* sexual behavior. In B. C. Jones & P. Mormede (Eds.), *Neurobehavioral genetics: Methods and applications* (pp. 365–372). Boca Raton, FL: CRC Press.

King, D. P., & Takahashi, J. S. (2000). Molecular genetics of circadian rhythms in mammals. *Annual Review of Neuroscience, 23,* 713–742.

King, D. P., Zhao, Y., Sangoram, A. M., Wilsbacher, L. D., Tanaka, M., Antoch, M. P., Steeves, T. D. L., Vitaterna, M. H., Kornhauser, J. M., Lowery, P. L., Turek, F. W., & Takahashi, J. S. (1997). Positional cloning of the mouse circadian Clock gene. *Cell, 89,* 641–643.

Kronhauser, J. M., Mayo, K. E., & Takahashi, J. S. (1996). Light, immediate early-genes, and circadian rhythms. *Behavior Genetics, 26,* 221–240.

LeRoy, I., Pothion, S., Mortaud, S., Chabert, C., Nicolas, L., Cherfouh, A., & Roubertoux, P. L. (2000). Loss of aggression after transfer onto a C57BL/6J background in mice carrying a targeted disruption of the neuronal nitric oxide synthase gene. *Behavior Genetics, 30,* 367–373.

Lewin, B. (1997). *Genes* (Vol. 6). Oxford, UK: Oxford University Press.

Lynch, C. B. (1994). Evolutionary inferences from genetic analyses of cold adaptation in laboratory and wild populations of the house mouse. In C. R. B. Boake (Ed.), *Quantitative genetic studies of behavioral evolution* (pp. 278–301). Chicago: University of Chicago Press.

Manning, A. (1961). The effect of artificial selection for mating speed in *Drosophila melanogaster. Animal Behavior, 9,* 82–92.

Maxson, S. C. (1992). Methodological issues in genetic analyses of an agonistic behavior (offense) in mice. In D. Goldowitz, D. Wahlsten, & R. Wimer (Eds.), *Techniques for the analysis of brain and behavior: Focus on the mouse* (pp. 349–373). New York: Elsevier.

Maxson, S. C. (1999). Aggression: Concepts and methods relevant to genetic analyses in mice and humans. In B. C. Jones & P. Mormede (Eds.), *Neurobehavioral genetics: Methods and applications* (pp. 293–300). Boca Raton, FL: CRC Press.

Maxson, S. C., Roubetoux, P. L., Guillot, P.-V., & Goldman, D. (2001). The genetics of aggression: From mice to humans. In M. Martinez (Ed.), *Prevention and control of aggression and the impact on its victims* (pp. 71–81). New York: Kluwer.

Maxson, S. C., Trattner, A., & Ginsburg (1979). Interaction of Y-chromosomal and autosomal genes in the development of aggression in mice. *Behavior Genetics, 9,* 219–226.

Meaney, M. J. (2001). Maternal care, gene expression and the transmission of individual differences in stress reactivity across generations. *Annual Review of Neuroscience, 24,* 1161–1192.

Mello, C., Vicario, D. S., & Clayton, D. F. (1992). Song presentation induces gene expression in the songbird forebrain. *Proceedings of the National Academy of Sciences, USA, 89,* 6819–6822.

Miczek, K. A., Maxson, S. C., Fish, E. W., & Faccidomo, S. (2001). Aggressive behavioral phenotypes in mice. *Behavioral Brain Research, 125,* 167–181.

Mirnics, K., Middleton, F. A., Lewis, D. A., & Levitt, P. (2001). Analysis of complex brain disorders with gene expression microarrays: Schizophrenia as a disease of the synapse. *Trends in Neuroscience, 24,* 479–486.

Nathans, J., Merbs, S. L., Sung, C.-H., Weitz, C. J., & Wang, Y. (1992). Molecular genetics of human visual pigments. *Annual Review of Genetics, 26,* 403–424.

Nathans, J., Thomas, D., & Hogness, D. S. (1986). Molecular genetics of human color vision: The genes encoding blue, green, and red pigments. *Science, 232,* 193–202.

Nelson, R. J. (1997). The use of genetic "knock-out" mice in behavioral endocrinology research. *Hormones and Behavior, 31,* 188–196.

Nelson, R. J., & Chiavegatto, S. (2001). Molecular basis of aggression. *Trends in Neuroscience, 24,* 713–719.

Nelson, R. J., Demas, G. E., Huang, P., Fishman, M. C., Dawson, V., Dawson, T. M., & Snyder, S. H. (1995). Behavioural abnormalities in male mice lacking neuronal nitric oxide synthase. *Nature, 378,* 383–386.

Nelson, R. J., & Young, K. A. (1998). Behavior in mice with targeted disruption of single genes. *Neuroscience and Biobehavioral Reviews, 22,* 453–462.

Nisenbaum, L. K. (2002). The ultimate chip shot: Can microarray technology deliver for neuroscience? *Genes, Brain, and Behavior, 1,* 27–34.

Page, R. D. M., & Holmes, E. C. (1998). *Molecular evolution: A phylogenetic approach.* Malden: Blackwell.

Pitkow, L. J., Sharer, C. A., Ren, X., Insel, T. R., Terwilliger, E. F., & Young, L. J. (2001). Facilitation of affiliation and pair-bond formation by vasopressin receptor gene transfer into the ventral forebrain of a monogamous vole. *Journal of Neuroscience, 21,* 7392–7396.

Plomin, R., & Caspi, A. (1998). DNA and personality. *European Journal of Personality, 12,* 387–407.

Plomin, R., & Crabbe, J. (2000). DNA. *Psychological Bulletin, 126,* 806–828.

Plomin, R., DeFries, J. C., McClearn, G. E., & McGuffin, P. (2000). *Behavioral genetics* (4th ed.). New York: Worth.

Sandberg, R., Yasuda, R., Pankratz, D. G., Carter, T. A., Del Rio, J. A., Wodicka, L., Mayford, M., Lockhart, D., & Barlow, C. (2000). Regional and strain-specific gene expression mapping in the adult mouse brain. *Proceedings of the National Academy of Sciences, USA, 97,* 11039–11043.

Segalat, L. (1999). Genetic analysis of behavior in the nematode, *Caenorhabditis elegans.* In B. C. Jones & P. Mormede (Eds.), *Neurobehavioral genetics: Methods and applications* (pp. 373–381). Boca Raton, FL: CRC Press.

Smith, C. U. M. (1991). *Elements of molecular neurobiology* (2nd ed.). New York: Wiley.

Sokolowski, M. B. (1999). Genetic analysis of food search behavior in the fruit fly, *Drosphilia melanogaster.* In B. C. Jones & P. Mormede (Eds.), *Neurobehavioral genetics: Methods and applications* (pp. 357–364). Boca Raton, FL: CRC Press.

Sokolowski, M. B., & Riedl, C. A. L. (1999). Behavior-genetic and molecular analysis of naturally occurring variation in *Drospophila* larval foraging behavior. In W. E. Crusio & R. T. Gerlai (Eds.), *Handbook of molecular-genetic techniques for brain and behavior research* (pp. 496–511). Amsterdam: Elsevier.

Squire, L. R., & Kandel, E. R. (2000). *Memory: From mind to molecules.* New York: Scientific American Library.

Takahashi, J. S., Pinto, L. H., & Vitaterna, M. H. (1994). Forward and reverse genetic approaches to behavior in the mouse. *Science, 264,* 1724–1732.

Talbot, C. J., Nicod, A., Cherny, S. S., Fulker, D. W., Collins, A. C., & Flint, J. (1999). High resolution mapping of quantitative trait loci in outbred mice. *Nature Genetics, 21,* 305–308.

Tsien, J. Z. (1999). Brain region-specific and temporally restricted gene knockout using the Cre recombinase system. In W. E. Crusio & R. T. Gerlai (Eds.), *Handbook of molecular-genetic techniques for brain and behavior research* (pp. 282–290). Amsterdam: Elsevier.

Vitaterna, M. H., King, D. P., Chang, A. M., Kornhauser, J. M., Lowrey, P. L., McDonald, J. D., Dove, W. F., Turek, F. W., & Takahashi, J. S. (1994). Mutagenesis and mapping of a mouse gene, Clock, essential for circadian behavior. *Science, 264,* 719–725.

Wahlsten, D. (1999). Single-gene influences on brain and behavior. *Annual Review of Psychology, 50,* 599–624.

Wallace, D. C. (1999). Mitochondrial diseases of man and mouse. *Science, 238,* 1482–1488.

Watson, J. D., & Crick, F. H. C. (1953a). Molecular structure of nucleic acids: A structure for deoxyribose nucleic acid. *Nature, 171,* 737–738.

Watson, J. D., & Crick, F. H. C. (1953b). Genetical implications of the structure of deoxyribosenucleic acid. *Nature, 171,* 964–967.

Winslow, J., Hastings, N., Carter, C. S., Harbaugh, C., & Insel, T. R. (1993). A role of central vasopressin in pair bonding in monogamous prairie voles. *Nature, 365,* 545–548.

Wheeler, D. A., Kyriacou, C. P., Greenacre, M. L., Yu, Q., Rutila, J. E., Rosbash, M., & Hall, J. C. (1991). Molecular transfer of a species-specific behavior from *Drospohila simulans* to *Drosophila melanogaster. Science, 251,* 1082–1085.

Young, L. J., Nilsen, R., Waymire, K. G., MacGregor, G. R., & Insel, T. R. (1999). Increased affiliative response in vasopressin mice expressing the V_1a receptor from a monogamous vole. *Nature, 400,* 766–768.

Young, L. J., Winslow, J. T., Nilsen, R., & Insel, T. R. (1997). Species differences in V_1a receptor gene expression in monogamous and nonmanogamous voles: Behavioral consequences. *Behavioral Neuroscience, 111,* 599–605.

CHAPTER 3

Comparative Psychology of Vision

GERALD H. JACOBS

Animals have accumulated an impressive array of sensory capacities to support the critical choices of life, but for most species vision provides an unparalleled source of information allowing access to sustenance, safe havens, and mates. Quite simply, vision is important for most species and paramount for many. Among the latter group are the members of our own order—the primates—and no doubt because of this there has long been a vigorous interest in studying vision. The fruits of this labor are represented in thousands of published studies detailing virtually every aspect of vision. A significant fraction of this work involves studies of nonhuman subjects, and this research, though often motivated by an interest in simply using results from other animals to infer aspects of human vision, has done much to reveal the details of visual processing across very disparate species. In addition, a smaller (but no less committed) group of investigators has pursued comparative studies of vision as an end that is useful and important in its own right. In this chapter I appropriate results drawn from both of these approaches in order to summarize some comparative features of vision with the intent of revealing examples of common solutions achieved by evolutionary experiments in seeing and of noting cases where visual diversity allows solutions to particular environmental opportunities. Let us start by considering some basic features of photic environments and eyes.

Preparation of this chapter was facilitated by a grant from the National Eye Institute (EY02052).

ENVIRONMENTS AND EYES

Fundamental Features of Photic Environments

Animals have evolved a range of photoreceptive mechanisms that allow the harvest of light to be employed toward multiple ends—for instance, in biological timing and navigation, as well as in seeing. In natural environments sunlight is the principle source of photic energy. Solar radiation is heavily filtered as it passes into earth's atmosphere such that the radiation spectrum of light reaching the planet surface encompasses only a relatively narrow range of wavelengths, from approximately 300 nm to 1100 nm. As a result of some additional limitations that are inherent in biological light detectors, this range becomes further truncated. In particular, longer wavelength lights contain insufficient energies to trigger effectively a change in photopigment molecules while the eyes of many species contain spectral filters of one sort or another that greatly attenuate short wavelength lights and accordingly make them unavailable for further visual processing. The result is that vision in animals is effectively limited to a span of wavelengths that lay somewhere in the range from approximately 300 nm to 700 nm, and most species do not see well over this entire range. Within this interval, variations in natural conditions can produce virtually infinite variations both in the overall amount of light (the total radiance) and in the relative distribution of light at different wavelengths (the radiance spectrum). These possibilities are illustrated in Figure 3.1, which shows radiance spectra measured for direct sunlight, for clouds, and for blue sky. Note, for example, that

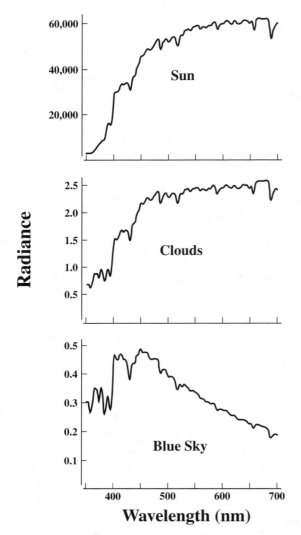

Figure 3.1 Radiance spectra measured for three sources of ambient light. The units of measurement for radiance are μmol/meter²/second/steradian/nanometer. (The data are from Endler, 1993.)

direct sunlight and blue sky differ not only in their relative distributions of spectral energy but also in peak radiance, in this case by more than five orders of magnitude. Examinations of spectra like these suggest that it would be useful to design visual systems that both allow for an analysis of variations in the spectral distribution of light and operate efficiently over an expanded range of overall radiance.

The variations in the spectral distribution and overall radiance of ambient light are enhanced even more as a result of fluctuations in light at different times of the daily cycle and as a result of the physical properties of matter intervening in the light path. For example, sunlight filtered through a canopy of foliage is preferentially absorbed by plant pigments and consequently presents a very different radiance spectrum from that of the same sunlight viewed in an open field. Filtering processes like these yield a wide variety of potential photic habitats and serve to provide important constraints on the nature of vision best suited to exploit local conditions. Probably nowhere is that fact more clearly evident than in aquatic habitats. Long-wavelength radiation is preferentially absorbed by water, the result being that as one moves downward from the surface of a body of water, the total radiance decreases, and the spectrum of available lights also shifts toward the shorter wavelengths. The filtering is such that in the ocean at depths of 200 m or so the total radiance has been greatly decreased and the remaining light is more nearly monochromatic and has energy centered near 500 nm. Systematic measurements have been made on the nature of available light in some important aquatic and terrestrial habitats (Endler, 1993; Jerlov, 1976).

Of course, vision results mostly not from directly viewing light sources, but rather from observing objects in the environment. For visual purposes objects can be characterized by the efficiency with which they reflect light as a function of wavelength (the reflectance spectrum). As illustrated in Figure 3.2, the light reaching the eye of a viewer is the product of the spectrum of the illuminant and the reflectance spectrum of the object. Accordingly, visual stimuli may be dramatically

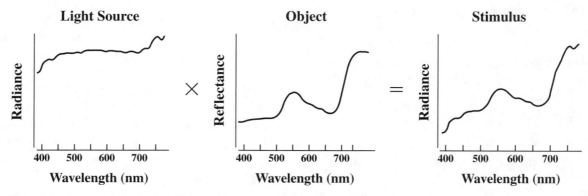

Figure 3.2 The spectral distribution of light reaching the eye of a viewer (right) is the product of the radiance spectrum of the source (left) and the reflectance spectrum of the viewed object (middle). Scaling on the ordinate axis is arbitrary. (After Sumner & Mollon, 2000a.)

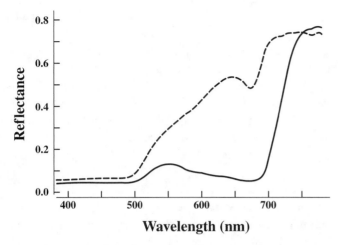

Figure 3.3 Reflectance measurements made on unripe (solid line) and ripe (broken line) specimens of Sapotaceae, a fruit that forms part of the diet of a number of different nonhuman primates. To a human eye the unripe fruit appears greenish and turns to yellow as it ripens. (After Sumner & Mollon, 2000b.)

altered by changes in the quality of the illuminant, as for instance at different times of the day, or by changes in the reflectance properties of the object. These alterations can be employed as a means for changing the nature of signals exchanged between animals or between an animal and a food source. A common example is that of fruiting plants. As fruits change from unripe to ripe, their reflectance properties are often dramatically shifted (Figure 3.3). For people and other species with the appropriate visual capacities (including various species of insects, nonhuman primates, fishes, and birds), this shift yields a large color change, and that information can allow a viewer to evaluate quickly and easily the potential palatability of fruit, perhaps thus guiding a decision as to whether it is worthy of the effort of harvesting.

In addition to overall radiance and spectral variation, there is another feature of light that can potentially provide useful information to an animal. Light radiated from the sun is unpolarized; that is, the electric vector (e-vector) of such light vibrates in all directions in the plane perpendicular to the direction of propagation. However, as light passes through the atmosphere, it becomes polarized so that the e-vector is oriented in a particular direction at each point in the sky relative to the position of the sun. It has long been appreciated that some species can analyze e-vector information to orient the animal relative to these polarization patterns. For example, honeybees are known to analyze patterns of polarized skylight to provide directional maps that can be used to chart the location of food sources (Rossel, 1993). Polarization sensitivity has been claimed to exist to varying degrees in many insects and birds, as well as in some fishes (Hawryshyn, 1992; Labhart & Meyer, 1999; Shashar & Cronin, 1996; Waterman, 1984). The biological mechanisms

present in the visual systems of these animals that allow for an analysis of the plane of polarization of light are absent from the eyes of mammals; thus, mammals are unable to exploit this potential source of visual information.

Eyes: Basic Design Features and Evolution

Although primitive devices that can detect light abound in simple organisms in the form of eyespots and eyecups, structures that are effectively not much more than localized accumulations of light-sensitive pigments on the surface of the body, the eyes with which we are most familiar are prominent organs that serve to collect light and focus it onto photosensitive cells. The consensus is that such eyes first appeared in great numbers during the Cambrian period, a time that saw an explosive divergence of metazoan phyla (Fernald, 2000). Examination of fossils from the middle Cambrian period (about 515 million years ago, or MYA) reveals irregularities on the body surface that have the form of a series of closely aligned parallel ridges or grooves, perhaps permitting them to serve as diffraction gratings. If so, these structures could have made the animals appear iridescent in the ambient light of their watery habitats. It has been proposed that this structural feature may have enabled for the first time the exchange of informative visual signals between individuals (Parker, 1998). Whether this adaptation was a trigger for a rapid evolution of eyes remains a matter for discussion, but in any case a number of phyla, including mollusks, arthropods, and chordates, emerged from the Cambrian period with functional eyes (Land, 1991).

Contemporary species provide examples of a variety of different eye designs. In essence, an eye images the outside world on a two-dimensional sheet of photoreceptor cells. Photoreceptors form immediate neural networks with other cells to make up the retina, and that structure constitutes the first stage of the visual nervous system. Two basically different kinds of optical systems have emerged to handle the task of image formation. In one, the retina is concave in shape; in the other, it is convex. If the retina is concave, a single optical element can be used to form an image across the retinal surface. This is the sort of arrangement found in the camera-type eyes of vertebrates. If the retina is convex, however, individual photoreceptive elements will be sensitive only to a narrow beam of incoming light, and this limitation is accommodated by the use of small lenses that are replicated again and again across the surface of the eye. The latter is characteristic of the compound eyes of arthropods (Goldsmith, 1990). Within these two design constraints are a number of qualitatively different imaging strategies. Several of these are illustrated schematically in Figure 3.4 (Land, 1991).

The top half of Figure 3.4 shows alternative versions of retinas that maintain a basic concave shape. In each case the

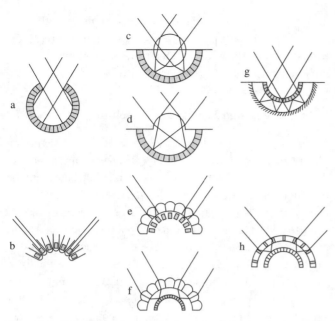

Figure 3.4   Principal mechanisms for image formation in animal eyes. The photosensitive portions of the eyes are shaded, and light rays are drawn to illustrate the image formation scheme. Further explanation is given in the text. (After Land, 1991.)

photosensitive portion of the eye appears as shaded, and light rays have been drawn to illustrate the image formation scheme. A possible precursor to the more elaborate versions of a concave retina is a simple pit (Figure 3.4, panel A), the bottom surface of which is pigmented so that shadowing of light allows the animal to gain an indication of the directionality of a light source. Two successors to this plan are illustrated in the middle. They each employ large refracting elements to form a retinal image. In one (panel C) this is done with a spherical lens (as is typical of the eyes of fishes and others); in the other (panel D), principal refraction of light is accomplished by the cornea. The latter arrangement is the one found in human eyes, as indeed it is in all terrestrial vertebrates. The eye schematized in panel G ingenuously accommodates the concave retina by reflecting light back from a concave surface (a mirror) onto the photoreceptor cells. Mirrored eyes like this are rare; the eyes of scallops provide a well-studied contemporary example (Land, 1965).

The bottom half of Figure 3.4 illustrates various optical arrangements that have evolved in conjunction with a convex retina. The scheme shown in panel B, in which the individual elements are tube-like structures with a photopigment accumulation at the base of the tube, is again a possible primitive precursor for more sophisticated convex retina designs. In the middle are the two common optical arrangements found in compound eyes. One (panel E) uses so-called apposition optics, in which each of the lenses forms an image on photosensitive pigment in individual structures called

rhabdoms. In the other version of the compound eye (panel F), the image is formed by the superposition of rays coming through many of the optical elements. Most insects have one or the other of these arrangements, and a usual generalization is that superposition eyes are found in diurnal insects whereas apposition eyes are found mostly in nocturnal insects. Finally, a reflecting-mirror version of the superposition eye (panel H) is found in decapod crustacea (shrimps, prawns, crayfish, and lobsters). All in all, animal eyes have managed to exploit an impressive array of image formation schemes—in the words of one of the foremost students of the matter, "It does seem that nearly every method of producing an image that exists has been tried somewhere in the animal kingdom" (Land, 1991, p. 133).

The main business of the visual system is to detect and analyze the spatial structure of the environment. Consequently, the details and relative merits of various types of eyes as devices for resolving images have been the subject of intense scrutiny (for extensive reviews of this topic see Goldsmith, 1990; Hughes, 1977; Land, 1999a). The principles governing the potential resolution of eyes are well understood. For instance, in single-lens eyes image resolution is conditioned by the focal length of the lens and the physical separation of the individual receptors. This is because a longer focal length yields higher magnification of the image whereas a denser packing of the receptors increases the spatial sampling of the image. A limitation on increasing the packing density of receptors is that as they are pushed closer together, they must necessarily become smaller. This is a problem because smaller receptors would enhance spatial sampling; but because they are smaller, they also become less efficient devices for trapping light. The consequence is the inevitable tradeoff between these two features. The trade is such that, in general, the portions of vertebrate receptors responsible for absorbing light (the outer segments) have diameters of not less than about 1 μm and a receptor-receptor spacing of not less than about 2 μm (Goldsmith, 1990). Examinations of single-lens eyes suggest that the packing density of receptors has been optimized so as to take the fullest advantage of the optical quality of the image provided by the anterior portion of the eye.

Compound eyes have a design problem not inherent in single-lens eyes. In compound eyes, the small sizes of the optical elements suffer a loss of resolution from diffraction of the focused light. This loss of resolution could be counteracted by an increase in the size of individual lenses and in the number of individual elements. Such increases in size are, however, difficult to accommodate in small-bodied animals. Just how difficult can be appreciated by a calculation suggesting that if a compound eye were designed to yield the same spatial resolution as that produced by the single-lens human eye, it would have to be about 1 m in diameter

(Kirschfeld, 1976)! This is obviously impractical, but one means that has evolved to increase spatial resolution in compound eyes without having to increase overall eye size is to adapt small regions of compound eyes so that they can provide for localized regions of higher acuity. For example, preferential increases in the sizes of some individual facets allow some flying insects to have a zone of increased spatial acuity that is directed toward the horizon (Land, 1999a).

Regional specializations designed to support zones of higher acuity are common to many types of eyes whether they are of the compound or single-lens type (Collin, 1999). For example, in vertebrate eyes the density of retinal ganglion cells (the output cells from the retina) can provide a rough guide as to the way in which visual acuity varies across the visual field, with ganglion cell density highest in those regions of most acute vision. Figure 3.5 shows a map of the retinal

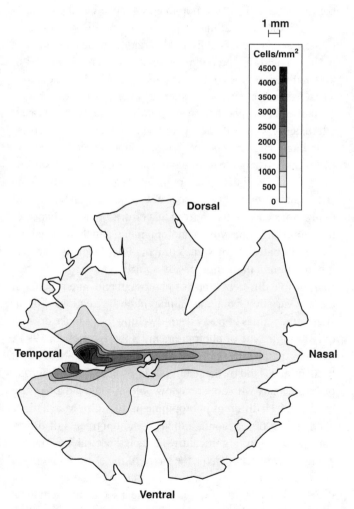

Figure 3.5 Ganglion-cell isodensity map for the retina of the spotted hyena. The tracing is of a retinal flat mount where each contour encloses the ganglion-cell densities that are indicated in the reference bar to the right. Note the presence of clear retinal streak with maximum ganglion-cell density located along the horizontal meridian in the temporal portion of the retina (Calderone, Reese, & Jacobs, 1995).

distribution of ganglion cells in a large carnivore, the spotted hyena (*Crocuta crocuta*). The hyena has a pronounced horizontal streak that stretches across the retina and is made up of densely packed ganglion cells. Visual streaks of this sort appear in the eyes of a number of mammals, often in animals that live in open terrain and that may therefore be thought to require heightened acuity along a plane parallel to the surface of the ground where most objects of interest will appear (Hughes, 1977). Cell distributions like those of Figure 3.5 can be used to generate quantitative estimates of the spatial resolution capacity of the animal. This can prove useful for predicting visual acuity and thus avoiding having to ask the animal to serve as a subject in a behavioral test of acuity, an invitation one might issue only with some reluctance in the case of subjects like the spotted hyena.

Another example of regional eye specialization is a little closer to home. Primate retinas have a fovea, a central region that contains a heightened packing of cones, the daylight photoreceptors. The foveal region is also free of blood vessels, and these structural adaptations, in conjunction with the superior optical quality that derives for light rays that pass through the center of the lens as well as a robust representation of this region in the nervous system, yields a central visual field in which visual acuity is unusually high. Studies of structural features in the eyes of the kinds described here for fly, hyena, and man have been used to infer the presence of specialized visual capacities in many other animals (Ahnelt & Kolb, 2000; Hughes, 1977).

Photosensitivity

Photopigments

The translation of energy from light into nerve signals is initiated by the activation of photopigments. Photopigments are intrinsic membrane proteins called opsins that are covalently bound to retinoid chromophores. Light causes an isomerization of the chromophore, and that shape change initiates a biochemical cascade culminating in photoreceptor activation (Baylor, 1996). Photopigments can be characterized according to the efficiency with which they absorb light (the spectral absorption curve), and it has been known for well more than a century that the absorption properties of photopigments contain important implications for understanding vision (Jacobs, 1998b). The essential point is that only light that is absorbed by photopigments contributes to sight.

An example of the intimate linkage that exists between photopigment absorption characteristics and vision is given in Figure 3.6, which shows results obtained from the Syrian golden hamster, a small rodent that is somewhat unusual in having only a single type of photopigment active under

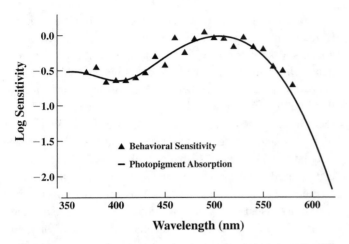

Figure 3.6 Comparison of photopigment and a behavioral sensitivity. The continuous line is the absorption spectrum for the single type of cone photopigment found in the eye of the Syrian golden hamster (peak value = 505 nm). The triangles show average threshold sensitivity obtained from two animals in a behavioral test. The two sets of data are shifted on the vertical axis so that they best superimpose. (After Jacobs, 1998b.)

daylight (photopic) conditions (Calderone & Jacobs, 1999). The solid line is the absorption spectrum of the hamster cone photopigment. Like all photopigments, that of the hamster has broad spectral absorption, but the efficiency with which it absorbs light varies greatly as a function of wavelength with peak sensitivity at about 500 nm. This species has also been the subject of direct tests of vision, and the triangles in Figure 3.6 plot those results, indicating the sensitivity of this species to lights of different wavelengths. It is apparent that the spectral absorption characteristics of the hamster cone photopigment almost perfectly predict the spectral sensitivity of the behaving animal. Various assumptions and corrections are usually required in order to compare photopigment absorption characteristics and different measurements of vision legitimately, but as the example of Figure 3.6 suggests, photopigment measurements per se may be used to derive strong inferences about the nature of vision. It is partially because of that fact that enormous effort has been directed toward measuring and understanding photopigments in a wide range of different animals.

The spectral absorption properties of photopigments depend on both of the essential components of photopigments. The width of the absorption curve is determined by the structure of the chromophore. In this case nature has been economical because only four different types of chromophores are used to construct all animal photopigments. These pigment chromophores are (a) retinal, the chromophore widely used in the photopigments of many vertebrates and invertebrates; (b) 3-dehydroretinal, used by most freshwater fishes, amphibians, and reptiles; (c) 3-hydroxyretinal, found in the photopigments of certain insects such as flies, moths, and butterflies;

and (d) 4-hydroxyretinal, a chromophore apparently used exclusively by a bioluminescent squid. Some animals are able to utilize two different chromophores to make photopigments, and this can (and often does) yield mixtures of photopigments in the retina based on these different chromophores. In addition, some switch from one chromophore to another at different stages in their life cycle (e.g., during metamorphosis in some anurans and during the migration between freshwater and marine environments for some fishes). Changing the chromophore can alter spectral sensitivity, sometimes drastically, and thus chromophore substitutions may significantly impact an animal's vision.

The spectral positioning of the absorption curve of the photopigment depends on the structure of the opsin. As was noted earlier, opsins are membrane-spanning proteins. Figure 3.7 is a schematic of a human cone photopigment opsin. It is composed of seven α-helices that weave back and forth through the membrane. The chromophore is attached to the opsin at the site indicated. All photopigments share this general configuration, but there is individual variation in the total number of amino acids in the polypeptide chain (from about 350 to 400 in different types of photopigment) and in their sequence. These sequence variations determine the spectral absorption properties of the photopigment; thus, because there are many alternate versions of the opsin molecule, there is a correspondingly large number of different photopigments.

Over the years measurements have been made of dozens of different animal photopigments (for summaries see Bowmaker, 1991, 1995; Briscoe & Chittka, 2001). Some generalizations can be drawn from this effort. First, most species have more than one type of photopigment, and their visual behavior is controlled by some combination of signals originating in different pigment types. It is fairly typical to find three, four, or five different kinds of photopigments in a retina, but there is variation from that number in both directions. For instance, the retinas of many deep-dwelling fishes make do with only a single type of photopigment (Bowmaker et al., 1994), whereas, at the other extreme, the current record for pigment production is held by the mantis shrimps, members of a group of crustaceans who are somehow able to make adaptive use of at least 11 different photopigments (Cronin, Marshall, & Caldwell, 2000). Second, although photopigments of different species vary significantly in their spectral positioning along the wavelength axis, the shape of the absorption curves changes in a lawful manner as a function of the location of their peak sensitivity (λ_{max}). This means that mathematical expressions can be derived to produce templates to account economically for the absorption spectra of any photopigment (Baylor, Nunn, & Schnapf, 1987; Carroll, McMahon, Neitz, & Neitz, 2000; Govardovskii, Fyhrquist, Reuter, Kuzmin, &

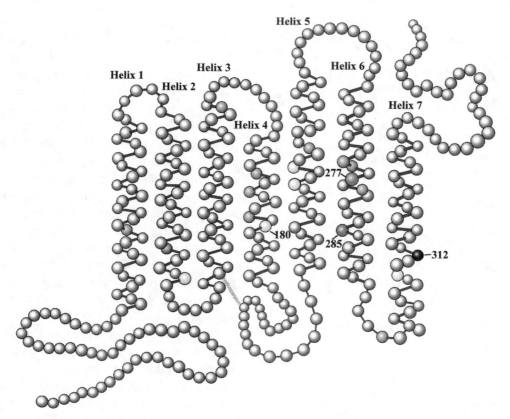

Figure 3.7 Schematic diagram of the opsin molecule for the human middle (M) and long (L) wavelength sensitive photopigment. Each of the 364 small circles represents an amino acid, and these pass back and forth through the receptor membrane in the form of seven helical palisades. The chromophore is attached at position 312 (clear circle). The other darkened sites represent the only amino acids that differ between the M and L versions of this opsin. The amino acids at the positions numbered 180, 277 and 285 are principally responsible for establishing the difference in spectral absorption of primate M and L pigments. (After Jacobs, 1998b.)

Donner, 2000; Lamb, 1995; Palacios, Varela, Srivastava, & Goldsmith, 1998; Stavenga, Smits, & Hoenders, 1993). Finally, pigments from different animals are frequently positioned at the same spectral locations. For example, in all cercopithecine primates (Old World monkeys, apes, and humans) two of the classes of cone photopigment have spectral locations that are virtually the same for all of the species in this group. This reflects the fact that structural variations in opsins specifying particular pigment positions are often conservatively maintained during the evolution of an animal line.

The absorption spectra for the daylight pigments of three species (goldfish, honeybee, and macaque monkey) appear in Figure 3.8. They exemplify the kind of variations in photopigments found among animals. These species have three or four different types of such pigment. In addition, goldfish and monkey have a population of rods subserving vision in low light, and this adds another pigment type to their retinal mix. The pigments from two of these, the honeybee and the macaque monkey, are based on retinal chromophores; goldfish pigments use 3-dehydroretinal. Note that the latter allows one of the fish pigments to be shifted much further into the long wavelengths than can be achieved for pigments built with retinal chromophores and that the spectral absorption bandwidth is greater for these 3-dehydroretinal pigments. Both goldfish and honeybee have photopigments that absorb maximally in the ultraviolet (UV) part of the spectrum. Some mammals (all rodents as far as is now known) have UV pigments, but primates are not among them (Jacobs, 1992). The results of variations in photopigment complements of these kinds are to provide spectral windows to the world that can vary greatly for different animal species. They also set the stage for significant variations in the color vision of different animals.

Opsins are produced by actions of single genes, and the past 15 years have witnessed significant progress in studying and understanding these genes. Opsin genes belong to a large family of cell surface receptors (which include a significant number of hormone and neurotransmitter receptors as well as other sensory receptors) and are believed to derive from a single ancestor in this family. Many different opsin gene

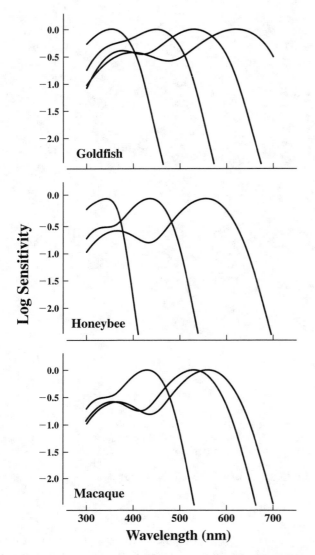

Figure 3.8 Absorption spectra for the cone photopigments found in three different species. The chromophore for the photopigments of honeybee and macaque monkey is retinal; the chromophore for goldfish photopigments is 3-dehydroretinal.

sequences have been derived: As of this writing, over 1500 primary sequence for opsins have been deposited in GenBank, a database maintained by the National Center for Biotechnology Information (http://www.ncbi.nlm.nih.gov80/). This accumulation of opsin gene sequences for diverse species in turn permits sequence comparisons from which ideas about the evolution of opsins can be derived. One caution in this enterprise is that the timing of evolutionary events derived from sequence comparisons depends on assumptions about the rate of molecular evolution (the so-called "molecular clock"), and that issue has generated considerable controversy. In particular, there is evidence that the mutation rates commonly used to calibrate such clocks differ for different groups of animals and thus that the assumption of a single clock rate appropriate for

all cases is unrealistic (Li, 1995). A consequence is that dates given for various events in photopigment evolution are quite provisional.

The eyespots of green algae contain opsins that bear significant sequence similarity to opsins of both invertebrate and vertebrate animals, suggesting that motile microorganisms like them might have been the first to develop photopigments (Deininger, Fuhrmann, & Hegemann, 2000). For historical context, the bacteria that employ pigments for photosynthesis can be traced back at least 3 billion years (Des Marais, 2000). In vertebrates, a single cone photopigment appeared first. Subsequently, this progenitor pigment gene duplicated, and the two diverged in structure, yielding two types of cone pigment having respective maximum sensitivity somewhere in the short and in the long wavelengths. This early divergence has been estimated to have occurred sometime between 400 MYA and 1,000 MYA (Bowmaker, 1998; Nathans, Thomas, & Hogness, 1986; Neitz, Carroll, & Neitz, 2001). This timing implies that two separate photopigments would have been available for use during the explosive expansion of eyes of the Cambrian period. Rod photopigments evolved from these early cone pigments following another gene duplication and four families of cone pigments also later emerged. A phylogenetic tree summarizing the inferred relationships among the vertebrate photopigments is shown in Figure 3.9. Note that whereas all contemporary vertebrates have rod pigments with only slightly variant spectral absorption properties, cone pigments have evolved to have maximum sensitivity over a much greater portion of the visible spectrum. Phylogenies for insect photopigments based on similar comparisons of opsin sequences are available elsewhere (Briscoe & Chittka, 2001).

Examination of the vertebrate opsin phylogeny of Figure 3.9 reveals the important fact that photopigments are both gained and lost during evolution. Thus, representatives of all four families of cone photopigments appear in modern animals from several groups (e.g., birds, fishes), but mammals have maintained pigments from only two of these families. How did this occur? One interpretation is that early mammals were nocturnal, and given that lifestyle, it may have been adaptive to increase the representation of rods in the retina in order to maximize sensitivity to the low light levels available during peak activity periods. Perhaps this change was at the expense of losing some daylight (cone-based) vision. Reflecting this loss, most contemporary mammals have only two types of cone pigment (Jacobs, 1993). As we shall see, some primates have added pigments and provide a notable exception to this rule. At the same time, other mammals have moved in the opposite direction; that is, they have lost a photopigment and thus a class of photoreceptors as a direct result

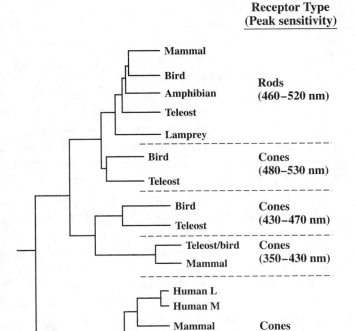

Figure 3.9 A proposed phylogeny for vertebrate photopigments. The interrelationships are derived from comparisons of opsin gene sequences. Illustrated are the relationships between four cone opsin gene families and a single rod opsin gene family. The peak sensitivity is a range given for photopigments measured in contemporary representatives of each of the named groups. See text for further discussion. (Modified from Bowmaker, 1998.)

of mutational changes in short-wavelength sensitive (S) cone opsin genes. Animals that have suffered this fate include some rodents and nocturnal primates, as well as many (perhaps all) marine mammals (Calderone & Jacobs, 1999; Crognale, Levenson, Ponganis, Deegan, & Jacobs, 1998; Fasick, Cronin, Hunt, & Robinson, 1998; Jacobs, Neitz, & Neitz, 1996; Peichl, Behrmann, & Kroger, 2001). It is not known why all these species have lost this particular cone pigment. Even so, the very presence of these nonfunctional genes makes clear that some ancestors of these animals must have had functional versions of these genes and the pigments they produce, and consequently these mutated genes stand as signposts that can guide us to a better understanding of the evolution of photosensitivity and vision. In any case, one major lesson learned from photopigment phylogenies is that the evolution of photopigments is not a one-way street.

Ocular Filtering

Light has to be absorbed by photopigments to contribute to vision, but light must reach the photopigments in order to be absorbed. The retinas of most animals contain photopigments that have the potential to absorb significant amounts of light well below 400 nm (see Figure 3.8), but that potential often goes unrealized because of intraocular filtering. These filters take many forms and can occur in any anatomical region of both vertebrate and invertebrate eyes (for an extensive review see Douglas & Marshall, 1999). Thus, the corneas or lenses of many species contain pigments that preferentially absorb short-wavelength radiation. An example is given in Figure 3.10, which shows transmission curves measured for lenses taken from the eyes of a number of different mammals. Lenses of this sort are nearly transparent to longer wavelength lights, but they begin to attenuate very steeply at some short-wavelength location, becoming progressively more optically dense and effectively opaque at still shorter wavelengths. The spectral location of the transmission cutoff varies among the species shown in Figure 3.10 such that, for instance, a light of 350 nm will be very heavily attenuated by the squirrel lens but hardly attenuated at all by the hamster lens.

In some cases photoreceptors contain screening pigments. These are called *oil droplets,* and they are positioned directly in the light path to the photopigment. Many birds and reptiles, as well as some amphibians and fishes, have oil droplets, and frequently there are several different varieties of oil droplets in a single retina (Douglas & Marshall, 1999). Like lens pigments oil droplets serve to attenuate short-wavelength lights, but unlike lens pigments the region of the attenuation may

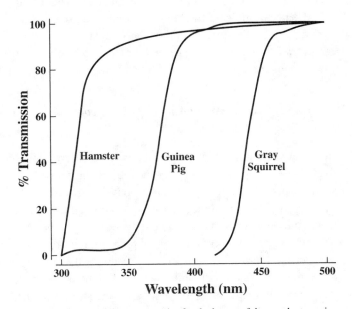

Figure 3.10 Transmission properties for the lenses of three rodent species. Note that all three transmit light with high efficiency for wavelengths longer than about 500 nm, but that they vary greatly in the spectral location where each begins to attenuate a significant amount of light. (Data from Douglas & Marshall, 1999.)

extend well out into the visible spectrum. As a consequence, a person viewing a fresh piece of retina sees these oil droplets as having a deeply colored appearance (red, orange, yellow, and so on). These pigments can serve to change drastically the absorption efficiency of the photopigment lying behind the droplet. There are a wide variety of other intraocular filters found in various animals. Considered as a group, these filters obviously greatly condition the extent to which environmental light contributes to sight.

Intraocular filters serve to reduce the influence that light can have on the visual system, and at first glance this might seem maladaptive. From his studies of the eyes of many different animals, Gordon Walls (1942), one of the great comparative vision specialists of the last century, famously suggested that "everything in the vertebrate eye means something" (p. iii). Following Walls's dictum, many investigators have felt impelled to try to understand what positive role intraocular filters might play. A variety of possibilities has been suggested. Among the more popular are these: (a) Intraocular filters might serve to protect the retina from high-energy (and potentially injurious) short-wavelength lights, and this may be particularly important for animals behaviorally active at high light levels; (b) intraocular filters could enhance the quality of the image formed on the photoreceptors by reducing the effects of chromatic aberrations, which are especially troublesome for short-wavelength lights; and (c) for oil droplets particularly, intraocular filters can effectively narrow the spectral sensitivities of photopigments and hence may serve to increase the number of spectral channels. There is little evidence to indicate whether any or all of these ideas are correct, but the presence of intraocular filters in so many different species makes it quite certain that they must play a variety of adaptive roles.

Drawing Inferences About Animal Vision From Photopigment Measurements

In recent years it has become possible to characterize objectively the photopigments of a species by using procedures such as spectrophotometry and electrophysiology, as well as by applying various molecular genetic approaches. These techniques have proven invaluable in identifying the number of types of photopigments in a given retina and in predicting their spectral absorption properties. Paradoxically, it is usually a much more difficult and time-consuming task to make direct measurements of vision in most animals in a way that permits an understanding of how these pigments are used to allow an animal to see (Jacobs, 1981, 1993). A consequence is that there is a near universal tendency to go directly from measurements of photopigments to conclusions about how an

animal sees. Although there are plenty of logical and compelling linkages between pigments and vision (as Figure 3.6 reveals), there is also need for caution in trying to establish these links.

One difficulty in making the jump from pigment specification to predictions about vision is that the techniques used for measurement typically do not give information about the prevalence of the receptors containing these photopigments or of their distributions within the retina. Obviously, a small number of receptors containing a particular photopigment that happen to be tucked away in some corner of the retina will have a very different potential impact than if this same photopigment is present in large numbers of receptors liberally spread across the retinal surface. Even when there is some information about photopigment prevalence and distribution, interpretational problems may persist, as they do in the following example. In recent years it has become possible to use immunostaining of opsins to identify and chart the spatial distribution of photopigments contained within a retina (Szel, Rohlich, Caffe, & van Veen, 1996), and when this technique was applied to a marsupial, the South American opossum (*Didelphis marsupialis aurita*), it was discovered that the animal's retina contains two classes of cones, one with maximum sensitivity in the short wavelengths and the other in the middle-to-long wavelengths (Ahnelt, Hokoc, & Rohlich, 1995). The presence of two classes of cone pigments would ordinarily be interpreted to suggest the possibility of dichromatic color vision. However, opossum cones were found to be scarce, never reaching a density greater than about $3,000/mm^2$ (by comparison, rod densities in this same retina may reach $400,000/mm^2$), and of these cones there are only a handful of S cones (never more than $300/mm^2$). An obvious concern is whether there are sufficient cone photoreceptors to capture the light needed to generate neural signals that can lead to color vision. Perhaps even more to the point would be to ask whether a devoutly nocturnal species like the opossum would often be active at light levels high enough to ensure such inputs.

A second example of the difficulty in arguing from pigment information to visual capacity comes from study of the coelacanth (*Latimeria chalumnae*), a fish that lives at depths of 200 m or so in the Indian ocean and that has attracted much attention over the years because it is considered a living fossil, having been little altered over the course of the last 400 million years. Recently, investigators ingeniously succeeded in isolating two opsin genes from the coelacanth, producing photopigment from these genes in an artificial expression system and then measuring the absorption characteristics of these pigments (Yokoyama, Zhang, Radlwimmer, & Blow, 1999). The coelacanth has two photopigments with closely spaced absorption spectra (peaks of 478 nm and 485 nm). These pigments are apparently housed in cone and rod receptors, respectively. What inferences can be drawn about vision in the coelacanth from these observations? By analogy to cases in mammals where feeble color vision may be derived from neural comparisons of rod and cone signals, the authors suggested that the pigments may give the coelacanth some color vision. But how likely is that? For one thing, the coelacanth has only a very small number of cone photoreceptors (Locket, 1980), so neural signals generated from one of the sets of receptors will be minimal at best. A similar reservation comes from the fact that the spectra for two pigments are very close together. In vertebrates, the signals used for color vision reflect a neural computation of the differences in spectral absorption between photopigments. Those differences will be very small for pigments whose spectra are so greatly overlapped, and an unavoidable consequence is that a considerable amount of light will be required to generate reliable difference signals (De Valois & Jacobs, 1984). Would the restricted amount of light available at the ocean depths that mark the home of the coelacanth be sufficient to generate such neural difference signals?

The point to be drawn from these examples is not that measurements of photopigments are unimportant for understanding animal vision. To the contrary, they are quite essential. What should be appreciated, however, is that frequently it is not straightforward to go from photopigment information to an understanding of how and what an animal sees. Care is always required in this step, and whenever possible it is useful to know something about visual behavior in the species under consideration.

The Role of the Nervous System

This section has dealt with a consideration of eyes and what can be learned about comparative vision by examining their structures and functions. Of course, for most animals the processing of information that leads to vision does not end with the eye, but rather with the networks of a visual nervous system that lie beyond the eye. These visual systems can be compact and simple or extensive and highly elaborate, comprised of anywhere from dozens to billions of nerve cells. The variations in structure and organization of visual systems across phyla are so profound as to make impractical any compact summary. Indeed, unlike the optical portions of eyes, where the components and their principals of operation are well understood, much of the detail of the function of visual systems remains still poorly understood, thus making comparison difficult.

Certainly there are many organizational features common to the visual nervous systems of different animals. For example, most visual systems have point-to-point topographic mappings between the visual field and various target structures in the visual system. Thus, topographic maps of this sort are found in mammalian visual cortex, in fish optic tecta, and in the optic lobes of insects. Such organization allows neural economy in the sense that information about contour boundaries in the visual world can be processed using only short-range neural interactions. Although perhaps less universal across phyla, there is also frequently some sort of parallel processing in the visual system that allows for a structural segregation of functional information. In mammalian visual systems, for instance, separate cortical regions are at least partially specialized for the analysis of different aspects of the visual scene. In insects an analogous segregation can be seen in the utilization of subregions of the nervous system for analysis of movement information. Finally, species having restricted nervous systems generally accomplish much of the filtering of environmental information using peripheral mechanisms, whereas relatively less preprocessing is done for species with more expansive nervous systems. The ultimate expansion is in the primate central visual system, where a large fraction of the neocortex is dedicated to the analysis of visual information. This extra processing capacity allows for richness in visual behavior that seems largely absent from animals with smaller and more hardwired visual systems. Indeed, it has been argued that the large expansion of primate visual cortex principally reflects a need for an increase in the processing of complex social-cognitive signals that can be inferred uniquely from examination of the visual world (Barton, 1998). See Cronly-Dillon and Gregory (1991) for detailed information about the visual systems of different animal groups.

Measuring Animal Vision

Two general strategies have been used in the study of animal vision. One probes animal vision to explore capacities that seem important based on our understanding of human vision or those that would be useful to establish in order to understand better some biological feature of the visual system. The stimuli in such applications usually isolate some dimension of the visual input (e.g., movement, contour orientation), and visual behavior is most often assessed by measuring thresholds using discrimination-learning paradigms of the sort developed over the years by animal behaviorists (Blake, 1998; Jacobs, 1981). An illustration of results from a study of this kind is shown in Figure 3.11. The goal of this particular experiment was to establish the temporal sensitivity of a small diurnal rodent, the California ground squirrel (*Spermophilus beecheyi*). The stimuli were sinusoidally flickering lights that were varied in frequency (cycles/second) and in luminance

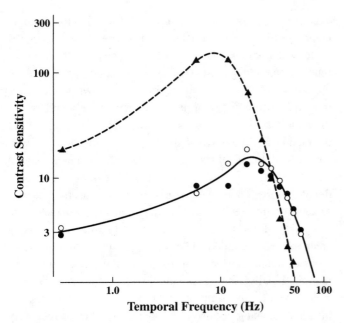

Figure 3.11   Temporal contrast sensitivity functions obtained from behavioral measurements made on two ground squirrels (symbols and solid line) and an equivalently tested human observer (triangles and dashed line). All three subjects were required to discriminate the presence of a sinusoidally flickering light varying in frequency and in luminance contrast. (After Jacobs et al., 1980.)

contrast. Through an operant conditioning procedure, ground squirrels were trained to detect the presence of such stimuli. The solid line in Figure 3.11 shows the sensitivity of ground squirrels to stimulus contrast as a function of the frequency of flicker; the dashed line shows discrimination results obtained from a human subject who was equivalently tested. The experiment indicates that although people are superior at detecting flickering lights of low to moderate frequency, for very fast flicker ground squirrels become superior and, indeed, people are quite blind to rapidly flickering lights that can be seen by ground squirrels. As for most experiments of this kind, these results were interpreted in light of details of the biology of the visual system and, to a lesser extent, as a step toward a better understanding of the normal visual behavior of this species (Jacobs, Blakeslee, McCourt, & Tootell, 1980).

A second general strategy for measuring animal vision relies on the use of natural behaviors. These are most frequently behaviors that are reliably elicited by some set of stimulus conditions and that therefore do not require that the animal be trained to perform an arbitrary response. Two examples illustrate this approach. The first involves an analysis of feeding behavior in a teleost fish, the black bream (*Acanthopagrus butcheri;* Shand, Chin, Harman, & Collin, 2000). In fish like this there are developmental changes in the position of the portion of the retina that has the highest ganglion-cell density (the area centralis) so that as the fish grows, the area centralis migrates from the central retina to a more dorsal location. As noted earlier, high ganglion-cell density is a regional retinal adaptation associated with the presence of heightened visual acuity. The question was whether this developmental change is paralleled by changes in visual behavior. To provide an answer, fish were offered food on the surface, at middepth, and on the bottom of an aquarium. It was discovered that as the fish grew, the preferred feeding location changes in accord with the position of its area centralis; that is, fish exploit that portion of the field that can be scanned with the highest visual acuity. A second example involves the predatory behavior of an insect, the praying mantis (*Sphodromantis viridis*). These insects sit in wait and skillfully dispatch passing flies by flicking out a leg and striking the prey in flight. The praying mantis has large forward-looking eyes that allow considerable binocular overlap between the two eyes. Rossel (1986) conducted a series of clever experiments involving the mantis's ability to strike flies accurately. By positioning prisms in front of the eye he was able to demonstrate that accuracy in striking behavior depends on the ability of the mantis's visual system to compare the angular extent of the target at the two eyes. Both of these examples illustrate the use of natural behaviors to understand better visual problems faced by particular species. Each also yields strong inferences about the relationships between the visual system and behavior.

THREE ISSUES IN COMPARATIVE VISION

A significant amount of research done on human subjects involves measurement of the limits of vision (e.g., the minimal amount of light required for detection, the highest temporal modulations that can be seen, the smallest wavelength change that can be registered, etc.). This approach can have a number of goals—for instance, to provide insights into visual mechanisms or to serve as a prerequisite for the development of practical applications. Studies of vision in other species are also frequently designed to assess the limits of vision, and these often have the goal of understanding the biology of vision as well. Studies of nonhuman species, however, also serve to focus attention sharply on the utility of vision. If two insect species differ significantly in their abilities to detect moving targets or if two rodent species have very different absolute thresholds, it is quite natural to seek an explanation of that fact in differences in the visual worlds of the respective species. Investigators studying animals that have more stereotypic visual behaviors, and correspondingly more simply organized visual systems, have been particularly avid in championing this kind of approach. In recent years the influence of this way of studying vision (sometimes subsumed under the phrase *ecology of vision*) has been steadily expanding to encompass a wider range of species, up to and including the primates. Here I cite some examples drawn from the comparative vision literature that are intended both to illustrate variations in animal vision and, where possible, to indicate how these variations relate to the visual demands placed on that animal. For convenience, these illustrations are divided according to three general problems that visual systems must solve.

Detecting Change

From a rodent searching the sky for a flying predator to a driver scanning a crosswalk for the presence of an errant pedestrian, success in seeing requires that novel events in the visual world be quickly detected and accurately appreciated. It is hardly surprising then that biological machinery appropriate for detection of stimulus change is an integral feature of visual systems. The importance of visual change (i.e., space-time alterations in the distribution of light) was dramatically underlined by early observations on human vision showing that when there is no change in the pattern of light falling on the photoreceptor array (a condition achieved by stabilizing the image of an object formed on the retinal surface), the visual scene simply fades from view after a few seconds to be replaced by a formless percept (Riggs, Ratliff, Cornsweet, & Cornsweet, 1953). In that sense, and at least for people, change and its detection are not just important—they are absolute prerequisites for sight.

Good examples of the ability of animal visual systems to detect change come from studies examining how animals use movement to control behavior. Consider the visual problems encountered by an insect in flight where image motion across the retina is a combination of inputs from stationary

backgrounds that are initiated by self-movement and from other moving objects in the field of view. Both of these generate complex input patterns that alter rapidly in configuration, have very high angular velocities, and can change direction unpredictably. Some of these flight behaviors have been well studied. Among these, observations have been made on how houseflies pursue one another (Land & Collett, 1974; Wagner, 1986). The aerial pursuits of flies are quite spectacular, characterized by quick turns made at high angular velocities often separated by periods of little or no turning. A clear implication is that the fly visual system must be capable of responding to very rapid change. Particularly intriguing is the observation that there are characteristic differences in flight behavior between the two sexes. Although both male and female houseflies pursue targets, males are pursuit specialists. This is because males avidly pursue females in flight, frequently intercepting and then mating with them.

The differences in pursuit behavior of male and female houseflies are uniquely paralleled by anatomical differences in the eye. In male houseflies, a region located in the fronto-dorsal portion of the eye contains enlarged ommatidia, each of which has a correspondingly larger facet lens (Land & Eckert, 1985). As was noted earlier, enlargement of the lens is an evolutionary strategy that allows a local increase in the acuity of compound eyes. There are other differences in the structure of these ommatidia in eyes of males and females, and there are also wiring differences in the visual nervous systems unique to the two sexes. The result is that the visual systems of houseflies show a significant sexual dimorphism that appears to correlate with the differences in aerial pursuit behavior. The portion of the eye in the male housefly that is adapted for initiating visual pursuit behavior has been fittingly dubbed the "love spot," and direct recordings made from photoreceptors in this region show clear differences between males and females (Hornstein, O'Carroll, Anderson, & Laughlin, 2000). Figure 3.12 illustrates some of these differences. The left

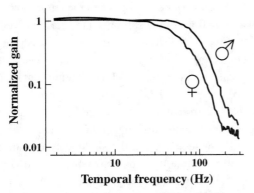 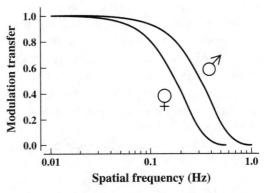

Figure 3.12 Temporal (left panel) and spatial (right panel) resolution properties of the photoreceptors of male and female houseflies. (After Hornstein et al., 2000.)

panel shows an index of temporal resolution of the photoreceptors of male and female houseflies. The curves effectively compare how efficiently receptors code information about lights presented at different temporal frequencies. In general, fly photoreceptors respond very well to high-frequency temporal change (e.g., they detect changes in visual stimuli at temporal frequencies of better than 100 Hz, a rate above what the human eye can discern), but male photoreceptors are clearly superior in this regard, showing about a 60% improvement above that achieved by the receptors from female eyes. The right panel of Figure 3.12 shows measurements made of the spatial resolution of these same fly photoreceptors. Again, the specialized photoreceptors of the male flies are significantly better than the corresponding female receptors at resolving spatial change. These clear differences in photoreceptor organization give males superior spatial and temporal resolution, and this in turn better enables them to locate and pursue small targets, such as females in flight.

Specialized visual adaptations always incur some cost, and the case of the housefly provides an example. Specifically, the faster responses of the male fly photoreceptors, involving as they do shorter time constants and higher membrane conductances, will require greater metabolic energy. There is likewise the burden of increasing the size of the facet lens to support higher acuity. It has been suggested that the better vision these adaptations give male flies are balanced by the energetic demands that are uniquely placed on female flies in reproduction, including activities such as egg production and laying (Hornstein et al., 2000).

Animals employ a variety of means to shift their direction of gaze—direct eye movements of various kinds, movements of the head, or indeed movements of the whole body. It is been argued that the goal of these movements is not to scan the surroundings continuously, as one might imagine, but rather to try to keep an image relatively fixed on the retina by employing rapid adjustments of eye position followed by a period of smooth tracking before further adjustments are initiated. In this view animals obtain a sampling of a series of more or less stationary images, as for instance many animals do during the fixations that are separated by rapid saccadic eye movements. In a recent review Land emphasized the commonality of this strategy across many different species and pointed out several reasons why it is advantageous to sample more or less stationary images than to allow continuous image movement across the eye (Land, 1999b). For one thing, fast movement of an image across the receptors leads to blurring. The occurrence of motion blurring depends both on the response speed of the eye and its spatial resolution. Eyes with higher response speeds and lower spatial resolution can tolerate movement at higher speeds without losing resolution. For example, at

movement speeds of only 3 deg/s much spatial detail disappears from human vision, whereas insects, having lower spatial resolution and receptors with faster response speeds, show little loss of resolution for objects moving with velocities of up to 100 deg/s (Land, 1999b). Second, measurements show that it is easier to detect moving objects if the retinal image of the background is held stationary, as can be achieved through the use of compensatory eye movements. There are other, more complicated, reasons for why it may be important to achieve a relatively stable fixation of an object of interest. What is remarkable is that even though the nature of their visual systems may differ drastically, most animals employ some combination of mechanisms to reach this same goal (Land, 1999b).

Resolving Spatial Structure

A number of features determine whether an animal will see an object. Among these, the size of the target and the degree to which the target contrasts with its surroundings are centrally important. Following the trend set by studies of human vision, early research on other animals concentrated on the utilization of object size as a cue to detection. This was mostly accomplished by assessing visual acuity through measurement of the smallest target that could seen or, more usually, the minimal size differences that could be detected (e.g., the smallest separation between two parallel lines). In recent years the contrast dimension has begun to receive equal scrutiny. With the widespread application of linear systems analysis to vision and the visual system, a typical contemporary experiment involves the determination of detection threshold for sinusoidal grating patterns that are jointly variant in size (spatial frequency, specified in cycles per degree of visual angle and thus directly translatable into retinal dimensions) and contrast (the difference in luminance or chromaticity between the peak and trough of the sinusoid). The results are plotted as spatial contrast sensitivity functions, a depiction quite analogous to the temporal contrast sensitivity functions of the sort presented earlier (Figure 3.11).

Figure 3.13 shows spatial contrast sensitivity functions obtained from five types of mammals. These include diurnal (man) and nocturnal (owl monkey) primates, a nocturnal carnivore (cat), and diurnal (ground squirrel) and nocturnal (rat) rodents. In each case, the animal was asked to detect the presence of a stationary sinusoidal luminance grating; the curve plots the reciprocal of threshold contrast required to see each grating. These functions have an inverted U shape such that some intermediate-size grating is detectable at lowest contrast and then visibility declines, precipitously for higher spatial frequencies and more gradually for lower spatial frequencies.

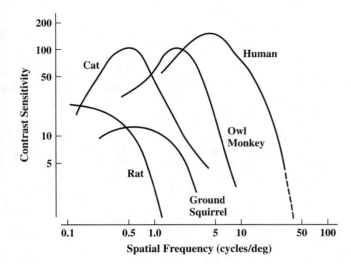

Figure 3.13 Spatial contrast sensitivity functions obtained from five types of mammal in behavioral tests. The continuous lines plot for each species the sensitivity to contrast in sinusoidal grating patterns determined over a wide range of spatial frequencies. (Data from Petry, Fox, & Casagrande, 1984.)

It has been argued that when properly scaled, contrast sensitivity functions from all species have the same common shape (Uhlrich, Essock, & Lehmkule, 1981). There is obvious large variation in the range of spatial frequencies these species can detect such that if viewed from the same distance, a high-frequency grating plainly visible to primate subjects is completely invisible to the rodents. Given the shapes of these functions, the inverse conclusion also holds; that is, a low spatial frequency target seen by a cat may go undetected by a human observer. The spatial frequency value obtained from extrapolation of the upper limb of the curve down to maximum contrast (indicated by the dashed line for the human observer) defines the high-frequency cutoff. It approximates the single value obtained from standard acuity tests like the familiar eye charts in which all the stimuli are presented at maximum contrast.

Contrast sensitivity functions are heavily influenced by the details of the test situation. In particular, (a) for technical reasons it is hard to arrange an adequate test at the very low spatial frequencies; (b) the shape and height of the function depend on the average light level of the target; and (c) because all retinas are to some extent heterogeneous, the details of how the subject views the targets are important. Therefore, detailed comparisons of functions of the sort shown in Figure 3.13 require caution. One useful feature in comparative experiments of these types is to include a reference standard—for instance, results from human observers tested in the same situation as the animal of interest. In any case, there is a clear relationship between the ranges of spatial frequencies to which an animal is sensitive and its visual world—many objects of interest to a primate will appear at a distance so that much of the object

will consist of higher spatial frequencies whereas for rodents similar objects will be viewed at close range and thus have their energies concentrated at lower spatial frequencies.

Table 3.1 provides estimates of spatial acuity in a range of common vertebrates. Included are single values that express (in cycles/deg) the limit of resolution in each species. These were obtained either by extracting the cutoff frequency of the spatial contrast sensitivity function or from a direct measure of visual acuity. Most were derived from behavioral tests, although a few were inferred from electrophysiological measurements. Even though the comparability of these results is subject to the reservations noted earlier, it obvious that there is a huge (>8 octaves) variation in the spatial acuity of these various animals.

The wedge-tailed eagle (*Aquila audax*) represents the upper end of the acuity distribution of Table 3.1. Like other raptors, this bird has phenomenal visual acuity, in this case about two and one-half times better than that of an equivalently tested human (Reymond, 1985). Raptor retinas are bifoveate, having a deep central fovea pointing about 45 deg away from the head axis and a shallower temporal fovea that points within 15 deg of the head axis. Distant objects are principally viewed with the deep foveae; near objects are principally viewed with shallow foveae (Tucker, 2000). A number of adaptations in the eye of this bird support high spatial acuity. First, cone photoreceptors are very densely packed together in the deep fovea. Second, the axial length of the eagle eye is long (about 35 mm vs. 24 mm in the human eye), allowing for a large retinal image. Finally, with the fully constricted pupil produced by high ambient light levels, the eagle eye shows only minimal evidence of optical aberrations (Reymond, 1985). These features combine to allow eagles to specialize in resolving high-frequency targets, such as would be presented by a small prey viewed from great heights. An interesting limitation on eagle visual acuity is its extreme dependence on light level. As acuity targets are dimmed, there is a precipitous decline in visual acuity so that eagle acuity actually becomes poorer than that of human observers at low light levels.

Among the species of Table 3.1 with relatively poor spatial vision is the opossum, a marsupial whose visual acuity barely exceeds 1 cycle/deg. The differences between eagle and opossum spatial vision and their visual worlds are instructive. As high-flying predators that alter their position rapidly and have to detect small targets, eagles require excellent spatial and temporal resolution. The visual adaptations that yield these properties (minimal spatial and temporal summation) require bright visual environments. As noted, one cost to the eagle for good spatial vision is much diminished capacity at low light levels. As a slow-moving omnivorous creature with a foreshortened visual world, the opossum has almost the opposite

TABLE 3.1   Spatial Acuity in Some Common Vertebrates

Class	Species	Cutoff Frequency/Visual Acuity (cycle/deg)	Method	Reference
Mammalia	Macaque monkey	50	Beh.	(De Valois, Morgan, & Snodderly, 1974)
	Squirrel monkey	17–35	Beh.	(Merigan, 1976)
	Owl monkey	10	Beh.	(Jacobs, 1977)
	Bush baby	4.3	Beh.	(Langston, Casagrande, & Fox, 1986)
	Cat	6	Beh.	(Blake, Cool, & Crawford, 1974)
	Lynx	5–6	Elec.	(Maffei, Fiorentini, & Bisti, 1990)
	Dog	11.6	Elec.	(Odom, Bromberg, & Dawson, 1983)
	Horse	23.3	Beh.	(Timney & Keil, 1992)
	Cow	2.6	Beh.	(Rehkamper, Perrey, Werner, Opfermann-Rungeler, & Gorlach, 2000)
	Sea lion (underwater)	3	Beh.	(Schusterman & Balliet, 1971)
	Tree squirrel	3.9	Beh.	(Jacobs, Birch, & Blakeslee, 1982)
	Ground squirrel	4	Beh.	(Jacobs et al., 1980)
	Rat (pigmented)	1.2	Beh.	(Birch & Jacobs, 1979)
	Rat (albino)	0.4	Beh.	(Birch & Jacobs, 1979)
	Mouse	0.5	Beh.	(Gianfranceschi, Fiorentini, & Maffei, 1999)
	Tree shrew	1.2–2.4	Beh.	(Petry et al., 1984)
	Opossum	1.3	Elec.	(Silveira et al., 1982)
	Wallaby	2.7	Beh.	(Hemmi & Mark, 1998)
	Numbat	5.2	Beh.	(Aresse et al., 1999)
Amphibia	Frog	2.8	Beh.	(Aho, 1997)
Reptilia	Turtle	4.4–9.9	Elec.	(Northmore & Granda, 1991)
Aves	Pigeon	12.6	Beh.	(Hodos, Bessette, Macko, & Weiss, 1985)
	Owl	8–10	Beh.	(Martin & Gordon, 1974)
	Eagle	140	Beh.	(Reymond, 1985)
	Falcon	73	Beh.	(Reymond, 1987)
Pisces	Goldfish	1.5–2.5	Beh.	(Northmore & Dvorak, 1979)

Note. Beh.: behavioral; elec.: electrophysiological.

problem. Its nocturnal environment offers only a small amount of light. To harvest photons efficiently, the pupillary aperture is opened wide, and the retinal wiring is arranged to support increased spatial summation of neural signals. The result is diminished spatial acuity but the ability to see under very low light levels. Interestingly, unlike the eagle, spatial acuity in the opossum changes little over a considerable range of luminance differences (Silveira, Picanco, & Oswaldo-Cruz, 1982). Whether nocturnal species like the opossum require increased spatial or temporal summation or some specific combination of the two is a complex question, the answer to which appears to depend on the details of their behavior (Warrant, 1999).

Here we have considered the spatial resolution abilities of various vertebrates. As indicated previously, compound eyes present an entirely different set of restrictions and opportunities. Visual acuity in compound eyes is determined principally by the angular spacing of the ommatidia, and on average this limits visual acuity to about 0.5 cycle/deg. Measurements of acuity of a number of insects reveal that some exceed this

value through regional specializations of the compound eye of the sort described earlier. On the other hand, many nocturnal insects also have much poorer visual acuity than this value. In a number of cases direct correspondences can be seen between insect spatial vision and their visual behaviors (Land, 1997).

Exploiting Chromatic Cues

At the beginning of this chapter I noted that there is virtually infinite variation in the spectral energy distributions from light sources and objects and that light thus offers an immense amount of potential information to a viewer. How much of this potential is realized? Photopigments effectively serve as counters that initiate a photoreceptor signal whose magnitude reflects the number of captured photons. That signal is transformed by the visual system into a visual sensation correspondingly varying in magnitude. If the eye has only a single photopigment, the resulting sensation lies along a single dimension. In the case of human vision this is the dimension of brightness or lightness. For human viewers tested at any single state of light adaptation, there are only 100 or so discriminable steps along this (achromatic) dimension. Having had only a single photopigment, it is a reasonable guess that our earliest seeing ancestors likely were similarly limited. An early step in the evolution of eyes was the addition of a second type of photopigment (Figure 3.9). This provides potential benefits because it expands significantly the size of the spectral window through which photons can be captured and thus yields a considerable visual advantage given the broad spectral patterns of most naturally occurring stimuli. If the outputs from receptors containing the two types of pigments are simply added together, the number of discriminable brightness steps will not increase. On the other hand, if signals originating from the two photopigments are compared in the nervous system in a fashion that computes the relative effectiveness of any light on the two pigments, a new dimension of sensation can emerge: color.

The mechanism allowing this new (chromatic) dimension is the presence in the nervous system of spectrally opponent neurons. These cells effectively subtract the (log transformed) inputs from afferents carrying signals that originated in the two types of pigments. Such information allows one to distinguish between variations in the wavelength and radiance content of a stimulus. So, for example, color vision allows discrimination between stimuli having their peak radiances in the long and short wavelengths respectively (like the sun and blue sky of Figure 3.1) regardless of their absolute radiance levels. The effect of this arrangement is to add a second, orthogonal, dimension to the animals' discrimination space, and because this chromatic dimension adds information at each of the span-of-brightness steps, the net result is enormous expansion in the number of radiance-wavelength combinations that can be effectively discriminated one from another. The presence of spectrally opponent cells in the visual systems of virtually all animals attests to the great advantage that accrues from both adding a second pigment and then using such mechanisms to gain a dimension of color vision. An alternative argument offered for the early evolution of spectrally opponent mechanisms is that they are relatively insensitive to fast flickering lights and thus that they may have served to remove the perception of flicker resulting from wave action that is inherent in shallow water environments. Such flicker, it is argued, would have made it difficult to detect the presence of potential predators (Maximov, 2000).

In the course of evolution, opsin gene changes added pigments to the original two with the result that, for instance, contemporary vertebrates may have three or four separate types of cone pigments. Through additional spectral opponency, the presence of a third pigment type can potentially provide another dimension of color vision. This allows for much finer discriminations among stimuli that vary in spectral content, and the net result is that the number of differences that can be discerned among stimuli that vary in wavelength and radiance climbs very significantly. Humans have three cone photopigments and two dimensions of chromatic experience (red/green and yellow/blue) in addition to an achromatic dimension. What this does for discrimination can be inferred from a recent estimate suggesting that people should be able to discern as many as 2.3 million different colors (Pointer & Attridge, 1998). This is a staggering number, and whether or not this estimate is accurate, it underlines one of the great advantages of acquiring a color vision capacity.

The relationship between number of photopigments and color vision dimensionality just described was firmly established through studies of normal and defective human color vision. Most people have three types of cone pigments and trichromatic color vision. Those individuals reduced to two types of cone pigments through gene changes have a single chromatic dimension (dichromatic color vision). Pigment complements are now known for many species, and a basic question is how well these relationships between pigments and color vision hold for other animals. Studies sufficient to establish the dimensionality of color vision have been reported for a number of nonhuman species (for reviews, see Jacobs, 1981; Menzel & Backhaus, 1991; Neumeyer, 1998). The general outcome is that the number of photopigment types can indeed predict the dimensionality of color vision. Thus, for example, of the species whose pigments are represented in Figure 3.8, the honeybee and macaque monkey have three photopigments and are trichromatic, whereas the goldfish with four pigments has acquired an added dimension of color vision and is tetrachromatic. Although results from pigment measurements and tests of color vision often line up well, there are instances where human color vision does not provide a very good model for color vision in other species. One example of this comes from behavioral studies of insects showing that although the utilization of signals from different photopigment types are processed through opponent mechanisms, they may be compulsively linked to specific aspects of behavior; for example, feeding responses and egg laying in butterflies are triggered by the activity of different combinations of photopigment signals (Menzel & Backhaus, 1991). Color vision in these species simply does not have the generality across stimulus conditions of the kind characteristic of human color vision.

Although knowledge of the number of photopigments may provide insight into the dimensionality of an animals' color vision, that fact by itself does not predict how acute the resulting color vision will be. That property will depend on the number the cones containing different pigments types, on their spectral properties and spatial distributions in the retina, and on the nature of chromatic opponent circuits formed from their outputs. Domestic cats and human deuteranopes both have two types of cone pigments with spectral properties that are not greatly different for the two species, and both formally have dichromatic color vision. However, with many more cones and much more robust spectral opponency, the human dichromat will have much better color vision than the cat. The point is that the quality of the resulting color vision, and likely the centrality of its role in vision, can be established only through appropriate behavioral examinations.

The human model gives us great familiarity with trichromatic color vision, but at least among vertebrates it seems possible that tetrachromatic color vision may be at least as widespread as trichromatic color vision. Many teleost fish have four types of cone pigments, as do many birds, and they could all be tetrachromats (Bowmaker, 1995; Bowmaker, Heath, Wilkie, & Hunt, 1997; Vorobyev, Osorio, Bennett, Marshall, & Cuthill, 1998). The question of why some animals have dichromatic color while others are trichromats or even tetrachromats remains unanswered. One suggested answer is based on the nature of photopigment spectra and the spectral band over which animals see (Kevan & Backhaus, 1998). The spectral span covered by the photopigments of tetrachromats is larger than that of trichromats (compare goldfish photopigments to those of the other species shown in Figure 3.8). The generation of color signals by spectral opponency requires that the spectral sensitivities of the pigments being compared overlap. Because the bandwidths of pigment spectra are fixed, in order to assure sufficient overlap to yield usable color signals one necessarily requires additional pigments to cover a broader spectral window. Some calculations suggest that for optimal color discrimination one pigment is required for about every 100 nm of spectral range (Kevan & Backhaus, 1998). This argument may seem a bit circular in the sense that it does not answer the question of why one needs an expanded spectral range to begin with. The answer to that question presumably lies in the details of how individual species use their color vision.

If adding more cone types and more dimensions in color spaces greatly expands the range of discriminations that can be made, why have all animals not become, say, pentachromats? This, too, undoubtedly reflects the nature of discriminations that are important for survival in any particular animal line. More generally, however, there are inevitable costs associated with adding cone types to support a new color vision capacity. For one thing, adding a new class of cone reduces the number of cones containing the previous pigment types and hence reduces the signal to noise ratio of each of the cone types. This could make the color vision less efficient (Vorobyev & Osorio, 1998; Vorobyev et al., 1998). For

another, in many visual systems the neural circuits required to yield spectral opponency are quite specific, so acquiring new color capacity may require elaborate nervous system changes as well as pigment addition.

Opsin genes were apparently lost during the early history of mammals (Figure 3.9), and as a result the baseline condition for contemporary mammals is the presence of two different types of cone photopigment in the retina. This allows many mammals to have dichromatic color vision, although even that capacity is often somewhat feeble because most animals of this group do not have large numbers of cones (Jacobs, 1993). Primates provide a striking exception to this picture: Their retinas typically contain lots of cones, and many of them have excellent trichromatic color vision. Because good color vision must somehow have reemerged among the primates, the story of color vision in this group can provide a good example of the utility of exploiting chromatic cues.

Some 90 species of catarrhine primates (Old World monkeys, apes, and people) share in common their color vision capacities (Jacobs & Deegan, 1999). It appears now that all of these animals have keen trichromatic color vision based on the presence of three classes of cone containing pigments absorbing maximally in the short (S), middle (M), and long (L) wavelengths and an associated visual system that supports spectrally opponent comparisons of signals from these three. The genes specifying the three opsins are located on Chromosome 7 (S) and at neighboring locations on the X chromosome (M and L), the latter two being almost structurally identical (Nathans et al., 1986). New World (platyrrhine) monkeys present a very different picture. Most of these species have polymorphic color vision with individual animals having any of several versions of trichromatic or dichromatic color vision so that there may be as many as six discretely different forms of color vision within a species (Jacobs, 1998a). The polymorphism reflects variations in the array of cone pigments found in individual animals that in turn arise from opsin gene variations. Like the catarrhines, the S-opsin gene in these monkeys is on Chromosome 7, but unlike the Old World primates the platyrrhine monkeys have only a single X-chromosome opsin gene. There is M/L gene polymorphism at that locus, accounting for the individual variations in color vision. As indicated in Figure 3.14, all these monkeys share in common the S pigment, but individuals have either any one of the three M/L pigments or any pair of the three, leading to six different color vision phenotypes. An important feature of the polymorphism is that because males have only a single X chromosome, they will inevitably have only a single M/L pigment and, thus, dichromatic color vision. With the benefit of two X chromosomes, females may become heterozygous at the pigment gene locus, and if they do, they have two different M/L pigments and trichromatic color vision (Jacobs, 1984).

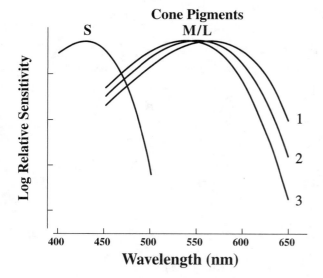

Figure 3.14 Schematic representation of the photopigment basis for the polymorphic color vision of most New World monkeys. At the top are the spectral absorption functions of four classes of cone photopigments characteristic of the species. The box at the bottom shows the six combinations of these photopigments. Each is found in some individual animals, and each yields a different type of color vision. (After Jacobs, 1998a.)

There is even further variation in color vision of the New World monkeys. Earlier I noted that some mammals have lost functional S-cone pigments through opsin gene mutation. One such animal is the nocturnal owl monkey (*Aotus*) that, by having only a single M/L cone pigment and no S pigment, ends up with no color vision at all (Jacobs, Deegan, Neitz, Crognale, & Neitz, 1993). A second exception to this polymorphic theme is seen among howler monkeys (*Alouatta*). Instead of being polymorphic, these monkeys have a gene/photopigment/color vision arrangement that is effectively the same as that of the Old World monkeys (i.e., they are universally trichromatic). Finally, Figure 3.14 illustrates a polymorphism that is based on three M/L opsin genes, but the fact is that some species of New World monkey have only two such genes while others may exceed three (Jacobs, 1998a).

Figure 3.15 summarizes the color vision variations so far described among the anthropoid primates. The figure includes results from species drawn from about half of the

43 genera that make up this group. This information, along with comparisons of primate opsin gene sequences, can provide scenarios for the evolution of primate color vision. One is that our earliest primate ancestors had two cone pigments (an S and a single M/L pigment) similar to that seen in most other mammals. Perhaps about 30 MYA to 40 MYA that single X-chromosome gene duplicated and the newly produced gene subsequently diverged in structure so that the pigment it specified differed in spectral absorption from the product of the original gene. This would allow for separate M and L pigments and set the stage for routine trichromatic color vision. The fact that the details of color vision are so similar among all of the catarrhine primates is evidence that these gene changes occurred early in catarrhine evolution. It further seems likely that the lines to modern platyrrhines and catarrhines diverged at a time prior to the point of gene duplication (Arnason, Gullberg, & Janke, 1998). An implication of this conclusion is that the polymorphism that allows some individuals to have trichromatic color vision was entirely a platyrrhine invention.

Tests of dichromatic and trichromatic humans show that there are enormous visual advantages in being trichromatic, and the same conclusion is supported by the fact that trichromacy has been conservatively maintained in all of the Old World monkeys and apes. Given that, why haven't the New World monkeys moved beyond the polymorphic arrangement that allows only about half of the individuals to have a trichromatic capacity? It may be nothing more than a matter of bad timing. The gene duplication that was required to convert catarrhines from dichromats to trichromats is a low probability event. It occurred early in catarrhine history, well before the great burst of speciation in that line, and thus all succeeding animals were able to profit from the change. X-chromosome opsin gene duplication has also happened at least once in platyrrhines (in the howler monkeys, as mentioned earlier). Unfortunately, this duplication occurred subsequent to much of the divergence that has led to modern day platyrrhines (perhaps only about 13 MYA), and thus no other New World monkeys have been able to take advantage of the color vision arrangement that the howler monkeys invented.

Studies such as those of primate color vision provide excellent examples of evolutionary changes in an important feature of animal vision. It is clear that color vision can increase dramatically an animal's capability to discriminate differences in its visual world, and it is useful to consider briefly the ends to which this enhanced capacity is directed. There is much contemporary discussion of the practical utility of color vision, of how a particular color capacity fits into local need. Thus, for example, the relationships between floral coloring and insect color vision (Kevan & Backhaus, 1998), between bird plumage characteristics and avian color vision

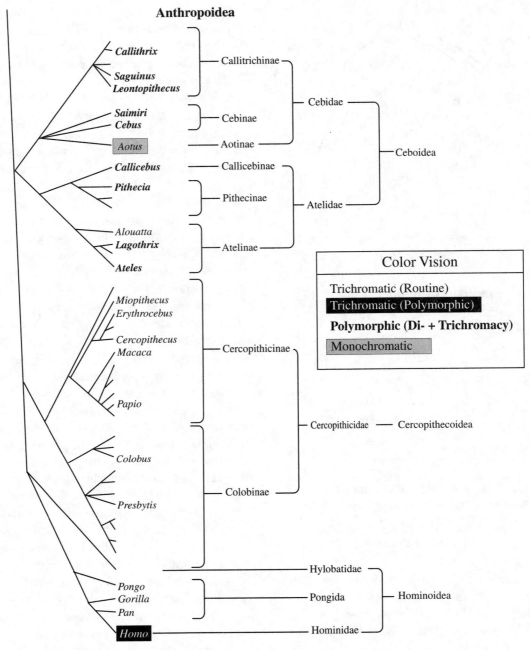

Figure 3.15   A tentative phylogeny of color vision for various anthropoid primates. Information is currently available for animals from about half of the total number of genera in this group (listed in the column at the left). Keyed are four different patterns of color vision: trichromatic (routine)—virtually all individuals share the same trichromatic color vision; trichromatic (polymorphic)—most individuals are trichromatic, but there is variation in the nature of the trichromacy and there are significant numbers of dichromatic individuals; polymorphic (di- + trichromacy)—large-scale individual variations in color vision with both dichromatic and trichromatic individuals; monochromatic—lacks a color vision capacity.

(Vorobyev et al., 1998), and between fish color vision and fish coloration (Marshall, 2000) have all been examined. For the primates, a common hypothesis is that many primates are frugivorous and must find fruit—a target that is often embedded in a sea of foliage—and therefore must determine whether that fruit is properly ripe (Figure 3.3). The principal cues for these tasks are the differences in the spectral reflectance properties of the fruit and their surroundings, and, as the argument goes, an ability to detect such differences could be materially aided by a trichromatic color capacity (Jacobs, 1999; Mollon, 1991). Thus, it may be that this relationship supported the evolution of primate trichromatic color vision. A number of recent studies that consider direct measurements of the spectral properties of target fruits in the context of the details of monkey vision do find that primate trichromacy is well suited for these fruit-harvesting tasks (Osorio & Vorobyev, 1996; Regan et al., 1998; Sumner & Mollon, 2000b). A problem is that most trichromatic primates are not exclusive frugivores, and some even eschew fruits almost completely. To account for them, it is suggested that trichromatic color vision is also particularly well suited for the detection and evaluation of leaves that make up a principal part of the diet of many species (Lucas, Darvell, Lee, Yuen, & Choong, 1998), and there is evidence for that possibility as well (Dominy & Lucas, 2001; Sumner & Mollon, 2000a).

CONCLUDING REMARKS

Proverbs (29:8) instructs us, "Where there is no vision, the people perish." In its literal sense this famous biblical citation is incorrect, both for people and for other species. It is clearly possible to survive and prosper without any vision at all, as for instance some species of cave fish and burrowing rodents are able to do. But these are clear exceptions, and the vast majority of animals has evolved and carefully maintained the biological machinery required to extract meaning from light. Comparative studies of vision and the visual system of the sort covered in this review have proven invaluable in revealing the impressive range of mechanisms that can be used to support sight. Understanding these adaptations provides a key to our appreciation of the natural world and is utterly indispensable in illuminating our own vision.

REFERENCES

Ahnelt, P. K., Hokoc, J. N., & Rohlich, P. (1995). Photoreceptors in a primitive mammal, the South American opossum, *Didelphis marsupalis aurita:* Characterization with anti-opsin immunolabeling. *Visual Neuroscience, 12,* 793–804.

Ahnelt, P. K., & Kolb, H. (2000). The mammalian photoreceptor mosaic-adaptive design. *Progress in Retinal and Eye Research, 19,* 711–770.

Aho, A. C. (1997). The visual acuity of the frog (*Rana pipiens*). *Journal of Comparative Physiology, 180A,* 19–24.

Aresse, C., Dunlop, S. A., Harman, A. M., Brackevelt, C. R., Ross, W. M., Shand, J., & Beazley, L. D. (1999). Retinal structure and visual acuity in a polyprotodont marsupial, the fat-tailed dunnart (*Sminthopsis crassicaudata*). *Brain, Behavior, and Evolution, 53,* 111–126.

Arnason, U., Gullberg, A., & Janke, A. (1998). Molecular timing of primate divergences as estimated by two nonprimate calibration points. *Journal of Molecular Evolution, 47,* 718–727.

Barton, R. A. (1998). Visual specialization and brain evolution in primates. *Proceedings of the Royal Society of London, 265B,* 1933–1937.

Baylor, D. A. (1996). How photons start vision. *Proceedings of the National Academy of Sciences, USA, 93,* 560–565.

Baylor, D. A., Nunn, B. J., & Schnapf, J. L. (1987). Spectral sensitivity of cones of the monkey *Macaca fascicularis. Journal of Physiology, 357,* 145–160.

Birch, D. G., & Jacobs, G. H. (1979). Spatial contrast sensitivity in albino and pigmented rats. *Vision Research, 19,* 933–937.

Blake, R. (1998). The behavioural analysis of animal vision. In J. G. Robson & R. H. S. Carpenter (Eds.), *Vision research: A practical approach* (pp. 137–160). Oxford, UK: Oxford University Press.

Blake, R., Cool, S. J., & Crawford, M. L. J. (1974). Visual resolution in the cat. *Vision Research, 19,* 933–937.

Bowmaker, J. K. (1991). Visual pigments, oil droplets and photoreceptors. In P. Gouras (Ed.), *The perception of colour* (pp. 108–127). Boca Raton, FL: CRC Press.

Bowmaker, J. K. (1995). The visual pigments of fish. *Progress in Retinal and Eye Research, 15,* 1–31.

Bowmaker, J. K. (1998). Evolution of colour vision in vertebrates. *Eye, 12,* 541–547.

Bowmaker, J. K., Govardovskii, V. I., Shukolyukov, S. A., Zueva, L. B., Hunt, D. M., Sideleva, V. G., & Smirnova, O. G. (1994). Visual pigments and the photic environment: The Cottoid fish of Lake Baikal. *Vision Research, 34,* 591–605.

Bowmaker, J. K., Heath, L. A., Wilkie, S. E., & Hunt, D. M. (1997). Visual pigments and oil droplets from six classes of photoreceptor in the retinas of birds. *Vision Research, 37,* 2183–2194.

Briscoe, A. D., & Chittka, L. (2001). The evolution of color vision in insects. *Annual Review of Entomology, 46,* 471–510.

Calderone, J. B., & Jacobs, G. H. (1999). Cone receptor variations and their functional consequences in two species of hamster. *Visual Neuroscience, 16,* 53–63.

Calderone, J. B., Reese, B. E., & Jacobs, G. H. (1995). Retinal ganglion cell distribution in the spotted hyena, *Crocuta crocuta. Society for Neuroscience Abstracts, 21,* 1418.

Carroll, J., McMahon, C., Neitz, M., & Neitz, J. (2000). Flicker-photometric electroretinogram estimates of L:M cone photoreceptor ratio in men with photopigment spectra derived from genetics. *Journal of the Optical Society of America, 17A,* 499–509.

Collin, S. P. (1999). Behavioural ecology and retinal cell topography. In S. N. Archer, M. B. A. Djamgoz, E. R. Loew, J. C. Partridge, & S. Vallerga (Eds.), *Adaptive mechanisms in the ecology of vision* (pp. 509–535). Dordrecht, The Netherlands: Kluwer.

Crognale, M. A., Levenson, D. H., Ponganis, P. J., Deegan, J. F., II, & Jacobs, G. H. (1998). Cone spectral sensitivity in the harbor seal (*Phoca vitulina*) and implications for color vision. *Canadian Journal of Zoology, 76,* 2114–2118.

Cronin, T. W., Marshall, N. J., & Caldwell, R. L. (2000). Spectral tuning and the visual ecology of mantis shrimps. *Philosophical Transactions of the Royal Society, London, 355B,* 1263–1268.

Cronly-Dillon, J. R., & Gregory, R. L. (1991). *Evolution of the eye and visual system* (Vol. 2). Boca Raton, FL: CRC Press.

Deininger, W., Fuhrmann, M., & Hegemann, P. (2000). Opsin evolution: Out of the wild green yonder? *Trends in Genetics, 16,* 158–159.

Des Marais, D. J. (2000). When did photosynethsis emerge on earth? *Science, 289,* 1703–1704.

De Valois, R. L., & Jacobs, G. H. (1984). Neural mechanisms of color vision. In I. Darian-Smith (Ed.), *Handbook of physiology: Vol. 3. Sensory processes.* Baltimore: Williams and Wilkins.

De Valois, R. L., Morgan, H. C., & Snodderly, D. M. (1974). Psychophysical studies of monkey vision: III. Spatial contrast sensitivity of macaque and human observers. *Vision Research, 14,* 75–81.

Dominy, N. J., & Lucas, P. W. (2001). Ecological importance of trichromatic colour vision to primates. *Nature, 410,* 363–365.

Douglas, R. H., & Marshall, N. J. (1999). A review of vertebrate and invertebrate ocular filters. In S. N. Archer, M. B. A. Djamgoz, E. R. Loew, J. C. Partridge, & S. Vallerga (Eds.), *Adaptive mechanisms in the ecology of vision* (pp. 95–162). Dordrecht, The Netherlands: Kluwer.

Endler, J. A. (1993). The color of light in forests and its implications. *Ecological Monographs, 63,* 1–27.

Fasick, J. I., Cronin, T. W., Hunt, D. M., & Robinson, P. R. (1998). The visual pigments of the bottlenose dolphin (*Tursiops truncatus*). *Visual Neuroscience, 15,* 643–651.

Fernald, R. D. (2000). Evolution of eyes. *Current Opinion in Neurobiology, 10,* 444–450.

Gianfranceschi, L., Fiorentini, A., & Maffei, L. (1999). Behavioural visual acuity of wild type and bc12 transgenic mice. *Vision Research, 39,* 569–574.

Goldsmith, T. H. (1990). Optimization, constraint, and history in the evolution of eyes. *Quarterly Review of Biology, 65,* 281–322.

Govardovskii, V. I., Fyhrquist, N., Reuter, T., Kuzmin, D. G., & Donner, K. (2000). In search of the visual pigment template. *Visual Neuroscience, 17,* 509–528.

Hawryshyn, C. W. (1992). Polarization vision in fish. *American Scientist, 80,* 164–175.

Hemmi, J. M., & Mark, R. F. (1998). Visual acuity, contrast sensitivity and retinal magnification in a marsupial, the tammar wallaby (*Macropus eugenii*). *Journal of Comparative Physiology, 183A,* 379–387.

Hodos, W., Bessette, B. B., Macko, K. A., & Weiss, S. R. (1985). Normative data for pigeon vision. *Vision Research, 25,* 1525–1527.

Hornstein, E. P., O'Carroll, D. C., Anderson, J. C., & Laughlin, S. B. (2000). Sexual dimorphism matches photoreceptor performance to behavioural requirements. *Proceedings of the Royal Society of London, 267B,* 2111–2117.

Hughes, A. (1977). The topography of vision in mammals of contrasting life style: Comparative optics and retinal organization. In F. Crescitelli (Ed.), *The visual system in vertebrates* (Vol. 7, pp. 613–756). Berlin: Springer-Verlag.

Jacobs, G. H. (1977). Visual capacities of the owl monkey (*Aotus trivirgatus*): II. Spatial contrast sensitivity. *Vision Research, 17,* 821–825.

Jacobs, G. H. (1981). *Comparative color vision.* New York: Academic Press.

Jacobs, G. H. (1984). Within-species variations in visual capacity among squirrel monkeys (*Saimiri sciureus*): Color vision. *Vision Research, 24,* 1267–1277.

Jacobs, G. H. (1992). Ultraviolet vision in vertebrates. *American Zoologist, 32,* 544–554.

Jacobs, G. H. (1993). The distribution and nature of colour vision among the mammals. *Biological Reviews, 68,* 413–471.

Jacobs, G. H. (1998a). A perspective on color vision in platyrrhine monkeys. *Vision Research, 38,* 3307–3313.

Jacobs, G. H. (1998b). Photopigments and seeing: Lessons from natural experiments. *Investigative Ophthalmology and Visual Science, 39,* 2205–2216.

Jacobs, G. H. (1999). Vision and behavior in primates. In S. N. Archer, M. B. A. Djamgoz, E. R. Loew, J. C. Partridge, & S. Vallerga (Eds.), *Adaptive mechanisms in the ecology of vision* (pp. 629–650). Dordrecht, The Netherlands: Kluwer.

Jacobs, G. H., Birch, D. G., & Blakeslee, B. (1982). Visual acuity and contrast sensitivity in tree squirrels. *Behavioural Processes, 7,* 367–375.

Jacobs, G. H., Blakeslee, B., McCourt, M. E., & Tootell, R. B. H. (1980). Visual sensitivity of ground squirrels to spatial and temporal luminance variations. *Journal of Comparative Physiology, 136,* 291–299.

Jacobs, G. H., & Deegan, J. F., II. (1999). Uniformity of colour vision in Old World monkeys. *Proceedings of the Royal Society of London, 266B,* 2023–2028.

Jacobs, G. H., Deegan, J. F., II, Neitz, J. A., Crognale, M. A., & Neitz, M. (1993). Photopigments and color vision in the nocturnal monkey, *Aotus. Vision Research, 33,* 1773–1783.

Jacobs, G. H., Neitz, M., & Neitz, J. (1996). Mutations in S-cone pigment genes and the absence of colour vision in two species of nocturnal primate. *Proceedings of the Royal Society of London, 263B,* 705–710.

Jerlov, N. G. (1976). *Marine optics.* Amsterdam: Elsevier.

Kevan, P. G., & Backhaus, W. G. K. (1998). Color vision: Ecology and evolution in making the best of the photic environment. In W. G. K. Backhaus, R. Kliegl, & J. S. Werner (Eds.), *Color vision: Perspectives from different disciplines* (pp. 163–183). Berlin: Walter de Gruyter.

Kirschfeld, K. (1976). The resolution of lens and compound eyes. In F. Zettler & R. Weiler (Eds.), *Neural principles in vision* (pp. 354–370). Berlin: Springer-Verlag.

Labhart, T., & Meyer, E. P. (1999). Detectors for polarized skylight in insects: A survey of ommatidial specializations in the dorsal rim area of the compound eye. *Microscopy Research and Technique, 47,* 368–379.

Lamb, T. D. (1995). Photoreceptor spectral sensitivities: Common shape in the long-wavelength range. *Vision Research, 35,* 3083–3091.

Land, M. F. (1965). Image formation by a concave reflector in the eye of the scalop, *Pecten maximus. Journal of Physiology, 179,* 138–153.

Land, M. F. (1991). Optics of the eyes of the animal kingdom. In J. R. Cronly-Dillon & R. L. Gregory (Eds.), *Evolution of the eye and visual system* (Vol. 2, pp. 118–135). London: Macmillan Press.

Land, M. F. (1997). Visual acuity in insects. *Annual Review of Entomology, 42,* 147–177.

Land, M. F. (1999a). Compound eye structure: Matching eye to environment. In S. N. Archer, M. B. A. Djamgoz, E. R. Loew, J. C. Partridge, & S. Vallerga (Eds.), *Adaptive mechanisms in the ecology of vision* (pp. 51–71). Dordrecht, The Netherlands: Kluwer.

Land, M. F. (1999b). Motion and vision: Why animals move their eyes. *Journal of Comparative Physiology, 185A,* 341–352.

Land, M. F., & Collett, T. F. (1974). Chasing behaviour of houseflies (*Fannia canicularis*). *Journal of Comparative Physiology, 89,* 331–357.

Land, M. F., & Eckert, H. (1985). Maps of the acute zones of fly eyes. *Journal of Comparative Physiology, 156A,* 525–538.

Langston, A., Casagrande, V. A., & Fox, R. (1986). Spatial resolution of the galago. *Vision Research, 26,* 791–796.

Li, W.-H. (1995). So, what about the molecular clock hypothesis? *Current Opinion in Genetics and Development, 3,* 896–901.

Locket, N. A. (1980). Some advances in coelacanth biology. *Proceedings of the Royal Society, London, 208B,* 265–307.

Lucas, P. W., Darvell, B. W., Lee, P. K. D., Yuen, T. D. B., & Choong, M. F. (1998). Colour cues for leaf food selection by long-tailed macaques (*Macaca fascicularis*) with a new suggestion for the evolution of trichromatic colour vision. *Folia Primatologica, 69,* 139–152.

Maffei, L., Fiorentini, A., & Bisti, S. (1990). The visual acuity of the lynx. *Vision Research, 30,* 527–528.

Marshall, N. J. (2000). Communication and camouflage with the same "bright" colours in reef fishes. *Philosophical Transactions of the Royal Society, London, 355B,* 1243–1248.

Martin, G. R., & Gordon, I. E. (1974). Visual acuity in the tawny owl (*Strix aluco*). *Vision Research, 14,* 1393–1397.

Maximov, V. V. (2000). Environmental factors which may have led to the appearance of colour vision. *Philosophical Transactions of the Royal Society, London, 355B,* 1239–1242.

Menzel, R., & Backhaus, W. (1991). Colour vision in insects. In P. Gouras (Ed.), *The perception of colour* (pp. 262–293). Boca Raton, FL: CRC Press.

Merigan, W. H. (1976). The contrast sensitivity of the squirrel monkey (*Saimiri sciureus*). *Vision Research, 16,* 375–379.

Mollon, J. D. (1991). Uses and evolutionary origins of primate colour vision. In J. R. Cronly-Dillon & R. L. Gregory (Eds.), *Evolution of the eye and visual system* (pp. 306–319). Boca Raton, FL: CRC Press.

Nathans, J., Thomas, D., & Hogness, D. S. (1986). Molecular genetics of human color vision: the genes encoding blue, green and red pigments. *Science, 232,* 193–202.

Neitz, J., Carroll, J., & Neitz, M. (2001). Color vision: Almost reason enough for having eyes. *Optics and Photonics News, 12,* 26–33.

Neumeyer, C. (1998). Color vision in lower vertebrates. In W. G. K. Backhaus, R. Kliegl, & J. S. Werner (Eds.), *Color vision: Perspectives from different disciplines* (pp. 149–162). Berlin: Walter de Gruyter.

Northmore, D. P., & Dvorak, C. A. (1979). Contrast sensitivity and acuity of the goldfish. *Vision Research, 19,* 255–261.

Northmore, D. P., & Granda, A. M. (1991). Refractive state, contrast sensitivity, and resolution in the freshwater turtle, *Pseudemys scripta elegans,* determined by tectal visual-evoked potentials. *Visual Neuroscience, 7,* 619–625.

Odom, J. V., Bromberg, N. M., & Dawson, W. W. (1983). Canine visual acuity: Retinal and cortical field potentials evoked by pattern stimulation. *American Journal of Physiology, 245,* R637–R641.

Osorio, D., & Vorobyev, M. (1996). Colour vision as an adaptation to frugivory in primates. *Proceedings of the Royal Society of London, 263B,* 593–599.

Palacios, A. G., Varela, F. J., Srivastava, R., & Goldsmith, T. H. (1998). Spectral sensitivity of cones in the goldfish, *Carassius auratus. Vision Research, 38,* 2135–2146.

Parker, A. R. (1998). Colour in Burgess shale animals and the effect of light on evolution in the Cambrian. *Proceedings of the Royal Society of London, 265B,* 967–972.

Peichl, L., Behrmann, G., & Kroger, R. H. H. (2001). For whales and seals the ocean is not blue: A visual pigment loss in marine mammals. *European Journal of Neuroscience, 13,* 1520–1528.

Petry, H. M., Fox, R., & Casagrande, V. A. (1984). Spatial contrast sensitivity of the tree shrew. *Vision Research, 24,* 1037–1042.

Pointer, M. R., & Attridge, G. G. (1998). The number of discernable colours. *Color Research and Application, 23,* 52–54.

Regan, B. C., Julliot, C., Simmen, B., Vienot, F., Charles-Dominique, P., & Mollon, J. D. (1998). Frugivory and colour vision in *Alouatta seniculus,* a trichromatic platyrrhine monkey. *Vision Research, 38,* 3321–3327.

Rehkamper, G., Perrey, A., Werner, C. W., Opfermann-Rungeler, C., & Gorlach, A. (2000). Visual perception and stimulus orientation in cattle. *Vision Research, 40,* 2489–2497.

Reymond, L. (1985). Spatial visual acuity of the eagle *Aguila audax*: A behavioural, optical and anatomical investigation. *Vision Research, 25,* 1477–1491.

Reymond, L. (1987). Spatial acuity of the falcon, *Falco berigora*: A behavioural, optical and anatomical investigation. *Vision Research, 27,* 1859–1874.

Riggs, L. A., Ratliff, F., Cornsweet, J. C., & Cornsweet, T. N. (1953). The disappearance of steadily fixated test objects. *Journal of the Optical Society of America, 43*, 495–501.

Rossel, S. (1986). Binocular spatial localization in the praying mantis. *Journal of Experimental Biology, 120*, 265–281.

Rossel, S. (1993). Navigation by bees using polarized skylight. *Comparative and Biochemical Physiology, 104A*, 695–708.

Schusterman, R. J., & Balliet, R. F. (1971). Aerial and underwater visual acuity in the California sea lion (*Zalophus californianus*) as a function of luminance. *Annual of the New York Academy of Sciences, 188*, 37–46.

Shand, J., Chin, S. M., Harman, A. M., & Collin, S. P. (2000). The relationship between the position of the retinal area centralis and feeding behaviour in juvenile black bream *Acanthopagarus butcheri* (Sparidae: Teleostei). *Philosophical Transactions of the Royal Society, London, 355B*, 1183–1186.

Shashar, N., & Cronin, T. W. (1996). Polarization contrast vision in Octopus. *Journal of Experimental Biology, 199*, 999–1004.

Silveira, L. C., Picanco, C. W., & Oswaldo-Cruz, E. (1982). Contrast sensitivity function and visual acuity of the opossum. *Vision Research, 22*, 1371–1377.

Stavenga, D. G., Smits, R. P., & Hoenders, B. J. (1993). Simple exponential functions describing the absorbance bands of visual pigment spectra. *Vision Research, 33*, 1011–1017.

Sumner, P., & Mollon, J. D. (2000a). Catarrhine photopigments are optimized for detecting targets against a foliage background. *Journal of Experimental Biology, 203*, 1963–1986.

Sumner, P., & Mollon, J. D. (2000b). Chromaticity as a signal of ripeness in fruits taken by primates. *Journal of Experimental Biology, 203*, 1987–2000.

Szel, A., Rohlich, P., Caffe, A. R., & van Veen, T. (1996). Distribution of cone photoreceptors in the mammalian retina. *Microscopy Research and Technique, 35*, 445–462.

Timney, B., & Keil, K. (1992). Visual acuity in the horse. *Vision Research, 32*, 2289–2293.

Tucker, V. A. (2000). The deep fovea, sideways vision and spiral flight paths in raptors. *Journal of Experimental Biology, 203*, 3745–3754.

Uhlrich, D. J., Essock, E. A., & Lehmkule, S. (1981). Cross-species correspondence of spatial contrast sensitivity functions. *Behavioural Brain Research, 2*, 291–299.

Vorobyev, M., & Osorio, D. (1998). Receptor noise as a determinant of colour thresholds. *Proceedings of the Royal Society of London, 265B*, 351–358.

Vorobyev, M., Osorio, D., Bennett, A. T. D., Marshall, N. J., & Cuthill, I. C. (1998). Tetrachromacy, oil droplets and bird plumage colours. *Journal of Comparative Physiology, 183A*, 621–633.

Wagner, H. (1986). Flight performance and visual control of flight of the free-flying house (*Musca domestica L.*): II. Pursuit of targets. *Philosophical Transactions of the Royal Society, London, 312B*, 553–579.

Walls, G. L. (1942). *The vertebrate eye and its adaptive radiation*. Bloomfield Hills, Michigan: Cranbrook Institute of Science.

Warrant, E. J. (1999). Seeing better at night: Life style, eye design and the optimum strategy of spatial and temporal summation. *Vision Research, 39*, 1611–1630.

Waterman, T. H. (1984). Natural polarized light and vision. In M. A. Ali (Ed.), *Photoreception and vision in invertebrates* (pp. 63–114). New York: Plenum Press.

Yokoyama, S., Zhang, H., Radlwimmer, F. B., & Blow, N. S. (1999). Adaptive evolution of color vision of the Comoran coelacanth (*Latimeria chalumnae*). *Proceedings of the National Academy of Sciences, USA, 96*, 6279–6284.

CHAPTER 4

Comparative Psychology of Audition

CYNTHIA F. MOSS AND CATHERINE E. CARR

The first author was supported by MH56366, and the second author was supported by DCD 000436. Both authors gratefully acknowledge A. Coffin for help with fish evolution and Amy Kryjak for careful editorial work. In addition, the authors thank Kari Bohn, Amy Kryjak, and Robyn Zakalik for assistance with figure preparation. C. F. Moss is deeply indebted to the Wissenschaftskolleg zu Berlin for fellowship support that afforded her time and extraordinary library resources to work on this manuscript.

The world is filled with acoustic vibrations, sounds used by animals for communication, predator evasion, and, in the case of humans, also for artistic expression through poetry, theater, and music. Hearing can complement vision and other senses by enabling the transfer of acoustic information from one animal to the next. In some instances, acoustic signals offer distinct advantages over visual, tactile, and chemical signals. Sound can be effectively transmitted in complete darkness, quickly and over long distances. These advantages may explain why hearing is ubiquitous in the animal world, in air and underwater.

The ability to detect and process acoustic signals evolved many times throughout the animal kingdom, from insects and fish to birds and mammals. Even within some animal groups, there is evidence that hearing evolved independently several times. Ears appear not only on opposite sides of the head, but also on a variety of body parts. Out of this diversity, one finds fascinating specializations but also a surprising number of general principles of organization and function. Comparative studies of hearing attempt to bring order to these findings and to deepen our understanding of sound processing and perception.

Research on comparative hearing includes a vast number of behavioral measures of auditory function, as well as elaborate neuroanatomical and neurophysiological studies of the auditory structures and signal processing. To review all common measures of auditory function, anatomy, and physiology in all species studied to date is far beyond the scope of this chapter. Instead, we review selected data from representative species, which allow us to highlight general principles and noteworthy specializations. We begin with a brief introduction to acoustic stimuli, followed by a review of ears and auditory systems in a large sample of species, and we conclude with a comparative presentation of auditory function in behavioral tasks. Due to the breadth of this topic, we have omitted most biophysical observations. For the reader who wishes to follow up on any or all topics covered here in more detail, we recommend Fay, Popper, and colleagues.

Overview of Acoustic Stimuli

Many features of hearing organs are simple consequences of the nature of sound waves. These are fluctuations in pressure propagating away from the source with a certain velocity. Therefore, devices sensitive to pressure, either pressure receivers or pressure gradient receivers, may detect sound. Because movement of particles in a medium is directional, receivers sensitive to this component of sound are inherently directional. Both types of detectors have evolved in the animal kingdom.

Sound behaves in a complicated manner close to a sound source (the near field) because sources are rarely the ideal small pulsating sphere. Further away in the far field (about 1 wavelength) sound behaves more simply, especially if there are no reflections. Sound waves can be characterized by their intensity or sound pressure level, frequency, and wavelength, all of which impact the detection, discrimination, and localization of acoustic signals.

Sound transmission distance is influenced by the characteristics of the acoustic signal and the environment (e.g., Wiley & Richards, 1978). These data, together with psychophysical measures of auditory function, can be used to estimate the communication range of a given species (see Figure 4.1). For a detailed discussion of acoustics and their constraints on hearing in different environments, we refer the reader to comprehensive books by Beranek (1988) and Pierce (1989).

AUDITORY PERIPHERY

Auditory hair cell bundles must be displaced for sensory transduction to occur. Although the basics of mechanoelectrical transduction are very similar among vertebrates, there are many ways to achieve movement of hair cell cilia because there are different physical constraints on the animals that detect sound in air or water. In water, soft tissues are acoustically transparent. Therefore, sound waves traveling through the body in water cause little direct displacement of hair cell bundles. Fish and amphibians solve this problem through relative motion between the hair cells and a denser overlying structure called an otolith (Lewis & Narins, 1999; Popper & Fay, 1999). In air, tympanic membranes and middle ear bones of terrestrial vertebrates compensate for the impedance mismatch between air and the water-filled inner ear cavities (Fritzsch, Barald, & Lomax, 1998).

Hearing is an evolutionarily ancient sense because vertebrate fossils possess an inner ear. Furthermore, such "primitive" vertebrates as lampreys and the coelacanth have inner ears (Popper & Fay, 1999). Modern vertebrates are thought to have evolved from a primitive group of jawless fishes. These early fishes gave rise to two separate evolutionary lines, the cartilaginous fishes (Chondrichthyes) and the bony fishes (Osteichthyes), as well as to the modern jawless fish. Early in bony fish evolution, the crossopterygian fishes are thought to have split off, to give rise eventually to the tetrapods. This lineage gave rise to the amphibians and then the stem reptiles. These early reptiles then diverged, leading to the evolution of two groups, the birds and crocodilians and the mammals. There have been significant modifications to the ear in all lineages.

Insects

Insect ears appear often in evolution and generally have three major features: (a) thinning of cuticle over the organ to form tympanum that is moved by air pressure, (b) formation of an air cavity of tracheal origin sometimes expanded into a chamber, and (c) innervation of this complex by sensory cells. Sound vibrates the tympanum and transmits motion to the sensory cell. Thus unlike vertebrate ears, where airborne vibrations are converted into vibrations in fluid by middle ear bones, no such conversion is required in insects. Most insect ears do not have many receptor cells, but tonotopic organization has developed where there are many receptors. For

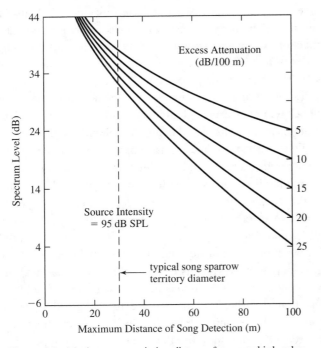

Figure 4.1 Maximum transmission distance for a songbird, calculated for given background noise levels at different values of excess attenuation (dB/100 m). Background noise level is given as a spectrum level (from Dooling et al., 2000).

example, crickets have relatively large ears, with 60 to 70 auditory receptor neurons divided into two groups. The proximal group is sensitive to lower frequencies, whereas the larger distal population is tuned over a frequency range from the best frequency of cricket song (~5 kHz) to ultrasound. Another strategy has been to develop different ears with different sensitivities: Mantis ears exhibit sensitivity to low frequencies in their mesothoracic ear and sensitivity to high (ultrasonic) frequencies in the metathoracic ear (Yager, 1999).

Fishes

The auditory organs of fishes are the saccule, lagena, and utricle. Each has sensory tissue containing hair cells and support cells overlain by an otolith. The otolith organ most used in hearing varies among species. In the herrings the utricle is specially adapted for receiving acoustic input, but in most fishes the saccule is the primary auditory organ. Most bony fishes have a swim bladder or other gas-filled "bubble" in the abdominal cavity or head. As sound pressure fluctuations occur, the bubble expands and contracts according to the amplitude of motion characteristic of the enclosed gas. The swim bladder thus becomes a monopole sound source. The motions of the swim bladder walls may reach the ears of some species and cause relative motion between the otoliths and underlying hair cells. In this case, the sound pressure amplitude determines hair cell stimulation. In most fishes response of the ear to sound is determined simultaneously by the ear detecting particle motion in its "accelerometer" mode and by the ear detecting sound pressure via the swim bladder response. In some species the swim bladder is specifically linked to the ear via specialized mechanical pathways. The best known such pathway is the Weberian ossicle system, a series of four bones connecting the anterior swim bladder wall to the ears. Fishes with such ossicles are considered to be "hearing specialists" in that their sensitivity and bandwidth of hearing is generally greater than for animals lacking such a system. The herrings and the mormyrids have gas bubbles near the ears in the head and are thus also considered to be hearing specialists (Popper & Fay, 1999).

Frogs

With the movement to land, all the major features of the amniote ear appeared, including the tympanum, middle ear, impedance-matching ossicles inserted in the oval window, a tectorial body overlying the hair cells, and specialized auditory end organs (Lewis & Narins, 1999). The ossicles act as an impedance transformer because they transmit motion of the tympanic membrane to the fluid-filled inner ear. Differential shearing between the membranes and hair cell cilia stimulates the hair cells. The sensory hair cells of the frog (*Rana*) have been used to identify the cellular basis of transduction, mechanosensitive channels located at the tips of the stereocilia (Hudspeth, Choe, Mehta & Martin, 2000). Hair cells are depolarized by movement of the stereocilia and release neurotransmitter onto their primary afferents.

Frogs have very specialized peripheral auditory systems, with two end organs, the amphibian and basilar papillae. This duplication may increase the frequency range because the basilar papilla is sensitive to lower frequencies than is the amphibian papilla (Lewis & Narins, 1999). The discovery of a papilla structure in the coelacanth similar to the amniotic basilar papilla suggests that this organ arose before the evolution of tetrapods (Fritzsch, 1998). There is debate about the homology of the amphibian papilla with the basilar papilla or cochlea of amniotic vertebrates (see Lewis & Narins, 1999). The amphibian papilla is functionally similar to the amniote papilla, but a lack of structural similarity suggests that these organs arose in parallel, with the common function reflecting a basic auditory role. Paleotological evidence suggests that the amniote tympanic ear may have evolved independently at least 5 times, in synapsids, lepidosauromorph diapsids, archosauromorph diapsids, probably turtles and amphibians (Clack, 1997).

In frogs the air spaces of the middle ear open widely to the mouth cavity via large eustachian tubes. This wide pathway of communication between the two ears and the mouth and lungs (and possibly the endolymphatic sac, which is located dorsally on the animal's neck and upper back) makes possible several potential pathways of sound both to the outer and inner surface of the tympanic membrane. Evidence exists that the ears of some anurans operate both as pressure receivers and as pressure gradient receivers in certain frequency ranges. Because pressure gradients are vector quantities, the ear operating in this mode is inherently directional (Lewis & Narins, 1999).

Reptiles

The reptilian ear has a new feature: a basilar membrane, a thin partition in the fluid partition along which alternating pressures are transmitted (Wever, 1978). Despite the uncertainty surrounding the amphibian ear, and the parallel evolution of the middle ear in amniotes, the evolution of the stereotypical basilar papilla of modern amniotes begins with the stem reptiles (Manley, 2000; M. R. Miller, 1980). The key features of this auditory organ are seen in turtles. The turtle basilar papilla is a flat strip of membrane populated by approximately

1,000 hair cells (Köppl & Manley, 1992). Salient features in papilla evolution include lengthening and curvature of the sensory epithelia, features thought to both enhance sensitivity and extend the audible frequency range (Gleich & Manley, 2000). The avian-crocodilian and mammalian lineages are thought to have diverged from the stem reptiles quite early, and the papillae of these groups are believed to have evolved in parallel. Elongation relative to the turtle papilla is seen in all groups. In addition, lizards display a unique population of freestanding hair cells that are sensitive to higher frequencies. How is frequency tuning achieved? Recordings from turtle hair cells show that a major part of the peripheral tuning mechanism resides in the individual hair cells; that is, they display electric tuning (Fettiplace, Ricci, & Hackney, 2001). Other mechanisms may also apply (Manley, 2000).

Birds

The outer ear of birds includes an external canal and a middle ear similar to those of the amphibians and reptiles in having a single major ossicle, the columella. The efficiency and frequency response of this system is not unlike that of mammals in the frequency range below about 2000 Hz. The columellar middle ear probably should not be considered the major factor limiting the frequency range of hearing because at least one species (the barn owl) has extended its range considerably without abandoning the columella design (Gleich & Manley, 2000). The inner ear of birds includes a cochlea in addition to an associated lagena. A cross section of the bird basilar membrane and papilla shows many rows of hair cells that vary in height across the membrane. There are not two types of hair cells, like there are in mammals, but the tall hair cells closest to the neural edge of the papilla provide the most afferent input to the auditory nerve dendrites, whereas short hair cells furthest from the neural edge receive purely efferent innervation. In general, the height of the hair cell stereocilia varies smoothly from one end of the papilla to the other. Long stereocilia have been associated with low frequency sensitivity, and short with high frequency sensitivity. It is likely that a frequency analysis occurs along the basilar membrane of the bird ear in much the same way that it occurs among mammals (Fuchs, 1992).

Mammals

Mammals have three middle ear bones that work together as a lever system to amplify the force of sound vibrations. The inner end of the lever moves through a shorter distance but exerts a greater force than the outer end. In combination the bones double or triple the force of the vibrations at the eardrum. The muscles of the middle ear also modify the amplification of this lever system and can act to protect the ear from large vibrations. The stapes passes the vibrations to the oval window or opening in the bony case of the cochlea. The oval window is 15 to 20 times smaller than the eardrum, which produces some of the amplification needed to match impedances between sound waves in the air and in the cochlear fluid and set up the traveling wave in the inner ear.

In mammals, sensory cells are organized on the basilar membrane into one row of inner hair cells (inner because they are closer to the central core of the cochlear) and three to five rows of outer hair cells (Dallos, 1996). Inner hair cells innervate Type 1 primary afferents and are innervated by a very few efferents. Outer hair cells are sparsely innervated by Type 2 primary afferents and receive more efferent terminals. Type 1 afferents comprise 95% of total afferents, and they convey the frequency, intensity, and phase of signal to the auditory nerve. Sound frequency is encoded by place on the cochlea; intensity is encoded by the DC component of receptor potential; and timing is encoded by the AC component. Such a system must act as a low pass filter, which places limits on phase locking. There are two main theories about the function of outer hair cells. One is that the traveling wave is boosted by a local electromechanical amplification process; that is, the outer hair cells act as a cochlear amplifier. The other theory is that the outer hair cells mechanically affect the movement of the tectorial membrane. If outer hair cells are destroyed, frequency tuning is greatly diminished.

CENTRAL AUDITORY PATHWAYS

Auditory information is encoded in the activity of both single neurons and arrays of neurons. This activity can be divided into four major codes: rate, temporal, ensemble, and the labeled line-place principle (Brugge, 1992; Figure 4.2). These codes assume the existence of a sensitive receiver or set of neurons whose activity changes in response to the code. None of the codes appear capable of transmitting the entire array of spectral and temporal information (Brugge, 1992). Instead, they appear to operate in various combinations depending on the acoustic environment. Coding strategies also appear to change at different levels of the central auditory pathway, for example, when the phase-locked spikes of the temporal code are converted to the place code output of neurons sensitive to interaural time differences (ITDs). There is no evidence that coding strategies differ among animals.

High-level neurons selective for complex stimulus features have been found in every auditory system. These include

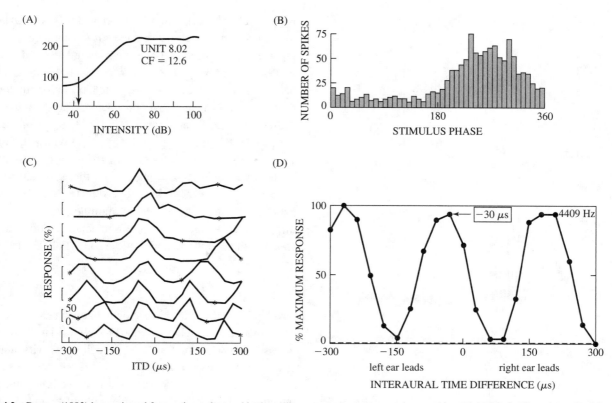

(A)

UNIT 8.02
CF = 12.6

INTENSITY (dB)

(B)

NUMBER OF SPIKES

STIMULUS PHASE

(C)

RESPONSE (%)

ITD (μs)

(D)

% MAXIMUM RESPONSE

−30 μs   4409 Hz

left ear leads   right ear leads

INTERAURAL TIME DIFFERENCE (μs)

Figure 4.2   Brugge (1992) has reviewed four major codes used in the auditory system: rate, temporal, ensemble, and the labeled line-place principle.

A. Rate: In the auditory nerve, sound intensity is encoded by the number of action potentials, which increase linearly with sound intensity over some range before reaching a plateau. This plot shows a rate-intensity function for a cat cochlear afferent to a tone at best frequency. The y-axis plots discharge rate in spikes/second (from Sachs & Abbas, 1974).

B. Temporal: Action potentials phase-lock to the waveform of the acoustic stimulus. Spikes occur most frequently at a particular phase of the tone, although not necessarily in every tonal cycle. Thus the discharge pattern of a cochlear nerve fiber can encode the phase of a tone with a frequency above 1000 Hz even though the average discharge rate is lower. Recording from a barn owl cochlear nucleus magnocellularis neuron plots the timing of action potentials with respect to stimulus phase in a period histogram. The best frequency of this neuron was 5.2 kHz. From Sullivan and Konishi (1984). Copyright 1984 by the Society for Neuroscience.

C. Ensemble: The existence of an ensemble code may be inferred or recorded with an array of microelectrodes. In the central nucleus of the inferior colliculus of the barn owl, an array of neurons is individually sensitive to interaural phase differences, and their responses show phase ambiguity. The ensemble encodes interaural time difference. From Wagner, Takahashi, and Konishi (1987). Copyright 1987 by the Society for Neuroscience.

D. Place: Within both the nucleus laminaris and the medial superior olive, inputs from left and right ears encode the timing of the stimulus at the two ears. This temporal code is converted into a place code for interaural phase difference by circuit composed of delay lines and coincidence detectors (see text). Position or place within the nucleus confers sensitivity to particular interaural phase differences (from Carr & Konishi, 1990).

the song-specific responses found in the song birds, pulse-interval-specific neurons in the midbrain of the mormyrid electric fish, and space-specific neurons in the space-mapped region of the inferior colliculus of the barn owl (Figure 4.3). It is not always clear what combination of inputs and intrinsic properties conveys such specificity.

The basic anatomical organization of the central auditory system does not differ greatly among vertebrates. These connections are reviewed in chapters in *The Mammalian Auditory Pathway: Neuroanatomy* (Webster, Popper, & Fay, 1993), in *Neurobiology of Hearing* (Altschuler, Hoffman, Bobbin, &

Clopton, 1991), and in *The Central Auditory System* (Ehret & Romand, 1997). The primary auditory nuclei send a predominantly contralateral projection to the auditory midbrain and in some vertebrates to second-order (olivary) nuclei and lemniscal nuclei. The auditory midbrain generally projects bilaterally to dorsal thalamus and then to hypothalamus and telencephalon. Major differences among central auditory structures appear seldom in evolution. Selective forces driving these changes have been ascribed to the development of new end organs in the auditory periphery and to the increased use of sound (Wilczynski, 1984).

(A)

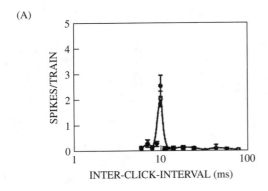

(B)

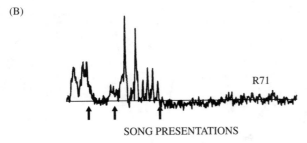

(C)

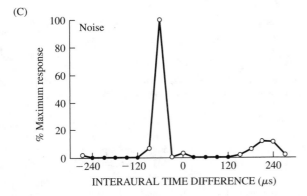

Figure 4.3 High-level neurons are sensitive or selective for complex stimulus features. A combination of auditory inputs, plus cellular features of these neurons, underlies this emergent sensitivity.

A. Selective neuron in the torus semicircularis of the mormyrid fish responds to the temporal features of complex sounds used in acoustic displays. This neuron was sensitive to particular interclick intervals found in the grunt element of the courtship signal (from J. D. Crawford, 1997).

B. Selective neuron in the higher vocal center of the white crown sparrow responds to the bird's own song. The song has three phrases: an introductory whistle, a buzz, and a trill. Multiunit neuronal activity was elicited by five repetitions of the bird's own song. Arrows mark the end of each phrase (from Margoliash & Konishi, 1985).

C. Selective response of a space-specific neuron in the external nucleus of the inferior colliculus of the barn owl, plotted as a function of interaural time difference. These neurons are also selective for particular interaural level differences (not shown). When stimulated with noise, this neuron responds to a characteristic delay of –60 μs (from Takahashi, 1989).

Insects

Insects hear to obtain information about their environment, so moths and mantises hear the echolocating sounds of bats, whereas crickets localize their mates (see Hoy, Popper, &

Fay, 1998). The tasks of the insect auditory system are to filter important signals out of the environmental noise including specific frequencies, patterns, and loudness and to determine the location of the sound source. Behavioral studies have shown that crickets can phonotax, or orient toward, sound (as shown later in Figure 3.13). These studies have shown that crickets are sensitive to a wide range of frequencies, with intraspecific signals being most important (Pollack, 1998). They recognize cricket song, particularly pulse period. In the cricket central nervous system, there are neurons that encode the frequency, intensity, direction, and temporal patterns of song. These include multiple pairs of identified interneurons, including the intrasegmental neurons that respond to the temporal pattern of the song (Pollack, 1998).

Fishes

Psychophysical studies have shown that fish hear in the same sense that other vertebrates hear (Fay, 1988). This conclusion is based on behavioral studies of their sensitivity and discriminative acuity for sound. The best sensitivity for hearing specialists is –40 to –50 dB (re 1 dyne per cm^2) units, between 200 Hz and 1500 Hz. Fishes without swim bladders or without clear connections between the swim bladder and the ear have best sensitivities between –35 dB and about 10 dB, between 50 Hz and 500 Hz. Sound pressure thresholds for fish that do not use the swim bladder in hearing are inadequate descriptors of sensitivity. The sensitivity of these animals is thus dependent on sound source distance and is better described in terms of acoustic particle motion. Fish ears are also inherently directional (Popper & Fay, 1999).

In all vertebrates the auditory nerve enters the brain and divides into two (ascending and descending) branches. In bony fish the ancestral pattern is for auditory and vestibular inputs to project to the anterior, magnocellular, descending and posterior nuclei of the ventral octaval column. Within fish that are auditory specialists, new more-dorsal auditory areas arise from the ventral column (McCormick, 1999). Auditory projections to the descending and anterior octaval nuclei have appeared independently many times in hearing specialists. Both the anterior and descending nuclei project to the auditory area of the central nucleus of the midbrain torus. This area is located medial to the lateral line area. In hearing specialists, secondary octaval and paralemniscal nuclei appear in the hindbrain. The secondary octaval nuclei receive input from the descending nucleus and project to the central nucleus. Many toral neurons phase-lock to the auditory stimulus, and some exhibit sharp frequency tuning, although the majority of toral units are more broadly tuned (Feng & Schellart, 1999). Some fish use sound for communication, and there are neurons in the central nucleus that are sensitive to the grunts, moans, and howls produced by vocalizing mormyrids (J. D. Crawford, 1997; see Figure 4.3, panel A). The central nucleus has major ascending projections to the dorsal thalamus (central posterior and sometimes anterior). It also projects to the ventromedial nucleus of the ventral thalamus, the posterior tuberculum, and the hypothalamus (McCormick, 1999). The central nucleus and hypothalamus are reciprocally interconnected, which may be related to the role of sound in reproductive and aggressive behavior in some fish. The telencephalon in bony fish is divided into dorsal and ventral areas, with the dorsal area proposed to be homologous to the pallium of other vertebrates, and the ventral area to the subpallium. Two dorsal areas have been shown to respond to sound (within dorsal medial pallium (DM) and dorsal central pallium (DC); see Figure 4.4), but little is know about auditory processing rostral to the midbrain.

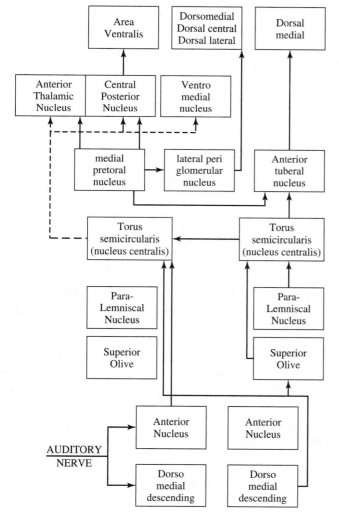

Figure 4.4 Simplified summary of possible acoustic circuits in otophysan fish, modified from McCormick (1999). A secondary octaval population appears in otophysan fish and in some other bony fish. This population projects to the midbrain, as do the anterior and descending nuclei. The major ascending projections from the midbrain is to the central posterior nucleus of the thalamus.

Frogs (Anurans)

Psychophysical hearing data exist only for the frogs. Many frogs vocalize during mating and other social interactions, and they are able to detect, discriminate, and localize species-specific vocalizations. Behavioral studies have exploited the natural tendency of frogs to orient to sounds broadcast in a more or less natural setting (Zelick, Mann, & Popper, 1999). In frogs afferents project to the specialized dorsal medullary nucleus, and ventrally and laterally to the vestibular column. The dorsal nucleus is tonotopically organized with high-frequency responses from the basilar papilla medial and lower best-frequency responses from the amphibian papilla mapped laterally (McCormick, 1999), as well as typical V-shaped tuning curves (Feng & Schellart, 1999). A major transformation in the signal representation takes place in the dorsal nucleus, with primary like, onset, pauser, and chopper discharge patterns recorded (Feng & Schellart, 1999). These four discharge patterns may correspond to different processing streams or neural codes. The dorsal nucleus projects both directly and indirectly to the auditory midbrain torus, with projections to the superior olive and superficial reticular nucleus (Figure 4.5). The superior olive receives bilateral input from the dorsal nucleus, and many neurons there respond to a wide range of amplitude-modulated stimuli. The ventral zone of the torus receives most of the ascending inputs. It is tonotopically organized; its neurons are often selective to amplitude-modulated stimuli; and more neurons respond to complex sounds than in the medulla (Feng & Schellart, 1999). The torus projects to the central and posterior nuclei of the thalamus and to the striatum. Recordings from the posterior nucleus show sensitivity to the frequency combination present in the frog advertisement calls, and many neurons in central thalamus are broadly tuned and sensitive to specific temporal features of the call (Feng & Schellart, 1999). The central thalamus projects to the striatum, the anterior preoptic area, and the ventral hypothalamus. These connections may mediate control of reproductive and social behavior in frogs (Wilcyznski et al., 1993). The anterior thalamic nucleus supplies ascending information to the medial pallium, although little is known about pallial auditory processing.

Reptiles

The auditory central nervous system is organized in a common plan in both birds and reptiles, presumably due to the conserved nature of the auditory sense and their close phylogenetic relationship (Carr & Code, 2000; Figure 4.6). The auditory nerve projects to two cochlear nuclei, the nucleus magnocellularis and the nucleus angularis, and sometimes to

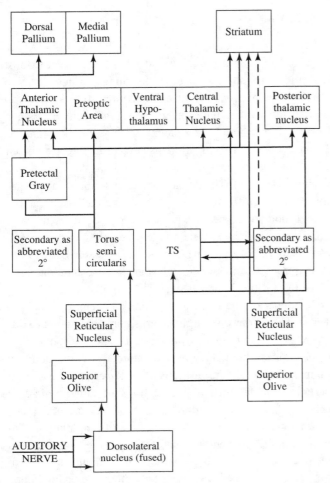

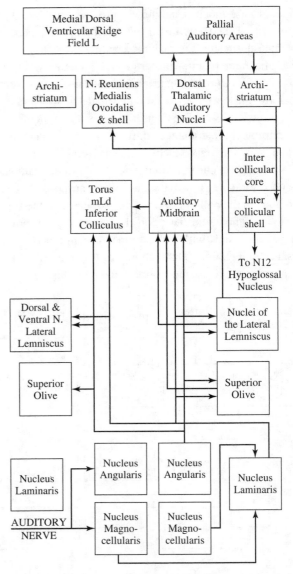

Figure 4.5 Simplified summary of possible acoustic circuits in ranid frogs, modified from McCormick (1999). The midline dorsolateral nucleus projects to the torus, the superior olive, and the superficial reticular nucleus. The torus contains three subdivisions: dorsal, principal, and ventral. The ventral zone is the main recipient of ascending auditory information. The nuclei of the forebrain are only shown on the one side. The caudal region of the central thalamic nucleus is concerned with auditory input and projects to the striatum, anterior preoptic area, and ventral hypothalamus.

Figure 4.6 Connections of the auditory system in birds and reptiles, modified from Carr and Code (2000). The laterality of the connections is generally indicated, with nuclei on the right given the generic terms (i.e., auditory midbrain) and the box on the left given the terms used in the literature (i.e., torus, mLd, inferior colliculus). Nucleus angularis projects to the contralateral auditory midbrain, with a smaller ipsilateral projection. Nucleus angularis also projects bilaterally to the superior olive and dorsal nucleus of the lateral lemniscus and to the contralateral ventral nucleus of the lateral lemniscus. Projections from nucleus laminaris were demonstrated to the ipsilateral superior olive, to the contralateral lemniscal nuclei, and to a small medial region in the auditory midbrain bilaterally with the contralateral projection being much denser than the ipsilateral one. Other nuclei having ascending connections with the midbrain include the contralateral superior olive, the ipsilateral dorsal nucleus of the lateral lemniscus, the contralateral ventral nucleus of the lateral lemniscus, and the contralateral midbrain. The ipsilateral superior olive and ventral nucleus of the lateral lemniscus also project sparsely to the midbrain (Conlee & Parks, 1986). The midbrain projects to the nucleus ovoidalis, which projects to Field L in the neostriatum. In songbirds Field L projects to the higher vocal center (HVC), which in turn projects to the robust nucleus of the archistriatum (RA). The descending archistriatal projections do not project to the core of the hindbrain and midbrain auditory nuclei, but rather terminate in the surrounding shell (Wild, Karten, & Frost, 1993).

the second-order nucleus laminaris. The nucleus magnocellularis projects to the nucleus laminaris that in turn projects to the superior olive, to the lemniscal nuclei, and to the central nucleus of the auditory midbrain (torus semicircularis, nucleus mesencephalicus lateralis dorsalis, inferior colliculus). The nucleus angularis projects to the superior olive, to the lemniscal nuclei, and to the central nucleus of the auditory midbrain. The parallel ascending projections of angularis and laminaris may or may not overlap with one another, and probably do overlap in the primitive condition. Hindbrain auditory connections are generally bilateral, although contralateral projections predominate. The lemniscal nuclei project to midbrain, thalamic, and forebrain targets. The central nucleus of the auditory midbrain projects bilaterally to its dorsal thalamic target (nucleus medialis or reuniens in reptiles, nucleus ovoidalis in birds). The auditory thalamus projects to the auditory region of the forebrain (medial dorsal ventricular ridge in reptiles, Field L in birds). Field L projects to other forebrain nuclei that may be involved in the control of song and other vocalizations. Descending projections from the archistriatum to the intercollicular area (and directly to the hypoglossal nucleus in some) appear to mediate vocalization.

The organization of the central auditory pathways in the turtles is considered to be close to the ancestral plan, whereas the brainstem auditory nuclei of lizards and snakes differ somewhat from other reptiles and birds (Gleich & Manley, 2000). This may be because lizards usually have two types of hair cell, tectorial and freestanding. Tectorial hair cells resemble those found in birds and mammals. Auditory nerve fibers that innervate them encode low center frequencies (100–800 Hz) and have sharp asymmetric tuning curves. Fibers from freestanding hair cells have high center frequencies (900–4000 Hz), high spontaneous rates, and broad symmetric tuning curves. Freestanding hair cells may be a uniquely derived feature of lizards that enables this group to respond to higher frequencies. Auditory nerve fibers from tectorial hair cells project to the nucleus magnocellularis and the lateral nucleus angularis. Neurons that contact freestanding hair cells project primarily to the nucleus angularis medialis. There have been very few physiological investigations of the cochlear nuclei in reptiles, although the auditory periphery has been studied extensively (Carr & Code, 2000).

Birds

Birds use sound for communication and hear higher frequencies than turtles, snakes, and lizards (Dooling, Lohr, & Dent, 2000; Klump, 2000). Most birds hear up to 5 kHz to 6 kHz, and the barn owl has exceptional high-frequency hearing, with characteristic frequencies of 9 kHz to 10 kHz in the auditory nerve (Konishi, 1973). Some land birds such as pigeons, chickens, and guinea fowl are also sensitive to infrasound, below 20 Hz (Carr, 1992). Infrasound signals may travel over great distances, and pigeons may use them for orientation.

Cochlear Nuclei Encode Parallel Ascending Streams of Auditory Information

The auditory nerve projects to nucleus magnocellularis and nucleus angularis in the pattern described for the bird and reptile morphotype (as discussed earlier; see Figure 4.6). In the owl, nucleus magnocellularis is the origin of a neural pathway that encodes timing information, while a parallel pathway for encoding sound level and other aspects of the auditory stream originates with nucleus angularis (Takahashi, 1989). Auditory responses include primary like, onset, chopper, and complex Type IV responses (Köppl, Carr, & Soares, 2001). Recordings in the chicken cochlear nuclei have found a similar but less clear segregation of function (Warchol & Dallos, 1990). The similarities between the owl and the chicken suggest that the functional separation of time and level coding is a common feature of the avian auditory system. The auditory system uses phase-locked spikes to encode the timing of the stimulus (Figure 4.2, panel B). In addition to precise temporal coding, behavioral acuity is also assumed to depend on the activity of neural ensembles (Figure 4.2, panel C). Phase locking underlies accurate detection of temporal information, including ITDs (Klump, 2000) and gap detection (Dooling, Lohr, & Dent, 2000). Neural substrates for phase locking include the specialized end-bulb terminal in the nucleus magnocellularis, termed an *end-bulb of Held*. This large synapse conveys the phase-locked discharge of the auditory nerve fibers to its postsynaptic targets in the nucleus magnocellularis (Trussell, 1997, 1999). AMPA-type (a-Amino-3-hydroxy-5-methyl-4-isoxazole propionic acid) glutamate receptors contribute to the rapid response of the postsynaptic cell by virtue of their rapid desensitization kinetics (Parks, 2000).

Detection of Interaural Time Difference in Nucleus Laminaris

Nucleus magnocellularis projects to the nucleus laminaris (Rubel & Parks, 1988; Carr & Konishi, 1990). The projections from the nucleus magnocellularis to the nucleus laminaris resemble the Jeffress model for encoding ITDs (see Joris, Smith, & Yin, 1998). The Jeffress model has two elements: delay lines and coincidence detectors. A Jeffress circuit is an array of coincidence detectors, each element of which has a different relative delay between its ipsilateral and contralateral excitatory inputs. Thus, ITD is encoded into the position (a place code) of the coincidence detector whose delay lines best cancel out the acoustic ITD (for reviews, see Joris et al., 1998; Konishi, 2000). Neurons of the nucleus laminaris phase-lock to both monaural and binaural stimuli but respond maximally when phase-locked spikes from each side arrive simultaneously, that is, when the difference in the conduction delays compensates for the ITD (Carr & Konishi, 1990). The cochlear nuclei also receive descending GABAergic inputs from the superior olive that may function as gain control elements or a negative feedback to protect nucleus laminaris neurons from losing their sensitivity to ITDs at high sound intensities (Peña, Viete, Albeck, & Konishi, 1996).

Efferent Control

Efferent innervation of the ear characterizes all vertebrates (Roberts & Meredith, 1992). Cochlear efferent neurons near the superior olive innervate the avian basilar papilla (Code, 1997). Differences in the organization of the avian cochlear efferent and the mammalian olivocochlear systems suggest that there may be significant differences in how these two systems modulate incoming auditory information. Abneural short hair cells in birds have only efferent endings, and these efferents appear act to inhibit responses of the auditory nerve and raise auditory thresholds.

Lemniscal Nuclei

The lemniscal nuclei are ventral to the auditory midbrain. There are two identified lemniscal nuclei in reptiles (dorsal and ventral) and three in birds (dorsal, intermediate, and ventral). These names are the same as those of the lemniscal nuclei in mammals, but the nuclei should not be considered homologous. The dorsal nucleus (LLDp) mediates detection of interaural level differences (ILDs) in the barn owl (Carr & Code, 2000). Interaural level differences are produced by the shadowing effect of the head when a sound source originates from off the midline (Klump, 2000). Some owls experience larger than predicted differences because their external ears are also oriented asymmetrically in the vertical plane. Because of this asymmetry, ILDs vary more with the elevation of the sound source than with azimuth. This asymmetry allows owls to use ILDs to localize sounds in elevation, and they use ITDs to determine the azimuthal location of a sound. The level pathway begins with the cochlear nucleus angularis, which responds to changing sound levels over about a 30-dB range (Carr & Code, 2000). Each nucleus angularis projects to contralateral LLDp. The cells of LLDp are excited by stimulation of the contralateral ear and inhibited by stimulation of the ipsilateral ear. Mapping of ILDs begins in LLDp, with neurons organized according to their preferred ILD. LLDp neurons do not encode elevation unambiguously and may be described as *sensitive* to ILD, but not *selective* because they are not immune to changes in sound level. The encoding of elevation improves in the auditory midbrain.

Midbrain and Emergence of Relevant Stimulus Features

The auditory midbrain receives ascending input and projects to the thalamus. It is surrounded rostrally and laterally by an intercollicular area that receives descending input from the forebrain archistriatum (Puelles, Robles, Martinez-de-la-Torre, & Martinez, 1994). The auditory midbrain mediates auditory processing, whereas the intercollicular area appears to mediate vocalization and other auditory-motor behaviors. The auditory midbrain is divided into an external nucleus and a central nucleus. The nucleus angularis, LLDp, and nucleus laminaris project to regions of the central nucleus (Conlee & Parks, 1986; Takahashi, 1989). Interaural time difference and ILD signals are combined, and the combinations are conveyed to the external nucleus, which contains a map of auditory space (Knudsen, 1980; Konishi, 1986). Studies of the owl auditory midbrain have shown that most neurons are binaural, excited by inputs from the contralateral ear and inhibited by the ipsilateral ear, although bilateral excitation and contralateral excitation are also present. Many neurons are sensitive to changes in interaural level and time difference. The tonotopic organization is consistent with the tonotopy observed in lizards and crocodiles, and low best frequencies are dorsal (Carr & Code, 2000).

Space-specific responses in the barn owl appear to be created through the gradual emergence of relevant stimulus responses in the progression across the auditory midbrain. Information about both interaural time and level differences project to the external nucleus, and each space-specific neuron receives inputs from a population of neurons tuned to different frequencies (Takahashi, 1989). The nonlinear interactions of these different frequency channels act to remove phase ambiguity in the response to ITDs. The representation of auditory space is ordered, with most of the external nucleus devoted to the contralateral hemifield (Knudsen, 1980). The external nucleus projects topographically to the optic tectum that contains maps of visual and auditory spaces that are in register. Activity in the tectum directs the rapid head movements made by the owl in response to auditory and visual stimuli (Knudsen, du Lac, & Esterly, 1987).

Thalamus and Forebrain

The central nucleus projects to both the external nucleus and the nucleus ovoidalis of the thalamus. Nucleus ovoidalis in turn projects ipsilaterally to Field L. Nucleus ovoidalis has been homologized to the mammalian medial geniculate nucleus (MGv; Karten & Shimizu, 1989). Nucleus ovoidalis is tonotopically organized, with high best frequencies located dorsally and low best frequencies ventrally (Proctor & Konishi, 1997). In the barn owl all divisions of the central nucleus project to ovoidalis, and the physiological responses in ovoidalis reflect this diverse array of inputs. Most neurons had responses to ITD or ILD, at stimulus frequencies similar to those found in the midbrain. In contrast to the mapping found in the midbrain, however, no systematic representation of sound localization cues was found in ovoidalis (Proctor &

Konishi, 1997). Nevertheless, sound localization and gaze control are mediated in parallel in the midbrain and forebrain of the *barn owl* (Carr & Code, 2000).

Field L is the principal target of ascending input from ovoidalis. It is divided into three parallel layers, L1, L2, and L3, with L2 further divided into L2a and L2b. Auditory units in L2 generally have narrow tuning curves with inhibitory sidebands, which might be expected from their direct input from dorsal thalamus, whereas the cells of L1 and L3 exhibit more complex responses in the guinea fowl (Scheich, Langer, & Bonke, 1979). The general avian pattern is that Field L projects to the adjacent hyperstriatum and to other nuclei of the caudal neostriatum. Auditory neostriatal targets of Field L (direct and indirect) include dorsal neostriatum in the pigeon, the higher vocal center (HVC) in songbirds, and ventrolateral neostriatum in budgerigars. These neostriatal nuclei project to the auditory areas of the archistriatum (intermediate archistriatum, ventro medial part (AIVM) and the robust nucleus of the archistriatum, or RA), which project back down to the auditory thalamus and midbrain (Carr & Code, 2000).

Song System Is Composed of Two Forebrain Pathways

Many animals make elaborate communication sounds, but few of them learn these sounds. The exceptions are humans and the many thousands of songbird species, as well as parrots and hummingbirds, that acquire their vocal repertoire by learning (Doupe & Kuhl, 1999). Both humans and songbirds learn their vocal motor behavior early in life, with a strong dependence on hearing, both of the adults that they will imitate and of themselves as they practice.

The song system is composed of an anterior and a posterior pathway. The posterior forebrain or motor pathway is composed of a circuit from HVC to the RA and then to the motor nuclei that control the syrinx and respiration (Brainard & Doupe, 2000; Konishi, 1985; Nottebohm, 1980). The posterior pathway is required throughout life for song production. The anterior forebrain pathway is needed during song learning, but not for normal adult song production, and is made up of a projection from HVC to X to DLM (dorsolateral part of the medial thalamus) to LMAN (lateral magnocellular nucleus of the anterior neostriatum) to RA. The posterior pathway is the presumed site where the motor program underlying the bird's unique song is stored, whereas the anterior pathway contains neurons that respond to song stimuli, consistent with the idea that this pathway is a possible site of template storage and song evaluation (Margoliash, 1997; Brenowitz, Margoliash, & Nordeen, 1997). The anterior pathway projects to the posterior pathway and is well positioned to provide a guiding influence on the developing motor

program. It is also homologous to cortical basal-ganglia circuits in other species (Bottjer & Johnson, 1997).

Mammals

Mammals hear high frequencies and use sound for communication. Humans hear up to 20 kHz, while microchiropteran bats have evolved high-frequency hearing for use in sonar, with characteristic frequencies of 50 kHz to 120 kHz. Some large mammals (elephants) are also sensitive to infrasound, which they use for communication (K. B. Payne, Langbauer, & Thomas, 1986).

Auditory Nerve

There are two types of auditory nerve afferents in mammals, Type 1 and Type 2. Type 1 afferents receive sharply tuned inputs from inner hair cells and send thick myelinated axons into the brain, where they divide into two. The ascending branch goes to the anterior region of the ventral cochlear nucleus and the descending branch to the posterior region of the ventral cochlear nucleus and to the new dorsal cochlear nucleus. Type 2 afferents are assumed to be unique to mammals, are innervated by outer hair cells, and have thin, unmyelinated axons. They project to granule cell caps of ventral cochlear nucleus (VCN) and dorsal cochlear nucleus (DCN) and are involved in the efferent feedback to the cochlea (Ryugo, 1993). See Figure 4.7.

Tonotopy is preserved in the projections of the auditory nerve. In mammals, the ventral part of each cochlear nucleus receives low center frequency (CF) (apical) input, and dorsal areas receive high CF input. These tonotopic projections are not point to point because each point on the basilar membrane projects to an isofrequency plane across the extent of the cochlear nucleus. Thus the cochlear place representation is expanded into a second dimension in the brain, unlike the visual and somatosensory systems, which are point to point. These tonotopic sheets are preserved all the way to cortex, although it is not clear what features are processed in these isofrequency slabs. Divergent and convergent connections within isofrequency planes may be observed at all levels. The auditory nerve forms different types of terminals onto different cell types in the cochlear nucleus (Ryugo, 1993). End bulbs of Held terminals are formed on bushy cells (as discussed later), whereas more varicose or bouton-like terminals are formed on other cell types in the cochlear nuclei. The auditory nerve appears to use glutamate as a transmitter, often with the postsynaptic cell expressing "fast" AMPA-type glutamate receptors that can mediate precise temporal coding (Oertel, 1999; Parks, 2000; Trussell, 1999).

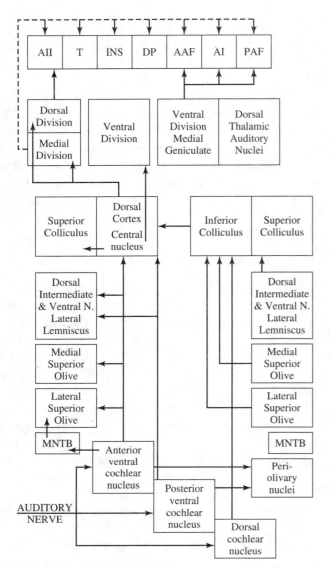

Figure 4.7 Connections of the auditory system in mammals, simplified from Winer (1991), Oliver and Huerta (1992), and de Rebaupierre (1997). The laterality of the connections is not indicated because of the large numbers of structures to be shown, and many connections have been simplified. The divisions of the cochlear nucleus are shown, not the cell types, although individual cell types have distinct projections (see text). The projection of the cochlear nuclei to the lemniscal nuclei and midbrain is predominantly contralateral. The projections of the superior colliculus are not shown (see Oliver & Huerta, 1992), nor are the projections of the efferent system. There is variation in the number of cortical areas and in their terminology.

The Cochlear Nucleus Produces Ascending Parallel Projections

There are four major cell types in the ventral cochlear nucleus (Rhode & Greenberg, 1992; Rouiller, 1997; Young, 1998). First, bushy cells respond in a primary- or auditory-nerve-like fashion to the auditory stimulus. Second, octopus cells respond to onsets or stimulus transients; and third,

two classes of multipolar neurons respond principally with "chopper" firing patterns. Bushy cells receive end-bulb inputs from the auditory nerve and exhibit accurate temporal coding. There are two forms of bushy cells, spherical and globular. Spherical cells dominate the anterior ventral cochlear nucleus, respond to lower best frequencies, and project to the medial superior olive, which is sensitive to ITDs. Globular bushy cells by comparison sometimes chop or exhibit onset responses to the stimulus, respond to higher frequencies, and project to the lateral superior olive and the medial nucleus of the trapezoid body. These projections may mediate detection of ILDs. Octopus cells in the posterior ventral cochlear nucleus are multipolar, with thick dendrites that extend across the nerve root (Oertel, Bal, Gardner, Smith, & Joris, 2000). This morphology enables them to integrate auditory nerve inputs across a range of frequencies. Octopus cells encode the time structure of stimuli with great precision and exhibit onset responses to tonal stimuli (Oertel et al., 2000). Onsets play an important role in theories of speech perception and segregation and grouping of sound sources (Bregman, 1990). Two classes of multipolar neurons respond to tones principally with "chopper" firing patterns (Doucet & Ryugo, 1997).

The dorsal cochlear nucleus appears for the first time in mammals, perhaps associated with the development of high-frequency hearing and motile external ears. It is composed of a cerebellum-like circuit in the superficial layers, with projection cells below that receive auditory nerve inputs (Berrebi & Mugnaini, 1991; Young, 1998). Dorsal cochlear nucleus cells exhibit a wide variety of response types, with one theory of function relating to echo suppression. The granule cells in the superficial layers receive ascending somatosensory input that may convey information about head and ear position. The deep portion of the dorsal cochlear nucleus contains fusiform and stellate cell types. Fusiform cells exhibit complex (Type IV) frequency tuning curves, with small areas of excitation at best frequency and at sides. This response is well suited to detecting the notches in sound level created by the pinnae that provide cues for locating sound in elevation (May, 2000).

Binaural Interactions and Feedback to the Cochlea Originate in Periolivary and Olivocochlear Nuclei

The superior olivary complex consists of the lateral and medial superior olivary nuclei and a large number of smaller cell groups known as the periolivary nuclei, which are sources of both ascending and descending projections (Helfert & Aschoff, 1997). All receive input from the cochlear nuclei.

Their functions are largely unknown, except for efferent control of the cochlea and encoding sound level (Warr, 1992). The medial nucleus of the trapezoid body (MNTB) projects to the lateral superior olive, ventral nucleus of the lateral lemniscus, medial superior olive, and other periolivary nuclei. Responses of MNTB cells were similar to their primary excitatory input, the globular bushy cell, which connects to the MNTB via end-bulb synapse. The MNTB cell output forms an important inhibitory input to a number of ipsilateral auditory brain stem nuclei, including the lateral superior olive. MNTB neurons are characterized by voltage-dependent potassium conductances that shape the transfer of auditory information across the bushy cell to MNTB cell synapse and allow high-frequency auditory information to be passed accurately across the MNTB relay synapse (Trussell, 1999).

Two populations of olivary neurons project to the cochlea: lateral and medial (Warr, 1992). Thin olivocochlear fibers arise from the lateral olivocochlear group located ipsilaterally in the lateral superior olive. Thick olivocochlear fibers arise from the medial olivocochlear group located bilaterally in the periolivary nuclei. Although they project primarily to the cochlea, olivocochlear neurons also give off branches to a variety of nuclei in the brainstem, and to inferior colliculus, thus involving auditory and nonauditory nuclei in the olivocochlear reflex system. Olivocochlear neurons can be activated by sound, whereas activation of the medial olivocochlear bundle results in suppression of spontaneous and tone-evoked activity in the auditory nerve.

Olivary Nuclei and Interaural Interactions

The olivary nuclei regulate the binaural convergence of acoustic information and mediate spatial hearing. Neural computations of sound location take place at this first site of binaural convergence. The lateral superior olive encodes ILD, whereas the medial superior olive encodes time differences. Thus an important transformation takes place here. Information conveyed by temporal and rate codes is transformed in the olivary nuclei into labeled line-place principle codes for location.

The lateral superior olive principal cells receive excitatory inputs from ipsilateral globular bushy cells, as well as inhibitory glycinergic inputs onto their cell bodies and proximal dendrites, relayed from the contralateral ear via the MNTB. The MNTB input acts to reverses the sign of bushy cell input from excitatory to inhibitory to make an EI response—that is, excited (E) by the ipsilateral ear and inhibited (I) by the contralateral ear. Traditionally, the lateral superior olive has been assigned the role of extracting azimuthal angle information of high-frequency sound from ILD. Some sensitivity to time differences has also been observed. Almost all lateral superior olive responses have monotonic rate-level functions, typically with sigmoidal ILD sensitivity functions. In general, as the strength of the contralateral input increases with increasing loudness in the contralateral ear, the maximum rate decreases. Thus the lateral superior olive rate signals a range of ILDs (Kuwada, Batra, & Fitzpatrick, 1997).

Sensitivity to ITDs originates in the medial superior olive. The organization of the medial superior olive circuit appears to conform to the requirements of the Jeffress model for transforming ITDs into a place code (Joris et al., 1998). The Jeffress model is made up of delay lines and coincidence detectors. Each coincidence detector in the array has a different relative delay between its ipsilateral and contralateral excitatory inputs. Interaural time difference is encoded into the position or place in the array whose delay lines best cancels out the ITD. Neurons of the medial superior olive act as coincidence detectors. They phase-lock to both monaural and binaural stimuli and respond maximally when phase-locked spikes from each side arrive simultaneously, that is, when the difference in the conduction delays compensates for the ITD (Joris et al., 1998). The overall result of this scheme is the creation of an array of cells tuned to specific ITDs and arranged according to their best azimuth. The azimuth of a sound source is coded by the location of maximal activity in the array (Joris et al., 1998).

Auditory Midbrain: Inferior Colliculus and the Emergence of Biologically Important Parameters

The inferior colliculus is the midbrain target of ascending auditory information. It has two major divisions, the central nucleus and dorsal cortex, and both divisions are tonotopically organized. The inputs from brainstem auditory nuclei are either distributed across or superimposed on maps to form what are believed to be locally segregated functional zones for processing different aspects of the auditory stimulus (Ehret, 1975; Oliver & Huerta, 1992). The central nucleus receives both direct monaural input and indirect binaural input. Physiological studies show both binaural and monaural responses (Ehret, 1975).

Casseday and Covey (1996) proposed that tuning processes in the inferior colliculus are related to the biological importance of sounds. Their ideas are summarized here. There is a change in timing properties at the inferior colliculus, from rapid input to slowed output, and they propose that this transformation is related to the timing of specific behaviors. The framework proposed by Casseday and Covey is useful because at least some neurons in the inferior colliculus are tuned to behaviorally relevant stimuli that trigger species-specific behavior, and the processing of these sign stimuli triggers action patterns for hunting, escape, or vocal communication. Evidence for the theory comes from the convergence of parallel auditory pathways at the inferior colliculus, the interaction of the inferior colliculus with motor systems, tuning of auditory midbrain neurons to biologically important sounds, the slow pace of neural processing at the inferior colliculus, and the slow pace of motor output.

Thalamus

Three major features characterize the auditory forebrain (de Rebaupierre, 1997; Winer, 1991). First, there is a primary, lemniscal pathway from the cochlear nuclei to primary auditory cortex (A1) with a systematic representation of tonotopy, binaural signals, and level. Second, a parallel nonprimary pathway arises in midbrain tegmentum, dorsal medial geniculate body, and nonprimary auditory cortex with broad tuning curves and nontopical representation predominate. Third, an even more broadly distributed set of connections and affiliations link auditory forebrain with cortical and subcortical components of the limbic forebrain and associated autonomic areas, as well as elements of the motor system that organize behavioral responses to biologically significant sounds (Winer, 1991).

The primary target of the inferior colliculus in dorsal thalamus is the medial geniculate. This nucleus has three subdivisions: medial, ventral, and dorsal. The ventral division receives major ascending input from the central nucleus of the inferior colliculus and contains sharply tuned cells like those of the inferior colliculus. The ventral division is tonotopically organized although the organization is not simple (there is a concentric component with low frequencies in the center; Imig & Morel, 1988). The cells of the dorsal and medial divisions are fairly unresponsive to tones or noise and respond with long latencies, consistent with major projection back from perirhinal cortex. The functional role of the dorsal and medial divisions is not clear, except to note that nonmonotonic (i.e., selective) responses are common there. In the mustached bat (*Pteronotus*), both medial and dorsal divisions contain fine delay-tuned neurons (Olsen & Suga, 1991; Suga, 1988). Recent studies on the bat's auditory system indicate that the corticofugal system mediates a highly focused positive feedback to physiologically "matched" subcortical neurons, and widespread lateral inhibition to physiologically "unmatched" subcortical neurons, to adjust and improve information processing (Suga, Gao, Zhang, Ma, & Olsen, 2000). Suga proposed that the processing of complex sounds

by combination-sensitive neurons is heavily dependent on the corticofugal system.

Auditory Cortex

The greatest difference between mammals and other vertebrates is the evolution of the cortex in place of the nuclear organization of the forebrain (Karten & Shimizu, 1989). Whether or not this new structure has facilitated the creation of new auditory areas, new areas are a feature of the mammalian auditory specialists. Whereas primitive mammals like tenrecs have few auditory areas (Krubitzer, Kunzle, & Kaas, 1997), there are at least seven tonotopic maps in the cat and the mustached bat. In the cat these areas include A1; secondary auditory cortex (A2); the anterior auditory field; posterior, ventral, and ventral posterior areas as well as insular; Te; and other anterior ectosylvian fields with uncertain tonotopy (de Rebaupierre, 1997). A1 and A2 share physiological features of alternating bands of EE and EI neurons that are mapped orthogonal to the tonotopic axis. In primary auditory cortex responses tend to be more transient than auditory nerve responses, and they show inhibition away from their best frequency. Most responses are binaural and similar to responses from brainstem. These binaural responses are generated by short latency excitatory input from contra ear, and ipsilateral input that might be E, I, or mixed, with the best frequency matched to the input from the contralateral ear.

In the mustached bat there are at least seven cortical areas, many of which are related to processing echolocation signal components. A1 systematically represents frequency with an enlarged representation of the Doppler shift compensation region (pulse frequency range), mapping not just frequency, but amplitude as well. There are several maps of echo delay, for delays that represent near, midrange, and far targets. There is also a map of the contralateral azimuth and a second Doppler shift region. Suga (1988) used these data to construct a parallel-hierarchical scheme for signal processing. Because the different constant-frequency and frequency-modulated components differ in frequency, they are processed in parallel channels in the auditory system by virtue of their tonotopy. In the cortex, however, combination-sensitive neurons may be created by comparing across frequency channels (Suga, 1988).

AUDITORY FUNCTION AND BEHAVIOR

Absolute Auditory Thresholds

A fundamental behavioral measure of hearing sensitivity is the audiogram, a plot of detection thresholds for pure tones across the audible spectrum, which provides an estimate of the frequency range and limits of an animal's hearing. These parameters are influenced by the features of the peripheral auditory system (Wever, 1949), and in mammals these features include the size and impedance-matching characteristics of the middle ear system (Dallos, 1973; Geisler & Hubbard, 1975; Guinan & Peake, 1967; Møller, 1983; Nedzelnitsky, 1980; Rosowski, 1994), the length and stiffness of the basilar membrane (Békésy, 1960; Echteler, Fay, & Popper, 1994; Manley, 1972), the size of the helicotrema (a small opening at the cochlear apex; Dallos, 1970), the density of hair cells (Burda & Voldrich, 1980; Ehret & Frankenreiter, 1977), and the density of hair cell innervation (Guild, Crowe, Bunch, & Polvogt, 1931) along the basilar membrane. In other animals, features of the auditory periphery also play a role in defining the limits and range of hearing in birds (Gleich & Manley, 2000), fish (Popper & Fay, 1999), anurans (Capranica &

Moffat, 1983; Lewis, Baird, Leverenz, & Koyama, 1982), and insects (Yager, 1999).

For most vertebrates, the audiogram is a smooth U-shaped function; thresholds are high at the lower and upper frequency boundaries compared to intermediate frequencies where thresholds are lowest (see, e.g., Masterton, Heffner, & Ravizza, 1969). Mammals differ greatly in the octave range over which they can hear, from as little as 3.5 octaves in the mouse and horseshoe bat to over 8 octaves in the dolphin, raccoon, cat, and kangaroo rat. The smaller octave range of hearing in the mouse and bat nonetheless covers a large frequency bandwidth, as these animals hear ultrasound, in which a single octave (frequency doubling) spans a minimum of 40 kHz. Humans show greatest sensitivity between 1 kHz and 4 kHz and hear over a range of about seven octaves (Sivian & White, 1933; see Figure 4.8).

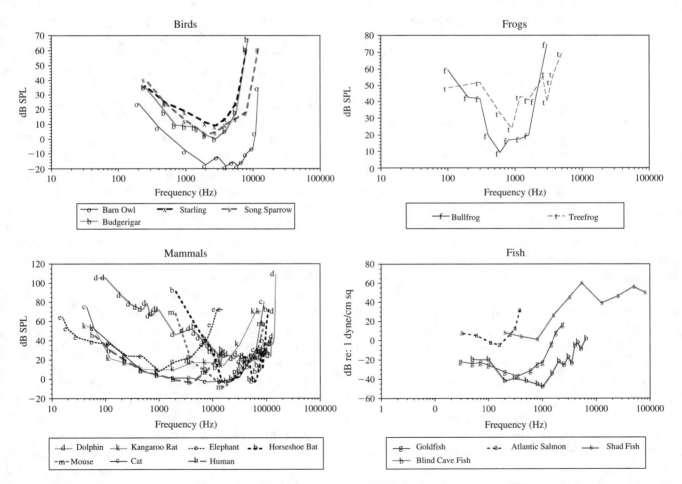

Figure 4.8   Comparative audiograms of selected birds, anurans, mammals, and fishes (data from: budgerigar, Dooling & Saunder, 1975; barn owl, Konishi, 1973; starling, Dooling, Okanoya, Downing, & Hulse, 1986; song sparrow, Okanoya & Dooling, 1987; bullfrog and treefrog, Megela-Simmons et al., 1985; dolphin, Johnson, 1967; mouse and kangaroo rat, H. E. Heffner & Masterton, 1980; cat, R. S. Heffner & Heffner, 1985; elephant, R. S. Heffner & Heffner, 1982; human, Sivian & White, 1933; horseshoe bat, Long & Schnitzler, 1975; goldfish, Fay, 1969; blind cave fish, Popper, 1970; Atlantic salmon, A. D. Hawkins & Johnstone, 1978; shad fish, Mann et al., 1998). Sound level is for detection of pure tones (Hz). The y-axis scale shows dB SPL, except for fish, in which sound pressure is plotted re 1 dyne/cm².

Some animals show enhanced sensitivity nested within their range of hearing. For instance, the audiogram of the echolocating horseshoe bat is highly irregular in shape (Long & Schnitzler, 1975). Between 10 kHz and 40 kHz, a plot of threshold change with frequency resembles the standard U-shaped function of most vertebrates, but the range of this animal's hearing extends far above 40 kHz. Threshold declines gradually at higher frequencies between 40 kHz and 70 kHz before rising rapidly at approximately 81 kHz. The audiogram then shows a very sharp peak in sensitivity at about 83 kHz; the auditory threshold at neighboring lower and upper bounding frequencies (81 kHz and 90 kHz) is elevated by about 30 dB. This bat emits echolocation signals adjusted to return at 83 kHz and has evolved a highly specialized auditory system to detect this biologically important sound frequency. The basilar membrane of the horseshoe bat shows considerable expansion of its frequency map in the region that responds to frequencies around 83 kHz, and this magnification is preserved in the tonotopic organization of the ascending auditory pathway. Thus, the unusual shape of this animal's audiogram reflects an adaptation to facilitate the reception of species-specific acoustic signals (Neuweiler, Bruns, & Schuller, 1980).

Adaptations in the auditory periphery also support specializations for low-frequency hearing. Examples are the kangaroo rat, mole rat, and Mongolian gerbil, small mammals that have evolved enlarged external ears and middle ear cavities that serve to collect and amplify low-frequency sounds (A. Ryan, 1976; H. E. Heffner & Masterton, 1980; Ravicz, Rosowski, & Voight, 1992). In fact, these organs take up roughly two thirds of the cross section of the Mongolian gerbil's head. These animals rely on low-frequency hearing to receive warning signals from conspecifics that must carry over long distances (Ravicz et al., 1992). Elephants also hear very low frequencies (65 dB SPL at 16 Hz; R. S. Heffner & Heffner, 1982), which is presumably important to long-distance communication through infrasound (K. B. Payne et al., 1986).

In vertebrate animals whose hearing sensitivity spans a narrow frequency range, a communication receiver may appear to dominate the auditory system. The frequency range of maximum sensitivity in birds is about 1 kHz to 5 kHz, with absolute hearing sensitivity approaching 0 dB SPL (Dooling, 1980; Dooling et al., 2000). There appears to be a general correspondence between a bird's peak auditory sensitivity and the average power spectrum of its species-specific song (e.g., canary, budgerigar, field sparrow, red-winged blackbird; Dooling, Mulligan, & Miller, 1971; Dooling & Saunders, 1975; Heinz, Sinnott, & Sachs, 1977; Konishi, 1970), suggesting the relative importance of a communication receiver in the avian auditory system. Nocturnal predators (hawks and owls) generally have lower thresholds than songbirds and nonsongbirds, and they use acoustic signals in part to detect and localize prey. Hearing sensitivity in birds falls off dramatically at 8 kHz to 12 kHz, depending on the species.

Behavioral measures of hearing in anurans (frogs and toads) also suggest that a communication receiver dominates the auditory system of these animals, but most data come from experiments that have relied on behavioral responses that the animals normally make in the context of vocal communication. One such technique, evoked calling, exploits the observation that male frogs will vocalize in response to recordings of natural or synthetic conspecific mating calls, while recordings of other species' calls fail to elicit vocalizations. In the bullfrog the sound pressure level of a species-specific call must be approximately 60 dB SPL to evoke calling (Megela, 1984). Another technique commonly used to measure hearing in frogs is selective phonotaxis, which exploits the observation that a gravid female will approach a speaker that broadcasts either natural or synthetic conspecific mating calls in preference to one that broadcasts other acoustic stimuli. The female green tree frog exhibits selective phonotaxis to pure tone stimuli at frequencies corresponding to the two major spectral peaks of the mating call, 900 Hz and 3000 Hz (Gerhardt, 1974). The minimum sound pressure level that elicits selective phonotaxis from the female green tree frog is approximately 55 dB SPL for a 900-Hz pure tone and 90 dB SPL for a 3000-Hz pure tone (Gerhardt, 1976). With a synthetic mating call (900- and 3000-Hz tones presented together), the phonotaxis threshold is 48 dB SPL (Gerhardt, 1981).

Using a neutral psychophysical technique that does not require behavior in the context of acoustic communication, Megela-Simmons, Moss, and Daniel (1985) measured hearing sensitivity in the bullfrog and green tree frog at frequencies within and outside those used by these animals for species-specific communication. The bullfrog's audiogram, like many other vertebrates, is a U-shaped function, ranging between about 300 Hz and 3000 Hz, with highest sensitivity between 600 Hz and 1000 Hz, where this species's mating call contains peak spectral energy. By contrast, the green tree frog's audiogram is a W-shaped function, with highest hearing sensitivity at 900 Hz and 3000 Hz, frequencies where spectral energy in the species-specific mating call is greatest. The differences between the audiograms of the bullfrog and the green tree frog can be attributed to a larger separation of frequency tuning of the two hearing organs in the frog's auditory periphery. In both species the amphibian papillae respond to frequencies up to about 1200 Hz, but the basilar papilla of the green tree frog resonates to approximately 3000 Hz, higher than that of the bullfrog's basilar papilla, which resonates to approximately 1800 Hz (Lewis, Baird, et al., 1982).

The frequency range of hearing is generally largest in mammals, followed by birds, frogs, fish, and insects (e.g., see the goldfish audiogram plotted in Figure 4.8). However, there are some noteworthy exceptions to this trend. One example is the American shad, a fish species that shares its habitat with the echolocating dolphin. The shad can hear sounds over a frequency range from 100 Hz to an astonishing 180 kHz. While this fish's threshold is higher in the ultrasonic range than in the audible range, this species can detect 100-kHz signals at about 140 dB re 1 Pa (Mann, Lu, Hastings, & Popper, 1998). Although a variety of fish species is subject to predation by dolphins, the shad has apparently evolved ultrasonic hearing to detect the sonar signals of its predator.

The importance of audition for the evasion of predators is well illustrated by insects that have evolved hearing for the evasion of echolocating bats. The hearing range and sensitivity in insects are often inferred from responses of auditory neurons, and many hear ultrasonic frequencies, which are produced by echolocating bats as they hunt insect prey (see Figure 4.9). Examples of insects that hear ultrasound include the praying mantis (a single ear located on the midline of the ventral thorax; Yager & Hoy, 1986), green lacewings (ears on the wings; L. A. Miller, 1970, 1984), noctuid moths (ears on the dorsal thorax; Roeder & Treat, 1957), hawk moths (ear built into mouthparts; Roeder, Treat, & Vandeberg, 1970), Hedyloidea butterflies (ears at the base of the forewings; Yack & Fullard, 1999), crickets (prothoracic tibia; Moiseff, Pollack, & Hoy, 1978; Oldfield, Kleindienst, & Huber, 1986), and tiger beetles (ears on the abdomen; Spangler, 1988; Yager, Cook, Pearson, & Spangler, 2000; Yager & Spangler, 1995). Generally, insect auditory thresholds in the ultrasonic range are high, at or above 50 dB SPL, and the frequency range of hearing is typically one to two octaves (Yager, 1999).

Examples also exist for insect sound detection in the human audio range, and often (but not exclusively), low-frequency hearing supports species-specific acoustic communication. Crickets and bush crickets have ears on the proximal tibiae of the prothoracic legs, and the low-frequency range of a large set of auditory receptors corresponds with the spectral content of their species-specific communication calls, generally between 2 kHz and 6 kHz (Imaizumi & Pollack, 1999; Michelsen, 1992; Pollack, 1998).

Masked Auditory Thresholds

When an acoustic signal coincides with interfering background noise, its detection may be partially or completely impaired. The process by which one sound interferes with the detection of another is called *masking*. Several stimulus parameters influence the extent to which masking occurs, including the relation among the temporal structure, amplitude, and frequency composition of the signal and the masker (e.g., Jeffress, 1970; Scharf, 1970). Predictably, the more similar the temporal and spectral characteristics of the masker are to those of the signal, the more effectively it interferes with the detection of the signal (e.g., Jesteadt, Bacon, & Lehman, 1982; Small, 1959; Vogten, 1974, 1978; Wegel & Lane, 1924). And when the sound pressure level of the masker increases, so does the detection threshold of the signal (e.g., Egan & Hake, 1950; Greenwood, 1961a; J. Hawkins & Stevens, 1950; B. C. J. Moore, 1978; Vogten, 1978; Zwicker & Henning, 1984).

If a masking stimulus is broadband white noise, only a portion of the noise band actually contributes to the masking of a pure tone stimulus. This was originally demonstrated by Fletcher (1940), who measured detection thresholds in humans for pure tones against white noise of varying bandwidths. In this experiment, noise bands were geometrically centered at the frequency of a test tone. The spectrum level of the noise (i.e., the power of the noise in a 1-Hz band) remained constant, but as the bandwidth varied, so did its total power. Because the total power of white noise is proportional to its bandwidth, it is perhaps not surprising that the threshold for detecting the pure tone increased as the noise band widened. The interesting observation was, however, that the detection threshold for the pure tone increased as the noise band increased only up to a critical value, beyond which the threshold remained constant. Fletcher termed this value the *critical band*—the frequency region about a pure tone that is effective in masking that tone. This effect is illustrated in Figure 4.10, panel A.

Figure 4.10 presents a schematic representation of the stimulus conditions in a critical band experiment. The solid bar in each graph (a–e) represents a pure tone of a fixed

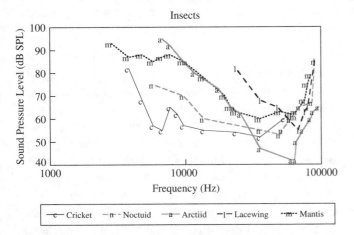

Figure 4.9 Comparative neural audiograms from several insect species (data from: mantis, Yager & Hoy, 1989; arctiid, Fullard & Barclay, 1980; noctuid, L. A. Miller, 1983; cricket, Nolen & Hoy, 1987; lacewing, L. A. Miller, 1975). After Yager and Hoy (1989).

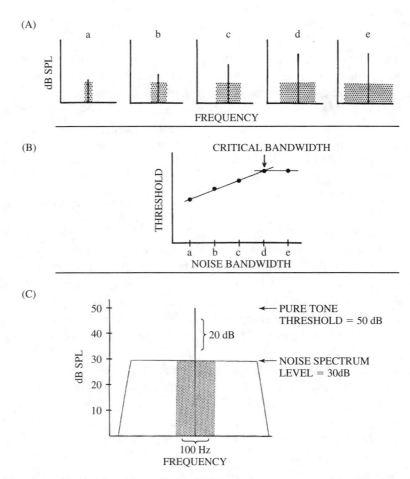

Figure 4.10   *A.* Stimulus conditions for a critical band experiment. Each solid line represents a pure tone, and each shaded region represents white noise whose frequency is centered on the tone. The height of the solid line indicates the sound pressure level of the tone at threshold when measured against a particular noise band. The height of each noise band represents the spectrum level, and this remains constant in a–e. The width of the noise band, however, increases from a to e. *B.* Detection thresholds for the pure tone are plotted as a function of the noise bandwidths (a–e). Note that threshold rises from a to d. The critical band (illustrated here at bandwidth d) is the frequency band about a pure tone which is effective in masking. Beyond the critical band, masked threshold remains constant. *C.* Schematic representation of Fletcher's hypothesis, which states that the power of the noise integrated over the critical band equals the power of the pure tone signal at threshold. The solid bar represents a pure tone, and the box (both open and shaded portions) represents broadband noise. The height of the bar represents the sound pressure level of the tone at threshold, when measured against the noise. The difference between the sound pressure level of the tone at threshold (50 dB) and the spectrum level of the noise (i.e., the power in a 1-Hz band: 30 dB/Hz) yields a ratio of 20 dB. This means that the level of the tone is 100 times greater than the spectrum level of the noise ($10 \log_{10} 100 = 20$). It then follows that 100 cycles of the noise must be summed to equal the power of the pure tone. The shaded region of the noise denotes this 100-Hz band.

frequency, and the shaded area represents white noise, centered at the frequency of the tone. The spectrum level of the noise in each graph is the same; however, the bandwidth increases from a to e. Accordingly, the total power of the noise also increases from a to e. The height of each bar indicates the level of the pure tone at threshold, when measured against the noise. From a to d the height of the bar increases, indicating that a higher amplitude tone is required for detection as the noise band widens. However, in e the height of the bar is the same as that in d, even though the bandwidth of the noise has again increased. Below (B) the amplitude of the pure tone at threshold is plotted for each of the five noise bandwidths. This figure summarizes the data presented earlier, showing

that threshold increases up to bandwidth d and thereafter remains constant. The breakpoint in the function at bandwidth d represents the critical band.

The importance of the results of critical band experiments rests on the implication that the ear sums the noise power or energy over a limited frequency region. A large critical band indicates that the noise must be summed over a wide frequency band in order to mask the signal and therefore indicates relatively poor frequency resolution of the auditory system. By contrast, a small critical band indicates relatively high frequency resolution.

Fletcher (1940) included in the concept of the critical band a hypothesis proposing that the power of the noise integrated over the critical band equals the power of the pure tone signal at threshold. This implies that a critical band can be determined indirectly by measuring the detection threshold for a pure tone against broadband masking noise, rather than directly by measuring the threshold against a variety of noise bandwidths. If one knows the level of the tone at threshold and the spectrum level of the noise, the ratio of the two provides the necessary information to determine the critical bandwidth based on Fletcher's assumptions. The level of the tone and the spectrum level of the noise are expressed in logarithmic units (dB); therefore, the ratio of the two is simply dB tone – dB noise spectrum level. Given this ratio, one can then calculate the frequency band over which the noise must be integrated to equal the power of the pure tone. Figure 4.10, panel C, illustrates this analysis.

In Figure 4.10, panel C, the solid line represents a pure tone, and the boxed-in area (both open and shaded portions) represents broadband white noise. The height of the bar denotes the amplitude of the pure tone at threshold (50 dB SPL) when measured against the background noise (spectrum level 30 dB SPL/Hz), and the difference between the two is 20 dB. This ratio of 20 dB, in linear units, equals a ratio of 100 ($10 \log_{10} 100 = 20$ dB). That is, the power of the pure tone is 100 times greater than the power in one cycle of noise; therefore, 100 cycles of the noise must be added together to equal the power of the tone. The shaded portion of the noise represents the

100-Hz frequency region about the pure tone that contributes to the masking. If Fletcher's assumptions were correct, this value (100 Hz) should equal the critical band, as measured directly; in accordance with this logic, the ratio of the pure tone at threshold to the spectrum level of the broadband noise has been termed the *critical ratio* (Zwicker, Flottorp, & Stevens, 1957).

Fletcher's assumptions have been tested, and it is now well established that critical bands (measured directly) are in fact approximately 2.5 times larger than estimates made from critical ratios (Saunders, Denny, & Bock, 1978; Zwicker et al., 1957). This outcome indicates that Fletcher's assumptions were not entirely correct; however, the two measures do follow almost parallel patterns of change with signal frequency. Figure 4.11 illustrates this relation, summarizing data collected from several vertebrate species, including humans. The critical ratios have been transformed to estimates of critical bands, following Fletcher's assumption that the power of the pure tone at threshold equals the power integrated over the critical band of noise. For most species tested, both critical bands and critical ratios increase systematically as a function of signal frequency, and the proportionality between the critical band and the critical ratio exists across a wide range of frequencies. In fact, had Fletcher assumed that the critical band contained 2.5 times the power of the masked tone at threshold (rather than equal power), the two functions would overlap for human listeners at frequencies above 300 Hz.

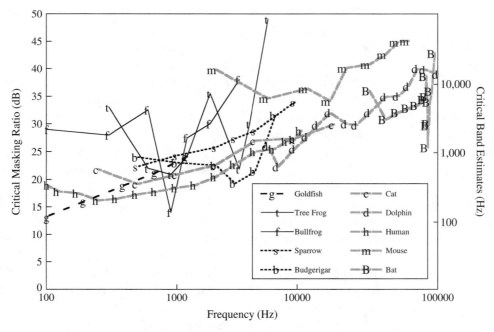

Figure 4.11   Critical ratios in dB (left y-axis) and corresponding critical band estimates in Hz (right y-axis; after Fletcher, 1940) plotted across test signal frequency. Data shown for a number of vertebrate species (data from: goldfish, Fay, 1974; tree frog, Moss & Megela-Simmons, 1986; bullfrog, Megela-Simmons, 1988; song sparrow, Okanoya & Dooling, 1987, 1988; budgerigar, Dooling & Saunders, 1975; cat, Costalupes, 1983; dolphin, Johnson, 1968; human, J. Hawkins & Stevens, 1950; mouse, Ehret, 1976; horseshoe bat, Long, 1977).

There are other empirically determined parallels between critical bands and critical ratios. Results of both critical band and critical ratio experiments show that the threshold for detecting a pure tone signal varies with the spectrum level of the masking noise. As the power of the noise increases, there is a proportionate increase in detection threshold (e.g., J. Hawkins & Stevens, 1950; Zwicker et al., 1957). Moreover, experimental findings also indicate that estimates of both the critical band and the critical ratio are invariant with the level of the masking stimulus, except at high noise spectrum levels (exceeding 60–70 dB; Greenwood, 1961a; J. Hawkins & Stevens, 1950).

Prior to Fletcher's study of the critical band, research on the peripheral auditory system revealed the existence of a frequency map along the cochlear partition (Guild et al., 1931; Steinberg, 1937). High frequencies are coded at the base of the basilar membrane, and lower frequencies are coded progressively toward the apex. This place coding arises from changes in the stiffness of the basilar membrane from base to apex. At the base, where the membrane is stiffest, high frequencies produce maximal displacement; and toward the apex, where relative stiffness decreases, lower frequencies produce maximal displacement (Békésy, 1960).

Fletcher approached his work on the critical band with the assumption that this measure would permit psychophysical estimates of the frequency coordinates of the basilar membrane. Indeed, he found that the function relating stimulus frequency to position along the basilar membrane paralleled the function relating stimulus frequency to the width of the critical band. Both the range of frequencies encoded by a fixed distance along the basilar membrane and the size of the critical band increase as an exponential function of sound frequency (Fletcher, 1940; Greenwood, 1961b; Liberman, 1982). This observation led to the hypothesis that a critical band represents a constant distance along the basilar membrane over which the neural response is integrated (Fletcher, 1940; Zwicker et al., 1957).

Following the early psychophysical studies of critical ratios and critical bands in humans, auditory masking research began on other vertebrate species. These experiments have permitted a comparative approach to the study of frequency selectivity in the auditory system. Remarkably, in a variety of vertebrates (e.g., cat: Watson, 1963; Costalupes, 1983; Pickles, 1975; mouse: Ehret, 1975; chinchilla: J. D. Miller, 1964; rat: Gourevitch, 1965), measures of critical bands and critical ratios show similar frequency-dependent trends, and this pattern resembles that observed in humans—that is, increasing systematically with signal frequency (3 dB/octave). This general pattern has led to the suggestion that frequency selectivity in the auditory systems of vertebrates depends on a common mechanism, the mechanical response of the cochlea (Greenwood, 1961b).

Direct measures of frequency selectivity in single VIIIth nerve fibers differ from those obtained psychophysically, indicating that critical ratios and critical bands are not simple correlates of the tuning curves of primary fibers (Pickles & Comis, 1976). This finding does not rule out the possibility that neural integration along the cochlear partition lays the foundation for frequency selectivity, although it does suggest that other processes, such as the distribution and temporal pattern of neural discharge in the central auditory system, may be involved in frequency discrimination.

Although critical bands and critical ratios increase systematically with signal frequency in most vertebrates, there are noteworthy exceptions. The parakeet shows a U-shaped function; critical ratios are lowest at an intermediate frequency of this animal's hearing range, and this frequency region corresponds to the dominant frequency components of its vocalizations. Also in this frequency region, the parakeet's absolute detection thresholds are lowest (Dooling & Saunders, 1975). A second example can be found in the echolocating horseshoe bat, which shows a sharp decline in critical ratio (i.e., a marked increase in frequency resolution) at 83 kHz, relative to neighboring frequencies (Long, 1977). This specialization for frequency resolution at 83 kHz parallels that observed for absolute sensitivity described earlier (Neuweiler et al., 1980).

In the parakeet and the horseshoe bat, the spectral regions of greatest frequency selectivity and absolute sensitivity coincide; however, it is important to emphasize that these two measures of auditory function are not typically related. The shapes of the audiogram and the critical ratio function differ markedly in most animals; at frequencies where absolute sensitivity is relatively high, frequency selectivity is not necessarily also high. Nonetheless, measures of hearing in the parakeet and horseshoe bat suggest that auditory specializations (possibly, e.g., the mechanical response of the cochlea, hair cell density and innervation patterns, tonotopic representation in the central auditory system, etc.) do occur to facilitate discrimination of biologically significant signals from noise.

The shape of the green tree frog's critical ratio function departs from that of most vertebrates. This animal shows a W-shaped critical ratio function, with lowest critical ratios at 900 Hz and 3000 Hz, corresponding to the dominant spectral peaks of its mating call. The smallest critical ratios obtained in the green tree frog are approximately 22 dB, indicating good resolving power of this animal's ear at biologically salient frequencies, 900 Hz and 3000 Hz. These data compare closely with estimates from other vertebrates at 900 Hz and 3000 Hz and suggest that the ear of the anuran, despite its distinct morphology, can filter frequency as well as that of other vertebrates, including those that possess basilar membranes (Moss & Simmons, 1986).

The mechanical response of the tonotopically organized cochlea can adequately account for measures of frequency selectivity among most vertebrates, and this implies that frequency selectivity is mediated by the spatial distribution of neural activity in the auditory system. However, data obtained from fish (e.g., goldfish: Fay, 1970, 1974; cod: A. D. Hawkins & Chapman, 1975) present a challenge to this commonly accepted notion. There is no biophysical evidence that the auditory receptor organ of the fish, the sacculus (also lacking a basilar membrane), operates on a place principle of frequency coding like the cochlea (Fay & Popper, 1983). Yet fish exhibit the same pattern of frequency-dependent changes in critical ratios as do other vertebrates whose peripheral auditory systems show place coding of frequency. Instead, frequency selectivity in fish has been explained in terms of temporal coding of neural discharge (Fay, 1978a, 1978b, 1983). That is, the temporal pattern of neural discharge in primary auditory fibers, regardless of their innervation sites along the sacculus, may carry the code for frequency selectivity. At present, differences and similarities in the mechanisms of frequency selectivity between fish and other vertebrates are not well understood.

Frequency Difference Limens

The discrimination of sounds on the basis of signal frequency is a common acoustic problem solved by species throughout the animal kingdom. In laboratory studies of frequency discrimination, reference and comparison tones are typically presented in sequence, and the listener is required to report when there is a change in frequency (see Figure 4.12). The data are plotted as the change in frequency required for discrimination as a function of the test frequency. Frequency difference thresholds (limen) measured in mammals, birds, and fishes show a common trend: $\Delta F/F$ is approximately constant (Weber's law holds), with thresholds tending to rise steadily with test frequency. In most animal groups tested (but see the exception noted later), individual species tend to fall within the same range, from less than 1% to about 10%. A low-frequency specialist is the pigeon, and it is hypothesized that this animal uses infrasound for homing (Quine & Kreithen, 1981). The bottlenose dolphin shows well-developed frequency discrimination from 1000 Hz to 140 kHz (Thompson & Herman, 1975).

A cross-species comparison of sound frequency discrimination illustrates that common patterns in the data can arise through different mechanisms. Frequency discrimination in insects arises from different auditory receptors that are tuned

to different sound frequencies (Michelsen, 1966; Oldfield et al., 1986). Mechanical tuning of the basilar papilla may support frequency discrimination in birds, but other mechanisms may also operate (Gleich & Manley, 2000). In the case of frogs and toads, the tectorial membrane over the amphibian papilla appears to support a traveling wave (Hillery & Narins, 1984; Lewis, Leverenz, & Koyama, 1982), and its mechanical tuning may contribute to frequency discrimination (Fay & Simmons, 1999), but temporal processing or hair cell tuning may also play a role. The fish ear lacks a hearing organ that could support a mechanical place principle of frequency analysis (Békésy, 1960; Fay & Simmons, 1999), but nonetheless fish show a pattern of frequency discrimination that resembles mammals and most birds. Hair cell micromechanics (Fay, 1997), hair cell tuning (A. C. Crawford & Fettiplace, 1980), and time-domain processing (Fay, 1978b) have been proposed as mechanisms for frequency discrimination in fish. Frequency discrimination in mammals is generally assumed to depend on the mechanical tuning of the basilar membrane (Békésy, 1960), but the variety of mechanisms that presumably operate in nonmammalian species challenges us to look more closely at this problem in these animals as well.

In anurans no psychophysical studies have yet measured frequency discrimination across the audible spectrum, as have been conducted in mammals, birds, and fishes. However, frequency discrimination data warrant mention. Evoked calling and selective phonotaxis methods have been used to estimate frequency discrimination in several different anuran species, each of which was tested only over a narrow frequency range that was appropriate for the methods that required behavioral responses in the context of acoustic communication behavior. Most threshold estimates were between 9% and 33%, generally higher than those taken from other species (e.g., Doherty & Gerhardt, 1984; Gerhardt, 1981; Narins & Capranica, 1978; M. J. Ryan, 1983; Schwartz & Wells, 1984). The higher threshold estimates may reflect the methods employed or differences in the frequency resolving power of the anuran ear (Fay & Simmons, 1999). The psychophysical data on critical ratios measured in the green tree frog (Moss & Simmons, 1986), which fall within the range of birds, mammals, and fishes, speak against the latter interpretation, but direct psychophysical studies of frequency discrimination in anurans would address the question more effectively.

Positive and negative phonotaxis have been used to measure frequency discrimination in insects. For example, the cricket (*Teleogryllus oceanicus*) steers toward a 5-kHz model of a conspecific calling song broadcast through a loud speaker and steers away from a 40-kHz model of a bat echolocation call. By systematically manipulating the stimulus frequency between that of the conspecific call and that of

(A)

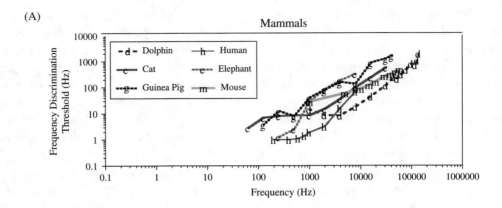

(B)

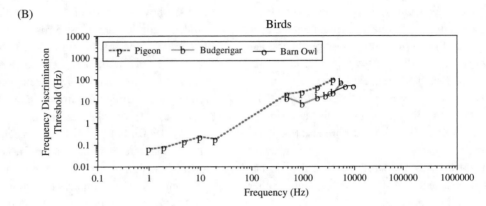

(C)

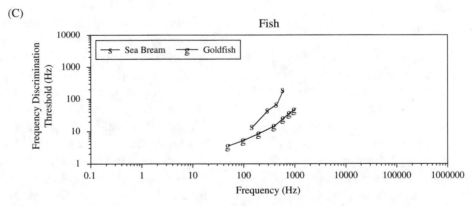

Figure 4.12   Frequency discrimination performance (ΔF/F), plotted for a number of vertebrate species, as a function of sound frequency. *A.* Mammals (data from: bottlenose dolphin, Thompson & Herman, 1975; human, Weir, Jesteadt, & Green, 1976; cat, Elliott, Stein, & Harrison, 1960; elephant, R. S. Heffner & Heffner, 1982; guinea pig, R. Heffner, H. Heffner, & Masterton, 1971; mouse, Ehret, 1975). *B.* Birds (data from: pigeon, Quine & Kreithen, 1981, for 1–20 Hz and Price, Dalton, & Smith, 1967, for 500–4000 Hz; barn owl, Quine & Konishi, 1974; budgerigar, Dooling & Saunders, 1975). *C.* Fish (data from: sea bream, Dijkgraaf, 1952; goldfish, Fay, 1970).

the echolocation signal, the cricket shows a shift in its phono-taxis behavior, which is related to its frequency discrimination of these sound frequencies (Moiseff et al., 1978). This is shown in Figure 4.13.

Temporal Resolution

Temporal processing of sound stimuli is an important aspect of hearing that contributes to the perception of complex signals and the localization of sound sources (discussed

later). There are many different approaches to the study of temporal processing in the auditory system, but not all have been widely applied to the study of different animal species. Because we emphasize comparative hearing in this chapter, we selected for discussion in this section two measures of temporal resolution that have been studied in several animal groups: temporal modulation transfer function (TMTF) and gap detection. Both measures require the subject to detect changes in the envelope of acoustic stimuli. Abrupt onset or offset of pure tones produces spectral smearing of the

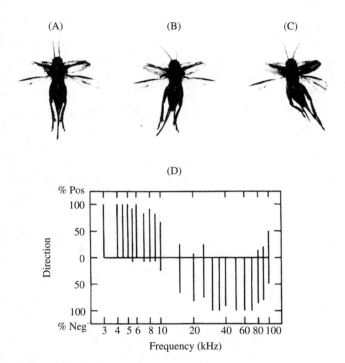

Figure 4.13 Phonotactic response of a cricket to sound frequencies used for communication and those used for bat evasion. After Moiseff et al. (1978).

stimulus that could provide unintended cues to the subject, and therefore experimenters generally study temporal resolution of the auditory system using noise stimuli.

Temporal Modulation Transfer Function

Detection of the sinusoidal amplitude modulation of broadband noise depends on the rate and depth of stimulus modulation. Measurements of the minimum amplitude modulation depth required for modulation detection across a range of modulation rates can be used to estimate a TMTF. Behavioral data taken from the human, chinchilla, and parakeet all yield TMTFs with low-pass characteristics. The rate at which temporal modulation detection falls to half power (-3dB) is 50 Hz for the human (Viemeister, 1979), 270 Hz for the chinchilla (Salvi, Giraudi, Henderson, & Hamernik, 1982), and 92 Hz for the parakeet (Dooling & Searcy, 1981). At higher rates, detection of temporal modulation requires increasing depths of amplitude modulation up to around 1000 Hz, and thresholds remain high up to about 3000 Hz (Fay, 1992), after which the auditory system can no longer resolve the temporal modulation. By contrast, the TMTF of the goldfish does not resemble a low pass filter but rather remains relatively constant across modulation rates between 2.5 Hz and 400 Hz (see Figure 4.14).

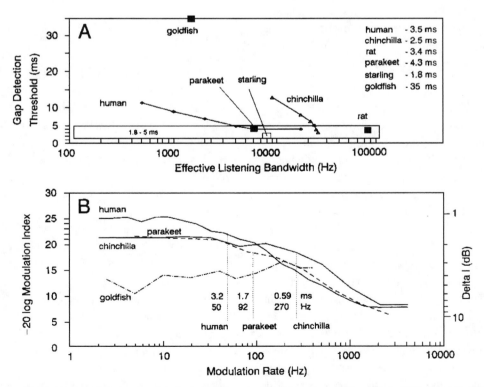

Figure 4.14   Gap detection thresholds (A) and temporal modulation transfer functions (data from: human, Fitzgibbons, 1983; chinchilla, Salvi & Arehole, 1985; rat, Ison, 1982; parakeet, Dooling & Searcy, 1981; starling, Klump & Maier, 1989; goldfish, Fay, 1985). (B) Selected vertebrate species (data from: human, Viemeister, 1979; chinchilla, Salvi et al., 1982, and Henderson, Salvi, Pavek, & Hamernik, 1984; parakeet, Dooling & Searcy, 1981; goldfish, Fay, 1985). After Fay (1992).

In mammals, data show that detection of temporal modulation of broadband noise depends on hearing bandwidth. High-frequency hearing loss in the chinchilla produces a rise in threshold of amplitude modulation detection across rates and a drop in the half-power temporal modulation rate (Salvi et al., 1982).

Gap Detection

The shortest silent interval that an animal can detect in an acoustic signal is referred to as the gap detection threshold, and in mammals this measure has been shown to depend on noise bandwidth (see Figure 4.14). In both the human (Fitzgibbons, 1983) and the chinchilla, gap detection thresholds are over 10 ms for narrowband noise and systematically decrease with noise bandwidth to a minimum of about 3.5 ms for the human (Fitzgibbons, 1983) and 2.5 ms for the chinchilla (Salvi & Arehole, 1985). The minimum gap detection threshold in the rat is 3.4 ms (Ison, 1982) and in the parakeet it is 4.3 ms (Dooling & Searcy, 1981). Experimentally induced hearing loss above 1 kHz in the chinchilla can raise the gap detection threshold to 23 ms (Salvi & Arehole, 1985). The goldfish shows a gap detection threshold of 35 ms (Fay, 1985). Striking is the very small gap detection threshold of the starling: only 1.8 ms (Klump & Maier, 1989).

Gap detection, like the TMTF, depends on bandwidth, which suggests an influence of frequency tuning in the auditory periphery on performance of these temporal tasks. Comparative hearing loss data are not, however, entirely consistent with this notion. Both gap detection and TMTF may also reflect limitations of neural time processing in the CNS (Fay, 1992).

Localization

Sound source localization plays a central role in the lives of many animals: to find conspecifics, to find food, and to avoid predators. A large number of species use acoustic signals for social communication, and commonly such signals convey the message, "Here I am. Come find me." For example, the advertisement calls of male frogs attract gravid females to their position along the pond (Capranica, 1976). Calls of birds serve a similar function. Thus, localization of the sender is an important function of acoustic communication in social animals. Some animals detect and localize prey from the acoustic signals they produce. The barn owl, for example, listens to rustling sounds generated by mice that move over the ground. The owl can track and capture the prey in complete darkness (R. S. Payne, 1971) by localizing the sounds generated by its movements through the grass and leaves on the ground. Another example of an animal that uses sound to localize prey is the echolocating bat. The bat transmits ultrasonic acoustic signals

that reflect off the prey and uses the features of the reflected echo to localize and capture small flying insects, and it can do so in the absence of vision (Griffin, 1958). The acoustic signals produced by predators can also serve as a warning to prey, and the localization of predator-generated signals can aid in the evasion of predators. For example, moths, crickets, and praying mantises can detect and localize the ultrasound of an echolocating bat, which can guide its flight away from the predator (Moiseff et al., 1978; R. S. Payne, Roeder, & Wallman, 1966; Yager & Hoy, 1986, 1989). Playing several crucial functions, it is not surprising that the capacity to localize sound sources occurs widely throughout the animal kingdom.

In most animals sound localization is enabled by the presence of two ears and a central auditory system that can compare the direction-dependent signals that each receives. The comparison of the signal arrival time (onset, amplitude peaks in the envelope, and ongoing phase) and amplitude spectrum at the two ears provides the basis for sound source localization in most vertebrates, referred to as ITD and interaural intensity difference cues (see Figure 4.15). Directional hearing in some animals, however, depends on directionality of hair cells of the auditory receptor organ (e.g., fish) or directionality of the external ear (e.g., Michelsen, 1998).

The acoustic cues used by mammals for horizontal sound localization depends on the time-frequency structure of the signals. Ongoing phase differences between signals received at the two ears can be discriminated unambiguously only if the period of the signal is longer than the interaural distance. In humans the distance between the two ears is roughly 17 cm, and the maximum interaural time delay is therefore about 0.5 ms (sound travels in air at a speed of approximately 344 m/s). Humans can use the phase difference of a pure tone signal to localize sound if the frequency is below 1400 Hz (Mills, 1958). At higher frequencies humans use interaural intensity differences for sound localization. In all land vertebrates, interaural intensity difference cues become available when wavelength of the sound is smaller than the dimensions of the animal's head, so that sufficient sound shadowing occurs to produce amplitude differences of the signal at the two ears (see Figure 4.15). Masterton et al. (1969), H. E. Heffner and Masterton (1980), and R. S. Heffner and Heffner (1992) reported a negative correlation between interaural distance and high-frequency hearing and suggested that high-frequency hearing evolved in animals with small heads to enable sound localization using interaural intensity cues.

There are many different approaches to measuring the accuracy with which a listener can localize a sound source. The listener may indicate the direction of a sound source by pointing or aiming the head. Here, the accuracy of the listener's

1.

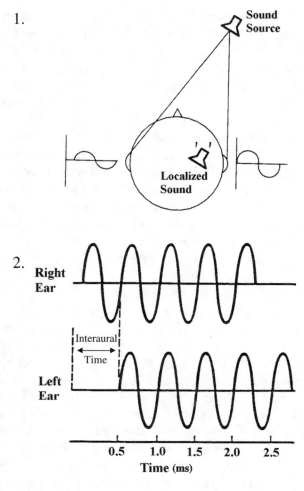

2.

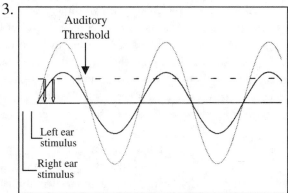

Figure 4.15 Schematic of acoustic cues used for binaural sound localization in the horizontal plane. Adapted from Yost and Hafter (1987). *1.* Illustration of a sound source to the right of the listener's midline, resulting in a signal level that is greater and arrives earlier at the listener's right ear. *2.* Illustration of interaural time differences for a signal that arrives at the right ear before the left ear. For this sine wave stimulus only the first cycle provides a reliable interaural time difference cue, after which the temporal offset of the signal at the two ears becomes ambiguous. This ambiguity occurs for sine wave stimuli with wavelengths shorter than the listener's interaural separation. *3.* Illustration of level differences at the right and left ears. Because the signal is stronger at the right ear than the left ear, it exceeds auditory threshold earlier in time. This shows how interaural intensity differences can translate into interaural time differences.

motor behavior is included in the localization measure. Some tasks simply require the subject to lateralize a sound source relative to a reference point. In many psychophysical experiments, the subject is asked to indicate whether a sound source location changed over successive presentations. Localization resolution measured in this way is referred to as the *minimum audible angle* (MAA; Mills, 1958). The MAA depends on the sound stimulus, with pure tones generally yielding higher thresholds than broadband signals. In mammals MAA can be very small: about 0.8 deg in the human (Mills, 1958), 1.2 deg in the elephant (R. S. Heffner & Heffner, 1982), and 0.9 deg in the bottlenose dolphin (Renaud & Popper, 1975). The macaque monkey has an MAA of 4.4 deg (R. S. Heffner & Masterton, 1978), similar to the opossum with an MAA of 4.6 deg (Ravizza & Masterton, 1972). Data from the horse show a surprisingly large MAA of 37 deg (R. S. Heffner & Heffner, 1984). The pallid bat, an echolocating species that is also known to use passive listening for prey capture, has an MAA of 2 deg (Fuzessery, Buttenhoff, Andrews, & Kennedy, 1993), whereas the echolocating big brown bat has an MAA of 14 deg in a passive listening paradigm (Koay, Kearns, Heffner, & Heffner, 1998). Estimates of azimuthal localization accuracy in the actively echolocating big brown bat are considerably lower: 1 deg to 3 deg (Masters, Moffat, & Simmons, 1985; Simmons et al., 1983). See Figure 4.15, panel B.

Vertical localization in mammals depends largely on spectral cues, created by the direction-dependent filtering of acoustic signals by the external ears, head, and torso (Yost & Gourevitch, 1987). The vertical position of a sound source influences the travel path of the sound through the pinna, which in turn shapes the signal spectrum (Batteau, 1967; R. S. Heffner, Heffner, & Koay, 1995, 1996). Human listeners can discriminate the vertical position of a sound source with accuracy of about 3 deg, but performance falls apart when pinna cues are disturbed (Batteau, 1967; R. S. Heffner et al., 1996). Vertical localization performance in mammals is typically poorer than horizontal localization, with thresholds of about 2 deg in dolphin (Renaud & Popper, 1975), 3 deg in humans (Wettschurek, 1973), 3 deg in rhesus pig tailed monkey (Brown, Schessler, Moody, & Stebbins, 1982), 3 deg in bats (Lawrence & Simmons, 1982), 4 deg in cat (Martin & Webster, 1987), 13 deg in opossum (Ravizza & Masterton, 1972), and 23 deg in chinchilla (R. S. Heffner et al., 1995). Certainly, free movement of the head and pinnae can aid in an animal's localization of a sound source.

The echolocating bat's foraging success depends on accurate localization of prey in azimuth, elevation, and distance. The bat uses the same acoustic cues described earlier for sound source localization in azimuth and elevation. The bat determines target distance from the time delay between its sonar vocalizations and the returning echoes and uses the three-dimensional information about target location to guide the features of its sonar vocalizations and to position itself to grasp insect prey with its wing or tail membrane (Erwin, Wilson, & Moss, 2001). Psychophysical studies of echo-delay difference discrimination report thresholds as low as 30 μs, corresponding to a range difference of 0.5 cm (reviewed in Moss & Schnitzler, 1995).

Behavioral studies demonstrate that birds also use interaural time and intensity differences to localize a sound source in the horizontal plane; however, there is some debate over the mechanisms. Researchers have argued that the bird's ears are too closely spaced to use ITDs from two independent pressure receivers, and the sound frequencies that they hear are too low for their small heads to generate sufficient sound shadowing to use interaural intensity differences. This problem can be solved if one assumes that the bird's ears act as *pressure difference receivers* (Kühne & Lewis, 1985). A pressure difference receiver is distinct from a direct pressure receiver in that the left and right ears are acoustically coupled through an interaural canal, allowing stimulation of the tympanic membrane from both directions (i.e., from the outside of the head and through the opposite ear via the interaural canal). The interaural intensity and time cues available to the animal are enhanced through a pressure-difference receiver, and substantial data support this hypothesized mechanism for sound localization in birds. However, owing largely to methodological difficulties in fully testing this hypothesis, some researchers continue to challenge the notion (Klump, 2000).

The minimum resolvable angle (MRA) measures the absolute localization performance of an animal, as opposed to relative localization tasks that only require the subject to detect a change in sound source location (e.g., MAA). The MRA has been studied in a number of bird species, and thresholds range from 1 deg to 3 deg in the barn owl (Knudsen & Konishi, 1979; Rice, 1982), saw-whet owl (Frost, Baldwin, & Csizy, 1989), and marsh hawk (Rice, 1982) to over 100 deg in the zebra finch (Park & Dooling, 1991) and the bobwhite quail (Gatehouse & Shelton, 1978). (See Figure 4.16.) It is not clear whether the very high thresholds reported for some species reflect poor localization ability or limitations in the psychophysical methods used to study localization performance. The great horned owl has an MRA of 7 deg (Beitel, 1991), the red-tailed hawk 8 deg to 10 deg, and the American kestrel 10 deg to 12 deg (Rice, 1982). The budgerigar shows an MRA of 27 deg (Park & Dooling, 1991), and the great tit 23 deg (Klump, Windt, & Curio, 1986).

It is not surprising that the smallest MRAs have been measured in raptors. The barn owl, for example, is a nocturnal predator that depends largely on hearing to find prey and has developed exceptional sound localization abilities. It hears higher frequency sounds than most birds (see Figure 4.8), and it shows specializations for temporal processing in the central auditory system that presumably supports its horizontal sound localization (see Figure 4.15). The dominant cue used by the barn owl for vertical sound localization is interaural intensity cues, created by the asymmetrical positions of its right and left ear canals. In addition, the barn owl's feather ruff enhances elevation-dependent changes in signal intensity (Moiseff, 1989). Vertical sound localization thresholds, like MRA in the horizontal plane, are lowest for broadband signals, as small as 2.2 deg for a 1,000-s noise burst (Knudsen & Konishi, 1979).

Minimum audible or resolvable angles have not been measured in frogs, but binaural hearing is required for sound localization in anurans (Feng, Gerhardt, & Capranica, 1976). Selective phonotaxis studies have been conducted to examine the female frog's localization accuracy in approaching a speaker that broadcasts a species-specific advertisement call. Taking the mean error between the frog's position and the position of the sound source averaged across all jumps during phonotactic approaches has yielded estimates of sound localization accuracy in several species: dendrobatid frog, 23 deg (Gerhardt & Rheinlaender, 1980); green tree frog, 15.1 deg (Rheinlaender, Gerhardt, Yager, & Capranica, 1979); painted reed frog, 22 deg in two dimensions, 43 deg in three dimensions (Passmore, Capranica, Telford, & Bishop, 1984); and gray tree frog, 23 deg in three dimensions (Jørgenson & Gerhardt, 1991). Sound localization by the frog derives from a combination pressure-pressure difference system (Feng & Shofner, 1981; Michelsen, 1992; Michelsen, Jørgenson, Christensen-Dalsgaard, & Capranica, 1986).

Fish can localize sound underwater, as they are sensitive to the acoustic particle motion that changes with the sound source direction. Cod can make angular discriminations of sound source location on the order of 20 deg in the horizontal plane and 16 deg in the vertical plane (Chapman & Johnstone, 1974), and sound localization depends on the integrity of both ears (Schuijf, 1975). It appears that vector coding within and across auditory receptor organs in the fish ear supports sound localization: Although the underwater acoustics that impact sound localization in fish differ from those for sound localization in terrestrial animals, it is interesting to note that similar organizational principles appear to operate; namely, binaural cues are used by fish for azimuthal

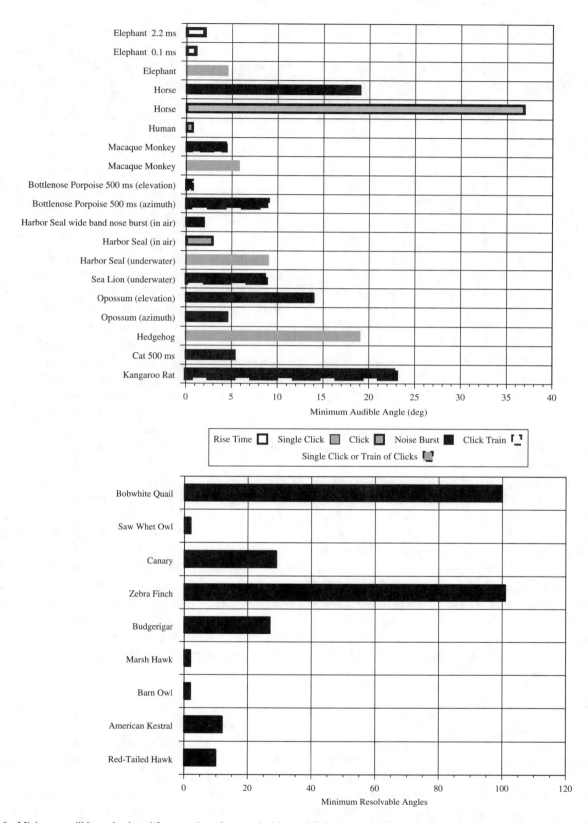

Figure 4.16   Minimum audible angle plotted for a number of mammals (above). Minimum resolvable angle plotted for a number of bird species (below; data from: elephant, R. S. Heffner & Heffner, 1982; horse and human, R. S. Heffner & Heffner, 1984; macaque monkey, R. S. Heffner & Masterton, 1978; dolphin, Renaud & Popper, 1975; harbor seal, Terhune, 1974; sea lion, P. W. B. Moore, 1975; opossum, Ravizza & Masterton, 1972; hedgehog, Chambers, 1971; cat, Casseday & Neff, 1975; kangaroo rat, H. E. Heffner & Masterton, 1980; bobwhite quail, Gatehouse & Shelton, 1978; saw whet owl, Frost et al., 1989; canary, zebra finch, and budgerigar, Park & Dooling, 1991; marsh hawk, barn owl, American kestrel, and red-tailed hawk, Rice, 1982).

localization and monaural cues for elevational localization (Fay & Edds-Walton, 2000).

Studies of some insect species show that despite their small size they are able to localize sound sources. Localization of acoustic sources is important to social communication and predator evasion in many insect species, which is achieved largely through pressure difference receivers and movement receivers (Autrum, 1940; Michelsen, 1998), although experimental evidence shows that acoustic cues are also available for some insect species to use pressure receivers (R. S. Payne et al., 1966). Pressure difference receivers are more sensitive than movement receivers in acoustic far fields. As in other animals that apparently use pressure difference receivers (e.g., frogs and birds, as discussed earlier), sound waves reach both surfaces of the tympanal membrane, and the directional cues are enhanced by the different paths of acoustic activation. Long, lightly articulated sensory hairs protruding from the body surface of an insect are inherently directional, and the activation pattern of these movement receivers can be used to determine sound source location, particularly at close range, where their sensitivity may be comparable to that of a pressure difference receiver (Michelsen, 1992, 1998).

Some insects are capable not only of lateralizing the direction of a sound source but also scaling the direction of a phonotactic response according to the angular position of the sound source. For example, crickets placed in an arena adjust the angle of each turn toward a loudspeaker broadcasting a conspecific call (Bailey & Thomson, 1977; Latimer & Lewis, 1986; Pollack, 1998). It is noteworthy that behavioral studies of sound localization in crickets using a treadmill apparatus that can elicit and track phonotactic behavior, while keeping the distance from the sound source fixed, have found that localization ability is still intact after removal of one ear or the tracheal connections between the ears. New data show that crickets retain 1 dB to 2 dB of directionality after surgical removal of one ear, which appears to be adequate for localization tasks in simplified laboratory tasks (Michelsen, 1998).

Auditory Scene Analysis

Auditory scene analysis involves the organization of complex acoustic events that allows the listener to identify and track sound sources in the environment. For example, at the symphony individuals in the audience may be able to hear out separate instruments or differentiate between music played from different sections of the orchestra. At the same time, each listener may also track a melody that is carried by many different sections of the orchestra together. In effect, the listener groups and segregates sounds, according to similarity or differences in pitch, timbre, spatial location, and temporal patterning, to organize perceptually the acoustic information from the auditory scene. In animal communication systems, auditory scene analysis allows an individual to segregate and interpret the acoustic signals of conspecifics that may overlap other environmental signals in frequency and time. The same principle holds for identifying and tracking the signals produced by predators. Auditory scene analysis thus allows the listener to make sense of dynamic acoustic events in a complex auditory world (Bregman, 1990), which is essential to the lives of all hearing animals.

Only recently have studies of animal auditory perception examined the principles of scene analysis in nonhuman species. Experiments with European starlings (Braaten & Hulse, 1993; Hulse, MacDougall-Shackleton, & Wisniewski, 1997; MacDougall-Shackleton, Hulse, Gentner, & White, 1998) and goldfish (Fay, 1998, 2000) have demonstrated that spectral and temporal features of acoustic patterns influence the perceptual organization of sound in these animals. Using conditioning and generalization procedures, these researchers provided empirical evidence that both fish and birds can hear out complex acoustic patterns into auditory streams. The use of biologically relevant stimuli in the study of auditory scene analysis has not been widely applied, but this approach was adopted by Wisniewski and Hulse (1997), who examined the European starling's perception of conspecific song and found evidence for stream segregation of biologically relevant acoustics in this bird species. Neurophysiological studies have also recently begun to examine the neural correlates of scene analysis in the primate auditory system (Fishman, Reser, Arezzo, & Steinschneider, 2001). Although the detection, discrimination, and localization of signals lay the building blocks for audition, it is clear that auditory systems across the phylogenetic scale must also organize this information for scene analysis to support species-specific acoustic behaviors that are central to social behaviors and predator evasion.

SUMMARY AND CONCLUSIONS

This chapter takes a comparative approach in its review of neurophysiological, anatomical, and behavioral studies of auditory systems. Selective pressures to encode the salient features of the auditory stream have produced a suite of convergent physiological and morphological features that contribute to auditory coding. All auditory systems, from those of insects to those of mammals, are organized along similar lines, with peripheral mechanisms responsive to acoustic vibrations that serve to activate neurons in the ascending auditory pathway. Most auditory systems also contain efferent systems that can modulate activity in the periphery and stations of the ascending pathway. It is also noteworthy that both invertebrate and vertebrate auditory systems appear to use comparable neural codes to carry information about sound source spectrum, amplitude, and location in space.

Behavioral studies of auditory systems reveal many common patterns across species. For example, hearing occurs over a restricted frequency range, often spanning several octaves. Absolute hearing sensitivity is highest over a limited frequency band, typically of biological importance to the animal, and this low-threshold region is commonly flanked by regions of reduced sensitivity at neighboring frequencies. Absolute frequency discrimination generally decreases with an increase in sound frequency, as does frequency selectivity. Some animals, however, show specializations in hearing sensitivity and frequency selectivity for biologically relevant sounds, with two regions of high sensitivity or frequency selectivity. Often, but not always, the specializations for sound processing can be traced to adaptations in the auditory periphery.

In sum, this chapter reviewed the basic organization of the auditory systems in a host of animal species. We detailed the anatomical and physiological features of the auditory system and described how these features support a broad range of acoustic behaviors. We presented data from auditory generalists and specialists to illustrate both common principles and species-specific adaptations for acoustic communication, sound source localization, predator evasion, and echolocation. The topic of this review is so broad that we also attempted to provide some direction for individuals who wish to read more in-depth coverage of research in comparative studies of audition.

REFERENCES

Altschuler, R. D., Hoffman, D., Bobbin, D., & Clopton, B. (Eds.). (1991). *Neurobiology of hearing: Vol. 3: The central auditory system.* New York: Raven Press.

Autrum, H. (1940). Über Lautäusserungen und Schallwahrnehmung bei Arthoropoden. II. Das Richtungshören von Locusta und Versuch einer Hörtheorie für Tympanalorgane vom Locustidentyp. *Zeitschrift fur Vergleichende Physiologie, 28,* 326–352.

Bailey, W. J., & Thomson, P. (1977). Acoustic orientation in the cricket *Teleogryllus oceanicus* (Le Guillou). *Journal of Experimental Biology, 67,* 61–75.

Batteau, D. W. (1967). The role of the pinna in human localization. *Proceedings of the Royal Society of London, 168B,* 158–180.

Beitel, R. E. (1991). Localization of azimuthal sound direction by the great horned owl. *Journal of the Acoustical Society of America, 90,* 2843–2846.

Békésy, G. von. (1960). *Experiments in hearing.* New York: McGraw-Hill.

Beranek, L. (1988). *Acoustical measurements.* New York: Acoustical Society of America Publication.

Berrebi, A. S., & Mugnaini, E. (1991). Distribution and targets of the cartwheel cell axon in the dorsal cochlear nucleus of the guinea pig. *Anatomy and Embryology, Berlin, 183*(5), 427–454.

Bottjer, S. W., & Johnson, F. (1997). Circuits, hormones, and learning: Vocal behavior in songbirds. *Journal of Neurobiology, 33,* 602–618.

Braaten, R. F., & Hulse, S. H. (1993). Perceptual organization of temporal patterns in European starlings (*Sturnus vulgaris*). *Perception and Psychophysics, 54,* 567–578.

Brainard, M. S., & Doupe, A. J. (2000). Auditory feedback in learning and maintenance of vocal behaviour. *Nature Reviews. Neuroscience, 1*(1), 31–40.

Bregman, A. S. (1990). *Auditory scene analysis: The perceptual organization of sound.* Cambridge, MA: MIT Press.

Brenowitz, E. A., Margoliash, D., & Nordeen, K. W. (1997). An introduction to birdsong and the avian song system. *Journal of Neurobiology, 33,* 495–500.

Brown, C. H., Schessler, T., Moody, D., & Stebbins, W. (1982). Vertical and horizontal sound localization in primates. *Journal of the Acoustical Society of America, 72,* 1804–1811.

Brugge, J. (1992). An overview of central auditory processing. In A. N. Popper & R. R. Fay (Eds.), *The mammalian auditory pathway: Neurophysiology* (pp. 1–33). New York: Springer-Verlag.

Burda, H., & Voldrich, L. (1980). Correlations between hair cell density and auditory threshold in the white rat. *Hearing Research, 3,* 91–93.

Capranica, R. R. (1976). Morphology and physiology of the auditory system. In R. Llinás & W. Precht (Eds.), *Frog neurobiology* (pp. 551–575). New York: Springer-Verlag.

Capranica, R. R., & Moffat, A. M. (1983). Neurobehavioral correlates of sound communication in anurans. In J. P. Ewert, R. R. Capranica, & D. J. Ingle (Eds.), *Advances in vertebrate neuroethology* (pp. 701–730). New York: Plenum Press.

Carr, C. E. (1992). Evolution of the central auditory system in reptiles and birds. In D. B. Webster, R. R. Fay, & A. N. Popper (Eds.), *The evolutionary biology of hearing* (pp. 511–543). New York: Springer-Verlag.

Carr, C. E., & Code, R. A. (2000). The central auditory system of reptiles and birds. In R. J. Dooling, R. R. Fay, & A. N. Popper (Eds.), *Comparative hearing: Birds and reptiles* (pp. 197–248). New York: Springer-Verlag.

Carr, C. E., & Konishi, M. (1990). A circuit for detection of interaural time differences in the brainstem of the barn owl. *Journal of Neuroscience, 10,* 3227–3246.

Casseday, J. H., & Covey, E. (1996). A neuroethological theory of the operation of the inferior colliculus. *Brain, Behavior, and Evolution, 147,* 311–336.

Casseday, J. H., & Neff, W. D. (1975). Auditory localization: Role of auditory pathways in brain stem of the cat. *Journal of Neurophysiology, 38,* 842–858.

Chapman, C. J., & Johnstone, A. D. F. (1974). Some auditory discrimination experiments on marine fish. *Journal of Experimental Biology, 61,* 521–528.

Chambers, R. E. (1971). Sound localization in the hedgehog (*Paraechinus hypomelas*). Unpublished doctoral dissertation, Florida State University, Tallahassee.

Clack, J. A. (1997). The evolution of tetrapod ears and the fossil record. *Brain, Behavior, and Evolution, 50,* 198–212.

Code, R. A. (1997). The avian cochlear efferent system. *Poultry and Avian Biology: Reviews, 8*(1), 1–8.

Conlee, J. W., & Parks, T. N. (1986). Origin of ascending auditory projections to the nucleus mesencephalicus lateralis pars dorsalis in the chicken. *Brain Research, 367,* 96–113.

Costalupes, J. A. (1983). Broadband masking noise and behavioral pure tone thresholds in cats. *Journal of the Acoustical Society of America, 74,* 758–764.

Crawford, A. C., & Fettiplace, R. (1980). The frequency selectivity of auditory nerve fibers and hair cells in the cochlea of the turtle. *Journal of Physiology, 306,* 79–125.

Crawford, J. D. (1997). Feature-detecting auditory neurons in the brain of a sound producing fish. *Journal of Comparative Physiology, 180,* 439–450.

Dallos, P. (1970). Low-frequency auditory characteristics: Species dependence. *Journal of the Acoustical Society of America, 48*(2), 489–499.

Dallos, P. (1973). *The auditory periphery: Biophysics and physiology.* New York: Academic Press.

Dallos, P. (1996). Overview: Cochlear neurobiology. In P. Dallos, A. N. Popper, & R. R. Fay (Eds.), *The cochlea* (pp. 1–43). New York: Springer-Verlag.

de Rebaupierre, F. (1997). Acoustical information processing in the auditory thalamus and cerebral cortex. In G. Ehret & R. Romand (Eds.), *The central auditory system* (pp. 317–398). New York: Oxford University Press.

Dijkgraaf, S. (1952). Uber die Schallwharnehmung bei Meeresfishen. *Zeitschrift fur Vergleichende Physiologie, 34,* 104–122.

Doherty, J. A., & Gerhardt, H. C. (1984). Evolutionary and neurobiological implications of selective phonotaxis in the spring peeper (*Hyla crucifer*). *Animal Behavior, 32,* 875–881.

Dooling, R. J. (1980). Behavior and psychophysics of hearing in birds. In A. N. Popper & R. R. Fay (Eds.), *Studies of hearing in vertebrates* (pp. 261–288). New York: Springer-Verlag.

Dooling, R. J., Lohr, B., & Dent, M. L. (2000). Hearing in birds and reptiles. In R. J. Dooling, R. R. Fay, & A. N. Popper (Eds.), *Comparative hearing: Birds and reptiles* (pp. 308–359). New York: Springer-Verlag.

Dooling, R. J., Mullingan, J. A., & Miller, J. D. (1971). Auditory sensitivity and song spectrum of the common canary (*Serinus canarius*). *Journal of the Acoustical Society of America, 50,* 700–709.

Dooling, R. J., Okanoya, K., Downing, J., & Hulse, S. (1986). Hearing in the starling (*Sturnus vulgaris*): Absolute thresholds and critical ratios. *Bulletin of the Psychonomic Society, 24,* 462–464.

Dooling, R. J., & Saunders, J. C. (1975). Hearing in the parakeet (*Melopsittacus undulatus*): Absolute thresholds, critical ratios, frequency difference limens and vocalizations. *Journal of Comparative and Physiological Psychology, 88,* 1–20.

Dooling, R. J., & Searcy, M. D. (1981). Amplitude modulation thresholds for the parakeet (*Melopsittacus undulatus*). *Journal of Comparative Physiology, 143,* 383–388.

Doucet, J. R., & Ryugo, D. K. (1997). Projections from the ventral cochlear nucleus to the dorsal cochlear nucleus in rats. *Journal of Comparative Neurology, 385,* 245–264.

Doupe, A. J., & Kuhl, P. K. (1999). Birdsong and human speech: Common themes and mechanisms. *Annual Review of Neuroscience, 22,* 567–631.

Echteler, S. M., Fay, R. R., & Popper, A. N. (1994). Structure of the mammalian cochlea. In R. R. Fay & A. N. Popper (Eds.), *Comparative hearing: Mammals* (pp. 134–171). New York: Springer-Verlag.

Egan, J. P., & Hake, H. W. (1950). On the masking pattern of a simple auditory stimulus. *Journal of the Acoustical Society of America, 22,* 622–630.

Ehret, G. (1975). Masked auditory thresholds, critical ratios, and scales of the basilar membrane of the housemouse (*Mus musculus*). *Journal of Comparative Physiology, 114,* 1–12.

Ehret, G. (1976). Critical bands and filter characteristics of the ear of the housemouse (*Mus musculus*). *Biological Cybernetics, 24,* 35–42.

Ehret, G., & Frankenreiter, M. (1977). Quantitative analysis of cochlear structures in the house mouse in relation to mechanics of acoustical information processing. *Journal of Comparative Physiology, 122,* 65–85.

Ehret, G., & Romand, R. (Eds.). (1997). *The central auditory system.* New York: Oxford University Press.

Elliott, D., Stein, L., & Harrison, M. (1960). Determination of absolute intensity thresholds and frequency difference thresholds in cats. *Journal of the Acoustical Society of America, 32,* 380–384.

Erwin, H., Wilson, W. W., & Moss, C. F. (2001). A computational model of sensorimotor integration in bat echolocation. *Journal of the Acoustical Society of America, 110,* 1176–1187.

Fay, R. R. (1969). Behavioral audiogram for the goldfish. *Journal of Auditory Research, 9,* 112–121.

Fay, R. R. (1970). Auditory frequency discrimination in the goldfish (*Carassius auratus*). *Journal of Comparative Physiology and Psychology, 73,* 175–180.

Fay, R. R. (1974). Masking of tones by noise for the goldfish (*Carassius auratus*). *Journal of Comparative Physiology and Psychology, 87,* 708–716.

Fay, R. R. (1978a). Coding of information in single auditory-nerve fibers of the goldfish. *Journal of the Acoustical Society of America, 63,* 136–146.

Fay, R. R. (1978b). Phase locking in goldfish saccular nerve fibers accounts for frequency discrimination capacities. *Nature, 275,* 320–322.

Fay, R. R. (1985). Sound intensity processing by the goldfish. *Journal of the Acoustical Society of America, 78,* 1296–1309.

Fay, R. R. (1988). *Hearing in vertebrates: A psychophysics databook.* Winnetka, IL: Hill-Fay Associates.

Fay, R. R. (1992). Structure and function in sound discrimination among vertebrates. In D. Webster, R. Fay, & A. Popper (Eds.), *The evolutionary biology of hearing* (pp. 229–263). New York: Springer-Verlag.

Fay, R. R. (1997). Frequency selectivity of saccular afferents of the goldfish revealed by revcor analysis. In G. R. Lewis, R. F. Lyons, P. M. Nairns, C. R. Steele, & E. Hecht-Poinar (Eds.), *Diversity in auditory mechanics* (pp. 69–75). Singapore: World Scientific.

Fay, R. R. (1998). Auditory stream segregation in goldfish (*Carassius auratus*). *Hearing Research, 120,* 69–76.

Fay, R. R. (2000). Spectral contrasts underlying auditory stream segregation in goldfish (*Carassius auratus*). *Journal of the Association for Research in Otolaryngology.*

Fay, R. R., & Edds-Walton, P. L. (2000). Directional encoding by fish auditory systems. *Philosophical Transactions of the Royal Society of London, 355B,* 1181–1284.

Fay, R. R., & Popper, A. N. (1983). Hearing in fishes: Comparative anatomy of the ear and the neural coding of auditory information. In R. R. Fay & G. Gourevitch (Eds.), *Hearing and other senses: Presentations in honor of E. G. Wever* (pp. 123–148). Groton, CT: Amphora Press.

Fay, R. R., & Simmons, A. M. (1999). The sense of hearing in fishes and amphibians. In R. R. Fay & A. N. Popper (Eds.), *Comparative hearing: Fishes and amphibians* (pp. 269–318). New York: Springer-Verlag.

Feng, A. S., Gerhardt, H. C., & Capranica, R. R. (1976). Sound localization behavior of the green treefrog (*Hyla cinerea*) and the barking treefrog (*H. gratiosa*). *Journal of Comparative Physiology, 107A,* 241–252.

Feng, A. S., & Schellart, N. A. M. (1999). Central auditory processing in fish and amphibians. In R. R. Fay & A. N. Popper (Eds.), *Comparative hearing: Fish and amphibians* (pp. 218–268). New York: Springer-Verlag.

Feng, A. S., & Shofner, W. P. (1981). Peripheral basis of sound localization in anurans. Acoustic properties of the frog's ear. *Hearing Research, 5,* 201–216.

Fettiplace, R., Ricci, A. J. & Hackney, C. M. (2001). Clues to the cochlear amplifier from the turtle ear. *Trends in Neuroscience, 24*(3), 169–175.

Fishman, Y. I., Reser, D. H., Arezzo, J. C., & Steinschneider, M. (2001). Neural correlates of auditory stream segregation in primary auditory cortex of the awake monkey. *Hearing Research, 151,* 167–187.

Fitzgibbons, P. F. (1983). Temporal gap detection in noise as a function of frequency, bandwidth, and level. *Journal of the Acoustical Society of America, 74,* 67–72.

Fletcher, H. (1940). Auditory patterns. *Review Modern Physiology, 12,* 47–65.

Fritzch, B., Barald, K. F., & Lomax, M. I. (1998). Early embryology of the vertebrate ear. In E. W. Rubel, A. N. Popper, & R. R. Fay (Eds.), *Development of the auditory system* (pp. 80–145). New York: Springer-Verlag.

Frost, B. J., Baldwin, P. J., & Csizy, M. L. (1989). Auditory localization in the northern saw-whet owl, *Aegolius acadicus. Canadian Journal of Zoology, 67*(8), 1955–1959.

Fuchs, P. A. (1992). Development of frequency tuning in the auditory periphery. *Current Opinions in Neurobiology, 2*(4), 457–461.

Fullard, J. H., & Barclay, R. M. R. (1980). Audition in spring species of arctiid moths as a possible response to differential levels of insectivorous bat predation. *Canadian Journal of Zoology, 58,* 1745–1750.

Fuzessery, Z. M., Buttenhoff, P., Andrews, B., & Kennedy, J. M. (1993). Passive sound localization of prey by the pallid bat (*Antrozous p. pallidus*). *Journal of Comparative Physiology, 171A,* 767–777.

Gatehouse, R. W., & Shelton, B. R. (1978). Sound localization in bobwhite quail (*Colinus virginianus*). *Behavioral Biology, 22,* 533–540.

Geisler, D. C., & Hubbard, A. M. (1975). The compatibility of various measurements on the ear as related by a simple model. *Acustica, 33,* 220–222.

Gerhardt, H. C. (1974). The significance of some spectral features in mating call recognition in the green treefrog. *Nature, 261,* 692–694.

Gerhardt, H. C. (1976). Significance of two frequency bands in long distance vocal communication in the green treefrog. *Nature, 261,* 692–694.

Gerhardt, H. C. (1981). Mating call recognition in the green treefrog (*Hyla cinerea*): Importance of two frequency bands as a function of sound pressure level. *Journal of Comparative Physiology, 144,* 9–16.

Gerhardt, H. C., & Rheinlaender, J. (1980). Accuracy or sound localization in a miniature dendrobatid frog. *Naturwissenschaften, 67,* 362–363.

Gleich, O., & Manley, G. A. (2000). The hearing organ of birds and crocodilia. In R. J. Dooling, R. R. Fay, & A. N. Popper (Eds.), *Comparative hearing: Birds and reptiles* (pp. 70–138). New York: Spring-Verlag.

Gourevitch, H. C. (1965). Auditory masking in the rat. *Journal of the Acoustical Society of America, 37,* 439–443.

Greenwood, D. D. (1961a). Auditory masking and the critical band. *Journal of the Acoustical Society of America, 33,* 484–502.

Greenwood, D. D. (1961b). Critical bandwidth and the frequency coordinates of the basilar membrane. *Journal of the Acoustical Society of America, 33,* 1344–1356.

Griffin, D. (1958). *Listening in the dark.* New Haven, CT: Yale University Press.

Guild, S. R., Crowe, S. J., Bunch, C. C., & Polvogt, L. L. (1931). Correlations of differences in the density of innervation of the organ of Corti with differences in the acuity of hearing, including evidence as to the location in the human cochlea of the receptors for certain tones. *Acta oto-laryngologica, 15,* 269–308.

Guinan, J. J., & Peake, W. T. (1967). Middle-ear characteristics of anesthetized cats. *Journal of the Acoustical Society of America, 41,* 1237–1261.

Hawkins, A. D., & Chapman, C. J. (1975). Masked auditory thresholds in the cod, *Gadus morhua L. Journal of Comparative Physiology, 103,* 209–226.

Hawkins A. D., & Johnstone, A. D. F. (1978). The hearing of the Atlantic salmon, *Salmo salar. Journal of Fish Biology, 13,* 655–673.

Hawkins, J., & Stevens, S. (1950). The masking of pure tones and of speech by white noise. *Journal of the Acoustical Society of America, 22,* 6–13.

Heffner, H. E., & Masterton, B. (1980). Hearing in Glires: Domestic rabbit, cotton rat, house mouse, and kangaroo rat. *Journal of the Acoustical Society of America, 68,* 1584–1599.

Heffner, R. S., & Heffner, H. E. (1982). Hearing in the elephant (*Elephas maximus*): Absolute sensitivity, frequency discrimination, and sound localization. *Journal of Comparative Psychology, 96,* 926–944.

Heffner, R. S., & Heffner, H. E. (1984). Sound localization in large mammals: Localization of complex sounds by horses. *Behavioral Neuroscience, 98,* 541–555.

Heffner, R. S., & Heffner, H. E. (1985). Hearing range of the domestic cat. *Hearing Research, 19,* 85–88.

Heffner, R. S., & Heffner, H. E. (1992). Evolution of sound localization in mammals. In D. B. Webster, R. R. Fay, & A. N. Popper (Eds.), *The evolutionary biology of hearing* (pp. 691–716). New York: Springer-Verlag.

Heffner, R. S., Heffner, H. E., & Koay, G. (1995). Sound localization in chinchillas: II. Front/back and vertical localization. *Hearing Research, 88,* 190–198.

Heffner, R. S., Heffner, H. E., & Koay, G. (1996). Sound localization in chinchillas: III. Effect of pinna removal. *Hearing Research, 99,* 13–21.

Heffner, R., Heffner, H., & Masterton, R. B. (1971). Behavioral measurement of absolute and frequency difference thresholds in guinea pig. *Journal of the Acoustical Society of America, 49,* 1888–1895.

Heffner, R. S., & Masterton, B. (1978). Contribution of auditory cortex to hearing in the monkey (*Macaca mulatta*). In D. J. Chivers & J. Herbert (Eds.), *Recent advances in primatology* (Vol. 1, pp. 735–754). New York: Academic Press.

Heinz, R. D., Sinnott, J. M., & Sachs, M. B. (1977). Auditory sensitivity of the red-winged blackbird (*Agelaius phoeniceus*) and brown-head cowbird (*Molothrus ater*). *Journal of Comparative Physiology and Psychology, 91,* 1365–1376.

Helfert, R., & Aschoff, A. (1997). Superior olivary complex and nuclei of the lateral lemniscus. In G. Ehret & R. Romand (Eds.), *The central auditory system* (pp. 193–258). New York: Oxford University Press.

Henderson, D., Salvi, R., Pavek, G., & Hamernik, R. P. (1984). Amplitude modulation thresholds in chinchillas with high-frequency hearing loss. *Journal of the Acoustical Society of America, 75,* 1177–1183.

Hillery, C. M., & Narins, P. M. (1984). Neurophysiological evidence for a traveling wave in the amphibian inner ear. *Science, 225,* 1037–1039.

Hoy, R. R., Popper, A. N., & Fay, R. R. (1998). *Comparative hearing: Insects.* New York: Springer.

Hudspeth, A. J., Choe, Y., Mehta, A. D., & Martin, P. (2000). Putting ion channels to work: Mechanoelectrical transduction, adaptation, and amplification by hair cells. *Proceedings of the National Academy of Sciences, USA, 97*(22), 11765–11772.

Hulse, S. H., MacDougall-Shackleton, S. A., & Wisniewski, A. B. (1997). Auditory scene analysis by songbirds: Stream segregation of birdsong by European starlings (*Sturnus vulgaris*). *Journal of Comparative Psychology, 111,* 3–13.

Imaizumi, K., & Pollack, G. S. (1999). Neural coding of sound frequency by cricket auditory receptors. *Journal of Neuroscience, 19,* 1508–1516.

Imig, T., & Morel, A. (1988). Organization of the cat's auditory thalamus. In G. M. Edelman, W. E. Gall, & W. M. Cowan (Eds.), *Auditory function: Neurobiological bases of hearing* (pp. 457–484). New York: Wiley.

Ison, J. R. (1982). Temporal acuity in auditory function in the rat: Reflex inhibition by brief gaps in noise. *Journal of Comparative and Physiological Psychology, 96,* 945–954.

Jeffress, L. A. (1970). Masking. In J. V. Tobias (Ed.), *Foundations of modern auditory theory* (Vol. 1, pp. 85–114). New York: Academic Press.

Jesteadt, W., Bacon, S., & Lehman, J. R. (1982). Forward masking as a function of frequency, masker level, and signal delay. *Journal of the Acoustical Society of America, 71,* 950–962.

Johnson, C. S. (1967). Sound detection thresholds in marine mammals. In W. N. Tavolga (Ed.), *Marine bio-acoustics* (Vol. 2, pp. 247–260). Oxford, UK: Pergamon.

Johnson, C. S. (1968). Masked tonal thresholds in the bottle-nosed porpoise. *Journal of the Acoustical Society of America, 44,* 965–967.

Jørgenson, M. B., & Gerhardt, H. C. (1991). Directional hearing in the gray tree frog *Hyla versicolor* eardrum vibrations and phonotaxis. *Journal of Comparative Physiology, 169A,* 177–183.

Joris, P. X., Smith, P. H., & Yin, T. C. (1998). Coincidence detection in the auditory system: 50 years after Jeffress. *Neuron, 21,* 1235–1238.

Karten, H. J., & Shimizu, T. (1989). The origins of neocortex: Connections and lamination as distinct events in evolution. *Journal of Cognitive Neuroscience, 1,* 291–301.

Klump, G. M. (2000). Sound localization in birds. In R. J. Dooling, R. R. Fay, & A. N. Popper (Eds.), *Comparative hearing: Birds and reptiles* (pp. 249–307). New York: Springer-Verlag.

Klump, G. M., & Maier, E. H. (1989). Gap detection in the starling (*Sturnus vulgaris*): I. Psychophysical thresholds. *Journal of Comparative Physiology, 164,* 531–538.

Klump, G. M., Windt, W., & Curio, E. (1986). The great tit's (*Parus major*) auditory resolution in azimuth. *Journal of Comparative Physiology, 158,* 383–390.

Knudsen, E. I. (1980). Sound localization in birds. In A. N. Popper & R. R. Fay (Eds.), *Comparative studies of hearing in vertebrates* (pp. 287–322). Berlin: Springer-Verlag.

Knudsen, E. I., du Lac, S., & Esterly, S. D. (1987). Computational maps in the brain. *Annual Review of Neuroscience, 10,* 41–65.

Knudsen, E. I., & Konishi, M. (1979). Mechanisms of sound localizations in the barn owl (*Tyto alba*). *Journal of Comparative Physiology, 133,* 13–21.

Koay, G., Kearns, D., Heffner, H. E., & Heffner, R. S. (1998). Passive sound-localization ability of the big brown bag (*Eptesicus fuscus*). *Hearing Research, 119,* 37–48.

Konishi, M. (1970). Comparative neurophysiological studies of hearing and vocalization in songbirds. *Journal of Comparative Physiology, 66,* 257–272.

Konishi, M. (1973). How the owl tracks its prey. *American Scientist, 61,* 414–424.

Konishi, M. (1985). Birdsong: From behavior to neuron. *Annual Review of Neuroscience, 8,* 125–170.

Konishi, M. (1986). Centrally synthesized maps of sensory space. *Trends in Neuroscience, 9,* 163–168.

Konishi, M. (2000). Study of sound localization by owls and its relevance to humans. *Comparative Biochemistry & Physiology, 126,* 459–469.

Köppl, C., Carr, C. E., & Soares, D. (2001). Diversity of response patterns in the cochlear nucleus angularis (NA) of the barn owl. *Association for Research Otolaryngology Abstract, 21,* 709.

Köppl, C., & Manley, G. A. (1992). Functional consequences of morphological trends in the evolution of lizard hearing organs. In D. B. Webster, R. R. Fay, & A. N. Popper (Eds.), *The evolutionary biology of hearing* (pp. 489–510). New York: Springer-Verlag.

Krubitzer, L., Kunzle, H., & Kaas, J. (1997). Organization of sensory cortex in a Madagascan insectivore, the tenrec (*Echinops telfairi*). *Journal of Comparative Neurology, 379,* 399–414.

Kühne, R., & Lewis, B. (1985). External and middle ears. In A. S. King & J. McLelland (Eds.), *Form and function in birds* (Vol. 3, pp. 227–271). London: Academic Press.

Kuwada, S., Batra, R., & Fitzpatrick, D. C. (1997). Neural processing of binaural temporal cues. In R. H. Gilkey & T. R. Andersen (Eds.), *Binaural and spatial hearing* (pp. 399–425). Hillsdale, NJ: Erlbaum.

Latimer, W., & Lewis, D. B. (1986). Song harmonic content as a parameter determining acoustic orientation behavior in the cricket *Teleogryllus oceanicus* (Le Guillou). *Journal of Comparative Physiology, 158A,* 583–591.

Lawrence, B. D., & Simmons, J. A. (1982). Echolocation in bats: The external ear and perception of the vertical positions of targets. *Science, 218,* 481–483.

Lewis, E. R., Baird, R. A., Leverenz, E. L., & Koyama, H. (1982). Inner ear: Dye injection reveals peripheral origins of specific sensitivities. *Science, 215,* 1641–1643.

Lewis, E. R., Leverenz, E. L., & Koyama, H. (1982). The tonatopic organization of the bullfrog amphibian papilla, an auditory organ lacking a basilar membrane. *Journal of Comparative Physiology, 145,* 437–445.

Lewis, E. R., & Narins, P. M. (1999). The acoustic periphery of amphibians: Anatomy and physiology. In R. R. Fay & A. N. Popper (Eds.), *Comparative hearing: Fish and amphibians* (pp. 101–154). New York: Springer-Verlag.

Liberman, M. C. (1982). The cochlear frequency map for the cat: Labeling auditory-nerve fibers of known characteristic frequency. *Journal of the Acoustical Society of America, 72,* 1441–1449.

Long, G. R. (1977). Masked auditory thresholds from the bat, *Rhinolophus ferrumequinum. Journal of Comparative Physiology, 100,* 211–220.

Long, G. R., & Schnitzler, H. U. (1975). Behavioral audiograms from the bat (*Rhinolophus ferrumequinum*). *Journal of Comparative Physiology, 100,* 211–219.

MacDougall-Shackleton, S. A., Hulse, S. H., Gentner, T. Q., & White, W. (1998). Auditory scene analysis by European starlings (*Sturnus vulgaris*): Perceptual segregation of tone sequences. *Journal of the Acoustical Society of America, 103,* 3581–3587.

Manley, G. A. (1972). A review of some current concepts of the functional evolution of the ear in terrestrial vertebrates. *Evolution, 26,* 608–621.

Manley, G. A. (2000). The hearing organs of lizards. In R. J. Dooling, R. R. Fay, & A. N. Popper (Eds.), *Comparative hearing: Birds and reptiles* (pp. 139–196). New York: Springer-Verlag.

Mann, D. A., Lu, Z., Hastings, M. C., & Popper, A. N. (1998). Detection of ultrasonic tones and simulated dolphin echolocation clicks by a teleost fish, the American Shad (*Alosa sapidissima*). *Journal of the Acoustical Society of America, 104*(1), 562–568.

Margoliash, D. (1997). Functional organization of forebrain pathways for song production and perception. *Journal of Neurobiology, 33,* 671–693.

Margoliash, D., & Konishi, M. (1985). Auditory representation of autogenous song in the song system of white crowned sparrows. *Proceedings of the National Academy of Sciences, USA, 82,* 5997–6000.

Martin, R. L., & Webster, W. R. (1987). The auditory spatial acuity of the domestic cat in the interaural horizontal and median vertical planes. *Hearing Research, 30,* 239–252.

Masters, W. M., Moffat, A. J. M., & Simmons, J. A. (1985). Sonar tracking of horizontally moving targets by the big brown bat *Eptesicus fuscus. Science, 228,* 1331.

Masterton, B., Heffner, H., & Ravizza, R. (1969). The evolution of human hearing. *Journal of the Acoustical Society of America, 45,* 966–985.

May, B. J. (2000). Role of the dorsal cochlear nucleus in the sound localization behavior of cats. *Hearing Research, 148,* 74–87.

McCormick, C. A. (1999). Anatomy of the central auditory pathways of fish and amphibians. In R. R. Fay & A. N. Popper (Eds.), *Comparative hearing: Fish and amphibians* (pp. 155–217). New York: Springer-Verlag.

Megela, A. L. (1984). Diversity of adaptation patterns in responses of eighth nerve fibers in the bullfrog, *Rana catesbeiana. Journal of the Acoustical Society of America, 75,* 1155–1162.

Megela-Simmons, A. (1988). Masking patterns in the bullfrog (*Rana catesbeiana*): I. Behavioral effects. *Journal of the Acoustical Society of America, 83,* 1087–1092.

Megela-Simmons, A., Moss, C. F., & Daniel, K. M. (1985). Behavioral audiograms of the bullfrog (*Rana catesbeiana*) and the green treefrog (*Hyla cinerea*). *Journal of the Acoustical Society of America, 78,* 1236–1244.

Michelsen, A. M. (1966). Pitch discrimination in the locust ear: Observations on single sense cells. *Journal of Insect Physiology, 12,* 1119–1131.

Michelsen, A. M. (1992). Hearing and sound communication in small animals: Evolutionary adaptations to the laws of physics. In D. B. Webster, R. R. Fay, & A. N. Popper (Eds.), *The evolutionary biology of hearing* (pp. 61–77). New York: Springer-Verlag.

Michelsen, A. M. (1998). Biophysics of sound localization in insects. In R. R. Hoy, A. N. Popper, & R. R. Fay (Eds.), *Comparative hearing: Insects* (pp. 18–62). New York: Springer-Verlag.

Michelsen, A. M., Jorgenson, M., Christensen-Dalsgaard, J., & Capranica, R. R. (1986). Directional hearing of awake, unrestrained treefrogs. *Naturwissenschaften, 73,* 682–683.

Miller, J. D. (1964). Auditory sensitivity of the chinchilla. *Journal of the Acoustical Society of America, 36,* 2010.

Miller, L. A. (1970). Structure of the green lacewing tympanal organ (*Chrysopa carnca,* Neuroptera). *Journal of Morphology, 181,* 359–382.

Miller, L. A. (1975). The behaviour of flying green lacewings, *Chrysopa carnea,* in the presence of ultrasound. *Journal of Insect Physiology, 21,* 205–219.

Miller, L. A. (1983). How insects detect and avoid bats. In F. Huber & H. Markl (Eds.), *Neuroethology and behavioral physiology* (pp. 251–266). Berlin: Springer.

Miller, L. A. (1984). Hearing in green lacewings and their responses to the cries of bats. In M. Canard, Y. Séméria, & T. R. New (Eds.), *Biology of chysopidae* (pp. 134–149). Boston: W. Junk.

Miller, M. R. (1980). The reptilian cochlear duct. In A. N. Popper & R. R. Fay (Eds.), *Comparative studies of hearing in vertebrates* (pp. 169–204). Berlin: Springer Verlag.

Mills, A. W. (1958). On the minimum audible angle. *Journal of the Acoustical Society of America, 30,* 237–246.

Moiseff, A. (1989). Bi-coordinate sound localization by the barn owl. *Journal of Comparative Physiology, 64A,* 637–644.

Moiseff, A., Pollack, G. S., & Hoy, R. R. (1978). Steering responses of flying crickets to sound and ultrasound: Mate attraction and predator avoidance. *Proceedings of the National Academy of Sciences, USA, 75*(8), 4052–4056.

Møller, A. R. (1983). *Auditory physiology.* New York: Academic Press.

Moore, B. C. J. (1978). Psychophysical tuning curves measured in simultaneous and forward masking. *Journal of the Acoustical Society of America, 63,* 524–532.

Moore, P. W. B. (1975). Underwater localization of pulsed pure tones by the California sea lion (*Zalophus californianus*). *Journal of the Acoustical Society of America, 58,* 721–727.

Moss, C. F., & Schnitzler, H.-U. (1995). Behavioral studies of auditory information processing. In A. N. Popper & R. R. Fay (Eds.), *Hearing by bats* (pp. 87–145). Berlin: Springer-Verlag.

Moss, C. F., & Simmons, A. M. (1986). Frequency selectivity of hearing in the green treefrog, *Hyla cinerea. Journal of Comparative Physiology, 159,* 257–266.

Narins, P. M., & Capranica, R. R. (1978). Communicative significance of the two-note call of the treefrog *Eleutherodactylus coqui. Journal of Comparative Physiology, 127A,* 1–9.

Nedzelnitsky, V. (1980). Sound pressures in the basal turn of the cochlea. *Journal of the Acoustical Society of America, 68,* 1676–1689.

Neuweiler, G., Bruns, V., & Schuller, G. (1980). Ears adapted for the detection of motion, or how echolocating bats have exploited the capacities of the mammalian auditory system. *Journal of the Acoustical Society of America, 68,* 741–753.

Nolen, T. G., & Hoy, R. R. (1987). Postsynaptic inhibition mediates high-frequency selectivity in the cricket *Teleogryllus oceanicus*: Implications for flight phonotaxis behavior. *Journal of Neuroscience, 7,* 2081–2096.

Nottebohm, F. (1980). Brain pathways for vocal learning in birds: A review of the first 10 years. *Progressive Pyschobiology Physiology Psychology, 9,* 85–124.

Oertel, D. (1999). The role of timing in the brainstem auditory nuclei. *Annual Review of Physiology, 61,* 497–519.

Oertel, D., Bal, R., Gardner, S. M., Smith, P. H., & Joris, P. X. (2000). Detection of synchrony in the activity of auditory nerve fibers by octopus cells of the mammaliancochlear nucleus. *Proceedings of the National Academy of Sciences, USA, 97*(22), 11773–11779.

Okanoya, K., & Dooling, R. J. (1987). Hearing in passerine and psittacine birds: A comparative study of absolute and masked auditory thresholds. *Journal of Comparative Psychology, 101,* 7–15.

Oldfield, B. P., Kleindienst, H. U., & Huber, F. (1986). Physiology and tonotopic organization of auditory receptors in the cricket *Gryllus bimaculatus* DeGeer. *Journal of Comparative Physiology, 159A,* 457–464.

Oliver, D., & Huerta, M. (1992). Inferior and superior colliculi. In D. B. Webster, A. N. Popper, & R. R. Fay (Eds.), *The mammalian auditory pathway: Neuroanatomy* (pp. 169–221). New York: Springer-Verlag.

Olsen, J. F., & Suga, N. (1991). Combination-sensitive neurons in the medial geniculate body of the mustached bat: Encoding of target range information. *Journal of Neurophysiology, 65,* 1275–1296.

Park, T. J., & Dooling, R. J. (1991). Sound localization in small birds: Absolute localization in azimuth. *Journal of Comparative Psychology, 105*(2), 25–133.

Parks, T. N. (2000). The AMPA receptors of auditory neurons. *Hearing Research, 147,* 77–91.

Passmore, N. I., Capranica, R. R., Telford, S. R., & Bishop, P. J. (1984). Phonotaxis in the painted reed frog (*Hyperolius marmoratus*). *Journal of Comparative Physiology, 154,* 189–197.

Payne, R. S. (1971). Acoustic location of prey by barn owls (*Tyto alba*). *Journal of Experimental Biology, 54,* 535–573.

Payne, R. S., Roeder, K. D., & Wallman, J. (1966). Directional sensitivity of the ears of noctuid moths. *Journal of Experimental Biology, 44,* 17–31.

Payne, K. B., Langbauer, W. R., Jr., & Thomas, E. M. (1986). Infrasonic calls of the Asian elephant (*Elephas maximus*). *Behavior Ecology and Sociobiology, 18,* 297–301.

Peña, J. L., Viete, S., Albeck, Y., & Konishi, M. (1996). Tolerance to sound intensity of binaural coincidence detection in the nucleus laminaris of the owl. *Journal of Neuroscience, 16,* 7046–7054.

Pickles, J. O. (1975). Normal critical bands in the cat. *Acta otolaryngology, 80,* 245–254.

Pickles, J. O., & Comis, S. D. (1976). Auditory-nerve fiber bandwidths and critical bandwidths in the cat. *Journal of the Acoustical Society of America, 60,* 1151–1156.

Pierce, A. D. (1989). *Acoustics: An introduction to its physical principles and applications.* New York: Acoustical Society of America.

Pollack, G. S. (1998). Neural processing of acoustic signals. In R. R. Hoy, A. N. Popper, & R. R. Fay (Eds.), *Comparative hearing: Insects* (pp. 139–196). New York: Springer-Verlag.

Popper, A. N. (1970). Auditory capacities of the Mexican blind cave fish (*Astyanax jordani*) and its eyed ancestor (*Astyanax mexicanus*). *Animal Behavior, 18,* 552–562.

Popper, A. N., & Fay, R. R. (1999). The auditory periphery in fishes. In R. R. Fay & A. N. Popper (Eds.), *Comparative hearing: Fishes and amphibians* (pp. 139–198). New York: Springer-Verlag.

Price, L. L., Dalton, L. W., Jr., & Smith, J. C. (1967). Frequency DL in the pigeon as determined by conditioned suppression. *Journal of Auditory Research, 7,* 229–239.

Proctor, L., & Konishi, M. (1997). Representation of sound localization cues in the auditory thalamus of the barn owl. *Proceedings of the National Academy of Sciences, USA, 94,* 10421–10425.

Puelles, L., Robles, C., Martinez-de-la-Torre, M., & Martinez, S. (1994). New subdivision schema for the avian torus semicircularis: Neurochemical maps in the chick. *Journal of Comparative Neurology, 340,* 98–125.

Quine, D. B., & Konishi, M. (1974). Absolute frequency discrimination in the barn owl. *Journal of Comparative and Physiological Psychology, 94,* 401–415.

Quine, D. B., & Kreithen, M. L. (1981). Frequency shift discrimination: Can homing pigeons locate infrasounds by doppler shifts? *Journal of Comparative Physiology, 141,* 153–155.

Ravicz, M. E., Rosowski, J. J., & Voigt, H. F. (1992). Sound power collection by the auditory periphery of the Mongolian gerbil *Meriones unguiculatus:* I. Middle ear input impedance. *Journal of the Acoustical Society of America, 92,* 157–177.

Ravizza, R. J., & Masterton, B. (1972). Contribution of neocortex to sound localization in opossum (*Didelphis virginiana*). *Journal of Neurophysiology, 35,* 344–356.

Renaud, D. L., & Popper, A. N. (1975). Sound localization by the bottlenose purpoise *Tursiops truncatus. Journal of Experimental Biology, 63,* 569–585.

Rheinlaender, J., Gerhardt, H. C., Yager, D. D., & Capranica, R. R. (1979). Accuracy of phonotaxis by the green treefrog (*Hyla cinerea*). *Journal of Comparative Physiology, 133,* 247–255.

Rhode, W. S., & Greenberg, S. (1992). Physiology of the cochlear nuclei. In A. N. Popper & R. R. Fay (Eds.), *The mammalian auditory pathway: Neurophysiology* (pp. 53–120). Heidelberg, Germany: Springer-Verlag.

Rice, W. R. (1982). Acoustical location of prey by the marsh hawk: Adaptation to concealed prey. *The Auk, 99*(3) 403–413.

Roberts, B. L., & Meredith, G. E. (1992). The efferent innervation of the ear: Variations on an enigma. In D. B. Webster, R. R. Fay, & A. N. Popper (Eds.), *The evolutionary biology of hearing* (pp. 185–210). New York: Springer-Verlag.

Roeder, K. D., & Treat, A. E. (1957). Ultrasonic reception by the lympanic organ of noctuid moths. *Journal of Experimental Zoology, 134,* 127–158.

Roeder, K. D., Treat, A. E., & Vandeberg, J. S. (1970). Auditory sensation in certain hawkmoths. *Science, 159,* 331–333.

Rosowski, J. J. (1994). Outer and middle ears. In R. R. Fay & A. N. Popper (Eds.), *Comparative hearing: Mammals* (pp. 172–247). New York: Springer-Verlag.

Rouiller, E. (1997). Functional organization of auditory pathways. In G. Ehret & R. Romand (Eds.), *The central auditory system* (pp. 3–96). New York: Oxford University Press.

Rubel, E. W., & Parks, T. N. (1988). Organization and development of the avian brainstem auditory system. In G. M. Edelman, W. E. Gall, & W. M. Cowan (Eds.), *Auditory function: Neurobiological bases of hearing* (pp. 3–92). New York: Wiley.

Ryan, A. (1976). Hearing sensitivity of the mongolian gerbil, *Meriones unguiculatus. Journal of the Acoustical Society of America, 59,* 1222–1226.

Ryan, M. J. (1983). Sexual selection and communication in a neotropical frog, *Physalaemus pustulosus. Evolution, 37,* 261–272.

Ryugo, D. K. (1993). The auditory nerve: Peripheral innervation, cell body morphology and central projections. In D. B. Webster, A. N. Popper, & R. R. Fay (Eds.), *The mammalian auditory pathway: Neuroanatomy* (pp. 23–65). New York: Springer-Verlag.

Sachs, M. B., & Abbas, P. J. (1974). Rate versus level functions for auditory-nerve fibers in cats: Tone-burst stimuli. *Journal of the Acoustical Society of America, 56,* 1835–1847.

Salvi, R. J., & Arehole, S. (1985). Gap detection in chinchillas with temporary high-frequency hearing loss. *Journal of the Acoustical Society of America, 77,* 1173–1177.

Salvi, R. J., Giraudi, D. M., Henderson, D., & Hamernik, R. P. (1982). Detection of sinusoidal amplitude modulated noise by the chinchilla. *Journal of the Acoustical Society of America, 71,* 424–429.

Saunders, J. C., Denny, R. M., & Bock, G. R. (1978). Critical bands in the parakeet (*Melopsittacus undulatus*). *Journal of Comparative Physiology, 125,* 359–365.

Scharf, B. (1970). Critical bans. In J. V. Tobias (Ed.), *Foundations of modern auditory theory* (pp. 159–202). New York: Academic Press.

Scheich, H., Langer, G., & Bonke, D. (1979). Responsiveness of units in the auditory neostriatum of the guinea fowl (*Numida meleagris*) to species specific calls and synthetic stimuli: II. discrimination of iambus-like calls. *Journal of Comparative Physiology, 32,* 257–276.

Schuijf, A. (1975). Directional hearing of cod (*Gadus morhua*) under approximate free field conditions. *Journal of Comparative Physiology, 98,* 307–332.

Schwartz, J. J., & Wells, K. D. (1984). Interspecific acoustic interactions of the neotropical treefrog, *Hyla ebraccata. Behavior Ecology Sociobiology, 14,* 211–224.

Simmons, J. A., Kick, S. A., Lawrence, B. D., Hale, C., Bard, C., & Escudie, B. (1983). Acuity of horizontal angle discrimination by the echolocating bat, *Eptesicus fuscus. Journal of Comparative Physiology, 153A,* 321–330.

Sivian, L. J., & White, S. J. (1933). On minimum audible sound fields. *Journal of the Acoustical Society of America, 4,* 288–321.

Small, A. M., Jr. (1959). Pure-tone masking. *Journal of the Acoustical Society of America, 31,* 1619–1625.

Spangler, H. G. (1988). Hearing in tiger beetles (*Cicindelidae*). *Physiogical Entomology, 13,* 447–452.

Steinberg, J. C. (1937). Positions of stimulation in the cochlea by pure tones. *Journal of the Acoustical Society of America, 8,* 176–180.

Suga, N. (1988). Auditory neuroethology and speech processing: complex sound processing by combination sensitive neurons. In G. M. Edelman, W. E. Gall, & W. M. Cowan (Eds.), *Auditory function: Neurobiological bases of hearing* (pp. 679–720). New York: Wiley.

Suga, N., Gao, E., Zhang, Y., Ma, X., & Olsen, J. F. (2000). The corticofugal system for hearing: Recent progress. *Proceedings of the National Academy of Sciences, USA, 97,* 11807–11814.

Sullivan, W. E., & Konishi, M. (1984). Segregation of stimulus phase and intensity coding in the cochlear nucleus of the barn owl. *Journal of Neuroscience, 4,* 1787–1799.

Takahashi, T. T. (1989). The neural coding of auditory space. *Journal of Experimental Biology, 146,* 307–322.

Terhune, J. M. (1974). Directional hearing of a harbor seal in air and water. *Journal of the Acoustical Society of America, 56,* 1862–1865.

Thompson, R. K., & Herman, L. M. (1975). Underwater frequency discrimination in the bottlenose dolphin (1–140 kHz) and the human (1–8 kHz). *Journal of the Acoustical Society of America, 57,* 943–948.

Trussell, L. O. (1997). Cellular mechanisms for preservation of timing in central auditory pathways. *Current Opinion in Neurobiology, 7,* 487–492.

Trussell, L. O. (1999). Synaptic mechanisms for coding timing in auditory neurons. *Annual Review of Neuroscience, 61,* 477–496.

Viemeister, N. F. (1979). Temporal modulation transfer functions based upon modulation thresholds. *Journal of the Acoustical Society of America, 66,* 1364–1380.

Vogten, L. L. M. (1974). Pure-tone masking: A new result from a new method. In E. Zwicker & E. Terhardt (Eds.), *Psychophysical models and physiological facts in hearing* (pp. 142–155). Tutzing, Germany: Springer-Verlag.

Vogten, L. L. M. (1978). Simultaneous pure tone masking: The dependence of masking asymmetries on intensity. *Journal of the Acoustical Society of America, 63,* 1509–1519.

Wagner, H., Takahashi, T., & Konishi, M. (1987). Representation of interaural time difference in the central nucleus of the barn owl's inferior colliculus. *Journal of Neuroscience, 7,* 3105–3116.

Warchol, M. E., & Dallos, P. (1990). Neural coding in the chick cochlear nucleus. *Journal of Comparative Physiology, 166,* 721–734.

Warr, W. B. (1992). Organization of olivocochlear efferent systems in mammals. In D. B. Webster, A. N. Popper, & R. R. Fay (Eds.), *The mammalian auditory pathway: Neuroanatomy* (pp. 410–448). New York: Springer-Verlag.

Watson, C. (1963). Masking of tones by noise for the cat. *Journal of the Acoustical Society of America, 35,* 167–172.

Webster, D. B., Popper, A. N., & Fay, R. R. (Eds.). (1993). *The mammalian auditory pathway: Neuroanatomy.* New York: Springer-Verlag.

Wegel, R. L., & Lane, C. E. (1924). The auditory masking of one pure tone by another and its probable relation to the dynamics of the inner ear. *Physical Review, 23,* 266–285.

Weir, C., Jesteadt, W., & Green, D. (1976). Frequency discrimination as a function of frequency and sensation level. *Journal of the Acoustical Society of America, 61,* 178–184.

Wettschurek, R. G. (1973). Die absoluten Unterschiedswellen der Richtungswahrnehmung in der Medianebene beim natürlichen Hören, sowie heim Hören über ein Kunstkopt-Übertragungssystem. *Acoustica, 28,* 97–208.

Wever, E. G. (1949). *Theory of hearing.* New York: Wiley.

Wever, E. G. (1978). *The reptile ear.* Princeton, NJ: Princeton University Press.

Wilczynski, W. (1984). Central neural systems subserving a homoplasous periphery. *American Zoology, 24,* 755–763.

Wilczynski, W., Allison, J. D., & Marlev, C. A. (1993). Sensory pathways linking social and environmental cues to endocrine control regions of amphibian forebrains. *Brain, Behavior, and Evolution, 42,* 252–264.

Wild, J. M., Karten, H. J., & Frost, B. J. (1993). Connections of the auditory forebrain in the pigeon (*Columba livia*). *Journal of Comparative Neurology, 337,* 32–62.

Wiley, R. H., & Richards, D. G. (1978). Physical constraints on acoustic communication in the atmosphere: Implications for the evolution of animal vocalizations. *Behavioral Ecology and Sociobiology, 3,* 69–94.

Winer, J. A. (1991). The functional architecture of the medial geniculate body and the primary auditory cortex. In D. B. Webster, A. N. Popper, & R. R. Fay (Eds.), *The mammalian auditory pathway: Neuroanatomy* (pp. 222–409). New York: Springer-Verlag.

Wisniewski, A. B., & Hulse, S. H. (1997). Auditory scene analysis in European starlings (*Sturnus vulgaris*): Discrimination of song segments, their segregation from multiple and reversed conspecific songs, and evidence for conspecific categorization. *Journal of Comparative Psychology, 111,* 337–350.

Yack, J. E., & Fullard, J. H. (1999). Ultrasonic hearing in nocturnal butterflies. *Nature, 403,* 265–266.

Yager, D. D. (1999). Hearing. In F. R. Prete, H. Wells, P. H. Wells, & L. E. Hurd (Eds.), *The praying mantids* (pp. 93–113). Baltimore: Johns Hopkins University Press.

Yager, D. D., & Hoy, R. R. (1986). The cyclopean ear: A new sense for the Praying Mantis. *Science, 231,* 647–772.

Yager, D. D., Cook, A. P., Pearson, D. L., & Spangler, H. G. (2000). A comparative study of ultrasound-triggered behaviour in tiger beetles (*Cicindelidae*). *Journal of Zoology, London, 251,* 355–368.

Yager, D. D., & Hoy, R. R. (1989). Audition in the praying mantis, *Mantis religiosa L.*: Identification of an interneuron mediating ultrasonic hearing. *Journal of Comparative Physiology, 165,* 471–493.

Yager, D. D., & Spangler, H. G. (1995). Characterization of auditory afferents in the tiger beetle, *Cicindela marutha* Dow. *Journal of Comparative Physiology, 176A,* 587–600.

Yost, W. A., & Gourevitch, G. (Eds.). (1987). *Directional hearing.* New York: Springer-Verlag.

Yost, W. A., & Hafter, E. R. (1987). Lateralization. In W. A. Yost & G. Gourevitch (Eds.), *Directional hearing* (pp. 49–84). New York: Springer-Verlag.

Young, E. D. (1998). The cochlear nucleus. In G. M. Shepherd (Ed.), *Synaptic organization of the brain* (pp. 131–157). New York: Oxford University Press.

Zelick, R., Mann, D., & Popper, A. N. (1999). Acoustic communication in fishes and frogs. In R. R. Fay & A. N. Popper (Eds.), *Comparative hearing: Fish and amphibians* (pp. 363–411). New York: Springer-Verlag.

Zwicker, E., Flottorp, G., & Stevens, S. (1957). Critical bandwidths in loudness summation. *Journal of the Acoustical Society of America, 29,* 548–557.

Zwicker, E., & Henning, G. B. (1984). Binaural masking level differences with tones masked by noises of various bandwidths and levels. *Hearing Research, 14,* 179–183.

CHAPTER 5

Comparative Psychology of Motor Systems

KARIM FOUAD, HANNO FISCHER, AND ANSGAR BÜSCHGES

LOCOMOTOR NETWORKS: INTRODUCTION AND HISTORY

In the animal kingdom, various kinds of locomotion—such as swimming, walking, flight, and crawling—have evolved. Understanding locomotor function is of vital scientific interest, because locomotion serves as multipurpose behavior in various more complex behavioral programs and issues. Understanding the neuronal mechanisms underlying locomotion has long attracted scientists as a case study well suited to understanding nervous system function in general and for medical use and robotics.

To understand locomotor systems requires a multilevel approach ranging from the cellular level (i.e., identifying the neurons involved, their intrinsic properties, the properties of their synaptic connections, and the role of particular

transmitters and neuromodulators) to the system level (i.e., determining the functional integration of these networks in complete motor programs). Our current understanding of locomotor networks is the outcome of investigating and comparing various invertebrate and vertebrate locomotor systems in which rhythmic behaviors can be studied on multiple levels, ranging from the interactions between identifiable neurons in identified circuits to the analysis of gait. This review will focus on (a) the principles of cellular and synaptic construction of central pattern-generating networks for locomotion, (b) their location and coordination, (c) the role of sensory signals in generating a functional network output, (d) the main mechanisms underlying their ability to adapt through modifications, and (e) basic features in modulating the network function.

Due to the limited space available for this introduction to this lively and fast-developing field in neurosciences, the authors will restrict citations mostly to recent, in-depth reviews on individual aspects mentioned and will refer to original articles only as specifically needed.

We would like to thank M. Cohen from the Institute for Advanced Study in Berlin for carefully editing the manuscript.

Understanding the Act of Progression: Historical Aspects

The problem of how locomotion is generated has been considered for more than 2,400 years, starting in the time of Aristotle (about 400 B.C.). Between the second and third centuries A.D., the Aristotelian concept of a *vital pneuma* (transformed from the omnipresent *ether* by the lungs and transported by the bloodstream to the muscles) as the ultimate cause underlying locomotor ability was first modified by Galen, who discovered that nerves originating in the brain and spinal cord innervate the muscles. In the seventeenth century, Descartes and Borelli integrated Galen's discoveries in a more mechanically based theory, suggesting that muscles contract by a corpuscular *animal spirit* released from the nervous system. In the mid-nineteenth century (and based on the work in the eighteenth century by Schwammerdam, Galvani, and others), Matteucci, Helmholtz, and du Bios-Reymond discovered the electrical properties of axons and their implication for neuromuscular transmission (the modern term *synapse* was adopted much later by Sherrington in 1897). Benefiting from the general progress in detailed anatomical knowledge and with a new basic concept (Cajal's neuron doctrine), late nineteenth-century physiology initiated a common understanding of the nervous system's function and its role in the generation and control of behavior (for an in-depth review of the early history, see Bennett, 1999).

The Neural Basis of Locomotor Pattern Generation: A First Concept

At the end of the nineteenth century, the discovery of proprioceptive pathways in the nervous system (e.g., by Bell, Golgi, and Kühne in the mid- nineteenth century; early review: Sherrington, 1900), the description of numerous different reflex responses in the limbs of monkeys, dogs, and cats after skin or nerve stimulation (establishing what are called *reflex laws;* Pflüger, 1853) and the apparent resemblance of these reflex responses, including *scratch reflexes* and *spinal stepping,* to parts of the limb-movement cycle during real locomotion led to the idea that the antagonistic activation of effector organs during locomotion might be triggered by feedback from sense organs in the skin and the moving parts of the body. Coordinated limb movement during locomotion was thought to be the result of a chain arrangement of these *reflex arcs.* Remarkably, this concept already included the principle of a reciprocal innervation of antagonistic muscles (Sherrington, 1905a, 1905b) and the demonstration of postural reflexes (Sherrington, 1900a).

Toward a Concept of Central Control of Locomotion

In the early twentieth century, the putative role of the spinal cord in the basic generation of locomotion was established by experiments in mammals, mainly in the dog and the cat, that could still produce alternating leg movements after the brain was disconnected (Brown, 1911, 1912; Sherrington, 1905a, 1905b). In cats, Brown (1911) demonstrated that the spinal cord was capable of producing locomotor patterns after complete deafferentation of the moving limb. He concluded that alternating rhythmic movements derive from a central spinal process and proposed a simple *half-center model* as the basis of the alternating activity of flexors and extensors during walking: Each half-center is responsible for activating either flexors or extensors, and both half-centers are connected by reciprocal inhibition in order to silence one center while the other is active. Much later, when reciprocal inhibition was first shown on the interneuron level in the spinal cord (Jankowska, Jukes, Lund, & Lundberg, 1967a, 1967b), the suggested spinal network organization incorporated the basic features of Brown's half-center model.

The Concept of a Central Pattern Generator (CPG)

The combined evidence from the first half of the twentieth century suggested that the central nervous system does not necessarily require sensory feedback to generate rhythmic movement resembling repetitive behaviors such as locomotion. This conclusion emerged from experiments in a variety of invertebrate and vertebrate species, in which the ability to generate a patterned rhythmic activity was not abolished by (a) paralysis using neuromuscular blockers to prevent proprioceptive input evoked by movements, (b) deafferentation, or (c) the complete physical isolation of the nervous system from all sources of possible feedback (for a review, see Grillner, 1985; see also Delcomyn, 1980). The ensemble of neuronal elements necessary and sufficient for the production of locomotor patterns was defined as a *central pattern generator (CPG;* Grillner & Zangger, 1975; Wilson, 1961). However, since the motor patterns observed after deafferentation are often imprecise and sometimes even lack important elements of motor output as compared to intact conditions (e.g., Grillner & Zangger, 1979; Pearson, 1985; Sillar, Clarac, & Bush, 1987), the validity of such a concept for *completely* central locomotor pattern generation was questioned (e.g., Bässler, 1987, 1988; Pearson, 1985). At present it is clear that, in the majority of locomotor systems, sensory feedback and CPG networks interact to generate the functional locomotor program, whereby sense organs form integral elements of the pattern-generating mechanisms (e.g., see the review in Büschges & El Manira, 1998; Pearson, 1995; Prochazka & Mushahwar, 2001) with only few exceptions (e.g., Arshavsky, Orlovsky, Panchin, Roberts, & Soffe, 1993).

ORGANIZATION OF NEURAL NETWORKS FOR LOCOMOTION

Most locomotor patterns have in common that they are based on rhythmic movements (i.e., cyclic motor patterns). Each cycle can be generally divided into two phases, a *power stroke* and a *return stroke*. During the *power stroke,* locomotor organs exert force against the surrounding medium and move the organism relative to its environment; during the *return stroke,* the locomotor organs are moved back to their starting position for the next power stroke. In walking, for example, the power stroke of the locomotor cycle is the stance phase, when the limb is on the ground and generates force to propel the body relative to the ground, either forward or backward. The return stroke of the leg is the swing phase, during which the leg is moved back to its starting position. In

general, antagonistic muscles of leg joints exhibit phases of alternating activity during the generation of stepping movements. In vertebrates like fish or agnaths, swimming is generated by a rostral-caudally or caudal-rostrally directed undulating contraction wave, depending on the direction of swimming. This contraction wave wanders along the trunk musculature. In every cycle, the myotomal musculature of both sides of each segment contracts in an alternating fashion.

In the next section we will review the main features of current knowledge of the construction of neural networks and the mechanisms underlying the generation of locomotor patterns in vertebrates and in invertebrates.

When considering the generation of locomotor programs, several different aspects and levels of nervous control are important (Figure 5.1). For a very detailed review of this, see Orlovsky, Deliagina, and Grillner (1999), where the following summary of present knowledge was presented. The highest level of control is represented in the *decision to locomote*. Activation of this system is mediated by external or internal cues, such as sensory stimuli or motivation. The decision to locomote activates two different systems of descending control. One system has command-like features and controls the

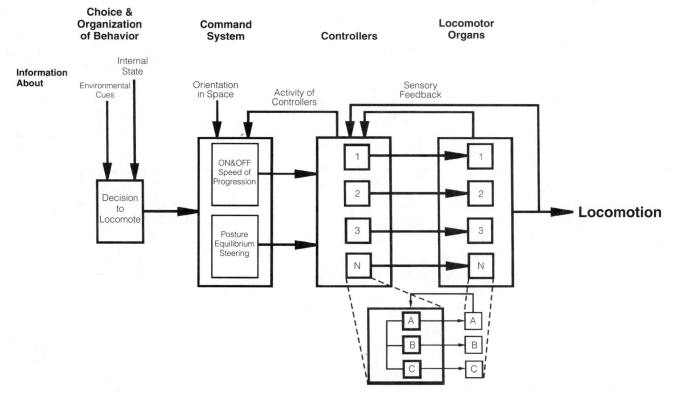

Figure 5.1   Schematic summary of the components and functional organization of a generalized system for generation and control of locomotion (see text for details and explanation) adapted from Orlovsky et al. (1999). Note that for multijointed locomotor organs, the controllers of the individual locomotor organs may be composed of several separate but interacting modules responsible for motor pattern generation at the different joints (see inset to the bottom right).

starting and stopping of the locomotor program as well as the intensity (e.g., speed) of locomotion. In vertebrates, the reticulospinal pathways, receiving signals from the mesencephalic locomotor region and the subthalamic locomotor region and sending their axons into the spinal cord, are elements of this system (e.g., Armstrong, 1988; Jordan, Brownstone, & Noga, 1992; Mori, Matsuyama, Kohyama, Kobayashi, & Takakusaki, 1992; Orlovsky et al., 1999).

In invertebrates, groups of interneurons or individual descending interneurons have been identified that serve command-like functions in the initiation and maintenance of motor programs (e.g., Bowerman & Larimer, 1974a, 1974b; Brodfuehrer & Friesen, 1986a, 1986b, 1986c; Gamkrelidze, Laurienti, & Blankenship, 1995; Kupfermann & Weiss, 1978). The second system is in charge of generating and controlling the animal's posture and equilibrium during locomotion, as well as its direction of locomotion. In vertebrates, the cerebellum, brainstem, and spinal cord serve this system; in invertebrates, this system is distributed among various ganglia. The information from these two systems is fed into the neuronal networks of the locomotor system itself, the *controllers,* located downstream close to the *locomotor organs* in spinal segments (vertebrates) or ganglia (invertebrates). The construction and action of these controllers will be our main focus in the following chapters. The *controllers* (Figure 5.1) encompass the neuronal networks, including the CPGs that generate activity of the *locomotor organs* by driving specific sets of motoneurons. These motoneurons form the neuronal output stage and innervate the muscles moving the *locomotor organs.* Rhythmic motoneuron activity is generated by alternating excitatory and inhibitory synaptic impulses from the premotor neural networks, the *controllers,* to the motoneurons. The generation of functional locomotor programs often relies on *feedback* about the executed action from each level to the next higher level. Information about the activity of the *controllers* is fed back to the command level. Sensory information reporting the actual movement generated by the locomotor organs is fed back to the *controllers.* Therefore, in many locomotor systems, *sense organs* have to be considered important elements enabling the systems to generate functional locomotor programs (see also Orlovsky et al., 1999). Finally, locomotor systems consisting of a multitude of locomotor organs need to generate coordinating mechanisms to adjust and time the sequence of movements among the individual locomotor organs (e.g., Cruse, 1990).

Marked differences appear to exist in the degree of coupling between the actions of individual controllers for locomotor systems, on the one hand, and a multitude of locomotor organs, on the other. For example, evidence suggests that the wing-control system in the locust flight system acts in general as one integrated common pattern generator for driving all four wings (Robertson & Pearson, 1983; Waldron, 1967). However, more recent evidence gathered from various vertebrate and invertebrate organisms suggests that each locomotor organ may indeed have its own controller—that is, each segment of a lamprey for swimming (Grillner et al., 1995), each leg of a vertebrate or invertebrate (Bässler & Büschges, 1998; Orlovsky et al., 1999) and each leg of a human (Gurfinkel, Levik, Kazennikov, & Selionov, 1998) for walking, and each wing of an insect for flying (Ronacher, Wolf, & Reichert, 1988). The construction of such controllers has been well studied for the generation of the swimming motor pattern in mollusks and lower vertebrates (Arshavsky et al., 1993; Grillner et al., 1995) and annelids (Brodfuehrer, Debski, O'Hara, & Friesen, 1995) and for walking pattern generation in crustaceans (Cattaert & LeRay, 2001), insects (Bässler & Büschges, 1998), anurans (Cheng et al., 1998), and mammals (Orlovsky et al., 1999). In humans, less evidence is presently available on the construction principles of the limb controllers themselves, but present data suggest that the main features in the organization of the walking control system of humans has similarities to those of both cats and arthropods (for a recent summary and comparison, see Orlovsky et al., 1999).

The complexity of the controllers' construction depends on (a) the complexity of the locomotor organs and (b) the requirements of the locomotor behavior to be generated out. Thus, the complexity of the controllers increases with the segmentation of the locomotor organs, from unitary wings to multisegmented legs. For example, in *Clione,* a mollusk, the swimming motor activity is generated by elevation and depression of wing-like appendages (Arshavsky et al., 1998). In invertebrates and vertebrates, however, walking is generated by the movements of multijointed limbs, which requires the coordination of the activities of several individual leg joints (Bässler, 1983; Grillner, 1979; Orlovsky et al., 1999). Controllers that need minimal sensory feedback, such as the one controlling locomotion in *Clione,* are constructed more simply than are controllers governing locomotor programs that depend on sensory feedback, such as walking systems. Pattern generation in the latter locomotor systems relies heavily on sensory signals about movements of the joints and the limbs, signals about forces or strain exerted on each segment of the limb, and coordinating signals between adjacent limbs (e.g., Bässler & Büschges, 1998; Pearson, 1995; Prochazka, 1996a). This also applies to the walking system of humans (Dietz, 1992; Gurfinkel et al., 1998; Sinkjaer, Andersen, Ladouceur, Christensen, & Nielsen, 2000).

Construction Principles of Pattern-Generating Networks for Locomotion

Central neuronal networks have been identified that are capable of generating ongoing rhythmic activity in motoneurons that contribute to the cyclic locomotor output generated for swimming, walking, and flying in vertebrates and invertebrates (described previously). These networks can also be activated in very reduced preparations either by the application of drugs, by sensory stimulation, or by stimulation of higher order centers in the central nervous system (for a comparative review, see Orlovsky et al., 1999). Using these approaches, more or less complete patterns of a locomotor program can be generated, allowing their detailed investigation. Neuronal networks have been analyzed on several levels: first, the *operational level,* focusing within the systems level on mechanisms for the generation of functional motor programs (e.g., Bässler & Büschges, 1998; Grillner, 1979); second, the level of the *neuronal networks* themselves, analyzed by investigating the topologies of the neural network and the synaptic interactions among its elements (e.g., Arshavsky et al., 1993; Bässler & Büschges, 1998; Grillner et al., 1995; Kiehn, Housgaard, & Sillar, 1997; Roberts, 2000); and third, a subject that has drawn a lot of attention lately: the *cellular and subcellular levels* and the cellular properties of individual neurons or neuron classes within the networks and their role in generating rhythmic locomotor activity (e.g., Dale, 1997; Grillner, Wallen, Hill, Cangiano, & El Manira, 2001). Finally, in the past two decades, simulation studies using artificial neural networks or computer models have increasingly helped to investigate the necessity and sufficiency of neuronal mechanisms and the construction of the neuronal networks underlying the generation of locomotor patterns as presently understood (e.g., reviews in Cruse et al., 1995; Grillner et al., 1995).

Despite differences among phyla, species, and locomotor tasks, it has become clear by now that there are some specific common outlines of networks generating rhythmic locomotor activity. Two prominent basic neural network topologies have been identified: *mutual inhibition* and *forward excitation–reciprocal inhibition.*

Mutual Inhibition

This construction principle found in various locomotor systems is based on mutual inhibition between neurons or groups of neurons within the neuronal networks (Figure 5.2, panel A). Each group of neurons is in charge of generating one phase of the locomotor activity. Through this mechanism, only one group of neurons is active at any given time once the activity

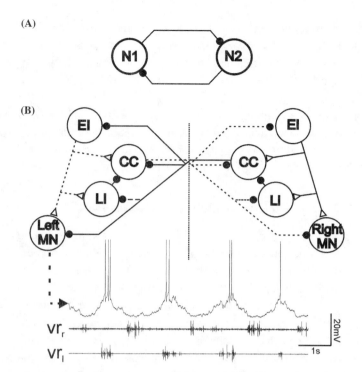

Figure 5.2   A. Reciprocal inhibition as building block for pattern generation in neural networks for locomotion. Filled circles = inhibitory synapse. Note that some tonic background excitation is needed to induce oscillatory activity of this network. **B.** Wiring diagram of the CPG for swimming in the lamprey spinal cord, based on data from Grillner and coworkers (see Grillner et al., 1995). Each circle denotes an identified class of interneurons in the spinal cord. EI, excitatory interneuron; LI, lateral inhibitory interneuron; CC, contralateral crossing inhibitory interneuron. *Open triangles:* excitatory synapse; *filled circle,* inhibitory synapse; MN, myotomal motoneuron. Connections from neurons of the right half of the segment are drawn with solid lines, connections from neurons of the right half of the segment are drawn with broken lines. The vertical stippled line denotes the midline of the spinal cord. The motor output of the pattern generator for swimming is exemplified at the bottom by an intracellular recording from a left myotomal motoneuron together with extracellular recordings from both ventral roots of the segment, in which the motoneuron is located. Note the strictly alternating activity between both sides of the segment. Activity was initiated and maintained by super fusion of the cord with the glutamate agonist NMDA (150 μM).

of the network has been started. Transition between the activity of the two neurons or groups of neurons emerges through mechanisms that either generate fatigue in the activity of the currently active group of neurons or enable the silent, inactive group of neurons to escape inhibition. Such topology is called *half-center construction,* and, long before experimental verification was possible, Brown (1911) conceived it for the generation of alternating activity during stepping in the cat. Mutual inhibition has been identified as a building block underlying the generation of alternating motor activity in the neuronal networks for swimming in vertebrates (lampreys [Buchanan, 1982; Grillner, 1985] and tadpoles [Roberts, Dale, Evoy, & Soffe, 1985; Soffe, Clarke, & Roberts, 1984]) and for swimming and other locomotor behaviors, such as crawling, in invertebrates (mollusks [Arshavsky, Beloozerova, Orlovsky, Panchin, & Pavlova, 1985a, 1985b, 1985c, 1985d; Getting, 1981; Getting, Lennard, & Hume, 1980; Katz, Getting, & Forst, 1994] and annelids [Friesen & Hocker, 2001; Friesen, Poon, & Stent, 1978; Stent et al., 1978]). For example, in the lamprey, swimming-network alternating activity of both sides of each segment is based on mutual inhibition between groups of crossed inhibitory neurons on each side of the spinal cord (Figure 5.2, panel B; Buchanan, 1982; Grillner, 1985).

Forward Excitation and Reciprocal Inhibition

Another identified network interaction is forward excitation from one neuron to another neuron via a delay and reciprocal inhibition from the second neuron to the first neuron (Figure 5.3, panel A). In the CPG network for locust flight, this element has been found to underlie alternating activation of wing elevator and depressor motoneurons, representing some kind of switch-off mechanism (Figure 5.3, panel B; Robertson & Pearson, 1983, 1985). For example, activity of one neuron (type 301) increases and excites another neuron (type 501) through the action of an excitatory influence with a certain delay. At some point, neuron 501 is pushed past its spike threshold and activated. Its activity then in turn terminates the activity of 301 through the inhibitory synapse (Robertson & Pearson, 1985). Ongoing rhythmic activity in such a circuit relies on some mechanism that enables neuron 301 to have pacemaker or burst-producing properties (described presently).

Finally, it is now known that other locomotor systems also combine different types of building blocks for the generation of rhythmic motor patterns, as with the locomotor network of the nudibranch *Tritonia,* which includes both elements previously described (Getting, 1981; Getting et al., 1980; Katz et al., 1994).

Although no definite information on network topology is available at this time, the finding that spinalized primates can produce locomotor patterns provides evidence that CPGs for locomotor activity also exist in the spinal cords of higher mammals (Fedirchuck, Nielsen, Petersen, & Hultborn, 1998). Evidence is also growing for the existence of spinal CPGs' controlling locomotion in humans (Calancie et al., 1994; Dimitrijevic, Gerasimenko, & Pinter, 1998).

In general, locomotor networks are constructed redundantly—that is, they contain multitudes of these small neuronal circuits (e.g., five in case of the locust flight CPG; Grimm & Sauer, 1995). They thereby gain substantial robustness against synaptic noise or functional failure in individual neuronal elements.

The pattern of activity generated by locomotor networks need not be two-phased, as the motor output often suggests.

Locomotor networks can be constructed and operate in a way that leads them to generate a rhythm with more than the two phases that are obvious from the locomotor program. For example, the locust flight system generating a two-phase motor output for wing elevation and depression is driven by the output of a three-phase neuronal network (Robertson & Pearson, 1985).

As the previous description makes clear, synaptic interactions within neuronal networks are important prerequisites for generating the rhythmic motor activity underlying locomotion. In addition, intrinsic properties of neurons contribute to and cooperate with the network topology in the generation of rhythmic motor activity. Intrinsic properties of neurons are generated within neurons themselves and have been studied in great detail. Some of the most prominent ones are summarized in Figure 5.4 and will be briefly introduced here:

- *Plateau potentials.* Besides the generation of action potentials, neurons can be capable of generating plateau potentials, which are spike-like, quasi-stable operating characteristics. A plateau potential is basically a prolonged, rather slow regenerative depolarization (Hille, 1991). It usually results from a voltage-dependent inward current mechanism: Sufficient depolarization initiates an inward current flow, which causes further depolarization, leading to a self-sustained depolarized state of the neuron. The membrane potential remains in this depolarized state for some time. Since the membrane potential of the plateau is usually above spike threshold, the plateau phase is characterized by burst activity of the neuron. A sufficient hyperpolarizing synaptic input or a mechanism for burst termination (discussed next) can terminate the plateau by turning off the voltage-dependent inward current. In-depth reviews on the role of this property for pattern generation are found in Kiehn et al. (1997), Marder and Calabrese (1996), and Pearson and Ramirez (1992).

- *Burst termination properties.* In addition to inhibitory synaptic inputs, intrinsic properties of neurons can contribute to terminating bursts of activity. One example is the calcium-dependent potassium (K_{Ca}) channel (Hille, 1991). During strong bursts of action potentials, calcium ions enter a neuron through cation channels underlying the depolarization and the burst of activity. Over time, this leads to an accumulation of Ca^{2+} ions in the neuron, which in turn activate K_{Ca} channels. The potassium outward current initiates a hyperpolarization of the neuron below its spike threshold and thereby terminates its depolarization and activity (e.g., Grillner & Wallen, 1985; in-depth review by Grillner et al., 1995).

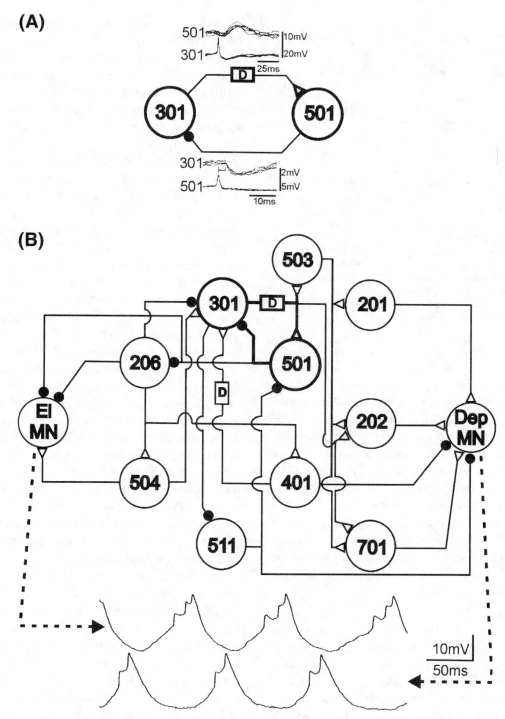

Figure 5.3 **A.** Forward excitation and backward inhibition as building block for pattern generation in neural networks for locomotion. *Open triangle:* excitatory synapse; *filled circle,* inhibitory synapse; D, delay of unknown origin. Note that some tonic background excitation is needed to induce oscillatory activity of this network. **B.** Wiring diagram of the CPG for flight in the locust thoracic ganglia, based on data from Pearson and coworkers (see Pearson & Ramirez, 1997; Robertson & Pearson, 1985), utilizing the building block from panel A. Each circle denotes an identified interneuron in the nervous system of the locust. The numbers denote certain types of identified interneurons. *Open triangles:* excitatory synapse; *filled circle,* inhibitory synapse; D, delay of unknown origin. El MN, wing elevator motoneuron; Dep MN, wing depressor motoneuron. The motor output of this pattern generator is exemplified at the bottom by a paired intracellular recording from hind wing elevator and depressor motoneurons during activity of the flight CPG. Note that the membrane potential oscillations also carry action potentials (arrowheads). Due to the fact that the recordings were made from the soma, these are very small in amplitude in invertebrates. Activity was initiated and maintained by a wind stimulus to the head of the locust.

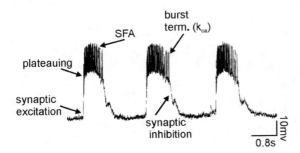

Figure 5.4   Recording from a motoneuron in an invertebrate locomotor network exemplifying schematically the contribution of some of the known synaptic and intrinsic factors (i.e., building blocks) for locomotor pattern generation. Activity in the neuron is initiated by depolarizing, excitatory synaptic inputs (synaptic excitation); burst activity in the neuron is then supported and maintained by bistable properties of the neuronal membrane (plateauing of the neuron); over time, spike activity of the neuron decays due to spike frequency adaptation (SFA), a mechanism reducing excitability of the neuron; activity of the neuron can be terminated by inhibitory synaptic inputs (synaptic inhibition) and intrinsic burst-termination properties (burst term. (K_{Ca})), both inducing repolarization of the membrane potential below spike threshold. For detailed description, see text.

- *Spike frequency adaptation (SFA).* There are presently many examples of the activity of neurons adapting over time to a given depolarization in membrane potential. The mechanism behind this phenomenon is often the *slow after-hyperpolarization* (sAHP) that follows each action potential (Hille, 1991; Schwindt & Crill, 1984). The sAHP is generated by K_{Ca} channels. With the generation of action potentials, not only Na^+ but also Ca^{2+} ions enter a neuron. These Ca^{2+} ions activate a K_{Ca} channel, which initiates an sAHP of the neuron following spike activity. sAHPs accumulate over time and can thereby reduce the excitability of a neuron and thus its activity (in-depth review in Grillner et al., 2000).

- *Intrinsic oscillations or endogenous bursting.* Neurons can be capable of steadily producing phases of alternating activity consisting of bursts and silence. This property is called *endogenous bursting* or *intrinsic oscillation* (Hille, 1991). The underlying ionic mechanisms are diverse here, as well. For example, the active phase of a neuron can display similarities to plateau potentials. There are also *automatic ionic mechanisms,* that is, conductances in the neuron that terminate activity after some time by opening ion channels (e.g., K^+ channels). These allow an outward current to hyperpolarize the membrane potential below spike threshold. The next cycle of activity is then started either by rebound properties of the neuron or by a tonic background excitation (Grillner & Wallen, 1985; Hochman, Jordan, & Schmidt, 1994; Sigvardt, Grillner, Wallen, & Van, 1985; Sillar & Simmers, 1994b).

Through the action of premotor neuronal networks, a basic rhythmic activity is generated that must be modified for a functional locomotor pattern, depending on the complexity of the locomotor organs and the locomotor task executed. Getting (1989) coined the term *building block* for identified types of network connections, synaptic properties, and intrinsic neuronal properties in charge of generating rhythmic motor activity.

The controllers of the locomotor organs can contain a multitude of such pattern-generating networks. Where the locomotor organ is segmented (e.g., for walking), the number of pattern-generating networks can be increased as well (Büschges, Schmitz, & Bässler, 1995; Cheng et al., 1998; Edgerton, Grillner, Sjöström, & Zangger, 1976). For example, in the stick insect walking system, each of the three main joints of each leg is driven by an individual neural network capable of generating rhythmic motor activity (Büschges et al.). The activity of the individual pattern generators can be coupled by sensory signals (e.g., Hess & Büschges, 1999; summary in Bässler & Büschges, 1998; and discussed later in this paper). Similar results have recently been presented for the cervical spinal cord controlling the forelimb of a vertebrate, the mudpuppy (Cheng et al.). In this investigation, evidence was presented that the motoneuron pools innervating the elbow joint, that is, the flexor and extensor, are driven by one central pattern-generating network for each of the two antagonistic muscle groups moving the tibia—the flexor and the extensor. These findings verified an old hypothesis, the *unit-burst generator concept* initially proposed by Edgerton et al., who suggested that there are unitary central pattern-generating networks present in the vertebrate spinal cord for each muscle group of the limb.

The basic rhythmic activity of the pattern-generating networks is shaped for a functional locomotor output by sensory signals from the locomotor organs and synaptically transmitted to the output elements of the locomotor system, the motoneurons. There are only a few examples of locomotor systems in which motoneurons themselves are elements of the pattern-generating networks, for example, in crustaceans (Chrachri & Clarac, 1989), annelids (Poon, Friesen, & Stent, 1978), and a lower vertebrate, the tadpole (Perrins & Roberts, 1995a, 1995b, 1995c).

LOCATION OF PATTERN-GENERATING NETWORKS FOR LOCOMOTION

As stated previously, rhythmic locomotor activity is generated within the controllers of the locomotor organs. These controllers are the neuronal networks located in the central nervous system (CNS), mostly in close apposition to locomotor organs (i.e., in the segments from which the locomotor organs arise and from where they are innervated). Segmental organization of the organism or segmental structure of the locomotor organs has no prejudicative meaning for the localization of the pattern-generating networks in the nervous system. Let us consider the generation of locomotor patterns on the level of rhythmic activity that drives one locomotor organ, for example, the chain of myotomal segments in swimming in the lamprey and the tadpole, each wing in flying (or swimming), or each limb in terrestrial locomotion.

With few exceptions, the controllers for locomotion are distributed across several segments of the CNS. The pattern-generating network for locust flight is a distributed neuronal network encompassing the three thoracic ganglia and some condensed abdominal neuromeres attached to the metathoracic ganglion (Robertson & Pearson, 1985). Distribution is also present in the walking-pattern-generating networks of vertebrates, for example, for the forelimb in the cervical spinal cord (Cheng et al., 1998) and for the hindlimb in the lumbar spinal cord (e.g., Cazalets, Borde, & Clarac, 1995; Kjaerulff & Kiehn, 1996). In the lamprey and the tadpole, the CPG for swimming that drives the chains of myotomal segments is distributed along the segments of the spinal cord (as discussed previously). Similarly, the pattern-generating networks for crawling and swimming in the leech are distributed along the chain of segmental ganglia (comparative summary in Orlovsky et al., 1999). However, these locomotor systems are special in the sense that, for swimming, the motor pattern results from the coordinated action of the subsequent segments of the organism; that is, the locomotor organ is the organism itself. For all controllers generating swimming movements, it is known that the nervous system of each individual segment contains neural networks capable of generating a rhythmic motor output for the segment. This is most obvious in the CPG for swimming in *Clione,* which is generated by a network of interneurons, most of which are located in the pedal ganglia of the nonsegmented organism (Arshavsky et al., 1985a, 1985b, 1985c, 1985d, 1985e). Only in arthropod walking systems has a clear segmental organization been found, with the controller of each leg restricted mainly to the segmental ganglion of the locomotor organ, which has been studied in great detail for the stick insect (summary in Bässler & Büschges, 1998).

Regarding mammalian locomotion, important new findings were recently presented on the organization and location of the pattern-generating networks for the individual limbs. Individual neuronal networks for the generation of rhythmic motor activity for both elbow flexor and elbow extensor motoneuron pools were identified in the mudpuppy forelimb

(Cheng et al., 1998). The data presented support the unit-burst generator concept of locomotion described earlier. Similarly, lesion experiments in the neonatal rat lumbar spinal cord have revealed that the CPGs controlling hindlimb movements are distributed throughout the hindlimb enlargement and most likely also in the lower thoracic cord (Cazalets et al., 1995; Kjaerulff & Kiehn, 1996). Together with additional evidence, this suggests that in mammals, too, the CPG for the hindlimb is not a unitary entity, but is again composed of several unit-burst generators controlling single muscles or joints. Between the lumbar segments, the capability to generate rhythmic activity declines from rostral to caudal (summary in Kiehn & Kjaerulff, 1998). In patients with spinal cord injuries, it was reported that the higher the level of the injury was, the more normal the locomotor pattern appeared (Dietz, Nakazawa, Wirz, & Erni, 1999). This indicated that, also in humans, the CPGs for locomotion are not restricted to specific levels of the spinal cord.

SENSORY SIGNALS CONTROLLING LOCOMOTOR ACTIVITY

In the majority of locomotor systems, sensory signals are utilized, first, to generate a functional locomotor pattern, and second, to stabilize the locomotor pattern, by adapting to biomechanical changes and responding to unexpected events. Third, sensory information plays a crucial role in controlling the posture and equilibrium of the locomotor system during the behavioral task (Macpherson, Fung, & Jacobs, 1997; Orlovski et al., 1999). Such information is gathered from multiple sensory systems and integrated in the networks controlling locomotion and related to the current position and condition of the body and the limbs (e.g., the phase of a movement). The dependence of motor control systems on proprioceptive signals has been well characterized in a statement by Prochazka (1996b): "You can only control what you sense." Proprioceptors located in muscles and joints characterize the positions of the limbs, and together with exteroreceptors they sense contact with the ground or obstacles and the load carried by the limb. Their general role is to establish the temporal order of the locomotor pattern and to reinforce ongoing activity (Bässler & Büschges, 1998; Duysens, Clarac, & Cruse, 2000; Grillner, 1979; Pearson, 1995; Pearson & Ramirez, 1997; Prochazka).

Other sensory information involved in the generation and control of locomotor behavior itself is provided by visual cues. Visual cues play a decisive role in controlling goal direction in locomotion, allowing the preadjustment of the locomotor activity and the interpretation of visual flow that yields information on walking speed and direction (review in Rossignol, 1996b). Furthermore, together with the vestibular apparatus or comparable gravity-sensor systems in invertebrates, visual input is involved in controlling the body's orientation in space. This is especially important for animals locomoting in a three-dimensional environment (i.e., flying or swimming; Orlovsky et al., 1992; Reichardt, 1969; Ullen, Deliagina, Orlovsky, & Grillner, 1995).

The following sections briefly review the major sensory systems and their roles in the control of locomotion.

Visual Regulation of Locomotion

Visual control of locomotion is very powerful. Apparently, visual input is used to direct locomotion, to avoid obstacles on the way to reach a target, and for orientation. Due to its complex nature, very little was known until recently about the visual control of locomotion; however, advances in computer technology allowing artificial simulation of the optical system (as with virtual reality; Warren, Kay, Zosh, Duchon, & Sahuc, 2001) provided deeper insight into the mechanisms of visuomotor control.

As introduced by Gibson (1958), movements of the body in space generate a continuously changing pattern of motion on the retina, a pattern referred to as *optic flow*. This self-induced optic flow must be distinguished in speed and direction from the optic flow induced by moving objects. Confusion about this distinction is typically experienced by a person who is sitting in one train and observing another train, and is unable to identify which train is moving. Generally, optical flow is used to assess the velocity of the locomotion and the direction of self-movement. Consequently, information gained from visual flow is used to control multiple aspects of locomotion, including goal-directed spatial behavior, locomotor speed, and gross adaptation to environmental changes. The association of changes in optic flow with changes in movement is so strong that artificially induced or perturbed optic flow can modulate the velocity and direction of locomotion or even initiate locomotor behavior. This is an observation commonly found throughout the animal kingdom, for example in lobsters and crayfish. A front-to-rear optokinetic stimulation provided by horizontal stripes on an underlying treadmill can trigger forward locomotion with the velocity depending on the velocity of the stripes (Davis & Ayers, 1972). Insects flying tethered inside a striped drum will tend to turn in the direction in which the drum is rotated (Reichardt, 1969), and expanding the size of a target during the time a gerbil is walking (giving the impression that the target is getting closer) causes the animal to decrease its velocity (Sun, Carey, & Goodale, 1992).

Powerful effects of changes in visual flow have also been reported in humans. For example, during forward walking in a room in which the walls can be displaced, moving them forward (instead of backward as it would appear during forward locomotion) will create the impression of walking backward, despite contradictory proprioceptive signals from the limbs (Lee & Thompson, 1982). Toddlers who have just learned to walk will tip over if the walls are set in motion (Stoffregen, Schmuckler, & Gibson, 1987). Comparable experimental approaches showed that, as in animals, walking velocity in humans is adjusted to visually perceived walking speed (Konczak, 1994; Prokop, Schubert, & Berger, 1997). Thus, visual input during locomotion in vertebrates and invertebrates is used not only to avoid obstacles, but also to guide locomotor direction and velocity.

In the field of visual locomotor control, there is an ongoing discussion whether visual flow is the dominant optical influence on target-directed locomotion or whether the walking direction is simply determined by the current body orientation and the perceived direction of the target. In light of this dispute, it has recently been demonstrated that humans do not guide locomotion by relying either on visual flow alone or on egocentric direction alone. Both components are probably used in a complementary way—for example, when the optical flow is reduced or distorted: On a grass lawn or at night, behavior tends to be governed by egocentric direction (Harris & Carre, 2001; Rushton, Harris, Lloyd, & Wann, 1998; Warren et al., 2001; Wood, Harvey, Young, Beedie, & Wilson, 2000).

Visual information is also essential to perform anticipatory foot placement in order to avoid obstacles. To avoid bumping into an object, it is crucial to calculate how much time is left for corrective action. The distance to the obstacle is relevant only in relation to the speed of self-motion. Thus, visual information is used in a feed-forward rather than an on-line control mode to regulate locomotion. Humans do not fixate on obstacles as they step over them, but perform a planning in the steps before (Hollands & Marple Horvat, 1996, 2001; Patla, Adkin, Martin, Holden, & Prentice, 1996; Patla & Vicker, 1996). This feed-forward information is very important in the control of walking, and it is not possible to walk more than 8 s or 5 m without visual feedback (Lee & Thompson, 1982).

Compared to our knowledge of invertebrate systems, knowledge about the mechanisms of visual locomotor control in vertebrates is rather incomplete. The approach of recording cortical cells during visually guided locomotion in cats demonstrated increased firing in pyramidal cells when modification of the step cycle was required to clear an obstacle (Drew, Jiang, Kably, & Lavoie, 1996). It has been suggested that the increased discharge is used to modify the step cycle, since it has been shown that inactivation of these cortical areas results in the inability to clear visible obstacles. A comparable feed-forward mechanism to anticipate collision was recently described in locusts (Hatsopoulos, Gabbiani, & Laurent, 1995). The *lobula giant motion detectors (LGMD)* in the locust optic lobe (Strausfeld & Nässel, 1981) are neurons that receive inputs from afferents that are sensitive to local motion over the entire visual hemifield (Rowell, O'Shea, & Williams, 1977) and that respond most strongly to objects approaching the eye (Rind & Simmons, 1992). LGMD synapse directly to a large neuron *(descending contralateral motion detector,* or *DCMD),* which is involved in the generation and control of flight and jump maneuvers (Pearson, Heitler, & Steeves, 1980; Robertson & Pearson, 1983). In the visual system of the fly, a number of processing stages have been identified and several interneurons with sensitivity to various directions of motion have been found (Borst & Egelhaaf, 1989), making the visual system of flies the best-described model in visual processing (reviewed in Krapp, 2000).

Proprioceptive Regulation of Locomotion

The question of how proprioceptive signals regulate locomotor activity has been an intensive field of research, including studies in humans, cats, and various arthropods (reviewed in Büschges & El Manira, 1998; Duysens et al., 2000; Pearson, 1995; Pearson & Ramirez, 1997; Prochazka, 1996b). These studies made it clear that there are common principles in the proprioceptive control of locomotion throughout the entire animal kingdom, indicating their general importance in the generation of functionally relevant locomotor movements (Pearson, 1993). A prominent example providing evidence that local proprioceptive reflex pathways are strongly involved in the control of stepping is the finding that spinalized cats walking with their hindlimbs on a treadmill are able to adapt the speed of stepping to the speed of the treadmill belt (Brown, 1911). The only explanation for this ability is that sensory feedback from proprioceptors in the limbs is involved in controlling the step cycle. Generally, proprioceptive feedback serves two separate functions in the control of locomotion: (a) the control of phase transition and (b) the regulation of the magnitude of muscle activity.

A common principle in sensory control of locomotion is the task- or phase-dependency of sensory feedback. Transmission in proprioceptive reflex pathways, for example, strongly depends on the motor task and the phase of the movement (reviewed in Büschges & El Manira, 1998; Pearson, 1995). For example, reflex pathways can generate opposite motor outputs of varying strength or gain, depending on the

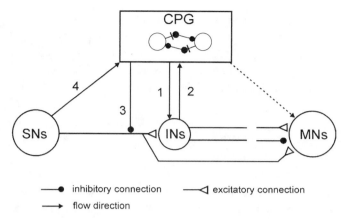

Figure 5.5 Summary of the mechanisms involved in the control of locomotor output by central and proprioceptive signals. When the CPG is active, phase- or state-depending priming of mono- and polysynaptic sensory-motor paths via interneurons (INs) between sensory neurons (SNs) and motoneurons (MNs) takes place. Arrow 1 symbolizes the state- or phase-dependent alterations in the processing of sensory information. Arrow 2 represents the influence of premotor interneurons in sensory-motor pathways on the CPG. Arrow 3 represents the presynaptic inhibition of afferent terminals in the CNS. Arrow 4 represents the pathway from sensory neurons that can affect the timing of the locomotor output. Modified from Büschges and El Manira (1998).

actual behavior or the phase of the movement (e.g., standing compared with walking; Figure 5.5). This phenomenon has been termed *reflex reversal* and is found in vertebrates (Pearson, 1993, 1995; Prochazka, 1996b) as well as in invertebrates (Bässler & Büschges, 1998; Cattaert & LeRay, 2001; Clarac, Cattaert, & LeRay, 2000). This flexibility of reflex pathways ensures that the motor output is adjusted properly to the actual behavioral task, depending on the behavioral and the biomechanical states of the locomotor apparatus.

Proprioceptive Control of Phase Transition

Sherrington (1910) already introduced the concept that somatosensory afferents from the limbs are involved in the regulation of the step cycle during walking in vertebrates. One mechanism regulating the duration of the stance phase in vertebrates is hip extension, since preventing hip extension in a limb prevents the onset of the swing phase and thus of stepping in cats and rats (e.g., Fouad & Pearson, 1997a; Grillner & Rossignol, 1978). The afferents responsible for signaling the hip angle and subsequently for the initiation of the swing phase are probably muscle spindles in hip flexor muscles (Hiebert, Whelan, Prochazka, & Pearson, 1996). Another signal in the control of the step cycle in vertebrates arises from Golgi tendon organs and muscle spindles from extensor muscles (Conway, Hultborn, & Kiehn, 1987; Whelan, Hiebert, & Pearson, 1995b). Both sensors are active during stance, with the Golgi tendon organs providing a gauge of the load carried by the leg (reviewed in Dietz & Duysens, 2000). The excitatory activity during walking is opposite to its inhibiting action during standing (reflex reversal). The functional consequence is that the swing phase is not initiated until the load is taken off the limb (otherwise, balance would be lost), as occurs at the end of the stance phase when the weight of the animal is borne by the other limbs.

The fact that, at the end of the stance phase, signals both about joint and limb displacement and about load on the limb are involved in the initiation of the swing phase is a general rule in vertebrate and invertebrate walking systems. It has been commonly found in stick insects, cockroaches, lobsters, cats, and humans (Figure 5.6; Anderson & Grillner, 1983; Bässler & Büschges, 1998; Clarac, 1982; Pang & Yang, 2000; Pearson, 1993; Wendler, 1974). In the stick insect, for example, two types of proprioceptors have been found to influence

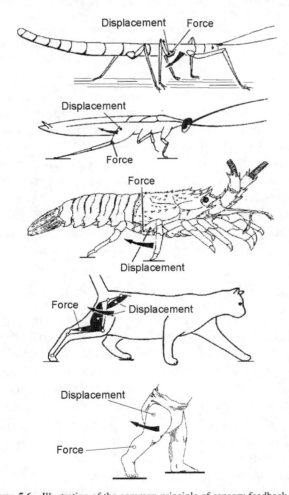

Figure 5.6   Illustration of the common principle of sensory feedback controlling the initiation of the swing phase in invertebrates (stick insect, cockroach, and crayfish) and vertebrates (cat and infant). When the limb is unloaded, and thus no force is detected in the limb, and the limb is extended, the swing phase will be initiated. Modified from Prochazka (1996b) and Pang and Yang (2000).

the timing of the onset of the swing phase. These sensors are (a) the campaniform sensillae, which measure load on a limb or strain on the cuticle, in a manner analogous to the Golgi tendon organs in vertebrates, and (b) the femoral chordotonal organ, which, by being stretch-sensitive in a manner analogous to muscle spindles in vertebrates, signals the movement and position of the femur-tibia joint (Bässler & Büschges).

Prochazka (1996b) has formulated a general rule for the transition from the stance phase to the swing phase during stepping in vertebrates:

IF extensor force low
AND hip extended
THEN initiate swing.

However, phase transitions controlled by proprioceptive signals are not only found in walking systems (reviewed in Pearson, 1993; Pearson & Ramirez, 1997). In the flight system of insects, especially well studied in locusts, sensory information about movements of the wings is also utilized for phase transition in motor activity. Two wing-sensory systems—that is, the wing tegulae—a hinge mechanoreceptor, and the stretch receptors control the initiation and duration of elevator activity during flight motor activity (Wolf & Pearson, 1988). Similarly, in vertebrate swimming (e.g., in the lamprey spinal locomotor network), sensory signals that report bending of the spinal cord contribute to the alternation of motor activity between the myotomal motoneuron pools of both sides of the spinal cord (Grillner et al., 1995).

The functional significance of regulating phase transition by means of afferent pathways might be to limit a movement, such as the amount of leg extension (Whelan et al., 1995b) or the amplitude of wing depression during flight (Wolf & Pearson, 1988), to a range compatible with effective function. A second advantage of afferent phase control is to ensure that a certain phase of the movement is not initiated until a defined biomechanical state has been reached. This allows the transition without destabilization of the system.

Regulation of the Magnitude of Muscle Activity

The second principle of locomotor control found in vertebrates and invertebrates is the control of motor activity via afferent feedback (Duysens et al., 2000; Pearson, 1993). A generalization emerging from studies in various walking systems is that afferent feedback from leg proprioceptors contributes to the generation of stance-phase activity (see Figure 5.6). For example, in invertebrates such as the stick insect, the chordotonal organ in the femur of the front leg signals flexion of the femur-tibia joint during the stance phase.

In walking animals, these sensory signals reinforce the activity in flexor motoneurons (Bässler, 1986) as a result of the action of a parallel and distributed neuronal network driving the leg motoneurons (Büschges, Sauer, & Bässler, 2000). Also, in the walking system of the crayfish, sensory signals are utilized to reinforce motor activity during stance (El Manira, DiCaprio, Cattaert, & Clarac, 1991; Sillar, Skorupski, Elson, & Bush, 1986). In vertebrates, sensory signals underlying the reinforcement of motor activity arise both from Golgi tendon organs and primary muscle spindle afferents (Guertin, Angel, Perreault, & McCrea, 1995; McCrea, Shefchyk, Stephens, & Pearson, 1995; Whelan et al., 1995b). At least three excitatory reflex pathways transmit proprioceptive information from extensor muscles to motoneurons or the CPG (Figure 5.7): (a) the well-known monosynaptic pathway from muscle spindles to motoneurons; (b) a disynaptic pathway from spindles and Golgi tendon organs that is opened during the stance phase; and (c) a polysynaptic pathway. The latter pathway includes the extensor half-center in a way that also controls the timing of the stepping pattern (Pearson & Ramirez, 1997). The neural mechanisms that contribute to the modulation of sensory pathways in the control of

locomotion have been investigated in great detail in the past decade. Two key factors are currently known: (a) In many locomotor systems the actual motor output is the result of the action of a distributed neural network that can modulate the magnitude of motor activity generated by differentially weighting (or opening and closing) individual parallel (sometimes opposing) interneuronal pathways between sense organs and motoneurons (Bässler & Büschges, 1998; Büschges et al., 2000; Cattaert & LeRay, 2001; Pearson, 1995; also refer to Figure 5.5). Phase dependency of this mechanism in the locomotor cycle is generated by the action of the central pattern generators. (b) Phasic modulation of efficacy of the individual pathways from sense organs onto motoneurons are the target of pre- and postsynaptic modulatory mechanisms at the intercalated synapses, for example, presynaptic inhibition (Clarac, El Manira, & Cattaert, 1992; Nusbaum, El Manira, Gossard, & Rossignol, 1997; Rossignol, 1996a; and Figure 5.5). In humans, as well, the load carried by the extensor muscles increases the magnitude of their activity (Dietz & Duysens, 2000; Stephens & Yang, 1999). In cats, removing feedback from these afferents reduces extensor activity by more than 50% and, in humans, the contribution to extensor muscle activity has been estimated to be about 30% (Yang, Stein, & James, 1991).

The general integration of proprioceptive feedback in locomotor systems throughout the animal kingdom strongly indicates the functional necessity of such a feature. The benefits are the appropriate and effective control of motor rhythm, integrating biomechanical changes and external perturbations in the system.

Role of Exteroceptive Input

Compared to proprioceptive control, much less knowledge has been gathered on the role of *exteroceptive inputs* (e.g., cutaneous afferents in vertebrates) in the control of locomotion. Exteroceptors in the skin have a strong influence on the central pattern generator for walking (Forssberg, 1979) and on brainstem areas controlling locomotion (Drew, Cabana, & Rossignol, 1996). One important function is to respond to unpredicted perturbations from obstacles on the ground. To be functionally meaningful, these reflexes are strongly modulated during the gait cycle, as has been demonstrated in cats (Abraham, Marks, & Loeb, 1985; Andersson, Forssberg, Grillner, & Lindquist, 1978; Duysens, Loeb, & Weston, 1980; Forssberg, 1979) and humans (Duysens, Trippel, Horstmann, & Dietz, 1990; Yang & Stein, 1990). A mechanical stimulus applied to the dorsal part of a paw in cats or to a cutaneous nerve in humans during the onset and middle of the swing phase produces a strong, short latency

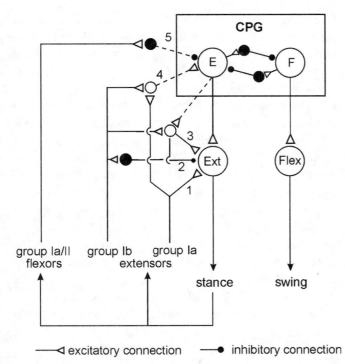

— excitatory connection   — inhibitory connection

Figure 5.7 Summary of the reflex circuits regulating the timing and magnitude of extensor activity during walking in the cat. 1 symbolizes the excitatory monosynaptic and 2 the disynaptic inhibitory pathway. Pathways 3 to 5 are opened only during locomotion. Transmission in the disynaptic pathway 3 occurs during extension and reinforces ongoing extensor activity. One function of excitatory pathways 4 and 5 is to regulate the duration of extensor activity. Modified from Pearson (1995).

excitement of flexor motoneurons and inhibition of extensor motoneurons to increase elevation of the limb and clear the obstacle. Forssberg introduced this reflex pattern as the *stumbling corrective response*. In contrast, the same stimulus applied during the end of the swing phase and during the stance phase produces the opposite response; the limb cannot be lifted at this phase in the step cycle because otherwise the animal or person would fall. However, the stimulus evokes increased flexor activity in the subsequent step. This state-dependent modulation has been found to be mediated by the convergence of primary afferents and the output from the CPG to premotor interneurons (Degtyarenko, Simon, & Burke, 1996).

Exteroceptive signals, such as cutaneous stimuli, are also known to trigger swimming or turning in animals. A well-defined system has been described for swimming behavior in tadpoles: A brief stimulus to the skin, (e.g., of the head) can trigger sustained swimming or struggling sequences, depending on stimulus intensity and duration (Soffe, 1991). This response is mediated via a single skin-sensory pathway directly accessing the CPGs in the spinal cord: the *Rohon-Beard sensory neurons*.

In conclusion, in many locomotor systems, sensory input plays a prominent role in shaping the motor output of the *controllers* toward functional locomotor behavior. The major tasks of sensory signals are (a) to control the direction of locomotion, (b) to control posture and equilibrium, (c) to control phase transitions in the step cycle, (d) to control the magnitude of muscle activity, (e) to avoid obstacles, and finally, (f) to respond to perturbations.

PLASTICITY IN MOTOR SYSTEMS

For many years, the central nervous system in adult mammals has been seen as a hardwired and rigid structure. The same was believed about the nervous systems of invertebrates, whose relatively short life spans were thought to make adaptive processes in the nervous system unnecessary. This view has changed, and today it is accepted that the CNS in vertebrates and invertebrates is capable of major reorganizations in response to injury or loss of parts of the nervous system under experimental or pathological conditions (Meinertzhagen, 2001; Raineteau & Schwab, 2001). Theoretically, reorganization can occur on multiple levels in preexisting neural circuits: by changing synaptic strength (referred to as *synaptic plasticity*), by anatomical reorganization through the sprouting of uninjured axonal branches and dendrites (referred to as *anatomical plasticity*), or by changes in neuronal properties. Because axonal plasticity after injuries to the CNS is frequently associated with functional recovery, ongoing research

in adult vertebrates focuses on understanding the mechanism of plasticity, which could lead to new treatments for patients suffering from stroke or traumatic injuries of the brain or spinal cord.

This chapter will introduce examples of plastic rearrangements in locomotor systems of the nervous system and discuss possible mechanisms of spontaneous recovery after injuries to the nervous system. Lately, this topic has been extensively reviewed by Bizzi, Tresch, Saltiel, and d'Avella (2000), Pearson (2000), and Raineteau and Schwab.

Injury-Induced Adaptations of Central Pattern-Generating Networks

A prominent example of plasticity in a locomotor system is the finding that cats with complete thoracic spinal cord transection can be trained to walk on a treadmill with their hind limbs (Barbeau & Rossignol, 1994; De Leon, Hodgson, Roy, & Edgerton, 1998; Lovely, Gregor, Roy, & Edgerton, 1990; and reviewed in Rossignol, 2000). Directly after spinalization, cats that had their forelimbs placed on a platform could not self-support their hindquarters during stepping movements on a treadmill. Within 2 weeks, these cats gained partial weight control and were sometimes even able to place the plantar surface of the paws on the treadmill belt. After about four weeks, the movement of the treadmill belt was able to trigger locomotion, and the cats could transiently support their own weight (Barbeau & Rossignol; Lovely et al.; De Leon et al.). Consistent with the idea of the activity-dependent acquisition of a motor task, the training effects persist. With longer delays in training, however, the effects of the treadmill training cease (De Leon et al., 1999). In humans, too, treadmill training has proven its validity in the rehabilitation phase of patients with spinal cord injuries (Behrman & Harkema, 2000; Dietz, Colombo, & Jensen, 1994; Wernig & Muller, 1992). Regular training with partial weight support by suspending patients in a parachute belt over a treadmill increased the return of rhythmic muscle activation, improved weight support capability, and decreased spasticity in patients with anatomically incomplete spinal cord injury. A mechanism probably involved in training-induced functional recovery is the enhanced excitability of spinal pattern-generating networks after spinal cord injury (De Leon et al., 1999; Tillakaratne et al., 2000).

Plasticity in Afferent Pathways Controlling Locomotion

The finding that treadmill training in spinalized cats enhances locomotor recovery indicated that adaptive changes in the pattern-generating networks are driven by sensory signals from the stepping limbs. A good example that afferent pathways are modifiable is the conditioning of the well-known *H-reflex* in a learning task in rats, monkeys, and humans (Segal & Wolf, 1994; Wolpaw, 1997). It is also known that, after injuries to the CNS (especially the spinal cord), reflexes are exaggerated (Burke, Gillies, & Lance, 1970; Hochman & McCrea, 1994; Nelson & Mendell, 1979). One factor in the increased reflex gain is the sprouting of sensory afferents and a simultaneous increase in their effectiveness.

Another example of injury-induced reflex plasticity is the finding that afferent pathways that are involved in the initiation of the swing phase and in reinforcing extensor activity are enhanced by partial denervation of extensor muscles (Gritsenko, Mushahwar, & Prochazka, 2001; Pearson, Fouad, & Misiaszek, 1999; Whelan et al., 1995a). Increases in proprioceptive reflex strength occur within a week and are paralleled by the recovery of stepping. The location of the adaptive changes is probably in the lumbar spinal cord, since the amplitudes of group I (rising from Golgi tendon organs and muscle spindles) field potentials from a spared synergistic muscle are increased in the intermediate nucleus of lumbar segments (Fouad & Pearson, 1997b). The finding that a comparable increase in the effectiveness of group I input from this muscle can also be found in chronically spinalized cats also indicates that reflex adaptations are occurring at the level of the spinal cord (Bouyer, Whelan, Pearson, & Rossignol, 2001). In the light of the adaptive capabilities of the spinal cord, Pearson (2001) recently reviewed the role of plasticity in reflex function and in the recovery of locomotion after injuries to the CNS.

The fact that plasticity can occur on several levels (e.g., that spinal reflex pathways are able to learn) has been also demonstrated by Lou and Bloedel (1988), who showed that decerebrated walking ferrets were able to change the trajectory of the swing phase when an obstacle was interjected into the step cycle during the swing phase.

In insects as well, the removal of sensory organs involved in the regulation of locomotion or even amputation of a limb can be compensated. For example, in the locust flight system, complete or partial removal of the tegulae (mechanoreceptors at the wing base) leads to compensatory anatomical and synaptic rearrangements resulting in functional recovery of flight motor behavior within 2 weeks following the lesion (Büschges, Ramirez, Driesang, & Pearson, 1992a, 1992b; Fischer & Ebert, 1999; Gee & Robertson, 1996; Wolf & Büschges, 1997). Interestingly, it is reported that this recovery occurs spontaneously and does not depend on training or activity. The plasticity of locomotor systems can also be expressed on an immediate short-term scale. An example of such injury-induced plasticity is the recovery of walking after leg amputation in cockroaches. The walking pattern adapts to the loss of the limb by switching interleg locomotor coordination from hexapods to that of tetrapods (Hughes, 1957; Wilson, 1966).

Injury-Induced Plasticity in the Corticospinal Tract

Due to limited self-repair after traumatic injuries to the CNS in higher vertebrates, it is believed that functional recovery, too, is rather limited. However, significant functional recovery occurs after stroke (Ferrucci et al., 1993; Speach & Dombovy, 1995) traumatic head injury (Sbordone et al., 1995), or spinal cord injury (Bracken et al., 2000). The underlying mechanisms of this spontaneous recovery are rather unclear. A phenomenon often observed in patients and animal models after such injuries and intensive rehabilitative training conducted parallel to functional recovery or in training paradigms is found at the cortical level in rearrangements of the sensory and motor representation maps (Bruehlmeier et al., 1998; Levy, Amassian, Traad, & Caldwell, 1990; Nudo, Milliken, Jenkins, & Merzenich, 1996; Wu & Kaas, 1999; and see Klintsova & Greenough, 1999, for a review). The underlying mechanisms of these rearrangements are probably multiple and rather unclear. It has been suggested that unmasking horizontal connections between the cortical subregions may play a crucial role (Chen, Corwell, Yaseen, Hallett, & Cohen, 1998; Huntley, 1997; Jacobs & Donoghue, 1991). A possible contribution of structural plasticity in descending corticospinal tract (CST) axons has been discussed since the recent finding that the CST in adult rats has a greater potential for anatomical rearrangements than was previously believed. Injury-induced sprouting and increased collateralization was found in severed CST fibers rostral to the lesion, in parallel with shifts in hindlimb motor cortex representations (Fouad, Pedersen, Schwab, & Brösamle, 2001). Structural adaptations have also been reported in spared CST fibers. Significant anatomical plasticity was correlated with spontaneous functional recovery in a grasping task in adult rats (Weidner, Ner, Salimi, & Tuszynski, 2001). It is thus currently speculated that such spontaneous growth of lesioned and unlesioned axons contributes to changes in cortical motor representations and to functional recovery after incomplete spinal cord lesions.

Functional and anatomical studies clearly show that the potential for adaptive reorganization in the adult nervous system in vertebrates and invertebrates has been underestimated. Adaptive changes can occur on several levels of the nervous system and are often activity dependent. Current approaches to experimentally increase the plastic capabilities of the nervous system, together with the progress in understanding rehabilitative strategies, might open new avenues in the treatment of injuries to the nervous system.

MODULATION OF LOCOMOTOR ACTIVITY

In order to initiate, maintain, adapt, or terminate locomotor activity to meet the requirements of the current environmental conditions, neuronal networks for motor control must be flexible. Whereas the fast, task-dependent, cycle-by-cycle adaptation of locomotor activity is achieved by sensory feedback, which, in a broad sense, can be viewed as being an integral part of the pattern-generating networks, neuromodulatory inputs can reshape the motor output by affecting intrinsic network properties of motor circuits and thus provide the general flexibility observed in motor behavior. The term *neuromodulation* has been in common usage for more than two decades and was originally defined as the alteration of the cellular or synaptic properties of a neuron mediated by a substance released from another neuron (Kaczmarek & Levitan, 1987; Kupfermann, 1979). However, this definition no longer strictly conforms to many other definitions of neuromodulation used in scientific literature, primarily because in many systems neurotransmission and neuromodulation apparently involve common mechanisms and address common targets (for an overview of the large variety of phenomena nowadays referred to as *neuromodulation,* see Katz, 1999). This section introduces the main mechanism of generating locomotor flexibility, the modulation of locomotor network function by neural active substances (neuromodulators).

Sources of Neuromodulators

In vertebrates and invertebrates, neuromodulators are mostly released from cell groups consisting of relatively few neurons located in the CNS, but outside the specific locomotor circuits and not participating in the basic locomotor rhythm generation (referred to as *extrinsic neuromodulation;* Katz, 1999). Most of the modulators of vertebrate locomotor networks are synthesized in distinct cell clusters in the brainstem that produce, among other things, the biogenic amines serotonin (5-HT, nucleus raphe), noradrenaline (norepinephrine, locus coeruleus), or dopamine. In many vertebrate systems, the axonal projections of these relatively few cells however, can supply large areas of the brain and spinal cord (Kuypers & Huisman, 1982; van Mier, Joosten, van Rheden, & ten Donkelaar, 1986). Invertebrate neuromodulators, such as the neuropeptide proctolin, are normally released from neurosecretory cells either clustered in cerebral ganglia regions or from single, paired, or small groups of cells spread over the whole ventral nerve cord (Beltz & Kravitz, 1987; Keshishian & O'Shea, 1985; Stevenson & Sporhase-Eichmann, 1995). This not only enables the coordinated release of neuromodulators to defined targets within a particular CPG, but also underlies the simultaneous control of locomotor networks consisting of multiple CPGs (e.g., networks driving leg joints or spinal networks for swimming). For vertebrates and invertebrates, classic neuromodulators associated with locomotor systems and their controllers—that is, the spinal cord in vertebrates and the segmental ganglia in invertebrates—are summarized in Table 5.1.

Effects of Neuromodulators on the Output of Locomotor Networks

In principle, neuromodulators alter the expression of motor patterns by affecting the controllers of a locomotor system that drives the effector organs, such as the muscles in the body wall or within limbs or wings. The best-recognized function of neuromodulators in vertebrate and invertebrate motor control is the alteration of ongoing motor activity. Such alterations in the intensity of locomotor activity are important, for instance, in adjusting the instantaneous speed of locomotion, which involves acceleration as well as deceleration and termination, or in changing locomotor intensity. Furthermore, in a variety of vertebrate and invertebrate species, neuromodulators are able to initiate locomotor activity (Table 5.1).

Initiation of Locomotor Activity

In the simplest examples, initiation of long-lasting periods of locomotor activity often requires no more than a short external stimulus that triggers long-lasting, self-sustained network activity (e.g., escape swimming in tadpoles; Roberts, 1990). However, locomotor activity can also be initiated by administration of neuromodulators. Intravenous injection of dopamine (L-DOPA) elicits locomotor activity in spinalized cats on a treadmill (Forssberg & Grillner, 1973; Jankovska et al., 1967a, 1967b). As well as in rabbits (Viala & Buser, 1969) and decerebrated adult rats (Iles & Nicolopoulos-Stournaras, 1996). Intrathecal application of noradrenaline (Kiehn, Hultborn, & Conway, 1992) or intravenous injection of adrenoreceptor agonists to acutely (Forssberg & Grillner) or chronically spinalized cats (e.g., Barbeau & Rossignol, 1991) also evokes locomotor activity (reviewed in Rossignol et al., 1998). Sublesional transplantation of noradrenergic embryonic neurons from the locus coeruleus into the spinal cord (i.e., close to the locomotor networks) is also able to trigger automatic locomotion in spinalized cats (Yakovleff et al., 1989). In addition, noradrenaline or dopamine, when applied to *in vitro* spinal cords of vertebrates, activate the locomotor networks (Kiehn & Kjaerulff, 1996; Kiehn, Sillar, Kjaerulff, & McDearmid, 1999; Squalli-Houssaini & Cazalets, 2000).

TABLE 5.1   Neuromodulators Contributing to the Initiation and Modulation of Locomotor Network Activity

Type	Motor System	Function	Species	Selected References
Vertebrate systems				
Dopamine	spinal CPGs	initiation	rabbit	Viala & Buser (1969)
	spinal CPGs	initiation	cat	Forssberg & Grillner (1973)
	spinal CPGs	initiation	neonatal rat	Kiehn & Kjaerulff (1996)
	spinal networks	modulation	lamprey	Schotland, Shupliakov, Wikström, Brodin, Srinivasan, You, Herrera-Marschitz, Zhang, Hökfeld, & Grillner (1995)
Serotonin (5-HT)	spinal networks	modulation	lamprey	Harris-Warrick & Cohen (1985)
	spinal network	modulation	tadpole	Sillar et al. (1992)
	spinal CPGs	initiation/modulation	neonatal rat	Kiehn & Kjaerulff (1996)
	spinal CPGs	initiation	mouse	Jiang, Carlin, & Brownstone (1999)
	spinal CPGs	initiation	rabbit	Viala & Buser (1969)
	spinal CPGs	modulation	mudpuppy	Jovanovic, Petrov, Greer, & Stein (1996)
Noradrenaline	spinal CPGs	modulation	neonatal rat	Squalli-Houssaini & Cazalets (2000)
	spinal network	modulation	tadpole	McDearmid et al. (1997)
Noradrenergic agonists	spinal CPGs	initiation/modulation	cat	Barbeau & Rossignol (1991)
Substance P[a]	spinal CPGs	modulation	neonatal rat	Barthe & Clarac (1997)
	spinal networks	modulation	lamprey	Parker & Grillner (1999)
Invertebrate systems				
Dopamine	escape motor system	modulation	cockroach	Goldstein & Camhi (1991)
	swimmeret networks	initiation	lobster	Barthe, Mons, Cattaert, Geffard, & Clarac (1989)
Octopamine	swimmeret networks	initiation/modulation	crayfish	Mulloney, Acevedo, & Bradbury (1987)
	swim network	modulation	medicinal leech	Mesce, Crisp, & Gilchrist (2001)
	flight motor system	initiation	locust	Ramirez & Pearson (1991a, 1991b)
	leg locomotor networks	modulation	locust	Sombati & Hoyle (1984)
	escape motor system	modulation	cockroach	Goldstein & Camhi (1991)
Proctolin	swimmeret network	initiation/modulation	crayfish	Mulloney et al. (1987)
Serotonin (5-HT)	escape motor system	modulation	cockroach	Goldstein & Camhi (1991)
	swim network	modulation	medicinal leech	Mangan, Cometa, & Friesen (1994)
	swim network	initiation	mollusc *Tritonia*	Katz et al. (1994)
	leg locomotor networks	modulation	locust	Parker (1995)
	swimmeret network	modulation	crayfish	Barthe, Bevengut, & Clarac (1993)
Pilocarpine[b]	leg locomotor networks	initiation	locust	Ryckebusch & Laurent (1993)
	leg locomotor networks	initiation	stick insect	Büschges et al. (1995)
	swimmeret networks	initiation	crayfish	Chrachri & Clarac (1989)
	locomotor networks	initiation	tobacco hornworm	Johnston & Levine (1996)

[a]Often colocalized with 5-HT or close to serotonergic neurons. [b]Muscarinic cholinergic agonist, used as a tool to activate rhythmic motor networks in invertebrates to study locomotor pattern generation.

Serotonin (5-HT) is a neuromodulator that can initiate locomotion in some vertebrates, but not in others. In the rabbit (Viala & Buser, 1969) and the neonatal rat (Cazalets, Squalli-Houssaini, & Clarac, 1992; Kiehn & Kjaerulff, 1996), 5-HT induces alternating rhythmic activity in muscle antagonists. Furthermore, sublesional transplantation of serotonergic brain stem cells into the spinal cord of chronically spinalized rats was shown to activate spinal locomotor networks and to improve locomotion (Feraboli-Lohnherr, Orsal, Yakovleff, Gimenez y Ribotta, & Privat, 1997). However, 5-HT cannot initiate locomotion in the cat (Barbeau & Rossignol, 1991), the lamprey (Harris-Warrick & Cohen, 1985), or the tadpole (Sillar, Wedderburn, & Simmers, 1992). Finally, in some

vertebrates, acetylcholine can cause a strong activation of spinal pattern generators (Cowley & Schmidt, 1994; Panchin, Perrins, & Roberts, 1991). In invertebrates, injection or bath application of neuromodulators to isolated nervous systems elicits locomotion or locomotor-like pattern (summary in Table 5.1). However, we do not at present fully understand what mechanisms underlie such an initiation or whether neuromodulators function to activate locomotor networks *in vivo* (e.g., Pearson, 1993). Evidence from invertebrate systems suggests that neuromodulators might either directly alter cellular properties of specific network neurons (Kleinhaus & Angstadt, 1995; Ramirez & Pearson, 1991a, 1991b), resulting in locomotor activity onset, or activate modulatory pathways external to the locomotor network, successively initiating pattern generation (Katz & Frost, 1995).

Modulation of Ongoing Locomotor Activity

In general, a neuromodulator can alter ongoing locomotor activity by affecting three major parameters of the locomotor pattern: (a) It can change the cycle period of the locomotor pattern; (b) it can change muscle force within each activity cycle by altering the duration and intensity of motoneuronal activity bursts; and (c) it can change the coordination of the activity cycles, not only between different neuron pools driving particular muscles (e.g., within one limb during walking) but also the longitudinal coordination of body segments (e.g., during swimming in aquatic animals).

In vertebrates, noradrenergic pathways particularly affect the duration of the movement cycle. For example, administration of noradrenergic agonists increases spinalized cats' step-cycle length during walking (reviewed in Ribotta et al., 1998). Noradrenaline and its agonists consistently lengthen cycle periods during swimming in amphibian tadpoles (Fischer, Merrywest, & Sillar, 2001; McDearmid, Scrymgeour-Wedderburn, & Sillar, 1997). However, an increased duration of the movement cycles is also mediated by 5-HT and dopamine (Grillner et al., 1995; Kiehn & Kjaerulff, 1996). In a wide range of vertebrates, 5-HT increases the duration and intensity of the activity bursts within each movement cycle—not only in swimming animals, such as the lamprey (Harris-Warrick & Cohen, 1985) and amphibian tadpoles (Sillar et al., 1992), but also in the locomotor systems of walking animals, such as rabbits (Viala & Buser, 1969), rats (Kiehn & Kjaerulff, 1996; Squalli-Houssaini et al., 1993), and cats (Barbeau & Rossignol, 1991). Finally, modulators such as noradrenaline, 5-HT, and dopamine not only influence the longitudinal coordination of the locomotor pattern between successive body segments in swimming animals (Fischer et al., 2001; Grillner et al., 1995), but also shift the activation of particular muscles within a step cycle and thus may alter the complete movement pattern of the limb (Kiehn & Kjaerulff).

In many systems, the effects of neuromodulators are mediated via numerous pharmacologically distinct receptor subclasses (for 5-HT see, e.g., Wedderburn & Sillar, 1994; Wikstrom, Hill, Hellgren, & Grillner, 1995), enabling a multimodal control of the motor pattern. In vertebrates, direct pharmacological activation of, for example, the *adrenoreceptors,* which are defined as putative target receptors for catecholamines such as noradrenaline (e.g., Hirst & Nield, 1980), can modulate motor output (Barbeau & Rossignol, 1991; Forssberg & Grillner, 1973; Kiehn et al.,

1992), with each subclass affecting particular facets of the motor pattern (Fischer et al.; Squalli-Houssaini & Cazalets, 2000).

Neuromodulators Affect Cellular Properties and the Synaptic Efficacy of Network Neurons

Most of the classic neuromodulators exert their effects by changing intrinsic properties of one or a few network neurons or of one or more particular synaptic connections, which affects the overall network output, resulting in a more or less extensive alteration of the motor pattern (discussed previously). For many motor systems, more than one neuromodulatory substance is known (e.g., Grillner, Parker, & El Manira, 1998; Schotland et al., 1995), each of which has distinct effects on the network output (Kiehn & Kjaerulff, 1996; Sillar, Keith, & McDearmid, 1998) and must be coordinated for proper pattern modulation. However, in the majority of motor systems, we are just beginning to understand how such multiple and sometimes even contradictory modulatory inputs are processed and integrated and thus enable a functional pattern modulation. The following sections summarize the most common elementary effects of neuromodulators acting extrinsically on particular cellular and synaptic properties of neurons within locomotor networks (for an in-depth review, see Kiehn & Katz, 1999).

Alteration of Intrinsic Cellular Properties of Network Neurons

Features of neuronal activity such as action potential formation, spike rate, and activity threshold of neurons may vary widely among the different classes of neurons within a network. The shape of a particular type of neuron's characteristic activity pattern in response to synaptic drive depends on intrinsic biophysical membrane parameters, that is, on its set of steady and transient voltage-dependent ionic conductances within the membrane. These intrinsic cellular properties determine (a) membrane resting potential (i.e., the state of excitability of a neuron); (b) burst activity, including SFA (i.e., codetermining the activity period of a neuron); (c) mechanisms underlying membrane bistability (i.e., the ability of plateau potential generation to maintain a prolonged period of activity); and (d) the mechanisms enabling a postinhibitory rebound (PIR) of a neuron (helping to escape a phase of strong inhibition)—all of which may contribute to the basic shaping of the network output. Most of the classic neuromodulators alter such intrinsic cellular properties by affecting one or more transient ionic conductances. An overview is given in Table 5.2.

TABLE 5.2   Effects of Common Neuromodulators on Intrinsic Cellular Properties of Neurons in Locomotor Networks.

Neuromodulator	Cellular Properties Affected	Motor System	Selected References
Serotonin (5-HT)	Membrane resting potential	rat	Hochman & Schmidt (1998)
		embryonic chick	Hayashi et al. (1997)
		tadpole	Sillar & Simmers (1994b)
		molluscs	Straub & Benjamin (2001)
		locust	Parker (1995)
	Spike afterhyperpolarisation (AHP)	lamprey	Wallen et al. (1989)
		locust	Parker (1995)
	Spike narrowing during burst	mollusc	Satterlie et al. (2000)
	Intrinsic oscillatory properties	cat	Hounsgaard et al. (1988)
	and plateau formation	rat	Hochman et al. (1994)
		lamprey	Sigvardt et al. (1985)
		turtle	Hounsgaard & Kiehn (1989)
		tadpole	Sillar & Simmers (1994)
Noradrenaline	Membrane resting potential	rat	Squalli-Houssaini & Cazalets (2000)
		frog	Wohlberg et al. (1986)
Dopamine	Membrane resting potential	mollusc	Lotshaw & Levitan (1988)
	Spike afterhyperpolarisation (AHP)	lamprey	Kemnitz (1997)
	Intrinsic oscillatory properties	cat	Schomburg & Steffens (1996)
	and plateau formation		Conway et al. (1988)
Octopamine	Membrane resting potential	crayfish	Skorupski (1996)
		locust	Sombati & Hoyle (1984)
	Spike afterhyperpolarisation (AHP)	locust	Parker (1996)
	spike ratio	locust	Matheson (1997)
			Bräunig & Eder (1998)
	Plateau formation	locust	Ramirez & Pearson (1991a, 1991b)
Proctoline	spike ratio	crayfish	Barthe et al. (1993)
	Intrinsic oscillatory properties	crayfish	Murchison et al. (1993)

Alteration of Synaptic Transmission Between Network Neurons

Besides their effects on intrinsic cellular properties, neuromodulators can affect synaptic transmission either by targeting presynaptic neurons (i.e., resulting in an altered amount of transmitter release; e.g., Shupliakov, Pieribone, Gad, & Brodin, 1995) or by changing the responses of the postsynaptic cell to a transmitter (e.g., by alterating particular membrane properties; Parker, 1995). In spinal locomotor networks, biogenic amines such as 5-HT and noradrenaline can control locomotor intensity by increasing or decreasing the amount of the inhibitory transmitter released from neurons responsible for the reciprocal coupling between antagonistic motoneuron pools. Strengthening (or weakening) an inhibitory phase between two consecutive movement cycles causes a delayed (or an earlier) onset of activity in the succeeding cycle and thus modulates the cycle duration during ongoing locomotor activity (e.g., Sillar et al., 1998). During locomotor activity, the properties of the synaptic transmission between neurons in a locomotor network can also depend on the connection's activity history (i.e., on the previous cycles of movement in the same episode of locomotion, so-called activity-dependent synaptic plasticity; e.g., Parker & Grillner, 2000). Neuromodulators can affect these activity-dependent properties of a synaptic connection, enabling synaptic *metaplasticity* (reviewed in, e.g., Parker, 2001), which adds a further degree of functional flexibility to the network output. In some cases, neuromodulators can even reverse the sign of a particular synaptic connection (Johnston, Peck, & Harris-Warrick, 1993).

CONCLUSIONS

Research in the field of locomotor control has greatly benefited from studies in lower vertebrates and invertebrates, such as the lamprey and tadpole for swimming pattern generation and the crayfish and stick insect for walking pattern generation. These animal models, in being experimentally well accessible, helped to unravel basic principles for neuronal networks controlling locomotion. However, a major outcome of the past research in various lower and higher animal species is that many of the mechanisms described also contribute to locomotor pattern generation in higher vertebrates (including humans) that are often less accessible experimentally, indicating that common principles appear to underlie the design of locomotor networks in the entire animal kingdom. However, it must be acknowledged that we are still far from completely understanding the mechanisms underlying locomotor network function, even in the few networks that have been characterized in detail on the cellular level. Important issues that must be addressed in the future are (a) the mechanisms underlying descending control and action selection (e.g., changes in gait or locomotor speed and selection of particular locomotor responses); (b) the structure and functioning of pattern-generating networks for terrestrial locomotion, such as walking, including the level of cell-to-cell interaction and mechanisms of coupling limbs, joints, and segments; and (c) interactions among neuromodulatory influences on locomotor patterns and neuronal activity.

Another major outcome of recent locomotor research is that networks are by no means hardwired but are flexible regarding their topology and the properties of the connections between their components. This not only enables a functional flexibility during ongoing behavior but also underlies the ability of these networks to establish locomotor ability during the development of an individual, to maintain locomotion throughout its life span as well as to enable a certain degree of functional recovery (following, e.g., the damage of peripheral nerves and muscles or the CNS). Discovering the mechanisms underlying such adaptive rearrangements in the adult mammalian nervous system is of immediate clinical interest because they are frequently related to functional recovery, and might offer a key to the treatment of patients with injuries of the CNS.

New techniques that were recently established offer experimental access to locomotor systems on levels required to address all these questions. For example, the development of *in vitro* preparations of the spinal cord for mammals opened new perspectives in exploring their complex neuronal networks. Recent advances in neurogenetics, in particular the availability of so-called *knockout mutants,* offer new approaches to studying a wide range of functional levels within motor systems ranging from the role of single molecules (e.g., receptors or transmitters) to much higher levels (e.g., supraspinal processes involved in the generation and control of locomotion).

REFERENCES

Abraham, L. D., Marks, W. B., & Loeb, G. E. (1985). The distal hindlimb musculature of the cat: Cutaneous reflexes during locomotion. *Experimental Brain Research, 58,* 594–603.

Andersson, O., Forssberg, H., Grillner, S., & Lindquist, M. (1978). Phasic gain control of the transmission in cutaneous reflex pathways to motoneurons during "fictive" locomotion. *Brain Research, 149*(2), 503–507.

Andersson, O., & Grillner, S. (1983). Peripheral control of the cat's step cycle. II: Entrainement of the central pattern generators for locomotion by sinusiodal hip movements during fictive locomotion. *Acta Pysiologica Scandinavica, 118,* 229–239.

Armstrong, D. M. (1988). The supraspinal control of mammalian locomotion. *Journal of Physiology, 405,* 1–37.

Arshavsky, Y., Beloozerova, I. N., Orlovsky, G. N., Panchin, Y., & Pavlova, G. A. (1985a). Control of locomotion in marine mollusc *Clione limacina.* I: Efferent activity during actual and fictitious swimming. *Experimental Brain Research, 58*(2), 255–262.

Arshavsky, Y., Beloozerova, I. N., Orlovsky, G. N., Panchin, Y., & Pavlova, G. A. (1985b). Control of locomotion in marine mollusc *Clione limacina.* II: Rhythmic neurons of pedal ganglia. *Experimental Brain Research, 58*(2), 263–272.

Arshavsky, Y., Beloozerova, I. N., Orlovsky, G. N., Panchin, Y., & Pavlova, G. A. (1985c). Control of locomotion in marine mollusc *Clione limacina.* III: On the origin of locomotor rhythm. *Experimental Brain Research, 58*(2), 273–284.

Arshavsky, Y., Beloozerova, I. N., Orlovsky, G. N., Panchin, Y., & Pavlova, G. A. (1985d). Control of locomotion in marine mollusc *Clione limacina.* IV: Role of type 12 interneurons. *Experimental Brain Research, 58*(2), 285–293.

Arshavsky, Y., Beloozerova, I. N., Orlovsky, G. N., Panchin, Y., & Pavlova, G. A. (1985e). Control of locomotion in marine mollusc *Clione limacina.* V: Photoinactivation of efferent neurons. *Experimental Brain Research, 59*(1), 203–205.

Arshavsky, Y., Deliagina, T. G., Orlovsky, G. N., Panchin, Y., Popova, L. B., & Sadreyev, R. I. (1998). Analysis of the central pattern generator for swimming in the mollusk *Clione. Annals of the New York Academy of Sciences, 860,* 51–69.

Arshavsky, Y., Orlovsky, G. N., Panchin, Y., Roberts, A., & Soffe, S. R. (1993). Neuronal control of swimming locomotion: Analysis of the pteropod mollusc *Clione* and embryos of the amphibian *Xenopus. Trends in Neuroscience, 16*(6), 227–233.

Barbeau, H., & Rossignol, S. (1991). Initiation and modulation of the locomotor pattern in the adult chronic spinal cat by noradrenergic, serotonergic and dopaminergic drugs. *Brain Research, 546,* 250–260.

Barbeau, H., & Rossignol, S. (1994). Enhancement of locomotor recovery following spinal cord injury. *Current Opinion in Neurology, 7*(6), 517–524.

Barthe, J. Y., Bevengut, M., & Clarac, F. (1993). In vitro, proctolin and serotonin induced modulations of the abdominal motor system activities in crayfish. *Brain Research, 623,* 101–109.

Barthe, J. Y., & Clarac, F. (1997). Modulation of the spinal network for locomotion by substance P in the neonatal rat. *Experimental Brain Research, 115,* 485–492.

Barthe, J. Y., Mons, N., Cattaert, D., Geffard, M., & Clarac, F. (1989). Dopamine and motor activity in the lobster *Homarus gammarus. Brain Research, 497,* 368–373.

Bässler, U. (1983). *Neural basis of elementary behavior in stick insects.* Berlin: Springer-Verlag.

Bässler, U. (1986). On the definition of central pattern generator and its sensory control. *Biological Cybernetics, 24,* 47–49.

Bässler, U. (1987). Timing and shaping influences on the motor output for walking in the stick insect. *Biological Cybernetics, 55,* 397–401.

Bässler, U. (1988). Functional principles of pattern generation for walking movements of stick insect forelegs: The role of femoral chordotonal organ afferences. *The Journal of Experimental Biology, 136,* 125–147.

Bässler, U. (1993). The femur-tibia control system of stick insects: A model system for the study of the neural basis of joint control. *Brain Research Reviews, 18,* 207–226.

Bässler, U., & Büschges, A. (1998). Pattern generation for stick insect walking movements: Multisensory control of a locomotor program. *Brain Research Reviews, 27*(1), 65–88.

Behrman, A. L., & Harkema, S. J. (2000). Locomotor training after human spinal cord injury: A series of case studies. *Physical Therapy, 80*(7), 688–700.

Beltz, B. S., & Kravitz, E. A. (1987). Physiological identification, morphological analysis, and development of identified serotonin-proctolin containing neurons in the lobster ventral nerve cord. *Journal of Neuroscience, 7,* 533–546.

Bennett, M. R. (1999). The early history of the synapse: From Plato to Sherrington. *Brain Research Bulletin, 50*(2), 95–118.

Bizzi, E., Tresch, M. C., Saltiel, P., & d'Avella, A. (2000). New perspectives on spinal motor systems. *Nature Reviews Neuroscience, 1,* 101–108.

Borst, A., & Egelhaaf, M. (1989). Principles of visual motion detection. *Trends in Neuroscience, 12,* 297–306.

Bouyer, L. J., Whelan, P. J., Pearson, K. G., & Rossignol, S. (2001). Adaptive locomotor plasticity in chronic spinal cats after ankle extensors neurectomy. *Journal of Neuroscience, 21*(10), 3531–3541.

Bowerman, R. F., & Larimer, J. L. (1974a). Command fibres in the circumoesophageal connectives of crayfish. I: Tonic fibres. *The Journal of Experimental Biology, 60,* 95–117.

Bowerman, R. F., & Larimer, J. L. (1974b). Command fibres in the circumoesophageal connectives of crayfish. II: Phasic fibres. *The Journal of Experimental Biology, 60,* 119–134.

Bracken, M. B., Aldrich, E. F., Herr, D. L., Hitchon, P. W., Holford, T. R., Marshall, L. F., Nockels, R. P., Pascale, V., Shepard, M. J., Sonntag, V. K., Winn, H. R., & Young, W. (2000). Clinical measurement, statistical analysis, and risk-benefit: Controversies from trials of spinal injury. *Journal of Trauma 48*(3), 558–561.

Bräunig, P., & Eder, M. (1998). Locust dorsal unpaired median (DUM) neurons directly innervate and modulate hindleg proprioceptors. *The Journal of Experimental Biology, 201,* 3333–3338.

Brodfuehrer, P. D., Debski, E. A., O'Gara, B. A., & Friesen, W. O. (1995). Neuronal control of leech swimming. *Journal of Neurobiology, 27*(3), 403–418.

Brodfuehrer, P. D., & Friesen, W. O. (1986a). Initiation of swimming activity by trigger neurons in the leech subesophageal ganglion. I: Output of Tr1 and Tr2. *Journal of Comparative Physiology A, 159*(4), 489–502.

Brodfuehrer, P. D., & Friesen, W. O. (1986b). Initiation of swimming activity by trigger neurons in the leech subesophageal ganglion. II: Role of segmental swim-initiating interneurons. *Journal of Comparative Physiology A, 159*(4), 503–510.

Brodfuehrer, P. D., & Friesen, W. O. (1986c). Initiation of swimming activity by trigger neurons in the leech subesophageal ganglion. III: Sensory inputs to Tr1 and Tr2. *Journal of Comparative Physiology A, 159*(4), 511–519.

Brown, G. T. (1911). The intrinsic factors in the act of progression in mammals. *Proceedings of the Royal Society of London, B, 84,* 308–319.

Brown, G. T. (1912). The factors in rhythmic activity of the nervous system. *Proceedings of the Royal Society of London, Series B, 85,* 278–289.

Bruehlmeier, M., Dietz, V., Leenders, K. L., Roelcke, U., Missimer, J., & Curt, A. (1998). How does the human brain deal with a spinal cord injury? *European Journal of Neuroscience, 10*(12), 3918–3922.

Buchanan, J. T. (1982). Identification of interneurons with contralateral, caudal axons in the lamprey spinal cord: Synaptic interactions and morphology. *Journal of Neurophysiology, 47*(5), 961–975.

Burke, D., Gillies, J. D., & Lance, J. W. (1970). The quadriceps stretch reflex in human spasticity. *Journal of Neurology, Neurosurgery and Psychiatry, 33*(2), 216–223.

Büschges, A., & El Manira, E. (1998). Sensory pathways and their modulation in the control of locomotion. *Current Opinion in Neurobiology, 8*(6), 733–739.

Büschges, A., Ramirez, J.-M., & Pearson, K. G. (1992). Reorganization of sensory regulation of locust flight after partial deafferentation. *Journal of Neurobiology, 23,* 31–43.

Büschges, A., Ramirez, J.-M., Driesang, R., & Pearson, K. G. (1992). Connections of the forewing tegulae in the locust flight system and their modification following partial deafferentation. *Journal of Neurobiology, 23,* 44–60.

Büschges, A., Sauer, A. E., & Bässler, U. (2000). Adaptive behavior and intelligent systems without symbols and logic. In H. Cruse, J. Dean, & H. Ritter (Eds.), *Prerational intelligence* (Vol. 1, pp. 267–296). Boston: Kluwer.

Büschges, A., Schmitz, J., & Bässler, U. (1995). Rhythmic patterns in the thoracic nerve cord of the stick insect induced by pilocarpine. *The Journal of Experimental Biology, 198,* 435–456.

Büschges, A., & Wolf, H. (1999). Phase-dependent presynaptic modulation of mechanosensory signals in the locust flight system. *Journal of Neurophysiology, 81,* 959–962.

Calancie, B., Needham-Shropshire, B., Jacobs, P., Willer, K., Zych, G., & Green, B. A. (1994). Involuntary stepping after chronic spinal cord injury. *Brain, 117,* 1143–1159.

Cattaert, D., & Le Ray, D. (2001). Adaptive motor control in crayfish. *Progress in Neurobiology, 63*(2), 199–240.

Cazalets, J. R., Borde, M., & Clarac, F. (1995). Localisation and organisation of the central pattern generator for hindlimb locomotion in newborn rats. *Journal of Neurophysiology, 15,* 4943–4951.

Cazalets, J.-R., Squalli-Houssaini, Y., & Clarac, F. (1992). Activation of the central pattern generators for locomotion by serotonin and excitatory aminoacids in neonatal rat. *Journal of Physiology, 455,* 187–204.

Chen, R., Corwell, B., Yaseen, Z., Hallett, M., & Cohen, L. G. (1998). Mechanisms of cortical reorganization in lower-limb amputees. *Journal of Neuroscience, 18*(9), 3443–3450.

Cheng, J., Stein, R. B., Jovanovic, K., Yoshida, K., Bennett, D. J., & Han, Y. (1998). Identification, localization, and modulation of neural networks for walking in the mudpuppy (*Necturus maculatus*) spinal cord. *Journal of Neuroscience, 18*(11), 4295–4304.

Chrachri, A., & Clarac, F. (1989). Induction of rhythmic activity in motoneurons of crayfish thoracic ganglia by cholinergic agonists. *Neuroscience Letters, 77*(1), 49–54.

Chrachri, A., & Clarac, F. (1989). Synaptic connections between motor neurons and interneurons in the fourth thoracic ganglion of the crayfish, *Procambarus clarkii. Journal of Neurophysiology, 62*(6), 1237–1250.

Clarac, F. (1982). Proprioceptive functions of invertebrates. *Journal of Physiology (Paris), 78*(7), 665–680.

Clarac, F., Cattaert, D., & Le Ray, D. (2000). Central control components of a "simple" stretch reflex. *Trends in Neuroscience, 23*(5), 199–208.

Clarac, F., El Manira, A., & Cattaert, D. (1992). Presynaptic control as a mechanism of sensory-motor integration. *Current Opinion in Neurobiology, 2*(6), 764–769.

Conway, B. A., Hultborn, H., & Kiehn, O. (1987). Proprioceptive input resets central locomotor rhythm in the spinal cat. *Experimental Brain Research, 68*(3), 643–656.

Conway, B. A., Hultborn, H., Kiehn, O., & Mintz, I. (1988). Plateau potentials in alpha-motoneurons induced by intravenous injection of L-dopa andclonidine in the spinal cat. *Journal of Physiology, 405,* 369–384.

Cowley, K. C., & Schmidt, B. J. (1994). A comparison of motor patterns induced by N-methyl-D-aspartate, acetylcholine and serotonin in the in vitro neonatal rat spinal cord. *Neuroscience Letters, 171,* 147–150.

Cruse, H. (1990). What mechanisms coordinate leg movement in walking arthropods? *Trends in Neurosciences, 13*(1), 15–21.

Cruse, H., Bartlin, C., Breifert, M., Schmitz, J., Brunn, D. E., Dean, J., & Kindermann, T. (1995). Walking: A complex behaviour controlled by simple networks. *Adaptive Behavior, 3,* 385–418.

Dale, N. (1997). Role of ionic currents in the operation of motor circuits in the *Xenopus.* In P. S. G. Stein, S. Grillner, A. I. Selverston, & D. G. Stuart (Eds.), *Neurons, Networks and Motor Behavior* (pp. 92–96). Cambridge: MIT Press.

Davis, W. J., & Ayers, J. L., Jr. (1972). Locomotion: Control by positive feedback optokinetic responses. *Science, 177,* 183–185.

Degtyarenko, A. M., Simon, E. S., & Burke, R. E. (1996). Differential modulation of disynaptic cutaneous inhibition and excitation in ankle flexor motoneurons during fictive locomotion. *Journal of Neurophysiology, 76*(5), 2972–2985.

De Leon, R. D., Hodgson, J. A., Roy, R. R., & Edgerton, V. R. (1998). Locomotor capacity attributable to step training versus spontaneous recovery after spinalization in adult cats. *Journal of Neurophysiology, 79*(3), 1329–1340.

De Leon, R. D., Hodgson, J. A., Roy, R. R., & Edgerton, V. R. (1999). Retention of hindlimb stepping ability in adult spinal cats after the cessation of step training. *Journal of Neurophysiology, 81*(1), 85–94.

Delcomyn, F. (1980). Neural basis of rhythmic behaviour in animals. *Science, 210,* 492–498.

Dietz, V. (1992). Human neuronal control of automatic functional movements: Interaction between central programs and afferent input. *Physiological Reviews, 72*(1), 33–69.

Dietz, V., Colombo, G., & Jensen, L. (1994). Locomotor activity in spinal man. *Lancet, 344*(8932), 1260–1263.

Dietz, V., & Duysens, J. (2000). Significance of load receptor input during locomotion: A review. *Gait Posture, 11*(2), 102–110.

Dietz, V., Nakazawa, K., Wirz, M., & Erni, T. (1999). Level of spinal cord lesion determines locomotor activity in spinal man. *Experimental Brain Research, 128*(3), 405–409.

Dimitrijevic, M. R., Gerasimenko, Y., & Pinter, M. M. (1998). Evidence for a spinal central pattern generator in humans. *Annals of the New York Academy of Science, 860,* 360–376.

Drew, T., Cabana, T., & Rossignol, S. (1996). Responses of medullary reticulospinal neurons to stimulation of cutaneous limb nerves during locomotion in intact cats. *Experimental Brain Research, 111*(2), 153–168.

Drew, T., Jiang, W., Kably, B., & Lavoie, S. (1996). Role of the motor cortex in the control of visually triggered gait modifications. *Canadian Journal of Physiology and Pharmacology, 74*(4), 426–442.

Duysens, J., Clarac, F., & Cruse, H. (2000). Load-regulating mechanisms in gait and posture: Comparative aspects. *Physiological Reviews, 80*(1), 83–133.

Duysens, J., Loeb, G. E., & Weston, B. J. (1980). Crossed flexor reflex responses and their reversal in freely walking cats. *Brain Research, 197*(2), 538–542.

Duysens, J., Trippel, M., Horstmann, G. A., & Dietz, V. (1990). Gating and reversal of reflexes in ankle muscles during human walking. *Experimental Brain Research, 82*(2), 351–358.

Edgerton, V. R., Grillner, S., Sjöström, A., & Zangger, P. (1976). Central generation of locomotion in vertebrates. In R. M.

Herman, S. Grillner, & D. G. Stuart (Eds.), *Neural control of locomotion* (pp. 439–464). New York: Plenum Press.

El Manira, A., DiCaprio, R. A., Cattaert, D., & Clarac, F. (1991). Monosynaptic interjoint reflexes and their central modulation during fictive locomotion in crayfish. *European Journal of Neuroscience, 3,* 1219–1232.

Fedirchuck, J. R., Nielsen, J., Petersen, N., & Hultborn, H. (1998). Pharmacologically evoked fictive motor patterns in the acutely spinalized marmoset monkey (*Callithrix jacchus*). *Experimental Brain Research, 122,* 351–361.

Feraboli-Lohnherr, D., Orsal, D., Yakovleff, A., Gimenez y Ribotta, M., & Privat, A. (1997). Recovery of locomotor activity in the adult chronic spinal rat after sublesional transplantation of embryonic nervous cells: Specific role of serotonergic neurons. *Experimental Brain Research, 113,* 443–454.

Ferrucci, L., Bandinelli, S., Guralnik, J. M., Lamponi, M., Bertini, C., Falchini, M., & Baroni, A. (1993). Recovery of functional status after stroke: A postrehabilitation follow-up study. *Stroke, 24*(2), 200–205.

Fischer, H., & Ebert, E. (1999). Tegula function during free locust flight in relation to motor pattern, flight speed and aerodynamic output. *The Journal of Experimental Biology, 202,* 711–721.

Fischer, H., Merrywest, S. D., & Sillar, K. T. (2001). Adrenoreceptor-mediated modulation of the spinal locomotor pattern during swimming in *Xenopus laevis* tadpoles. *European Journal of Neuroscience, 13,* 977–986.

Forssberg, H. (1979). Stumbling corrective reaction: A phase-dependent compensatory reaction during locomotion. *Journal of Neurophysiology, 42,* 936–953.

Forssberg, H., & Grillner, S. (1973). The locomotion of the acute spinal cat injected with clonidine i.v. *Brain Research, 50,* 184–186.

Fouad, K., & Pearson, K. G. (1997a). Effects of extensor muscle afferents on the timing of locomotor activity during walking in adult rats. *Brain Research, 749*(2), 320–328.

Fouad, K., & Pearson, K. G. (1997b). Modification of group I field potentials in the intermediate nucleus of the cat spinal cord after chronic axotomy of an extensor nerve. *Neuroscience Letters, 236*(1), 9–12.

Fouad, K., Pedersen, V., Schwab, M. E., & Brösamle, C. (2001). Cervical sprouting of corticospinal fibers after thoracic spinal cord injury accompanies shifts in evoked motor responses. *Current Biology, 11,* 1766–1770.

Friesen, W. O., & Hocker, C. G. (2001). Functional analyses of the leech swim oscillator. *Journal of Neurophysiology, 86*(2), 824–835.

Friesen, W. O., Poon, M., & Stent, G. S. (1978). Neuronal control of swimming in the medicinal leech. IV: Identification of a network of oscillatory interneurons. *The Journal of Experimental Biology, 75,* 25–43.

Gamkrelidze, G. N., Laurienti, P. J., & Blankenship, J. E. (1995). Identification and characterization of cerebral ganglion neurons that induce swimming and modulate swim-related pedal ganglion neurons in *Aplysia brasiliana. Journal of Neurophysiology, 74*(4), 1444–1462.

Gee, C. E., & Robertson, R. M. (1996). Recovery of the flight system following ablation of the tegulae in immature adult locusts. *The Journal of Experimental Biology, 199,* 1395–1403.

Getting, P. A. (1981). Mechanisms of pattern generation underlying swimming in *Tritonia*. I: Neuronal network formed by monosynaptic connections. *Journal of Neurophysiology, 46*(1), 65–79.

Getting, P. A. (1989). Emerging principles governing the operation of neural networks. *Annual Reviews in Neuroscience, 12,* 185–204.

Getting, P. A., Lennard, P. R., & Hume, R. I. (1980). Central pattern generator mediating swimming in *Tritonia*. I: Identification and synaptic interactions. *Journal of Neurophysiology, 44*(1), 151–164.

Gibson, J. J. (1958). Visually controlled locomotion and visual orientation in animals. *British Journal of Psycology, 49,* 182–189.

Goldstein, R. S., & Camhi, J. M. (1991). Different effects of the biogenic amines dopamine, serotonin and octopamine on the thoracic and abdominal portions of the escape circuit in the cockroach. *Journal of Comparative Physiology A, 168,* 103–112.

Grillner, S. (1979). Interaction between central and peripheral mechanisms in the control of locomotion. *Progress in Brain Research, 50,* 227–235.

Grillner, S. (1985). Neurobiological bases of rhythmic motor acts in vertebrates. *Science, 228,* 143–149.

Grillner, S., Cangiano, L., Hu, G., Thompson, R., Hill, R., & Wallen, P. (2000). The intrinsic function of a motor system: From ion channels to networks and behavior. *Brain Research, 886*(1-2), 224–236.

Grillner, S., Deliagina, T., Ekeberg, O., El Manira, A., Hill, R. H., Lansner, A., Orlovsky, G. N., & Wallen, P. (1995). Neural networks that co-ordinate locomotion and body orientation in lamprey. *Trends in Neurosciences, 18*(6), 270–279.

Grillner, S., Parker, D., & El Manira, A. (1998). Vertebrate locomotion: A lamprey perspective. *Annals of the New York Academy of Sciences, 860,* 1–18.

Grillner, S., & Rossignol, S. (1978). On the initiation of the swing phase of locomotion in chronic spinal cats. *Brain Research, 146,* 269–277.

Grillner, S., & Wallen, P. (1985). The ionic mechanisms underlying N-methyl-D-aspartate receptor-induced, tetrodotoxin-resistant membrane potential oscillations in lamprey neurons active during locomotion. *Neuroscience Letters, 60*(3), 289–294.

Grillner, S., Wallen, P., Hill, R., Cangiano, L., & El Manira, A. (2001). Ion channels of importance for the locomotor pattern generation in the lamprey brainstem-spinal cord. *Journal of Physiology, 533*(1), 23–30.

Grillner, S., & Zangger, P. (1975). How detailed is the central pattern generation for locomotion? *Brain Research, 88*(2), 367–371.

Grillner, S., & Zangger, P. (1979). On the central generation of locomotion in the low spinal cat. *Experimental Brain Research, 34*(2), 241–261.

Grimm, K., & Sauer, A. E. (1995). The high number of neurons contributes to the robustness of the locust flight: CPG against parameter variation. *Biological Cybernetics, 72,* 329–335.

Gritsenko, V., Mushahwar, V., & Prochazka, A. (2001). Adaptive changes in locomotor control after partial denervation of triceps surae muscles in the cat. *Journal of Physiology, 533*(1), 299–311.

Guertin, P., Angel, M. J., Perreault, M. C., & McCrea, D. A. (1995). Ankle extensor group I afferents excite extensors throughout the hindlimb during fictive locomotion in the cat. *Journal of Physiology, 487*(1), 197–209.

Gurfinkel, V. S., Levik, Y. S., Kazennikov, O. V., & Selionov, V. A. (1998). Locomotor-like movements evoked by leg muscle vibration in humans. *European Journal of Neuroscience, 10*(5), 1608–1612.

Harris, M. G., & Carre, G. (2001). Is optic flow used to guide walking while wearing a displacing prism? *Perception, 30,* 811–818.

Harris-Warrick, R. M., & Cohen, A. H. (1985). Serotonin modulates the central pattern generator for locomotion in the isolated lamprey spinal cord. *The Journal of Experimental Biology, 116,* 27–46.

Hatsopoulos, N., Gabbiani, F., & Laurent, G. (1995). Elementary computation of object approach by a wide-field visual neuron. *Science, 270,* 1000–1003.

Hayashi, T., Mendelson, B., Phelan, K. D., Skinner, R. D., & Garcia-Rill, E. (1997). Developmental changes in serotonergic receptor-mediated modulation of embryonic chick motoneurons in vitro. *Brain Research and Developmental Brain Research, 10,* 21–33.

Hess, D., & Büschges, A. (1999). Role of proprioceptive signals from an insect femur-tibia joint in patterning motoneuronal activity of an adjacent leg joint. *Journal of Neurophysiology, 81*(4), 1856–1865.

Hiebert, G. W., Whelan, P. J., Prochazka, A., & Pearson, K. G. (1996). Contribution of hind limb flexor muscle afferents to the timing of phase transitions in the cat step cycle. *Journal of Neurophysiology, 75*(3), 1126–1137.

Hille, B. (1991). *Ionic channels of excitable membranes* (3rd ed.). New York: Sinauer Associates.

Hirst, G. D., & Neild, T. O. (1980). Evidence for two populations of excitatory receptors for noradrenaline on arteriolar smooth muscle. *Nature, 283,* 767–768.

Hochman, S., Jordan, L. M., & Schmidt, B. J. (1994). TTX-resistant NMDA-receptor mediated voltage oscillations in mammalian lumbar motoneurons. *Journal of Neurophysiology, 72,* 2559–2562.

Hochman, S., & McCrea, D. A. (1994). Effects of chronic spinalization on ankle extensor motoneurons. II: Motoneuron electrical properties. *Journal of Neurophysiology, 71*(4), 1468–1479.

Hochman, S., & Schmidt, B. J. (1998). Whole cell recordings of lumbar motoneurons during locomotor-like activity in the in vitro neonatal rat spinal cord. *Journal of Neurophysiology, 79,* 743–752.

Hollands, M. A., & Marple-Horvat, D. E. (1996). Visually guided stepping under conditions of step cycle–related denial of visual information. *Experimental Brain Research, 109,* 343–356.

Hollands, M. A., & Marple-Hovat, D. E. (2001). Coordination of eye and leg movements during visually guided stepping. *Journal of Motor Behavior, 33,* 205–216.

Hounsgaard, J., Hultborn, H., Jespersen, B., & Kiehn, O. (1988). Bistability of alpha-motoneurons in the decerebrate cat and in the acute spinal cat after intravenous 5-hydroxytryptophan. *Journal of Physiology, 405,* 345–367.

Hounsgaard, J., & Kiehn, O. (1989). Serotonin-induced bistability of turtle motoneurons caused by a nifedipine-sensitive calcium plateau potential. *Journal of Physiology, 414,* 265–282.

Hughes, G. M. (1957). The co-ordination of insect movements. II: The effect of limb amputation and the cutting of commissures in the cockroach (*Blatta orientalis*). *The Journal of Experimental Biology, 34,* 306–333.

Huntley, G. W. (1997). Correlation between patterns of horizontal connectivity and the extend of short-term representational plasticity in rat motor cortex. *Cerebral Cortex, 7,* 143–156.

Iles, J. N., & Nicolopoulos-Stournaras, S. (1996). Fictive locomotion in the decerebrated rat. *Experimental Brain Research, 109,* 393–398.

Jacobs, K. M., & Donoghue, J. P. (1991). Reshaping the cortical motor map by unmasking latent intracortical connections. *Science, 251,* 944–957.

Jankowska, E., Jukes, M. G., Lund, S., & Lundberg, A. (1967a). The effect of DOPA on the spinal cord. 5: Reciprocal organization of pathways transmitting excitatory action to alpha motoneurons of flexors and extensors. *Acta Physiologica Scandinavica, 70*(3), 369–388.

Jankowska, E., Jukes, M. G., Lund, S., & Lundberg, A. (1967b). The effect of DOPA on the spinal cord. 6: Half-centre organization of interneurons transmitting effects from the flexor reflex afferents. *Acta Physiologica Scandinavica, 70*(3), 389–402.

Jiang, Z., Carlin, K. P., & Brownstone, R. M. (1999). An in vitro functionally mature mouse spinal cord preparation for the study of spinal motor networks. *Brain Research, 816,* 493–499.

Johnston, B. R., Peck, J. H., & Harris-Warrick, R. M. (1993). Dopamine induces sign reversal at mixed chemical-electrical synapses. *Brain Research, 625,* 159–164.

Johnston, R. M., & Levine, R. B. (1996). Crawling motor patterns induced by pilocarpine in isolated larval nerve cords of *Manduca sexta. Journal of Neurophysiology, 76*(5), 3178–3195.

Jordan, L. M., Brownstone, R. M., & Noga, B. R. (1992). Control of functional systems in the brainstem and spinal cord. *Current Opinion in Neurobiology, 2,* 794–801.

Jovanovic, K., Petrov, T., Greer, J. J., & Stein, R. B. (1996). Serotonergic modulation of the mudpuppy (*Necturus maculatus*) locomotor pattern in vitro. *Experimental Brain Research, 111,* 57–67.

Kaczmarek, L. K., & Levitan, I. B. (1987). *Neuromodulation: The biochemical control of neuronal excitability.* New York: Oxford University Press.

Katz, P. S. (1999). What are we talking about? Modes of neuronal communication. In P. S. Katz (Ed.), *Beyond Neurotransmission: Neuromodulation and its importance for information processing* (pp. 1–28). Oxford: Oxford University Press.

Katz, P. S., & Frost, W. N. (1995). Intrinsic neuromodulation in the *Tritonia* swim CPG: Serotonin mediates both neuromodulation and neurotransmission. *Journal of Neurophysiology, 74,* 2281–2294.

Katz, P. S., Getting, P. A., & Frost, W. N. (1994). Dynamic neuromodulation of synaptic strength intrinsic to a central pattern generator circuit. *Nature, 367,* 729–731.

Kemnitz, C. P. (1997). Dopaminergic modulation of spinal neurons and synaptic potentials in the lamprey spinal cord. *Journal of Neurophysiology, 77,* 289–298.

Keshishian, H., & O'Shea, M. (1985). The distribution of a peptide neurotransmitter in the postembryonic grasshopper central nervous system. *Journal of Neuroscience, 5,* 992–1004.

Kiehn, O., Housgaard, J., & Sillar, K. T. (1997). Basic building blocks of vertebrate spinal central pattern generators. In P. S. G. Stein, S. Grillner, A. I. Selverston, & D. G. Stuart (Eds.), *Neurons, networks and motor behaviour* (pp. 47–59). Cambridge: MIT Press.

Kiehn, O., Hultborn, H., & Conway, B. A. (1992). Spinal locomotor activity in acutely spinalized cats induced by intrathecal application of noradrenaline. *Neuroscience Letters, 143,* 243–246.

Kiehn, O., & Katz, P. S. (1999). Making circuits dance: Neuromodulation of motor systems. In P. S. Katz (Ed.), *Beyond neurotransmission* (pp. 275–317). New York: Oxford University Press.

Kiehn, O., & Kjaerulff, O. (1996). Spatiotemporal characteristics of 5-HT and dopamine-induced rhythmic hindlimb activity in the in vitro neonatal rat. *Journal of Neurophysiology, 75,* 1472–1482.

Kiehn, O., & Kjaerulff, O. (1998). Distribution of central pattern generators for rhythmic motor outputs in the spinal cord of limbed vertebrates. *Annals of the New York Academy of Sciences, 860,* 110–129.

Kiehn, O., Sillar, K. T., Kjaerulff, O., & McDearmid, J. R. (1999). Effects of noradrenaline on locomotor rhythm-generating networks in the isolated neonatal rat spinal cord. *Journal of Neurophysiology, 82,* 741–746.

Kjaerulff, O., & Kiehn, O. (1996). Distribution of networks generating and coordinating locomotor activity in the neonatal rat spinal cord. *Journal of Neurophysiology, 775,* 1472–1482.

Kleinhaus, A. L., & Angstadt, J. D. (1995). Diversity and modulation of ionic conductances in leech neurons. *Journal of Neurobiology, 27,* 419–433.

Klintsova, A. Y., & Greenough, W. T. (1999). Synaptic plasticity in cortical systems. *Current Opinion in Neurobiology, 9*(2), 203–208.

Konczak, J. (1994). Effects of optic flow on the kinematics of human gait: A comparison of young and older adults. *Journal of Motor Behavior, 26,* 225–236.

Krapp, H. G. (2000). Neuronal matched filters for optic flow processing in flying insects. In M. Lappe (Ed.), International review of Neurobiology, 44: *Neuronal processing of optic flow.* New York: Academic Press.

Kupfermann, I. (1979). Modulatory actions of neurotransmitters. *Annual Review of Neuroscience, 2,* 447–465.

Kupfermann, I., & Weiss, K. R. (1978). The command neuron concept. *The Behavioral and Brain Sciences, 1,* 3–39.

Kuypers, H. G. J. M., & Huisman, A. M. (1982). The new anatomy of the descending brain pathways. In B. Sjölund & A. Björklund (Eds.), *Brain stem control of spinal mechanisms* (pp. 29–54). Amsterdam: Elsevier Biomedical Press.

Lee, D. N., & Thomson, J. A. (1982). Vision in action: The control of locomotion. In D. J. Ingle, M. A. Goodale, & R. J. W. Mansfield (Eds.), *Analysis of visual behavior* (pp. 411–433). Cambridge: MIT Press.

Levy, W. J., Amassian, V. E., Traad, M., & Cadwell, J. (1990). Focal magnetic coil stimulation reveals motor cortical system reorganized in humans after traumatic quadriplegia. *Brain Research, 510*(1), 130–134.

Lou, J. S., & Bloedel, J. R. (1988). A new conditioning paradigm: Conditioned limb movements in locomoting decerebrate ferrets. *Neurosci Lett, 84,* 185–190.

Lotshaw, D. P., & Levitan, I. B. (1988). Reciprocal modulation of calcium current by serotonin and dopamine in the identified Aplysia neuron R15. *Brain Research, 439,* 64–76.

Lovely, R. G., Gregor, R. J., Roy, R. R., & Edgerton, V. R. (1990). Weight-bearing hindlimb stepping in treadmill-exercised adult spinal cats. *Brain Research, 514*(2), 206–218.

Macpherson, J. M., Fung, J., & Jacobs, R. (1997). Postural orientation, equilibrium, and the spinal cord. *Advances in Neurology, 72,* 227–232.

Mangan, P. S., Cometa, A. K., & Friesen, W. O. (1994). Modulation of swimming behavior in the medicinal leech. IV: Serotonin-induced alteration of synaptic interactions between neurons of the swim circuit. *Journal of Comparative Physiology A, 175,* 723–736.

Marder, E., & Calabrese, R. L. (1996). Principles of rhythmic motor pattern generation. *Physiological Reviews, 76*(3), 687–717.

Matheson, T. (1997). Octopamine modulates the responses and presynaptic inhibition of proprioceptive sensory neurons in the locust *Schistocerca gregaria. The Journal of Experimental Biology, 200,* 1317–1325.

McCrea, D. A., Shefchyk, S. J., Stephens, M. J., & Pearson, K. G. (1995). Disynaptic group I excitation of synergists ankle extensor motoneurons during fictive locomotion in the cat. *Journal of Physiology, 487*(2), 527–539.

McDearmid, J. R., Scrymgeour-Wedderburn, J. F., & Sillar, K. T. (1997). Aminergic modulation of glycine release in a spinal network controlling swimming in *Xenopus laevis. Journal of Physiology, 503,* 111–117.

Meinertzhagen, I. A. (2001). Plasticity in the insect nervous system. *Advances in Insect Physiology, 28,* 84–167.

Mesce, K. A., Crisp, K. M., & Gilchrist, L. S. (2001). Mixtures of octopamine and serotonin have nonadditive effects on the CNS of the medicinal leech. *Journal of Neurophysiology, 85,* 2039–2046.

Mori, S., Matsuyama, K., Kohyama, J., Kobayashi, Y., & Takakusaki, K. (1992). Neuronal constituents of postural and locomotor control systems and their interactions in cats. *Brain Development, 14*(20), 109–120.

Mulloney, B., Acevedo, L. D., & Bradbury, A. G. (1987). Modulation of the crayfish swimmeret rhythm by octopamine and the neuropeptide proctolin. *Journal of Neurophysiology, 58,* 584–597.

Murchison, D., Chrachri, A., & Mulloney, B. (1993). A separate local pattern-generating circuit controls the movements of each swimmeret in crayfish. *Journal of Neurophysiology, 70,* 2620–2631.

Nelson, S. G., & Mendell, L. M. (1979). Enhancement in Ia-motoneuron synaptic transmission caudal to chronic spinal cord transection. *Journal of Neurophysiology, 42,* 642–654.

Nudo, R. J., Milliken, G. W., Jenkins, W. M., & Merzenich, M. M. (1996). Use-dependent alterations of movement representations in primary motor cortex of adult squirrel monkeys. *Journal of Neuroscience, 16,* 785–807.

Nusbaum, M. P., El Manira, A., Gossard, J.-P., & Rossignol, S. (1997). Presynaptic mechanisms during rhythmic activity in vertebrates and invertebrates. In P. S. G. Stein, S. Grillner, A. I. Serlverston, & D. G. Stuart (Eds.), *Neurons, networks, and behavior* (pp. 225–235). Cambridge: MIT Press.

Orlovsky, G. N., Deliagina, T. G., & Grillner, S. (1999). *Neuronal control of locomotion.* Oxford: Oxford University Press.

Orlovsky, G. N., Deliagina, T. G., & Wallen, P. (1992). Vestibular control of swimming in lamprey. I: Responses of reticulospinal neurons to roll and pitch. *Experimental Brain Research, 90*(3), 479–488.

Panchin, Y., Perrins, R. J., & Roberts, A. (1991). The action of acetylcholine on the locomotor central pattern generator for swimming in *Xenopus* embryos. *The Journal of Experimental Biology, 161,* 527–531.

Pang, M. Y. C., & Yang, J. F. (2000). The initiation of the swing phase in human infant stepping: Importance of hip position and leg loading. *Journal of Physiology, 528.2,* 389–404.

Parker, D. (1995). Serotonergic modulation of locust motor neurons. *Journal of Neurophysiology, 73,* 923–932.

Parker, D. (2001). Spinal cord plasticity: Independent and interactive effects of neuromodulator and activity-dependent plasticity. *Molecular Neurobiology, 22,* 55–80.

Parker, D., & Grillner, S. (1999). Long-lasting substance-P-mediated modulation of NMDA-induced rhythmic activity in the lamprey locomotor network involves separate RNA- and protein-synthesis-dependent stages. *European Journal of Neuroscience, 11,* 1515–1522.

Parker, D., & Grillner, S. (2000). The activity-dependent plasticity of segmental and intersegmental synaptic connections in the lamprey spinal cord. *European Journal of Neuroscience, 12,* 2135–2146.

Patla, A. E., Adkin, A., Martin, C., Holden, R., & Prentice, S. (1996). Characteristics of voluntary visual sampling of the environment for safe locomotion over different terrains. *Experimental Brain Research, 112,* 513–522.

Patla, A. E., & Vickers, J. N. (1997). Where and when do we look as we approach and step over an obstacle in the travel path? *Neuroreport, 8,* 3661–3665.

Pearson, K. G. (1985). Are there central pattern generators for walking and flight in insects? In W. J. P. Barnes & M. Gladden (Eds.), *Feedback and motor control in invertebrates and vertebrates* (pp. 307–316). London: Croom-Helm.

Pearson, K. G. (1993). Common principles of motor control in vertebrates and invertebrates. *Annual Reviews in Neuroscience, 16,* 265–297.

Pearson, K. G. (1995). Proprioceptive regulation of locomotion. *Current Opinion in Neurobiology, 5*(6), 786–791.

Pearson, K. G. (2000). Neural adaptation in the generation of rhythmic behavior. *Annual Reviews of Physiology, 62*(1), 723–753.

Pearson, K. G. (2001). Could enhanced reflex function contribute to improving locomotion after spinal cord repair? *Journal of Physiology, 533*(1), 75–81.

Pearson, K. G., & Duysens, J. E. J. (1976). Functions of segmental reflexes in the control of stepping in cockroaches and cats. In R. E. Herman, S. Grillner, D. Stuart, & P. Stein (Eds.), *Neural control in locomotion* (pp. 519–538). New York: Plenum Press.

Pearson, K. G., Fouad, K., & Misiaszek, J. E. (1999). Adaptive changes in motor activity associated with functional recovery following muscle denervation in walking cats. *Journal of Neurophysiology, 82*(1), 370–381.

Pearson, K. G., Heitler, W. J., & Steeves, J. D. (1980). Triggering of locust jump by multimodal inhibitory interneurons. *Journal of Neurophysiology, 43,* 257–278.

Pearson, K. G., & Ramirez, J.-M. (1992). Parallels with other invertebrate and vertebrate motor systems. In R. M. Harris-Warrick, E. Marder, A. I. Selverston, & M. Moulins (Eds.), *Dynamic biological networks* (pp. 263–281). Cambridge: MIT Press.

Pearson, K. G., & Ramirez, J.-M. (1997). Sensory modulation of pattern-generating circuits. In P. S. G. Stein, S. Grillner, A. I. Serlverston, & D. G. Stuart (Eds.), *Neurons, networks, and behavior* (pp. 225–235). Cambridge: MIT Press.

Perrins, R., & Roberts, A. (1995a). Cholinergic contribution to excitation in a spinal locomotor central pattern generator in *Xenopus* embryos. *Journal of Neurophysiology, 73,* 1005–1012.

Perrins, R., & Roberts, A. (1995b). Cholinergic and electrical motoneuron-to-motoneuron synapses contribute to on-cycles excitation during swimming in Xenopus embryos. *Journal of Neurophysiology, 73,* 1013–1019.

Perrins, R., & Roberts, A. (1995c). Cholinergic and electrical synapses between synergistic spinal motoneurons in the Xenopus *laevis* embryo. *Journal of Physiology, 485,* 135–144.

Pflüger, A. (1853). *Die sensorischen Funktionen des Rückenmarks der Wirbelthiere nebst einer neuen Lehre über die Leitungsgesetze der Reflexionen.* Berlin.

Poon, M., Friesen, W. O., & Stent, G. S. (1978). Neuronal control of swimming in the medicinal leech. V: Connexions between the oscillatory interneurons and the motor neurons. *The Journal of Experimental Biology, 75,* 45–63.

Prochazka, A. (1996a). The fuzzy logic of visuomotor control. *Canadian Journal of Physiology and Pharmacology, 74*(4), 456–462.

Prochazka, A. (1996b). Proprioceptive feedback and movement regulation. In L. Rowell & J. T. Shepherd (Eds.), *Handbook of physiology* (pp. 89–127). New York: Oxford University Press.

Prochazka, A., & Mushahwar, V. K. (2001). Spinal cord function and rehabilitation: An overview. *Journal of Physiology, 533*(1), 3–4.

Prokop, T., Schubert, M., & Berger, W. (1997). Visual influence on human locomotion: Modulation of changes in optic flow. *Experimental Brain Research, 114,* 63–70.

Raineteau, O., & Schwab, M. E. (2001). Plasticity of motor systems after incomplete spinal cord injury. *Nature Reviews Neuroscience, 2*(4), 263–273.

Ramirez, J.-M., & Pearson, K. G. (1991a). Octopamine induces bursting and plateau potentials in insect neurons. *Brain Research, 549,* 332–337.

Ramirez, J.-M., & Pearson, K. G. (1991b). Octopaminergic modulation of interneurons in the flight system of the locust. *Journal of Neurophysiology, 66,* 1522–1537.

Reichardt, W. (1969). Movement perception in insects. In W. Reichardt (Ed.), *Processing of optical data by organisms and by machines* (pp. 465–493). New York: Academic Press.

Ribotta, M. G., Orsal, D., Ferboli-Lohnherr, D., & Privat, A. (1998). Recovery of locomotion following transplantation of mono-aminergic neurons in the spinal cord of paraplegic rats. *Annals of the New York Academy of Sciences, 860,* 393–411.

Rind, F. C., & Simmons, P. J. (1992). Orthopteran DCMD neurons: A reevaluation of responses to moving objects. I. Selective responses to approaching objects. *Journal of Neurophysiology, 68,* 1654–1682.

Roberts, A. (1990). How does a nervous system produce behaviour? A case study in neurobiology. *Scientific Progress (Oxford), 74,* 31–51.

Roberts, A. (2000). Early functional organization of spinal neurons in developing lower vertebrates. *Brain Research Bulletin, 53*(5), 585–593.

Roberts, A., Dale, N., Evoy, W. H., & Soffe, S. R. (1985). Synaptic potentials in motoneurons during fictive swimming in spinal Xenopus embryos. *Journal of Neurophysiology, 54*(1), 1–10.

Robertson, R. M., & Pearson, K. G. (1983). Interneurons in the flight system of the locust: Distribution, connections, and resetting properties. *Journal of Comparative Neurology, 215*(1), 33–50.

Robertson, R. M., & Pearson, K. G. (1985). Neural circuits in the flight system of the locust. *Journal of Neurophysiology, 53*(1), 110–128.

Ronacher, B., Wolf, H., & Reichert, H. (1988). Locust flight behaviour after hemisection of individual thoracic ganglia: Evidence for hemiganglionic premotor centers. *Journal of Comparative Physiology A, 163,* 749–759.

Rossignol, S. (1996a). Neural control of stereotypic limb movements. In L. B. Rowell & J. T. Sheperd (Eds.), *Handbook of physiology* (pp. 173–216). New York: Oxford University Press.

Rossignol, S. (1996b). Visuomotor regulation of locomotion. *Journal of Physiology and Pharmacology, 74,* 418–425.

Rossignol, S. (2000). Locomotion and its recovery after spinal injury. *Current Opinion in Neurobiology, 10*(6), 708–716.

Rossignol, S., Chau, C., Brunstein, E., Giroux, N., Boyer, L., Barbeau, H., & Reader, T. A. (1998). Pharmacological activation and modulation of the central pattern generator for locomotion in the cat. *Annals of the New York Academy of Sciences, 860,* 346–359.

Rowell, C. H. F., O'Shea, M., & Williams, J. L. D. (1977). The neuronal basis of a sensory analyser: The acridid movement detector system. *The Journal of Experimental Biology, 68,* 157–185.

Rushton, S. K., Harris, J. M., Lloyd, M. R., & Wann, J. P. (1998). Guidance of locomotion of foot uses perceived target location rather than optic flow. *Current Biology, 8,* 1191–1194.

Ryckebusch, S., & Laurent, G. (1993). Rhythmic patterns evoked in locust leg motor neurons by the muscarinic agonist pilocarpine. *Journal of Neurophysiology, 69,* 1583–1595.

Satterlie, R. A., Norekian, T. P., & Pirtle, T. J. (2000). Serotonin-induced spike narrowing in a locomotor pattern generator permits increases in cycle frequency during accelerations. *Journal of Neurophysiology, 83,* 2163–2170.

Satterlie, R. A., & Spencer, A. N. (1985). Swimming in the Pteropod Mollusk, Clione-Limacina. 2. Physiology. *The Journal of Experimental Biology, 116,* 205–232.

Sbordone, R. J., Liter, J. C., & Pettler-Jennings, P. (1995). Recovery of function following severe traumatic brain injury: A retrospective 10-year follow-up. *Brain Injury, 9*(3), 285–299.

Schomburg, E. D., & Steffens, H. (1996). Bistable characteristics of motoneuron activity during DOPA induced fictive locomotion in spinal cats. *Neuroscience Research, 26,* 47–56.

Schotland, J., Shupliakov, O., Wikstrom, M., Brodin, L., Srinivasan, M., You, Z. B., Herrera-Marschitz, M., Zhang, W., Hokfelt, T., & Grillner, S. (1995). Control of lamprey locomotor neurons by colocalized monoamine transmitters. *Nature, 374,* 266–268.

Schwindt, P. C., & Crill, W. E. (1984). Membrane properties of the cat spinal motoneurons. In R. A. Davidoff (Ed.), *Handbook of the spinal cord* (pp. 199–242). New York: Marcel Dekker.

Segal, R. L., & Wolf, S. L. (1994). Operant conditioning of spinal stretch reflexes in patients with spinal cord injuries. *Experimental Neurology, 130*(2), 202–213.

Sherrington, C. S. (1900a). The muscular sense. In E. A. Schäfer (Ed.), *Textbook of physiology* (Vol. 2, pp. 1002–1025). Edinburgh:

Sherrington, C. S. (1900b). On the innervation of antagonistic muscles (sixth note). *Proceedings of the Royal Society, 66,* 60–67.

Sherrington, C. S. (1905a). On reciprocal innervation of antagonistic muscles (seventh note). *Proceedings of the Royal Society, 76B,* 160–163.

Sherrington, C. S. (1905b). On the reciprocal innervation of antagonistic muscles (eighth note). *Proceedings of the Royal Society, 76B,* 269–279.

Sherrington, C. S. (1910). Flexor reflex of the limb, crossed extension reflex, and reflex stepping and standing. *Journal of Physiology (London), 40,* 28–121.

Shupliakov, O., Pieribone, V. A., Gad, H., & Brodin, L. (1995). Synaptic vesicle depletion in reticulospinal axons is reduced by 5-hydroxytryptamine: Direct evidence for presynaptic modulation of glutamatergic transmission. *European Journal of Neuroscience, 7,* 1111–1116.

Sigvardt, K. A., Grillner, S., Wallen, P., & Van, D. P. (1985). Activation of NMDA receptors elicits fictive locomotion and bistable membrane properties in the lamprey spinal cord. *Brain Research, 336,* 390–395.

Sillar, K. T., Clarac, F., & Bush, B. M. H. (1987). Intersegmental coordination of central neural oscillators for rhythmic movements of the walking legs of crayfish, *P. lenisculus. The Journal of Experimental Biology, 131,* 245–264.

Sillar, K. T., Reith, C. A., & McDearmid, J. R. (1998). Development and aminergic neuromodulation of a spinal locomotor network controlling swimming in *Xenopus* larvae. *Annals of the New York Academy of Sciences, 860,* 318–332.

Sillar, K. T., & Simmers, A. J. (1994a). 5HT induces NMDA receptor-mediated intrinsic oscillations in embryonic amphibian spinal neurons. *Proceedings of the Royal Society of London B, 255,* 139–145.

Sillar, K. T., & Simmers, A. J. (1994b). Oscillatory membrane properties of spinal cord neurons that are active during fictive swimming in *Rana temporaria* embryos. *European Journal of Morphology, 32,* 185–192.

Sillar, K. T., Skorupski, P., Elson, R. C., & Bush, B. M. H. (1986). Two identified afferent neurons entrain a central locomotor rhythm generator. *Nature, 323,* 440–443.

Sillar, K. T., Wedderburn, J. F., & Simmers, A. J. (1992). Modulation of swimming rhythmicity by 5-hydroxytryptamine during post-embryonic development in *Xenopus laevis. Proceedings of the Royal Society London B, 250,* 107–114.

Sinkjaer, T., Andersen, J. B., Ladouceur, M., Christensen, L. O., & Nielsen, J. B. (2000). Major role for sensory feedback in soleus EMG activity in the stance phase of walking in man. *Journal of Physiology, 523*(3), 817–827.

Skorupski, P. (1996). Octopamine induces steady-state reflex reversal in crayfish thoracic ganglia. *Journal of Neurophysiology, 76,* 93–108.

Soffe, S. R. (1991). Triggering and gating of motor responses by sensory stimulation: Behavioral selection in *Xenopus* embryos. *Proceedings of the Royal Society of London B, Biological Sciences, 246,* 197–203.

Soffe, S. R., Clarke, J. D., & Roberts, A. (1984). Activity of commissural interneurons in spinal cord of *Xenopus* embryos. *Journal of Neurophysiology, 51*(6), 1257–1267.

Sombati, S., & Hoyle, G. (1984). Generation of specific behaviors in a locust by local release into neuropil of the natural neuromodulator octopamine. *Journal of Neurobiology, 15,* 481–506.

Speach, D. P., & Dombovy, M. L. (1995). Recovery from stroke: Rehabilitation. *Baillieres Clinical Neurology, 4*(2), 317–338.

Squalli-Houssaini, Y., & Cazalets, J.-R. (2000). Noradrenergic control of locomotor networks in the vitro spinal cord of the neonatal rat. *Brain Research, 852,* 100–109.

Squalli-Houssaini, Y., Cazalets, J. R., & Clarac, F. (1993). Oscillatory properties of the central pattern generator for locomotion in neonatal rats. *Journal of Neurophysiology, 70,* 803–813.

Stent, G. S., Kristan, W. B., Jr., Friesen, W. O., Ort, C. A., Poon, M., & Calabrese, R. L. (1978). Neuronal generation of the leech swimming movement. *Science, 200,* 1348–1357.

Stephens, M. J., & Yang, J. F. (1999). Loading during the stance phase of walking in humans increases the extensor EMG amplitude but does not change the duration of the step cycle. *Experimental Brain Research, 124*(3), 363–370.

Stevenson, P. A., & Sporhase-Eichmann, U. (1995). Localization of octopaminergic neurons in insects. *Comparative Biochemistry and Physiology A, Physiology, 110*(3), 203–215.

Stoffregen, T. A., Schmuckler, M. A., & Gibson, E. J. (1987). Use of central and peripheral optical flow in stance and locomotion in young walkers. *Perception, 16*(1), 113–119.

Straub, V. A., & Benjamin, P. R. (2001). Extrinsic modulation and motor pattern generation in a feeding network: A cellular study. *Journal of Neuroscience, 21,* 1767–1778.

Strausfeld, N. J., & Nässel, D. R. (1981). Neuroarchitecture of brain regions that subserve the compound eyes of crustacea and insects. In H. Autrum (Ed.), *Comparative physiology and evolution of vision in invertebrates* (Vol. 2, part 6B, pp. 1–132). Berlin: Springer.

Sun, H.-J., Carey, D. P., & Goodale, M. A. (1992). A mammalian model of optic-flow utilization in the control of locomotion. *Experimental Brain Research, 91,* 171–175.

Tillakaratne, N. J., Mouria, M., Ziv, N. B., Roy, R. R., Edgerton, V. R., & Tobin, A. J. (2000). Increased expression of glutamate decarboxylase (GAD(67)) in feline lumbar spinal cord after complete thoracic spinal cord transection. *J Neurosci Res, 60*, 219–230.

Ullen, F., Deliagina, T. G., Orlovsky, G. N., & Grillner, S. (1996). Visual potentiation of vestibular responses in lamprey reticulospinal neurons. *European Journal of Neuroscience, 8*(11), 2298–2307.

van Mier, P., Joosten, H. W., van Rheden, R., & ten Donkelaar, H. J. (1986). The development of serotonergic raphespinal projections in *Xenopus laevis. International Journal of Developmental Neurosciences, 4*, 465–475.

Viala, D., & Buser, P. (1969). The effects of DOPA and 5-HTP on rhythmic efferent discharges in hindlimb nerves in the rabbit. *Brain Research, 12*, 437–443.

Waldron, I. (1967). Mechanisms for the production of the motor output pattern in flying locusts. *The Journal of Experimental Biology, 47*, 201–212.

Wallen, P., Buchanan, J. T., Grillner, S., Hill, R. H., Christenson, J., & Hokfelt, T. (1989). Effects of 5-hydroxytryptamine on the afterhyperpolarization, spike frequency regulation, and oscillatory membrane properties in lamprey spinal cord neurons. *Journal of Neurophysiology, 61*, 759–768.

Warren, H. W., Kay, B. A., Zosh, W. D., Duchon, A. P., & Sahuc, S. (2001). Optic flow is used to control human walking. *Nature Neuroscience, 4*(2), 213–216.

Wedderburn, J. F., & Sillar, K. T. (1994). Modulation of rhythmic swimming activity in post-embryonic *Xenopus laevis* tadpoles by 5-hydroxytryptamine acting at 5HT1a receptors. *Proceedings of the Royal Society of London B, 257*, 59–66.

Weidner, N., Ner, A., Salimi, N., & Tuszynski, M. H. (2001). Spontaneous corticospinal axonal plasticity and functional recovery after adult central nervous system injury. *Proceedings of the National Academy of Science, 98*(6), 3513–3518.

Wendler, G. (1964). Laufen und Stehen der Stabheuschrecke Carausius morosus: Sinnesborstenfelder in den Beingelenken als Glieder von Regelkreisen. *Z. vergl. Physiol., 48*, 198–250.

Wernig, A., & Muller, S. (1992). Laufband locomotion with body weight support improved walking in persons with severe spinal cord injuries. *Paraplegia, 30*(4), 229–238.

Whelan, P. J., Hiebert, G. W., & Pearson, K. G. (1995a). Plasticity of the extensor group I pathway controlling the stance to swing transition in the cat. *Journal of Neurophysiology, 74*(6), 2782–2787.

Whelan, P. J., Hiebert, G. W., & Pearson, K. G. (1995b). Stimulation of the group I extensor afferents prolongs the stance phase in walking cats. *Experimental Brain Research, 103*, 20–30.

Wikstrom, M., Hill, R., Hellgren, J., & Grillner, S. (1995). The action of 5-HT on calcium-dependent potassium channels and on the spinal locomotor network in lamprey is mediated by 5-HT1A-like receptors. *Brain Research, 678*, 191–199.

Wilson, D. M. (1961). The central nervous control of flight in a locust. *The Journal of Experimental Biology, 38*, 471–490.

Wilson, D. M. (1966). Insect walking. *Annual Review of Entomology, 11*, 103–122.

Wohlberg, C. J., Hackman, J. C., & Davidoff, R. A. (1987). Epinephrine and norepinephrine modulate neuronal responses to excitatory amino acids antagonists in frog spinal cord. *Synapse, 1*, 202–207.

Wolf, H., & Büschges, A. (1997). Plasticity of synaptic connections in sensory-motor pathways of the adult locust flight system. *Journal of Neurophysiology, 78*, 1276–1284.

Wolf, H., & Pearson, K. G. (1988). Proprioceptive input patterns elevator activity in the locust flight system. *Journal of Neurophysiology, 59*, 1831–1853.

Wolpaw, J. R. (1997). The complex structure of a simple memory. *Trends in Neuroscience, 20*(12), 588–594.

Wood, R. M., Harvey, M. A., Young, C. E., Beedie, A., & Wilson, T. (2000). Weighting to go with the flow? *Current Biology, 10*, 545–546.

Wu, C. W., & Kaas, J. H. (1999). Reorganization in primary motor cortex of primates with long-standing therapeutic amputations. *Journal of Neuroscience, 19*(17), 7679–7697.

Yakovleff, A., Roby-Brami, A., Guezard, B., Mansour, H., Bussel, B., & Privat, A. (1989). Locomotion in rats transplanted with noradrenergic neurons. *Brain Research Bulletin, 22*, 115–121.

Yang, J. F., & Stein, R. B. (1990). Phase-dependent reflex reversal in human leg muscles during walking. *Journal of Neurophysiology, 63*(5), 1109–1117.

Yang, J. F., Stein, R. B., & James, K. B. (1991). Contribution of peripheral afferents to the activation of the soleus muscle during walking in humans. *Experimental Brain Research, 87*(3), 679–687.

Zhao, F.-Y., & Roberts, A. (1998). Assessing the roles of glutamatergic and cholinergic synaptic drive in the control of fictive swimming frequency in young *Xenopus* tadpoles. *Journal of Comparative Physiology A, 183*, 753–758.

CHAPTER 6

Visual Processing in the Primate Brain

TATIANA PASTERNAK, JAMES W. BISLEY, AND DAVID CALKINS

The visual system is the most widely studied and perhaps the best understood mammalian sensory system. Not only have the details of its anatomical features been well described, but the behavior of its neurons have also been characterized at many stages of the neural pathway. For this reason, the visual system has also become the system of choice for the study of sensory coding and of such higher cognitive processes as memory and attention. In this chapter we focus on the visual system of nonhuman primates, because in the past 10–15 years it has been extensively studied and because nonhuman primates provide an excellent animal model for understanding human vision.

THE RETINA

Our visual world is complex and dynamic. To successfully interpret this world the visual system performs the analysis of various attributes of the visual image and then integrates these attributes into a percept of a visual scene. The most fundamental characteristic of our visual world is that it is not uniform in time and space, and the visual system is well designed to analyze these nonuniformities. Such fundamental dimensions of visual stimuli as spatial and temporal variations in luminance and chromaticity are encoded at the level of the retina, whereas the encoding of other more complex stimulus features such as motion, complex forms, and depth emerge at the level of the visual cortex.

The Retinal Image

The retina is the sheet of neural tissue—some 0.3–0.4 mm thick (300–400 μm) and about 520 mm^2 in area—that lines the back portion of the eye where the image of light rays focused through the cornea and lens is formed. Because the eye is first and foremost an optical system, this image on the retina is measured in terms of visual angle, which is the angle formed by rays emanating from an object to their point of focus near the back surface of the lens (the so-called *nodal point;* for review, see Rodieck, 1998; Wandell, 1995). Rays diverging from the nodal point form the same angle as they impinge on the retina. Thus, the length and height of the retinal image formed by objects of different size and distance in the physical world will be the same if the visual angles formed by those objects are the same. These dimensions depend critically on the size of the eye. The macaque eye is roughly 67% of the size of the human eye, and the distance on the retina that corresponds to one degree of visual angle is therefore about 67% of that for the human retina—200 μm versus 290 μm (Drasdo & Fowler, 1974). Thus, how far eccentric an object on the retina is from the point of central fixation can be described using this simple conversion either by the angle in visual degrees that object makes with the fixation point or by its distance from this point in μm (or mm). The point of central fixation on the retina corresponds to the *fovea,* an area about 1.5 mm (or 7°) in diameter, specialized for the best possible optical path and high acuity (discussed later in this chapter). Eccentricity on the retina is therefore measured with respect to the center point of the fovea. The conversion between linear distance and visual angle depends somewhat on eccentricity due to changes in the eye's optics, especially for eccentricities greater than 50° or so (Drasdo & Fowler, 1974).

Retinal Design

Because of its location in the eye, the retina is often misconstrued as a peripheral structure—more a part of the eye than of the brain. In fact, the retina is an extension of the central nervous system, much like the olfactory bulb. Like the rest of the brain, the retina comprises a great diversity of neuronal cell types (approximately 60–70) distributed across five classes of neuron within six primary layers (Figure 6.1). A tremendous degree of specialization for functional circuitry is therefore obtained by permuting these types in different combinations (reviewed in Masland & Raviola, 2000).

The basic architecture of the vertebrate retina includes (a) an array of *photoreceptors* (the input element) that transduces absorbed light into electrical activity and (b) an array of *ganglion cells* that encodes this activity as a train of action potentials carried along axonal fibers of the optic nerve. The macaque retina contains about 50 million photoreceptors that converge through layers of retinal circuitry upon some 1.5 million ganglion cells (Curcio, Packer, & Hendrickson, 1989; Rodieck, 1988). The output of the photoreceptor mosaic is carried to the ganglion cells via parallel and iterative circuits composed of serial connections between a variety of both excitatory and inhibitory interneurons (Figure 6.2). The activity of a ganglion cell at a particular moment in its physiological history is therefore the confluence of all excitation and inhibition in its presynaptic circuitry. Excitation in and from the retina is conveyed primarily through the so-called

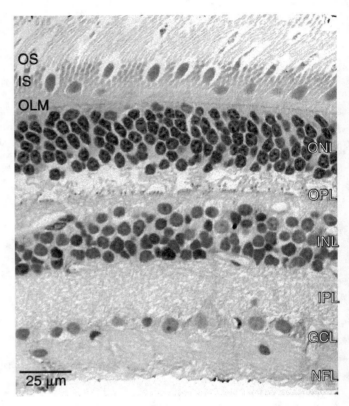

Figure 6.1 Photomicrograph of radial section through macaque (*Macaca fascicularis*) retina demonstrating major cellular layers and structures. The thin, pigment-containing outer segment (OS) and thicker, light-funneling inner segment (IS) of each photoreceptor is separated from the cell body by the outer limiting membrane (OLM), which stabilizes the photoreceptor layer as it penetrates the retinal pigment epithelium (not shown). The outer (closest to the brain) and inner (closest to the lens of the eye) retina are each comprised of a *nuclear* layer, containing cell bodies, and a *plexiform* layer, containing intermingled axons and dendrites of cells forming synaptic contacts with one another. The outer nuclear layer (ONL) contains the cell bodies of the photoreceptors, which send their axon terminals to the outer plexiform layer (OPL) to contact the postsynaptic processes of bipolar and horizontal cells. The inner nuclear layer (INL) contains the cell bodies of horizontal cells—closest to the OPL—and the cell bodies of bipolar and amacrine cells, which send their axonal processes to the inner plexiform layer (IPL), where they contact one another and the dendrites of ganglion cells. The ganglion cell layer (GCL) contains the cell bodies of the ganglion cells (and some displaced amacrine cells), whereas the nerve fiber layer (NFL) contains the axons of the ganglion cells on their way to the optic nerve.

feed-forward circuit from photoreceptors to ganglion cells via a class of intermediate neurons called *bipolar cells.* In mammalian retina, this circuit is entirely *glutamatergic*—each element transmits information from its axon terminal to the next level of processing by the release of glutamate (Massey, 1990). Inhibition within the retina, in contrast, is conveyed primarily through two levels of so-called feedback circuits. In the outer retina, *horizontal cells* collect excitation from a large number of photoreceptors (discussed later in this chapter) and provide inhibition proportionally back to the photoreceptors

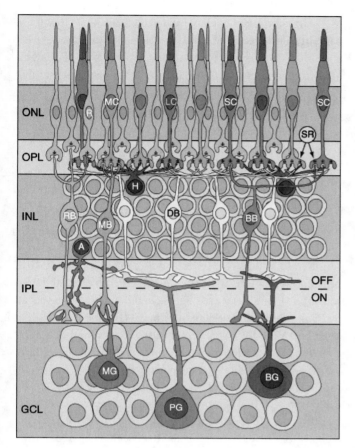

Figure 6.2 Schematic diagram of a macaque retina indicating major cell types and their circuits. Each photoreceptor synapse is marked by a dense synaptic ribbon that facilitates the release of glutamate from the axon terminal. Rod photoreceptors (R) send their signals to a specialized amacrine cell (A) via a single type of rod bipolar cell (RB). Middle-wavelength sensitive cones (MC) and long-wavelength sensitive cones (LC) both contact midget ganglion cells (MG) via a narrow-field midget bipolar cell (MB) and parasol ganglion cells (PG) via large-field diffuse bipolar cells (DB). Short-wavelength cones (SC) send signals for blue color vision to a specialized bistratified ganglion cell (BG) via the so-called blue cone bipolar cell (BB). Inhibitory horizontal cells (H) collect signals from photoreceptors over a large area and make feedback contacts both to the photoreceptors and to the bipolar cells. The IPL is subdivided into an OFF region—for contacts between cells used in signaling light decrements from the mean—and an ON region—for contacts between cells used in signaling light increments from the mean. Other abbreviations are the same as those in Figure 6.1.

processing. Cells within a type form a continuous mosaic that determines the spacing between cells and their sampling density (typically expressed as cells mm^{-2} or as cells deg^{-2}) as a function of eccentricity. With increasing eccentricity, the density of the mosaics for most retinal neurons decreases (with some notable exceptions) as the spacing between neurons increases. For example, ganglion cell density peaks in the fovea at about 60,000 cells mm^{-2} and falls to 10,000 cells mm^{-2} at 20° and to 1,000 cells mm^{-2} at 40° (Wässle, Grünert, Röhrenbeck, & Boycott, 1990). Cells within a particular mosaic cover the retina so that signals from each location in the photoreceptor mosaic are represented at least once within that mosaic; this implies that as the density of a particular cell type decreases with increasing eccentricity, the area covered by that cell's processes (the so-called *collecting aperture*) becomes larger to accommodate the greater spacing between photoreceptors. For example, as the density of horizontal cells decreases from 20,000 cells mm^{-2} in the fovea to 2,000 cells mm^{-2} at 30° eccentricity, the area of the photoreceptor mosaic from which their processes collect increases by a factor of 25 (Wässle, Grünert, Röhrenbeck, & Boycott, 1989). Generally, the anatomical area covered by an individual retinal neuron increases at a rate greater than the rate of decrease in density of any retinal mosaic. This implies that the convergence of presynaptic neurons to a particular cell increases with increasing eccentricity (Calkins & Sterling, 1999). Consequently, in moving from the fovea to the periphery, both the spatial tuning of any single retinal neuron and the spatial resolution of that neuron's mosaic decrease dramatically. From a functional perspective, this natural property of retinal cell types establishes the first limit for the well-known decrease in spatial resolution for psychophysical channels with increasing retinal eccentricity.

Retinal Cell Types

Each of the five classes of neurons in the retina is specialized for a broad function in encoding visual information, loosely delineated between excitation and inhibition. However, our visual world contains a diverse spectrum of spatial, temporal, and spectral variations, spanning a large range of contrasts and frequencies. The most efficient means to encode such diverse information with the highest possible fidelity is to partition the task among different circuits, each specialized for serving a particular portion of the visual dynamic range (Sterling, 1998). To accommodate this need for specialization, each class of retinal neuron is comprised of several cell types, each type demonstrating a unique combination of morphology, connectivity, neurochemistry, and physiology (Masland & Raviola, 2000). It is the precise connectivity between different

themselves and to the dendritic trees of bipolar cells (Dacey et al., 2000). This inhibition modulates the release of glutamate by the photoreceptor and its excitatory effect on bipolar cells. In the inner retina, *amacrine cells* collect more localized excitation from bipolar cells and provide inhibition back to the bipolar cell axon and to the dendritic trees of ganglion cells (Sterling, 1998). The role of inhibition in the retina is therefore to modulate the degree of excitation both at the release sites for glutamate and at its postsynaptic targets.

Certain fundamental properties of retinal cell populations have bearing on the organization of higher levels of visual types that render each retinal circuit uniquely tuned to different aspects of visual information.

Photoreceptors

About 94% of the photoreceptors are rods, each sufficiently sensitive to signal the absorption of even a single photon at the absolute threshold of vision. Rods dominate the photoreceptor population over most of the retina, with a peak density of 170,000 rods mm^{-2} at 15° eccentricity, which drops to 50,000–70,000 rods mm^{-2} at 45°. The fovea contains a small region, about 150 μm in diameter, that is rod-free, completely avascular, and devoid of all postphotoreceptor elements of the retina, which are displaced laterally to form the foveal wall. This region contains the highest density of cone photoreceptors, which comprise the remaining 6%; each is capable of operating at light levels eliciting as many as 10 million photon absorptions per cone each second. The cone density peaks at about 210,000 cones mm^{-2} and drops precipitously to about 5000 cones mm^{-2} at 20° (Curcio et al., 1989; Wässle et al., 1990). For both rods and cones, the light-funneling inner segment of the photoreceptor increases in diameter the further it is from the fovea, with a fivefold increase for cones and a threefold increase for rods; thus, the collecting aperture of each photoreceptor increases with eccentricity as it does for other retinal neurons.

Light funneled through the photoreceptor inner segment enters the outer segment where—if it is absorbed by the light-sensitive photopigment—it elicits a biochemical cascade called *phototransduction*. The two classes of photoreceptors, *rods* and *cones,* show both similarities and differences in their response to light. In the dark, rods and cones are relatively depolarized to a resting potential of about −40 mV due to the net influx of positive ions through cyclic-G-gated channels in the outer segment (for review, see chapter 6 in Rodieck, 1998). When photons are absorbed, a G-protein coupled cascade is initiated that ultimately results in the closure of these ion channels, thus hyperpolarizing the photoreceptor. Despite these similarities, there are notable differences between this cascade for rods and cones that render several distinctions in their physiological responses to light. Key among these differences is the more rapid activity of an enzyme in the outer segment of the cone to maintain a steady concentration of cyclic-G. This enhanced activity is likely to underlie the faster response of the cone to light and its faster recovery; thus, the pathways collecting signals from cones will be faster than are those collecting from rods. Furthermore, unlike rods, cones will not saturate in bright lights, and they demonstrate different rates of adaptation to light (for review, see Baylor, Nunn, & Schnapf, 1987).

The proportion of cyclic-G-gated channels that close for a particular photoreceptor, and the amplitude of this hyperpolarization depends upon the rate of photon absorption. The number of photons funneled through the inner segment and the wavelength of these photons determines this rate; therefore, the key variable in phototransduction is the spectral sensitivity of the photopigment. Rods all contain a single photopigment called *rhodopsin* with a peak sensitivity near 500 nm. Cones, on the other hand, distribute into three types defined by differences in the photopigments they express. Cones sensitive to short (S) wavelengths contain a pigment that peaks in sensitivity around 430 nm, near the region of the spectrum where we perceive violet and blue. These cones comprise on average only about 5% of all cones (reviewed in Calkins, 2001). Cones sensitive to middle (M) wavelengths contain a pigment that peaks at 535 nm, near where we perceive green, and cones sensitive to long (L) wavelengths contain a pigment peaks at 567 nm, near where we perceive orange (Baylor et al., 1987). Together, M and L cones comprise the remaining fraction of cones and in macaque retinas are present in about equal numbers (Packer, Williams, & Bensinger, 1996).

The expression of different types of cones in the photoreceptor mosaic allows primates to discriminate surfaces based on differences in spectral reflectance. The difference between signals from M and L cones is fed to a mechanism underlying discrimination between red and green (red-green), whereas the difference between S cones and the summed signal from M and L cones is fed to a mechanism providing the basis for discriminating blue from yellow (blue-yellow). The combined activity within the red-green and the blue-yellow channels ultimately provides the wide range of colors we experience (Wandell, 1995).

Horizontal Cells

In the dark, the relative depolarization of the photoreceptor—like depolarization in other neurons—promotes an influx of Ca^{2+} ions into the axon terminal and a release of glutamate from the photoreceptor synapse. Retinal neurons—with the exception of ganglion cells—are unmyelinated and do not produce action potentials. Instead, voltage fluctuations are conveyed through the electrotonic spread of ions in grades of current flow. Thus, the release of glutamate from the photoreceptor synapse is correspondingly graded from its highest release rate in the dark to lower rates with increasing light absorption and hyperpolarization of the photoreceptor. Each cone photoreceptor is coupled electrically to its neighbors and to neighboring rods via small junctions of shared membrane of the axon terminal called *gap junctions* (Tsukamoto, Masarachia, Schein, & Sterling, 1992). These junctions are essentially electrical resistors and are thought to allow a limited degree of spread of current from one cone to another or from cone to rod (and vice versa). Gap junctions probably serve to average or electrotonically smooth the conjoint activity of the photoreceptor mosaic (Sterling, 1998). Therefore, the release of glutamate from a photoreceptor reflects mostly the rate of light absorption not only within its own outer segment, but also (to a lesser extent) the level of light activity in its neighbors.

Closest to the point of glutamate release from the photoreceptor synapse are the processes of horizontal cells (Figure 6.2), which are thought to collect excitation from the synapse and provide inhibitory (GABAergic; from gamma-aminobutyric acid) feedback to the photoreceptor axon terminal (Sterling, Smith, Rao, & Vardi, 1995; Vardi, Kaufman, & Sterling, 1994; Vardi, Masarachia, & Sterling, 1992). This feedback is thought to drive the photoreceptor membrane potential towards its resting or *dark* value, thereby reducing the release of glutamate (Kamermans & Spekreijse, 1999). There are two types of horizontal cells in the primate retina, named simply "HI" and "HII" and generally designated as such (Wässle & Boycott, 1991). The HI cell has one arbor that collects from (and feeds back to) M and L cones, but not S cones, and a second arbor that is separated from the main arbor by a long axon-like process that contacts rods. The HII cell has a main arbor and a smaller arbor that both collect from all cone types but not from rods; therefore, the spectral sensitivity of both HI and HII cells is broadband (Dacey, 2000). Each horizontal cell collects from multiple photoreceptors. For example, the HI cell collects from some 15–25 cones in the fovea and from 10–15 further in the periphery as the spacing between cones increases (calculated from Wässle et al., 1989). However, HI cells couple electrotonically to one another via gap junctions, and HII cells are likewise interconnected. This connectivity produces a large network of horizontal cells that effectively enlarges laterally the photoreceptor input to any one cell. Consequently, the feedback to any single photoreceptor reflects not only its own activity, but also the average activity pooled across two independent networks of horizontal cells. Because of the intercell coupling between horizontal cells, the feedback is not only spatially but also temporally low-pass: The inhibition is broad and slow (V. C. Smith, Pokorny, Lee, & Dacey, 2001).

Bipolar Cells

The release of glutamate at the photoreceptor axon terminal fluctuates up and down from some baseline rate set by the average activity in the outer retina (for review, see Rodieck, 1998). These fluctuations constitute information, so ultimately both directions of change in glutamate release need to be encoded as excitation at the photoreceptor to bipolar cell synapse. Roughly half of the 10–12 types of bipolar cell respond with excitation (depolarization) to increments in local light activity (*on* cells), whereas the remainder responds to decrements in activity (*off* cells; Boycott & Hopkins, 1991). This division of labor is accomplished by a simple molecular trick at the bipolar cell dendritic tree. *On* bipolar cells express *metabotropic* glutamate receptors that gate cation channels with decreasing glutamate (i.e., increasing light), whereas *off* bipolar cells express *ionotropic* receptors that gate cation channels with increasing glutamate (decreasing light; Morigiwa & Vardi, 1999). In this way, only a single neurotransmitter (glutamate) is required to encode both increments and decrements from the average photoreceptor activity. The physiological division into *on* and *off* also correlates with a morphological division. *On* bipolar cells send long axons into the proximal half of the inner plexiform layer, closest to the ganglion cell layer, whereas *off* bipolar cells have shorter axons that stratify in the distal half of the inner plexiform layer (Boycott & Hopkins, 1991; also see Figure 6.2).

Rod Bipolar Cells.   Each rod diverges to two to three representatives of a single type of *on* bipolar cell. Each of these so-called rod bipolar cells collects signals from 12–15 rods in the central retina, increasing gradually to 50–60 rods in the periphery (Grünert & Martin, 1991). At night, both the absolute level of light and the contrast from a reflective surface are far less. Thus, the retinal circuit for rod or *scotopic* vision—like the rod itself—is designed to transmit with the highest possible sensitivity. The convergence of so many rods to the rod bipolar cell increases this sensitivity so that the signal from the absorption of even a single photon of light is preserved and transmitted with great fidelity (Makous, 1990). We find it interesting that the collected excitatory signal from this pool of rods is conveyed indirectly to different types of ganglion cells via a specialized amacrine cell (the AII amacrine) that contacts both *on* and *off* bipolar cells (Strettoi, Dacheux, & Raviola, 1990). The functional significance of this divergence is not known, but it probably serves to send copies of the signal from rare photon events in the dark to the multiple types of ganglion cells.

Cone Bipolar Cells.   Cones diverge to the remaining 9–11 types of bipolar cell. Each of these types has a unique expression of particular subunits of glutamate receptor (DeVries, 2000). This pattern bestows upon each type a unique physiology that in turn contributes to the particular spectral, spatial, and temporal properties of the ganglion cells to which they connect. To a first approximation, for a particular *on* type there is an analogous *off* bipolar cell type. Because in the mammalian retina bipolar cells are likely to only use glutamate as their neurotransmitter (Massey, 1990), their response polarity (*on* or *off*) is conserved in the synapse to the ganglion cell. Thus, some 85–90% of the ganglion cells are either *on* or *off,* while the rest are both (Dacey & Lee, 1994; Watanabe & Rodieck, 1989). Most morphological types of ganglion cells therefore also distribute into separate *on* and *off* mosaics that respond, respectively, to light increments or light decrements (Famiglietti & Kolb, 1976). Cone bipolar cells distribute into two main categories, *midget* and *diffuse,* defined by differences in the morphology of their dendritic trees and the number of cones contacting them (for a review, see Boycott & Hopkins, 1997). These subsystems have distinct roles in early visual processing.

The primate retina is highly specialized for supporting the highest possible spatial acuity. In the fovea, discrimination of spatial patterns is limited in resolution only by the spacing of the cone photoreceptors (Williams, 1986). This corresponds to about 40 cycles deg^{-1} spatially in the macaque monkey retina and at 60 cycles deg^{-1} in the human retina (Samy & Hirsch, 1989). To support this acuity, each cone contacts a single *on* and a single *off midget bipolar cell* and—over most of the retina—each midget cell collects from only a single cone (Calkins & Sterling, 1999; see Figure 6.2). Far in the periphery, beyond about 45°, up to three to five cones may contact each midget bipolar cell (Wässle, Grünert, Martin, & Boycott, 1994). In contrast, each of the six or so types of diffuse bipolar cells (named simply DB1–DB6 for "*d*iffuse *b*ipolar") collect from 8–12 cones over the entire retina, with cell types named DB1–DB3 providing *off* signals to the inner retina and the types named DB4–DB6 providing *on* signals (Boycott & Hopkins, 1991). We know very little about the separate mosaics and physiology of these diffuse cells. With so many cones converging on each, however, the diffuse system appears to have sacrificed spatial resolution for higher contrast sensitivity, and with higher sensitivity comes a sharper temporal response (DeVries, 2000). These differences between the midget and diffuse bipolar cells are apparent in the responses of ganglion cells to which they provide input (discussed in the next part of this chapter). Thus, the first segregation of functional pathways in vision occurs where the cone synapse diverges to different types of bipolar cell.

Ganglion Cells

Receptive Fields.   The response of a particular retinal neuron to a given pattern of light impinging on the photoreceptor array depends on the distribution of spectral, spatial, and temporal energy within that pattern. The quality and degree of tuning to this energy depends upon the structure of the *receptive field* of the neuron—consisting of (a) an excitatory *center* arising from the photoreceptor to the bipolar cell to the ganglion cell circuitry and (b) an inhibitory *surround* arising from the lateral circuitry of horizontal and amacrine cells (reviewed in Sterling, 1998). A neuron responds, therefore, with increased activity to an appropriate stimulus imaged upon its receptive field center and with decreased activity when that same stimulus is imaged upon the surround.

The precise physiology of the center and surround for a particular retinal neuron depends on the circuitry providing its presynaptic input and on where that neuron is in the retinal hierarchy. For example, the center of the receptive field of a photoreceptor is formed primarily by that photoreceptor plus the excitation pooled from its neighbors via gap junctions (R. G. Smith & Sterling, 1990). On the other hand, the center for a bipolar cell is comprised of the contributions from overlying photoreceptors (Dacey et al., 2000). Similarly, the excitatory center of a ganglion cell arises from the convergence within the photoreceptor to the bipolar cell circuitry that contacts its dendritic tree, whereas much (but probably not all) of the inhibitory surround arises in the lateral connections from horizontal cells to photoreceptors (and bipolar cell dendrites; Freed, Smith, & Sterling, 1992; Vardi et al., 1994). Thus, spatially the center and surround are quantified in reference to the area of the photoreceptor mosaic contributing to each.

The response amplitudes of the center and surround are spatially nonuniform; each is roughly Gaussian in shape and depends upon the spatial distribution of the synaptic contributions from the cells contributing to each (Croner & Kaplan, 1995). Also, because of anatomical and physiological differences between the cells that comprise them, the center of the receptive field is spatially narrower, temporally quicker, and spectrally sharper (i.e., more wavelength dependent) than the surround is. The center also tends to be greater in amplitude than the surround is, generally by 35–40% for ganglion cells (Croner & Kaplan, 1995); thus, when a stimulus fills the entire receptive field, the center response dominates. In this sense, the surround can be considered as a spatial and temporal filter for subtracting the redundancy that inevitably is present in a typical natural scene, while the center conveys the signal for whatever spatial and temporal contrast remains. In other words, the surround essentially filters the background activity, and what is transmitted at the photoreceptor axon is the contrast or edge provided by modulation of light activity above or below this background.

Because each retinal neuron derives its input from overlying photoreceptors, most often the receptive field is quantified spatially with reference to the region of the photoreceptor mosaic that elicits a modulation of the cell's activity. However, because stimuli are multidimensional, it is equally important to understand the spectral and temporal characteristics of the receptive field. Because receptive fields of retinal neurons are tuned to different types of information receptive field function as a *filter,* passing certain bandwidths of information while filtering out others. For example, the horizontal cell contribution to the surround is often referred to as a *low-pass* spatiotemporal filter because it is broad spatially, slow temporally, and therefore tuned to low spatial and temporal signals (Srinivasan, Laughlin, & Dubs, 1982).

Ganglion Cell Mosaics.   Even though the fovea only comprises 1–2% of the retinal surface area, it contains more than 35% of all retinal ganglion cells (calculated from Wässle et al., 1989). Although the peak density of ganglion cells (about 60,000 cells mm^{-2}) is less than the peak cone density by more than a factor of three, the tight packing of cells within the fovea renders the effective sampling of the ganglion cell mosaic much higher, with three to four ganglion cells per cone (Wässle et al., 1989). This is sufficient to provide each cone access to several parallel ganglion cell circuits serving different visual functions; it also explains—at least in part— the expansion of the foveal representation in the primary visual cortex (V1; discussed later in this chapter). The functionality of these circuits correlates strongly with ganglion cell morphology, which in turn reflects the nature of its presynaptic inputs. The number of these types depends critically upon species. For the primate retina, the number is probably 15–20, each with a distinct pattern of presynaptic input, physiology, and central projection into the thalamus (Leventhal, Rodieck, & Dreher, 1981; Rodieck & Watanabe, 1993). The circuits for most of these and their role in visual information processing are unknown. Nevertheless, there are a few circuits in the primate retina about whose function we can say a great deal, although it is probably imprudent to call them solved. These divide broadly first into *on* and *off,* following the pairing of *on* and *off* bipolar cell types, and this is reflected by the level of stratification of the ganglion cell dendritic tree in the inner retina (see Figure 6.2; Dacey & Lee, 1994). These circuits also divide broadly according to whether the bipolar cell input is midget or diffuse; this determines the spatiotemporal and spectral responses of the ganglion cell.

What the cortex ultimately reads as retinal output are spectral, spatial, and temporal signals filtered through the receptive fields of individual ganglion cells. Because the filter properties of ganglion cells are determined by their presynaptic circuitry, this circuitry determines what specific types of visual information are filtered at the first stage of visual processing.

Midget or P Ganglion Cells.   Midget bipolar cells collect from a single cone over most of the retina, and each cone diverges to a single *on* and single *off* midget bipolar cell (Wässle et al., 1994). In and around the fovea, each *on* and *off* midget bipolar cell contacts a single *on* or *off* midget ganglion cell, and no midget ganglion cell collects from more than one midget bipolar cell (Calkins & Sterling, 1999). In this way, the greatest possible spatial resolution—that of a single cone—is afforded to the receptive field center of the midget pathway for both light increments and decrements. Midget ganglion cells comprise about 80% of the ganglion cells in the foveal region (Perry, Oehler, & Cowey, 1984), so the expansion of the foveal representation in V1 is in large part due to the presence of the midget system (Wässle et al., 1989). Outside the fovea, as the optics of the eye worsen and the spacing between cones increases (Hirsch, 1984), the dendritic tree of the midget ganglion cell expands considerably, and each cell collects from increasing numbers of midget bipolar cells and cones (Calkins & Sterling, 1999). Even so, these ganglion cells remain the smallest and most numerous, with the least convergence of cones.

Midget ganglion cells provide the dominant retinal input to the parvocellular region of the lateral geniculate nucleus (LGN; discussed later in this chapter). For this reason, midget cells are often referred to as *P cells,* as are the parvocellular relay neurons to which they connect. For the most part, the physiological properties of P cells in the LGN mimic those of the midget/P cell in the retina. Thus, the LGN P cell also demonstrates a small receptive field center that corresponds to the small dendritic tree of the midget ganglion cell. In fact, despite inevitable variation between different sets of experiments, the physiological measurements of the spatial extent of the P cell center match very well the anatomical convergence of cones to the midget ganglion cell across retinal eccentricities (Figure 6.3). Thus, for this circuit, the anatomy reasonably predicts the spatial properties of the receptive field center.

Over the entire retina, the receptive field center of the midget cell is the most narrow of all ganglion cell receptive fields and the sampling density of the midget cell mosaic establishes the limit of spatial acuity (Croner & Kaplan, 1995; Dacey, 1993). However, because the convergence of cones to the midget cell is minimal, its spatial contrast sensitivity is relatively poor (Croner & Kaplan, 1995). For reasons we do not yet understand—but no doubt arising in part from the small number of cones converging upon it—the midget ganglion cell is also temporally sluggish and responds to light in a sustained fashion. Thus, the spatiotemporal contrast sensitivity of the midget cell is distributed across high spatial but lower temporal frequencies (see Figure 6.5 later in this chapter for the equivalent properties in the LGN).

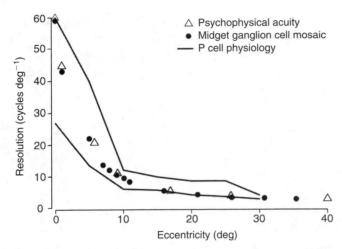

Figure 6.3 Spatial resolution of the high acuity system. The high-frequency cutoff for spatial resolution in cycles deg^{-1} is plotted against retinal eccentricity for three independent measures. Psychophysical acuity for human observers (triangles) is replotted from S. A. Anderson, Mullen, and Hess (1991), who used the drifting grating protocol to measure the upper limit of spatial resolution. Acuity for the center fovea was adopted from Williams (1986). Resolution of the midget ganglion cell mosaic in human retina (circles) was measured using intercell spacing and replotted from Dacey (1993). Resolution of physiological measurements from P cells in the macaque retina and LGN (lines) was calculated from the diameter of the P cell receptive field center. Cell density was estimated from the diameter assuming a coverage factor of unity (Watanabe & Rodieck, 1989), and resolution was calculated as the Nyquist limit assuming triangular packing (Williams, 1986). A range of physiological measurements of macaque P cell receptive field centers in retina and LGN was used to calculate lower and upper bounds (Derrington & Lennie, 1984).

The mosaic of M and L cones in the primate retina is patchy, with cones of like type distributing into small clusters. Because each midget ganglion cell collects from only a single cone in and near the fovea, their excitatory connections are by definition finely tuned spectrally, conferring upon the midget cell high *chromatic contrast sensitivity*. As the number of cones increases, some cells remain finely tuned to M and L cone modulation (Martin, Lee, White, Solomon, & Ruttiger, 2001), while others begin to respond preferentially to luminance (M + L) modulation. Whether the cortex uses whatever chromatic sensitivity is present in the midget mosaic as the basis for red-green color discrimination across the retina is a matter of debate (Calkins & Sterling, 1999). What is undeniable is that midget cells—because of their fine spatial apertures (discussed previously)—are highly specialized and probably evolved primarily as a system to support foveal acuity limited only by the spacing of the cones.

Parasol or M Ganglion Cells. Like the midget ganglion cell, the *parasol* ganglion cell comes in both *on* and *off* types, both of which have a broad, circularly symmetric dendritic tree that resembles a parasol one might carry to keep the rain off. At a given retinal eccentricity, the area covered by the

dendritic tree of the parasol cell is some 20 times the area covered by a midget cell (Watanabe & Rodieck, 1989), and the parasol mosaic is accordingly sparser, comprising some 5–8% of all ganglion cells (Grünert, Greferath, Boycott, & Wässle, 1993). As a consequence of its size, the convergence of cones to the parasol cell is also a factor of 20 greater. For example, in the fovea, the parasol cell collects from 20–25 cones via four to five diffuse bipolar cells (Calkins, 1999). Physiologically, this contributes to a broader receptive field center with higher contrast sensitivity, about six times greater on average than that of the midget ganglion cell (Croner & Kaplan, 1995). It is likely that the nature of its bipolar cell input, diffuse versus midget, also contributes to its characteristic transient response to light—the response fades for stationary stimuli and is optimal for stimuli moving across the photoreceptor mosaic (Kaplan et al., 1990; Kaplan, Purpura, & Shapley, 1988; Kaplan & Shapley, 1986). Thus, the parasol cell responds best to lower spatial frequencies, higher temporal frequencies, and differences in retinal luminance. In terms of their projections to the brain, parasol ganglion cells provide the dominant retinal input to the magnocellular region of the LGN (Perry et al., 1984). Thus, they are generally called *M cells*. Like their retinal counterparts, M cells in the LGN have a receptive field center that is much broader than that of P cells, corresponding to the larger dendritic tree of the parasol ganglion cell. Some evidence also suggests that some parasol cells may send axon collaterals to the superior colliculus (for review, see Rodieck & Watanabe, 1993).

The retinal image is constantly in motion, due to small eye movements (for review, see Rodieck, 1998). Superposed upon this inherent movement is the actual translation of objects in a natural scene, or *stimulus motion*. This movement of stimuli across the photoreceptor mosaic at once blurs the spatial information contained in those stimuli while introducing light contrast at higher temporal frequencies. Some mammalian retinas (e.g., rabbit retinas; see Vaney, 1994; Vaney, Peichl, & Boycott, 1981) have ganglion cells tuned to specific directions of moving stimuli. The primate retina (to our knowledge) does not have this type of directional selectivity. However, what ultimately becomes a motion signal higher in the cortical streams is likely to originate at least in part from the transient responses propagating through the mosaic of the parasol cells as a stimulus moves across the photoreceptor array.

Other Ganglion Cells and Their Circuits. The primary ganglion cell input to the LGN, in terms of numbers of cells, is provided jointly by the midget (P) and parasol (M) mosaics (Perry et al., 1984). Nevertheless, it is incorrect to associate only retinal midget cells with the parvocellular LGN and only parasol cells with the magnocellular LGN. Despite the convenience of this simplification, it remains just that—a simplification. Retrograde labeling of ganglion cells following injections of markers into the LGN reveal a diverse array of more sparsely populating ganglion cells, each with a unique morphology and (presumably) retinal circuitry (Rodieck & Watanabe, 1993). Although we know little about the function of these cells, we now appreciate that some of them are likely to project not to the primary P and M layers of the LGN, but rather to the intercalated or koniocellular layers in between (discussed later in this chapter). One of these is the small bistratified ganglion cell that is implicated in color vision used to discriminate blues from yellows. The receptive field of this cell is such that signals from S cones oppose those from M and L cones in an antagonistic fashion. This antagonism is spatially overlapping, so the small bistratified cell is tuned sharply to spectral (chromatic) differences and very little to spatial edges (Calkins, Tsukamoto, & Sterling, 1998; Dacey, 1996).

What the Retina Responds To

In laying out a basic understanding of the retina, it is important to point out that there is a difference between a perceptual attribute and the physical stimulus that elicited it; the latter has very much to do with the retina, which interfaces the brain with the external visual world, whereas the former is something more ambiguous—ascribed to the stimulus by a host of (we presume) physiological interactions working in concert through higher visual areas of the brain. The former has to fit into our internal representation of the visual world that is built upon an earlier, more rudimentary representation in the output of the retina. For example, color is an attribute of the internal representation of a surface that arises from the retinal representation of the spectral reflectance of that surface. Similarly, motion is an attribute our internal representation provides for the displacement of an object in space and time that arises from local differences in the activity of ganglion cells as the image of that object steps across the retinal array. Motion is—in simple terms—something that is computed by the cortex based on changes in retinal firing patterns in response to the changing image upon the photoreceptor array. Certain ganglion cells in the primate retina may indeed respond favorably to a moving stimulus, but this does not imply that motion is encoded within the retina—the stage for what will become the perception of motion is merely set in the retina. Other cells will respond to a stimulus that to the human observer appears colored, but color is not itself assigned by retinal activity; thus, the complexity of the retinal wiring has less to do with perception and more to do with encoding the critical events that the cortex interprets as vision.

It is also critical to emphasize that although each of the circuits shown in Figure 6.2 underlies tuning of ganglion cell receptive fields for particular spatial, temporal, or spectral

frequencies, most types of ganglion cells respond in some measure to more than one attribute of a visual stimulus. For example, a midget ganglion cell will respond to a light moving across its receptive field, provided that movement is within the temporal sensitivity profile of the receptive field (see Figure 6.5 later in this chapter). Also, a parasol cell will respond to a fine spatial pattern, even though its broad receptive field is not necessarily specialized to convey the highest frequencies within that pattern. The point is that what we ultimately experience as vision arises from the confluence of activity across the mosaic of each type of ganglion cell, and rarely is any one type completely silent in that mass contribution.

Parallel Visual Pathways From the Retina

Visual pathways comprise a massive sensory component that involves about 90% of the retinal ganglion cells, those that project into the LGN of the thalamus and from there to the primary visual cortex (Figure 6.4; Hendrickson, Wilson, & Ogren, 1978; Rodieck & Watanabe, 1993). Another component involves the remaining 10% or so, mostly large ganglion cells that sample the photoreceptor mosaic more sparsely than do the major types involved in acquiring sensory information (Rodieck & Watanabe, 1993). Relatively little is known about the circuitry and receptive fields of these ganglion cells in primates. Most involve complex dendritic trees that integrate both *on* and *off* information about light contrast, and their central projections are similar to those of other mammalian species. No fewer than nine subcortical nuclei are distributed within six major regions that provide recipient zones

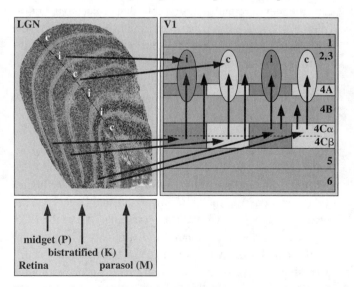

Figure 6.4   Schematic of early visual pathways from retina to V1. In retina, three main types of ganglion cell project to the P (dashed), M (solid) and K (dotted) regions of the LGN. The six primary M and P layers of the LGN are segregated by eye input; the input to each K layer generally reflects the input to the primary layer just dorsal to it. See insert for color version of this figure.

for axon collaterals leaving the retina (reviewed in Leventhal et al., 1981; also see Rodieck & Watanabe, 1993). Some of these ganglion cells may send collaterals to multiple nuclei, many of which provide projections back to the muscles of the eye for a variety of functions, including the coordination of eye movements and the setting of the circadian rhythm that contributes to the modulation of retinal physiology. In this section we focus on the retino-geniculate-cortical pathway. For comprehensive information concerning areas outside this pathway, the reader is referred to more specialized reviews (Kaas & Huerta, 1988; Rodieck, 1979; Rodieck, 1998).

LATERAL GENICULATE NUCLEUS (LGN)

Anatomy

The LGN is about the size and shape of large peanut, situated in the posterior-most quarter of the thalamus. The LGN on each side of the thalamus receives input about the contralateral visual hemifield from the retina of both eyes, ipsilaterally from the temporal retina and contralaterally from the nasal retina (for general overview, see Wurtz & Kandel, 2000). This input is anatomically segregated into six primary layers, each about 500 μm thick, with Layers 1, 4, and 6 (numbered ventral to dorsal) receiving contralateral input and Layers 2, 3, and 5 receiving (Spear, Kim, Ahmad, & Tom, 1996) ipsilateral input. The number of LGN neurons that receive retinal input and project to striate cortex is 1.0–1.5 million (Blasco, Avendano, & Cavada, 1999; Hendry & Reid, 2000), about the same number of retinal ganglion cells that project to the LGN. Thus, a 1:1 relationship between retinal ganglion cell and LGN relay neuron is usually presumed, although this is difficult to assess due to large variability in the numbers of ganglion cells and LGN cells between animals (Spear et al., 1996). Layers 1–2 comprise the ventral one third of the LGN and contain about 10% of the cortical-projecting neurons to striate cortex. Because the bodies of these neurons are large, Layers 1–2 are called *magnocellular* (or simply M). In contrast, Layers 3–6 comprise the dorsal two thirds of the LGN and contain about 80% of the LGN relay neurons. The bodies of these neurons are small by comparison, and Layers 3–6 are termed *parvocellular* (or P). The remaining 10% of the LGN relay neurons distribute nonuniformly, mostly within the intercalated layers sandwiched just ventral to each of the six primary M and P layers but also within small clusters within the primary layers. These cells can be visualized by neurochemical means (Hendry & Yoshioka, 1994) and are termed *koniocellular* (or K) because of their small size (Casagrande & Kaas, 1994; Hendry & Reid, 2000).

The relative number of M, P, and K cells in the LGN reflects the nature of their retinal inputs. The population of P cells is the most numerous because most of these receive input from a midget ganglion cell, whereas the population of M cells is more sparse because many (but probably not all) receive input from a parasol ganglion cell (Perry et al., 1984). The small number of K cells, probably 3–5% (Calkins & Sterling, 1999), receives input from the small bistratified ganglion cell (Martin, White, Goodchild, Wilder, & Sefton, 1997). Other types of ganglion cell project to each of the M, P, and K populations, each with a unique morphology and presynaptic circuitry (Rodieck & Watanabe, 1993).

Functional Properties

The receptive fields of LGN neurons have center-surround organization reflecting the characteristics of the ganglion receptive fields providing its input (Hubel, 1960; Kaplan et al., 1990). Thus, neurons in the magnocellular layers of the LGN differ from those in the parvocellular layers; the neurons in the magnocellular layers have faster conduction velocities, greater luminance contrast sensitivity, and greater contrast gain control (Derrington & Lennie, 1984). Furthermore, the parvocellular neurons show high spatial resolution, prefer lower temporal frequencies (Derrington & Lennie, 1984; Levitt, Schumer, Sherman, Spear, & Movshon, 2001), and have concentric color-opponent receptive fields, whereas the magnocellular neurons respond better to higher temporal and lower spatial frequencies, and their responses are spectrally broadband and not affected by chromatic stimulus modulations (Derrington, Krauskopf, & Lennie, 1984; Schiller & Colby, 1983; Schiller & Malpeli, 1978; Wiesel & Hubel, 1966). Thus, the main distinguishing characteristics between these neurons are chromatic opponency and differences in the spatiotemporal range of response properties (Figure 6.5). It should be pointed out that there is a large degree of overlap in spatiotemporal properties of the two subdivisions of the LGN, and under many conditions the two classes of neurons give very similar responses to the same stimuli (Levitt et al., 2001; Spear, Moore, Kim, & Xue, 1994).

For years, similarities between the properties of retinal and LGN receptive fields have been used to categorize LGN as a passive relay station for signals on their way to cortex. However, recent physiological studies suggest that LGN is not a simple, passive relay of information to cortex but instead is involved in many dynamic processes that could affect the nature of the information relayed to cortex (Sherman & Guillery, 1996). They showed that LGN and other thalamic relay neurons exhibit two response modes: *tonic* and *burst* (Sherman, 1996). Basing his ideas on the properties of the two response

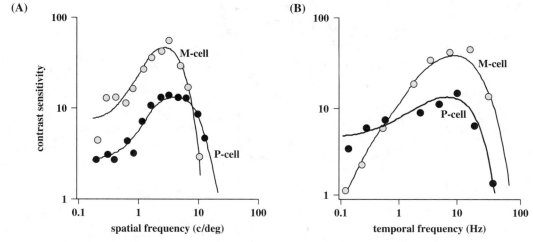

Figure 6.5 Spatiotemporal sensitivity of P and M neurons recorded from the LGN of the macaque monkey. Spatial (A) and temporal (B) contrast sensitivity of representative parvocellular (P cell) and magnocellular (M cell) neurons. Contrast sensitivity was taken as the reciprocal of the contrast that produced a criterion modulation of discharge on 50% of trials (usually about 10 spikes/s). Each spatial and temporal sensitivity function was measured with sinusoidal gratings set at an optimal temporal or spatial frequency, respectively. The M cells have higher peak sensitivity to contrast and respond to higher temporal frequencies than the P cells do. On the other hand, the P cells respond to higher spatial frequencies and show higher sensitivity at the lowest temporal frequencies. Note substantial overlap in the range of spatial and temporal frequencies to which the two classes of neurons respond. Replotted from Derrington and Lennie, 1984.

modes, Sherman proposed that the burst mode is better suited for stimulus detection, whereas the tonic mode is suited for faithful transmission of visual stimuli (Sherman, 2001). He also proposed that the mechanism for switching between the two modes is under the control of afferents from the visual cortex, the brain stem, or both, and that the LGN contains the necessary intrinsic circuitry to accomplish this switch. This circuitry consists of a large number of inhibitory interneurons (Wilson, 1993), excitatory inputs from Layer 6 of striate cortex (Casagrande & Kaas, 1994), as well as inputs from the parabrachial region of the brain stem and the thalamic reticular nucleus (Erisir, Van Horn, & Sherman, 1997). This organization allows LGN to play a more active role in transmitting and gating the information reaching the visual cortex.

Effects of Selective Lesions

Effects of lesions restricted to the P or M layers in the LGN reflect the spatiotemporal properties of the affected regions. For example, lesions restricted to the magnocellular zone produce dramatic deficits in luminance contrast sensitivity for higher temporal and lower spatial frequencies (Merigan, Byrne, & Maunsell, 1991; Schiller, Logothetis, & Charles, 1990) measured with flickering or moving gratings (Figure 6.6) but do not produce any loss in sensitivity for chromatic stimuli (Merigan, Byrne, et al., 1991; Merigan & Maunsell, 1990) or for luminance contrast sensitivity when measured with stationary stimuli (see Figure 6.6). These results correlate with the physiological studies of individual parasol cells in the retina and M cells in the LGN that show high contrast

sensitivity for high temporal and low spatial frequencies. Although the effects of M lesions did not appear to have a specific effect on motion perception (Merigan, Byrne, et al., 1991), the spatiotemporal characteristics of the deficit support a role for the magnocellular pathway in feeding signals to cortical streams for motion processing (Merigan & Maunsell, 1993).

In contrast, selective lesions of the parvocellular zone produce a fourfold decrease in visual acuity, cutting off sensitivity to higher spatial frequencies (Merigan, Katz, & Maunsell, 1991). Furthermore, the parvocellular lesion also results in a dramatic loss of both red-green and blue-yellow chromatic sensitivity (Merigan, 1989; Schiller et al., 1990) confirming the unique role of parvocellular neurons in carrying chromatic signals to cortex. However, one must keep in mind that the lesions included the population of K cells embedded within the dorsal two thirds of the LGN, some of which are likely to receive inputs from the small bistratified ganglion cell implicated in processing of blue-yellow signals (Calkins & Sterling, 1999). The loss of these neurons could have contributed to the profound loss of chromatic contrast sensitivity reported by Merigan (1989).

CORTICAL PROCESSING

The information provided by the three major types of ganglion cells arrives in the visual cortex largely segregated. The functionally distinct magnocellular and parvocellular fibers from the LGN project to different sublamina of Layer 4 in striate cortex and this anatomical segregation of processing of

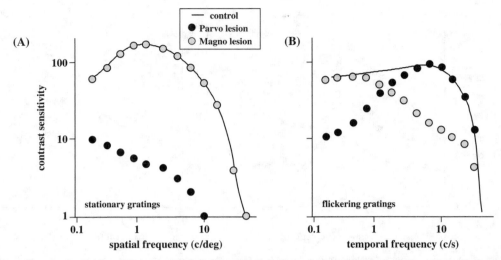

Figure 6.6 Visual loss after selective lesions of the magnocellular and parvocellular layers in the LGN. Monkeys discriminated between vertical and horizontal sinusoidal gratings presented in a portion of the visual field affected by the lesion. Contrast sensitivity (reciprocal of contrast threshold) was measured over a range of spatial and temporal frequencies. When the measurements were performed with stationary gratings (A), the parvocellular lesion resulted in a substantial loss in sensitivity to a wide range of spatial frequencies, which increased with spatial frequencies and a large loss in visual acuity. Under these conditions, the monkeys with the magnocellular lesions showed no sensitivity loss. When contrast sensitivity was measured with gratings flickering at various temporal frequencies (B), the magnocellular but not the parvocellular lesions resulted in a loss in sensitivity, but only at intermediate and higher temporal frequencies. Adapted from Merigan and Maunsell, 1993.

different aspects of visual information continues to a greater or lesser extent throughout the visual cortex. Neocortex contains at least 32 distinct areas identified as areas involved in processing of visual information (Felleman & Van Essen, 1991). A subset of these areas and a simplified diagram of major visual cortical pathways are shown in Figure 6.7.

The information about visual motion and spatial location generated at the earliest stages of cortical processing is directed for further elaboration into the *dorsal visual stream,* whereas shape, color, and texture information flow into the *ventral visual stream.* The two visual pathways originate in segregated subregions of primary visual cortex (V1) and continue to be largely distinct at the next stage of processing, in Area V2, until they separate into the pathway streaming dorsally toward the parietal cortex and the pathway streaming ventrally towards the temporal lobe. The former has been termed the *motion* or *where* pathway; the latter is called the *color and form* or *what* pathway (Ungerleider & Mishkin, 1982). In the following discussion we outline the functional organization and properties of the most important and best understood components of the two pathways.

Primary Visual Cortex (Striate Cortex; V1)

Anatomy

The first stage of cortical processing of visual signals takes place in the area called V1 also called striate cortex because of the prominent stripe of white matter (*stria Gennari* or the *line of Gennari*) running through Layer 4. It is a large region that in

the macaque monkey occupies an area of 1,200 mm^2 in the occipital lobe or about 12% of entire neocortex (Felleman & Van Essen, 1991). The three types of inputs from the LGN to V1 (parvocellular, magnocellular, and koniocellular) terminate in separate subdivisions within Layer 4 (see Figure 6.4). The

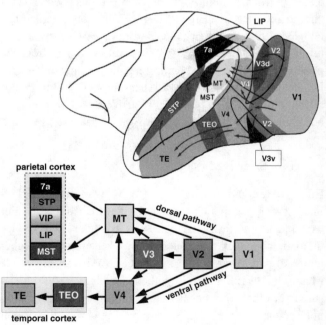

Figure 6.7 Visual areas in monkey cortex. The diagram of the monkey brain shows the location of cortical areas and their primary connections. The *dorsal* and the *ventral visual pathways* streaming towards the parietal and temporal lobes are shown in a simplified diagram. All the connections between cortical areas are largely reciprocal. The diagram of the monkey brain has been adapted from Farah, Humphreys, and Rodman, 1999. See insert for color version of this figure.

magnocellular and parvocellular fibers project to separate sub-lamina within Layer 4C, Layers 4Cα and 4Cβ respectively (Blasdel & Lund, 1983; Hendrickson et al., 1978), thus maintaining their anatomical segregation. The koniocellular neurons from the intercalated laminae in the LGN terminate in Layers 2/3 in regions with characteristic pattern of labeling for enzyme cytochrome oxidase, termed *blobs* (Horton, 1984; Livingstone & Hubel, 1984), as well as in Layer 1 (Hendry & Reid, 2000).

Most of V1 output is directed to the adjacent area, V2 (Livingstone & Hubel, 1983; Rockland & Pandya, 1979), although it also sends direct projections to MT (the middle temporal area; Boyd & Casagrande, 1999; Maunsell & Van Essen, 1983a), an area specialized for processing visual motion (discussed later in this chapter). V1 sends projections back to the LGN, to the pulvinar (a visual thalamic region implicated in control of attention), and to the superior colliculus (Casagrande & Kaas, 1994; Ungerleider, Galkin, & Mishkin, 1983). In addition, V1 maintains connections with a wide range of other cortical and subcortical regions (Kennedy & Bullier, 1985).

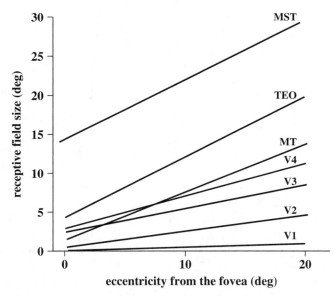

Figure 6.8 Receptive field sizes in visual cortical areas along the dorsal and ventral streams. Receptive fields are smallest in the foveal region in Area V1 and increase with distance from the fovea. At subsequent stages of cortical analysis, receptive fields become larger and also increase with eccentricity from fovea. The data are taken from Desimone and Ungerleider, 1986; Dow et al., 1981; and Felleman and Van Essen, 1987.

Functional Properties

V1 contains a retinotopic representation of the entire contralateral visual field with a disproportionately large number of neurons devoted to processing of information provided by the foveal region of the retina (Azzopardi & Cowey, 1993; Dow, Snyder, Vautin, & Bauer, 1981). Thus, six to nine cones located near the fovea are represented by 1 mm of cortex, whereas the same number of cones located 20° from the fovea are represented by a region of cortex that is about five times smaller (Dow et al., 1981; Van Essen, Newsome, & Maunsell, 1984). This expansion of the foveal representation, referred to as *cortical magnification,* is characteristic of many cortical visual areas and indicates allocation of additional neural circuitry for processing of information in the central portion of the visual field. This magnification may in part be a reflection of the great number of ganglion cells serving foveal cones (Wässle et al., 1989).

Receptive fields in V1 representing the fovea are quite small and increase with eccentricity in a manner that is roughly inversely proportional to cortical magnification (Dow et al., 1981; Hawken & Parker, 1991). Thus, foveal receptive fields can be as small as 1–2 min of arc, about the diameter of a single cone, and as large as 60 min of arc at 20° eccentricity (Figure 6.8).

Although the size of a cortical receptive field has always been considered one of its most stable features, recent studies have revealed that it can be modulated by some properties of its optimal stimulus (e.g., contrast), as well as by the visual

and behavioral context in which this stimulus is presented (e.g., Bakin, Nakayama, & Gilbert, 2000; Ito & Gilbert, 1999; Sceniak, Ringach, Hawken, & Shapley, 1999; Figure 6.9). Such effects demonstrate the dynamic nature of cortical neurons, a phenomenon most likely mediated by the feedback projections arriving in V1 from subsequent levels of cortical analysis (Ito & Gilbert, 1999).

A number of features not seen in the preceding stages of analysis emerge in striate cortex. These features include selectivity for stimulus orientation, size, depth, and the direction of stimulus motion; they represent the first stage of processing leading to the perception of form and motion.

Sensitivity to Contrast and Spatiotemporal Filtering

One of the fundamental properties of retinal ganglion cells is center-surround organization, a feature that allows the detection of variations in luminance or chromatic contrast across space. Neurons in the magnocellular pathway are exquisitely sensitive and show reliable responses to contrasts as low as 1%, whereas parvocellular neurons require higher contrasts (Derrington & Lennie, 1984; see Figure 6.5). These properties are reflected in the cortical layers receiving inputs from the two pathways, with neurons in 4Cα receiving inputs from the magnocelluar neurons showing higher sensitivity to contrast than neurons in 4Cβ. This segregation of regions of low and high sensitivity to contrast is also present in neurons

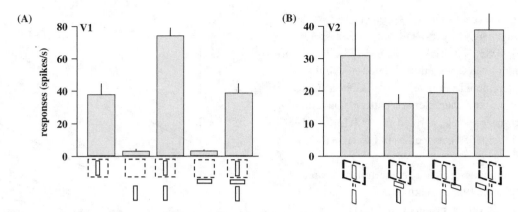

Figure 6.9   Stimuli outside the classical receptive field affect responses of orientation-selective cortical neurons.

A. Responses of a V1 neuron to a bar of preferred orientation placed inside the receptive field (dashed square) are facilitated when a stimulus of the same orientation is placed outside of the receptive field. When the horizontal bar interrupts the contour formed by the two separated bars of the same orientation, the effect of facilitation induced by the bar outside the receptive field is blocked.

B. Responses of a V2 neuron to a bar of preferred orientation in the receptive field are also facilitated by the stimulus of the same orientation placed outside the receptive field. However, this facilitation is blocked only when the horizontal bar is placed in the same depth plane or in the far depth plane (0.16° uncrossed disparity) relative to the two vertical bars. However, when the orthogonal bar is placed in the near depth plane (0.16° uncrossed disparity), facilitation by the peripheral vertical bar is reinstated. This effect illustrates that depth cues provided by stimuli from outside of the receptive field can have strong modulatory effects on responses of cortical neurons at early stages of cortical processing and implicates neurons in Area V2 in three-dimensional representation of surfaces. Adapted from Bakin et al., 2000.

located in more superficial layers, projecting outside of striate cortex. Thus, although most neurons in Layers 2/3 have relatively low contrast sensitivity, there is a small population of cells clustering near the centers of the blobs (discussed later in this chapter) with high contrast sensitivity, reminiscent of magnocellular LGN neurons (Edwards, Purpura, & Kaplan, 1995). These cells are likely to receive inputs from the K cells, which have been shown to have contrast sensitivity close to that of M cells (Xu et al., 2000). This larger dynamic range in the population of neurons within the blobs suggests that these regions are well equipped for signaling stimulus contrast.

Measurements of contrast response are usually performed with drifting or flickering sinusoidal gratings presented at spatial and temporal frequencies that are optimal for a given neuron. Careful selection of spatial and temporal stimulus parameters is necessary because visual neurons in the cortex respond to a limited range of spatial and temporal frequencies—that is, they behave like spatiotemporal filters. With respect to the spatial parameters, V1 neurons show sharp attenuation at both low and high frequencies (see Figure 6.10; De Valois, Albrecht, & Thorell, 1982)—unlike LGN neurons, which show high-frequency cutoff but more modest attenuation at low frequencies (Derrington & Lennie, 1984).

There is a correlation between the eccentricity, optimal spatial frequency, high frequency cutoff, and size of the receptive field of a given neuron. For example, an increase in eccentricity that results in a twofold increase in receptive field size is accompanied by a twofold decrease in the optimal spatial

frequency (Foster, Gaska, Nagler, & Pollen, 1985). However, not all regions in V1 have similar spatial tuning at a given eccentricity. For instance, neurons in the blobs appear to be tuned to low spatial frequencies, and the optimal spatial frequency increases with distance from the blob (Born & Tootell, 1991; Edwards et al., 1995). Preferences for lower spatial

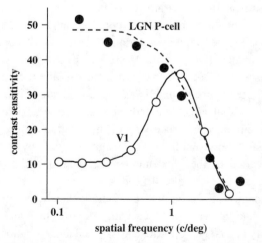

Figure 6.10   Spatial frequency selectivity of a neuron in LGN and V1. Responses of a LGN parvocellular neuron and a V1 simple color-luminance cell to equiluminant red-green gratings of different spatial frequencies. Note that whereas the P cell shows no low spatial frequency attenuation, the V1 cell is tuned to a narrow range of spatial frequencies. This spatial selectivity of color-selective neurons illustrates the integration of color and spatial information in V1. From E. N. Johnson, Hawken, and Shapley (2001). The spatial transformation of color in the primary visual cortex of the macaque monkey. *Nature Neuroscience, 4,* 409–416.

frequencies have also been found in the subregions containing the majority of directionally selective neurons, upper Layer 4 and Layer 6 (Hawken, Parker, & Lund, 1988). These neurons also show high sensitivity to contrast, a property characteristic of directionally selective neurons in MT (Sclar, Maunsell, & Lennie, 1990), the region that receives direct inputs from V1 (Hawken et al., 1988).

With respect to temporal characteristics, cortical neurons are similar to neurons encountered in the retina and the LGN and show broad tuning to temporal frequencies. However, whereas LGN neurons show preferences for relatively high frequencies of temporal modulation, 10–20 Hz (Hicks, Lee, & Vidyasagar, 1983), cortical cells respond better to lower temporal modulations (3–8 Hz), showing little attenuation at low temporal frequencies (Foster et al., 1985).

Binocular Interactions

Information from the two eyes—segregated into separate layers in the LGN—remains segregated upon their arrival in Layer 4C of striate cortex (Hubel & Wiesel, 1977). At this stage of cortical processing, the signals from the two eyes are processed separately, and the neurons are grouped according to their eye of origin. These groupings, termed *oculodominance columns* (Figure 6.11), are most prominent in Layer 4C, but can be visualized as alternating bands across the entire thickness of cortex, becoming less apparent in layers above and below because of the intermixing of inputs from the two eyes. The amount of cortex devoted to processing the information from each eye is nearly equal for the central 20° of the visual field, and the width of the alternating columns representing each eye is about 0.5 mm. The representation of the ipsilateral eye declines at greater eccentricity and eventually disappears—only the contralateral eye is represented (LeVay, Connolly, Houde, & Van Essen, 1985). The intermixing of the inputs from the two eyes in layers above and below Layer 4 is reflected in the properties of neurons in these regions, many of which respond best when both eyes are stimulated. Furthermore, many of these neurons are sensitive to the absolute retinal disparity or the difference in the position of a single stimulus in the two eyes (Cumming & Parker, 1999; Livingstone & Tsao, 1999; Poggio, Gonzalez, & Krause, 1988), an early stage of processing that leads to stereoscopic depth perception (Cumming & Parker, 2000).

Orientation Selectivity

Neurons in the input layers of striate cortex retain a concentric center-surround organization similar to that observed in the retina and LGN, whereas in other layers receptive fields

(A)

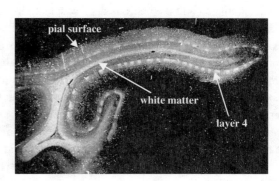

(B)

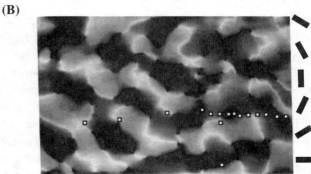

(C)

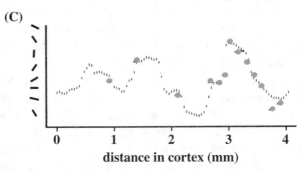

distance in cortex (mm)

Figure 6.11 Organization of eye and orientation preferences in Area V1. See insert for color version of this figure.

A. Ocular dominance columns in monkey cortex seen as alternating bright and dark patches in Layer 4 in a section cut perpendicularly to the surface. One eye of a monkey was injected with a radioactively labeled amino acid, which was taken up by cell bodies in the retina and transported to the LGN, whose axons terminate in Layer 4 in the striate cortex. Areas in the cortex that receive input from the injected eye are labeled and appear bright; the alternating unlabeled patches receive input from the uninjected eye. The white matter has a bright appearance because it contains labeled axons of LGN neurons. Adapted from Hubel and Wiesel, 1979.

B. Orientation columns in monkeys V1 revealed by optically imaging and comparing local changes in reflectance, which indicate activation. Imaging of the cortical surface was performed in anesthetized monkeys presented with stimuli of various orientations. Areas that were most active during the presentation of a particular orientation are indicated by the color bars. Complementary colors represent orthogonal orientations: Red and green indicate maximal activity for vertical and horizontal orientations, and blue and yellow indicate maximal activity for right and left obliques. Adapted from Blasdel and Salama, 1986.

C. Preferred orientation of neurons recorded with the microelectrode along the track indicated by the white squares in the optical image shown in B. The preferred orientations of the recorded neurons corresponds to those revealed with optical imaging. Adapted from Blasdel and Salama, 1986.

become elongated and the neurons display selectivity for the orientation of the stimulus. Among orientation-selective neurons, a subset of cells termed *simple cells* have receptive fields consisting of distinct excitatory and inhibitory subregions, whereas receptive fields of *complex cells* contain excitatory and inhibitory subregions that are intermixed (Hubel & Wiesel, 1968). Some orientation selective neurons, termed *hypercomplex cells* (or special complex cells) are also sensitive to the length of the optimally oriented stimuli and show inhibition if the bar extends outside its receptive field (Hubel & Wiesel, 1977).

This inhibition—produced by the stimulus extending outside the classical receptive field—is not the only indication of active processes in the area surrounding the classical receptive field. A number of recent studies have shown that responses to stimuli placed in the receptive field are strongly modulated by the context in which this stimulus is presented. Most of these studies used oriented patterns centered on the classical receptive field surrounded by a large texture and found inhibitory or excitatory effects of the surrounding texture dependent on whether the elements in the surround matched the properties of the elements in the center (Knierim & Van Essen, 1992; Nothdurft, Gallant, & Van Essen, 1999). In some cases, these influences were produced only by texture boundaries located close to the borders of the receptive field, suggesting a role for V1 neurons in the detection of texture boundaries but arguing against the contribution of these neurons to the process of figure-ground segregation (Rossi, Desimone, & Ungerleider, 2001). Because this contextual modulation often emerges a relatively long time after the stimulus onset, it is likely to be the product of the influences of subsequent stages of cortical processing sending feedback projections to V1 (Nothdurft et al., 1999). These observations suggest that the mechanisms underlying texture segmentation and possibly figure-ground segregation may already be in place at a very early stage of cortical processing.

As for neurons with similar eye preferences, neurons with similar orientation preferences cluster into narrow columns extending perpendicularly from the cortical surface to the white matter (Hubel & Wiesel, 1977). Each column is about 30–100 μm wide and 2 mm deep. Neurons in these columns respond not only to the same orientation, but also to stimulation of the same portion of the visual field. Along the cortical surface all axes of orientations are represented, and the points where neurons with different orientations meet form a characteristic pinwheel pattern (Obermayer & Blasdel, 1993; Figure 6.11). On average, a region of 1 mm² on the surface of cortex contains all orientation preferences for a given point of visual space. This periodic pattern of orientation columns is interrupted by the cytochrome oxydase blob regions prominent in Layers 2/3 which contain cells that are not ori-

entation selective and show some selectivity for color and respond to low spatial frequencies (Edwards et al., 1995; Livingstone & Hubel, 1984).

Together, columns representing each eye, orientation columns, and the blobs for a given portion of the visual field form a unit termed a *hypercolumn* (Hubel & Wiesel, 1977); each hypercolumn occupies 1 mm² of striate cortex. There is evidence that many columns and blobs with similar preferences are linked by long horizontal connections, although there are also connections that would allow for the interactions between the compartments with different preferences (Yoshioka, Blasdel, Levitt, & Lund, 1996). These horizontal connections between individual compartments are believed to play a role in the integration of information over many millimeters of cortex (Gilbert, Ito, Kapadia, & Westheimer, 2000).

Direction Selectivity

A feature emerging in V1 that has major implications for the ability to see object movement is selectivity for the direction of stimulus motion (Hubel & Wiesel, 1968). Directionally selective neurons fire vigorously to one direction of motion of an optimally oriented bar or grating and fire less or not at all when the same bar moves in the opposite direction. In the monkey, directionally selective neurons are present predominantly in Layer 4Cα and Layer 4B, which sends projections to MT (Hawken et al., 1988). Like the magnocellular neurons in the LGN (Derrington & Lennie, 1984), these neurons are sensitive to low contrasts and have relatively poor spatial resolution (Hawken et al., 1988; Movshon & Newsome, 1996).

Response to Color

Chromatic signals from the three cone types, combined in an opponent fashion in the retina, arrive in Layer 4Cβ in striate cortex from the parvocellular layers in the LGN; thus, it is not surprising that chromatic properties of cortical neurons resemble those found in parvocellular neurons in the LGN (Derrington et al., 1984). Like the P cells, nearly all neurons in the striate cortex show some degree of chromatic and spatial opponency, which is most commonly found in Layers 4A and 4Cβ, as well as in the blobs (Lennie, Krauskopf, & Sclar, 1990; Livingstone & Hubel, 1984; Ts'o & Gilbert, 1988). A less numerous group of color responsive neurons are those sensitive exclusively to stimuli defined by color differences (E. N. Johnson, Hawken, & Shapley, 2001). These cells are largely nonoriented, respond to low spatial frequencies, and are commonly found in blobs (Johnson et al., 2001; Lennie et al., 1990; Leventhal, Thompson, Liu, Zhou,

& Ault, 1995). A larger proportion of neurons respond robustly to stimuli defined both by color differences and by luminance (E. N. Johnson et al., 2001). This group of neurons—most commonly found in Layers 2/3—is highly selective for stimulus form and is equipped to carry spatial information about color and luminance to other cortical areas (E. N. Johnson et al., 2001; see Figure 6.10). Thus, these V1 neurons not only retain color information provided by the LGN, but also add spatial selectivity that enables the detection of color boundaries.

There is recent evidence that V1 neurons not only retain but also amplify chromatically opponent signals arriving from the LGN producing a gradual change in color tuning (Cottaris & De Valois, 1998). This dynamic process, which is likely to involve intracortical circuitry, is reminiscent of a change in orientation tuning—taking place about 30–45 ms after stimulus presentation—observed in neurons located in the output layers of striate cortex (Ringach, Hawken, & Shapley, 1997).

Effects of V1 Lesions

In the primate, most of the visual information is carried to cortex via the retino-geniculate-striate pathway, so it is not surprising that damage to V1 results in a profound visual loss (Merigan, Nealey, & Maunsell, 1993; Miller, Pasik, & Pasik, 1980; Weiskrantz & Cowey, 1967). Although the loss appears to be nearly complete and humans with damage to striate cortex report inability to see anything in the affected portion of the visual field (Glickstein, 1988), rudimentary visual capacities appear to persist. Monkeys with V1 lesions can detect rapid flicker (Humphrey & Weiskrantz, 1967), discriminate simple colors (Keating, 1979; Schilder, Pasik, & Pasik, 1972), track moving lights (Humphrey & Weiskrantz, 1967), and discriminate simple forms (Dineen & Keating, 1981). This residual visual function most likely depends on alternative projections that reach the cortex via the superior colliculus and thalamus. For example, the minimal color vision that survives may depend on color-opponent P ganglion cells projecting to cortex through the pulvinar (Cowey, Stoerig, & Bannister, 1994). On the other hand, the coarse localization of light after V1 lesions may be maintained by the cortical areas receiving projections from the superior colliculus (Walker, Fitzgibbon, & Goldberg, 1995).

Area V2

Anatomy

Area V2 is a narrow strip of cortex located anterior and adjacent to area V1; it is on the surface of and inside the lunate sulcus (Essen & Zeki, 1978; Zeki & Sandeman, 1976). It contains topographically organized representations of the contralateral visual field (Gattass, Gross, & Sandell, 1981) and receives its major inputs from striate cortex (Kennedy & Bullier, 1985; Rockland, 1992; Van Essen, Newsome, Maunsell, & Bixby, 1986). Although it also receives some projections from the LGN (Bullier & Kennedy, 1983) and pulvinar (Curcio & Harting, 1978), its activity appears to be driven mainly by the inputs provided by V1 neurons (Girard & Bullier, 1989; Schiller & Malpeli, 1977). As in Area V1, the representation of the central 10° of the visual field is substantially expanded (Gattass et al., 1981). Area V2 projects topographically back to Area V1 and to Areas V3, MT, and V4, as well as to regions within parietal cortex, including the medial superior temporal area (MST), posterior occipital area (PO), and the ventral intraparietal area (VIP; Gattass, Sousa, Mishkin, & Ungerleider, 1997).

Functional Properties

Although many V2 receptive field properties resemble those found in V1, a number of new features emerge. Common to the two areas is the presence of selectivity for stimulus orientation and direction (Burkhalter & Van Essen, 1986). However, neurons in V2 have larger receptive fields (Gattass et al., 1981; see Figure 6.8), prefer lower spatial frequencies, and have a spatial frequency tuning somewhat broader than that of V1 neurons (Foster et al., 1985; Levitt, Kiper, & Movshon, 1994). Although selectivity for stimulus orientation is present in more than half of V2 neurons (Zeki, 1978b), only a small proportion (15%) are selective for the direction of stimulus motion (Burkhalter & Van Essen, 1986; Levitt, Kiper, et al., 1994). These directionally selective neurons are localized largely to the thick stripes (discussed later in this chapter) and show somewhat higher contrast sensitivity (Levitt, Kiper, et al., 1994), suggesting influences of the M pathway.

Many neurons in V2 are sensitive to chromatic modulations (Burkhalter & Van Essen, 1986) and some show strong color opponent responses (Levitt, Kiper, et al., 1994; Zeki, 1978b). There are similarities in chromatic sensitivity of V2 neurons with that observed in Area V1, although some differences in tuning have been reported (Levitt, Kiper, et al., 1994). There are also a greater proportion of color-oriented cells—as well as neurons that exhibit color and disparity selectivity—in comparison with V1 (Roe & Ts'o, 1997).

In contrast to cells in Area V1, most V2 cells are binocularly driven, and many of these neurons are tuned to retinal disparity (Hubel & Livingstone, 1987; Poggio, 1995; Zeki, 1979). Although most of these neurons are sensitive only to the absolute disparity, some respond to the *relative disparity* between different locations in the visual field, a property absent from V1 neurons (Cumming & Parker, 1999). The emergence of neurons sensitive to relative disparity, a property upon which stereopsis depends, suggests that some V2 neurons may be providing signals to support depth perception (Cumming & DeAngelis, 2001).

Another feature to emerge in V2 neurons is a robust response to illusory contours, first observed by Peterhans and von der Heydt (1989), although there is some evidence of neuronal responses to illusory contours in V1 (Grosof, Shapley, & Hawken, 1993). Such responses are indicative of neurons' filling in the information about missing contours—a process requiring some level of contour integration. V2 neurons have also been shown to respond to illusory contours induced by depth cues; these responses are present even with cues located beyond the classical receptive field, suggesting a role of long-range horizontal connections within Area V2 (Bakin et al., 2000; see example in Figure 6.9).

In addition to these properties, a selectivity of V2 for complex shapes has also been reported, suggesting that an amount of integration of stimulus features encoded in Area V1 is likely to take place in V2 neurons (Hegde & Van Essen, 2000; Kobatake & Tanaka, 1994). All these features suggest that the information provided by V2 neurons may play a role in coding of surface properties, including contours, opacity, transparency, and relative depths.

Functional and Anatomical Segregation

The spatial segregation and clustering of receptive field properties characteristic of V1 is also present in V2. The first insights into the anatomical and functional organization of this region were provided by the metabolic marker *cytochrome oxydase,* which revealed a characteristic pattern of labeling consisting of a series of stripes (DeYoe & Van Essen, 1985; Hubel & Livingstone, 1987; Livingstone & Hubel, 1984; Olavarria & Van Essen, 1997). These stripes, consisting of dark thin and thick regions separated by lightly stained pale stripes, have also been visualized by optical imaging (Malach, Tootell, & Malonek, 1994; Roe & Ts'o, 1995). The visual map of V2 consists of three distinct maps, with every location represented once in each of the thin, pale, and thick stripes associated with neurons selective for color, orientation, and disparity respectively (Roe & Ts'o, 1995; Zeki & Shipp, 1987). This anatomical segregation of the three modalities is not entirely complete, as demonstrated by the presence of neurons selective for more than one modality. In fact, studies utilizing optical imaging combined with single-neuron recordings revealed subcompartments within individual stripes, specific for color, form, and disparity (Ts'o, Roe, & Gilbert, 2001). These

findings argue against the notion that processing of color, orientation, and disparity is strictly localized to specific types of stripes; this is supported by the fact that the thick stripes in V2, known to receive inputs from Layer 4B in V1 (the magnocellular output layer) also receives inputs from Layer 4A, the parvocellular output layer. Another interesting feature of projections supplied by pyramidal V1 neurons is their relatively extensive spread across V2 and the possibility that they interconnect individual stripe-like compartments in V2, providing an anatomical substrate for interactions between segregated channels in V1 (Levitt, Yoshioka, & Lund, 1994). Furthermore, the intrinsic organization within V2 is such that all three cytochrome-oxydase-rich compartments are interconnected by horizontal connections (Levitt, Yoshioka, et al., 1994; Malach et al., 1994). This anatomical intermixing of signals from the two pathways suggests that V2 may play a role in combining these signals, a notion supported by many receptive field properties encountered in this region.

Effects of V2 Lesions

Although a number of studies have examined the effects of lesions on prestriate cortex—a region that in addition to V2 includes a number of other cortical areas—only one study examined the effects of lesions limited to Area V2 (Merigan et al., 1993). This study reported depressed contrast sensitivity for orientation discrimination (measured with gratings defined by luminance or color) but not for the discrimination of the direction of motion (tested with rapidly moving stimuli). In addition, V2 lesions also profoundly and permanently disrupted the discrimination of complex forms. This profile of visual loss is consistent with receptive field properties characteristic to that area and suggests that neurons in Area V2 play an important role in processing of complex form and color but have a lesser role in motion perception.

Area V3

Anatomy

Area V3, a narrow strip of cortex located immediately anterior to V2, contains a representation of the central 40° of the contralateral visual field split into the ventral (V3v) and the dorsal (V3d) portions, representing the upper and lower quadrants, respectively (see Figure 6.7; Essen & Zeki, 1978; Zeki, 1978d). Although the ventral and dorsal subdivisions of V3 encompass a single representation of the visual field, they differ in their pattern of connectivity (Van Essen et al., 1986) as well as in their receptive field properties, with V3d having a higher incidence of directionally selective neurons but lower number of color-selective cells (Burkhalter & Van Essen, 1986). Because of these differences, Burkhalter and Van Essen (1986) argued that these areas should be treated as separate visual areas; they termed the dorsal region *V3* and the ventral region *ventral posterior area* (VP). Recently, Kaas and Lyon (2001) disputed the idea of splitting these regions into separate visual areas and proposed an alternative scheme that included a single but redefined Area V3. Although the issue of what specifically constitutes Area V3 is important, the details of this controversy are outside the scope of this chapter; we focus here on the results of recordings performed in this general region, treating V3d and V3v together.

This region receives major inputs from Layer 4B of V1 and projects to Areas MT, MST, and VIP (Beck & Kaas, 1999; Felleman, Burkhalter, & Van Essen, 1997), suggesting an association with the dorsal visual stream. However, V3 also receives inputs from V2 and is strongly interconnected with V4, the major component of the ventral visual stream (Beck & Kaas, 1999). Because of this pattern of connectivity, V3 is in a good position to serve as a site where the integration of various visual signals can occur.

Functional Properties

The properties of V3 neurons support the notion that this region may be one of the sites of integration between the visual signals carried by the two major functional streams. Unfortunately, only a small number of physiological studies examining visual receptive field properties have been performed on this region, and those that did recorded from anesthetized animals (e.g., Gegenfurtner, Kiper, & Levitt, 1997). Although the receptive fields of V3 neurons are larger than those found in V2 (Felleman & Van Essen, 1987; Gattass, Sousa, & Gross, 1988), they share a number of similar properties with V2 neurons, including a high incidence of orientation selectivity (80%) and similar orientation tuning (Gegenfurtner et al., 1997). On the other hand, V3 neurons prefer lower spatial and higher temporal frequencies and exhibit a higher sensitivity to contrast than do V2 neurons (Gegenfurtner et al., 1997). These properties—together with the relatively high incidence of directional selectivity (nearly 60%) and the presence of selectivity for binocular disparity (Felleman & Van Essen, 1987)—suggest a role in processing of motion information. Indeed, Gegenfurtner et al. (1997) found that some directionally selective neurons in V3 respond to the motion of a plaid pattern rather to its components, a feature characteristic of many MT neurons and indicative of higher-level motion processing (Movshon, Adelson, Gizzi, & Newsome, 1985).

In addition to motion and depth analysis, nearly half of all neurons in V3 show selectivity for color (Burkhalter & Van Essen, 1986; Gegenfurtner et al., 1997). It is noteworthy that many of the neurons responding to color also show directional selectivity, and a substantial number of V3 neurons responds show directional selectivity to isoluminant gratings. This interaction between color and motion—in addition to motion integration—suggests that V3 represents an important stage in processing of visual information. These properties and the connections with Areas MT and V4, the key midlevel components of the dorsal and the ventral cortical pathways, places V3 at an important stage in the analysis of the visual scene.

Area V3A

Van Essen and Zeki (1978) described a distinct region located between Areas V3 and V4 containing separate visual field representation; they labeled this region *V3A*. This region receives projections from Area V2, projects to Area V4, contains a representation of both the upper and lower visual quadrants, and has also been referred to as the *posterior intraparietal area* (PIP; Colby, Gattass, Olson, & Gross, 1988; Felleman, Burkhalter, et al., 1997).

Very few functional differences have been found between Areas V3 and V3A. These differences include the finding that neurons in V3 become unresponsive to visual stimuli when V1 is removed, whereas a third of neurons in V3A remain responsive (Girard, Salin, & Bullier, 1991). The activity of neurons in V3A has been shown to be modulated by the direction of gaze (Galletti & Battaglini, 1989), and some of the direction-selective neurons respond better to real motion across the retina rather than to motion induced by a stationary stimulus when the eye moved (Galletti, Battaglini, & Fattori, 1990).

Parallel Functional Streams

The inputs from the P and M pathways are segregated into different cortical layers in the striate cortex, and an anatomical segregation of neurons with similar properties is also apparent in Area V2. However, the segregation within the visual system becomes most pronounced at the subsequent stage of cortical processing, in Areas V4 and MT. At this stage, the two areas give rise to two distinct cortical streams, the ventral and dorsal pathways. The *ventral pathway* has been termed the *color and form* or the *what* pathway (Maunsell & Newsome, 1987) because in earlier studies both color and shape selectivity appeared to be most prominent in the physiological responses of neurons in the two main components of this stream—Area V4 and the inferotemporal cortex. The *dorsal pathway,* consisting of MT and the areas within the posterior parietal cortex, has been termed the *motion* or the *where* pathway because of the prevalence of directionally selective neurons and the evidence for encoding of spatial location within this pathway. In the following discussion we provide a brief overview of the major properties of the regions within the ventral and dorsal streams and discuss the current view of their role in visual function.

VENTRAL VISUAL STREAM

Area V4

Anatomy

Area V4, first identified by Zeki (1971), is located in a region anterior to the lunate sulcus. It receives direct projections from Areas V1, V2, and V3 (Nakamura, Gattass, Desimone, & Ungerleider, 1993; Yukie & Iwai, 1985; Zeki, 1978c), sends strong projections to temporal area (TEO) in the inferotemporal cortex, and has reciprocal connections with a number of other areas across the visual system (Distler, Boussaoud, Desimone, & Ungerleider, 1993; Tanaka, Lindsley, Lausman, & Creutzfeldt, 1990). Anatomical modularity, prevalent in V2 in the form of thin, thick, and pale stripe regions, is not as apparent, although the projections from the thin and pale stripe subdivisions of V2 are distinct and there is evidence of a modular organization within V4 that reflect these inputs (Felleman, Xiao, & McClendon, 1997; Y. Xiao, Zych, & Felleman, 1999). There is also evidence of clustering of neurons with similar preferred orientation and size (Ghose & Ts'o, 1997).

Functional Properties

Area V4 contains a complete representation of the contralateral visual field with an expanded representation of its central portion (Gattass et al., 1988). The receptive fields are well defined but are larger than those encountered in Areas V1, V2, and V3 (Desimone & Schein, 1987; Gattass et al., 1988). Many of the properties encountered in V4 are reminiscent of those found in the primary visual cortex; thus, many V4 neurons are tuned for stimulus orientation and show selectivity for the length and the width of oriented bars (Cheng, Hasegawa, Saleem, & Tanaka, 1994; Desimone & Schein, 1987). In addition, about a third of V4 neurons show selectivity for the direction of stimulus motion (Desimone & Schein, 1987; Ferrera, Rudolph, & Maunsell, 1994), and the majority are selective to binocular disparity (Hinkle & Connor, 2001). Although V4 neurons respond selectively to many of the same features as V1 neurons, a number of more complex properties emerge that suggest specialization for the analysis of complex forms. For example, Gallant, Connor, Rakshit, Lewis, and Van

Essen (1996) reported that V4 neurons not only are selective for conventional Cartesian gratings, but many also respond preferentially to more complex polar and hyperbolic stimuli. Pasupathy and Connor (1999) found strong selectivity for specific stimulus contours such as angles and curves and showed a bias toward convex contours—a feature that could account for perceptual preferences for convex forms—and a recently reported sensitivity to texture and selectivity to shading suggests the involvement of V4 neurons in the extraction of shape from shading (Hanazawa & Komatsu, 2001). An example of selective responses of V4 neurons to complex textures is shown in Figure 6.12. Together with sensitivity to binocular disparity, these features could enable V4 neurons to use stereoscopic cues to extract object information.

From the time Area V4 was first described, it had been thought of as the color-processing area (Zeki, 1971). However, subsequent work has argued against this specialization. Although many V4 neurons show some wavelength sensitivity and a small proportion are color-biased or color-opponent, similar properties have been observed in neurons in other areas of the visual cortex (Desimone, Schein, Moran, & Ungerleider, 1985). It remains to be seen whether V4 neurons show color constancy, one of the critical features of color vision.

Effects of V4 Lesions

A number of studies have examined the effects of lesions of this area on form and color discrimination; the results—for the most part—support its unique contribution to processing of form, as suggested by single-unit recordings. These studies have shown that the loss of Area V4 results in relatively modest and often transitory deficits in the discrimination of size and shape of simple forms (Heywood & Cowey, 1987; Schiller, 1993; Walsh, Butler, et al., 1992). Monkeys with V4 lesions can discriminate the orientation of simple gratings at normal levels as long as the gratings are at relatively high contrasts, are not masked by noise, and are defined by luminance or color (De Weerd, Desimone, & Ungerleider, 1996; Merigan, 1996). However, the same lesions produce severe and permanent deficits in tasks involving discrimination of illusory contours, three-dimensional forms, textures, and groupings (De Weerd et al., 1996; Merigan, 1996, 2000). These effects are quite selective because when the contours are defined by motion, luminance, or color, the effects of V4 lesions were minimal (De Weerd et al., 1996).

Lesions of V4 also affect some aspects of color vision, although these effects are relatively modest. Walsh and colleagues reported largely transient deficits of color discrimination and modest deficits in color constancy (Walsh, Kulikowski, Bulter, & Carden, 1992; Walsh, Carden, Butler, &

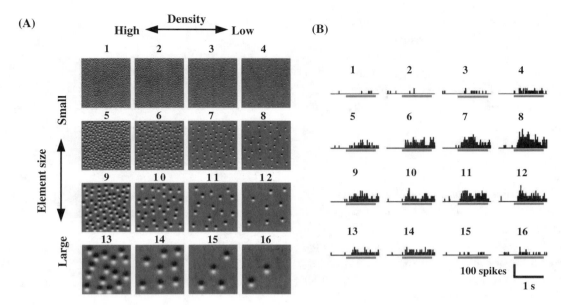

Figure 6.12 Responses of V4 neurons to texture patterns.

A. Texture stimuli. In each row, the density of the elements doubled with each step. In each column, the size of the elements doubled and the density decreased by one fourth with each step from top to bottom. Across all stimuli the spacing of the elements remained constant.

B. Responses of a V4 cell tuned to density and size of the elements. Histograms show the responses to stimuli corresponding to those shown in A. Bars below histograms indicate the period of stimulus presentation. This neuron shows selectivity for textures with medium-sized elements of relatively low density, suggesting integration. From Hanazawa and Komatsu, 2001.

Kulikowski, 1993). They also reported that perception of color categories was unaffected by the absence of V4 neurons and suggested that these categories are established by chromatic mechanisms at earlier stages of cortical processing. Other studies have also reported relatively minor disruptions of hue-discrimination thresholds and modest deficits in chromatic contrast sensitivity (Dean, 1979; Heywood, Gadotti, & Cowey, 1992; Merigan, 1996). These results support the notion that although V4 represents an important step in processing of complex shape and texture, it is less likely to play a key role in processing of information about color.

Inferotemporal Cortex

Anatomy

Inferotemporal (IT) cortex is the final processing stage of the ventral visual stream and is believed to play a key role in processing shape information. It consists of a posterior portion, Area TEO, which in turn projects to the adjacent, more anterior portion, Area TE. Area TEO receives its major inputs from V4 as well as from Areas V2 and V3 (Distler et al., 1993). From there, visual information is sent to TEO, which also receives a direct projection from V4 and from a number of areas in the ventral and anterior portions of the temporal lobe, including

the hippocampus (Yukie & Iwai, 1988). This region also is reciprocally interconnected with ventral portions of prefrontal cortex (Bullier, Schall, & Morel, 1996; Seltzer & Pandya, 1989), with the superior temporal polysensory area (STPa)—which also receives projections from the dorsal pathway (discussed later in this chapter)—with parahippocampal regions (Shiwa, 1987), with the basal ganglia (Middleton & Strick, 1996), and with subcortical areas—notably, the pulvinar (Baleydier & Morel, 1992), and portions of the amygdala (Amaral & Price, 1984; Cheng, Saleem, & Tanaka, 1997).

Functional Properties: Area TEO

Area TEO contains an orderly representation of the entire contralateral visual field with receptive fields that are somewhat larger than those in Area V4, increasing with eccentricity from about 5° near the fovea to 60° in the far periphery (Boussaoud, Desimone, & Ungerleider, 1991). Inputs from V4 cluster to produce an apparent modular segregation within TEO with respect to color and shape selectivity (Felleman, Xiao, et al., 1997). Many characteristics of TEO receptive fields are reminiscent of those found in V4 and earlier stages of cortical processing; many of its cells respond selectively to simple features such as length, width, orientation, and wavelength (Kobatake & Tanaka, 1994). However, selectivity for more complex patterns is also quite common (Desimone et al., 1984; Kobatake & Tanaka, 1994). The nature of this selectivity appears to be different from that encountered in TE (discussed in the next part of this chapter) because neurons show less invariance in their response to changes in the size and orientation of objects (Hikosaka, 1999).

Functional Properties: Area TE

In contrast to TEO, this region contains neurons with very large receptive fields that almost always include the fovea and extend into both visual hemifields covering as much as 40° of the visual field (Boussaoud et al., 1991; Desimone & Gross, 1979). Its dorsal (TEad) and ventral (TEav) portions have slightly different connections and show some subtle differences in response properties (Martin-Elkins & Horel, 1992; Tamura & Tanaka, 2001), although for the purposes of this review we treat them as a single area. The incidence of neurons responding strongly to complex stimulus features increases dramatically in Area TE (Tanaka, 1997), and although some TE neurons show extreme selectivity for complex structures such as faces (Desimone, Albright, Gross, & Bruce, 1984; Figure 6.13), other neurons are much less discriminating and respond strongly to a variety of complex patterns. Tanaka (1997) has shown that TE neurons with preferences for similar stimulus features cluster into overlapping columns perpendicular to the cortical surface and extending across all cortical layers. There are about 1,300 of such columns, each extending over about 400 μm (Tanaka, 1993; Figure 6.13).

Among novel features emerging in TE—and not present at earlier stages of cortical analysis—is response invariance. For example, there are neurons in TE with responses to complex stimuli that are not affected by large changes in the location of the stimulus in the visual (and receptive) field or in retinal image size (Desimone et al., 1984; Hikosaka, 1999; Ito, Tamura, Fujita, & Tanaka, 1995). Neurons in TE also respond to three-dimensional objects and develop selectivity for specific views of those objects, particularly for those that the monkey learned to recognize the familiar views of those objects (Logothetis & Pauls, 1995).

There is accumulating evidence that TE neurons acquire preferences to specific stimulus features through learning (Kobatake, Wang, & Tanaka, 1998; Logothetis, Pauls, & Poggio, 1995; Sakai & Miyashita, 1994). For example, it has been shown that exposure to a set of patterns during discrimination training increases the probability that that TE neurons will respond maximally to these stimuli (Kobatake, Wang, & Tanaka, 1998). The finding by Logothetis et al. (1995)—that the selectivity of TE neurons is most pronounced for objects the monkey is able to recognize—suggests that new receptive

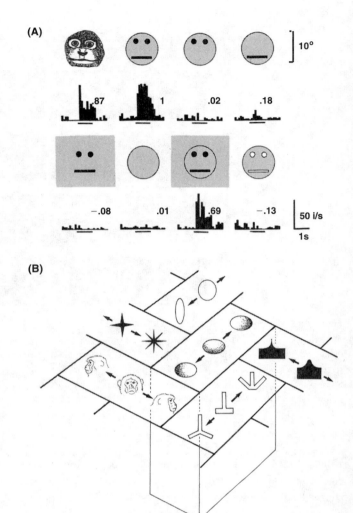

Figure 6.13   A. Response of a neuron in the anterior portion of inferotemporal cortex (TEO) to complex stimuli. The histograms show responses of the cell to each of the stimuli shown. The line below each histogram indicates the time of stimulus presentation. The cell responded strongly to the face of a toy monkey and to a pattern consisting of two dots and a horizontal line arranged in a gray circle, a configuration resembling the face. Other stimuli consisting of some but not all elements of these stimuli were ineffective in producing a response.

B. Schematic drawing of columnar organization in TE. This cortical region consists of columns in which cells respond to similar but not identical features. Cells in different columns respond to different features and each column extends across all cortical layers. The width of each column is greater than 400 μm, and it has been estimated that there are 1,300 columns across the entire surface of TE. From Tanaka, K. (1997). Columnar organization in inferotemporal cortex. In K. S. Rockland, J. H. Kaas, & A. Peters (Eds.), *Extrastriate cortex in primates.* Copyright 1997, Plenum Press.

field properties can be acquired during active learning. This apparent ability of TE neurons to acquire new properties with learning has also been demonstrated in tasks designed specifically to test long-term memory for complex patterns (Sakai & Miyashita, 1994).

Another striking feature of TE neurons was revealed in experiments by Sheinberg and Logothetis (1997), who used perceptually ambiguous stimuli induced by binocular rivalry.

They showed that the activity of the majority of IT neurons is determined by the perceptually dominant stimulus, a phenomenon only rarely observed at earlier stages of cortical analysis (Leopold & Logothetis, 1996). This activity—together with the complex response properties described previously—reinforces the importance of IT neurons in the processing and perception of complex shape and form.

Effects of IT Lesions

The role of IT in object recognition was first revealed in studies involving damage to this region over 50 years ago (Mishkin, 1954; Mishkin & Pribram, 1954) and in numerous lesion studies performed since (for a review, see Merigan & Pasternak, in press). Many of these studies reported deficits in the discrimination of complex forms as well as in the learning of new discriminations (e.g., Britten, Newsome, & Saunders, 1992; Huxlin, Saunders, Marchionini, Pham, & Merigan, 2000). These deficits were often transient, and only a few persisted after extensive retraining. A number of studies also examined the effects of IT lesions on color vision and found deficits in color discriminations that ranged from profound to relatively modest (e.g., Buckley, Gaffan, & Murray, 1997; Huxlin et al., 2000). As is the case with form discriminations, postlesion training often resulted in improvements in color vision. On the whole, the effects of IT lesions are reminiscent of effects of V4 lesions (see previous discussion of this area), although in the case of color vision the deficits appear to be a bit more pronounced.

DORSAL VISUAL STREAM

Area MT

Although the dorsal visual stream originates in specific layers of striate cortex and occupies well-defined subregions (thick cytochrome oxidase (CO) stripes) within V2, it becomes truly distinct—both anatomically and functionally—at the level of the middle temporal area (MT) located in the superior temporal sulcus (STS). During the past 10–15 years, MT has become one of the most studied midlevel processing areas in the visual system of primates. Because most of the physiological recordings from this area are carried out in monkeys performing behavioral tasks, this area has become a fertile ground for establishing links between neural activity, behavior, and perception.

Anatomy

Area MT was first described and named by Allman and Kaas (1971) in the owl monkey. Subsequently, Zeki (1974)

identified an equivalent area in the macaque monkey and—because of the selectivity of neurons in this area to image motion—named it the *motion area of the superior temporal sulcus* and later *V5* (Zeki, 1978a). In the macaque monkey, MT is located in the medial part of the posterior bank of the STS. It receives strong projections from Layer 4B of the striate cortex (Hawken et al., 1988), the recipient zone of the magnocellular pathway, and from the thick stripes of Area V2 (DeYoe & Van Essen, 1985; Shipp & Zeki, 1989); both regions contain a high incidence of directionally selective neurons. MT projects to the adjacent area, MST (Desimone & Ungerleider, 1986)—also rich in directionally selective cells—and provides inputs to other regions of the parietal cortex (Boussaoud, Ungerleider, & Desimone, 1990; Gattass & Gross, 1981). Together with these associated areas, MT constitutes an important component of the dorsal visual stream specialized for processing of visual motion and spatial information. MT also maintains reciprocal connections with Area V4 (Ungerleider & Desimone, 1986), allowing direct communication between the two streams; furthermore, it interconnects with some areas in prefrontal cortex (Schall, Morel, King, & Bullier, 1995) as well as with a number of subcortical structures, including the superior colliculus and pulvinar (Ungerleider, Desimone, Galkin, & Mishkin, 1984).

Functional Properties

MT contains a complete representation of the contralateral visual field, with a disproportionately large area devoted to central vision (Van Essen, Maunsell, & Bixby, 1981). Its neurons have relatively large receptive fields similar in size to those of V4 (Desimone & Ungerleider, 1986; see Figure 6.8). Selectivity for the direction and speed of stimulus motion is the defining characteristic of the majority of MT neurons (e.g., Albright, 1984; Maunsell & Van Essen, 1983b; Figure 6.14), and neurons with similar directional tuning are organized in columns (Albright, 1984). The majority of MT neurons respond best to the stimulation of both eyes and are selective for retinal disparity (DeAngelis & Newsome, 1999; Maunsell & Van Essen, 1983b; Tanaka et al., 1986); neurons with similar disparities cluster into columns, which extend over the thickness of cortex (Figure 6.15). The two sets of columns, direction and disparity, seem to occupy the same subregions in MT, but the relationship between them is still unclear (DeAngelis & Newsome, 1999).

Motion Integration

MT neurons display directional selectivity to smooth and sampled motion of random dots, bars (Figure 6.14), and gratings (Maunsell & Van Essen, 1983c; Mikami, Newsome, & Wurtz, 1986), as well as to more complex motion consisting

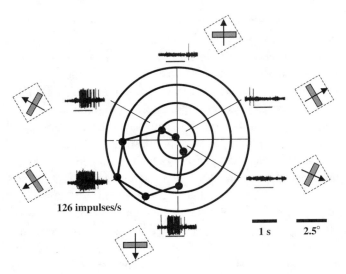

Figure 6.14 Direction-selective neuron in MT. Small slits of light (gray bars) were moved in various directions across the receptive field (dashed squares), and responses to individual presentations of each direction of motion were recorded. The polar plot shows average firing rates in response to each direction. The horizontal line below each response trace represents the stimulus duration. This neuron shows strong preference for the motion to the left and down (firing rate = 126 impulses/s) and did not respond to the opposite direction (to the right and up). Over 90% of neurons in MT show strong selectivity to stimulus direction, similar to that shown here. Adapted from Maunsell and Van Essen, 1983b.

of multiple motion vectors at the same part of the visual space (Albright, 1984; Britten, Shadlen, Newsome, & Movshon, 1992). This property of MT neurons was first demonstrated by Movshon et al. (1985) and later by Rodman and Albright (1989), who compared responses to moving gratings of different orientations to plaid patterns consisting of two component gratings. They found that although some MT neurons

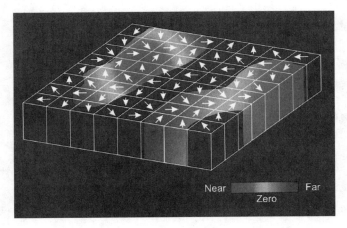

Figure 6.15 Columnar organization of direction and binocular disparity selectivity in MT. The surface of this slab corresponds to the surface of MT, and its height represents the thickness of cortex. Arrows denote the preferred direction of motion of MT neurons in each direction column. Preferred disparity is color coded, with green representing near disparities, red representing far disparities, and yellow indicating zero disparity. Blue regions denote portions of MT that have poor disparity tuning. From DeAngelis and Newsome, 1999. See insert for color version of this figure.

responded only to the motion of the individual components of the plaid, other neurons appeared capable of coding the direction of the whole plaid pattern—independent of the motions of component gratings. In contrast, direction-selective neurons in the striate cortex responded exclusively to the motion of the components of the plaid rather to the direction of plaid motion. It is interesting that the behavior of these pattern-selective neurons in MT responding to the direction of the plaid matched the percept reported by human observers viewing the plaid stimuli (Adelson & Movshon, 1982). These experiments demonstrate the emergence of neuronal properties that could be tied more directly to perception.

Subsequent studies have examined the responses of MT neurons to other types of complex motion, also consisting of multiple motion vectors presented in the same part of the visual space. For example, in contrast to V1 neurons, which respond equally well to nontransparent and transparent motion, responses of MT neurons to the motion of transparent surfaces formed by random dots moving in different directions are suppressed (Snowden, Treue, Erickson, & Andersen, 1991). Similar suppression has been observed with a smaller number of elements moving in different directions within an MT receptive field (Recanzone, Wurtz, & Schwartz, 1997). This suppression is reminiscent of the perception of motion transparency observed in human psychophysical experiments (Qian, Andersen, & Adelson, 1994) and is an example of the way MT neurons deal with multiple directional vectors at the same spatial location.

Another example illustrating the integrative properties of MT neurons comes from studies utilizing stochastic random-dot stimuli consisting of coherently and randomly moving dots (e.g., Britten, Shadlen, et al., 1992), in which the strength of motion is controlled by the proportion of spatiotemporally correlated dots. Britten, Shadlen, Newsome, and Movshon (1993) showed that the responses of MT neurons to such stimuli vary linearly with stimulus correlation, suggesting linear pooling of local directional signals provided by earlier stages of motion analysis—most likely by striate cortex neurons. Another study involving random-dot stimuli containing multiple directions showed that responses of direction-selective neurons in MT reflect the sum of their responses to the individual motion components (Treue, Hol, & Rauber, 2000).

Finally, direction-selective MT receptive fields have strong antagonistic surrounds, which—when stimulated by the same direction, speed, or both as the excitatory center—show strong inhibition (Allman, Miezin, & McGuinness, 1985; D. K. Xiao, Raiguel, Marcar, Koenderink, & Orban, 1995). This property illustrates the ability of MT neurons to integrate local motion signals with the context in which this motion appears, suggesting a role in the detection of relative motion and in figure-ground segregation.

Processing of Depth

A large proportion of neurons in MT are tuned for depth (DeAngelis & Newsome, 1999; Maunsell & Van Essen, 1983b; Tanaka et al., 1986) and are found clustered according to preferred disparity (see Figure 6.15). These neurons appear to contribute to stereoscopic depth perception; microstimulation of similarly tuned cells can bias the monkey's perceptual judgment of depth towards the preferred disparity (DeAngelis, Cumming, & Newsome, 1998). Apart from depth perception, the disparity tuning of these neurons appears to be relevant to other perceptual phenomena. For example, a difference in disparity of the display consisting of sheets of random dots creates the percept of transparent motion (Bradley, Quian, & Andersen, 1995; Qian et al., 1994), and changing the disparity in the surround of the classical receptive field modulates not only the response of MT neurons to motion, but also the percept of the direction of motion (Bradley, Chang, & Andersen, 1998; Duncan, Albright, & Stoner, 2000). It has also been suggested that MT may be involved in extracting shape from motion (Buracas & Albright, 1996; Dodd, Krug, Cumming, & Parker, 2001); furthermore, although there is evidence of the interaction between motion and disparity signals in the same neurons (Bradley et al., 1995), MT neurons do not appear to be tuned to motion in depth (Maunsell & Van Essen, 1983b).

Processing of Color

Although the activity of MT neurons is strongly influenced by the magnocellular pathway (Maunsell, Nealey, & DePreist, 1990)—not known to carry color-opponent signals—many MT neurons maintain significant responses to motion of isoluminant stimuli (Gegenfurtner et al., 1994; Seidemann, Poirson, Wandell, & Newsome, 1999; Thiele, Dobkins, & Albright, 2001). Furthermore, the presence of chromatic information has been shown to increase neuronal direction discrimination (Croner & Albright, 1999). Although chromatic signals reaching MT are much weaker than the luminance signals are, the activity in MT to isoluminant gratings appears to be sufficient to explain the performance of monkeys in a color-based motion discrimination task (Thiele et al., 2001).

Relating Activity of MT Neurons to Perception

Newsome and colleagues have used stochastic random-dot stimuli (discussed previously) as a tool to study the relationship between the activity of single neurons and behavioral performance (Britten, Shadlen, et al., 1992; Newsome, Britten, & Movshon, 1989). They have found that single MT neurons are able to detect the direction of motion in such stimuli at nearly the same level as the monkeys performing the task. They concluded that only a small number of MT neurons are needed to explain the perceptual judgments made by the monkeys. Subsequently, Britten and Newsome (1998) examined directional tuning of MT neurons near psychophysical threshold and modified this view, concluding that direction discrimination near threshold is likely to depend on a population of MT neurons with a wide range of preferred directions.

Other powerful evidence that monkeys use signals from MT during the performance of this task comes from microstimulation experiments (Bisley, Zaksas, & Pasternak, 2001; Salzman, Britten, & Newsome, 1990; Seidemann, Zohary, & Newsome, 1998). In these studies, low-current stimulation of physiologically identified directional columns in MT applied during the presentation of random dots at various levels of coherence biased the animals' decisions toward the preferred direction of the stimulated directional column (Salzman et al., 1990; Salzman, Murasagi, Britten, & Newsome, 1992). Bisley et al. (2001) recently applied higher current stimulation during the performance of a discrimination task in which the monkey compared two directions of motion separated in time (see Figure 6.16). When stimulation was applied during the presentation of the first of the two stimuli, the monkeys consistently reported that the stimulus was moving in the direction preferred by the stimulated neurons—regardless of the true stimulus direction (Figure 6.16, Panels B and C). Furthermore, the monkeys reported motion in the preferred direction of the stimulated column even when the stimulus consisted of stationary dots. Thus, MT neurons appear to be the main source of information used by the monkeys to judge the directions of stimulus motion.

Effects of MT Lesions

Studies involving lesions of MT have confirmed to a large degree the ideas about the role of MT in motion perception, as suggested by the neurophysiological and microstimulation experiments. Although some of the lesion effects were transient and showed substantial postlesion recovery with training (Newsome & Pare, 1988; Rudolph & Pasternak, 1999), they were selective for the properties characteristic of MT neurons. Thus, direction and speed discrimination, motion integration, and the ability to extract motion from noise were selectively affected by the damage to MT (Bisley & Pasternak, 2000; Newsome & Pare, 1988; Pasternak & Merigan, 1994; Rudolph & Pasternak, 1999). Deficits in processing of speed information were also revealed by measuring saccades and smooth pursuit of the moving targets (Dursteler, Wurtz, & Newsome, 1987; Newsome, Wurtz, Dursteler, & Mikami, 1985; Schiller & Lee, 1994).

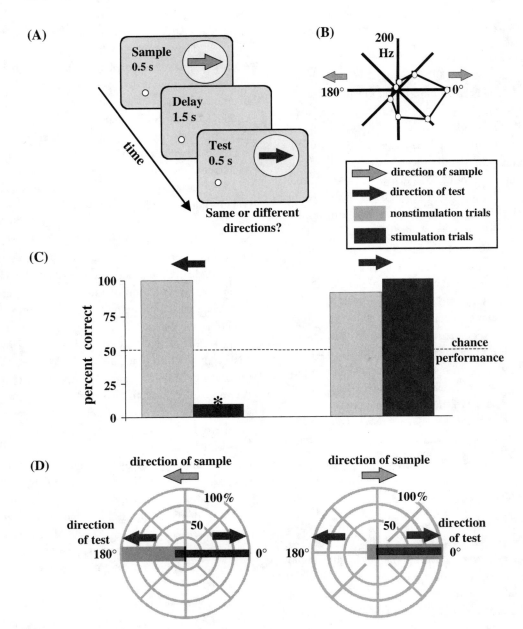

Figure 6.16 Microstimulation of a directionally selective column in MT.

A. Behavioral task. The monkeys compared two directions of moving random-dot stimuli presented in sequence and separated by a brief (1.5 s) delay. They were rewarded for correctly reporting the two stimuli as moving in the same or different directions by pressing one of two buttons. The two stimuli always moved either in the same or in opposite directions, and the directions of sample motion were selected on the basis of the preferred direction of the stimulated site in MT.

B. Direction selectivity profile of a representative site in MT measured by recording multiunit activity. Note that this site responds best to rightward-moving stimuli.

C. Effect of microstimulation of the site in MT shown in B. Stimulation was applied during the entire duration of the *sample* on 25% of the trials. The performance during nonstimulation trials (gray columns) was nearly perfect for the sample moving to the right (preferred direction) or to the left (null direction). During stimulation trials (blue columns) the monkeys performed at 100% correct when the sample moved rightward (columns on the right) but near 0% correct when sample moved leftward.

D. Analysis of trials in which the monkey equated the direction of the sample with the direction of the test (*same* trials). The axes on the polar plot indicate the direction of motion of the test stimulus. The distance from the origin shows the percent of trials in which sample direction was equated with test direction. During nonstimulation trials, the monkeys equated sample and test almost every time the sample and test both moved to the right or to the left. During stimulation trials, the monkey always equated the sample with the rightward-moving test regardless of the true direction of the sample; this suggests that the monkey interpreted signals produced by stimulation of the rightward directional column as directional motion signals.

Area MST

Anatomy

Area MST, the medial superior temporal area, was first identified as the MT-recipient zone by Maunsell and Van Essen (1983a). It communicates with the far-peripheral-field representations of Areas V1 and V2 as well as with the parieto-occipital visual area of the dorsal pathway (Boussaoud et al., 1990; Maunsell & Van Essen, 1983a). MST consists of two functionally and anatomically distinct regions: dorsal (MSTd) and ventrolateral (MSTv or MSTl; Tanaka, Fukada, & Saito, 1989; Tanaka & Saito, 1989).

Functional Properties

Neurons in MSTd have very large receptive fields and prefer motion of full-field stimuli (Desimone & Ungerleider, 1986; Saito et al., 1986; Tanaka et al., 1986), whereas cells in MSTl generally have smaller receptive fields and respond preferentially to motion of small objects (Tanaka, 1998). Properties of MSTd neurons suggest a role in integrating visual motion signals—generated during the observer's movement through the environment—with eye-movement and vestibular signals (Andersen, 1997). On the other hand, neurons in MSTl are more likely to be involved in the analysis of object motion in the environment (Tanaka, 1998) and in the maintenance of pursuit eye movements associated with this motion (Komatsu & Wurtz, 1988).

Processing of Optic Flow

MSTd neurons have been implicated in the processing of *optic flow,* the motion of the visual world perceived by observers during their own movement through the environment. This type of visual motion can be a source of information about the direction of self-motion (Gibson, 1994).

Neurons in MSTd respond to various types of motion of large-field flow patterns, such as expansion, contraction, rotation, translation, or a combination of these (Duffy & Wurtz, 1991; Lagae, Maes, Raiguel, Xiao, & Orban, 1994; Tanaka & Saito, 1989). In response to full-field optic flow stimuli, many of these neurons have a preferred location of the focus of expansion (FOE), which may serve as a cue of the direction of heading (Duffy & Wurtz, 1997; Page & Duffy, 1999; Upadhyay, Page, & Duffy, 2000; see Figure 6.17). These neurons often do not discriminate between the optic flow created by the movement of a subject and simulated optic flow (Duffy, 1998); their responses are largely unaffected by eye or head movements (Bradley, Maxwell, Andersen, Banks, & Shenoy, 1996; Page & Duffy, 1999; Shenoy, Bradley, & Andersen, 1999).

Although it is still not clear how the visual cues resulting from self-motion are utilized, it appears that the computation of the direction of heading is likely to be represented in the population of MST neurons rather than at level of single neurons (Paolini, Distler, Bremmer, Lappe, & Hoffmann, 2000).

Thus, MSTd has the machinery needed to extract and signal the direction of heading from optic flow stimuli (Lappe, Bremmer, Pekel, Thiele, & Hoffmann, 1996; van den Berg & Beintema, 2000). The evidence that the use of such information may depend on MST has been provided by Britten and van Wezel (1998), who took advantage of clustering of neurons preferring the same direction of heading and applied electrical microstimulation to them. This manipulation produced biased decisions about direction of heading provided by from optic flow stimuli. It should be pointed out, however, that there is no direct evidence that this mechanism is actually utilized during self-motion. Although some evidence indicates that humans use optic flow to control walking (Warren, Kay, Zosh, Duchon, & Sahuc, 2001), much more conclusive data suggest that rather than using optic flow, humans usually aim towards an object and correct their aim as they walk (Rushton, Harris, Lloyd, & Wann, 1998).

Retinal Disparity and Object Motion

Some properties of MSTl neurons are reminiscent of neurons in MT. For example, in addition to similarly sized receptive fields, many neurons in MSTl are tuned for retinal disparity, and some show a change in direction selectivity when disparity is changed (Eifuku & Wurtz, 1999; Roy, Komatsu, & Wurtz, 1992; Takemura, Inoue, Kawano, Quaia, & Miles, 2001). Also similar to MT is that neurons in this region have antagonistic surrounds and respond very strongly to object motion when the motion in the surround is in the opposite direction (Eifuku & Wurtz, 1998). This sensitivity to relative motion of objects suggests that these neurons may play a role in segmenting moving objects from backgrounds.

Involvement in Eye Movements

MSTd neurons have also been shown to participate in mechanisms underlying both voluntary and involuntary eye movements. They are active during smooth-pursuit eye movements (Komatsu & Wurtz, 1988), and the ability to match the speed of the target during pursuit is affected by lesioning (Dursteler & Wurtz, 1988) and by electrical stimulation of these neurons (Komatsu & Wurtz, 1989). MSTd neurons are also active prior to the ocular following response (OFR), an involuntary short-latency tracking eye movement evoked by a sudden movement of a stable environment (Kawano, Shidara, Watanabe, &

(A)

(B)

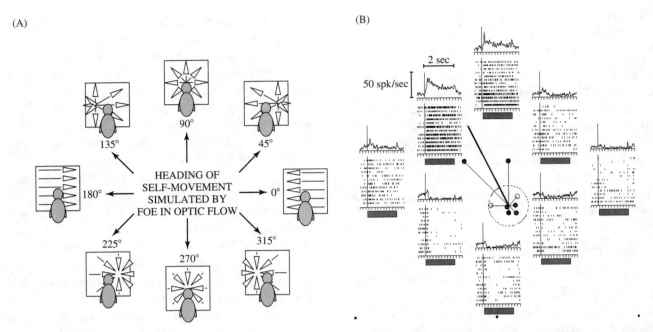

Figure 6.17   Neuronal responses to optic flow in MST. Responses of a single neuron recorded in the medial superior temporal area (MST) of an awake rhesus monkey.

A. Eight optic flow stimuli were presented in a pseudorandom sequence. Each frame represents the 90° × 90° rear-projection screen as viewed by a monkey (shaded figure) that is fixating a point at the center of the screen. The arrows in each frame illustrate the local direction of white dot movement on the otherwise black background of the screen. The focus of expansion (FOE) at the junction of the arrows is a cue about the simulated direction of self-movement. The large arrows indicate the heading direction of self-movement that is simulated by the adjacent optic flow pattern.

B. The responses of a neuron that showed a strong preference for the left-forward direction of simulated self-movement. Responses to repeated presentations of the optic flow stimuli are shown as spike rasters in which each vertical deflection indicates the occurrence of a neuronal action potential. Spike density histograms graph the average firing rate across the presentation period (shaded bar) for the stimulus at the corresponding position in A. The polar plot at the center includes eight limbs (narrow lines) with directions that indicate the simulated heading direction in a stimulus; the lengths indicate the relative firing rate evoked by that stimulus. The control firing rate, recorded during trials in which no optic flow stimulus was presented, is indicated by the radius of the circle. The balls at the end of each polar limb indicate whether the response represented by that limb was significantly different from the control firing rate. The net vector (bold line) is the sum of the stimulus vectors and indicates the preferred direction of that response and the strength of that directional preference. Courtesy of C. J. Duffy, 2001.

Yamane, 1994; Miles, Kawano, & Optican, 1986; Takemura, Inoue, & Kawano, 2000). Because these responses are also affected by MST lesions (Dursteler & Wurtz, 1988), it is likely that this area serves a role in the circuitry subserving OFR.

In sum, the properties of this important component of the dorsal visual stream point to its role in the processing of motion information in active observers. Neurons in MSTd are capable of integrating visual information extracted during movement of the observer with signals related to eye and head movements (Andersen, Shenoy, Syder, Bradley, & Crowell, 1999). On the other hand, MSTl may contribute to the ability to detect and pursue motion of small objects in complex environments.

Area LIP

Anatomy

The lateral intraparietal area (LIP) and its contribution to visually guided behavior have received a lot of attention in recent

years. Studies examining the properties of LIP neurons have focused on its role in the encoding of a representation of visual space, in planning eye movements, and in spatial attention. It receives inputs from a number of cortical regions, including V2, V3, V3A, V4, MT, MST, TEO, and TE (Andersen, Asanuma, & Cowan, 1985; Andersen, Asanuma, et al., 1990; Blatt, Andersen, & Stoner, 1990). It is reciprocally interconnected with Areas VIP and 7a in the parietal cortex (Blatt et al., 1990; Seltzer & Pandya, 1986), with the prefrontal and premotor cortex, and with the superior colliculus and pulvinar (Cavada & Goldman-Rakic, 1989; Schall et al., 1995).

Functional Properties

LIP contains a representation of the contralateral visual field; more than half of its neurons are devoted to processing stimuli in a region of about 6° around the fovea (Ben Hamed, Duhamel, Bremmer, & Graf, 2001). Receptive fields in LIP are larger than those in MT, although they are well defined and increase in size with eccentricity from about 5° near the fovea (Ben Hamed et al., 2001).

Neurons in LIP have a number of properties not seen at earlier levels of visual processing. Although they respond to the onset of visual stimuli (Robinson, Goldberg, & Stanton, 1978), they also show memory activity in tasks requiring saccadic eye movements to remembered spatial locations (Barash, Bracewell, Fogassi, Gnadt, & Andersen, 1991a, 1991b; Gnadt & Andersen, 1988). There is also evidence that the activity of LIP neurons is modulated by the position of the eye in the orbit (Andersen, Bracewell, Barash, Gnadt, & Fogassi, 1990) and that these neurons store information not only in eye-centered (Duhamel, Colby, & Goldberg, 1992), but also in body-centered coordinates (Snyder, Grieve, Brotchie, & Andersen, 1998). Another intriguing feature of LIP neurons is that the spatial representation of the remembered stimulus is dynamic and shifts to the corresponding retinal location around the time of a saccade (Duhamel et al., 1992; see Figure 6.18). Thus, neurons in the parietal cortex update the retinal coordinates of remembered stimuli to anticipate the upcoming eye movement. This remapping—important for maintaining continuous representation of the

visual world during eye movements—is not unique to LIP; it has also been observed in other visual areas, including V2, V3, and V3A (Nakamura & Colby, 2000, 2002).

These properties—together with observations showing that LIP neurons fire in preparation for a saccade—lead to the hypothesis that the memory activity preceding the saccade represents an intention to make a saccade to the remembered location (Andersen, Snyder, Bradley, & Xing, 1997; Mazzoni, Bracewell, Barash, & Andersen, 1996; Platt & Glimcher, 1997; Snyder, Batista, & Andersen, 1997). According to this hypothesis, LIP activity is indicative of the role of LIP in sensorimotor transformations that take place in preparation for action. An alternative hypothesis is based on results showing that the visual and memory responses are modulated by the salience and behavioral significance of visual stimuli (Colby, Duhamel, & Goldberg, 1996; Gottlieb, Kusunoki, & Goldberg, 1998; Powell & Goldberg, 2000). This hypothesis suggests that the level of activity in LIP is used by the brain to allocate attention to the region of greatest activity—whether it is driven by a salient stimulus, such as a saccade target, or by top-down mechanisms. Whether LIP is involved in motor planning, attention, or both, the activity of these neurons

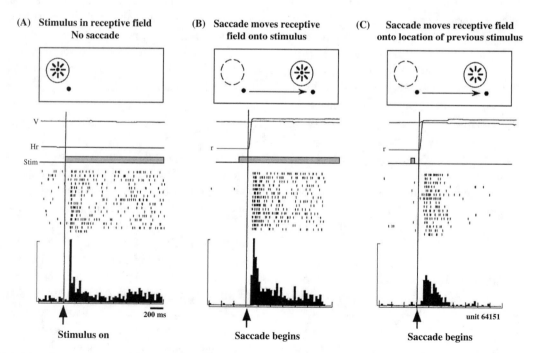

Figure 6.18 Remapping of memory trace activity in Area LIP. The top of each panel shows the task, followed by the vertical and horizontal eye traces. The thick gray bar shows the duration of the visual stimulus. The activity in single trials is illustrated by the tick marks, and the histogram shows the mean activity in 25-ms bins.

A. During fixation, this LIP neuron responds to the stimulus in the receptive field.

B. The response following a saccade that moves the stimulus onto the receptive field.

C. The response following a saccade that moves the location where the stimulus had flashed onto the receptive field. The stimulus was presented for 50 ms and is extinguished before the saccade begins. The response is thus to a memory trace that has been remapped from the coordinates of the initial eye position to those of the final eye position. Adapted from Colby and Olson, 1999.

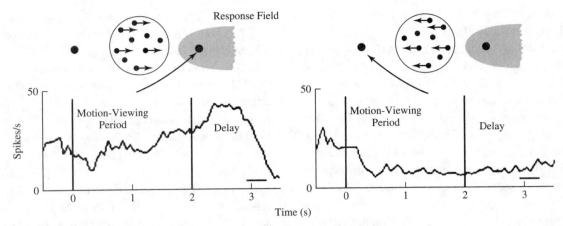

Figure 6.19 Responses of a LIP neuron during the performance of a direction discrimination task. The monkey judged the direction of motion of a dynamic random-dot stimulus by making saccadic eye movements to one of two targets (black spots). The targets were placed either in the LIP receptive field or in a remote location. The plots show the activity of an LIP neuron during the presentation of the visual motion stimulus and during the delay prior to the saccade. The authors suggest that this activity represents a neural correlate of the decision process that involves integration of sensory signals toward a decision appropriate for guiding movement. Reprinted from *Neuron, 21,* M. I. Leon and M. N. Shadlen, Exploring the neurophysiology of decisions, 669–672, Copyright 1998, with permission from Elsevier Science.

provides the opportunity to study neural correlates of cognitive behavior (Leon & Shadlen, 1998; Platt & Glimcher, 1999; Shadlen & Newsome, 1996; Shadlen & Newsome, 2001; also see Figure 6.19).

Some neurons in LIP also display properties more common in other visual areas; these areas include selectivity for stimulus shape (Sereno & Maunsell, 1998) and the direction of stimulus motion (Eskandar & Assad, 1999). However, it is not clear whether these response properties represent a role in processing this information, or whether these are just the remnants of signals from the multitude of areas that project to LIP. In summary, LIP neurons appear to carry visual-, memory-, and saccade-related signals that are modulated by the behavioral significance of the stimulus, suggesting that they are involved in sensorimotor transformations taking place in preparation for goal-oriented eye movements and possibly involved in the allocation of visual attention.

Area VIP

The ventral intraparietal area (VIP) has prominent connections from MT, MST, and FST; unlike LIP, however, it receives few (if any) inputs from the ventral pathway (Boussaoud et al., 1990; Colby, Duhamel, & Goldberg, 1993). This evidence and its interactions with other parietal areas suggest that VIP plays a role exclusively in the dorsal stream. Receptive fields of neurons in this area are similar in size to those found in LIP (Duhamel, Colby, & Goldberg, 1998) and show selectivity for optic flow (Colby et al., 1993; Schaafsma & Duysens, 1996). The responses of many VIP neurons are modulated by eye position, and individual neurons can encode information in

eye-centered coordinates through to head-centered coordinates (Bremmer, Graf, Ben Hamed, & Duhamel, 1999; Duhamel, Bremmer, Ben Hamed, & Graf, 1997). Some neurons have been found to prefer stimuli that are close to the animal (Colby et al., 1993); most of these cells also respond to tactile stimuli in congruent locations on the head to the visual receptive fields (Duhamel et al., 1998). This has lead to the suggestion that this region is involved in a construction of a multisensory head-centered representation of near personal space (Duhamel et al., 1998).

Area STPa

STPa receives inputs from both visual streams (Baizer, Ungerleider, & Desimone, 1991; Boussaoud et al., 1990) and has been proposed to be a region of convergence and integration of form and motion signals (Oram & Perrett, 1996). Its neurons respond to visual as well as to somatosensory and auditory stimuli (Bruce, Desimone, & Gross, 1981); they have large, gaze centered, receptive fields, and they show selectivity to visual motion similar to that observed in Areas MT and MST (K. C. Anderson & Siegel, 1999; Oram, Perrett, & Hietanen, 1993). Some neurons also respond particularly well to biological motion, such as that made by a walking person (K. C. Anderson & Siegel, 1998; Perrett et al., 1985; Oram & Perrett, 1996).

Area 7a

Area 7a constitutes the final stage in the hierarchy within the dorsal visual stream and is interconnected with a wide

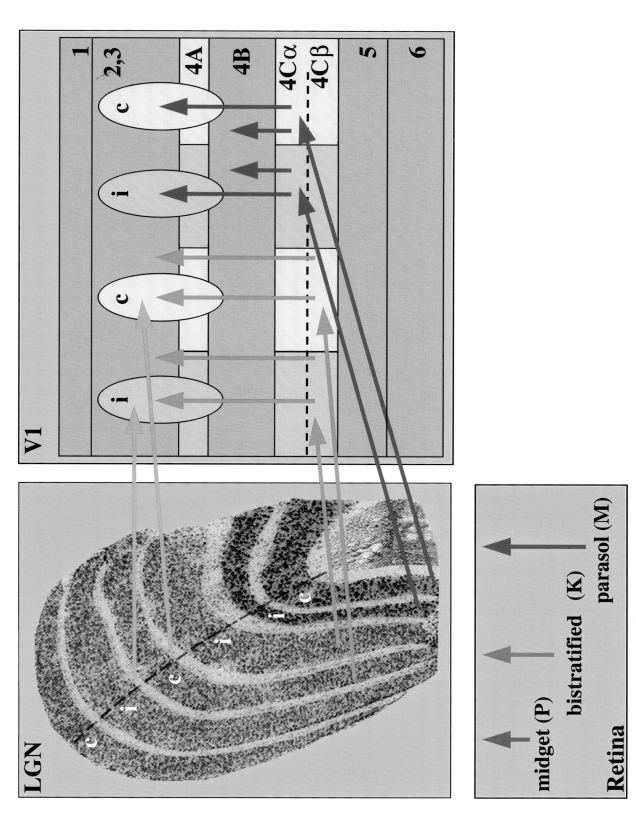

Figure 6.4 Schematic of early visual pathways from retina to V1. In retina, three main types of ganglion cell project to the P (dashed), M (solid) and K (dotted) regions of the LGN. The six primary M and P layers of the LGN are segregated by eye input; the input to each K layer generally reflects the input to the primary layer just dorsal to it.

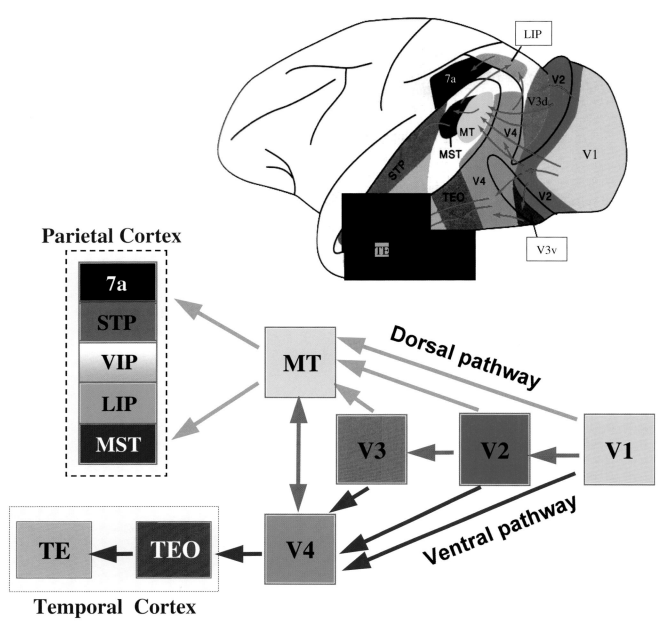

Figure 6.7 Visual areas in monkey cortex. The diagram of the monkey brain shows the location of cortical areas and their primary connections. The *dorsal* and the *ventral visual pathways* streaming towards the parietal and temporal lobes are shown in a simplified diagram. All the connections between cortical areas are largely reciprocal. The diagram of the monkey brain has been adapted from Farag, Humphreys, and Rodman, 1999.

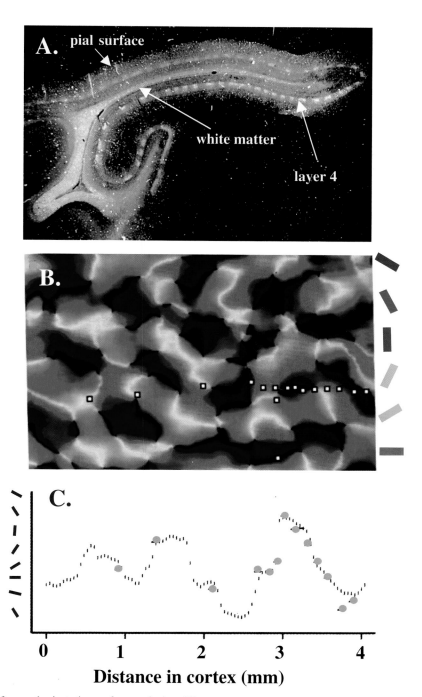

Figure 6.11 Organization of eye and orientation preferences in Area V1.

A. Ocular dominance columns in monkey cortex seen as alternating bright and dark patches in Layer 4 in a section cut perpendicularly to the surface. One eye of a monkey was injected with a radioactively labeled amino acid, which was taken up by cell bodies in the retina and transported to the LGN, whose axons terminate in Layer 4 in the striate cortex. Areas in the cortex that receive input from the injected eye are labeled and appear bright; the alternating unlabeled patches receive input from the uninjected eye. The white matter has a bright appearance because it contains labeled axons of LGN neurons. Adapted from Hubel and Wiesel, 1979.

B. Orientation columns in monkeys V1 revealed by optically imaging and comparing local changes in reflectance, which indicate activation. Imaging of the cortical surface was performed in anesthetized monkeys presented with stimuli of various orientations. Areas that were most active during the presentation of a particular orientation are indicated by the color bars. Complementary colors represent orthogonal orientations: Red and green indicate maximal activity for vertical and horizontal orientations, and blue and yellow indicate maximal activity for left and right obliques. Adapted from Blasdel and Salama, 1986.

C. Preferred orientation of neurons recorded with the microelectrode along the track indicated by the white squares in the optical image shown in B. The preferred orientations of the recorded neurons corresponds to those revealed with optical imaging. Adapted from Blasdel and Salama, 1986.

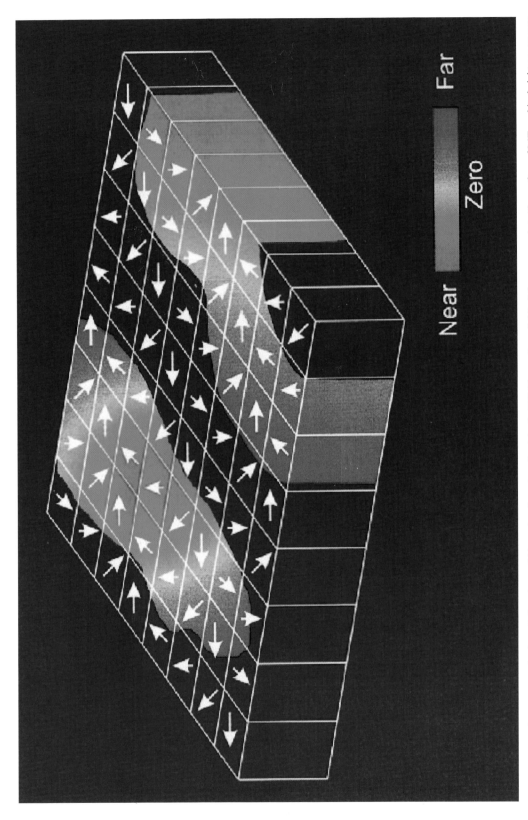

Figure 6.15 Columnar organization of direction and binocular disparity selectivity in MT. The surface of this slab corresponds to the surface of MT, and its height represents the thickness of cortex. Arrows denote the preferred direction of motion of MT neurons in each direction column. Preferred disparity is color coded, with green representing near disparities, red representing far disparities, and yellow representing zero disparity. Blue regions denote portions of MT that have poor disparity tuning. From De Angelis and Newsome, 1999.

range of cortical and subcortical regions providing visual and visuomotor signals important for the execution of visually guided behavior. It receives inputs from Areas LIP and MST, as well as from other visually responsive areas in the parietal cortex (Andersen, Asanuma, et al., 1990; Cavada & Goldman-Rakic, 1989). It sends ascending projections to the prefrontal cortex (Cavada & Goldman-Rakic, 1989; Neal, Pearson, & Powell, 1990; Selemon & Goldman-Rakic, 1988) as well as to the inferotemporal cortex, LIP, STPa, and the basal ganglia (for review, see Siegel & Read, 1997). Neurons in Area 7a have large receptive fields that are often bilateral (Blatt et al., 1990). They respond to visual stimuli (Mountcastle, Lynch, Georgopoulos, Sakata & Acuna, 1975; Robinson et al., 1978) and are active during fixation and visual tracking eye movements (Bremmer, Distler, & Hoffmann, 1997; Kawano, Sasaki, & Yamashita, 1984; Sakata, Shibutani, & Kawano, 1983). Because the activity of these neurons is largely not affected by changes in body or head position during saccades to specific retinal locations, it is likely that these cells encode information in world-referenced coordinates (Snyder et al., 1998).

Some neurons in Area 7a possess properties similar to those encountered at preceding stages of processing in the dorsal visual stream. These neurons are sensitive to complex visual motion, exhibiting selectivity to rotational motion (Sakata, Shibutani, Ito, & Tsurugai, 1986; Sakata, Shibutani, Ito, Tsurugai, Mine, & Kusunoki, 1994), to the optic flow patterns, and to rotational motion components (Phinney & Siegel, 2000; Read & Siegel, 1997; Siegel & Read, 1997).

A number of studies have shown that responses of 7a neurons are modulated by the behavioral relevance of the stimulus appearing in the receptive field (Mountcastle, Andersen, & Motter, 1981; Robinson et al., 1978). A salient or behaviorally relevant object appearing in a nonattended location can enhance the activity of a neuron, whereas the same object appearing in the attended region often reduces its activity (Constantinidis & Steinmetz, 2001; Steinmetz, Connor, Constantinidis, & McLaughlin, 1994). This phenomenon— also observed in LIP neurons (Powell & Goldberg, 2000)— suggests that Area 7a together with LIP may play a role in the control of spatial attention.

Other Vision-Related Areas in Parietal Cortex

There are a number of less studied visually responsive areas in the parietal cortex; little is known about their role in visually guided behavior. Some of these areas appear to be associated with somatosensory and motor-cortical areas. Among these areas are V6 and V6A (Galletti, Fattori, Battaglini, Shipp, & Zeki, 1996; Nakamura, Chung, Graziano, & Gross, 1999), the medial intraparietal area (area MIP), the medial

dorsal parietal area (MDP), and Area 7m (Ferraina et al., 1997; P. B. Johnson, Ferraina, Bianchi, & Caminiti, 1996; Luppino, Murata, Govoni, & Matelli, 1999).

Area FST contains visually responsive neurons with large receptive fields at the center of gaze and—unlike STPa—has limited directional selectivity (Desimone & Ungerleider, 1986). Little is known about the function of this area, which appears to lie at a level similar to that of MST within the visual hierarchy.

COGNITIVE MODULATION OF CORTICAL ACTIVITY: VISUAL ATTENTION

With the use of a number of simple but effective behavioral paradigms such as change blindness and attentional blindness (Rensink, 2000), it has become clear that visual attention is necessary for the construction of the visual world we perceive. These behavioral paradigms demonstrate that without the ability to allocate attention, detecting even large changes in the visual world becomes difficult. In the laboratory, directing attention to a specific location of the visual field speeds up detection and increases sensitivity to visual stimuli presented at that location (Bashinski & Bacharach, 1980; Bowman, Brown, Kertzman, Schwarz, & Robinson, 1993; Posner, 1980; Yantis & Jonides, 1984). Neurophysiological correlates of this enhancement have been found in many visual areas, including V1 (Ito & Gilbert, 1999; Roelfsema, Lamme, & Spekreijse, 1998), V2 (Luck, Chelazzi, Hillyard, & Desimone, 1997; Reynolds, Chelazzi, & Desimone, 1999), V3A (Nakamura & Colby, 2000), V4 (Fischer & Boch, 1981; McAdams & Maunsell, 1999; Moran & Desimone, 1985; Reynolds, Pasternak, & Desimone, 2000), MT, and MST (Seidemann & Newsome, 1999; Treue & Maunsell, 1996).

Effects of attention on processing of visual stimuli have been found already at the V1 level. For example, Ito and Gilbert (1999) have shown that although the attentional state of an animal has no detectable effect on responses to oriented stimuli placed in the receptive field, it affects neuronal activity when these stimuli are surrounded by flanking lines placed outside the receptive field. The authors proposed that this modulation is accomplished by feedback connections from higher-order cortical areas.

The enhancement of neural activity associated with the demand of the behavioral task has been studied most extensively in Area V4. Neurons in this area show enhanced responses to visual stimuli when they become the target of a saccade (Fischer & Boch, 1981; Moore, Tolias, & Schiller, 1998) or when a single stimulus used by the monkey in the discrimination task is placed in the receptive field (McAdams &

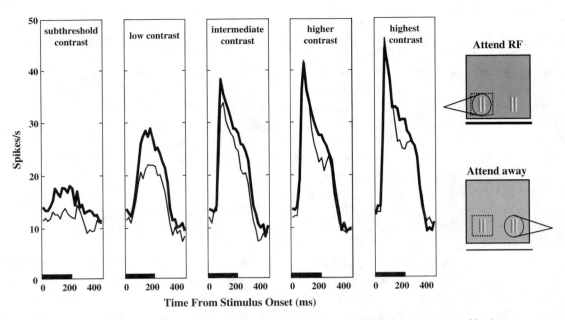

Figure 6.20 Effect of attention on sensitivity to contrast in Area V4. Responses of V4 neurons to stimuli across a range of luminance contrasts were recorded while the monkey discriminated a target stimulus appearing in a sequence of nontargets. The bar-shaped patches of grating were simultaneously presented at two locations—one in the receptive field (indicated by a dashed square) and the other at an equally eccentric position in the opposite hemifield. The monkey performed a discrimination task either with stimuli in the receptive field (*attend RF*) or with stimuli away from the receptive field (*attend away*). Each panel shows the response at a particular contrast, averaged across the population of 84 neurons. Black lines show average response to the attended stimuli; gray lines show response to the ignored stimuli. Attention caused a greater increase in the response at low contrast than at high contrast. Thus, attention increased sensitivity of V4 neurons to contrast. Adapted from Reynolds et al., 2000.

Maunsell, 1999; Motter, 1994; Reynolds, Pasternak, & Desimone, 2000). This attentional enhancement is greatest when the discriminative stimulus is presented at near-threshold contrasts, resulting in an increase in neuronal sensitivity to contrast (Reynolds et al., 2000; Figure 6.20). Attentional effects on neuronal firing are even more pronounced when two stimuli are placed within the receptive field of a V4 neuron; in this case, the response is primarily driven by the attended stimulus (Moran & Desimone, 1985; Reynolds et al., 1999). These observations lead to the hypothesis that within the circuitry of extrastriate cortex, there is a mechanism that gates out the unattended stimulus (Desimone, 1998)—and that this gating may be due to the interaction between neighboring receptive fields (Connor, Preddie, Gallant, & Van Essen, 1997). In animals with lesions in V4, attention appears to be automatically allocated to the most salient stimulus, suggesting that the mechanism that controls the gating may include neurons within V4 (De Weerd, Peralta, Desimone, & Ungerleider, 1999; Schiller, 1993).

Although earlier studies identified V4 and the ventral visual stream as one of the main sites of attentional influences on visual processing, a number of recent studies have demonstrated similar influences in visual cortical areas within the dorsal visual stream. For example, Treue and Maunsell (1999) have shown that directing attention to the receptive field in Areas MT and MST results in an increase in neuronal firing. This effect was more pronounced when two spots moving in the preferred and the nonpreferred direction were placed in the receptive field; attention was directed from the nonpreferred to the preferred direction. In a subsequent study, Treue and Martinez Trujillo (1999) have demonstrated that attention increases the gain of direction-selective neurons. These effects are similar to those found in V4 and show that attention enhances the representation of the attended stimuli and reduces the influence of unattended stimuli.

COGNITIVE MODULATION OF CORTICAL ACTIVITY: VISUAL MEMORY

Traditionally, sensory cortical areas have not been viewed as regions that play a role in retaining information about the stimuli they process. However, there is now accumulating evidence of the active involvement of sensory areas in neuronal circuitry underlying temporary storage of this information (Fuster, 1997). This type of storage—often referred to as *working memory*—remains active for only a few seconds and is distinct from long-term memory (Squire, 1987). Its major function is to briefly retain information to be used in specific tasks, a function fundamental to the successful execution of visually guided behaviors.

Much of the neurophysiological work studying the neural mechanisms of visual working memory has focused on IT, which represents a relatively advanced stage of processing within the ventral visual stream (Merigan & Maunsell, 1993). Such studies have reported that IT neurons of monkeys trained to remember visual properties of objects and maintain an elevated firing rate during the delay after a specific color, shape, or location is presented (e.g. Fuster, 1990; Miller, Li, & Desimone, 1993; Miyashita & Chang, 1988). These results have been interpreted as evidence that these neurons may be involved in the short-term storage of information about stimulus form, color, or location. Neurons in V4, which provide a major input to IT, also show enhanced responses to previously cued visual stimuli (e.g., Ferrera et al., 1994; Motter, 1994). Furthermore, there is also some evidence that lesions of V4 affect performance of some memory-related tasks (Desimone, Lehky, Ungerleider, & Mishkin, 1990; Walsh, Le Mare, Blaimire, & Cowey, 2000).

Within the dorsal visual stream, memory-related activity has been reported in Area 7a for motion (Ferrera et al., 1994) and in spatial memory tasks in Areas 7a and LIP (Barash et al., 1991b; Constantinidis & Steinmetz, 1996), although it is not clear whether this latter activity represents short-term memory per se or whether it is a neural mechanism used to track the spatial locations of previously identified objects of importance. Neurons in MT do not show the same sustained pattern of memory-related activity as neurons in 7a, V4, or IT (Ferrera et al., 1994). However, there is accumulating evidence that this area shows a pattern of activation during the delay that is indicative of its participation in storage of visual information (Droll, Bisley, & Pasternak, 2000). This observation is consistent with the suggestion provided by lesion and microstimulation studies that MT may be involved in storing the information it encodes (Bisley & Pasternak, 2000; Bisley et al., 2001).

CONCLUDING REMARKS

In recent years the visual system of nonhuman primates has become the system of choice in the study of neural mechanisms underlying visual perception. One reason is the apparent similarity in visual function between old-world monkeys and humans. The second reason is that the development of behavioral and neurophysiological procedures has provided an opportunity to record neural activity in monkeys that can be directly related to visually guided behavior. These techniques have provided new insights into the properties of visually responsive neurons at various stages of cortical analysis. The first—and perhaps most important—realization that emerged from these studies is that visual cortical (and probably thalamic) neurons are not simply passive processors of any stimulus that appears on the retina as long as the stimulus matches the preferences of its receptive field. There is now evidence that as early in processing as the primary visual cortex, responses of neurons are defined not only by the properties of the visual stimulus, but also by its behavioral significance. The modulation of neuronal responses by the behavioral significance of a stimulus has been well documented in Areas V2 and V4, in MT, and in the posterior parietal cortex. The results reported by many of these studies suggest that some of the characteristics of cortical receptive fields established in experiments performed with anesthetized animals may have to be reexamined. Another feature of visual cortical neurons that emerged from combining neurophysiological recordings with behavioral testing is their ability to change their receptive fields as a result of training. This plasticity has until recently been considered to be the property of a developing brain; however, it appears to be present in the adult inferotemporal cortex (Kobatake et al., 1998) and has been documented in striate cortex (Crist, Li, & Gilbert, 2001). There is also accumulating evidence that visual cortical neurons—particularly those at middle and later stages of analysis—not only are involved in processing visual information, but also participate in circuits underlying its storage (see Fuster, 1995). These results further emphasize the dynamic and plastic nature of neural circuitry underlying processing of visual information. They also point to the continued participation of this circuitry in more cognitive processes (e.g., memory and learning)—processes that until recently have been thought to be localized to regions outside of traditionally defined sensory systems.

These developments call for the application of approaches that would allow examination of the neural basis of visually guided behaviors by simultaneously monitoring the activity of wider brain regions. Functional magnetic resonance imaging (fMRI), is one such technique. Introduced only about 10 years ago, fMRI has become widely used in the study of neural activity-related signals associated with visual processing in humans (Courtney & Ungerleider, 1997; Wandell, 1999). The development of this approach with nonhuman primates should provide an important tool for simultaneously examining neural activity in multiple brain regions during the performance of visual-guided behaviors; several laboratories have recently begun successful efforts in that direction (Dubowitz et al., 1998; Logothetis, Guggenberger, Peled, & Pauls, 1999; Stefanacci et al., 1998). Another important approach to examining the activity of neuronal ensembles in multiple brain regions is simultaneous microelectrode recordings from multiple brain regions. This valuable tool has already been applied in several laboratories with some success (see Nowak, Munk, James, Girard, & Bullier, 1999; Varela, Lachaux, Rodriguez, & Martinerie, 2001) and holds great promise.

REFERENCES

Adelson, E. H., & Movshon, J. A. (1982). Phenomenal coherence of moving visual patterns. *Nature, 300,* 523–525.

Albright, T. D. (1984). Direction and orientation selectivity of neurons in visual area MT of the macaque. *Journal of Neurophysiology, 52,* 1106–1130.

Allman, J. M., & Kaas, J. H. (1971). A representation of the visual field in the caudal third of the middle tempral gyrus of the owl monkey (*Aotus trivirgatus*). *Brain Research, 31,* 85–105.

Allman, J. M., Miezin, F., & McGuinness, E. (1985). Direction- and velocity-specific responses from beyond the classical receptive field in the middle temporal visual area (MT). *Perception, 14,* 105–126.

Amaral, D. G., & Price, J. L. (1984). Amygdalo-cortical projections in the monkey (*Macaca fascicularis*). *Journal of Comparative Neurology, 230,* 465–496.

Andersen, R. A. (1997). Multimodal integration for the representation of space in the posterior parietal cortex. *Philosophical Transactions of the Royal Society, London, 352B,* 1421–1428.

Andersen, R. A., Asanuma, C., & Cowan, W. M. (1985). Callosal and prefrontal associational projecting cell populations in area 7A of the macaque monkey: A study using retrogradely transported fluorescent dyes. *Journal of Comparative Neurology, 232,* 443–455.

Andersen, R. A., Asanuma, C., Essick, G., & Siegel, R. M. (1990). Corticocortical connections of anatomically and physiologically defined subdivisions within the inferior parietal lobule. *Journal of Comparative Neurology, 296,* 65–113.

Andersen, R. A., Bracewell, R. M., Barash, S., Gnadt, J. W., & Fogassi, L. (1990). Eye position effects on visual, memory, and saccade-related activity in areas LIP and 7a of macaque. *Journal of Neuroscience, 10,* 1176–1196.

Andersen, R. A., Shenoy, K. V., Snyder, L. H., Bradley, D. C., & Crowell, J. A. (1999). The contributions of vestibular signals to the representations of space in the posterior parietal cortex. *Annals of the New York Academy of Sciences, 871,* 282–292.

Andersen, R. A., Snyder, L. H., Bradley, D. C., & Xing, J. (1997). Multimodal representation of space in the posterior parietal cortex and its use in planning movements. *Annual Review of Neuroscience, 20,* 303–330.

Anderson, K. C., & Siegel, R. M. (1998). Lack of selectivity for simple shapes defined by motion and luminance in STPa of the behaving macaque. *Neuroreport, 9,* 2063–2070.

Anderson, K. C., & Siegel, R. M. (1999). Optic flow selectivity in the anterior superior temporal polysensory area, STPa, of the behaving monkey. *Journal of Neuroscience, 19,* 2681–2692.

Anderson, S. A., Mullen, K. T., & Hess, R. F. (1991). Human peripheral spatial resolution for achromatic and chromatic stimuli: Limits imposed by optical and retinal factors. *Journal of Physiology, 442,* 47–64.

Azzopardi, P., & Cowey, A. (1993). Preferential representation of the fovea in the primary visual cortex. *Nature, 361,* 719–721.

Baizer, J. S., Ungerleider, L. G., & Desimone, R. (1991). Organization of visual inputs to the inferior temporal and posterior parietal cortex in macaques. *Journal of Neuroscience, 11,* 168–190.

Bakin, J. S., Nakayama, K., & Gilbert, C. D. (2000). Visual responses in monkey areas V1 and V2 to three-dimensional surface configurations. *Journal of Neuroscience, 20,* 8188–8198.

Baleydier, C., & Morel, A. (1992). Segregated thalamocortical pathways to inferior parietal and inferotemporal cortex in macaque monkey. *Visual Neuroscience, 8,* 391–405.

Barash, S., Bracewell, R. M., Fogassi, L., Gnadt, J. W., & Andersen, R. A. (1991a). Saccade-related activity in the lateral intraparietal area: I. Temporal properties; comparison with area 7a. *Journal of Neurophysiology, 66,* 1095–1108.

Barash, S., Bracewell, R. M., Fogassi, L., Gnadt, J. W., & Andersen, R. A. (1991b). Saccade-related activity in the lateral intraparietal area: II. Spatial properties. *Journal of Neurophysiology, 66,* 1109–1124.

Bashinski, H. S., & Bacharach, V. R. (1980). Enhancement of perceptual sensitivity as the result of selectively attending to spatial locations. *Perception and Psychophysics, 28,* 241–248.

Baylor, D. A., Nunn, B. J., & Schnapf, J. L. (1987). Spectral sensitivity of cones of the monkey *Macaca fascicularis*. *Journal of Physiology, 390,* 145–160.

Bear, M. F., Connors, B., & Paradiso, M. A. (1996). *Neuroscience: Exploring the brain.* New York: Williams and Wilkins.

Beck, P. D., & Kaas, J. H. (1999). Cortical connections of the dorsomedial visual area in old world macaque monkeys. *Journal of Comparative Neurology, 406,* 487–502.

Ben Hamed, S., Duhamel, J.-R., Bremmer, F., & Graf, W. (2001). Representation of the visual field in the lateral intraparietal area of macaque monkeys: A quantitative receptive field analysis. *Experimental Brain Research, 140,* 127–144.

Bisley, J. W., & Pasternak, T. (2000). The multiple roles of visual cortical areas MT/MST in remembering the direction of visual motion. *Cerebral Cortex, 10,* 1053–1065.

Bisley, J. W., Zaksas, D., & Pasternak, T. (2001). Microstimulation of cortical area MT affects performance on a visual working memory task. *Journal of Neurophysiology, 85,* 187–196.

Blasco, B., Avendano, C., & Cavada, C. (1999). A stereological analysis of the lateral geniculate nucleus in adult *Macaca nemestrina* monkeys. *Visual Neuroscience, 16,* 933–941.

Blasdel, G. G., & Lund, J. S. (1983). Termination of afferent axons in macaque striate cortex. *Journal of Neuroscience, 3,* 1389–1413.

Blasdel, G. G., & Salama, G. (1986). Voltage-sensitive dyes reveal a modular organization in monkey striate cortex. *Nature, 321,* 579–585.

Blatt, G. J., Andersen, R. A., & Stoner, G. R. (1990). Visual receptive field organization and cortico-cortical connections of the lateral intraparietal area (area LIP) in the macaque. *Journal of Comparative Neurology, 299,* 421–445.

Born, R. T., & Tootell, R. B. (1991). Spatial frequency tuning of single units in macaque supragranular striate cortex. *Proceedings of the National Academy of Sciences, USA, 88,* 7066–7070.

Boussaoud, D., Desimone, R., & Ungerleider, L. G. (1991). Visual topography of area TEO in the macaque. *Journal of Comparative Neurology, 306,* 554–575.

Boussaoud, D., Ungerleider, L. G., & Desimone, R. (1990). Pathways for motion analysis: Cortical connections of the medial superior temporal and fundus of the superior temporal visual areas in the macaque. *Journal of Comparative Neurology, 296,* 462–495.

Bowman, E. M., Brown, V. J., Kertzman, C., Schwarz, U., & Robinson, D. L. (1993). Covert orienting of attention in macaques: I. Effects of behavioral context. *Journal of Neurophysiology, 70,* 431–443.

Boycott, B. B., & Hopkins, J. M. (1991). Cone bipolar cells and cone synapses in the primate retina. *Visual Neuroscience, 7,* 49–60.

Boycott, B. B., & Hopkins, J. M. (1997). The cone synapses of cone bipolar cells of primate retina. *Journal of Neurocytology, 26,* 313–325.

Boyd, J. D., & Casagrande, V. A. (1999). Relationships between cytochrome oxidase (CO) blobs in primate primary visual cortex (V1) and the distribution of neurons projecting to the middle temporal area (MT). *Journal of Comparative Neurology, 409,* 573–591.

Bradley, D. C., Chang, G. C., & Andersen, R. A. (1998). Encoding of three-dimensional structure-from-motion by primate area MT neurons. *Nature, 392,* 714–717.

Bradley, D. C., Maxwell, M., Andersen, R. A., Banks, M. S., & Shenoy, K. V. (1996). Mechanisms of heading perception in primate visual cortex. *Science, 273,* 1544–1547.

Bradley, D. C., Qian, N., & Andersen, R. A. (1995). Integration of motion and stereopsis in middle temporal cortical area of macaques. *Nature, 373,* 609–611.

Bremmer, F., Distler, C., & Hoffmann, K. P. (1997). Eye position effects in monkey cortex: II. Pursuit-and fixation- related activity in posterior parietal areas LIP and 7A. *Journal of Neurophysiology, 77,* 962–977.

Bremmer, F., Graf, W., Ben Hamed, S., & Duhamel, J. R. (1999). Eye position encoding in the macaque ventral intraparietal area (VIP). *Neuroreport, 10,* 873–878.

Britten, K. H. (1998). Clustering of response selectivity in the medial superior temporal area of extrastriate cortex in the macaque monkey. *Visual Neuroscience, 15,* 553–558.

Britten, K. H., & Newsome, W. T. (1998). Tuning bandwidths for near-threshold stimuli in area MT. *Journal of Neurophysiology, 80,* 762–770.

Britten, K. H., Newsome, W. T., & Saunders, R. C. (1992). Effects of inferotemporal cortex lesions on form-from-motion discrimination in monkeys. *Experimental Brain Research, 88,* 292–302.

Britten, K. H., Shadlen, M. N., Newsome, W. T., & Movshon, J. A. (1992). The analysis of visual motion: A comparison of neuronal and psychophysical performance. *Journal of Neuroscience, 12,* 4745–4765.

Britten, K. H., Shadlen, M. N., Newsome, W. T., & Movshon, J. A. (1993). Responses of neurons in macaque MT to stochastic motion signals. *Visual Neuroscience, 10,* 1157–1169.

Britten, K. H., & van Wezel, R. J. (1998). Electrical microstimulation of cortical area MST biases heading perception in monkeys. *Nature Neuroscience, 1,* 59–63.

Bruce, C., Desimone, R., & Gross, C. G. (1981). Visual properties of neurons in a polysensory area in superior temporal sulcus of the macaque. *Journal of Neurophysiology, 46,* 369–384.

Buckley, M. J., Gaffan, D., & Murray, E. A. (1997). Functional double dissociation between two inferior temporal cortical areas: Perirhinal cortex versus middle temporal gyrus. *Journal of Neurophysiology, 77,* 587–598.

Bullier, J., & Kennedy, H. (1983). Projection of the lateral geniculate nucleus onto cortical area V2 in the macaque monkey. *Experimental Brain Research, 53,* 168–172.

Bullier, J., Schall, J. D., & Morel, A. (1996). Functional streams in occipito-frontal connections in the monkey. *Behavioural Brain Research, 76,* 89–97.

Buracas, G. T., & Albright, T. D. (1996). Contribution of area MT to perception of three-dimensional shape: A computational study. *Vision Research, 36,* 869–887.

Burkhalter, A., & Van Essen, D. C. (1986). Processing of color, form and disparity information in visual areas VP and V2 of ventral extrastriate cortex in the macaque monkey. *Journal of Neuroscience, 6,* 2327–2351.

Calkins, D. J. (1999). Synaptic organization of cone pathways in the primate retina. In K. Gegenfurtner & L. Sharpe (Eds.), *Color vision: From molecular genetics to perception.* New York: Cambridge University Press.

Calkins, D. J. (2001). Seeing with S cones. *Progress in Retinal and Eye Research, 20,* 255–287.

Calkins, D. J., & Sterling, P. (1999). Evidence that circuits for spatial and color vision segregate at the first retinal synapse. *Neuron, 24,* 313–321.

Calkins, D. J., Tsukamoto, Y., & Sterling, P. (1998). Microcircuitry and mosaic of a blue-yellow ganglion cell in the primate retina. *Journal of Neuroscience, 18,* 3373–3385.

Casagrande, V. A., & Kaas, J. H. (1994). The afferent, intrinsic, and efferent connections of primary visual cortex in primates. In E. G. Jones, A. Peters (Series Eds.), A. Peters, & K. S. Rockland (Vol. Eds.), *Cerebral cortex: Vol. 10. Primary visual cortex in primates* (pp. 201–259). New York: Plenum Press.

Cavada, C., & Goldman-Rakic, P. S. (1989). Posterior parietal cortex in rhesus monkey: I. Parcellation of areas based on distinctive limbic and sensory corticocortical connections. *Journal of Comparative Neurology, 287,* 393–421.

Cheng, K., Hasegawa, T., Saleem, K. S., & Tanaka, K. (1994). Comparison of neuronal selectivity for stimulus speed, length, and contrast in the prestriate visual cortical areas V4 and MT of the macaque monkey. *Journal of Neurophysiology, 71,* 2269–2280.

Cheng, K., Saleem, K. S., & Tanaka, K. (1997). Organization of corticostriatal and corticoamygdalar projections arising from the anterior inferotemporal area TE of the macaque monkey: A *Phaseolus vulgaris* leucoagglutinin study. *Journal of Neuroscience, 17,* 7902–7925.

Colby, C. L., Duhamel, J. R., & Goldberg, M. E. (1993). Ventral intraparietal area of the macaque: Anatomic location and visual response properties. *Journal of Neurophysiology, 69,* 902–914.

Colby, C. L., Duhamel, J. R., & Goldberg, M. E. (1996). Visual, presaccadic, and cognitive activation of single neurons in monkey lateral intraparietal area. *Journal of Neurophysiology, 76,* 2841–2852.

Colby, C. L., Gattass, R., Olson, C. R., & Gross, C. G. (1988). Topographical organization of cortical afferents to extrastriate visual area PO in the macaque: A dual tracer study. *Journal of Comparative Neurology, 269,* 392–413.

Colby, C. L., & Olson, C. R. (1999). Spatial cognition. In M. J. Zigmond, F. E. Bloom, S. C. Landis, & L. R. Squire (Eds.), *Fundamental neuroscience* (pp. 1363–1383). London: Academic Press.

Connor, C. E., Preddie, D. C., Gallant, J. L., & Van Essen, D. C. (1997). Spatial attention effects in macaque area V4. *Journal of Neuroscience, 17,* 3201–3214.

Constantinidis, C., & Steinmetz, M. A. (1996). Neuronal activity in posterior parietal area 7a during the delay periods of a spatial memory task. *Journal of Neurophysiology, 76,* 1352–1355.

Constantinidis, C., & Steinmetz, M. A. (2001). Neuronal responses in area 7a to multiple stimulus displays: II. Responses are suppressed at the cued location. *Cerebral Cortex, 11,* 592–597.

Cottaris, N. P., & De Valois, R. L. (1998). Temporal dynamics of chromatic tuning in macaque primary visual cortex. *Nature, 395,* 896–900.

Courtney, S. M., & Ungerleider, L. G. (1997). What fMRI has taught us about human vision. *Current Opinion in Neurobiology, 7,* 554–561.

Cowey, A., Stoerig, P., & Bannister, M. (1994). Retinal ganglion cells labelled from the pulvinar nucleus in macaque monkeys. *Neuroscience, 61,* 691–705.

Crist, R. E., Li, W., & Gilbert, C. D. (2001). Learning to see: Experience and attention in primary visual cortex. *Nature Neuroscience, 4,* 519–525.

Croner, L. J., & Albright, T. D. (1999). Segmentation by color influences responses of motion-sensitive neurons in the cortical middle temporal visual area. *Journal of Neuroscience, 19,* 3935–3951.

Croner, L. J., & Kaplan, E. (1995). Receptive fields of P and M ganglion cells across the primate retina. *Vision Research, 35,* 7–24.

Cumming, B. G., & DeAngelis, G. C. (2001). The physiology of stereopsis. *Annual Review of Neuroscience, 24,* 203–238.

Cumming, B. G., & Parker, A. J. (1999). Binocular neurons in V1 of awake monkeys are selective for absolute, not relative, disparity. *Journal of Neuroscience, 19,* 5602–5618.

Cumming, B. G., & Parker, A. J. (2000). Local disparity not perceived depth is signaled by binocular neurons in cortical area V1 of the macaque. *Journal of Neuroscience, 20,* 4758–4767.

Curcio, C. A., & Harting, J. K. (1978). Organization of pulvinar afferents to area 18 in the squirrel monkey: Evidence for stripes. *Brain Research, 143,* 155–161.

Curcio, C. A., Packer, O., & Hendrickson, A. E. (1989). Photoreceptor topography of the retina in the adult pigtail macaque (*Macaca nemestrina*). *The Journal of Comparative Neurology, 288,* 165–183.

Dacey, D. M. (1993). The mosaic of midget ganglion cells in the human retina. *Journal of Neuroscience, 13,* 5334–5355.

Dacey, D. M. (1996). Circuitry for color coding in the primate retina. *Proceedings of the National Academy of Sciences, USA, 93,* 582–588.

Dacey, D. M. (2000). Parallel pathways for spectral coding in primate retina. *Annual Review of Neuroscience, 23,* 743–775.

Dacey, D. M., & Lee, B. B. (1994). The blue-on opponent pathway in primate retina originates from a distinct bistratified ganglion cell type. *Nature, 367,* 731–735.

Dacey, D. M., Packer, O. S., Diller, L., Brainard, D., Peterson, B., & Lee, B. (2000). Center surround receptive field structure of cone bipolar cells in primate retina. *Vision Research, 40,* 1801–1811.

Dean, P. (1979). Visual cortex ablation and thresholds for successively presented stimuli in rhesus monkeys: II. Hue. *Experimental Brain Research, 35,* 69–83.

DeAngelis, G. C., Cumming, B. G., & Newsome, W. T. (1998). Cortical area MT and the perception of stereoscopic depth. *Nature, 394,* 677–680.

DeAngelis, G. C., & Newsome, W. T. (1999). Organization of disparity-selective neurons in macaque area MT. *Journal of Neuroscience, 19,* 1398–1415.

Derrington, A. M., Krauskopf, J., & Lennie, P. (1984). Chromatic mechanisms in lateral geniculate nucleus of macaque. *Journal of Physiology, 357,* 241–265.

Derrington, A. M., & Lennie, P. (1984). Spatial and temporal contrast sensitivities of neurones in lateral geniculate nucleus of macaque. *Journal of Physiology, 357,* 219–240.

Desimone, R. (1998). Visual attention mediated by biased competition in extrastriate visual cortex. *Philosophical Transactions of the Royal Society, London, 353B,* 1245–1255.

Desimone, R., Albright, T. D., Gross, C. G., & Bruce, C. (1984). Stimulus-selective properties of inferior temporal neurons in the macaque. *Journal of Neuroscience, 4,* 2051–2062.

Desimone, R., & Gross, C. G. (1979). Visual areas in the temporal cortex of the macaque. *Brain Research, 178,* 363–380.

Desimone, R., Li, L., Lehky, S., Ungerleider, L. G., & Mishkin, M. (1990). Effects of V4 lesions on visual discrimination performance and responses of neurons in inferior temporal cortex. *Neuroscience Abstracts, 16,* 621.

Desimone, R., & Schein, S. J. (1987). Visual properties of neurons in area V4 of the macaque: Sensitivity to stimulus form. *Journal of Neurophysiology, 57,* 835–868.

Desimone, R., Schein, S. J., Moran, J., & Ungerleider, L. G. (1985). Contour, color and shape analysis beyond the striate cortex. *Vision Research, 25,* 441–452.

Desimone, R., & Ungerleider, L. G. (1986). Multiple visual areas in the caudal superior temporal sulcus of the macaque. *Journal of Comparative Neurology, 248,* 164–189.

De Valois, R. L., Albrecht, D. G., & Thorell, L. G. (1982). Spatial frequency selectivity of cells in macaque visual cortex. *Vision Research, 22,* 545–559.

DeVries, S. H. (2000). Bipolar cells use kainate and AMPA receptors to filter visual information into separate channels. *Neuron, 28,* 847–856.

De Weerd, P., Desimone, R., & Ungerleider, L. G. (1996). Cue-dependent deficits in grating orientation discrimination after V4 lesions in macaques. *Visual Neuroscience, 13,* 529–538.

De Weerd, P., Peralta, M. R., III, Desimone, R., & Ungerleider, L. G. (1999). Loss of attentional stimulus selection after extrastriate cortical lesions in macaques. *Nature Neuroscience, 2,* 753–758.

DeYoe, E. A., & Van Essen, D. C. (1985). Segregation of efferent connections and receptive field properties in visual area V2 of the macaque. *Nature, 317,* 58–61.

Dineen, J., & Keating, E. G. (1981). The primate visual system after bilateral removal of striate cortex: Survival of complex pattern vision. *Experimental Brain Research, 41,* 338–345.

Distler, C., Boussaoud, D., Desimone, R., & Ungerleider, L. G. (1993). Cortical connections of inferior temporal area TEO in macaque monkeys. *Journal of Comparative Neurology, 334,* 125–150.

Dodd, J. V., Krug, K., Cumming, B. G., & Parker, A. J. (2001). Perceptually bistable three-dimensional figures evoke high choice probabilities in cortical area MT. *Journal of Neuroscience, 21,* 4809–4821.

Dow, B. M., Snyder, A. Z., Vautin, R. G., & Bauer, R. (1981). Magnification factor and receptive field size in foveal striate cortex of the monkey. *Experimental Brain Research, 44,* 213–228.

Drasdo, N., & Fowler, C. W. (1974). Non-linear projection of the retinal image in a wide-angle schematic eye. *British Journal of Opthalmology, 58,* 709–714.

Droll, J. A., Bisley, J. W., & Pasternak, T. (2000). Delay activity in area MT neurons during a visual working memory task. *Investigative Ophthalmology and Visual Science Supplement (Abstracts), 41,* S70.

Dubowitz, D. J., Chen, D. Y., Atkinson, D. J., Grieve, K. L., Gillikin, B., Bradley, W. G., et al. (1998). Functional magnetic resonance imaging in macaque cortex. *Neuroreport, 9,* 2213–2218.

Duffy, C. J. (1998). MST neurons respond to optic flow and translational movement. *Journal of Neurophysiology, 80,* 1816–1827.

Duffy, C. J., & Wurtz, R. H. (1991). Sensitivity of MST neurons to optic flow stimuli: I. A continuum of response selectivity to large-field stimuli. *Journal of Neurophysiology, 65,* 1329–1345.

Duffy, C. J., & Wurtz, R. H. (1997). Planar directional contributions to optic flow responses in MST neurons. *Journal of Neurophysiology, 77,* 782–796.

Duhamel, J. R., Bremmer, F., Ben Hamed, S., & Graf, W. (1997). Spatial invariance of visual receptive fields in parietal cortex neurons. *Nature, 389,* 845–848.

Duhamel, J. R., Colby, C. L., & Goldberg, M. E. (1992). The updating of the representation of visual space in parietal cortex by intended eye movements. *Science, 255,* 90–92.

Duhamel, J. R., Colby, C. L., & Goldberg, M. E. (1998). Ventral intraparietal area of the macaque: Congruent visual and somatic response properties. *Journal of Neurophysiology, 79,* 126–136.

Duncan, R. O., Albright, T. D., & Stoner, G. R. (2000). Occlusion and the interpretation of visual motion: Perceptual and neuronal effects of context. *Journal of Neuroscience, 20,* 5885–5897.

Dursteler, M. R., & Wurtz, R. H. (1988). Pursuit and optokinetic deficits following chemical lesions of cortical areas MT and MST. *Journal of Neurophysiology, 60,* 940–965.

Dursteler, M. R., Wurtz, R. H., & Newsome, W. T. (1987). Directional pursuit deficits following lesions of the foveal representation within the superior temporal sulcus of the macaque monkey. *Journal of Neurophysiology, 57,* 1262–1287.

Edwards, D. P., Purpura, K. P., & Kaplan, E. (1995). Contrast sensitivity and spatial frequency response of primate cortical neurons in and around the cytochrome oxidase blobs. *Vision Research, 35,* 1501–1523.

Eifuku, S., & Wurtz, R. H. (1998). Response to motion in extrastriate area MSTl: Center-surround interactions. *Journal of Neurophysiology, 80,* 282–296.

Eifuku, S., & Wurtz, R. H. (1999). Response to motion in extrastriate area MSTl: Disparity sensitivity. *Journal of Neurophysiology, 82,* 2462–2475.

Erisir, A., Van Horn, S. C., & Sherman, S. M. (1997). Relative numbers of cortical and brainstem inputs to the lateral geniculate nucleus. *Proceedings of the National Academy of Sciences, USA, 94,* 1517–1520.

Eskandar, E. N., & Assad, J. A. (1999). Dissociation of visual, motor and predictive signals in parietal cortex during visual guidance. *Nature Neuroscience, 2,* 88–93.

Essen, D. C., & Zeki, S. M. (1978). The topographic organization of rhesus monkey prestriate cortex. *Journal of Physiology, 277,* 193–226.

Famiglietti, E. V., Jr., & Kolb, H. (1976). Structural basis for ON- and OFF-center responses in retinal ganglion cells. *Science, 194,* 193–195.

Farah, M. J., Humphreys, G. W., & Rodman, H. R. (1999). Object and face recognition. In M. J. Zigmond, F. E. Bloom, S. C. Landis, J. L. Roberts, & L. R. Squire (Eds.), *Fundamental neuroscience* (pp. 1339–1361). London: Academic Press.

Felleman, D. J., Burkhalter, A., & Van Essen, D. C. (1997). Cortical connections of areas V3 and VP of macaque monkey extrastriate visual cortex. *Journal of Comparative Neurology, 379,* 21–47.

Felleman, D. J., & Van Essen, D. C. (1987). Receptive field properties of neurons in area V3 of macaque monkey extrastriate cortex. *Journal of Neurophysiology, 57,* 889–920.

Felleman, D. J., & Van Essen, D. C. (1991). Distributed hierarchical processing in the primate cerebral cortex. *Cerebral Cortex, 1,* 1–47.

Felleman, D. J., Xiao, Y., & McClendon, E. (1997). Modular organization of occipito-temporal pathways: Cortical connections between visual area 4 and visual area 2 and posterior inferotemporal ventral area in macaque monkeys. *Journal of Neuroscience, 17,* 3185–3200.

Ferraina, S., Garasto, M. R., Battaglia-Mayer, A., Ferraresi, P., Johnson, P. B., Lacquaniti, F., et al. (1997). Visual control of hand-reaching movement: Activity in parietal area 7 m. *European Journal of Neuroscience, 9,* 1090–1095.

Ferrera, V. P., Rudolph, K. K., & Maunsell, J. H. (1994). Responses of neurons in the parietal and temporal visual pathways during a motion task. *Journal of Neuroscience, 14,* 6171–6186.

Fischer, B., & Boch, R. (1981). Selection of visual targets activates prelunate cortical cells in trained rhesus monkey. *Experimental Brain Research, 41,* 431–433.

Foster, K. H., Gaska, J. P., Nagler, M., & Pollen, D. A. (1985). Spatial and temporal frequency selectivity of neurones in visual cortical areas V1 and V2 of the macaque monkey. *Journal of Physiology, 365,* 331–363.

Freed, M. A., Smith, R. G., & Sterling, P. (1992). Computational model of the on-alpha ganglion cell receptive field based on bipolar circuitry. *Proceedings of the National Academy of Sciences, USA, 89,* 236–240.

Fuster, J. M. (1990). Inferotemporal units in selective visual attention and short-term memory. *Journal of Neurophysiology, 64,* 681–697.

Fuster, J. M. (1995). *Memory in the cerebral cortex.* Cambridge, MA: MIT Press.

Fuster, J. M. (1997). Network memory. *Trends in Neurosciences, 20,* 451–459.

Gallant, J. L., Connor, C. E., Rakshit, S., Lewis, J. W., & Van Essen, D. C. (1996). Neural responses to polar, hyperbolic, and Cartesian gratings in area V4 of the macaque monkey. *Journal of Neurophysiology, 76,* 2718–2739.

Galletti, C., & Battaglini, P. P. (1989). Gaze-dependent visual neurons in area V3A of monkey prestriate cortex. *Journal of Neuroscience, 9,* 1112–1125.

Galletti, C., Battaglini, P. P., & Fattori, P. (1990). "Real-motion" cells in area V3A of macaque visual cortex. *Experimental Brain Research, 82,* 67–76.

Galletti, C., Fattori, P., Battaglini, P. P., Shipp, S., & Zeki, S. (1996). Functional demarcation of a border between areas V6 and V6a in the superior parietal gyrus of the macaque monkey. *European Journal of Neuroscience, 8,* 30–52.

Gattass, R., & Gross, C. G. (1981). Visual topography of striate projection zone (MT) in posterior superior temporal sulcus of the macaque. *Journal of Neurophysiology, 46,* 621–638.

Gattass, R., Gross, C. G., & Sandell, J. H. (1981). Visual topography of V2 in the macaque. *Journal of Comparative Neurology, 201,* 519–539.

Gattass, R., Sousa, A. P., & Gross, C. G. (1988). Visuotopic organization and extent of V3 and V4 of the macaque. *Journal of Neuroscience, 8,* 1831–1845.

Gattass, R., Sousa, A. P., Mishkin, M., & Ungerleider, L. G. (1997). Cortical projections of area V2 in the macaque. *Cerebral Cortex, 7,* 110–129.

Gegenfurtner, K. R., Kiper, D. C., Beusmans, J. M., Carandini, M., Zaidi, Q., & Movshon, J. A. (1994). Chromatic properties of neurons in macaque MT. *Visual Neuroscience, 11,* 455–466.

Gegenfurtner, K. R., Kiper, D. C., & Levitt, J. B. (1997). Functional properties of neurons in macaque area V3. *Journal of Neurophysiology, 77,* 1906–1923.

Ghose, G. M., & Ts'o, D. Y. (1997). Form processing modules in primate area V4. *Journal of Neurophysiology, 77,* 2191–2196.

Gibson, J. J. (1994). The visual perception of objective motion and subjective movement: 1954. *Psychology Review, 101,* 318–323.

Gilbert, C., Ito, M., Kapadia, M., & Westheimer, G. (2000). Interactions between attention, context and learning in primary visual cortex. *Vision Research, 40,* 1217–1226.

Girard, P., & Bullier, J. (1989). Visual activity in area V2 during reversible inactivation of area 17 in the macaque monkey. *Journal of Neurophysiology, 62,* 1287–1302.

Girard, P., Salin, P. A., & Bullier, J. (1991). Visual activity in areas V3a and V3 during reversible inactivation of area V1 in the macaque monkey. *Journal of Neurophysiology, 66,* 1493–1503.

Glickstein, M. (1988). The discovery of the visual cortex. *Scientific American, 259,* 118–127.

Gnadt, J. W., & Andersen, R. A. (1988). Memory related motor planning activity in posterior parietal cortex of macaque. *Experimental Brain Research, 70,* 216–220.

Gottlieb, J. P., Kusunoki, M., & Goldberg, M. E. (1998). The representation of visual salience in monkey parietal cortex. *Nature, 391,* 481–484.

Grosof, D. H., Shapley, R. M., & Hawken, M. J. (1993). Macaque V1 neurons can signal "illusory" contours. *Nature, 365,* 550–552.

Grünert, U., Greferath, U., Boycott, B. B., & Wässle, H. (1993). Parasol (P alpha) ganglion-cells of the primate fovea:

Immunocytochemical staining with antibodies against GABAa-receptors. *Vision Research, 33,* 1–14.

Grünert, U., & Martin, P. R. (1991). Rod bipolar cells in the macaque monkey retina: Immunoreactivity and connectivity. *Journal of Neuroscience, 11,* 2742–2758.

Hanazawa, A., & Komatsu, H. (2001). Influence of the direction of elemental luminance gradients on the responses of V4 cells to textured surfaces. *Journal of Neuroscience, 21,* 4490–4497.

Hawken, M. J., & Parker, A. J. (1991). Spatial receptive field organization in monkey V1 and its relationship to the cone mosaic. In M. S. Landy & J. A. Movshon (Eds.), *Computational models of visual processing* (pp. 83–93). Cambridge, MA: MIT Press.

Hawken, M. J., Parker, A. J., & Lund, J. S. (1988). Laminar organization and contrast sensitivity of direction-selective cells in the striate cortex of the old world monkey. *Journal of Neuroscience, 8,* 3541–3548.

Hegde, J., & Van Essen, D. C. (2000). Selectivity for complex shapes in primate visual area V2. *Journal of Neuroscience, 20,* RC61.

Hendrickson, A. E., Wilson, J. R., & Ogren, M. P. (1978). The neuroanatomical organization of pathways between the dorsal lateral geniculate nucleus and visual cortex in old world and new world primates. *Journal of Comparative Neurology, 182,* 123–136.

Hendry, S. H., & Reid, R. C. (2000). The koniocellular pathway in primate vision. *Annual Reviews in Neuroscience, 23,* 127–153.

Hendry, S. H., & Yoshioka, T. (1994). A neurochemically distinct third channel in the macaque dorsal lateral geniculate nucleus. *Science, 264,* 575–577.

Heywood, C. A., & Cowey, A. (1987). On the role of cortical area V4 in the discrimination of hue and pattern in macaque monkeys. *Journal of Neuroscience, 7,* 2601–2617.

Heywood, C. A., Gadotti, A., & Cowey, A. (1992). Cortical area V4 and its role in the perception of color. *Journal of Neuroscience, 12,* 4056–4065.

Hicks, T. P., Lee, B. B., & Vidyasagar, T. R. (1983). The responses of cells in macaque lateral geniculate nucleus to sinusoidal gratings. *Journal of Physiology, 337,* 183–200.

Hikosaka, K. (1999). Tolerances of responses to visual patterns in neurons of the posterior inferotemporal cortex in the macaque against changing stimulus size and orientation, and deleting patterns. *Behavioral Brain Research, 100,* 67–76.

Hinkle, D. A., & Connor, C. E. (2001). Disparity tuning in macaque area V4. *Neuroreport, 12,* 365–369.

Hirsch, J. (1984). Quality of the primate photoreceptor lattice and limits of spatial vision. *Vision Research, 24,* 347–355.

Horton, J. C. (1984). Cytochrome oxidase patches: A new cytoarchitectonic feature of monkey visual cortex. *Philosophical Transactions of the Royal Society, London, 304B,* 199–253.

Hubel, D. H. (1960). Single unit activity in lateral geniculate body and optic tract of unrestrained cats. *Journal of Physiology, 150,* 91–104.

Hubel, D. H. (1979). The brain. *Scientific American, 241,* 44–53.

Hubel, D. H., & Livingstone, M. S. (1987). Segregation of form, color, and stereopsis in primate area 18. *Journal of Neuroscience, 7,* 3378–3415.

Hubel, D. H., & Wiesel, T. N. (1968). Receptive fields and functional architecture of monkey striate cortex. *Journal of Physiology, 195,* 215–243.

Hubel, D. H., & Wiesel, T. N. (1977). Ferrier lecture: Functional architecture of macaque monkey visual cortex. *Proceedings of the Royal Society, London, 198B,* 1–59.

Humphrey, N. K., & Weiskrantz, L. (1967). Vision in monkeys after removal of the striate cortex. *Nature, 215,* 595–597.

Huxlin, K. R., Saunders, R. C., Marchionini, D., Pham, H. A., & Merigan, W. H. (2000). Perceptual deficits after lesions of inferotemporal cortex in macaques. *Cerebral Cortex, 10,* 671–683.

Ito, M., & Gilbert, C. D. (1999). Attention modulates contextual influences in the primary visual cortex of alert monkeys. *Neuron, 22,* 593–604.

Ito, M., Tamura, H., Fujita, I., & Tanaka, K. (1995). Size and position invariance of neuronal responses in monkey inferotemporal cortex. *Journal of Neurophysiology, 73,* 218–226.

Johnson, E. N., Hawken, M. J., & Shapley, R. (2001). The spatial transformation of color in the primary visual cortex of the macaque monkey. *Nature Neuroscience, 4,* 409–416.

Johnson, P. B., Ferraina, S., Bianchi, L., & Caminiti, R. (1996). Cortical networks for visual reaching: Physiological and anatomical organization of frontal and parietal lobe arm regions. *Cerebral Cortex, 6,* 102–119.

Kaas, J. H., & Huerta, M. F. (1988). The subcortical visual system of primates. In H. D. Steklis (Ed.), *Neurosciences: Vol. 4. Comparative primate biology* (pp. 327–391). New York: Alan R. Liss.

Kaas, J. H., & Lyon, D. C. (2001). Visual cortex organization in primates: Theories of V3 and adjoining visual areas. *Progress in Brain Research, 134,* 285–295.

Kamermans, M., & Spekreijse, H. (1999). The feedback pathway from horizontal cells to cones: A mini review with a look ahead. *Vision Research, 39,* 2449–2468.

Kaplan, E., Lee, B. B., & Shapley, R. M. (1990). New views of primate retinal function. In N. Osborne & J. Chader (Eds.), *Progress in retinal research: Vol. 9.* (pp. 273–336). Oxford: Pergamon Press.

Kaplan, E., Purpura, K., & Shapley, R. M. (1988). Background light and the contrast gain of primate P and M retinal ganglion cells. *Proceedings of the National Academy of Sciences, USA, 85,* 4534–4537.

Kaplan, E., & Shapley, R. M. (1986). The primate retina contains two types of ganglion cells, with high and low contrast sensitivity. *Proceedings of the National Academy of Sciences, USA, 83,* 2755–2757.

Kawano, K., Sasaki, M., & Yamashita, M. (1984). Response properties of neurons in posterior parietal cortex of monkey during visual-vestibular stimulation: I. Visual tracking neurons. *Journal of Neurophysiology, 51,* 340–351.

Kawano, K., Shidara, M., Watanabe, Y., & Yamane, S. (1994). Neural activity in cortical area MST of alert monkey during ocular following responses. *Journal of Neurophysiology, 71,* 2305–2324.

Keating, E. G. (1979). Rudimentary color vision in the monkey after removal of striate and preoccipital cortex. *Brain Research, 179,* 379–384.

Kennedy, H., & Bullier, J. (1985). A double-labeling investigation of the afferent connectivity to cortical areas V1 and V2 of the macaque monkey. *Journal of Neuroscience, 5,* 2815–2830.

Knierim, J. J., & Van Essen, D. C. (1992). Neuronal responses to static texture patterns in area V1 of the alert macaque monkey. *Journal of Neurophysiology, 67,* 961–980.

Kobatake, E., & Tanaka, K. (1994). Neuronal selectivities to complex object features in the ventral visual pathway of the macaque cerebral cortex. *Journal of Neurophysiology, 71,* 856–867.

Kobatake, E., Wang, G., & Tanaka, K. (1998). Effects of shape-discrimination training on the selectivity of inferotemporal cells in adult monkeys. *Journal of Neurophysiology, 80,* 324–330.

Komatsu, H., & Wurtz, R. H. (1988). Relation of cortical areas MT and MST to pursuit eye movements: I. Localization and visual properties of neurons. *Journal of Neurophysiology, 60,* 580–603.

Komatsu, H., & Wurtz, R. H. (1989). Modulation of pursuit eye movements by stimulation of cortical areas MT and MST. *Journal of Neurophysiology, 62,* 31–47.

Lagae, L., Maes, H., Raiguel, S., Xiao, D. K., & Orban, G. A. (1994). Responses of macaque STS neurons to optic flow components: A comparison of areas MT and MST. *Journal of Neurophysiology, 71,* 1597–1626.

Lappe, M., Bremmer, F., Pekel, M., Thiele, A., & Hoffmann, K. P. (1996). Optic flow processing in monkey STS: A theoretical and experimental approach. *Journal of Neuroscience, 16,* 6265–6285.

Lennie, P., Krauskopf, J., & Sclar, G. (1990). Chromatic mechanisms in striate cortex of macaque. *Journal of Neuroscience, 10,* 649–669.

Leon, M. I., & Shadlen, M. N. (1998). Exploring the neurophysiology of decisions. *Neuron, 21,* 669–672.

Leopold, D. A., & Logothetis, N. K. (1996). Activity changes in early visual cortex reflect monkeys' percepts during binocular rivalry. *Nature, 379,* 549–553.

LeVay, S., Connolly, M., Houde, J., & Van Essen, D. C. (1985). The complete pattern of ocular dominance stripes in the striate cortex and visual field of the macaque monkey. *Journal of Neuroscience, 5,* 486–501.

Leventhal, A. G., Rodieck, R. W., & Dreher, B. (1981). Retinal ganglion cell classes in the old world monkey: Morphology and central projections. *Science, 213,* 1139–1142.

Leventhal, A. G., Thompson, K. G., Liu, D., Zhou, Y., & Ault, S. J. . (1995). Concomitant sensitivity to orientation, direction, and color of cells in layers 2, 3, and 4 of monkey striate cortex. *Journal of Neuroscience, 15,* 1808–1818.

Levitt, J. B., Kiper, D. C., & Movshon, J. A. (1994). Receptive fields and functional architecture of macaque V2. *Journal of Neurophysiology, 71,* 2517–2542.

Levitt, J. B., Schumer, R. A., Sherman, S. M., Spear, P. D., & Movshon, J. A. (2001). Visual response properties of neurons in the LGN of normally reared and visually deprived macaque monkeys. *Journal of Neurophysiology, 85,* 2111–2129.

Levitt, J. B., Yoshioka, T., & Lund, J. S. (1994). Intrinsic cortical connections in macaque visual area V2: Evidence for interaction between different functional streams. *Journal of Comparative Neurology, 342,* 551–570.

Livingstone, M. S., & Hubel, D. H. (1983). Specificity of cortico-cortical connections in monkey visual system. *Nature, 304,* 531–534.

Livingstone, M. S., & Hubel, D. H. (1984). Anatomy and physiology of a color system in the primate visual cortex. *Journal of Neuroscience, 4,* 309–356.

Livingstone, M. S., & Tsao, D. Y. (1999). Receptive fields of disparity-selective neurons in macaque striate cortex. *Nature Neuroscience, 2,* 825–832.

Logothetis, N. K., Guggenberger, H., Peled, S., & Pauls, J. (1999). Functional imaging of the monkey brain. *Nature Neuroscience, 2,* 555–562.

Logothetis, N. K., & Pauls, J. (1995). Psychophysical and physiological evidence for viewer-centered object representations in the primate. *Cerebral Cortex, 5,* 270–288.

Logothetis, N. K., Pauls, J., & Poggio, T. (1995). Shape representation in the inferior temporal cortex of monkeys. *Current Biology, 5,* 552–563.

Luck, S. J., Chelazzi, L., Hillyard, S. A., & Desimone, R. (1997). Neural mechanisms of spatial selective attention in areas V1, V2, and V4 of macaque visual cortex. *Journal of Neurophysiology, 77,* 24–42.

Luppino, G., Murata, A., Govoni, P., & Matelli, M. (1999). Largely segregated parietofrontal connections linking rostral intraparietal cortex (areas AIP and VIP) and the ventral premotor cortex (areas F5 and F4). *Experimental Brain Research, 128,* 181–187.

Makous, W. (1990). Absolute sensitivity. In R. F. Hess, L. T. Sharpe, & K. Nordby (Eds.), *Night vision: Basic, clinical and applied aspects* (pp. 146–176). New York: Cambridge University Press.

Malach, R., Tootell, R. B., & Malonek, D. (1994). Relationship between orientation domains, cytochrome oxidase stripes, and intrinsic horizontal connections in squirrel monkey area V2. *Cerebral Cortex, 4,* 151–165.

Martin, P. R., Lee, B. B., White, A. J., Solomon, S. G., & Ruttiger, L. (2001). Chromatic sensitivity of ganglion cells in the peripheral primate retina. *Nature, 410,* 933–936.

Martin, P. R., White, A. J., Goodchild, A. K., Wilder, H. D., & Sefton, A. E. (1997). Evidence that blue-on cells are part of the third geniculocortical pathway in primates. *European Journal of Neuroscience, 9*, 1536–1541.

Martin-Elkins, C. L., & Horel, J. A. (1992). Cortical afferents to behaviorally defined regions of the inferior temporal and parahippocampal gyri as demonstrated by WGA-HRP. *Journal of Comparative Neurology, 321*, 177–192.

Masland, R. H., & Raviola, E. (2000). Confronting complexity: Strategies for understanding the microcircuitry of the retina. *Annual Review of Neuroscience, 23*, 249–284.

Massey, S. C. (1990). Cell types using glutamate as a neurotransmitter in the vertebrate retina. In N. N. Osborne & G. Chader (Eds.), *Progress in retinal research: Vol. 9.* (pp. 399–425). London: Pergamon Press.

Maunsell, J. H., Nealey, T. A., & DePriest, D. D. (1990). Magnocellular and parvocellular contributions to responses in the middle temporal visual area (MT) of the macaque monkey. *Journal of Neuroscience, 10*, 3323–3334.

Maunsell, J. H., & Newsome, W. T. (1987). Visual processing in monkey extrastriate cortex. *Annual Review of Neuroscience, 10*, 363–401.

Maunsell, J. H., & Van Essen, D. C. (1983a). The connections of the middle temporal visual area (MT) and their relationship to a cortical hierarchy in the macaque monkey. *Journal of Neuroscience, 3*, 2563–2586.

Maunsell, J. H., & Van Essen, D. C. (1983b). Functional properties of neurons in middle temporal visual area of the macaque monkey: I. Selectivity for stimulus direction, speed, and orientation. *Journal of Neurophysiology, 49*, 1127–1147.

Maunsell, J. H., & Van Essen, D. C. (1983c). Functional properties of neurons in middle temporal visual area of the macaque monkey: II. Binocular interactions and sensitivity to binocular disparity. *Journal of Neurophysiology, 49*, 1148–1167.

Mazzoni, P., Bracewell, R. M., Barash, S., & Andersen, R. A. (1996). Motor intention activity in the macaque's lateral intraparietal area: I. Dissociation of motor plan from sensory memory. *Journal of Neurophysiology, 76*, 1439–1456.

McAdams, C. J., & Maunsell, J. H. (1999). Effects of attention on orientation-tuning functions of single neurons in macaque cortical area V4. *Journal of Neuroscience, 19*, 431–441.

Merigan, W. H. (1989). Chromatic and achromatic vision of macaques: Role of the P pathway. *Journal of Neuroscience, 9*, 776–783.

Merigan, W. H. (1996). Basic visual capacities and shape discrimination after lesions of extrastriate area V4 in macaques. *Visual Neuroscience, 13*, 51–60.

Merigan, W. H. (2000). Cortical area V4 is critical for certain texture discriminations, but this effect is not dependent on attention. *Visual Neuroscience, 17*, 949–958.

Merigan, W. H., Byrne, C. E., & Maunsell, J. H. (1991). Does primate motion perception depend on the magnocellular pathway? *Journal of Neuroscience, 11*, 3422–3429.

Merigan, W. H., Katz, L. M., & Maunsell, J. H. (1991). The effects of parvocellular lateral geniculate lesions on the acuity and contrast sensitivity of macaque monkeys. *Journal of Neuroscience, 11*, 994–1001.

Merigan, W. H., & Maunsell, J. H. (1990). Macaque vision after magnocellular lateral geniculate lesions. *Visual Neuroscience, 5*, 347–352.

Merigan, W. H., & Maunsell, J. H. (1993). How parallel are the primate visual pathways? *Annual Review of Neuroscience, 16*, 369–402.

Merigan, W. H., Nealey, T. A., & Maunsell, J. H. (1993). Visual effects of lesions of cortical area V2 in macaques. *Journal of Neuroscience, 13*, 3180–3191.

Merigan, W. H., & Pasternak, T. (in press). Lesions in primate visual cortex leading to deficits of perception. In M. Fahle & M. Greenlee (Eds.), *Neuropsychology of vision: Vol.*: Oxford University Press.

Middleton, F. A., & Strick, P. L. (1996). The temporal lobe is a target of output from the basal ganglia. *Proceedings of the National Academy of Sciences, USA, 93*, 8683–8687.

Mikami, A., Newsome, W. T., & Wurtz, R. H. (1986). Motion selectivity in macaque visual cortex: I. Mechanisms of direction and speed selectivity in extrastriate area MT. *Journal of Neurophysiology, 55*, 1308–1327.

Miles, F. A., Kawano, K., & Optican, L. M. (1986). Short-latency ocular following responses of monkey: I. Dependence on temporospatial properties of visual input. *Journal of Neurophysiology, 56*, 1321–1354.

Miller, E. K., Li, L., & Desimone, R. (1993). Activity of neurons in anterior inferior temporal cortex during a short-term memory task. *Journal of Neuroscience, 13*, 1460–1478.

Miller, M., Pasik, P., & Pasik, T. (1980). Extrageniculostriate vision in the monkey: VII. Contrast sensitivity functions. *Journal of Neurophysiology, 43*, 1510–1526.

Mishkin, M. (1954). Visual discrimination performance following partial ablations of the temporal lobe: II. Ventral surface vs. hippocampus. *Journal of Comparative & Physiological Psychology, 47*, 187–193.

Mishkin, M., & Pribram, K. H. (1954). Visual discrimination performance following partial ablations of the temporal lobe: I. Ventral vs. lateral. *Journal of Comparative & Physiological Psychology, 47*, 14–20.

Miyashita, Y., & Chang, H. S. (1988). Neuronal correlate of pictorial short-term memory in the primate temporal cortex. *Nature, 331*, 68–70.

Moore, T., Tolias, A. S., & Schiller, P. H. (1998). Visual representations during saccadic eye movements. *Proceedings of the National Academy of Sciences, USA, 95*, 8981–8984.

Moran, J., & Desimone, R. (1985). Selective attention gates visual processing in the extrastriate cortex. *Science, 229,* 782–783.

Morigiwa, K., & Vardi, N. (1999). Differential expression of iono-tropic glutamate receptor subunits in the outer retina. *Journal of Comparative Neurology, 405,* 173–184.

Motter, B. C. (1994). Neural correlates of feature selective memory and pop-out in extrastriate area V4. *Journal of Neuroscience, 14,* 2190–2199.

Mountcastle, V. B., Andersen, R. A., & Motter, B. C. (1981). The influence of attentive fixation upon the excitability of the light-sensitive neurons of the posterior parietal cortex. *Journal of Neuroscience, 1,* 1218–1225.

Mountcastle, V. B., Lynch, J. C., Georgopoulos, A., Sakata, H., & Acuna, C. (1975). Posterior parietal association cortex of the monkey: Command functions for operations within extrapersonal space. *Journal of Neurophysiology, 38,* 871–908.

Movshon, J. A., Adelson, E. H., Gizzi, M. S., & Newsome, W. T. (1985). The analysis of moving visual patterns. In C. Chagas, R. Gattas, & C. G. Gross (Eds.), *Pattern recognition mechanisms* (pp. 117–151). Vatican City: Ponticifica Academia Scientiarum.

Movshon, J. A., & Newsome, W. T. (1996). Visual response properties of striate cortical neurons projecting to area MT in macaque monkeys. *Journal of Neuroscience, 16,* 7733–7741.

Nakamura, H., Gattass, R., Desimone, R., & Ungerleider, L. G. (1993). The modular organization of projections from areas V1 and V2 to areas V4 and TEO in macaques. *Journal of Neuroscience, 13,* 3681–3691.

Nakamura, K., Chung, H. H., Graziano, M. S., & Gross, C. G. (1999). Dynamic representation of eye position in the parieto-occipital sulcus. *Journal of Neurophysiology, 81,* 2374–2385.

Nakamura, K., & Colby, C. L. (2000). Visual, saccade-related, and cognitive activation of single neurons in monkey extrastriate area V3a. *Journal of Neurophysiology, 84,* 677–692.

Nakamura, K., & Colby, C. L. (2002). Updating of the visual representation in monkey striate and extrastriate areas during saccades. *PNAS, 99,* 4026–4031.

Neal, J. W., Pearson, R. C., & Powell, T. P. (1990). The connections of area PG, 7a, with cortex in the parietal, occipital and temporal lobes of the monkey. *Brain Research, 532,* 249–264.

Newsome, W. T., Britten, K. H., & Movshon, J. A. (1989). Neuronal correlates of a perceptual decision. *Nature, 341,* 52–54.

Newsome, W. T., & Pare, E. B. (1988). A selective impairment of motion perception following lesions of the middle temporal visual area (MT). *Journal of Neuroscience, 8,* 2201–2211.

Newsome, W. T., Wurtz, R. H., Dursteler, M. R., & Mikami, A. (1985). Deficits in visual motion processing following ibotenic acid lesions of the middle temporal visual area of the macaque monkey. *Journal of Neuroscience, 5,* 825–840.

Nothdurft, H. C., Gallant, J. L., & Van Essen, D. C. (1999). Response modulation by texture surround in primate area V1: Correlates of "popout" under anesthesia. *Visual Neuroscience, 16,* 15–34.

Nowak, L. G., Munk, M. H., James, A. C., Girard, P., & Bullier, J. (1999). Cross-correlation study of the temporal interactions between areas V1 and V2 of the macaque monkey. *Journal of Neurophysiology, 81,* 1057–1074.

Obermayer, K., & Blasdel, G. G. (1993). Geometry of orientation and ocular dominance columns in monkey striate cortex. *Journal of Neuroscience, 13,* 4114–4129.

Olavarria, J. F., & Van Essen, D. C. (1997). The global pattern of cytochrome oxidase stripes in visual area V2 of the macaque monkey. *Cerebral Cortex, 7,* 395–404.

Oram, M. W., & Perrett, D. I. (1996). Integration of form and motion in the anterior superior temporal polysensory area (STPa) of the macaque monkey. *Journal of Neurophysiology, 76,* 109–129.

Oram, M. W., Perrett, D. I., & Hietanen, J. K. (1993). Directional tuning of motion-sensitive cells in the anterior superior temporal polysensory area of the macaque. *Experimental Brain Research, 97,* 274–294.

Packer, O. S., Williams, D. R., & Bensinger, D. G. (1996). Photopigment transmittance imaging of the primate photoreceptor mosaic. *Journal of Neuroscience, 16,* 2251–2260.

Page, W. K., & Duffy, C. J. (1999). MST neuronal responses to heading direction during pursuit eye movements. *Journal of Neurophysiology, 81,* 596–610.

Paolini, M., Distler, C., Bremmer, F., Lappe, M., & Hoffmann, K. P. (2000). Responses to continuously changing optic flow in area MST. *Journal of Neurophysiology, 84,* 730–743.

Pasternak, T., & Merigan, W. H. (1994). Motion perception following lesions of the superior temporal sulcus in the monkey. *Cerebral Cortex, 4,* 247–259.

Pasupathy, A., & Connor, C. E. (1999). Responses to contour features in macaque area V4. *Journal of Neurophysiology, 82,* 2490–2502.

Perrett, D. I., Smith, P. A. J., Mistlin, A. J., Chitty, A. J., Head, A. S., Potter, D. D., et al. (1985). Visual analysis of body movements by neurons in the temporal cortex of the macaque monkey: A preliminary report. *Behavioral Brain Research, 16,* 153–170.

Perry, V. H., Oehler, R., & Cowey, A. (1984). Retinal ganglion cells that project to the dorsal lateral geniculate nucleus in the macaque monkey. *Neuroscience, 12,* 1101–1123.

Peterhans, E., & von der Heydt, R. (1989). Mechanisms of contour perception in monkey visual cortex: II. Contours bridging gaps. *Journal of Neuroscience, 9,* 1749–1763.

Phinney, R. E., & Siegel, R. M. (2000). Speed selectivity for optic flow in area 7a of the behaving macaque. *Cerebral Cortex, 10,* 413–421.

Platt, M. L., & Glimcher, P. W. (1997). Responses of intraparietal neurons to saccadic targets and visual distractors. *Journal of Neurophysiology, 78,* 1574–1589.

Platt, M. L., & Glimcher, P. W. (1999). Neural correlates of decision variables in parietal cortex. *Nature, 400,* 233–238.

Poggio, G. E. (1995). Mechanisms of stereopsis in monkey visual cortex. *Cerebral Cortex, 5,* 193–204.

Poggio, G. F., Gonzalez, F., & Krause, F. (1988). Stereoscopic mechanisms in monkey visual cortex: Binocular correlation and disparity selectivity. *Journal of Neuroscience, 8,* 4531–4550.

Posner, M. I. (1980). Orienting of attention. *Quarterly Journal of Experimental Psychology, 32,* 3–25.

Powell, K. D., & Goldberg, M. E. (2000). Response of neurons in the lateral intraparietal area to a distractor flashed during the delay period of a memory-guided saccade. *Journal of Neurophysiology, 84,* 301–310.

Qian, N., Andersen, R. A., & Adelson, E. H. (1994). Transparent motion perception as detection of unbalanced motion signals: I. Psychophysics. *Journal of Neuroscience, 14,* 7357–7366.

Read, H. L., & Siegel, R. M. (1997). Modulation of responses to optic flow in area 7a by retinotopic and oculomotor cues in monkey. *Cerebral Cortex, 7,* 647–661.

Recanzone, G. H., Wurtz, R. H., & Schwarz, U. (1997). Responses of MT and MST neurons to one and two moving objects in the receptive field. *Journal of Neurophysiology, 78,* 2904–2915.

Rensink, R. A. (2000). Visual search for change: A probe into the nature of attentional processing. *Visual Cognition, 7,* 345–376.

Reynolds, J. H., Chelazzi, L., & Desimone, R. (1999). Competitive mechanisms subserve attention in macaque areas V2 and V4. *Journal of Neuroscience, 19,* 1736–1753.

Reynolds, J. H., Pasternak, T., & Desimone, R. (2000). Attention increases sensitivity of V4 neurons. *Neuron, 26,* 703–714.

Ringach, D. L., Hawken, M. J., & Shapley, R. (1997). Dynamics of orientation tuning in macaque primary visual cortex. *Nature, 387,* 281–284.

Robinson, D. L., Goldberg, M. E., & Stanton, G. B. (1978). Parietal association cortex in the primate: Sensory mechanisms and behavioral modulations. *Journal of Neurophysiology, 41,* 910–932.

Rockland, K. S. (1992). Laminar distribution of neurons projecting from area V1 to V2 in macaque and squirrel monkeys. *Cerebral Cortex, 2,* 38–47.

Rockland, K. S., & Pandya, D. N. (1979). Laminar origins and terminations of cortical connections of the occipital lobe in the rhesus monkey. *Brain Research, 179,* 3–20.

Rodieck, R. W. (1979). Visual pathways. *Annual Review of Neuroscience, 2,* 193–225.

Rodieck, R. W. (1988). The primate retina. In H. D. Steklis (Ed.), *Neurosciences: Vol. 4. Comparative primate biology* (pp. 203–278). New York: Alan R. Liss.

Rodieck, R. W. (1998). *The first steps in seeing.* Sunderland, MA: Sinauer Associates.

Rodieck, R. W., & Watanabe, M. (1993). Survey of the morphology of macaque retinal ganglion cells that project to the pretectum, superior colliculus, and parvicellular laminae of the lateral geniculate nucleus. *Journal of Comparative Neurology, 338,* 289–303.

Rodman, H. R., & Albright, T. D. (1989). Single-unit analysis of pattern-motion selective properties in the middle temporal visual area (MT). *Experimental Brain Research, 75,* 53–64.

Roe, A. W., & Ts'o, D. Y. (1995). Visual topography in primate V2: Multiple representation across functional stripes. *Journal of Neuroscience, 15,* 3689–3715.

Roe, A. W., & Ts'o, D. Y. (1997). The functional architecture of area V2 in the macaque monkey: Physiology, topography, connectivity. In E. G. Jones, A. Peters (Series Eds.), K. S. Rockland, J. H. Kaas, & A. Peters (Vol. Eds.), *Cerebral cortex: Vol. 12. Extrastriate cortex in primates* (pp. 295–333). New York: Plenum Press.

Roelfsema, P. R., Lamme, V. A., & Spekreijse, H. (1998). Object-based attention in the primary visual cortex of the macaque monkey. *Nature, 395,* 376–381.

Rossi, A. F., Desimone, R., & Ungerleider, L. G. (2001). Contextual modulation in primary visual cortex of macaques. *Journal of Neuroscience, 21,* 1698–1709.

Roy, J. P., Komatsu, H., & Wurtz, R. H. (1992). Disparity sensitivity of neurons in monkey extrastriate area MST. *Journal of Neuroscience, 12,* 2478–2492.

Rudolph, K., & Pasternak, T. (1999). Transient and permanent deficits in motion perception after lesions of cortical areas MT and MST in the macaque monkey. *Cerebral Cortex, 9,* 90–100.

Rushton, S. K., Harris, J. M., Lloyd, M. R., & Wann, J. P. (1998). Guidance of locomotion on foot uses perceived target location rather than optic flow. *Current Biology, 8,* 1191–1194.

Saito, H., Yukie, M., Tanaka, K., Hikosaka, K., Fukada, Y., & Iwai, E. (1986). Integration of direction signals of image motion in the superior temporal sulcus of the macaque monkey. *Journal of Neuroscience, 6,* 145–157.

Sakai, K., & Miyashita, Y. (1994). Neuronal tuning to learned complex forms in vision. *Neuroreport, 5,* 829–832.

Sakata, H., Shibutani, H., Ito, Y., & Tsurugai, K. (1986). Parietal cortical neurons responding to rotary movement of visual stimulus in space. *Experimental Brain Research, 61,* 658–663.

Sakata, H., Shibutani, H., Ito, Y., Tsurugai, K., Mine, S., & Kusunoki, M. (1994). Functional properties of rotation-sensitive neurons in the posterior parietal association cortex of the monkey. *Experimental Brain Research, 101,* 183–202.

Sakata, H., Shibutani, H., & Kawano, K. (1983). Functional properties of visual tracking neurons in posterior parietal association cortex of the monkey. *Journal of Neurophysiology, 49,* 1364–1380.

Salzman, C. D., Britten, K. H., & Newsome, W. T. (1990). Cortical microstimulation influences perceptual judgements of motion direction. *Nature, 346,* 174–177.

Salzman, C. D., Murasugi, C. M., Britten, K. H., & Newsome, W. T. (1992). Microstimulation in visual area MT: Effects on direction discrimination performance. *Journal of Neuroscience, 12,* 2331–2355.

Samy, C. N., & Hirsch, J. (1989). Comparison of human and monkey retinal photoreceptor sampling mosaics. *Visual Neuroscience, 3,* 281–285.

Sceniak, M. P., Ringach, D. L., Hawken, M. J., & Shapley, R. (1999). Contrast's effect on spatial summation by macaque V1 neurons. *Nature Neuroscience, 2,* 733–739.

Schaafsma, S. J., & Duysens, J. (1996). Neurons in the ventral intraparietal area of awake macaque monkey closely resemble neurons in the dorsal part of the medial superior temporal area in their responses to optic flow patterns. *Journal of Neurophysiology, 76,* 4056–4068.

Schall, J. D., Morel, A., King, D. J., & Bullier, J. (1995). Topography of visual cortex connections with frontal eye field in macaque: Convergence and segregation of processing streams. *Journal of Neuroscience, 15,* 4464–4487.

Schilder, P., Pasik, P., & Pasik, T. (1972). Extrageniculostriate vision in the monkey: III. Circle VS triangle and "red VS green" discrimination. *Experimental Brain Research, 14,* 436–448.

Schiller, P. H. (1993). The effects of V4 and middle temporal (MT) area lesions on visual performance in the rhesus monkey. *Visual Neuroscience, 10,* 717–746.

Schiller, P. H., & Colby, C. L. (1983). The responses of single cells in the lateral geniculate nucleus of the rhesus monkey to color and luminance contrast. *Vision Research, 23,* 1631–1641.

Schiller, P. H., & Lee, K. (1994). The effects of lateral geniculate nucleus, area V4, and middle temporal (MT) lesions on visually guided eye movements. *Visual Neuroscience, 11,* 229–241.

Schiller, P. H., Logothetis, N. K., & Charles, E. R. (1990). Functions of the colour-opponent and broad-band channels of the visual system. *Nature, 343,* 68–70.

Schiller, P. H., & Malpeli, J. G. (1977). The effect of striate cortex cooling on area 18 cells in the monkey. *Brain Research, 126,* 366–369.

Schiller, P. H., & Malpeli, J. G. (1978). Functional specificity of lateral geniculate nucleus laminae of the rhesus monkey. *Journal of Neurophysiology, 41,* 788–797.

Sclar, G., Maunsell, J. H., & Lennie, P. (1990). Coding of image contrast in central visual pathways of the macaque monkey. *Vision Research, 30,* 1–10.

Seidemann, E., & Newsome, W. T. (1999). Effect of spatial attention on the responses of area MT neurons. *Journal of Neurophysiology, 81,* 1783–1794.

Seidemann, E., Poirson, A. B., Wandell, B. A., & Newsome, W. T. (1999). Color signals in area MT of the macaque monkey. *Neuron, 24,* 911–917.

Seidemann, E., Zohary, E., & Newsome, W. T. (1998). Temporal gating of neural signals during performance of a visual discrimination task. *Nature, 394,* 72–75.

Selemon, L. D., & Goldman-Rakic, P. S. (1988). Common cortical and subcortical targets of the dorsolateral prefrontal and posterior parietal cortices in the rhesus monkey: Evidence for a distributed neural network subserving spatially guided behavior. *Journal of Neuroscience, 8,* 4049–4068.

Seltzer, B., & Pandya, D. N. (1986). Posterior parietal projections to the intraparietal sulcus of the rhesus monkey. *Experimental Brain Research, 62,* 459–469.

Seltzer, B., & Pandya, D. N. (1989). Frontal lobe connections of the superior temporal sulcus in the rhesus monkey. *Journal of Comparative Neurology, 281,* 97–113.

Sereno, A. B., & Maunsell, J. H. (1998). Shape selectivity in primate lateral intraparietal cortex. *Nature, 395,* 500–503.

Shadlen, M. N., & Newsome, W. T. (1996). Motion perception: Seeing and deciding. *Proceedings of the National Academy of Sciences, USA, 93,* 628–633.

Shadlen, M. N., & Newsome, W. T. (2001). Neural basis of a perceptual decision in the parietal cortex (area LIP) of the rhesus monkey. *Journal of Neurophysiology, 86,* 1916–1936.

Sheinberg, D. L., & Logothetis, N. K. (1997). The role of temporal cortical areas in perceptual organization. *Proceedings of the National Academy of Sciences, USA, 94,* 3408–3413.

Shenoy, K. V., Bradley, D. C., & Andersen, R. A. (1999). Influence of gaze rotation on the visual response of primate MSTd neurons. *Journal of Neurophysiology, 81,* 2764–2786.

Sherman, S. M. (1996). Dual response modes in lateral geniculate neurons: Mechanisms and functions. *Visual Neuroscience, 13,* 205–213.

Sherman, S. M. (2001). Tonic and burst firing: Dual modes of thalamocortical relay. *Trends in Neurosciences, 24,* 122–126.

Sherman, S. M., & Guillery, R. W. (1996). Functional organization of thalamocortical relays. *Journal of Neurophysiology, 76,* 1367–1395.

Shipp, S., & Zeki, S. (1989). The organization of connections between areas V5 and V2 in macaque monkey visual cortex. *European Journal of Neuroscience, 1,* 333–354.

Shiwa, T. (1987). Corticocortical projections to the monkey temporal lobe with particular reference to the visual processing pathways. *Archive Ital Biol, 125,* 139–154.

Siegel, R. M., & Read, H. L. (1997). Analysis of optic flow in the monkey parietal area 7a. *Cerebral Cortex, 7,* 327–346.

Smith, R. G., & Sterling, P. (1990). Cone receptive field in cat retina computed from microcircuitry. *Visual Neuroscience, 5,* 453–461.

Smith, V. C., Pokorny, J., Lee, B. B., & Dacey, D. M. (2001). Primate horizontal cell dynamics: An analysis of sensitivity regulation in the outer retina. *Journal of Neurophysiology, 85,* 545–558.

Snowden, R. J., Treue, S., Erickson, R. G., & Andersen, R. A. (1991). The response of area MT and V1 neurons to transparent motion. *Journal of Neuroscience, 11,* 2768–2785.

Snyder, L. H., Batista, A. P., & Andersen, R. A. (1997). Coding of intention in the posterior parietal cortex. *Nature, 386,* 167–170.

Snyder, L. H., Grieve, K. L., Brotchie, P., & Andersen, R. A. (1998). Separate body- and world-referenced representations of visual space in parietal cortex. *Nature, 394,* 887–891.

Spear, P. D., Kim, C. B. Y., Ahmad, A., & Tom, B. W. (1996). Relationship between numbers of retinal ganglion cells and lateral geniculate neurons in the rhesus monkey. *Visual Neuroscience, 13,* 199–203.

Spear, P. D., Moore, R. J., Kim, C. B. Y., Xue, J.-T., & Tumosa, N., (1994). Effects of aging on the primate visual system: Spatial and temporal processing by lateral geniculate neurons in young adult and old rhesus monkeys. *Journal of Neurophysiology, 72,* 402–420.

Squire, L. R. (1987). *Memory and brain.* New York: Oxford University Press.

Srinivasan, M. V., Laughlin, S. B., & Dubs, A. (1982). Predictive coding: A fresh view of inhibition in the retina. *Proceedings of the Royal Society, London, 216B,* 427–459.

Stefanacci, L., Reber, P., Costanza, J., Wong, E., Buxton, R., Zola, S., et al. (1998). FMRI of monkey visual cortex. *Neuron, 20,* 1051–1057.

Steinmetz, M. A., Connor, C. E., Constantinidis, C., & McLaughlin, J. R. (1994). Covert attention suppresses neuronal responses in area 7a of the posterior parietal cortex. *Journal of Neurophysiology, 72,* 1020–1023.

Sterling, P. (1998). "Knocking out" a neural circuit. *Neuron, 21,* 643–644.

Sterling, P., Smith, R. G., Rao, R., & Vardi, N. (1995). Functional architecture of mammalian outer retina and bipolar cells. In S. Archer, M. B. Djamgoz, & S. Vallerga (Eds.), *Neurobiology and clinical aspects of the outer retina* (pp. 325–348). London: Chapman & Hall.

Strettoi, E., Dacheux, R. F., & Raviola, E. (1990). Synaptic connections of rod bipolar cells in the inner plexiform layer of the rabbit retina. *Journal of Comparative Neurology, 295,* 449–466.

Takemura, A., Inoue, Y., & Kawano, K. (2000). The effect of disparity on the very earliest ocular following responses and the initial neuronal activity in monkey cortical area MST. *Neuroscience Research, 38,* 93–101.

Takemura, A., Inoue, Y., Kawano, K., Quaia, C., & Miles, F. A. (2001). Single-unit activity in cortical area MST associated with disparity-vergence eye movements: Evidence for population coding. *Journal of Neurophysiology, 85,* 2245–2266.

Tamura, H., & Tanaka, K. (2001). Visual response properties of cells in the ventral and dorsal parts of the macaque inferotemporal cortex. *Cerebral Cortex, 11,* 384–399.

Tanaka, K. (1993). Neuronal mechanisms of object recognition. *Science, 262,* 685–688.

Tanaka, K. (1996). Inferotemporal cortex and object vision. *Annual Review of Neuroscience, 19,* 109–139.

Tanaka, K. (1997). Columnar organization in inferotemporal cortex. In E. G. Jones, A. Peters (Series Eds.), K. S. Rockland, J. H. Kaas, & A. Peters (Vol. Eds.), *Cerebral cortex: Vol. 12.*

Extrastriate cortex in primates (pp. 469–498). New York: Plenum Press.

Tanaka, K. (1998). Representation of visual motion in the extrastriate visual cortex. In T. Watanabe (Ed.), *High-level motion processing: Computational, neurobiological, and psychophysical perspectives* (pp. 295–313). Cambridge, MA: MIT Press.

Tanaka, K., Fukada, Y., & Saito, H. A. (1989). Underlying mechanisms of the response specificity of expansion/contraction and rotation cells in the dorsal part of the medial superior temporal area of the macaque monkey. *Journal of Neurophysiology, 62,* 642–656.

Tanaka, K., Hikosaka, K., Saito, H., Yukie, M., Fukada, Y., & Iwai, E. (1986). Analysis of local and wide-field movements in the superior temporal visual areas of the macaque monkey. *Journal of Neuroscience, 6,* 134–144.

Tanaka, K., & Saito, H. (1989). Analysis of motion of the visual field by direction, expansion/contraction, and rotation cells clustered in the dorsal part of the medial superior temporal area of the macaque monkey. *Journal of Neurophysiology, 62,* 626–641.

Tanaka, M., Lindsley, E., Lausmann, S., & Creutzfeldt, O. D. (1990). Afferent connections of the prelunate visual association cortex (areas V4 and DP). *Anatomy and Embryology, Berlin, 181,* 19–30.

Thiele, A., Dobkins, K. R., & Albright, T. D. (2001). Neural correlates of chromatic motion perception. *Neuron, 32,* 351–358.

Treue, S., Hol, K., & Rauber, H.-J. (2000). Seeing multiple directions of motion: Physiology and psychophysics. *Nature Neuroscience, 3,* 270–276.

Treue, S., & Martinez Trujillo, J. C. (1999). Feature-based attention influences motion processing gain in macaque visual cortex. *Nature, 399,* 575–579.

Treue, S., & Maunsell, J. H. (1996). Attentional modulation of visual motion processing in cortical areas MT and MST. *Nature, 382,* 539–541.

Treue, S., & Maunsell, J. H. (1999). Effects of attention on the processing of motion in macaque middle temporal and medial superior temporal visual cortical areas. *Journal of Neuroscience, 19,* 7591–7602.

Ts'o, D. Y., & Gilbert, C. D. (1988). The organization of chromatic and spatial interactions in the primate striate cortex. *Journal of Neuroscience, 8,* 1712–1727.

Ts'o, D. Y., Roe, A. W., & Gilbert, C. D. (2001). A hierarchy of the functional organization for color, form and disparity in primate visual area V2. *Vision Research, 41,* 1333–1349.

Tsukamoto, Y., Masarachia, P., Schein, S. J., & Sterling, P. (1992). Gap junctions between the pedicles of macaque foveal cones. *Vision Research, 32,* 1809–1815.

Ungerleider, L. G., & Desimone, R. (1986). Cortical connections of visual area MT in the macaque. *Journal of Comparative Neurology, 248,* 190–222.

Ungerleider, L. G., Desimone, R., Galkin, T. W., & Mishkin, M. (1984). Subcortical projections of area MT in the macaque. *Journal of Comparative Neurology, 223,* 368–386.

Ungerleider, L. G., Galkin, T. W., & Mishkin, M. (1983). Visuotopic organization of projections from striate cortex to inferior and lateral pulvinar in rhesus monkey. *Journal of Comparative Neurology, 217,* 137–157.

Ungerleider, L. G., & Mishkin, M. (1982). Two cortical visual systems. In D. J. Ingle, R. J. Mansfield, & M. S. Goodale (Eds.), *The analysis of visual behavior* (pp. 549–586). Cambridge, MA: MIT Press.

Upadhyay, U. D., Page, W. K., & Duffy, C. J. (2000). MST responses to pursuit across optic flow with motion parallax. *Journal of Neurophysiology, 84,* 818–826.

van den Berg, A. V., & Beintema, J. A. (2000). The mechanism of interaction between visual flow and eye velocity signals for heading perception. *Neuron, 26,* 747–752.

Van Essen, D. C., & Zeki, S. M. (1978). The topographic organization of rhesus monkey prestriate cortex. *The Journal of Physiology, 277,* 193–226.

Van Essen, D. C., Maunsell, J. H., & Bixby, J. L. (1981). The middle temporal visual area in the macaque: Myeloarchitecture, connections, functional properties and topographic organization. *Journal of Comparative Neurology, 199,* 293–326.

Van Essen, D. C., Newsome, W. T., & Maunsell, J. H. (1984). The visual field representation in striate cortex of the macaque monkey: Asymmetries, anisotropies, and individual variability. *Vision Research, 24,* 429–448.

Van Essen, D. C., Newsome, W. T., Maunsell, J. H., & Bixby, J. L. (1986). The projections from striate cortex (V1) to areas V2 and V3 in the macaque monkey: Asymmetries, areal boundaries, and patchy connections. *Journal of Comparative Neurology, 244,* 451–480.

Vaney, D. I. (1994). Territorial organization of direction-selective ganglion cells in rabbit retina. *Journal of Neuroscience, 14,* 6301–6316.

Vaney, D. I., Peichl, L., & Boycott, B. B. (1981). Matching populations of amacrine cells in the inner nuclear and ganglion cell layers of the rabbit retina. *Journal of Comparative Neurology, 199,* 373–391.

Vardi, N., Kaufman, D. L., & Sterling, P. (1994). Horizontal cells in cat and monkey retina express different isoforms of glutamic acid decarboxylase. *Visual Neuroscience, 11,* 135–142.

Vardi, N., Masarachia, P., & Sterling, P. (1992). Immunoreactivity to GABAa receptor in the outer plexiform layer of the cat retina. *Journal of Comparative Neurology, 320,* 394–397.

Varela, F., Lachaux, J. P., Rodriguez, E., & Martinerie, J. (2001). The brainweb: Phase synchronization and large-scale integration. *Nature Reviews Neuroscience, 2,* 229–239.

Walker, M. F., Fitzgibbon, E. J., & Goldberg, M. E. (1995). Neurons in the monkey superior colliculus predict the visual result of impending saccadic eye movements. *Journal of Neurophysiology, 73,* 1988–2003.

Walsh, V., Butler, S. R., Carden, D., & Kulikowski, J. J. (1992). The effects of V4 lesions on the visual abilities of macaques: Shape discrimination. *Behavioural Brain Research, 50,* 115–126.

Walsh, V., Carden, D., Butler, S. R., & Kulikowski, J. J. (1993). The effects of V4 lesions on the visual abilities of macaques: Hue discrimination and colour constancy. *Behavioural Brain Research, 53,* 51–62.

Walsh, V., Kulikowski, J. J., Butler, S. R., & Carden, D. (1992). The effects of lesions of area V4 on the visual abilities of macaques: Colour categorization. *Behavioural Brain Research, 52,* 81–89.

Walsh, V., Le Mare, C., Blaimire, A., & Cowey, A. (2000). Normal discrimination performance accompanied by priming deficits in monkeys with V4 or TEO lesions. *Neuroreport, 11,* 1459–1462.

Wandell, B. A. (1995). *Foundations of vision.* Sunderland, MA: Sinauer Associates.

Wandell, B. A. (1999). Computational neuroimaging of human visual cortex. *Annual Review of Neuroscience, 22,* 145–173.

Warren, W. H., Kay, B. A., Zosh, W. D., Duchon, A. P., & Sahuc, S. (2001). Optic flow is used to control human walking. *Nature Neuroscience, 4,* 213–216.

Wässle, H., & Boycott, B. B. (1991). Functional architecture of the mammalian retina. *Physiological Reviews, 71,* 447–480.

Wässle, H., Grünert, U., Martin, P. R., & Boycott, B. B. (1994). Immunocytochemical characterization and spatial distribution of midget bipolar cells in the macaque monkey retina. *Vision Research, 34,* 561–579.

Wässle, H., Grünert, U., Röhrenbeck, J., & Boycott, B. B. (1989). Cortical magnification factor and ganglion cell density of the primate retina. *Nature, 341,* 643–646.

Wässle, H., Grünert, U., Röhrenbeck, J., & Boycott, B. B. (1990). Retinal ganglion cell density and cortical magnification factor in the primate. *Vision Research, 30,* 1897–1911.

Watanabe, M., & Rodieck, R. W. (1989). Parasol and midget ganglion cells of the primate retina. *Journal of Comparative Neurology, 289,* 434–454.

Weiskrantz, L., & Cowey, A. (1967). Comparison of the effects of striate cortex and retinal lesions on visual acuity in the monkey. *Science, 155,* 104–106.

Wiesel, T. N., & Hubel, D. H. (1966). Spatial and chromatic interactions in the lateral geniculate body of the rhesus monkey. *Journal of Neurophysiology, 29,* 1115–1156.

Williams, D. R. (1986). Seeing through the photoreceptor mosaic. *Trends in Neuroscience, 9,* 193–198.

Wilson, J. R. (1993). Circuitry of the dorsal lateral geniculate nucleus in the cat and monkey. *Acta Anatomica, 147,* 1–13.

Wurtz, R. H., & Kandel, E. R. (2000). Central visual pathways. In E. R. Kandel, J. H. Schwartz, & T. M. Jessell (Eds.), *Principles of neural science* (4th ed., pp. 523–547). New York: McGraw-Hill.

Xiao, D. K., Raiguel, S., Marcar, V., Koenderink, J., & Orban, G. A. (1995). Spatial heterogeneity of inhibitory surrounds in the middle temporal visual area. *Proceedings of the National Academy of Sciences, USA, 92,* 11303–11306.

Xiao, Y., Zych, A., & Felleman, D. J. (1999). Segregation and convergence of functionally defined V2 thin stripe and interstripe compartment projections to area V4 of macaques. *Cerebral Cortex, 9,* 792–804.

Xu, X., Ichida, J. M., Allison, J. D., Boyd, J. D., Bonds, A. B., & Casagrande, V. A. (2000). A comparison of koniocellular, magnocellular and parvocellular receptive field properties in the lateral geniculate nucleus of the owl monkey (*Aotus trivirgatus*). *Journal of Physiology, 531,* 203–218.

Yantis, S., & Jonides, J. (1984). Abrupt visual onsets and selective attention: Evidence from visual search. *Journal of Experimental Psychology and Human Perception and Performance, 10,* 601–621.

Yoshioka, T., Blasdel, G. G., Levitt, J. B., & Lund, J. S. (1996). Relation between patterns of intrinsic lateral connectivity, ocular dominance, and cytochrome oxidase-reactive regions in macaque monkey striate cortex. *Cerebral Cortex, 6,* 297–310.

Yukie, M., & Iwai, E. (1985). Laminar origin of direct projection from cortex area V1 to V4 in the rhesus monkey. *Brain Research, 346,* 383–386.

Yukie, M., & Iwai, E. (1988). Direct projections from the ventral TE area of the inferotemporal cortex to hippocampal field CA1 in the monkey. *Neuroscience Letters, 88,* 6–10.

Zeki, S. M. (1971). Cortical projections from two prestriate areas in the monkey. *Brain Research, 34,* 19–35.

Zeki, S. M. (1974). Functional organization of a visual area in the posterior bank of the superior temporal sulcus of the rhesus monkey. *Journal of Physiology (London), 236,* 549–573.

Zeki, S. M. (1978a). The cortical projections of foveal striate cortex in the rhesus monkey. *Journal of Physiology, 277,* 227–244.

Zeki, S. M. (1978b). Functional specialisation in the visual cortex of the rhesus monkey. *Nature, 274,* 423–428.

Zeki, S. M. (1978c). The third visual complex of rhesus monkey prestriate cortex. *Journal of Physiology, 277,* 245–272.

Zeki, S. M. (1978d). Uniformity and diversity of structure and function in rhesus monkey prestriate visual cortex. *Journal of Physiology, 277,* 273–290.

Zeki, S. M. (1979). Functional specialization and binocular interaction in the visual areas of rhesus monkey prestriate cortex. *Proceedings of the Royal Society, London, 204B,* 379–397.

Zeki, S. M., & Sandeman, D. R. (1976). Combined anatomical and electrophysiological studies on the boundary between the second and third visual areas of rhesus monkey cortex. *Proceedings of the Royal Society, London, 194B,* 555–562.

Zeki, S. M., & Shipp, S. (1987). Functional segregation within area V2 of macaque monkey visual cortex. In J. J. Kulikowski, C. M. Dickinson, & I. J. Murray (Eds.), *Seing contour and color* (pp. 120–124). Oxford: Pergamon Press.

CHAPTER 7

Auditory Processing in the Primate Brain

TROY A. HACKETT AND JON H. KAAS

For all mammals, including primates, the auditory system makes it possible to obtain information from the environment that may or may not be detected by other sensory modalities. Sounds can be perceived, localized, and identified, often at great distances, without confirmation by the other senses. Depending on the species, input to the auditory system may be crucial for navigation, evasion of predators, location of food and water, and communication between other members of the same species. Some species of bats, for example, rely on auditory input for both navigating and finding food. Primates, by comparison, are not dependent on audition for these activities but have specializations that enable vocal communication between individuals (Ghazanfar & Hauser, 1999). Auditory-related specializations such as these equip each species with unique mechanisms that ultimately enhance survival and propagation.

To accomplish these tasks, the auditory system must encode the relevant acoustic cues and distribute this information to the auditory and multisensory areas of the brain that make use of it. This complex process involves a wide variety of neuronal cell types, specialized circuitry, and vast networks of subcortical nuclei and cortical fields. These pathways and their elements are only partially understood, but the available data allow us to describe certain processes competently. For the purposes of this chapter, therefore, we discuss auditory-related processing and behaviors in terms of the two major tasks of the auditory system: *object recognition* and *sound localization*. We highlight the subcortical and cortical mechanisms that underlie these aspects of audition, in general, with special emphasis given to the organization of the auditory system in primates.

THE AUDITORY PATHWAYS

In mammals the major components of the auditory system are the *outer ear, middle ear, inner ear,* and *central pathways,* including the *cerebral cortex*. Peripherally, the outer and middle ears are responsible for the conduction of sound energy to the inner ear, where the signal is encoded by specialized sensory receptors (hair cells) and the eighth cranial nerve (CN VIII). The central auditory pathways consist of an elaborate network of interconnected nuclear complexes in the brain stem and thalamus and a number of cortical areas or fields (Figure 7.1). Serial and parallel inputs to each level are processed and passed on to other nuclei or fields, where additional processing occurs. In addition to the ascending network for the processing of sensory input, there is an extensive descending network that modulates activity at all levels, including the cochlea, enabling neurons to modify their input.

Subcortical Auditory Processing

Compared to the somatosensory and visual systems, the organization of the subcortical auditory pathways is exceptionally complex. The pathways involve five major nuclear groups, each of which can be parceled into discrete subdivisions. In addition, the pathways from each ear cross the midline shortly after entering the brain stem; thus, input from both ears is available to both sides of the brain at nearly every level of processing. This complexity creates an abundance of opportunities for signal processing below the level of cortex; thus our discussion of auditory processing would be incomplete without the inclusion of this information.

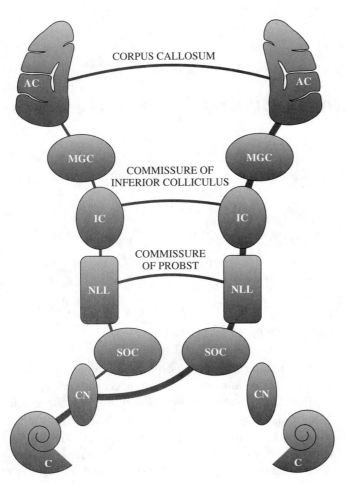

Figure 7.1   Schematic diagram of major ascending auditory pathways from one cochlea. Subdivisions of nuclear complexes and minor pathways are not shown. Dominant contralateral pathways are indicated by wide lines. C, cochlea; CN, cochlear nucleus; SOC, superior olivary complex; NLL, nuclei of the lateral lemniscus; IC, inferior colliculus; MGC, medial geniculate complex; AC, auditory cortex.

Compared with some other mammals, anatomical and physiological studies of subcortical auditory structures in primates are relatively few in number. Most of what is known about subcortical auditory processing in mammals comes from studies of nonprimates, especially cats, bats, and rodents. The findings from primate studies largely complement those of other mammals; thus it has been common to generalize principles of auditory subcortical organization across taxonomic groups, including humans. The extent to which this is valid depends on the presence of species-dependent specializations are expressed in the organization of the subcortical auditory pathways. Because of the lack of relevant primate data, however, such differences cannot be ruled out, so we must rely on data from nonprimates to discuss subcortical auditory processing in primates. In contrast, functional specializations are well known in the organization of auditory cortex, where the number of cortical fields devoted to a given sensory modality varies across taxa, and animals with larger

brains tend to have more neocortical areas (Kaas, 1993, 2000). We must remind ourselves, however, that the identification of species differences in cortical organization does not rule out attendant subcortical differentiation. It may be that technical limitations hinder identification of the subcortical substrates that underlie, or contribute to, cortical specializations. Nevertheless, for our purposes we assume that the functional organization of subcortical auditory structures in primates corresponds to that of species for which data are more abundant. We begin with an overview of the sensory transduction process in the cochlea, followed by a brief description of auditory processing associated with each nuclear complex. Although much of the information is based on findings in nonprimates, we make reference to relevant primates studies where appropriate.

Cochlea

The cochlea is a coiled fluid-filled tubular structure carved out of the petrous portion of the temporal bone. The sensory receptors responsible for neural transduction of the acoustic signal, the *hair cells,* are located in the cochlea within the organ of Corti. The organ of Corti rests on the *basilar membrane,* which runs the entire length of the cochlear spiral. In primates the length of the basilar membrane is about 20 mm (Fernandez, Butler, Konishi, & Honrubia, 1962; Rose, Hind, Anderson, & Brugge, 1971). Deflection of the basilar membrane by fluid movements within the cochlea depolarizes the hair cells, giving rise to the neural signal. Afferent innervation of the cochlea is mediated by bipolar neurons located in the *spiral ganglion* of the cochlea within its central bony core. The distal (peripheral) processes of these neurons terminate on the hair cells. The proximal (central) processes comprise the auditory portion of CN VIII and synapse with neurons of the ipsilateral cochlear nucleus in the medulla. A single row of *inner hair cells* is the principal source of afferent information in the auditory system. Each inner hair cell is innervated by approximately 10 to 20 myelinated afferent fibers (Type I). The three rows of *outer hair cells* are innervated by a different class of afferent neurons (Type II). Type II neurons are unmyelinated, and collaterals of a single fiber innervate many outer hair cells; thus, the afferent contribution of the outer hair cells is minor compared with that of the inner hair cells. A more important function of the outer hair cells may be related to their efferent innervation. Efferent modulation of outer hair cell properties affects the physical attributes of the organ of Corti and appears to serve as a mechanism for fine tuning the afferent output of the cochlea (discussed later).

One important property of the cochlea concerns the arrangement of hair cells along the basilar membrane. Because of the physical properties of the cochlear structures, hair cells at the base of the cochlea (i.e., nearest the stapes bone and middle ear) are maximally responsive to high-frequency sounds, whereas hair cells at the apex of the cochlea respond to low-frequency sounds. This feature enables the cochlea to separate a complex acoustic signal into its component frequencies. The resulting *tonotopic organization* of the cochlea is preserved in CN VIII and subsequent stages of central auditory processing and therefore represents an important organizational feature of the auditory system.

Eighth Cranial Nerve

Also known as the vestibulocochlear nerve, CN VIII has two divisions containing fibers from the *vestibular* and *cochlear* structures of the inner ear. CN VIII passes through the temporal bone via the internal auditory canal in the skull base, exiting medially at the junction of the medulla, pons, and cerebellum. Alving and Cowan (1971) estimated that the number of fibers in the macaque monkey ranges from about 28,000 to 33,500, considerably less than the 50,000 to 55,000 estimated for cats (Gacek & Rasmussen, 1961). The auditory division of CN VIII is comprised of two classes of bipolar neurons. Type I auditory neurons comprise 90% to 95% of the total fiber population and carry most of the afferent information from the inner hair cells of the cochlea. Type II afferent and efferent neurons make up the rest. Type I neurons can be subclassified on the basis of spontaneous activity, activation threshold, and spectral response profile. The spectral and temporal features of the acoustic signal are preserved in the firing patterns and topography of CN VIII neurons. Consistent with the tonotopic organization of the cochlea, units that innervate hair cells in the basal segment of the cochlea respond best to high-frequency stimuli, whereas those that innervate the apical portion of the cochlea are most sensitive to low-frequency stimuli. Typically, CN VIII neurons respond to a narrow range of frequencies over a broad intensity range. The spectral response profile of each neuron is commonly referred to as its *receptive field*. The frequency to which the neuron is most sensitive (i.e., lowest threshold) is known as the *characteristic frequency* (CF). The unit also responds to frequencies above and below the CF, but response thresholds are higher (i.e., greater intensity is required to elicit a response). By plotting response frequency as a function of threshold intensity, the receptive field of the unit can be represented in the form of a *tuning curve* (Figure 7.2). Tuning curves can be obtained from auditory-responsive neurons at all levels of the central auditory system, and the distributions of CFs are used to construct tonotopic maps of a given nucleus or cortical field.

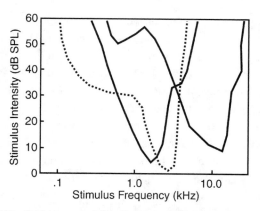

Figure 7.2 Tuning curves from neurons in the inferior colliculus (solid lines) and auditory core (dashed line) of the marmoset monkey. Receptive field properties vary by stimulus intensity.

Cochlear Nucleus

The cochlear nucleus represents only the first stage of subcortical auditory processing, yet the anatomical and physiological diversity of this structure indicates that substantial auditory processing is mediated at this level. The cochlear nuclei contain several subdivisions and a wide variety of cell types (Figure 7.3). The tonotopic organization of CN VIII is maintained in the orderly pattern of projections of Type I

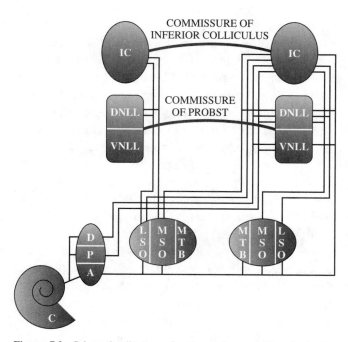

Figure 7.3 Schematic diagram of major and some minor brain-stem pathways from one cochlea to the level of the inferior colliculus. Subdivisions of nuclear complexes and some of their connections are shown. C, cochlea; D, dorsal cochlear nucleus; P, posteroventral cochlear nucleus; A, anteroventral cochlear nucleus; LSO, lateral superior olive; MSO, medial superior olive; MTB, medial nucleus of the trapezoid body; VNLL, ventral nucleus lateral lemniscus; DNLL, dorsal nucleus lateral lemniscus; IC, inferior colliculus.

and II fibers among the various subdivisions of the cochlear nucleus, which bifurcate on entering the brain stem. The ascending branches innervate the anteroventral division of the cochlear nucleus (AVCN). The posterior branches synapse in the posteroventral (PVCN) and/or dorsal (DCN) divisions. Neurons in the cochlear nuclei project to nearly every auditory nucleus on both sides of the brain stem, including the reticular formation. Each division exhibits a distinct pattern of projections to higher auditory centers and also receives patterned modulatory projections from higher auditory and nonauditory centers. Three major fiber bundles form the principal output connections of the cochlear nuclei. The largest band from the AVCN forms the *trapezoid body* with bilateral projections to the superior olivary complexes (SOCs), and contralateral projections to the lateral lemniscus and inferior colliculus (IC). Fibers from the PVCN form the *intermediate acoustic stria of Held* with projections to the contralateral lateral lemniscus and IC. The *dorsal acoustic stria of von Monakow* is formed by fibers of the DCN that also project primarily to the contralateral lateral lemniscus and IC. The anatomical features of the cochlear nuclei are generally consistent across primate species (Barnes, Magoun, & Ranson, 1943; Moskowitz & Liu, 1972; Strominger & Strominger, 1971; Strominger, Nelson, & Dougherty, 1977) and compare well with nonprimates, although some structural variations have been found (e.g., J. K. Moore, 1980).

In the cochlear nucleus each of the major cell types is associated with a unique response profile reflecting particular attributes of the original acoustic signal. Different populations of neurons appear to be specialized to extract particular aspects of the encoded auditory stimulus for delivery to other centers for further processing (Romand & Avan, 1997). In the AVCN, for example, only the globular and bushy spherical cells exhibit a primary-like response similar to that of CN VIII fibers (Smith, Joris, Carney, & Yin, 1991). By comparison, certain pyramidal cells in the DCN respond only after a variable delay (Oertel & Wu, 1989; Rhode, Smith, & Oertel, 1983). The distribution and connectivity of each cell type varies among the subdivisions of the cochlear nucleus and contributes to the range of response properties observed; thus each subdivision has a unique anatomical and physiological profile. The diverse cell populations also give rise to a number of segregated pathways that are functionally distinct (Figure 7.3). Division of the auditory pathways into multiple subsystems has been observed at all levels of subcortical processing; however, one pathway may not be functionally independent of the others at any level, nor must a pathway be strictly hierarchical across levels. The complex network of connections between auditory nuclei provides numerous opportunities for interaction between pathways at all levels.

Superior Olivary Complex

The next major level of auditory brain-stem processing involves the SOC. The primary ascending pathway from the contralateral AVCN synapses in the SOC and then projects to the ipsilateral central nucleus of the IC (ICc; see Figure 7.3). Additional ascending pathways also synapse in the SOC, whereas others bypass the SOC with targets in the lateral lemniscus or IC. The SOC consists of several nuclei that vary morphologically among mammals, birds, reptiles, and amphibians. In mammals the three main subnuclei are the lateral (LSO) and medial (MSO) superior olivary nuclei and the medial nucleus of the trapezoid body (MNTB). These nuclei are surrounded by a variable number of *periolivary* nuclei, depending on the species. Anatomical studies in several primate species recognize the three major divisions, but descriptions of the periolivary nuclei reveal some variations (Barnes et al., 1943; Harrison & Irving, 1966; Irving & Harrison, 1967; J. K. Moore & Moore, 1971; J. K. Moore, 2000). The major divisions of the SOC are tonotopically organized and can be distinguished on the bases of their anatomy and physiology; however, their small size has limited their study to some extent, and only anatomical data are available for primates.

One of the primary functions associated with the SOC is the encoding of auditory cues pertaining to sound location. The SOC is the lowest level of central auditory processing at which inputs from both ears are represented on both sides of the brain stem. Tonotopic inputs to the MSO and LSO originate bilaterally in the AVCN and MNTB. The interaural differences associated with the location of a sound source can be resolved by the circuitry of the LSO and MSO. The LSO can detect interaural differences in time and intensity. The majority of LSO neurons sensitive to these differences are inhibited (I) by contralateral stimulation and excited (E) by ipsilateral stimulation (Type IE; Caird & Klinke, 1983; Tsuchitani, 1977). By comparison, most of the neurons in the MSO are excited by ipsilateral and contralateral stimulation (Type EE) and sensitive to interaural differences in time or phase (Guinan, Guinan, & Norris, 1972; Guinan, Norris, & Guinan, 1972; Yin & Chan, 1990) but relatively insensitive to differences in intensity. The interaural differences encoded by the LSO and MSO are the primary auditory cues used by later stages of processing to identify the location of a sound source in three-dimensional space. The principal cells in the LSO project tonotopically to the ICc bilaterally via the lateral lemniscus (Glendenning & Masterton, 1983; Henkel & Brunso-Bechtold, 1993). These projections are inhibitory to the ipsilateral ICc (Saint-Marie & Baker, 1990; Saint-Marie, Ostapoff, Morest, & Wenthold, 1989) and excitatory to the contralateral ICc (Glendenning, Baker, Hutson, & Masterton, 1992). Significant projections also target the dorsal nucleus of the lateral lemniscus (DNLL). The majority of MSO neurons project tonotopically to the ipsilateral ICc and DNLL, whereas minor projections target the contralateral ICc (Brunso-Bechtold, Thompson, & Masterton, 1981; Goldberg & Moore, 1967; Henkel & Spangler, 1983). Subsequent projections to the superior colliculus and motor nuclei in the brain stem mediate various reflexive and nonreflexive movements of the eyes, head, and limbs in response to particular types of auditory stimuli.

A second important function of the SOC is related to its centrifugal projections. There is evidence for the modulation of ascending activity by descending inputs at nearly every level of the central and peripheral auditory system. One of the most well-studied pathways involves direct projections from the periolivary region of the SOC to the cochlea. The *olivocochlear bundle* (OCB) was originally described by Rasmussen (1946, 1953) and has since been the subject of intense study. Activation of the OCB produces a variety of inhibitory effects on the cochlea thought to protect the cochlea from acoustic trauma and possibly improve auditory acuity in the presence of background (masking) noise. Two primary pathways comprise the olivocochlear system (for a review, see Warr, 1992). The lateral olivocochlear system (LOS) is largely uncrossed and involves projections from cells in the vicinity of the LSO to the ipsilateral cochlea. Most of these fibers terminate on the dendrites of Type I auditory neurons innervating the inner hair cells. The medial olivocochlear system (MOS) includes projections from medial periolivary neurons to the contralateral (approximately two thirds) and ipsilateral (approximately one third) cochleas. These fibers terminate primarily at the base of outer hair cells. The LOS and MOS systems of cochlear projections are tonotopic (Guinan, Warr, & Norris, 1983; Guinan, Warr, & Norris, 1984; Robertson, Anderson, & Cole, 1987). The modulation of OHC activity is thought to alter cochlear mechanics in a manner that decreases the sensitivity of inner hair cells (M. C. Brown, Nuttall, & Masta, 1983; Brownell, Bader, Bertrand, & de Ribaupierre, 1985). Activation of the crossed OCB projections by electrical or acoustic stimulation raises response thresholds and reduces the spontaneous activity of Type I afferents (Buno, 1978; Galambos, 1956; Guinan & Gifford, 1988; Liberman, 1989; Wiederhold & Kiang, 1970). In the presence of continuous background noise, OCB activation suppresses responses to the noise but enhances responses to transients by decreasing adaptation in the auditory nerve (Kawase & Liberman, 1993; Kawase, Delgutte, & Liberman,

1993). This antimasking mechanism could actually improve auditory discrimination in noise (Winslow & Sachs, 1987, 1988). OCB-mediated response suppression has also been shown to protect the inner ear from certain types of acoustic trauma (Rajan, 1988a, 1988b, 2000; Rajan & Johnstone, 1988a, 1988b, 1988c, 1989; Reiter & Liberman, 1995; Trahiotis & Elliott, 1970).

Nuclei of the Lateral Lemniscus

The lateral lemniscus is the principal fiber tract between the SOC and IC. In most species at least two primary subnuclei are recognized. The ventral nucleus (VNLL) receives inputs primarily from the contralateral ventral cochlear nuclei (Adams & Warr, 1976; Friauf & Ostwald, 1988; Glendenning, Brunso-Bechtold, Thompson, & Masterton, 1981). Output projections target mainly the ipsilateral ICc (Brunso-Bechtold et al., 1981; Covey & Casseday, 1986; Kudo, 1981). The dorsal nucleus (DNLL) receives bilateral inputs from the AVCN and LSO, an ipsilateral projection from the MSO, and additional inputs from the contralateral DNLL (Adams & Warr, 1976; Glendenning et al., 1981; Henkel & Spangler; 1983: Schneiderman, Oliver, & Henkel, 1988). The major DNLL projections are tonotopically organized and target the ICc bilaterally, with minor outputs to the deep layers of the superior colliculus bilaterally and the ipsilateral medial geniculate complex (Bajo, Merchan, Lopez, & Rouiller, 1993; Brunso-Bechtold et al., 1981; Coleman & Clerici, 1987; Hackett, Neagu, & Kaas, 1999; Hutson, Glendenning, & Masterton, 1991; Kudo, 1981; Merchan, Saldana, & Plaza, 1994; Schneiderman et al., 1988).

The VNLL is one of the few auditory nuclei that does not appear to be tonotopically organized (Aitkin, Anderson, & Brugge, 1970; Glendenning & Hutson, 1998; Whitley & Henkel, 1984). Most neurons in the VNLL are monaural and respond only to contralateral stimulation (Aitkin et al., 1970; Guinan, Norris, et al., 1972). Neurons in the DNLL are tonotopically organized, and most are of the EI type (Aitkin et al., 1970; Markovitz & Pollak, 1993, 1994; Merchan et al., 1994). Brugge, Andersen, and Aitkin (1970) reported that 88% of DNLL neurons sampled were responsive to binaural stimulation. Many units were sensitive to interaural differences in either intensity or phase, reflecting the projections of the LSO and MSO. The DNLL performs a wide range of integrative functions (see Pollak, 1997) and has an important influence on the activity of neurons in the IC (Kelly & Li, 1997; van Adel, Kidd, & Kelly, 1999). Its anatomical and physiological profile is consistent with a role in binaural auditory processing, but the precise functions of the lateral lemnisens remain unclear.

Inferior Colliculus

Multiple ascending and descending auditory pathways converge in the IC (Figures 7.3 and 7.4). Nearly all projections from the cochlear nuclei, SOC, and lateral lemniscus terminate in the IC, as do descending inputs from superior colliculus, thalamus, and cortex (for reviews, see Ehret, 1997; Huffman & Henson, 1990; Spangler & Warr, 1991). Accordingly, the IC is the principal source of ascending input to the medial geniculate complex (MGC) and descending projections to lower levels of the brain stem. As the connection patterns indicate, the IC plans a major role in the integration of monaural and binaural information processed by lower and higher auditory centers, including cortex.

The IC is most commonly divided into three subnuclei: central (ICc), external (ICx), and pericentral (ICp) or dorsal cortex (ICdc). Ipsilateral and contralateral inputs to the ICc originate in the cochlear nuclei, SOC, and lateral lemniscus, as described earlier. Most major projections to the ICc are tonotopically organized. Within the ICc neurons are narrowly tuned and topographically arranged by CF (Aitkin, Webster, Veale, & Crosby, 1975; Fitzpatrick, 1975; Merzenich & Reid, 1974; Rose, Greenwood, Goldberg, & Hind, 1963; Webster, Serviere, Crewther, & Crewther, 1984). Manley and Muller-Preuss (1981) studied single-unit responses to tones, clicks, white noise, and species-specific vocalizations in the squirrel monkey IC. Most of the neurons sampled (>90%) were responsive to all classes of stimuli. One review of the literature

(Irvine, 1986) indicated that about 75% of the units in the ICc are binaural (types EE and EI) and sensitive to interaural differences in level and phase. By comparison, tuning curves in the ICdc and ICx are broad and variable in shape (Aitkin et al., 1975; Merzenich & Reid, 1974) and tend to be more sensitive to complex sounds than pure tones. Some units in the ICx respond to both auditory and somatic stimulation (Aitkin, Dickhaus, Schulz, & Zimmerman, 1978). Experiments in the barn owl (Knudsen & Konishi, 1978a, 1978b) and guinea pig (Binns, Grant, Withington, & King, 1992) have shown that the auditory midbrain contains a representation of auditory space that is computed from the map of stimulus frequency. In the ICx spatial cues are combined across frequency channels and transformed into a topographic code of auditory space where neurons are tuned for location instead of frequency (for reviews, see Cohen & Knudsen, 1999; Knudsen, du Lac, & Esterly, 1987). As shown in Figure 7.5, the output of these neurons targets the superior colliculus, where there is a coregistration of auditory and visual space (e.g., Hyde & Knudsen, 2000; King & Palmer, 1983). Descending inputs to the IC target the dorsomedial and pericentral regions. The ventrolateral ICc is virtually devoid of descending inputs; thus the ascending and descending tracks in the IC are largely segregated (see Huffman & Henson, 1990; Spangler & Warr, 1991). The major ascending projections of the IC target the MGC bilaterally. Other outputs target the superior colliculi, reticular formation, periaqueductal gray, contralateral IC, and lower auditory nuclei.

The integration of inputs is a key feature of signal processing in the IC, reflected in the wide variety of response patterns among its neurons. Patterns vary with the frequency, intensity, temporal, and binaural characteristics of the sound and reflect a broad range of acoustic features. In addition to stimulus frequency some of these features, including latency, response threshold, tuning bandwidth, and best azimuth, appear to be arranged topographically in distinct maps in the ICc (Aitkin, Pettigrew, Calford, Phillips, & Wise, 1985; Schreiner & Langner, 1988; Stiebler, 1986). Thus, different acoustic stimuli would be expected to activate unique spatial domains in each feature map, and the resulting pattern of activation would constitute an abstraction of the original stimulus. At higher levels of processing the integration of coactivation patterns across maps could underlie the formation of feature combination maps (see Kohonen & Hari, 1999; Suga, 1988).

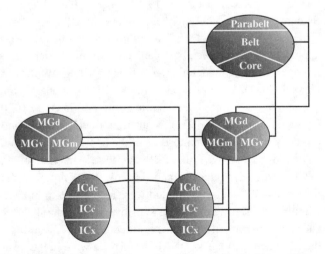

Figure 7.4 Schematic diagram of major ascending auditory pathways between the inferior colliculus and auditory cortex (subcollicular input from one cochlea). Subdivisions of nuclear complexes and some minor pathways are shown. ICc, central nucleus inferior colliculus; ICx, external nucleus inferior colliculus; ICdc, dorsal cortex, inferior colliculus; MGv, ventral division medial geniculate complex; MGm, medial/magnocellular division medial geniculate complex; MGd, dorsal division medial geniculate complex; Core, Belt, Parabelt, major regions of auditory cortex.

Medial Geniculate Complex

The MGC is the final stage of subcortical processing of ascending auditory information. The primary input to the MGC

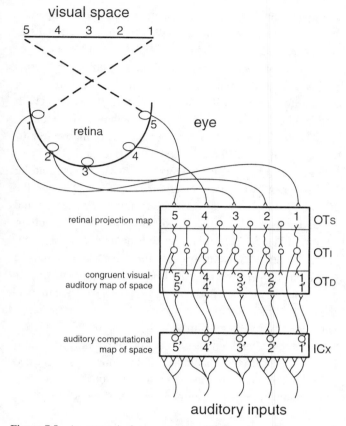

Figure 7.5 An anatomic framework for calibrating the auditory map of spatial location with the visual map. The superficial layers of the optic tectum (OTS) or superior colliculus receive an orderly, topographic pattern of connections from the retina (1–5) of the contralateral eye, and, to species-varying extents, the ipsilateral eye, to form a retinotopic map (1–5) of visual space. Auditory inputs to the external nucleus of the inferior colliculus (ICx) form a map of auditory space (1'–5') that matches the retinal map in the OTS. The deep layers of the optic tectum (OTD) form a multimodal premotor map that mediates head and eye movements. Neurons in the intermediate layers of the optic tectum (OTI) detect mismatches in the auditory and visual maps and bring the maps into congruence via feedback projections to the ICx. Adapted from Kaas and Hackett (2000a) based on the findings of Hyde and Knudsen (2000).

arises bilaterally from the IC (Figure 7.4). Outputs target primary and nonprimary auditory cortical fields. In primates the MGC is commonly divided into three or four divisions: ventral (MGv), dorsal (MGd; anterodorsal, MGad; posterodorsal, MGpd), and magnocellular or medial (MGm; Burton & Jones, 1976; Fitzpatrick & Imig, 1978; Jordan, 1973). These divisions are distinguished on the bases of their unique architecture, patterns of cortical and subcortical connections, and neurophysiological properties. In addition to the MGC, the connection patterns of the suprageniculate nucleus (Sg), posterior nucleus (PO), and medial pulvinar (PM) indicate that these nuclei, among others, also play a role in thalamic auditory processing, although their significance is more uncertain. The functional organization of the MGC incorporates

multiple parallel pathways in which distinct aspects of auditory processing appear to be mediated (Andersen, Knight, & Merzenich, 1980; Calford & Aitkin, 1983; Morest, 1965).

The principal target of the primary ascending pathway through the ICc is the MGv. Neurons in the MGv are arranged in distinct laminae corresponding to the tonotopic organization of the MGv and ICc (Calford & Aitkin, 1983; Morest, 1965). The input from the ipsilateral ICc is much stronger than the contralateral projection (monkeys: Hackett, Neagu, et al., 1999; cats: Andersen, Roth, Aitkin, & Merzenich, 1980; Rouiller & de Ribaupierre, 1985). In primates the thalamocortical projections of the MGv target areas in the primary auditory region, known as the core, while the surrounding narrow belt of cortex adjacent to the core has few connections with the MGv (see Hackett, Stepniewska, & Kaas, 1998b, for review). The MGad and MGpd receive inputs from the ICdc (Andersen, Roth, et al., 1980; Calford & Aitkin, 1983; Kudo & Niimi, 1980) and project primarily to the belt and parabelt regions surrounding the core (Molinari et al., 1995; Morel, Garraghty, & Kaas, 1993). The MGm receives projections from the ICc and ICx (Calford & Aitkin, 1983; Kudo & Niimi, 1980). In contrast to the ventral and dorsal divisions of the MGC, the MGm projects diffusely to the core, belt, and parabelt fields of the primate auditory cortex (see Hackett, Stepniewska, et al., 1998b). The heterogeneous cell populations of the MGm project to the supragranular layers of cortex (Oliver, 1984), and there is some evidence that different classes of neurons project to different cortical layers (Hashikawa, Molinari, Rausell, & Jones, 1995; Molinari et al., 1995).

Neurons in the MGv are tonotopically arranged in distinct laminae (Gross, Lifschitz, & Anderson, 1974). Tuning curve configurations vary widely among MGv cells (Morel, Rouiller, de Ribaupierre, & de Ribaupierre, 1987) and with anesthetic conditions (Allon, Yeshurun, & Wollberg, 1981; see also Rouiller, 1997), thus a range of response types has been observed. Symmes, Alexander, and Newman (1980) found that units in the squirrel monkey MGv were responsive to tones, clicks, white noise, and species-specific vocalizations. Neurons were most responsive to vocalizations that contained significant spectral energy at the CF of the unit, but neurons were generally not selective for particular vocal stimuli. The majority of cells are binaural (EE or EI) and are sensitive to interaural differences in intensity or time (Heierli, de Ribaupierre, & de Ribaupierre, 1987; Imig & Adrian, 1977; Ivarsson, de Ribaupierre, & de Ribaupierre, 1988), but there is no evidence for a map of auditory space in the MGC. As in the ICc, response features such as stimulus frequency, tuning bandwidth, latency, and binaural class are distributed as gradients within isofrequency laminae in the MGv (Rodrigues-Dagaeff et al., 1989). Thus, the MGv appears capable of simultaneous processing of complex signals. In the MGm neuron response properties vary widely, and patterns of organization are difficult to identify. There is some evidence of tonotopic organization rostrally (Rouiller et al., 1989), but tuning curves are often broad or multi-peaked, and response latencies are highly variable (Aitkin, 1973; Gross et al., 1974; Symmes et al., 1980). Some units in the MGm respond also to vestibular and somatic stimulation (Blum, Abraham, & Gilman, 1979; Curry, 1972; Love & Scott, 1969; Wepsic, 1966), reflecting connections with multisensory nuclei such as the ICx; however, it is unclear how these inputs influence the processing of auditory information. The dorsal nuclei of the MG have not been found to be tonotopically organized. Most units are broadly tuned and do not respond well to simple acoustic stimuli like pure tones (Calford & Aitkin, 1983; Toros-Morel, de Ribaupierre, & Rouiller, 1981), and many units respond selectively to complex sounds (e.g., Buchwald, Dickerson, Harrison, & Hinman, 1988).

Serial and Parallel Processing in Subcortical Pathways

Although it may be tempting to ascribe a specific function to individual nuclei, it is important to emphasize that in the SOC, like most other auditory structures, each nuclear subdivision contains a variety of cell types that contribute to major and minor pathways. Most participate in diverse circuits involving feed-forward and feedback connections linking multiple levels of processing. Thus, the full scope of auditory processing mediated by any given nucleus is indefinite because comprehensive descriptions are lacking.

The picture of auditory processing that emerges is that each major stage of hierarchical processing in the brain stem and thalamus initiates and integrates multiple segregated parallel pathways involving functionally distinct populations of neurons. These pathways are responsible for the distribution of specialized acoustic information to higher centers, including cortex, and to lower stages, including the cochlea. Thus, the modulation and integration of auditory input occurs in multiple pathways at all levels, indicating that the system is not strictly hierarchical. Although the unique anatomical and physiological features of these pathways support their segregation into functionally distinct subsystems, interpretations vary. Poljak (1926) proposed that the pathways originating in the ventral and dorsal cochlear nuclei may mediate processing related to auditory localization and discrimination, respectively. Subsequent anatomical and physiological studies were used to support the notion that separate pathways were specialized for the extraction of features important for sound localization and pattern recognition (see Evans, 1974).

Parallel channels were also included in subsequent proposals, but less emphasis was placed on their putative functional significance. Andersen, Knight, et al. (1980) identified two segregated pathways in their study of the thalamic connections with auditory cortex in cats: a *cochleotopic system* involving AI (auditory area 1), MGv, and ICc; and a *diffuse system* with uncertain cochleotopic organization involving AII (auditory area 2), medial geniculate divisions outside of the ventral division, and ICp. Calford and Aitkin (1983) identified four tectothalamic pathways through the MGv, MGd, MGm, and Sg in cats. Their proposal included a *core* pathway through the ICc and MGv and a *diffuse* pathway involving the ICp and subdivisions of the MGC surrounding the MGv. Rouiller, Simm, Villa, de Ribaupierre, and de Ribaupierre (1991) organized the auditory pathways into three parallel channels: a *tonotopic system* involving the MGv, a *nontonotopic/diffuse system* involving the MGd, and a *polysensory system* involving the MGm. The various proposals share obvious anatomical and physiological similarities, but it remains unclear whether spatial and nonspatial auditory functions, for example, are mediated by separate parallel channels, as suggested by Poljak. Some clues may lie in the functional organization of the auditory cortex, described in the next section.

Cortical Auditory Processing

The organization of the auditory cortex in humans and nonhuman primates has received sporadic attention for more than 100 years (for reviews, see Aitkin, 1990; Hackett, 2002; Kaas & Hackett, 1998; Newman, 1988; Woolsey & Walzl, 1982). Early anatomical and lesion studies were useful in identifying the location of the auditory cortex in the brain, and subsequent studies have refined and expanded certain details of its organization. Studies of auditory cortex in other mammals, however, have outpaced work in primates both in number and in scope. Consequently, more is known about the organization of auditory cortex in cats and bats, for example, than in any primate species. Fortunately, interest in primate auditory cortex is rising, and considerable progress has been made in recent years. In the following sections we present what is currently known about the functional organization of the primate auditory cortex and relate these details to more general issues of auditory processing in the brain.

Anatomical Organization

In humans and nonhuman primates the auditory cortex occupies a large portion of the superior temporal region in which a network of interconnected fields processes information in parallel three or more serial stages. Corticocortical connections of these areas include auditory-related fields in frontal, parietal, and temporal cortex, whereas corticofugal projections target numerous subcortical nuclei. Based on anatomical and physiological data from several primate species, including our own recent studies, we have developed a working model of auditory cortical processing in primates to provide a platform for more detailed investigation (Hackett, Stepniewska, & Kaas, 1998a; Hackett, Preuss, & Kaas, 2001; Kaas & Hackett, 1998; Kaas, Hackett, & Tramo, 1999). In the schematic diagram of this model (Figure 7.6) auditory cortex contains three hierarchically arranged regions: core, belt, and parabelt. The *core region* is comprised of two or three primary-like areas (AI, R, [RT]), each of which has independent parallel inputs from the MGv. The core is surrounded by a *belt region* of possibly seven or eight areas (CM, CL, ML, AL, RTL, RTM, RM) at a second level of processing with major inputs from the core, MGd, MGm, Sg, and uncertain inputs from the MGv. The lateral portion of the belt region is bordered by a *parabelt region* of at least two divisions (RP, CP) located on the exposed superior temporal gyrus. The parabelt receives direct projections from the belt, MGd, MGm, Sg, and PM, but not the core or MGv; thus, it represents a third stage of auditory cortical processing. The

patterns of thalamocortical and corticocortical connections suggest that areas within a region may process information in parallel before output to a later stage. This parallel arrangement is not known to constrain activity to the simultaneous processing of identical information; rather, significant differences are likely given the topographically distinct patterns of cortical connections noted among areas at all levels.

Adjacent areas within and between regions tend to share the densest connections (Figure 7.6). AI, for example, appears to have denser connections with R, CM, CL, and ML than with nonadjacent areas RT, RM, AL, RTM, and RTL. Similarly, the caudal belt areas (CM, CL, ML) have stronger connections with areas in the caudal belt and parabelt (CPB) than with fields in the rostral belt and parabelt (RPB; Hackett et al., 1998a). The topographical differences between the rostral and caudal auditory fields is maintained in their projections to other cortical regions, including the prefrontal cortex (Hackett, Stepniewska, & Kaas, 1999; Romanski, Bates, & Goldman-Rakic, 1999; Romanski, Tian, et al., 1999) and ventral intraparietal cortex (Lewis & Van Essen, 2000). The orderly topography of auditory cortical connections among functionally distinct cortical regions has been used to support the hypothesis that there are two streams of processing in primate auditory cortex: one devoted

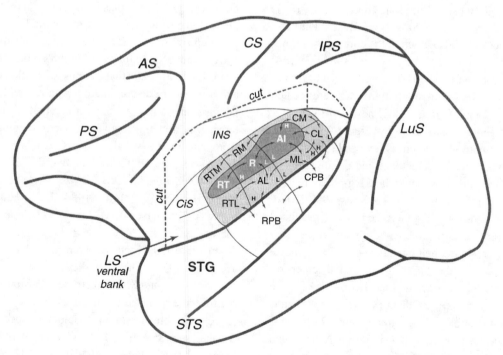

Figure 7.6 Schematic view of the macaque left hemisphere showing the location and intrinsic connections of auditory cortex. The dorsal bank of the lateral sulcus has been removed (*cut*) to expose the superior temporal plane (*LS ventral bank*). The floor and outer bank of the circular sulcus (*CiS*) have been flattened to show the medial auditory fields. The core region (dark shading) contains three subdivisions (AI, R, RT). In the belt region (light shading) seven subdivisions are proposed (CM, CL, ML, AL, RTL, RTM, RM). The parabelt region (no shading) occupies the exposed surface of the superior temporal gyrus (STG). The core fields project to surrounding belt areas (arrows). Inputs to the parabelt arise from the lateral and medial belt subdivisions. Connections between the parabelt and medial belt fields are not illustrated to improve clarity. Tonotopic gradients in the core and lateral belt fields are indicated by the letters H (*high frequency*) and L (*low frequency*). Adapted from Hackett et al. (2001).

to spatial processing, the other involved with nonspatial auditory processing (Colombo, Rodman, & Gross, 1996; Hackett, Stepniewska, et al., 1999; Kaas & Hackett, 1998, 2000b; Rauschecker, 1998; Rauschecker, Tian, Pons, & Mishkin, 1997; Romanski, Bates, et al., 1999; Romanski, Tian, et al., 1999). This idea is analogous to the ventral "what" and dorsal "where" pathways of the visual system (Mishkin, Ungerleider, & Macko, 1983; Ungerleider & Mishkin, 1982). In the visual system these functionally distinct pathways originate in visual area 1 (VI) and form dual streams through ventral and dorsal visual cortical areas subserving visual object (what) and visual spatial (where) processing, respectively. The evidence for the segregation of auditory function into dual processing streams is discussed later.

Functional Organization

Microelectrode mapping studies of auditory cortex have focused primarily on the tonotopic organization of the core and belt regions (Aitkin, Merzenich, Irvine, Clarey, & Nelson, 1986; Brugge, 1982; Imig, Ruggero, Kitzes, Javel, & Brugge, 1977; Kosaki, Hashikawa, He, & Jones, 1997; Luethke et al., 1989; Merzenich & Brugge, 1973; Morel & Kaas, 1992; Morel et al., 1993; Pfingst & O'Connor, 1981; Rauschecker, Tian, & Hauser, 1995; Rauschecker et al., 1997; Recanzone, Guard, & Phan, 2000; Tian, Reser, Durham, Kustov, & Rauschecker, 2001). Each of the core areas is tonotopically organized, and the tuning curves of single neurons tend to be narrow, especially when compared with units in adjacent belt fields. In AI, neurons with higher CFs are located caudomedially in curved isofrequency lines, and lower frequencies are represented rostrolaterally (Figure 7.6). At the border with R the tonotopic gradient is reversed such that AI and R share a low CF border. The tonotopic organization of RT is not clear, but another reversal in the CF gradient may be present at the border of R and RT (Morel & Kaas, 1992). Mapping in the belt areas surrounding the core has also produced evidence of tonotopic organization. Although less responsive to pure tones, neurons in the belt can also be driven by noise bands (e.g., 1/3 octave, 1/2 octave) with a defined center frequency. Experiments using tones and narrow bands of noise have shown that the tonotopic gradient in a given belt area is parallel to that of the adjacent core area (Figure 7.6). Thus, tonotopic organization represents an underlying functional property that is maintained in the auditory cortex through the second major stage of processing in the belt.

Other aspects of functional organization have also been explored in the core and belt regions using stimuli other than pure tones and noise bands. Many of these findings have been interpreted as relevant to the processing of either spatial or nonspatial auditory information, as neurons in some areas are more responsive to certain classes of acoustic stimuli than to others. Accordingly, these findings relate in various ways to the dual-streams hypothesis pertaining to functional segregation in auditory cortex.

Nonspatial Processing

Primates produce a repertoire of species-specific calls that, for at least some species, may refer to objects or events in the environment and may thus convey "what" information about food, predators, social relationships, the caller's identity, and the caller's emotional state (Ghazanfar & Hauser, 1999). Calls produced by other animals and a wide range of environmental sounds are also likely to provide useful "what" information. For these sounds to be meaningful, they must ultimately be associated with a specific entity or event. However, because the acoustic structure of a given auditory object (e.g., a "grunt" call) varies significantly within and between sources, the auditory system must be able to extract and make use of the invariant acoustic cues that convey meaning (see Beecher, Petersen, Zoloth, Moody, & Stebbins, 1979; Green, 1975; May, Moody, & Stebbins, 1989; Wang, 2000; Zoloth et al., 1979). The dynamic nature of the natural acoustic environment suggests that both hardwired and plastic mechanisms contribute to this process in development and throughout life.

Attempts to understand these mechanisms have produced a wide range of findings. Ablation studies of primate auditory cortex indicate that lesions of auditory cortex disrupt auditory pattern discrimination. Animals with unilateral or bilateral ablation of core, belt, or parabelt regions exhibit problems discriminating between sounds ranging in complexity from pure tones to vocalizations (Colombo et al., 1996; Cowey & Dewson, 1972; Cowey & Weiskrantz, 1976; Dewson, Pribram, & Lynch, 1969; Dewson, Cowey, & Weiskrantz, 1970; Heffner & Heffner, 1984, 1986; Hupfer, Jurgens, & Ploog, 1977; Iversen & Mishkin, 1973; Jerison & Neff, 1953; Massopust, Wolin, Meder, & Frost, 1967; Massopust, Wolin, & Frost, 1970; Pratt & Iversen, 1978; Symmes, 1966; Wegener, 1976), although they are still able to detect an auditory stimulus. Microelectrode recordings within the core region have revealed neurons responsive to a similar broad range of acoustic stimuli, including species-specific calls (Funkenstein & Winter, 1973; Glass & Wollberg, 1983; Lu & Wang, 2000; Manley & Muller-Preuss, 1978; Newman, 1978a, 1978b; Newman & Symmes, 1979; Newman & Wollberg, 1973a, 1973b; Pelleg-Toiba & Wollberg, 1991; Wang, Merzenich, Beitel, & Schreiner, 1995; Winter & Funkenstein, 1973; Wollberg & Newman, 1972). Because many neurons in the core were found to be responsive to vocalizations, it was initially proposed that these neurons may also be selective for a particular vocalization (i.e., "call detectors"), but this hypothesis was not supported by subsequent studies. Based on the wide range of response types encountered in AI, for example, Newman (1978b, 1979) classified neurons into seven categories: (a) *tuned filters,* responsive to stimuli restricted to a particular bandwidth; (b) *specialists,* responsive only to a single vocalization; (c) *class detectors,* responsive to all tonal or atonal calls, but not both; (d) *complex-feature detectors,* responsive to tonal, atonal, and mixed vocalizations; (e) *generalists,* responsive to all vocalizations and possibly responsive to tones or noise; (f) *amplitude modulation (AM) detectors,* responsive to most stimuli and with a response pattern that matches the temporal pattern of the stimulus; and (g) *variant detectors,* discriminately responsive to variants within a class of vocalizations. The specialists and class detectors represented 33% and 20% of the sampled population, respectively. In later studies (Glass & Wollberg, 1983; Pelleg-Toiba & Wollberg, 1991; Wang et al., 1995), however, most AI neurons were found to be equally responsive to vocalizations presented normally and in reverse temporal order. These results suggest that only subpopulations of neurons at the first stage of cortical processing in the core function as call detectors in the representation of complex vocalizations. Their contribution is augmented by the activity of synchronized cell assemblies that are spatially distributed along and across the tonotopic axis, as described in marmoset monkeys by Wang et al. (1995). Their findings suggest that the spectral and temporal discharge pattern of a large population of AI neurons forms an abstract representation of the acoustic pattern of the vocalization. Although abrupt changes in complex waveforms can be followed for some stimuli (Bieser & Muller-Preuss, 1996; Steinschneider, Arezzo, & Vaughan, 1980; Steinschneider, Reser, Fishman, Schroder, & Arezzo, 1998; Steinschneider, Reser, Schroeder, & Arezzo, 1995; Steinschneider, Schroeder, Arezzo, & Vaughan, 1995), precise replication of the spectrotemporal acoustic pattern is not preserved because few cortical neurons are able to follow rapid temporal changes faster than 20 ms to 30 ms (Lu & Wang, 2000). The collective findings indicate that a smaller population of neurons in AI is more selective to specific calls or callers and that a larger nonselective population is responsive to a wide range of sounds (Wang, 2000). The selective population could signal the detection of a specific call or caller, whereas the nonselective population processes and distributes detailed information about the sound (Suga, 1994).

Outside of the core, neuron response profiles are notably different, and greater selectivity has been observed. Symmes, Newman, and Alexander (1976) reported that neurons in cortex lateral to AI of squirrel monkeys were generally less responsive to acoustic stimulation, but the incidence of call-selective units was two to three times higher than in AI. This may be related to spectrotemporal integration by neurons in the belt areas, where tuning has been found to be broader (Kosaki et al., 1997; Merzenich & Brugge, 1973; Morel et al., 1993; Rauschecker et al., 1995, 1997; Recanzone, Guard, & Phan, 2000). Recording from fields in the lateral belt region of macaques, Rauschecker et al. (1995) reported that neurons were generally much more responsive to narrow bands of noise with a defined center frequency than to pure tones. Moreover, neurons were found to be cochleotopically arranged by best center frequency (BFc). On the basis of reversals in BFc, Rauschecker et al. identified three lateral belt areas (AL, ML, CL) adjacent to areas R, AI, and CM, respectively. The tonotopic gradient in each lateral belt field matched that of the adjacent core field (see Figure 7.6). The anterior (AL) and caudal (CL) fields of the lateral belt could also be distinguished by preference for frequency modulated (FM) sweep rates (Tian & Rauschecker, 1995). Neurons in AL responded better to lower sweep rates (approximately 10 kHz/s), whereas units in CL preferred higher rates (approximately 100 kHz/s). Most lateral belt neurons also responded better to species-specific vocalizations than to energy-matched tones or noise bands and preferred certain calls to others. Call preferences could often be predicted from the spectral composition of the call given the frequency response area (receptive field) of the neuron. In addition, temporal integration was found to characterize the responses of some neurons. For example, response strength was greater when both syllables of a two-syllable vocalization were presented in their correct temporal sequence than when either syllable was presented alone. Although response specificity for calls might be expected to increase as a result of spectral and temporal integration, most neurons in the lateral belt responded to several calls, and few responded exclusively to a single call or to all calls. Support for the dual streams hypothesis can be found in a recent study of the lateral belt fields (Tian et al., 2001). Neurons in AL were found to be more selective for a particular call than were neurons in CL, which are more selective for the spatial location (azimuth) of the call. However, neurons rarely responded to a single call. Further integration and greater specificity may be found at later stages of processing (e.g., parabelt, superior temporal sulcus, insula) or among networks of neurons in one or more areas.

In the multimodal insular cortex of squirrel monkeys, neurons respond to simple and complex auditory stimuli, including species-specific vocalizations (Bieser, 1998; Bieser & Muller-Preuss, 1996; Pribram, Rosner, & Rosenblith, 1954; Sudakov, MacLean, Reeves, & Marino, 1971). There is some evidence for cochleotopic organization in the granular insula (Bieser & Muller-Preuss, 1996;). Neurons in AI and the insula exhibited phase-locked encoding of periodic FM stimuli (e.g., tones and twitter calls) at repetition rates up to about 16 Hz (Bieser, 1998). Using AM stimuli, the temporal resolution of AI neurons had a mean best modulation frequency of 17.8 Hz, compared to a mean of 9.9 Hz for insular neurons (Bieser & Muller-Preuss, 1996). These results suggest that complex sound integration in squirrel monkeys occurs in a time window of about 50 ms and that the temporal resolution of insular neurons is sufficient to encode the transient features of a complex call. Interestingly, in AI, R, and the insula, the phase-locked response to the natural call, which is comprised of both AM and FM elements, was better than the response to an FM stimulus alone. These results are comparable to human psychophysical data showing that mixed AM-FM modulated stimuli were easier to detect than were AM or FM stimuli alone, suggesting related mechanisms of detection (B. C. J. Moore & Sek, 1992; Sek & Moore, 1994). Overall, then, these findings indicate that insular neurons are involved in the processing of complex auditory stimuli. Further, as found for most mammals, these auditory cortical neurons appear best suited to process slow temporal modulations of simple and complex acoustic stimuli (see Langner, 1992).

Spatial Processing

Like most mammals, primates are able to localize sounds in space with high precision (C. H. Brown, Beecher, Moody, & Stebbins, 1978; C. H. Brown, Beecher, Moody, & Stebbins, 1980; C. H. Brown, Schessler, Moody, & Stebbins, 1982). In addition to the contribution of subcortical mechanisms of spatial encoding, numerous studies suggest that the auditory cortex plays a role in sound localization. Lesion studies have shown that bilateral (Heffner & Heffner, 1990; Heffner & Masterton, 1975; Ravizza & Diamond, 1974) and unilateral (Thompson & Cortez, 1983) ablation of the auditory cortex caused deficits in sound localization. Unilateral lesions cause greater deficits for sounds presented in the hemisphere contralateral to the lesion, whereas bilateral lesions have more global effects. The deficits observed across studies are somewhat task dependent, and lesions involved multiple fields; thus, the functional implications are uncertain, but it seems clear that lesions of auditory cortex tend to reduce spatial acuity and performance in tasks requiring accurate sound localization. Spatial discrimination of sounds near the midline may be less affected by a bilateral cortical lesion than sounds in the same hemifield further from midline (Heffner & Heffner, 1990).

In experiments using microelectrode recordings, Brugge and Merzenich (1973) found that cells in the core and belt regions of macaque monkeys were sensitive to interaural differences in time and intensity, and many units were most sensitive to a particular stimulus intensity or interaural delay. Recording from the caudal superior temporal gyrus in the area known as the temporoparietal area (Tpt), Leinonen, Hyvarinen, and Sovijarvi (1980) found neurons responsive to auditory, somatosensory, and visual stimuli. Unimodal and bimodal units were encountered for each modality. Most of the auditory responsive neurons in this area were selective for a particular azimuth of the sound source, typically in the contralateral hemifield. In a survey of 196 single units, Benson, Hienz, and Goldstein (1981) found that a majority of units sampled in cortex outside of the core were spatially tuned, but there was no correlation between tuning properties and the cortical field in which the neuron was isolated. More recently, however, the connections of auditory fields in the caudal belt and parabelt regions were correlated with prefrontal (see Hackett, Stepniewska, et al., 1999; Romanski, Bates, et al., 1999; Romanski, Tian, et al., 1999) and parietal (Lewis & Van Essen, 2000) areas involved in auditory and multimodal spatial processing. Such findings have generated renewed interest in the possibility that certain areas of primate auditory cortex are specialized for the processing of spatial information (for reviews, see Rauschecker & Tian, 2000; Recanzone, 2000; Tian et al., 2001). One of these areas is the caudomedial area, CM, adjacent to the caudal and medial borders of AI. Single- and multiple-unit recordings in CM have consistently reported that neurons in CM are generally broadly tuned and respond more variably to pure tones than to complex acoustic stimuli (Imig et al., 1977; Morel & Kaas, 1992; Kosaki et al., 1997; Merzenich & Brugge, 1973; Morel, Garraghty, & Kaas, 1993; Rauschecker et al., 1997; Recanzone, Guard, & Phan, 2000). In addition, Rauschecker et al., 1997 demonstrated that CM is dependent on inputs from AI for responsiveness to tonal stimuli. In these experiments ablation of AI abolished tonal responses in CM, but not the adjacent core field. Rauschecker (1998) reported finding neurons tuned to specific spatial locations in CM, suggesting that CM may represent the beginning of the spatial pathway in auditory cortex. Support for this hypothesis can be found in a recent study correlating single-unit activity of neurons in AI and CM with sound localization in awake behaving macaque monkeys (Recanzone, Guard, Phan, & Su, 2000). The responses of about 80% of the neurons sampled in AI and CM were correlated with a particular azimuth or elevation (spatially sensitive), usually in the contralateral hemifield. On the psychophysical detection task performance was best for broadband stimuli, and compared with neurons in AI, a slightly greater percentage of neurons in CM were sensitive to the spatial location of both tone and noise stimuli. Further, neurons in AI and CM could predict behavioral thresholds for spatial location, but neurons in CM were generally better predictors of performance. The CM area is also unique among auditory belt fields for its bimodal response properties. Several studies have shown that neurons in CM are responsive to auditory and somatosensory stimulation (Fu et al., 2001; Robinson & Burton, 1980a, 1980b; Schroeder et al., 2001). The significance of bimodal convergence in CM with respect to its role in spatial localization is currently unclear as there is not yet evidence for a correspondence in spatial tuning among the auditory and somatosensory responsive neurons. One possibility is that such convergence would be useful in networks computing head and body position from somatosensory, auditory, visual, and vestibular inputs because neurons in this region have been shown to be responsive to vestibular stimulation (for review, see Gulden & Grusser, 1998). Another caudal auditory field has been shown to demonstrate spatial selectivity. Tian et al. (2001) found a clear dissociation of auditory spatial tuning between neurons in the anterolateral (AL) and caudolateral (CL) auditory belt fields. Neurons in CL were much more selective for spatial location of species-specific vocalizations than were neurons in AL, which responded equally to calls at any azimuth but were more selective for the type of call than were neurons in CL.

Auditory Processing in Prefrontal Cortex

Anatomical and functional connections between nonprimary auditory cortex and the frontal lobe are well established in primates, dating back to some early studies of macaque monkeys (Hurst, 1959; Mettler, 1935; Sugar, French, & Chusid, 1948; Ward, Peden, & Sugar, 1946). Pandya and Kuypers (1969) and Pandya, Hallett, and Mukherjee (1969) subsequently showed that the rostral and caudal auditory regions projected to different domains of frontal cortex. The distinctive patterns of prefrontal projections from rostral and caudal auditory regions have since been elucidated in greater detail (see Hackett, Stepniewska, et al., 1999; Romanski, Bates, et al., 1999; Romanski, Tian, et al., 1999). Rostral belt and parabelt fields are most densely connected with orbitofrontal cortex and Areas 10, 12, 45, and rostral 46 within the inferior convexity and frontopolar cortex (Figure 7.7). By comparison, caudal belt and parabelt fields are primarily connected with the dorsolateral periprincipal region (e.g., caudal 46) and prearcuate cortex (e.g., Area 8). The rostrocaudal topography of auditory corticofrontal connections has been used to support the dual-streams hypothesis (Hackett, Stepniewska, et al., 1999a; Kaas & Hackett, 1998, 2000b; Rauschecker, 1998; Rauschecker et al., 1997; Romanski, Bates, et al., 1999; Romanski, Tian, et al., 1999). Rostral auditory fields

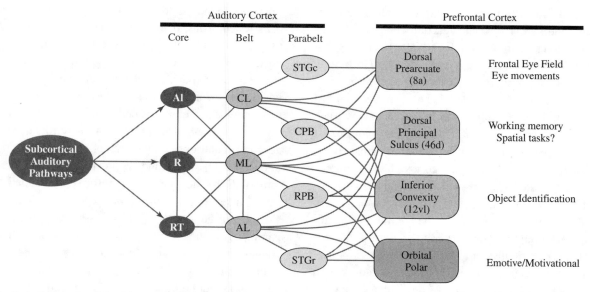

Figure 7.7 Projections to the prefrontal cortex from auditory cortex and auditory-related fields of the superior temporal gyrus. The three subdivisions of the auditory core (RT, R, AI) receive parallel subcortical auditory inputs. Inputs to the lateral belt fields (AL, ML, CL) arise from adjacent areas of the core. Topographically organized outputs of the lateral belt target the auditory parabelt region (RPB, CPB) and auditory-related fields on the superior temporal gyrus (STGr, STGc). Subdivisions of lateral belt and parabelt/STG fields (colored lines) project topographically to distinct regions of prefrontal cortex. Connectional patterns indicate a propensity for rostral auditory fields to target nonspatial domains and caudal auditory fields to favor spatial domains, with mixed projections from some fields. Proposed functional roles for divisions of frontal cortex are indicated. Abbreviations: RT, rostrotemporal core; R, rostral core; AI, auditory core area I; AL, anterolateral belt; ML, middle lateral belt; CL, caudolateral belt; STGr, rostral superior temporal gyrus; RPB, rostral parabelt; CPB, caudal parabelt; STGc, caudal superior temporal gyrus. Adapted from Kaas and Hackett (1999).

target inferior, polar, and orbital prefrontal domains involved in auditory memory, discrimination, and language processing, whereas the caudal auditory fields target dorsolateral and periarcuate prefrontal areas involved in multimodal spatial tasks. The segregation of pathways is not complete, however, as there are connections between rostral and caudal auditory domains and notable overlapping projections from auditory cortex to the dorsal superior temporal sulcus and prefrontal Area 46 (principal sulcus region). Thus, there are numerous opportunities for interaction between streams and for other streams, as well (see Kaas & Hackett, 1999). Nevertheless, there is compelling support for the segregation of spatial and nonspatial processing in some form as revealed by anatomical and physiological studies of the frontal lobe.

Microelectrode recordings have uncovered unimodal and multimodal neurons responsive to auditory, visual, and somatic stimulation throughout the frontal lobe of monkeys (e.g., Tanila, Carlson, Linnankoski, & Kahila, 1993). Some but not all of these studies used methods and produced data relevant to the dual-streams hypothesis. Newman and Lindsley (1976) recorded from the periarcuate and periprincipalis regions in squirrel monkeys. They obtained responses in both regions to pure tones, clicks, and species-specific vocalizations, although a greater proportion of cells around the principal sulcus responded to vocalizations. Units responsive to clicks and tones were more evenly distributed between the two regions. Ito (1982) studied unit activity in the prearcuate and caudal principalis regions of macaque monkeys during auditory and visual reaction time tasks. Unimodal and bimodal neurons were found in both regions, but unimodal units tended to exhibit a phasic onset response, whereas a tonic response profile characterized most bimodal units. It was suggested that unimodal phasic units modulated activity of multimodal tonic units to initiate behaviors such as gaze control. Azuma and Suzuki (1984) and Suzuki (1985) recorded from neurons in the caudal principal sulcus and prearcuate regions of prefrontal cortex. The frontal eye field (FEF), associated with visual saccade initiation, is located within the prearcuate cortex. Most of the units they encountered responded maximally in the contralateral hemifield within an azimuthal range of less than 45 deg. Vaadia, Benson, Heinz, and Goldstein (1986) studied the responses of neurons in the periarcuate region of rhesus monkeys in passive and active localization tasks using auditory and visual stimulation. They found that it was more common for units to respond to both auditory and visual modalities in the active tasks. Further, during active localization many units were tuned to one or more spatial locations (i.e., 0, 30, 60, or 90 deg contralateral), whereas the same units exhibited little spatial tuning in the passive detection task. These findings suggest that location-encoding mechanisms in this region are not necessarily based on location-specific units, but on the coordinated activity of multiple neurons that have broad spatial tuning. In a subsequent report expanding on the former, Vaadia (1989) described a large population of bimodal periarcuate units with similar visual and auditory spatial tuning that were not responsive to passive auditory or visual stimulation but exhibited enhanced responses during an active localization task. Russo and Bruce (1994) found that neurons in the FEF that exhibited movement activity prior to saccades to a visual target were also active prior to saccades made to auditory targets, suggesting that targeting signals from both modalities converge at or before this level of processing (see also Hyde & Knudsen, 2000; Kaas & Hackett, 2000b; Schall, 1991; Schall, Morel, King, & Bullier, 1995).

Such results provide strong support for auditory and visual spatial processing in these prefrontal regions; however, unimodal and bimodal units active in passive and nonspatial tasks have been found within fields of the periprincipalis, prearcuate, postarcuate, and inferior convexity regions (Watanabe, 1992; Wollberg & Sela, 1980). Under passive listening conditions in awake squirrel monkeys, Wollberg and Sela (1980) found units responsive to clicks, species-specific vocalizations, and visual stimuli in pre- and postarcuate cortex. Vocalizations and light flashes were the most effective stimuli in generating a response. About 50% of the cells responded to only one or two vocalizations, and the researchers found just one cell responsive to all seven of the calls tested. Thus, there was some selectivity for particular calls. In a study of units in the periprincipal, prearcuate, postarcuate, and inferior prefrontal cortex, Watanabe (1992) studied the encoding of the associative significance (i.e., whether the stimulus was associated with a reward) of auditory and visual stimuli. Bimodal units were found in all four regions, but the highest proportions were found in postarcuate cortex anterior to primary motor cortex. The second highest proportion was found in prearcuate cortex. About one third of the bimodal units were sensitive to associative significance independent of the stimulus properties and were considered to be involved in cross-modal coding of this parameter. Although the paradigms used in both of these studies were not designed to test the spatial properties of auditory stimuli, the influence of spatial cues on neuronal responses cannot be ruled out because directional information was inherent in the acoustic stimuli. Indeed, the location of a species-specific vocalization is a behaviorally important component of the auditory percept that cannot be reliably ignored or discounted under those experimental conditions.

Other studies of rostral, inferior, and orbital prefrontal regions utilizing auditory stimuli are few in number, so little is known about auditory function in areas with connections favoring the rostral auditory fields of the temporal lobe. Benevento, Fallon, Davis, and Rezak (1977) reported that many units in the orbitofrontal cortex respond to auditory or visual stimuli. Over half of these were bimodal and often showed auditory-visual interactions. For example, presentation of an auditory stimulus resulted in inhibition of excitation produced by concurrent visual stimulation and vice versa. Subsequently, Thorpe, Rolls, and Maddison (1983) showed that the selectivity of bimodal neurons in the orbitofrontal cortex could be matched. A unit that responded selectively to the sight of a banana also could exhibit the same selectivity for the taste of the banana (i.e., cross-modal matching). All of these functional data, coupled with the distinctive connectional patterns described earlier, suggest that the inferior and orbital prefrontal cortex may play a role in the processing of nonspatial information involving several sensory modalities, including audition. However, a role in the processing of spatial-related information cannot be ruled out at this time.

Auditory Processing in Parietal Cortex

The posterior parietal cortex contains several functionally distinct areas that contribute to a multimodal representation of space used by motor structures to guide movements. One of these areas, the lateral intraparietal area (LIP), has connections with extrastriate visual cortex and projections to prefrontal and motor areas involved in movements of the eyes, including the frontal eye field (for review, see Andersen, Snyder, Bradley, & Xing, 1997). Connections between the caudal superior temporal gyrus and the LIP region have been known for many years (Divac, Lavail, Rakic, & Winston, 1977; Hyvarinen, 1982; Lewis & Van Essen, 2000; Pandya & Kuypers, 1969). Physiological investigations of LIP were not able to locate auditory responsive neurons (Hyvarinen, 1982; Koch & Fuster, 1989; Mountcastle et al., 1975). In more recent studies, however, auditory responsive neurons have been identified in macaque monkeys performing auditory and auditory-visual spatial tasks (Grunewald, Linden, & Andersen, 1999; Linden, Grunewald, & Andersen, 1999; Mazzoni, Bracewell, Barash, & Andersen, 1996; Stricanne, Andersen, & Mazzoni, 1996). Grunewald et al. (1999) demonstrated that auditory responses appear in LIP only after training on spatial tasks requiring saccades to a remembered location after a variable delay. In a companion study, Linden et al. (1999) showed that neurons exhibited greater response strength during the memory-saccade task than during a simple fixation task. Thus, auditory responses in LIP appear to be dependent on both training and the behavioral task. These findings led the investigators to conclude that the auditory

responses in LIP are supramodal (cognitive or motor) and not modality-specific sensory responses. Thus, it seems clear that the cortical processing of spatial-related auditory information involves circuitry linking the caudal auditory belt and parabelt fields, the lateral intraparietal area, and prefrontal cortex (Rauschecker & Tian, 2000). The extent to which these circuits constitute a "where" pathway for audition is the subject of ongoing investigations.

REFERENCES

Adams, J. C., & Warr, W. B. (1976). Origins of axons in the cat's acoustic striae determined by injection of horseradish peroxidase into severed tracts. *Journal of Comparative Neurology, 170,* 107–121.

Aitkin, L. M. (1973). Medial geniculate body of cat: Responses to tonal stimuli of neurons in medial division. *Journal of Neurophysiology, 36,* 275–283.

Aitkin, L. M. (1990). *The auditory cortex: Structural and functional bases of auditory perception.* London: Chapman and Hall.

Aitkin, L. M., Anderson, D. J., & Brugge, J. F. (1970). Tonotopic organization and discharge characteristics of neurons in the nuclei of the lateral lemniscus. *Journal of Neurophysiology, 33,* 421–440.

Aitkin, L. M., Dickhaus, H., Schulz, W., & Zimmermann, M. (1978). External nucleus of inferior colliculus: Auditory and spinal somatosensory afferents and their interactions. *Journal of Neurophysiology, 41,* 837–847.

Aitkin, L. M., Merzenich, M. M., Irvine, D. R., Clarey, J. C., & Nelson, J. E. (1986). Frequency representation in auditory cortex of the common marmoset (*Callithrix jacchus jacchus*). *Journal of Comparative Neurology, 252,* 175–185.

Aitkin, L. M., Pettigrew, J. D., Calford, M. B., Phillips, S. C., & Wise, L. Z. (1985). Representation of stimulus azimuth by low-frequency neurons in inferior colliculus of the cat. *Journal of Neurophysiology, 53,* 43–59.

Aitkin, L. M., Webster, W. R., Veale, J. L., & Crosby, D. C. (1975). Inferior colliculus: I. Comparison of response properties of neurons in central, pericentral, and external nuclei of adult cat. *Journal of Neurophysiology, 38,* 1196–1207.

Allon, N., Yeshurun, Y., & Wollberg, Z. (1981). Responses of single cells in the medial geniculate body of awake squirrel monkeys. *Experimental Brain Research, 41,* 222–232.

Alving, B. M., & Cowan, W. M. (1971). Some quantitative observations on the cochlear division of the eighth nerve in the squirrel monkey (*Saimiri sciureus*). *Brain Research, 25,* 229–239.

Andersen, R. A., Knight, P. J., & Merzenich, M. M. (1980). The thalamocortical and corticothalamic connections of AI, AII, and the anterior auditory field (AAF) in the cat: Evidence for two largely segregated systems of connections. *Journal of Comparative Neurology, 194,* 663–701.

Andersen, R. A., Roth, G. L., Aitkin, L. M., & Merzenich, M. M. (1980). The efferent projections of the central nucleus and the pericentral nucleus of the inferior colliculus in the cat. *Journal of Comparative Neurology, 194*(3), 649–662.

Andersen, R. A., Snyder, L. H., Bradley, D. C., & Xing, J. (1997). Multimodal representation of space in the posterior parietal cortex and its use in planning movements. *Annual Review of Neuroscience, 20,* 303–330.

Azuma, M., & Suzuki, H. (1984). Properties and distribution of auditory neurons in the dorsolateral prefrontal cortex of the alert monkey. *Brain Research, 90,* 57–73.

Bajo, V. M., Merchan, M. A., Lopez, D. E., & Rouiller, E. M. (1993). Neuronal morphology and efferent projections of the dorsal nucleus of the lateral lemniscus in the rat. *Journal of Comparative Neurology, 334,* 241–262.

Barnes, W. T., Magoun, H. W., & Ranson, S. W. (1943). The ascending auditory pathway in the brain stem of the monkey. *Journal of Comparative Neurology, 79,* 129–152.

Beecher, M. D., Petersen, M. R., Zoloth, S. R., Moody, D. B., & Stebbins, W. C. (1979). Perception of conspecific vocalizations by Japanese macaques. *Brain Behavior and Evolution, 16,* 443–460.

Benevento, L. A., Fallon, J. H., Davis, B. J., & Rezak, M. (1977). Auditory-visual interaction in single cells of the superior temporal sulcus and orbitofrontal cortex of the macaque monkey. *Experimental Neurology, 57,* 849–872.

Benson, D. A., Hienz, R. D., & Goldstein, M. H., Jr. (1981). Single-unit activity in the auditory cortex of monkeys actively localizing sound sources: Spatial tuning and behavioral dependency. *Brain Research, 219*(2), 249–267.

Bieser, A. (1998). Processing of twitter-call fundamental frequencies in insula and auditory cortex of squirrel monkeys. *Experimental Brain Research, 122,* 139–148.

Bieser, A., & Muller-Preuss, P. (1996). Auditory responsive cortex in the squirrel monkey: Neural responses to amplitude-modulated sounds. *Experimental Brain Research, 108,* 273–284.

Binns, K. E., Grant, S., Withington, D. J., & King, M. J. (1992). A topographic representation of auditory space in the external nucleus of the inferior colliculus of the guinea-pig. *Brain Research, 589,* 231–242.

Blum, P. S., Abraham, L. D., & Gilman, S. (1979). Vestibular, auditory and somatic input to the posterior thalamus of the cat. *Experimental Brain Research, 34,* 1–9.

Brown, C. H., Beecher, M. D., Moody, D. B., & Stebbins, W. C. (1978). Localization of primate calls by Old World monkeys. *Science, 201*(4357), 753–754.

Brown, C. H., Beecher, M. D., Moody, D. B., & Stebbins, W. C. (1980). Localization of noise bands by Old World monkeys. *Journal of the Acoustical Society of America, 68*(1), 127–132.

Brown, C. H., Schessler, T., Moody, D., & Stebbins, W. (1982). Vertical and horizontal sound localization in primates. *Journal of the Acoustical Society of America, 72*(6), 1804–1811.

Brown, M. C., Nuttall, A. L., & Masta, R. I. (1983). Intracellular recordings from cochlear inner hair cells: Effects of stimulation of the crossed olivo-cochlear efferents. *Science, 222,* 69–71.

Brownell, W. E., Bader, C. R., Bertrand, D., & de Ribaupierre, Y. (1985). Evoked mechanical responses of isolated cochlear outer hair cells. *Science, 227,* 194–197.

Brugge, J. F. (1982). Auditory cortical areas in primates. In C. N. Woolsey (Ed.), *Cortical sensory organization: Vol. 3. Multiple auditory areas* (pp. 97–111). New York: Raven Press.

Brugge, J. F., Andersen, D. J., & Aitkin, L. M. (1970). Responses of neurons in the dorsal nucleus of the lateral lemniscus of cat to binaural tonal stimulation. *Journal of Neurophysiology, 33,* 441–458.

Brugge, J. F., & Merzenich, M. M. (1973). Responses of neurons in auditory cortex of the macaque monkey to monaural and binaural stimulation. *Journal of Neurophysiology, 36,* 1138–1158.

Brunso-Bechtold, J. K., Thompson, G. C., & Masterton, R. B. (1981). HRP study of the organization of auditory afferents ascending to the central nucleus of the inferior colliculus in cat. *Journal of Comparative Neurology, 197,* 705–722.

Buchwald, J., Dickerson, L., Harrison, J., & Hinman, C. (1988). Medial geniculate body responses to cat cries. In J. Syka & R. B. Masterton (Eds.), *Auditory pathway, structure and function* (pp. 319–322). New York: Plenum Press.

Buno, W. (1978). Auditory nerve activity influenced by contralateral ear sound stimulation. *Experimental Neurology, 59,* 62–74.

Burton, H., & Jones, E. G. (1976). The posterior thalamic region and its cortical projection in New World and Old World monkeys. *Journal of Comparative Neurology, 168,* 249–302.

Caird, D., & Klinke, R. (1983). Processing of binaural stimuli by cat superior olivary complex neurons. *Experimental Brain Research, 52,* 385–399.

Calford, M. B., & Aitkin, L. M. (1983). Ascending projections to the medial geniculate body of the cat: Evidence for multiple, parallel auditory pathways through thalamus. *Journal of Neuroscience, 3,* 2365–2380.

Cohen, Y. E., & Knudsen, E. I. (1999). Maps versus clusters: Different representations of auditory space in the midbrain and forebrain. *Trends in Neuroscience, 22,* 128–135.

Coleman, J. R., & Clerici, W. J. (1987). Sources of projections to subdivisions of the inferior colliculus in the rat. *Journal of Comparative Neurology, 262,* 215–226.

Colombo, M., Rodman, H. R., & Gross, C. G. (1996). The effects of superior temporal cortex lesions on the processing and retention of auditory information in monkeys (*Cebus apella*). *Journal of Neuroscience, 16,* 4501–4517.

Covey, E., & Casseday, J. H. (1986). Connectional basis for frequency representation in the nuclei of the lateral lemniscus of the bat, *Eptesicus fuscus. Journal of Neuroscience, 6,* 2926–2940.

Cowey, A., & Dewson, J. H. (1972). Effects of unilateral ablation of superior temporal cortex on auditory sequence discrimination in *Macaca mulatta. Neuropsychologia, 10,* 279–289.

Cowey, A., & Weiskrantz, L. (1976). Auditory sequence discrimination in *Macaca mulatta*: The role of the superior temporal cortex. *Neuropsychologia, 14,* 1–10.

Curry, M. J. (1972). The exteroceptive properties of neurones in the somatic part of the posterior group (PO). *Brain Research, 44,* 439–462.

Dewson, J. H., Cowey, A., & Weiskrantz, L. (1970). Disruptions of auditory sequence discrimination by unilateral and bilateral cortical ablations of superior temporal gyrus in the monkey. *Experimental Neurology, 28,* 529–548.

Dewson, J. H., Pribram, K. H., & Lynch, J. C. (1969). Effects of ablations of temporal cortex upon speech sound discrimination in the monkey. *Experimental Neurology, 24,* 579–591.

Divac, I., Lavail, J. H., Rakic, P., & Winston, K. R. (1997). Heterogeneous afferents to the inferior parietal lobule of the rhesus monkey revealed by the retrograde transport method. *Brain Research,* 197–207.

Ehret, G. (1997). The auditory midbrain, a "shunting yard" of acoustical information processing. In G. Ehret & R. Romand (Eds.), *The central auditory system* (pp. 259–316). New York: Oxford University Press.

Evans, E. F. (1974). Neural processes for the detection of acoustic patterns and for sound localization. In F. O. Schmitt & F. G Worden (Eds.), *The neurosciences* (pp. 131–145). Cambridge, MA: MIT Press.

Fernandez, C., Butler, R., Konishi, T., & Honrubia, V. (1962). Cochlear potentials in the rhesus and squirrel monkey. *Journal of the Acoustical Society of America, 34,* 1411–1417.

Fitzpatrick, K. A. (1975). Cellular architecture and topographic organization of the inferior colliculus of the squirrel monkey. *Journal of Comparative Neurology, 164,* 185–208.

Fitzpatrick, K. A., & Imig, T. J. (1978). Projections of auditory cortex upon the thalamus and midbrain in the owl monkey. *Journal of Comparative Neurology, 177,* 537–556.

Friauf, E., & Ostwald, J. (1988). Divergent projections of physiologically characterized rat ventral cochlear nucleus neurons as shown by intra-axonal injection of horseradish peroxidase. *Experimental Brain Research, 73,* 263–284.

Fu, K. G., Johnston, T. A., Shah, A. S., Arnold, L., Smiley, J., Hackett, T. A., Garraghty, P. E., & Schroeder, C. E. (2001). Characterization of somatosensory input to auditory association cortex in macaques. *Society for Neuroscience Abstracts, 27.*

Funkenstein, H. H., & Winter, P. (1973). Responses to acoustic stimuli of units in the auditory cortex of awake squirrel monkeys. *Experimental Brain Research, 18,* 464–488.

Gacek, R. R., & Rasmussen, G. L. (1961). Fiber analysis of the statoacoustic nerve of guinea pig, cat, and monkey. *Anatomical Record, 139,* 455–463.

Galambos, R. (1956). Suppression of auditory nerve activity by stimulation of efferent fibers to cochlea. *Journal of Neurophysiology, 19,* 424–437.

Ghazanfar, A. A., & Hauser, M. C. (1999). The neuroethology of primate vocal communication: Substrates for the evolution of speech. *Trends in Cognitive Sciences, 3,* 377–384.

Glass, I., & Wollberg, Z. (1983). Responses to cells in the auditory cortex of awake squirrel monkeys to normal and reversed species-specific vocalizations. *Hearing Research, 9,* 27–33.

Glendenning, K. K., Baker, B. N., Hutson, K. A., & Masterton, R. B. (1992). Acoustic chiasm V: Inhibition and excitation in the ipsilateral and contralateral projections of LSO. *Journal of Comparative Neurology, 318,* 100–122.

Glendenning, K. K., Brunso-Bechtold, J. K., Thompson, G. C., & Masterton, R. B. (1981). Ascending auditory afferents to the nuclei of the lateral lemniscus. *Journal of Comparative Neurology, 197,* 673–703.

Glendenning, K. K., & Hutson, K. A. (1998). Lack of topography in the ventral nucleus of the lateral lemniscus. *Microscopy Research and Technique, 41*(4), 298–312.

Glendenning, K. K., & Masterton, R. B. (1983). Acoustic chiasm: Efferent projections to the lateral superior olive. *Journal of Neuroscience, 3,* 1521–1537.

Goldberg, R. B., & Moore, R. Y. (1967). Ascending projections of the lateral lemniscus in the cat and monkey. *Journal of Comparative Neurology, 129,* 143–156.

Green, S. (1975). Auditory sensitivity and equal loudness in the squirrel monkey (*Saimiri sciureus*). *Journal of the Experimental Analysis of Behavior, 23,* 255–264.

Gross, N. B., Lifschitz, W. S., & Anderson, D. J. (1974). The tonotopic organization of the auditory thalamus of the squirrel monkey (*Saimiri sciureus*). *Brain Research, 65,* 323–332.

Grunewald, A., Linden, J. F., & Andersen, R. A. (1999). Responses to auditory stimuli in macaque lateral intraparietal area: I. Effects of training. *Journal of Neurophysiology, 82,* 330–342.

Guinan, J. J., & Gifford, M. L. (1988). Effects of electrical stimulation of efferent olivocochlear neurons on cat auditory-nerve fibers: III. Tuning curves and thresholds at CF. *Hearing Research, 37,* 29–46.

Guinan, J. J., Guinan, S. S., & Norris, B. E. (1972). Single auditory units in the superior olivary complex: I. Responses to sound and classifications based on physiological properties. *International Journal of Neuroscience, 4,* 101–120.

Guinan, J. J., Norris, B. E., & Guinan, S. S. (1972). Single auditory units in the superior olivary complex: II. Locations of unit categories and tonotopical organization. *International Journal of Neuroscience, 4,* 147–166.

Guinan, J. J., Warr, W. B., & Norris, B. E. (1983). Differential olivocochlear projections from lateral versus medial zones of the superior olivary complex. *Journal of Comparative Neurology, 221,* 358–370.

Guinan, J. J., Warr, W. B., & Norris, B. E. (1984). Topographic organization of the olivocochlear projections from the lateral and medial zones of the superior olivary complex. *Journal of Comparative Neurology, 226,* 21–27.

Guldin, W. O., & Grusser, O. J. (1998). Is there a vestibular cortex? *Trends in Neuroscience, 21,* 254–259.

Hackett, T. A. (2002). The comparative anatomy of the primate auditory cortex. In A. Ghazanfar (Ed.), *Primate audition: Ethology and neurobiology* (pp. 199–225). Boca Raton: CRC Press.

Hackett, T. A., Neagu, T. A., & Kaas, J. H. (1999). Subcortical connections of the inferior colliculus in primates. *Association for Research in Otolaryngology Abstracts, 22,* 222.

Hackett, T. A., Preuss, T. M., & Kaas, J. H. (2001). Architectonic identification of the core region in auditory cortex of macaques, chimpanzees, and humans. *Journal of Comparative Neurology, 441,* 197–222.

Hackett, T. A., Stepniewska, I., & Kaas, J. H. (1998a). Subdivisions of auditory cortex and ipsilateral cortical connections of the parabelt auditory cortex in macaque monkeys. *Journal of Comparative Neurology, 394,* 475–495.

Hackett, T. A., Stepniewska, I., & Kaas, J. H. (1998b). Thalamocortical connections of parabelt auditory cortex in macaque monkeys. *Journal of Comparative Neurology, 400,* 271–286.

Hackett, T. A., Stepniewska, I., & Kaas, J. H. (1999). Prefrontal connections of the auditory parabelt cortex in macaque monkeys. *Brain Research, 817,* 45–58.

Harrison, J. M., & Irving, R. (1966). Visual and nonvisual auditory systems in mammals. *Science, 154,* 738–743.

Hashikawa, T., Molinari, M., Rausell, E., & Jones, E. G. (1995). Patchy and laminar terminations of medial geniculate axons in monkey auditory cortex. *Journal of Comparative Neurology, 362,* 195–208.

Heffner, H. E., & Heffner, R. S. (1984). Temporal lobe lesions and perception of species-specific vocalizations by macaques. *Science, 226,* 75–76.

Heffner, H. E., & Heffner, R. S. (1986). Effect of unilateral and bilateral auditory cortex lesions on the discrimination of vocalizations by Japanese macaques. *Journal of Neurophysiology, 56,* 683–701.

Heffner, H. E., & Heffner, R. S. (1990). Effect of bilateral auditory cortex lesions on sound localization in Japanese macaques. *Journal of Neurophysiology, 64*(3), 915–931.

Heffner, H., & Masterton, B. (1975). Contribution of auditory cortex to sound localization in the monkey (*Macaca mulatta*). *Journal of Neurophysiology, 38,* 1340–1358.

Heierli, P., de Ribaupierre, F., & de Ribaupierre, Y. (1987). Functional properties and interactions of neuron pairs simultaneously recorded in the medial geniculate body of the cat. *Hearing Research, 25,* 209–225.

Henkel, C. K., & Brunso-Bechtold, J. K. (1993). Laterality of superior olivary projections to the inferior colliculus in adult and developing ferret. *Journal of Comparative Neurology, 331,* 458–468.

Henkel, C. K., & Spangler, K. M. (1983). Organization of the efferent projections of the medial superior olivary nucleus in the cat as revealed by HRP and autoradiographic tracing methods. *Journal of Comparative Neurology, 221,* 416–428.

Huffman, R. F., & Henson, O. W. (1990). The descending auditory pathway and acousticomotor systems: Connections with the inferior colliculus. *Brain Research Reviews, 15,* 245–323.

Hupfer, K., Jurgens, U., & Ploog, D. (1977). The effect of superior temporal lesions on the recognition of species specific calls in the squirrel monkey. *Experimental Brain Research, 30,* 75–87.

Hurst, E. M. (1959). Some cortical association systems related to auditory functions. *Journal of Comparative Neurology, 112,* 103–119.

Hutson, K. A., Glendenning, K. K., & Masterton, R. B. (1991). Acoustic chiasm IV: Eight midbrain decussations of the auditory system in the cat. *Journal of Comparative Neurology, 312,* 105–131.

Hyde, P. S., & Knudsen, E. I. (2000). Topographic projection from the optic tectum to the auditory space map in the inferior colliculus of the barn owl. *Journal of Comparative Neurology, 421,* 146–160.

Hyvarinen, J. (1982). Posterior parietal lobe of the primate brain. *Physiological Reviews, 62,* 1060–1129.

Imig, T. J., & Adrian, H. O. (1977). Binaural columns in the primary field (AI) of cat auditory cortex. *Brain Research, 138,* 241–257.

Imig, T. J, Ruggero, M. A., Kitzes, L. M., Javel, E., & Brugge, J. F. (1977). Organization of auditory cortex in the owl monkey (*Aotus trivirgatus*). *Journal of Comparative Neurology, 171,* 111–128.

Irvine, D. R. F. (1986). The auditory brainstem. In D. Ottoson (Ed.), *Progress in sensory physiology: Vol. 7* (pp. 1–279). Berlin: Springer-Verlag.

Irving, R., & Harrison, J. M. (1967). The superior olivary complex and audition: A comparative study. *Journal of Comparative Neurology, 130,* 77–86.

Ito, S.-I. (1982). Prefrontal unit activity of macaque monkeys during auditory and visual reaction time tasks. *Brain Research, 247,* 39–47.

Ivarsson, C., de Ribaupierre, Y., & de Ribaupierre, F. (1988). Influence of auditory localization cues on neuronal activity in the auditory thalamus of the cat. *Journal of Neurophysiology, 59,* 586–606.

Iversen, S. D., & Mishkin, M. (1973). Comparison of superior temporal and inferior prefrontal lesions on auditory and nonauditory tasks in rhesus monkeys. *Brain Research, 55,* 355–367.

Jerison, H. J., & Neff, W. D. (1953). Effect of cortical ablation in the monkey on discrimination of auditory patterns. *Federation Proceedings, 12,* 73–74.

Jordan, H. (1973). The structure of the medial geniculate nucleus (MGN): A cyto- and myeloarchitectonic study in the squirrel monkey. *Journal of Comparative Neurology, 148,* 469–480.

Kaas, J. H. (1993). Evolution of multiple areas and modules within neocortex. *Perspectives on Developmental Neurobiology, 1,* 101–107.

Kaas, J. H. (2000). Why is brain size so important? Design problems and solutions as neocortex gets bigger or smaller. *Brain and Mind, 1,* 7–23.

Kaas, J. H., & Hackett, T. A. (1998). Subdivisions and levels of processing in primate auditory cortex. *Audiology and Neurootolology, 3,* 73–85.

Kaas, J. H., & Hackett, T. A. (1999). "What" and "where" processing in auditory cortex. *Nature Neuroscience, 2*(12), 1045–1047.

Kaas, J. H., & Hackett, T. A. (2000a). How the visual projection map instructs the auditory computational map. *Journal of Comparative Neurology, 421,* 143–145.

Kaas, J. H., & Hackett, T. A. (2000b). Subdivisions of auditory cortex and processing streams in primates. *Proceedings of the National Academy of Science, USA, 97*(22), 11793–11799.

Kaas, J. H., Hackett, T. A., & Tramo, M. J. (1999). Auditory processing in primate cerebral cortex. *Current Opinion in Neurobiology, 9*(2), 164–170.

Kawase, T., Delgutte, B., & Liberman, M. C. (1993). Antimasking effects of the olivocochlear reflex: II. Enhancement of auditory-nerve response to masked tones. *Journal of Neurophysiology, 70,* 2533–2549.

Kawase, T., & Liberman, M. C. (1993). Antimasking effects of the olivocochlear reflex: I. Enhancement of compound action potentials to masked tones. *Journal of Neurophysiology, 70,* 2519–2532.

Kelly, J. B., & Li, L. (1997). Two sources of inhibition affecting binaural evoked responses in the rat's inferior colliculus: The dorsal nucleus of the lateral lemniscus and the superior olivary complex. *Hearing Research, 104,* 112–126.

King, A. J., & Palmer, A. R. (1983). Cells responsive to free-field auditory stimuli in guinea-pig superior colliculus: Distribution and response properties. *Journal of Physiology, 342,* 361–381.

Knudsen, E. I., du Lac, S., & Esterly, S. D. (1987). Computational maps in the brain. *Annual Review of Neuroscience, 10,* 41–65.

Knudsen, E. I., & Konishi, M. (1978a). Center-surround organization of auditory receptive fields in the owl. *Science, 202,* 778–780.

Knudsen, E. I., & Konishi, M. (1978b). Space and frequency are represented separately in auditory midbrain. *Journal of Neurophysiology, 41,* 870–884.

Koch, K. W., & Fuster, J. M. (1989). Unit activity in monkey parietal cortex related to haptic perception and temporary memory. *Experimental Brain Research, 76,* 292–306.

Kohonen, T., & Hari, R. (1999). Where the abstract feature maps of the brain might come from. *Trends in Neuroscience, 22,* 135–139.

Kosaki, H., Hashikawa, T., He, J., & Jones, E. G. (1997). Tonotopic organization of auditory cortical fields delineated by parvalbumin immunoreactivity in macaque monkeys. *Journal of Comparative Neurology, 386,* 304–316.

Kudo, M. (1981). Projections of the nuclei of the lateral lemniscus in the cat: An autoradiographic study. *Brain Research, 221,* 57–71.

Kudo, M., & Niimi, K. (1980). Ascending projections of the inferior colliculus in the cat: An autoradiographic study. *Journal of Comparative Neurology, 191,* 545–556.

Langner, G. (1992). Periodicity coding in the auditory system. *Hearing Research, 60,* 115–142.

Leinonen, L., Hyvarinen, J., & Sovijarvi, A. R. (1980). Functional properties of neurons in the temporo-parietal association cortex of awake monkey. *Experimental Brain Research, 39,* 203–215.

Lewis, J. W., & Van Essen, D. C. (2000). Corticocortical connections of visual, sensorimotor, and multimodal processing areas in the parietal lobe of the macaque monkey. *Journal of Comparative Neurology, 428,* 112–137.

Liberman, M. C. (1989). Rapid assessment of sound-evoked olivocochlear feedback: Suppression of compound action potentials by contralateral sound. *Hearing Research, 38,* 47–57.

Linden, J. F., Grunewald, A., & Andersen, R. A. (1999). Responses to auditory stimuli in macaque lateral intraparietal area: II. Behavioral modulation. *Journal of Neurophysiology, 82,* 343–358.

Love, J. A., & Scott, J. W. (1969). Some response characteristics of cells of the magnocellular division of the medial geniculate body of the cat. *Canadian Journal of Physiology and Pharmacology, 47,* 881–888.

Lu, T., & Wang, X. (2000). Temporal discharge patterns evoked by rapid sequences of wide- and narrowband clicks in the primary auditory cortex of cat. *Journal of Neurophysiology, 84,* 236–246.

Luethke, L. E., Krubitzer, L. A., & Kaas, J. H. (1989). Connections of primary auditory cortex in the New World monkey, *Saguinus. Journal of Comparative Neurology, 285,* 487–513.

Manley, J. A., & Muller-Preuss, P. (1978). Response variability of auditory cortex cells in the squirrel monkey to constant acoustic stimuli. *Experimental Brain Research, 32,* 171–180.

Manley, J. A., & Muller-Preuss, P. A. (1981). A comparison of the responses evoked by artificial stimuli and vocalizations in the inferior colliculus of squirrel monkeys. In J. Syka & L. Aitkin (Eds.), *Neuronal mechanisms of hearing* (pp. 307–310). New York: Plenum Press.

Markovitz, N. S., & Pollak, G. D. (1993). The dorsal nucleus of the lateral lemniscus in the mustache bat: monaural properties. *Hearing Research, 71,* 51–63.

Markovitz, N. S., & Pollak, G. D. (1994). Binaural processing in the dorsal nucleus of the lateral lemniscus. *Hearing Research, 73,* 121–140.

Massopust, L. C., Jr., Wolin, L. R., & Frost, V. (1970). Increases in auditory middle frequency discrimination thresholds after cortical ablations. *Experimental Neurology, 28,* 299–307.

Massopust, L. C., Jr., Wolin, L. R., Meder, R., & Frost, V. (1967). Changes in auditory frequency discrimination thresholds after temporal cortex ablations. *Experimental Neurology, 19,* 245–255.

May, B., Moody, D. B., & Stebbins, W. C. (1989). Categorical perception of conspecific communication sounds by Japanese macaques, *Macaca fuscata. Journal of the Acoustical Society of America, 85*(2), 837–847.

Mazzoni, P., Bracewell, R. M., Barash, S., & Andersen, R. A. (1996). Spatially tuned auditory responses in area LIP of macaques performing delayed memory saccades to acoustic targets. *Journal of Neurophysiology, 75*, 1233–1241.

Merchan, M. A., Saldana, E., & Plaza, I. (1994). Dorsal nucleus of the lateral lemniscus in the rat: Concentric organization and tonotopic projection to the inferior colliculus. *Journal of Comparative Neurology, 342*, 259–278.

Merzenich, M. M., & Brugge, J. F. (1973). Representation of the cochlear partition on the superior temporal plane of the macaque monkey. *Brain Research, 50*, 275–296.

Merzenich, M. M., & Reid, M. D. (1974). Representation of the cochlea within the inferior colliculus of the cat. *Brain Research, 77*, 397–415.

Mettler, F. A. (1935). Corticofugal fiber connections of the cortex of *Macaca mulatta*: The temporal region. *Journal of Comparative Neurology, 61*, 25–47.

Mishkin, M., Ungerleider, L. G., & Macko, K. A. (1983). Object vision and spatial vision: Two cortical pathways. *Trends in Neuroscience, 6*, 414–417.

Molinari, M., Dell'Anna, M. E., Rausell, E., Leggio, M. G., Hashikawa, T., & Jones, E. G. (1995). Auditory thalamocortical pathways defined in monkeys by calcium-binding protein immunoreactivity. *Journal of Comparative Neurology, 362*, 171–194.

Moore, B. C. J., & Sek, A. (1992). Detection of combined frequency and amplitude modulation. *Journal of the Acoustical Society of America, 92*, 3119–3131.

Moore, J. K. (1980). The primate cochlear nuclei: Loss of lamination as a phylogenetic process. *Journal of Comparative Neurology, 193*, 609–629.

Moore, J. K. (2000). Organization of the human superior olivary complex. *Microscopy Research and Technique, 51*, 403–412.

Moore, J. K., & Moore, R. Y. (1971). A comparative study of the superior olivary complex in the primate brain. *Folia Primatologia, 16*, 35–51.

Morel, A., Garraghty, P. E., & Kaas, J. H. (1993). Tonotopic organization, architectonic fields, and connections of auditory cortex in macaque monkeys. *Journal of Comparative Neurology, 335*, 437–459.

Morel, A., & Kaas, J. H. (1992). Subdivisions and connections of auditory cortex in owl monkeys. *Journal of Comparative Neurology, 318*, 27–63.

Morel, A., Rouiller, E., de Ribaupierre, Y., & de Ribaupierre, F. (1987). Tonotopic organization in the medial geniculate body (MGB) of lightly anesthetized cats. *Experimental Brain Research, 69*, 24–42.

Morest, D. K. (1965). The lateral tegmental system of the midbrain and the medial geniculate body: A study with Golgi and Nauta methods in cat. *Journal of Anatomy, 99*, 611–634.

Moskowitz, N., & Liu, J.-C. (1972). Central projections of the spiral ganglion of the squirrel monkey. *Journal of Comparative Neurology, 144*, 335–344.

Newman, J. D. (1988). Primate hearing mechanisms. In H. D. Steklis & J. Erwin (Eds.), *Neurosciences: 4. Comparative primate biology* (pp. 469–499). New York: Liss.

Newman, J. D. (1978a). Detection of biologically significant sounds by single neurons. In D. Chivers & J. Herbert (Eds.), *Recent advances in primatology* (Vol. 1, pp. 755–762). London: Academic Press.

Newman, J. D. (1978b). Perception of sounds used in species-specific communication: The auditory cortex and beyond. *Journal of Medical Primatology, 7*, 98–105.

Newman, J. D. (1979). Central nervous system processing of sounds in primates. In H. Steklis & M. Raleigh (Eds.), *Neurobiology of social communication in primates* (pp. 69–109). New York: Academic Press.

Newman, J. D., & Lindsley, D. F. (1976). Single unit analysis of auditory processing in squirrel monkey auditory cortex. *Experimental Brain Research, 25*, 169–181.

Newman, J. D., & Symmes, D. (1979). Feature detection by single units in squirrel monkey auditory cortex. *Experimental Brain Research Supplement, 2*, 140–145.

Newman, J. D., & Wollberg, Z. (1973a). Multiple coding of species-specific vocalizations in auditory cortex of squirrel monkeys. *Brain Research, 54*, 287–304.

Newman, J. D., & Wollberg, Z. (1973b). Responses of single neurons in the auditory cortex of squirrel monkeys to variants of a single call type. *Experimental Neurology, 40*, 821–824.

Oertel, D., & Wu, S. H. (1989). Morphology and physiology of cells in slice preparations of the dorsal cochlear nucleus of mice. *Journal of Comparative Neurology, 283*, 228–247.

Oliver, D. L. (1984). Neuron types in the central nucleus of the inferior colliculus that project to the medial geniculate body. *Neuroscience, 11*, 409–424.

Pandya, D. N., Hallett, M., & Mukherjee, S. K. (1969). Intra- and interhemispheric connections of the neocortical auditory system in the rhesus monkey. *Brain Research, 14*, 49–65.

Pandya, D. N., & Kuypers, H. G. J. M. (1969). Cortico-cortical connections in the rhesus monkey. *Brain Research, 13*, 13–36.

Pelleg-Toiba, R., & Wollberg, Z. (1991). Discrimination of communication calls in the squirrel monkey: "Call detectors" or "cell ensembles"? *Journal of Basic Clinical Physiology and Pharmacology, 2*, 257–272.

Pfingst, B. E., & O'Connor, T. A. (1981). Characteristics of neurons in auditory cortex of monkeys performing a simple auditory task. *Journal of Neurophysiology, 45*, 16–34.

Poljak, S. (1926). The connections of the acoustic nerve. *Journal of Anatomy, 60*, 465–469.

Pollak, G. D. (1997). Roles of GABAergic inhibition for the binaural processing of multiple sound sources in the inferior colliculus. *Annals of Otology, Rhinology, and Laryngology, 168*(Suppl.), 44–54.

Pratt, S. R., & Iversen, S. D. (1978). Selective cortical lesions and auditory behaviour in the monkey. In D. Chievers & J. Herbert (Eds.), *Recent advances in primatology* (pp. 807–809). London: Academic Press.

Pribram, K. H., Rosner, B. S., & Rosenblith, W. A. (1954). Electrical responses to acoustic clicks in monkey: Extent of neocortex activated. *Journal of Neurophysiology, 17,* 336–344.

Rajan, R. (1988a). Effect of electrical stimulation of the crossed olivocochlear bundle on temporary threshold shifts in auditory sensitivity: I. Dependence on electrical stimulation parameters. *Journal of Neurophysiology, 60,* 549–568.

Rajan, R. (1988b). Effect of electrical stimulation of the crossed olivocochlear bundle on temporary threshold shifts in auditory sensitivity: II. Dependence on the level of temporary threshold shifts. *Journal of Neurophysiology, 60,* 569–579.

Rajan, R. (2000). Centrifugal pathways protect hearing sensitivity at the cochlea in noisy environments that exacerbate the damage induced by loud sound. *Journal of Neuroscience, 20,* 6684–6693.

Rajan, R., & Johnstone, B. M. (1988a). Binaural acoustic stimulation exercises protective effects at the cochlea that mimic the effects of electrical stimulation of an auditory efferent pathway. *Brain Research, 459,* 241–255.

Rajan, R., & Johnstone, B. M. (1988b). Electrical stimulation of cochlear efferents at the round window reduces auditory desensitization in guinea pigs: I. Dependence on electrical stimulation parameters. *Hearing Research, 36,* 53–73.

Rajan, R., & Johnstone, B. M. (1988c). Electrical stimulation of cochlear efferents at the round window reduces auditory desensitization in guinea pigs: II. Dependence on level of temporary threshold shifts. *Hearing Research, 36,* 75–88.

Rajan, R., & Johnstone, B. M. (1989). Contralateral cochlear destruction mediates protection from monaural loud sound exposures through the crossed olivocochlear bundle. *Hearing Research, 39,* 263–277.

Rasmussen, G. L. (1946). The olivary peduncle and other fiber connections of the superior olivary complex. *Journal of Comparative Neurology, 84,* 141–219.

Rasmussen, G. L. (1953). Further observations on the efferent cochlear bundle. *Journal of Comparative Neurology, 99,* 61–74.

Rauschecker, J. P. (1998). Parallel processing in the auditory cortex of primates. *Audiology and Neurootology, 3,* 86–103.

Rauschecker, J. P., & Tian, B. (2000). Mechanisms and streams for processing of "what" and "where" in auditory cortex. *Proceedings of the National Academy of Science, USA, 97,* 11800–11806.

Rauschecker, J. P., Tian, B., & Hauser, M. (1995). Processing of complex sounds in the macaque nonprimary auditory cortex. *Science, 268,* 111–114.

Rauschecker, J. P., Tian, B., Pons, T., & Mishkin, M. (1997). Serial and parallel processing in rhesus monkey auditory cortex. *Journal of Comparative Neurology, 382,* 89–103.

Ravizza, R., & Diamond, I. T. (1974). Role of auditory cortex in sound localization: A comparative ablation study of hedgehog and bush-baby. *Federation Proceedings, 33,* 1915–1919.

Recanzone, G. H. (2000). Spatial processing in the auditory cortex of the macaque monkey. *Proceedings of the National Academy of Science, USA, 97,* 11829–11835.

Recanzone, G. H., Guard, D. C., & Phan, M. L. (2000). Frequency and intensity response properties of single neurons in the auditory cortex of the behaving macaque monkey. *Journal of Neurophysiology, 83,* 2315–2331.

Recanzone, G. H., Guard, D. C., Phan, M. L., & Su, T. I. K. (2000). Correlation between the activity of single auditory cortical neurons and sound-localization behavior in the macaque monkey. *Journal of Neurophysiology, 83,* 2723–2739.

Reiter, E. R., & Liberman, M. C. (1995). Efferent-mediated protection from acoustic overexposure: Relation to slow effects of olivocochlear stimulation. *Journal of Neurophysiology, 73,* 506–514.

Rhode, W. S., Smith, P. H., & Oertel, D. (1983). Physiological response properties of cells labeled intracellularly with horseradish peroxidase in cat dorsal cochlear nucleus. *Journal of Comparative Neurology, 213,* 426–447.

Robertson, D., Anderson, C. J., & Cole, K. S. (1987). Segregation of efferent projections to different turns of the guinea pig cochlea. *Hearing Research, 25,* 69–76.

Robinson, C. J., & Burton, H. (1980a). Organization of somatosensory receptive fields in cortical areas 7b, retroinsula, postauditory, and granular insula of *M. fascicularis. Journal of Comparative Neurology, 192,* 69–92.

Robinson, C. J., & Burton, H. (1980b). Somatic submodality distribution within the second somatosensory (SII), 7b, retroinsular, postauditory, and granular insular cortical areas of *M. fascicularis. Journal of Comparative Neurology, 192,* 93–108.

Rodrigues-Dagaeff, C., Simm, G., de Ribaupierre, Y., Villa, A., & de Ribaupierre, F., Rouiller, E. M. (1989). Functional organization of the ventral division of the medial geniculate body of the cat: Evidence for a rostro-caudal gradient of response properties and cortical projections. *Hearing Research, 39,* 103–125.

Romand, R., & Avan, P. (1997). Anatomical and functional aspects of the cochlear nucleus. In G. Ehret & R. Romand (Eds.), *The central auditory system* (pp. 97–191). New York: Oxford University Press.

Romanski, L. M., Bates, J. F., & Goldman-Rakic, P. S. (1999). Auditory belt and parabelt projections to the prefrontal cortex in the rhesus monkey. *Journal of Comparative Neurology, 403,* 141–157.

Romanski, L. M., Tian, B., Fritz, J., Mishkin, M., Goldman-Rakic, P., & Rauschecker, J. P. (1999). Dual streams of auditory afferents target multiple domains in the primate prefrontal cortex. *Nature Neuroscience, 2*(12), 1131–1136.

Rose, J. E., Greenwood, D. D., Goldberg, J. M., & Hind, J. E. (1963). Some discharge characteristics of single neurons in the inferior colliculus of the cat: I. Tonotopical organization, relation of spike-counts to tone intensity, and firing patterns of single elements. *Journal of Neurophysiology, 26,* 294–320.

Rose, J. E., Hind, J. E., Anderson, D. J., & Brugge, J. F. (1971). Some effects of stimulus intensity on response of auditory nerve fibers in the squirrel monkey. *Journal of Neurophysiology, 34,* 685–699.

Rouiller, E. M. (1997). Functional organization of the auditory pathways. In G. Ehret & R. Romand (Eds.), *The central auditory system* (pp. 3–96). New York: Oxford University Press.

Rouiller, E. M., & de Ribaupierre, F. (1985). Origin of afferents to physiologically defined regions of the medial geniculate body of the cat: Ventral and dorsal divisions. *Hearing Research, 19,* 97–114.

Rouiller, E. M., Rodrigues-Dagaeff, C., Simm, G., de Ribaupierre, Y., Villa, A., & de Ribaupierre, F. (1989). Functional organization of the medial division of the medial geniculate body of the cat: Tonotopic organization, spatial distribution of response properties and cortical connections. *Hearing Research, 39,* 127–142.

Rouiller, E. M., Simm, G. M., Villa, A. E. P., de Ribaupierre, Y., & de Ribaupierre, F. (1991). Auditory corticocortical interconnections in the cat: Evidence for parallel and hierarchical arrangement of the auditory cortical areas. *Experimental Brain Research, 86,* 483–505.

Russo, G. S., & Bruce, C. J. (1994). Frontal eye field activity preceding aurally guided saccades. *Journal of Neurophysiology, 71,* 1250–1253.

Saint-Marie, R. L., & Baker, R. A. (1990). Neurotransmitter-specific uptake and retrograde transport of [3H] glycine from the inferior colliculus by ipsilateral projections of the superior olivary complex and nuclei of the lateral lemniscus. *Brain Research, 524,* 244–253.

Saint-Marie, R. L., Ostapoff, E. M., Morest, D. K., & Wenthold, J. R. (1989). Glycine immunoreactive projection of the cat lateral superior olive: Possible role in midbrain ear dominance. *Journal of Comparative Neurology, 279,* 382–396.

Schall, J. D. (1991). Neuronal activity related to visually guided saccades in the frontal eye fields of rhesus monkeys: Comparison with supplementary eye fields. *Journal of Neurophysiology, 66,* 559–579.

Schall, J. D., Morel, A., King, D. J., & Bullier, J. (1995). Topography of visual cortex connections with frontal eye field in macaque: Convergence and segregation of processing streams. *Journal of Neuroscience, 15,* 4464–4487.

Schneiderman, A., Oliver, D. L., & Henkel, D. K. (1988). Connections of the dorsal nucleus of the lateral lemniscus: An inhibitory parallel pathway in the ascending auditory system? *Journal of Comparative Neurology, 276,* 188–208.

Schreiner, C. E., & Langner, G. (1988). Periodicity coding in the inferior colliculus of the cat: II. Topographical organization. *Journal of Neurophysiology, 60,* 1823–1840.

Schroeder, C. E., Lindsley, R. W., Specht, C., Marcovici, A., Smiley, J. F., & Javitt, D. C. (2001). Somatosensory input to auditory association cortex in the macaque monkey. *Journal of Neurophysiology, 85*(3), 1322–1327.

Sek, A., & Moore, B. C. J. (1994). Detection of mixed modulation using correlated and uncorrelated noise modulators. *Journal of the Acoustical Society of America, 95,* 3511–3517.

Smith, P. H., Joris, P. X., Carney, L. H., & Yin, T. C. T. (1991). Projections of physiologically characterized globular bushy cell axons from the cochlear nucleus of the cat. *Journal of Comparative Neurology, 304,* 387–407.

Spangler, K. M., & Warr, W. B. (1991). The descending auditory system. In R. A. Altschuler, R. P. Bobbin, B. M. Clopton, & D. W. Hoffman (Eds.), *Neurobiology of hearing: The central auditory system* (pp. 27–45). New York: Raven Press.

Stiebler, I. (1986). Tone threshold mapping in the inferior colliculus of the house mouse. *Neuroscience Letters, 65,* 336–340.

Steinschneider, M., Arezzo, J., & Vaughan, H. G., Jr. (1980). Phase-locked cortical responses to a human speech sound and low-frequency tones in the monkey. *Brain Research, 198,* 75–84.

Steinschneider, M., Reser, D. H., Fishman, Y. I., Schroeder, C. E., & Arezzo, J. C. (1998). Click train encoding in primary auditory cortex of the awake monkey: Evidence for two mechanisms subserving pitch perception. *Journal of the Acoustical Society of America, 104,* 2935–2955.

Steinschneider, M., Reser, D., Schroeder, C. E., & Arezzo, J. C. (1995). Tonotopic organization of responses reflecting stop consonant place of articulation in primary auditory cortex (A1) of the monkey. *Brain Research, 674,* 147–152.

Steinschneider, M., Schroeder, C. E., Arezzo, J. C., & Vaughan, H. G., Jr. (1995). Physiologic correlates of the voice onset time boundary in primary in auditory cortex (A1) of the awake monkey: Temporal response patterns. *Brain and Language, 48,* 326–340.

Stricanne, B., Andersen, R. A., & Mazzoni, P. (1996). Eye-centered, head-centered, and intermediate coding of remembered sound locations in area LIP. *Journal of Neurophysiology, 76,* 2071–2076.

Strominger, N. L., Nelson, L. R., & Dougherty, W. J. (1977). Second order auditory pathways in the chimpanzee. *Journal of Comparative Neurology, 172,* 349–366.

Strominger, N. L., & Strominger, A. I. (1971). Ascending brainstem projections of the anteroventral cochlear nucleus in the rhesus monkey. *Brain Research, 252,* 353–365.

Sudakov, K., MacLean, P. D., Reeves, A., & Marino, R. (1971). Unit study of exteroceptive inputs to claustrocortex in awake, sitting, squirrel monkey. *Brain Research, 28,* 19–34.

Suga, N. (1988). Auditory neuroethology and speech processing: Complex sound processing by combination-sensitive neurons. In G. M. Edelman, W. E. Gall, & W. M. Cowan (Eds.), *Auditory function: Neurobiological bases of hearing* (pp. 679–720). New York: Wiley.

Suga, N. (1994). Multi-function theory for cortical processing of auditory information: Implications of single-unit and lesion data for future research. *Journal of Comparative Physiology, 175,* 135–144.

Sugar, O., French, J. D., & Chusid, J. G. (1948). Corticocortical connections of the superior surface of the temporal operculum in the monkey (*Macaca mulatta*). *Journal of Neurophysiology, 11*, 175–184.

Suzuki, H. (1985). Distribution and organization of visual and auditory neurons in the monkey prefrontal cortex. *Vision Research, 25*, 465–469.

Symmes, D. (1966). Discrimination of intermittent noise by macaques following lesions of the temporal lobe. *Experimental Neurology, 16*, 201–214.

Symmes, D., Alexander, G. E., & Newman, J. D. (1980). Neural processing of vocalizations and artificial stimuli in the medial geniculate body of squirrel monkey. *Brain Research, 3*, 133–146.

Symmes, D., Newman, J. D., & Alexander, G. E. (1976). Comparison of temporal auditory areas with respect to reception of species specific sounds. *Society for Neuroscience Abstracts, 2*, 696.

Tanila, H., Carlson, S., Linnankoski, I., & Kahila, H. (1993). Regional distribution of functions in dorsolateral prefrontal cortex of the monkey. *Behavioral Brain Research, 53*, 63–71.

Thompson, G. C., & Cortez, A. M. (1983). The inability of squirrel monkeys to localize sound after unilateral ablation of auditory cortex. *Behavioral Brain Research, 8*, 211–216.

Thorpe, S. J., Rolls, E. T., & Maddison, S. (1983). The orbitofrontal cortex: Neuronal activity in the behaving monkey. *Experimental Brain Research, 49*, 93–115.

Tian, B., & Rauschecker, J. P. (1995). FM-selectivity of neurons in the lateral areas of rhesus monkey auditory cortex. *Society for Neuroscience Abstracts, 21*, 269.

Tian, B., Reser, D., Durham, A., Kustov, A., & Rauschecker, J. P. (2001). Functional specialization in rhesus monkey auditory cortex. *Science, 292*, 290–293.

Toros-Morel, A., de Ribaupierre, F., & Rouiller, E. (1981). Coding properties of the different nuclei of the cat's medial geniculate body. In J. Syka & L. Aitkin (Eds.), *Neuronal mechanisms of hearing* (pp. 239–243). New York: Plenum Press.

Trahiotis, C., & Elliott, D. N. (1970). Behavioral investigation of some possible effects of sectioning the crossed olivocochlear bundle. *Journal of the Acoustical Society of America, 47*, 592–596.

Tsuchitani, C. (1977). Functional organization of lateral cell groups of the cat superior olivary complex. *Journal of Neurophysiology, 40*, 296–318.

Ungerleider, L. G., & Mishkin, M. (1982). Two cortical visual systems. In D. J. Ingle, M. A. Goodale, & R. J. W. Mansfield (Eds.), *Analysis of visual behaviour* (pp. 549–586). Cambridge, MA: MIT Press.

Vaadia, E. (1989). Single-unit activity related to active localization of acoustic and visual stimuli in the frontal cortex of the rhesus monkey. *Brain Behavior and Evoluation, 33*, 127–131.

Vaadia, E., Benson, D. A., Heinz, R. D., & Goldstein, M. H., Jr. (1986). Unit study of monkey frontal cortex: Active localization of auditory and of visual stimuli. *Journal of Neurophysiology, 56*, 934–952.

van Adel, B. A., Kidd, S. A., & Kelly, J. B. (1999). Contribution of the commissure of Probst to binaural evoked responses in the rat's inferior colliculus: interaural time differences. *Hearing Research, 130*, 115–130.

Wang, X. (2000). On cortical coding of vocal communication sounds in primates. *Proceedings of the National Academy of Science, USA, 97*, 11843–11849.

Wang, X., Merzenich, M. M., Beitel, R., & Schreiner, C. E. (1995). Representation of a species-specific vocalization in the primary auditory cortex of the common marmoset: Temporal and spectral characteristics. *Journal of Neurophysiology, 74*, 2685–2706.

Ward, A. A., Jr., Peden, J. K., & Sugar, O. (1946). Cortico-cortical connections in the monkey with special reference to area 6. *Journal of Neurophysiology, 9*, 453–461.

Warr, W. B. (1992). Organization of olivocochlear efferent systems in mammals. In D. B. Webster, A. N. Popper, & R. R. Fay (Eds.), *The mammalian auditory pathway: Neuroanatomy* (pp. 410–448). New York: Springer-Verlag.

Watanabe, M. (1992). Frontal units of the monkey coding the associative significance of visual and auditory stimuli. *Experimental Brain Research, 89*, 233–247.

Webster, W. R., Serviere, J., Crewther, D., & Crewther, S. (1984). Iso-frequency 2-DG contours in the inferior colliculus of the awake monkey. *Experimental Brain Research, 56*, 425–437.

Wegener, J. G. (1976). Auditory and visual discrimination following lesions of the anterior supratemporal plane in monkeys. *Neuropsychologia, 14*, 161–173.

Wepsic, J. G. (1966). Multimodal sensory activation of cells in the magnocellular medial geniculate nucleus. *Experimental Neurology, 15*, 299–318.

Whitley, J. M., & Henkel, C. K. (1984). Topographical organization of the inferior collicular projection and other connections of the ventral nucleus of the lateral lemniscus in the cat. *Journal of Comparative Neurology, 229*, 257–270.

Wiederhold, M. L., & Kiang, N. Y. S. (1970). Effects of electric stimulation of the crossed olivocochlear bundle on single auditory-nerve fibers in the cat. *Journal of the Acoustical Society of America, 48*, 950–965.

Winslow, R. L., & Sachs, M. B. (1987). Effect of electrical stimulation of the crossed olivocochlear bundle on auditory nerve response to tones in noise. *Journal of Neurophysiology, 57*, 1002–1021.

Winslow, R. L., & Sachs, M. B. (1988). Single-tone intensity discrimination based on auditory nerve responses in backgrounds of quiet, noise, and with stimulation of the crossed olivocochlear bundle. *Hearing Research, 44*, 161–178.

Winter, P., & Funkenstein, H. H. (1973). The effect of species-specific vocalization on the discharge of auditory cortical cells in the awake squirrel monkey (*Saimiri sciureus*). *Experimental Brain Research, 18*, 489–504.

Wollberg, Z., & Newman, J. D. (1972). Auditory cortex of squirrel monkey: Response patterns of single cells to species-specific vocalizations. *Science, 175,* 212–214.

Wollberg, Z., & Sela, J. (1980). Frontal cortex of the awake squirrel monkey: Responses of single cells to visual and auditory stimuli. *Brain Research, 198,* 216–220.

Woolsey, C. N., & Walzl, E. M. (1982). Cortical auditory area of *Macaca mulatta* and its relation to the second somatic sensory area (Sm II). In C. N. Woolsey (Ed.), *Cortical sensory organiza-tion: Vol. 3. Multiple auditory areas* (pp. 231–256). Clifton, New Jersey: Humana.

Yin, T. C. T., & Chan, J. C. K. (1990). Interaural time sensitivity in medial superior olive of cat. *Journal of Neurophysiology, 64,* 465–488.

Zoloth, S. R., Petersen, M. R., Beecher, M. D., Green, S., Marler, P., Moody, D. B., & Stebbins, W. (1979). Species-specific percep-tual processing of vocal sounds by monkeys. *Science, 204,* 870–873.

CHAPTER 8

Processing of Tactile Information in the Primate Brain

STEVEN HSIAO, KEN JOHNSON, AND TAKASHI YOSHIOKA

In this chapter, we discuss the neural mechanisms of tactile perception. In each of the sensory systems, information about the external world is analyzed into separate processing streams. In the somatosensory system, that division begins at the very first stage of sensory processing. Nociceptors, thermoreceptors, proprioceptors, and cutaneous mechanoreceptors transduce different stimulus features and channel their information into separate, parallel streams. We focus here on the four cutaneous mechanoreceptors that are responsible for tactile perception. Evidence from psychophysical and neurophysiological studies, reviewed here, suggests that they serve distinctly separate functions. We first describe the four mechanoreceptor types and discuss their roles in tactile perception. Then we discuss the anatomy and functions of the central pathways. We end with a discussion of the role of attention in tactile information processing. Throughout the chapter we focus on the processing of information about surface features and object form.

PERIPHERAL NEURAL MECHANISMS
OF TACTILE PERCEPTION

Mechanoreception

Tactile perception is based on four cutaneous mechanoreceptive afferent neuron types: slowly adapting type 1 (SA1),

rapidly adapting (RA), Pacinian (PC), and slowly adapting type 2 (SA2) afferents (see Table 8.1). Two of the four, the RA and PC afferents, respond only to skin motion; they are classed as *rapidly adapting* because they respond transiently to sudden indentation. The other two, the SA1 and SA2 afferents, are classed as *slowly adapting* because they respond to sustained skin deformation with a sustained discharge that declines slowly, although they (particularly SA1 afferents) are more sensitive to skin movement than to static deformation. The neural response properties of these cutaneous afferents have been studied extensively in both human and nonhuman primates, and—except for the SA2 afferents, which are not found in nonhuman primates—there are no interspecies differences. We use the terms SA1, SA2, RA, and PC systems throughout this chapter (Johnson & Hsiao, 1992). By *SA1 system,* for example, we mean the SA1 receptors (the Merkel-neurite complex), the SA1 afferent nerve fiber population, and all the ascending and central neuronal pathways that convey the SA1 signal used for memory and perception. We do not mean to imply that there is no central convergence between these systems or that the systems do not overlap.

SA1 afferent fibers branch repeatedly before they lose their myelin and terminate in the basal layer of the epidermis. There, they are enveloped by specialized (Merkel) epidermal cells that enfold the unmyelinated ends of the SA1 axons (Iggo & Andres, 1982). Although there are synapse-like junctions between the Merkel cells and the axon terminals, action potentials appear to arise as the result of mechanosensitive ion channels in the bare nerve endings (Diamond, Mills, &

Supported by National Institutes of Health Grants NS34086 and NS18787.

Table 8.1   Properties of mechanoreceptors that innervate the hand

Afferent Type	Receptor	Adaptation to Steady Deformation	RF Size	Spatial Resolution	Temporal Sensitivity (Hz)	Function
SA1	Merkel	slow	small	0.5 mm	0–100	form & texture perception
RA	Meissner	rapid	small	3–5 mm	2–100	motion perception, grip control
PC	Pacinian	rapid	large	2 cm	10–1000	transmitted vibration, tool use
SA2	Ruffini	slow	large	1 cm	0–20	lateral force, hand shape, motion direction

Mearow, 1988; Ogawa, 1996). SA1 afferents innervate the skin of the fingerpad densely and have small receptive fields. As a consequence of these two properties, they transmit a high-resolution spatial neural image of a stimulus contacting the fingerpad. A striking response property of these afferents is surround suppression (Vega-Bermudez & Johnson, 1999b), which is similar to surround inhibition. In the central nervous system, surround inhibition in the receptive field of visual or somatosensory neurons is the result of an excitatory center and an inhibitory surround produced by inhibitory synaptic mechanisms. Surround inhibition makes a neuron sensitive to local curvature and—depending on the balance between excitation and inhibition—insensitive to uniform stimulation. In touch, surround suppression confers similar response properties to SA1 afferents; instead of being based on synaptic mechanisms, however, it is based entirely on mechanoreceptor sensitivity to a specific component of tissue strain near the nerve ending (strain energy density or a closely related component of strain; Phillips & Johnson, 1981; Srinivasan & Dandekar, 1996). As a consequence, SA1 afferents fire vigorously to points, edges, and curvature, and these responses are suppressed by the presence of stimuli in the surrounding skin (illustrated in Figure 8.2). Also, because of surround suppression, SA1 afferents are minimally responsive to uniform skin indentation; therefore, local spatial features such as edges and curves are represented strongly in the neural image conveyed by the peripheral SA1 population response. Combined psychophysical and neurophysiological experiments (reviewed later in this chapter) indicate that the SA1 system is responsible for form and texture perception.

RA afferent fibers also branch repeatedly as they near the epidermis. Each RA afferent ends in 30–80 Meissner's corpuscles (Johnson, Yoshioka, & Vega-Bermudez, 2000), which occur in dermal pockets between the sweat duct and adhesive ridges (Guinard, Usson, Guillermet, & Saxod, 2000; Munger & Ide, 1988). This puts Meissner's corpuscles, which lie in the dermis, as close to the surface of the epidermis as is possible (Quilliam, 1978); this may account, in part, for the RA's greater sensitivity to minute skin deformation relative to SA1 afferents, whose receptors are located on the tips of

the sweat-duct ridges. RA afferents innervate the skin of the fingerpad more densely than do the SA1 afferents. Based on combined data from humans and monkeys (Darian-Smith & Kenins, 1980; Johansson & Vallbo, 1976; Johansson & Vallbo, 1979b), which are not significantly different, the best estimates at the fingertip are 100 SA1 and 150 RA afferents/cm^2. This greater innervation density suggests a role for RA afferents in the two-dimensional representation of stimulus form, but RA afferents resolve the spatial details of tactile stimuli more poorly than do SA1 afferents. Their receptive field sizes depend strongly on stimulus intensity and are much larger than SA1 receptive fields at indentation levels that occur in ordinary tactile experience. The striking feature of RA responses is their sensitivity to minute skin motion. The effective operating range of indentations for RAs is about 4–400 μm; the comparable SA1 range is about 15–1,500 μm or more (Blake, Johnson, & Hsiao, 1997; Johansson, 1979; Mountcastle, Talbot, & Kornhuber, 1966; Vega-Bermudez & Johnson, 1999a). Thus, the SA1 and RA response properties are complementary. The RA and SA1 systems are in some ways like the scotopic and photopic systems in vision. The RA system, like the scotopic system, has greater sensitivity but poorer spatial resolution and limited dynamic range. The SA1 system, like the photopic system, is less sensitive but has higher spatial resolution and operates over a wider dynamic range. The neural response properties of RA afferents make them ideally suited for motion perception. In fact, combined psychophysical and neurophysiological studies show that the RA system is responsible for the perception of events that produce low-frequency, low-amplitude skin motion; that includes the detection of microscopic surface features, the detection of low-frequency vibration, and the detection of slip, which is critical for grip control (reviewed in Johnson et al., 2000).

Each PC afferent terminates in a single Pacinian corpuscle, which occurs in the dermis or the deeper tissues. The history, structure, and electrophysiological properties of this receptor are reviewed by Bell, Bolanowski, and Holmes (1994). The most striking feature of the PC response is its extreme sensitivity, which derives from mechanosensitive ion channels located in the unmyelinated ending within the corpuscle. Pacinian corpuscles respond with action potentials to vibratory amplitudes as small as 3 nm applied directly to the corpuscle (Bolanowski & Zwislocki, 1984) and 10 nm applied to the skin (Brisben, Hsiao, & Johnson, 1999). The corpuscles comprise multiple layers of fluid-filled sacs; these sacs act as a cascade of high-pass filters that shield the unmyelinated ending from the large, low-frequency deformations that accompany most manual tasks (Hubbard, 1958; Loewenstein & Skalak, 1966). If not for this intense filtering, the transducer, which is two orders of magnitude more sensitive than the other mechanoreceptive transducers, would be overwhelmed by most cutaneous stimuli. Because of their extreme sensitivity, receptive field boundaries are difficult to define. Some PCs have receptive fields that encompass an entire hand or even an entire arm; other PC's have receptive fields restricted to a single phalanx. There are about 2,500 Pacinian corpuscles in the human hand and they are about twice as numerous in the fingers as in the palm (about 350 per finger and 800 in the palm; reviewed in Brisben et al., 1999). Because of its small numbers and its large receptive fields, the PC population transmits little (if any) useful information about the spatial properties of a stimulus. Instead, it transmits very effectively information communicated by vibrations in objects, tools, or probes held in the hand (reviewed in Johnson et al., 2000).

SA2 afferents are distinguished from SA1 afferents by four properties: (a) Their receptive field areas are about five times larger than SA1 receptive fields and have borders that are not clearly demarcated (Johansson & Vallbo, 1980); (b) they are about six times less sensitive to skin indentation (Johansson & Vallbo, 1979a; Johansson, Vallbo, & Westling, 1980); (c) they are two to four times more sensitive to skin stretch (Edin, 1992); and (d) their interspike intervals are more uniform (Chambers, Andres, von Duering, & Iggo, 1972; Edin, 1992). SA2 afferents are thought to end in Ruffini complexes (Iggo & Andres, 1982), although the association of afferents with these response properties with a specific receptor is not as secure as it is with other cutaneous mechanoreceptors. Both SA1 and SA2 afferents respond to forces orthogonal and parallel to the skin surface, but between them the SA1 afferents are biased toward responsiveness to orthogonal forces, and SA2 afferents are biased toward parallel forces (Macefield, Hager-Ross, & Johansson, 1996). The poor SA2 responses to raised dot patterns (e.g., Braille patterns in Figure 8.4) and to curved surfaces suggest that they play no role in form perception (Phillips, Johansson, & Johnson, 1990). Because of SA2 responses to curved surfaces, Goodwin, Macefield, and Bisley (1997, p. 2887) conclude that "SA2 responses are unlikely to signal information to the brain about the local shape of an object." Because of their sensitivity to skin stretch, SA2s are well suited to signaling lateral forces such as active forces pulling on an object held in the hand. An interesting possibility is that they send a neural image of the pattern of skin stretch to the central nervous system when the hand moves about and that this neural image plays a significant or possibly even the dominant role in our perception of hand conformation (reviewed in Johnson et al., 2000) and of the direction of motion of an object moving across the skin (Olausson, Wessberg, & Kakuda, 2000).

Form and Texture Perception

The distinction between form and texture perception is that form perception concerns perception of the geometric structure of a surface or object, whereas texture perception corresponds to the subjective feel of a surface or object. Form perception depends on the specific geometry of a surface or object; texture perception depends on its distributed, statistical properties. Form perception has many dimensions; texture perception has only two or possibly three dimensions (see this chapter's section entitled "Texture Perception"). Form perception can be studied with objective methods (i.e., the subject's responses can be scored for accuracy); texture perception cannot. A sheet of Braille text provides an example of the distinction. After scanning a Braille passage with the fingertip, a Braille reader can be asked to report the content of the passage or to report how rough it felt. The subject's character- or word-recognition abilities can be scored for accuracy; the report of roughness cannot. Similarly, reports about the spacing or density of the Braille dots would be a product of form and not of texture perception.

Form Perception

Form perception is constant over a wide range of stimulus conditions. The ability to discriminate object or surface features and the capacity for pattern recognition at the fingertip are the same whether the object is contacted by active touch or is applied to the passive hand. Form perception is affected only marginally by whether the object is stationary or moving relative to the skin; it is unaffected by scanning speed up to 40 mm/s; it is unaffected by contact force, at least over the range from 0.2–1.0 N; and it is affected only marginally by the height (relief) of spatial features over a wide range of heights (Johnson & Lamb, 1981; Loomis, 1981, 1985; Phillips, Johnson, & Browne, 1983; Vega-Bermudez, Johnson, & Hsiao, 1991). The evidence presented in the following discussion shows that the SA1 system is responsible for form perception.

Figure 8.1 shows the results of three psychophysical studies of the human ability to discriminate stimuli with the distal pad

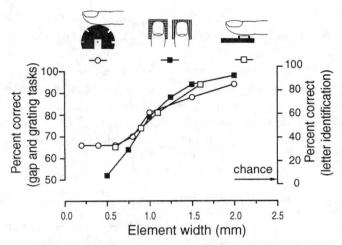

Figure 8.1 Human performance in gap detection (open circles), grating orientation discrimination (filled squares), and letter recognition (open squares) tasks. The abscissa represents the fundamental element width for each task, which was gap size for the gap detection task, bar width (half the grating period) for the grating orientation discrimination task, and the average bar and gap width within letters (approximately one fifth the letter height) for the letter recognition task. Threshold is defined as the element size producing performance midway between chance (50% correct for the gap and grating tasks, 1/26 for letter recognition) and perfect performance. Adapted from Johnson and Phillips, 1981.

of the index finger. In all three studies, the element width that resulted in performance midway between chance and perfect discrimination was between 0.9 and 1.0 mm, which is close to the theoretical limit set by the innervation density of SA1 and RA primary afferents at the fingertip. Acuity declines progressively from the index finger to the fifth finger (Vega-Bermudez & Johnson, 2001) and it declines progressively with age (Sathian, Zangaladze, Green, Vitek, & DeLong, 1997; J. C. Stevens & Choo, 1996; Wohlert, 1996). Whether these declines are due to differences in innervation density is not known. Spatial acuity at the lip and tongue is significantly better than that at the fingertip (Essick, Chen, & Kelly, 1999; Sathian & Zangaladze, 1996; Van Boven & Johnson, 1994). Tactile spatial acuity is the same in human and nonhuman primates (Hsiao, O'Shaughnessy, & Johnson, 1993).

The ability to discriminate gratings and letters with element widths around 1 mm means that at least one of the afferent systems must sustain a neural image with 1 mm resolution or better. That requires an innervation density of at least one afferent per square mm; it also requires that individual afferents be able to resolve the spatial details with a resolution that accounts for human discrimination performance. Neither the PC system nor the SA2 system comes close on either score (Johansson & Vallbo, 1979b). Note that the human performance illustrated in Figure 8.1 begins to rise above chance at element sizes around 0.5 mm, which means that either the SA1 or RA system must begin to resolve

spatial detail at about 0.5 mm. Evidence that only the SA1 afferents account for the human performance illustrated in Figure 8.1 comes from neurophysiological experiments in which SA1 and RA afferents were studied with periodic gratings. SA1 responses to a periodic grating convey information about spatial structure when the groove and ridge widths are 0.5 mm wide (Figure 8.2). When the grooves and ridges are 1 mm wide, SA1s provide a robust neural image of the stimulus. In contrast, RAs require grooves that are 3 mm wide or more before their responses begin to distinguish a grating from a flat surface; most RAs fail even to register

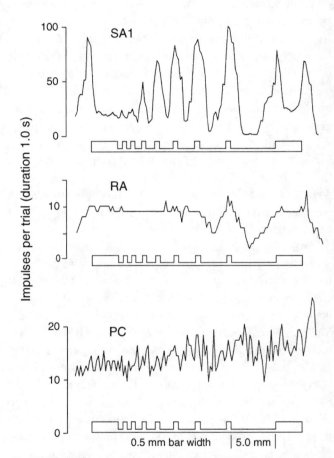

Figure 8.2 Responses of monkey SA1, RA, and PC afferents to a grating pressed into the skin. The grating is shown in cross-section beneath each response profile. The bars are 0.5 mm wide; the grooves are deeper than illustrated (2.0 mm deep) and are 0.5, 0.5, 0.75, 1.0, 1.5, 2.0, 3.0, and 5.0 mm wide. The responses displayed in each profile were obtained by indenting the skin to a depth of 1 mm, holding the indentation for 1 s, raising the grating, and then moving it laterally by 0.2 mm before the next indentation. The horizontal dimension of the response profile represents the location of the center of the receptive field relative to the grating; for example, the left peak in the SA1 response profile (approximately 95 imp/s) occurred when the center of the SA1 receptive field was directly beneath the left edge of the grating. The RA illustrated here was the most sensitive to the spatial structure of the grating of the 12 RA afferents that were studied. Some RAs barely registered the presence of the 5 mm gap even though they responded vigorously at all grating positions. Adapted from Phillips and Johnson, 1981.

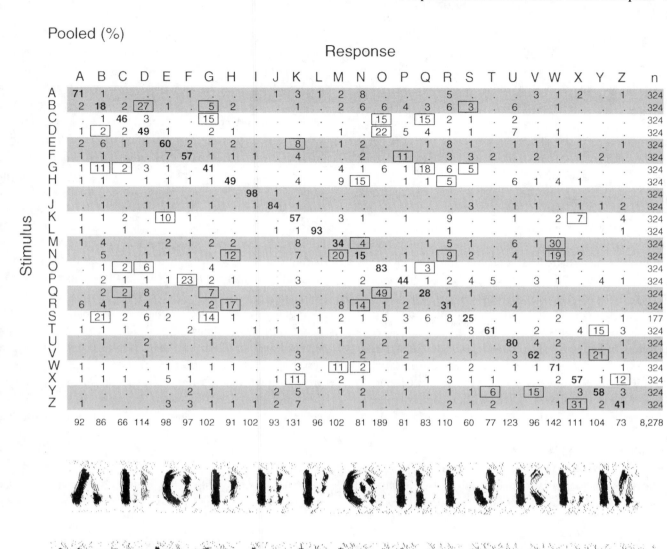

Figure 8.3 Confusion matrix of responses obtained from human letter recognition task (top) and responses of a monkey SA1 afferent to letter stimuli (*A–Z*), which approximates the neural image of letter stimuli conveyed to the brain (bottom). The confusion matrix is derived from the pooled results of 64 subjects who performed either the active or passive letter identification task. The letters were raised 0.5 mm above the background and were 6 mm high. Matrix entries represent the frequencies of all possible responses to each letter (e.g., the letter *A* was called *N* on 8% of presentations). The numbers in the bottom row represent column sums. The numbers in the rightmost column represent the number of presentations for each stimulus. Boxes around entries represent letter pairs whose mean confusion rates exceed 8%. For example, the mean confusion rate for *B* and *G* is 8% because *G* is called *B* on 11% of trials and *B* is called *G* on 5% of trials. The neural image (bottom) was derived from action potentials recorded from a single SA1 afferent fiber in a monkey. The stimuli consisted of the same embossed letters as in the letter recognition task scanned repeatedly from right to left across the receptive field of the neuron. Each black tick in the raster represents the occurrence of an action potential (see caption in Figure 8.4 for details). Adapted from Vega-Bermudez et al., 1991.

grooves 3 mm wide. The RA response illustrated in Figure 8.2 was the most sensitive to spatial detail of the 12 RAs that were studied. PC afferents were unable to resolve grooves that were 5 mm wide (Figure 8.2). Kops and Gardner (1996) obtained nearly identical results with an Optacon, which is a dense array of vibrotactile probes designed as a reading aid for the blind (Bliss, 1969).

The human ability to recognize raised letters of the alphabet when the letter heights are near threshold is illustrated in Figure 8.3. In this figure, we also show the response of a typical SA1 afferent to repeated scans of the same raised letters (Vega-Bermudez et al., 1991). In that study, Vega-Bermudez et al. (1991) showed that there was no detectable difference in human performance between active and passive touch and that the confusion matrix shown in Figure 8.3 is characteristic of human letter recognition performance across a wide range of stimulus conditions. Even the detailed patterns of identifications and errors were identical between active and passive touch. Accuracies in letter recognition ranged from 15% (N) to 98% (I) and more than 50% of the confusions were confined to 7% of all possible confusion pairs (22 out of 325 possible confusion pairs), which are enclosed in boxes in Figure 8.3. The confusions in all but 5 of those 22 pairs are highly asymmetric ($p < 0.001$). The frequency of occurrence of letters in English bears no relationship to the rates of correct responses, false positives, or total responses. Furthermore, excluding I, J, and L, which had high hit rates and low false-positive rates, there was no relationship between hit and false-positive rates. All of this evidence suggests that the response patterns are not the result of cognitive biases.

The pattern of confusions seems to be explained by the response of SA1 afferents to the letters, which is illustrated at the bottom of Figure 8.3. For example, B is identified as B on only 18% of trials; instead, it is called D 50% more often than it is called B. Conversely, D is virtually never called B (Figure 8.3 top). This pattern of confusion can be explained by the SA1 surround suppression mechanism discussed earlier, which suppresses the response to the central, horizontal bar of the B. The neural representation of the B resembles a D more than it does a B (see rasters at bottom of Figure 8.3), which accounts for the strong bias in the psychophysical studies towards the letter D. For another example, C is often

called G or Q, but G and Q are almost never called C. An explanation is that the participant learns quickly that internal and trailing features are often represented weakly or not at all; therefore, when the participant is presented with the letter C, lack of the features expected of a G or a Q in the neural representation is not a strong reason to not respond G or Q. Conversely, the strong representation of the distinctive features of the G and Q make confusion with a C unlikely. The performance illustrated in Figure 8.3 is for naive subjects in their first testing session. Performance improves steadily on repeated testing (Vega-Bermudez et al., 1991). One possible reason for the improvement is that subjects may learn the idiosyncracies of the neural representations (e.g., as soon as a participant recognizes the distinctive feature of the G in the neural representation, he or she is less likely to mistake a C for a G).

Figure 8.4 shows the responses of typical human cutaneous afferent responses to Braille symbols (top row) scanned over their receptive fields (Phillips et al., 1990). The responses of human afferents to these raised-dot patterns are indistinguishable from the responses of monkey afferents to similar patterns (Johnson & Lamb, 1981). SA1 afferents provide a sharp, isomorphic representation of the Braille patterns, RA provide a less sharply defined isomorphic representation, and PCs and SA2's provide no useful spatial information.

Neurophysiological studies with the Optacon show that it activates the RA and PC systems well but not the SA1

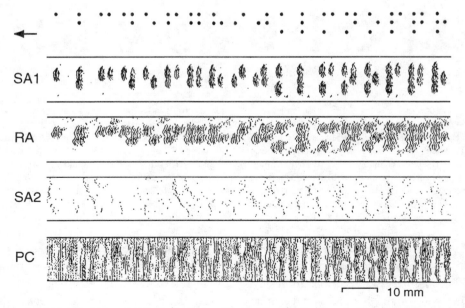

Figure 8.4   Responses of human SA1, RA, SA2, and PC afferent fibers to the Braille symbols corresponding to the letters *A–R*. The Braille symbols were scanned (60 mm/s) repeatedly from right to left over the afferent fibers' receptive fields (in effect, the receptive fields scanned from left to right). After each scan, the Braille pattern was shifted 0.2 mm at right angles to the scanning direction. Each black tick in the impulse rasters represents the occurrence of an action potential. Each row of the raster represents the response to a separate scan. The receptive fields were all on the distal fingerpads. Adapted from Phillips et al., 1990.

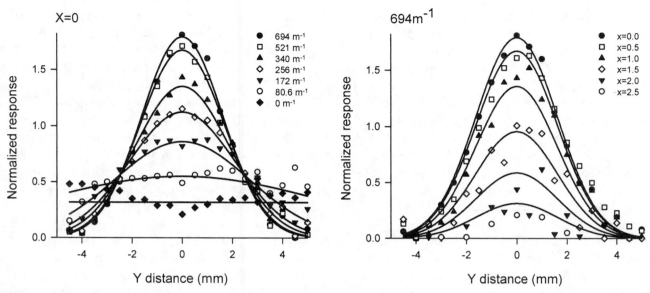

Figure 8.5 Population response of peripheral SA1 afferents to indentation with spheres of varying curvature. The left plot shows the mean responses of SA1 afferents as a function of proximal-distal distance from the center of indentation. Data are shown for seven curved surfaces with radii ranging from 1.4 mm (curvature = 694 m^{-1}) to a flat surface (curvature = 0 m^{-1}). The right plot shows population response profiles in proximal-distal slices at varying distances from the center of indentation. Adapted from Goodwin et al., 1995.

system; furthermore, these studies demonstrate that only the RA system can account for spatial pattern recognition performance with the Optacon (Gardner & Palmer, 1989; Palmer & Gardner, 1990). Therefore, the psychophysical studies employing the Optacon (J. C. Craig & Rollman, 1999) are studies of the form-processing capacity of the RA system. The results of those studies are exactly what one would predict based on the RA responses illustrated in Figure 8.2. For example, humans cannot discriminate the orientation of an Optacon grating pattern until the gaps in the grating exceed 5 mm width (Kops & Gardner, 1996).

Studies of curvature perception also implicate the SA1 system in form processing (Goodwin, Browning, & Wheat, 1995; Goodwin, John, & Marceglia, 1991; Goodwin & Wheat, 1992a, 1992b). Those studies show that estimates of curvature are unaffected by changes in contact area and force, and—conversely—estimates of force are unaffected by changes in curvature. This latter finding is particularly surprising, considering that SA1 firing rates are strongly affected by curvature and that SA1 mean firing rates are the most likely neural code for the perception of force (Goodwin et al., 1995; LaMotte & Srinivasan, 1993; Srinivasan & LaMotte, 1987). The psychophysical observations showing that curvature perception is unaffected by changes in contact area or force suggest that the spatial profile of neural activity is used for the perception of curvature and that a different neural code (e.g., total discharge rate) is used for the perception of force. Only the SA1 population response provides a

veridical representation of curvature that can account for the psychophysical observations (Dodson, Goodwin, Browning, & Gehring, 1998; Goodwin et al., 1995). The SA1 population responses to a wide range of curvatures are shown in Figure 8.5. RAs respond poorly to such stimuli and provide no signal that might account for the ability of humans to discriminate curvature (Goodwin et al., 1995; Khalsa, Friedman, Srinivasan, & LaMotte, 1998; LaMotte, Friedman, Lu, Khalsa, & Srinivasan, 1998).

Texture Perception

Multidimensional scaling studies have shown that texture perception includes soft-hard and smooth-rough as independent perceptual dimensions—surface hardness and roughness can occur in almost any combination, and they account for most or all of texture perception (Hollins, Bensmaïa, Karlof, & Young, 2000; Hollins, Faldowski, Rao, & Young, 1993). A third dimension (sticky-slippery) improves the multidimensional scaling fit in some subjects. Thus, it appears that texture perception has two strong dimensions and possibly a third weaker dimension.

Roughness. Roughness perception has been studied extensively (Blake, Hsiao, & Johnson, 1997; Connor, Hsiao, Phillips, & Johnson, 1990; Connor & Johnson, 1992; Hollins et al., 2000; Lederman, 1974; Meenes & Zigler, 1923; Meftah, Belingard, & Chapman, 2000; Sathian, Goodwin,

John, & Darian-Smith, 1989; S. S. Stevens & Harris, 1962; Yoshioka, Dorsch, Hsiao, & Johnson, 2001). These studies demonstrate that roughness perception is unidimensional (the test of unidimensionality being the ability to assign numbers on a unidimensional continuum and to make greater-than and less-than judgments); that it depends on element height, diameter, shape, compliance, and density; and that the relationship between roughness and the different element parameters is complex and nonlinear. Important early observations were that scanning velocity, contact force, and friction between the finger and a surface have minor or no effects on roughness magnitude judgments (Lederman, 1974; Taylor & Lederman, 1975).

The neural mechanisms of roughness perception have been studied in a series of combined psychophysical and neurophysiological studies (reviewed in Johnson et al., 2000). These studies suggest strongly that the neural mechanisms underlying roughness perception depend on the spatial variation (mean absolute difference) in firing rates between SA1 afferents with receptive field centers separated by 2–3 mm. This conclusion was derived through the use of the method of successive falsification (Platt, 1964; Popper, 1959), whereby psychophysical data from human participants were tested against neurophysiological data recorded from monkeys using the exact same stimuli and stimulus conditions. In this method, multiple working hypotheses are proposed, and a hypothesis is rejected only when there is no consistent (one-to-one) relationship between the neural measure and human performance. The favored hypothesis is the one that survives the hypothesis testing. The first study (Connor et al., 1990) rejected neural codes based on mean firing rate; the second study (Connor & Johnson, 1992) rejected all neural codes that depend on the temporal fluctuations in firing rates of the afferent fibers; the third study (Blake, Hsiao, et al., 1997) rejected all neural codes based on the firing of RA afferent fibers; the fourth study (Yoshioka et al., 2001) rejected all neural codes based on the firing of PC afferent fibers. The only neural code that consistently accounts for human roughness perception over surfaces with individual elements spaced from 0.1 to 6.2 mm apart and heights from 0.28 to 2.0 mm is one based on spatial variation of firing among SA1 afferent fibers. The correlation between the psychophysical roughness magnitude estimates and spatial variation in the SA1 discharge was greater than 0.97 in all four studies (see Figure 8.6).

Recent studies, reviewed in the following discussion, have shown that a subpopulation of neurons in area 3b of primary somatosensory cortex (SI) have receptive fields composed of spatially separated regions of excitation and inhibition. These neurons have discharge rates that are proportional to the difference in discharge rates that one would

expect between SA1 afferent fibers with receptive fields separated by 2–3 mm (DiCarlo & Johnson, 2000)—that is, the mechanism underlying their firing rates is exactly the one that was discussed earlier as the neural basis for roughness judgments. The mean firing rate of a population of such neurons would correspond closely to subjects' roughness judgments; moreover, like roughness perception, the mean firing rate would be affected only secondarily by scanning velocity and contact force (DiCarlo & Johnson, 1999). These results suggest that roughness perception may be based on the responses of a subpopulation of neurons in area 3b.

Softness. Softness (or its reciprocal, hardness) is the second major dimension of texture (Hollins et al., 2000). Softness is the subjective impression of the progressive change in conformation of a surface to the contours of the fingers that accompanies changes in contact force. The perception of softness is not to be confused with the perception of compliance. Although both are dependent on changes in contact force, compliance is a physical property of the surface being touched—consequently, discrimination of compliance, like dot spacing, is objective (i.e., can be scored for accuracy). In contrast, softness, like roughness, is a subjective sense. Perceived softness does not depend on the relationship between force and object displacement—the fact that the space bar on a computer keyboard gives way easily (is compliant) does not make it soft. A soft object conforms to the finger or hand as it is manipulated, but conformation is not sufficient; the keyboard keys that are molded to conform to the skin of a fingertip feel as hard as flat keys. A working hypothesis is that softness is signaled by the rate of growth of contact area with contact force and by the uniformity of pressure across the contact area.

The neural mechanisms of softness perception have not been studied systematically. Except for a study by Harper and Stevens (1964), most psychophysical studies have focused on the objective ability to discriminate compliance. Harper and Stevens showed that subjective softness judgments were related to the compliance of their test objects by a power function and that hardness and softness judgments were reciprocally related. The most extensive study of the ability of humans to discriminate compliance is by Srinivasan and LaMotte (1995), who used cutaneous anesthesia and various modes of stimulus contact to show that cutaneous information alone is sufficient to discriminate the compliance of objects with deformable surfaces. Subjects discriminate softness when an object is applied to the passive, immobile finger as accurately as they do when they actively palpate the object. Moreover, the study showed that this ability is unaffected when the velocity and force of application are randomized.

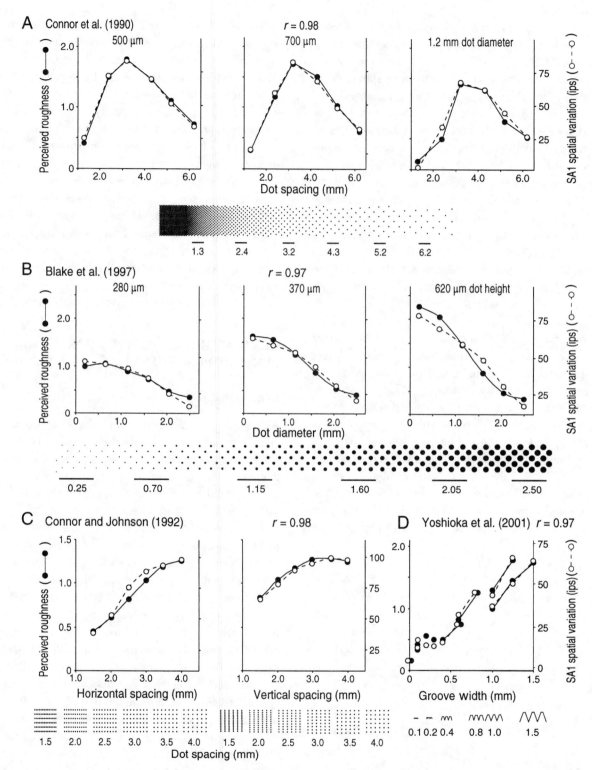

Figure 8.6 Human subjective magnitude roughness estimates and measures of spatial variation in firing rates among SA1 afferents of the monkey in four studies that used different textured surfaces. The left ordinate in each graph is the mean reported roughness. The right ordinate is the spatial variation in SA1 firing rates. The surface pattern used in each study is illustrated below the data to which it applies. The top row (A) shows results from Connor et al. (1990), who used 18 raised dot patterns with different dot spacings and diameters. The middle row (B) shows results from Blake, Hsiao, et al. (1997), who used 18 raised dot patterns with different dot heights and diameters. The two left graphs in the bottom row (C) show results from Connor and Johnson (1992), who varied pattern geometry to distinguish temporal and spatial neural coding mechanisms. The right graph shows data from Yoshioka et al. (2001), who used fine gratings with spatial periods ranging from 0.1 to 2.0 mm. The lines connect stimulus patterns with constant spatial periods.

There are no combined psychophysical and neurophysiological experiments that systematically address the neural mechanisms of softness perception, but the likely mechanism can be inferred from what we know about the response properties of each of the afferent types. Just as in roughness perception, the a priori possibilities are intensive, temporal, or spatial neural codes in one or more of the cutaneous afferent populations. Intensive codes are unlikely because random changes in velocity and force, which do not affect discrimination performance, have strong effects on afferent impulse rates (Srinivasan & LaMotte, 1996). Purely temporal codes seem unlikely because perceived softness (or hardness) is based on perceived changes in object form with changing contact force. Hence, the most likely mechanism is that softness is based on the dynamic changes in the profile of the population response of the SA1 afferents that occur when the finger comes into contact with a surface.

Texture Perception With a Probe.   When we use a tool or probe, we perceive distant events almost as if our fingers were present at the working surfaces of the tool or probe. An early demonstration of this was made by Katz (1925/1989), who showed that we can discriminate one textured surface from another as well with a probe as with a finger applied directly to the surfaces. He showed further that this capacity is lost when vibrations in the probe are damped. A recent study (Brisben et al., 1999) has shown that when subjects grasp a probe, transmitted vibrations with amplitudes less than 10 nm at the hand can be detected (the mean is 30 nm; see Figure 8.7). Only the PC system can account for this capacity.

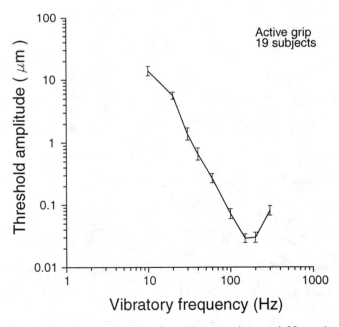

Figure 8.7 Vibratory detection for subjects grasping a rod 35 mm in diameter. Adapted from Brisben et al., 1999.

The hypothesis that the PC system is responsible for the perception of vibrations transmitted through an object held in the hand supposes not only that Pacinian receptors detect the transmitted vibration, but also that the PC population transmits a neural representation of the vibratory signal sufficient to account for this perceptual capacity. Work on the human ability to detect and discriminate complex vibratory stimuli supports this idea by showing that we are sensitive to the temporal structure of high-frequency stimuli that only activate PC afferents (Formby, Morgan, Forrest, & Raney, 1992; Lamore, Muijser, & Keemink, 1986; Weisenberger, 1986); for example, humans can discriminate the frequency with which a 250-Hz carrier stimulus is modulated for modulation frequencies as high as 60 Hz (Formby et al., 1992). In contrast, Bensmaïa and Hollins (2000) have shown that the discrimination of complex waveforms composed of high frequencies is poor; they have suggested that RA afferents may play a role in temporal coding.

CENTRAL MECHANISMS OF FORM AND TEXTURE PERCEPTION

Central Pathways

A principle of organization within the somatosensory system is that neurons responsible for the different aspects of sensory perception are separated into separate anatomical pathways that are modality specific. The division begins at the level of the peripheral nerves and continues as axons leaving the dorsal root ganglion send their projections into the spinal cord. Axons entering the spinal cord separate into two parallel paths (Figure 8.8). One—the *dorsal-column-medial-lemniscal pathway*—contains large- and medium-diameter myelinated fibers that ascend in the ipsilateral dorsal column to synapse on neurons in the dorsal column nuclei (DCN). This pathway is responsible for conveying information concerning both mechanoreceptive and proprioceptive function. The other pathway—the spinothalamic tract (STT)—conveys information from unmyelinated C fibers and small myelinated A-delta fibers that enter and terminate in the dorsal horn of the spinal cord. From there, the axons of the STT cross the midline to ascend in the anterolateral quadrant of the spinal cord. This pathway is primarily responsible for conveying information about pain and temperature. The division of function continues as second-order neurons in the DCN and dorsal horn send their axons to the thalamic nuclei (A. D. Craig & Dostrovsky, 1999; Jones, 1990; Jones & Friedman, 1982; Perl, 1998; Poggio & Mountcastle, 1960). For the dorsal-column-medial-lemniscal pathway, the second-order neurons terminate at the contralateral ventral posterior lateral nucleus of the thalamus (VPL), where afferents from the deep tissues are segregated from the cutaneous inputs (Jones & Friedman, 1982). Neurons

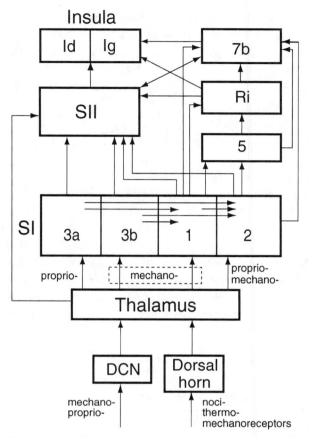

Figure 8.8   Schematic diagram of the somatosensory system. Arrowheads represent feed-forward projections (i.e., projections terminating in Layer IV of the target area). The two arrowheads in the connection between SII and 7b indicate that both areas have been reported to receive feed-forward projections. Feedback projections are not shown.

in VPL then send their projections to primary (SI) somatosensory cortex, whereas neurons in ventral posterior inferior nucleus (VPI) project to secondary (SII) somatosensory cortex (Friedman, Murray, O'Neill, & Mishkin, 1986; Jones & Burton, 1976; Jones & Friedman, 1982).

SI cortex is composed of four cytoarchitectonic areas (3a, 3b, 1, and 2) that receive the majority of their inputs from VPL. The connectivity is highly specific, with neurons in 3a and 2 receiving inputs from neurons in VPL that respond to proprioceptive stimuli and neurons in 3b and 1 receiving inputs from neurons in VPL that respond to cutaneous stimuli. The four areas of SI are also interconnected; neurons in 3a send a large projection to area 2 and a small projection to 1, neurons in 3b send their outputs to 1 and 2, and 1 sends its outputs to 2 (for a review, see Felleman & Van Essen, 1991). Based on these connections alone, one can infer that areas 3b and 1 are important for mechanoreceptive functions and that neurons in 3a and 2 are important for functions like stereognosis that require proprioceptive information (Landgren, Silfvenius, & Olsson, 1984).

There are two main projections from SI. One is toward areas 5, Ri, and 7b; the other is toward SII. SII also receives inputs from Ri and 7b and along with these areas sends its outputs to two separate divisions of the insula. Although in Figure 8.8 we have depicted SII as a single area, it is composed of two or more areas (reviewed later in this chapter). A working hypothesis with extensive support from both neurophysiological and ablation studies is that the main pathway underlying form and texture perception proceeds from the thalamus to SI cortex, then to SII cortex, and finally to the insula (Schneider, Friedman, & Mishkin, 1993).

SI Cortex

The segregation of function between the SA1, RA, SA2, and PC systems suggests that these afferent systems remain segregated to some degree in the central nervous system. However, considering how distinctly separate are the functions of the four afferent systems, it is surprising that there is little evidence to support the notion that these systems are segregated within SI cortex. One of the few definite claims that can be made is that 3b is important for form perception. In the remainder of this section on SI cortex, we review the neural mechanisms of form processing in area 3b.

Area 3b.   Removal of area 3b produces profound behavioral deficits in all somatosensory tasks tested, whereas removal of other SI areas appears to produce more specific deficits in the tactile discrimination of textures (area 1) and three-dimensional forms (area 2; Randolph & Semmes, 1974). Neurophysiological studies have shown that 3b has smaller receptive fields (Paul, Goodman, & Merzenich, 1972; Sur, Garraghty, & Bruce, 1985; Sur, Merzenich, & Kaas, 1980) and a higher proportion of cells responding to static skin indentation (Paul et al., 1972; Sur, Wall, & Kaas, 1984) than do other SI cortical areas. However, none of these observations is especially indicative of 3b playing a role in spatial information processing. The smaller receptive fields in 3b are almost certainly a consequence of 3b being at an earlier stage of processing within the somatosensory pathways (Bankman, Johnson, & Hsiao, 1990; Johnson, Hsiao, & Twombly, 1995). A continued response to sustained, steady indentation does imply that neurons in 3b receive inputs from slowly adapting afferents, but the converse is not true—a transient response may result from lack of slowly adapting input or, just as likely, delayed inhibition that shuts off the response to a sustained input (Andersson, 1965; DiCarlo & Johnson, 2000; Gardner & Costanzo, 1980; Innocenti & Manzoni, 1972; Sur et al., 1984).

A clue that 3b is specialized for processing spatial information comes from the relative expansions of the representations of the digits in areas 3b and 1. The cortical magnification factors (unit cortical area per unit body surface area) in areas 3b and 1 are approximately equal over most of the postcentral gyrus, except in the finger region, where spatial acuity is highest and the magnification in 3b climbs to approximately five times that in area 1 (Sur et al., 1980). Another clue comes from the response properties of neurons in 3b. When neurons with receptive fields on the fingerpads are stimulated with scanned, complex spatial stimuli, almost all of them yield responses that are more complex than can be accounted for by simple, excitatory receptive fields. It is evident from these responses that many neurons in 3b are responding to specific spatial features of the stimuli (Bankman et al., 1990; Hsiao, Johnson, Twombly, & DiCarlo, 1996; Johnson et al., 1995; Phillips, Johnson, & Hsiao, 1988). Responses of two SA neurons in area 3b are illustrated in Figure 8.9. The neuron illustrated in the top two rows of Figure 8.9 is clearly responding to the orientations of letter segments. The neuron illustrated in the bottom two rows has a complex response that is not easily

interpreted; for example, the central response to the letters appears to be completely suppressed by the horizontal bars within the *B*, *E*, and *F* but not the *H*. Thus, the neuronal responses in 3b suggest specialization for form processing rather than (for example) motion processing.

Receptive Fields in Area 3b. A recent series of studies with controlled, scanned stimuli has confirmed that there is little or no directional selectivity in area 3b and that 3b neuronal discharge rates are affected only mildly by changes in stimulus velocity across the skin (DiCarlo & Johnson, 1999, 2000; DiCarlo, Johnson, & Hsiao, 1998). They also show, however, that all neurons in 3b are selectively responsive to particular spatial patterns of stimulation, that they are sensitive to the orientation of these patterns, and that this selectivity is shaped as much by inhibition as it is by excitation. Previous studies have generally failed to identify this inhibition using a simple probe because it is manifested only as

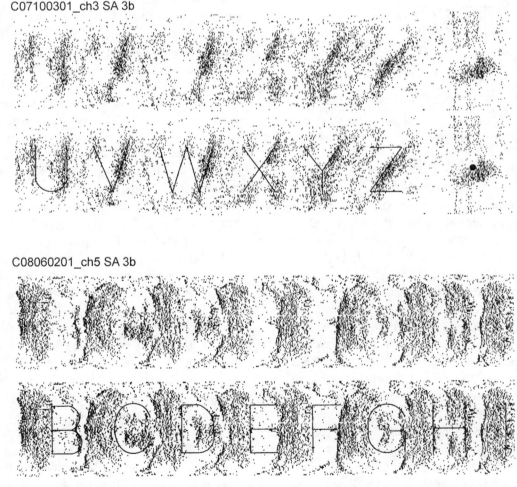

Figure 8.9 Responses of two SA neurons to letter stimuli (*U–Z:* top neuron; *B–H:* bottom neuron) recorded from Area 3b of the awake monkey. Letter height: 8.5 mm; scanning velocity: 50 mm/s; contact force: 60 g. Shown for each neuron are the neural responses without (top row) and with the stimulus letters. Details are the same as those in Figure 8.4.

a reduction of the response to a stimulus that simultaneously contacts both the excitatory and inhibitory parts of the receptive field. Ninety-five percent of 3b neuronal receptive fields have three components: (a) a single, central excitatory region of short duration (10 ms at most), (b) one or more inhibitory regions that are adjacent to and synchronous with the excitation, and (c) a larger inhibitory region that overlaps the excitation partially or totally and is delayed with respect to the first two components (by 30 ms on average). The remaining 5% have two or more regions of excitation.

The receptive fields of 247 area 3b neurons mapped with scanned, random-dot stimuli are illustrated in Figure 8.10, which shows that virtually all receptive fields are characterized by a single central region of excitation with inhibition on

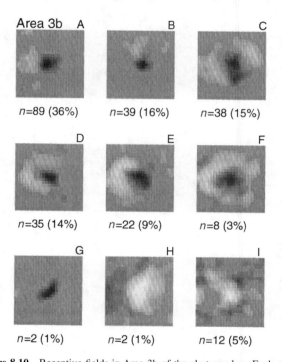

Figure 8.10 Receptive fields in Area 3b of the alert monkey. Each panel illustrates a typical example of a receptive field type, the total number of receptive fields of that type, and their percentage of the total receptive field sample (n = 247) from distal fingerpads. The gray scale represents the grid of excitation and inhibition (25 × 25 bins = 10 × 10 mm) that best described the neuron's response to a random stimulus pattern. Dark regions represent excitatory regions; lighter regions represent inhibitory regions. The uniform background gray level represents the region where stimuli had no effect. The types are shown in decreasing order of frequency: A. a single inhibitory region located on the trailing (distal) side of the excitatory region (left); B. a region of inhibition located on one of the three nontrailing sides of the excitatory region; C. two regions of inhibition on opposite sides of the excitatory region; D. inhibition on three sides of the excitatory region; E. inhibition on two contiguous sides of the excitatory region; F. a complete inhibitory surround; G. an excitatory region only; H. receptive field dominated by inhibition; and I. receptive fields not easily assigned to one of the preceding categories. Reprinted by permission from DiCarlo, J. J., Johnson, K. O., and Hsiao, S. S. (1998). Structure of receptive fields in area 3b of primary somatosensory cortex in the alert monkey. *Journal of Neuroscience, 18,* 2626–2645. Copyright 1998 by the Society for Neuroscience.

one, two, or three sides. Surround inhibition occurred rarely. The inhibitory area was, on average, about 30% larger than the excitatory area (means were 18 and 14 mm²) and—like the excitatory area—varied greatly (from 1–47 mm²). The inhibitory mass (absolute value of inhibition integrated over the entire inhibitory field), like the excitatory mass (comparable definition), varied by 50 to 1 between neurons (125–6,830 mass units; mean 1,620 mass units). There was no evidence of clustering into distinct receptive field types. The distributions of excitatory and inhibitory areas and masses were all Gaussian in logarithmic coordinates (i.e., lognormal); the excitatory and inhibitory masses were more closely correlated ($\rho = 0.56$) than were the areas ($\rho = 0.26$). Receptive fields mapped in this way accurately predict neuronal responses to stimulus features such as orientation (DiCarlo & Johnson, 2000).

Delayed Inhibition.   Area 3b neurons have two striking response properties that are not evident in Figure 8.10. The first is that the spatiotemporal structure of their neuronal responses and the spatial structures of their receptive fields are virtually unaffected by the velocity with which a stimulus moves across the skin or (conversely) how rapidly a finger is scanned over a surface for velocities up to at least 80 mm/s (DiCarlo & Johnson, 1999)—that is, the spatial structure of responses like the ones illustrated in Figure 8.9 are unaffected by changes in scanning velocity. Increasing scanning velocity causes a marked increase in the intensities of the excitatory and inhibitory subfields without affecting their geometries; this results in increased firing rates without any loss of the response selectivity conferred by the receptive field geometry. The mechanism of this increased responsiveness with increased velocity lies in an interaction between the excitation and the delayed inhibition (DiCarlo & Johnson, 1999).

The delayed inhibition confers a second property, which causes the geometry of the receptive field to be strongly scanning-direction-dependent (DiCarlo & Johnson, 2000). A typical example of a response that is dependent on scanning direction is shown in Figure 8.11. The receptive field at the left of each group of three receptive field diagrams is the receptive field obtained directly from the neuron's responses to random-dot stimuli scanned in one of the eight directions. This figure illustrates that regardless of scanning direction, there is a fixed region of inhibition distal and left of the central region of excitation. It can also be seen that there is a region of inhibition displaced in the scanning direction (opposite to the finger motion) from the region of excitation. To visualize this more clearly, each neuron's response was fitted with a three-component receptive field model comprising a Gaussian excitatory region and two Gaussian inhibitory

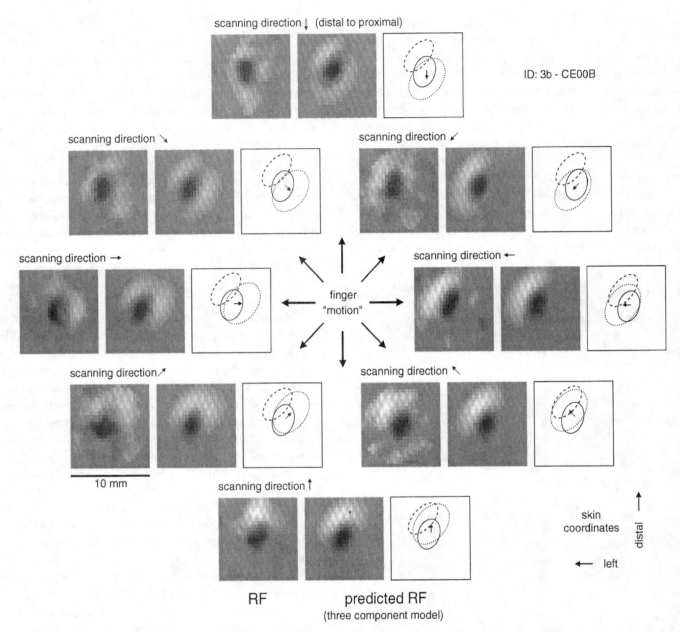

Figure 8.11 Receptive fields from a single Area 3b neuron of the alert monkey determined with the stimulus scanned in eight directions. The three squares in each group display the receptive field estimated from the raw data (left), the receptive field predicted by the three-component model (middle), and the positions of the model Gaussian components (right). The ellipses in the right square in each group are isoamplitude contours at 1.5 *SD*. The scanning direction is shown above each group. Each receptive field is plotted as if it were viewed through the dorsum of the finger with the finger pointed toward the top of the figure; the effect of relative motion between the finger and the stimulus pattern on the receptive field can be visualized by placing a fingerpad in the center of the figure and sliding it along the arrow labeled *finger motion* toward the receptive field of interest. Note how the locations of the model's excitatory (solid ellipse) and fixed inhibitory components (dashed ellipse) are unaffected by scanning direction and—similarly—how the lagged inhibitory component (dotted ellipse) trails the lag center by a fixed distance in each direction (the lag distance is the same in all directions because the scanning velocity was constant, 40 mm/s). The arrow in each right-hand square shows the displacement of the lagged inhibitory component due to scanning. The degree to which the model accounts for receptive field structure in each direction can be seen by comparing the left and middle panels in each group. Reprinted by permission from DiCarlo, J. J., and Johnson, K. O. (2000). Spatial and temporal structure of receptive fields in primate somatosensory area 3b: Effects of stimulus scanning direction and orientation. *Journal of Neuroscience, 20,* 495–510. Copyright 2000 by the Society for Neuroscience.

regions—one to simulate the region of fixed, synchronous inhibition and one to simulate the region of delayed inhibition. This model is illustrated by the simulated receptive field in the central panel in each group of three panels and by the corresponding diagram in the right panel. The degree to which the model description accounts for the observed receptive fields can be seen by comparing the model receptive field in the central panel and the actual receptive field in the left panel. This comparison shows that the three-component model explains the effect of scanning direction on receptive field shape well. The correlation between the model and observed receptive fields averaged 0.81 in 62 neurons studied with four or more scanning directions. Neurons with lower correlations all had a third, fixed region of inhibition not accounted for by the three-component model (i.e., they would have been described by the three components enumerated previously if the model had allowed for more than one region of fixed inhibition).

Functional Implications.   The wide range of receptive field geometries and the wide range of responses to complex, scanned stimuli found in 3b shows that the initial, isomorphic neural representation of spatial form that prevails in the periphery gives way to an altered form of representation in which neuronal responses represent the presence of specific features. The more complex responses observed in SII cortex (Hsiao et al., 1996) suggest that 3b is an intermediate step in a series of transformations leading to a more complex form of representation (Bankman et al., 1990; DiCarlo et al., 1998; Johnson et al., 1995).

The fixed inhibitory components of each neuron's receptive field interacts with the central excitation to act as a spatial filter, conferring selectivity for particular spatial features or patterns regardless of scanning direction and velocity. For example, when the fixed inhibition lies on two adjacent sides, the neuron is more responsive to corners that protrude into the excitatory subfield without activating the inhibitory subregions. When the fixed inhibitory subfield occupies a single location on one side of the excitatory subfield, both tend to be elongated and to lie parallel to one another; as a result, the neuron is more responsive to edges oriented parallel to the two subregions (DiCarlo & Johnson, 2000; DiCarlo et al., 1998).

The delayed inhibitory component serves three functions. First, it confers sensitivity to stimulus gradients in the scanning direction, regardless of that direction. The delayed inhibition suppresses the response to uniform surfaces and thereby emphasizes the effects of spatial or temporal novelty. When scanning the finger over a surface, features first activate the regions of excitation and fixed inhibition and then 30 ms later activate the lagged inhibition. Second, when the delayed inhibition is centered on the excitation it produces a progressive increase in discharge rate with increasing scanning velocity. The acquisition of tactile spatial information by scanning one's finger over a surface compensates for the very limited field of view provided by a single fingerpad. It is clearly an advantage to be able to scan one's fingers over an object or a surface rapidly without loss of information. Psychophysical experiments demonstrate that performance in pattern recognition is unaffected as scanning rate increases from 20 to 40 mm/s, and then only a small loss is observed as the rate is

increased to 80 mm/s (Vega-Bermudez et al., 1991). In the absence of a compensatory mechanism, rapid scanning has a substantial cost. As scanning velocity increases, each stimulus element spends less time within the receptive field (reduced dwell time) and the element is represented by fewer action potentials. The delayed inhibition provides a compensatory mechanism that increases the firing rate with increasing scanning velocity. As velocity increases, the delayed inhibition lags progressively to expose more excitation. Consequently, the excitatory and inhibitory components of the receptive field grow rapidly in intensity, with no effect on receptive field geometry. The result is a representation of spatial form that is invariant with scanning velocity and that is more intense than it would be without this mechanism (DiCarlo & Johnson, 1999). Third—and least significant—is that direction sensitivity occurs when the delayed inhibition is displaced from the center of excitation (Barlow & Levick, 1965; DiCarlo & Johnson, 2000; Gardner & Costanzo, 1980; Warren, Hämäläinen, & Gardner, 1986); this is because motion in the direction of the displacement exposes progressively more excitation, which produces a progressively greater discharge rate. Motion in the opposite direction shifts the delayed inhibition over the center of excitation, thereby reducing the discharge rate. The center of the delayed inhibition in area 3b is, with few exceptions, close to the center of excitation, which may explain why so few neurons in 3b exhibit directional selectivity. When the center of the delayed inhibition is displaced from the center of excitation, it predicts the neuron's directional selectivity accurately (DiCarlo & Johnson, 2000).

SII Cortex

SII was first described in the early 1940s. Adrian (1941) reported a second tactile area in the ectosylvian gyrus of the cat; he hypothesized that this area was specialized for processing information from the animal's paw. Woolsey (1943) studied this area more extensively and reported that it also existed in both dogs and monkeys; furthermore, he found that it contained a complete somatotopically organized representation of the body surface. Since those initial studies, the functional role and detailed organization of SII has remained elusive. Neurophysiological mapping studies (Robinson & Burton, 1980c; Whitsel, Petrucelli, & Werner, 1969), anatomical tracer studies in macaque monkeys (Burton, Fabri, & Alloway, 1995; Friedman & Murray, 1986; Krubitzer, Clarey, Tweedale, Elston, & Calford, 1995), and recent neural imaging studies in humans (Disbrow, Roberts, & Krubitzer, 2000) show that SII cortex extends approximately 10 mm across the upper bank of the lateral sulcus and that what was initially identified as SII cortex comprises two separate areas—SII and parietal ventral cortex (Krubitzer et al., 1995), which are also called SIIp and

SIIr (Burton & Sinclair, 1996; Whitsel et al., 1969). Although these areas have separate somatotopic maps, the functional roles that they play in tactile perception are not known.

Evidence from anatomical tracer studies (Friedman & Murray, 1986) and from studies in which areas of cortex were selectively deactivated by cooling suggest that SI and SII process information in parallel (G. M. Murray, Zhang, Kaye, Sinnadurai, Campbell, & Rowe, 1992; Zhang et al., 1996), whereas lesion (Pons, Garraghty, Friedman, & Mishkin, 1987) and neurophysiological studies (Burton & Sinclair, 1990; Hsiao et al., 1993) suggest otherwise. In the cooling studies, Rowe and his colleagues were unable to abolish SII responses by cooling SI cortex, which suggests that SI and SII process information in parallel (Zhang et al., 1996). In contrast, Pons et al. (1987) provided strong evidence for serial processing. When SI is ablated, neurons in SII become silent; when SII is ablated, neurons in SI remain active (Pons, Wall, Garraghty, Cusick, & Kaas, 1987). In other studies they showed that selective lesions in the subregions that constitute SI result in modality-selective deficits in the response properties of neurons in SII (Garraghty, Pons, & Kaas, 1990; Pons, Garraghty, & Mishkin, 1992). Neurophysiological evidence from single-cell studies supports the hypothesis that SII lies at a processing stage higher than that of SI. Neurons in SI tend to have small, simple receptive fields confined to one (area 3b) or a few digits on a single hand (Iwamura, Tanaka, Sakamoto, & Hikosaka, 1983; Sur et al., 1984). In contrast, neurons in SII tend to have larger and more complex receptive fields that span multiple digits on one or both hands (reviewed in the next section of this chapter). A third line of evidence supporting the serial hypothesis is that almost all of the neurons in SII are strongly affected by the animal's focus of attention, suggesting that this area is closely related to higher cognitive aspects of tactile perception.

Role of SII in Tactile Processing.   SII cortex plays an important role in texture and two- and three-dimensional shape processing. Ettlinger and his colleagues demonstrated that monkeys with ablations of SII were unable to perform almost all tactile tasks that required touch (Garcha & Ettlinger, 1978; Ridley & Ettlinger, 1976). In addition, they found that animals that had SII cortex ablated were impaired in their ability to learn new tasks and were unable to do tasks that required intermanual transfer of information. Murray and Mishkin (1984) showed that when SII was ablated, monkeys were unable to discriminate texture (hard vs. soft and rough vs. smooth), form (square vs. diamond and convex vs. concave shapes), and object orientation (horizontal vs. vertical) and were significantly impaired in size discrimination (small

vs. large objects). Furthermore, they showed that SII and not area 5 is important for these functions because animals with lesions confined to area 5 showed no deficits on the same tasks (Murray & Mishkin, 1984).

Neurophysiological studies support the idea that SII is further along the pathways responsible for processing tactile form. Neurons in SII tend to have large receptive fields that often span multiple digits on the same hand (receptive fields < 10 cm^2, Robinson & Burton, 1980a) and respond to stimulation of both hands (Burton & Carlson, 1986; Cusick, Wall, Felleman, & Kaas, 1989; Robinson & Burton, 1980a; Whitsel et al., 1969; Sinclair & Burton, 1993). Stimulus selectivity varies widely in SII cortex. Some SII neurons are activated by light touch, whereas others require complex stimuli (Burton & Sinclair, 1990, 1991; Chapman, Zompa, Williams, Shenasa, & Jiang, 1996; Ferrington & Rowe, 1980; Fitzgerald, Lane, Yoshioka, Nakama, & Hsiao, 1999; Hsiao et al., 1993; Pruett, Sinclair, & Burton, 2000; Robinson & Burton, 1980b; Sinclair & Burton, 1993).

Recently Fitzgerald et al. (1999) used oriented bars as stimuli and found that approximately 30% of the neurons in SII cortex showed orientation-tuned responses. The preferred orientations of these neurons were approximately uniformly distributed across the eight orientations that were tested. In addition, they found that most of those neurons showed similar orientation tuning preferences between phalanges and between digits. They hypothesized that these orientation-sensitive neurons could be part of a network that is involved in generating a positionally invariant representation of tactile stimuli or could be involved in representing shape information for objects that span multiple digits. The results from studies in SII using embossed letters suggest that SII lies at a processing stage higher than that of SI. First, unlike neurons in SI, none of the neurons in SII show isomorphic responses. Instead, the responses tend to be highly nonisomorphic and feature selective. Examples of two neuronal responses to scanned letters are shown in Figure 8.12. These neurons responded well to trailing features and to specific local features such as the leading parts of the letters *C* and *D* but not to the leading parts of the letters *B* and *E* (Figure 8.12).

Several studies have investigated the responses of neurons in SII to vibration and to textured patterns. Two separate studies that used vibratory stimuli report that many neurons in SII show phase-locking to both low- and high-frequency vibrations (Burton & Sinclair, 1991; Ferrington & Rowe, 1980). The degree of phase-locking was greater for SII neurons than for SI neurons, suggesting that vibratory information may bypass SI cortex (Ferrington & Rowe, 1980). Studies using active and passive scanning of gratings suggest that neurons in SII are sensitive to textured stimuli (Jiang,

SII-SA (C12170304_ch4, 8.0 mm, 20 mm/s)

SII-SA (C12180204_ch4, 8.0 mm, 20 mm/s)

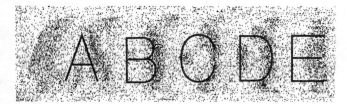

Figure 8.12   Responses of two SA neurons in Area SII of the alert monkey to letters 8 mm high, scanned at 20 mm/s. Superimposed over the rasters are the stimulus letters *ABCDE*. Adapted from Hsiao, S. S., Johnson, K. O., Twombly, I. A., & DiCarlo, J. J. (1996). Form processing and attention effects in the somatosensory system. In O. Franzén, R. S. Johansson, & L. Terenius (Eds.), *Somesthesis and the neurobiology of the somatosensory cortex* (pp. 229–247). Basel, Switzerland: Birkhäuser Verlag.

Tremblay, & Chapman, 1997; Pruett et al., 2000; Sinclair & Burton, 1993). These studies demonstrated that the firing rates of many neurons in SII show monotonic increases (or decreases) in firing rate as the spatial period of a grating is increased. One of these studies (Jiang et al., 1997) reported that the majority of the neurons in SII that responded to the textured surfaces showed responses that were more related to the differences in spatial periods than to the spatial periods themselves.

ATTENTION

Psychophysics of Tactile Attention

Selective attention plays an important role in sensory processing. Cross-modal studies in which attention is switched between touch and a visual or auditory stimulus suggest that attention has a limited capacity. In one series of studies, Chapman and her colleagues asked participants to direct or divide their focus of attention between the onset of either a 40-Hz vibration or a light (Post & Chapman, 1991) or detect the occurrence of a textured stimulus and a light (Zompa & Chapman, 1995). In both studies, the stimuli were preceded with cues that directed participants' attention either toward or away from the correct stimulus or directed their attention to both stimuli (divided attention task). They found that the

attentional resources are limited and that subjects had the shortest reaction times when cued correctly, intermediate reaction times when given the neutral cue, and the longest reaction times when cued incorrectly. Different results are found when attention is switched between tactile stimuli at multiple skin sites. Shiffrin, Craig, and Cohen (1973) had participants detect the occurrence of vibrations presented at three different locations on the body (thenar eminence of the right hand, tip of left index finger, and the forearm); participants were cued either to direct their attention to the correct site or to divide their attention between the three sites. In contrast to the cross-modal studies, they found that there was no difference in performance in the directed and divided conditions. Similarly, J. C. Craig (1985) found that there were minimal differences in performance when attention was directed to a single hand or was divided between the two hands. These studies suggest that under certain circumstances the capacity of attention may be large.

Focus of Attention

Several studies show that attention may function like a cognitive spotlight, so to speak. Lakatos and Shepard (1997) reported that the time it takes to discriminate the presence or absence of a tactile stimulus depends on the distance between the cued site and the test locations. A surprising finding was that the critical distance was not related to the somatotopic distance (i.e., anatomical distance along the body surface between the tested sites) but instead was related to the straight-line distance between the two test sites (Lakatos & Shepard, 1997). Driver and Grossenbacher (1996) reported similar results in studies in which they delivered vibrotactile stimuli to hands that were either together or spread apart. They also showed that reaction times for detecting stimuli on the relevant hand decreased when participants oriented their heads toward the hand; these results were unaffected when the participants were blindfolded. These studies indicate that the coordinate system for attention is based on an internal representation of extrapersonal space and that proprioception plays a role in selective attention.

The spotlight of attention appears to have a minimum aperture size. The fundamental finding is that vibrotactile stimuli presented on a single hand tend to interact. For example, J. C. Craig (1985) showed that there is a decrement in performance when individuals are told to attend to a single finger and competing stimuli are presented on other fingers of the same hand; if identical stimuli are presented on target and nontarget fingers, then performance is improved. Similar results were reported by Franzén, Markowitz, and Swets (1970), who showed that vibrotactile stimuli presented to two fingers on the same hand interact. These studies suggest that the hand may be under a single attentional focus. In contrast, there appears to be minimal interference when stimuli are presented simultaneously to both hands. Evans and Craig (1991) reported that nontarget distractors have minimal effects when stimuli are presented to fingers on different hands. Similarly, J. C. Craig (1985) asked participants to combine pattern fragments presented to two fingers on the same or opposite hands. He found that individuals integrated the pattern fragments with greater accuracy when they were presented to two fingers on opposite hands than when they were presented to adjacent fingers of the same hand. He also showed that the participants' performance on tasks in which the stimuli were presented on fingers on opposite hands was unaffected by the spatial separation between the two hands.

Using a search task, Klatzky, Lederman, and O'Neil (1996) showed that features based on surface properties (e.g., rough-smooth, hard-soft, and cool-warm) and surface discontinuities tended to have flat reaction time slopes (RT slopes < 30 ms per distractor item), whereas other features such as bar orientation have steep reaction time slopes. Features based on three-dimensional contours had intermediate reaction times. Whang, Burton, and Shulman (1991) and Sathian and Burton (1991) performed similar studies using vibratory and textured stimuli; they showed that selective attention is only minimally required to detect a change in texture or vibration (Sathian & Burton, 1991; Whang et al., 1991). Recently Sinclair, Kuo, and Burton (2000) showed that attention can selectively separate vibration frequency and roughness from stimulus duration.

Effects of Attention on Responses of Neurons in the Somatosensory System

The focus of attention has been shown to affect even the earliest stages of information processing within the somatosensory system. Hayes, Dubner, and Hoffman (1981) reported that the neuronal responses in the dorsal horn of the spinal cord were modulated by the attentional focus of animals performing thermal and light discrimination tasks. Although Poranen and Hyvärinen (1982) reported no effects of attention on neurons in the ventral posterior area of the thalamus (VP), other studies have reported that attention has small but significant effects on the response of these neurons. Bushnell, Duncan, Dubner, Fang, and He (1984) found a small number of neurons that were affected by the animal's attentional focus, and recently Morrow and Casey (2000) showed that a small but significant number of neurons (7/18) in VPL showed attention-modulated responses.

Similar descriptions of attention-modulated responses have been reported in SI cortex. In an early study, Hyvärinen, Poranen, and Jokinen (1980) recorded from neurons in SI cortex of animals trained to perform a vibration detection task; they found that about 8% of the neurons in area 3b and about 22% of the neurons in area 1 were affected by the animals' focus of attention. Furthermore, they reported that all of these neurons showed enhanced responses. In another study, Poranen and Hyvärinen (1982) found that the attentional state had minimal effects on the neural responses. In both of those studies, the effects could have been due to arousal because the effects were assessed by comparing neural responses when the animals were performing the detection task with responses while the animal sat passively. Hsiao et al. (1993) controlled for arousal effects by recording from animals trained to perform a tactile letter discrimination task and a visual detection task. During both tasks, the same tactile stimuli were scanned across the distal pads of the animals' hands, and the effects of attention were assessed by comparing the responses recorded during the two attentional states. They found that 50% of SI neurons had increased firing rates when the animal attended to the tactile stimulus. Furthermore, the firing rates were increased only during the presentation of letters that counted toward receiving a reward. For example, during the reward period or during timeout periods triggered by a false-positive response, the neural response rates were the same as they were when the animal was performing the visual task. Figure 8.13 shows examples of the effect of attention on the responses of neurons in SI and SII cortex. This figure shows the responses of neurons to a target letter (*) and the following nontarget letter that the animal learned was behaviorally irrelevant (i.e., the animal learned it could not receive a reward for letters following target letters). Both neurons showed a significant increase in neural activity when the animal performed the tactile task relative to the visual task. The effect was not simply a change in gain; it was also a change in the form of the neural response to the stimulus (Figure 8.13). Burton and Sinclair (2000) recorded from neurons in animals trained to detect a change in vibratory amplitude. They also reported that about 50% of neurons in SI cortex are affected by the animal's focus of attention.

Recent studies indicate that neurons in SI cortex have altered responses during the delay period in a memory-related task (Zhou & Fuster, 1996, 1997). In those studies, animals were trained to perform either a tactile-tactile match or a cross-modal visual-tactile match. They found that during the delay period between the stimuli, many neurons in all four areas of SI cortex showed sustained rate changes. These

A. SII - SA : C13110201_ch0

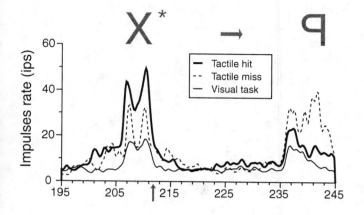

B. SI - SA : C13290201_ch5

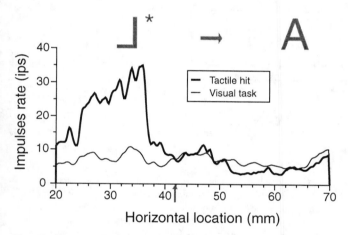

Figure 8.13 Effects of attention on neural responses of neuron in SI (B) and SII cortex (A) of an awake, behaving monkey. The animal is engaged in either a tactile letter discrimination task or visual detection task. In the tactile task, the animal was rewarded for responding to the target letters (indicated by *) that scanned across its distal fingerpad. In the visual task, the animal was rewarded for responding when a light dimmed. The abscissa in each panel represents the linear positions of the raised letters within the entire stimulus pattern (mm). The pattern was scanned repeatedly across the neuron's receptive field (15 mm/s) while the animal's attention was directed back and forth between the tactile and visual tasks at 3-min intervals. The ordinate represents mean impulse rate evoked by the letters during repeated scans of the drum. The thick solid, dashed, and thin solid lines represent impulse rates during and after hits and misses and during the visual task. The arrow on each abscissa represents the mean location of the monkey's response to the target letters in the tactile task. Adapted from Hsiao et al. (1993).

studies suggest that neurons in SI may participate in the short-term memory of tactile stimuli.

Studies in SII show that attention has more profound effects on the responses of neurons in SII than in SI cortex. Based on multiunit recordings, Poranen and Hyvärinen (1982) found that whereas attention had minimal effects on

the responses of neurons in SI, all of the neurons in SII were affected. Similarly, Hsiao et al. (1993) reported that 80% of the neurons in SII were affected by attention and that the effects were divided between increased (58%) and decreased (22%) neural firing rates. Burton, Sinclair, Hong, Pruett, and Whang (1997) studied animals performing a vibration detection task and found that 45% of the neurons in SII cortex were affected by the animal's focus of attention. They showed that the responses were generally suppressed during the early phases and enhanced during the late phases of a trial.

A modification of impulse rate is only one of the ways that attention might affect the responses of a neuron. Studies in SI and SII cortex employing multiple electrodes have shown that synchronous firing between neurons may play an important role in tactile information processing (A. Roy, Steinmetz, Hsiao, Johnson, & Niebur, 2001; S. Roy & Alloway, 1999; Steinmetz et al., 2000). S. Roy and Alloway (1999) observed that more than 60% of the neuron pairs in SI fired synchronously and that the degree of synchronous firing increased when stimuli were moved across the skin. Steinmetz et al. (2000) investigated the synchrony of neuronal discharge in SII cortex in animals trained to switch their attention between a visual task and a tactile discrimination task. They reported that a large fraction of the neuron pairs in SII cortex fired synchronously and—more important—that the degree of synchrony was affected by the animal's focus of attention (Figure 8.14). On average 17% of the neuron pairs that fired synchronously showed changes in the degree of synchrony when the animal switched its focus of attention from the visual to the tactile task. In addition, the percentage of neurons that showed changes in synchrony differed between the three animals in a predictable way. Thirty-five percent of the neuron pairs showed changes in synchrony in the animal performing the most difficult tactile task, whereas only 9% of the neuron pairs were affected in the animal performing the easiest task.

These findings suggest that attention may operate by changing the synchrony of firing of selected neurons. Synchronous firing between neurons that have a common target produces larger excitatory postsynaptic potentials in the target neuron than does asynchronous firing and is therefore more effective at driving the target neuron. Hence, when the firing in a subpopulation is made more synchronous by attention, the message contained in that subpopulation is selected preferentially for further processing. Changes in firing synchrony may be the neural correlate of selective attention.

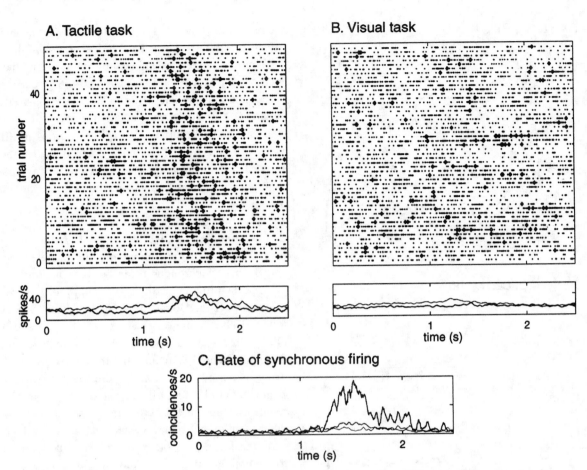

A. Tactile task

B. Visual task

C. Rate of synchronous firing

Figure 8.14   Effect of attention on synchrony in firing of a typical neuron pair (red and green in A and B) in monkey cortical SII. The response rasters are triggered at the onsets of 50 tactile stimulus periods while the monkey performs the tactile letter discrimination task (A) and the visual dim detection task (B; see legend for Figure 8.13). Each row in the raster represents one stimulus period, 2.5 s long, corresponding to the presentation of one letter. The letter enters the receptive field at about 1.25 s. Red and green dots represent the action potentials of the two neurons. Peristimulus time histograms are shown below each raster plot with corresponding colors. Synchronous events, defined as spikes from each neuron within 2.5 ms of each other, are represented as blue diamonds. The number of synchronous events is much higher when attention is directed towards the tactile stimuli. This change in synchrony is also apparent in plots of rates of synchronous events shown in C: blue curve—tactile task, red curve—visual task, violet curve—coincidences expected by chance. Reprinted by permission from *Nature, 404,* Steinmetz et al., Attention modulates synchronized neuronal firing in primate somatosensory cortex, 187–190. Copyright 2000 Macmillan Magazines Ltd.

SUMMARY

In this chapter we have reviewed the peripheral neural mechanisms of tactile sensation, the neural mechanisms in SI and SII cortex, and the effects of attention on information processing in the somatosensory pathways. Three decades of combined psychophysical and neurophysiological experiments suggest a sharp division of function among the four cutaneous afferent systems that innervate the human hand. The SA1 system provides a high-quality neural image of the spatial structure of objects and surfaces that contact the skin; this is the basis of form and texture perception. The RA system provides a neural image of motion signals from the whole hand. From this image, the brain extracts information that is critical for grip control and also information about the motion of objects contacting the skin. The PC system provides a neural image of

vibrations transmitted from objects grasped in the hand. The SA2 system provides a neural image of skin stretch, which changes as hand conformation changes. The evidence is less secure, but the most likely hypothesis is that the brain extracts information from the SA2 population response about hand conformation and the direction of motion of objects moving across the skin. SI and SII cortex transform information from the four afferent systems to an altered form of representation that is still not well understood.

This review concentrated on the processing of spatially patterned stimuli. Neurons in Area 3b of SI cortex, which is the first cortical somatosensory processing area, have small receptive fields restricted to a single finger. These neurons have responses that are selective for the local spatial features of a stimulus. Neurons in SII cortex have more complex responses and often have receptive fields that span multiple fingers or both hands. Neurons in SII cortex are—like neurons in SI cortex—orientation selective, and the orientation selectivity is consistent over multiple fingers on the same hand. These responses may represent a mechanism that confers position invariance (i.e., responses to a stimulus are the same regardless of position), or they may indicate a mechanism that integrates information across multiple fingers, which is necessary for object recognition. Selective attention is an important mechanism in sensory processing. Neurophysiological studies show that attention affects neuronal responses at the very first level of processing within the somatosensory pathways (the dorsal horn of the spinal cord) and becomes progressively more important at higher levels within the system. In SII cortex, the focus of attention has a profound affect on the responses of single neurons and on the temporal patterning of neural activity between neurons.

REFERENCES

Adrian, E. D. (1941). Afferent discharges to the cerebral cortex from peripheral sense organs. *Journal of Physiology, 100,* 159–191.

Andersson, S. A. (1965). Intracellular postsynaptic potentials in the somatosensory cortex of the cat. *Nature, 205,* 297–298.

Bankman, I. N., Johnson, K. O., & Hsiao, S. S. (1990). Neural image transformation in the somatosensory system of the monkey: Comparison of neurophysiological observations with responses in a neural network model. *Cold Spring Harbor Symposia on Quantitative Biology, 55,* 611–620.

Barlow, H. B., & Levick, W. R. (1965). The mechanism of directionally selective units in rabbit's retina. *Journal of Physiology, 178,* 477–504.

Bell, J., Bolanowski, S. J., & Holmes, M. H. (1994). The structure and function of Pacinian corpuscles: A review. *Progress in Neurobiology, 42,* 79–128.

Bensmaïa, S. J., & Hollins, M. (2000). Complex tactile waveform discrimination. *Journal of the Acoustical Society of America, 108,* 1236–1245.

Blake, D. T., Hsiao, S. S., & Johnson, K. O. (1997). Neural coding mechanisms in tactile pattern recognition: The relative contributions of slowly and rapidly adapting mechanoreceptors to perceived roughness. *Journal of Neuroscience, 17,* 7480–7489.

Blake, D. T., Johnson, K. O., & Hsiao, S. S. (1997). Monkey cutaneous SAI and RA responses to raised and depressed scanned patterns: Effects of width, height, orientation, and a raised surround. *Journal of Neurophysiology, 78,* 2503–2517.

Bliss, J. C. (1969). A relatively high-resolution reading aid for the blind. *IEEE Transactions on Man-Machine Systems, 10,* 1–9.

Bolanowski, S. J., & Zwislocki, J. J. (1984). Intensity and frequency characteristics of Pacinian corpuscles: Pt. 1. Action potentials. *Journal of Neurophysiology, 51,* 793–811.

Brisben, A. J., Hsiao, S. S., & Johnson, K. O. (1999). Detection of vibration transmitted through an object grasped in the hand. *Journal of Neurophysiology, 81,* 1548–1558.

Burton, H., & Carlson, M. (1986). Second somatic sensory cortical area (SII) in a prosimian primate, *Galago crassicaudatus. Journal of Comparative Neurology, 247,* 200–220.

Burton, H., Fabri, M., & Alloway, K. D. (1995). Cortical areas within the lateral sulcus connected to cutaneous representations in areas 3b and 1: A revised interpretation of the second somatosensory area in macaque monkeys. *Journal of Comparative Neurology, 355,* 539–562.

Burton, H., & Sinclair, R. J. (1990). Second somatosensory cortical area in macaque monkeys: I. Neuronal responses to controlled, punctate indentions of glabrous skin on the hand. *Brain Research, 520,* 262–271.

Burton, H., & Sinclair, R. J. (1991). Second somatosensory cortical area in macaque monkeys: II. Neuronal responses to punctate vibrotactile stimulation of glabrous skin on the hand. *Brain Research, 538,* 127–135.

Burton, H., & Sinclair, R. J. (1996). Somatosensory cortex and tactile perceptions. In L. Kruger (Ed.), *Pain and touch* (pp. 105–177). San Diego, CA: Academic Press.

Burton, H., & Sinclair, R. J. (2000). Tactile-spatial and cross-modal attention effects in the primary somatosensory cortical areas 3b and 1-2 of rhesus monkeys. *Somatosensory and Motor Research, 17,* 213–228.

Burton, H., Sinclair, R. J., Hong, S. Y., Pruett, J. R., & Whang, K. C. (1997). Tactile-spatial and cross-modal attention effects in the second somatosensory and 7b cortical areas of rhesus monkeys. *Somatosensory and Motor Research, 14,* 237–267.

Bushnell, M. C., Duncan, G. H., Dubner, R., Fang, L., & He, L. F. (1984). Activity of trigeminothalamic neurons in medullary dorsal horn of awake monkeys trained in a thermal discrimination task. *Journal of Neurophysiology, 52,* 170–187.

Chambers, M. R., Andres, K. H., von Duering, M., & Iggo, A. (1972). The structure and function of the slowly adapting type II mechanoreceptor in hairy skin. *Quarterly Journal of Experimental Physiology, 57,* 417–445.

Chapman, C. E., Zompa, I. C., Williams, S. R., Shenasa, J., & Jiang, W. (1996). Factors influencing the perception of tactile stimuli during movement. In O. Franzén, R. S. Johansson, & L. Terenius (Eds.), *Somesthesis and the neurobiology of the somatosensory cortex* (pp. 307–320). Basel, Switzerland: Birkhäuser Verlag.

Connor, C. E., Hsiao, S. S., Phillips, J. R., & Johnson, K. O. (1990). Tactile roughness: neural codes that account for psychophysical magnitude estimates. *Journal of Neuroscience, 10,* 3823–3836.

Connor, C. E., & Johnson, K. O. (1992). Neural coding of tactile texture: comparisons of spatial and temporal mechanisms for roughness perception. *Journal of Neuroscience, 12,* 3414–3426.

Craig, A. D., & Dostrovsky, J. O. (1999). Medulla to thalamus. In P. D. Wall & R. Melzack (Eds.), *Textbook of pain* (pp. 183–214). Hong Kong: Harcourt.

Craig, J. C. (1985). Attending to two fingers: two hands are better than one. *Perception and Psychophysics, 38,* 496–511.

Craig, J. C., & Rollman, G. B. (1999). Somesthesis. *Annual Review of Psychology, 50,* 305–331.

Cusick, C. G., Wall, J. T., Felleman, D. J., & Kaas, J. H. (1989). Somatotopic organization of the lateral sulcus of owl monkeys: Area 3b, S-II, and a ventral somatosensory area. *Journal of Comparative Neurology, 282,* 169–190.

Darian-Smith, I., & Kenins, P. (1980). Innervation density of mechanoreceptive fibers supplying glabrous skin of the monkey's index finger. *Journal of Physiology, 309,* 147–155.

Diamond, J., Mills, L. R., & Mearow, K. M. (1988). Evidence that the Merkel cell is not the transducer in the mechanosensory Merkel cell-neurite complex. *Progress in Brain Research, 74,* 51–56.

DiCarlo, J. J., & Johnson, K. O. (1999). Velocity invariance of receptive field structure in somatosensory cortical area 3b of the alert monkey. *Journal of Neuroscience, 19,* 401–419.

DiCarlo, J. J., & Johnson, K. O. (2000). Spatial and temporal structure of receptive fields in primate somatosensory area 3b: Effects of stimulus scanning direction and orientation. *Journal of Neuroscience, 20,* 495–510.

DiCarlo, J. J., Johnson, K. O., & Hsiao, S. S. (1998). Structure of receptive fields in area 3b of primary somatosensory cortex in the alert monkey. *Journal of Neuroscience, 18,* 2626–2645.

Disbrow, E., Roberts, T., & Krubitzer, L. (2000). Somatotopic organization of cortical fields in the lateral sulcus of Homo sapiens: evidence for SII and PV. *Journal of Comparative Neurology, 418,* 1–21.

Dodson, M. J., Goodwin, A. W., Browning, A. S., & Gehring, H. M. (1998). Peripheral neural mechanisms determining the orientation of cylinders grasped by the digits. *Journal of Neuroscience, 18,* 521–530.

Driver, J., & Grossenbacher, P. G. (1996). Multimodal spatial constraints on tactile selective attention. In T. Inui & J. McClelland (Eds.), *Attention and performance: Vol. 16. Information integration in perception and communication (attention and performance).* Cambridge, MA: MIT Press, 209–235.

Edin, B. B. (1992). Quantitative analysis of static strain sensitivity in human mechanoreceptors from hairy skin. *Journal of Neurophysiology, 67,* 1105–1113.

Essick, G. K., Chen, C. C., & Kelly, D. G. (1999). A letter-recognition task to assess lingual tactile acuity. *Journal of Oral and Maxillofacial Surgery, 57,* 1324–1330.

Evans, P. M., & Craig, J. C. (1991). Tactile attention and the perception of moving tactile stimuli. *Perception and Psychophysics, 49,* 355–364.

Felleman, D. J., & Van Essen, D. C. (1991). Distributed hierarchical processing in the primate cerebral cortex. *Cerebral Cortex, 1,* 1–47.

Ferrington, D. G., & Rowe, M. J. (1980). Differential contributions to coding of cutaneous vibratory information by cortical somatosensory areas I and II. *Journal of Neurophysiology, 43,* 310–331.

Fitzgerald, P. J., Lane, J. W., Yoshioka, T., Nakama, T., & Hsiao, S. S. (1999). Multidigit receptive field structures and orientation tuning properties of neurons in SII cortex of the awake monkey [Abstract]. *Society for Neuroscience Abstracts, 25,* 1684.

Formby, C., Morgan, L. N., Forrest, T. G., & Raney, J. J. (1992). The role of frequency selectivity in measures of auditory and vibrotactile temporal resolution. *Journal of the Acoustical Society of America, 91,* 293–305.

Franzén, O., Markowitz, J., & Swets, J. A. (1970). Spatially-limited attention to vibrotactile stimulation. *Perception and Psychophysics, 7,* 193–196.

Friedman, D. P., & Murray, E. A. (1986). Thalamic connectivity of the second somatosensory area and neighboring somatosensory fields of the lateral sulcus of the macaque. *Journal of Comparative Neurology, 252,* 348–373.

Friedman, D. P., Murray, E. A., O'Neill, J. B., & Mishkin, M. (1986). Cortical connections of the somatosensory fields of the lateral sulcus of macaques: Evidence for a corticolimbic pathway for touch. *Journal of Comparative Neurology, 252,* 323–347.

Garcha, H. S., & Ettlinger, G. (1978). The effects of unilateral or bilateral removals of the second somatosensory cortex (area SII): A profound tactile disorder in monkeys. *Cortex, 14,* 319–326.

Gardner, E. P., & Costanzo, R. M. (1980). Temporal integration of multiple-point stimuli in primary somatosensory cortical receptive fields of alert monkeys. *Journal of Neurophysiology, 43,* 444–468.

Gardner, E. P., & Palmer, C. I. (1989). Simulation of motion on the skin: I. Receptive fields and temporal frequency coding by cutaneous mechanoreceptors of Optacon pulses delivered to the hand. *Journal of Neurophysiology, 62,* 1410–1436.

Garraghty, P. E., Pons, T. P., & Kaas, J. H. (1990). Ablations of areas 3b (SI proper) and 3a of somatosensory cortex in marmosets deactivate the second and parietal ventral somatosensory areas. *Somatosensory and Motor Research, 7,* 125–135.

Goodwin, A. W., Browning, A. S., & Wheat, H. E. (1995). Representation of curved surfaces in responses of mechanoreceptive afferent fibers innervating the monkey's fingerpad. *Journal of Neuroscience, 15,* 798–810.

Goodwin, A. W., John, K. T., & Marceglia, A. H. (1991). Tactile discrimination of curvature by humans using only cutaneous information from the fingerpads. *Experimental Brain Research, 86,* 663–672.

Goodwin, A. W., Macefield, V. G., & Bisley, J. W. (1997). Encoding of object curvature by tactile afferents from human fingers. *Journal of Neurophysiology, 78,* 2881–2888.

Goodwin, A. W., & Wheat, H. E. (1992a). Human tactile discrimination of curvature when contact area with the skin remains constant. *Experimental Brain Research, 88,* 447–450.

Goodwin, A. W., & Wheat, H. E. (1992b). Magnitude estimation of force when objects with different shapes are applied passively to the fingerpad. *Somatosensory and Motor Research, 9,* 339–344.

Guinard, D., Usson, Y., Guillermet, C., & Saxod, R. (2000). PS-100 and NF 70-200 double immunolabeling for human digital skin Meissner corpuscle 3D imaging. *Journal of Histochemistry and Cytochemistry, 48,* 295–302.

Harper, R., & Stevens, S. S. (1964). Subjective hardness of compliant materials. *Quarterly Journal of Experimental Psychology, 16,* 204–215.

Hayes, R. L., Dubner, R., & Hoffman, D. S. (1981). Neuronal activity in medullary dorsal horn of awake monkeys trained in a thermal discrimination task: II. Behavioral modulation of responses to thermal and mechanical stimuli. *Journal of Neurophysiology, 46,* 428–443.

Hollins, M., Bensmaïa, S. J., Karlof, K., & Young, F. (2000). Individual differences in perceptual space for tactile textures: Evidence from multidimensional scaling. *Perception and Psychophysics, 62,* 1534–1544.

Hollins, M., Faldowski, R., Rao, S., & Young, F. (1993). Perceptual dimensions of tactile surface texture: A multidimensional-scaling analysis. *Perception and Psychophysics, 54,* 697–705.

Hsiao, S. S., Johnson, K. O., Twombly, I. A., & DiCarlo, J. J. (1996). Form processing and attention effects in the somatosensory system. In O. Franzén, R. S. Johansson, & L. Terenius (Eds.), *Somesthesis and the neurobiology of the somatosensory cortex* (pp. 229–247). Basel, Switzerland: Birkhäuser Verlag.

Hsiao, S. S., O'Shaughnessy, D. M., & Johnson, K. O. (1993). Effects of selective attention of spatial form processing in monkey primary and secondary somatosensory cortex. *Journal of Neurophysiology, 70,* 444–447.

Hubbard, S. J. (1958). A study of rapid mechanical events in a mechanoreceptor. *Journal of Physiology, 141,* 198–218.

Hyvärinen, J., Poranen, A., & Jokinen, Y. (1980). Influence of attentive behavior on neuronal responses to vibration in primary somatosensory cortex of the monkey. *Journal of Neurophysiology, 43,* 870–882.

Iggo, A., & Andres, K. H. (1982). Morphology of cutaneous receptors. *Annual Review of Neuroscience, 5,* 1–31.

Innocenti, G. M., & Manzoni, T. (1972). Response patterns of somatosensory cortical neurones to peripheral stimuli: An intracellular study. *Archives Italiennes de Biologie, 110,* 322–347.

Iwamura, Y., Tanaka, M., Sakamoto, M., & Hikosaka, O. (1983). Functional subdivisions representing different finger regions in area 3 of the first somatosensory cortex of the conscious monkey. *Experimental Brain Research, 51,* 315–326.

Jiang, W., Tremblay, F., & Chapman, C. E. (1997). Neuronal encoding of texture changes in the primary and the secondary somatosensory cortical areas of monkeys during passive texture discrimination. *Journal of Neurophysiology, 77,* 1656–1662.

Johansson, R. S. (1979). Tactile afferent units with small and well demarcated receptive fields in the glabrous skin area of the human hand. In D. R. Kenshalo (Ed.), *Sensory function of the skin in humans* (pp. 129–145). New York: Plenum.

Johansson, R. S., & Vallbo, Å. B. (1976). Skin mechanoreceptors in the human hand: An inference of some population properties. In Y. Zotterman (Ed.), *Sensory functions of the skin in primates* (pp. 171–184). Oxford, England: Pergamon Press.

Johansson, R. S., & Vallbo, Å. B. (1979a). Detection of tactile stimuli: Thresholds of afferent units related to psychophysical thresholds in the human hand. *Journal of Physiology, 297,* 405–422.

Johansson, R. S., & Vallbo, Å. B. (1979b). Tactile sensibility in the human hand: Relative and absolute densities of four types of mechanoreceptive units in glabrous skin. *Journal of Physiology, 286,* 283–300.

Johansson, R. S., & Vallbo, Å. B. (1980). Spatial properties of the population of mechanoreceptive units in the glabrous skin of the human hand. *Brain Research, 184,* 353–366.

Johansson, R. S., Vallbo, Å. B., & Westling, G. (1980). Thresholds of mechanosensitive afferents in the human hand as measured with von Frey hairs. *Brain Research, 184,* 343–351.

Johnson, K. O., & Hsiao, S. S. (1992). Neural mechanisms of tactual form and texture perception. *Annual Review of Neuroscience, 15,* 227–250.

Johnson, K. O., Hsiao, S. S., & Twombly, I. A. (1995). Neural mechanisms of tactile form recognition. In M. S. Gazzaniga (Ed.), *The cognitive neurosciences* (pp. 235–268). Cambridge, MA: MIT Press.

Johnson, K. O., & Lamb, G. D. (1981). Neural mechanisms of spatial tactile discrimination: Neural patterns evoked by Braille-like dot patterns in the monkey. *Journal of Physiology, 310,* 117–144.

Johnson, K. O., & Phillips, J. R. (1981). Tactile spatial resolution: I. Two-point discrimination, gap detection, grating resolution, and letter recognition. *Journal of Neurophysiology, 46,* 1177–1191.

Johnson, K. O., Yoshioka, T., & Vega-Bermudez, F. (2000). Tactile functions of mechanoreceptive afferents innervating the hand. *Journal of Clinical Neurophysiology, 17,* 539–558.

Jones, E. G. (1990). *The thalamus.* New York: Plenum.

Jones, E. G., & Burton, H. (1976). Areal differences in the laminar distribution of thalamic afferents in cortical fields of the insular, parietal and temporal reigons of primates. *Journal of Comparative Neurology, 168,* 197–248.

Jones, E. G., & Friedman, D. P. (1982). Projection pattern of functional components of thalamic ventrobasal complex upon monkey somatic sensory cortex. *Journal of Neurophysiology, 48,* 521–544.

Katz, D. (1989). *The world of touch* (L. E. Krueger, Trans.). Hillsdale, NJ: Erlbaum. (Original work published 1925)

Khalsa, P. S., Friedman, R. M., Srinivasan, M. A., & LaMotte, R. H. (1998). Encoding of shape and orientation of objects indented into the monkey fingerpad by populations of slowly and rapidly adapting mechanoreceptors. *Journal of Neurophysiology, 79,* 3238–3251.

Klatzky, R. L., Lederman, S. J., & O'Neil, C. O. (1996). Haptic object processing: I. Early perceptual features. In O. Franzén, R. S. Johansson, & L. Terenius (Eds.), *Somesthesis and the neurobiology of the somatosensory cortex* (pp. 147–152). Basel, Switzerland: Birkhäuser Verlag.

Kops, C. E., & Gardner, E. P. (1996). Discrimination of simulated texture patterns on the human hand. *Journal of Neurophysiology, 76,* 1145–1165.

Krubitzer, L. A., Clarey, J., Tweedale, R., Elston, G., & Calford, M. B. (1995). A redefinition of somatosensory areas in the lateral sulcus of macaque monekeys. *Journal of Neuroscience, 15,* 3821–3839.

Lakatos, S., & Shepard, R. N. (1997). Time-distance relations in shifting attention between locations on one's body. *Perception and Psychophysics, 59,* 557–566.

Lamore, P. J. J., Muijser, H., & Keemink, C. J. (1986). Envelope detection of amplitude-modulated high-frequency sinusoidal signals by skin mechanoreceptors. *Journal of the Acoustical Society of America, 79,* 1082–1085.

LaMotte, R. H., Friedman, R. M., Lu, C., Khalsa, P. S., & Srinivasan, M. A. (1998). Raised object on a planar surface stroked across the fingerpad: Responses of cutaneous mechanoreceptors to shape and orientation. *Journal of Neurophysiology, 80,* 2446–2466.

LaMotte, R. H., & Srinivasan, M. A. (1993). Responses of cutaneous mechanoreceptors to the shape of objects applied to the primate fingerpad. *Acta Psychologica, 84,* 41–51.

Landgren, S., Silfvenius, H., & Olsson, K. A. (1984). The sensorimotor integration in area 3a of the cat. *Experimental Brain Research, 9*(Suppl.), 359–375.

Lederman, S. J. (1974). Tactile roughness of grooved surfaces: The touching process and the effects of macro- and microsurface structure. *Perception and Psychophysics, 16,* 385–395.

Loewenstein, W. R., & Skalak, R. (1966). Mechanical transmission in a Pacinian corpuscle: An analysis and a theory. *Journal of Physiology, 182,* 346–378.

Loomis, J. M. (1981). On the tangibility of letters and Braille. *Perception and Psychophysics, 29,* 37–46.

Loomis, J. M. (1985). Tactile recognition of raised characters: A parametric study. *Bulletin of the Psychonomic Society, 23,* 18–20.

Macefield, V. G., Hager-Ross, C., & Johansson, R. S. (1996). Control of grip force during restraint of an object held between finger and thumb: Responses of cutaneous afferents from the digits. *Experimental Brain Research, 108,* 155–171.

Meenes, M., & Zigler, M. J. (1923). An experimental study of the perceptions of roughness and smoothness. *American Journal of Psychology, 34,* 542–549.

Meftah, E. M., Belingard, L., & Chapman, C. E. (2000). Relative effects of the spatial and temporal characteristics of scanned surfaces on human perception of tactile roughness using passive touch. *Experimental Brain Research, 132,* 351–361.

Morrow, T. J., & Casey, K. L. (2000). Attention-related, cross-modality modulation of somatosensory neurons in primate ventrobasal (VB) thalamus. *Somatosensory and Motor Research, 17,* 133–144.

Mountcastle, V. B., Talbot, W. H., & Kornhuber, H. H. (1966). The neural transformation of mechanical stimuli delivered to the monkey's hand. In A. V. de Reuck & J. Knight (Eds.), *Touch, heat, pain and itch* (pp. 325–351). London: Churchill.

Munger, B. L., & Ide, C. (1988). The structure and function of cutaneous sensory receptors. *Archives of Histology and Cytology, 51,* 1–34.

Murray, E. A., & Mishkin, M. (1984). Relative contributions of SII and area 5 to tactile discrimination in monkeys. *Behavioural Brain Research, 11,* 67–85.

Murray, G. M., Zhang, H. Q., Kaye, A. N., Sinnadurai, T., Campbell, D. H., & Rowe, M. J. (1992). Parallel processing in rabbit first (SI) and second (SII) somatosensory cortical areas: Effects of reversible inactivation by cooling of SI on responses in SII. *Journal of Neurophysiology, 68,* 703–710.

Ogawa, H. (1996). The Merkel cell as a possible mechanoreceptor cell. *Progress in Neurobiology, 49,* 317–334.

Olausson, H., Wessberg, J., & Kakuda, N. (2000). Tactile directional sensibility: peripheral neural mechanisms in man. *Brain Research, 866,* 178–187.

Palmer, C. I., & Gardner, E. P. (1990). Simulation of motion on the skin: IV. Responses of Pacinian corpuscle afferents innervating the primate hand to stripe patterns on the OPTACON. *Journal of Neurophysiology, 64,* 236–247.

Paul, R. L., Goodman, H., & Merzenich, M. M. (1972). Alterations in mechanoreceptor input to Brodmann's areas 1 and 3 of the postcentral hand area of Macaca mulatta after nerve section and regeneration. *Brain Research, 39,* 1–19.

Perl, E. R. (1998). Getting a line on pain: is it mediated by dedicated pathways? *Nature Neuroscience, 1,* 177–178.

Phillips, J. R., Johansson, R. S., & Johnson, K. O. (1990). Representation of Braille characters in human nerve fibers. *Experimental Brain Research, 81,* 589–592.

Phillips, J. R., & Johnson, K. O. (1981). Tactile spatial resolution: II. Neural representation of bars, edges, and gratings in monkey primary afferents. *Journal of Neurophysiology, 46,* 1192–1203.

Phillips, J. R., Johnson, K. O., & Browne, H. M. (1983). A comparison of visual and two modes of tactual letter resolution. *Perception and Psychophysics, 34,* 243–249.

Phillips, J. R., Johnson, K. O., & Hsiao, S. S. (1988). Spatial pattern representation and transformation in monkey somatosensory cortex. *Proceedings of the National Academy of Sciences, USA, 85,* 1317–1321.

Platt, J. R. (1964). Strong inference. *Science, 146,* 347–353.

Poggio, G. F., & Mountcastle, V. B. (1960). A study of the functional contributions of the lemniscal and spinothalamic systems to somatic sensibility. *Bulletin of the Johns Hopkins Hospital, 106,* 266–316.

Pons, T. P., Garraghty, P. E., Friedman, D. P., & Mishkin, M. (1987). Physiological evidence for serial processing in somatosensory cortex. *Science, 237,* 417–420.

Pons, T. P., Garraghty, P. E., & Mishkin, M. (1992). Serial and parallel processing of tactual information in somatosensory cortex of rhesus monkeys. *Journal of Neurophysiology, 68,* 518–527.

Pons, T. P., Wall, J. T., Garraghty, P. E., Cusick, C. G., & Kaas, J. H. (1987). Consistent features of the representation of the hand in area 3b of macaque monkeys. *Somatosensory Research, 4,* 309–331.

Popper, K. (1959). *The logic of scientific discovery.* New York: Basic Books.

Poranen, A., & Hyvärinen, J. (1982). Effects of attention on multiunit responses to vibration in the somatosensory regions of the monkey's brain. *Electroencephalography and Clinical Neurophysiology, 53,* 525–537.

Post, L. J., & Chapman, C. E. (1991). The effects of cross-modal manipulations of attention on the detection of vibrotactile stimuli in humans. *Somatosensory and Motor Research, 8*(2), 149–157.

Pruett, J. R., Sinclair, R. J., & Burton, H. (2000). Response patterns in second somatosensory cortex (SII) of awake monkeys to passively applied tactile gratings. *Journal of Neurophysiology, 84,* 780–797.

Quilliam, T. A. (1978). The structure of finger print skin. In G. Gordon (Ed.), *Active touch* (pp. 1–18). Oxford, UK: Pergamon Press.

Randolph, M., & Semmes, J. (1974). Behavioral consequences of selective ablations in the postcentral gyrus of *Macaca mulatta. Brain Research, 70,* 55–70.

Ridley, R. M., & Ettlinger, G. (1976). Impaired tactile learning and retention after removal of the second somatic sensory cortex (SII) in the monkey. *Brain Research, 109,* 656–660.

Robinson, C. J., & Burton, H. (1980a). Organization of somatosensory receptive fields in cortical areas 7b, retroinsula, postauditory and granular insula of *M. fascicularis. Journal of Comparative Neurology, 192,* 69–92.

Robinson, C. J., & Burton, H. (1980b). Somatic submodality distribution within the second somatosensory (SII), 7b, retroinsular, postauditory, and granular insular cortical areas of *M. fascicularis. Journal of Comparative Neurology, 192,* 93–108.

Robinson, C. J., & Burton, H. (1980c). Somatotopographic organization in the second somatosensory area of *M. fascicularis. Journal of Comparative Neurology, 192,* 43–67.

Roy, A., Steinmetz, P. N., Hsiao, S. S., Johnson, K. O., & Niebur, E. (2001). *Synchrony: A neural correlate of somatosensory attention.* Manuscript submitted for publication.

Roy, S., & Alloway, K. D. (1999). Synchronization of local neural networks in the somatosensory cortex: A comparison of stationary and moving stimuli. *Journal of Neurophysiology, 81,* 999–1013.

Sathian, K., & Burton, H. (1991). The role of spatially selective attention in the tactile perception of texture. *Perception and Psychophysics, 50,* 237–248.

Sathian, K., Goodwin, A. W., John, K. T., & Darian-Smith, I. (1989). Perceived roughness of a grating: Correlation with responses of mechanoreceptive afferents innervating the monkey's fingerpad. *Journal of Neuroscience, 9,* 1273–1279.

Sathian, K., & Zangaladze, A. (1996). Tactile spatial acuity at the human fingertip and lip: Bilateral symmetry and interdigit variability. *Neurology, 46,* 1464–1466.

Sathian, K., Zangaladze, A., Green, J., Vitek, J. L., & DeLong, M. R. (1997). Tactile spatial acuity and roughness discrimination: Impairments due to aging and Parkinson's disease. *Neurology, 49,* 168–177.

Schneider, R. J., Friedman, D. P., & Mishkin, M. (1993). A modality-specific somatosensory area within the insula of the rhesus monkey. *Brain Research, 621,* 116–120.

Shiffrin, R. M., Craig, J. C., & Cohen, E. (1973). On the degree of attention and capacity limitation in tactile processing. *Perception and Psychophysics, 13,* 328–336.

Sinclair, R. J., & Burton, H. (1993). Neuronal activity in the second somatosensory cortex of monkeys (*macaca mulatta*) during active touch of gratings. *Journal of Neurophysiology, 70,* 331–350.

Sinclair, R. J., Kuo, J. J., & Burton, H. (2000). Effects on discrimination performance of selective attention to tactile features. *Somatosensory and Motor Research, 17,* 145–157.

Srinivasan, M. A., & Dandekar, K. (1996). An investigation of the mechanics of tactile sense using two-dimensional models of the primate fingertip. *Journal of Biomechanical Engineering, 118,* 48–55.

Srinivasan, M. A., & LaMotte, R. H. (1987). Tactile discrimination of shape: Responses of slowly and rapidly adapting mechanoreceptive afferents to a step indented into the monkey fingerpad. *Journal of Neuroscience, 7,* 1682–1697.

Srinivasan, M. A., & LaMotte, R. H. (1995). Tactual discrimination of softness. *Journal of Neurophysiology, 73,* 88–101.

Srinivasan, M. A., & LaMotte, R. H. (1996). Tactual discrimination of softness: Abilities and mechanisms. In O. Franzén, R. S. Johansson, & L. Terenius (Eds.), *Somesthesis and the neurobiology of the somatosensory cortex* (pp. 123–135). Basel, Switzerland: Birkhäuser Verlag.

Steinmetz, P. N., Roy, A., Fitzgerald, P. J., Hsiao, S. S., Johnson, K. O., & Niebur, E. (2000). Attention modulates synchronized neuronal firing in primate somatosensory cortex. *Nature, 404,* 187–190.

Stevens, J. C., & Choo, K. K. (1996). Spatial acuity of the body surface over the life span. *Somatosensory and Motor Research, 13,* 153–166.

Stevens, S. S., & Harris, J. R. (1962). The scaling of subjective roughness and smoothness. *Journal of Experimental Psychology, 64,* 489–494.

Sur, M., Garraghty, P. E., & Bruce, C. J. (1985). Somatosensory cortex in macaque monkeys: Laminar differences in receptive field size in areas 3b and 1. *Brain Research, 342,* 391–395.

Sur, M., Merzenich, M. M., & Kaas, J. H. (1980). Magnification, receptive-field area, and hypercolumn size in areas 3b and 1 of somatosensory cortex in owl monkeys. *Journal of Neurophysiology, 44,* 295–311.

Sur, M., Wall, J. T., & Kaas, J. H. (1984). Modular distribution of neurons with slowly adapting and rapidly adapting responses in area 3b of somatosensory cortex in monkeys. *Journal of Neurophysiology, 51,* 724–744.

Taylor, M. M., & Lederman, S. J. (1975). Tactile roughness of grooved surfaces: A model and the effect of friction. *Perception and Psychophysics, 17,* 23–36.

Van Boven, R. W., & Johnson, K. O. (1994). The limit of tactile spatial resolution in humans: Grating orientation discrimination at the lip, tongue and finger. *Neurology, 44,* 2361–2366.

Vega-Bermudez, F., & Johnson, K. O. (1999a). SA1 and RA receptive fields, response variability, and population responses mapped with a probe array. *Journal of Neurophysiology, 81,* 2701–2710.

Vega-Bermudez, F., & Johnson, K. O. (1999b). Surround suppression in the responses of primate SA1 and RA mechanoreceptive afferents mapped with a probe array. *Journal of Neurophysiology, 81,* 2711–2719.

Vega-Bermudez, F., & Johnson, K. O. (2001). Differences in spatial acuity between digits. *Neurology, 56,* 1389–1391.

Vega-Bermudez, F., Johnson, K. O., & Hsiao, S. S. (1991). Human tactile pattern recognition: Active versus passive touch, velocity effects, and patterns of confusion. *Journal of Neurophysiology, 65,* 531–546.

Warren, S., Hämäläinen, H. A., & Gardner, E. P. (1986). Objective classification of motion- and direction-sensitive neurons in primary somatosensory cortex of awake monkeys. *Journal of Neurophysiology, 56,* 598–622.

Weisenberger, J. M. (1986). Sensitivity to amplitude-modulated vibrotactile signals. *Journal of the Acoustical Society of America, 80,* 1707–1715.

Whang, K. C., Burton, H., & Shulman, G. L. (1991). Selective attention in vibrotactile tasks: Detecting the presence and absence of amplitude change. *Perception and Psychophysics, 50,* 157–165.

Whitsel, B. L., Petrucelli, L. M., & Werner, G. (1969). Symmetry and connectivity in the map of the body surface in somatosensory area II of primates. *Journal of Neurophysiology, 32,* 170–183.

Wohlert, A. B. (1996). Tactile perception of spatial stimuli on the lip surface by young and older adults. *Journal of Speech and Hearing Research, 39,* 1191–1198.

Woolsey, C. N. (1943). 'Second' somatic receiving areas in the cerebral cortex of cat, dog, and monkey. *Federation Proceedings, 2,* 55.

Yoshioka, T., Dorsch, A. K., Hsiao, S. S., & Johnson, K. O. (2001). Neural coding mechanisms underlying perceived roughness of finely textured surfaces. *Journal of Neuroscience, 21,* 6905–6916.

Zhang, H. Q., Murray, G. M., Turman, A. B., Mackie, P. D., Coleman, G. T., & Rowe, M. J. (1996). Parallel processing in cerebral cortex of the marmoset monkey: Effect of reversible SI inactivation on tactile responses in SII. *Journal of Neurophysiology, 76,* 3633–3655.

Zhou, Y. D., & Fuster, J. M. (1996). Mnemonic neuronal activity in somatosensory cortex. *Proceedings of the National Academy of Sciences, USA, 93,* 10533–10537.

Zhou, Y. D., & Fuster, J. M. (1997). Neuronal activity of somatosensory cortex in a cross-modal (visuo-haptic) memory task. *Experimental Brain Research, 116,* 551–555.

Zompa, I. C., & Chapman, C. E. (1995). Effects of cross-modal manipulations of attention on the ability of human subjects to discriminate changes in texture. *Somatosensory and Motor Research, 12,* 87–102.

CHAPTER 9

The Biological Psychology of Pain

TERENCE J. CODERRE, JEFFREY S. MOGIL, AND M. CATHERINE BUSHNELL

Pain has been defined by the International Association for the Study of Pain as "an unpleasant sensory and emotional experience associated with actual or potential tissue damage, or described in terms of such damage." However, like many other sensations, pain is subjective; its quality, intensity, and emotional effects can only be truly realized by the perceiver. Biologists recognize that those stimuli that cause pain normally are likely to damage tissue. However, an individual learns the application of the word through experiences related to injury in early life and beyond. Pain is unquestionably a sensation within the body, but it is also unpleasant and therefore reflects an emotional experience. Although pain is often directly associated with tissue injury, it is also true that

T. J. C. and M. C. B. receive grant support from the Canadian Institutes of Health Research (CIHR); J. S. M. receives grant support from the National Institutes of Health (USA). T. J. C. is a CIHR Investigator.

pain cannot be equated with or predicted by the amount of tissue injury. Some individuals with severe injuries experience little pain, and some with minor injury experience excruciating pain. Indeed, pain often persists long after damaged tissue has healed (Merskey & Bogduk, 1994).

Recently, it has been proposed that pain be considered as two separate sensory entities: (a) physiological pain and (b) pathological pain (Woolf, 1991). Physiological pain reflects a normal reaction of the somatosensory system to noxious stimulation, which alerts the individual to actual or potential tissue damage. It serves a protective function of informing organisms of injury or disease and usually remits when healing is complete or the condition is cured. The importance of physiological pain to the health and integrity of the individual is illustrated by the rare syndrome of congenital insensitivity to pain. These individuals lack small-diameter primary afferent fibers that transmit information about tissue-damaging stimuli. People with this syndrome frequently injure themselves and are unaware of internal injury or disease, when the sole symptom alerting these conditions is pain. These individuals often become disfigured, develop severe joint deformities, and have a significantly shortened life span.

Pathological pain occurs with the development of abnormal sensitivity in the somatosensory system, usually precipitated by inflammatory injury or nerve damage. Pathological pain is characterized by one or more of the following: pain in the absence of a noxious stimulus (spontaneous pain), increased duration of response to brief stimulation (hyperpathia), perception of pain in response to normally nonpainful stimulation (allodynia), increased responsiveness to noxious stimulation (hyperalgesia), and spread of pain and hyperalgesia to uninjured tissue (referred pain and secondary hyperalgesia). The abnormality that underlies pathological pain may reside in any of numerous sites along the neuronal pathways that both relay and modulate somatosensory inputs. Indeed, the most intractable pains are those that result from injury to the nerves (neuropathic pain) and central nervous system (CNS) structures (central pain) that subserve somatosensory processing.

This chapter provides a comprehensive review of the current knowledge concerning the anatomical, physiological, and neurochemical substrates that underlie both physiological and pathological pain; thus, we describe in detail the pathways that underlie the transmission of inputs from the periphery to the CNS, the physiological properties of the neurons activated by painful stimuli, and the neurochemicals that have been found to mediate or modulate synaptic transmission in somatosensory pathways. Much like the field of pain research itself, we have broken down our review into separate sections on the peripheral nervous system and the CNS, with a further breakdown of the CNS into sections on the spinal cord dorsal horn and the brain. A special effort has been made to identify critical advances in the field of pain research, which point to the processes by which pathological pain develops following tissue or nerve injury, as well as how pain is modulated by various brain mechanisms. In our review of the peripheral nervous system, we have concentrated on differences in the properties of the primary afferent neurons that transduce and relay painful messages to the CNS; we also discuss how their responses are affected by injuries that produce inflammation. In our review of the spinal cord dorsal horn, we concentrate on what is known about the neurochemical influences on synaptic transmission and how neurochemical processes are affected by inflammatory and nerve injuries in the periphery. Our review of pain processing in the brain focuses on the role of various brain regions in the determination of the multidimensional nature of pain, as discerned by anatomical connectivity, physiological function,

and brain imaging. Finally, we provide some insights into the future of pain research—with a focus on molecular biology and behavioral genetics—as a means to understand individual differences in pain sensitivity and expression.

THE PERIPHERAL NERVOUS SYSTEM

Primary Afferent Fibers

Under normal circumstances, nociceptive inputs are transmitted to the spinal cord dorsal horn or brain stem trigeminal nuclei (for inputs from the neck, face, and head) by primary afferent nerve fibers in skin, muscle, joint, viscera, and vasculature (see Figure 9.1). Each individual fiber extends from

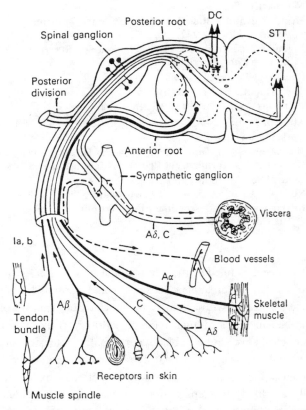

Figure 9.1 Schematic diagram illustrating the projection of primary afferent fibers (Aβ, Aδ, C, group Ia,b) from their site of origin in the skin, muscle, and viscera to their target cells in the dorsal horn of the spinal cord. Primary afferent fibers with their cell bodies (dorsal root ganglion cells) in the spinal ganglion project through the dorsal or posterior roots. The peripheral axon branch originates in skin receptors, muscle spindles, tendon bundles, and so on. The central axon branch terminates on spinal cord neurons that project to the thalamus and brain through various ascending tracts, including the spinothalamic tract (STT), or ascend to the caudal medulla through the dorsal columns (DC). Also shown is the ventral or anterior root through which efferent motor fibers (Aα) project to skeletal muscle and sympathetic efferent (C) fibers project through the sympathetic ganglion to blood vessels and viscera. Reprinted with permission from Bonica, J. J. (1990). *The management of pain:* Vol. 1. Copyright 1990, Lea and Febiger.

its tissue of origin (e.g., skin, joint, etc.) to its CNS target (e.g., spinal cord dorsal horn), and makes its first synapse at that level. The cell bodies of these neurons are grouped together to form the dorsal root ganglia, with the peripheral axonal branch extending to the tissue of origin, and the central axonal branch extending to the CNS. Primary afferent fibers are bundled together to form nerves that are often combined with efferent (or descending) fibers (muscle and sympathetic) to form mixed nerves.

Primary afferent fibers in the skin include large-diameter (>10 μM) myelinated Aβ fibers that conduct impulses quickly (30–100 m/s); medium-diameter (2–6 μM) myelinated Aδ fibers with an intermediate conduction velocity (12–30 m/s); and small-diameter (0.4–1.2 μM) unmyelinated C fibers that are slowly conducting (0.5–2.0 m/s; Willis & Coggeshall, 1991). Primary afferent fibers in muscle and joint are subdivided into three groups of myelinated axons with the corresponding conduction velocities in parentheses: I (72–120 m/s), II (24–71 m/s), III (6–23 m/s), and IV, which are unmyelinated axons (<2.5). Group II fibers in muscle and joint are analogous to Aβ in skin, whereas Group III and Group IV are comparable to Aδ and C fibers, respectively. Group I fibers, of which there are few in joints, do not have analogous skin fibers, but they are comparable to Aα muscle efferent fibers. They are also separated into Ia and Ib, which contribute to the stretch or myotatic reflex and the inverse myotatic reflex, respectively. Visceral nerves share the same terminology as cutaneous nerve fibers (Bonica, 1990; Willis & Coggeshall, 1991).

Aβ fibers are linked with various cutaneous mechanoreceptors (Type I, Type II, D hair, G_1, G_2 hair, T hair, Field, G1, G2, Krause's end-bulbs, Merkel's cells, Meissner's corpuscles, Pacinian corpuscles) and a small number of visceral mechanoreceptors (mesenteric Pacinian corpuscles), whereas Group I and II large-diameter myelinated fibers are linked with muscle mechanoreceptors (primary and secondary muscle spindles, Golgi tendon organs), and joint mechanoreceptors (Ruffini endings, Golgi tendon organs, Paciniform endings, Golgi-Mazzoni endings). Normally, Aβ and Group I and II axons are low-threshold fibers that carry somatosensory inputs that encode nonnoxious cutaneous mechanical (e.g., skin indentation, skin or hair movement, vibrations of the skin and hair) and nonnoxious stimulation in muscle (normal changes in length, tension, contraction, or vibration), joint (normal flexion, extension, pressure, or vibration), and viscera (normal distension, contraction, or vibration; Burgess & Perl, 1973).

Aδ and C cutaneous fibers as well as Group III muscle-joint and Group IV muscle fibers are free nerve endings, and they are typically high threshold (higher intensity stimulation

is required to activate these fibers). It is believed that Aδ fibers evoke a rapid early pain response that is sharp in nature, whereas C fibers elicit a later, dull, burning "second" pain (Bishop, 1946; Burgess & Perl, 1973). Aδ fibers include separate classes of cutaneous fibers or cutaneous nociceptors—that is, receptors that encode noxious mechanical (Types I and II), heat, and cold stimulation of the skin. C fibers include separate cutaneous nociceptors that encode noxious mechanical, heat, or cold stimulation of the skin, as well as C polymodal nociceptors (also known as CMH fibers, for noxious *cold, mechanical,* and *heat* stimuli) that respond to noxious heat, severe cold, mechanical damage, and noxious chemical stimulation of the skin.

In addition to transmitting inputs centrally or orthodromically to signal pain (afferent function), heat-sensitive C nociceptors and polymodal C nociceptors have an efferent function as well; thus, these fibers propagate impulses antidromically (towards the periphery) within their branches and mediate a phenomenon known as *neurogenic inflammation,* which is responsible for the axon flare response elicited by tissue injury. Aδ and C fibers also act as cutaneous thermoreceptors, with cold receptors innervated by Aδ and C fibers and warm receptors innervated by C fibers. Group III small myelinated and Group IV unmyelinated joint fibers respond to extreme bending or probing of joints, but many also respond to innocuous movements of the joint. Group III and IV muscle fibers respond to intense pressure, ischemia, or damage to the muscle. However, both Group III and IV muscle fibers encode polymodal inputs (including chemical stimulation), and many respond also to nonnoxious muscle stretch, contractions, and pressure (Groups III and IV) and thermal stimuli (Group IV; Burgess & Perl, 1973; Willis & Coggeshall, 1991).

It is important to note that the aforementioned classifications are only relative; exceptions do exist. The classifications and their descriptions are complicated by various factors including differences between species, differences in the terminology used, and different properties of similar fibers in various tissues, including hairy versus nonhairy or glabrous skin. The response characteristics of individual fibers can also change following tissue or nerve injury. For example, repetitive thermal stimulation will sensitize Aδ fiber mechanoreceptors (discussed later in this chapter) so that they respond to heat as well as respond more vigorously to noxious mechanical stimulation (LaMotte, Thalhammer, Torebjörk, & Robinson, 1982). In contrast, repetitive heat stimulation often leads to a decreased responsiveness in C polymodal nociceptors (Meyer & Campbell, 1981). It is important to note that although Aβ fibers are low threshold and typically transmit inputs signaling the perception of touch, after tissue or nerve injury these fibers change their phenotype and may become important in the signaling of abnormal pain inputs in response to normally nonnoxious stimuli (Neumann, Doubell, Leslie, & Woolf, 1996; Woolf, 1996).

Inflammation and Peripheral Sensitization

Following an injury to cutaneous tissue, a series of defensive reactions serve as a protective mechanism against further skin injury. Lewis (1942) described a triple response of injured skin—a local reddening at the site of injury; followed by a weal characterized by swelling, tenderness, and redness just around the injury; and a subsequent flare or spreading of redness to surrounding tissue. These reactions demonstrate the four classic signs of inflammation: redness, heat, swelling, and pain. The redness and heat are caused by a dilation of blood vessels (vasodilitation) and by the large amounts of warm blood close to the skin surface. Swelling or *edema* is due to plasma extravasation (the leakage of fluids) from the blood vessels into the tissue. Pain is caused by a direct activation of peripheral nociceptors by the noxious stimulus, as well as by stimulation from substances released in response to the injury.

Along with inflammation, the cutaneous tissue becomes hyperalgesic or more sensitive to cutaneous stimulation. Painful responses to both noxious mechanical and thermal stimuli are enhanced. The hyperalgesia is present not only at the site of injury (primary hyperalgesia), but also spreads to surrounding uninjured tissue (secondary hyperalgesia). Whereas primary hyperalgesia depends entirely on peripheral sensitization, secondary hyperalgesia probably depends on both peripheral and central sensitization (Meyer, Campbell, & Raja, 1994).

Nociceptor Sensitization

Following tissue injury there is an increase in the excitability of high-threshold primary afferent fibers, which is known as *peripheral* or *nociceptor sensitization.* Nociceptor sensitization is reflected by one or more of the following changes in the properties of neuronal firing: a decrease in threshold, an increase in impulse frequency to the same stimulus, a decrease in latency of the first impulse, an afterdischarge following extended or intense stimulation, and the appearance of spontaneous firing in primary afferent fibers (Beitel & Dubner, 1976). Repeated heat stimulation produces sensitization that develops within 1 min and lasts for hours. Following heating of the skin, sensitization to further heat stimuli has been demonstrated in C fiber polymodal nociceptors, Aδ fiber high-threshold mechanoreceptors, and cold receptors. Cutaneous nociceptors have also been found to be sensitized to mechanical stimulation following injury of the skin by scraping. However, it has been suggested that both C polymodal

nociceptors and high-threshold mechanoreceptors do not become sensitized to mechanical stimuli following heat injury, although this idea has been questioned (Meyer et al., 1994; Treede, Meyer, Raja, & Campbell, 1992).

Various studies have attempted to demonstrate a correlation between nociceptor sensitization and reports of hyperalgesia following a cutaneous injury. Initially this was performed by comparing magnitude estimations of hyperalgesia in humans with neurophysiological recordings in nerve fibers of monkeys (see Figure 9.2). More recent studies have examined the correlation between human sensory judgements and evoked responses from primary afferent fibers in the same subjects using percutaneous recording techniques (microneurography). The results of these studies have been controversial. Whereas Meyer and Campbell (1981) reported that hyperalgesia is associated with a sensitization of Aδ fibers and a desensitization of C fibers, LaMotte, Thalhammer, and Robinson (1983) and Torebjörk, LaMotte, and Robinson (1984) suggested that hyperalgesia is related to a sensitization of C fibers and not Aδ fibers. This discrepancy may depend on either the type of skin (hairy vs. glaborous) injured or the intensity of the stimulus producing the injury.

Silent Nociceptors

It has recently been found that there are nociceptors that are normally unresponsive to acute noxious stimuli but that become capable of responding to noxious stimulation following injury or inflammation. These C fiber nociceptors have been called *silent* or *sleeping nociceptors* and have been detected in skin, joints, and viscera. Nociceptors typically have a small, restricted receptive field (i.e., the tissue area in which noxious stimulation activates the fiber). It has been argued that the reported expansion of the receptive fields of primary afferent fibers, which occurs after injury or inflammation, reflects the recruitment of previously silent branches of the fiber. Clearly, the recruitment of additional fibers not previously contributing to the afferent signal would enhance the opportunity for temporal and spatial summation and enhance the afferent barrage transmitted to the spinal cord dorsal horn (Treede et al., 1992).

Neuroactive Substances

Evidence suggests that nociceptor sensitization and hyperalgesia at the site of injury are partly mediated by the release of neuroactive substances from cells damaged by the injury (see Figure 9.3). Exposure to severe or prolonged noxious stimulation results in tissue damage. The damage is reflected by a destruction of cells as well as nerve endings at the site of injury. The chemicals potassium (K^+) and adenosine triphosphate (ATP), which are contained in the cells of tissue, are

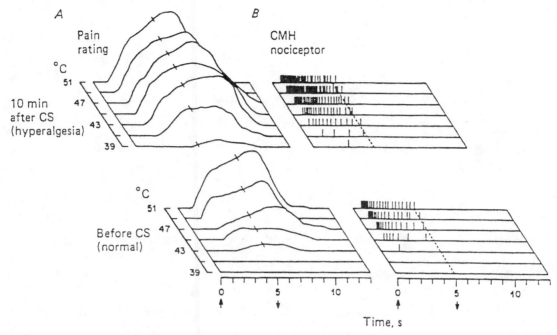

Figure 9.2 Magnitude estimates of pain in human subjects and responses of a C fiber mechanoheat (CMH) nociceptor in a monkey to graded noxious heat stimuli before and after heat injury. The heat injury was produced by 50 °C heating for 100 s. The tests shown were made before and 10 min after the injury. The human subject was stimulated on the volar forearm. The receptive field of the monkey afferent fiber was on the hairy skin of a finger. A. Hyperalgesia had developed by 10 min, as indicated by a lowering of pain threshold from 43 °C to 39 °C and enhanced ratings of suprathreshold stimuli. B. The nociceptor had become sensitized, as evidenced by a lowering of threshold and enhanced frequency of discharge to suprathreshold stimuli. Reprinted with permission from LaMotte, R. H., Thalhammer, J. G., and Robinson, C. J. (1983), Peripheral neural correlates of magnitude of cutaneous pain and hyperalgesia: A comparison of neural events in monkey with sensory judgment in human, *Journal of Neurophysiology*.

released following injury. The release of K$^+$ and ATP causes a sensitization of nerve endings and likely produces pain sensations because each chemical has been found to produce pain when applied to the exposed base of a blister. There is also an accumulation of protons (H$^+$) in injured tissue, which lowers the pH of the tissue and activates primary afferent fibers by stimulating various ion channels discussed later in this chapter. Protons contribute to inflammation and hyperalgesia following tissue injury. Blood and damaged tissue locally release serotonin and bradykinin, and damaged mast cells release histamine and serotonin. Bradykinin and histamine sensitize C fiber nociceptive units and produce pain following intradermal injection. Serotonin causes a sensitization of cutaneous nociceptors and pain sensations when applied to a blister base (Coderre, 1992; Rang, Bevan, & Dray, 1994).

Tissue damage is also followed by the production and accumulation of arachidonic acid metabolites in inflammatory perfusate. The cyclooxygenase products of arachidonic acid metabolism (prostaglandins and prostacyclins) as well as the lipoxygenase products (leukotrienes and dihydroxy-eicosatetraenoic acid; diHETE), cause a sensitization of C fiber nociceptors and produce pain or hyperalgesia when administered intradermally or subcutaneously. Furthermore, during inflammation there is an upregulation of an inducible form of cyclooxygenase (COX-2), which produces large amounts of prostaglandins (Hla & Neilson, 1992). The importance of prostaglandins to the sensitization of primary afferent fibers during inflammation is highlighted by the significant anti-inflammatory and analgesic effects of aspirin and other nonsteroidal anti-inflammatory drugs (NSAIDs), which inhibit the synthesis of prostaglandins by blocking the cyclooxygenase metabolism of arachidonic acid. The promise of new NSAIDs that selectively block COX-2 is that they will produce analgesia without producing stomach ulcers, a side effect that has been attributed mostly to inhibition of COX-1 (Masferrer et al., 1994).

Primary afferent fibers can also be activated or sensitized by products from activated immune cells that are either resident or attracted to the site of injury or infection. Keratinocytes and fibroblasts in the skin produce and release a precursor of interleukin-1 (pro-IL-1), which is cleaved by the chymase released from damaged mast cells to produce interleukin-1β (IL-1β). Damaged mast cells also release the pro-inflammatory cytokines IL-1β, IL-6, and tumor necrosis factor alpha (TNFα; L. R. Watkins, Maier, & Goehler, 1995). These cytokines activate primary afferent fibers and stimulate the release of substance P. The substance P released from primary afferent fibers further stimulates mast cells and attracts macrophages from the

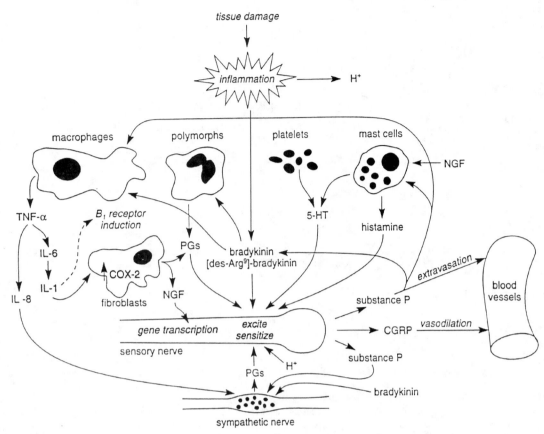

Figure 9.3   Simplified scheme showing some of the local mediators that may act on nociceptive nerve terminals under conditions of tissue damage and inflammation, as discussed in text. Abbreviations: B_1, bradykinin$_1$ receptor; COX-2, cyclooxygenase-2; CGRP, calcitonin gene-related peptide; H+, hydrogen ions; IL, interleukin, NGF, nerve growth factor; PGs, prostaglandins; TNF, tumor necrosis factor, 5HT, 5-hydroxytryptamine (serotonin). [Reprinted with permission from Dray, A., and Bevan, S. (1993), Inflammation and Hyperalgesia: Highlighting the team effort. *Trends in Pharmacological Sciences, 14,* 287–290. Copyright 1993, Elsevier Science].

bloodstream to release even more IL-1β, IL-6, and TNFα (L. R. Watkins et al., 1995). These inflammatory cytokines are known to facilitate pain transmission and blocking their activity reduces hyperalgesia associated with various inflammatory stimuli (Cunha, Lorenzetti, Poole, & Ferreira, 1991; Ferreira, Lorenzetti, & Poole, 1993).

It has also been shown that the neurotrophin nerve growth factor (NGF) is up-regulated in inflamed skin in response to the increase in inflammatory cytokines. NGF is released by Schwann cells and fibroblasts in inflamed skin and produces thermal and mechanical hyperalgesia either by direct activating tyrosine kinase A (trkA) or p75 receptors on primary afferent fibers or by stimulating the release of inflammatory mediators from mast cells (Shu & Mendell, 1999). Additional neurotrophins, brain-derived neurotrophic factor (BDNF), and neurotrophin-4 (NT-4) also are found to sensitize primary afferent fibers and evoke thermal hyperalgesia most likely by activating trkB receptors on mast cells (Shu & Mendell, 1999). NGF also stimulates the enhanced synthesis of neuropeptides such as substance P and calcitonin gene-related peptide (CGRP) in primary afferent fibers.

Mediators that stimulate primary afferent fibers not only cause a facilitation of nociceptive signals, but also enhance the release of neuropeptides from the peripheral terminals of C fibers in skin, viscera, muscle, or joints. Neuropeptides such as substance P, CGRP, and neurokinin A (NKA) induce vasodilatation and plasma extravasation as well as nociceptor activation (or sensitization) and pain (or hyperalgesia; Dray & Urban, 1996). Glutamate is also released from the peripheral terminals of activated primary afferent fibers and can contribute to injury-induced sensory changes (Jackson, Graff, Durnett-Richardson, & Hargreaves, 1995).

Heat, Acid, and Voltage-Gated Ion Channels in Primary Afferent Fibers

Recent evidence suggests there are specific receptors and ion channels that enable Aδ and C fibers to detect and transmit nociceptive stimuli (see Figure 9.4). Ion channels are either regulated by receptors (heat, acid, or ligand-gated) or by the voltage of the neuron (voltage-gated) and allow ions such as sodium (Na+), calcium (Ca^{2+}), or potassium (K+) to flow in

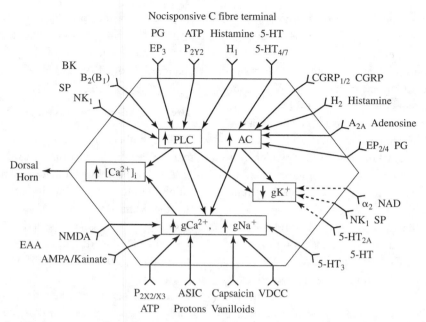

Figure 9.4   Roles of diverse receptors and intracellular signals (ionic conductance or second messenger activation) in mediating the actions of pronociceptive mediators at nocisponsive, polymodal C fiber terminals. Abbreviations are defined in the text of this chapter. The mechanisms indicated relate to common modes of action and not necessarily to common loci of action. For example, Ca^{2+}-permeable ion channels coupled to vanilloid receptors are distinct from Ca^{2+}-permeable ion channels coupled to NMDA receptor. Dotted lines are given where interactions may be indirect, remain uncertain, or both. Actions of ATP at metabotropic P_{2Y2} receptors, potentially involved in mediating mechanical allodynia, are exerted at $A\beta$ rather than C fibers but are included for comparative purposes. Reprinted from *Progress in Neurobiology, 57,* M. J. Millan, The induction of pain: An integrative review, 1–164. Copyright 1999, with permission from Elsevier Science.

or out of the cell. Many of these receptors and channels are modified during tissue injury and contribute to increased sensitivity of primary afferent fibers; thus, the vanniloid receptor (VR-1), which mediates the nociceptive response to capsaicin (the active ingredient in hot chili peppers), is activated naturally by intense heat stimulation (Caterina et al., 1997). Heat stimuli cause an exaggerated activation of this receptor after tissue injury, when the pH of the tissue is low. ASIC (acid-sensing ionic channel) and DRASIC (dorsal root acid-sensing ionic channel) are also sensitive to low pH (when protons collect and increase the acidity of the tissue) and account for the chemosensitivity of some C polymodal nociceptors (Waldmann & Lazdunski, 1998).

Voltage-gated Na^+ channels are responsible for the initial phase of the nerve's action potential and play an essential role (along with K^+ channels) in determining the excitability of primary afferent fibers, and the transfer of the action potential along its axon. Voltage-gated Ca^{2+} channels—along with Na^+ channels—are critical to the process of *exocytosis,* or transmitter release from the presynaptic terminal, and they also contribute to the depolarization and increases in excitability of the postsynaptic neuron. Na^+ channels with varying properties are differentially expressed in normal conditions or following tissue or nerve injury; this leads to differences in the excitability of various primary afferent fibers. Indeed, some evidence suggests that following nerve damage, Na^+ channels

accumulate at the site of injury and may underlie the development of abnormal spontaneous activity (ectopic firing) and mechanical sensitivity of the damaged nerve fibers (England et al., 1996; Novakovic et al., 1988).

Ligand-Gated Receptors, G Protein-Coupled Receptors, and the Phosphorylation of Ion Channels

There are also receptors on primary afferent fibers that are sensitive to chemical stimulation associated with the aforementioned neuroactive substances—that is, excitatory amino acids (EAAs), histamine, serotonin, bradykinin, purines (ATP), prostaglandins, cytokines, and neurotrophins. These substances typically activate receptors on primary afferent fibers that increase neuronal excitability by increasing flow or currents through ligand-gated ion channels (i.e., the ion channel is opened or closed directly by the substance). Alternatively, they may act at G protein-coupled receptors, which increase the affect of ion channels directly or affect the production of second messengers that phosphorylate either ligand-gated or voltage-gated ion channels. Phosphorylation results in changes in the properties of ligand- or voltage-gated ion channels increasing or decreasing ion currents across the channel (Woolf & Costigan, 1999).

Thus, it has recently been demonstrated that various substances (EAAs, ATP, serotonin) act at specific receptors

$((\pm)$-α-amino-3-hydroxy-5-methlisoxazole-4-propionic acid (AMPA)/kainate/N-methyl-D-aspartate or NMDA, $P_{2X2/X3}$, and 5-HT_3, respectively) to enhance ion flow through Na^+ and Ca^{2+} channels in primary afferent fibers. Other substances (substance P, bradykinin, prostaglandin, ATP, histamine) act at specific receptors (NK_1, $BK_{1/2}$, EP_3, P_{2Y2}, and H_1, respectively) that are positively coupled to phospholipase C (PLC). The enzyme PLC triggers an increased release of intracellular Ca^{2+} and protein kinase C (PKC), which produces a phosphorylation of neuronal membranes leading to increased Na^+ and Ca^{2+} currents and decreased K^+ currents in the primary afferent fibers.

Other substances (adenosine, calcitonin gene-related peptide (CGRP), histamine, prostaglandin, and serotonin) act at additional receptors ($A2_A$, $CGRP_{1/2}$, H_2, $EP_{2/4}$, and 5-$HT_{4/7}$, respectively) that are positively coupled to adenylate cyclase. The enzyme adenylate cyclase increases cyclic-adenosine monophosphate (cAMP), which also causes membrane phosphorylation that enhances Na^+ and Ca^{2+} currents and decreases K^+ currents in primary afferent fibers. Finally, substances including substance P and serotonin may also act at additional receptors (neurokinin-1; NK_1, 5-HT_{2A}) to decrease K^+ channels currents in primary afferent fibers (Millan, 1999; Wood & Docherty, 1997).

Phenotype Changes

Changes in the sensitivity of primary afferent fibers after tissue injury or inflammation may also depend on alteration in the phenotype (i.e., a change in gene expression) of the neurons. An up-regulation of various transmitters (substance P, CGRP, glutamate, nitric oxide), receptors (NK_1, galanin-1, neuropeptide Y_1; NPY_1), ion channels (VR1, sensory neuron-specific (SNS) Na^+ channels), and growth factors (NGF, brain derived neurotrophic factor (BDNF)) has been demonstrated in primary afferent fibers in response to inflammation (Millan, 1999). In addition, various peptides—including substance P, CGRP, and somatostatin—are down-regulated, while others including galanin, NPY, vasoactive intestinal polypeptide (VIP), pituitary adenylate cyclase activating peptide (PACAP), and cholecystokinin (CCK) are up-regulated in dorsal root ganglion cells after nerve injury (Hökfelt, Zhang, & Wiesenfeld-Hallin, 1994; as is discussed later in this chapter).

Recently it has been demonstrated that specific primary afferent fibers may even be able to switch their phenotype; thus, it has been shown that after inflammatory injury, Aβ fibers begin to produce and release substance P (which they normally do not contain)—a phenomenon that has important implications for the development of mechanical allodynia

(believed to be mediated largely by Aβ fibers). Evidence suggests that growth factors or neurotrophins may play a critical role in the development of these injury-induced phenotype changes (Woolf, 1996).

The Sympathetic Nervous System

The sympathetic nervous system consists of efferent fibers that are critical in the control of the body's blood flow. For years it has been known that the sympathetic nervous system influences chronic pain and inflammation. Evidence indicates that the primary transmitter released from sympathetic fibers, *noradrenaline,* enhances the activity of primary afferent fibers in inflamed tissue, despite its vasoconstrictive actions that reduce inflammation. Primary afferent fibers damaged by traumatic nerve lesions are also activated either by sympathetic stimulation or by noradrenaline (Sato & Perl, 1991). Noradrenaline contributes to inflammatory hyperalgesia through its actions on α_1 receptors (coupled to PLC) and may contribute to neuropathic pain by an action at upregulated α_2 receptors (coupled positively to Na^+ channels and negatively to K^+ channels) on primary afferent fibers. Sympathetic neurons are also known to release ATP, neuropeptide Y (NPY), nitric oxide, and prostaglandin—substances known to directly or indirectly sensitize primary afferent fibers (Raja, 1995).

THE SPINAL CORD DORSAL HORN

Afferent Input

The majority of primary afferent fiber axons project from the dorsal root ganglion to the spinal cord through the dorsal root (see Figure 9.1). As the root approaches the spinal cord, the small-diameter myelinated Aδ and unmyelinated C fibers segregate from the larger diameter Aβ fibers. The Aβ fibers send central processes ascending and descending in the dorsal columns, with collateral branches penetrating the spinal cord dorsal horn. The small-diameter fibers also send ascending and descending branches in the tract of Lissauer, but these only extend one or two spinal segments (Coggeshall, Chung, Chung, & Langford, 1981). Primary afferent fiber input to the spinal cord dorsal horn is for the most part ipsilateral (projecting to the dorsal horn on the same side of the body). However, there are also some contralateral inputs (to the dorsal horn on the opposite side of the body), which may underlie a phenomenon known as *mirror image pain* and may explain bilateral neurochemical, anatomical, and functional changes that can occur after unilateral stimulation of peripheral tissue and nerves (Willis & Coggeshall, 1991).

Primary afferent fibers from the neck, face, and head that make up the cranial nerves (including the trigeminal or Vth cranial nerve) carry somatosensory inputs to the main sensory nucleus of V in the pons, or the spinal trigeminal nucleus, which is partly in the cervical spinal cord (C1 and C2) and partly in the medulla (known as the medullary dorsal horn). This region plays a role similar to that of the spinal cord dorsal horn—receiving, processing, and transmitting somatosensory and nociceptive inputs (Dubner & Bennett, 1983).

The dendrites and cell bodies of spinal cord neurons constitute the grey matter of the spinal cord, which has a characteristic butterfly-like shape when observed on cross-section. Primary afferent fibers terminate and make synapses with spinal cord neurons that are in the two regions (left and right) at the back (humans) or top (animals) of the grey matter (i.e., the posterior or dorsal horns). The grey matter of the spinal cord is divided into 10 laminae that can be distinguished morphologically. The *dorsal horn* consists of Lamina I (marginal layer), II (substantia gelatinosa), III and IV (nucleus proprius), and V and VI (deep layers). Lamina VII is referred to as the *intermediate grey matter,* Laminae VIII and IX are called the *medial* and *lateral ventral horns,* and Lamina X is the region surrounding the central canal. The shape of these laminae vary considerably throughout the length of the spinal cord along the cervical, thoracic, lumbar, and sacral spinal segments, and Lamina VI is only clearly defined in the lumbar and cervical segments of the spinal cord (Rexed, 1952; Willis & Coggeshall, 1991).

Nociceptive inputs are for the most part received in Lamina I and the outer part of Lamina II (IIo), known together as the *superficial dorsal horn,* as well as the deeper laminae, V, VI, and X (see Figure 9.5). Generally, cutaneous C fibers terminate predominantly in Lamina IIo and to a lesser extent in Laminae I and V, whereas cutaneous Aδ fibers terminate largely in Laminae I and V and sparsely in Laminae IIo and X. C fibers from viscera, joints, and muscle terminate mostly in Laminae I, V, and VI (Christensen & Perl, 1970).

Individual dorsal horn neurons may receive converging inputs from primary afferent fibers originating in cutaneous tissue and those originating in viscera or muscle. This convergence probably underlies a phenomenon known as *referred pain,* whereby inputs from injured viscera are mistakenly interpreted as coming from skin regions with primary afferent fibers that converge on the same neurons as the primary afferent fibers from the injured viscera. A familiar example of referred pain is the pain of myocardial infarction, in which many patients report pain not only in the chest and upper abdomen, but also along the ulnar aspect of the left arm. Nonnociceptive inputs from Aβ fibers mostly terminate in Laminae III and IV, although there are limited projections to Laminae I, IIi (inner), V, and VI. The ventral horn (Laminae VIII and IX) contains predominantly motoneurons, which transmit efferent motor activity required for reflex and voluntary movements (Besson & Chaouch, 1987; Dubner & Bennett, 1983).

Dorsal Horn Neurons

There are three classes of dorsal horn neurons that receive input from primary afferent fibers. Nonnociceptive neurons (NON-N)—found primarily in Laminae II, III, and IV—receive input from Aβ fibers. These neurons are activated by nonnoxious mechanical and thermal stimuli. Nociceptive-specific (NS) neurons, found mostly in Laminae I and IIo but also in V and VI receive inputs from Aδ and C fibers. Normally, these neurons respond only to high-intensity, noxious stimuli. The small receptive fields and specific response properties of these neurons render them suitable to signal the location and physical characteristics of noxious stimuli. Wide dynamic range (WDR) neurons—found predominantly in Lamina V—receive inputs from Aβ fibers as well as from Aδ and C fibers. These neurons respond in a graded fashion to nonnoxious as well as noxious mechanical, thermal, and chemical stimuli. WDR neurons, which are important for encoding stimulus intensity, often receive convergent input from cutaneous, muscle, and visceral tissue and are heavily implicated in central sensitization following tissue or nerve injury (discussed later in this chapter; Dubner & Bennett, 1983; Willis & Coggeshall, 1991).

Neurotransmitters and Neuromodulators Released From the Central Terminals of Primary Afferent Fibers

Primary afferent fibers release a variety of substances that act either as neurotransmitters or as neuromodulators in the spinal cord dorsal horn (see Figure 9.6). Neurotransmitters and neuromodulators involved in synaptic transmission include EAAs (aspartate, glutamate), neuropeptides (substance P, NKA, CGRP, NPY, galanin, VIP, CCK, endomorphin-2), purines (ATP, adenosine), neurotrophins (NGF, BDNF), and second messengers that include gas molecules (nitric oxide), arachidonic acid metabolites (prostaglandin), phospholipases (PLs; PLA_2, PLC), cyclic nucleotides (adenylate cyclase, cAMP) and protein kinases (PKs; PKA, PKC, PKG).

EAAs, neuropeptides, and purines act at receptors that are coupled to ion channels, G proteins, or both; they alter ionic currents or the activity of second messengers and affect the neuronal excitability in various ways. Generally, neuronal excitability is enhanced by activity at receptors that increase Na^+ or Ca^{2+} currents or decrease K^+ currents across ion

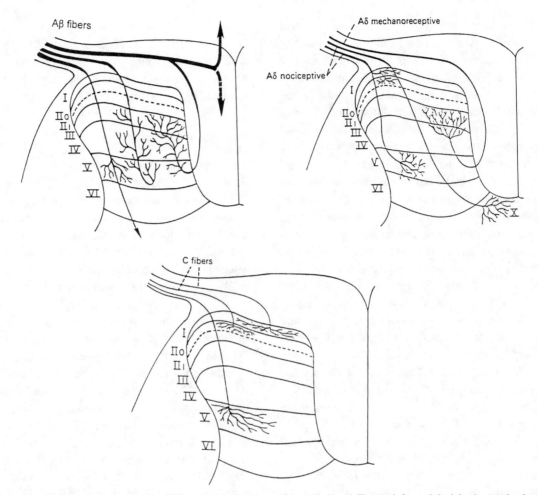

Figure 9.5 Organization of cutaneous, primary afferent input to the dorsal horn of the spinal cord. The top left panel depicts the termination of Aβ fibers. On entering the spinal cord these fibers proceed medially and bifurcate into short descending and long ascending branches in the dorsal columns. Before entering the dorsal column, they give off collaterals, some of which penetrate the dorsal horn and terminate largely in Laminae IIi, III, and IV and to a lesser extend in Lamina V. The top right panel depicits the termination of Aδ fibers. On entering the spinal cord, these fibers run laterally into the medial aspect of the tract of Lissauer, where they divide into short ascending and descending branches that run for one or two segments. Collaterals of the Aδ nociceptors penetrate the lateral aspect of the dorsal horn and terminate in Laminae I, IIo, V, and X. The bottom panel depicts the termination of C fibers. Collaterals of C fibers penetrate the dorsal gray matter from the medial tract of Lissauer and appear to terminate exclusively in Laminae I, IIo, and V of the dorsal horn. Reprinted with permission from Bonica, J. J. (1990). *The management of pain:* Vol. 1. Copyright 1990, Lea and Febiger.

channels or that are positively coupled to G proteins, which enhance activity of the various second messengers mentioned previously. Conversely, decreases in neuronal excitability generally occur after activation of receptors that increase K^+ currents, decrease Na^+ or Ca^{2+} currents, or are negatively coupled with the second messenger adenylate cyclase and decrease cAMP. Second messengers typically alter neuronal excitability for prolonged periods by phosphorylating voltage- or ligand-gated ion channels (often resulting in increased Na^+ or Ca^{2+} currents across the channels).

Excitatory Amino Acids

Aspartate and glutamate are released from the central terminals of primary afferent fibers in response to noxious thermal and chemical stimulation and act at both ionotropic and metabotropic glutamate receptors in the spinal cord dorsal horn. Ionotropic glutamate receptors are ligand-gated ion channels and include subtypes of receptors that have been classified according to synthetic agents that selectively activate these receptors—that is, (±)-alpha-amino-3-hydroxy-5-methlisoxazole-4-propionic acid (AMPA), kainate and N-methyl-D-aspartate (NMDA). Metabotropic glutamate receptors (mGluR) are directly coupled via G proteins to intracellular second messengers and include eight subtypes that have been grouped into three classes—Group I (mGluR1 and 5), Group II (mGluR2–3), and Group III (mGluR4 and mGluR6–8; Coderre, 1993; J. C. Watkins & Evans, 1981).

AMPA and kainate receptors are for the most part only permeable to Na^+ ions and are believed to act as fast transmitters

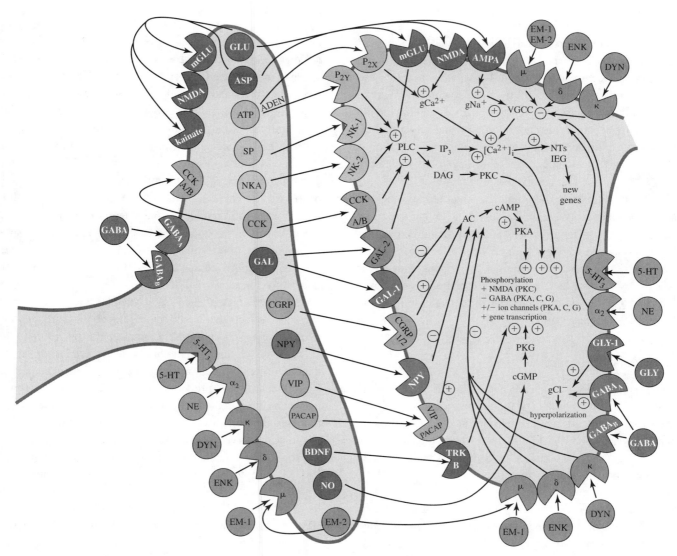

Figure 9.6 Neurotransmitters, neuromodulators, and signal transduction in the spinal cord dorsal horn. See text for details on neurotransmitters, neuromodulators, and second messengers. Also included in the figure is a schema illustrating the ability of neurotrophins and increased intracellular Ca^{2+} to trigger the induction of immediate early genes (IEG), whose protein products are instrumental in the gene transcription needed for the production of new gene products. This gene transcription is required for the up-regulation of transmitters and receptors and for changes in neuronal phenotype that occur after tissue injury leading to pathological pain. Intracellular actions indicated on the postsynaptic neuron occur also on the presynaptic neuron but are not shown. Also not discussed is the role of phosphatases counteracting the effects of kinases which phosphorylate various ion channels. Modified and reprinted from *Progress in Neurobiology, 57,* M. J. Millan, The induction of pain: An integrative review, 1–164, Copyright 1999, with permission from Elsevier Science.

because they are inactivated quickly. For this reason, it is believed that activation of AMPA and kainate receptors is involved in the transmission of nonnoxious and acute noxious stimulation. In contrast, NMDA receptors have high permeability to Ca^{2+} as well as Na^+ and are slowly inactivated. They are also subject to voltage-sensitive Mg^+ block of the ion channel, such that the receptors are not able to respond fully until the neuron is partially depolarized; thus, NMDA receptors are not fully activated until there is excessive aspartate or glutamate release, which by repeatedly stimulating AMPA and kainate receptors, produces enough depolarization of the

neuron to free the NMDA channels from their Mg^+ block. As a result, NMDA receptors play a critical role in persistent pain, which is associated with excessive release of aspartate and glutamate. Also, the high permeability to Ca^{2+} ensures that NMDA receptor activation leads to long-term cellular changes that result when various excitatory second messengers (nitric oxide, prostaglandin, PKC) are activated by high intracellular Ca^{2+} concentrations. Indeed, considerable evidence suggests that NMDA receptors play a critical role in persistent pain and in central sensitization that contributes to hyperalgesia (Coderre, 1993; Watkins & Evans, 1981).

Metabotropic glutamate receptors are also believed to have long-lasting effects through their stimulation of intracellular second messengers. However, the overall effects are dependent on specific class of mGluRs that are activated. Thus, cellular excitation occurs following activation of Group I mGluRs that are positively coupled to PLC, an enzyme that catalyzes phosphotidylinositol hydrolysis and activates PKC. However, cellular inhibition occurs following activation of Group II and III mGluRs, which are negatively coupled to adenylate cyclase and reduce the production of cAMP. It is believed that aspartate and glutamate act at Group I mGluRs to enhance nociceptive transmission but also that they regulate this process through actions at Group II and III mGluRs. It is important to note that Group III mGluRs have a significant role as autoreceptors in many CNS regions; thus, aspartate and glutamate act at Group III mGluRs on primary afferent fibers to inhibit their own further release (Coderre, Fisher, & Fundytus, 1997).

Neuropeptides

The neuropeptides substance P, neurokinin A, and CGRP are colocalized with aspartate and glutamate in a subset of small-diameter primary afferent fibers. Substance P and neurokinin A act primarily at NK_1 and NK_2 receptors in the spinal cord, respectively, and are coupled by G proteins to PLC. These neuropeptides have been found to produce a slow, long-lasting depolarization of dorsal horn neurons; they are generally believed to act as neuromodulators, which enhance the response of dorsal horn neurons to excitatory input. These excitatory neuropeptides may act to relieve NMDA receptors of their voltage-gated block and may enhance the release of aspartate and glutamate from primary afferent fibers. Preventing the activation of substance P at NK_1 receptors effectively alleviates nociception in various experimental models of persistent pain, hyperalgesia, or both. CGRP, which exists in two isoforms (α and β), acts at two known receptors $CGRP_1$ and $CGRP_2$. These are also G protein-coupled receptors but are positively linked with adenylate cyclase, the enzyme that stimulates the production of cAMP, which has excitatory effects (Dray, 1996; Millan, 1999).

Additional neuropeptides that have been shown to have significant effects in the spinal cord dorsal horns include NPY, galanin, VIP, and CCK. The levels of these neuropeptides are affected by both tissue or nerve injury and probably influence the hyperalgesia and allodynia associated with injury. Thus, the spinal level of NPY, which is normally quite low, is dramatically increased after peripheral nerve injury (particularly in Aβ fibers; Hökfelt et al., 1994). NPY acts at several receptor subtypes that are negatively coupled to adenylate cyclase and by lowering cAMP, it tends to decrease nociception. Nociception is also decreased by the action of NPY at receptors coupled to ion channels that enhance K^+ currents or decrease Ca^{2+} currents. Galanin is found in both Aβ and C fibers and normally contributes to spinal nociception. Conversely, after nerve injury there is an up-regulation of galanin in primary afferent fibers, and galanin appears to have an antinociceptive effect in neuropathic rats (Xu, Wiesenfeld-Hallin, Villar, Fahrenkrug, & Hökfelt, 1990). The separate nociceptive and antinociceptive effects may depend partly on galanin's action at two separate receptors. It is likely that galanin produces its nociceptive effects at a Gal-2 receptor, which is coupled by a G protein to PLC, and results in increases in intracellular Ca^{2+} and PKC (Ahren, 1996). In contrast, galanin's action at a Gal-1 receptor may be antinociceptive because activity at this receptor produces an inhibition of voltage-gated Ca^{2+} channels and increased K^+ currents—effects that would hyperpolarize the target neuron, and reduce its activity (Kask, Langel, & Bartfai, 1995).

VIP is also found both in A and C fibers, but is more abundant in visceral primary afferent fibers than it is in cutaneous ones. Generally, it produces nociceptive effects on spinal neurons, although these effects are attenuated in neuropathic rats, despite the fact that there is an up-regulation of VIP in Aδ and C fibers (Hökfelt et al., 1994). VIP is structurally similar to PACAP and shares actions with PACAP at two VIP-PACAP receptor subtypes. These receptors are positively coupled to adenylate cyclase, and their activation causes increases in cAMP, which tends to have nociceptive effects (Rawlings & Hezarch, 1996). CCK is also normally quite low in primary afferent fibers and is markedly increased following nerve injury. It is believed that CCK produces antiopioid effects, reducing the release of endogenous opioids or their postsynaptic effects on spinal neurons, possibly after stimulating PLC. The reduced effects of opiates in neuropathic rats have been attributed in part to the increased levels of spinal CCK and may be influenced by other peptides such as Phe-Met-Arg-Phe-amide (FMRFamide) and Phe-Leu-Phe-Gln-Pro-Gln-Arg-Phe-amide (neuropeptide FF, NPFF). In contrast, the increased potency of opiates in rats with peripheral inflammation has been attributed to inflammation-induced decreases in spinal CCK (Stanfa, Dickenson, Xu, & Wiesenfeld-Hallin, 1994).

Endomorphin-1 and 2 are recently discovered peptides that act selectively at the μ-opioid receptor, which is the primary receptor that mediates the analgesia effects of opiates. Endomorphin-2 is highly expressed in primary afferent fibers and is released into the spinal cord dorsal horn after stimulation of the dorsal roots (Dun, Dun, Wu, Williams, & Kwok, 2000). It has been found that endomorphin-2 acts back on primary afferent fibers to suppress transmitter release, as well as on postsynaptic neurons causing a hyperpolarization. Activation of the μ-opioid receptor inhibits Ca^{2+} currents, enhances K^+ currents, and inhibits the production of cAMP by suppressing adenylate cyclase activity—all effects that hyperpolarize the target neuron (Zadina et al., 1999). Enkephalins acting at δ-opioid receptors and dynorphins acting at κ-opioid receptors produce similar effects, although actions at these receptors do not have as potent analgesic effects.

Purines

Purines active in the spinal cord dorsal horn include ATP and its metabolite adenosine. ATP may act in the spinal cord dorsal—similar to its action at the peripheral terminal of primary afferent fibers—to produce excitatory or nociceptive effects (Gu & MacDermott, 1997; Li & Perl, 1995). These excitatory effects are mediated through a variety of receptor subtypes that include both ionotropic (P_{2X}) and metabotropic (P_{2Y}) receptors. The P_{2X} receptors are coupled to Ca^{2+} channels, and excitatory effects follow increased influx of Ca^{2+}. The P_{2Y} receptors are coupled to PLC and have excitatory effects by enhancing glutamate transmission in the dorsal horn. In contrast to ATP, spinal adenosine tends to produce antinociceptive effects at an A_1 receptor that is negatively coupled to adenylate cyclase and whose activation inhibits and enhances Ca^{2+} and K^+ currents, respectively (Sawynok & Sweeney, 1989).

Neurotrophins

Neurotrophins are growth factors that stimulate neuronal growth in embryonic development and maintain neuronal viability in adult tissues. Neurotrophins include NGF, which acts selectively at trkA receptors; BDNF, NT-4, and NT-5, which act at trkB receptors; and NT-3, which acts at trkC receptors in spinal cord. An additional neurotrophin, glial derived neurotrophic factor (GDNF) binds to the receptor GDNF family receptor-alpha1. Small-diameter unmyelinated primary afferent fibers generally fall into two groups: One contains CGRP, substance P, and trkA receptors and depends on NGF for its development; a second contains the lectin isolectin B-4 and trkB receptors and is dependent on GDNF for its development (McMahon, Armanini, Ling, & Philips, 1994). These neurotrophic factors are required not only for neuronal development; they also continue to be produced by numerous types of cells, produce excitatory effects on primary afferent fibers, and are required to maintain normal neuronal function of primary afferent fibers. BDNF has been found to be expressed in primary afferent fibers (particularly C fibers containing CGRP and substance P) and to act in the spinal cord to enhance neuronal excitability.

It has been hypothesized that hyperalgesia after inflammatory injury is influenced by an up-regulation of BDNF in primary afferent fibers that occurs in response to peripheral stimulation of primary afferent fibers with NGF. Thus, inflammation leads to increased production of NGF in peripheral tissue, which stimulates trkA receptors on the first group of primary afferent fibers described previously. The stimulation of trkA receptors results in increased BDNF production in this group of C fibers and precipitates enhanced BDNF release and a subsequent sensitization of dorsal horn neurons (Thompson, Bennett, Kerr, Bradbury, & McMahon, 1999).

Second Messengers

As noted previously, excitatory amino acids, neuropeptides, and purines act at receptors that are coupled to G proteins and alter the activity of second messengers affecting neuronal excitability in various ways. Some also have associated ion channels that are permeable to Ca^{2+}, which itself is an important activator of various second messengers; thus, receptors positively coupled by G proteins to adenylate cyclase tend to have excitatory effects associated with the increase in intracellular cAMP, whereas those negatively coupled to adenylate cyclase have the opposite effect. Receptors coupled to PLC also tend to have excitatory effects associated with increases in the release of Ca^{2+} from intracellular stores and with the activation of PKC. An increase in the flux of Ca^{2+} through receptor-operated Ca^{2+} channels—like NMDA receptor channels—also stimulates PLC and results in increased release of Ca^{2+} from internal stores as well as an increased activation of PKC.

Increases in Ca^{2+} influx also stimulate PLA_2, which metabolizes arachidonic acid into prostaglandins, which produce excitatory effects in the dorsal horn. Finally, increased Ca^{2+} influx also stimulates nitric oxide synthase to breakdown arginine into the gas molecule nitric oxide. Nitric oxide produces excitatory effects either by stimulating the production of cGMP in the postsynaptic cell and phosphorylating ion channels or by acting as a retrograde transmitter that diffuses into the presynaptic neuron to enhance synaptic release directly or by stimulating cGMP. Generally, each of these second messengers (PKC, prostaglandins, nitric oxide, cAMP, cGMP) alter neuronal excitability for prolonged periods by phosphorylating voltage- or ligand-gated ion channels (often resulting in increased Na^+ or Ca^{2+} currents across the channels). Each of these second messengers has been found to play a role either in pain transmission or the development of sensitization in spinal cord dorsal horn neurons (Coderre, 1993; Millan, 1999).

Central Sensitization

Various studies indicate that following injury, noxious stimulation, or C fiber afferent electrical stimulation, there is a sensitization of neurons in the dorsal horn of the spinal cord and other areas in the somatosensory pathway. This sensitization is reflected by increased spontaneous activity, reduced thresholds or increased responsiveness to afferent inputs, prolonged after-discharges to repeated stimulation, the expansion of the peripheral receptive field of CNS neurons, and an increased excitability of flexion reflexes. After repeated high-frequency, C fiber strength inputs, spinal cord dorsal horn neurons also develop a cumulative depolarization that results in bursts of firing known as *windup,* a phenomenon that may contribute to some pathological pains that are paroxysmal (shock-like) in nature (Coderre, Katz, Vaccarino, & Melzack, 1993).

Central sensitization and the neuroplasticity it reflects are dependent on neurochemical, cellular, and molecular events in the CNS systems described previously in this chapter (Coderre et al., 1993). The discovery of long-term changes in the CNS after acute injury has led to the use of *preemptive analgesia,* in which a local anesthetic, analgesic agents, or both are given before surgery—even when a general anesthetic is used—with the aim of preventing central sensitization. Studies in animals and humans show that postoperative pain is reduced when nociceptive input is blocked during the surgical procedure (Richmond, Bromley, & Woolf, 1993).

Neuronal Changes Underlying Neuropathic Pain

Damage to peripheral nerves can result in spontaneous pain, hyperalgesia, and allodynia (when innocuous stimulation is felt as noxious), that persists for years or decades after the original injury. Syndromes such as causalgia, postherpetic neuralgia, painful diabetic neuropathy, and phantom limb pain are all associated with damage to peripheral nerves and with abnormal pain sensations. Evidence suggests that although sensitized primary afferent fibers or ectopic firing in neuromas can account for some symptoms, other symptoms depend on plastic changes in the CNS. For example, the phenomenon of dynamic mechanical allodynia, in which excruciating pain is evoked by lightly brushing the skin, is mediated by Aβ fibers, which normally transmit tactile information acting on sensitized central neurons (Gracely, Lynch, & Bennett, 1992).

Two categories of changes have been proposed to occur at the level of the spinal cord dorsal horn: (a) *central sensitization,* whereby the neuronal response to normal pain input is augmented, producing hyperalgesia; and (b) *structural reorganization,* whereby previously nonexistent connections are formed between Aβ fibers and nociceptive neurons, producing allodynia (Woolf, Shortland, & Coggeshall, 1992). Furthermore, as described previously, there are considerable changes in the expression of various peptides contained in primary afferent fibers that determine the excitability of those fibers and their net effect on spinal projection neurons (see Figure 9.7).

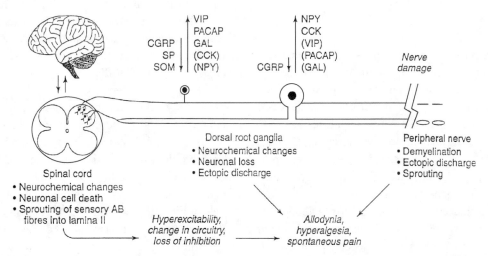

Figure 9.7   Plastic changes following nerve injury. Within the small and large sensory neurons of the dorsal root ganglia (DRG), a number of neurochemical changes occur. Within the large-diameter DRG cells there is a particularly marked increase in the levels of neuropeptide Y (NPY) and cholecystokinin (CCK), whereas the levels of calcitonin gene-related peptide (CGRP) are seen to decrease. In small-diameter DRG cells, the levels of substance P (SP), CGRP, and somatostatin (SOM) decrease, while the levels of galanin, vasoactive intestinal polypeptide (VIP), and pituitary adenylate cyclase-activating polypeptide (PACAP) are all markedly increased. Several morphological and phenotypic changes can also be observed within the spinal cord and the injured peripheral nerve, including alterations in the expression of a number of neuropeptide receptors. These various neurochemical changes coincide with various morphological (demyelination, peripheral and central sprouting, neuronal cell death) and physiological (ectopic discharge in neuroma and DRG) changes that underlie hyperexcitability and loss of inhibition, and contribute to the development of allodynia, hyperalgesia, and spontaneous pain. Reprinted from *Trends in Pharmacological Sciences, 20,* T. Dickinson and S. M. Fleetwood-Walker, VIP and PACAP: Very important in pain? 324–330, Copyright 1999, with permission from Elsevier Science.

Interneurons and Descending Fibers Within the Dorsal Horn

In addition to the previously described classification of dorsal horn neurons based on the inputs they receive (i.e., NON-N, NS, and WDR), dorsal horn neurons can also be classified by their output destination. Generally, there are projection neurons, which transmit information supraspinally, and interneurons (excitatory or inhibitory), which project inputs locally or within the spinal cord. Projection neurons are found predominantly in Laminae I, V, and VI, whereas interneurons are concentrated in Lamina II. Although some projection neurons are contacted directly (monosynaptically) by primary afferent fibers, others receive indirect (polysynaptic) input from excitatory interneurons. It has been suggested that excitatory interneurons play a large role in allowing WDR neurons to receive inputs from both $A\beta$ and C fibers. These excitatory interneurons are believed to use neuropeptides such as substance P, VIP, and CCK, and purines (ATP) or second messengers (nitric oxide, prostaglandins) as their neurotransmitters-modulators. (Cervero & Iggo, 1980; Willis & Coggeshall, 1991).

Inhibitory Interneurons

Various classes of inhibitory interneurons have been identified that regulate nociceptive transmission by targeting postsynaptic neurons (i.e., NS and WDR projection neurons) or presynaptic neurons (i.e., the central terminals of primary afferent fibers). These classes include interneurons that release gamma-aminobutyric acid (GABA), glycine, opioid peptides, or acetycholine (ACh). GABA is a major inhibitory transmitter that binds at two receptor subtypes ($GABA_A$ and $GABA_B$). $GABA_A$ receptors have a chloride-(Cl^-) permeable ion channel that when activated hyperpolarizes the neuron causing inhibition. $GABA_B$ receptors are negatively coupled by G proteins to adenylate cyclase and inhibit cAMP; they also reduce Ca^{2+} currents and increase K^+ currents, which hyperpolarizes the neuron and decreases transmitter release. Like GABA, glycine is a major inhibitory transmitter that is linked to a Cl^--permeable ion channel. Although glycine acts primarily at Gly_1 (strychnine-sensitive) receptors to hyperpolarize neurons by increasing flux through Cl^- channels, it also acts at Gly_2 (strychnine-insensitive) receptors as a cotransmitter at the NMDA receptor, enabling aspartate and glutamate to produce excitatory effects at this site (Hammond, 1997).

Enkephalin and dynorphin are opioid peptides contained within inhibitory interneurons in the spinal cord dorsal horn. These peptides act primarily at δ- and κ-opioid receptors, respectively (but also at μ-opioid receptors), and produce inhibitory effects on both primary afferent fibers and spinal cord neurons. Like the endormorphin released from primary afferent fibers, these opioid peptides cause hyperpolarization of target neurons by enhancing K^+ currents and decreasing Ca^{2+} currents and adenylate cyclase activity. Additional interneurons release ACh, which acts at both muscarinic and nicotinic receptors to hyperpolarize primary afferent fibers and spinal cord neurons (Fields & Basbaum, 1994).

Descending Fibers

Spinal cord dorsal horn neurons and the central terminals of primary afferent fibers also receive inhibitory input from fibers that descend from supraspinal structures (cortex, midbrain, and brain stem). Fibers that descend from the periaqueductal gray (PAG) activate serotoninergic neurons in the rostroventral medulla or noradrenergic neurons in the dorsolateral pontine reticular formation. These neurons descend to the spinal cord and release serotonin and noradrenaline, respectively. Serotonin and noradrenaline act directly, or they act indirectly through enkephalinergic and possibly GABAergic inhibitory interneurons to inhibit the release of transmitters from primary afferent fibers or to inhibit the activation of spinal cord projection neurons (see Figure 9.8 and this chapter's section titled "Pain Modulation"). Although these descending fiber tracts play a large role in the inhibitory modulation of input to the spinal cord, there is also evidence that parallel fibers are capable of producing a descending facilitation of spinal transmission. However, the actions of serotonin and noradrenalin are dependent on the subtypes of the receptors on which they act. Thus, whereas inhibition occurs through actions at α_2 and 5-serotonin1A ($5-HT_{1A}$) receptors, facilitation occurs at α_1 and $5-HT_{2/3}$ receptors (Millan, 1999).

The Gate Control Theory of Pain

Much of the research underlying the discovery of the descending pain modulation system was prompted by theoretical pain-gating mechanisms that were proposed in the gate control theory of pain proposed by Melzack and Wall in 1965 (see Figure 9.9). This theory basically proposed that the transmission of nerve impulses from spinal cord nociceptive projection neurons are modulated by a spinal gating mechanism in the dorsal horn. According to Melzack and Wall, the gating mechanism is influenced by the relative amount of activity in large-diameter and small-diameter primary afferent fibers, with large-fiber activity tending to close the gate and small-fiber activity opening the gate.

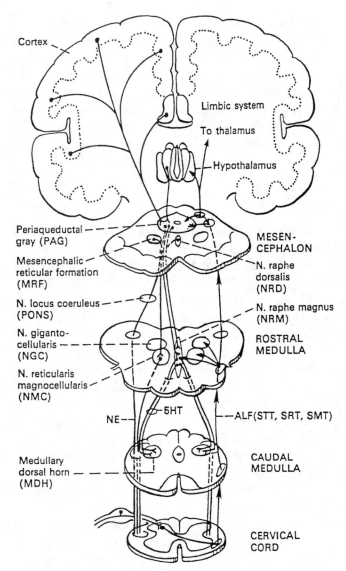

Figure 9.8 Descending endogenous pain control (inhibitory systems). The most extensively studied and probably the most important descending system is composed of four tiers, including the mesencephalon (midbrain), rostral medulla, caudal medulla, and cervical spinal cord. The ascending anterolateral fasciculus (ALF), composed of the spinothalamic (STT), spinoreticular (SRT) and spinomesencephalic (SMT) tracts, has important inputs into the nucleus raphe magnus (NRM), nucleus magnocellularis (NMC), nucleus reticularis gigantocellularis (NGC), and periaqueductal gray (PAG). The ALF also has input to the medullary-pontine reticular formation (MRF). The PAG receives important input from such rostral structures as the frontal and insular cortex (and other parts of the cerebrum involved in cognition) and from the limbic system, the thalamus, and—most important—the hypothalamus, which sends beta-endorphin axons to the PAG. The locus coeruleus in the pons is a major source of noradrenergic (NE) input to the PAG and dorsal horn (tract labeled NE). These mesencephalic structures (PAG, NRD, MRF) contain enkephalin (ENK), dynorphin (DYN), serotonin (5HT), and neurotensin (NT) neurons, but only the latter two send axons that project to NRM and NGC. Here they make synapses with neurons that are primarily serotonergic, whose axons project to the medullary dorsal horn and descend in the dorsolateral funiculus to the spinal cord. Modified and reprinted with permission from Bonica, J. J. (1990). *The management of pain:* Vol. 1. Copyright 1990, Lea and Febiger.

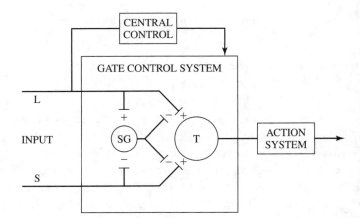

Figure 9.9 Gate control theory of pain. Circuit proposed by Melzack and Wall (1965) for a gating system that might determine the output of the "action system." Large (L) fiber inputs close the gate and hyperpolarize transmission (T) cells by activating inhibitory interneurons in the substantia gelatinosa (SG), while small (S) fibers open the gate and depolarize T cells by suppressing the activation of inhibitory neurons in the SG. Reprinted with permission from Melzack, R., and Wall, P. D. (1965). Pain mechanisms: A new theory. *Science, 150,* 971–979. Copyright 1965 American Association for the Advancement of Science.

In order to explain the powerful influence of cognitive processes on pain perception, Melzack and Wall also proposed that the spinal gating mechanism was influenced by descending modulation (or central control) from the brain; indeed, they proposed that a large fiber pathway (called the *central control trigger*) rapidly conveyed inputs to the brain and allowed for activation of this descending modulatory system. This theory has provided a justification for the development of transcutaneous electrical nerve stimulation (to stimulate large fibers and close the gate), dorsal column stimulation (to activate the central control trigger), and deep brain stimulation (to activate the descending modulatory system) as means to alleviate intractable pain by modulating inputs from the spinal cord (Melzack & Wall, 1965).

THE BRAIN

Transmission of Nociceptive Inputs to Supraspinal Centers

Axons of projection neurons in the spinal cord dorsal horn project to the brain along a number of different fiber tracts (see Figure 9.10). The spinothalamic tract is the main spinal cord pathway for pain transmission. Its cells of origin are located primarily in Laminae IV and V; the majority of axons cross within the spinal segment they originate, and they ascend in the contralateral anterolateral quadrant of the spinal cord. Many spinothalamic fibers terminate in a somatotopic fashion in the ventral posterior (VP) thalamic nucleus, which also

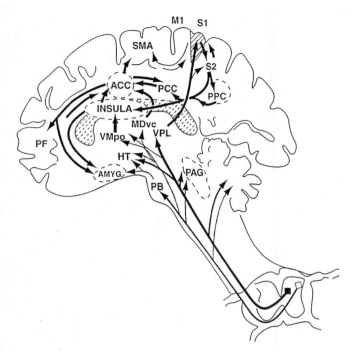

Figure 9.10 Schematic of ascending pathways, subcortical structures, and cerebral cortical structures involved in processing pain. PAG, periaqueductal gray; PB, parabrachial nucleus of the dorsolateral pons; VMpo, ventromedial part of the posterior nuclear complex; MDvc, ventrocaudal part of the medial dorsal nucleus; VPL, ventroposterior lateral nucleus; ACC, anterior cingulate cortex; PCC, posterior cingulate cortex; HT, hypothalamus; S-1 and S-2, first and second somatosensory cortical areas; PPC, posterior parietal complex; SMA, supplementary motor area; AMYG, amygdala; PF, prefrontal cortex. Reprinted with permission from Price, D. D. (2000). Psychological and neural mechanisms of the affective dimension of pain. *Science, 288,* 1769–1772. Copyright 1965 American Association for the Advancement of Science.

receives the main output of tactile information from the dorsal column nuclei. Cells in VP, including those responsive to noxious stimuli, send axons to the somatosensory cortex in the postcentral gyrus. Generally, these inputs carry information about the intensity and specific location of the pain stimulus (Bushnell, 1995). Other spinothalamic fibers terminate in the posterior thalamus. A nucleus in the posterior thalamus (ventromedial posterior thalamus, VMpo) has recently been identified that receives specific pain and temperature information from Lamina I of the dorsal horn and sends projections to the insular cortex (Craig, Bushnell, Zhang, & Blomqvist, 1994).

Spinothalamic fibers also terminate in medial thalamic intralaminar nuclei, including parafascicularis (Pf) and the ventrocaudal portion of the medialis dorsalis (MDvc). Whereas nociceptive neurons in VP have small receptive fields and are highly somatotopic, those in medial thalamus have large receptive fields and little somatotopic organization. Neurophysiological studies in awake monkeys indicate that the responsiveness of medial thalamic neurons to noxious stimuli is influenced by behavioral state. When a monkey is attending to a noxious stimulus, the activity of these neurons is greater than that when the monkey is distracted (Bushnell & Duncan, 1989). Neurons in the VMpo may be particularly important for determining stimulus modality and may be important for the determination of whether a stimulus is potentially harmful (Bushnell, 1995). Regions of medial thalamus that receive nociceptive input project to a diversity of cortical and subcortical sites, including limbic and motor regions. The diversity of these projections may reflect the rich variety of emotional and motoric responses that pain evokes.

Although the spinothalamic tract is the best understood pain pathway, nociceptive information reaches the brain by a number of other routes. Two such pathways, the spinoreticular and spinomesencephalic tracts, are located in the anterolateral quadrant of the spinal cord, along with the spinothalamic tract. Some spinoreticular neurons terminate on cells involved in descending pain modulation pathways (described previously), but most terminate in the brain stem reticular formation and play a role in the affective or emotional response to pain. Other spinoreticular neurons make up the spinoreticulothalamic tract, which terminates in medial thalamus, along with the spinothalamic neurons. The spinomesencephalic tract terminates primarily in the superior colliculus and the PAG. Nociceptive activity in the superior colliculus could be involved in multisensory integration, behavioral reactions, and orienting to painful stimuli. Projections to the PAG terminate in a region critical to the endogenous pain-modulating system (Bushnell, 1995).

A surgical procedure used for almost a century for the treatment of severe intractable pain is the anterior cordotomy, in which the anterolateral quadrant of the spinal cord is lesioned and the spinothalamic, spinoreticular, and spinomesencephalic pathways are interrupted. Although this neurosurgical procedure is one of the most successful, frequently the patient's pain returns after months or years. This delayed return of pain can best be explained by functional changes in other pathways that convey nociceptive information to the brain. One pathway by which nociceptive input could reach the thalamus, bypassing the anterolateral quadrant, is via the dorsal columns to the DCN in the caudal medulla. Although the vast majority of fibers ascending in the dorsal columns are axon collaterals of large-diameter primary afferents, some nociceptive neurons in Lamina V project axons in this pathway to the cuneate and gracile (dorsal column) nuclei.

Recent evidence suggests that the DCN may be particularly important for the transmission of visceral pain. Another pathway often spared after anterolateral cordotomy is the spinocervical tract, which terminates in the thalamus after synapsing in the lateral cervical nucleus (LCN) in the cervical spinal cord. The dorsal columns and the spinocervical tract are not affected by anterolateral cordotomy because these tracts project ipsilaterally to their relay centers in the DCN and LCN, respectively, before crossing over to the contralateral side and ascending to the thalamus (Berkley, 1997). Projections of these pathways to the lateral thalamus (VP) are believed to be involved in the sensory-discriminative aspects of pain, whereas those to the medial thalamus and VMpo are proposed to influence the motivational-affective dimension of pain (Melzack & Casey, 1968; see Figure 9.11).

Another important pain pathway is the spinopontoamygdaloid system, originating in Laminae I and V of the dorsal horn, ascending in the dorsolateral funiculus (DLF) and synapsing in the parabrachial area of the pons before reaching the amygdaloid complex. Besson, Bernard, and colleagues, who have studied the pathway extensively, suggest that this system normally is involved in the fear and memory of pain as well as in behavioral and autonomic reactions to noxious events, such as vocalization, flight, freezing, pupil dilation, and cardiorespiratory responses (Bernard & Besson, 1990). A parallel pathway is the spinoparabrachiohypothalamic tract that also ascends via the DLF to the parabrachial area but carries on to the hypothalamus. This pathway—along with the spinohypothalamic tract, which projects

directly to the hypothalamus—is also involved in the affective or emotional reaction to pain. Due to connections of the hypothalamus with the pituitary, ascending inputs in both of these tracts may be critical in the triggering of endocrine and adrenocortical responses to painful stimuli.

Cortical Processing of Pain

Until recently, there has been little consensus about the role of the cerebral cortex in pain processing. Early in the twentieth century, Head and Holmes (1911) observed that soldiers who had extensive injuries of the cerebral cortex continued to perceive pain, leading Head and Holmes to conclude that the cortex played only a minimal role in pain perception. Penfield and Boldrey (1937) reached a similar conclusion based on findings that patients rarely reported sensations of pain upon electrical stimulation of their exposed cerebral cortex during surgery to remove brain tissue with epileptic seizure foci. Despite these observations, anatomical and physiological data show that nociceptive information reaches a number of cortical areas. Recent studies of the human brain using positron-emission tomography (PET) to measure the relative cerebral blood flow (rCBF)—and more recently, functional magnetic resonance imaging (fMRI) to show changes in

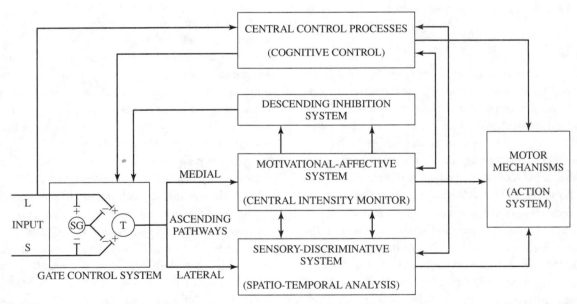

Figure 9.11 Conceptual model of the structures underlying the multidimensional nature of pain, according to Melzack and Casey (1968). The output of the T cell in the dorsal horn projects to the sensory-discriminative system via the lateral ascending system and to the motivational-affective system via the medial ascending system. The central control trigger—composed of the dorsal column and the dorsolateral projection systems—is represented by a line running from the large fibers (L) to the central control processes in the brain. These central processes project back to the dorsal horn as well as to the sensory-discriminative and motivational-affective systems. Added to the scheme of Melzack and Casey is the brain stem inhibitory control system (see Figure 9.8), which provides descending control on the dorsal horn. As indicated by arrows, there is also an interaction between the motivational-affective and the sensory-discriminative systems. The net effect of these interacting systems is activation of the motor (action) system. From Melzack, R., and Casey, K. L. Sensory, motivational and central control determinants of pain. In D. R. Kenshalo (Ed.), *The skin senses* (pp. 423–443), 1968. Courtesy of Charles C Thomas, Ltd., Springfield, Illinois.

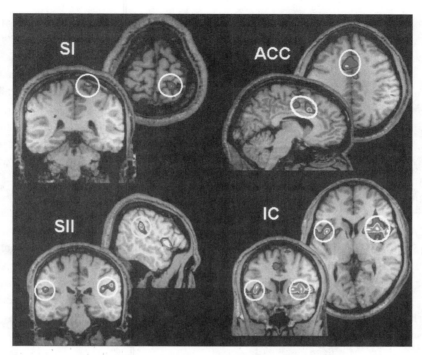

Figure 9.12 Functional magnetic resonance imaging (fMRI) data from a single subject. Each image shows a slice of the anatomical MRI data with the super-imposed functional data. Statistical activation maps are generated and presented using color codes from blue to red, with neural activity subtracted from pain-related activity. Sites of pain-related activation are circled. These sites include the anterior cingulate (ACC) and anterior insular (Ant. Ins.) cortices of the frontal lobe and the primary and sensory somatosensory cortices of the parietal lobe (SI and SII). Painful heat (46 °C) and neutral (36 °C) stimuli were applied to the left calf using a 9-cm^2 aluminium heating block. Adapted with permission from Bushnell, M. C., Duncan, G. H., Hofbauer, R. K., Ha, B., Chen, J., and Carrier, B. (1999). Pain perception: Is there a role for primary somatosensory cortex? *Proceedings of the National Academy of Sciences, U.S.A, 96,* 7705–7709.

blood oxygenation—now reveal that a number of cortical regions are activated during pain. PET studies show that even during the simple presentation of a noxious heat pulse, numerous cortical and subcortical brain regions are activated (Casey, Minoshima, Morrow, & Koeppe, 1996; Jones, Brown, Friston, Qi, & Frackowiak, 1991; Talbot et al., 1991).

Figure 9.12 shows an fMRI revealing four cortical regions that were activated by noxious heat repeatedly presented to the calf during 6-min sequences. Areas activated by noxious heat include the primary and secondary somatosensory cortex (SI and SII), anterior cingulate cortex, and rostral (anterior) insular cortex, all contralateral to the stimulated limb. Other recent investigations demonstrate cerebral blood flow changes related to a number of different noxious stimuli, including persistent noxious cold and heat stimulation, electrical muscle stimulation, cutaneous capsaicin or ethanol injection, and esophageal or colonic distention and ischemia, as well as cutaneous pain described as an illusion produced by adjacent combinations of innocuous hot and cold temperatures (thermal grill illusion; Bushnell, Duncan, Ha, Chen, & Olausson, 2000; Coghill et al., 1994). Although various differences were found in the results of these studies, contralateral SI, SII, anterior cingulate (ACC), and insular (IC) cortices were

consistently activated by a variety of painful stimuli, thus strongly implicating these regions in pain processing.

Although other cortical regions—including parts of pre-frontal cortex and premotor areas such as the supplemental motor cortex—are activated in some pain studies (Craig, Chen, Bandy, & Reiman, 2000; Derbyshire, 2000; Derbyshire et al., 1994), these responses are less reliable, suggesting that their activation may not be directly related to the essential pain experience. Neurophysiological and anatomical studies further support a direct role of S1, S2, ACC, and IC in pain perception. Data from anesthetized animals reveal neurons in each of these regions that respond best when noxious stimuli, such as pinching or heating the skin, are presented (Burkey, Carstens, Wenniger, Tang, & Jasmin, 1996; Dong et al., 1989; Kenshalo & Isensee 1983). Similar nociceptive neurons have been recorded in the ACC of awake human subjects undergoing neurosurgical procedures (Hutchison, Davis, Lozano, Tasker, & Dostrovsky, 1999).

The distributed cerebral activation probably reflects the complex nature of pain, involving discriminative, affective, autonomic, and motoric components. Anatomical connectivity suggests that SI and SII cortices may contribute primarily to spatial, temporal, and intensity discrimination of painful stimuli. Indeed, evidence suggests that lesions to SI may reduce only the ability to judge the intensity of a noxious stimulus but not affect clinical pain (Devinsky, Morrell, & Vogt, 1995). The rostral insular cortex may be involved in pain affect by integrating somatosensory information with memory, whereas the anterior cingulate cortex may be implicated in both pain affect and the modulation of motoric and autonomic reactions to pain. Both the insular cortex and anterior cingulate cortex have extensive connections to the limbic system and therefore probably play an important role in the effects of painful stimulus on attention, cognition, and mood (Casey & Minoshima, 1995).

Anatomical data show a high degree of connectivity among these cortical areas, and discrete lesions to any of these regions do not produce a precise, permanent deficit in pain perception. Chronic pain may initially be alleviated by lesions to SI, SII, ACC, or IC, but usually the pain returns after several months. These findings suggest that pain is processed by complex cortical and subcortical networks. Furthermore, the resilience of chronic pain may involve plasticity in pain pathways, whereby functions usually performed by one region are taken over by another. Such redundancy and resiliency are of obvious evolutionary value because nociception is essential for survival. However, this resiliency may contribute to the refractoriness of various chronic pain syndromes (Bushnell et al., 1999).

Role of the Cerebral Cortex in Aberrant Pain Processing

Brain imaging studies now allow us to ask questions about pain that is experienced in the absence of peripheral nociceptor stimulation. Is central pain real or imaginary? Does the pain of fibromyalgia have a neurophysiological basis? Is the illusion of pain produced by the thermal grill real? Human brain imaging studies show that there is a neurophysiological basis for such aberrant pain states. For example, PET studies reveal that when people experience the thermal grill pain illusion (produced by stimulating the skin with an alternating grid of warm and cool bars), regions of the cerebral cortex normally activated by noxious stimulation are activated during the illusion of pain (Craig, Reiman, Evans, & Bushnell, 1996).

Several investigators have used PET in patients with peripheral neuropathic pain or central pain to examine changes in pain processing that could account for such symptoms as ongoing pain, hyperalgesia, and allodynia. Abnormal forebrain responsiveness include decreased spontaneous thalamic activity (Iadarola et al., 1995) and increases in blood flow to a number of pain-related cortical regions, including ACC and IC (Hsieh, Belfrage, Stone-Elander, Hansson, & Ingvar, 1995). In studies of patients with central pain,

hyperexcitability has been observed in the thalamus (Cesaro et al., 1991) and the cerebral cortex (Canavero et al., 1993).

Some data suggest that allodynia—whether related to neuropathic pain or to capsaicin application to the skin—is processed differently in the cerebral cortex from nociceptive pain. Whereas the ACC is almost always activated in PET or fMRI studies of nociceptive pain, Peyron et al. (1998, 2000) failed to find ACC activation during allodynia in patients with central pain. Similarly, Baron, Baron, Disbrow, and Roberts (1999) failed to observe ACC activation during dynamic tactile allodynia after capsaicin application in normal subjects and suggested that Aβ-mediated pain has a unique cortical presentation. Nevertheless, other data suggest that pain arising from aberrant or normal processes ultimately activates the same cortical structures. For example, ACC has been reported to be activated during dynamic tactile allodynia produced by capsaicin injection in normal subjects (Iadarola et al., 1998), as well as by a large cortical lesion in patients with central pain (Olausson et al., 2001).

PAIN MODULATION

As complex as the systems mediating the transmission of nociceptive information are now known to be, it is clear that the perception of pain is a function not only of activity in these ascending systems but also of that in a number of modulatory systems. To account for the influence of cognitive and emotional processes on pain, the gate control theory postulated the influence of central control (i.e., from the brain) on spinal nociceptive gating mechanisms. This prediction has been clearly confirmed and the underlying mechanisms widely studied, because many clinical analgesics are thought to exert their actions on descending pain-inhibitory pathways.

Opiate Analgesia, Stimulation-Produced Analgesia, and Stress-Induced Analgesia

It was discovered in 1969 that electrical stimulation of the midbrain periaqueductal gray matter (PAG) produced potent analgesia in laboratory rats (Reynolds, 1969). Comprehensive study of this phenomenon, dubbed *stimulation-produced analgesia* (SPA; e.g., Mayer, Wolfle, Akil, Carder, & Liebeskind, 1971), revealed a number of parallels with opiate analgesia—for example, its sensitivity to blockade by naloxone, the opioid receptor antagonist (Akil, Mayer, & Liebeskind, 1976). It seemed clear that SPA revealed the existence of neural circuits providing the central control predicted by gate control theory—circuits that morphine and its congeners can activate. The subsequent isolation of opioid receptors (Pert & Snyder, 1973) and endogenous opioid peptides (e.g., endorphins and enkephalins; Hughes et al., 1975) solidified the notion that morphine's analgesic action was explained at least partly by activation of these descending circuits. What remained unclear were the circumstances that would cause the release of the endogenous opioids, but it was soon demonstrated that environmental stressors could produce analgesia via the activation of these same mechanisms, a phenomenon known as *stress-induced analgesia* (SIA; Kelly, 1982). The adaptive value of temporarily inhibiting pain perception in an animal facing life-or-death circumstances is obvious, although SIA can be reliably elicited in the laboratory by a number of more modest stressors (Bodnar, 1984). It is now clear that stress need not always produce analgesia, sometimes producing short- or long-lasting hyperalgesia instead (Jorum, 1988; Quintero et al., 2000). Also, pain modulation systems can be affected by psychological factors other than stress per se, including attention, anxiety, and pain itself (probably explaining the clinical phenomenon of counter-irritation).

Neuroanatomy and Neurochemistry of Pain Inhibition

The neuroanatomy and neurochemistry of these descending pain inhibition systems are now known in some degree of detail (see Basbaum & Fields, 1984; Willis & Westlund, 1997; see Figure 9.8). Cortical and limbic system structures such as the amygdala are critically involved (e.g., Manning, 1998). Although ascending modulatory systems are known to exist (see Andersen & Dafny, 1983; Gear, Aley, & Levine, 1999; Morgan, Sohn, & Liebeskind, 1989), the most well-characterized is the descending midbrain to brain stem to spinal cord circuit involving the midbrain PAG and the brain stem rostroventral medulla (RVM) or dorsolateral pontine reticular formation. Activation of these brain stem sites results in release of serotonin or norepinephrine, respectively, in the dorsal horn of the spinal cord (via the dorsolateral funiculus). These monoamines act directly, or they can act indirectly through enkephalinergic or GABAergic inhibitory interneurons to inhibit the firing of spinal cord projection neurons, or may inhibit transmitter release from primary afferent fibers. The participation of serotonin and norepinephrine in descending pain inhibition mechanisms may explain the clinical efficacy of antidepressants (monoamine reuptake inhibitors) and intrathecal clonidine, an α_2-adrenergic receptor agonist. The relevant circuitry is known in greatest detail in the RVM, where elegant work by Fields and colleagues has characterized the local action of μ-opioids like morphine as a combination of direct inhibition of descending fibers whose firing is correlated with nocifensive responses (i.e., *on* cells, facilitating pain) and disinhibition of descending fibers whose firing is correlated with the absence of such responses (i.e., *off* cells, producing analgesia; e.g., Heinricher, Morgan, Tortorici, & Fields, 1994; Pan & Fields, 1996). Even at this level of analysis, the influence of psychological factors is evident because the RVM has been shown to modulate nociception in restrained (i.e., stressed) but not unrestrained rats (Milne & Gamble, 1990; Mitchell, Lowe, & Fields, 1998).

Although neural circuits involving opioid peptides and receptors are comparatively well studied, it was clear from the earliest research into both SPA and SIA that parallel nonopioid mechanisms exist. By altering the anatomical location of the electrodes in SPA (e.g., dorsal vs. ventral PAG; Cannon, Prieto, Lee, & Liebeskind, 1982) or the precise parameters of the stressor in SIA (Lewis, Cannon, & Liebeskind, 1980), one can selectively elicit either naloxone-sensitive or naloxone-insensitive analgesia. Nonopioid SIA may be selectively mediated by $GABA_A$ receptors (L. R. Watkins et al., 1997), histamine H_2 receptors (Gogas, Hough, Glickl, & Su, 1986), serotonin $5-HT_{1A}$ or $5-HT_3$ receptors (Rodgers & Shepherd, 1989; Rodgers, Shepherd, & Randall, 1990), NMDA receptors (Marek, Mogil, Sternberg, Panocka, & Liebeskind, 1992; Marek, Page, Ben-Eliyahu, & Liebeskind, 1991), and may occur in parallel to activation of opioid receptors (μ, δ, κ; L. R. Watkins, Wiertelak, Grisel, Silbert, & Maier, 1992). There is evidence pointing to major sex differences in the neurochemical mediation of nonopioid SIA, in that females do not appear to use NMDA receptors to mediate this phenomenon as males do (Kavaliers & Galea, 1995; Mogil, Sternberg, Kest, Marek, & Liebeskind, 1993). The elucidation of the neurochemistry of nonopioid analgesia could have major clinical implications because the efficacy of this system is known to exceed that of its opioid counterpart (e.g., Mogil, Sternberg, Balian, Liebeskind, & Sadowski, 1996).

Tonic Activation?

One intriguing and elusive question regarding endogenous pain inhibitory systems is whether they are tonically active— that is, are these systems contributing to pain sensitivity at all times, providing an analgesic tone—or only when activated, for example, by stress? This question has been addressed by considering whether administration of broad-spectrum opioid receptor antagonists, naloxone or naltrexone, produces a relative hyperalgesic state. Generally speaking, such experiments have failed to demonstrate a reliable effect of these drugs (see, however, Buchsbaum, Davis, & Bunney, 1977), although interpretation may be confounded by the "paradoxical" analgesia that naloxone and naltrexone can produce (see Crain & Shen, 2000; Gillman & Lichtigfeld, 1989). Recent evidence with cannabinoid (CB) receptor antagonists have revived the notion of analgesic tone, however, suggesting that CB1 receptors may be filling this role (Richardson, Aanonsen, &

Hargreaves, 1997; Zimmer, Zimmer, Hohmann, Herkenham, & Bonner, 1999).

Conditioning, Antianalgesia Mechanisms, and Descending Facilitation

Although endogenous analgesic mechanisms probably evolved to participate in emergent, fight-or-flight situations, they play a broader role by virtue of the efficient one-trial learning that stress exposure can engender. Previously neutral stimuli paired with painful stressors may acquire the ability to produce conditioned fear and analgesia, and this type of learning can guide adaptive species-specific defensive reactions (Fanselow, 1986). Just as so-called danger signals can be conditioned to evoke analgesia, an intriguing experiment by Wiertelak, Maier, and Watkins (1992) demonstrated that previously neutral safety signals can be conditioned to evoke antianalgesia. The ability of certain peptides to block opioid analgesia had been known for some time (e.g., Faris, Komisaruk, Watkins, & Mayer, 1983; Friedman, Jen, Chang, Lee, & Loh, 1981; Gispen, Buitellar, Wiegant, Terenius, & De Wied, 1976), but it now seems clear that antianalgesia is produced by activation of a separate circuit rather than simply by modulating the analgesia circuitry per se. Antianalgesic mechanisms have been implicated in the phenomena of opiate tolerance and dependence, which limit the clinical utility of this class of drugs. This hypothesis posits that repeated administration of an analgesic elicits increasing release of antianalgesic peptides, whose opposing actions make it appear that the analgesic is losing efficacy (Rothman, 1992). Peptides so implicated include adrenocorticotrophic hormone (ACTH), cholecystokinin, dynorphin, FMRFamide, α-melanocyte stimulating hormone (α-MSH), Tyr-Pro-Leu-Gly-NH$_2$ (Tyr-MIF), NPFF, neurotensin, and tyrosine-releasing hormone (TRH; Rothman, 1992).

Cognitive Modulation of Pain Perception

Clinical and experimental evidence shows that an individual's cognitive state has a profound influence on pain perception. Diverse studies show that cognitive manipulations, such as hypnosis, behavioral modification, relaxation training, biofeedback, operant conditioning, and cognitive-behavioral therapy alter a person's experience of pain. One simple variable that is common to many of these psychological procedures is attentional state. Experimental studies reveal that people report lower pain when they are distracted from the pain and higher pain when they attend closely to the nociceptive stimulus (Leventhal, Brown, Shacham, & Engquist, 1979; Levine, Gordon, Smith, & Fields, 1982; McCaul & Haugtvedt, 1982).

Cognitive processes other than distraction also can enhance or reduce pain perception. Hypnosis has been used as a cognitive intervention to produce analgesia in a variety of settings. Experimental studies of hypnotic analgesia show not only that hypnosis reduces pain, but also that different hypnotic suggestions can be used to reduce independently the perceived intensity of a painful stimulus (sensory dimension) and its perceived unpleasantness (affective dimension; Rainville, Duncan, Price, Carrier, & Bushnell, 1997; Hofbauer, Rainville, Duncan, & Bushnell, 2001).

Human brain imaging studies reveal that there is a clear neurophysiological basis for psychological modulation of pain. When attention is directed away from a painful heat stimulus presented on a person's arm, his or her evaluation of the intensity of the pain is decreased, and the activity of SI cortex elicited by the painful stimulus is dramatically reduced (Bushnell et al., 1999; also see Figure 9.13). Other studies have found attention-related modulation of pain induced activity in other brain areas, such as the thalamus, ACC, and IC (Petrovic, Petersson, Ghatan, Stone-Elander, & Ingvar, 2000;

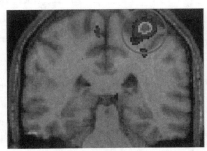
Attention to pain

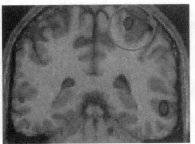
Attention to tones

Figure 9.13 Pain-related activity when attention was directed to a painful heat stimulus (left) or to an auditory stimulus (right) is revealed by subtracting PET data recorded when a warm stimulus (32–38 °C) was presented from those recorded when a painfully hot stimulus (46.5–48.5 °C) was presented during each attentional state. PET data, averaged across 9 subjects, is illustrated against an MRI from 1 subject. Coronal slices through SI cortex are centered at the activation peaks. Red circles surround the region of SI. There was a significantly greater pain-evoked SI activation when subjects attended to the pain than when they attended to the auditory stimuli. Adapted with permission from Bushnell, M. C., Duncan, G. H., Hofbauer, R. K., Ha, B., Chen, J., and Carrier, B. (1999). Pain perception: Is there a role for primary somatosensory cortex? *Proceedings of the National Academy of Sciences, U.S.A, 96,* 7705–7709.

Peyron et al., 1999). These findings are consistent with other evidence suggesting that the afferent nociceptive signals are reduced by a cognitively activated descending control system in the brain.

Other imaging data show that hypnotic suggestions alter pain-evoked cortical activity and that this alteration depends on the nature of the hypnotic suggestions (Rainville et al., 1997; Hofbauer et al., 2001). Hypnotic suggestions can be given that reduce how much a painful stimulus bothers the person (i.e., the unpleasantness), while the person still feels a pain sensation, such as burning. When subjects are given such suggestions, activity in the ACC is reduced, but activity in the SI is not. In contrast, when suggestions are given to reduce the intensity of the burning pain sensation, SI activity is dramatically reduced, just as it is when subjects are distracted.

Cognitive factors other than attention or hypnotic suggestion—such as mood, emotional state, attitudes, and expectations—also have been shown to alter pain perception. Clinical studies reveal that emotional state and attitudes of patients have an effect on postsurgical analgesic requirements and pain associated with chronic diseases (Fernandez & Milburn, 1994; Haythornthwaite & Benrud-Larson, 2000; Kvaal & Patodia, 2000). In the experimental context, manipulations that alter mood or emotional state, such as pleasant music or humorous films, reduce pain perception (Good, 1996; Magill-Levreault, 1993; Zillmann, De Wied, King-Jablonski, & Jenzowsky, 1996). The neural circuitry underlying such pain modulation is not known, although ACC and prefrontal cortex might be important regions for hedonic modulation of pain.

Thus, in stark contrast to the Cartesian view of pain processing as simply involving the faithful passage of information from the periphery to the brain via the spinal cord, a modern view needs to account for the powerful modulatory influences exerted by endogenous mechanisms of analgesia and antianalgesia. The situation becomes yet more complicated after tissue or nerve injury. We have described at great length how plastic changes in the neural circuitry subserving pain transmission can result in hyperalgesia and allodynia. Recent data have shown that injury can also cause the inappropriate tonic activation of descending pain *facilitatory* mechanisms in the brain stem. These mechanisms may or may not be similar to the antianalgesic systems described above. The importance of descending pain facilitatory systems is shown by the demonstration that lesions of the DLF—the pathway by which pain-modulatory information descends to the spinal cord—block neuropathic pain after spinal nerve injury (Ossipov, Sun, Malan, Lai, & Porreca, 2000). Thus, it seems that the DLF provides a pathway for descending facilitation as well as inhibition. *On* cells in the RVM are probably involved in this facilitation (Porreca et al., 2001), as are cholecystokinin

CCK_B receptors (Kovelowski et al., 2000) and dynorphin acting at NMDA receptors (Wang et al., 2001). Descending facilitation may hold the key to explaining a number of puzzling features of neuropathic pain, including the greatly prolonged time course of the pain relative to that of the ectopic discharge of injured afferents and the poor efficacy of opioids against neuropathic pain.

NEW DIRECTIONS IN PAIN RESEARCH

Most pain research has been conducted at the level of the protein (i.e., receptors, neurotransmitters, second messengers), using pharmacological, physiological, and anatomical approaches. Largely due to the availability of new techniques, many of the new directions in pain research involve the study of pain phenomena at higher (systems-wide), and lower (molecular genetic) levels. Results from modern fMRI studies, wherein the impact of pain on multiple cortical and subcortical nervous system structures can be evaluated simultaneously, have been provided. We turn now to the implications of the ability to clone and manipulate individual pain-relevant genes.

Molecular Studies of Pain

The development of large-capacity cloning vectors and the polymerase chain reaction have made it possible to isolate and sequence any of the 30,000 genes in the mammalian genome. After this is accomplished, two very powerful experimental strategies become feasible: (a) to measure the expression, in particular tissues and under particular conditions, of the messenger RNAs of these genes; and (b) to render these genes nonfunctional by transgenesis or antisense oligonucleotide administration.

The study of gene expression has revealed the existence of a few genes in the dorsal root ganglion (DRG) that appear to be expressed selectively in small-diameter nociceptors. For example, mRNAs encoding the SNS and NaN/SNS2 tetrodotoxin-resistant Na^+ channel subunits are found nowhere else but the DRG and may play a critical role in chronic pain (see McCleskey & Gold, 1999). Other pain-relevant proteins that were identified largely by molecular genetic techniques include the capsaicin-sensitive, heat transducer channel VR-1 (Caterina et al., 1997), the ATP-gated purinersic receptor (P2X3) (Cook, Vulchanova, Hargreaves, Elde, & McCleskey, 1997) and the *acid-sensing ion channel* ASIC1 (Waldmann, Champigny, Bassilana, Heurteaux, & Lazdunski, 1997). In addition to these examples of expression cloning, in which novel genes are identified via a defined physiological screening assay, molecular techniques can be applied to the identification of all genes whose expressions are altered in a particular pain-related state. The power of this latter strategy to identify the molecular "players" in pain is enhanced by the development of microarrays, in which virtually all genes—known and unknown—can be studied *simultaneously* (Schena, Shalon, Davis, & Brown, 1995). Such gene expression profiling will no doubt lead to major advances. At this point in time, however, there exist no published studies of this strategy as applied to pain.

In contrast, upwards of 500 studies have been published since 1996 describing the effects of *knocking out* (i.e., by producing transgenic mutant mice) or *knocking down* (i.e., by administering antisense) the expression of particular genes (see Mogil & Grisel, 1998; Mogil & McCarson, 2000; Mogil, Yu, & Basbaum, 2000). Although these techniques cannot identify truly novel pain-related genes, they are proving very useful in elucidating the role of known genes in pain, especially in cases in which pharmacological tools are lacking or unsatisfactory. The great advantage of transgenic and antisense studies is their unsurpassed specificity on the molecular level, and although these approaches are associated with certain interpretational challenges (Lariviere, Chesler, & Mogil, 2001; Mogil & McCarson, 2000), many recent experiments could not have been performed any other way. The utility of transgenic and antisense techniques will only increase, as inducible knockout technology limits the problems of compensation in the former (e.g., Kuhn, Schwenk, Aguet, & Rajewsky, 1995), and new chemical modifications reduce the toxicity of the latter (e.g., Wahlestedt et al., 2000).

Individual Differences in Pain

Pain—probably more than most sensory systems, but similar to many complex biobehavioral phenomena—exhibits robust individual differences. The seminal demonstration that responders and nonresponders to pain exist was probably that of Libman (1934), who reported that pressure applied to the mastoid bone towards the styloid process produced marked pain in 60–70% of his patients, whereas the remainder felt little or no pain from the same stimulus. The existence of pain-sensitive and pain-resistant individuals has subsequently been demonstrated with more modern algesiometric assays (Chen, Dworkin, & Haug, 1989) and may be reflected in variable cortical imaging data (Zubieta et al., 2001). Also showing marked individual differences are analgesic responses to opiates (Galer, Coyle, Pasternak, & Portenoy, 1992; Lasagna & Beecher, 1954) and NSAIDs (Walker, Sheather-Reid,

Carmody, Vial, & Day, 1997). Most strikingly, less than 15% of peripheral nerve injuries develop into chronic pain syndromes (Richards, 1967).

Such interindividual variability is frustrating to the clinician and puzzling to the scientist. Until very recently, however, the topic was ignored in pain research, with experimental results from particular populations of rat generalized to all rats and then to all humans. Just as the advent of molecular genetic tools have facilitated the bottom-up study of pain genes (e.g., knockout mice), they have also allowed the top-down study of classical (Mendelian) pain genetics.

The application of Mendelian genetics to a pain trait requires a prior determination that the trait is heritable. It is important to remember that the demonstration that a pain trait runs in families is *not* prima facie evidence of heritability because familial modeling (e.g., learned illness behavior) may be a sufficient explanation (see Turk, Flor, & Rudy, 1987). A wide range of heritability estimates has been reported in humans for clinical pain. Inherited genetic variation accounts for most of the overall variance in migraine, menstrual pain, back pain, and fibromyalgia (Bengtsson & Thorson, 1991; Buskila, Neumann, Hazanov, & Carmi, 1996; Peroutka, 1998; Treloar, Martin, & Heath, 1998). At the other end of the spectrum, variability in experimental pressure pain sensitivity and in the prevalence of trigeminal neuralgia and myofacial temporomandibular disorder has been reported to be almost exclusively environmental in origin (MacGregor, Griffiths, Baker, & Spector, 1997; Raphael, Marbach, Gallagher, & Dohrenwend, 1999; Rasmussen, 1990).

A number of inherited pain-related pathologies have recently been explained on the genetic level. For example, congenital insensitivity to pain with anhidrosis (hereditary sensory neuropathy Type IV) is now known to be due to any one of a number of single base-pair mutations of the NTRK1 gene (Indo et al., 1996), which encodes the high-affinity, nerve growth factor-specific tyrosine kinase receptor. Hereditary sensory neuropathies Type I and III, also featuring abnormalities in pain perception, have been attributed to mutations in the SPTLC1 and IKAP genes, respectively (Anderson et al., 2001; Bejaoui et al., 2001; Dawkins, Hulme, Brahmbhatt, & Auer-Grumbach, 2001; Slaugenhaupt et al., 2001). An inherited form of hemiplegic migraine is now known to be due to mutations in the gene encoding the P/Q-type, *calcium channel* α_1 *subunit*, CACNL1A4 (Ophoff, Terwindt, Frants, & Ferrari, 1998).

As impressive as these demonstrations are, there is little evidence that any of these genes are involved in variability in pain responses in the normal range. For research in this domain and for progress in the pharmacogenetics of analgesics, animal models are necessary. The mouse in particular is a useful model species, largely because of the existence of over 30 major inbred strains in which each mouse is a clone of every other. The nociceptive sensitivity of a large number of inbred mouse strains on multiple algesiometric assays in this species has been documented (Lariviere, Wilson, et al., 2001; Mogil et al., 1999). Impressive strain differences were noted in every assay, corresponding to rough heritability estimates (i.e., the proportion of variance accounted for by inherited genes) of 28–76% depending on the measure, with an average heritability of 46%.

Such strain differences have been exploited toward the genomic localization and eventually the identification of the genes responsible for the genetic component of these strain differences. Progress has been reported for thermal nociception (Mogil, Richards, O'Toole, Helms, Mitchell, & Belknap, 1997), chemical-inflammatory nociception (Wilson et al., 2001), neuropathic pain behavior (Seltzer, Wu, Max, & Diehl, 2001), stress-induced analgesia (Mogil, Richards, O'Toole, Helms, Mitchell, Kest, et al., 1997) and morphine analgesia (Belknap et al., 1995; Bergeson et al., 2001; Hain, Belknap, & Mogil, 1999). Morphine analgesia is a notable case because pharmacological evidence has been provided to support particular candidate genes in genomic regions statistically associated with the trait, including the *Oprm* gene encoding the mouse μ-opioid receptor (Belknap et al., 1995), and the *Htr1b* gene encoding the serotonin-1B receptor (Hain et al., 1999).

Although considerable progress is being made in identifying so-called pain genes, it should be borne in mind that the majority of the observed variability is environmental in origin. Such factors may include past pain experience, age, diet, demographic status, and culture. Some of the variance is likely explained by factors influenced by (and interacting with) genetics but not pain genes per se; such factors include sex, hormonal status, personality, coping styles, cognition, and stress. A true understanding of individual differences in pain—and of the full complexities of the biopsychology of pain more generally—will require the identification of all factors affecting the phenomenon, both intrinsic and extrinsic to the organism.

REFERENCES

Ahren, B. (1996). Galanin increases cytoplasmic calcium in insulin-producing RINm5F cells by activating phospholipase C. *Biochemical and Biophysical Research Communications, 221,* 89–94.

Akil, H., Mayer, D. J., & Liebeskind, J. C. (1976). Antagonism of stimulation-produced analgesia by naloxone, a narcotic antagonist. *Science, 191,* 961–962.

Andersen, E., & Dafny, N. (1983). Dorsal raphe stimulation reduces responses of parafascicular neurons to noxious stimulation. *Pain, 15,* 323–331.

Anderson, S. L., Coli, R., Daly, I. W., Kichula, E. A., Rork, M. J., Volpi, S. A., Ekstein, J., & Rubin, B. Y. (2001). Familial dysautonomia is caused by mutations of the IKAP gene. *American Journal of Human Genetics, 68,* 753–758.

Baron, R., Baron, Y., Disbrow, E., & Roberts, T. P. (1999). Brain processing of capsaicin-induced secondary hyperalgesia: A functional MRI study. *Neurology, 53,* 548–557.

Basbaum, A. I., & Fields, H. L. (1984). Endogenous pain control systems: Brainstem spinal pathways and endorphin circuitry. *Annual Review of Neuroscience, 7,* 309–338.

Beitel, R. E., & Dubner, R. (1976) Response of unmyelinated (c) polymodal nociceptors to thermal stimuli applied to monkey's face. *Journal of Neurophysiology, 39,* 1160–1175.

Bejaoui, K., Wu, C., Scheffler, M. D., Haan, G., Ashby, P., Wu, L., de Jong, P., & Brown, R. H., Jr. (2001). SPTLC1 is mutated in hereditary sensory neuropathy, type 1. *Nature Genetics, 27,* 261–262.

Belknap, J. K., Mogil, J. S., Helms, M. L., Richards, S. P., O'Toole, L. A., Bergeson, S. E., & Buck, K. J. (1995). Localization to proximal Chromosome 10 of a locus influencing morphine-induced analgesia in crosses derived from C57BL/6 and DBA/2 mouse strains. *Life Sciences, 57,* 117–124.

Bengtsson, B., & Thorson, J. (1991). Back pain: A study of twins. *Acta Genetics Medical Gemmellologiae, 40,* 83–90.

Bergeson, S. E., Helms, M. L., O'Toole, L. A., Jarvis, M. W., Hain, H. S., Mogil, J. S., & Belknap, J. K. (2001). Quantitative trait loci influencing morphine antinociception in four mapping populations. *Mammalian Genome, 12,* 546–553.

Berkley, K. J. (1997). On the dorsal columns: Translating basic research hypotheses to the clinic. *Pain, 70,* 103–107.

Bernard, J. F., & Besson, J. M. (1990). The spino(trigemino)pontoamygdaloid pathway: Electrophysiological evidence for an involvement in pain processes. *Journal of Neurophysiology, 63,* 473–490.

Besson, J.-M., & Chaouch, A. (1987). Peripheral and spinal mechanisms of nociception. *Physiological Reviews, 67,* 67–186.

Bishop, G. H. (1946). Neural mechanisms of cutaneous sense. *Physiological Review, 26,* 77–102.

Bodnar, R. J. (1984). Types of stress which induce analgesia. In M.D. Tricklebank & G. Curzon (Eds.), *Stress-induced analgesia* (pp. 19–32). New York: Wiley.

Bonica, J. J. (Ed.). (1990). *The management of pain* (2nd ed.). Philadelphia: Lea and Febiger.

Buchsbaum, M. S., Davis, G. C., & Bunney, W. E., Jr. (1977). Naloxone alters pain perception and somatosensory evoked potentials in normal subjects. *Nature, 270,* 620–622.

Burgess, P. R., & Perl, E. R. (1973). Cutaneous mechanoreceptors and nociceptors. In A. Iggo (Ed.), *Handbook of sensory physiology: Vol. 2. Somatosensory system* (pp. 29–78). New York: Springer.

Burkey, A. R., Carstens, E., Wenniger, J. J., Tang, J. W., & Jasmin, L. (1996). An opioidergic cortical antinociception triggering site in the agranular insular cortex of the rat that contributes to morphine antinociception. *Journal of Neuroscience, 16,* 6612–6623.

Bushnell, M. C. (1995). Thalamic processing of sensory-discriminative and affective-motivational dimensions of pain. In J.-M. Besson, G. Guilbaud, & H. Ollat (Eds.). *Forebrain areas involved in pain processing* (pp. 63–68). Paris: John Libbey Eurotext.

Bushnell, M. C., & Duncan, G. H. (1989). Sensory and affective aspects of pain perception: Is medial thalamus restricted to emotional issues? *Experimental Brain Research, 78,* 415–418.

Bushnell, M. C., Duncan, G. H., Ha, B., Chen, J.-I., & Olausson, H. (2000). Non-invasive brain imaging during experimental and clinical pain. In M. Devor, M. C. Rowbotham, & Z. Wiesenfeld-Hallin (Eds.), *Proceedings of the 9th world congress on pain: Progress in pain research and management: Vol. 16* (pp. 485–495). Seattle, WA: IASP Press.

Bushnell, M. C., Duncan, G. H., Hofbauer, R. K., Ha, B., Chen, J., & Carrier, B. (1999). Pain perception: Is there a role for primary somatosensory cortex? *Proceedings of the National Academy of Sciences, USA, 96,* 7705–7709.

Buskila, D., Neumann, L., Hazanov, I., & Carmi, R. (1996). Familial aggregation in the fibromyalgia syndrome. *Seminars in Arthritis and Rheumatism, 26,* 605–611.

Canavero, S., Pagni, C. A., Castellano, G., Bonicalzi, V., Bello', M., Duca, S., & Podio, V. (1993). The role of cortex in central pain syndromes: Preliminary results of a long-term technetium-99 hexamethylpropyleneamineoxime single photon emission computed tomography study. *Neurosurgery, 32,* 185–191.

Cannon, J. T., Prieto, G. J., Lee, A., & Liebeskind, J. C. (1982). Evidence for opioid and non-opioid forms of stimulation-produced analgesia in the rat. *Brain Research, 243,* 315–321.

Casey, K. L., & Minoshima, S. (1995). The forebrain network for pain: An emerging image. In J.-M. Besson, G. Guilbaud, & H. Ollat (Eds.), *Forebrain areas involved in pain processing* (pp. 213–228). Paris: John Libbey Eurotext.

Casey, K. L., Minoshima, S., Morrow, T. J., & Koeppe, R. A. (1996). Comparison of human cerebral activation patterns during cutaneous warmth, heat pain and deep cold pain. *Journal of Neurophysiology, 76,* 571–581.

Caterina, M. J., Schumacher, M. A., Tominaga, M., Rosen, T. A., Levine, J. D., & Julius, D. (1997). The capsaicin receptor: A heat-activated ion channel in the pain pathway. *Nature, 389,* 816–824.

Cervero, F., & Iggo, A. (1980). The substantia gelatinosa of the spinal cord. *Brain, 103,* 717–772.

Cesaro, P., Mann, M. W., Moretti, J. L., Defer, G., Roualdès, B., Nguyen, J. P., & Degos, J. D. (1991). Central pain and thalamic hyperactivity: A single photon emission computerized tomographic study. *Pain, 47,* 329–336.

Chen, A. C. N., Dworkin, S. F., & Haug, J. (1989). Human pain responsivity in a tonic pain model: Psychological determinants. *Pain, 37,* 143–160.

Christensen, B. N., & Perl, E. R. (1970). Spinal neurons specifically excited by noxious or thermal stimuli: Marginal zone of the spinal cord. *Journal of Neurophysiology, 33,* 293–307.

Coderre, T. J. (1992). Physiologic consequences of tissue injury and acute pain. In A. N. Sandler & J. L. Benumof (Eds.), *Current concepts in acute pain control: Anesthesiology clinics of North America: Vol. 10* (pp. 247–269). Philadephia: W. B. Saunders.

Coderre, T. J. (1993). The role of excitatory amino acid receptors and intracellular messengers in persistent nociception after tissue injury in rats. *Molecular Neurobiology, 7,* 229–246.

Coderre, T. J., Fisher, K., & Fundytus, M. E. (1997). The role of ionotropic and metabotropic glutamate receptors in persistent nociception. In T. S. Jensen, T. A. Turner, & Z. Wiesenfeld-Hallin (Eds.), *Proceedings of the 8th world congress on pain: Progress in pain research and management: Vol. 8* (pp. 259–275). Seattle, WA: IASP Press.

Coderre, T. J., Katz, J., Vaccarino, A. L., & Melzack, R. (1993). Contribution of central neuroplasticity to pathological pain: Review of clinical and experimental evidence. *Pain, 52,* 259–285.

Coggeshall, R. E., Chung, K., Chung, J. M., & Langford, L. A. (1981). Primary afferent axons in the tract of Lissauer in the monkey. *Journal of Comparative Neurology, 196,* 431–442.

Coghill, R. C., Talbot, J. D., Evans, A. C., Meyer, E., Gjedde, A., Bushnell, M. C., & Duncan, G. H. (1994). Distributed processing of pain and vibration by the human brain. *Journal of Neuroscience, 14,* 4095–4108.

Cook, S. P., Vulchanova, L., Hargreaves, K. M., Elde, R., & McCleskey, E. W. (1997). Distinct ATP receptors on pain-sensing and stretch-sensing neurons. *Nature, 387,* 505–506.

Craig, A. D., Bushnell, M. C., Zhang, E.-T., & Blomqvist, A. (1994). A thalamic nucleus specific for pain and temperature sensation. *Nature, 372,* 770–773.

Craig, A. D., Chen, K., Bandy, D., & Reiman, E. M. (2000). Thermosensory activation of insular cortex. *Nature Neuroscience, 3,* 184–190.

Craig, A. D., Reiman, E. M., Evans, A. C., & Bushnell, M. C. (1996). Functional imaging of an illusion of pain. *Nature, 384,* 258–260.

Crain, S. M., & Shen, K.-F. (2000). Antagonists of excitatory opioid receptor functions enhance morphine's analgesic potency and attenuate opioid tolerance/dependence liability. *Pain, 84,* 121–131.

Cunha, F. Q., Lorenzetti, B. B., Poole, S., & Ferreira, S. H. (1991). Interleukin-8 as a mediator of sympathetic pain. *British Journal of Pharmacology, 104,* 765–767.

Dawkins, J. L., Hulme, D. J., Brahmbhatt, S. B., Auer-Grumbach, M., & Nicholson, G. A. (2001). Mutations in SPTLC1, encoding serine palmitoyltransferase, long chain base subunit-1, cause hereditary sensory neuropathy type I. *Nature Genetics, 27,* 309–312.

Derbyshire, S. W. (2000). Exploring the pain "neuromatrix." *Current Reviews on Pain, 4,* 467–477.

Derbyshire, S. W., Jones, A. K., Devani, P., Friston, K. J., Feinmann, C., Harris, M., Pearce, S., Watson, J. D., & Frackowiak, R. S. (1994). Cerebral responses to pain in patients with atypical facial pain measured by positron emission tomography. *Journal of Neurology Neurosurgery and Psychiatry, 57,* 1166–1172.

Devinsky, O., Morrell, M. J., & Vogt, B. A. (1995). Contributions of anterior cingulate cortex to behavior. *Brain, 118,* 279–306.

Dong, W. K., Salonen, L. D., Kawakami, Y., Shiwaku, T., Kaukoranta, E. M., & Martin, R. F. (1989). Nociceptive responses of trigeminal neurons in SII-7b cortex of awake monkeys. *Brain Research, 484,* 314–324.

Dray, A. (1996). Neurogenic mechanisms and neuropeptides in chronic pain. In G. Carli & M. Zimmermann (Eds.), *Progress in brain research: Vol. 110* (pp. 85–94). Amsterdam: Elsevier.

Dray, A., & Urban, L. (1996). New pharmacological strategies for pain relief. *Annual Review of Pharmacology and Toxicology, 36,* 253–280.

Dubner R., & Bennett, G. J. (1983). Spinal and trigeminal mechanisms of nociception. *Annual Review of Neuroscience, 6,* 381–418.

Dun, N. J., Dun, S. L., Wu, S. Y., Williams, C. A., & Kwok, E. H. (2000). Endomorphins: Localization, release and action on rat dorsal horn neurons. *Journal of Biomedical Science, 7,* 213–220.

England, S., Happel, L. T., Kline, D. G., Gamboni, F., Thouron, C. L., Liu, Z. P., & Levinson, S. R. (1996). Sodium channel accumulation in humans with painful neuromas. *Neurology, 47,* 272–276.

Fanselow, M. S. (1986). Conditioned fear-induced opiate analgesia: A competing motivational state theory of stress-induced analgesia. *Annals of the New York Academy of Sciences, 467,* 40–54.

Faris, P. L., Komisaruk, B. R., Watkins, L. R., & Mayer, D. J. (1983). Evidence for the neuropeptide cholecystokinin as an antagonist of opiate analgesia. *Science, 219,* 310–312.

Fernandez, E., & Milburn, T. W. (1994). Sensory and affective predictors of overall pain and emotions associated with affective pain. *Clinical Journal of Pain, 10,* 3–9.

Ferreira, S. H., Lorenzetti, B. B., & Poole, S. (1993). Bradykinin initiates cytokine-mediated inflammatory hyperalgesia. *British Journal of Pharmacology, 110,* 1227–1231.

Fields, H. L., & Basbaum, A. I. (1994). Central nervous system mechanisms of pain modulation. In P. D. Wall & R. Melzack (Eds.), *Textbook of pain* (pp. 243–257). Edinburgh: Churchill-Livingstone.

Friedman, H. J., Jen, M.-F., Chang, J. K., Lee, N. M., & Loh, H. H. (1981). Dynorphin: A possible modulatory peptide on morphine or ß-endorphin analgesia in mouse. *European Journal of Pharmacology, 69,* 357–360.

Galer, B. S., Coyle, N., Pasternak, G. W., & Portenoy, R. K. (1992). Individual variability in the response to different opioids: Report of five cases. *Pain, 49,* 87–91.

Gear, R. W., Aley, K. O., & Levine, J. D. (1999). Pain-induced analgesia mediated by mesolimbic reward circuits. *Journal of Neuroscience, 19,* 7175–7181.

Gillman, M. A., & Lichtigfeld, F. J. (1989). Naloxone analgesia: An update. *International Journal of Neuroscience, 48,* 321–324.

Gispen, W. H., Buitellar, J., Wiegant, V. M., Terenius, L., & De Wied, D. (1976). Interaction between ACTH fragments, brain opiate receptors and morphine-induced analgesia. *European Journal of Pharmacology, 39,* 393–397.

Gogas, K. R., Hough, L. B., Glickl, S. D., & Su, K. (1986). Opposing actions of cimetidine on naloxone-sensitive and naloxone-insensitive forms of footshock-induced analgesia. *Brain Research, 370,* 370–374.

Good, M. (1996). Effects of relaxation and music on postoperative pain: A review. *Journal of Advances in Nursing, 24,* 905–914.

Gracely, R. H., Lynch, S. A., & Bennett, G. J. (1992). Painful neuropathy: Altered central processing maintained dynamically by peripheral input. *Pain, 51,* 175–194.

Gu, J. G., & MacDermott, A. B. (1997). Activation of ATP P_{2X} receptors elicits glutamate release from sensory neuron synapses. *Nature, 389,* 749–753.

Hain, H. S., Belknap, J. K., & Mogil, J. S. (1999). Pharmacogenetic evidence for the involvement of 5-hydroxytryptamine (serotonin)-1B receptors in the mediation of morphine antinociceptive sensitivity. *Journal of Pharmacology and Experimental Therapeutics, 291,* 444–449.

Hammond, D. L. (1997). Inhibitory neurotransmitters and nociception: Role of GABA and glycine. In A. Dickenson & J.-M. Besson (Eds.), *Handbook of experimental pharmacology: Vol. 130. The pharmacology of pain* (pp. 361–384). Berlin: Springer-Verlag.

Haythornthwaite, J. A., & Benrud-Larson, L. M. (2000). Psychological aspects of neuropathic pain. *Clinical Journal of Pain, 16,* S101–S105.

Head, H., & Holmes, G. (1911). Sensory disturbances from cerebral lesions. *Brain, 34,* 102–254.

Heinricher, M. M., Morgan, M. M., Tortorici, V., & Fields, H. L. (1994). Disinhibition of off-cells and antinociception produced by an opioid action within the rostral ventromedial medulla. *Neuroscience, 63,* 279–288.

Hla, T., & Neilson, K. (1992). Human cyclooxygenase-2 cDNA. *Proceedings of the National Academy of Sciences USA, 89,* 7389–7398.

Hofbauer, R. K., Rainville, P., Duncan, G. H., & Bushnell, M. C. (2001). Cortical representation of the sensory dimension of pain. *Journal of Neurophysiology, 86,* 402–411.

Hökfelt, T., Zhang, X., & Wiesenfeld-Hallin, Z. (1994). Messenger plasticity in primary sensory neurons following axotomy and its functional implications. *Trends in Neurosciences, 17,* 22–30.

Hsieh, J. C., Belfrage, M., Stone-Elander, S., Hansson, P., & Ingvar, M. (1995). Central representation of chronic ongoing neuropathic pain studied positron emission tomography. *Pain, 63,* 225–236.

Hughes, J., Smith, T. W., Kosterlitz, H. W., Fothergill, L. A., Morgan, B. A., & Morris, H. R. (1975). Identification of two related pentapeptides from the brain with potent opiate agonist activity. *Nature, 258,* 577–579.

Hutchison, W. D., Davis, K. D., Lozano, A. M., Tasker, R. R., & Dostrovsky, J. O. (1999). Pain-related neurons in the human cingulate cortex. *Nature Neuroscience, 2,* 403–405.

Iadarola, M. J., Berman, K. F., Zeffiro, T. A., Byas-Smith, M. G., Gracely, R. H., Max, M. B., & Bennett, G. J. (1998). Neural activation during acute capsaicin-evoked pain and allodynia assessed with PET. *Brain, 121*(Pt. 5), 931–947.

Iadarola, M. J., Max, M. B., Berman, K. F., Byas-Smith, M. G., Coghill, R. C., Gracely, R. H., & Bennett, G. J. (1995). Unilateral decrease in thalamic activity observed with positron emission tomography in patients with chronic neuropathic pain. *Pain, 63,* 55–64.

Indo, Y., Tsurata, Y., Karim, M. A., Ohta, K., Kawano, T., Mitsubuchi, H., Tonoki, H., Awaya, Y., & Matsuda, I. (1996). Mutations in the TRKA/NGF receptor gene in patients with congenital insensitivity to pain with anhidrosis. *Nature Genetics, 13,* 485–488.

Jackson, D. L., Graff, C. B., Durnett-Richardson, J., & Hargreaves, K. M. (1995). Glutamate participates in the peripheral modulation of thermal hyperalgesia in rats. *European Journal of Pharmacology, 284,* 321–325.

Jones, A. K. P., Brown, W. D., Friston, K. J., Qi, L. Y., & Frackowiak, R. S. J. (1991). Cortical and subcortical localization of response to pain in man using positron emission tomography. *Proceedings of the Royal Society of London [Biology], 244,* 39–44.

Jorum, E. (1988). Analgesia or hyperalgesia following stress correlates with emotional behavior in rats. *Pain, 32,* 341–348.

Kask, K., Langel, U., & Bartfai, T. (1995). Galanin: A neuropeptide with inhibitory actions. *Cellular and Molecular Neurobiology, 15,* 653–673.

Kavaliers, M., & Galea, L. A. M. (1995). Sex differences in the expression and antagonism of swim stress-induced analgesia in deer mice vary with the breeding season. *Pain, 63,* 327–334.

Kelly, D. D. (1982). The role of endorphins in stress-induced analgesia. *Annals of the New York Academy of Sciences, 398,* 260–271.

Kenshalo, D. R., Jr., & Isensee, O. (1983). Responses of primate SI cortical neurons to noxious stimuli. *Journal of Neurophysiology, 50,* 1479–1496.

Kovelowski, C. J., Ossipov, M. H., Sun, H., Lai, J., Malan, T. P., Jr., & Porreca, F. (2000). Supraspinal cholecystokinin may drive tonic descending facilitation mechanisms to maintain neuropathic pain in the rat. *Pain, 87,* 265–273.

Kuhn, R., Schwenk, F., Aguet, M., & Rajewsky, K. (1995). Inducible gene targeting in mice. *Science, 269,* 1427–1429.

Kvaal, S. A., & Patodia, S. (2000). Relations among positive affect, negative affect and somatic symptoms in a medically ill patient sample. *Psychological Reports, 87,* 227–233.

LaMotte, R. H., Thalhammer, J. G., & Robinson, C. J. (1983). Peripheral neural correlates of magnitude of cutaneous pain and hyperalgesia: A comparison of neural events in monkey with sensory judgment in human. *Journal of Neurophysiology, 50,* 1–25.

LaMotte, R. H., Thalhammer, J. G., Torebjörk, H. E., & Robinson, C. J. (1982). Peripheral neural mechanisms of cutaneous hyperalgesia following mild injury by heat. *Journal of Neuroscience, 2,* 765–781.

Lariviere, W. R., Chesler, E. J., & Mogil, J. S. (2001). Transgenic studies of pain and analgesia: Mutation or background phenotype? *Journal of Pharmacology Experimental Therapeutics, 297,* 467–473.

Lariviere, W. R., Wilson, S. G., Laughlin, T. M., Kokayeff, A., West, E. E., Adhikari, S. M., Wan, Y., & Mogil, J. S. (2001). *Heritability of nociception: III. Genetic relationships among commonly used assays of nociception and hypersensitivity.* Manuscript submitted for publication.

Lasagna, L., & Beecher, H. K. (1954). The optimal dose of morphine. *Journal of the American Medical Association, 156,* 230–234.

Leventhal, H., Brown, D., Shacham, S., & Engquist, G. (1979). Effects of preparatory information about sensations, threat of pain and attention on cold pressor distress. *Journal of Personality and Social Psychology, 37,* 688–714.

Levine, J. D., Gordon, N. C., Smith, R., & Fields, H. L. (1982). Post-operative pain: Effect of extent of injury and attention. *Brain Research, 234,* 500–504.

Lewis, J. W., Cannon, J. T., & Liebeskind, J. C. (1980). Opioid and non-opioid mechanisms of stress analgesia. *Science, 208,* 623–625.

Lewis, T. (1942). *Pain.* New York: MacMillan.

Li, J., & Perl, E. J. (1995). ATP modulation of synaptic transmission in the spinal substantia gelatinosa. *Journal of Neuroscience, 15,* 3357–3365.

Libman, E. (1934). Observations on individual sensitiveness to pain. *Journal of the American Medical Association, 102,* 335–341.

MacGregor, A. J., Griffiths, G. O., Baker, J., & Spector, T. D. (1997). Determinants of pressure pain threshold in adult twins:

Evidence that shared environmental influences predominate. *Pain, 73,* 253–257.

Magill-Levreault, L. (1993). Music therapy in pain and symptom management. *Journal of Palliative Care, 9,* 42–48.

Manning, B. H. (1998). A lateralized deficit in morphine antinociception after unilateral inactivation of the central amygdala. *Journal of Neuroscience, 18,* 9453–9470.

Marek, P., Mogil, J. S., Sternberg, W. F., Panocka, I., & Liebeskind, J. C. (1992). N-methyl-D-aspartic acid (NMDA) receptor antagonist MK-801 blocks non-opioid stress-induced analgesia: II. Comparison across three swim stress paradigms in selectively bred mice. *Brain Research, 578,* 197–203.

Marek, P., Page, G. G., Ben-Eliyahu, S., & Liebeskind, J. C. (1991). NMDA receptor antagonist MK-801 blocks non-opioid stress-induced analgesia: I. Comparison of opiate receptor-deficient and opiate receptor-rich strains of mice. *Brain Research, 551,* 293–296.

Masferrer, J. L., Zweifel, B. B., Manning, P. T., Hauser, S. D., Leahy, K. M., & Smith, W. G. (1994). Selective inhibition of inducible cyclooxygenase 2 in vivo is antiinflammatory and nonulcerogenic. *Proceedings of the National Academy of Sciences, USA, 91,* 3228–3232.

Mayer, D. J., Wolfle, T. L., Akil, H., Carder, B., & Liebeskind, J. C. (1971). Analgesia from electrical stimulation in the brainstem of the rat. *Science, 174,* 1351–1354.

McCaul, K. D., & Haugtvedt, C. (1982). Attention, distraction and cold-pressor pain. *Journal of Personality and Social Psychology, 43,* 154–162.

McCleskey, E. W., & Gold, M. S. (1999). Ion channels of nociception. *Annual Review of Physiology, 61,* 835–856.

McMahon, S. B., Armanini, M. P., Ling, L. H., & Philips, H. S. (1994). Expression and co-expression of trk receptors in subpopulations of adult primary sensory neurons projecting to identified peripheral targets. *Neuron, 12,* 1161–1171.

Melzack, R., & Casey, K. L. (1968). Sensory, motivational and central control determinants of pain: A new conceptual model. In D. R. Kenshalo (Ed.), *The skin senses* (pp. 423–443). Springfield, IL: Thomas.

Melzack, R., & Wall, P. D. (1965). Pain mechanisms: A new theory. *Science, 150,* 971–979.

Merskey, H., & Bogduk, N. (1994). *Classification of chronic pain, IASP task force on taxonomy.* Seattle, WA: IASP Press.

Meyer, R. A., & Campbell, J. N. (1981). Myelinated nociceptive afferents account for the hyperalgesia that follows a burn to the hand. *Science, 213,* 1527–1529.

Meyer, R. A., Campbell, J. N., & Raja, S. N. (1994). Peripheral neural mechanisms of nociception. In P. D. Wall & R. Melzack (Eds.), *Textbook of pain* (pp. 13–44). Edinburgh, UK: Churchill-Livingstone.

Millan, M. J. (1999). The induction of pain: An integrative review. *Progress in Neurobiology, 57,* 1–164.

Milne, R. J., & Gamble, G. D. (1990). Behavioural modification of bulbospinal serotonergic inhibition and morphine analgesia. *Brain Research, 521,* 167–174.

Mitchell, J. M., Lowe, D., & Fields, H. L. (1998). The contribution of the rostral ventromedial medulla to the antinociceptive effects of systemic morphine in restrained and unrestrained rats. *Neuroscience, 87,* 123–133.

Mogil, J. S., & Grisel, J. E. (1998). Transgenic studies of pain. *Pain, 77,* 107–128.

Mogil, J. S., & McCarson, K. E. (2000). Finding pain genes: Bottom-up and top-down approaches. *Journal of Pain, 1*(Suppl. 1), 66–80.

Mogil, J. S., Richards, S. P., O'Toole, L. A., Helms, M. L., Mitchell, S. R., & Belknap, J. K. (1997). Genetic sensitivity to hot-plate nociception in DBA/2J and C57BL/6J inbred mouse strains: Possible sex-specific mediation by d2-opioid receptors. *Pain, 70,* 267–277.

Mogil, J. S., Richards, S. P., O'Toole, L. A., Helms, M. L., Mitchell, S. R., Kest, B., & Belknap, J. K. (1997). Identification of a sex-specific quantitative trait locus mediating nonopioid stress-induced analgesia in female mice. *Journal of Neuroscience, 17,* 7995–8002.

Mogil, J. S., Sternberg, W. F., Balian, H., Liebeskind, J. C., & Sadowski, B. (1996). Opioid and non-opioid swim stress-induced analgesia: A parametric analysis in mice. *Physiology and Behavior, 59,* 123–132.

Mogil, J. S., Sternberg, W. F., Kest, B., Marek, P., & Liebeskind, J. C. (1993). Sex differences in the antagonism of swim stress-induced analgesia: Effects of gonadectomy and estrogen replacement. *Pain, 53,* 17–25.

Mogil, J. S., Wilson, S. G., Bon, K., Lee, S. E., Chung, K., Raber, P., Pieper, J. O., Hain, H. S., Belknap, J. K., Hubert, L., Elmer, G. I., Chung, J. M., & Devor, M. (1999). Heritability of nociception: I. Responses of eleven inbred mouse strains on twelve measures of nociception. *Pain, 80,* 67–82.

Mogil, J. S., Yu, L., & Basbaum, A. I. (2000). Pain genes? Natural variation and transgenic mutants. *Annual Review of Neuroscience, 23,* 777–811.

Morgan, M. M., Sohn, J.-H., & Liebeskind, J. C. (1989). Stimulation of the periaqueductal gray matter inhibits nociception at the supraspinal as well as spinal level. *Brain Research, 502,* 61–66.

Neumann, S., Doubell, T. P., Leslie, T., & Woolf, C. J. (1996). Inflammatory pain hypersensitivity mediated by phenotypic switch in myelinated primary sensory neurons. *Nature, 384,* 360–364.

Novakovic, S. D., Tzoumaka, E., McGivern, J. G., Haraguchi, M., Sangameswaran, L., Gogas, K. R., Eglen, R. M., & Hunter, J. C. (1998). Distribution of the tetrodotoxin-resistant sodium channel PN3 in rat sensory neurons in normal and neuropathic conditions. *Journal of Neuroscience, 15,* 2174–2187.

Olausson, H., Marchand, S., Bittar, R. G., Bernier, J., Ptito, A., & Bushnell, M. C. (2001). Central pain in a hemispherectomized patient. *European Journal of Pain, 5,* 209–218.

Ophoff, R. A., Terwindt, G. M., Frants, R. R., & Ferrari, M. D. (1998). P/Q-type Ca^{2+} channel defects in migraine, ataxia and epilepsy. *Trends in Pharmacological Sciences, 19,* 121–127.

Ossipov, M. H., Sun, H., Malan, T. P., Jr., Lai, J., & Porreca, F. (2000). Mediation of spinal nerve injury induced tactile allodynia by descending facilitatory pathways in the dorsolateral funiculus in rats. *Neuroscience Letters, 290,* 129–132.

Pan, Z. Z., & Fields, H. L. (1996). Endogenous opioid-mediated inhibition of putative pain-modulating neurons in rat rostral ventromedial medulla. *Neuroscience, 74,* 855–862.

Penfield, W., & Boldrey, E. (1937). Somatic motor and sensory representation in the cerebral cortex of man as studied by electrical stimulation. *Brain, 60,* 389–443.

Peroutka, S. J. (1998). Genetic basis of migraine. *Clinical Neuroscience, 5,* 34–37.

Pert, C. B., & Snyder, S. H. (1973). Opiate receptor: Demonstration in nervous tissue. *Science, 179,* 1011–1013.

Petrovic, P., Petersson, K. M., Ghatan, P. H., Stone-Elander, S., & Ingvar, M. (2000). Pain-related cerebral activation is altered by a distracting cognitive task. *Pain, 85,* 19–30.

Peyron, R., Garcia-Larrea, L., Gregoire, M. C., Convers, P., Lavenne, F., Veyre, L., Froment, J. C., Mauguiere, F., Michel, D., & Laurent, B. (1998). Allodynia after lateral-medullary (Wallenberg) infarct: A PET study. *Brain, 121,* 345–356.

Peyron, R., Larrea, L., Goire, M. C., Convers, P., Richard, A., Lavenne, F., Barral, F. G., Mauguiere, F., Michel, D., & Laurent, B. (2000). Parietal and cingulate processes in central pain: A combined positron emission tomography (PET) and functional magnetic resonance imaging (fMRI) study of an unusual case. *Pain, 84,* 77–87.

Peyron, R., Larrea, L., Goire, M. C., Costes, N., Convers, P., Lavenne, F., Mauguiere, F., Michel, D., & Laurent, B. (1999). Haemodynamic brain responses to acute pain in humans: Sensory and attentional networks. *Brain, 122,* 1765–1780.

Porreca, F., Burgess, S. E., Gardell, L. R., Vanderah, T. W., Malan, T. P., Jr., Ossipov, M. H., Lappi, D. A., & Lai, J. (2001). Inhibition of neuropathic pain by selective ablation of brainstem medullary cells expressing the m-opioid receptor. *Journal of Neuroscience, 21,* 5281–5288.

Quintero, L., Moreno, M., Avila, C., Arcaya, J., Maixner, W., & Suarez-Roca, H. (2000). Long-lasting delayed hyperalgesia after subchronic swim stress. *Pharmacology, Biochemistry and Behavior, 67,* 449–458.

Rainville, P., Duncan, G. H., Price, D. D., Carrier, B., & Bushnell, M. C. (1997). Pain affect encoded in human anterior cingulate but not somatosensory cortex. *Science, 277,* 968–971.

Raja, S. N. (1995). Role of the sympathetic nervous system in acute pain and inflammation. *Annals of Medicine, 27,* 241–246.

Rang, H. P., Bevan, S. J., & Dray, A. (1994). Nociceptive peripheral neurones: Cellular properties. In P. D. Wall & R. Melzack (Eds.), *Textbook of pain* (pp. 57–78). Edinburgh, UK: Churchill-Livingstone.

Raphael, K. G., Marbach, J. J., Gallagher, R. M., & Dohrenwend, B. P. (1999). Myofascial TMD does not run in families. *Pain, 80,* 15–22.

Rasmussen, P. (1990). Facial pain: I. A prospective survey of 1052 patients with a view of definition, delimitation, classification, general data, genetic factors and previous diseases. *Acta Neurochirgery, 107,* 112–120.

Rawlings, S. R., & Hezarch, M. (1996). Pituitary adenylate cyclase-activating polypeptide (PACAP) and PACAP/vasoactive intestinal polypeptide receptors: Actions on the anterior pituitary gland. *Endocrine Review, 17,* 4–29.

Rexed, B. (1952). The cytoarchitectonic organization of the spinal cord in the rat. *Journal of Comparative Neurology, 96,* 415–466.

Reynolds, D. V. (1969). Surgery in the rat during electrical analgesia induced by focal brain stimulation. *Science, 164,* 444–445.

Richards, R. L. (1967). Causalgia: A centennial review. *Archives of Neurology, 16,* 339–350.

Richardson, J. D., Aanonsen, L., & Hargreaves, K. M. (1997). SR 14176A, a cannabinoid receptor antagonist, produces hyperalgesia in untreated mice. *European Journal of Pharmacology, 319,* 3–4.

Richmond, C. E., Bromley, L. M., & Woolf, C. J. (1993). Preoperative morphine preempts postoperative pain. *Lancet, 342,* 73–75.

Rodgers, R. J., & Shepherd, J. K. (1989). 5-HT1A agonist, 8-hydroxy-2-(DI-n-propylamino) tetralin (8-OH-DPAT), inhibits non-opioid analgesia in defeated mice: Influence of route of administration. *Psychopharmacology, 97,* 163–165.

Rodgers, R. J., Shepherd, J. K., & Randall, J. I. (1990). Highly potent inhibitory effects of 5-HT3 receptor antagonist, GR38032F, on non-opioid defeat analgesia in male mice. *Neuropharmacology, 29,* 17–23.

Rothman, R. B. (1992). A review of the role of anti-opioid peptides in morphine tolerance and dependence. *Synapse, 12,* 129–138.

Sato, J., & Perl, E. R. (1991). Adrenergic excitation of cutaneous pain receptors induced by peripheral nerve injury. *Science, 251,* 1608–1610.

Sawynok, J., & Sweeney, M. I. (1989). The role of purines in nociception. *Neuroscience, 32,* 557–569.

Schena, M., Shalon, D., Davis, R. W., & Brown, P. O. (1995). Quantitative monitoring of gene expression patterns with a complimentary DNA microarray. *Science, 270,* 467–470.

Seltzer, Z., Wu, T., Max, M. B., & Diehl, S. R. (2001). Mapping a gene for neuropathic pain-related behavior following peripheral neurectomy in the mouse. *Pain, 93,* 101–106.

Shu, X.-Q., & Mendell, L. M. (1999). Neurotrophic and hyperalgesia. *Proceedings of the National Academy of Sciences, USA, 96,* 7693–7696.

Slaugenhaupt, S. A. B. A., Gill, S. P., Leyne, M., Mull, J., Cuajungco, M. P., Liebert, C. B., Chadwick, B., Idelson, M., Reznik, L., Robbins, C., Makalowska, I., Brownstein, M., Krappmann, D., Scheidereit, C., Maayan, C., Axelrod, F. B., & Gusella, J. F. (2001). Tissue-specific expression of a splicing mutation in the IKBKAP gene causes familial dysautonomia. *American Journal of Human Genetics, 68,* 598–605.

Stanfa, L. C., Dickenson, A. H., Xu, X.-J., & Wiesenfeld-Hallin, Z. (1994). Cholecystokinin and morphine analgesia: variations on a theme. *Trends in Pharmacological Sciences, 15,* 65–66.

Talbot, J. D., Marrett, S., Evans, A. C., Meyer, E., Bushnell, M. C., & Duncan, G. H. (1991). Multiple representations of pain in human cerebral cortex. *Science, 251,* 1355–1358.

Thompson, S. W. N., Bennett, D. L. H., Kerr, B. J., Bradbury, E. J., & McMahon, S. B. (1999). Brain-derived neurotrophic factor is an endogenous modulator of nociceptive responses in the spinal cord. *Proceedings of the National Academy of Sciences, USA, 96,* 7714–7718.

Torebjörk, H. E., LaMotte, R. H., & Robinson, C. J. (1984). Peripheral neural correlation of magnitude of cutaneous pain and hyperalgesia: Simultaneous recordings in humans of sensory judgments of pain and evoked response in nociceptors with C-fibres. *Journal of Neurophysiology, 51,* 325–339.

Treede, R. D., Meyer, R. A., Raja, S. N., & Campbell, J. N. (1992). Peripheral and central mechanisms of cutaneous hyperalgesia. *Progress in Neurobiology, 38,* 397–421.

Treloar, S. A., Martin, N. G., & Heath, A. C. (1998). Longitudinal genetic analysis of menstrual flow, pain and limitation in a sample of Australian twins. *Behavioral Genetics, 28*(2), 107–116.

Turk, D. C., Flor, H., & Rudy, T. E. (1987). Pain and families: I. Etiology, maintenance and psychosocial impact. *Pain, 30,* 3–27.

Wahlestedt, C., Salmi, P., Good, L., Kela, J., Johnsson, T., Hokfelt, T., Broberger, C., Porreca, F., Lai, J., Ren, K., Ossipov, M. H., Koshkin, A., Jakobsen, N., Skouv, J., Oerum, H., Jacobsen, M. H., & Wengel, J. (2000). Potent and nontoxic antisense oligonucleotides containing locked nucleic acids. *Proceedings of the National Academy of Sciences, USA, 97,* 5633–5638.

Waldmann, R., Champigny, G., Bassilana, F., Heurteaux, C., & Lazdunski, M. (1997). A proton-gated cation channel involved in acid-sensing. *Nature, 386,* 173–177.

Waldmann, R., & Lazdunski, M. (1998). $H^{(+)}$-gated cation channels: Neuronal acid sensors in the NaC/DEG family of ion channels. *Current Opinion in Neurobiology, 8,* 418–424.

Walker, J. S., Sheather-Reid, R. B., Carmody, J. J., Vial, J. H., & Day, R. O. (1997). Nonsteroidal antiinflammatory drugs in rheumatoid arthritis and osteoarthritis. *Arthritis and Rheumatism, 40,* 1944–1954.

Wang, Z., Gardell, L. R., Ossipov, M. H., Vanderah, T. W., Brennan, M. B., Hochgeschwender, U., Hruby, V. J., Malan, T. P., Jr., Lai, J., & Porreca, F. (2001). Pronociceptive actions of dynorphin maintain chronic neuropathic pain. *Journal of Neuroscience, 21,* 1779–1786.

Watkins, J. C., & Evans, R. H. (1981). Excitatory amino acid transmitters. *Annual Review of Pharmacology and Toxicology, 21,* 165–204.

Watkins, L. R., Maier, S. F., & Goehler, L. E. (1995). Immune activation: The role of pro-inflammatory cytokines in inflammation, illness responses and pathological pain states. *Pain, 63,* 289–302.

Watkins, L. R., McGorry, M., Schwartz, B., Sisk, D., Wiertelak, E. P., & Maier, S. F. (1997). Reversal of spinal cord non-opiate analgesia by conditioned anti-analgesia in the rat. *Pain, 71,* 237–247.

Watkins, L. R., Wiertelak, E. P., Grisel, J. E., Silbert, L. H., & Maier, S. F. (1992). Parallel activation of multiple spinal opiate systems appears to mediate "non-opiate" stress-induced analgesias. *Brain Research, 594,* 99–108.

Wiertelak, E. P., Maier, S. F., & Watkins, L. R. (1992). Cholecystokinin antianalgesia: Safety cues abolish morphine analgesia. *Science, 256,* 830–833.

Willis, W. D., Jr., & Coggeshall, R. E. (1991). *Sensory mechanisms of the spinal cord* (2nd ed.). New York: Plenum Press.

Willis, W. D., Jr., & Westlund, K. N. (1997). Neuroanatomy of the pain system and of the pathways that modulate pain. *Journal of Clinical Neurophysiology, 14,* 2–31.

Wilson, S. G., Chesler, E. J., Hain, H. S., Rankin, A. L., Schwarz, J. Z., Call, S. B., Murray, M. R., West, E. E., Teuscher, C., Rodriquez-Zas, S., Belknap, J. K., & Mogil, J. S. (2001). *Identification of quantitative trait loci for chemical/inflammatory nociception in mice.* Manuscript submitted for publication.

Wood, J. N., & Docherty, R. J. (1997). Chemical activators of sensory neurons. *Annual Review of Physiology, 59,* 457–482.

Woolf, C. J. (1991). Central mechanisms of acute pain. In M. R. Bond, J. E. Charlton, & C. J. Woolf (Eds.), *Proceedings of the 6th world congress on pain* (pp. 25–34). Amsterdam: Elsevier Science.

Woolf, C. J. (1996). Phenotypic modification of primary sensory neurons: The role of nerve growth factor in the production of persistent pain. *Philosophical Transactions of the Royal Society of London [Biology], 351,* 441–448.

Woolf, C. J., & Costigan, M. (1999). Transcriptional and posttranslational plasticity and the generation of inflammatory pain. *Proceedings of the National Academy of Sciences, USA, 96,* 7723–7730.

Woolf, C. J., Shortland, P., & Coggeshall, R. E. (1992). Peripheral nerve injury triggers central sprouting of myelinated afferents. *Nature, 355,* 75–77.

Xu, X. J., Wiesenfeld-Hallin, Z., Villar, M. J., Fahrenkrug, P., & Hökfelt, T. (1990). On the role of galanin, substance P and other neuropeptides in primary sensory neurons of the rat: Studies on spinal reflex excitability and peripheral axotomy. *European Journal of Neuroscience, 2,* 733–743.

Zadina, J. E., Martin-Schild, S., Gerall, A. A., Kastin, A. J., Hackler, L., Ge, L. J., & Zhang, X. (1999). Endomorphins: Novel endogenous mu-opiate receptor agonists in regions of high mu-opiate receptor density. *Annals of the New York Academy of Sciences, 897,* 136–144.

Zillmann, D., De Wied, M., King-Jablonski, C., & Jenzowsky, S. (1996). Drama-induced affect and pain sensitivity. *Psychosomatic Medicine, 58,* 333–341.

Zimmer, A., Zimmer, A. M., Hohmann, A. G., Herkenham, M., & Bonner, T. I. (1999). Increased mortality, hypoactivity and hypoalgesia in cannabinoid CB1 receptor knockout mice. *Proceedings of the National Academy of Sciences, USA, 96,* 5780–5785.

Zubieta, J.-K., Smith, Y. R., Bueller, J. A., Xu, Y., Kilbourn, M. R., Jewett, D. M., Meyer, C. R., Koeppe, R. A., & Stohler, C. S. (2001). Regional mu opioid receptor regulation of sensory and affective dimensions of pain. *Science, 293,* 311–315.

CHAPTER 10

Olfaction and Taste

PATRICIA M. DI LORENZO AND STEVEN L. YOUNGENTOB

The ability to detect and interpret the chemicals in our environment affects nearly every aspect of our survival. Most important, perhaps, is the central role of chemical sensation in the detection of what is edible and where it is located. It is well known, for example, that the flavor of our food (i.e., the combination of its taste and smell) is a major determinant of ingestion. One need consider only what happens to our appetite and our affect (see Toller, 1999) when these sensibilities are lost or altered to realize just how essential the chemical senses are to our well-being. Conversely, we utilize our chemical senses to protect us from ingesting or inhaling toxins that can harm us.

Historically, the study of taste and olfaction has progressed at a relatively slow pace when compared to the study of the other sensory modalities such as vision or audition. The reason has been in part the difficulty in defining the dimensions of the stimulus domain of the chemical senses. The original hypotheses regarding chemical structure as a predictor of perceptual quality have at times led to some anomalous results. Likewise, psychophysical analysis of tastes and smells has sometimes produced controversy. Without adequate confidence that any given array of stimuli would span the limits of chemical sensibility, investigators have been slow to agree on schemes with which taste and olfactory stimuli are encoded by the nervous system. However, as the present review of the recent scientific literature hopefully reveals, technological advances, particularly in the realm of molecular neurobiology, are providing the tools for unraveling some of the long-standing mysteries of the chemical senses.

TASTE

Taste Stimuli

Before one can define a *taste stimulus,* one must define what constitutes a *taste sensation.* From a purely literal view a taste sensation is the sum of the neural activity in a taste-related pathway in the nervous system. Obviously, this definition is circular in that taste-related pathways are defined by the observation that their activation produces a taste sensation. The chemosenses have this tautology in common with all sensory systems. Thus, the definition of a taste stimulus is a stimulus that evokes a taste sensation or, by extension, any stimulus that evokes activity in a taste-related portion of the nervous system. Historically, some sensations that we think of as taste, such as metallic or alkaline, have turned out not to be taste sensations at all, but rather arise from the concurrent stimulation of trigeminal or olfactory pathways. In fact, most of what we think of ordinarily as taste sensations are actually combinations of taste, olfactory, tactile, and thermal sensations; there are very few purely *taste* sensations. In part, that accounts for the observation that an individual can lose a large part of his or her sense of taste and not be aware of any loss at all (Kveton & Bartoshuk, 1994).

From a practical point of view taste stimuli are chemicals that are capable of dissolving in saliva because saliva is the medium that conveys the stimulus to the taste receptors. Taste stimuli express a variety of chemical structures but, as some would argue, evoke only a handful of different sensations.

TABLE 10.1   Examples of Stimuli That Are Commonly Used in Taste Experiments

Salty Salts	Bitter Salts	Sour	Sweet	Bitter	Other
NaCl	KCl	HCl	sucrose	quinine HCl	monosodium glutamate
LiCl	$CaCl_2$	citric acid	fructose	quinine SO_4	maltose
Na_2SO_4	NH_4Cl	malic acid	glucose	urea	polycose
$NaNO_3$	NH_4Br	HNO_3	dl-alanine	Sucrose octa-acetate	ethanol
	$MgCl_2$	NaOH	glycine	caffeine	
		tartaric acid			
		lactic acid			

These are commonly known as the four basic taste qualities: sweet, sour, salty, and bitter. Prototypical stimuli associated with these basic qualities are sucrose (sugars) for sweet, citric or hydrochloric acid for sour, sodium chloride (NaCl) for salty, and quinine for bitter. Many have argued that another taste, called umami and exemplified by monosodium glutamate (MSG) and L-aspartate, is unique enough to be considered a fifth basic taste quality. Although it was discovered nearly 100 years ago, investigation of umami in this regard has intensified only in the last two decades (Brand, 2000; Kurihara & Kashiwayanagi, 2000; Yamaguchi, 1991). Table 10.1 shows a list of chemicals that have been used in experiments on the gustatory system.

Defining what constitutes a taste stimulus is not a trivial exercise because it affects an entire cascade of research on the taste system. For example, if one argues that a group of chemicals taste alike, say salty, then psychophysicists will study the "salty" sensation of fluids; chemists will look for molecular similarities that define whether a chemical tastes salty; cell biologists will look for salt receptors on the taste receptor cells; physiologists will look for nerve fibers and neurons that respond well to salt; and theorists will devise schemes for how salt is encoded. To provide guidance as to how the taste world is organized, students of gustation have turned to the field of psychophysics.

A Word About Psychophysics

Early psychophysicists set about to examine the inherent organization of the world of sapid (defined as having a taste) stimuli. They quickly discovered that there were groups of stimuli that tasted alike and that each group could be characterized by a single descriptor (e.g., sweet or salty). From these observations came the idea of *taste primaries,* defined as qualities that in combination could reconstruct any gustatory experience. The most active challenge to this idea has been offered by Erickson (2000) and Schiffman (2000), who argued that the taste world is organized as a continuum, rather than parceled into discrete groups. Their argument, in part, is that the historical categorization into four taste qualities is an artifact of our language, in that the English lan-

guage has a limited number of words available to describe a taste and that most of us have a long history of describing what we taste using just these few words. It has been shown, for example, that in Asian cultures umami is a commonly recognized taste whereas in the United States the taste of umami is described as salty-bitter (O'Mahony & Ishii, 1986).

In general, the problem of reconciling language with function is thorny and not easily solved, though many have tried. Many studies of the organization of the taste world ask subjects to describe the taste stimulus presented to them without giving any specific suggestions. In that case, one cannot divorce the subject's history from the likelihood of his or her choices of descriptors. This inherent conflict may be reinforced in studies where subjects are asked to choose from among a list of descriptors that are restricted to those associated with the four or five basic taste qualities. Erickson (2000) discussed this point in detail in a recent review.

One of the more persuasive paradigms that has been used to study the idea that there are four (or five) independent taste qualities is that of adaptation. The phenomenon of adaptation is defined as a response decrement following prolonged exposure to a given stimulus. The overall strategy is to adapt the tongue to one stimulus and test for a response to another; if the adapting and test stimuli share a common receptor mechanism, the response to the test stimulus should be attenuated. If the two stimuli are independent in the sense that they evoke independent (i.e., nonoverlapping) sensations, adaptation to one will not alter the perception of the other. In general, results of this kind of experiment have concluded that, psychophysically, there is little cross-adaptation among the four basic taste qualities and, conversely, much cross-adaptation among stimuli classified as belonging to the same class of taste quality (e.g., McBurney & Bartoshuk, 1973).

In addition to producing an outline of the taste world, modern psychophysicists have identified several areas of research where their contributions can have potentially significant medical and societal impact. One of these areas is in the genetic variability of taste as a marker for people who are at risk for a variety of disorders. For example, it has been known since the 1930s that the ability to perceive phenylthio-carbamide (PTC) and the chemically related 6-*n*-propylthio-uracil (PROP) as bitter is genetically transmitted through a dominant gene (Bartoshuk, Duffy, Reed, & Williams, 1996). More recently, the study of people who taste PROP, called tasters, has suggested that there is a subset of tasters who experience PROP as extremely bitter (i.e., more bitter than most other tasters do). This group of supertasters has not only an enhanced perception of PROP but also a greater number of fungiform taste papillae than do medium tasters or nontasters, as well as an enhanced perception for other bitter compounds, for salty, sweet, fatty, and viscous substances, and for oral burn produced by capsaicin (Bartoshuk, Duffy, Lucchina, Prutkin, & Fast, 1998). In the United States about 25% of the public are nontasters; 50% are medium tasters; and 25% are supertasters. There is some evidence that the ability to perceive PROP may be a genetic marker for the propensity to become alcoholic (DiCarlo & Powers, 1998; Pelchat & Danowski, 1992), although this remains controversial (see Kranzler, Moore, & Hesselbrock, 1996). In any case, these studies suggest that genetic variability in taste perception may prove to be a useful marker for at-risk populations for a variety of behavioral problems.

Another application for the study of taste psychophysics has been in the study of the relationship of taste perception to the molecular biology of signal transduction. In general, there is an interplay between the perceptual phenomena that psychophysicists can define (i.e., commonalities among the things we taste) and the transduction mechanisms that molecular biologists search for and study to account for these commonalities. A good example of this is the study of the perception of saltiness. When the amiloride-sensitive sodium channels were discovered, it was widely hypothesized that the direct entry of Na^+ ions through these channels could account entirely for salt perception (see Halpern, 1998, for a review). However, when it turned out that amiloride mixed with a NaCl solution did not eliminate the perception of saltiness entirely, it became apparent that additional transduction mechanisms for NaCl must be present. Indeed, it is now known that NaCl can affect neurotransmitter release from receptor cells through other pathways (as discussed later).

Transduction of Taste Stimuli

Some of the most exciting discoveries in the field of taste in recent years have been in the study of transduction mechanisms. A thorough treatment of these advances is beyond the scope of the present chapter; however, the reader is referred to some excellent reviews (Brand, 2000; Gilbertson, Damak, & Margolskee, 2000; Herness & Gilbertson, 1999; Kinnamon & Margolskee, 1996; Lindemann, 1996; Miyamoto, Fujiyama, Okada, & Sato, 2000; Spielman, 1998; R. E. Stewart, DeSimone, & Hill, 1997).

Most treatments of the subject of taste transduction mechanisms are divided into sections according to taste quality. That is, there are usually separate sections for encoding of sweet, sour, salty, and bitter substances. This is partly a natural extension of the results from psychophysical work, as mentioned earlier, and it has proven a fruitful strategy, all things considered. However, as this work has unfolded, it has become clear that there may be more than one transduction mechanism for each of the basic tastes. The fact that multiple transduction pathways contribute to a taste experience may underlie the singular taste experiences.

Saltiness

The sensation of saltiness in its purest form is produced by NaCl or lithium chloride (LiCl; Murphy, Cardello, & Brand, 1981). Other salts produce taste qualities (e.g., bitter or sour) in addition to saltiness. The rather narrow spectrum of pure tastants associated with saltiness endows the system with the ability to pick out NaCl specifically when needed, as in the case of Na^+ deprivation (Fitzsimmons, 1979). This ability may be beneficial to survival because NaCl is essential for a variety of biological functions, including nervous function and homeostatic regulation of water in the body.

The transduction of NaCl is thought to involve the entry of Na^+ ions directly into the taste receptor cell (TRC) through two separate pathways. The first is through Na^+ channels that are reversibly blockable by the diuretic amiloride. These amiloride-sensitive channels (ASCs) are located on the apical portion of the TRC. There are large species differences in the effectiveness of amiloride to block these channels, and these differences are reflected in the varying effectiveness of amiloride to block the perception of saltiness (see Halpern, 1998, for a review). Na^+ is thought to enter the TRC through these channels and depolarize the TRC membrane, causing voltage-sensitive Na^+, K^+, and Ca^{++} channels to open. The entry of Ca^{++} into the TRC then causes the release of transmitter from the TRC onto the taste nerve endings. The second transduction pathway for NaCl is by Na^+ entry through Na^+ channels located on the basolateral TRC membrane below the tight junctions.

There is also a role for the anion in the transduction and subsequent perception of saltiness. Small anions such as Cl^- act through a paracellular shunt by diffusing past the tight junctions. This produces a negative region at the basal portion of the TRC that further promotes the influx of positive ions. The tight junctions control this diffusion and current flow; they pass small cations more freely than they do larger ones. This accounts for the observation that salts with larger cations (e.g., sodium gluconate) do not taste as salty as do those with smaller ones (e.g., NaCl).

Sourness

The sensation of sourness is produced by acids. Sourness is thought to be associated with rotting fruit and, by extension, with toxicity. Its detection is therefore important for survival.

The perception of sourness appears to be directly related to the concentration of the hydrogen ion (Ganzevles & Kroeze, 1987). A variety of transduction mechanisms have been studied for sourness, and it appears that there are large species differences in the mechanisms that are present. For example, in the mud puppy (Kinnamon, Dionne, & Beam, 1988) and tiger salamander (Sugimoto & Teeter, 1991), H^+ ions block a normally open K^+ channel located on the apical region of the TRC. This then depolarizes the TRC, resulting in the eventual entry of Ca^{++} and subsequent release of neurotransmitter. In the hamster there is good evidence that H^+ enters the TRC through amiloride-blockable channels that may be identical to those involved in Na^+ transduction (Gilbertson, Avenet, Kinnamon, & Roper, 1992); however, this mechanism is not present in the rat (DeSimone, Calahan, & Heck, 1995). Still other mechanisms that have been proposed include a proton exchange mechanism, a stimulus-gated Ca^{++} channel, and the direct entry through a H^+ channel that has yet to be identified (see Lindemann, 1996). Clearly, there is much work yet to be done in this area.

Bitterness

As is the case for sweet substances, a wide variety of chemicals produces a bitter sensation. These include some plant alkaloids such as the prototypical bitter substance quinine, nicotine, strychnine, and caffeine, as well as hydrophilic salts of Ca^{++}, Mg^{++}, Ba^{++}, Cs^+, K^+, and NH_4 (R. E. Stewart et al., 1997). Other compounds such as urea, sucrose octa-acetate (SOA), denatonium, and many of the D-isomers of amino acids also taste bitter. The variety of chemical structures represented by bitter substances has led investigators to conclude that many different receptors must be involved in their transduction. Furthermore, observations that some bitter tastants utilize more than one transduction pathway (see R. E. Stewart et al., 1997) only complicate the question of how bitterness is encoded at the TRC level.

Fortunately, some dramatic discoveries in the last decade have significantly advanced our knowledge of the transduction of bitterness. These began with the cloning of a

G protein called gustducin, which is localized exclusively in TRCs (Spielman, 1998) and was reported by McLaughlin, McKinnon, and Margolskee in 1992. Gustducin shares an 80% homology with transducin, the G protein once thought to be restricted to the retina. In fact, transducin has also been found in TRCs (McLaughlin, McKinnon, Spickofsky, Danho, & Margolskee, 1994). Because of the gustducin's similarity to transducin, the former is thought to work in much the same way: Binding of a bitter substance to a receptor (discussed later) would cause gustducin to activate phosphodiesterase, which would then decrease the level of a cyclic nucleotide. Lower levels of cyclic nucleotides would affect a cyclic nucleotide-activated membrane channel and thereby depolarize the membrane potential. Conversely, high levels of cyclic nucleotides in frog TRCs produce a decrease in conductance (Kolesnikov & Margolskee, 1995).

In addition to the cyclic nucleotide pathway for bitter transduction, other transduction mechanisms are also under investigation. For example, there is evidence that some bitter substances, such as SOA (Spielman, Huque, Nagai, Whitney, & Brand, 1994) and denatonium (Akabus, Dodd, & Al-Awqati, 1988), stimulate the inositol triphosphate (IP_3) system to increase Ca^{++} levels derived from intracellular stores. SOA is also known to block K^+ channels directly (Spielman, Huque, Whitney, & Brand, 1992), as does quinine at low concentrations (Ozeki, 1971).

Sweetness

A wide variety of compounds produces a sweet sensation, including mono-, di-, and polysaccharides, polyalcohols, amino acids, peptides, and some proteins. In addition to the variety of chemical structures, there are wide species differences in sensitivity to sweet-tasting substances. For example, it is well known that gerbils are about 40 times more sensitive to sucrose than are humans. However, some chemicals that taste sweet to humans, such as aspartame, probably do not taste sweet to rats. For example, Sclafani and Abrams (1986) demonstrated that rats showed only a weak preference for aspartame over water when aspartame was presented at a variety of concentrations in a two-choice paradigm. It is interesting to note that cats do not have any sweet taste receptors and thus are completely insensitive to sweetness.

Considering the diversity of the molecular structure of this group of chemicals, it is not surprising that a number of transduction mechanisms exist. There is growing evidence that natural sweeteners like sucrose activate the production of cAMP through a receptor–G protein interaction. The production of cyclic adenosine monophosphate (cAMP) would then activate protein kinase A, leading to the closure of

K^+ channels. The subsequent depolarization would result in Ca^{++} entry through voltage-activated Ca^{++} channels and eventual neurotransmitter release. There is also evidence that a decrease in cAMP may be involved in sweet taste transduction. This evidence is derived from the observation by Wong, Gannon, and Margolskee (1996) that knockout mice that are lacking gustducin are also deficient in their sensitivity to sweet-tasting compounds. As with bitter compounds, gustducin may activate a phosphodiesterase and thereby decrease the concentration of cyclic nucleotides. The resolution of evidence implying both an increase and a decrease in cyclic nucleotides in response to sweet substances requires additional investigation.

Yet another transduction mechanism for sweet tastes involves the IP_3 cascade. Sweet chemicals such as saccharin and amino acids also close K^+ channels but do not activate cAMP. These substances stimulate Ca^{++} release from intracellular stores (Bernhardt, Naim, Zehavi, & Lindemann, 1996). There is evidence (Behe, DeSimone, Avenet, & Lindemann, 1990) that TRCs may contain the molecular machinery for both cAMP and IP_3 transduction pathways.

Finally, there is evidence that sugars stimulate an influx of cations through an ASC in dogs but not in rats (Simon, Labarca, & Robb, 1989).

Umami

Although still controversial to some, it has been argued that the taste of umami is just as distinct as that of salty, sweet, bitter, or sour and should therefore be considered a fifth basic taste quality. The prototypical stimulus for umami is MSG, although L-aspartate also evokes umami. Other amino acids evoke umami as well.

The transduction of MSG as a tastant is presumably accomplished through a glutamate receptor. Although much of the work on glutamate receptors related to gustation has been done in the channel catfish (see Caprio et al., 1993, for a review), studies in mammalian systems have also begun to bear fruit. In this context there is evidence for both ionotropic and metabotropic receptors in TRCs. Recently, a G-protein coupled receptor for MSG that is localized to mouse TRCs (Chaudhari, Landin, & Roper, 2000) has been identified, and evidence has been provided implicating it as a taste receptor for MSG.

The Search for Taste Receptors

Researchers have only recently begun to identify candidate genes and their respective proteins that may serve as taste receptors. The first of these is a small family of two G-protein coupled receptors, T1R-1 and T1R-2, which have been localized specifically to TRCs (Hoon et al., 1999). Each of these has a differential spatial distribution across the receptive fields of the oropharyngeal area: T1R-1 is expressed primarily in the fungiform papillae and palatal taste buds, and T1R-2 is expressed more prominently in foliate and circumvallate taste buds. This regional specificity led Hoon et al. (1999) to suggest that these putative receptors encode sweet and bitter modalities; however, this idea remains speculative at present. It is interesting that these proteins are absent from TRCs expressing gustducin.

Another recent report has identified a family of putative taste receptors, called T2Rs, that are specifically localized to TRCs in the mouse (Adler et al., 2000). Further evidence suggested that TRCs may express a large repertoire of T2Rs, which may account for the ability to perceive a wide variety of substances as bitter (Chandrashekar et al., 2000). This line of research is quite recent and can certainly be expected to progress rapidly in the next few years.

Anatomy of the Taste System

Peripheral Nervous System

Taste buds are located in the oropharyngeal area in structures called *papillae*. Papillae can be seen as bumps on the surface of the tongue. Filliform papillae do not contain any taste buds and are located on the dorsal middle of the tongue. Fungiform papillae, found on the tip and sides of the tongue, resemble mushrooms in shape. In the rat only one taste bud is located in each fungiform papilla, and nearly all fungiform papillae have taste buds in them (Mistretta & Oakley, 1986). In humans, however, fungiform papillae contain on average one to four taste buds each (Arvidson, 1979; Miller, 1986). In general, only about one third of these papillae contain any taste buds (Cheng & Robinson, 1991). The great majority of fungiform papillae and the taste buds contained in them are located on the tip of the tongue in both rat (Miller & Preslar, 1975) and human (Cheng & Robinson, 1991). Circumvallate papillae are located at the rear of the tongue and look like flattened disks; taste buds are also located in surrounding trenches as with fungiform papillae. In the human they are arranged in an inverted V with the apex oriented toward the back of the tongue. Foliate papillae are located along the sides of the tongue behind the molar teeth. They appear as parallel folds and ridges with taste buds buried in the folds. There are also taste buds on the soft palate and epiglottis.

In general, there is a good deal of variation from person to person in the number of papillae and in the number of taste buds per papillae; this variation may be genetically determined and may be related to taste sensitivity (Bartoshuk, 2000a, 2000b). For an excellent review of the location and distribution of papillae and taste buds in the human, see Miller and Bartoshuk (1991). Stimulation of individual taste papillae and individual taste buds can evoke all four taste qualities (Bealer & Smith, 1975).

One of the most common misconceptions about taste is that different parts of the tongue are differentially sensitive to the various taste qualities. For example, it is usually stated that the tip of the tongue is most sensitive to sweet, the back to bitter, and so on. These assertions are based on work in the nineteenth century showing that there are differences in taste thresholds for the basic taste qualities across different regions of the tongue. In truth, these differences are slight, and all of the basic taste qualities may be perceived everywhere there are taste buds (Collings, 1974).

The sensory organ that contains the receptor cells for taste is the taste bud. The arrangement of the spindle-shaped TRCs within the taste bud is usually described as resembling the slices of an orange (see Figure 10.1). Slender cilia protrude from the apical end of TRCs into the oral environment through the taste pore. Tight junctions between TRCs prevent taste stimuli from entering the taste bud. There are generally three types of TRCs described in mammalian taste buds: Type I (dark), Type II (light), and Type III, which synapse on the gustatory nerves. These types are generally considered to represent different developmental stages; TRCs are known to have a life span of about 10 days. In the mouse all types of taste cells receive synapses from gustatory nerve fibers (Royer & Kinnamon, 1994). In the basal portion of the taste bud in the rat, nerve fibers form a dense plexus, sending thin beaded branches between the taste cells to synapse on Type III cells (Kanazawa & Yoshie, 1996; Muller & Jastrow, 1998). It is now known that TRCs can contain the transduction mechanisms for all four taste qualities, can produce action potentials themselves, and can thus respond broadly across the basic taste qualities. For a recent review of this topic see Herness (2000).

Three cranial nerves innervate taste buds. The first is the facial (VII) with the greater superficial petrosal branch innervating taste buds within the nasoincisor ducts and the chorda tympani (CT) innervating the rostral two thirds of the tongue. The rat CT contains about 1,500 fibers (Ferrell, Tsuetaki, & Chole, 1985), whereas the human CT contains about 5,500 fibers (Ylikoski, Gamoletti, & Galey, 1983). The second is the glossopharyngeal (IX), or GP, with the lingual branch innervating the caudal third of the tongue. The remaining taste buds are innervated by the superior laryngeal branch of the vagus (X) nerve. The VIIth, IXth, and Xth nerve innervations of the oropharyngeal area project to the medulla via the geniculate, petrosal, and nodose ganglia, respectively.

Central Taste Pathways

Figure 10.2 is a schematic diagram of the central neural pathways associated with gustation in the rodent.

The three cranial nerves associated with taste terminate centrally in a roughly topographical arrangement within the rostral portion of the nucleus of the solitary tract (NTS), although there is considerable overlap (Halsell, Travers, & Travers, 1993; McPheeters et al., 1990; S. P. Travers & Norgren, 1995). These primary afferents form excitatory synapses on the distal dendrites and spines of cells in the

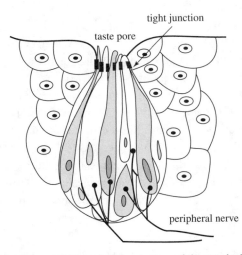

Figure 10.1 Schematic diagram of the structure of the taste bud showing light and dark taste receptor cells, surrounding epithelial cells, and peripheral nerve innervation. Adapted from Brand (1997).

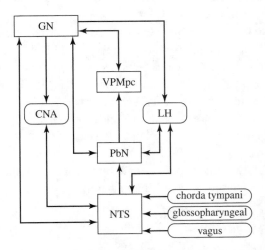

Figure 10.2 Schematic diagram of the anatomical pathways associated with taste in the rodent brain. Abbreviations are as follows: NTS, nucleus of the solitary tract; PbN, parabrachial nucleus of the pons; VPMpc, ventroposteromedial nucleus of the thalamus, parvocellular region; GN, gustatory neocortex; CNA, central nucleus of the amygdala; LH, lateral hypothalamus.

rostral central and rostral lateral subdivisions of the NTS (Whitehead, 1986; Whitehead & Frank, 1983). They terminate in glomeruli in which a variety of synaptic relationships is located (Davis, 1998; Whitehead & Frank, 1983). These include both axodendritic (possibly inhibitory) and dendrodendritic connections (Whitehead & Frank, 1983).

Most investigations of the morphological characteristics of neurons in the gustatory NTS have identified three cell types: fusiform (elongate), stellate (multipolar), and ovoid. Fusiform cells have at least two primary dendrites that are preferentially oriented in the mediolateral plane, are perpendicular to the solitary tract, and can extend distances of several hundred micrometers (Whitehead, 1986; Whitehead & Frank, 1983). (More recent evidence using three-dimensional reconstruction of neurobiotin-labeled cells suggests that very few NTS cells are actually bipolar; Renehan, Jin, Zhang, & Schweitzer, 1994.) It has been suggested that this arrangement maximizes the opportunity to synapse with a large number of incoming fibers (Davis & Jang, 1986; Whitehead, 1986; Whitehead & Frank, 1983). A more recent analysis of the morphology of NTS cells has defined six cell types, based on a cluster analysis of six morphological features (Renehan et al., 1994). One of these features, cell size, may correlate with immunohistochemical features (i.e., large cells are associated with immunoreactivity to tyrosine hydroxylase; Davis, 1998), and small cells are immunoreactive to gamma-aminobutyric acid (GABA; Davis, 1993; Lasiter, & Kachele, 1988b) and may be inhibitory interneurons (Whitehead, 1986).

A significant proportion of cells in the rostral central and rostral lateral subdivisions of the NTS are responsive to exogenously applied GABA (Davis, 1993; Liu, Behbehani, & Smith, 1993; Smith & Li, 1998, 2000). Evidence that both GABA$_A$ and GABA$_B$ receptors are present has been reported (Liu et al., 1993; Smith & Li, 1998). These observations have fueled speculation that inhibitory processes may be important in the neural processing of gustatory stimuli in the NTS.

From the NTS the gustatory pathway in the rodent is known to project mainly to the parabrachial nucleus of the pons (PbN; Norgren, 1974; Saper & Loewy, 1980). Some taste-sensitive projections from the NTS, however, may bypass the PbN and terminate in the lateral hypothalamus (LH), central nucleus of the amygdala (CNA), and the gustatory neocortex (GN; Horst, de Boer, Luiten, & van Willigen, 1989; Ricardo & Koh, 1978). (In the primate, the main projection of the taste-related pathway from the NTS is directly to the thalamus without a synapse in the PbN; see Pritchard, 1991.) Approximately one third of the taste-responsive NTS cells send axons to the PbN (Monroe & Di Lorenzo, 1995; Ogawa, Imoto, & Hayama, 1984; Ogawa, Imoto, Hayama, & Kaisaku, 1982; Ogawa & Kaisaku, 1982). Anatomical studies

have shown that only fusiform and stellate cells send axons to the gustatory portions of the PbN (Whitehead, 1990). These cells receive input also from primary gustatory afferents and are therefore second-order neurons in the gustatory pathway.

In the PbN taste-responsive cells are found in the medial and lateral subdivisions and scattered among the fibers of the brachium, in the so-called waist area (Davis, 1991; Lasiter & Kachele, 1988a). Two types of cells in the areas that receive afferents from the gustatory portions of the NTS have been described: fusiform and multipolar cells (Davis, 1991; Lasiter & Kachele, 1988a). Compared with cells in the NTS, neurons in gustatory subdivisions of the PbN apparently show more elaborate dendritic arborizations that do not extend large distances (Davis, 1991).

From the PbN gustatory neurons project rostrally in the central tegmental bundle and terminate bilaterally in the parvicellular region of the ventromedial thalamus (VPMpc; Bester, Bourgeais, Villanueva, Besson, & Bernard, 1999; Karimnamazi & Travers, 1998; Krout & Loewy, 2000; Norgren, 1974). In addition, ascending fibers from the PbN project also to the GN (Saper, 1982), the LH (Bester, Besson, & Bernard, 1997), the CNA (Bernard, Alden, & Besson, 1993; Karimnamazi & Travers, 1998), the substantia innominata (Karimnamazi & Travers, 1998), and the bed nucleus of the stria terminalis (Alden, Besson, & Bernard, 1994). From the VPMpc there is a reciprocal connection with the GN (Norgren & Grill, 1976; Wolf, 1968). The GN in the rodent is located in the agranular and dysgranular insular cortex, on either side of the middle cerebral artery, just above the rhinal fissure. (See also the later discussion of the location of the GN in primates.)

Centrifugal Influence in Relation to Gustation

Like all sensory systems, the gustatory system is characterized by a rich centrifugal influence. In addition to projections to the VPMpc (Norgren & Grill, 1976; Shi & Cassell, 1998; Wolf, 1968), the GN projects to the CNA (Norgren & Grill, 1976; Shi & Cassell, 1998) and to the PbN (Lasiter, Glanzman, & Mensah, 1982; Norgren & Grill, 1976; Wolf, 1968). The LH (Bereiter, Berthoud, & Jeanrenaud, 1980; Hosoya & Matsushita, 1981) also sends direct input to the PbN. Direct projections from the LH (Bereiter et al., 1980; Hosoya & Matsushita, 1981; Whitehead, Bergula, & Holliday, 2000), the CNA (Whitehead et al., 2000), and the GN (Norgren & Grill, 1976; Whitehead et al., 2000) to the NTS have been described. Additionally, projections from the contralateral NTS have recently been discovered in the hamster (Whitehead et al., 2000).

Although centrifugal input to gustatory neural structures has been described anatomically, little is known of the physiological mechanisms involved or of their functional significance. A few studies, however, have been reported. For example, Yamamoto, Matsuo, and Kawamura (1980) investigated the effects of electrical stimulation of the GN on the VPMpc. They found two types of changes in excitability of thalamic cells: inhibitory (for about 60 ms) and inhibitory (for about 10 ms)-facilitory (for about 60 ms). The researchers suggested that their results could be partially explained by a corticofugal feedback loop. In an earlier study, Ganchrow and Erickson (1972) recorded synaptic activation from the GN of some cells in the VPMpc, which might involve thalamic interneurons.

Corticofugal input to the CNA has also been investigated. Although anatomical evidence suggests a direct input from the GN to the CNA (Norgren & Grill, 1976; Shi & Cassell, 1998), Yamamoto, Azuma, and Kawamura (1984) found evidence only for a mutual polysynaptic relationship between these structures. They reported that 13 out of 18 CNA units showed facilitation or inhibition to electrical shocks in the GN. These effects occurred with a mean latency of 16 ms. Behavioral data suggested that interruption of the cortico-amygdaloid projection impairs conditioned taste-aversion retention. A polysynaptic influence of the GN on the LH has also been reported (Kita & Oomura, 1981), which showed two types of responses in the LH following GN stimulation: initial excitation followed by inhibition and inhibition alone.

The GN is also known to affect the processing of taste stimuli in the brain stem. When taste responses were recorded in the NTS before and after infusions of procaine (a local, short-acting anesthetic) into the GN on both sides of the brain, 22 of 30 units (73%) were affected by infusions on at least one side of the brain (Di Lorenzo & Monroe, 1995). Both infusions had the effect of decreasing the number of taste stimuli to which a unit responded. It is interesting that the most profound effects of the elimination of GN input were seen in taste responses in those units that did not evidence projections to the PbN (as determined by the lack of an antidromically driven response to electrical stimulation of the PbN). It is therefore likely that the influence of the GN in the NTS is on interneurons, many of which may be inhibitory.

More recently, Smith and Li (2000) recorded from taste-responsive cells in the NTS following stimulation of the ipsilateral GN. They found that spontaneous activity was both enhanced and attenuated by cortical input in 34% of 50 cells in the NTS. Infusion of bicuculline, a $GABA_A$ antagonist, into the NTS blocked only the inhibition. This inhibitory influence was found to be most often associated with NaCl best cells. These results confirm previous reports (Smith & Li, 1998) showing that GN input is selective in that it affects neither all taste-responsive NTS cells nor the responses to all

taste stimuli within a cell (Di Lorenzo, 1990; Di Lorenzo & Monroe, 1995).

In a similar experiment 40 of 42 (95%) of the taste-responsive units in the PbN were affected by procaine infusions into the ipsilateral GN (Di Lorenzo, 1990). As in the NTS, taste responses could be either enhanced or attenuated, and the effects were stimulus selective within the response profile of a given cell. Only about one third of the taste-responsive units in the PbN could be directly activated by electrical stimulation of the GN (Di Lorenzo & Monroe, 1992). These results imply that much of the corticofugal influence of the GN on the PbN is relayed through the NTS.

Physiology of Taste

Studies of the physiology of the taste system show that participants are multisensitive at all levels of processing from receptor cell to cortex. That is, they respond to more than one of the representatives of the four basic taste qualities. However, within each structure the breadth of tuning across taste qualities can vary widely among the responsive elements, as well as the preponderance of sensitivity to one taste quality or another. For example, the majority of fibers in the CT of the rat generally respond well to NaCl and to acid (Frank, 1973, 1974; Frank, Bieber, & Smith, 1988; Frank, Contreras, & Hettinger, 1983) and less well to sucrose and quinine. The GP nerve also responds well to salt and acid but is more sensitive to quinine than are the other nerves (Frank, 1991; Hanamori, Miller, & Smith, 1988). In the monkey there is a similar division of sensitivity between the CT and GP nerves (Hellekant, Danilova, & Ninomiya, 1997). The greater superficial petrosal nerve, on the other hand, is relatively more sensitive to sucrose and NaCl (S. P. Travers & Norgren, 1991; S. P. Travers, Pfaffmann, & Norgren, 1986). Collectively, it appears that although the peripheral nerves that convey taste information are multisensitive, some specialization in their sensitivity among taste qualities is apparent. These specializations are reflected in the effects of selective nerve cuts on the perceptual capabilities of animals.

For example, behavioral assessments of taste perception have suggested that damage to the facial nerve (VII), composed of the greater superficial ptrosal (GSP) and CT branches, or to the GP nerve has distinctly different effects. In both hamsters (Barry, Larson, & Frank, 1996) and rats (Spector & Grill, 1992), transection of the CT nerve disrupts the discrimination of NaCl versus KCl. Recovery of this task depends on the regeneration of the CT (St. John, Markison, & Spector, 1995). Damage to the GP nerve had no effect on discrimination between NaCl and KCl (Spector & Grill, 1992). Transection of the CT nerve in hamsters (Barry,

Larson, & Frank, 1993) has been shown to disrupt conditioned taste aversions to NaCl but not KCl. The opposite finding has been reported in rats (St. John, Markison, & Spector, 1997). However, sensitivity to low concentrations of NaCl, but not sucrose, was disrupted (O'Keefe, Schumm, & Smith, 1994), and the threshold for detection of NaCl, but not sucrose, was elevated in rats with CT damage (Spector, Schwartz, & Grill, 1990). NaCl appetite was also impaired after CT, but not GP, transection (Markison, St. John, & Spector, 1995). Whereas these studies point to a role of the CT nerve in the perception of salt, other work suggests that a combined CT and GSP transection is required to disrupt the sensitivity to sweet tastes (Spector, Markison, St. John, & Garcea, 1997; Spector, Redman, & Garcea, 1996; Spector, Travers, & Norgren, 1993). Likewise, combined CT and GP transection is most effective in disrupting the perception of quinine (St. John & Spector, 1996; St. John, Garcea, & Spector, 1994).

There is some evidence that GP nerve damage alone has disruptive effects on the processing of quinine. For example, Markison, St. John, and Spector (1999) showed that rats without any preexposure to quinine drank more of high-concentration quinine solutions after GP transection than did sham-operated controls. Furthermore, recent work in rats has shown that GP damage eliminates the expression of *fos* produced by quinine in the NTS (King, Travers, Rowland, Garcea, & Spector, 1999) and that this returns after GP regeneration (King, Garcea, & Spector, 2000).

Several reports in the literature point to the idea that input from the CT can affect the responses produced by GP stimulation, and vice versa, at their central projection sites in the brain stem. Perhaps the first hint of such an interaction was published by Halpern and Nelson (1965), who reported that anesthetization of the CT in rats enhanced taste responses in the NTS produced by stimulation of the posterior tongue. They interpreted their results as indicating a general inhibitory influence of the CT input on the input from the GP. This interpretation has been buttressed by psychophysical studies using anesthesia of the CT in humans (Kroeze & Bartoshuk 1985; Lehman, Bartoshuk, Catalanotto, Kveton, & Lowlocht, 1995). The appearance of *taste phantoms* following such a procedure has prompted these authors to suggest also that the input from the CT inhibits the input from the GP. Since the early work of Halpern and Nelson (1965), several other physiological studies in rodents have reported results here and there that have been consistent with the idea that such an interaction occurs (e.g., Sweazy & Smith, 1987).

However, in a study designed to test the idea of CT inhibition of GP input directly, Dinkins and Travers (1998) failed to replicate Halpern and Nelson's (1965) earlier findings.

Dinkins and Travers recorded the multiunit and single-unit responses to a cocktail of taste stimuli before and after anesthetization of the CT. Receptive fields within the oropharyngeal area innervated by different taste nerves were tested individually. Results showed that CT anesthesia produced pervasive attenuation, rather than enhancement, of taste responses in NTS cells that received input from the CT and the GP. These data suggest that, rather than input from the CT inhibiting input from the GP, these inputs may instead be additive.

Grabauskas and Bradley (1996) showed that electrical stimulation of the solitary tract at levels where either the CT or GP input terminate produced both excitatory postsynaptic potentials (EPSPs) or inhibitory postsynaptic potentials (IPSPs) in NTS cells in vitro. Their evidence suggests that both excitatory and inhibitory input from both the CT and GP are combined in complex ways.

In the brain stem, taste responses reflect convergence of input from the various peripheral taste fields. Neurons in the NTS, for example, are more broadly tuned than are those of peripheral nerve fibers that drive them (see J. B. Travers, Travers, & Norgren, 1987, for a review). In addition, the overall magnitude of response is magnified in the NTS compared with peripheral nerve responses (Ganchrow & Erickson, 1970). In the rat only about one third of the taste-responsive NTS neurons project directly to the PbN (Monroe & Di Lorenzo, 1995; Ogawa et al., 1984; Ogawa et al., 1982). PbN cells with a given response profile (e.g., NaCl best or HCl best) receive direct input from cells in the NTS with a variety of response profiles, both those with the same and those with different best stimuli (Di Lorenzo & Monroe, 1997). This suggests that there is a convergence of cell types at the level of the PbN. Taste responses in the PbN are again amplified with respect to the NTS (Di Lorenzo & Monroe, 1997), but this amplification is already apparent in the enhanced responses of NTS-PbN relay neurons. This implies that taste responses are enhanced before they are relayed to the PbN.

Similarly, taste responses in PbN-thalamic relay neurons (about 60% of all PbN taste-responsive cells) were larger than were nonrelay neurons (Ogawa, Hayama, & Ito, 1987). PbN-thalamic relay neurons respond to taste stimuli at about a threefold amplification compared with NTS-PbN neurons.

At the level of the thalamus, taste-responsive cells retain their broad sensitivity across taste qualities. In the rat, taste-evoked response magnitude is attenuated with respect to the PbN (Nomura & Ogawa, 1985; Scott & Erickson, 1971). This deamplification results in more similar response magnitudes for all taste stimuli as well as broader tuning compared with cells in the PbN (Scott & Erickson, 1971). In the monkey, electrophysiological data suggest that taste stimuli are processed similarly in the thalamus and brain stem (Pritchard, Hamilton, & Norgren, 1989). In both rat (Scott & Erickson, 1971) and monkey (Pritchard et al., 1989) there appears to be a more prominent response to sucrose in the thalamus compared with lower centers; however, the relatively small sensitivity of the brain stem to sucrose may be a by-product of anesthetics. Recordings from the NTS (Nakamura & Norgren, 1991, 1993) and PbN (Nishijo & Norgren, 1997) from awake, unanesthetized rats show a significantly larger proportion of sucrose best cells and an overall larger response magnitude associated with sucrose compared with recordings from anesthetized rats. Approximately 56% of the taste-responsive neurons in the thalamus project to the GN (Ogawa & Nomura, 1988). Thalamocortical relay neurons do not differ from nonrelay neurons in their response properties (Ogawa & Nomura, 1988).

Reponses of GN neurons in rats show a trend toward equalization of effectiveness among the four basic taste qualities. As a result, cells in the GN are more broadly tuned than taste-responsive cells at lower levels (reviewed in Ogawa, 1994). Two areas within the GN have been identified: the granular insula, where fine gustatory discrimination is thought to occur, and the dysgranular insula, where integration of taste information occurs (Ogawa, Hasegawa, & Murayama, 1992). Cells in the dysgranular insula have larger receptive fields in the oral cavity than do those in the granular insula, although no evidence of orotopic mapping was found in either area of cortex (Ogawa, Murayama, & Hasegawa, 1992). Attempts to discover a columnar organization within the GN have revealed that adjacent neurons can show overlapping sensitivities (Kosar & Schwartz, 1990). Cross-correlational analyses of simultaneously recorded pairs of cortical neurons have, however, provided some evidence for the existence of functional columns measuring about 50 µm in diameter (T. Nakamura & Ogawa, 1997).

In the macaque monkey two cortical areas have been identified that process information about taste. In the primary GN (rostrodorsal insula and frontal opercular cortex) only a small percentage of cells (6%) respond to gustatory stimuli, and their response profiles are more narrowly tuned than those in lower structures (Scott & Plata-Salaman, 1999; Yaxley, Rolls, & Sienkiewicz, 1990). Cells in the secondary GN (caudolateral orbitofrontal cortex) are the first in the gustatory pathway to reflect motivational variables associated with food (Rolls, Yaxley, & Sienkiewicz, 1990).

The investigation of taste processing in the human cortex is ongoing (see Small et al., 1999, for a review). In general, a primary GN has been located in the insula and the parietal and opercular region of the neocortex using magnetic imaging (Faurion et al., 1999; Faurion, Cerf, Le Bihan, & Pillias, 1998;

Kobayakawa et al., 1999; Small et al. 1999) and positron-emission tomography (PET) scans (Frey & Petrides, 1999; Kinomura et al., 1994). An area that may correspond to the secondary GN described in monkey cortex has been localized to the caudolateral orbitofrontal cortex in the right hemisphere (Small et al., 1999). There seems to be some lateralization associated with the cortical representation of gustation in the human (Faurion et al. 1999; Pritchard, Macaluso, & Eslinger, 1999).

Theories of Taste Coding

In the study of the gustatory system two main theories of neural coding have dominated the literature. Both of these theories were originally based on observations of the taste sensitivity of single fibers in the CT nerve of the rodent. Both are based on the observation that nearly all fibers are multisensitive. That is, they respond to tastants representing more than one taste quality when stimuli are presented at midrange concentrations. (The relative response rates evoked by the spectrum of taste stimuli representing the various taste qualities define a unit's response profile.) Because other studies have shown that neural elements at all levels of the taste pathway—from the TRCs to the cortex—are generally multisensitive, these two theories have also been used to account for taste coding in all parts of the system (see Scott & Giza, 2000, for a recent review).

One theory, called the *labeled line (LL) theory*, emphasizes the commonalities among response profiles. That is, given a fixed array of taste stimuli, cells that respond most vigorously to a particular stimulus will tend to respond similarly to the other tastants in the array. Cells may then be grouped according to their best stimuli. For example, knowing that a taste cell responds to sucrose as its best stimulus will predict that its second best stimulus will be NaCl. In effect, the implication of these observations is that groups of units that share the same best stimulus represent unit "types" that are functionally homogeneous in that they serve the same role in the coding process. Original conceptualizations identified four groups or neuron types, each labeled by one of the four tastants that are prototypical of the four basic taste qualities (e.g., NaCl for salty, sucrose for sweet, HCl for sour, and quinine for bitter). In its extreme incarnation each neuron type was posited to be exclusively responsible for encoding the taste quality represented by its best stimulus.

More recent investigations have divided fiber types in the CT (see Frank, 2000; M. Sato, Ogawa, & Yamashita, 1994) and cell types in the geniculate ganglion (Lundy & Contreras, 1999) into *specialists* and *generalists*. Specialists, as one might imagine, respond nearly exclusively to a single class of taste stimuli representing a single basic taste quality. Generalists respond well to several tastants but are named for their best stimuli. In the rat and hamster CT there are sucrose and NaCl specialists and HCl and quinine generalists (see Frank, 2000, for a review). Contreras and Lundy (2000) have recently identified a class of NaCl generalists in the rat geniculate ganglion.

In aid of the LL theory many studies have aimed at identifying functional characteristics, other than the response properties under normal conditions, that would correlate with a neuron's best stimulus and thus contribute to the definition of these types as distinct. Some manipulations, such as salt deprivation (Contreras, 1977; Contreras & Frank, 1979; Jacobs, Mark, & Scott, 1988; McCaughey, Giza, & Scott, 1996; Shimura, Komori, & Yamamoto, 1997; Tamura & Norgren, 1997) and conditioned taste aversion (Chang & Scott, 1984; McCaughey, Giza, Nolan, & Scott, 1997), have effects on only one best-stimulus neuron type, whereas others, such as hormonal manipulations (Di Lorenzo & Monroe, 1989, 1990) and adaptation (Di Lorenzo & Lemon, 2000), have more widespread effects across these putative neuron types. At present there seems to be ample evidence that not all units behave in the same way under all experimental conditions. That implies that there are *types* of units, defined functionally. Although most investigators still use the best-stimulus nomenclature to define these types, other, less theoretically laden labels may be more appropriate.

The second major theory of taste coding, the *across-fiber* (or -neuron) *pattern (AFP) theory* emphasizes the differences or varieties among response profiles. Proponents of this theory suggest that the perception of a given tastant is captured by the pattern of firing across the population of fibers or neurons. To compare AFPs generated by two taste stimuli, most investigators have used the Pearson correlation coefficient. Support for the AFP theory has been derived from the observation that correlation coefficients of AFPs generated by similar-tasting stimuli tend to be larger than those generated by dissimilar tastants (e.g., Doetsch & Erickson, 1970; Ganchrow & Erickson, 1970; Woolston & Erickson, 1979). The observation that tastants evoking similar AFPs also evoke similar behavioral reactivity (Scott, 1974; Yamamoto & Yuyama, 1987; Yamamoto, Yuyama, Kato, & Kawamura, 1985) has lent further support to this theory.

In its purest form the AFP theory assumes that all neural elements within a taste-related nerve or neural structure contribute equivalently to the neural code for a taste stimulus. That includes both fibers and neurons that respond and those that do not. In a slight variation of this idea, Erickson and Gill (Erickson, 1986; Gill & Erickson, 1985) proposed that the discrimination between two taste stimuli is encoded by the difference in the amount of neural activity produced by both tastants across neurons. They called this quantity the *neural mass dif-* *ference.* It is calculated as the difference between the responses evoked by two taste stimuli for each unit in a sample, averaged across units. In the description of the rationale behind this metric, the authors proposed that the absolute amount, rather than the relative amount, of neural activity produced by a taste stimulus is an important feature of the neural code.

Despite several decades of research, there is still debate over whether the LL or AFP theories are closer to the truth. Recent studies have produced interpretations that incorporate some aspects of both theories. One of these lines of research has involved the use of amiloride, a Na^+ channel blocker. Because it is believed that NaCl is transduced through these amiloride-sensitive Na^+ channels (as discussed earlier), it has been argued that recording the electrophysiological responses to NaCl before and after blocking these channels can provide insight into how NaCl is encoded. Whereas some reports concluded that only NaCl responses in NaCl best neurons in the NTS were affected by amiloride (Giza & Scott, 1991; Scott & Giza, 1990), more recent studies in the hamster concluded that NaCl responses in both NaCl best and sucrose best NTS neurons were modified by amiloride (Boughter & Smith, 1998; Smith, Liu, & Vogt, 1996). The upshot of these studies is that the neural code for NaCl is represented by the neural activity that is distributed across both types of neurons (Smith, St. John, & Boughter, 2000). The idea of neuron types is retained, but it is the pattern of activity across these types that conveys the information.

A third aspect of the neural code for taste is based on the observation that different taste stimuli appear to produce different temporal patterns of response. The first strategy for the investigation of temporal patterns has been to find ways to quantify the time-dependent aspects of the response (Bradley, Stedman, & Mistretta, 1983; Nagai & Ueda, 1981; Ogawa, Sato, & Yamashita, 1973; Ogawa, Yamashita, & Sato, 1974). In most cases this process combines some sort of standardization with various methods of comparison of sequences of increases and decreases in firing rate across the time course of the response. The results of these studies, although suggestive, have not definitively determined that information contained in the temporal pattern of response can be used unambiguously to identify a taste stimulus (Di Lorenzo & Schwartzbaum, 1982; Nagai & Ueda, 1981). As an alternative, some accounts suggest that the temporal pattern may signal the hedonic properties of taste stimuli (Di Lorenzo & Schwartzbaum, 1982). That is, those tastants that are rejected (expelled from the mouth) by an organism may produce a different temporal pattern of response than do those that are accepted (ingested).

Two experiments thus far have produced evidence that the temporal pattern of a taste response may have some function in determining the type of behavioral reactivity to a taste stimulus. The first is the work in which Covey (1980) first recorded the electrophysiological responses to a variety of tastants in the NTS. She then used the temporal patterns of response evoked by each tastant to produce electrical pulse trains that followed these temporal patterns. These unique pulse trains were then delivered to the CT of an awake decerebrate rat. Results showed that these rats displayed orofacial reactions that were appropriate to the taste stimuli whose temporal patterns of response were used to drive the electrical pulse trains.

The second example of a study of the functional significance of temporal patterns of response (Di Lorenzo & Hecht, 1993) involved the presentation of lick-contingent electrical pulse trains to the NTS through chronically implanted microelectrodes in awake, intact rats. In that experiment the electrophysiological response to sucrose recorded from the NTS of an anesthetized animal was used as a template for the temporal arrangement of electrical pulses in a 1-s train of electrical stimulation. Animals learned to avoid lick-contingent electrical stimulation when it was paired with injections of LiCl in a conditioned aversion paradigm. When the temporal pattern of electrical stimulation was switched from one that mimicked a sucrose response to one that mimicked a quinine response, the animals avoided the lick-contingent stimulation without any prior training. Collectively, these studies imply that the temporal pattern of response may provide some information that may be used as a guide for behavioral reactivity. Whether the temporal pattern of response is used also to identify more precisely a taste stimulus remains an open question.

Conclusions

To conclude this survey of the study of the gustatory system, it is perhaps fitting to highlight the frontiers of the field because they will undoubtedly be the subject of future reviews. First is the study of the biology of the TRC, aided in recent times by stunning advances in molecular biology. These advances have opened the door to studies on the transduction mechanisms associated with taste and have, for the first time, enabled the study of the genetics of chemoreception. Future research will define the structure and physiology of taste receptor molecules, the interrelationship of the various transduction pathways within the receptor cells and the neurotransmitters that are released. Second, the study of the regeneration of TRCs and their innervation is already a very active and exciting field of study, and it promises to become even more so in the future. Again, molecular biology has finally provided the tools for examining how old receptor cells die and how new ones are born,

mature, and are innervated to replace the old ones. Finally, there is the study of the relationship of psychophysics to health and disease. In this regard, psychophysicists have already begun to link the genetic variability in chemical receptivity to a variety of behavioral and physical conditions and abnormalities (see Bartoshuk, 2000b; Reed et al., 1999). The further study of what our individual receptive profiles can tell us about our susceptibility to disease and the normal functioning of the body will certainly yield some exciting developments.

OLFACTION

Overview

The Role of the Olfactory System

Of the senses we possess, the olfactory system is, in evolutionary terms, an ancient sensory system capable of detecting and discriminating among thousands of different odorants. It is well established that olfaction is critical to the survival of many lower animals ranging from insects to mammals. Proper olfactory function is basic to the maintenance of life in a variety of ways, namely, the regulation of reproductive physiology, food intake, and social behaviors (Brown, 1979; Doty, 1986; Hudsen & Distel, 1983). It is essential for finding food, and it is the first line of defense from becoming food. Even the basic foundation of animal communication is chemical, relying on odors produced by body glands, feces, and urine (Mech & Peters, 1977; Muller-Schwartz, 1977; Yahr, 1977). For example, the male gypsy moth uses olfactory cues to find his mate many miles away (D. Schneider, 1969), as does the adult salmon to return to its spawning ground (Harden-Jones, 1968). Several species as diverse as cats, dogs, and deer mark their territory with urine or other secretions (Mech & Peters, 1977; Muller-Schwartz, 1977; Yahr, 1977). These chemical signatures provide the animal sampling the scent mark with information regarding whether it came from a conspecific, whether the depositor was male or female, and even the social and reproductive status of the animal.

Studies in a number of different species have also shown a well-documented dependency of reproductive and sexual behavior on olfactory cues. Odors are involved at almost all stages of mammalian reproduction, from initial attraction of the sexes to induction of estrus, maintenance or termination of pregnancy, and maternal-neonate imprinting. For example, introducing the odor of a male mouse or his urine can induce and even accelerate the estrus cycle of a female (Whitten, 1956). In addition, appropriate odor cues from a female are important in attracting the male's interest during estrus and promoting copulation. Male hamsters will display mating behavior, even with anesthetized males, when presented with vaginal discharge from receptive females (Darby, Devor, & Chorover, 1975).

The importance of this type of chemical communication cannot be overstated. In some animals a reduction or loss of olfaction can result in sexual dysfunction and even altered sexual development (Brown, 1979; Doty, 1986; Hudsen & Distel, 1983). Although not as extensively documented as in lower animals, a relationship between olfaction and sex has been demonstrated in humans. Olfactory acuity in women appears better at ovulation than during menstruation (Henkin, 1974; Schneider & Wolf, 1955), and there is emerging strong evidence that olfactory cues (i.e., human pheromones) among women can synchronize the menstrual cycle (McClintock, 1983; Stern & McClintock, 1998). Similarly, odors in humans may play a role in attracting the opposite sex (Gangestad & Thornhill, 1998).

In humans the sense of smell is generally considered less critical to survival, even though there are times when the detection of odors associated with a potential danger such as smoke, gas, or decaying food can prevent bodily injury. In contrast to the lower animals, the potential importance of this sense should be given consideration because of the tremendous impact it has on our quality of life. In other words, modern society seems to emphasize the hedonic effect of olfaction. As examples of the positive hedonic effect, people add a variety of spices to their foods, often creating dishes with complex aromas and flavors (as discussed later), perfume their bodies, and add pleasing odors to a variety of things such as their cars, homes, and even shopping malls. In contrast, the importance of the negative effect is illustrated by the vast number of commercial products available today that are directed toward eliminating offensive odors. These preferences, of course, depend on a number of variables such as age, sex, socioethnic background, and prior odor experience (Wysocki, Pierce, & Gilbert, 1991).

One instance in which olfaction has been shown to play a major role is in *flavor* perception (i.e., the integration of taste and smell) and the recognition of *tastes* (Mozell, Smith, Smith, Sullivan, & Swender, 1969). In fact, people are actually *smelling* much of what they think they are tasting. That is, individuals often confuse the concept of taste perception (i.e., the identification of salty, sour, bitter, and sweet) with flavor perception. In the Mozell et al. study (1969) subjects were asked to identify 21 common food substances placed on the tongue. The results were rather intriguing in that there was a decrease from an average of 60% correct to 10% correct when, experimentally, no odor vapors given off by the test stimuli were allowed to reach the nasal cavity (i.e., there was no access in either the ortho- or retronasal direction).

Even coffee and chocolate, which were correctly identified by greater than 90% of the test subjects when odorant molecules had access to the nasal cavity, were not identified correctly when the nose was made inaccessible. Thus, at least for humans, olfaction appears to have a tremendous impact on the quality of life, and anything that interferes with proper functioning can be very distressing. Consider what happens to simple food appreciation when people have colds or nasal allergies.

Basic Anatomy

The olfactory organ of vertebrates is a complex structure designed to collect odorant molecules and direct them to the sensory neurons. Although the chemoreceptive endings and neural projections of the olfactory nerve carry the primary information of the sense of smell, other cranial nerves are involved, namely, the trigeminal, GP, and vagus. These cranial nerves, which innervate different regions of the respiratory tract (i.e., nose, pharynx, and larynx) give rise to the pungent or irritating quality often experienced as part of an odor sensation (Cain, 1976, 1990). In addition, they also mediate a variety of reflexes in response to chemical stimulation (James & Daley, 1969). These reflexes serve to minimize the effects of noxious stimuli and protect the animal from continued exposure.

The primary olfactory receptive area is the region of the nasal cavity subserved by the olfactory nerve (cranial nerve I). In humans the olfactory receptors lie deep within the nasal cavity and are confined to a patch of specialized epithelium, the olfactory epithelium, covering roughly 5 cm^2 of the dorsal posterior recess of the nasal cavity (Moran, Rowley, & Jafek, 1982). In other lower mammals, such as rats and mice, the olfactory epithelium extends throughout the rostrocaudal extent of the nasal cavity occupying the superior and lateral portions of all nasal turbinates (Pedersen, Jastreboff, Stewart, & Shepherd, 1986; W. B. Stewart & Pedersen, 1987).

Figure 10.3 illustrates that the olfactory epithelium proper is a pseudostratified structure comprised of three principal cell types: (a) receptor cells, (b) supporting cells, and (c) basal cells. The olfactory receptor is a bipolar neuron that has a short peripheral process and a long central process. The short peripheral process or dendrite extends to the surface of the epithelium (which is in contact with the air space of the nasal cavity), where it ends in an expanded olfactory knob. This knob, in turn, gives rise to several cilia that, along with the cilia from other receptor cells, form a dense mat at the epithelial surface (Moran et al., 1982; Morrison & Costanzo, 1990). Odor transduction is initiated in these cilia as a result of the interaction of odorant molecules with specialized receptor proteins within the ciliary membrane

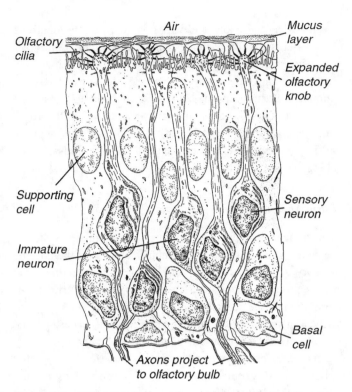

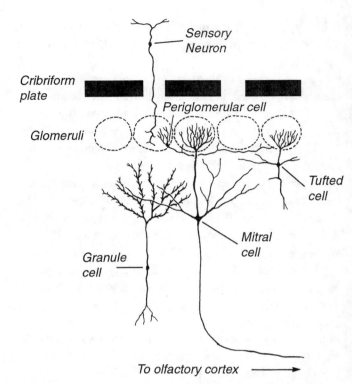

Figure 10.3 Schematic of the vertebrate olfactory epithelium illustrating that mature sensory neurons are imbedded among supporting cells, basal cells, and immature developing neurons. The cilia of the mature neurons form a dense mat at the epithelial surface, which is bathed in mucus. To reach the specialized receptor proteins in the ciliary membrane, odorant molecules must move from the air phase above the cilia into the liquid phase of the mucus. Adapted from Andres (1966).

Figure 10.4 The vertebrate olfactory bulb is a laminated structure containing both secondary projection neurons and a highly ordered microcircuitry. The axons of the sensory neurons contact the primary dendrites of mitral and tufted cells (the output neurons of the bulb), as well as periglomerular cells, in a specialized neuropil structure called the glomerulus. Periglomerular cells and granule cells are inhibitory interneurons that participate in the sharpening of information at the level of the output neurons. Adapted from Shepherd (1972).

(Buck & Axel, 1991). The longer central process of the olfactory receptor is an unmyelinated axon that projects through the cribriform plate to synapse in the olfactory bulb. In contrast to the receptor cells, supporting cells do not have an axon, nor are they believed to mediate any sensory information. The supporting cells, as their name implies, surround the receptor cells in a columnar fashion. In addition to their role as supporting elements, they also have secretory properties (M. L. Getchell, Zelinski, & Getchell, 1988). Basal cells or stem cells, on the other hand, are found either singly or in clusters next to the basal lamina of the epithelium. Basal cells are mitotically active and give rise to new neurons and supporting cells throughout life and at a markedly increased rate after injury (Huard, Youngentob, Goldstein, Luskin, & Schwob, 1998; Schwob, Youngentob, & Mezza, 1995). This process for self-renewal is quite remarkable because the developing receptor cell must send its newly formed dendrite toward the surface of the epithelium and its axon in the opposite direction to synapse appropriately in the olfactory bulb.

The first relay station in the olfactory pathway is the olfactory bulb, a distinctly laminated structure that receives direct axonal projections from the peripheral sensory neurons (Figure 10.4; Shepherd, 1972). The unmyelinated axons of the olfactory nerve synapse on secondary projection neurons (i.e., mitral and tufted cells) within the bulb. In addition to the massive input from the periphery, the olfactory bulb contains a highly ordered synaptic microcircuitry. Following interaction with local circuits within the olfactory bulb (Shepherd & Greer, 1990), the mitral and tufted cell axons project to higher cortical regions including the piriform cortex, olfactory tubercle, anterior olfactory nucleus, amygdala, and entorhinal cortex (Price, 1987).

Analytical Problem

The olfactory system is a molecular detector of great sensitivity. It has the capacity to discriminate among literally millions of different odorants and can often detect them at concentrations well below the levels of physical instrumentation. It has not been an easy task to understand the mechanisms by which the olfactory system encodes odorant quality information due to the absence of a clear physical energy continuum to describe and control odorant stimuli. In contrast to other sensory systems such as vision and audition, there is no metric analogous to wavelength for color or frequency for pitch. Moreover, unlike mixtures of light or sound, odorant mixtures do not result in predictable perceptions. The situation is further confounded by the knowledge that essentially identical chemical substances can have different quality perceptions. For example, the enantiomers d-carvone and l-carvone have very different odors (Pike, Enns, & Hornung, 1988). D-carvone smells like caraway, whereas l-carvone smells like spearmint. Enantiomers are stereoisomers; that is, their formulas are the same, but the two molecules are mirror images. Precisely why these odorants smell perceptually different still remains unanswered. In contrast, some substances with very different chemical formulas, such as carborane, trisallylrhodium, and cyclopentadienyl-tricarbon monoxide-manganese, all have perceptually the same odor (i.e., camphor; Beets, 1971). How does the olfactory system handle the transduction and encoding of odorant information?

Processing of Odorant Stimuli

Signal Recognition and Transduction

In terrestrial animals, in order for airborne odorant molecules to gain access to the olfactory receptors, these molecules must first traverse the mucus layer covering the olfactory epithelium. The time it takes for odorant molecules to enter and exit the epithelium, as well as the dwell time within the receptor environment, is considered to be an important part of the initial reception process (T. V. Getchell, Margolis, & Getchell, 1984). The discovery of abundant small, water-soluble proteins in the mucus of the vertebrate nasal cavity led to the hypothesis that odorant-binding proteins (OBPs) may accommodate and enhance the access of odorant molecules to the receptors (Pevsner & Snyder, 1990). To date, however, no direct physiological demonstration of function has been reported for vertebrate OBPs. Nonetheless, given the time frame in which olfactory events occur, translocation of odorants from the mucus surface to the receptors must be achieved either by some kind of carrier-bound delivery system or by facilitated diffusion.

The mechanism by which thousands of different odorants that vary widely in structure are readily detected and identified has long been a key problem in understanding the encoding of odorants. However, it is now well established that odorant receptors are G-protein coupled receptors, encoded by a large olfactory-specific multigene family numbering between 500 and 1,000 genes (Buck & Axel, 1991). In addition to being large in number, molecular sequence comparison among members of the receptor gene family has indicated that they are highly divergent. Therefore, it appears that the extremely large size and diversity of this gene family provide the necessary breadth to interact with an immense number of different odorants. Unfortunately, although vigorously characterized, most of these odorant receptors have remained, for the most part, functionally anonymous. That is, there has been a paucity of information regarding the relationship between individual odorant receptors and that portion of the odorant universe to which they respond. One recent study, however, established a relationship between one rat odorant receptor, I7, and the transduction of a restricted odorant set (Zhao et al., 1998). This particular odorant receptor appears to be sensitive to a small subset of aldehydes with chain lengths between 7 and 10 carbons. Aldehydes with both longer and shorter chain lengths failed to elicit responses. Thus, odorant receptors may be highly selective for particular molecular features of an odorant, including chain length.

The expression pattern of the large multigene family of receptors also likely plays an important role in the encoding process. In situ hybridization studies examining spatial expression patterns of olfactory receptors in the epithelium indicate that each olfactory receptor gene is expressed by a small subset of sensory neurons (Ressler, Sullivan, & Buck, 1993; Strotmann, Wanner, Helfrich, Beck, & Breer, 1994). On average, each olfactory receptor gene is expressed in approximately 0.1% to 0.2% of the total olfactory sensory neuronal population (or approximately 5,000–10,000 neurons). In addition, neurons expressing a given olfactory receptor are restricted to one of four expression zones within the epithelium (Figure 10.5). Each expression zone occupies a different anatomical domain within the nasal cavity, and each encompasses approximately 25% of the epithelial surface area. In general, within a zone each of the different odorant receptors is homogeneously distributed with each receptor neuron surrounded by other sensory neurons expressing a different receptor type, although exceptions to this rule have been observed (Kubick, Strotmann, Andreini, & Breer, 1997; Strotmann, Wanner, Krieger, Raming, & Breer, 1992). Thus, each receptor zone forms a mosaic of different subtypes of sensory neurons expressing different odorant receptor proteins.

Binding of odorant molecules to the odorant receptor protein sets into motion an intracellular signal cascade leading to the depolarization of olfactory sensory neurons. This depolarization, in turn, is converted into action potentials that are transmitted via olfactory axons to the olfactory bulb.

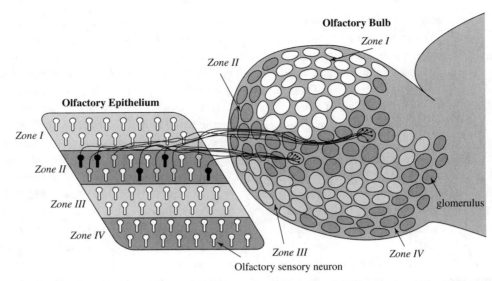

Figure 10.5 Schematic representation of olfactory information processing. Information coming from the receptors is broadly organized into four spatial expression zones within the epithelium. Within an expression zone neurons expressing the same odorant receptor gene (indicated by shading) are widely distributed. The zonal organization of incoming information is preserved in the olfactory bulb, and each expression zone projects to a corresponding zone in the bulb. Axons of sensory neurons expressing the same odorant receptor converge onto one or a few defined glomeruli. Adapted from Mori, Nagao, and Yoshihara (1999).

Figure 10.6 illustrates that two different intracellular messengers, cAMP and IP$_3$, have been implicated in the transduction process that follows odorant stimulation, with cAMP generating the response to some odorants (Breer, Boekoff, & Tareilus, 1990; Lowe, Nakamura, & Gold, 1989) and IP$_3$ mediating the response to others (Breer & Boekoff, 1991; Restrepo et al., 1992). At present, the duality of the second messenger system in mammals remains somewhat controversial (Firestein, Darrow, & Shepherd, 1991; Lowe & Gold, 1993; T. Nakamura, Lee, Kobayashi, & Sato, 1996), with recent evidence suggesting that the cyclic nucleotide-gated channel subserves excitatory olfactory signal transduction and that cAMP is the sole second messenger mediating the process (Brunet, Gold, & Ngai, 1996). Nonetheless, in either cascade, odorant ligand receptor interactions lead to the activation of G-protein coupled cascades with the former producing cAMP and the latter producing IP$_3$. In turn, these cascades open calcium channels on the plasma membrane, resulting in membrane depolarization and axon potential generation.

In vertebrates, olfactory receptor neurons differ in the number and profile of odorants to which they respond (Firestein, Picco, & Menini, 1993; T. V. Getchell & Shepherd, 1978; Revial, Sicard, Duchamp, & Holley, 1982, 1983). The earliest single-cell recordings showed that individual sensory neurons typically responded to a range of odorants that varied from cell to cell. For example, one such study of single neuron responses to 20 different stimuli demonstrated that individual neurons responded to as few as two of the odorants

(A)

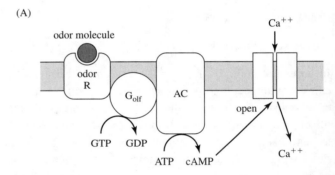

(B)

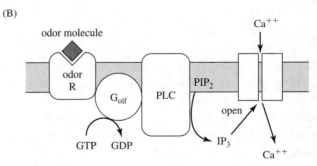

Figure 10.6 Dual transduction pathways have been implicated in the intracellular events that follow odorant stimulation. On binding of odorant ligands, the specialized receptor proteins in the ciliary membrane (odor R) act through G proteins (activation of G$_{olf}$ results in the dephosphorylation of guanosine triphosphate, or GTP) to stimulate either (A) an olfactory-specific adenylate cyclase (AC) generating cyclic adenosine monophosphate (cAMP) or (B) phospholipase C (PLC), which converts membrane-bound phosphotidyl inositol biphosphate (PIP$_2$) into the second messenger inositol triphosphate (IP$_3$). Both cAMP and IP$_3$ open different ion channels permitting calcium to enter the cell, thereby changing membrane potential. Adapted from Mori and Yoshihara (1995).

within the panel (Gesteland, Lettvin, Pitts, & Rojas, 1963). Furthermore, even though more than 50 neurons were sampled, each had a distinct odorant response profile. Thus, it would appear that olfactory neuronal responses define the range of odorants that can elicit a response in a given cell (termed its *molecular receptive range,* or MRR, and analogous to the spatial receptive field in the visual, auditory, or somatosensory systems; Mori, Imamura, & Mataga, 1992; Mori & Shepherd, 1994; Mori & Yoshihara, 1995).

Emerging evidence further suggests that a cell's MRR reflects interactions with particular ligand determinants. Studies of olfactory sensory neurons using homologous series of odorants have demonstrated regular patterns of neuronal responses to compounds with a similar organization of carbon atoms or functional groups (T. Sato, Hirano, Tonoike, & Takebayashi, 1994). The importance of ligand determinants to the encoding of odorant quality was further extended by the work of Malnic, Hirano, Sato, and Buck (1999) using calcium imaging and single-cell reverse transcription-polymerase chain reaction (RT-PCR). In keeping with prior electrophysiology (Firestein et al., 1993; T. V. Getchell & Shepherd, 1978; Revial et al., 1982, 1983), this study demonstrated, at a molecular level, that different odorants are recognized by different combinations of odorant receptors.

In short, the body of evidence suggests that the features of an odorant are dissected and encoded by the types of odorant receptors with which they interact and by the sensory neurons expressing those receptors. Accordingly, if receptor neurons are to be classified as to type on the basis of their response to the odorant universe, then the number of categories might very well approximate the number of different odorant receptors types encoded by the large multigene family (Buck & Axel, 1991).

Processing of Information in the Epithelium and Bulb

In other sensory systems (i.e., audition, vision, and somesthesis), receptor cells encode specificity about the sensory stimulus by virtue of their exact placement in the receptor sheet. In contrast, the receptor sheet in olfaction does not form a spatial map about the environment. Instead, as previously noted, the responsivity of olfactory neurons results from the affinity of their receptors for a particular odorant ligand. So, how is this molecular information mapped into the nervous system? Studies of the ensemble properties of the olfactory epithelium suggest that odorant quality information is encoded in large-scale spatial patterns of neural activity. That is, direct presentation of odorants to the exposed olfactory epithelium revealed intrinsic spatial and temporal differences in the sensitivity to different odorants across this neural tissue

(MacKay-Sim & Kesteven, 1994; MacKay-Sim & Kubie, 1981; Moulton, 1976; Mozell et al., 1987; Youngentob, Kent, Sheehe, Schwob, & Tzoumaka, 1995).

In exploring these differential patterns of sensitivity to different odorants, one approach has utilized optical recordings from rat olfactory epithelium stained with a voltage-sensitive dye (Kent, Mozell, Murphy, & Hornung, 1996; Kent, Youngentob, & Sheehe, 1995; Youngentob et al., 1995). The strategy in each of these studies was simultaneously to monitor 100 mucosal sites in an optical matrix and to record the fluorescence changes in response to different odorants. As illustrated in Figure 10.7, different odorants gave their maximal responses at different mucosal regions, even though they

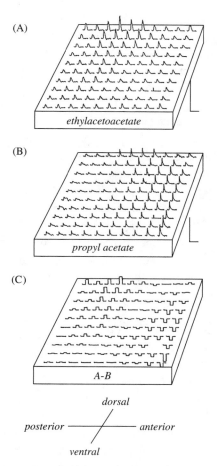

Figure 10.7 Using a 10 × 10 photodiode array matrix, fluorescence responses were recorded from a 6-mm by 6-mm area of the olfactory epithelium lining a rat's nasal septum in response to ethylacetoacetate (A) and propyl acetate (B). Array C is the pixel-by-pixel subtraction of response heights of A–B. As noted in the text, all regions of the septal epithelium responded to stimulation with either odorant. Nonetheless, as highlighted in array C, for each odorant there existed a distinct spatial distribution pattern of activity with each having a unique region of maximum sensitivity. The positive bars indicate the relative area of increased sensitivity for ethylacetoacetate, whereas the negative bars indicate this for propyl acetate. Adapted from Youngentob et al. (1995).

gave at least some response in all regions. These activity patterns, which reflect the differential odorant responsiveness of the receptor cell in different regions, were termed *inherent activity patterns* by Moulton (1976), who initially observed them on the olfactory epithelium of the salamander.

At a molecular level, the underlying mechanism by which these spatial patterns are established appears to be based on the differential responsiveness of different odorant receptor types to different odorants (Malnic et al., 1999) and on the observation that some odorant receptors have topographically distinct clustered patterns of expression, unlike the generally described broad expression zones (Dear, Boehm, Keverne, & Rabbitts, 1991; Kubick et al., 1997; Nef et al., 1992; Strotmann et al., 1992).

Even though the vertebrate olfactory system does not process information about odors by virtue of a single type of receptor neuron's placement in the receptor sheet, a degree of rhinotopy (analogous to retinotopy in the visual system) does exist in the organization of the central projection. The foundation for this rhinotopy lies in the topographical organization of bulbar glomeruli (neuropil structures comprised of olfactory receptor neuron axon terminals and the distal dendrites of mitral, tufted, and periglomerular cells) in relation to the expression of odorant receptor type in the epithelium. As illustrated in Figure 10.5, an entire subset of olfactory sensory neurons expressing a particular odorant receptor sends its axons to converge on one medially and one laterally positioned glomerulus in each olfactory bulb (Mombaerts et al., 1997; Vassar et al., 1994). With input ratios on the order of, for example, 25,000 receptors to 1 glomerulus in rabbits (Allison, 1952), mammalian glomeruli therefore represent a very large input convergence of information.

More important, this convergence of axons from neurons expressing the same odorant receptor type results in a precise spatial map of olfactory information within the glomerular layer of the bulb, with information gathered by thousands of neurons in the epithelium projecting to precise foci in each bulb. As a result, the odorant information contained in the large-scale differential activation of subsets of olfactory sensory neurons seen in the periphery can be encoded by producing differential spatial patterns of activity across the glomerular layer of the olfactory bulb. Indeed, several lines of evidence using physiologic (Cinelli & Kauer, 1994) and metabolic (Johnson & Leon, 2000; Johnson, Woo, & Leon, 2000) techniques indicate that glomeruli are functional units in odor processing and that each odorant produces a unique pattern of glomerular activation. This activity is further sharpened in the relay neurons of the bulb via complicated local circuits that act both locally and laterally on the signals impinging on the bulb (Mori & Shepherd, 1994; Mori & Takagi, 1978).

In the simplest terms, then, the extraction of odorant features begins with the differential binding affinities of the odorant receptors, which in turn are reflected in the differential activation of the epithelium by different odorants. This information is directly reflected spatially in the olfactory bulb through the existence of anatomically and functionally distinct glomeruli and their associated output neurons, the mitral and tufted cells, dedicated to receiving information from a single receptor type. Studies of the electrophysiological response properties of bulbar output neurons are consistent with this model, indicating that mitral cells are highly selective for particular odorant determinants and respond to similar odorants that have these determinants in common (Imamura, Mataga, & Mori, 1992; Katoh, Koshimoto, Tani, & Mori, 1993; Mori et al., 1992). More important, through the activation of lateral inhibitory mechanisms, the contrast between strongly activated and weakly activated glomeruli is enhanced, thereby sharpening the tuning specificity of individual mitral and tufted cell output neurons to odorant molecules (Buoniviso & Chaput, 1990; Kashiwadani, Sasaki, Uchida, & Mori, 1999; Yokoi, Mori, & Nakanishi, 1995). The second-order mitral and tufted cells may therefore be more sharply tuned to specific molecular features than the sensory neurons themselves. As a result, the ability of the olfactory bulb glomeruli and their output neurons to encode the features of an odorant may allow for an exceedingly large number of odorants to be discriminated.

From Molecules to Perception

In the final analysis, the reception of odorant molecules in the nasal cavity must be translated into a psychological perception. One approach to this problem was directed toward understanding the perceptual coding of olfactory information by comparing the structure of chemical compounds that smelled alike. On the basis of Henning's (1922) success with primary tastes, the hope was that after ordering a large series of substances into as few groups as possible, based on the perceptual similarity of their odors, one would be able to specify the physical or chemical similarity of the substances in each class. Amoore (1962a, 1962b) examined over 600 different odorants and, on the basis of this work, proposed a stereochemical classification model for describing odor quality and similarity. In this model odorants with similar odors have similar molecular configurations. Amoore first proposed to explain all odor qualities on the basis of a set of seven primary odors or odor dimensions: ethereal, camphoraceous, musky, floral, minty, pungent, and putrid. His concept was that the sense of smell operated on the basis of a limited number of discrete primary odor sensations that can be combined in different proportions to give a large range of distinguishable odors. In this manner, smell would be analogous to taste with its four classic primaries of salty, sour, bitter, and sweet or to color vision with its three primaries of red, yellow, and blue. This would be in contrast to audition, which depends on a continuum of frequencies and has no primary elements.

The evidence for primary odors was provided by a detailed study of smell blindness or specific anosmias (unfortunately misnamed because they actually represented a reduced sensitivity to one or a very limited number of odors in the presence of otherwise normal olfactory functioning; Amoore, 1967, 1977). Amoore believed that these observations were genetic in origin and involved primary odors transduced by specific receptors. Subsequent psychophysical research has, in fact, suggested that a larger number of primaries are needed to account for all of the different perceptual qualities we appreciate and that the number of specific anosmias is far greater than seven (Amoore, 1977). This later observation was consistent with the finding that although many odors fell within the original seven categories, there were, nonetheless, many exceptions. So the original notion of seven primaries appeared to be wrong even though the basic concept might be correct. In this regard, recall that molecular biological techniques have been used to identify a large family of receptor proteins in the olfactory epithelium, which numbers somewhere on the order of 500 to 1,000 (Buck & Axel, 1991). In fact, there may be as many as 500 to 1,000 different odor primaries, each corresponding to a particular receptor protein. Why such a complex system may have developed is unclear. Once again, it can be suggested that in order to detect a wide range of compounds with the necessary high sensitivity, a large number of primary odor receptor types would be necessary.

Others have attempted to understand the perception of odorant quality by presenting stimuli and monitoring both neurophysiological and behavioral responses. The question of course is whether a relationship exists between a candidate coding mechanism, such as the large-scale distributed patterns of neural activity outlined earlier, and the perception of the animal.

To explore this hypothesis, Kent et al. (1995) trained rats to report differentially (i.e., identify) either a qualitatively unrelated set of five odorants or a homologous series of aldehydes. Once trained, the animals were tested using a confusion matrix design, and the resultant data were used to measure the degree of perceptual dissimilarity between any pair of the five odorants in each set (Youngentob, Markert, Mozell, & Hornung, 1990). The dissimilarity measures were, in turn, subjected to multidimensional scaling analysis in order to establish a perceptual odor space for each animal. At the completion of behavioral testing, optical recording tech-

niques were used to monitor the large-scale activity patterns across a large expanse of epithelium in response to the same odorants. Comparison of these patterns of neural excitation also yielded dissimilarity measures that were subjected to multidimensional scaling analysis in order to establish a neural odorant space for each animal.

Analysis of the behavioral and neurophysiological data indicated a highly significant predictive relationship between the relative position of an odorant's location in neural space and the relative position of the same odorant in a psychophysically determined perceptual odor space. In other words, the more similar the large-scale activity patterns of two odorants were, the greater was their perceptual similarity. Conversely, the more different the activity patterns of two odorants were, the greater was their degree of perceptual dissimilarity. Thus, on the basis of these data it was suggested that the epithelial representation of an odorant is indeed distributed such that large-scale spatial patterns of activation serve as the basis of odor perceptual space. The results also suggested that the *relational* information encoded in the odorant-induced mucosal activity patterns were preserved through further neural processing. These conclusions were consistent with observations outlined earlier that there is an organized and stereotyped patterning of information that occurs at the level of the peripheral projection from the olfactory epithelium onto the bulb. That is, a fixed map of bulbar activation would permit the relational information laid down at the level of the epithelium to be transmitted to the brain.

Conclusions

Growing awareness of the importance of olfaction in the lives of many animals, including humans, has led to an increased interest in the study of odor perception and its neural basis. With regard to the olfactory stimulus itself, the olfactory system is faced with a unique problem, namely, the large diversity and potentially unpredictable nature of the odorant universe. As outlined in the foregoing, the basic principles underlying the encoding of odorant quality perception at the level of the olfactory epithelium and bulb are slowly beginning to emerge. The fundamental units of odorant information appear to be contained in the determinants on the odorant molecule. Using a combinatorial code, the molecular features of an odorant are dissected and encoded by the types of odorant receptors with which they interact and the sensory neurons expressing those receptors. The odorant receptors, being members of a large olfactory-specific multigene family, provide the necessary diversity to interact with the breadth of molecular features required to define an immensely large number of odorants. The differential response of the epithelium to different odorants, in turn, can be traced through successive stages of processing in the olfactory bulb. In these processing steps the molecular features of an odorant molecule are first mapped onto bulbar glomeruli and their associated output neurons, constructing a spatial map of activity that is unique for each odorant. Further, the synaptic circuits of the bulb contain mechanisms for fine-tuning the responses of the output neurons and also for comparing the responses of different subsets.

In short, the prevailing data suggest that the differential activation of different subsets of sensory neurons forms the basis for neural coding and further processing by higher centers in the olfactory pathway. Unfortunately, to date, no direct behavioral tests of this emerging model of odorant quality coding have been performed, although a relationship between dissimilarities in epithelial activity patterns and perceptual dissimilarities among odorants has been demonstrated. Nonetheless, it is clear that the integration of data from anatomical, molecular biological, neurophysiological, and behavioral studies are beginning to unravel the basic principles of processing and organization in this phylogenetically ancient sensory system.

REFERENCES

Adler, E., Hoon, M. A., Mueller, K. L., Chandrashekar, J., Ryba, N. J., & Zuker, C. S. (2000). A novel family of mammalian taste receptors. *Cell, 100*(6), 693–702.

Akabus, M. H., Dodd, J., & Al-Awqati, Q. (1988). A bitter substance induces a rise in intracellular calcium in a subpopulation of rat taste cells. *Science, 242,* 1047–1050.

Alden, M., Besson, J. M., & Bernard, J. F. (1994). Organization of the efferent projections from the pontine parabrachial area to the bed nucleus of the stria terminalis and neighboring regions: A PHA-L study in the rat. *Journal of Comparative Neurology, 341*(3), 289–314.

Allison, A. C. (1952). The morphology of the olfactory system in vertebrates. *Biological Reviews, 28,* 195–244.

Amoore, J. E. (1962a). The stereochemical theory of olfaction: I. Identification of seven primary odors. *Proceedings of the Scientific Section the Toilet Goods Association, 37*(Suppl.), 1–12.

Amoore, J. E. (1962b). The stereochemical theory of olfaction: II. Elucidation of the stereochemical properties of the olfactory receptor sites. *Proceedings of the Scientific Section the Toilet Goods Association, 37*(Suppl.), 13–23.

Amoore, J. E. (1967). Specific anosmia: A clue to the olfactory code. *Nature, 214,* 1095–1098.

Amoore, J. E. (1977). Specific anosmia and the concept of primary odors. *Chemical Senses and Flavor, 2,* 267–281.

Andres, K. H. (1966). Der Feinbau der Regio Olfactoria von Makrosmatikern (*The microstructure of the olfactory area of the xxx*). *Zeitschrift fur Zellforschung, 69,* 140–154.

Arvidson, K. (1979). Location and variation in number of taste buds in human fungiform papillae. *Scandinavian Journal of Dental Research, 87*(6), 435–442.

Barry, M. A., Larson, D. C., & Frank, M. E. (1993). Loss and recovery of sodium-salt taste following bilateral chorda tympani nerve crush. *Physiology and Behavior, 53,* 75–80.

Barry, M. A., Larson, D. C., & Frank, M. E. (1996). Effects of chorda tympani transection on long-term salt preference in hamsters. *Physiology and Behavior, 60,* 347–352.

Bartoshuk, L. M. (2000a). Psychophysical advances aid the study of genetic variation in taste. *Appetite, 34*(1), 105.

Bartoshuk, L. M. (2000b). Comparing sensory experiences across individuals: Recent psychophysical advances illuminate genetic variation in taste perception. *Chemical Senses, 25*(4), 447– 460.

Bartoshuk, L. M., Duffy, V. B., Lucchina, L. A., Prutkin, J., & Fast, K. (1998). PROP (6-n-propylthiouracil) supertasters and the saltiness of NaCl. *Annals of the New York Academy of Sciences, 855,* 793–796.

Bartoshuk, L. M., Duffy, V. B., Reed, D., & Williams, A. (1996). Supertasting, earaches and head injury: Genetics and pathology alter our taste worlds. *Neuroscience and Biobehavioral Reviews, 20*(1), 79–87.

Bealer, S. L., & Smith, D. V. (1975). Multiple sensitivity to chemical stimuli in single human taste papillae. *Physiology and Behavior, 14*(6), 795–799.

Beets, M. G. J. (1971). Olfactory response and molecular structure. In L. Beidler (Ed.), *Handbook of sensory physiology: Vol. 4. Chemical senses* (pp. 257–321). New York: Springer-Verlag.

Behe, P., DeSimone, J. A., Avenet, P., & Lindemann, B. (1990). Membrane currents in taste cells of the rat fungiform papilla: Evidence for two types of Ca currents and inhibition of K currents by saccharin. *Journal of General Physiology, 96,* 1061–1084.

Bereiter, D. A., Berthoud, H. R., & Jeanrenaud, B. (1980). Hypothalamic input to brain stem neurons responsive to oropharyngeal stimulation. *Experimental Brain Research, 39,* 33–39.

Bernard, J. F., Alden, M., & Besson, J. M. (1993). The organization of the efferent projections from the pontine parabrachial area to the amygdaloid complex: A Phaseolus vulgaris leucoagglutinin (PHA-L) study in the rat. *Journal of Comparative Neurology, 329*(2), 201–229.

Bernhardt, S. J., Naim, M., Zehavi, U., & Lindemann, B. (1996). Changes in IP3 and cytosolic Ca2+ in response to sugars and non-sugar sweeteners in transduction of sweet taste in the rat. *Journal of Physiology, 490*(Pt. 2), 325–336.

Bester, H., Besson, J. M., & Bernard, J. F. (1997). Organization of efferent projections from the parabrachial area to the hypothalamus: A Phaseolus vulgaris-leucoagglutinin study in the rat. *Journal of Comparative Neurology, 383*(3), 245–281.

Bester, H., Bourgeais, L., Villanueva, L., Besson, J. M., & Bernard, J. F. (1999). Differential projections to the intralaminar and gustatory thalamus from the parabrachial area: A PHA-L study in the rat. *Journal of Comparative Neurology, 405*(4), 421–449.

Boughter, J. D., & Smith, D. V. (1998). Amiloride blocks acid responses in NaCl-best gustatory neurons of the hamster solitary nucleus. *Journal of Neurophysiology, 80,* 1362–1372.

Bradley, R. M., Stedman, H. M., & Mistretta, C. M. (1983). Superior laryngeal nerve response patterns to chemical stimulation of sheep epiglottis. *Brain Research, 276*(1), 81–93.

Brand, J. G. (1997). Biophysics of taste. In G. K. Beauchamp & L. M. Bartoshuk (Eds.), *Tasting and smelling* (pp. 1–24). San Diego, CA: Academic Press.

Brand, J. G. (2000). Receptor and transduction processes for umami taste. *Journal of Nutrition, 130*(4, Suppl.), 942S–945S.

Breer, H., & Boekoff, I. (1991). Odorants of the same odor class activate different second messenger pathways. *Chemical Senses, 16,* 19–29.

Breer, H., Boekoff, I., & Tareilus, E. (1990). Rapid kinetics of second messenger formation in olfactory transduction. *Nature, 345,* 65–68.

Brown, R. E. (1979). Mammalian social odors: A critical review. *Advanced Study in Behavior, 10,* 104–162.

Brunet, L. J., Gold, G. H., & Ngai, J. (1996). General anosmia caused by a targeted disruption of the mouse olfactory cyclic nucleotide-gated cation channel. *Neuron, 17,* 681–693.

Buck, L., & Axel, R. (1991), A novel multigene family may encode odorant receptors: A molecular basis for odor recognition. *Cell, 65,* 175–187.

Buoniviso, N., & Chaput, M. A. (1990). Response similarity to odors in olfactory bulb output cells presumed to be connected to the same glomerulus: Electrophysiological study using simultaneous single unit recordings. *Journal of Neurophysiology, 63,* 447–454.

Cain, W. S. (1976). Olfaction and the common chemical sense: Some psychophysical contrasts. *Sensory Processes, 1,* 57–67.

Cain, W. S. (1990). Perceptual characteristics of nasal irritation. In B. G. Green, J. R. Mason, & M. R. Kare (Eds.), *Chemical senses: Vol. 2. Irritation* (pp. 43–58). New York: Marcel Dekker.

Caprio, J., Brand, J. G., Teeter, J. H., Valentincic, T., Kalinoski, D. L., Kohbara, J., Kumazawa, T., & Wegert, S. (1993). The taste system of the channel catfish: From biophysics to behavior. *Trends in Neuroscience, 16*(5), 192–197.

Chandrashekar, J., Mueller, K. L., Hoon, M. A., Adler, E., Feng, L., Guo, W., Zuker, C. S., & Ryba, N. J. (2000). T2Rs function as bitter taste receptors. *Cell, 100*(6), 703–711.

Chang, F.-C. T., & Scott, T. R. (1984). Conditioned taste aversions modify neural responses in the rat nucleus tractus solitarius. *Journal of Neuroscience, 4,* 1850–1862.

Chaudhari, N., Landin, A. M., & Roper, S. D. (2000). A metabotropic glutamate receptor variant functions as a taste receptor. *Nature Neuroscience, 3*(2), 113–119.

Cheng, L. H., & Robinson, P. P. (1991). The distribution of fungiform papillae and taste buds on the human tongue. *Archives of Oral Biology, 36*(8), 583–589.

Cinelli, A. R., & Kauer, J. S. (1994). Voltage-sensitive dyes and functional activity in the olfactory pathway. *Annual Review of Neuroscience, 15,* 321–351.

Collings, V. B. (1974). Human taste response as a function of the locus of stimulation on the tongue and soft palate. *Perception and Psychophysics, 15,* 169–174.

Contreras, R. J. (1977). Changes in gustatory nerve discharges with sodium deficiency: A single unit analysis. *Brain Research, 121,* 373–378.

Contreras, R. J., & Frank, M. E. (1979). Sodium deprivation alters neural responses to gustatory stimuli. *Journal of General Physiology, 73,* 569–594.

Contreras, R. J., & Lundy, R. F. (2000). Gustatory neuron types in the periphery: A functional perspective. *Physiology and Behavior, 69*(1-2), 41–52.

Covey, E. (1980). *Temporal coding in gustation.* Unpublished doctoral dissertation, Duke University, Durham, North Carolina.

Darby, E. M., Devor, M., & Chorover, S. L. (1975). A presumptive sex pheromone in the hamster: Some behavioral effects. *Journal of Comparative Physiological Psychology, 88,* 496–502.

Davis, B. J. (1991). The ascending gustatory pathway: A Golgi analysis of the medial and lateral parabrachial complex in the adult hamster. *Brain Research Bulletin, 27,* 63–73.

Davis, B. J. (1993). GABA-like immunoreactivity in the gustatory zone of the nucleus of the solitary tract in the hamster: Light and electron microscopic studies. *Brain Research Bulletin, 30,* 69–77.

Davis, B. J. (1998). Synaptic relationships between the chorda tympani and tyrosine hydroxylase-immunoreactive dendritic processes in the gustatory zone of the nucleus of the solitary tract in the hamster. *Journal of Comparative Neurology, 392*(1), 78–91.

Davis, B. J., & Jang, T. (1986). The gustatory zone of the solitary tract in the hamster: Light microscopic morphometric studies. *Chemical Senses, 11,* 213–228.

Dear, T. N., Boehm, T., Keverne, E. B., & Rabbitts, T. H. (1991). Novel genes for potential ligand-binding proteins in subregions of the olfactory mucosa. *The EMBO Journal, 10,* 2813–2819.

DeSimone, J. A., Calahan, E. M., & Heck, G. L. (1995). Chorda tympani taste responses of rat to hydrochloric acid subject to voltage-clamped lingual receptive field. *American Journal of Physiology, 268*(5, Pt. 1), C1295–C1300.

DiCarlo, S. T., & Powers, A. S. (1998). Propylthiouracil tasting as a possible genetic association marker for two types of alcoholism. *Physiology and Behavior, 64*(2), 147–152.

Di Lorenzo, P. M. (1990). Corticofugal influence on taste responses in the parabrachial pons of the rat. *Brain Research, 530*(1), 73–84.

Di Lorenzo, P. M., & Hecht, G. S. (1993). Perceptual consequences of electrical stimulation in the gustatory system. *Behavioral Neuroscience, 107,* 130–138.

Di Lorenzo, P. M., & Lemon, C. H. (2000). The neural code for taste in the nucleus of the solitary tract of the rat: Effects of adaptation. *Brain Research, 852,* 383–397.

Di Lorenzo, P. M., & Monroe, S. (1989). Taste responses in the parabrachial pons of male, female and pregnant rats. *Brain Research Bulletin, 23,* 219–227.

Di Lorenzo, P. M., & Monroe, S. (1990). Taste responses in the parabrachial pons of ovariectomized rats. *Brain Research Bulletin, 25,* 741–748.

Di Lorenzo, P. M., & Monroe, S. (1992). Corticofugal input to taste-responsive units in the parabrachial pons. *Brain Research Bulletin, 29*(6), 925–930.

Di Lorenzo, P. M., & Monroe, S. (1995). Corticofugal influence on taste responses in the nucleus of the solitary tract in the rat. *Journal of Neurophysiology, 74*(1), 258–272.

Di Lorenzo, P. M., & Monroe, S. (1997). Transfer of information about taste from the nucleus of the solitary tract to the parabrachial nucleus of the pons. *Brain Research, 763,* 167–181.

Di Lorenzo, P. M., & Schwartzbaum, J. S. (1982). Coding of gustatory information in the pontine parabrachial nuclei of the rabbit: Temporal patterns of neural response. *Brain Research, 251,* 245–257.

Dinkins, M. E., & Travers, S. P. (1998). Effects of chorda tympani nerve anesthesia on taste responses in the NST. *Chemical Senses, 23*(6), 661–673.

Doetsch, G. S., & Erickson, R. P. (1970). Synaptic processing of taste-quality information in the nucleus tractus solitarius of the rat. *Journal of Neurophysiology, 33,* 490–507.

Doty, R. L. (1986). Odor-guided behavior in mammals. *Experentia, 42,* 257–271.

Erickson, R. P. (1986). A neural metric. *Neuroscience and Biobehavioral Reviews, 10*(4), 377–386.

Erickson, R. P. (2000). The evolution of neural coding ideas in the chemical senses. *Physiology and Behavior, 69*(1-2), 3–16.

Faurion, A., Cerf, B., Le Bihan, D., & Pillias, A. M. (1998). fMRI study of taste cortical areas in humans. *Annals of the New York Academy of Sciences, 855*(12), 535–545.

Faurion, A., Cerf, B., Van De Moortele, P. F., Lobel, E., Mac Leod, P., & Le Bihan, D. (1999). Human taste cortical areas studied with functional magnetic resonance imaging: Evidence of functional lateralization related to handedness. *Neuroscience Letters, 277*(3), 189–192.

Ferrell, F., Tsuetaki, T., & Chole, R. A. (1985). Myelination in the chorda tympani of the postnatal rat: A quantitative electron microscope study. *Acta Anatomica, Basel, 123*(4), 224–229.

Firestein, S., Darrow, B., & Shepherd, G. M. (1991). Activation of the sensory current in salamander olfactory receptor neurons depends on a G-protein-mediated cAMP second messenger system. *Neuron, 6,* 825–835.

Firestein, S., Picco, C., & Menini, A. (1993). The relation between stimulus and response in the olfactory receptor cells of tiger salamander. *Journal of Physiology, London, 468,* 1–10.

Fitzsimmons, J. T. (1979). *The physiology of thirst and sodium appetite* (Physiological Society Monograph No. 35). London: Cambridge University Press.

Frank, M. E. (1973). An analysis of hamster afferent taste nerve response functions. *Journal of General Physiology, 61,* 588–618.

Frank, M. E. (1974). The classification of mammalian afferent taste fibers. *Chemical Senses, 1,* 53–60.

Frank, M. E. (1991). Taste-responsive neurons of the glossopharyngeal nerve of the rat. *Journal of Neurophysiology, 65*(6), 1452–1463.

Frank, M. E. (2000). Neuron types, receptors, behavior, and taste quality. *Physiology and Behavior, 69*(1-2), 53–62.

Frank, M. E., Bieber, S. L., & Smith, D. V. (1988). The organization of taste sensibilities in hamster chorda tympani nerve fibers. *Journal of General Physiology, 91,* 861–896.

Frank, M. E., Contreras, R., & Hettinger, T. (1983). Nerve fibers sensitive to ionic taste stimuli in chorda tympani of the rat. *Journal of Neurophysiology, 50*(4), 941–960.

Frey, S., & Petrides, M. (1999). Re-examination of the human taste region: A positron emission tomography study. *European Journal of Neuroscience, 11*(8), 2985–2988.

Ganchrow, D., & Erickson, R. P. (1970). Neural correlates of gustatory intensity and quality. *Journal of Neurophysiology, 33*(6), 768–783.

Ganchrow, D., & Erickson, R. P. (1972). Thalamocortical relations in gustation. *Brain Research, 36,* 289–305.

Gangestad, S. W., & Thornhill, R. (1998). Menstrual cycle variation in women's preferences for the scent of symmetrical men. *Proceedings of the Royal Society of London, 265B,* 927–933.

Ganzevles, P. G. J., & Kroeze, J. H. A. (1987). Effects of adaptation and cross-adaptation to common ions on sour intensity. *Physiology and Behavior, 40,* 641–646.

Gesteland, R. C., Lettvin, J. Y., Pitts, W. H., & Rojas, A. (1963). Odorant and autonomic regulation of secretion in the olfactory mucosa. In Y. Zotterman (Ed.), *Olfaction and taste* (pp. 19–44). Oxford, UK: Pergamon Press.

Getchell, M. L., Zelinski, B., & Getchell, T. V. (1988). Odorant and autonomic regulation of secretion in the olfactory mucosa. In F. L. Margolis & T. V. Getchell (Eds.), *Molecular biology of the olfactory system* (pp. 71–78). New York: Plenum Press.

Getchell, T. V., Margolis, F. L., & Getchell, M. L. (1984). Perireceptor and receptor events in vertebrate olfaction. *Progress in Neurobiology, 23,* 317–345.

Getchell, T. V., & Shepherd, G. M. (1978). Responses of olfactory receptor cells to step pulses of odour at different concentrations in salamander. *Journal of Physiology, 282,* 521–540.

Gilbertson, T. A., Avenet, P., Kinnamon, S. C., & Roper, S. D. (1992). Proton currents through amiloride-sensitive Na+ channels in hamster taste cells: Role in acid transduction. *Journal of General Physiology, 100,* 941–960.

Gilbertson, T. A., Damak, S., & Margolskee, R. F. (2000). The molecular physiology of taste transduction. *Current Opinions in Neurobiology, 10*(4), 519–527.

Gill, J. M., II, & Erickson, R. P. (1985). Neural mass differences in gustation. *Chemical Senses, 10,* 531–548.

Giza, B. K., & Scott, T. R. (1991). The effect of amiloride on taste-evoked activity in the nucleus tractus solitarius of the rat. *Brain Research, 550,* 247–256.

Grabauskas, G., & Bradley, R. M. (1996). Synaptic interactions due to convergent input from gustatory afferent fibers in the rostral nucleus of the solitary tract. *Journal of Neurophysiology, 76*(5), 2919–2927.

Halpern, B. P. (1998). Amiloride and vertebrate gustatory responses to NaCl. *Neuroscience and Biobehavioral Reviews, 23*(1), 5–47.

Halpern, B. P., & Nelson, L. M. (1965). Bulbar gustatory responses to anterior and to posterior tongue stimulation in the rat. *American Journal of Physiology, 209,* 105–110.

Halsell, C. B., Travers, J. B., & Travers, S. P. (1993). Gustatory and tactile stimulation of the posterior tongue activate overlapping but distinctive regions within the nucleus of the solitary tract. *Brain Research, 632,* 161–173.

Hanamori, T., Miller, I. J., & Smith, D. V. (1988). Gustatory responsiveness of fibers in the hamster glossopharyngeal nerve. *Journal of Neurophysiology, 60*(2), 478–498.

Harden-Jones, F. R. (1968). *Fish migration.* London: Edward Arnold.

Hellekant, G., Danilova, V., & Ninomiya, Y. (1997). Primate sense of taste: Behavioral and single chorda tympani and glossopharyngeal nerve fiber recordings in the rhesus monkey, *Macaca mulatta. Journal of Neurophysiology, 77*(2), 978–993.

Henkin, R. I. (1974). Sensory changes during the menstrual cycle. In M. Ferin, F. Halberg, R. M. Richart, & R. L. Vande Wiele (Eds.), *Biorhythms and human reproduction* (pp. 277–285). New York: Wiley.

Henning, H. (1922). Psychologische studien au geschmacksinn (*Psychological studies of taste*). *Handbuch der Biologische Arbeit-methoden* (6A, pp. 627–740). Berlin: Urban & Schwarzenberg.

Herness, S. (2000). Coding in taste receptor cells: The early years of intracellular recordings. *Physiology and Behavior, 69*(1-2), 17–28.

Herness, M. S., & Gilbertson, T. A. (1999). Cellular mechanisms of taste transduction. *Annual Review of Physiology, 61,* 873–900.

Hoon, M. A., Adler, E., Lindemeier, J., Battey, J. F., Ryba, N. J., & Zuker, C. S. (1999). Putative mammalian taste receptors: A class of taste-specific GPCRs with distinct topographic selectivity. *Cell, 96*(4), 541–551.

Horst, G. J. T., de Boer, P., Luiten, P. G. M., & van Willigen, J. D. (1989). Ascending projections from the solitary tract nucleus to the hypothalamus: A phaseolus vulgaris lectin tracing study in the rat. *Neuroscience, 31,* 785–797.

Hosoya, Y., & Matsushita, M. (1981). Brainstem projections from the lateral hypothalamic area in the rat, as studied with autoradiography. *Neuroscience Letters, 24,* 111–116.

Huard, J. M. T., Youngentob, S. L., Goldstein, B. J., Luskin, M. B., & Schwob, J. E. (1998). Adult olfactory epithelium contains multipotent progenitors that give rise to neurons and non-neuronal cells. *Journal of Comparative Neurology, 400,* 469–486.

Hudsen, R., & Distel, H. (1983). Nipple location by newborn rabbits: Behavioral evidence for pheromonal guidance. *Behavior, 85,* 260–275.

Imamura, K., Mataga, N., & Mori, K. (1992). Coding of odor molecules by mitral/tufted cells in rabbit olfactory bulb: I. Aliphatic compounds. *Journal of Neurophysiology, 68,* 1986–2002.

Jacobs, K. M., Mark, G. P., & Scott, T. R. (1988). Taste responses in the nucleus tractus solitarius of sodium-deprived rats. *Journal of Physiology, London, 406,* 393–410.

James, J. E. A., & Daly, M. de B. (1969). Nasal reflexes. *Proceedings of the Royal Society of Medicine, 62,* 1287–1293.

Johnson, B. A., & Leon, M. (2000). Modular representation of odorants in the glomerular layer of the rat olfactory bulb and effects of stimulus concentration. *Journal of Comparative Neurology, 422*(4), 496–509.

Johnson, B. A., Woo, C. C., & Leon, M. (2000). Spatial coding of odorant features in the glomerular layer of the rat olfactory bulb. *Journal of Comparative Neurology, 393,* 457–471.

Kanazawa, H., & Yoshie, S. (1996). The taste bud and its innervation in the rat as studied by immunohistochemistry for PGP 9.5. *Archives of Histology and Cytology, 59*(4), 357–367.

Karimnamazi, H., & Travers, J. B. (1998). Differential projections from gustatory responsive regions of the parabrachial nucleus to the medulla and forebrain. *Brain Research, 813*(2), 283–302.

Kashiwadani, H., Sasaki, Y. F., Uchida, N., & Mori, K. (1999). Synchronized oscillatory discharges of mitral/tufted cells with different molecular receptive ranges in the rabbit olfactory bulb. *Journal of Neurophysiology, 82,* 1786–1792.

Katoh, K., Koshimoto, H., Tani, A., & Mori, K. (1993). Coding of odor molecules by mitral/tufted cells in rabbit olfactory bulb: II. Aromatic compounds. *Journal of Neurophysiology, 70,* 2161–2165.

Kent, P. F., Mozell, M. M., Murphy, S. J., & Hornung, D. E. (1996). The interaction of imposed and inherent olfactory mucosal activity patterns and their composite representation in a mammalian species using voltage-sensitive dyes. *Journal of Neuroscience, 16,* 345–353.

Kent, P. F., Youngentob, S. L., & Sheehe, P. R. (1995). Odorant-specific spatial patterns in mucosal activity predict perceptual differences among odorants. *Journal of Neurophysiology, 74,* 1777–1781.

King, C. T., Garcea, M., & Spector, A. C. (2000). Glossopharyngeal nerve regeneration is essential for the complete recovery of quinine-stimulated oromotor rejection behaviors and central patterns of neuronal activity in the nucleus of the solitary tract in the rat. *Journal of Neuroscience, 20*(22), 8426–8434.

King, C. T., Travers, S. P., Rowland, N. E., Garcea, M., & Spector, A. C. (1999). Glossopharyngeal nerve transection eliminates quinine-stimulated fos-like immunoreactivity in the nucleus of the solitary tract: Implications for a functional topography of gustatory nerve input in rats. *Journal of Neuroscience, 19*(8), 3107–3121.

Kinnamon, S. C., Dionne, V. E., & Beam, K. G. (1988). Apical localization of K channels in taste cells provides the basis for sour taste transduction. *Proceedings of the National Academy of Sciences, USA, 85*(18), 7023–7027.

Kinnamon, S. C., & Margolskee, R. F. (1996). Mechanisms of taste transduction. *Current Opinion in Neurobiology, 6*(4), 506–513.

Kinomura, S., Kawashima, R., Yamada, K., Ono, S., Itoh, M., Yoshioka, S., Yamaguchi, T., Matsui, H., Miyazawa, H., Itoh, H., Goto, R., Fujiwara, T., Satoh, K., & Fukuda, H. (1994). Functional anatomy of taste perception in the human brain studied with positron emission tomography. *Brain Research, 659*(1-2), 263–266.

Kita, H., & Oomura, Y. (1981). Functional synaptic interconnections between the lateral hypothalamus and frontal and gustatory cortices in the rat. In Y. Katsuki, R. Norgren, & M. Sato (Eds.), *Brain mechanisms of sensation* (pp. 307–322). New York: Wiley.

Kobayakawa, T., Ogawa, H., Kaneda, H., Ayabe-Kanamura, S., Endo, H., & Saito, S. (1999). Spatio-temporal analysis of cortical activity evoked by gustatory stimulation in humans. *Chemical Senses, 24*(2), 201–209.

Kolesnikov, S. S., & Margolskee, R. F. (1995). A cyclic-nucleotide-suppressible conductance activated by transducin in taste cells. *Nature, London, 376,* 85–88.

Kosar, E., & Schwartz, G. J. (1990). Cortical unit responses to chemical stimulation of the oral cavity in the rat. *Brain Research, 513*(2), 212–224.

Kranzler, H. R., Moore, P. J., & Hesselbrock, V. M. (1996). No association of PROP taster status and paternal history of alcohol dependence. *Alcoholism: Clinical and Experimental Research, 20*(8), 1496–1500.

Kroeze, J. H., & Bartoshuk, L. M. (1985). Bitterness suppression as revealed by split-tongue taste stimulation in humans. *Physiology and Behavior, 35*(5), 779–783.

Krout, K. E., & Loewy, A. D. (2000). Parabrachial nucleus projections to midline and intralaminar thalamic nuclei of the rat. *Journal of Comparative Neurology, 428*(3), 475–494.

Kubick, S., Strotmann, J., Andreini, I., & Breer, H. (1997). Subfamily of olfactory receptors characterized by unique structural features and expression patterns. *Journal of Neurochemistry, 69,* 465–475.

Kurihara, K., & Kashiwayanagi, M. (2000). Physiological studies on umami taste. *Journal of Nutrition, 130*(4, Suppl.), 931S–934S.

Kveton, J. F., & Bartoshuk, L. M. (1994). The effect of unilateral chorda tympani damage on taste. *Laryngoscope, 104*(1, Pt. 1), 25–29.

Lasiter, P. S., Glanzman, D. L., & Mensah, P. A. (1982). Direct connectivity between pontine taste areas and gustatory neocortex in rat. *Brain Research, 234,* 111–121.

Lasiter, P. S., & Kachele, D. L. (1988a). Postnatal development of the parabrachial gustatory zone in rat: Dendritic morphology and mitochondrial enzyme activity. *Brain Research Bulletin, 21,* 79–94.

Lasiter, P. S., & Kachele, D. L. (1988b). Organization of GABA and GABA-transaminase containing neurons in the gustatory zone of the nucleus of the solitary tract. *Brain Research Bulletin, 21,* 623–636.

Lehman, C. D., Bartoshuk, L. M., Catalanotto, F. C., Kveton, J. F., & Lowlocht, R. A. (1995). Effect of anesthesia of the chorda tympani nerve on taste perception in humans. *Physiology and Behavior, 57*(5), 943–951.

Lindemann, B. (1996). Taste reception. *Physiological Review, 76*(3), 718–766.

Liu, H., Behbehani, M. M., & Smith, D. V. (1993). The influence of GABA on cells in the gustatory region of hamster solitary nucleus. *Chemical Senses, 18*(3), 285–305.

Lowe, G., & Gold, G. H. (1993). Contribution of ciliary cyclic nucleotide-gated conductance to olfactory transduction in the salamander. *Journal of Physiology, 462,* 175–196.

Lowe, G., Nakamura, T., & Gold, G. H. (1989). Adenylate cyclase mediates olfactory transduction for a wide variety of odorants. *Proceedings of the National Academy of Sciences, USA, 86,* 5641–5645.

Lundy, R. F., & Contreras, R. J. (1999). Gustatory neuron types in rat geniculate ganglion. *Journal of Neurophysiology, 82*(6), 2970–2988.

MacKay-Sim, A., & Kesteven, S. (1994). Topographic patterns of responsiveness to odorants in the rat olfactory epithelium. *Journal of Neurophysiology, 71,* 150–160.

MacKay-Sim, A., & Kubie, J. L. (1981). The salamander nose: A model system for the study of spatial coding of olfactory quality. *Chemical Senses, 6,* 249–257.

Malnic, B., Hirano, J., Sato, T., & Buck, L. B. (1999). Combinatorial receptor codes for odors. *Cell, 96,* 713–723.

Markison, S., St. John, S. J., & Spector, A. C. (1995). Glossopharyngeal nerve transection does not compromise the specificity of taste-guided sodium appetite in rats. *American Journal of Physiology, 269*(1, Pt. 2), R215–R221.

Markison, S., St. John, S. J., & Spector, A. C. (1999). Glossopharyngeal nerve transection reduces quinine avoidance in rats not given presurgical stimulus exposure. *Physiology and Behavior, 65*(4-5), 773–778.

McBurney, D. H., & Bartoshuk, L. M. (1973). Interactions between stimuli with different taste qualities. *Physiology and Behavior, 10*(6), 1101–1106.

McCaughey, S. A., Giza, B. K., Nolan, L. J., & Scott, T. R. (1997). Extinction of a conditioned taste aversion in rats: II. Neural effects in the nucleus of the solitary tract. *Physiology and Behavior, 61*(3), 373–379.

McCaughey, S. A., Giza, B. K., & Scott, T. R. (1996). Activity in rat nucleus tractus solitarius after recovery from sodium deprivation. *Physiology and Behavior, 60*(2), 501–506.

McClintock, M. (1983). Pheromonal regulation of the ovarian cycle: Enhancement, suppression and synchrony. In J. G. Vandenbergh (Ed.), *Pheromones and reproduction in mammals* (pp. 95–112). New York: Academic Press.

McLaughlin, S. K., McKinnon, P. J., & Margolskee, R. F. (1992). Gustducin is a taste-cell-specific G protein closely related to the transducins. *Nature, 357*(6379), 563–569.

McLaughlin, S. K., McKinnon, P. J., Spickofsky, N., Danho, W., & Margolskee, R. F. (1994). Molecular cloning of G proteins and phosphodiesterases from rat taste cells. *Physiology and Behavior, 56*, 1157–1164.

McPheeters, M., Hettinger, T., Nuding, S. C., Savoy, L. D., Whitehead, M. C., & Frank, M. E. (1990). Taste-responsive neurons and their locations in the solitary nucleus of the hamster. *Neuroscience, 34*(3), 745–758.

Mech, L. D., & Peters, R. P. (1977). The study of chemical communication in free-ranging mammals. In D. Muller-Schwartz & M. M. Mozell (Eds.), *Chemical signals in vertebrates* (pp. 321–333). New York: Plenum Press.

Miller, I. J. (1986). Variation in human fungiform taste bud densities among regions and subjects. *Anatomical Record, 216*(4), 474–482.

Miller, I. J., & Bartoshuk, L. M. (1991). Taste perception and taste bud distribution. In T. V. Getchell, L. M. Bartoshuk, R. L. Doty, & J. B. Snow (Eds.), *Smell and taste in health and disease* (pp. 205–234). New York: Raven Press.

Miller, I. J., & Preslar, A. J. (1975). Spatial distribution of rat fungiform papillae. *Anatomical Record, 181*(3), 679–684.

Mistretta, C. M., & Oakley, I. A. (1986). Quantitative anatomical study of taste buds in fungiform papillae of young and old Fischer rats. *Journal of Gerontology, 41*(3), 315–318.

Miyamoto, T., Fujiyama, R., Okada, Y., & Sato, T. (2000). Acid and salt responses in mouse taste cells. *Progress in Neurobiology, 62*(2), 135–157.

Mombaerts, P., Wang, F., Dulac, C., Chao, S. K., Nemes, A., Mendelsohn, M., Edmondson, J., & Axel, R. (1997). Visualizing an olfactory sensory map. *Cell, 87*, 675–686.

Monroe, S., & Di Lorenzo, P. M. (1995). Taste responses in neurons in the nucleus of the solitary tract that do and do not project to the parabrachial pons. *Journal of Neurophysiology, 74*(1), 249–257.

Moran, D. T., Rowley, J. C., & Jafek, B. W. (1982). Electron microscopy of human olfactory epithelium reveals a new cell type: The microvillar cell. *Brain Research, 253*, 39–46.

Mori, K., Imamura, K., & Mataga, N. (1992). Differential specificities in mitral cells in rabbit olfactory bulb for a homologous series of fatty acid molecules. *Journal of Neurophysiology, 67*, 786–789.

Mori, K., Nagao, H., & Yoshihara, Y. (1999). The olfactory bulb: Coding and processing of odor molecule information. *Science, 286*, 711–715.

Mori, K., & Shepherd, G. M. (1994). Emerging principles of molecular signal processing by mitral/tufted cells in the olfactory bulb. *Seminars in Cell Biology, 5*(1), 65–74.

Mori, K., & Takagi, S. F. (1978). An intracellular study of dendrodendritic inhibitory synapses on mitral cells in the rabbit olfactory bulb. *Journal of Physiology, London, 279*, 569–588.

Mori, K., & Yoshihara, Y. (1995). Molecular recognition and olfactory processing in the mammalian olfactory system. *Progress in Neurobiology, 45*, 585–619.

Morrison, E. E., & Costanzo, R. M. (1990). Morphology of the human olfactory epithelium. *Journal of Comparative Neurology, 297*, 1–13.

Moulton, D. G. (1976). Spatial patterning response to odors in the peripheral olfactory system. *Physiological Reviews, 56*, 578–593.

Mozell, M. M., Sheehe, P. R., Hornung, D. E., Kent, P. F., Youngentob, S. L., & Murphy, S. J. (1987). "Imposed" and "inherent" mucosal activity patterns: Their composite representation of olfactory stimuli. *Journal of General Physiology, 90*, 625–650.

Mozell, M. M., Smith, B. P., Smith, P. E., Sullivan, R. L., & Swender, P. (1969). Nasal chemoreception in flavor identification. *Archives of Otolaryngology, 90*, 131–137.

Muller, T., & Jastrow, H. (1998). The innervation of taste buds in the soft palate and circumvallate papilla of the rat as revealed by the zinc iodide-osmium tetroxide technique. *Archives of Histology and Cytology, 61*(4), 327–336.

Muller-Schwartz, D. (1977). Complex mammalian behavior and pheromone bioassay in the field. In D. Muller-Schwartz & M. M. Mozell (Eds.), *Chemical signals in vertebrates* (pp. 413–435). New York: Plenum Press.

Murphy, C., Cardello, A. V., & Brand, J. B. (1981). Tastes of fifteen halide salts following water and NaCl: Anion and cation effects. *Physiology and Behavior, 26*, 1083–1095.

Nagai, T., & Ueda, K. (1981). Stochastic properties of gustatory impulse discharges in rat chorda tympani fibers. *Journal of Neurophysiology, 45*(3), 574–592.

Nakamura, K., & Norgren, R. (1991). Gustatory responses of neurons in the nucleus of the solitary tract of behaving rats. *Journal of Neurophysiology, 66*(4), 1232–1248.

Nakamura, K., & Norgren, R. (1993). Taste responses of neurons in the nucleus of the solitary tract of awake rats: An extended stimulus array. *Journal of Neurophysiology, 70*(3), 879–891.

Nakamura, T., Lee, H. H., Kobayashi, H., & Sato, T. O. (1996). Gated conductances in native and reconstituted membranes from frog olfactory cilia. *Biophysical Journal, 70*, 813–817.

Nakamura, T., & Ogawa, H. (1997). Neural interaction between cortical taste neurons in rats: A cross-correlation analysis. *Chemical Senses, 22*(5), 517–528.

Nef, P., Hermans-Borgmeyer, I., Artieres, H., Beasely, L., Dionne, V. E., & Heinemann, S. F. (1992). Spatial pattern of receptor gene expression in the olfactory epithelium. *Proceedings of the National Academy of Sciences, USA, 89*, 8948–8952.

Nishijo, H., & Norgren, R. (1997). Parabrachial neural coding of taste stimuli in awake rats. *Journal of Neurophysiology, 78*(5), 2254–2268.

Nomura, T., & Ogawa, H. (1985). The taste and mechanical response properties of neurons in the parvicellular part of the thalamic posteromedial ventral nucleus of the rat. *Neuroscience Research, 3*(2), 91–105.

Norgren, R. (1974). Gustatory afferents to ventral forebrain. *Brain Research, 81*, 285–295.

Norgren, R., & Grill, H. J. (1976). Efferent distribution from the cortical gustatory area in rats. *Neuroscience Abstracts, 2,* 124.

Ogawa, H. (1994). Gustatory cortex of primates: Anatomy and physiology. *Neuroscience Research, 20*(1), 1–13.

Ogawa, H., Hasegawa, K., & Murayama, N. (1992). Difference in taste quality coding between two cortical taste areas, granular and dysgranular insular areas, in rats. *Experimental Brain Research, 91*(3), 415–424.

Ogawa, H., Hayama, T., & Ito, S. (1987). Response properties of the parabrachio-thalamic taste and mechanoreceptive neurons in rats. *Experimental Brain Research, 68*(3), 449–457.

Ogawa, H., Imoto, T., & Hayama, T. (1984). Responsiveness of solitario-parabrachial relay neurons to taste and mechanical stimulation applied to the oral cavity in rats. *Experimental Brain Research, 54*, 349–358.

Ogawa, H., Imoto, T., Hayama, T., & Kaisaku, J. (1982). Afferent connections to the pontine taste area: Physiologic and anatomic studies. In Y. Katsuki, R. Norgren, & M. Sato (Eds.), *Brain mechanisms of sensation* (pp. 161–176). New York: Wiley.

Ogawa, H., & Kaisaku, J. (1982). Physiological characteristics of the solitario-parabrachial relay neurons with tongue afferent inputs in rats. *Experimental Brain Research, 48*(3), 362–368.

Ogawa, H., Murayama, N., & Hasegawa, K. (1992). Difference in receptive field features of taste neurons in rat granular and dysgranular insular cortices. *Experimental Brain Research, 91*(3), 408–414.

Ogawa, H., & Nomura, T. (1988). Receptive field properties of thalamo-cortical taste relay neurons in the parvicellular part of the posteromedial ventral nucleus in rats. *Experimental Brain Research, 73*(2), 364–370.

Ogawa, H., Sato, M., & Yamashita, S. (1973). Variability in impulse discharges in rat chorda tympani fibers in response to repeated gustatory stimulations. *Physiology and Behavior, 11*(4), 469–479.

Ogawa, H., Yamashita, S., & Sato, M. (1974). Variation in gustatory nerve fiber discharge pattern with change in stimulus concentration and quality. *Journal of Neurophysiology, 37*(3), 443–457.

O'Keefe, G. B., Schumm, J., & Smith, J. C. (1994). Loss of sensitivity to low concentrations of NaCl following bilateral chorda tympani nerve sections in rats. *Chemical Senses, 19*(2), 169–184.

O'Mahony, M., & Ishii, R. (1986). A comparison of English and Japanese taste languages: Taste descriptive methodology, codability and the umami taste. *British Journal of Psychology, 77*(Pt. 2), 161–174.

Ozeki, M. (1971). Conductance change associated with receptor potentials of gustatory cells in rat. *Journal of General Physiology, 58*, 688–699.

Pedersen, P. E., Jastreboff, P. J., Stewart, W. B., & Shepherd, G. M. (1986). Mapping of an olfactory receptor population that projects to a specific region in the rat olfactory bulb. *Journal of Comparative Neurology, 250*, 93–108.

Pelchat, M. L., & Danowski, S. (1992). A possible genetic association between PROP-tasting and alcoholism. *Physiology and Behavior, 51*(6), 1261–1266.

Pevsner, J., & Snyder, S. H. (1990). Odorant binding protein: Odorant transport function in the vertebrate nasal epithelium. *Chemical Senses, 15*, 217–222.

Pike, L. M., Enns, M. P., & Hornung, D. E. (1988). Quality and intensity differences of carvone enantiomers when tested separately and in mixtures. *Chemical Senses, 13,* 307–309.

Price, J. L. (1987). The central and accessory olfactory systems. In T. E. Finger & W. L. Silver (Eds.), *Neurobiology of taste and smell* (pp. 179–204). New York: Wiley.

Pritchard, T. C. (1991). The primate gustatory system. In T. V. Getchell, L. M. Bartoshuk, R. L. Doty, & J. B. Snow (Eds.), *Smell and taste in health and disease* (pp. 109–126). New York: Raven Press.

Pritchard, T. C., Hamilton, R. B., & Norgren, R. (1989). Neural coding of gustatory information in the thalamus of *Macaca mulatta*. *Journal of Neurophysiology, 61*(1), 1–14.

Pritchard, T. C., Macaluso, D. A., & Eslinger, P. J. (1999). Taste perception in patients with insular cortex lesions. *Behavioral Neuroscience, 113*(4), 663–671.

Reed, D. R., Nanthakumar, E., North, M., Bell, C., Bartoshuk, L. M., & Price, R. A. (1999). Localization of a gene for bitter-taste perception to human chromosome 5p15. *American Journal of Human Genetics, 64*(5), 1478–1480.

Renehan, W. E., Jin, Z., Zhang, X., & Schweitzer, L. (1994). The structure and function of gustatory neurons in the nucleus of the solitary tract: I. A classification of neurons based on morphological features. *Journal of Comparative Neurology, 347*, 531–544.

Ressler, K. J., Sullivan, S. L., & Buck, L. B. (1993). A zonal organization of odorant receptor gene expression in the olfactory epithelium. *Cell, 73,* 597–609.

Restrepo, D., Teeter, J. H., Honda, E., Boyle, A. G., Marecek, J. F., Prestwich, G. D., & Kalinoski, D. L. (1992). Evidence for an InsP3-gated channel protein in isolated rat olfactory cilia. *American Journal of Physiology, 263,* C667–C673.

Revial, M. F., Sicard, G., Duchamp, A., & Holley, A. (1982). New studies on odour discrimination in the frog's olfactory receptor cells: I. Experimental results. *Chemical Senses, 7,* 175–190.

Revial, M. F., Sicard, G., Duchamp, A., & Holley, A. (1983). New studies on odour discrimination in the frog's olfactory receptor cells: II. Mathematical analysis of electrophysiological responses. *Chemical Senses, 8,* 179–194.

Ricardo, J. A., & Koh, E. T. (1978). Anatomical evidence of direct projections from the nucleus of the solitary tract to the hypothalamus amygdala and other forebrain structures in the cat. *Brain Research, 153,* 1–28.

Rolls, E. T., Yaxley, S., & Sienkiewicz, Z. J. (1990). Gustatory responses of single neurons in the caudolateral orbitofrontal cortex of the macaque monkey. *Journal of Neurophysiology, 64*(4), 1055–1066.

Royer, S. M., & Kinnamon, J. C. (1994). Application of serial sectioning and three-dimensional reconstruction to the study of taste bud ultrastructure and organization. *Microscopy Research and Technique, 29*(5), 381–407.

Saper, C. B. (1982). Reciprocal parabrachial-cortical connections in the rat. *Brain Research, 242,* 33–40.

Saper, C. B., & Loewy, A. D. (1980). Efferent connections of the parabrachial nucleus of the pons. *Brain Research, 197,* 291–317.

Sato, M., Ogawa, H., & Yamashita, S. (1994). Gustatory responsiveness of chorda tympani fibers in the cynomolgus monkey. *Chemical Senses, 19*(5), 381–400.

Sato, T., Hirano, J., Tonoike, M., & Takebayashi, M. (1994). Tuning specificity to aliphatic odorants in mouse olfactory receptor neurons and their local distribution. *Journal of Neurophysiology, 72,* 2980–2989.

Schiffman, S. S. (2000). Taste quality and neural coding: Implications from psychophysics and neurophysiology. *Physiology and Behavior, 69*(1-2), 147–160.

Schneider, D. (1969). Insect olfaction: Deciphering system for chemical messages. *Science, 163,* 1031–1036.

Schneider, R. A., & Wolf, S. (1955). Olfactory perception thresholds for citral utilizing a new type olfactorium. *Journal of Applied Physiology, 8,* 337–342.

Schwob, J. E., Youngentob, S. L., & Mezza, R. (1995). The reconstitution of the rat olfactory epithelium after methyl bromide-induced lesion. *Journal of Comparative Neurology, 359,* 15–37.

Sclafani, A., & Abrams, M. (1986). Rats show only a weak preference for the artificial sweetener aspartame. *Physiology and Behavior, 37*(2), 253–256.

Scott, T. R. (1974). Behavioral support for a neural taste theory. *Physiology and Behavior, 12*(3), 413–417.

Scott, T. R., & Erickson, R. P. (1971). Synaptic processing of taste-quality information in thalamus of the rat. *Journal of Neurophysiology, 34*(5), 868–883.

Scott, T. R., & Giza, B. (1990). Coding channels in the rat taste system. *Science, 249,* 1585–1587.

Scott, T. R., & Giza, B. (2000). Issues of gustatory neural coding: Where they stand today. *Physiology and Behavior, 69*(1-2), 65–76.

Scott, T. R., & Plata-Salaman, C. R. (1999). Taste in the monkey cortex. *Physiology & Behavior, 67*(4), 489–511.

Shepherd, G. M. (1972). Synaptic organization of the mammalian olfactory bulb. *Physiological Reviews, 52,* 864–917.

Shepherd, G. M., & Greer, C. A. (1990). Olfactory bulb. In G. M. Shepherd (Ed.), *The synaptic organization of the brain* (pp. 139–169). New York: Oxford University Press.

Shi, C. J., & Cassell, M. D. (1998). Cortical, thalamic, and amygdaloid connections of the anterior and posterior insular cortices. *Journal of Comparative Neurology, 399*(4), 440–468.

Shimura, T., Komori, M., & Yamamoto, T. (1997). Acute sodium deficiency reduces gustatory responsiveness to NaCl in the parabrachial nucleus of rats. *Neuroscience Letters, 236*(1), 33–36.

Simon, S. A., Labarca, P., & Robb, R. (1989). Activation by saccharides of a cation-selective pathway in canine lingual epithelium. *American Journal of Physiology, 256*(Regulatory Integrative Comparative Physiology 25), R394–R402.

Small, D. M., Zald, D. H., Jones-Gotman, M., Zatorre, R. J., Pardo, J. V., Frey, S., & Petrides, M. (1999). Human cortical gustatory areas: A review of functional neuroimaging data. *NeuroReport, 10*(1), 7–14.

Smith, D. V., & Li, C.-S. (1998). Tonic GABAergic inhibition of taste-responsive neurons in the nucleus of the solitary tract. *Chemical Senses, 23,* 159–169.

Smith, D. V., & Li, C.-S. (2000). GABA-mediated corticofugal inhibition of taste-responsive neurons in the nucleus of the solitary tract. *Brain Research, 858*(2), 408–415.

Smith, D. V., Liu, H., & Vogt, M. B. (1996). Responses of gustatory cells in the nucleus of the solitary tract of the hamster after NaCl or amiloride adaptation. *Journal of Neurophysiology, 76*(1), 47–58.

Smith, D. V., St. John, S. J., & Boughter, J. D. (2000). Neuronal cell types and taste quality coding. *Physiology and Behavior, 69*(1-2), 77–85.

Spector, A. C., & Grill, H. J. (1992). Salt taste discrimination after bilateral section of the chorda tympani or glossopharyngeal nerves. *American Journal of Physiology, 263*(1, Pt. 2), R169–R176.

Spector, A. C., Markison, S., St. John, S. J., & Garcea, M. (1997). Sucrose vs. maltose taste discrimination by rats depends on the input of the seventh cranial nerve. *American Journal of Physiology, 272*(4, Pt. 2), R1210–R1218.

Spector, A. C., Redman, R., & Garcea, M. (1996). The consequences of gustatory nerve transection on taste-guided licking of sucrose and maltose in the rat. *Behavioral Neuroscience, 110*(5), 1096–1109.

Spector, A. C., Schwartz, G. J., & Grill, H. J. (1990). Chemospecific deficits in taste detection after selective gustatory deafferentation in rats. *American Journal of Physiology, 258*(3, Pt. 2), R820–R826.

Spector, A. C., Travers, S. P., & Norgren, R. (1993). Taste receptors on the anterior tongue and nasoincisor ducts of rats contribute synergistically to behavioral responses to sucrose. *Behavioral Neuroscience, 107*(4), 694–702.

Spielman, A. I. (1998). Gustducin and its role in taste. *Journal of Dental Research, 77*(4), 539–544.

Spielman, A. I., Huque, T., Nagai, H., Whitney, G., & Brand, J. G. (1994). Generation of inositol phosphates in bitter taste transduction. *Physiology and Behavior, 56*, 1149–1155.

Spielman, A. I., Huque, T., Whitney, G., & Brand, J. G. (1992). The diversity of bitter taste signal transduction mechanisms. *Society of General Physiologists Series, 47*, 307–324.

St. John, S. J., Garcea, M., & Spector, A. C. (1994). Combined, but not single, gustatory nerve transection substantially alters taste-guided licking behavior to quinine in rats. *Behavioral Neuroscience, 108*(1), 131–140.

St. John, S. J., Markison, S., & Spector, A. C. (1995). Salt discriminability is related to number of regenerated taste buds after chorda tympani nerve section in rats. *American Journal of Physiology, 269*(1, Pt. 2), R141–R153.

St. John, S. J., Markison, S., & Spector, A. C. (1997). Chorda tympani nerve transection disrupts taste aversion learning to potassium chloride, but not sodium chloride. *Behavioral Neuroscience, 111*(1), 188–194.

St. John, S. J., & Spector, A. C. (1996). Combined glossopharyngeal and chorda tympani nerve transection elevates quinine detection thresholds in rats (*Rattus norvegicus*). *Behavioral Neuroscience, 110*(6), 1456–1468.

Stern, K., & McClintock, M. K. (1998). Regulation of ovulation by human pheromones. *Nature, 392*, 177–179.

Stewart, R. E., DeSimone, J. A., & Hill, D. L. (1997). New perspectives in a gustatory physiology: Transduction, development, and plasticity. *American Journal of Physiology, 272*(1, Pt. 1), C1–C26.

Stewart, W. B., & Pedersen, P. E. (1987). The spatial organization of the olfactory nerve projections. *Brain Research, 411*, 248–258.

Strotmann, J., Wanner, I., Helfrich, T., Beck, A., & Breer, H. (1994). Rostrocaudal patterning of receptor expressing olfactory neurones in the rat nasal cavity. *Cell and Tissue Research, 278*, 11–20.

Strotmann, J., Wanner, I., Krieger, J., Raming, K., & Breer, H. (1992). Expression of odorant receptors in spatially restricted subsets of chemosensory neurones. *NeuroReport, 3*, 1053–1056.

Sugimoto, K., & Teeter, J. H. (1991). Stimulus-induced currents in isolated taste receptor cells of the larval tiger salamander. *Chemical Senses, 16*, 1109–1122.

Sweazy, R. D., & Smith, D. V. (1987). Convergence onto hamster medullary taste neurons. *Brain Research, 408*, 173–184.

Tamura, R., & Norgren, R. (1997). Repeated sodium depletion affects gustatory neural responses in the nucleus of the solitary tract of rats. *American Journal of Physiology, 273*(4, Pt. 2), R1381– R1391.

Toller, S. V. (1999). Assessing the impact of anosmia: Review of a questionnaire's findings. *Chemical Senses, 24*(6), 705–712.

Travers, J. B., Travers, S. P., & Norgren, R. (1987). Gustatory neural processing in the hindbrain. *Annual Review of Neuroscience, 10*, 595–632.

Travers, S. P., & Norgren, R. (1991). Coding the sweet taste in the nucleus of the solitary tract: Differential roles for anterior tongue and nasoincisor duct gustatory receptors in the rat. *Journal of Neurophysiology, 65*(6), 1372–1380.

Travers, S. P., & Norgren, R. (1995). Organization of orosensory responses in the nucleus of the solitary tract of rat. *Journal of Neurophysiology, 73*(6), 2144–2162.

Travers, S. P., Pfaffmann, C., & Norgren, R. (1986). Convergence of lingual and palatal gustatory neural activity in the nucleus of the solitary tract. *Brain Research, 365*, 305–320.

Vassar, R., Chao, S. K., Sitcheran, R., Nunez, J. M., Vosshall, L. B., & Axel, R. (1994). Topographic organization of sensory projections to the olfactory bulb. *Cell, 79*, 981–991.

Whitehead, M. C. (1986). Anatomy of the gustatory system in the hamster: Synaptology of facial afferent terminals in the solitary nucleus. *Journal of Comparative Neurology, 224*, 1–24.

Whitehead, M. C. (1990). Subdivisions and neuron types of the nucleus of the solitary tract that project to the parabrachial nucleus in the hamster. *Journal of Comparative Neurology, 301*(4), 554–574.

Whitehead, M. C., Bergula, A., & Holliday, K. (2000). Forebrain projections to the rostral nucleus of the solitary tract in the hamster. *Journal of Comparative Neurology, 422*(3), 429–447.

Whitehead, M. C., & Frank, M. E. (1983). Anatomy of the gustatory system in the hamster: Central projections of the chorda tympani and the lingual nerve. *Journal of Comparative Neurology, 220*, 378–395.

Whitten, W. K. (1956). Modification of oestrus cycle of mouse by external stimuli associated with the male. *Journal of Endocrinology, 13*, 399–404.

Wolf, G. (1968). Projections of thalamic and cortical gustatory areas in the rat. *Journal of Comparative Neurology, 132*, 519–530.

Wong, G. T., Gannon, K. S., & Margolskee, R. F. (1996). Transduction of bitter and sweet taste by gustducin. *Nature, 381*(6585), 796–800.

Woolston, D. C., & Erickson, R. P. (1979). Concept of neuron types in gustation in the rat. *Journal of Neurophysiology, 42*, 1390–1409.

Wysocki, C. J., Pierce, J. D., & Gilbert, A. N. (1991). Geographic, cross-cultural and individual variation in human olfaction. In T. V. Getchell, R. L. Doty, L. M. Bartoshuk, & J. B. Snow (Eds.), *Smell and taste in health and disease* (pp. 287–314). New York: Raven Press.

Yahr, P. (1977). Central control of scent marking. In D. Muller-Schwartz & M. M. Mozell (Eds.), *Chemical signals in vertebrates* (pp. 549–563). New York: Plenum Press.

Yamaguchi, S. (1991). Basic properties of umami and effects on humans. *Physiology and Behavior, 49,* 843–841.

Yamamoto, T., Azuma, S., & Kawamura, Y. (1984). Functional relations between the cortical gustatory area and the amygdala: Electrophysiological and behavioral studies in rats. *Experimental Brain Research, 56,* 23–31.

Yamamoto, T., Matsuo, R., & Kawamura, Y. (1980). Corticofugal effects on the activity of thalamic taste cells. *Brain Research, 193,* 258–262.

Yamamoto, T., & Yuyama, N. (1987). On a neural mechanism for cortical processing of taste quality in the rat. *Brain Research, 400*(2), 312–320.

Yamamoto, T., Yuyama, N., Kato, T., & Kawamura, Y. (1985). Gustatory responses of cortical neurons in rats: III. Neural and behavioral measures compared. *Journal of Neurophysiology, 53*(6), 1370–1386.

Yaxley, S., Rolls, E. T., & Sienkiewicz, Z. J. (1990). Gustatory responses of single neurons in the insula of the macaque monkey. *Journal of Neurophysiology, 63*(4), 689–700.

Ylikoski, J., Gamoletti, R., & Galey, F. (1983). Chorda tympani nerve fibers in man. *Acta Otolaryngologica, 95*(3-4), 291–296.

Yokoi, M., Mori, K., & Nakanishi, S. (1995). Refinement of odor molecule tuning by dendrodendritic synaptic inhibition in the olfactory bulb. *Proceedings of the National Academy of Sciences, USA, 92,* 3371–3375.

Youngentob, S. L., Kent, P. F., Sheehe, P. R., Schwob, J. E., & Tzoumaka, E. (1995). Mucosal inherent activity patterns in the rat: Evidence from voltage sensitive dyes. *Journal of Neurophysiology, 73,* 387–398.

Youngentob, S. L., Markert, L. M., Mozell, M. M., & Hornung, D. E. (1990). A method for establishing a five odorant identification confusion matrix in rats. *Physiology and Behavior, 47,* 1053–1059.

Zhao, H., Ivic, L., Otaki, J. M., Hashimoto, M., Mikoshiba, K., & Firestein, S. (1998). Functional expression of a mammalian odorant receptor. *Science, 279,* 237–242.

CHAPTER 11

Food and Fluid Intake

TIMOTHY H. MORAN AND RANDALL R. SAKAI

Ingestive behaviors play primary roles in the maintenance of fluid homeostasis and energy balance. Feeding and drinking are intermittent behaviors that both renew and anticipate depletions. Their controls are complex and redundant. Early views of homeostasis focused on physiological mechanisms in the body for maintaining constant internal states. Claude Bernard (1859) and Walter Cannon (1932) put forth the concept of homeostasis as the maintenance of the internal milieu within fixed limits through the coordination of controlled physiological processes. Although Bernard and Cannon recognized a role for behavior in these processes, Curt Richter (1943) expanded the view of physiological defenses of the internal milieu to include behavior as a major regulating factor. For Richter, the role of behavioral regulators in homeostasis was broadly conceived and studied. A focus on the behavior itself has revealed that both food intake and water intake have multiple levels of control that interact to ensure that the body has adequate hydration and energy stores.

In the following sections we focus on the major physiological systems involved in the controls of food and fluid intake, identify the systems that monitor available nutrient and hydrational stores, discuss systems that respond to the consequences of food and fluid intake, and identify how interactions among these systems produce behavioral outcomes that result in adequate and appropriate food and fluid intake.

FOOD INTAKE AND ENERGY BALANCE

What and how much we eat depend on a wide variety of factors. These include factors related to palatability or taste, learning, social and cultural influences, environmental factors, and physiological controls. The relative contributions of these many factors to feeding control vary across species and testing situations. We concentrate on the roles of three interacting systems important in feeding control. These are systems that mediate (a) signals related to metabolic state, especially to the degree of adiposity; (b) affective signals related to taste and nutritional consequences that serve to reinforce aspects of ingestive behavior; and (c) signals that arise within an individual meal and produce satiety. We also identify the important interactions among these systems that permit the overall regulation of energy balance.

Metabolic Signals and Their Mediation

A role for signals related to the availability of energy stores in the control of food intake has long been postulated. Depletion-repletion models tied to carbohydrate availability (Mayer, 1953) and fat stores (Kennedy, 1953) have been proposed. Although neither of these individual models is sufficient to explain the multiple variations in food intake that occur throughout the life cycle, evidence for food intake controls that depend upon monitoring fuel availability and utilization is strong. Administration of metabolic inhibitors that act on differing metabolic pathways stimulate food intake. For example, treatment with either 2-deoxy-D-methyl glucose (2-DG), which inhibits glucose utilization, or methyl palmoxirate, which suppresses fatty acid oxidation, stimulates food intake in satiated animals. Sites of action in both the liver and brain have been identified (Ji, Graczyk-Milbrandt, & Friedman, 2000; Ritter, Dinh, & Zhang, 2000).

Alterations in circulating glucose have been tied to meal initiation in both rats and humans. Campfield and colleagues have shown that transient declines and partial restorations in blood glucose levels reliably predict meal initiation (Campfield & Smith, 1986; Melanson, Westerterp-Plantenga, Saris, Smith, & Campfield, 1999). Demonstrations that experimentally induced declines in blood glucose can result in meal initiation suggest that the relationship may be more than correlational (Smith & Campfield, 1993).

Studies of genetic obesity models had long suggested the importance of circulating factors in overall body weight control. Having identified two different mutations in mice that led to obesity, Coleman (1973) conducted parabiotic experiments involving two strains of obese (obese, ob/ob, and diabetic, db/db) and normal mice in which the blood supply between the two mice in a parabiotic pair was shared. The results showed that when paired with db/db mice, ob/ob mice became hypoglycemic, lost weight, and eventually died—a similar response to that seen in normal mice combined with db/db mice. In contrast, when combined with normal mice, ob/ob mice gained less weight than they otherwise would but were fully viable. The results led Coleman to conclude that the ob/ob mouse lacked a circulating satiety factor that, in its absence, results in hyperphagia and obesity whereas the db/db mouse produced the factor but lacked the ability to respond appropriately to it.

The positional cloning of leptin as the product of the ob gene (Zhang et al., 1994) and subsequent identification of the leptin receptor as the product of the db gene (Chua et al., 1996; Tartaglia et al., 1995) has provided the basis for Coleman's observations. Leptin not only normalizes food intake and body weight in ob/ob mice but also reduces food intake in normal mice and rats (Campfield, Smith, Guisez, Devos, & Burn, 1995; Seeley et al., 1996). Leptin is produced in white adipose tissue, and circulating leptin levels correlate positively with adipose mass as animals and humans become obese (Maffei et al., 1995). Thus, leptin signals the availability of body energy stores.

Leptin is currently viewed as the major adiposity factor important for the long-term control of energy balance. Leptin receptors are members of the cytokine-receptor superfamily. Multiple leptin receptor isoforms that arise from differential

splicing have been identified. The predominant form of the leptin receptor is the short form (Ob-Ra), which is widely expressed in multiple areas including the choroid plexus and brain microvasculature (Bjorbaek et al., 1998). These binding sites are likely to function as a part of a saturable transport system for circulating leptin to gain access into the brain. The long form of the leptin receptor (Ob-Rb) can activate Janus kinase (JAK) signal transduction and signal transducers and activators of transcription (STAT) elements to mediate leptin's cellular actions (Bjorbaek, Uotoni, da Silva, & Flier, 1997). Ob-Rb is highly expressed within hypothalamic nuclei with identified roles in energy balance. Highest concentrations of the long form of the leptin receptor are found within the arcuate, paraventricular, and dorsomedial hypothalamic nuclei as well as within the lateral hypothalamus (LH; Elmquist, Bjorbaek, Ahima, Flier, & Saper, 1998). Interactions of leptin with Ob-Rb receptors within these hypothalamic nuclei result in the activation or inactivation of hypothalamic pathways containing various orexigenic and anorexigenic peptides (M. W. Schwartz, Seeley, Campfield, Burn, & Baskin, 1996).

Hypothalamic Systems Involved in Food Intake

The role of the hypothalamus in food intake control was established through the classic experiments of Heatherington and Ranson (1940) and Anand and Brobesck (1951). Using stereotaxically placed lesions, they demonstrated that bilateral lesions of the medial hypothalamus resulted in hyperphagia and obesity whereas lesions of the LH produced profound anorexia and weight loss. Subsequent work demonstrated that stimulation of these hypothalamic regions had the opposite effects. Medial hypothalamic stimulation inhibited food intake whereas stimulation of the LH produced food intake. Results such as these led Stellar (1954) to propose the classic dual center hypothesis for the role of the hypothalamus in food intake. The ventromedial region (VMH) was viewed as a satiety center, and the LH was viewed as a feeding center.

The roles of various hypothalamic nuclei in food intake are now much better understood, and many of the peptide neurotransmitters through which these actions are mediated have been identified. Table 11.1 depicts the variety of the

TABLE 11.1   Hypothalamic Peptides That Affect Food Intake

Orexigenic	Anorexigenic
Neuropeptide Y (NPY)	Alpha-melanocyte stimulating hormone (α-MSH)
Agouti-related protein (AgRP)	
Galanin	Corticotrophin-releasing hormone (CRH)
Orexins or hypocretins	Urocortin
Melanin concentrating hormone (MCH)	Cocaine and amphetamine regulated transcript (CART)

hypothalamic peptides that have effects on food intake. These may be broadly classified as falling into two categories: orexigenic, or those that stimulate or increase food intake, and anorexigenic, or those that decrease food intake.

Among the orexigenic peptides, the one that has received the most attention is neuropeptide Y (NPY). Intracerebroventricular or direct hypothalamic injection of NPY potently stimulates feeding (Clark, Kalra, Crowley, & Kalra, 1984; Morley, Levine, Gosnell, Kneip, & Grace, 1987; Stanley, Krykouli, Lampert, & Leibowitz, 1986), and repeated or chronic NPY administration results in obesity (Stanley et al., 1986; Zarjevski, Cusin, Vetter, Rohner-Jeanrenaud, & Jeanrenaud, 1993). Hypothalamic NPY gene expression and secretion increase in response to food deprivation (Kalra, Dube, Sahu, Phelps, & Kalra, 1991; White & Kershaw, 1989) or exercise (Lewis et al., 1993) and decrease in response to overconsumption of a highly palatable high-energy diet (Widdowson et al., 1999). Cell bodies of neurons expressing NPY are found in multiple hypothalamic nuclei including the arcuate and dorsomedial hypothalamic nuclei (Chornwall et al., 1985). Important projection sites for these neurons in mediating the feeding stimulatory actions of NPY are the paraventricular nucleus and perifornical region of the LH (Stanley & Leibowitz, 1985; Stanley, Magdalin, Seirafi, Thomas, & Leibowitz, 1993). Whereas chronic treatment with NPY results in obesity, absence of NPY or its receptors does not result in the absence of food intake or wasting. Murine knockout models that do not express NPY or NPY receptors are viable (Erikson, Clegg, & Palmiter, 1996; Marsh, Hollopeter, Kafer, & Palmiter, 1998; Pedrazzini et al., 1998). Rather than suggesting that NPY does not play a role in food intake control and energy balance, these results should be interpreted as suggesting that there are multiple redundant systems available for stimulating food intake and that the absence of one is not sufficient to block this critical behavior significantly.

Other hypothalamic orexigenic peptides have been identified and their roles in food intake investigated. These include galanin, hypocretin 1 and 2 (also known as orexin A and B) and melanin concentrating hormone (MCH). Galanin stimulates food intake following either intraventricular or hypothalamic administration (Crawley et al., 1990; Kyrkouli, Stanley, & Leibowitz, 1986). Galanin levels and mRNA expression are elevated in rats consuming a high-fat diet but do not appear to be affected by food deprivation (Beck, Burlet, Nicolas, & Burlet, 1993; Mercer, Lawrence, & Atkinson, 1996). Whereas galanin antagonists block the actions of exogenous galanin on food intake, little effect of the antagonists alone have been demonstrated (Crawley, 1999).

Hypocretin 1 and 2 (i.e., orexin A and B) are recently identified peptides that are coded from same prepro-mRNA

(Sakurai et al., 1998). Both compounds increase food intake when centrally administered, but orexin A is much more potent (Sakurai et al., 1998; Sweet, Levine, Billington, & Kotz, 1999). Orexin-containing neurons are found in the perifornical area of the hypothalamus and project throughout the hypothalamus (Peyron et al., 1998). Prepro-orexin expression is increased in response to deprivation (Lopez et al., 2000), and administration of an orexin A antagonist has been demonstrated to inhibit food intake, suggesting a role for endogenous orexin A in food intake control (Haynes et al., 2000).

Intraventricular MCH administration increases food intake in a dose-related fashion in short-term tests but does not alter 24-hr food intake, and chronic administration does not result in significant weight gain (Rossi et al., 1997). MCH expression is increased in obesity, and levels are modulated by fasting (Qu et al., 1996). MCH neurons in the LH are a distinct population from those expressing hypocretin/orexin; like orexin neurons, however, they are innervated by arcuate nucleus NPY-containing fibers (Broberger, DeLecea, Sutcliffe, & Hokfelt, 1998).

Endogenous melanocortins have both feeding-stimulatory and feeding-inhibitory actions. Pro-opiomelanocortin (POMC) is the precursor for a variety of peptides. Among these is the anorexigenic peptide alpha-melanocyte stimulating hormone (-MSH). Central administration of -MSH or synthetic melanocortin agonists potently inhibits food intake (Benoit et al., 2000; Fan, Boston, Kesterson, Hruby, & Cone, 1997). The feeding inhibitory actions of central melanocortins are mediated primarily through interactions with the melanocortin-4 (MC-4) receptors. Within the hypothalamus, POMC expression is limited to the arcuate nucleus. Arcuate POMC expression decreases with food deprivation (Kim, Welch, Grace, Billington, & Levine, 1996) and increases with overfeeding (Hagan et al., 1999), suggesting a regulatory role for this peptide in feeding control. Important roles for melanocortin signaling in energy balance are demonstrated in experiments examining the effects of POMC (Yaswen, Diehl, Brennan, & Hochgeschwender, 1999) or MC-4 receptor (Huszar et al., 1997) knockouts. Unlike many other peptide-signaling systems that affect food intake, the melanocortin system has an endogenous receptor antagonist that is orexigenic. Agouti-related protein (AgRP) is localized to the arcuate nucleus, and its expression is up-regulated by fasting (Hahn, Breininger, Baskin, & Schwartz, 1998). AgRP or synthetic melanocortin antagonists increase food intake when administered centrally, and their effects are long lasting (Fan et al., 1997).

Other hypothalamic anorexigenic peptides have been identified. These include corticotrophin-releasing hormone

(CRH), urocortin, and cocaine and amphetamine regulated transcript (CART). Central administration of each of these peptides decreases food intake. The expression of each is decreased in response to food deprivation and increased in states of positive energy balance.

A number of these hypothalamic orexigenic and anorexigenic peptides have been implicated in the actions of leptin. Thus, a primary site of leptin action is within the arcuate nucleus. Ob-Rb receptors are localized to two distinct arcuate nucleus neuronal populations. Within the medial arcuate, Ob-Rb is expressed in cells that also express the orexigenic peptides NPY and AgRP. In more lateral aspects of the arcuate, Ob-Rb is expressed in cells containing the anorexigenic peptides CART and the anorexigenic peptide precursor POMC. Leptin up-regulates POMC- and CART-containing neurons and down-regulates NPY- and AgRP-containing neurons resulting in increased anorexigenic and decreased orexigenic activity (Kristensen et al., 1998; M. J. Schwartz et al., 1996, 1997). Leptin also affects the activity of MCH (Sahu, 1998), orexins (Beck & Richy, 1999) and CRH (van Dijk et al., 1999), down-regulating the expression of the orexigenic peptides and up-regulating the activity of CRH. Thus, as shown in Table 11.2, many of these hypothalamic signaling pathways are responsive to the overall level of adiposity as reflected by circulating leptin levels.

Although leptin is the adiposity signal that has received the most attention, insulin also acts in the hypothalamus as an adiposity signal. Insulin is secreted from pancreatic beta cells rather than adipose tissue. However, insulin levels increase with increased adiposity in response to growing insulin resistance. Insulin is transported from the circulation into the brain, and insulin receptors are localized to the hypothalamus with a high concentration in the arcuate nucleus (Corp et al., 1986). Central insulin inhibits food intake (Woods, Lotter, McKay, & Porte, 1979) and decreases NPY mRNA expression (M. W. Schwartz et al., 1992).

Whereas the hypothalamus has been the main focus of study for anorexigenic and orexigenic peptides, a number of these also have ingestive effects when delivered to the dorsal hindbrain. Thus, fourth-cerebroventricular administration of NPY (Corp, Melville, Greenberg, Gibbs, & Smith, 1990) or a melanocortin antagonist (Grill, Ginsburg, Seeley, & Kaplan, 1998) potently increases food intake, whereas a melanocortin agonist (Grill et al., 1998), CART (Aja, Sahandy, Ladenheim, Schwartz, & Moran, 2001), and urocortin (Grill, Markison, Ginsberg, & Kaplan, 2000) inhibit food intake when administered at this site. These hindbrain actions suggest that the central feeding regulatory system is a distributed one. How these hindbrain and hypothalamic systems interact with one another remains to be determined.

The Role of Reward in Food Intake Control

Taste and palatability play major roles in dietary choices and in the amount of a particular food that is consumed. The effects of taste on ingestion are best demonstrated under conditions in which the feedback effects of postingestional consequences are minimized. A number of paradigms that specifically assess the effects of palatability on ingestion have been commonly used. The first of these is the sham feeding paradigm in which animals have an esophageal or gastric fistula so that consumed liquid nutrients drain out of the fistula and do not accumulate in the stomach. Such a preparation was first employed by Pavlov (1910). Pavlov demonstrated that dogs with open esophageal fistulas did not develop satiety but continued to eat for hours. The sham feeding paradigm has clearly demonstrated the important role of orosensory stimuli in ingestion. Increasing the concentration of saccharide solutions or oil emulsions increases the amount consumed in a linear fashion over extensive concentration ranges (Grill & Kaplan, 1992; Mook, 1963; Weingarten & Watson, 1982).

A second method for assessing the effects of palatability on ingestion involves examining rates of ingestion when access is limited to a brief time period or examining ingestion rates at the very beginning of an ingestive bout. Both of these allow ingestion to be monitored at times during which the inhibitory effects of postoral feedback are minimized. In such tests, increasing concentrations of sugars or adding saccharin to sugar solutions can be shown to produce more rapid rates of licking in rats (Breslin, Davis, & Rosenak, 1996; Davis & Levine, 1977).

The effects of palatability on ingestion have both opioid and dopaminergic mediations. It has long been known that opiate agonists can increase feeding whereas antagonists decrease food intake. The effects of opioid ligands on ingestion appear to occur through alterations in palatability. Morphine enhances the intake of preferred over nonpreferred diets (Gosnell, Krahn, & Majchrzak, 1990) and enhances hedonic responses to sweet solutions as measured in taste reactivity tests (Doyle, Berridge, & Gosnell, 1993). In contrast, administration of the opiate antagonist naloxone specifically

TABLE 11.2 Leptin's Effects on Hypothalamic Orexigenic and Anorexigenic Peptides

Leptin Down-Regulates	Leptin Up-Regulates
NPY	POMC
AgRP	CART
MCH	CRH
Orexin	

reduces the intake of a preferred diet while not affecting the intake of a nonpreferred diet in a choice paradigm in 24-hr deprived rats (Glass et al., 1996).

Although there has been significant interest in the hypothesis that opioids specifically affect the intake of fats deriving from studies demonstrating specific increases or decreases in fat intake with morphine or naloxone in nutrient self-selection paradigms (Marks-Kaufman & Kanarek, 1990), analyses of baseline nutrient preferences have indicated that morphine stimulates fat intake in fat-preferring rats and carbohydrate intake in carbohydrate-preferring rats (Gosnell et al., 1990). Such results have led to the conclusion that opioid effects on macronutrient selection and overall food intake are mediated through their actions in modulating food reward (Glass, Billington, & Levine, 2000).

Dopaminergic mediation of aspects of palatability has also been documented. Low doses of dopamine agonists increase food intake (Sills & Vaccarino, 1996), and animals with severe neurotoxin-induced dopamine depletions (Ungerstedt, 1971) or dopamine deficiency through gene knockout (Zhou & Palmiter, 1995) fail to consume food independently. Feeding increases extracellular dopamine within the nucleus accumbens, and the increase is greater with the consumption of a highly palatable food (Martel & Fantino, 1996), suggesting a specific role for mesolimbic dopamine in mediating food reward. A specific role for dopamine in signaling the incentive value of foods is also supported by work with dopamine antagonists. Dopamine antagonists potently reduce the sham intake of palatable diets. An ID_{50} dose of the dopamine 2 (D2) antagonist raclopride produces the same effect on both overall intake and the microstructure of licking as does halving the sucrose concentration (Schneider, Davis, Watson, & Smith, 1990). The consumption of 10% sucrose with raclopride resembles the consumption of 5% sucrose without antagonist pretreatment. Such data have been interpreted as suggesting that dopamine plays a critical role in the hedonic processing of orosensory stimuli. However, unlike opioids that can be shown to shift the hedonic response to ingestants in taste reactivity tests, dopamine antagonists suppress both hedonic and aversive responses (Pecina, Berridge, & Parker, 1997), suggesting alterations in intake through a change in sensorimotor responses rather than through a shift in taste palatability. Such data have been interpreted to suggest that dopaminergic antagonists reduce ingestion of palatable diets by affecting the incentive salience rather than by shifting the hedonic value of palatable diets.

The nutrient consequences of ingestion can also serve to reinforce dietary choice. This is best demonstrated in experiments that pair a novel taste with an intragastric nutrient infusion. Rats prefer the taste that has been associated with

intragastric nutrient (Bolles, Hayward, & Crandall, 1981; Sclafani, 1991). Such nutrient conditioning has been demonstrated with simple and complex carbohydrates (Elizalde & Sclafani, 1990; Perez, Lucas, & Sclafani, 1998), proteins (Perez, Ackroff, & Sclafani, 1996), and fats (Lucas & Sclafani, 1989). Although the phenomena of flavor conditioning are well documented, the neural mediation is not well understood. There is some evidence that such preference conditioning can alter the taste responses to the paired flavor at the level of the nucleus of the solitary tract (Giza, Ackroff, McCaughey, Sclafani, & Scott, 1997). However, these effects are relatively weak. Potential opioid mediation of nutrient conditioning has also been investigated. The opioid antagonist naltrexone fails to block either the acquisition or the expression of a flavor preference conditioned by intragastric nutrients (Azzara, Bodnar, Delameter, & Sclafani, 2000), arguing for a nonopioid mediation of nutrient conditioning.

Satiety Signaling

In many species, including humans, food intake occurs in distinct bouts or meals. Meal initiation is determined by a variety of factors, especially food availability. During a meal, ingested nutrients contact a variety of receptors within the oral cavity and gastrointestinal tract, resulting in neural and hormonal signals that contribute to the determination of meal size. Meal size can be highly variable, and alterations in meal size appear to be a major determinant of overall food intake.

Taste plays an important role in determining meal size. Palatable or good-tasting substances are consumed more rapidly and in greater amounts than are unpalatable foods. Analyses of patterns of sham feeding not only have demonstrated effects of palatability on ingestion but also have revealed pregastric contributions to satiety. Sham feeding does eventually stop, and a number of processes have been proposed to contribute to the cessation of sham feeding, including oral metering (Mook, 1990), habituation (Swithers & Hall, 1994), and sensory-specific satiety (decreasing pleasantness of a specific food as more is ingested; B. J. Rolls, 1986). The amount that is sham fed depends also on the experience of the animal with the sham feeding paradigm. Although the rats' intakes double the first time that they sham feed, continued experience with sham feeding significantly increases intake over the next three or four tests. These data demonstrate the presence of a conditioned inhibition on food intake that is due to an association of the oral stimulation with postingestive negative feedback. Only with continued experience is this conditioned inhibition on intake overcome (Davis & Smith, 1990; Weingarten & Kulikovsky, 1989).

In normal ingestion, consumed nutrients contact mechano- and chemosensitive receptors that provide feedback information to the brain that is important to the control of meal size. The potential range of feedback mechanism that could be operating to lead to meal termination is dependent on the distribution of ingested nutrients during the meal. Kaplan, Spector, and Grill (1992) demonstrated in the rat that when the stomach is filled at rates mimicking normal ingestion rates, gastric emptying during the period of gastric fill is much more rapid than following fill, occurs at a constant rate for the duration of the fill period, and is not affected by nutrient concentration. Similar results were found whether the meal was infused or ingested by the rat (Kaplan, Seimers, & Grill, 1997). These data demonstrate that a significant portion of ingested nutrients (in the rat as much as 30%) enters the duodenum, contacts duodenal receptors, and is available for absorption. Similar dynamics of gastric emptying during fill have been demonstrated in rhesus monkeys; however, although volume is a main determinant, nutrient concentration also plays a significant role (Moran, Knipp, & Schwartz, 1999). Thus, the stomach and a significant proportion of the upper intestine are potential sites for within-meal generation of feedback signals.

The vagus nerve (Xth cranial nerve) is the major neuroanatomical link between the gastrointestinal tract and the brain. Vagal afferent fibers with cell bodies in the nodose ganglion arise from the digestive organs and project to the nucleus of the solitary tract (NTS) with a rough viscerotopic representation of the alimentary canal (Altschuler, Bao, Bieger, Hopkins, & Miselis, 1989). The response properties of vagal afferents depend in part on the target organ from which they arise. Although there are also significant spinal gut neural connections, the response properties of this system have not been well characterized.

Mechanosensitive gastric vagal afferents increase their firing in response to increasing gastric load volume. Slowly adapting mechanoreceptive fibers increase their response rate with increasing gastric volume (Andrews, Grundy, & Scratcherd, 1980). The fibers remain active while load volume is retained and show an off response in which activity briefly drops below baseline levels when the load volume is removed. Individual afferents are differentially tuned such that there are differences in their dynamic ranges (G. J. Schwartz, McHugh, & Moran, 1993). Some afferents reach their maximal activity at small intragastric volumes, whereas others do not begin to respond until a significant gastric load is present. Gastric mechanoreceptive vagal afferents do not respond directly to the chemical character of the gastric load. Response rate is similarly increased by nutrient and nonnutrient load volumes that are restricted to the stomach by a pyloric noose (Mathis, Moran, & Schwartz, 1998).

Duodenal vagal afferents are activated by both intraluminal load volume and nutrient character. Slowly adapting mechanoreceptive fibers in the duodenum have been identified. Similar to gastric mechanoreceptive fibers, activity increases with increases in load volume. Duodenal vagal afferents are also directly responsive to nutrient character. For example, both intestinal casein (Eastwood, Maubach, Kirkup, & Grundy, 1998) or lipid infusions (Randich et al., 2000) increase vagal afferent activity. Although gastric vagal activity is not directly responsive to intragastric nutrient character, gastric afferent responsivity can be altered by duodenal nutrient (G. J. Schwartz & Moran, 1998). Thus, gastric vagal afferent activity is modulated in the presence of duodenal nutrients.

These alterations in vagal afferent activity may reflect the actions of duodenal nutrient-induced release of gastrointestinal (GI) peptides. For example, the brain-gut peptide cholecystokinin (CCK) is released by the duodenal presence of nutrient digestion products. Local arterial CCK administration results in increases in vagal gastric mechanoreceptive afferent activity similar to those produced by intragastric load (G. J. Schwartz, McHugh, & Moran, 1991). Combinations of gastric load and CCK produce greater degrees of activity than either alone (G. J. Schwartz et al., 1991). CCK also modifies responses to subsequent intragastric load such that load volume results in greater degrees of activity following CCK administration than prior to it even at times when the initial response has disappeared (G. J. Schwartz et al., 1993). Duodenal vagal afferents also are activated by CCK; combinations of load and CCK combine to produce greater duodenal vagal afferent activity than either alone, and CCK affects the response to subsequent load volumes (G. J. Schwartz, Tougas, & Moran, 1995). CCK also plays a role in the response of duodenal afferents to nutrients. Administration of a CCK antagonist blocks the increase in vagal afferent activity produced by intraduodenal casein (Eastwood et al., 1998).

CCK-induced changes in gastric vagal afferent activity appear to result from a direct action of the peptide on the vagal afferent fibers. Vagal afferents contain CCK receptors (Moran, Norgren, Crosby, & McHugh, 1990), and CCK induces decreases in intragastric pressure that would not be expected to result in a secondary increase in vagal afferent activity (G. J. Schwartz, Moran, White, & Ladenheim, 1997). In contrast, gastrin-releasing peptide (GRP) induced increases in gastric vagal activity appear to be secondary to local peptide-induced changes in gastric motility. GRP increases gastric wall tension and intragastric pressure, and the increases in vagal afferent activity are correlated with these changes. In addition, GRP receptors are not found on vagal afferents (G. J. Schwartz et al., 1997).

Elimination of aspects of vagal afferent or peptide-induced feedback can result in significant alterations in the way that rats pattern their food intake. Surgical vagal deafferentation results in alterations in meal patterns in rats maintained on liquid diet in that such rats consume larger, less frequent meals than do sham-operated controls (G. J. Schwartz, Salorio, Skoglund, & Moran, 1999). Meal frequency is reduced in response to these increases in meal size such that overall food intake is unchanged. Similar alterations in meal size have been reported in response to capsaicin-induced chemical deafferentation. Following capsaicin treatment, rats consume larger meals on a novel diet (Chavez, Kelly, York, & Berthoud, 1997) or with calorically dilute sucrose access (Kelly, Morales, Smith, & Berthoud, 2000). These data demonstrate a role for vagal afferent feedback in the controls of meal size.

Peripheral Peptide Satiety Signaling

A number of peripherally acting peptides with roles in the controls of food intake have been identified. The best characterized of these is the brain-gut peptide CCK. Exogenously administered CCK was originally demonstrated to decrease food intake in rats (Gibbs, Young, & Smith, 1973). This feeding-inhibitory action of CCK and CCK agonists has been demonstrated in a variety of species including humans and nonhuman primates (Moran & McHugh, 1982; Pi-Sunyer et al., 1982). Exogenously administered CCK reduces meal size and results in an earlier appearance of a behavioral satiety sequence (Antin, Gibbs, Holt, Young, & Smith, 1975). A role for CCK in the control of the size of individual meals was confirmed by experiments examining the effects of repeated, meal-contingent CCK administration. CCK consistently reduced meal size without producing a significant change in overall daily food intake (West, Fey, & Woods, 1984).

The satiety actions of CCK depend on interactions with multiple receptor sites. CCK-A receptors, the receptor subtype through which the satiety actions of CCK are mediated, are found on vagal afferent fibers and on circular muscle cells within the pyloric sphincter. As discussed earlier, CCK activates vagal afferents. Surgical or chemical disruption of subdiaphragmatic vagal afferent innervation significantly affects the ability of CCK to inhibit food intake (Ritter & Ladenheim, 1985; Smith, Jerome, & Norgren, 1985; Moran, Baldessarini, Solorio, Lowerry, & Schwartz, 1997). The nature of this disruption is a reduction in CCK's potency. Low doses of CCK that inhibit food intake in intact rats are ineffective following vagal afferent lesions. Higher doses inhibit intake but to a smaller degree. In contrast, surgical removal of the pyloric sphincter does not affect the ability of low

doses of CCK to inhibit intake but truncates the dose-effect curve such that the additional suppression that normally accompanies higher CCK doses is eliminated (Moran, Shnayder, Hostetler, & McHugh, 1988). Results such as these have led to the proposal that the satiety actions of CCK are multifaceted and are, in part, secondary to its local gastrointestinal effects (Moran & McHugh, 1992).

A role for endogenous CCK in satiety is supported by data demonstrating that administration of CCK antagonists with specificity for the CCK-A receptor results in increases in food intake (Moran, Ameglio, Peyton, Schwartz, & McHugh, 1993; Reidelberger & O'Rourke, 1989). In the primate, the effects have been demonstrated to be dose related with a maximum increase of around 40% in daily food intake in monkeys with 4-hr daily food access. This increase is almost completely accounted for by an increase in the size of their first meal (Moran et al., 1993). Alterations in meal patterns are also evident in rats lacking CCK-A receptors. Otsuka Long Evans Tokushima Fatty (OLETF) rats have been demonstrated to have approximately a 6-kb (kilobase) deletion in the CCK-A receptor gene spanning the promotor region and the first and second exons. This deletion prevents protein expression resulting in a CCK-A receptor knockout rat (Takiguchi et al., 1997). OLETF rats are obese and hyperphagic. Characterization of their spontaneous solid food intake has revealed a 35% increase in daily food intake resulting from a 78% increase in meal size combined with an insufficient decrease in meal frequency. Similar results are obtained when OLETF rats are maintained on liquid diet. Meal size, expressed as the number of licks, is increased by 93% (Moran, Katz, Plata-Salaman, & Schwartz, 1998).

Satiety actions have also been demonstrated for the mammalian bombesin-like peptides GRP and neuromedin-B (NMB). These peptides reduce food intake following peripheral exogenous administration (Gibbs, Fauser, Rowe, Rolls, & Maddison, 1979; Ladenheim, Taylor, Coy, & Moran, 1994; Stein & Woods, 1982). Bombesin is the most potent—an effect that can be best explained by its high affinity for both GRP and NMB receptors. Bombesin activates both mammalian pathways and produces an effect similar in magnitude to combined GRP and NMB administration (Ladenheim, Wirth, & Moran, 1996). Both vagal and spinal afferents contribute to the mediation of the satiety actions of abdominal bombesin-like peptides. Either combined vagotomy, dorsal rhizotomy, and cord section or neonatal capsaicin administration are necessary to abolish the effects of bombesin on food intake (Stuckey, Gibbs, & Smith, 1985; Michaud, Anisman, & Merali, 1999). Bombesin-like peptides also inhibit food intake following central administration, and the site of action for this effect is within the caudal hindbrain (F. W. Flynn, 1989;

Ladenheim & Ritter, 1988). There does appear to be a relationship between the central and peripheral actions of these peptides because central antagonist administration can block the effect of peripherally administered peptides (Ladenheim, Taylor, Coy, Moore, & Moran, 1996). Such results suggest the possibility that peripherally administered bombesin-like peptides may exert some of their actions through a central site.

A role for endogenous mammalian bombesin-like peptides in satiety is supported by data demonstrating increases in food intake following antagonist administration. Central GRP (F. W. Flynn, 1992; Merali, Moody, & Coy, 1993) and NMB receptor antagonists (Ladenheim et al., 1997) have been demonstrated to increase food intake in a variety of feeding paradigms. These data provide further support for a central site of action as being important for the feeding effects of bombesin-like peptides and are consistent with a role for endogenous bombesin-like peptides in the controls of meal size.

Satiety actions for the pancreatic peptides glucagon and amylin have also been demonstrated. Rapidly eating elicits an increase in pancreatic glucagon secretion (Langhans, Pantel, Muller-Schell, Effengerger, & Scharrer, 1984). Because an increase in plasma glucagon is also stimulated by sham feeding, this appears to be a cephalic phase response (Nilsson & Uvnas-Wallenstien, 1977). Glucagon is rapidly cleared from the circulation by the liver (Langhans et al., 1984), which appears to be the site of glucagon's satiety action (Geary, 1998). Hepatic-portal infusion of glucagon at meal onset elicits a dose-related reduction in meal size (Geary & Smith, 1982a), and glucagon's satiety actions have been demonstrated in human subjects (Geary, Kissileff, Pi-Sunyer, & Hinton, 1992). Glucagon's satiety action requires the presence of other forms of ingestional consequences because glucagon does not affect sham feeding (Geary & Smith, 1982b). A role for endogenous glucagon in the control of meal size is supported by data demonstrating the ability of hepatic portal infusions of glucagon antibody to increase meal size (LeSauter, Noh, & Geary, 1991).

Amylin inhibits feeding in a dose-dependent and behaviorally specific manner following either peripheral or central administration (Lutz, Geary, Szabady, Del Prete, & Scharrer, 1995; Lutz, Rossi, Althaus, Del Prete, & Scharrer, 1998). Although meal-related amylin release has not been specifically shown, amylin is obligatorily cosecreted with insulin by pancreatic beta cells (Cooper, 1994). Thus, amylin levels rise rapidly with meal onset and remain elevated for a significant period of time during and following meals. Amylin's site of action is within the area postrema, a hindbrain structure lacking a blood-brain barrier. The area postrema contains amylin receptors, and lesions of the area postrema block the feeding-inhibitory actions of peripherally administered amylin (Lutz,

Senn, et al., 1998). A physiological role for endogenous amylin in feeding controls is supported by experiments demonstrating increases in food intake in response to administration of amylin antagonists (Rushing et al., 2001).

Unlike these peptides that play roles in limiting food intake, ghrelin, a brain-gut peptide that is primarily synthesized in the stomach, has recently been shown to stimulate food intake following peripheral or central administration (Tschop, Smiley, & Heiman, 2000; Wren et al., 2000). Ghrelin synthesis and plasma ghrelin levels are increased by food deprivation and reduced by refeeding (Tschop et al., 2000). Systemic and central ghrelin administration produce c-fos activation within the arcuate nucleus (Hewson & Dickson, 2000; Nakazato et al., 2001), and central ghrelin administration increases arcuate NPY expression (Shintani et al., 2001), suggesting a hypothalamic site of action. A physiological role for ghrelin in feeding initiation or maintenance is supported by data demonstrating that ghrelin antibodies suppress food intake (Nakazato et al., 2001). Together, these data suggest a novel action for a gastric peptide in stimulating food intake.

Interactions Among Control Systems

With food intake being influenced by these seemingly separate neural systems, the question of how they interact with one another is important. A number of the clearest demonstrations of interactions involve the adiposity signal leptin. As noted earlier, leptin circulates in direct relation to the degree of adiposity serving as a feedback signal for the overall regulation of energy balance. Both peripheral and central leptin administration reduce food intake, and a number of experiments have demonstrated that leptin's effects on feeding are specific to reducing meal size without changing meal frequency (Eckel et al., 1998; M. C. Flynn, Scott, Pritchard, & Plata-Salaman, 1998; Kahler et al., 1998).

How does a signal that is critically involved in regulating hypothalamic pathways involved in energy balance result in reductions in the size of individual meals? Recent experiments have suggested multiple mechanisms through which leptin may affect food intake. Leptin's actions may depend in part on its interactions with within-meal signals. For example, central administration of leptin at doses that are subthreshold for inhibiting feeding when administered alone enhance the satiating potential of peripheral CCK or an intragastric preload (Emond, Schwartz, Ladenheim, & Moran, 2001; Emond, Schwartz, & Moran, 1999). This action of leptin appears to depend on its ability to enhance the degree of NTS neural activation produced by these peripheral manipulations. That is, leptin enhances the dorsal hindbrain representation of ascending vagal afferent feedback signals arising from CCK or gastrointestinal stimulation induced by gastric preload.

Reducing leptin levels through food deprivation has the opposite result: The satiating potency of CCK is reduced (Billington, Levine, & Morley, 1983; McMinn, Sindelar, Havel, & Schwartz, 2000). This effect may be mediated through enhanced NPY signaling because NPY administration has the opposite effect to that of leptin on both the behavioral and neural activation potencies of CCK. NPY reduces the degree of NTS activation in response to CCK (McMinn et al., 2000).

Leptin also may result in reductions in meal size through its direct actions on taste sensitivity. Leptin specifically reduces chorda tympani and glossopharyngeal sensitivity to sweet stimuli without altering responses to other tastants (Kawai, Sugimoto, Nakashima, Mura, & Ninomiya, 2000). This appears to be a direct effect at the level of the taste bud because leptin hyperpolarizes the taste cell. Finally, leptin may decrease meal size by altering the reinforcing effects of ingestion. Leptin reduces the rewarding efficacy of electrical brain stimulation (Fulton, Woodside, & Shizgal, 2000). Thus, a signal derived from fat stores serving as a long-term regulator of energy balance has multiple actions. Many of these may contribute to its reductions in food intake in ways that enhance the negative feedback effects of ingestion while also reducing the positive feedback effects. Together these actions result in consistent reductions in meal sizes that over the long term serve to constrain energy intake and contribute to overall energy balance.

Satiety signals can also affect the efficacy of adiposity signals. For example, not only does leptin enhance the potency of CCK within an individual meal situation, but also CCK enhances the leptin's ability to reduce food intake and decrease body weight over the longer term (Matson, Reid, Cannon, & Ritter, 2000; Matson & Ritter, 1999). A dose of CCK that alone has no effect on 24-hr food intake or body weight significantly increases leptin's effects on food intake and body weight. The site of action for this effect is yet to be determined, but it may be hypothalamic because in a short-term test CCK significantly enhances the leptin-induced neural activation within the paraventricular nucleus (Emond, Schwartz, & Moran, 1998).

Other kinds of interactions have also been demonstrated. As ingestion continues, the perceived pleasantness or palatability of foods can change. That is, feedback signals arising from ingestion or ingestive consequences can alter aspects of taste processing. This may occur at multiple levels of the neural axis. For example, continued consumption of a single food results in that food's being perceived as less pleasant in comparison to other nonconsumed foods. Such a phenomenon is referred to a sensory-specific satiety (B. J. Rolls, 1986). These changes are rapid and do not depend on the nutritional value of the consumed food, indicating that they likely arise from the sensory properties of the food, or on cognitive processes involved in assessing that enough of a particular type of food has been consumed. Sensory-specific satiety has been proposed to be an important mechanism for ensuring that a variety of foods are consumed, increasing the likelihood that an organism will maintain nutritional balance (B. J. Rolls, 1986). Sensory-specific satiety has a neurophysiological basis in that LH neurons that have ceased to respond to the taste of one food will respond to a different food (E. T. Rolls, Murzi, Yaxley, Thorpe, & Simpson, 1986).

Perceived pleasantness or palatability can also be reduced by gastrointestinal nutrient stimulation—a phenomena that has been termed *alliesthesia* (Cabanac, 1971). Thus, human subjects rate a sweet solution as less pleasant following a gastric glucose load (Cabanac & Fantino, 1977). Similar findings have been obtained in rats, using orofacial responses as a measure of the perceived pleasantness of taste stimuli (see Grill & Norgren, 1978). Gastric or intestinal nutrient infusions reduce the incidence of positive orofacial responses and increase the incidence of negative responses to an oral sucrose infusion (Cabanac & LaFrance, 1992). Similar results are produced by exogenous CCK, and the phenomenon is blocked by vagotomy (Cabanac & Zhao, 1994). Thus, one of the ways that within-meal negative feedback signaling affects ingestion is through a change in the perceived pleasantness of ingestive stimuli. In primates, the orbitofrontal cortex appears to be the likely neural site where such effects are mediated. Taste-evoked activity in the orbitofrontal cortex is suppressed by gastrointestinal nutrients (Scott, Yan, & Rolls, 1995).

A final example of interactions among signaling systems suggests a role for central reinforcing pathways in mediating the feeding actions of hypothalamic signaling systems. The opiate antagonist naloxone blocks the feeding stimulatory action of NPY (Kotz, Grace, Briggs, Levine, & Billington, 1995). The site of action for naloxone for this effect is within the medial subnucleus of the NTS (Kotz, Glass, Levine, & Billington, 2000). The site of action for the interaction appears to be within the amygdala. Naloxone does not affect NPY's ability to induce *c-fos* within the hypothalamic paraventricular nucleus, but both NPY and naloxone induce *c-fos* within the central nucleus of the amygdala but do so in different cellular population (Pomonis, Levine, & Billington, 1997). Together, these data suggest that neural systems normally involved in palatability-induced feeding stimulation also play a modulatory role in the feeding induced by the hypothalamic signaling system's response to adiposity stores.

Summary

The body contains multiple systems for regulating overall energy balance. These systems derive from and control different aspects of ingestive behavior and its consequences. Although adiposity, satiety, and reinforcement signaling have different primary sites of mediation within the brain, they are interacting systems that together ensure that the organism consumes an adequate amount and variety of nutrients. Although such interactions can now be demonstrated, little is known about the underlying cellular mechanisms through which they are mediated. Furthermore, how these interactions at the level of individual neurons are translated into behavioral outcomes remains to be determined. These are the two major issues currently facing investigators involved in research on the controls of food intake.

Over the past 10 years our knowledge of the brain sites and signaling systems involved in energy balance has grown exponentially. This has provided multiple targets for potential treatment development in obesity and eating disorders. A more complete understanding of how these systems respond under multiple metabolic states and interact with one another will be necessary to provide a rational base for such eventual treatment development.

WATER INTAKE AND FLUID BALANCE

The amount of water that we drink, like the amount of food that we eat, depends on a rich variety of factors that include homeostatic controls, learning and experience, and environmental social and cultural influences. Although there is ample evidence that the contribution of each of these factors is neurally mediated in the control of water intake, we concentrate here on the role of three relatively well-characterized systems that interact among themselves and that are important in the control of water balance. These three systems include, respectively, (a) neural and hormonal signals related to the detection of plasma osmolality and extracellular fluid volume that influence the initiation of bouts of ingestion, (b) neural and hormonal signals related to myriad factors that lead to satiety and thus terminate bouts of drinking, and (c) brain sites that receive and integrate these signals and that elicit appropriate physiological and behavioral responses. We also discuss the important interactions among these systems that permit overall regulation of body fluid balance.

Osmotic and Hypovolemic Signals That Stimulate Water Intake

All physiological processes occur in one or another internal sea consisting of mild salt solutions, and maintenance of the appropriate volume and concentration of the various fluid compartments in the body is essential for these processes to occur. Regulation occurs at the cellular level, enabling normal intracellular processes to occur, as well as at the level of the fluids that interconnect the cells, such that the formation and maintenance of extracellular fluid is a high priority. In this regard, maintenance of adequate blood volume is particularly essential for the delivery of nutrients to tissues and for the removal of metabolites for excretion. Thus, when body fluid balance is compromised, both physiological and behavioral responses are initiated to defend further aberrations in body fluid balance and to replenish lost body fluid stores. This could occur when fluid is shifted between compartments within the body (as in edema), when excess fluid is lost from the body (as occurs following hemorrhage or extreme vomiting), or when insufficient water and minerals are available for consumption. If water or sodium is lacking, the antidiuretic hormone arginine vasopressin (AVP) and the antinatriuretic hormone aldosterone work together to promote renal conservation of both water and sodium, thus preventing further body fluid depletion and maintaining the best possible level of osmolality. The behavioral responses of thirst and sodium appetite can also be engaged to restore lost water or salt because this is the only mechanism by which the lost fluids and electrolytes can be replaced. Both the physiological and the behavioral responses to perturbations of body fluid balance are under tight control by the brain. Although the careful balance of ingesting both water and salt is necessary for maintenance of extracellular fluid volume and concentration, this chapter focuses on the endocrine and neural controls of water intake.

Contemporary understanding of the physiology of water intake began with Andersson's (1953; Andersson & Wyrwicka, 1957) report of the elicitation of drinking following the administration of hyperosmotic solutions to the brain of goats. Although the conscious goats had no apparent interest in water under basal conditions, they drank avidly when stimulated briefly within the anterior hypothalamus by small volumes of hypertonic saline. In later experiments drinking was elicited by weak electrical currents applied to the same anatomical sites. These reports demonstrated that water intake could be elicited by direct stimulation of the brain, and they thereby challenged the prevailing view that water intake was merely a sensation or a reflexive response to reduced salivary flow produced by dehydration (Cannon, 1918). In addition, these studies heralded the modern investigation of water intake by exploring its central neural basis and its instinctive (Lashley, 1938) and motivated (Stellar, 1954) origins. In the mid 1950s and early 1960s research focused on investigations of the water intake that accompanies cellular dehydration. This concept was initially proposed by Wettendorff (1901) and then established as a mechanism of water intake by Gilman's (1937) well-known experiments demonstrating that the administration of solutes that are excluded from cells (such as sodium) elicit cellular dehydration and are consequently highly effective dipsogens.

The more molar context of current research on the neural mechanisms of water intake was not achieved until Fitzsimons (1961) established hypovolemia (reduced blood volume) as an independent stimulus for thirst. He accomplished this by eliciting water intake in rats using several experimental manipulations that all resulted in reduced blood volume (e.g., hemorrhage, ligation of the inferior vena cava, hyperoncotic colloid dialysis). It is important that all of these paradigms resulted in reduced blood volume with no change of osmolarity of the remaining plasma, and hence with no change of cell volume. This essential point has been confirmed more clearly by the work of Tang (1976), who found (a) that these treatments reduce the plasma volume of rats without altering serum electrolytes or osmolarity and (b) that drinking is suppressed if the reduction in intravascular volume is prevented by intravenous infusion of an isotonic plasma substitute. Although earlier research had suggested that the causes of thirst are necessarily complex and that changes in extracellular volume, among others, must be considered (e.g., Adolph, Barker, & Hoy, 1954), the concept that hypovolemia is a second and potent cause of water intake—that hypovolemia operates under normal conditions of dehydration and has an independent sensory system utilizing detectors of reduced blood volume—was not considered. Rather, these concepts were elaborated by Fitzsimons (see Fitzsimons, 1979, for a full review) along with the subsequent proof of concept by Stricker (1968). Together, their work demonstrated that hypovolemia lowers the threshold for the initiation of drinking, that the water intake that is generated is a function of the magnitude of the reduction in blood volume, and that hypovolemia elicits drinking with the expected properties of motivation. In addition, the pioneering studies of hypovolemia-induced water intake also revealed the role of the renin angiotensin hormone system as an important systemic system that accesses the brain and stimulates water intake (Fitzsimons, 1969). Ultimately, the demonstration that cellular dehydration and extracellular volume loss can independently elicit water intake was suggested by the *double depletion hypothesis of thirst* (Epstein, Kissileff, & Stellar, 1973). Over a lengthy series of experiments, it was demonstrated that water intake in many naturalistic situations, and especially water deprivation, could be precisely predicted by this hypothesis. The bottom line is that cellular dehydration locally in the brain and systemic hypovolemia combine to produce the urge to drink, and the concurrent restoration of each deficit results in a summative

suppression of drinking. The nature of the two depletions, the portions of the brain devoted to their regulation, and the manner of their joint function in the control of spontaneous drinking behavior directed much of the subsequent research on the physiology of water intake.

Cellular Dehydration and Brain Osmosensors

Cellular dehydration-induced water intake requires that the brain somehow detect water loss from osmosensitive or volume-sensitive cells and to generate a signal that leads to drinking. Studies in the early 1970s focused on cells within the brain that could be sensors that arouse drinking as a consequence of cellular water loss. Experiments by Peck and Novin (1971) and Blass and Epstein (1971) demonstrated that cells in the lateral preoptic area of the hypothalamus contained a large concentration of osmosensitive cells. When hyperosmotic solutions were applied locally in the vicinity of these cells, water intake was elicited. Conversely, when the cell group in the lateral preoptic area was selectively lesioned, the animals demonstrated impaired drinking stimulated by sudden increases in the osmolarity of the blood reaching the brain, whereas drinking elicited by hypovolemia remained intact.

Although more recent data have continued to support a role of the lateral preoptic area as a major osmosensitive area in the brain that elicits drinking, there remains considerable uncertainty about the location of the specific osmosensitive neurons that stimulate vasopressin secretion to promote water retention by the kidney. Candidate brain areas for these osmoreceptors are other subnuclei of the hypothalamus (including the lamina terminalis and the supraoptic nucleus) and the circumventricular organs (CVOs). The latter are implicated because they lack a blood-brain barrier and hence are sensitive to both plasma and brain interstitial osmotic influences. Further, they have axonal connections to areas that control drinking behavior.

Circumventricular Organs and Hypovolemic Water Intake

The demonstration that hypovolemia-induced intake is independent of cellular dehydration-induced intake arose from experiments in which rats drank water in response to an isotonic reduction of blood volume (Fitzsimons, 1961; Stricker, 1969; Tang, 1976). Because the osmolarity of the plasma is not increased as a function of reduced blood volume per se, the water intake cannot be attributed to dehydration of cells. The discovery of a hormonal control over this kind of drinking came from Fitzsimons's (1964, 1969) demonstrations that the kidneys must be attached to the general circulation in order for hypovolemic treatments to have their full dipsogenic effects. This was demonstrated most clearly in following caval ligation, a procedure in which the inferior vena cava is occluded, preventing the return of the blood from the abdomen and lower limbs and thus reducing cardiac output by approximately 40%. The ensuing water intake that develops is dependent on access of the kidneys to the circulation. Because nephrectomy reduces caval ligation–induced intake, Fitzsimons reasoned not only that the kidney is necessary for eliciting hypovolemia-induced water intake but also that it does so as an endocrine rather than as an exocrine organ. The subsequent identification of renin, a peptide hormone produced by the kidney, and the demonstration that its levels are the rate-limiting step in the renin-angiotensin cascade that produces a powerful dipsogenic action, completed the story (Fitzsimons & Simons, 1969). It was subsequently found that renin acts as an enzyme that causes the formation of the peptide angiotensin II in the blood and that angiotensin II in turn gains access to the brain and stimulates drinking by acting on receptors in the CVOs.

The CVO that was initially observed to be particularly sensitive to the local application of angiotensin II in terms of eliciting a dipsogenic response was the subfornical organ (SFO; Simpson & Routtenberg, 1974). Using novel neuropharmacological application techniques, Simpson and his colleagues subsequently demonstrated that the SFO is exquisitely sensitive to the dipsogenic actions of angiotensin II as well as to other known dipsogenic agents such as the cholinomimetic carbachol. That group also found that lesions of the SFO rendered animals less responsive to hypovolemic stimuli as well as to intravenously administered angiotensin II, while still being responsive to cellular dehydration–induced stimuli (Simpson, Epstein, & Camardo, 1978). Subsequently, receptors that specifically bind angiotensin II have been localized in high concentrations in the SFO as well as in other brain areas. The distribution of angiotensin II receptors in the brain is of interest because many of the brain sites that contain high concentrations of these receptors receive direct projections from the SFO and are in other areas that lack a blood-brain barrier (Mendelsohn, Quirion, Saavedra, Aguiler, & Catt, 1984; Miselis, 1981).

The activation of these additional brain sites by angiotensin II is thought to occur by endogenous angiotensin II that is centrally generated because all of the components that are required to produce angiotensin II are present within the brain (Ganten, Hutchinson, Schelling, Ganten, & Fischer, 1975). Subsequent pharmacological studies have now revealed that there are at least two subtypes of angiotensin II receptors, designated angiotensin AT1 and AT2 receptors.

Although both receptor subtypes bind the native ligand angiotensin II with equal affinity, they differ in their amino acid sequences by over 70%. Based on this, the synthesis of nonpeptidergic ligands for each receptor subtype has become possible, and it is now recognized that the two receptors differ in binding affinity for these novel ligands and engage different second-messenger signaling systems once activated. Due in part to the widespread interest in these receptor subtypes in the control of various physiological functions, both AT1 and AT2 receptors have been cloned and sequenced. Subsequent research utilizing specific antisense oligodeoxynucleotide sequences has allowed both in vitro and in vivo receptor knockdown of each angiotensin receptor subtype. The bottom line from many experiments is that over 95% of the biological actions of angiotensin II appear to be mediated through its binding at the AT1 receptor. The physiological role of activation of the AT2 receptor subtype remains unclear. In sum, the SFO is a major site of action for peripherally generated angiotensin II in response to hypovolemia. The stimulation of the SFO, an area that contains high concentrations of angiotensin AT1 receptors, by systemic angiotensin II may also trigger the central angiotensin system to stimulate drinking as well as other physiological responses (such as the release of vasopressin) to maintain fluid homeostasis in response to hypovolemia.

Satiety Signals for Water Intake

The intake of water, like the intake of food, is under the control of diverse signals, some of which initiate the behavior and others of which stop it (i.e., *satiety signals*). Unlike the well-described satiety signals that terminate feeding, however, the satiety signals that terminate drinking are much less clear. A thirsty animal allowed the opportunity to drink water will rapidly consume sufficient water to restore the lost fluids. Although the animal may ingest a large quantity of fluid, satiation generally occurs several minutes prior to the time that substantial water is absorbed from the digestive system (Ramsay, Rolls, & Wood, 1977). Thus, the possibility that some sort of oral metering of ingested fluids provides a least one level of input to the satiation of thirst has been considered. Support for this concept derives from the data of Nicolaidis (1968), who demonstrated that infusions of water into the oral cavity of dehydrated rats produced rapid decreases in plasma vasopressin prior to any substantial absorption of the fluid by the digestive system. Although receptors in the mouth and throat can be demonstrated to influence the amount of water an animal ingests, receptors in the stomach, small intestine, and liver are also critically involved in the normal satiation of drinking. That is, preloads of water given by gastric gavage (thereby bypassing oral stimulation) also reduce drinking. Unlike the signals that lead to satiation of food intake, there is no clear evidence that receptors in the duodenum are involved in satiation of water intake.

The site of integration of the satiety signals for drinking is also unclear, although recent data have implicated the lateral parabrachial nucleus in the caudal brain stem as being important. This nucleus receives gustatory input from the tongue and appears to be an important site for the integration of signals that control fluid intake. Data from Menani and colleagues have demonstrated that this brain area may be producing a tonic serotonergic inhibitory tone on fluid intake (Menani, Colombari, Beltz, Thunhorst, & Johnson, 1998). During episodes of hypovolemia, parabrachial serotonergic tone is decreased, thus allowing the expression of drinking. Other neurotransmitters have also been found to inhibit fluid intake, including oxytocin, which is generated in forebrain areas and is projected to caudal brain sites to inhibit fluid ingestion. The identification of satiety signals for drinking awaits future research.

Interactions Among Other Control Systems

Besides being mediated by both osmotic and hypovolemic signals, the controls of water intake interact with other homeostatic control systems as well. Sodium homeostasis and its behavioral counterpart, sodium appetite, provide an important example of how the controls of water intake interact with other systems. Recall that for adequate reestablishment of extracellular fluid volume, electrolytes that act as osmotic agents are essential for maintaining water within the extracellular fluid compartment. There is ample evidence that the angiotensin II that is secreted in response to hypovolemic signals also stimulates a specific appetite for sodium as well as for water (Weisinger, Blair-West, Burns, Denton, & Tarjan, 1997). In addition, many of the same brain areas (SFO, other CVOs, several hypothalamic nuclei) at which the actions of angiotensin II regulate water intake also alter sodium appetite. For example, the expression of angiotensin II receptors can be differentially regulated by circulating levels of adrenal steroids such as aldosterone in sodium-depleted rats, and sex steroids such as estrogen can modulate the dipsogenic potency of angiotensin II in the normally cycling female rat (Kisley, Sakai, & Fluharty, 1999).

Summary

In summary, we have reviewed the multiple mechanisms known to influence the elicitation and cessation of drinking. Because the maintenance of blood volume and osmotic

pressure is so critical to the functioning of every organ system, and because even small deviations from the ideal can soon incapacitate an organism, the control system is exquisitely sensitive and fast to respond. In an ideal world, water and electrolytes would be consumed in the right volumes and concentrations to preclude having to monitor and adjust their levels constantly, and at one level of control this is what actually happens. Most individuals, when they are able, consume sufficient electrolytes and water with their food to ensure adequate regulation. In fact, estimates of the percentage of total daily water that is consumed when food is being eaten (i.e., at meal times) under conditions of ad libitum access range from 70% to 90% or more. Any excess water or electrolytes that are consumed during meals are rapidly and efficiently excreted from the body in the urine.

Unfortunately, few organisms live in such luxury and thus cannot rely on prandial consumption of sufficient water and electrolytes. As a result, they fall back on the control systems described in this chapter. In this process, the brain relies primarily on osmotic and volumetric signals arising in key sensory receptors in strategic locations in the body, as well as in the brain itself, to determine body fluid status. When deviations from the ideal are detected, the brain has a complex armamentarium of responses on which it can draw to reverse the problem and preclude its worsening. Hence, the brain can engage specific neurohormonal systems such as the renin-angiotensin system to restore fluid balance.

As with food intake, there are signals that stimulate drinking, as well as signals that terminate drinking; the two interacting types of signals maximize the likelihood of consuming adequate amounts of water and electrolytes. The normal integration of these stimuli ensures that behavioral and physiological responses occur, in many cases, in anticipation of need states such that the individual is protected from large demands to defend homeostatic processes. That is, in a predictable environment, when an inadequate supply of water and electrolytes is inevitable, animals learn to activate the appropriate regulatory responses in anticipation of the situation and hence circumvent problems of fluid balance before they arise. These vital and complex regulatory processes are controlled, in many cases, utilizing redundant systems such that even in the case of disease or injury the individual is still able to function and respond normally.

One area in fluid balance that is not yet well understood is the nature of the controls involved in prandial drinking (drinking in association with meals). We do not know whether prandial drinking is elicited by the osmotic load of the meal or if the drinking occurs in anticipation of the osmotic load. We also do not yet appreciate whether the neurotransmitters and hormones that we normally associate with controlling water intake specific to fluid balance are involved in prandial drinking or whether this represents a unique situation. These issues remain to be investigated.

The investigation of water and sodium ingestion has provided insights into how the brain controls motivated behavior. A number of points are obvious. The first is that the controls over fluid balance in the body parallel in many ways those involved in energy regulation. Just as the body monitors key parameters such as blood glucose and body adiposity, it tracks osmolarity and blood volume. The second is that the central control over all homeostatically regulated systems, including fluid balance, is integrated such that water and electrolyte intake and excretion do not occur in a vacuum. Rather, the brain takes into account all of the key systems, compromises where necessary, and ensures the long-term survival of the organism. The study of water intake has also provided a model system to examine how peptide and steroid hormones interact with neural signals in the control of behavior. Specific brain areas that are critical in the control of these behaviors, as well as specific chemical signals that mediate this control (hormones and neurotransmitters), have been identified through the incorporation of modern biochemical and molecular biological tools. Because of the explosion of new techniques available in the last decade, great advances into how this complex behavior is governed have been forthcoming. As we look to the future, studies examining the interactions among the controls over caloric, thermal, and fluid needs, including the various neurochemical systems that mediate them, will be more clearly examined. Finally and most important, given the increasing knowledge of the controls of ingestive behavior, we hope to begin to use this information to develop rational and viable treatments for common human disorders such as obesity and hypertension.

REFERENCES

Adolph, E. F., Barker, J. P., & Hoy, P. A. (1954). Multiple factors in thirst. *American Journal of Physiology, 178,* 538–562.

Aja, S., Sahandy, S., Ladenheim, E. E., Schwartz, G. J., & Moran, T. H. (2001). Intracerebroventricular CART peptide reduces food intake and alters motor behavior at a hindbrain site. *American Journal of Physiology, 281,* R1862–R1867.

Altschuler, S. M., Bao, X., Bieger, D., Hopkins, D. A., & Miselis, R. R. (1989). Viscerotopic representation of the upper gastrointestinal tract in the rat: Sensory ganglia and nuclei of the solitary and spinal trigeminal tracts. *Journal of Comparative Neurology, 243,* 248–268.

Anand, B. K., & Brobesck, J. R. (1951). Localization of a feeding center in the hypothalamus of the rat. *Proceedings of the Society for Experimental Biology and Medicine, 77,* 323–324.

Andersson, B. (1953). The effect of injections of hypertonic NaCl-solutions in different parts of the hypothalamus of goats. *Acta Physiologica Scandinavica, 28,* 188–201.

Andersson, B., & Wyrwicka, W. (1957). The elicitation of a drinking motor conditioned reaction by electrical stimulation of the hypothalamic "drinking area." *Acta Physiologica Scandinavica, 41,* 194–198.

Antin, J., Gibbs, J., Holt, J., Young, R. C., & Smith, G. P. (1975). Cholecystokinin elicits the complete behavioral satiety sequence in rats. *Journal of Comparative and Physiological Psychology, 89,* 784–790.

Azzara, A. V., Bodnar, R. J., Delameter, A. R., & Sclafani, A. (2000). Naltrexone fails to block the acquisition or expression of a flavor preference conditioned by intragastric carbohydrate infusions. *Pharmacology, Biochemistry, and Behavior, 67,* 545–557.

Beck, B., Burlet, A., Nicolas, J. P., & Burlet, C. (1993). Galanin in the hypothalamus of fed and fasted lean and obese Zucker rats. *Brain Research, 623,* 124–130.

Beck, B., & Richy, S. (1999). Hypothalamic hypocretin/orexin and neuropeptide Y: Divergent interaction with energy depletion and leptin. *Biochemical Biophysical Research Communications, 258,* 119–122.

Benoit, S. C., Schwartz, M. W., Lachey, J. L., Hagan, M. M., Rushing, P. A., Blake, K. A., Yagaloff, K. A., Kurylko, G., Franco, L., Danhoo, W., & Seeley, R. J. (2000). A novel selective melanocortin-4 receptor agonist reduces food intake in rats and mice without producing aversive consequences. *Journal of Neuroscience, 20,* 3442–3448.

Bernard, C. (1859). *Lecons sur les proprietes physiologiques et les alterations pathologiques de l'organisme.* Paris: Baillers.

Billington, C. J., Levine, A. S., & Morley, J. E. (1983). Are peptides truly satiety agents? A method for testing for neurohumoral satiety effects. *American Journal of Physiology, 245,* R920–R926.

Bjorbaek, C., Elmquist, J. K., Michl, P., Ahima, R. S., van Buer, A., McCall, A. L., & Flier, J. S. (1998). Expression of leptin receptor isoforms in rat brain microvessels. *Endocrinology, 139,* 3485–3491.

Bjorbaek, C., Uotoni, S., da Silva, B., & Flier, J. S. (1997). Divergent signaling capacities of the long and short isoforms of the leptin receptor. *Journal of Biochemistry, 272,* 32686–32695.

Blass, E. M., & Epstein, A. N. (1971). A lateral preoptic osmosensitive zone for thirst in the rat. *Journal of Comparative and Physiological Psychology, 76,* 378–394.

Bolles, R. C., Harward, L., & Crandall, C. (1981). Conditioned taste preferences based on caloric density. *Journal of Experimental Psychology (Animal Behavior Processes), 7,* 59–69.

Breslin, P. A. S., Davis, J. D., & Rosenak, R. (1996). Saccharin increase the effectiveness of glucose in stimulating ingestion in rats but has little effect on negative feedback. *Physiology and Behavior, 60,* 411–416.

Broberger, C., DeLecea, L., Sutcliffe, J. G., & Hokfelt, T. (1998). Hypocretin/orexin and melanin concentrating hormone expressing cells form distinct populations in the rodent lateral hypothalamus: Relationship to neuropeptide Y and agouti gene related protein systems. *Journal of Comparative Neurology, 402,* 460–474.

Cabanac, M. (1971). Physiological role of pleasure. *Science, 173,* 1103–1107.

Cabanac, M., & Fantino, M. (1977). Origin of olfacto-gustatory alliesthesia: Intestinal sensitivity to carbohydrate concentration? *Physiology and Behavior, 18,* 1039–1045.

Cabanac, M., & LaFrance, L. (1992). Duodenal preabsorptive origin of gustatory alliesthesia in rats. *American Journal of Physiology, 263,* R1013–R1017.

Cabanac, M., & Zhao, C. (1994). Postingestive alliesthesia produced by exogenous choloecystokinin and blocked by abdominal vagotomy. *American Journal of Physiology, 266,* R633–R637.

Campfield, L. A., & Smith, F. J. (1986). Functional coupling between transient declines in blood glucose and feeding behavior; Temporal relationships. *Brain Research Bulletin, 17,* 427–433.

Campfield, L. A., Smith, F. A., Guisez, Y., Devos, R., & Burn, P. (1996). Recombinant mouse ob protein: Evidence for a peripheral signal linking adiposity and central neural networks. *Science, 271,* 994–996.

Cannon, W. B. (1918). The physiological basis of thirst. *Proceedings of the Royal Society, London, 90B,* 283–301.

Cannon, W. B. (1932). *The wisdom of the body.* New York: Norton.

Chavez, M., Kelly, L., York, D. A., & Berthoud, H. R. (1997). Chemical lesion of visceral afferents causes transient overconsumption of unfamiliar high-fat diets in rats. *American Journal of Physiology, 272,* R1657–R1673.

Chornwall, B. M., Di Maggio, D. A., Massari, V. J., Pickel, S. M., Ruggiero, D. A., & O'Donohue, T. L. (1985). The anatomy of neuropeptide Y containing neurons in the rat brain. *Neuroscience, 15,* 1159–1181.

Chua, S. C., Chung, W. K., Wu-Peng, X. S., Zhang, Y., Liu, S. M., Tartaglia, L., & Liebel, R. L. (1996). Phenotypes of mouse diabetes and rat fatty due to mutations in the OB (leptin) receptor. *Science, 271,* 994–996.

Clark, J. T., Kalra, P. S., Crowley, W. R., & Kalra, S. P. (1984). Neuropeptide Y and human pancreatic polypeptide stimulate feeding behavior in rats. *Endocrinology, 115,* 427–429.

Coleman, D. L. (1973). Effects of parabiosis of obese and diabetes and normal mice. *Diabetologia, 9,* 294–298.

Cooper, G. J. (1994). Amylin compared with calcitonin gene-related peptide: Structure, biology and relevance to metabolic disease. *Endocrine Review, 15,* 163–201.

Corp, E. S., Melville, L. D., Greenberg, D., Gibbs, J., & Smith, G. P. (1990). Effect of 4th ventricular neuropeptide Y and peptide YY on ingestive and other behaviors. *American Journal of Physiology, 259,* R317–R323.

Corp, E. S., Woods, S. C., Porte, D., Jr., Dorsa, D. M., Figlewicz, D. P., & Baskin, D. G. (1986). Localization of 125I-insulin binding sites in the rat hypothalamus by quantitative autoradiography. *Neuroscience Letters, 70,* 17–22.

Crawley, J. N. (1999). The role of galanin in feeding behavior. *Neuropeptides, 33,* 369–375.

Crawley, J. N., Austin, M. C., Fiske, S. M., Martin, B., Consolo, S., Berthold, M., Langel, U., Fisone, G., & Bartfai, T. (1990). Activity of centrally administered galanin fragments on stimulation of feeding behavior and on galanin receptor binding in the rat hypothalamus. *Journal of Neuroscience, 10,* 3695–3700.

Davis, J. D., & Levine, M. (1977). A model for the control of ingestion. *Psychological Review, 84,* 379–412.

Davis, J. D., & Smith, G. P. (1990). Learning to sham feed: Behavioral adjustments to loss of physiological postingestive stimuli. *American Journal of Physiology, 259,* R1228–R1235.

Doyle, T. G., Berridge, K. C., & Gosnell, B. A. (1993). Morphine enhances hedonic taste palatability in rats. *Pharmacology, Biochemistry, and Behavior, 46,* 745–749.

Eastwood, C., Maubach, K., Kirkup, A. J., & Grundy, D. (1998). The role of endogenous cholecystokinin in the sensory transduction of luminal nutrient signaling in the rat jejunum. *Neuroscience Letters, 254,* 145–153.

Eckel, L. A., Langhans, W., Kahler, A., Campfield, L. A., Smith, F. J., & Geary, N. (1998). Chronic administration of OB protein decreases food intake by selectively meal size in female rats. *American Journal of Physiology, 275,* R186–R189.

Elizalde, G., & Sclafani, A. (1990). Flavor preferences conditioned by intragastric polycose; A detailed analysis using an electronic esophagus preparation. *Physiology and Behavior, 47,* 63–67.

Elmquist, J. K., Bjorbaek, C., Ahima, R. S., Flier, J. S., & Saper, C. B. (1998). Distribution of leptin receptor mRNA isoforms in the rat brain. *Journal of Comparative Anatomy, 395,* 535–547.

Epstein, A. N., Kissileff, H. R., & Stellar, E. (Eds.). (1973). *The neuropsychology of thirst.* Washington, DC: V. H. Winston & Sons.

Erikson, J. C., Clegg, K. E., & Palmiter, R. D. (1996). Sensitivity to leptin and susceptibility to seizures in mice lacking neuropeptude Y. *Nature, 381,* 415–418.

Fan, W., Boston, B. A., Kesterson, R. A., Hruby, V. J., & Cone, R. D. (1997). Role of melanocortinergic neurons in feeding and agouti obesity syndrome. *Nature, 385,* 165–168.

Fitzsimons, J. T. (1961). Drinking by rats depleted of body fluid without increase in osmotic pressure. *Journal of Physiology (London), 159,* 297–309.

Fitzsimons, J. T. (1964). Drinking caused by constriction of the inferior vena cava in the rat. *Nature, 204,* 479–480.

Fitzsimons, J. T. (1969). The role of renal thirst factor in drinking induced by extracellular stimuli. *Journal of Physiology (London), 201,* 349–369.

Fitzsimons, J. T. (1979). *The physiology of thirst and sodium appetite.* Cambridge, UK: Cambridge University Press.

Fitzsimons, J. T., & Simons, B. J. (1969). The effect on drinking in the rat of intravenous infusion of angiotensin, given alone or in combination with other stimuli of thirst. *Journal of Physiology (London), 203,* 45–57.

Flynn, F. W. (1989). Fourth ventricle bombesin injection suppresses ingestive behavior in rats. *American Journal of Physiology, 256,* R590–R596.

Flynn, F. W. (1992). Fourth ventricular injection of selective bombesin receptor antagonists facilitates feeding in rats. *American Journal of Physiology, 264,* R218–R221.

Flynn, M. C., Scott, T. R., Pritchard, T. C., & Plata-Salaman, C. R. (1998). Mode of action of OB protein (leptin) on feeding. *American Journal of Physiology, 275,* R174–R179.

Fulton, S., Woodside, B., & Shizgal, P. (2000). Modulation of brain reward circuitry by leptin. *Science, 287,* 125–128.

Ganten, D., Hutchinson, J. S., Schelling, P., Ganten, U., & Fischer, H. (1975). The isorenin angiotensin systems in extrarenal tissue. *Clinical Experimental Pharmacology and Physiology, 2,* 127–151.

Geary, N. (1998). Glucagon and the control of meal size. In G. P. Smith (Ed.), *Satiation: From gut to brain* (pp. 164–197). New York: Oxford University Press.

Geary, N., Kissileff, H. R., Pi-Sunyer, F. X., & Hinton, V. (1992). Individual, but not simultaneous, glucagon and cholecystokinin infusion inhibit feeding in men. *American Journal of Physiology, 262,* R975–R980.

Geary, N., & Smith, G. P. (1982a). Pancreatic glucagon and post-prandial satiety in the rat. *Physiology and Behavior, 28,* 313–322.

Geary, N., & Smith, G. P. (1982b). Pancreatic glucagon fails to inhibit sham feeding in the rat. *Peptides, 3,* 163–166.

Gibbs, J., Fauser, D. J., Rowe, E. A., Rolls, E. T., & Maddison, S. P. (1979). Bombesin suppresses feeding in rats. *Nature, 245,* 323–325.

Gibbs, J., Young, R. C., & Smith, G. P. (1973). Cholecystokinin decreases food intake in rats. *Journal of Comparative and Physiological Psychology, 84,* 488–495.

Gilman, A. (1937). The relation between blood osmotic pressure, fluid distribution and voluntary water intake. *American Journal of Physiology, 120,* 323–328.

Giza, A. K., Ackroff, K., McCaughey, S. A., Sclafani, A., & Scott, T. R. (1997). Preference conditioning alters taste responses in the nucleus of the solitary tract. *American Journal of Physiology, 273,* R1230–R1240.

Glass, M. J., Billington, C. J., & Levine, A. S. (2000). Opioids, food reward and macronutrient selection. In H.-R. Berthoud & R. J. Seeley (Eds.), *Neural and metabolic control of macronutrient intake* (pp. 407–423). Boca Raton, FL: CRC Press.

Glass, M. J., Grace, M., Cleary, J. P., Billington, C. J., & Levine, A. S. (1996). Potency of naloxone's anorectic effect in rats in dependent on diet preference. *American Journal of Physiology, 271,* R217–R221.

Gosnell, B. A., Krahn, D. D., & Majchrzak, M. J. (1990). The effects of morphine on diet selection are dependent on baseline diet preferences. *Pharmacology, Biochemistry, and Behavior, 37,* 207–212.

Grill, H. J., Ginsburg, A. B., Seeley, R. J., & Kaplan, J. M. (1998). Brainstem application of melanocortin receptor ligands produces long-lasting effects on feeding and body weight. *Journal of Neuroscience, 18,* 10128–10135.

Grill, H. J., & Kaplan, J. M. (1992). Sham feeding in intact and chronic decerebrate rats. *American Journal of Physiology, 262,* R1070–R1074.

Grill, H. J., Markison, S., Ginsberg, A., & Kaplan, J. M. (2000). Long term effects on feeding and body weight after stimulation of forebrain or hindbrain CRH receptors with urocortin. *Brain Research, 867,* 19–28.

Grill, H. J., & Norgren, (1978). The taste reactivity test: I. Mimetic responses to gustatory stimuli in neurologically normal rats. *Brain Research, 143,* 263–279.

Hagan, M. M., Rushing, P. A., Schwartz, M. W., Yagaloff, K. A., Burn, P., Woods, S. C., & Seeley, R. J. (1999). Role of CNS melanocortin system in the response to overfeeding. *Journal of Neuroscience, 19,* 2362–2367.

Hahn, T., Breininger, J., Baskin, D., & Schwartz, M. (1998). Coexpression of AgRP and NPY in fasting activated hypothalamic neurons. *Nature Neuroscience, 1,* 271–272.

Haynes, A. C., Jackson, B., Chapman, H., Tadyyon, M., Johns, A., Porter, R. A., & Arch, J. R. (2000). A selective orexin-1 receptor antagonist reduces food consumption in male and female rats. *Regulatory Peptides, 96,* 45–51.

Heatherington, A. W., & Ranson, S. W. (1940). Hypothalamic lesions and adiposity in the rat. *Anatomical Record, 78,* 149–172.

Hewson, A. K., & Dickson, S. L. (2000). Systemic administration of ghrelin induces Fos and Egr-1 proteins in the hypothalamus arcuate nucleus of fasted and fed rats. *Journal of Endocrinology, 12,* 1047–1049.

Huszar, D., Lynch, C. A., Fairchild-Huntress, V., Dunmore, J. H., Fang, Q., Berlemeier, L. R., Gu, W., Kesterson, R. A., Boston, B. A., Cone, R. D., Smith, F. J., Campfield, L. A., Burn, P., & Lee, F. (1997). Targeted disruption of the melanocortin-4 receptor results in obesity. *Cell, 88,* 131–141.

Ji, H., Graczyk-Milbrandt, G., & Friedman, M. I. (2000). Metabolic inhibitors synergistically decrease hepatic energy status and increase food intake. *American Journal of Physiology, 278,* R1579–R1582.

Kahler, A., Geary, N., Eckel, L. A., Campfield, L. A., Smith, F. J., & Langhans, W. (1998). Chronic administration of OB protein decreases food intake by selectively meal size in male rats. *American Journal of Physiology, 275,* R180–R185.

Kalra, S. P., Dube, M. G., Sahu, A., Phelps, C. P., & Kalra, P. (1991). Neuropeptide Y secretion increases in the paraventricular nucleus in association with increased appetite for food. *Proceedings of the National Academy of Sciences, 88,* 10931–10935.

Kaplan, J. M., Siemers, W. H., & Grill, H. J. (1997). Effect of oral versus gastric delivery on gastric emptying of corn oil emulsions. *American Journal of Physiology, 273,* R1263–R1270.

Kaplan, J. M., Spector, A. C., & Grill, H. J. (1992). Dynamics of liquid gastric emptying during and after stomach fill. *American Journal of Physiology, 263,* R813–R819.

Kawai, K., Sugimoto, K., Nakashima, K., Mura, H., & Ninomiya, Y. (2000). Leptin as a modulator of sweet taste sensitivities in mice. *Proceedings of the National Academy of Sciences, 97,* 11044–11049.

Kelly, L., Morales, S., Smith, B. K., & Berthoud, H. R. (2000). Capsaicin-treated rats permanently overingest low but not high concentration sucrose solutions. *American Journal of Physiology, 279,* R1805–R1812.

Kennedy, G. C. (1953). The role of depot fat in the hypothalamic control of food intake in the rat. *Proceedings of the Royal Society, London, 140,* 579–592.

Kim, E. M., Welch, C. C., Grace, M. K., Billington, C. J., & Levine, A. S. (1996). Chronic food restriction and acute food deprivation decrease mRNA levels of opioid peptides in the arcuate nucleus. *American Journal of Physiology, 270,* R1019–R1024.

Kisley, L. R., Sakai, R. R., Fluharty, S. J. (1999). Estrogen decreases hypothalamic angiotensin II AT1 receptor binding and mRNA in the female rat. *Brain Research, 844*(1-2), 34–42.

Kotz, C. M., Glass, M. J., Levine, A. S., & Billington, C. J. (2000). Regional effect of naltrexone in the nucleus of the solitary tract in blockade of NPY-induced feeding. *American Journal of Physiology, 278,* R499–R503.

Kotz, C. M., Grace, M. K., Briggs, J. E., Levine, A. S., & Billington, C. J. (1995). Effects of opiate antagonists naloxone and naltrexone on neuropeptide Y induced feeding and brown fat thermoregulation in the rat: Neural site of action. *Journal of Clinical Investigation, 96,* 163–170.

Kristensen, P., Judge, M. E., Thim, L., Ribel, U., Christjansan, K. N., Wulff, B. S., Clausen, J. T., Jensen, P. B., Madsen, O. D., Vrang, N., Larsen, P. J., & Hastrup, S. (1998). Hypothalamic CART is a new anorectic peptide regulated by leptin. *Nature, 393,* 72–76.

Ladenheim, E. E., & Ritter, R. C. (1988). Low-dose 4th ventricular bombesin selectively suppresses food intake. *American Journal of Physiology, 255,* R988–R992.

Ladenheim, E. E., Taylor, J. E., Coy, D. H., Carrigan, T. S., Wohn, A., & Moran, T. H. (1997). Caudal hindbrain neuromedin B-preferring receptors participate in the control of food intake. *American Journal of Physiology, 272,* R433–R437.

Ladenheim, E. E., Taylor, J. E., Coy, D. H., Moore, K. A., & Moran, T. H. (1996). Hindbrain GRP receptor blockade antagonizes feeding suppression by peripherally administered GRP. *American Journal of Physiology, 271,* R180–R184.

Ladenheim, E. E., Taylor, J. E., Coy, D. H., & Moran, T. H. (1994). Blockade of feeding inhibition by neuromedin B using a selective receptor antagonist. *European Journal of Pharmacology, 271,* R7–R9.

Ladenheim, E. E., Wirth, K., & Moran, T. H. (1996). Receptor subtype mediation of the feeding suppression by bombesin-like peptides. *Pharmacology, Biochemistry, and Behavior, 54,* 705–711.

Langhans, W., Pantel, K., Muller-Schell, W., Effengerger, E., & Scharrer, E. (1984). Hepatic handling of pancreatic glucagon and glucose during meals in rats. *American Journal of Physiology, 247,* R827–R832.

Lashley, K. S. (1938). The experimental analysis of instinctive behavior. *Psychological Review, 45,* 445–471.

LeSauter, J., Noh, U., & Geary, N. (1991). Hepatic portal infusion of glucagon antibodies increases spontaneous meal size in rats. *American Journal of Physiology, 261,* R154–R161.

Lewis, D. E., Shellard, L., Koeslag, D. C., Boer, D. E., McCarthy, H. D., McKibbin, P. E., Russell, J. C., & Williams, G. (1993). Intense exercise and food deprivation cause similar hypothalamic neuropeptide Y increases in rats. *American Journal of Physiology, 264,* E279–E284.

Lopez, M., Seoane, L., del Carmen Garcia, M., Lago, F., Casanueva, F. F., Senaris, R., & Dieguez, C. (2000). Leptin regulation of prepro-orexin and orexin receptor mRNA levels in the hypothalamus. *Biochemical and Biophysical Research Communications, 269,* 41–45.

Lucas, F., & Sclafani, A. (1989). Flavor preferences conditioned by intragastric fat infusions in the rat. *Physiology and Behavior, 46,* 403–412.

Lutz, T. A., Geary, N., Szabady, M. M., Del Prete, E., & Scharrer, E. (1995). Amylin deceases meal size in rats. *Physiology and Behavior, 58,* 1197–1202.

Lutz, T. A., Rossi, R., Althaus, J., Del Prete, E., & Sharrer, E. (1998). Amylin reduces food intake more potently than calcitonin gene-related peptide (CGRP) when injected into the lateral brain ventricle in rats. *Peptides, 19,* 1533–1540.

Lutz, T. A., Senn, M., Althaus, J., Del Prete, E., Ehrensperger, E., & Scharrer, E. (1998). Lesion of the area postema/nucleus of the solitary tract (AP/NTS) attenuates the anorectic effects of amylin and calcitonin gene related peptide (CGRP) in rats. *Peptides, 19,* 309–317.

Maffei, M., Halaas, E., Ravussin, E., Pratley, R. E., Lee, G. H., Zhang, Y., Fei, H., Kim, S., Lallone, R., Ranganathan, S., Kern, P. A., & Friedman, J. M. (1995). Leptin levels in human and rodent: Measurement of plasma leptin and ob RNA in obese and weight reduced subjects. *Nature Medicine, 1,* 1155–1161.

Marks-Kaufman, R., & Kanarek, R. B. (1990). Diet selection following chronic morphine and naloxone regimen. *Pharmacology, Biochemistry, and Behavior, 35,* 665–669.

Marsh, D. J., Hollopeter, G., Kafer, K. E., & Palmiter, R. D. (1998). Role of Y5 neuropeptide Y receptor in feeding and obesity. *Nature Medicine, 4,* 718–721.

Martel, P., & Fantinio, M. (1996). Mesolimbic dopaminergic system activity as a function of food reward: A microdialysis study. *Pharmacology, Biochemistry, and Behavior, 53,* 221–226.

Mathis, C., Moran, T. H., & Schwartz, G. J. (1998). Load sensitive rat gastric vagal afferents encode volume but not gastric nutrients. *American Journal of Physiology, 274,* R280–R286.

Matson, C. A., Reid, D. F., Cannon, T. A., & Ritter, R. C. (2000). Cholecystokinin and leptin act synergistically to reduce body weight. *American Journal of Physiology, 278,* R882–R890.

Matson, C. A., & Ritter, R. C. (1999). Long term CCK-leptin synergy suggests a role for CCK in the regulation of body weight. *American Journal of Physiology, 276,* R1038–R1045.

Mayer, J. (1953). Glucostatic mechanisms of regulation of food intake. *New England Journal of Medicine, 249,* 13–16.

McMinn, J. E., Sindelar, D. K., Havel, P. J., & Schwartz, M. W. (2000). Leptin deficiency induced by fasting impairs the satiety response to cholecystokinin. *Endocrinology, 141,* 4442–4448.

Melanson, K. J., Westerterp-Plantenga, M. S., Saris, W. H., Smith, F. J., & Campfield, L. A. (1999). Blood glucose patterns and appetite in time blinded humans: Carbohydrate vs fat. *American Journal of Physiology, 277,* R337–R345.

Menani, J. V., Colombari, D. S. A., Beltz, T. G., Thunhorst, R. L., & Johnson, A. K. (1998). Salt appetite: Interaction of forebrain angiotensinergic and hindbrain serotonergic mechanisms. *Brain Research, 801*(1-2), 29–35.

Mendelsohn, F. A. O., Quirion, R., Saavedra, J. M., Aguiler, G., & Catt, K. J. (1984). Autoradiographic localization of angiotensin II receptors in rat brain. *Proceeding of the National Academy of Sciences, USA, 81,* 1575–1579.

Merali, Z., Moody, T. W., & Coy, D. (1993). Blockade of brain bombesin/GRP receptors increases food intake in sated rats. *American Journal of Physiology, 264,* R1031–R1034.

Mercer, J. G., Lawrence, C. B., & Atkinson, T. (1996). Regulation of galanin gene expression in the hypothalamic paraventricular nucleus of the obese Zucker rat by manipulation of dietary macronutrient. *Molecular Brain Research, 43,* 202–208.

Michaud, D., Anisman, H., & Merali, Z. (1999). Capsaicin sensitive fibers are required for the anorexic action of systemic but not central bombesin. *American Journal of Physiology, 276,* R1617–R1622.

Miselis, R. R. (1981). The efferent projections of the subfornical organ of the rat: A circumventricular organ within a neural network subserving water balance. *Brain Research, 230,* 1–23.

Mook, D. G. (1963). Oral and postingestional determinants of the intake of various solutions in rats with esophagela fistulas. *Journal of Comparative and Physiological Psychology, 56,* 645–659.

Mook, D. G. (1990). Satiety, specifications and stop rules: Feeding as a voluntary act. In A. N. Epstein & A. R. Morrison (Eds.), *Progress in psychobiology and physiological psychology: Vol. 14.* (pp. 1–65). New York: Academic Press.

Moran, T. H., Ameglio, P. J., Peyton, H. J., Schwartz, G. J., & McHugh, P. R. (1993). Blockade of type A, but not type B, CCK receptors postpones satiety in rhesus monkeys. *American Journal of Physiology, 265,* R620–R624.

Moran, T. H., Baldessarini, A. R., Solorio, C. F., Lowerry, T., & Schwartz, G. J. (1997). Vagal afferent and efferent contributions to the inhibition of food intake by cholecystokinin. *American Journal of Physiology, 272,* R1245–R1251.

Moran, T. H., Katz, L. F., Plata-Salaman, C. R., & Schwartz, G. J. (1998). Disordered food intake and obesity in rats lacking CCKA receptors. *American Journal of Physiology, 274,* R618–R625.

Moran, T. H., Knipp, S., & Schwartz, G. J. (1999). Gastric and duodenal features of meals mediate controls of liquid gastric emptying during fill in rhesus monkeys. *American Journal of Physiology, 277,* R1282–R1290.

Moran, T. H., & McHugh, P. R. (1982). Cholecystokinin decreases food intake by inhibiting gastric emptying. *American Journal of Physiology, 242,* R491–R497.

Moran, T. H., & McHugh, P. R. (1992). Gastric mechanisms in CCK satiety. In C. T. Dourish, S. J. Cooper, S. D. Iversen, & L. L. Iversen (Eds.), *Multiple cholecystokinin receptors in the CNS* (pp. 183–205). Oxford: Oxford University Press.

Moran, T. H., Norgren, R., Crosby, R. J., & McHugh, P. R. (1990). Central and peripheral vagal transport of CCK binding sites occurs in afferent fibers. *Brain Research, 526,* 95–102.

Moran, T. H., Shnayder, L., Hostetler, A. M., & McHugh, P. R. (1988). Pylorectomy reduces the satiety actions of cholecystokinin. *American Journal of Physiology, 255,* R1059–R1063.

Morley, J. E., Levine, A. S., Gosnell, B. A., Kneip, J., & Grace, M. (1987). Effect of neuropeptide Y on ingestive behaviors in the rat. *American Journal of Physiology, 252,* R599–R609.

Nakazato, M., Murakami, N., Date, Y., Kojima, M., Matuso, H., Kanagawa, K., & Matsukara, S. (2001). A role for ghrelin in the central regulation of feeding. *Nature, 409,* 194–198.

Nilsson, G., & Uvnas-Wallenstein, K. (1977). Effect of teasing and sham feeding on plasma glucagon concentration in dogs. *Acta Physiologica Scandinavia, 100,* 298–302.

Pavlov, I. P. (1910). *The work of the digestive glands* (2nd ed.). London: Charles Griffin.

Pecina, S., Berridge, K. C., & Parker, L. A. (1997). Pimozide does not shift palatability: Separation of anhedonia from sensorimotor suppression of taste reactivity. *Pharmacology, Biochemistry, and Behavior, 58,* 801–811.

Peck, J. W., & Novin, D. (1971). Evidence that osmoreceptors mediating drinking in rabbits are in the lateral preoptic area. *Journal of Comparative and Physiological Psychology, 74,* 134–147.

Pedrazzini, T., Seydoux, J., Kunster, P., Aubert, J.-F., Grouzmann, E., Beerman, F., & Brunner, H.-R. (1998). Cardiovascular response, feeding behavior and locomotor activity in mice lacking the NPY Y1 receptor. *Nature Medicine, 4,* 722–726.

Perez, C., Ackroff, K., & Sclafani, A. (1996). Carbohydrate and protein conditioned flavor preferences: Effects of nutrient preloads. *Physiology and Behavior, 59,* 467–474.

Perez, C., Lucas, F., & Sclafani, A. (1998). Increased flavor acceptance and preference conditioned by the postingestive actions of glucose. *Physiology and Behavior, 64,* 483–492.

Peyron, C., Tighe, D. K., van den Pol, A. N., de Leces, L., Heller, H. C., Sutcliffe, J. G., & Kilduff, T. S. (1998). Neurons containing hypocretin (orexin) project to multiple neural systems. *Journal of Neuroscience, 18,* 9996–10015.

Pomonis, J. D., Levine, A. S., & Billington, C. J. (1997). Interaction of hypothalamic paraventricular nucleus and central nucleus of the amygdala in naloxone blockade of neuropeptide Y induced feeding revealed by c-fos expression. *Journal of Neuroscience, 17,* 5175–5182.

Qu, D., Ludwig, D. S., Gammeltolft, S., Piper, M., Pellymounter, M. A., Cullen, M. J., Mathes, W. F., Przypek, J., Kanarek, R., & Maratos-Flier, E. (1996). A role for melanin concentrating hormone in the central regulation of feeding behavior. *Nature, 380,* 243–247.

Ramsay, D. J., Rolls, B. J., & Wood, R, J. (1977). Thirst following water deprivation in dogs. *American Journal of Physiology, 232,* R93–R100.

Randich, A., Tyler, W. J., Cox, J. E., Meller, S. T., Kelm, G. R., & Bharaj, S. S. (2000). Responses of celiac and cervical vagal afferents to infusions of lipids in the jejunum or ileum of the rat. *American Journal of Physiology, 278,* R34–R43.

Reidelberger, R. D., & O'Rourke, M. F. (1989). Potent cholecystokinin antagonist L-364,718 stimulates food intake in rats. *American Journal of Physiology, 257,* R1512–R1518.

Richter, C. P. (1943). Total self regulatory functions in animals and human beings. *Harvey Lectures, 38,* 63–103.

Ritter, R. C., & Ladenhiem, E. E. (1985). Capsaicin pretreatment attenuates suppression of food intake by cholecystokinin. *American Journal of Physiology, 248,* R501–R504.

Ritter, S., Dinh, T. T., & Zhang, Y. (2000). Localization of hindbrain glucoreceptors sites controlling food intake and blood glucose. *Brain Research, 856,* 37–47.

Rolls, B. J. (1986). Sensory-specific satiety. *Nutrition Reviews, 44,* 93–101.

Rolls, E. T., Murzi, E., Yaxley, S., Thorpe, S. J., & Simpson, S. J. (1986). Sensory specific satiety: Food specific reduction in responsiveness of ventral forebrain neurons after feeding in the monkey. *Brain Research, 368,* 79–86.

Rossi, M., Choi, S. J., O'Shea, D., Miyoshi, T., Ghatei, M. A., & Bloom, S. R. (1997). Melanin-concentrating hormone acutely stimulates feeding, but chronic administration has no effect on body weight. *Endocrinology, 138,* 351–355.

Rushing, P. A., Haga, M. M., Seeley, R. J., Lutz, T. A., D'Alessio, D. A., Air, E. L., & Woods, S. C. (2001). Inhibition of central amylin signaling increases food intake and body adiposity in rats. *Endocrinology, 142,* 5035–5038.

Sahu, A. (1999). Evidence suggesting that galanin, melanin concentrating hormone, neurotensin, proopiomelanocortin and neuropeptide Y are targets of leptin signaling in the hypothalamus. *Endocrinology, 139,* 795–798.

Sakurai, T., Amemiya, A., Ishii, M., Matszaki, I., Chemelli, R. M., Tanaka, H., Williams, S. C., Richardson, J. A., Kozlowski, G. P., Wilson, S., Arch, J. R. S., Buckingham, R. E., Haynes, A. C., Carr, S. A., Annan, R. S., McNulty, D. E., Liu, W.-S., Terett, J. A., Elshourbagy, N. A., Bergsma, D. J., & Yanagisawa, M. (1998). Orexins and orexin receptors: A family of hypothalamic neuropeptides and G protein coupled receptors that regulate feeding behavior. *Cell, 92,* 573–585.

Schneider, L. H., Davis, J. D., Watson, C. W., & Smith, G. P. (1990). Similar effects of raclopride and reduced sucrose concentration on the microstructure of sucrose sham feeding. *European Journal of Pharmacology, 186,* 61–70.

Schwartz, G. J., McHugh, P. R., & Moran, T. H. (1991). Integration of vagal afferent responses to gastric load and CCK in rats. *American Journal of Physiology, 261,* R64–R69.

Schwartz, G. J., McHugh, P. R., & Moran, T. H. (1993). Gastric loads and CCK synergistically stimulate rat gastric vagal afferents. *American Journal of Physiology, 265,* R872–R876.

Schwartz, G. J., & Moran, T. H. (1998). Duodenal nutrient exposure elicits nutrient specific gut motility and vagal afferent signals in rats. *American Journal of Physiology, 274,* R1236–R1242.

Schwartz, G. J., Moran, T. H., White, W. O., & Ladenheim, E. E. (1997). Relationship between gastric motility and gastric vagal afferent responses to CCK and GRP in rats. *American Journal of Physiology, 272,* R1726–R1733.

Schwartz, G. J., Solorio, C. F., Skoglund, C., & Moran, T. H. (1999). Gut vagal afferent lesions increase meal size but do not block gastric preload induced feeding suppression. *American Journal of Physiology, 276,* R1629–R1999.

Schwartz, G. J., Tougas, G., & Moran, T. H. (1995). Integration of vagal afferent responses to duodenal loads and exogenous CCK. *Peptides, 16,* 707– 711.

Schwartz, M. W., Seeley, R. J., Campfield, L. A., Burn, P., & Baskin, D. G. (1996). Identification of targets of leptin action in rat hypothalamus. *Journal of Clinical Investigation, 98,* 1101–1106.

Schwartz, M. W., Seeley, R. J., Woods, S. C., Weigle, D. S., Campfield, L. A., Burn, P., & Baskin, D. G. (1997). Leptin increases hypothalamic proopiomelanocortin mRNA expression in the rostral arcuate nucleus. *Diabetes, 46,* 2119–2123.

Schwartz, M. W., Sipols, A. J., Marks, J. L., Sanacora, G., White, J. D., Scheurink, A., Kahn, S. E., Baskin, D. G., Woods, S. C., Figlewicz, D. P., & Porte, D. J., Jr. (1992). Inhibition of hypothalamic neuropeptide Y gene expression by insulin. *Endocrinology, 130,* 3608–3616.

Sclafani, A. (1991). Conditioned food preferences. *Bulletin of the Psychonomic Society, 29,* 256–260.

Scott, T. R., Yan, J., & Rolls, E. T. (1995). Brain mechanisms of satiety and taste in macaques. *Neurobiology, 3,* 281–292.

Seeley, R. J., van Dijk, G., Campfield, L. A., Smith, F. J., Burn, P., Nelligan, J. A., Baskin, D. G., & Woods, S. C. (1996).

Intraventricular leptin reduces food intake and body weight in lean rats but not obese Zucker rats. *Hormone and Metabolism Research, 28,* 664–668.

Shintani, M., Ogawa, Y., Ebihara, K., Aizawa-Abe, M., Miyanaga, F., Takaya, K., Hayashi, T., Inoue, G., Hosada, K., Kojima, M., Kanagawa, K., & Nakao, K. (2001). Ghrelin, an endogenous growth hormone secretagogue, is a novel orexigenic peptide that antagonizes leptin action through the activation of hypothalamic neuropeptide Y/Y1 receptor pathway. *Diabetes, 50,* 227–232.

Sills, T. L., & Vaccarino, F. J. (1996). Individual differences in sugar consumption following systemic or intraccumbens administration of low doses of amphetamine in deprived rats. *Pharmacology, Biochemistry and Behavior, 54,* 665–670.

Simpson, J. B., Epstein, A. N., & Camardo, J. S. (1978). The localization of receptors for the dipsogenic action of angiotensin II in the subfornical organ. *Journal of Comparative and Physiological Psychology, 92,* 581–608.

Simpson, J. B., & Routtenberg, A. (1974). Subfornical organ: Acetylcholine application elicits drinking. *Brain Research, 79,* 157–164.

Smith, F. J., & Campfield, L. A. (1993). Meal initiation occurs after experimental induction of transient declines in blood glucose. *American Journal of Physiology, 265,* R1423–R1429.

Smith, G. P., Jerome, C., & Norgren, R. (1985). Afferent axons in abdominal vagus mediate the satiety effect of cholecystokinin. *American Journal of Physiology, 249,* R638–R641.

Stanley, B. G., Kyrkouli, S. E., Lampert, S., & Leibowitz, S. F. (1986). Neuropeptide Y chronically injected into the hypothalamus: A powerful neurochemical inducer of hyperphagia and obesity. *Peptides, 7,* 1189–1192.

Stanley, B. G., & Leibowitz, S. F. (1985). Neuropeptide Y injected into the paraventricular hypothalamus: A powerful stimulant of feeding behavior. *Proceedings of the National Academy of Sciences, 82,* 3940–3943.

Stanley, B. G., Magdalin, W., Seirafi, A., Thomas, W. J., & Leibowitz, S. F. (1993). The perifornical area: The major focus of a patchily distributed hypothalamic neuropeptide Y sensitive feeding system(s). *Brain Research, 604,* 304–317.

Stein, L. J., & Woods, S. C. (1982). Gastrin releasing peptide reduces meal size in rats. *Peptides, 3,* 833–835.

Stellar, E. (1954). The physiology of motivation. *Psychological Review, 61,* 5–22.

Stricker, E. M. (1968). Some physiological and motivational properties of the hypovolemic stimulus for thirst. *Physiology and Behavior, 3,* 379–385.

Stricker, E. M. (1969). Osmoregulation and volume regulation in rats: Inhibition of hypovolemic thirst by water. *American Journal of Physiology, 217,* 98–105.

Stuckey, J. A., Gibbs, J., & Smith, G. P. (1985). Neural disconnection of the gut from brain blocks bombesin-induced satiety. *Peptides, 6,* 1249–1252.

Sweet, D. C., Levine, A. S., Billington, C. J., & Kotz, C. M. (1999). Feeding responses to central orexins. *Brain Research, 821,* 535–538.

Swithers, S. E., & Hall, W. G. (1994). Does oral experience terminate ingestion? *Appetite, 23,* 113–138.

Takiguchi, S., Takata, T., Funakoshi, K., Miyasaka, K., Kataoka, K., Fujimura, Y., Goto, T., & Kono, A. (1997). Disrupted cholecystokinin type-A receptor (CCK-AR) gene in OLETF rats. *Gene, 197,* 169–175.

Tang, M. (1976). Dependence of polyethylene glycol-induced dipsogenesis of intravascular fluid volume depletion. *Physiology and Behavior, 17,* 811–816.

Tartaglia, L. A., Demski, M., Weng, X., Deng, N., Culpepper, J., Devos, R., Richards, G. J., Campfield, L. A., Clarck, F. T., Deeds, J., Muir, C., Sanker, S., Moriarity, A., Moore, K. J., Smutko, J. S., Mays, G. G., Wolfe, E. A., Monroe, C. A., & Tepper, R. I. (1995). Identification and expression of a leptin receptor, OB-R. *Cell, 83,* 1–20.

Tschop, M., Smiley, D. L., & Heiman, M. L. (2000). Ghrelin induces adiposity in rodents. *Nature, 407,* 908–913.

van Dijk, G., Seeley, R. J., Theile, T. E., Freidman, M. I., Ji, H., Wikinson, C. W., Burn, P., Campfield, L. A., Tenenbaum, R., Baskin, D. G., Woods, S. C., & Schwartz, M. W. (1999). Metabolic, gastrointestinal and CNS neuropeptide effects of brain leptin administration in the rat. *American Journal of Physiology, 276,* R1425–R1433.

Weingarten, H. P., & Kulikovsky, O. T. (1989). Taste-to-postingestive consequence conditioning: Is the rise in sham feeding with repeated experience a learning phenomenon? *Physiology and Behavior, 45,* 471–476.

Weingarten, H. P., & Watson, S. D. (1982). Sham feeding as a procedure for assessing the influence of diet palatability on food intake. *Physiology and Behavior, 28,* 401–407.

Weisinger, R. S., Blair-West, J. R., Burns, P., Denton, D. A., & Tarjan, E. (1997). Role of Brain angiotensin in thirst and sodium appetite of rats. *Peptides, 18,* 977–984.

West, D. B., Fey, D., & Woods, S. C. (1984). Cholecystokinin persistently suppresses meal size but not food intake in free feeding rats. *American Journal of Physiology, 246,* R776–R787.

Wettendorff, H. (1901). Modifications de sang sous l'influence de la privation d'eau: Contribution a l'etude de la soif. *Travaux du Laboratoire de Physiologie, Institut de Physiologie, Instituts, Solvay, 4,* 353–384.

White, J. D., & Kershaw, M. (1989). Increased neuropeptide Y expression following food deprivation. *Molecular and Cellular Neuroscience, 1,* 41–48.

Widdowson, P. S., Henderson, L., Pickavance, L., Buckingham, R., Tadayyon, M., Arch, J. R. S., & Williams, G. (1999). Hypothalamic NPY status during positive energy balance and the effects of the NPY antagonist, BW1229U91, on the consumption of highly palatable energy rich diet. *Peptides, 20,* 367–372.

Woods, S. C., Lotter, E. C., McKay, L. D., & Porte, D., Jr. (1979). Chronic intracerebroventricular infusion of insulin reduces food intake and body weight in baboons. *Nature, 282,* 503–505.

Wren, A. M., Small, C. J., Ward, H. L., Murphey, K. G., Dakin, C. L., Taheri, S., Kennedy, A. R., Roberts, G. H., Morgan, D. G., Ghatei, M. A., & Bloom, S. R. (2000). The novel hypothalamic peptide ghrelin stimulates food intake and growth hormone secretion. *Endocrinology, 141,* 4325–4328.

Yaswen, J., Diehl, N., Brennan, M. B., & Hochgeschwender, U. (1999). Obesity in the mouse model of pro-opiomelanocortin deficiency responds to peripheral melanocortin. *Nature Medicine, 5,* 1066–1070.

Zarjevski, N., Cusin, I., Vetter, R., Rohner-Jeanrenaud, F., & Jeanrenaud, B. (1993). Chronic intracerebroventricular NPY administration to normal rats mimics hormonal and metabolic changes of obesity. *Endocrinology, 133,* 1753–1758.

Zhang, Y., Porcina, R., Maffei, M., Barone, M., Leopold, L., & Freidman, J. M. (1994). Positional cloning of the mouse obese gene and its human homologue. *Nature, 372,* 425–432.

Zhou, Q. Y., & Palmiter, R. D. (1995). Dopamine-deficient mice are severely hypoactive, adipsic and aphagic. *Cell, 83,* 1197–1209.

CHAPTER 12

Sex Behavior

ELAINE M. HULL AND JUAN M. DOMINGUEZ

In this review we summarize the progress that has been made in understanding sexual differentiation, as well as the hormonal and neural mechanisms that drive and direct male and female sexual behavior. We begin with the question of why sexual reproduction is by far the most common means of propagating multicellular species even though asexual reproduction is theoretically much faster and easier. We then describe copulatory patterns that are common across mammalian

Research for this chapter was conducted with the support of NIMH grants R01-MH-40826 and K02-01714 to E. M. H. and an NIMH Minority Supplement Grant to J. M. D.

species and summarize various laboratory tests of sexual behavior. Because hormones are important for sex differentiation in all mammalian and avian species, and because hormones also activate sexual behavior in adulthood, we discuss the means by which hormones exert their influence. We next describe the hormonal and neural control of female sexual behavior, followed by a similar treatment of the control of male sexual behavior. In each case, we first summarize the effects of systemically administered drugs and hormones or other treatments that affect more than one brain area. We then review the information concerning the specific brain areas that are implicated in the control of the behavior, including effects of lesions and stimulation, local application of drugs and hormones, and measures of neural activity. Finally, we observe that the hormonal and neural mechanisms that control sexual behavior are similar to the mechanisms that regulate other social behaviors. We close with a series of questions that remain unanswered and that may form a basis for future research. We hope that the reader will gain an understanding of the theoretical context in which sexual reproduction is embedded as well as an appreciation for both the similarities and the variations in the means by which sexual motivation is translated into successful reproduction.

Why Sex?

Why is sexual reproduction so prevalent? Asexual reproduction potentially results in twice as many offspring per generation and costs much less time and energy. Most multicellular animals spend large amounts of time and energy sizing up the field of potential mates and then preparing to copulate with the most desirable of the lot. The fact that sexual reproduction persists in the face of obvious disadvantages suggests that very important benefits accrue to sexually produced offspring. One advantage of sexual reproduction is that the recombination of genes promotes survival in times of environmental change. It also promotes differential adaptation to various niches in a time of relative constancy and decreases the ability of pathogens to exploit a single genotype. Another advantage is that some offspring will inherit fewer harmful mutations than either parent and will therefore be advantaged, whereas other offspring inherit more than the average number of harmful mutations and are more likely to die before reproducing, thereby carrying a large load of mutations to the grave (Kondrashov, 1988). In addition, meiotic recombination allows for repair of DNA. Lack of such recombination of the Y chromosome has resulted in evolutionary degeneration so that it is now only a shadow of its partner, the X chromosome, with which it now aligns only in the uppermost region.

Sex Differentiation

Fish and Reptiles

Sexual reproduction implies differentiation into different sexes. One might think that because of the importance of sex differentiation, evolutionarily early mechanisms for differentiation would have been conserved. However, a brief perusal of such mechanisms provides a richly varied list. Among fish there are both simultaneous and sequential hermaphrodites. Simultaneous hermaphrodites have ovotestes that produce both eggs and sperm; these fish alternate between masculine and feminine patterns of behavior. Sequential hermaphrodites begin life as one sex and then change to the other in response to environmental or genotypic influences. Among other species of fish, males are polymorphic; that is, there are two male phenotypes. For example, among plainfin midshipmen, Type I males are larger and are territorial, whereas Type II males resemble females and sneak into the nest sites of Type I males and release their sperm (reviewed in Nelson, 2000).

Among some species of reptiles, sex differentiation is determined genetically, as in birds and mammals. However, in many species of lizards, turtles, and crocodiles, the ambient temperature during incubation of the eggs determines whether offspring will be male or female. In some species, warmer temperatures produce females; in others, warm temperatures produce males. In snapping turtles and crocodiles, females are produced if temperatures are either very high or very low. Apparently, the temperature influences the differentiation of the embryonic gonad into either a testis or an ovary; however, the mechanism for this influence is not known (Crews, Bull, & Billy, 1988).

As in fish, the males of some species of lizards exhibit multiple phenotypes. High levels of both testosterone and progesterone during early posthatching development result in territorial males with orange and blue dewlaps (skin flaps) attached to their throats (Moore, Hews, & Knapp, 1998). Low levels of testosterone and progesterone produce nonterritorial males with plain orange dewlaps. The presence of high corticosterone as a result of stress in adulthood determines whether nonterritorial males are sedentary or nomadic. Thus, interactions between early and late hormonal influences and environmental factors determine the coloration and behavior of these lizards.

Birds

In birds a ZZ chromosomal configuration confers maleness, whereas females have a ZW chromosomal pattern. The homogametic sex (the sex with two of the same type of sex chromosomes) is the default sex for reproductive behavior patterns (Balthazart & Ball, 1995). Thus, birds with two Z chromosomes will develop male-typical reproductive behaviors in the absence of gonadal secretions. Secretion of estrogen by ovaries of ZW individuals organizes female-typical reproductive behavior patterns. However, for singing behavior, female-typical lack of singing is the default condition, unless testosterone masculinizes the song-producing neural circuits. For other types of behavior, neither the male- nor female-typical pattern is the default condition. The W chromosome directs the differentiation of the left primitive gonad to become an ovary, which secretes estrogen, causing the right Müllerian duct to degenerate. The lack of a W chromosome, and of the resultant production of estrogen, results in retention of both Müllerian ducts.

Mammals

In mammals the homogametic sex is the female, with an XX chromosomal pattern. In the absence of hormones, a phenotypic female develops. A gene on the Y chromosome, the sex-determining region of the Y chromosome (SRY), produces a locally acting protein that causes the primitive gonads to differentiate into testes. The testes then secrete androgens and peptide hormones that produce masculine differentiation. Differentiation of the external genitalia is mediated primarily by a metabolite of testosterone, 5-alpha-dihydrotestosterone (DHT), which binds with higher affinity than testosterone to the intracellular androgen receptor. Testosterone is converted to DHT by the enzyme 5-alpha-reductase, which is present in the genital skin of embryonic males and females. Under androgenic influence the genital folds that would become labia in females fuse into a scrotum; the genital tubercle enlarges into a penis, rather than a smaller clitoris; and the genital groove fuses to become a duct for both urine and semen.

Because females possess 5-alpha-reductase and androgen receptors, their genitalia may be partially masculinized if they are exposed to high concentrations of androgens during development, as in *congenital adrenal hyperplasia* (CAH). Individuals with CAH lack or have insufficient amounts of the enzyme that produces cortisol, the major glucocorticoid in humans. As a result of the lack of negative feedback from cortisol, blood concentrations of adrenocorticotropic hormone (ACTH) are high; they stimulate the adrenal cortex to produce excess adrenal androgens that partially masculinize a female fetus's genitalia. Conversely, if males lack 5-alpha-reductase, their genitalia will be incompletely masculinized, and they may be thought to be female at birth (Imperato-McGinley, Guerrero, Gautier, & Peterson, 1974). However, the pubertal surge of testosterone is sufficient to masculinize the genitals, and the individuals become phenotypically, as well as genotypically, male.

Another disorder of differentiation is *androgen insensitivity syndrome,* in which a genetic male (XY chromosome pattern) lacks androgen receptors. As a result, the testosterone produced by internal testes cannot masculinize the body, and the individual is phenotypically female. However, she lacks female internal genitalia and is sterile.

Individuals whose genitals are ambiguous at birth are called intersexes. Controversy has arisen over the medical and psychological treatment of intersexes. Often, babies born with small penises or large clitorises have been subjected to surgical "correction," usually reducing the size of the penis or clitoris and forming a vagina. It was thought that gender identity is very malleable and that an individual could easily adopt the gender role that was assigned. However, this surgical reconstruction usually left the individual with greatly diminished, or absent, genital sensations, and frequently with little information, counseling, or medical follow-up (Fausto-Sterling, 2000). Because of these problems, new guidelines for the management of intersexuality have been proposed (Diamond & Sigmundson, 1997).

In most male rodents, differentiation of brain mechanisms controlling sexual behavior and endocrine function is mediated by estradiol, which is produced from testosterone by the enzyme aromatase. Females usually are not masculinized by their own and their mother's estradiol because estradiol is bound to alpha-fetoprotein, which keeps estradiol circulating in the blood, rather than entering cells to bind to estrogen receptors. Exposure to excess estradiol during early development can masculinize female rodents so that they display masculine sexual preferences and behavior patterns if they are given estradiol or testosterone in adulthood (McCarthy, Schlenker, & Pfaff, 1993). Among primates and guinea pigs, androgens, rather than estradiol, are the primary masculinizing and defeminizing hormones (Goy & McEwen, 1980).

Although the neural bases of reproductive behavior are permanently differentiated early in life, hormones are required during adulthood in order to activate the patterns that were previously organized. This finding has been referred to as the *organizational-activational distinction.*

PATTERNS OF SEXUAL BEHAVIOR IN MAMMALS

Female Reproductive Cycles

Female reproductive cycles consist of a preovulatory follicular phase, during which the follicle surrounding the oocyte (immature egg) secretes increasing amounts of estrogen and promotes the development of the oocyte. Following ovulation, the remnant of the follicle, the corpus luteum, secretes progesterone, which prepares the uterus for implantation of a fertilized egg.

There are three types of reproductive cycles in female mammals. Type 1 cycles, characterized by spontaneous ovulation and a spontaneous luteal phase, are exhibited by primates (including women), dogs, and guinea pigs. As the follicle grows, it secretes more and more estrogen in response to follicle-stimulating hormone (FSH) from the anterior pituitary. When the level of estrogen rises high enough, it triggers a positive feedback response, in which a surge of luteinizing hormone (LH), accompanied by a smaller surge of FSH, is released from the anterior pituitary. Luteinizing hormone causes the oocyte to undergo its first meiotic division and to break free of the surrounding follicle. The follicle then becomes the corpus luteum (yellow body) and secretes progesterone and smaller amounts of estrogen, which increase the vascularization of the uterus. If the oocyte is fertilized by a sperm, it will undergo its second meiotic division, develop into a blastocyst in the fallopian tube or uterine horn, and implant in the highly vascularized uterus. If fertilization does not occur, the lining of the uterus is either sloughed off, as in humans and other great apes, or resorbed.

Type 2 cycles require the stimuli derived from copulation in order to induce ovulation, but when ovulation does occur, the luteal phase is spontaneous. Type 2 cycles are characteristic of animals that live solitary lives, including cats, rabbits, voles, and ferrets. Thus, ovulation, and in some cases behavioral estrus as well, occurs only when a male is present.

Animals with Type 3 cycles ovulate spontaneously but require copulatory stimuli to induce a luteal phase. Rats, mice, and hamsters exhibit Type 3 cycles. Both Type 2 and Type 3 cycles minimize the amount of time spent in a nonpregnant state and are seen in animals that tend to be short-lived and to produce a large number of offspring.

Because females are fertile for only a relatively brief period, it is usually important for them to advertise their sexual interest. Attractive chemosensory pheromones are released, and in some species physical changes in the genital region occur. In addition, the female may engage in a series of proceptive behaviors, which are defined as those that indicate the female's motivation to engage in sexual activity. These behaviors may include approaches to a male, alternating approaches and withdrawals, prolonged eye contact, vocalizations, and presentation of the genital region. The third component of female sexuality, in addition to attractivity and proceptivity, is receptivity. Behaviors associated with receptivity include postures that permit the male to copulate successfully. All three components of female sexuality (attractivity, proceptivity, and receptivity) are enhanced by estrogen, which also leads to ovulation and therefore fertility. It is not surprising that evolutionary processes ensure that the most attractive females, from a male's perspective, are those that are the most fertile and also those that display the greatest sexual motivation and responsiveness.

Copulatory Patterns Common Across Mammalian Species

Some patterns of copulation are common across species. In many mammals copulation is preceded by the male's investigation of the female's genitals, which allows him to determine whether she is receptive and provides him with sexually arousing stimuli. If the female is receptive, the male will mount from her rear, clasp her flanks with his forepaws, and begin a series of rapid, shallow thrusts with his pelvis. Usually, the male's penis is at least partially erect during this thrusting. In response to flank contact or the actual mount, the female will typically display lordosis, a rather rigid posture in which her back is flat or concave and her tail is deflected. By exposing the vagina, lordosis makes it possible for the male to achieve intromission (insertion of his penis into the female's vagina).

If the male does not detect the vagina with his penis soon after he begins thrusting, he usually dismounts and either reapproaches the female or engages in other activities. If a male rodent does detect the female's vagina, he typically performs a deeper, intravaginal thrust, followed immediately by a springing dismount. This springing dismount is usually used as the measure of intromission in rats and many other rodents because it is reliably associated with penile insertion (Sachs, 1983). After an intromission male rodents typically groom their genitals and wait for a minute or two before mounting again. Male rats ejaculate after about 10 such intromissions. Ejaculation is characterized by a deeper intravaginal thrust, a much slower dismount, prolonged genital grooming, and ultrasonic vocalizations during the postejaculatory interval of quiescence.

In other species, such as mice, the male maintains the intromission and shows repeated intravaginal thrusting before ejaculating (Mosig & Dewsbury, 1976). Male ungulates may ejaculate immediately after intromission (Lott, 1981). Dogs and other canids begin to ejaculate soon after penile insertion, but their penis swells to such an extent that it remains locked in the vagina for up to 30 min, thereby promoting sperm transport (Beach & LeBoeuf, 1967). Ejaculation is usually accompanied by rhythmic contractions of skeletal muscles and the striated muscles of the perineal area.

Ejaculation is typically followed by genital grooming and a period of sexual quiescence. The postejaculatory interval of quiescence may last for less than 30 s in Syrian hamsters (Bunnell, Boland, & Dewsbury, 1976), for 5 to 10 min in rats, or hours or days in other species (Dewsbury, 1972). During this time male rats make ultrasonic calls, and male gerbils stomp their feet. Toward the end of the period, introduction of a novel female may elicit renewed copulation. The lack of copulation during the postejaculatory interval does not result from erectile failure, at least in some species. In rats, for example, *ex copula* touch-based erections are actually enhanced following an ejaculation (O'Hanlon & Sachs, 1980). At the end of the postejaculatory interval, copulation is likely to occur again.

A male rat may achieve up to seven or eight ejaculations before reaching sexual satiety, which lasts for several days. After reaching satiety with one female, some males can be induced to begin copulating with a new female. This phenomenon is sometimes referred to as the *Coolidge effect,* a reference to an anecdote involving President and Mrs. Calvin Coolidge. When visiting a farm, Mrs. Coolidge observed that one rooster mated repeatedly during her visit to the chicken pen and asked the farmer to call Mr. Coolidge's attention to the rooster's activities when the President visited the facility. When the farmer relayed the message later that day, Mr. Coolidge asked the farmer to point out to Mrs. Coolidge that the repeated activity was directed toward many different hens.

Females with Type 2 or Type 3 reproductive cycles require the stimulation of copulation to trigger ovulation or a luteal phase, respectively. For example, spines on the male cat's penis scratch the female's vagina, a rather painful way to induce ovulation (Type 2 cycle). Female rats typically require five or six intromissions, separated by approximately 2-min intervals, to elicit a luteal phase (Type 3 cycle). In the wild, or in seminatural environments, female rats pace their interactions with males in order to achieve the correct timing and number of intromissions before ejaculation (McClintock, 1987). Indeed, there was a higher rate of pregnancy in females receiving 5 paced intromissions than in those receiving 10 nonpaced intromissions (Erskine, 1985). Females tested in a place-conditioning apparatus spent more time in the paced mating compartment, but not in the nonpaced mating compartment, compared to a neutral compartment (Paredes & Alonso, 1997). Females developed place preferences even if they were not actively pacing, if males were placed into their compartments at their preferred intervals (Jenkins & Becker, 2001b). Thus, copulation was rewarding only if it occurred at the female's preferred intercopulatory interval.

In addition to triggering a luteal phase, multiple intromissions or intravaginal thrusting may increase the number of sperm in the male's ejaculate and facilitate sperm transport in the female's reproductive tract (Adler & Toner, 1986), or promote male-female bonding (reviewed in Carter, DeVries, & Getz, 1995). On the other hand, copulation is energetically expensive, and lengthy copulation may expose the animals to predation. Therefore, copulatory behavior reflects a balance of selection pressures imposed by the physical, biological, and social environments.

Testing Paradigms

Use of a Limited Number of Species

As in other areas of biology, most research on sexual behavior has been done on a limited number of species, most of them rodents. The rat is a common model because it is relatively inexpensive and there is currently much information on its neural and endocrine systems. However, focusing on a limited number of species limits the opportunities to identify interesting variations and to correlate neural and behavioral variations.

Tests of Sexual Motivation

It is useful to distinguish between sexual motivation and copulatory performance. However, these concepts may be difficult to measure. Lesions or drugs may alter the ability to detect or interpret stimuli, perform copulatory movements, or remember stimuli associated with previous sexual encounters. Drugs or lesions may cause general malaise, and altered stimuli from one partner may inhibit the behavior of the other, thereby compounding the copulatory deficits.

Mount and intromission latencies are common measures of sexual motivation. However, intromission latency depends on the ability to achieve an erection, as well as on motivation. There are several tests of sexual motivation that are not based directly on copulatory behavior. In place-preference tests one partner is initially allowed to copulate in one of two interconnected areas and to be alone in the other area. The subject later spends time in the side previously associated with copulation or in the side it inhabited alone. In a second technique a subject must cross an obstruction in order to reach a sexual partner. Another test of sexual motivation is the X-maze or cross-maze, in which a sexual partner is placed into one of four interconnected goal boxes; the other three goal boxes contain different objects or remain empty. The number of choices of each goal box, the latencies to reach each goal box, and the number of no-choice trials are measured. A fourth technique uses a bilevel apparatus in which a male and female are initially allowed to copulate throughout the apparatus. The subject is later placed alone into the apparatus, and the number of times he or she changes levels, presumably in search of the partner, is tabulated. A final measure is lever pressing for a secondary reinforcer that has been paired with copulation. In several of these tasks motivational factors are confounded with motor ability or with the ability to learn the secondary reinforcement task. Therefore, care must be given to the choice of test to be used and to the interpretation of results.

Tests of Female Attractivity

Female attractivity is measured primarily by allowing a male to spend time with one female or another. In some tests the bedding from a female's home cage, which presumably contains the pheromones excreted either directly from the anogenital region or in the urine, is presented to a male, who spends time in contact with the bedding of the estrous female or that of a nonestrous female, a male, or clean bedding.

Tests of Female Proceptivity

Female proceptivity is measured by direct observation of behaviors that increase the likelihood of sexual contact. These include approach to the male, display of the genital region, and species-typical behaviors, such as hopping and darting by female rats and increased eye contact and tongue flicking by primates.

Tests of Female Receptivity

Female receptivity is usually measured as the number of receptive postures displayed divided by the number of mounts by a male (lordosis quotient). Some tests of receptivity include a quantification of lordosis quality, ranging from 0 (no lordosis behavior) to 1 (brief stationary posture with flat back), 2 (slightly concave back), 3 (markedly concave back), and 4 (markedly concave back, a posture that is held for several seconds).

Tests of Male Copulatory Behavior

Male copulatory behavior is usually quantified in tests that use both temporal and behavioral criteria to determine test length. In this way the initiation of sexual behavior can be distinguished from the ability to copulate to ejaculation after copulation has begun. Other test paradigms allow the male to mate until he achieves sexual satiety, defined as failure to resume copulation within a specified time after the last ejaculation.

Male rat copulatory behavior has been analyzed into four weakly correlated factors (Sachs, 1978). First, a copulatory rate factor includes the interintromission interval, the ejaculation latency, the time from an ejaculation to the termination of ultrasonic vocalization, and the postejaculatory interval before the next intromission. These four measures are highly correlated in tests of normal males, but they can be dissociated by experimental treatments; therefore, they may be controlled by separate physiological mechanisms. Three other factors included an initiation factor based primarily on mount and intromission latencies, an intromission ratio factor based on the number of intromissions divided by the number of mounts plus intromissions, and an intromission count factor based on the number of intromissions preceding ejaculation. A later factor analysis, based on copulation tests in bilevel chambers, identified an anticipatory factor, reflecting the number of times the male changed levels, in addition to the four factors just noted (Pfaus, Damsma, et al., 1990).

Tests of Penile Function

Erection, intromission, and ejaculation can be easily observed in studies of monkeys, dogs, cats, and many other species, including humans. However, in rodents these penile components of copulation are more often inferred than observed. In some experiments an angled mirror was placed under a clear floor of a test cage to facilitate observation of penile actions; in other experiments the female's vagina was inspected after copulation for evidence of sperm. Because genital reflexes are difficult to measure while the male is copulating, paradigms have been developed for monitoring them *ex copula*. However, different physiological mechanisms may control erection in different contexts (reviewed in Sachs, 2000).

Spontaneous erections can occasionally be observed when a male is alone in his home cage or in a neutral arena. Such erections can be increased by various drugs, in which case they are called drug-induced erections. The number of spontaneous erections is increased in the presence of an inaccessible estrous female (Sachs, Akasofu, Citron, Daniels, & Natoli, 1994) or the volatile odors of an estrous female (Kondo, Tomihara, & Sakuma, 1999). These noncontact erections are a model for psychogenic erections in humans and appear to have physiological bases similar to those of spontaneous and drug-induced erections.

Touch-based erections have been elicited by manually stimulating the penes of dogs or other species. However, tactile stimulation of the penis in rats and other rodents inhibits erection. Therefore, Hart developed a technique that exerts pressure at the base of the penis of rats (1968) or mice (Sachs, 1980). The male is restrained in a supine position, and the penile sheath is retracted, exposing the glans penis. The continuing pressure of the retracted sheath around the base of the penis elicits a series of erections. Penile anteroflexions (flips) may also occur. Occasionally, semen is emitted, usually as a result of drug administration. These *ex copula* reflexes are similar in form and mechanical basis to those used *in copula* (Holmes, Chapple, Leipheimer, & Sachs, 1991); however, the temporal relations are different, as are the hormonal mechanisms of control (Sachs, 1983).

The Urethrogenital Reflex

Another *ex copula* genital response is the urethrogenital reflex, which has been proposed as a model for the human orgasmic reflex. This reflex has been elicited in both male and female rats that had been anesthetized and spinally transected (McKenna, Chung, & McVary, 1991). Typically, the urethra is filled with saline under pressure, and then the pressure is rapidly released. The reflex consists of rhythmic contractions of the pelvic muscles, with similar timing as in human orgasm.

PRINCIPLES OF HORMONAL ACTION

Genomic Effects

Hormones are blood-borne chemical messengers that are produced and released by endocrine glands and that act on tissues located at some distance from the secreting gland. Because they circulate throughout the body, the specificity of their action depends on the presence of specialized receptors in the target tissues or organs. Most of the cellular receptors that are important for sexual behavior act by initiating or repressing transcription of certain genes. According to the most widely accepted model of hormonal action, a steroid hormone molecule binds to its cognate receptor in the cytoplasm of the cell. The hormone-receptor complex then enters the cell nucleus, where it dimerizes (links to another hormone-receptor complex); the dimer then binds to a hormone response element upstream of a structural gene and initiates transcription of the appropriate mRNA, which is in turn translated into a protein. The resultant protein may be a regulator of transcription of additional genes, or it may be an enzyme, a receptor, or a structural protein. Some hormonal effects may be exerted indirectly by increased activity impinging on downstream neurons.

The importance of steroid receptors has been demonstrated by profound deficits in masculine and feminine sexual behavior observed in male and female mice that lack the classic estrogen receptor (ERα). These knockout (ERαKO) animals usually exhibit little or no copulatory behavior (Ogawa et al., 1998; Wersinger et al., 1997). Administration of estradiol, with or without progesterone, to ovariectomized female ERαKO mice did not result in receptivity (Rissman, Early, Taylor, Korach, & Lubahn, 1997). Furthermore, male mice frequently behaved aggressively toward ERαKO female intruders but never to wild-type females, suggesting that attractivity was also impaired by the lack of estrogen receptors (Ogawa et al., 1996).

Animals lacking progesterone receptors (progesterone receptor knockout mice, or PRKOs) have also been produced. PRKO females do not ovulate, and after ovariectomy they do not respond behaviorally to estradiol or progesterone injections (Mani, Blaustein, & O'Malley, 1997). Similar results were obtained when estrogen-primed female rats were injected with antisense to the progesterone receptor into the ventromedial nucleus of the hypothalamus (VMH), an important area for the control of receptivity (Ogawa, Olazabal, Parhar, & Pfaff, 1994). (Antisense oligonucleotides bind to mRNA for the designated protein, thereby preventing

translation of the protein.) Male PRKO mice, however, showed a copulatory deficit only on their first copulatory tests (Phelps, Lydon, O'Malley, & Crews, 1998).

Rapid, Nongenomic Effects

Besides their slow, genomically mediated effects, steroid hormones may have rapid effects. For example, estrogen had very rapid effects on neuron membranes (Xiao & Becker, 1998). In addition, progesterone and its metabolites acted in an agonist-like manner to increase functioning of gamma-aminobutyric acid (GABA$_A$) receptors (Majewska, Harrison, Schwartz, Barker, & Paul, 1986), thereby increasing chloride influx and hyperpolarizing neurons. Testosterone has affected cell firing in the medial preoptic area (MPOA) of castrated male rats within minutes (Pfaff & Pfaffman, 1969) or seconds (Yamada, 1979). Furthermore, neurons in slices from the MPOA showed changes in firing rates within minutes of estrogen or testosterone administration via the perfusion medium (Silva & Boulant, 1986). On the other hand, hours or days of steroid hormone replacement are required to restore copulation in gonadectomized animals. Although rapid membrane effects of estrogen are not sufficient for induction of estrus in female rats and rapid effects of testosterone are not sufficient to restore sexual behavior of castrated male rats, they may contribute to such facilitation. For example, rapid effects of progesterone in the ventral tegmental area (VTA) of the midbrain prolonged lordosis in female rats and hamsters (Frye & Vongher, 1999).

There is evidence for a rapid effect of testosterone on erectile function (Sachs & Leipheimer, 1988). Electromyograph (EMG) recordings during tests of touch-based erections revealed penile muscle activity in some testosterone-treated castrated rats within 5 min after injection. However, testosterone did not restore erection at that time. Inhibition of protein synthesis by the antibiotic anisomycin did not affect the short-latency (within 24 hr) activation of touch-based erections by testosterone (Meisel, Leipheimer, & Sachs, 1986). Therefore, protein synthesis was not a necessary component of the hormonal activation of touch-based erections.

ACTIVATION OF FEMALE SEXUAL BEHAVIOR BY GONADAL HORMONES

Dependence of Most Nonprimate Species on Steroid Hormones

Females of virtually all nonmammalian species that have been tested mate only during a period of elevated blood estrogens (Crews & Silver, 1985). Most nonprimate female mammals are also completely dependent on hormones to elicit proceptive and receptive sexual behaviors. The estrous cycles of rats are typically four (occasionally five) days long. During two days of diestrus, plasma concentrations of estrogen and progesterone are low, although estrogen begins to rise during the second day of diestrus. On the day of proestrus, estrogen peaks in the afternoon, followed several hours later by progesterone. Hormone levels then fall precipitously, so that estrogen is at basal levels by the beginning of the day of estrus; progesterone declines to its nadir by the middle of the day of estrus. Female rats are receptive only during the evening of proestrus. Some ovariectomized female rats can be induced to become receptive following injections of low doses of estrogen alone, but most require a subsequent surge of progesterone. One function of the initial surge of estrogen is to up-regulate the production of progesterone receptors, stimulation of which then elicits the proceptive and receptive behaviors.

On the other hand, female sheep require progesterone before estrogen (Robinson, 1954). Other rodents, such as prairie voles (Carter, Witt, Auksi, & Casten, 1987) and hamsters (Wynne-Edwards, Terranova, & Lisk, 1987), require only estrogen for receptivity. Female musk shrews aromatize circulating testosterone to estradiol in the preoptic area and hypothalamus (Rissman, 1991). Thus, there is much variability in the pattern of hormone secretion, but females of most nonprimate species require hormones associated with ovulation in order to become sexually receptive.

Increased Likelihood of Copulation by Periovulatory Female Primates

Sexual behavior in female primates is less dependent on hormones. Female monkeys readily display proceptive and receptive behaviors throughout their 28-day cycle in laboratory tests with a single male partner. However, sexual interest is heightened during the periovulatory period. This increase is especially noticeable in female monkeys in the wild or in seminatural environments, where females are subjected to aggression and harassment by other females if they show proceptive behaviors toward a male (Wallen, 1990). As a result, females are willing to risk this aggression only around the time of ovulation, when high levels of estrogen increase sexual motivation.

In humans, too, there may be increased sexual interest around the time of ovulation. Among women in stable sexual relationships, there is relatively little variation in the frequency of copulation throughout the menstrual cycle (Adams, Gold, & Burt, 1978). However, there is a peak in erotic thoughts and in autoerotic activity around the time of ovulation and a smaller increase shortly before menstruation (Adams et al.,

1978; Slob, Bax, Hop, Rowland, & Van der Werff ten Bosch, 1996). This pattern of increased periovulatory sexual interest and of a secondary peak shortly before the onset of menstruation was also observed among lesbians (Matteo & Rissman, 1984).

Hormonal Control of Sensory Processes

One way in which hormones facilitate sexual behavior is by enhancing the processing of sensory information. Females have generally greater sensitivity for chemosensory stimuli, including species-specific pheromones, than do males (Doty, Applebaum, Zusho, & Settle, 1985). This sensitivity is further enhanced by increased periovulatory estrogen concentrations. Both female mice and women are able to use chemosensory stimuli to express preferences for males with certain immune system markers that are different from their own (reviewed in Wedekind & Penn, 2000). The resultant increase in ability of the offspring's immune system to recognize a greater variety of invaders contributes to their survival. Males are unable to detect these differences.

Somatosensory input from the flank area is also enhanced by estrogen in female rats. Pressure on the flank before and during a mount increases the likelihood or intensity of lordosis. The size of the receptive fields (the areas on the skin that elicit an electrophysiological response) of sensory nerves increases following estrogen administration to ovariectomized females (Kow, Montgomery & Pfaff, 1979). As a result, the flanks become more sensitive to the stimuli that elicit lordosis.

SYSTEMICALLY ADMINISTERED DRUGS AFFECT FEMALE SEXUAL BEHAVIOR

The slow, genomically mediated effects of steroid hormones on copulatory behavior are mediated primarily by up- or down-regulation of some aspect of neurotransmitter function. Because neurotransmitters often act synergistically in more than one site and because the site of action often is not known a priori, systemic administration of drugs can be advantageous. However, drugs can have interfering actions at different sites. Therefore, to gain a full understanding of neurotransmitter influences, some experiments should administer drugs widely throughout the system, whereas in other experiments drugs should be targeted to specific sites. Table 12.1 summarizes the effects on female sexual behavior of drugs and treatments that affect neurotransmitter function in more than one brain area.

TABLE 12.1   Effects of Systemically Administered Drugs or Treatments Affecting More Than One Brain Area on Female Sexual Behavior

Transmitter Altering Drugs	Effects on Sexual Behavior	References	Remarks
Dopamine			
Neurotoxic DA lesions	+	[2] [13]	The apparently contradictory effects may be related to
Systemic DA antagonists	+	[1]	the female's initial state of receptivity, or perhaps to
Systemic D_1/D_2 agonist	+	[5]	differential effects on different brain areas, which may
ICV D_1 agonist	+	[8]	reflect hormonal influences on receptors.
Norepinephrine			
Lesions of the VNAB	−	[6]	
Systemic NE antagonist	−	[7]	
Systemic NE agonist	+	[3]	
Serotonin			
Lesions of 5-HT cell bodies	+	Serotonergic	
Stimulation of 5-HT_{1A}	−	effects reviewed	
Stimulation of 5-HT_{1B}	−	in [14]	
Stimulation of 5-HT_2	+		
Stimulation of 5-HT_3	−		
Acetycholine			
Intraventricular M_2 agonists	+	[4]	This facilitation was independent of progesterone [12].
Intraventricular M_1 agonists	n/e		
GABA			
Inhibit GABA degradation	−	[11]	
$GABA_A$ agonist	−	[11]	
Opiates			
Systemic morphine (μ agonist)	−	[10]	
Peptide δ-receptor agonist	+	[10]	
Low levels of morphiceptin	−	[9] [15]	
Higher levels of morphiceptin	+	[9]	This facilitation was blocked by a δ antagonist, but not a μ antagonist [9].

Note. + = facilitation; − = inhibition; n/e, no effect; VNAB, ventral noradrenergic bundle, the major source of norepinephrine input to the hypothalamus. References: [1] Ahlenius, Engel, Eriksson, Modigh, & Sodersten (1972); [2] Caggiula et al. (1979); [3] Crowley, Nock, & Feder (1978); [4] Dohanich, McMullan, Cada, and Mangum, 1991; [5] Hamburger-Bar & Rigter (1975); [6] Hansen, Stanfield, & Everitt (1980); [7] Nock & Feder (1979); [8] Mani, Allen, Clark, Blaustein, & O'Malley (1994); [9] Pfaus, Pendleton, & Gorzalka (1986); [10] Pfaus & Gorzalka (1987); [11] Qureshi, Bednar, Forsberg, & Sodersten (1988); [12] Richmond & Clemens (1986); [13] Sirinathsinghji, Whittington, & Audsley (1986); [14] Uphouse (2000); [15] Wiesner & Moss (1986).

BRAIN AREAS IMPLICATED IN THE ACTIVATION OF FEMALE SEXUAL BEHAVIOR

Neural Control of Proceptivity

Medial Preoptic Area and Ventromedial Hypothalamus

Pfaff (1999) suggested that the MPOA is important for active proceptive behaviors; it then must decrease its activity during the stationary lordosis posture, which is promoted by the ventromedial hypothalamus (VMH). Estrogen increased the facilitative effect of the preoptic area on the midbrain locomotor region, thereby enhancing proceptive behaviors (Takeo & Sakuma, 1995).

Dopamine release in the MPOA of ovariectomized female rats increased with the onset of sexual receptivity following estrogen and progesterone injections (Matuszewich, Lorrain, & Hull, 2000). Dopamine concentrations increased further when a male was introduced and the animals copulated; however, a significant increase occurred only in a nonpacing environment, although dopamine metabolites increased in both pacing and nonpacing conditions. Perhaps the lack of an increase in dopamine was related to the smaller number of copulatory behaviors in the pacing environment.

Nucleus Accumbens

Dopamine release in the mesolimbic dopamine tract, which ends in the nucleus accumbens (NAcc) and several other limbic sites, may be critical for the rewarding aspects of paced mating. Dopamine is released in the NAcc and dorsal striatum of female rats (Mermelstein & Becker, 1995; Pfaus, Damsma, Wenkstern, & Fibiger, 1995) and hamsters (Meisel, Camp, & Robinson, 1993) during paced, but not during nonpaced, copulation. Furthermore, paced copulation is rewarding for female rats, but nonpaced copulation is not (Oldenburger, Everitt, & de Jonge, 1992; Paredes & Alonso, 1997). Even when the female is not actively in control of copulatory intervals and the male is removed and replaced at her preferred interval, dopamine is released (Becker, Rudick, & Jenkins, 2001), and the female develops a conditioned place preference for the copulatory arena (Jenkins & Becker, 2001b).

Neural Control of Receptivity

Pfaff and Schwartz-Giblin (1988) have provided a thorough and elegant model of the neural mechanisms that control lordosis (see Figure 12.1). The functions of the five modules that they identified range from slow hormone-mediated disinhibition of behavior to moment-to-moment postural adjustments.

The Forebrain Module

The forebrain exerts primarily inhibitory effects, but there are selective facilitative effects. Electrolytic lesions of the lateral septum increased receptivity in female rats (Nance, Shryne, Gordon, & Gorski, 1977), whereas electrical stimulation inhibited lordosis in female hamsters (Zasorin, Malsbury, & Pfaff, 1975). Thus, the septal area is generally inhibitory to receptivity in female rodents. Olfactory bulbectomy increased lordosis responses in hormone-primed female rats (Lumia, Meisel, & Sachs, 1981) and in gonadally intact, cycling female rats (Al Satli & Aron, 1977). However, removal

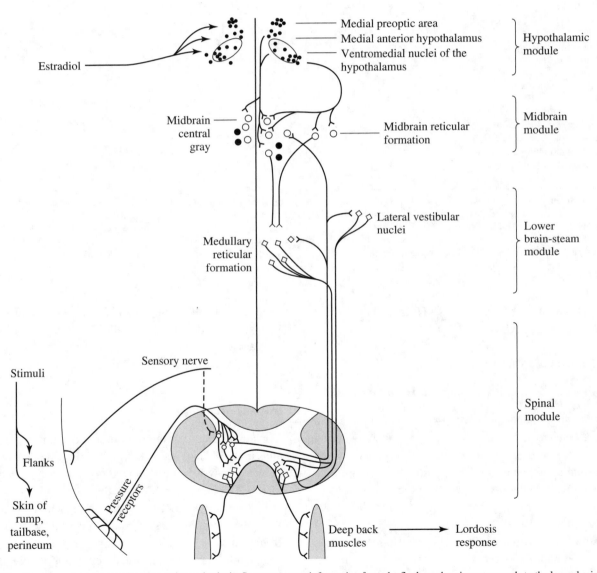

Figure 12.1 Summary of neural circuitry that activates lordosis. Somatosensory information from the flanks and perineum ascends to the lower brain stem and midbrain modules. Estrogen-concentrating neurons in the hypothalamic module disinhibit neurons in the midbrain module, enabling them to respond to the sensory input. Descending output from the midbrain facilitates the brain stem module, which organizes the rapid responses of motor neurons in the spinal cord that control the deep back muscles that produce the lordosis posture. The forebrain module, which is largely inhibitory to lordosis, is not shown. Adapted from Pfaff et al. (1994).

of only vomeronasal input inhibited responding in female hamsters (Mackay-Sim & Rose, 1986).

The Hypothalamic Module

The hypothalamic module is the primary site for slow hormone-mediated effects. Estradiol and progesterone bind to their respective receptors in the VMH and the preoptic area and initiate RNA transcription and protein synthesis. These hormones also alter the electrophysiological responsiveness of neurons in the hypothalamus. There are apparently contradictory reports concerning the role of the preoptic area in controlling lordosis behavior of female rats. On the one hand, lesions of the MPOA facilitated lordosis responding in hormonally primed females, and electrical stimulation inhibited lordosis (Takeo, Chiba, & Sakuma, 1993). However, in another study MPOA lesions inhibited lordosis (Bast, Hunts, Renner, Morris, & Quadagno, 1987). Even in animals whose receptive behavior was enhanced by MPOA lesions, proceptive behavior was suppressed (Hoshina, Takeo, Nakano, Sato, & Sakuma, 1994), suggesting that the intact MPOA inhibits receptivity and facilitates proceptivity. A single-neuron recording experiment suggests a resolution of the apparent contradiction: Different groups of neurons, located in slightly different subregions of the preoptic area, may promote proceptive behavior and lordosis (Kato & Sakuma, 2000).

Lesions of the VMH have consistently impaired lordosis responses and also increased male-typical behavior (Dörner, Döcke, & Götz, 1975). Conversely, electrical stimulation facilitated lordosis (Pfaff & Sakuma, 1979). Sequential implantation of estradiol and progesterone into the VMH was sufficient to restore receptivity in ovariectomized rats (Rubin & Barfield, 1983). Furthermore, estrogen injections in ovariectomized female rats induced transcription of RNA for the progesterone receptor selectively in the ventromedial hypothalamus of females, but not in males (Lauber, Romano, & Pfaff, 1991). Progesterone's ability to facilitate behavior was blocked by administration of antisense to the progesterone receptor into the VMH (Ogawa et al., 1994). Estradiol also increased mRNA for preproenkephalin (the precursor of enkephalin) in the VMH (Romano, Harlan, Shivers, Howells, & Pfaff, 1988). Enkephalin mRNA synthesis in the VMH was highly correlated with the female rat estrous cycle (Funabashi, Brooks, Kleopoulos, Grandison, Mobbs, & Pfaff, 1995).

Estradiol priming is essential for the release of norepinephrine in the VMH of female rats during copulation (Vathy & Etgen, 1988). Norepinephrine stimulates (α1 receptors, which are associated with increased neural activity of the VMH and with the activation of lordosis (Kow, Weesner, & Pfaff, 1992). Microinjection of an (α1 antagonist (prazosin) into the VMH inhibited receptivity (Etgen, 1990).

The effects of several other neurotransmitters on lordosis are mediated by the VMH. Acetylcholine, possibly acting via muscarinic M_3 receptors, and serotonin, acting via 5-HT$_{2C}$ receptors, increased neural activity in the VMH and increased lordosis; conversely, stimulation of 5-HT$_{1A}$ receptors inhibited VMH neural activity and lordosis (reviewed in Pfaff, Schwartz-Giblin, McCarthy, & Kow, 1994; Uphouse, 2000). Oxytocin also increased both VMH neural activity (Kow, Johnson, Ogawa, & Pfaff, 1991) and lordosis (Witt & Insel, 1991) and may override the inhibitory effects of stress (McCarthy, McDonald, Brooks, & Goldman, 1996). The oxytocinergic neurons that innervate the VMH are located in the paraventricular nucleus of the hypothalamus (PVN). Oxytocin neurons in the PVN also project to the spinal cord, where they promote lordosis responding.

The Midbrain Module

The primary role of the midbrain module is to transform the slow effects of hormonal stimulation of the hypothalamus into the rapid, behaviorally relevant activity that mediates receptive behavior. Major output neurons from the preoptic area and VMH to the midbrain central gray contain substance P, prolactin, and gonadotropin releasing hormone (GnRH), all of which are important facilitators of lordotic responding (reviewed in Pfaff et al., 1994). Microinjection of GnRH into the central gray facilitated lordosis, whereas microinjection of an antiserum to GnRH blocked lordosis (Sakuma & Pfaff, 1980). Similar results were observed with substance P (Dornan, Malsbury, & Penney, 1987) and prolactin (Harlan, Shivers, & Pfaff, 1983) and antibodies to these peptides. Within the central gray acetylcholine (Richmond & Clemens, 1986) and GABA (McCarthy, Pfaff, & Schwartz-Giblin, 1991) also contribute to the facilitation of lordosis. The central gray in turn sends output to the reticulospinal neurons of the lower brain stem module. Lesions of the central gray impair lordotic responding (Hennessey, Camak, Gordon, & Edwards, 1990) and abolish the facilitative effects of VMH stimulation (Sakuma & Pfaff, 1979).

The Lower Brain Stem Module

The lower brain stem module integrates sensory input from the spinal cord in order to perform moment-to-moment corrections of posture. The vestibular organs and proprioceptors throughout the body also provide input that is essential for maintaining the rigid lordotic posture and accommodating the weight of the male.

The Spinal Cord Module

The spinal cord receives and processes the relevant somatosensory input; it also receives descending facilitative input and generates the motor output. The characteristic dorsiflexion of lordosis requires intersegmental coordination. The important sensory stimuli are pressure applied to the flanks, posterior rump, and perineal area. Estrogen increases the size of the receptive fields of neurons in these areas (Kow et al., 1979). Because the combined sensory input from several nearby regions summates to elicit the lordosis response, this increase in receptive field size greatly increases the probability that mounting by the male will elicit lordosis.

The Urethrogenital Reflex

As noted earlier, the urethrogenital reflex has been proposed as a model for the human orgasmic reflex (McKenna et al., 1991). It can be elicited in both male and female rats and appears to have similar mechanisms of control in both sexes (Vathy & Marson, 1998).

Summary of Circuitry Controlling Female Proceptive and Receptive Behavior

In summary, most of the forebrain inhibits receptive behavior. The hypothalamus, especially the VMH, is the primary site at which estrogen and progesterone have their slow, genomically mediated facilitative effects on lordosis. Some neurons in the MPOA may facilitate proceptive behavior and inhibit lordosis, and others may do the opposite. The VMH communicates with the midbrain module, particularly the central gray, via axons carrying neuropeptides including GnRH, substance P, and prolactin. These neuropeptides alter the responsiveness of neurons to the rapid, behaviorally relevant stimuli that control the behavior. The central gray, in turn, interacts with the lower brain stem, which produces the postural changes of lordosis. The spinal cord both receives the somatosensory input that initiates the lordosis response and also transmits the motor signals to the deep back muscles that produce the response.

ACTIVATION OF MALE SEXUAL BEHAVIOR BY GONADAL HORMONES

Dependence of Copulation on Recent Exposure to Testosterone

Male sexual behavior is heavily dependent on hormones. Increasing production of testosterone at puberty increases sexual activity; after castration, sexual activity declines. There is usually more testosterone than is necessary to facilitate sexual behavior; the excess is necessary for sperm production in the testes. Thus, small reductions of testosterone typically do not affect behavior.

Time Course of Changes in Copulation Following Castration

Although androgens are almost completely eliminated from the body within 24 hr after castration (Krey & McGinnis, 1990), male rats often continue to copulate for days or weeks. The threshold for ejaculation (number of intromissions required to trigger ejaculation) actually decreases for some days after castration, whereas intromission latencies and postejaculatory intervals increase (Davidson, 1966).

The behavioral changes following castration occur in a characteristic sequence. Ejaculation is lost first, then intromission, and mounting last. This sequential loss occurs in part because the different behavioral elements depend on different peripheral target mechanisms. For example, unlike intromission, mounting is not dependent on tactile sensitivity of the penis or erectile function, and ejaculation requires even more sensory and motor competence than does intromission. The various elements may also depend on different central circuits, which have different hormonal requirements.

The effects of castration in men are more variable than in animals. Kinsey concluded, on the basis of anecdotal accounts, that castration had relatively little effect on sexual function in most men (Kinsey, Pomeroy, & Martin, 1948). However, a review of prospective studies of men castrated as "treatment" for sexual offenses revealed that half to two thirds of the men rapidly lost sexual interest, whereas the rest reported a gradual waning of sexual activity, with 10% continuing to have intercourse for up to 20 years (Heim & Hursch, 1979).

Time Course of Changes in Copulation Following Testosterone Restoration

After copulation has been lost, exogenous testosterone restores copulatory elements in the reverse order in which they were lost. Restoration occurs over 5 to 10 days (Putnam, Du, Sato, & Hull, 2001), which suggests that long-term genomic effects mediate the restoration of copulation. In support of this conclusion, inhibition of protein synthesis with anisomycin blocked the effects of testosterone on copulatory behavior (McGinnis & Kahn, 1997). However, anisomycin did not disrupt, and in some cases even facilitated, testerone's restoration of touch-based erections (Meisel et al., 1986).

The Role of Testosterone Metabolites in Maintaining and Restoring Copulation

Testosterone works primarily via metabolism to either estradiol or DHT. Unlike testosterone, DHT cannot be aromatized to estradiol; therefore, it can be used to differentiate androgenic versus estrogenic effects of testosterone. Some target cells produce both estradiol and DHT and have both estrogen and androgen receptors.

Estrogen and DHT differentially affect copulation and *ex copula* reflexes. In male rats estrogen maintained or restored most copulatory elements (Davidson, 1969). Furthermore, systemic inhibition of aromatase or administration of estrogen receptor antagonists inhibited restoration of copulation by testosterone (Vagell & McGinnis, 1997). Similar inhibitory effects of aromatase inhibition were found in castrated, testosterone-treated monkeys (Zumpe, Clancy, Bonsall, & Michael, 1996). Neither DHT (Beyer, Larsson, Perez-Palacios, & Morali, 1973) nor another nonaromatizable androgen (methlytrienolone, R1881; Baum, Kingsbury, & Erskine, 1987) restored or maintained copulation in castrated male rats. DHT and R1881 were also ineffective in male gerbils (Yahr & Stephens, 1987), hamsters (Christensen, Coniglio, Paup, & Clemens, 1973), pigs (Levis & Ford, 1989), and rams (Parrott, 1986). Finally, several synthetic androgens (5-alpha-androstanediols) that can be aromatized to estradiol, but not 5-alpha-reduced to DHT, were even more effective than testosterone in restoring sexual behavior in castrated rats (Morali et al., 1993) or mice (Ogawa et al., 1996). The effectiveness of estradiol, and the ineffectiveness of DHT, gave rise to the *aromatization hypothesis*. That is, the aromatization of testosterone to estradiol is the critical step in the maintenance or restoration of copulation in males of numerous species.

However, estrogen cannot maintain full copulatory behavior. Estrogen-treated castrates displayed fewer behavioral ejaculation patterns than did males treated with testosterone or a combination of estrogen and DHT (Putnam, Panos, & Hull, 1998; Vagell & McGinnis, 1997). Furthermore, estradiol alone was unable to restore partner preference, and the nonsteroidal aromatase inhibitor fadrozole failed to block the effects of testosterone on partner preference (Vagell & McGinnis, 1997). The estrogen receptor antagonist RU-58668 also did not block testosterone's restoration of copulation or partner preference in male rats, but it did inhibit restoration of scent marking (Vagell & McGinnis, 1998). Similar results were observed in male hamsters; fadrozole failed to inhibit testosterone's restoration of copulation or anogenital investigation of an estrous female hamster (Cooper, Clancy, Karom, Moore, & Albers, 2000). Therefore,

the activation of estrogen receptors is not always sufficient to stimulate copulation or partner preference in male rats or hamsters, and estrogen receptor antagonists do not always render testosterone ineffective.

Furthermore, stimulation of androgen receptors does sometimes contribute to testosterone's effects. For example, the nonsteroidal antiandrogen flutamide reduced testosterone's ability to restore copulation in castrated male rats (Vagell & McGinnis, 1998). It also inhibited the restoration of partner preference, scent marking, and 50-kHz ("attraction") vocalizations. An antiandrogen with greater affinity for the androgen receptor ($\alpha\alpha\alpha$-trifluoro-2-methyl-4′-nitro-m-lactoluidide, SCH-16423) eliminated all copulatory behavior in most male rats treated with a dose of testosterone that restored ejaculation in all control males (McGinnis & Mirth, 1986). Therefore, stimulation of estrogen receptors is not sufficient for full restoration of copulation in male rats or hamsters.

In a number of other species, the aromatization hypothesis has little or no support. DHT is sufficient for maintenance or restoration of copulation in mice (Luttge & Hall, 1973), deer mice (Clemens & Pomerantz, 1982), rabbits (Ågmo & Södersten, 1975), guinea pigs (Butera & Czaja, 1989), and monkeys (Phoenix, 1974).

Effects of Hormone Deprivation and Replacement on *Ex Copula* Penile Responses

Animal Studies

Compared to copulation, touch-based reflexes could be reinstated much more rapidly. In castrated male rats, touch-based erections were increased 24 hr after testosterone replacement, with normal levels of erections reached by 48 hr (Gray, Smith, & Davidson, 1980). The same males were tested for copulation 52 hr after testosterone replacement, and only 1 of 10 males mounted. Noncontact erections were also lost more rapidly after castration, and were restored sooner by testosterone, compared to copulation (Manzo, Cruz, Hernandez, Pacheco, & Sachs, 1999). Therefore, the hormonal stimulation of noncontact and touch-based erections may be similar but may differ from hormonal control of copulation, at least with regard to temporal factors.

Another difference in hormonal control of penile reflexes, compared to copulation, is the ineffectiveness of estrogen and the effectiveness of DHT in restoring or maintaining touch-based (Gray et al., 1980; Meisel, O'Hanlon, & Sachs, 1984) or noncontact (Manzo et al., 1999) erections in rats. DHT was the active androgen that also maintained nitric oxide–mediated erections in rats (Lugg, Rajfer, & Gonzalez-Cadavid,

1995), as discussed later. The DHT regimens that maintained or restored reflexes were ineffective in copulation tests (Gray et al., 1980; Meisel, O'Hanlon, et al., 1984). Furthermore, treatment of testosterone-replaced castrated rats with the androgen receptor antagonist flutamide (Gray et al., 1980) or with a 5-alpha-reductase inhibitor (Bradshaw, Baum, & Awh, 1981) blocked the restorative effects of testosterone. Therefore, as with temporal factors, the hormonal mechanisms that control *ex copula* erections are different from those that regulate copulation.

Although estrogen is ineffective in *ex copula* reflex tests, it can maintain erections during copulation. The fact that an erection actually occurred during copulation, and not just the behavioral pattern associated with intromission, was verified by placing nontoxic tempera paint into the female's vagina (O'Hanlon, Meisel, & Sachs, 1981). Estrogen-treated males had as high a percentage of intromission patterns in which they actually achieved insertion as did control males. Furthermore, EMG recordings from the bulbospongiosus muscle revealed that the duration, frequency, and average amplitude were at least as great in estrogen-treated castrates as in testosterone-treated castrates (Holmes & Sachs, 1992). Sachs (1983) suggested that a copulatory *behavioral cascade* was organized in the brain and included activation of reflexes that were not observable in noncopulatory contexts. Elicitation of reflexive erections may depend primarily on disinhibition of the lumbosacral spinal circuits. Whereas estrogen cannot disinhibit reflexes in *ex copula* tests, it can apparently activate those same reflexes in the context of copulation.

Studies on Human Males

There is usually little (Raboch, Mellan, & Starka, 1975) or no (Pirke, Kockott, Aldenhoff, Besinger, & Feil, 1979) difference in testosterone concentrations in men with erectile dysfunction compared with normally functioning men. However, testosterone replacement in hypogonadal men increased erectile function (Davidson, Camargo, & Smith, 1979; O'Carroll, Shapiro, & Bancroft, 1985). Furthermore, the loss of erection in hypogonadal men is restricted to nocturnal and spontaneous erections and not erections stimulated by fantasizing or viewing erotic films (Bancroft & Wu, 1983; LaFerla, Anderson & Schalch, 1978). Thus, the effect of androgen on erection in men is context-sensitive, as it is in rats.

Exogenous testosterone treatments in eugonadal men (which produced supraphysiological concentrations), as well as in hypogonadal men (which produced normal concentrations), increased subjective sexual arousal ratings in response to sexual audiotapes (Alexander et al., 1997). These treatments also increased the bias to attend to sexual auditory stimuli in a dichotic listening task. However, there did not appear to be a strong correlation between endogenous testosterone levels in eugonadal men and sexual behavior (Brown, Monti, & Corriveau, 1978).

Testosterone and DHT were equally effective in stimulating sexual activity in agonadal men, and in normal men treatment with an estrogen receptor blocker or an aromatase inhibitor had no effect on sexual function (Gooren, 1985). An exception to this finding comes from an unusual case of a man receiving combined estrogen and progesterone to alleviate menopausal-like symptoms after undergoing castration (Davidson et al., 1979). In this man a normal level of sexual activity was maintained without androgen treatment. However, because progesterone is a precursor of testosterone, a slight increase in testosterone may have been sufficient to stimulate sexual function.

EFFECTS OF SYSTEMICALLY ADMINISTERED DRUGS ON MALE SEXUAL BEHAVIOR

Table 12.2 summarizes the effects on male sexual behavior of systemically administered drugs and of treatments that affect neurotransmitter function in more than one brain area.

BRAIN AREAS IMPLICATED IN CONTROL OF MALE SEXUAL BEHAVIOR

Sensory Systems

Chemosensory Systems

The main and accessory olfactory bulbs receive chemosensory information from receptors in the nasal epithelium and vomeronasal organ, respectively. Generally, damage to the olfactory system impairs male sexual behavior. In male hamsters, bilateral bulbectomy abolished copulation (Murphy, 1980; Winans & Powers, 1974). When destruction of receptors in the nasal epithelium was combined with vomeronasal nerve cuts or deafferentation of the vomeronasal pump, copulation was also severely disrupted (Meredith, Marques, O'Connell, & Stem, 1980). In rats the primary effects of olfactory bulbectomies were a reduction in the percentage of rats that copulated to ejaculation and a slowing of copulation (reviewed in Meisel, Sachs, & Lumia, 1984). Early reports of sexual impairment by bulbectomy attributed the effects to anosmia alone. However, the olfactory bulbs also have nonsensory influences because peripheral deafferentation was often less debilitating than was olfactory bulbectomy (reviewed in Cain, 1974). Olfaction plays a less critical role in the control of male sexual behavior in nonrodent species (reviewed in Hull, Meisel, & Sachs, 2002).

TABLE 12.2 Effects on Male Sexual Behavior of Systemically Administered Drugs or Treatments Affecting More Than One Brain Area

Transmitter Altering Drugs	Effects on Sexual Behavior	References	Remarks
Dopamine			
DA agonists	+	[7] [17] [22]	DA agonists also facilitated copulation in short-term (Malmnas, 1976)
DA antagonists	−	[2] [5]	and long-term (Scaletta & Hull, 1990) castrated rats.
Norepinephrine			
NE agonists	+	[13] [14] [15] [33]	Although noradrenergic drugs appear to facilitative male sexual
NE antagonists	−	[13] [35]	behavior, high levels of peripheral NE activity inhibit erections (Stefanick, Smith, & Davidson, 1983) by vasoconstricting penile arteries.
Serotonin			
Lesions of 5-HT cell bodies	+	[6] [27]	
5-HT reuptake inhibitors	−	In rats, [11] [37]; in humans, reviewed in [34]	
Stimulation of 5-HT$_{1A}$	+/−	[16] [20]	Stimulation of 5-HT$_{1A}$ may promote ejaculation but inhibit erections.
Stimulation of 5HT$_{2C}$	+/−	[26] [31]	Stimulation of 5-HT$_{2C}$ may facilitate erections but inhibit ejaculations.
Acetylcholine			
Systemic ACh agonists	−	[1]	Systemically administered muscarinic agonists may facilitate copulation
Systemic ACh antagonists	−	[1] [10]	and erections, although contradictory results have been reported.
Stim. of muscarinic ACh rec.	+	[24] [32] [38]	These effects may be mediated in part by peripheral influences on
Inhibiting ACh degradation	+	[38]	penile muscle or the parasympathetic nervous system.
GABA			
Systemic GABA$_A$ agonist	−	[4]	Because GABA is so widespread, it is not clear that systemic
Systemic GABA$_B$ agonist	−	[29]	administration of GABA agonists or antagonists would affect sexual
Inhibit GABA catabolism	−	[30]	behavior in a specific manner.
Inhibit GABA synthesis	−	[30]	
Opiates			
Opiate agonists	−	[3] [23]	A possible explanation for these apparently contradictory effects is that
Opiate antagonists	+/−	[3] [25] [28] [36]	low to moderate levels of endogenous opioids may facilitate sexual motivation and genital reflexes; however, exogenous opiates or high levels of endogenous opioids may inhibit those same functions.
Nitric Oxide			
NO agonists	+	[12] [18] [19]	Although NO is a major facilitator of parasympathetically mediated
NO antagonists	−	[8] [9] [21]	erections, it may inhibit sympathetically mediated seminal emission and ejaculation (Moses & Hull, 1999).

Note. + =facilitation; − =inhibition; n/e = no effect. References: [1] Ågmo (1976); [2] Ågmo & Picker (1990); [3] Ågmo, Paredes, & Contreras (1994); [4] Ågmo, Paredes, Sierra, & Garces (1997); [5] Ahlenius & Larson (1990); [6] Albinsson, Andersson, Andersson, Vega-Matuszczyk, & Larsson (1996); [7] Barbeau (1969); [8] Benelli et al. (1995); [9] Bialy, Beck, Abramczyk, Trzebski, & Przybylski (1996); [10] Bignami (1966); [11] Cantor, Binik, & Pfaus (1999); [12] Christiansen, Guirguis, Cox, & Osterloh (2000); [13] Clark (1995); [14] Clark, Smith, & Davidson (1984); [15] Clark, Smith, & Davidson (1985); [16] Coolen et al. (1997); [17] Dula et al. (2000); [18] Giuliano, Montorsi, Mirone, Rossi, & Sweeney (2000); [19] Goldstein et al. (1998); [20] Haensel & Slob (1997); [21] Hull et al. (1994); [22] Lal et al. (1987); [23] Leyton & Stewart (1992); [24] Maeda, Matsuoka, & Yamaguchi (1994); [25] McIntosh, Vallano, & Barfield (1980); [26] Millan et al. (1997); [27] Monaghan et al. (1993); [28] Myers & Baum (1979); [29] Paredes & Ågmo (1995); [30] Paredes, Karam, Highland, & Ågmo (1997); [31] Pomerantz et al. (1993); [32] Retana-Marquez & Velasquez-Moctezuma (1997); [33] Rodriguez-Manzo (1999); [34] Rosen, Lane, & Menza (1999); [35] Tallentire, McRae, Spedding, Clark, & Vickery (1996); [36] van Furth & van Ree (1994); [37] Vega Matuszyk, Larsson, & Eriksson (1998); [38] Zarrindast, Mamanpush, & Rashidy-Pour (1994).

Cells in the olfactory bulbs are activated after copulation and after exposure to a sexually relevant olfactory stimulus. Fos immunoreactivity (ir) is used as a measure of region-specific cellular activity following a stimulus, in this case sexual behavior. (See Figure 12.2 for a diagram of the brain areas activated by sexual behavior in male or female rodents.) In the accessory olfactory bulb of male hamsters, Fos-ir increased after copulation; this increase was also observed in males whose main olfactory system was ablated with zinc sulfate (Fernandez-Fewell & Meredith, 1994). Thus, pheromonal stimulation of the vomeronasal organ and the accessory olfactory bulb is sufficient for cellular activation in the central vomeronasal pathway of male hamsters. In male rats, Fos-ir was increased in the accessory olfactory bulbs after exposure to bedding from an estrous female; an even higher amount of Fos-ir was observed after copulation (Kelliher, Liu, Baum, & Sachs, 1999).

Somatosensory Systems

Mechanoreceptors in the penis supply somatosensory information to the brain and contribute to sexual arousal. These receptors are more responsive when the penis is erect (Johnson, 1988) or near core body temperature, as it is during

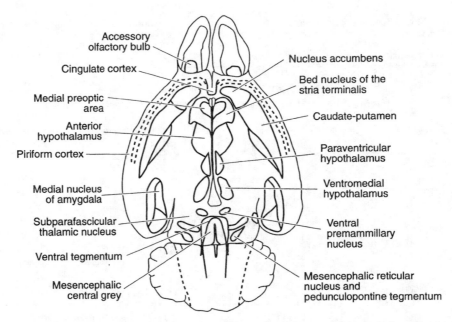

Figure 12.2 Regions in a horizontal section of rat brain in which Fos induction is observed after sexual behavior in females and males. With some exceptions, Fos has been observed in similar regions in hamsters and gerbils. Reprinted from *Brain Research Bulletin, 44*, J. G. Pfaus & M. M. Heeb, "Implications of immediate-early gene induction in the brain following sexual stimulation of female and male rodents," 397–407, Copyright 1997, with permission from Elsevier Science.

erection (Johnson & Kitchell, 1987). Major somatosensory input from the penile skin, prepuce, and glans penis enter the central nervous system in the spinal cord mainly via the dorsal nerve of the penis (reviewed in Steers, 2000).

Auditory System

Male and female rats produce ultrasonic vocalizations during copulation; these vocalizations are believed to facilitate copulation (reviewed in Barfield & Thomas, 1986). During mating, the male produces a 50-kHz vocalization, which is associated with arousal, and a 22-kHz vocalization following ejaculation (Barfield & Geyer, 1972). There is also increased vocalization by the female in response to the male's vocalizations (White, Gonzales, & Barfield, 1993).

Amygdala

Basolateral Nuclei

Lesions of the basolateral amygdala did not impair copulation in male rats (Kondo, 1992) or hamsters (Lehman & Winans, 1982), but did inhibit bar pressing for a secondary reinforcer that had been paired with access to a female (Everitt, 1990). Therefore, the basolateral amygdala may be important for the motivational aspects of male sexual behavior or for learning the appropriate associations, but not for copulatory performance.

Corticomedial Nuclei

Unlike lesions of the basolateral amygdala, lesions of the corticomedial nuclei clearly impaired male sexual behavior in rats (Dominguez, Riolo, Xu, & Hull, 2001; Kondo, 1992), hamsters (Lehman, Winans, & Powers, 1980), and gerbils (Heeb & Yahr, 2000). These animals required more time to reach an ejaculation and displayed fewer ejaculations than did control animals. Furthermore, medial amygdala lesions blocked the facilitative effects on copulation of preexposure to an estrous female (de Jonge, Oldenburger, Louwerse, & Van de Poll, 1992) and reduced the number of noncontact erections (Kondo, Sachs, & Sakuma, 1997). Thus, the medial amygdala facilitates the response to and assimilation of sexually exciting stimuli.

The medial and anterior cortical nuclei of the amygdala receive projections from the olfactory system (reviewed in McDonald, 1998). Both exposure to chemosensory stimuli from estrous female rats and increasing amounts of copulation elicited increasing amounts of Fos-ir in the medial amygdala and in several downstream sites that are important for male sexual behavior (Baum & Everitt, 1992; Robertson et al., 1991; Veening & Coolen, 1998). Chemosensory stimuli and copulation also induced increasing Fos-ir patterns in hamsters (Kollack-Walker & Newman, 1997), gerbils (Heeb & Yahr, 1996), prairie voles (Wang, Hulihan, & Insel, 1997), and musk shrews (Gill, Wersinger, Veney, & Rissman, 1998).

The posterodorsal region of the medial amygdala (MeApd) contains a high concentration of androgen receptors. Androgen-sensitive neurons in this region that project to the MPOA are activated selectively by ejaculation (Gréco, Edwards, Zumpe, & Clancy, 1998). The MeApd is part of an interconnected ejaculation-specific circuit that may promote sexual satiety in rats (Coolen, Olivier, Peters, & Veening, 1997), hamsters (Parfitt, Coolen, Newman, & Wood, 1996; Parfitt & Newman, 1998), and gerbils (Heeb & Yahr, 1996).

Bed Nucleus of the Stria Terminalis

The bed nucleus of the stria terminalis (BNST) has reciprocal connections with the medial amygdala and the MPOA. Lesions of the BNST increased the number of intromissions required to elicit an ejaculation, increased postejaculatory intervals, and decreased the number of ejaculations (Emery &

Sachs, 1976); these effects are similar to those observed following lesions of the medial amygdala. In addition, exposure to a sexually relevant olfactory stimulus, noncontact erections, or mating increased Fos-ir in the BNST of male rats (Kelliher et al., 1999) and hamsters (Fernandez-Fewell & Meredith, 1994).

Medial Preoptic Area

The MPOA is perhaps the most important integrative site for the regulation of male sexual behavior in all vertebrate species that have been tested. It receives indirect input from every sensory modality (Simerly & Swanson, 1986) and sends projections to structures that are critical for the initiation and patterning of copulation (Simerly & Swanson, 1988). See Figure 12.3 for interconnections of the MPOA and other areas important for the control of male sexual behavior.

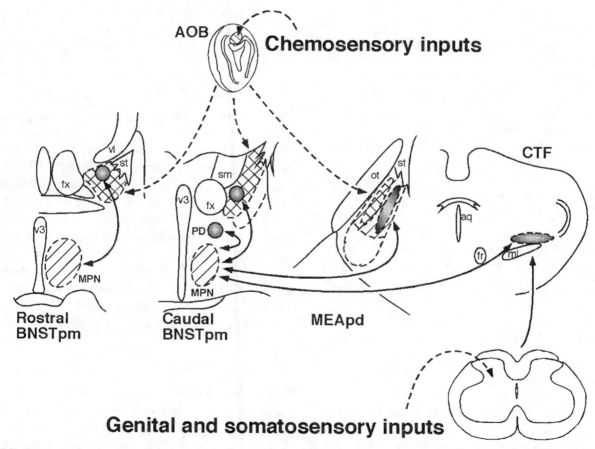

Figure 12.3   Schematic overview of neural activation in circuits underlying male sexual behavior. Areas where Fos is induced following exposure to chemosensory cues are illustrated by diagonal stripes from upper left to lower right. Areas where Fos is induced primarily following ejaculation are illustrated in dark shading. Areas where Fos is induced by all consummatory elements of behavior are illustrated by diagonal stripes from lower left to upper right. AOB, accessory olfactory bulbs; MPN, medial preoptic nucleus; PD, posterodorsal preoptic nucleus; BNSTpm, posteromedial bed nucleus of the stria terminalis; MEApd, posterodorsal medial amygdala; CTF, central tegmental field; LSSC, lumbosacral spinal cord; v3, third ventricle; fx, fornix; vl, lateral ventricle; st, stria terminalis; sm, stria medularis; ot, optic tract; aq, aqueduct; Fr, fasciculus retroflexus; ml, medial lemniscus. Figure courtesy of Lique Coolen, reprinted from Hull et al. (2002).

Effects of Lesions

Damage to the MPOA has consistently impaired male sexual behavior in rats, monkeys, goats, dogs, cats, mice, guinea pigs, hamsters, ferrets, gerbils, snakes, birds, lizards, and fish (reviewed in Hull et al., 2002). Because the nature of the sexually relevant stimuli and the motor patterns that express copulation vary greatly among species, the fact that MPOA damage impairs sexual behavior in all these different species confirms the MPOA's role as a central integrative node for the regulation of male sexual behavior. The severity of sexual impairment by MPOA lesions is dependent on the lesion's size and location. Smaller MPOA lesions have variable and less severe effects than do larger lesions (Arendash & Gorski, 1983; Heimer & Larsson, 1966/1967). Lesions of the caudal MPOA, including the rostral anterior hypothalamus, impaired copulation more severely than did those of the rostral MPOA (Van de Poll & van Dis, 1979).

There has been disagreement as to whether the MPOA is important for the appetitive as well as the consummatory aspects of male sexual behavior. Everitt (1990) suggested that the MPOA controls only copulatory performance and is not important for motivation. This was supported by reports that male rats with MPOA lesions pursued estrous females and investigated their anogenital regions (Hansen & Hagelsrum, 1984; Heimer & Larsson, 1966/1967). Similar patterns of behavior were observed in cats (Hart, Haugen, & Peterson, 1973) and dogs (Hart, 1974) with MPOA lesions. Furthermore, MPOA lesions did not affect the frequency of masturbation in monkeys (Slimp, Hart, & Goy, 1978) or noncontact erections in rats (Liu, Salamone, & Sachs, 1997b). On the other hand, MPOA lesions diminished preference for a female partner in rats (Edwards & Einhorn, 1986; Edwards, Walter, & Liang, 1996; Paredes, Tzschentke, & Nakach, 1998) and ferrets (Kindon, Baum, & Paredes, 1996; Paredes & Baum, 1995), decreased pursuit of a female by male rats (Paredes, Highland, & Karam, 1993), and precopulatory behavior in marmosets (Lloyd & Dixson, 1988), suggesting that the MPOA is indeed important for sexual motivation.

Effects of Stimulation

Stimulation of the MPOA enhances sexual activity. In rats, electrical stimulation of the MPOA reduced the number of intromissions preceding ejaculation, the ejaculation latency, and the postejaculatory interval (Malsbury, 1971; Rodriguez-Manzo, Pellicer, Larsson, & Fernandez-Guasti, 2000). However, MPOA stimulation did not restore copulation in males that had reached sexual satiety (Rodriguez-Manzo et al., 2000), suggesting that sexual inhibition due to satiety is not mediated by the MPOA. Stimulation of the MPOA has also elicited erection (Giuliano et al., 1997) and the urethrogenital reflex (Marson & McKenna, 1994b).

Fos Studies

Exposure to the odor of an estrous female and increasing amounts of copulation induced increasing amounts of Fos-ir in the MPOA of male rats (Baum & Everitt, 1992; Bressler & Baum, 1996; Robertson et al., 1991; Veening & Coolen, 1998), hamsters (Kollack-Walker & Newman, 1997), and gerbils (Heeb & Yahr, 1996). Noncontact erections and exposure to the bedding of an estrous female also induced Fos-ir in the MPOA of male rats, but the effects were less dramatic than those observed following copulation (Kelliher et al., 1999). Ejaculation-induced Fos-ir in the MPOA was decreased by a D_1 antagonist and by lack of previous sexual experience (Lumley & Hull, 1999). In one subregion, the posterodorsal preoptic nucleus, Fos-ir was significantly increased only following ejaculation in male rats (Coolen, Peters, & Veening, 1996), hamsters (Kollack-Walker & Newman, 1997), and gerbils (Heeb & Yahr, 1996).

Microinjection Studies

Microinjection of the classic dopamine agonist apomorphine into the MPOA of male rats facilitated copulation (Hull, Bitran, Pehek, Warner, & Band, 1986) and touch-based genital reflexes (Pehek, Thompson, & Hull, 1989a), whereas a dopamine antagonist impaired appetitive and consummatory measures of sexual behavior, as well as genital reflexes (Warner et al., 1991). Stimulation of D_1 receptors in the MPOA promoted parasympathetically mediated erections and speeded copulation, whereas stimulation of D_2 receptors shifted the autonomic balance to favor sympathetically mediated seminal emission and ejaculation (Hull, Eaton, Markowski, Moses, Lumley, & Loucks, 1992; Hull et al., 1989; Markowski, Eaton, Lumley, Moses, & Hull, 1994).

Microdialysis Studies

Extracellular dopamine increased in the MPOA of male rats during exposure to an estrous female and during copulation (Hull, Du, Lorrain, & Matuszewich, 1995). Both basal (Lorrain & Hull, 1993) and mating-induced (Lorrain, Matuszewich, Howard, Du, & Hull, 1996) dopamine levels were decreased by reverse dialysis of a nitric oxide synthase (NOS) inhibitor and by castration (Du, Lorrain, & Hull, 1998; Hull et al., 1995). Lesions of the medial amygdala blocked the mating-induced increase but did not affect basal dopamine levels in the MPOA; therefore, the mating-induced dopamine increase was mediated by input from the medial amygdala (Dominguez et al., 2001). These lesions also impaired copulation; microinjection of the dopamine agonist apomorphine into the MPOA restored copulatory ability (Dominguez et al., 2001).

Paraventricular Nucleus of the Hypothalamus

Effects of Lesions

Lesions of the parvocellular PVN inhibited noncontact erections (Liu, Salamone, & Sachs, 1997a) and decreased the quantity of seminal emission during ejaculation (Ackerman, Lange, & Clemens, 1997) but did not impair copulation (Ackerman et al., 1997; Liu et al., 1997a).

Microinjection and Microdialysis Studies

Microinjections of either oxytocin, the classic D_1/D_2 dopamine agonist apomorphine, or the D_2 agonist quinpirole into the PVN facilitated drug-induced and noncontact erections (Argiolas, Melis, Mauri, & Gessa, 1987; Melis, Argiolas, & Gessa, 1987). PVN microinjections of apomorphine (Pehek et al., 1989a) or the D_3/D_2 agonist quinelorane (Eaton et al., 1991) also increased touch-based erections and seminal emissions. These effects were blocked by intraventricular, but not PVN, administration of an oxytocin antagonist (Melis, Succu, Spano, & Argiolas, 1999b), suggesting that oxytocinergic axon terminals ending outside the PVN, perhaps in the hippocampus (Melis, Stancampiano, & Argiolas, 1992), promote noncontact erections.

Nitric oxide (NO) in the PVN also promotes erections. Microinjection of an NOS inhibitor (L-NAME) into the PVN decreased noncontact erections and impaired copulation (Melis, Succu, Mauri, & Argiolas, 1998). Both noncontact erections and copulation increased NO production in the PVN (Melis et al., 1998; Melis, Succu, Spano, & Argiolas, 1999a). However, reverse dialysis of a different NOS inhibitor (L-NMMA) into the PVN failed to impair copulation, although it did inhibit noncontact erections (Sato et al., 1999), and similar treatment in the MPOA did inhibit copulation (Sato, Horita, Kurohata, Adachi, & Tsukamoto, 1998). Systemic injections of either apomorphine or the D_2 agonist quinpirole increased NO production in the PVN and elicited drug-induced erections (Melis, Succu, & Argiolas 1996). Similarly, microinjections of the glutamate agonist N-methyl-D-aspartate (NMDA) into the PVN increased erections and increased NO production in the PVN (Melis, Succu, Iannuci, & Argiolas, 1997). Finally, oxytocin and NOS are colocalized in the PVN (Yamada, Emson, & Hokfelt, 1996).

These studies provide a consistent model of PVN function, in which dopamine (via D_2 receptors) or glutamate (via NMDA receptors) activates NO production in oxytocinergic neurons. This intracellular NO increases the release of oxytocin from axon terminals ending elsewhwere, perhaps the hippocampus, where they promote noncontact and drug-induced erections and may produce some facilitation of copulation. In addition, oxytocinergic neurons descending from the PVN to the spinal cord may promote seminal emission and ejaculation.

Anterior Lateral Hypothalamus

Important reciprocal connections between the MPOA and several more caudal sites pass through the lateral hypothalamus (Simerly & Swanson, 1988). Lesions that sever these connections are as destructive to copulation as are MPOA lesions (Scouten, Burrell, Palmer, & Cegavske, 1980). However, cell bodies in the anterior lateral hypothalamus (LHA) also influence sexual behavior. Serotonin is released in the LHA at the time of ejaculation, and a selective serotonin reuptake inhibitor (SSRI) microinjected into the LHA delayed the onset of copulation and delayed ejaculation after the male did begin to copulate (Lorrain, Matuszewich, Friedman, & Hull, 1997). Thus, the LHA appears to be one site at which SSRI antidepressants inhibit sexual motivation and ejaculation. One means by which SSRIs in the LHA inhibit sexual motivation may be by decreasing dopamine release in the mesolimbic tract, which is important for many motivated behaviors. Reverse dialysis of serotonin into the LHA resulted in a decrease in dopamine release in the NAcc, a major terminus of the mesolimbic dopamine tract (Lorrain, Riolo, Matuszewich, & Hull, 1999). Thus, serotonin release in the LHA may inhibit sexual motivation by inhibiting dopamine release in the NAcc.

Nucleus Accumbens and Ventral Tegmental Area

Effects of Lesions and Electrical Stimulation

The mesolimbic dopamine tract arises from cell bodies in the VTA and ascends to several forebrain structures, including the NAcc. It is important for behavioral activation, reward, and incentive learning for a variety of motivated behaviors. NAcc lesions decreased noncontact and apomorphine-stimulated erections (Liu, Sachs, & Salamone, 1998). Copulation was unaffected, except for increased intromission latency; amphetamine-stimulated locomotion was also decreased, suggesting a general deficit in behavioral activation. Lesions of the VTA increased the postejaculatory interval but did not affect other measures of copulation (Brackett, Iuvone, & Edwards, 1986). Conversely, electrical stimulation of the NAcc decreased the latencies to mount, intromit, and ejaculate and to resume copulation after ejaculating (Eibergen & Caggiula, 1973; Markowski & Hull, 1995).

Microinjection Studies

Stimulating inhibitory autoreceptors on mesolimbic cell bodies in the VTA delayed the start of copulation and slowed its rate (Hull, Bazzett, Warner, Eaton, & Thompson, 1990); however, it did not affect genital reflexes or the percentage of X-maze trials on which the male chose the goal box containing the female (Hull et al., 1991). Therefore, behavioral activation, rather than sexual motivation or reflexes, was affected by inhibition of mesolimbic activity. Similarly, microinjection of the opioid antagonist naloxone into the VTA decreased level changing in search of a female but did not affect copulation (van Furth & van Ree, 1996).

Manipulations of the NAcc resulted in similar conclusions. Amphetamine shortened the latency to begin copulating, and a dopamine antagonist (cis-flupenthixol) or selective neurotoxic lesions delayed it (reviewed in Everitt, 1990). Microinjection of a D_3/D_2 agonist (quinelorane) into the NAcc increased the number of trials on which the male did not leave the start area of the X maze but did not affect his choice of the female or copulation after the male reached the female (Moses, Loucks, Watson, Matuszewich, & Hull, 1995). It is not clear whether quinelorane's effects resulted from stimulation of inhibitory presynaptic autoreceptors or postsynaptic receptors in the NAcc. However, the pattern is consistent with a role for the mesolimbic dopamine system in activation of motivated behaviors, rather than specifically sexual motivation or the pattern of copulatory behavior.

Microdialysis Studies

Dopamine is released in the NAcc of male rats when they are exposed to the odor of a receptive female, but not that of a nonreceptive female or a male, and during copulation (Fumero, Fernandez-Vera, Gonzalez-Mora, & Mas, 1994; Mas, Gonzalez-Mora, Louilot, Sole, & Guadalupe, 1990; Mitchell & Gratton, 1991; Pfaus, Damsma, et al., 1990; Wenkstern, Pfaus, & Fibiger, 1993). Finer temporal analysis, achieved with in vivo voltammetry (Blackburn, Pfaus, & Phillips, 1992; Mas et al., 1990) or microdialysis with capillary chromatography (Lorrain et al., 1999), revealed that dopamine rose with the initial presentation of a female,

increased further during copulation, decreased during each postejaculatory interval, and increased again as copulation resumed. Reverse dialysis of serotonin into the LHA decreased extracellular dopamine in the NAcc and prevented the increase during copulation (Lorrain et al., 1999). Therefore, one factor promoting sexual quiescence after ejaculation may be the decreased dopamine release in the NAcc caused by serotonin in the LHA.

Sexually satiated males showed a slight increase in NAcc dopamine when they were presented with a novel female; dopamine rose further during copulation with the new female (Fiorino, Coury, & Phillips, 1997). In addition, repeated injections of amphetamine increased ("sensitized") the locomotor response to amphetamine and also increased the dopamine response to a female (Fiorino & Phillips, 1999). Sensitized males also had shorter intromission latencies and more copulatory behaviors. Therefore, sensitization to a stimulant drug cross-sensitized to a natural behavior.

Nigrostriatal Dopamine Tract

The nigrostriatal dopamine tract arises from cell bodies in the substantia nigra, adjacent to the VTA, and projects to the caudate-putamen (dorsal striatum). It contributes to the initiation and control of movement. Degeneration results in Parkinson's disease, which is characterized by difficulty initiating movements, slowing of movement, and tremor at rest. Bilateral lesions of the substantia nigra slowed copulation and decreased the number of ejaculations (Brackett et al., 1986). In contrast to the immediate release of dopamine in the NAcc when a receptive female was presented, dopamine in the dorsal striatum rose only with the onset of copulation (Damsma, Pfaus, Wenkstern, Phillips, & Fibiger, 1992). This pattern suggests that the nigrostriatal tract is more important for the motor aspects of copulation than for sexual motivation.

Thalamus and Brain Stem

Subparafascicular Nucleus of the Thalamus

The medial parvocellular portion of the subparafascicular nucleus of the thalamus (SPFp) is part of a circuit that responds specifically to ejaculation in rats (Coolen et al., 1996, 1997), hamsters (Kollack-Walker & Newman, 1997), and gerbils (Heeb & Yahr, 1996). Bilateral lesions of the SPFp in gerbils did not affect copulatory performance, suggesting that the SPFp is more important for processing the sensory information resulting from ejaculation than for control of the behavior (Heeb & Yahr, 1996).

Central Tegmental Field and Dorsolateral Tegmentum

The midbrain tegmentum receives sensory input from the genitals, which it relays to the MPOA and anterior hypothalamus; in turn, it receives input from the MPOA, which it sends to the brain stem and spinal cord (Simerly & Swanson, 1986, 1988). Subregions of the tegmentum have been referred to as the central tegmental field (CTF) or the dorsolateral tegmentum (DLT). Combined ipsilateral lesions of the medial amygdala and the CTF abolished copulation-induced Fos-ir in the MPOA, although lesion of either structure alone did not affect Fos-ir (Baum & Everitt, 1992). Unilateral MPOA lesions did not affect Fos-ir in either of those structures; thus, the main flow of information is from CTF and medial amygdala to the MPOA.

Periaqueductal Gray

The periaqueductal gray (PAG) has extensive reciprocal connections with the MPOA (Rizvi, Murphy, Ennis, Behbehani, & Shipley, 1996; Simerly & Swanson, 1986). Bilateral PAG lesions facilitated copulation (Bracket et al., 1986). The caudal two thirds of the PAG contain many androgen and estrogen receptors (Murphy, Shupnick, & Hoffman, 1999). Furthermore, projections from the MPOA terminated in close proximity to steroid-receptor containing PAG neurons, and almost half of the neurons that projected to the nucleus paragigantocellularis (nPGi; discussed next) contained androgen or estrogen receptors (Murphy & Hoffman, 2001).

Nucleus Paragigantocellularis

The nPGi of the medulla contributes to the tonic inhibitory control of spinal mechanisms that control erection and ejaculation. Bilateral lesions of the nPGi increased the number of sexually naive male rats that ejaculated during their first exposure to a receptive female (Yells, Hendricks, & Prendergast, 1992). These lesions also decreased the time and number of intromissions before ejaculation, increased copulatory efficiency, and delayed sexual satiety. Similar lesions decreased the latency to the first touch-based erection and increased the number of anteroflexions (Marson, List, & McKenna, 1992); they also disinhibited the urethrogenital reflex as effectively as did spinal transection (Marson & McKenna, 1990).

Spinal Cord

The spinal cord provides initial processing of somatic and visceral stimuli from the genitals and is the site of somatic and autonomic nuclei that control erection, ejaculation, and detumescence. Both local reflex loops and descending axons from the brain are important for these functions (reviewed in Giuliano & Rampin, 2000).

Effects of Lesions

Transection of the spinal cord dramatically increased touch-based erections (Sachs & Garinello, 1979) and disinhibited the urethrogenital reflex (McKenna et al., 1991). However, acute injections of a local anesthetic decreased the number and magnitude of touch-based erections, in addition to shortening the latency to the first erection (Sachs & Bitran, 1990). The decrease in latency probably resulted from the removal of a supraspinal inhibitory influence; however, the decrease in erections suggests that there is also a descending facilitative influence. The previously observed increase in erections following spinal transection probably resulted from neural reorganization within the spinal cord during the interval between the transection and the test.

Descending serotonergic axons mediate much of the inhibitory influence on touch-based erections and on the urethrogenital reflex. Either intrathecal (around the spinal cord) or intracerebroventricular injections of a serotonin neurotoxin (5,7-dihydroxytryptamine, or 5,7-DHT) disinhibited the urethrogenital reflex in otherwise intact male rats (Marson & McKenna, 1994a), and lesions of the median raphe nuclei (a major source of serotonin neurons) increased the number of touch-based erections (Monaghan, Arjomand, & Breedlove, 1993). In addition to the median raphe nuclei, the nPGi may contribute to the serotonergic inhibition of genital reflexes. A majority of the axons from the nPGi contain serotonin (Marson & McKenna, 1992), and as noted earlier, lesions of the nPGi disinhibited both the urethrogenital reflex and touch-based erections.

Serotonin Receptor Subtypes

Paradoxically, stimulation of 5-HT_{2C} receptors may facilitate erection. Immunoreactivity for 5-HT_{2C} receptors was found on all neurons that projected from the sacral parasympathetic nucleus to the corpus cavernosum and from the motor neurons to the striated penile muscles (Bancilla et al., 1999). Thus, the neurons that are known to control the hemodynamic and striated muscle actions that produce erections possess 5-HT_{2C} receptors, and a systemically administered 5-HT_{2C} agonist (mCPP) facilitated erections in monkeys (Pomerantz, Hepner, & Wurtz, 1993) and rats (Millan, Peglion, Lavielle, & Perrin-Monneyron, 1997).

Intrathecal administration of the 5-HT_{1A} agonist 8-OH-DPAT decreased the number of rats that displayed touch-based erections or seminal emissions; however, similar administration of 8-OH-DPAT resulted in a dramatic facilitation of copulation (Lee, Smith, Mas, & Davidson, 1990). The basis for this discrepancy is not clear; however, a similar discrepancy was observed with intrathecal administration of the dopamine agonist apomorphine, which inhibited touch-based erections but facilitated copulation (Pehek, Thompson, & Hull, 1989b). In addition, intrathecal administration of a $GABA_B$ agonist inhibited touch-based erections but had no effect on copulation; a $GABA_A$ agonist was almost completely ineffective (Bitran, Miller, McQuade, Leipheimer, & Sachs, 1988).

Oxytocin

Oxytocin, carried by axons from the PVN, provides a major facilitative influence on erection. Administration of oxytocin in the lumbosacral region increased intracavernous pressure (Giuliano, Bernabé, McKenna, Longueville, & Rampin, 2001). Section of the pelvic nerve, the major parasympathetic input to the pelvis, blocked the effect. However, blockade of striated muscle activation did not diminish oxytocin's effects, providing further evidence that those effects were mediated by the parasympathetic nervous system, rather than by striated penile muscles.

Summary of Circuitry Underlying Mammalian Male Sexual Behavior

The MPOA is the central hub for the control of male copulatory behavior. There are two main sources of sensory input to the MPOA of male rodents. Chemosensory information is processed by the main olfactory system and the vomeronasal system and is relayed via the medial amygdala to the MPOA, BNST, NAcc, and other sites. Somatosensory input from the genitals is processed initially in the dorsal horn of the spinal cord and ascends to the MPOA via the nPGi, CTF, SPFp, and PVN. One circuit, including the SPFp, the posterodorsal medial amygdala, and the posterodorsal preoptic nucleus, responds specifically to ejaculation and may contribute to sexual satiety. Output from the MPOA is routed via the medial forebrain bundle to the PVN, the midbrain PAG, the midline raphe nuclei, and the nPGi. Many of the neurons responding to sexually relevant sensory input and those providing output to downstream structures contain steroid hormone receptors. Therefore, hormones are able to increase sensitivity to sexually relevant stimuli and to increase responsiveness of motoric output. This circuitry has been highly conserved during evolution, as MPOA lesions in fishes, birds, lizards, and numerous mammals, including humans, impair or abolish male sexual behavior, and lesions

of input and output structures also produce similar effects across species.

SEXUAL BEHAVIOR IN THE CONTEXT OF MAMMALIAN SOCIAL BEHAVIOR

Brain areas that are important for male sexual behavior also contribute to female sexual behavior, aggression, and territorial marking (reviewed in Newman, 1999). Furthermore, these areas are richly interconnected, and most contain steroid hormone receptors. Perinatal and adult hormones predispose the network to produce particular patterns of behavior. It is not clear whether each cell contributes to multiple behaviors or whether labeled-line neurons specific for each type of behavior are intermingled within the same structures. Because all of these behaviors contribute to the survival of the species, it may be wise to attend to the common themes underlying these various social behaviors, as well as using analytic techniques for each behavior.

UNANSWERED QUESTIONS AND FUTURE DIRECTIONS OF RESEARCH

Both in spite of and as a result of the impressive advancements in understanding the physiological bases of sexual behavior, many questions remain partially or completely unanswered. First, there is much to be learned about the anatomical interconnections that control both female and male sexual behavior. Both the neural connections from one place to the next and the neurotransmitter signatures of those neurons are important pieces of the puzzle. There are also questions concerning neurotransmitter interactions. Which neuropeptides are released with classical neurotransmitters and under what circumstances? Which receptor subtypes mediate each effect? There are also questions concerning the intracellular mediators of neurotransmitter and hormonal effects. What changes in gene transcription are induced by specific steroid hormones? How do rapid membrane effects of steroids influence sexual behavior? What changes in gene transcription mediate the effects of previous sexual experience? How does activation of *c-fos* and other immediate-early genes influence sexual behavior? Finally, broader questions include the interrelationships among sexual and other social behaviors, how species-specific differences in behavior are related to their ecological niches, and how, exactly, motivational fervor elicits particular behavioral responses. These questions should provide the framework for research in the years to come.

REFERENCES

Ackerman, A. E., Lange, G. M., & Clemens, L. G. (1997). Effects of paraventricular lesions on sex behavior and seminal emissions in male rats. *Physiology and Behavior, 63,* 49–53.

Adams, D. B., Gold, A. R., & Burt, A. D. (1978). Rise in female-initiated sexual activity at ovulation and its suppression by oral contraceptives. *New England Journal of Medicine, 229,* 1145–1150.

Adler, N. T., & Toner, J. P. (1986). The effects of copulatory behavior on sperm transport and fertility in rats. *Annals of the New York Academy of Sciences, 474,* 21–32.

Ågmo, A. (1976). Cholinergic mechanisms and sexual behavior in the male rabbit. *Psychopharmacology, 51,* 43–45.

Ågmo, A., Paredes, R. G., & Contreras, J. L. (1994). Opioids and sexual behaviors in the male rabbit: The role of central and peripheral opioid receptors. *Journal of Neural Transmission, General Section, 97,* 211–223.

Ågmo, A., Paredes, R. G., Sierra, L., & Garces, I. (1997). The inhibitory effects on sexual behavior and ambulatory activity of the mixed $GABA_A/GABA_B$ agonist progabide are differentially blocked by GABA receptor antagonists. *Psychopharmacology, 129,* 27–34.

Ågmo, A., & Picker, Z. (1990). Catecholamines and the initiation of sexual behavior in male rats without sexual experience. *Pharmacology, Biochemistry, and Behavior, 35,* 327–334.

Ågmo, A., & Södersten, P. (1975). Sexual behaviour in castrated rabbits treated with testosterone, oestradiol, dihydrotestosterone or oestradiol in combination with dihydrotestosterone. *Journal of Endocrinology, 67,* 327–332.

Ahlenius, S., Engel, J., Eriksson, H., Modigh, K., & Sodersten, P. (1972). Importance of central catecholamines in the mediation of lordosis behaviour in ovariectomized rats treated with estrogen and inhibitors of monoamine synthesis. *Journal of Neural Transmission, 33,* 247–255.

Ahlenius, S., & Larsson, K. (1990). Effects of selective D_1 and D_2 antagonists on male rat sexual behavior. *Experientia, 46,* 1026–1028.

Albinsson, A., Andersson, G., Andersson, K., Vega-Matuszczyk, J., & Larsson, K. (1996). The effects of lesions in the mesencephalic raphe systems on male rat sexual behavior and locomotor activity. *Behavioural Brain Research, 80,* 57–63.

Alexander, G. M., Swerdloff, R. S., Wang, C., Davidson, T., McDonald, V., Steiner, B., & Hines, M. (1997). Androgen-behavior correlations in hypogonadal men and eugonadal men: I. Mood and response to auditory sexual stimuli. *Hormones and Behavior, 31,* 110–119.

Al Satli, M., & Aron, C. (1977). Influence of olfactory bulb removal on sexual receptivity in the rat. *Psychoneuroendocrinology, 2,* 399–407.

Arendash, G. W., & Gorski, R. A. (1983). Effects of discrete lesions of the sexually dimorphic nucleus of the preoptic area or other medial preoptic regions on the sexual behavior of male rats. *Brain Research Bulletin, 10,* 147–154.

Argiolas, A., Melis, M. R., Mauri, A., & Gessa, G. L. (1987). Paraventricular nucleus lesion prevents yawning and penile erection induced by apomorphine and oxytocin, but not by ACTH in rats. *Brain Research, 421,* 349–352.

Balthazart, J., & Ball, G. F. (1995). Sexual-differentiation of brain and behavior in birds. *Trends in Endocrinology and Metabolism, 6,* 21–29.

Bancila, M., Verge, D., Rampin, O., Backstrom, J. R., Sanders-Bush, E., McKenna, K. E., Marson, L., Calas, A., & Giuliano, F. (1999). 5-Hydroxytryptamine2C receptors on spinal neurons controlling penile erection in the rat. *Neuroscience, 92,* 1523–1537.

Bancroft, J., & Wu, F. C. (1983). Changes in erectile responsiveness during androgen replacement therapy. *Archives of Sexual Behavior, 12,* 59–66.

Barbeau, A. (1969). L-DOPA therapy in Parkinson's disease: A critical review of nine years' experience. *Canadian Medical Association Journal, 101,* 791–800.

Barfield, R. J., & Geyer, L. A. (1972) Sexual behavior: Ultrasonic postejaculatory song of the male rat. *Science, 176,* 1349–1350.

Barfield, R. J., & Thomas, D. A. (1986). The role of ultrasonic vocalizations in the regulation of reproduction in rats. *Annals of the New York Academy of Sciences, 474,* 33–43.

Bast, J. D., Hunts, C., Renner, K. J., Morris, R. K., & Quadagno, D. M. (1987). Lesions in the preoptic area suppressed sexual receptivity in ovariectomized rats with estrogen implants in the ventromedial hypothalamus. *Brain Research Bulletin, 18,* 153–158.

Baum, M. J., & Everitt, B. J. (1992). Increased expression of c-fos in the medial preoptic area after mating in male rats: Role of afferent inputs from the medial amygdala and midbrain central tegmental field. *Neuroscience, 50,* 627–646.

Baum, M. J., Kingsbury, P. A., & Erskine, M. S. (1987). Failure of the synthetic androgen 17 beta-hydroxyl-17alpha-methyl-estra-4,9,11-triene-3-one (methyltrienolone, R1881) to duplicate the activational effect of testosterone on mating in castrated male rats. *Journal of Endocrinology, 113,* 15–20.

Beach, F. A., & LeBoeuf, B. J. (1967). Coital behaviour in dogs: I. Preferential mating in the bitch. *Animal Behaviour, 15,* 546–558.

Becker, J. B., Rudick, C. N., & Jenkins, W. J. (2001). The role of dopamine in the nucleus accumbens and striatum during sexual behavior in the female rat. *The Journal of Neuroscience, 21,* 3236–3241.

Benelli, A., Bertolini, A., Poggioli, R., Cavazzuti, E., Calza, L., Giardino, L., & Arletti, R. (1995). Nitric oxide is involved in male sexual behavior of rats. *European Journal of Pharmacology, 294,* 505–510.

Beyer, C., Larsson, K., Perez-Palacios, G., & Morali, G. (1973). Androgen structure and male sexual behavior in the castrated rat. *Hormones and Behavior, 4,* 99–108.

Bialy, M., Beck, J., Abramczyk, P., Trzebski, A., & Przybylski, J. (1996). Sexual behavior in male rats after nitric oxide synthesis inhibition. *Physiology and Behavior, 60,* 139–143.

Bignami, G. (1966). Pharmacologic influences on mating behavior in the male rat: Effects of d-amphetamine, LSD-25, strychnine, nicotine, and various anticholinergic agents. *Psychopharmacologia, 10,* 44–58.

Bitran, D., Miller, S. A., McQuade, D. B., Leipheimer, R. E., & Sachs, B. D. (1988). Inhibition of sexual reflexes by lumbosacral injection of a GABA$_B$ agonist in the male rat. *Pharmacology, Biochemistry, and Behavior, 31,* 657–666.

Blackburn, J. R., Pfaus, J. G., & Phillips, A. G. (1992). Dopamine functions in appetitive and defensive behaviours. *Progress in Neurobiology, 39,* 247–279.

Brackett, N. L., Iuvone, P. M., & Edwards, D. A. (1986). Midbrain lesions, dopamine and male sexual behavior. *Behavioural Brain Research, 20,* 231–240.

Bradshaw, W. G., Baum, M. J., & Awh, C. C. (1981). Attenuation by a 5α-reductase inhibitor of the activational effect of testosterone propionate on penile erections in castrated male rats. *Endocrinology, 109,* 1047–1051.

Bressler, S. C., & Baum, M. J. (1996). Sex comparison of neuronal Fos immunoreactivity in the rat vomeronasal projection circuit after chemosensory stimulation. *Neuroscience, 71,* 1063–1072.

Brown, W. A., Monti, P. M., & Corriveau, D. P. (1978). Serum testosterone and sexual activity and interest in men. *Archives of Sexual Behavior, 7,* 97–103.

Bunnell, B. N., Boland, B. D., & Dewsbury, D. A. (1976). Copulatory behavior of the golden hamster (*Mesocricetus auratus*). *Behaviour, 61,* 180–206.

Butera, P. C., & Czaja, J. A. (1989). Effects of intracranial implants of dihydrotestosterone on the reproductive physiology and behavior of male guinea pigs. *Hormones and Behavior, 23,* 424–431.

Caggiula, A. R., Herndon, J. G., Jr., Scanlon, R., Greenstone, D., Bradshaw, W., & Sharp, D. (1979). Dissociation of active from immobility components of sexual behavior in female rats by central 6-hydroxydopamine: Implications for CA involvement in sexual behavior and sensorimotor responsiveness. *Brain Research, 172,* 505–520.

Cain, D. P. (1974). The role of the olfactory bulb in limbic mechanisms. *Psychological Bulletin, 81,* 654–671.

Cantor, J. M., Binik, Y. M., & Pfaus, J. G. (1999). Chronic fluoxetine inhibits sexual behavior in the male rat: Reversal with oxytocin. *Psychopharmacology, 144,* 355–362.

Carter, C. S., DeVries, A. C., & Getz, L. L. (1995). Physiological substrates of mammalian monogamy: The prairie vole model. *Neuroscience and Biobehavioral Reviews, 19,* 303–314.

Carter, C. S., Witt, D. M., Auksi, T., & Casten, L. (1987). Estrogen and the induction of lordosis in female and male prairie voles (*Microtus ochrogaster*). *Hormones and Behavior, 21,* 65–73.

Christensen, L. W., Coniglio, L. P., Paup, D. C., & Clemens, L. C. (1973). Sexual behavior of male golden hamsters receiving diverse androgen treatments. *Hormones and Behavior, 4,* 223–229.

Christiansen, E., Guirguis, W. R., Cox, D., & Osterloh, I. H. (2000). Long-term efficacy and safety of oral Viagra (sildenafil citrate) in men with erectile dysfunction and the effect of randomized treatment withdrawal. *International Journal of Impotence Research, 12,* 177–182.

Clark, J. T. (1995). Sexual arousal and performance are modulated by adrenergic-neuropeptide-steroid interactions. In J. Bancroft (Ed.), *The pharmacology of sexual function and dysfunction: Proceedings of the Esteve Foundation Symposium VI, Son Vida, Mallorca* (pp. 55–68). Amsterdam: Excerpta Medica.

Clark, J. T., Smith, E. R., & Davidson, J. M. (1984). Enhancement of sexual motivation in male rats by yohimbine. *Science, 225,* 847–849.

Clark, J. T., Smith, E. R., & Davidson, J. M. (1985). Evidence for the modulation of sexual behavior by α-adrenoceptors in male rats. *Neuroendocrinology, 41,* 36–43.

Clemens, L. G., & Pomerantz, S. M. (1982). Testosterone acts as a prohormone to stimulate male copulatory behavior in male deer mice (*Peromyscus maniculatus bairdi*). *Journal of Comparative and Physiological Psychology, 96,* 114–122.

Coolen, L. M., Olivier, B., Peters, H. J., & Veening, J. G. (1997). Demonstration of ejaculation-induced neural activity in the male rat brain using 5-HT$_{1A}$ agonist 8-OH-DPAT. *Physiology and Behavior, 62,* 881–891.

Coolen, L. M., Peters, H. J., & Veening, J. G. (1996). Fos immunoreactivity in the rat brain following consummatory elements of sexual behavior: A sex comparison. *Brain Research, 738,* 67–82.

Cooper, T. T., Clancy, A. N., Karom, M., Moore, T. O., & Albers, H. E. (2000). Conversion of testosterone to estradiol may not be necessary for the expression of mating behavior in male Syrian hamsters (*Mesocricetus auratus*). *Hormones and Behavior, 37,* 237–245.

Crews, D., Bull, J. J., & Billy, A. J. (1988). Sex determination and sexual differentiation in reptiles. In J. M. A. Sitsen (Ed.), *Handbook of sexology: Vol. 6. The pharmacology and endocrinology of sexual function* (pp. 98–121). New York: Elsevier.

Crews, D., & Silver, R. (1985). Reproductive physiology and behavior interactions in nonmammalian vertebrates. In N. T. Adler, D. Pfaff, & R. W. Goy (Eds.), *Handbook of behavioral neurobiology: Vol. 7. Reproduction* (pp. 101–182). New York: Plenum Press.

Crowley, W. R., Nock, B. L., & Feder, H. H. (1978). Facilitation of lordosis behavior by clonidine in female guinea pigs. *Pharmacology, Biochemistry, and Behavior, 8,* 207–209.

Damsma, G., Pfaus, J. G., Wenkstern, D., Philips, A. G., & Fibiger, H. C. (1992). Sexual behavior increases dopamine transmission in the nucleus accumbens and striatum of male rats: A comparison with novelty and locomotion. *Behavioral Neuroscience, 106,* 181–191.

Davidson, J. M. (1966). Characteristics of sex behaviour in male rats following castration. *Animal Behavior, 14,* 266–272.

Davidson, J. M. (1969). Effects of estrogen on the sexual behavior of male rats. *Endocrinology, 84,* 1365–1372.

Davidson, J. M., Camargo, C. A., & Smith, E. R. (1979). Effects of androgen on sexual behavior in hypogonadal men. *Journal of Clinical Endocrinology and Metabolism, 48,* 955–958.

de Jonge, F. H., Oldenburger, W. P., Louwerse, A. L., & Van de Poll, N. E. (1992). Changes in male copulatory behavior after sexual exciting stimuli: Effects of medial amygdala lesions. *Physiology and Behavior, 52,* 327–332.

Dewsbury, D. A. (1972). Patterns of copulatory behavior in male mammals. *Quarterly Review of Biology, 47,* 1–33.

Diamond, M., & Sigmundson, K. (1997). Management of intersexuality: Guidelines for dealing with persons with ambiguous genitalia. *Archives of Pediatric and Adolescent Medicine, 151,* 1046–1050.

Dohanich, G. P., McMullan, D. M., Cada, D. A., & Mangum, K. A. (1991). Muscarinic receptor subtypes and sexual behavior in female rats. *Pharmacology, Biochemistry, and Behavior. 38,* 115–124

Dominguez, J., Riolo, J. V., Xu, Z., & Hull, E. M. (2001). Regulation by the medial amygdala of copulation and medial preoptic dopamine release. *The Journal of Neuroscience, 21,* 349–355.

Dornan, W. A., Malsbury, C. W., & Penney, R. B. (1987). Facilitation of lordosis by injection of substance P into the midbrain central gray. *Neuroendocrinology, 45,* 498–506.

Dörner, G., Döcke, F., & Götz, F. (1975). Male-like sexual behaviour of female rats with unilateral lesions in the hypothalamic ventromedial nuclear region. *Endokrinologie, 65,* 133–137.

Doty, R. L., Applebaum, S., Zusho, H., & Settle, R. G. (1985). Sex differences in odor identification ability: A cross cultural analysis. *Neuropsychologia, 23,* 667–672.

Du, J., Lorrain, D. S., & Hull, E. M. (1998). Castration decreases extracellular, but increases intracellular, dopamine in medial preoptic area of male rats. *Brain Research, 782,* 11–17.

Dula, E., Keating, W., Siami, P. F., Edmonds, A., O'Neil, J., & Buttler, S. (2000). Efficacy and safety of fixed-dose and dose-optimization regimens of sublingual apomorphine versus placebo in men with erectile dysfunction: The Apomorphine Study Group. *Urology, 56,* 130–135.

Eaton, R. C., Markowski, V. P., Lumley, L. A., Thompson, J. T., Moses, J., & Hull, E. M. (1991). D$_2$ receptors in the paraventricular nucleus regulate genital responses and copulation in male rats. *Pharmacology, Biochemistry, and Behavior, 39,* 177–181.

Edwards, D. A., & Einhorn, L. C. (1986). Preoptic and midbrain control of sexual motivation. *Physiology and Behavior, 37,* 329–335.

Edwards, D. A., Walter, B., & Liang, P. (1996). Hypothalamic and olfactory control of sexual behavior and partner preference in male rats. *Physiology and Behavior, 60,* 1347–1354.

Eibergen, R. D., & Caggiula, A. R. (1973). Ventral midbrain involvement in copulatory behavior of the male rat. *Physiology and Behavior, 10,* 435–441.

Emery, D. E., & Sachs, B. D. (1976). Copulatory behavior in male rats with lesions in the bed nucleus of the stria terminalis. *Physiology and Behavior, 17,* 803–806.

Erskine, M. S. (1985). Effects of paced coital stimulation on estrus duration in intact cycling rats and ovariectomized and ovariectomized-adrenalectomized hormone-primed rats. *Behavioral Neuroscience, 99,* 151–161.

Etgen, A. M. (1990). Intrahypothalamic implants of noradrenergic antagonists disrupt lordosis behavior in female rats. *Physiology and Behavior, 48,* 31–36.

Everitt, B. J. (1990). Sexual motivation: A neural and behavioral analysis of the mechanisms underlying appetitive and copulatory responses of male rats. *Neuroscience and Biobehavioral Reviews, 14,* 217–232.

Fausto-Sterling, A. (2000). *Sexing the body: Gender politics and the construction of sexuality.* New York: Basic Books.

Fernandez-Fewell, G. D., & Meredith, M. (1994). C-fos Expression in vomeronasal pathways of mated or pheromone-stimulated male golden hamsters: Contribution from vomeronasal sensory input and expression related to mating performance. *The Journal of Neuroscience, 14,* 3643–3654.

Fiorino, D. F., Coury, A., & Phillips, A. G. (1997). Dynamic changes in nucleus accumbens dopamine efflux during the Coolidge effect in male rats. *The Journal of Neuroscience, 17,* 4849–4855.

Fiorino, D. F., & Phillips, A. G. (1999). Facilitation of sexual behavior and enhanced dopamine efflux in the nucleus accumbens of male rats after D-amphetamine-induced behavioral sensitization. *The Journal of Neuroscience, 19,* 456–463.

Frye, C. A., & Vongher, J. M. (1999). Progestins' rapid facilitation of lordosis when applied to the ventral tegmentum corresponds to efficacy at enhancing GABA(A) receptor activity. *Journal of Neuroendocrinology, 11,* 829–837.

Fumero, B., Fernandez-Vera, J. R., Gonzalez-Mora, J. L., & Mas, M. (1994). Changes in monoamine turnover in forebrain areas associated with masculine sexual behavior: A microdialysis study. *Brain Research, 662,* 233–239.

Funabashi, T., Brooks, P. J., Kleopoulos, S. P., Grandison, L., Mobbs, C. V., & Pfaff, D. W. (1995). Changes in preproenkephalin messenger-RNA level in the rat ventromedial hypothalamus during the estrous cycle. *Molecular Brain Research, 28,* 129–134.

Gill, C. J., Wersinger, S. R., Veney, S. L., & Rissman, E. F. (1998). Induction of c-fos-like immunoreactivity in musk shrews after mating. *Brain Research, 811,* 21–28.

Giuliano, F., Bernabé, J., Brown, K., Droupy, S., Benoit, G., & Rampin, O. (1997). Erectile response to hypothalamic stimulation in rats: Role of peripheral nerves. *American Journal of Physiology, 273,* R1990–R1997.

Giuliano, F., Bernabé, J., McKenna, K., Longueville, F., & Rampin, O. (2001). Spinal proerectile effect of oxytocin in anesthetized rats. *American Journal of Physiology: Regulatory, Integrative, and Comparative Physiology, 280,* R1870–R1877.

Giuliano, F., Montorsi, F., Mirone, V., Rossi, D., & Sweeney, M. (2000). Switching from intracavernous prostaglandin E1 injections to oral sildenafil citrate in patients with erectile dysfunction: Results of a multicenter European study. *Journal of Urology, 164,* 708–711.

Giuliano, F., & Rampin, O. (2000). Central neural regulation of penile erection. *Neuroscience and Biobehavioral Reviews, 24,* 517–533.

Goldstein, I., Lue, T. F., Padma-Nathan, H., Rosen, R. C., Steers, W. D., & Wicker, P. A. (1998). Oral sildenafil in the treatment of erectile dysfunction. *New England Journal of Medicine, 338,* 1397–1404.

Gooren, L. J. (1985). Human male sexual functions do not require aromatization of testosterone: A study using tamoxifen, testolactone, and dihydrotestosterone. *Archives of Sexual Behavior, 14,* 539–548.

Goy, R. W., & McEwen, B. S. (1980). *Sexual differentiation of the brain.* Cambridge, MA: MIT Press.

Gray, G. D., Smith, E. R., & Davidson, J. M. (1980). Hormonal regulation of penile erection in castrated male rats. *Physiology and Behavior, 24,* 463–468.

Gréco, B., Edwards, D. A., Zumpe, D., & Clancy, A. N. (1998). Androgen receptor and mating-induced Fos immunoreactivity are co-localized in limbic and midbrain neurons that project to the male rat medial preoptic area. *Brain Research, 781,* 15–24.

Haensel, S. M., & Slob, A. K. (1997). Flesinoxan: A prosexual drug for male rats. *European Journal of Pharmacology, 330,* 1–9.

Hamburger-Bar, R., & Rigter, H. (1975). Apomorphine: Facilitation of sexual behaviour in female rats. *European Journal of Pharmacology, 32,* 357–360.

Hansen, S., & Hagelsrum, L. J. (1984). Emergence of displacement activities in the male rat following thwarting of sexual behavior. *Behavioral Neuroscience, 98,* 868–883.

Hansen, S., Stanfield, E. J., & Everitt, B. J. (1980). The role of ventral bundle noradrenergic neurones in sensory components of sexual behaviour and coitus-induced pseudopregnancy. *Nature, 286,* 152–154.

Harlan, R. E., Shivers, B. D., & Pfaff, D. W. (1983) Midbrain microinfusions of prolactin increase the estrogen-dependent behavior, lordosis. *Science, 219,* 1451–1453.

Hart, B. L. (1968). Alteration of quantitative aspects of sexual reflexes in spinal male dogs by testosterone. *Journal of Comparative and Physiological Psychology, 66,* 726–730.

Hart, B. L. (1973). Effects of testosterone propionate and dihydrotestosterone on penile morphology and sexual reflexes of spinal male rats. *Hormones and Behavior, 4,* 239–246.

Hart, B. L. (1974). The medial preoptic-anterior hypothalamic area and sociosexual behavior of male dogs: A comparative neuropsychological analysis. *Journal of Comparative and Physiological Psychology, 86,* 328–349.

Hart, B. L., Haugen, C. M., & Peterson, D. M. (1973). Effects of medial preoptic-anterior hypothalamic lesions on mating behavior of male cats. *Brain Research, 54,* 177–191.

Heeb, M. M., & Yahr, P. (1996). C-fos immunoreactivity in the sexually dimorphic area of the hypothalamus and related brain regions of male gerbils after exposure to sex-related stimuli or performance of specific sexual behaviors. *Neuroscience, 72,* 1049–1071.

Heeb, M. M., & Yahr, P. (2000). Cell-body lesions of the posterodorsal preoptic nucleus or posterodorsal medial amygdala, but not the parvicellular subparafascicular thalamus, disrupt mating in male gerbils. *Physiology and Behavior, 68,* 317–331.

Heim, N., & Hursch, C. J. (1979). Castration for sex offenders: Treatment or punishment? A review and critique of recent European literature. *Archives of Sexual Behavior, 8,* 281–304.

Heimer, L., & Larsson, K. (1966/1967). Impairment of mating behavior in male rats following lesions in the preoptic-anterior hypothalamic continuum. *Brain Research, 3,* 248–263.

Hennessey, A. C., Camak, L., Gordon, F., & Edwards, D. A. (1990). Connections between the pontine central gray and the ventromedial hypothalamus are essential for lordosis in female rats. *Behavioral Neuroscience, 104,* 477–488.

Holmes, G. M., Chapple, W. D., Leipheimer, R. E., & Sachs, B. D. (1991). Electromyographic analysis of male rat perineal muscles during copulation and reflexive erections. *Physiology and Behavior, 49,* 1235–1246.

Holmes, G. M., & Sachs, B. D. (1992). Erectile function and bulbospongiosus EMG activity in estrogen-maintained castrated rats vary with behavioral context. *Hormones and Behavior, 26,* 406–419.

Hoshina, Y., Takeo, T., Nakano, K., Sato, T., & Sakuma, Y. (1994). Axon-sparing lesion of the preoptic area enhances receptivity and diminishes proceptivity among components of female rat sexual behavior. *Behavioural Brain Research, 61,* 197–204.

Hull, E. M., Bazzett, T. J., Warner, R. K., Eaton, R. C., & Thompson, J. T. (1990). Dopamine receptors in the ventral tegmental area modulate male sexual behavior in rats. *Brain Research, 512,* 1–6.

Hull, E. M., Bitran, D., Pehek, E. A., Warner, R. K., & Band, L. C. (1986). Dopaminergic control of male sex behavior in rats: Effects of an intracerebrally infused agonist. *Brain Research, 370,* 73–81.

Hull, E. M., Du, J., Lorrain, D. S., & Matuszewich, L. (1995). Extracellular dopamine in the medial preoptic area: Implications for sexual motivation and hormonal control of copulation. *The Journal of Neuroscience, 15,* 7465–7471.

Hull, E. M., Eaton, R. C., Markowski, V. P., Moses, J., Lumley, L. A., & Loucks, J. A. (1992). Opposite influence of medial preoptic D_1 and D_2 receptors on genital reflexes: Implications for copulation. *Life Sciences, 51,* 1705–1713.

Hull, E. M., Lumley, L. A., Matuszewich, L., Dominguez, J., Moses, J., & Lorrain, D. S. (1994). The roles of nitric oxide in sexual function of male rats. *Neuropharmacology, 33,* 1499–1504.

Hull, E. M., Meisel, R. L., & Sachs, B. D. (2002). Male sexual behavior. In D. W. Pfaff (Ed.), *Hormones, brain, and behavior* (pp. 3–137). New York: Academic Press.

Hull, E. M., Warner, R. K., Bazzett, T. J., Eaton, R. C., Thompson, J. T., & Scaletta, L. L. (1989). D₂/D₁ ratio in the medial preoptic area affects copulation of male rats. *Journal of Pharmacology and Experimental Therapeutics, 251,* 422–427.

Hull, E. M., Weber, M. S., Eaton, R. C., Dua, R., Markowski, V. P., Lumley, L., & Moses, J. (1991). Dopamine receptors in the ventral tegmental area affect motor, but not motivational or reflexive, components of copulation in male rats. *Brain Research, 554,* 72–76.

Imperato-McGinley, J., Guerrero, L., Gautier, T., & Peterson, R. E. (1974). Steroid 5-alpha-reductase deficiency in man: An inherited form of male pseudohermaphroditism. *Science, 186,* 1213–1215.

Jenkins, W. J., & Becker, J. B. (2001a). Role of the striatum and nucleus accumbens in paced copulatory behavior in the female rat. *Behavioural Brain Research, 121,* 119–128.

Jenkins, W. J., & Becker, J. B. (2001b). Sexual behavior that occurs at the female rat's preferred pacing interval is reinforcing [Abstract]. *Hormones and Behavior, 39,* 334.

Johnson, R. D. (1988). Efferent modulation of penile mechanoreceptor activity. In A. Iggo & W. Hamann, (Eds.), *Progress in brain research: Vol. 74. Transduction and cellular mechanisms in sensory receptors* (pp. 319–324). Amsterdam: Elsevier.

Johnson, R. D., & Kitchell, R. L. (1987). Mechanoreceptor response to mechanical and thermal stimuli in the glans penis of the dog. *Journal of Neurophysiology, 57,* 1813–1836.

Kato, A., & Sakuma, Y. (2000). Neuronal activity in female rat preoptic area associated with sexually motivated behavior. *Brain Research, 862,* 90–102.

Kelliher, K. R., Liu, Y. C., Baum, M. J., & Sachs, B. D. (1999). Neuronal Fos activation in olfactory bulb and forebrain of male rats having erections in the presence of inaccessible estrous females. *Neuroscience, 92,* 1025–1033.

Kindon, H. A., Baum, M. J., & Paredes, R. J. (1996). Medial preoptic/anterior hypothalamic lesions induce a female-typical profile of sexual partner preference in male ferrets. *Hormones and Behavior, 30,* 514–527.

Kinsey, A. C., Pomeroy, W. B., & Martin, C. E. (1948). *Sexual behavior in the human male.* Philadelphia: W. B. Saunders.

Kollack-Walker, S., & Newman, S. W. (1997). Mating-induced expression of c-fos in the male Syrian hamster brain: Role of experience, pheromones, and ejaculations. *Journal of Neurobiology, 32,* 481–501.

Kondo, Y. (1992). Lesions of the medial amygdala produce severe impairment of copulatory behavior in sexually inexperienced male rats. *Physiology and Behavior, 51,* 939–943.

Kondo, Y., Sachs, B. D., & Sakuma, Y. (1997). Importance of the medial amygdala in rat penile erection evoked by remote stimuli from estrous females. *Behavioural Brain Research, 91,* 215–221.

Kondo, Y., Tomihara, K., & Sakuma, Y. (1999). Sensory requirement for noncontact penile erection in the rat. *Behavioral Neuroscience, 113,* 1062–1070.

Kondrashov, A. S. (1988). Deleterious mutations and the evolution of sexual reproduction. *Nature, 336,* 435–440.

Kow, L. M., Johnson, A. E., Ogawa, S., & Pfaff, D. W. (1991). Electrophysiological actions of oxytocin on hypothalamic neurons in vitro: Neuropharmacological characterization and effects of ovarian steroids. *Neuroendocrinology, 54,* 526–535.

Kow, L. M., Montgomery, M. O., & Pfaff, D. W. (1979). Triggering of lordosis reflex in female rats with somatosensory stimulation: Quantitative determination of stimulus parameters. *Journal of Neurophysiology, 42,* 195–202.

Kow, L. M., Weesner, G. D., & Pfaff, D. W. (1992) Alpha 1-adrenergic agonists act on the ventromedial hypothalamus to cause neuronal excitation and lordosis facilitation: Electrophysiological and behavioral evidence. *Brain Research, 588,* 237–245.

Krey, L. C., & McGinnis, M. Y. (1990). Time-courses of the appearance/disappearance of nuclear androgen + receptor complexes in the brain and adenohypophysis following testosterone administration/withdrawal to castrated male rats: Relationships with gonadotropin secretion. *Journal of Steroid Biochemistry, 35,* 403–408.

LaFerla, J. L., Anderson, D. L., & Schalch, D. S. (1978). Psychoendocrine response to sexual arousal in human males. *Psychosomatic Medicine, 40,* 166–172.

Lal, S., Laryea, E., Thavundayil, J. X., Nair, N. P., Negrete, J., Ackman, D., Blundell, P., & Gardiner, R. J. (1987). Apomorphine-induced penile tumescence in impotent patients: Preliminary findings. *Progress in Neuropsychopharmacology and Biological Psychiatry, 11,* 235–242.

Lauber, A. H., Romano, G. J., & Pfaff, D. W. (1991). Sex difference in estradiol regulation of progestin receptor mRNA in rat mediobasal hypothalamus as demonstrated by in situ hybridization. *Neuroendocrinology, 53,* 608–613.

Lee, R. L., Smith, E. R., Mas, M., & Davidson, J. M. (1990). Effects of intrathecal administration of 8-OH-DPAT on genital reflexes and mating behavior in male rats. *Physiology and Behavior, 47,* 665–669.

Lehman, M. N., & Winans, S. S. (1982). Vomeronasal and olfactory pathways to the amygdala controlling male hamster sexual behavior: Autoradiographic and behavioral analyses. *Brain Research, 240,* 27–41.

Lehman, M. N., Winans, S. S., & Powers, J. B. (1980). Medial nucleus of the amygdala mediates chemosensory control of male hamster sexual behavior. *Science, 210,* 557–560.

Levis, D. G., & Ford, J. J. (1989). The influence of androgenic and estrogenic hormones on sexual behavior in castrated adult male pigs. *Hormones and Behavior, 23,* 393–411.

Leyton, M., & Stewart, J. (1992). The stimulation of central kappa opioid receptors decreases male sexual behavior and locomotor activity. *Brain Research, 594*, 56–74.

Liu, Y. C., Sachs, B. D., & Salamone, J. D. (1998). Sexual behavior in male rats after radiofrequency or dopamine-depleting lesions in nucleus accumbens. *Pharmacology, Biochemistry, and Behavior, 60*, 585–592.

Liu, Y. C., Salamone, J. D., & Sachs, B. D. (1997a). Impaired sexual response after lesions of the paraventricular nucleus of the hypothalamus in male rats. *Behavioral Neuroscience, 111*, 1361–1367.

Liu, Y. C., Salamone, J. D., & Sachs, B. D. (1997b). Lesions in medial preoptic area and bed nucleus of stria terminalis: Differential effects on copulatory behavior and noncontact erection in male rats. *The Journal of Neuroscience, 17*, 5245–5253.

Lloyd, S. A., & Dixson, A. F. (1988). Effects of hypothalamic lesions upon the sexual and social behaviour of the male common marmoset (Callithrix jacchus). *Brain Research, 463*, 317–329.

Lorrain, D. S., & Hull, E. M. (1993). Nitric oxide increases dopamine and serotonin release in the medial preoptic area. *NeuroReport, 5*, 87–89.

Lorrain, D. S., Matuszewich, L., Friedman, R. D., & Hull, E. M. (1997). Extracellular serotonin in the lateral hypothalamic area is increased during postejaculatory interval and impairs copulation in male rats. *The Journal of Neuroscience, 17*, 9361–9366.

Lorrain, D. S., Matuszewich, L., Howard, R. V., Du, J., & Hull, E. M. (1996). Nitric oxide promotes medial preoptic dopamine release during male rat copulation. *NeuroReport, 8*, 31–34.

Lorrain, D. S., Riolo, J. V., Matuszewich, L., & Hull, E. M. (1999). Lateral hypothalamic serotonin inhibits nucleus accumbens dopamine: Implications for sexual refractoriness. *The Journal of Neuroscience, 19*, 7648–7652.

Lott, D. F. (1981). Sexual behavior and intersexual strategies in American bison. *Zhurnal für Tierpsychologie, 56*, 97–114.

Lugg, J. A., Rajfer, J., & Gonzalez-Cadavid, N. F. (1995). Dihydrotestosterone is the active androgen in the maintenance of nitric oxide-mediated penile erection in the rat. *Endocrinology 136*, 1495–1501.

Lumia, A. R., Meisel, R. L., & Sachs, B. D. (1981). Induction of female and male mating patterns in female rats by gonadal steroids: Effects of neonatal or adult olfactory bulbectomy. *Journal of Comparative and Physiological Psychology, 95*, 497–509.

Lumley, L. A., & Hull, E. M. (1999). Effects of a D₁ antagonist and of sexual experience on copulation-induced Fos-like immunoreactivity in the medial preoptic nucleus. *Brain Research, 829*, 55–68.

Luttge, W. G., & Hall, N. R. (1973). Differential effectiveness of testosterone and its metabolites in the induction of male sexual behavior in two strains of albino mice. *Hormones and Behavior, 4*, 31–43.

Mackay-Sim, A., & Rose, J. D. (1986). Removal of the vomeronasal organ impairs lordosis in female hamsters: Effect is reversed by luteinising hormone-releasing hormone. *Neuroendocrinology, 42*, 489–493.

Maeda, N., Matsuoka, N., & Yamaguchi, I. (1994). Role of the dopaminergic, serotonergic and cholinergic link in the expression of penile erection in rats. *Japanese Journal of Pharmacology, 66*, 59–66.

Majewska, M. D., Harrison, N. L, Schwartz, R. D., Barker, J. L., & Paul, S. M. (1986). Steroid hormone metabolites are barbiturate-like modulators of the GABA receptor. *Science, 232*, 1004–1007.

Malmnas, C. O. (1976). The significance of dopamine, versus other catecholamines, for L-dopa induced facilitation of sexual behavior in the castrated male rat. *Pharmacology, Biochemistry, and Behavior, 4*, 521–526.

Malsbury, C. W. (1971). Facilitation of male rat copulatory behavior by electrical stimulation of the medial preoptic area. *Physiology and Behavior, 7*, 797–805.

Mani, S. K., Allen, J. M. C., Clark, J. H., Blaustein, J. D., & O'Malley, B. W. (1994). Convergent pathways for steroid hormone- and neurotransmitter-induced rat sexual behavior. *Science, 265*, 1246–1249.

Mani, S. K., Blaustein, J. D., & O'Malley, B. W. (1997). Progesterone receptor function from a behavioral perspective. *Hormones and Behavior, 31*, 244–255.

Manzo, J., Cruz, M. R., Hernandez, M. E., Pacheco, P., & Sachs, B. D. (1999). Regulation of noncontact erection in rats by gonadal steroids. *Hormones and Behavior, 35*, 264–270.

Markowski, V. P., Eaton, R. C., Lumley, L. A., Moses, J., & Hull, E. M. (1994). A D₁ agonist in the MPOA area facilitates copulation of male rats. *Pharmacology Biochemistry and Behavior, 47*, 483–486.

Markowski, V. P., & Hull, E. M. (1995). Cholecystokinin modulates mesolimbic dopaminergic influences on male rat copulatory behavior. *Brain Research, 699*, 266–274.

Marson, L., List, M. S., & McKenna, K. E. (1992). Lesions of the nucleus paragigantocellularis alter ex copula penile reflexes. *Brain Research, 592*, 187–192.

Marson, L., & McKenna, K. E. (1990). The identification of a brainstem site controlling spinal sexual reflexes in male rats. *Brain Research, 515*, 303–308.

Marson, L., & McKenna, K. E. (1992). A role for 5-hydroxytryptamine in descending inhibition of spinal sexual reflexes. *Experimental Brain Research, 88*, 313–320.

Marson, L., & McKenna, K. E. (1994a). Serotonergic neurotoxic lesions facilitate male sexual reflexes. *Pharmacology Biochemistry Behavior, 47*, 883–888.

Marson, L., & McKenna, K. E. (1994b). Stimulation of the hypothalamus initiates the urethrogenital reflex in male rats. *Brain Research, 638*, 103–108.

Mas, M., Gonzalez-Mora, J. L., Louilot, A., Sole, C., & Guadalupe, T. (1990). Increased dopamine release in the nucleus accumbens of copulating male rats as evidenced by in vivo voltammetry. *Neuroscience Letters, 110*, 303–308.

Matteo, S., & Rissman, E. F. (1984). Increased sexual activity during the midcycle portion of the human menstrual cycle. *Hormones and Behavior, 18,* 249–255.

Matuszewich, L., Lorrain, D. S., & Hull, E. M. (2000). Dopamine release in the medial preoptic area of female rats in response to hormonal manipulation and sexual activity. *Behavioral Neuroscience, 114,* 772–782.

McCarthy, M. M., McDonald, C. H., Brooks, P. J., & Goldman, D. (1996). An anxiolytic action of oxytocin is enhanced by estrogen in the mouse. *Physiology and Behavior, 60,* 1209–1215.

McCarthy, M. M, Pfaff, D. W., & Schwartz-Giblin, S. (1991). Midbrain central gray GABA-a receptor activation enhances, and blockade reduces, sexual-behavior in the female rat. *Experimental Brain Research, 86,* 108–116.

McCarthy, M. M., Schlenker, E. H., & Pfaff, D. W. (1993). Enduring consequences of neonatal treatment with antisense oligodeoxynucleotides to estrogen receptor messenger ribonucleic acid on sexual differentiation of rat brain. *Endocrinology, 133,* 433–439.

McClintock, M. K. (1987). A functional approach to the behavioral endocrinology of rodents. In D. Crews (Ed.), *Psychobiology of reproductive behavior: An evolutionary perspective* (pp. 176–203). Englewood Cliffs, NJ: Prentice Hall.

McDonald, A. J. (1998). Cortical pathways to the mammalian amygdala. *Progress in Neurobiology, 55,* 257–332.

McGinnis, M. Y., & Kahn, D. F. (1997). Inhibition of male sexual behavior by intracranial implants of the protein synthesis inhibitor anisomycin into the medial preoptic area of the rat. *Hormones and Behavior, 31,* 15–23.

McGinnis, M. Y., & Mirth, M. C. (1986). Inhibition of cell nuclear androgen receptor binding and copulation in male rats by an antiandrogen, Sch 16423. *Neuroendocrinology, 43,* 63–68.

McIntosh, T. K., Vallano, M. L., & Barfield, R. J. (1980). Effects of morphine, beta-endorphin and naloxone on catecholamine levels and sexual behavior in the male rat. *Pharmacology, Biochemistry, and Behavior, 13,* 435–441.

McKenna, K. E., Chung, S. K., & McVary, K. T. (1991). A model for the study of sexual function in anesthetized male and female rats. *American Journal Physiology, 30,* R1276–R1285.

Meisel, R. L., Camp, D. M., & Robinson, T. E. (1993). A microdialysis study of ventral striatal dopamine during sexual behavior in female Syrian hamsters. *Behavioural Brain Research, 55,* 151–157.

Meisel, R. L., Leipheimer, R. E., & Sachs, B. D. (1986). Anisomycin does not disrupt the activation of penile reflexes by testosterone in rats. *Physiology and Behavior, 37,* 951–956.

Meisel, R. L., O'Hanlon, J. K., & Sachs, B. D. (1984). Differential maintenance of penile responses and copulatory behavior by gonadal hormones in castrated male rats. *Hormones and Behavior, 18,* 56–64.

Meisel, R. L., Sachs, B. D., & Lumia, A. R. (1984). Olfactory bulb control of sexual function. In S. Finger & C. R. Almli (Eds.), *Early brain damage: Vol. 2. Neurobiology and behavior* (pp. 253–268). Orlando: Academic Press.

Melis, M. R., Argiolas, A., & Gessa, G. L. (1987). Apomorphine-induced penile erection and yawning: Site of action in brain. *Brain Research, 415,* 98–104.

Melis, M. R., Stancampiano, R., & Argiolas, A. (1992). Hippocampal oxytocin mediates apomorphine-induced penile erection and yawning. *Pharmacology, Biochemistry, and Behavior, 42,* 61–66.

Melis, M. R., Succu, S., & Argiolas, A. (1996). Dopamine agonists increase nitric oxide production in the paraventricular nucleus of the hypothalamus: Correlation with penile erection and yawning. *European Journal of Neuroscience, 8,* 2056–2063.

Melis, M. R., Succu, S., Iannucci, U., & Argiolas, A. (1997). N-methyl-D-aspartic acid-induced penile erection and yawning: Role of hypothalamic paraventricular nitric oxide. *European Journal of Pharmacology, 328,* 115–123.

Melis, M. R., Succu, S., Mauri, A., & Argiolas, A. (1998). Nitric oxide production is increased in the paraventricular nucleus of the hypothalamus of male rats during non-contact penile erections and copulation. *European Journal of Neuroscience, 10,* 1968–1974.

Melis, M. R., Succu, S., Spano, M. S., & Argiolas, A. (1999a). Morphine injected into the paraventricular nucleus of the hypothalamus prevents noncontact penile erections and impairs copulation involvement of nitric oxide. *European Journal of Neuroscience, 11,* 1857–1864.

Melis, M. R., Succu, S., Spano, M. S., & Argiolas, A. (1999b). The oxytocin antagonist d(CH2)5Tyr(ME)2-Om8-vasotocin reduces non-contact penile erections in male rats. *Neuroscience Letters, 265,* 171–174.

Meredith, M., Marques, D. M., O'Connell, R. J., & Stem, F. L. (1980). Vomeronasal pump: Significance for male hamster sexual behavior. *Science, 207,* 1224–1226.

Mermelstein, P. G., & Becker, J. B. (1995). Increased extracellular dopamine in the nucleus accumbens and striatum of the female rat during paced copulatory behavior. *Behavioral Neuroscience, 109,* 354–365.

Millan, M. J., Peglion, J. L, Lavielle, G., & Perrin-Monneyron, S. (1997). 5-HT$_{2C}$ receptors mediate penile erections in rats, actions of novel and selective agonists and antagonists. *European Journal of Pharmacology, 325,* 9–12.

Mitchell, J. B., & Gratton, A. (1991). Opioid modulation and sensitization of dopamine release elicited by sexually relevant stimuli: A high speed chronoamperometric study in freely behaving rats. *Brain Research, 551,* 20–27.

Monaghan, E. P., Arjomand, J., & Breedlove, S. M. (1993). Brain lesions affect penile reflexes. *Hormones and Behavior, 27,* 122–131.

Moore, M. C., Hews, D. K., & Knapp, R. (1998). Hormonal control and evolution of alternative male phenotypes: Generalizations of models for sexual differentiation. *American Zoologist, 38,* 133–151.

Morali, G., Lemus, A. E., Munguia, R., Arteaga, M., Perez-Palacios, G., Sundaram, K., Kumar, N., & Bardin, C. W. (1993). Induction of male sexual behavior in the rat by 7 alpha-methyl-19-nortestosterone, an androgen that does not undergo 5 alpha-reduction. *Biology of Reproduction, 49,* 577–581.

Moses, J., & Hull, E. M. (1999). A nitric oxide synthesis inhibitor administered into the medial preoptic area increases seminal emissions in an *ex copula* reflex test. *Pharmacology, Biochemistry, and Behavior, 63,* 345–348.

Moses, J., Loucks, J. A., Watson, H. L., Matuszewich, L., & Hull, E. M. (1995). Dopaminergic drugs in the medial preoptic area and nucleus accumbens: Effects on motor activity, sexual motivation, and sexual performance. *Pharmacology, Biochemistry, and Behavior, 51,* 681–686.

Mosig, D. W., & Dewsbury, D. A. (1976). Studies of the copulatory behavior of house mice (*Mus musculus*). *Behavioral Biology, 16,* 463–473.

Murphy, A. Z., & Hoffman, G. E. (2001). Distribution of gonadal steroid receptor-containing neurons in the preoptic-periaqueductal gray-brainstem pathway: A potential circuit for the initiation of male sexual behavior. *Journal of Comparative Neurology, 438,* 191–212.

Murphy, A. Z., Shupnik, M. A., & Hoffman, G. E. (1999). Androgen and estrogen (alpha) receptor distribution in the periaqueductal gray of the male rat. *Hormones and Behavior, 36,* 98–108.

Murphy, M. R. (1980). Sexual preferences of male hamsters: Importance of preweaning and adult experience, vaginal secretion, and olfactory or vomeronasal sensation. *Behavioral and Neural Biology, 30,* 323–340.

Myers, B. M., & Baum, M. J. (1979). Facilitation by opiate antagonists of sexual performance in the male rat. *Pharmacology, Biochemistry, and Behavior, 10,* 615–618.

Nance, D. M., Shryne, J. E., Gordon, J. H., & Gorski, R. A. (1977). Examination of some factors that control the effects of septal lesions on lordosis behavior. *Pharmacology, Biochemistry, and Behavior, 6,* 227–234.

Nelson, R. J. (2000). *An introduction to behavioral endocrinology* (2nd. ed.). Sunderland, MA: Sinauer.

Newman, S. W. (1999). The medial extended amygdala in male reproductive behavior: A node in the mammalian social behavior network. *Annals of the New York Academy of Sciences, 877,* 242–257.

Nock, B., & Feder, H. H. (1979). Noradrenergic transmission and female sexual behavior of guinea pigs. *Brain Research, 166,* 369–380.

O'Carroll, R., Shapiro, C., & Bancroft, J. (1985). Androgens, behaviour and nocturnal erection in hypogonadal men: The effects of varying the replacement dose. *Clinical Endocrinology, 23,* 527–538.

Ogawa, S., Olazabal, U. E., Parhar, I. S., & Pfaff, D. W. (1994). Effects of intrahypothalamic administration of antisense DNA for progesterone receptor mRNA on reproductive behavior and progesterone receptor immunoreactivity in female rat. *The Journal of Neuroscience, 14,* 1766–1774.

Ogawa, S., Robbins, A., Kumar, N., Pfaff, D. W., Sundaram, K., & Bardin, C. W. (1996). Effects of testosterone and 7 alpha-methyl-19-nortestosterone (MENT) on sexual and aggressive behaviors in two inbred strains of male mice. *Hormones and Behavior, 30,* 74–84.

Ogawa, S., Washburn, T. F., Taylor, J., Lubahn, D. B., Korach, K. S., & Pfaff, D. W. (1998). Modification of testosterone-dependent behaviors by estrogen receptor-alpha gene disruption in male mice. *Endocrinology, 139,* 5058–5069.

O'Hanlon, J. K., Meisel, R. L., & Sachs, B. D. (1981). Estradiol maintains castrated male rats' sexual reflexes in copula, but not ex copula. *Behavioral and Neural Biology, 32,* 269–273.

O'Hanlon, J. K., & Sachs, B. D. (1980). Penile reflexes in rats after different numbers of ejaculations. *Behavioral and Neural Biology, 29,* 338–348.

Oldenburger, W. P., Everitt, B. J., & de Jonge, F. H. (1992). Conditioned place preference induced by sexual interation in female rats. *Hormones and Behavior, 26,* 214–228.

Paredes, R. G., & Ågmo, A. (1995). The GABA$_B$ antagonist CGP 35348 inhibits the effects of baclofen on sexual behavior and motor coordination. *Brain Research Bulletin, 36,* 495–497.

Paredes, R. G., & Alonso, A. (1997). Sexual behavior regulated (paced) by the female induces conditioned place preference. *Behavioral Neuroscience, 111,* 123–128.

Paredes, R. G., & Baum, M. J. (1995). Altered sexual partner preference in male ferrets given excitotoxic lesions of the preoptic area/anterior hypothalamus. *The Journal of Neuroscience, 15,* 6619–6630.

Paredes, R. G., Highland, L., & Karam, P. (1993). Socio-sexual behavior in male rats after lesions of the medial preoptic area: Evidence for reduced sexual motivation. *Brain Research, 618,* 271–276.

Paredes, R. G., Karam, P., Highland, L., & Ågmo, A. (1997). GABAergic drugs and socio-sexual behavior. *Pharmacology, Biochemistry, and Behavior, 58,* 291–298.

Paredes, R. G., Tzschentke, T., & Nakach, N. (1998). Lesions of the medial preoptic area/anterior hypothalamus (MPOA/AH) modify partner preference in male rats. *Brain Research, 813,* 81–83.

Parfitt, D. B., Coolen, L. M., Newman, S. W., & Wood, R. I. (1996). Lesions of the posterior medial nucleus of the amygdala delay sexual satiety. *Society for Neuroscience Abstracts, 22,* 155.

Parfitt, D. B., & Newman, S. W. (1998). Fos-immunoreactivity within the extended amygdala is correlated with the onset of sexual satiety. *Hormones and Behavior, 34,* 17–29.

Parrott, R. F. (1986). Minimal effects of 17 beta-hydroxy-17 alpha-methyl-estra-4,9,11-triene-3-one (R1881) on sexual behaviour in prepubertally castrated rams. *Journal of Endocrinology, 110,* 481–487.

Pehek, E. A., Thompson, J. T., & Hull, E. M. (1989a). The effects of intracranial administration of the dopamine agonist apomorphine on penile reflexes and seminal emission in the rat. *Brain Research, 500*, 325–332.

Pehek, E. A., Thompson, J. T., & Hull, E. M. (1989b). The effects of intrathecal administration of the dopamine agonist apomorphine on penile reflexes and copulation in the male rat. *Psychopharmacology, 99*, 304–308.

Pfaff, D. W. (1999). *Drive: Neurobiological and molecular mechanisms of sexual motivation*. Cambridge, MA: MIT Press.

Pfaff, D. W., & Pfaffmann, C. (1969). Olfactory and hormonal influences on the basal forebrain of the male rat. *Brain Research, 15*, 137–156.

Pfaff, D. W., & Sakuma, Y. (1979). Facilitation of the lordosis reflex of female rats from the ventromedial nucleus of the hypothalamus. *Journal of Physiology, 288*, 189–202.

Pfaff, D. W., & Schwartz-Giblin, S. (1988). Cellular mechanisms of female reproductive behaviors. In E. Knobil, J. Neill, & D. W. Pfaff (Eds.), *The physiology of reproduction* (pp. 1487–1576). New York: Raven.

Pfaff, D. W., Schwartz-Giblin, S., McCarthy, M. M., & Kow, L. M. (1994). Cellular and molecular mechanisms of female reproductive behaviors. In E. Knobil & J. Neill (Eds.), *The physiology of reproduction* (2nd ed.). New York: Raven.

Pfaus, J. G., Damsma, G., Nomikos, G. G., Wenkstern, D. G., Blaha, C. D., Philips, A. G., & Fibiger, H. C. (1990). Sexual behavior enhances central dopamine transmission in the rat. *Brain Research, 530*, 345–348.

Pfaus, J. G., Damsma, G., Wenkstern, D., & Fibiger, H. C. (1995). Sexual activity increases dopamine transmission in the nucleus accumbens and striatum of female rats. *Brain Research, 693*, 21–30.

Pfaus, J. G., & Gorzalka, B. B. (1987). Selective activation of opioid receptors differentially affects lordosis behavior in female rats. *Peptides, 8*, 309–317.

Pfaus, J. G., & Heeb, M. M. (1997). Implications of immediate-early gene induction in the brain following sexual stimulation of female and male rodents. *Brain Research Bulletin, 44*, 397–407.

Pfaus, J. G., Mendelson, S. D., & Phillips, A. G. (1990). A correlational and factor analysis of anticipatory and consummatory measures of sexual behavior in the male rat. *Psychoneuroendocrinology, 15*, 329–340.

Pfaus, J. G., Pendleton, N., & Gorzalka, B. B. (1986). Dual effect of morphiceptin on lordosis behavior: Possible mediation by different opioid receptor subtypes. *Pharmacology, Biochemistry, and Behavior, 24*, 1461–1464.

Phelps, S. M., Lydon, J. P., O'Malley, B. W., & Crews, D. (1998). Regulation of male sexual behavior by progesterone receptor, sexual experience, and androgen. *Hormones and Behavior, 34*, 294–302.

Phoenix, C. H. (1974). Effects of dihydrotestosterone on sexual behavior of castrated male rhesus monkeys. *Physiology and Behavior, 12*, 1045–1055.

Pirke, K. M., Kockott, G., Aldenhoff, J., Besinger, U., & Feil, W. (1979). Pituitary gonadal system function in patients with erectile impotence and premature ejaculation. *Archives of Sexual Behavior, 8*, 41–48.

Pomerantz, S. M., Hepner, B. C., & Wertz, J. M. (1993). 5-HT$_{1A}$ and 5-HT$_{1C/1D}$ receptor agonists produce reciprocal effects on male sexual behavior of rhesus monkeys. *European Journal of Pharmacology, 243*, 227–234.

Putnam, S. K., Du, J., Sato, S., & Hull, E. M. (2001). Testosterone restoration of copulatory behavior correlates with medial preoptic dopamine release in castrated male rats. *Hormones and Behavior, 39*, 216–224.

Putnam, S. K., Panos, J. J., & Hull, E. M. (1998). Hormonal maintenance of copulation in male rat castrates: Association with MPOA dopamine response. *Society for Neuroscience Abstracts, 24*, 1705.

Qureshi, G. A., Bednar, I., Forsberg, B. G., & Södersten, P. (1988). GABA inhibits sexual behaviour in female rats. *Neuroscience, 27*, 169–174.

Raboch, J., Mellan, J., & Starka, L. (1975). Plasma testosterone in male patients with sexual dysfunction. *Archives of Sexual Behavior, 4*, 541–545.

Retana-Marquez, S., & Velazquez-Moctezuma, J. (1997). Cholinergic-androgenic interaction in the regulation of male sexual behavior in rats. *Pharmacology, Biochemistry, and Behavior, 56*, 373–378.

Richmond, G., & Clemens, L. G. (1986). Evidence for involvement of midbrain central gray in cholinergic mediation of female sexual receptivity in rats. *Behavioral Neuroscience, 100*, 376–380.

Rissman, E. F. (1991). Frank A. Beach Award: Behavioral endocrinology of the female musk shrew. *Hormones and Behavior, 25*, 125–127.

Rissman, E. F., Early, A. H., Taylor, J. A., Korach, K. S., & Lubahn, D. B. (1997). Estrogen receptors are essential for female sexual receptivity. *Endocrinology, 138*, 507–510.

Rizvi, T. A., Murphy, A. Z., Ennis, M., Behbehani, M. M., & Shipley, M. T. (1996). Medial preoptic area afferents to periaqueductal gray medullo-output neurons: A combined Fos and tract tracing study. *Journal of Neuroscience, 16*, 333–344.

Robertson, G. S., Pfaus, J. G., Atkinson, L. J., Matsumura, H., Phillips, A. G., & Fibiger, H. C. (1991). Sexual behavior increases *c-fos* expression in the forebrain of the male rat. *Brain Research, 564*, 352–357.

Robinson, T. J. (1954). The necessity for progesterone with estrogen for the induction of recurrent estrus in the ovariectomized ewe. *Endocrinology, 55*, 403–408.

Rodríguez-Manzo, G. (1999). Yohimbine interacts with the dopaminergic system to reverse sexual satiation: Further evidence for a role of sexual motivation in sexual exhaustion. *European Journal of Pharmacology, 372*, 1–8.

Rodríguez-Manzo, G., Pellicer, F., Larsson, K. & Fernandez-Guasti, A. (2000). Stimulation of the medial preoptic area facilitates sexual behavior but does not reverse sexual satiation. *Behavioral Neuroscience, 114,* 553–560.

Romano, G. J., Harlan, R. E., Shivers, B. D., Howells, R. D., & Pfaff, D. W. (1988). Estrogen increases proenkephalin messenger ribonucleic acid levels in the ventromedial hypothalamus of the rat. *Molecular Endocrinology, 2,* 1320–1328.

Rosen, R. C., Lane, R. M., & Menza, M. (1999). Effects of SSRIs on sexual function: A critical review. *Journal of Clinical Psychopharmacology, 19,* 67–85.

Rubin, B., & Barfield, R. (1983). Induction of estrous behavior in ovariectomized rats by sequential replacement of estrogen and progesterone to the ventromedial hypothalamus. *Neuroendocrinology, 37,* 218–224.

Sachs, B. D. (1978). Conceptual and neural mechanisms of masculine copulatory behavior. In T. E. McGill, D. A. Dewsbury, & B. D. Sachs (Eds.), *Sex and behavior* (pp. 267–295). New York: Plenum Press.

Sachs, B. D. (1980). Sexual reflexes of spinal male house mice. *Physiology and Behavior, 24,* 489–492.

Sachs, B. D. (1983). Potency and fertility: Hormonal and mechanical causes and effects of penile actions in rats. In J. Balthazart, E. Pröve, & R. Gilles (Eds.), *Hormones and behaviour in higher vertebrates* (pp. 86–110). Berlin: Springer-Verlag.

Sachs, B. D. (2000). Contextual approaches to the physiology and classification of erectile function, erectile dysfunction, and sexual arousal. *Neuroscience and Biobehavioral Reviews, 24,* 541–560.

Sachs, B. D., Akasofu, K., Citron, J. H., Daniels, S. B., & Natoli, J. H. (1994). Noncontact stimulation from estrous females evokes penile erection in rats. *Physiology and Behavior, 55,* 1073–1079.

Sachs, B. D., & Bitran, D. (1990). Spinal block reveals roles for brain and spinal cord in the mediation of reflexive erection in rats. *Brain Research, 528,* 99–108.

Sachs, B. D., & Garinello, L. D. (1979). Spinal pacemaker controlling sexual reflexes in male rats. *Brain Research, 171,* 152–156.

Sachs, B. D., & Leipheimer, R. E. (1988). Rapid effect of testosterone on striated muscle activity in rats. *Neuroendocrinology, 48,* 453–458.

Sakuma, Y., & Pfaff, D. W. (1979). Mesencephalic mechanisms for integration of female reproductive behavior in the rat. *American Journal of Physiology, 237,* R285–R290.

Sakuma, Y., & Pfaff, D. W. (1980). LH-RH in the mesenphalic central grey can potentiate lordosis reflex of female rats. *Nature, 283,* 566–567.

Sato, Y., Christ, G. J., Horita, H., Adachi, H., Suzuki, N., & Tsukamoto, T. (1999). The effects of alterations in nitric oxide levels in the paraventricular nucleus on copulatory behavior and reflexive erections in male rats. *Journal of Urology, 162,* 2182–2185.

Sato, Y., Horita, H., Kurohata, T., Adachi, H., & Tsukamoto, T. (1998). Effect of the nitric oxide level in the medial preoptic area on male copulatory behavior in rats. *American Journal of Physiology, 274,* R243–R247.

Scaletta, L. L., & Hull, E. M. (1990). Systemic or intracranial apomorphine increases copulation in long-term castrated male rats. *Pharmacology, Biochemistry, and Behavior, 37,* 471–475.

Scouten, C. W., Burrell, L., Palmer, T., & Cegavske, C. F. (1980). Lateral projections of the medial preoptic area are necessary for androgenic influence on urine marking and copulation in rats. *Physiology and Behavior, 25,* 237–243.

Silva, N. L., & Boulant, J. A. (1986). Effects of testosterone, estradiol, and temperature on neurons in preoptic tissue slices. *American Journal of Physiology, 250,* R625–R632.

Simerly, R. B., & Swanson, L. W. (1986). The organization of neural inputs to the medial preoptic nucleus of the rat. *Journal of Comparative Neurology, 246,* 312–342.

Simerly, R. B., & Swanson, L. W. (1988). Projections of the medial preoptic nucleus: A *Phaseolis vulgaris* leucoagglutinin anterograde tract-tracing study in the rat. *Journal of Comparative Neurology, 270,* 209–242.

Sirinathsinghji, D. J., Whittington, P. E., & Audsley, A. R. (1986). Regulation of mating behaviour in the female rat by gonadotropin-releasing hormone in the ventral tegmental area: Effects of selective destruction of the A10 dopamine neurones. *Brain Research, 374,* 167–173.

Slimp, J. C., Hart, B. L., & Goy, R. W. (1978). Heterosexual, autosexual and social behavior of adult male rhesus monkeys with medial preoptic-anterior hypothalamic lesions. *Brain Research, 142,* 105–122.

Slob, A. K., Bax, C. M., Hop, W. C., Rowland, D. L., & van der Werff ten Bosch, J. J. (1996). Sexual arousability and the menstrual cycle. *Psychoneuroendocrinology, 21,* 545–558.

Steers, W. D. (2000). Neural pathways and central sites involved in penile erection: Neuroanatomy and clinical implications. *Neuroscience and Biobehavioral Reviews, 24,* 507–516.

Stefanick, M. L., Smith, E. R., & Davidson, J. M. (1983). Penile reflexes in intact rats following anesthetization of the penis and ejaculation. *Physiology and Behavior, 31,* 63–65.

Takeo, T., Chiba, Y., & Sakuma, Y. (1993). Suppression of the lordosis reflex of female rats by efferents of the medial preoptic area. *Physiology and Behavior, 53,* 831–838.

Takeo, T., & Sakuma, Y. (1995). Diametrically opposite effects of estrogen on the excitability of female rat medial and lateral preoptic neurons with axons to the midbrain locomotor region. *Neuroscience Research, 22,* 73–80.

Tallentire, D., McRae, G., Spedding, R., Clark, R., & Vickery, B. (1996). Modulation of sexual behaviour in the rat by a potent and selective alpha 2-adrenoceptor antagonist, delequamine (RS-15385-197). *British Journal of Pharmacology, 118,* 63–72.

Uphouse, L. (2000). Female gonadal hormones, serotonin, and sexual receptivity. *Brain Research: Brain Research Reviews, 33,* 242–257.

Vagell, M. E., & McGinnis, M. Y. (1997). The role of aromatization in the restoration of male rat reproductive behavior. *Journal of Neuroendocrinology, 9,* 415–421.

Vagell, M. E., & McGinnis, M. Y. (1998). The role of gonadal steroid receptor activation in the restoration of sociosexual behavior in adult male rats. *Hormones and Behavior, 33,* 163–179.

van de Poll, N. E., & van Dis, H. (1979). The effect of medial preoptic-anterior hypothalamic lesions on bisexual behavior of the male rat. *Brain Research Bulletin, 4,* 505–511.

van Furth, W. R., & van Ree, J. M. (1996). Sexual motivation: Involvement of endogenous opioids in the ventral tegmental area. *Brain Research, 729,* 20–28.

Vathy, I., & Etgen, A. M. (1988). Ovarian steroids and hypothalamic norepinephrine release: Studies using in vivo brain microdialysis. *Life Sciences, 43,* 1493–1499.

Vathy, I., & Marson, L. (1998). Effects of prenatal morphine and cocaine exposure on spinal sexual reflexes in male and female rats. *Physiology and Behavior, 63,* 445–450.

Veening, J. G., & Coolen, L. M. (1998). Neural activation following sexual behavior in the male and female rat brain. *Behavioural Brain Research, 92,* 181–193.

Vega Matuszcyk, J., Larsson, K., & Eriksson, E. (1998). The selective serotonin reuptake inhibitor fluoxetine reduces sexual motivation in male rats. *Pharmacology, Biochemistry, and Behavior, 60,* 527–532.

Wallen, K. (1990). Desire and ability: Hormones and the regulation of female sexual behavior. *Neuroscience and Biobehavioral Reviews, 14,* 233–241.

Wang, Z., Hulihan, T. J., & Insel, T. R. (1997). Sexual and social experience is associated with different patterns of behavior and neural activation in male prairie voles. *Brain Research, 767,* 321–332.

Warner, R. K., Thompson, J. T., Markowski, V. P., Loucks, J. A., Bazzett, T. J., Eaton, R. C., & Hull, E. M. (1991). Microinjection of the dopamine antagonist cis-flupenthixol into the MPOA impairs copulation, penile reflexes and sexual motivation in male rats. *Brain Research, 540,* 177–182.

Wedekind, C., & Penn, D. (2000). MHC genes, body odours, and odour preferences. *Nephrology, Dialysis and Transplantation, 15,* 1269–1271.

Wenkstern, D., Pfaus, J. G., & Fibiger, H. C. (1993). Dopamine transmission increases in the nucleus accumbens of male rats during their first exposure to sexually receptive females rats. *Brain Research, 618,* 4 1–46.

Wersinger, S. R., Sannen, K., Villalba, C., Lubahn, D. B., Rissman, E. F., & De Vries, G. J. (1997). Masculine sexual behavior is disrupted in male and female mice lacking a functional estrogen receptor alpha gene. *Hormones and Behavior, 32,* 176–183.

White, N. R., Gonzales, R. N., & Barfield, R. J. (1993). Do vocalizations of the male rat elicit calling from the female? *Behavioral and Neural Biology, 59,* 76–78.

Wiesner, J. B., & Moss, R. L. (1986). Suppression of receptive and proceptive behavior in ovariectomized, estrogen-progesterone-primed rats by intraventricular beta-endorphin: Studies of behavioral specificity. *Neuroendocrinology, 43,* 57–62.

Winans, S. S., & Powers, J. B. (1974). Neonatal and two-stage olfactory bulbectomy: Effects on male hamster sexual behavior. *Behavioral Biology, 10,* 461–471.

Witt, D. M., & Insel, T. R. (1991). A selective oxytocin antagonist attenuates progesterone facilitation of female sexual behavior. *Endocrinology, 128,* 3269–3276.

Wolf, A., Caldarola-Pastuszka, M., DeLashaw, M., & Uphouse, L. (1999). 5-HT2C receptor involvement in female rat lordosis behavior. *Brain Research, 825,* 146–151.

Wynne-Edwards, K. E., Terranova, P. F., & Lisk, R. D. (1987). Cyclic Djungarian hamsters, *Phodopus campbelli,* lack the progesterone surge normally associated with ovulation and behavioral receptivity. *Endocrinology, 120,* 1308–1316.

Xiao, L., & Becker, J. B. (1998). Effects of estrogen agonists on amphetamine-stimulated striatal dopamine release. *Synapse, 29,* 379–391.

Yahr, P., & Stephens, D. R. (1987). Hormonal control of sexual and scent marking behaviors of male gerbils in relation to the sexually dimorphic area of the hypothalamus. *Hormones and Behavior, 21,* 331–346.

Yamada, K., Emson, P., & Hokfelt, T. (1996). Immunohistochemical mapping of nitric oxide synthase in the rat hypothalamus and colocalization with neuropeptides. *Journal of Chemical Neuroanatomy, 10,* 295–316.

Yamada, Y. (1979). The effects of testosterone on unit activity in rat hypothalamus and septum. *Brain Research, 172,* 165–169.

Yells, D. P., Hendricks, S. E., & Prendergast, M. A. (1992). Lesions of the nucleus paragigantocellularis: Effects on mating behavior in male rats. *Brain Research, 596,* 73–79.

Zarrindast, M. R., Mamanpush, S. M., & Rashidy-Pour, A. (1994). Morphine inhibits dopaminergic and cholinergic induced ejaculation in rats. *General Pharmacology, 25,* 803–808.

Zasorin, N. L., Malsbury, C., & Pfaff, D. W. (1975). Suppression of lordosis in the hormone-primed female hamster by electrical stimulation of the septal area. *Physiology and Behavior, 14,* 595–599.

Zumpe, D., Clancy, A. N., Bonsall, R. W., & Michael, R. P. (1996). Behavioral responses to Depo-Provera, Fadrozole, and estradiol in castrated, testosterone-treated cynomolgus monkeys (*Macaca fascicularis*): The involvement of progestin receptors. *Physiology and Behavior, 60,* 531–540.

CHAPTER 13

Sleep and Biological Clocks

FEDERICA LATTA AND EVE VAN CAUTER

One of the most remarkable characteristics of life on earth is the ability of almost all species to change their behavior on a 24-hour basis. Not only are daily rhythms observed in organisms as diverse as algae, fruit flies, rodents, and humans, but every aspect of the internal environment of the organism also undergoes pronounced fluctuations over the course of the 24-hour day. These fluctuations or oscillations are called *circadian rhythms.* Circadian, from the Latin *circa diem,* means approximately one day. An oscillation is defined by its period (i.e., the time interval after which the wave shape of the oscillation recurs), by its range (i.e., the difference between the maximal and minimal values within one period), and by its mean value (i.e., the arithmetic mean of all instantaneous values of the oscillating variable within one period). Half the range of oscillation is called the amplitude. The peak value is often referred to as the *acrophase,* and the lowest value is often called the nadir of the oscillation.

An immense variety of circadian rhythms have been observed in humans—from physiological variables such as body temperature, heart rate, and blood pressure to behavioral variables such as mood, vigilance, and cognitive performance. The temporal organization of behavioral and physiological variables across the 24-hour cycle ultimately results from the

activity of two interacting time-keeping mechanisms in the central nervous system: endogenous circadian rhythmicity and sleep-wake homeostasis. Depending on the parameter under consideration, the wave shape of the rhythm may also be affected by food intake, postural changes, changes in intensity of physical activity, and effects of stress. In mammals, endogenous circadian rhythmicity is generated by a pacemaker located in the paired suprachiasmatic nucleus (SCN) of the hypothalamus (Turek, 1998). Sleep-wake homeostasis refers to an hourglass-like mechanism relating the amount and quality of sleep to the duration of prior wakefulness (Borbély, 1998). Both processes interact to control temporal changes in essentially all behavioral and physiological variables across the 24-hour day, but the relative contributions of each of these factors vary from one variable to the other.

In the following three sections, we review current notions on the human circadian system, sleep regulation, and the interaction of circadian rhythmicity and sleep in the control of the 24-hour profiles of behavioral and physiological variables under normal conditions. The last section is dedicated to abnormal conditions of circadian rhythmicity, sleep, or both, either behaviorally induced or resulting from pathological alterations.

CIRCADIAN RHYTHMICITY

Overview

Circadian rhythms are endogenous—that is, they originate from within the organism and persist even under constant environmental conditions. The endogenous nature of human circadian rhythms has been established by experiments in which subjects were isolated with no access to the natural light-dark (LD) cycle and no time cues. Such experiments were first performed in natural caves, then in underground bunker laboratories, and finally in specially designed windowless soundproof chambers. The results of such experiments showed that circadian rhythms continue to be expressed even in the absence of external time-giving cues. However, under such constant environmental conditions, the period of the rhythm in humans has been commonly observed to be slightly longer than 24 hours. When a circadian rhythm is expressed in the absence of any 24-hour signals in the environment, it is said to be *free-running* (i.e., the rhythm is not synchronized or entrained by any cyclic change in the physical environment). The period length of a free-running rhythm varies between individuals.

The fact that the endogenous circadian period observed under constant conditions is not exactly equal to 24 hours implies that periodic changes in the physical environment must synchronize or entrain the internal-endogenous clock system regulating circadian rhythms. A clock with a period even only a few minutes shorter or longer than 24 hours would otherwise be soon out of synchrony with the environmental day. Factors that are capable of entraining or synchronizing circadian rhythms are called *zeitgebers,* a German word for time giver. For the vast majority of mammalian species, the LD cycle is the most powerful environmental factor that synchronizes the endogenous biological clock, but entrainment by other periodic factors in the environment (e.g., social cues, feeding schedules) has been demonstrated. In rodents and other mammals, social and behavioral cues that alter the rest-activity cycle—either by eliciting activity during the normal rest period or by preventing activity during the normal active period—result in phase shifts of circadian rhythms. In humans, there is evidence to indicate that exposure to dark or sleep during the usual active period and exposure to high levels of physical activity during the usual rest period can phase-shift circadian rhythms.

The direction and magnitude of the shifts resulting from exposure to a zeitgeber depend on the circadian time at which the zeitgeber is presented. A plot of the phase shift induced by an environmental perturbation as a function of the circadian time at which the perturbation is given is called a *phase*

response curve (PRC). The upper left panel of Figure 13.1 shows a typical response of the rhythm of locomotor activity to a pulse of bright light in a hamster. The animal is kept in constant darkness for 16 days and the rhythm of locomotor activity free-runs. A pulse of light presented at the end of the 17th subjective day results in a phase advance of the onset of locomotor activity. The lower panel of Figure 13.1 shows a typical PRC to pulses of bright light (closed symbols) in the hamster derived from experiments such as that illustrated in the upper left panel. The PRC to light pulses for all organisms share certain characteristics including the fact that light pulses presented near the onset of the subjective night induce phase delays, whereas light pulses presented in the late subjective night or early subjective day induce phase advances. Light pulses presented during most of the subjective day induce no phase shifts. The upper right panel of Figure 13.1 shows the phase advance of the onset of locomotor activity when a bout of activity is pharmacologically induced during the normal rest period. The PRC to this nonphotic zeitgeber is shown (open symbols) in the lower panel of Figure 13.1 (Van Cauter & Turek, 1995).

Circadian rhythms have evolutionary importance and functional significance because they provide synchronization with the pronounced periodic fluctuations in the external environment and organize the internal milieu so that there is coordination and synchronization of internal processes. The external synchronization is of obvious importance for the survival of the species and ensures that the organism does the right thing at the right time of the day. The internal synchronization ensures temporal organization between the myriad of biochemical and physiological systems in the body. The physical and mental malaise occurring following rapid travel across time zones (i.e., jet lag) and the pathologies associated with long-term shift work are assumed to be due in part to the misalignment between various internal rhythms.

The Organization of the Mammalian Circadian System

As previously noted, the endogenous component of mammalian 24-hour rhythms originates from a pacemaker located in the paired SCN of the anterior hypothalamus (Turek, 1998). The two halves of the SCN each contain about 8,000 neurons, and it appears that many SCN neurons are capable of independent oscillatory behavior (Dunlap, 2000). There is strong evidence to indicate that the SCN is the master pacemaker involved in the generation and entrainment of circadian rhythms. Indeed, when the SCN is destroyed in rodents, circadian rhythmicity is abolished or markedly disrupted. Circadian rhythmicity can be restored in adult arrhythmic SCN-lesioned rodents by transplanting fetal SCN tissue into

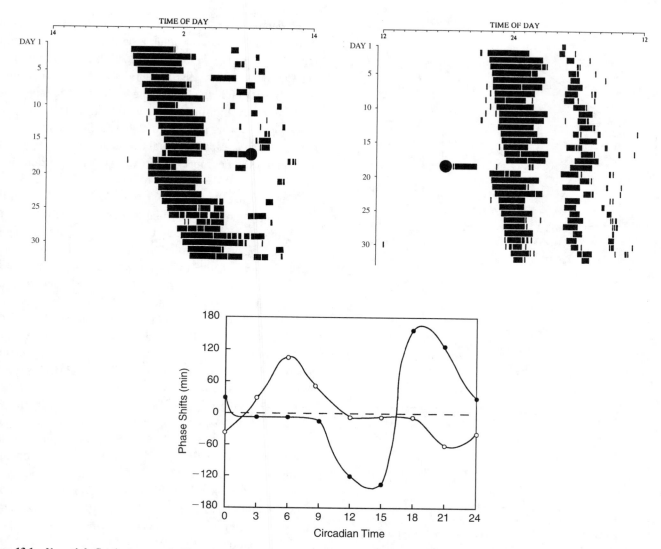

Figure 13.1 *Upper left:* Continuous record of locomotor activity in a hamster maintained under free-running conditions for 16 days and exposed to a pulse of bright light (indicated by a dark circle) at the end of the subjective day, resulting in an advance of about 2 hours in the rhythm of locomotor activity. *Upper right:* Continuous record of locomotor activity in a hamster maintained under free-running conditions for 16 days who received an intraperitoneal injection of triazolam (indicated by a dark circle) in the later part of the inactive period. Injection of the benzodiazepine was associated with a bout of activity and an approximate 2-hour advance of the rhythm of locomotor activity. *Lower panel:* Typical phase response curves to light (closed circles) and induced activity (open circles) in the hamster. Circadian time 12 corresponds to the onset of locomotor activity. From Van Cauter and Turek, 1995.

the region of the SCN. Moreover, if tissue from a fetus with a mutant clock (i.e., an animal that when adult shows an abnormal circadian rhythm) is used, the host animal will show the rhythm of the donor genotype (Ralph, Foster, Davis, & Menaker, 1990). Finally, a number of SCN rhythms persist in vitro, including those of neural firing, vasopressin release, and glucose metabolism.

Figure 13.2 provides a schematic representation of the current understanding of the organization of the mammalian circadian system (Van Cauter & Turek, 2001). The SCN receives light information from the retina via the retinohypothalamic tract (RHT) using glutamatergic neurotransmission. In addition to the RHT, the SCN also receives retinal

information indirectly from the intergeniculate leaflet (IGL) of the thalamus, which receives direct light input from the retina. Transmission from the IGL to the SCN involves both neuropeptide Y (NPY) and gamma-aminobutyric acid (GABA) inputs. Photic information received by the SCN is transmitted to the pineal gland, which does not receive any direct photic input in mammals. The pineal gland releases the hormone melatonin, which is secreted during the dark period only and has sedative properties. Some evidence indicates that melatonin exerts phase-setting effects on circadian function, and melatonin receptors have been identified in the SCN. The SCN also receives a direct serotoninergic (5-HT [5-hydroxytryptamine]) input from the raphe

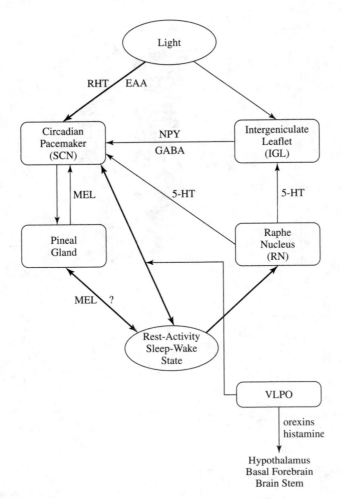

Figure 13.2 Schematic representation of the organization of the mammalian circadian system. SCN: suprachiasmatic nucleus; NPY: neuropeptide Y; 5-HT: serotonin; RHT: retino-hypothalamic tract; IGL: intergeniculate leaflet; VLPO: ventro-lateral preoptic area; LH: lateral hypothalamus; LC: locus coeruleus; EAA: excitatory amino acids; NPY: neuropeptide Y; MEL: melatonin; GABA: gamma-aminobutyric acid; RN: raphe nucleus.

nucleus (RN). The median and dorsal raphe nuclei send robust 5-HT projections to the ventrolateral SCN and the IGL. Recent studies indicate that photic information can influence the effects of 5-HT stimulation on circadian rhythmicity, and 5-HT inputs can alter the response of the clock to the entraining effects of light (Turek & Van Reeth, 1996). One of the pathways by which 5-HT information may mediate the effects of activity-inducing stimuli on the circadian clock may involve the NPY projection from the IGL to the SCN. Thus, the IGL is currently seen as a putative integrator of photic and nonphotic information in the circadian system.

Circadian control of the sleep-wake cycle is likely to involve several pathways. There is a prominent indirect projection from the SCN to the locus coeruleus (LC), a noradrenergic center that plays a major role in the control of arousal (Aston-Jones, Chen, Zhu, & Oshinsky, 2001). The ventrolateral preoptic (VLPO) area of the hypothalamus con-

tains sleep-active neurons, which provide GABAergic innervation to inhibit the ascending arousal monoamine systems, including the LC (Gallopin et al., 2000; Sherin, Shiromani, McCarley, & Saper, 1996). There is a circadian rhythm in *c-fos* expression in the VLPO, suggesting that this area could also be involved in the circadian control of sleep and wake states. Recent work also suggests that the SCN may modulate activity in an area of the lateral hypothalamus where neurons containing the neuropeptide orexin appear to participate in the regulation of sleep and wakefulness.

The past decade has seen a great deal of progress in the understanding of the molecular and genetic mechanisms underlying circadian rhythmicity. The first mammalian clock gene, *Clock,* was identified and cloned in the mouse. The identification of the other known mammalian circadian genes (*bmal, tim, cry1, cry2, per1, per2, per3*), and the study of the interactions of these genes and their protein products, led to the elucidation of a transcription-translation autoregulatory loop (King & Takahashi, 2000). This complex, negative feedback loop generates a remarkably precise oscillation of about 24-hour CLOCK and BMAL proteins bind together to activate expression of the *per1, per2, per3* genes. The PER proteins form dimers with other proteins (PER, TIM, CRY1, CRY2), reenter the nucleus, and in turn suppress the CLOCK and BMAL complex, eventually halting *per* gene production. As PER protein levels decline, the inhibition of CLOCK and BMAL is released and the loop begins anew. A recently discovered mammalian circadian gene, *casein kinase I epsilon* (Lowrey et al., 2000), modulates the timing of this feedback loop by phosphorylation and degradation of PER protein.

The plant photopigment-like molecules from the cryptochromes GENES (*cry1* and *cry2*) also appear to play a role in the light input pathway to the SCN (Sancar, 2000). The mechanisms by which the central circadian pacemaker drives downstream effector systems are poorly understood.

Ontogeny of Circadian Rhythms

The SCN is formed in the rat between embryonic day 14 (E14) and E17 (approximately 5 days before birth; Davis, Frank, & Heller, 1999; Turek & Van Reeth, 1996). Between E17 and postnatal day 10 (P10), the SCN enlarges and assumes its adult appearance. Synaptogenesis occurs primarily after birth, because it has been estimated that each adult SCN neuron has 300–1,200 synaptic contacts, and at E19 there appears to be less than one synapse per SCN neuron. This is particularly interesting in view of the fact that rhythmicity within the SCN is present before this time. In addition, the innervation of the SCN by the RHT is a postnatal event and becomes clearly present by P4.

In several mammalian species, circadian oscillations are present in the SCN already during fetal life (Reppert & Weaver, 1991). The fetal SCN is entrained by circadian signals from the mother, and although rhythms develop normally in pups born to SCN-lesioned mothers, fetal SCN rhythms cannot be entrained without the presence of the maternal SCN (Reppert & Weaver, 1991). It seems likely that the fetal SCN is entrained by multiple circadian signals from the mother, and at least in rats, the maternal influence on rhythmicity persists after birth for about a week. After a week, the pups become capable of responding to the entraining effects of the light-dark cycle.

Despite the early development of circadian rhythms within the SCN, the ability of the SCN to regulate overt behavioral and physiological rhythms does not occur until much later. For example, in rats, most endocrine and behavioral rhythms do not appear until the second or third weeks of life. Therefore, the circadian clock in the SCN becomes a circadian pacemaker when it develops sufficient afferent, intrinsic, and efferent neural connections to be entrained and to regulate effector systems (Moore, 1991). However, it has been demonstrated that the phase of specific rhythms can be set long before the appearance of the rhythms (Davis et al., 1999; Reppert & Weaver, 1991; Turek & Van Reeth, 1996).

Moore (1991) divided the development of circadian function regulated by the SCN into four components. First, the cells in the SCN are formed, they grow and mature, and rhythmic function is established within the nucleus before major synaptic contacts either between SCN cells or with the rest of the brain are formed. Second, there is the development of entrainment pathways to the SCN (that is primarily the RHT) with the resultant ability of the SCN to respond to environmental cues. Third, SCN projections develop, resulting in the coupling of the SCN to effector systems, often before the effector systems are able to express rhythms. Fourth, the maturation of the output systems reaches the point at which they can express circadian function.

Aging of the Circadian System

Age-related changes have been documented in metabolic, endocrine, and behavioral circadian rhythms in a variety of species, including humans (Brock, 1991; Carrier, Monk, Buysse, & Kupfer, 1996; Copinschi, Leproult, & Van Cauter, 2001; Czeisler, Chiasera, & Duffy, 1991; Kolker & Turek, 2001; McGinty & Stern, 1988). Among the observed age-related alterations are reduced amplitude, increased day-to-day variability, changes in intrinsic endogenous period, changes in the phase angle of entrainment, and diminished responses to synchronizing factors, including the light-dark cycle. The nature and severity of age-related disturbances appear to vary from one overt rhythm to another and there seem to be important species differ-

ences, in addition to the individual variability that is typical of age effects. The most frequently observed age-related alteration is a reduction in amplitude.

Changes in the waveshape or amplitude of a given circadian rhythm do not necessarily imply a change that is intrinsic to the circadian clock system itself. These changes could be explained by age-related changes that are either upstream (inputs to the pacemaker system) or downstream (outputs from the pacemaker system) from the circadian clock. For example, age-related changes in amplitude or entrainment of circadian rhythms can be caused by a decrease in the perception of light (as occurs in many older adults) or can reflect an alteration in the function of the effector system, such as a reduced ability to sustain locomotor activity, as has been observed in older laboratory rodents.

Nevertheless, there is evidence in rodents that the circadian pacemaker system itself is altered in aging. A number of studies have demonstrated that the free-running period of the circadian rhythms of locomotor activity, body temperature, or both becomes shorter with age in rats, field mice, and hamsters (reviewed in Kolker & Turek, 2001). It is possible that the shortening of the intrinsic period of the circadian clock with age underlies the advance of circadian phase that is observed under entrained conditions in a number of species, including humans. Evidence for age-related changes in the clock itself has also been provided by Wise and her colleagues (Wise, Cohen, Weiland, & London, 1988), who found that aging alters the circadian rhythms of glucose utilization in the SCN. In both rats and hamsters, there are age differences in the amplitude of the firing rhythms of the SCN (Satinoff et al., 1993), but the number of neurons within the SCN does not appear to decrease with advanced age. Such differences in amplitude of intrinsic SCN rhythmicity are best explained by an age-related alterations of the coupling of the individual neuronal oscillators within the SCN. In humans, the most recent estimations of the length of the endogenous circadian period have suggested that the period remains constant across adulthood, at least for individuals that are typical of successful aging (Czeisler et al., 1999). Therefore, the well-documented age-related phase-advances and decreases in amplitude of human circadian rhythms may reflect a modification of entrainment mechanisms, function of effector systems, or both.

In addition to intrinsic changes that may take place in the circadian pacemaker with senescence, there are also alterations in the response of the pacemaker to environmental stimuli. Old hamsters, rats, and mice show a decreased response to the phase-shifting effects of light pulses (Kolker & Turek, 2001). Aging also appears to attenuate the phase shifts induced by activity-inducing stimuli (Mrosovsky, 1996; Penev, Zee, Wallen, & Turek, 1995; Van Reeth, Zhang, Reddy, Zee, & Turek, 1993; Van Reeth, Zhang, Zee, & Turek, 1992).

Behavioral changes in older adults may also lead to changes in environmental inputs to the biological pacemaker system. In older persons, exposure to bright light and social cues is markedly diminished when compared with young adults (Ancoli-Israel, Kripke, Jones, Parker, & Hanger, 1991; Campbell, Kripke, Gillin, & Hrubovcak, 1988; Ehlers, Frank, & Kupfer, 1988). Absence of professional constraints, reduced mobility due to illness, and decreased socialization and outdoor activities are all hallmarks of old age. Therefore, diminished exposure to environmental stimuli that entrain circadian rhythms could contribute to the disruptions in circadian rhythmicity. The use of exposure to bright light in the elderly in order to reinforce circadian rhythmicity and to improve both daytime alertness and nighttime sleep has proved beneficial (Campbell, Dawson, & Anderson, 1993). Similarly, increases in physical and social activity have beneficial effects on daytime function and nighttime sleep (Naylor et al., 2000).

SLEEP

Sleep Regulation

The sleep-wake cycle is one of the circadian rhythms that is driven by the circadian pacemaker and synchronized to the day-night cycle. Sleep is a rhythmic behavioral and physiological process. Historically, sleep was long considered to be a passive brain state, resulting from the withdrawal of activity in waking centers. This concept was disproven by the pioneering experiments of Bremer in 1930 and by Morruzzi and Magoun in 1940–1950, and it was recognized that sleep is actively generated by activity in specific brain regions (Rechtschaffen & Siegel, 2000). In 1953, Nathaniel Kleitman, a professor of physiology at the University of Chicago, and his graduate student Eugene Aserinsky observed the occurrence of rapid eye movements in sleeping infants. This discovery lead to the identification of two separate states within sleep: rapid eye movement (REM) sleep and non-REM (NREM) sleep.

The electroencephalogram (EEG) to record brain waves, the electrooculogram (EOG) to record eye movements, and the electromyogram (EMG) to record chin muscle tension have become the primary means of monitoring the stages of human sleep. This set of recordings is called polysomnography. In 1968, Rechtschaffen and Kales defined standard criteria to score an epoch of polysomnographic recording in five stages, allowing for the determination of the macrostructure of sleep (Figure 13.3).

The EEG pattern in NREM is described as synchronous and it is conventionally subdivided into four stages. The four NREM stages can be considered as a continuum in depth of

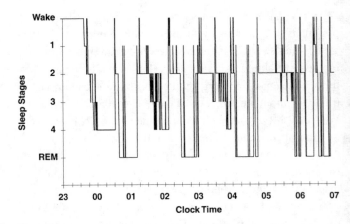

Figure 13.3   Typical polysomnogram of a normal young adult.

sleep, with the lowest arousal thresholds in Stage 1 and the highest in Stage 4. Often Stages 3 and 4 are lumped together and are called *slow wave sleep* (SWS) because the EEG is characterized by waves of high amplitude and low frequency (delta waves; 0.5–4.0 Hz). During SWS, the muscles are relaxed, and the autonomic system shows a parasympathetic dominance.

REM sleep is characterized by a desynchronized EEG pattern, defined by irregular waves of higher frequency and lower amplitude, similar to brain activity during waking or the lighter stage of NREM sleep. This brain pattern is associated with strong sympathetic activation, muscle atonia, and episodic bursts of rapid eye movements. The middle ear muscles are also phasically active, and both REM and middle ear muscle activity appear to be driven by phasic bursts of electrical activity that can be recorded in animals from the pons, oculomotor nuclei, thalamus, and visual cortex, and are referred to as pontine-geniculate-occipital (PGO) spikes (Rechtschaffen & Siegel, 2000).

The adult human enters sleep through NREM sleep, beginning with Stage 1, and continuing with Stages 2, 3, and 4 (Figure 13.3). Spindle activity appears in Stage 2 of NREM sleep. External stimuli can interrupt the progression from the lighter to the deeper stages of NREM sleep. About 60–80 minutes after going to sleep, the individual begins gradually to cycle back from Stage 4 through Stages 3 and 2, and then enters a period of REM. NREM and REM sleep continue to alternate through the night in cyclic fashion with a period of 90 to 110 minutes. REM sleep in the first cycle episode is usually quite short, lasting only a few minutes, but its length increases across the night; it is greatest towards the early morning hours. As the night progresses, NREM sleep becomes more shallow and REM sleep more prominent. In young adults, wakefulness after sleep onset normally accounts for less than 5% of the night, REM sleep occupies approximately 25% (about four to six discrete episodes per night), while SWS constitutes approximately 20%. Thus, 50% of the night is usually spent in the lighter stages of NREM sleep.

There are specific brain mechanisms that generate NREM and REM sleep (Rechtschaffen & Siegel, 2000). Studies using lesions, electrical stimulation, and chemical stimulation have shown that the major brain regions involved in NREM sleep generation are the anterior hypothalamus and the basal forebrain. These NREM sleep mechanisms involve GABAergic inhibitory neurons that inhibit waking centers in the hypothalamus and in the midbrain. The nucleus of the solitary tract and the VLPO also participate in NREM sleep regulation (Gallopin et al., 2000; Sherin et al., 1996). It thus appears that several widely separate brain regions are involved and interact to initiate and maintain NREM sleep. During NREM sleep, slow waves in the EEG reflect the synchronized firing of thalamocortical neurons. In contrast to those involved in NREM sleep, the brain mechanisms generating REM sleep appear to be critically located in a small area of the lateral pontine tegmentum. This area contains cholinergic cells that discharge at a high rate during REM sleep (REM-on cells) and inhibit serotonergic and noradrenergic activity as well as motor neurons. Although other brain regions distant from the pons appear to participate in the control of REM sleep, the small pontine area including the REM-on cells appears to be critical. It is important to note that the three characteristics of REM sleep (i.e., desynchronized EEG, PGO waves, and atonia) can be evoked separately by cholinergic stimulation of the pons.

Humans awakened during REM report dreaming 80–90% of the times, often including elaborate visual imagery and complicated plots (Hobson, 1995; Rechtschaffen & Siegel, 2000). Awakenings from SWS are less frequently associated with oniric activity than are awakenings from REM sleep, and the dreams are generally simpler and shorter than the dreams reported after REM sleep.

In addition to the alternation of NREM and REM states, sleep is regulated by two basic processes: (a) a homeostatic process determined by the prior duration of wakefulness and largely independent of the circadian system, and (b) a circadian process that modulates sleep propensity and duration independently of homeostatic sleep pressure. The homeostatic process is thought to involve one or several putative neural sleep factors (factor S), which rise during periods of wakefulness and decay exponentially during sleep (Borbély, 1998). Sleep propensity is increased when sleep is curtailed or absent, and it is decreased in response to sleep. The timing, the amount and the intensity of SWS are primarily under the control of the homeostatic process, whereas circadian rhythmicity plays an important role in sleep timing, sleep duration, sleep consolidation, and the distribution of REM sleep.

After sleep deprivation, NREM and REM sleep are enhanced; in particular, a remarkable increase in slow waves has been documented during recovery sleep in rodents, rabbits, cats, mice, and humans (Tobler, 2000). The neuroanatomical and neurochemical basis of homeostatic sleep regulation is not entirely understood; however, it appears to involve the basal forebrain cholinergic region and adenosine, a neuromodulator whose extracellular concentrations in this region rise during sustained wakefulness and decrease during sleep (Porkka-Heiskanen et al., 1997).

It is safe to assume that all mammals sleep, even though there are large variations in the amount of sleep exhibited by different species, and sleep may be difficult to observe or recognize in some species like cetaceans (Zepelin, 2000). Sleep can usually be identified by sustained quiescence in a species-specific posture accompanied by reduced responsiveness to external stimuli. For mammals, the definition of sleep requires the additional criteria of quick reversibility to the wakeful condition (unlike hibernation or coma) and characteristic changes in the EEG activity (Zepelin, 2000). Spindling and slow waves are the hallmarks of mammalian NREM sleep, but there are considerable interspecies variations in their amplitudes. REM sleep is clearly present in all mammals studied so far, but some of the characteristics of REM sleep (frequency of eye movements and muscular atonia) as well as the relative amount of REM sleep and the duration of the REM-NREM cycle vary widely across species (Zepelin, 2000). The amount of REM sleep is positively correlated with total sleep time, and total sleep time and NREM sleep are negatively correlated with body weight—that is, heavier animals sleep less. Altricial animals (animals born in a relatively immature state and unable to care for themselves) have large amounts of REM sleep at birth; furthermore, although these amounts decrease with maturity, the amount of REM sleep in adults of altricial species are remarkably higher than in adults of precocial species (Siegel, 1995, 1999). Zepelin (2000) showed that throughout life immaturity at birth is the single best predictor of REM sleep time. It appears that REM sleep time correlates with the security of the sleep site. Predators and animals with secure sleep have greater amounts of REM sleep.

The cyclic organization of sleep is also present in birds, although the sleep cycles are much shorter than in mammalian sleep. Behavioral and EEG criteria for sleep that apply to mammals can be applied to birds. However, avian sleep has no spindling activity and lacks the differentiation in NREM sleep stages. But the main difference that distinguishes avian from mammalian sleep is the much lower percentage of REM sleep (about 5% of sleep time on average for birds, versus 15–30% in mammals) and much shorter REM periods, often less than 10 s (Zepelin, 2000). Very little is known about the sleep of fish, amphibians, and reptiles.

Ontogeny of Sleep

Sleep changes dramatically during the course of development. For the first days of life, the sleep of infants is characterized by two different types of sleep: *active sleep* and *quiet sleep* (Hobson, 1995). In the first weeks of their lives, infants spend about half of their sleeping time in active sleep. The EEG pattern of active sleep in infants is similar to that seen in adult REM sleep. However, the appearance of rapid eye movements is not associated with a complete motor paralysis as it is in adults, because the cerebral inhibitory mechanisms that block the transmission of nerve impulses to the skeletal muscles are still immature. Thus, small body movements—particularly in the fingers and toes and facial muscles—are possible. Active sleep decreases gradually during the first year, stabilizing at about 25–30% at 1 year of age. At this age body movements during REM sleep gradually disappear, and muscle atonia is observed as in adults. Quiet sleep of infants is analogous to NREM sleep in adults, but well-defined delta waves and sleep spindles cannot be discerned during the first weeks of life because electrical brain activity is still irregular and disorganized at this time. REM sleep depends on the activity of the reticular neurons in the pons, which are already relatively mature at birth; however, it is only when the cells in the cortex become extensively interconnected and when their connections to and from the thalamus are developed that the typical EEG patterns of SWS are observed and distinct sleep Stages 2, 3, and 4 develop from quiet sleep (Hobson, 1995).

The cyclic alternation of NREM-REM sleep is present from birth, but the period in the newborn is of about 50–60 minutes. A consolidated nocturnal sleep cycle is gradually acquired, and the fully developed EEG patterns of NREM sleep stages emerge over the first 2–6 months of life. Another major difference between infant and adult sleep is that in newborns the transition from wake to sleep is often accomplished through active sleep.

The declining levels of REM sleep during the first year of life are in part the result of an increase in the noradrenergic and serotonergic inhibitory control of REM and in part the result of neurons becoming less sensitive to acetylcholine, a neurotransmitter that enhances REM sleep (Hobson, 1995).

When brain structure and function achieve a level that can support the high-voltage characteristic of SWS, then Stages 3 and 4 become quite prominent in young children. In addition, their SWS is much deeper than the SWS of older adults, with a very high arousal threshold. The amount of SWS achieved per night is maximal in young children but decreases markedly with age; it decreases by nearly 40% during the second decade of life (Carskadon & Dement, 1987).

Sleep and Aging

Decreased subjective sleep quality is one of the most common health complaints of older adults (Prinz, 1995). The most consistent alterations associated with normal aging include increased number and duration of awakenings and decreased amounts of deep SWS (Benca, Obermeyer, Thisted, & Gillin, 1992; Bliwise, 1994; Feinberg, Koresko, & Heller, 1967). REM sleep appears to be relatively better preserved during aging (Benca et al., 1992; Bliwise, 1994; Ehlers & Kupfer, 1989; Feinberg, 1976; Landolt, Dijk, Achermann, & Borbely, 1996). There are gender differences in sleep quality in normal adults; premenopausal women have more SWS than do men.

The results of a recent analysis of polygraphic sleep recordings from 149 normal men ages 16–83 years are shown in Figure 13.4 (Van Cauter, Leproult, & Plat, 2000). It can be seen that age-related changes in SWS and REM sleep occur with markedly different chronologies. SWS decreases markedly from early adulthood (16–25 years) to midlife (36–50 years) and is replaced by lighter sleep (Stages 1 and 2) without significant increases in sleep fragmentation or decreases in REM sleep. The transition from midlife to late life involved an increase in wake at the expense of both NREM and REM sleep. This age-related increase in awakenings appears primarily related to an inability of maintaining NREM sleep (Dijk, Duffy, & Czeisler, 2001). The decrease in REM sleep at night has been correlated with intellectual functioning in older persons; patients with a diagnosis of probable senile dementia of Alzheimer's type have very little REM sleep compared to healthy control subjects (Prinz et al., 1982).

Studies in laboratory rodents have also documented a decrease in SWS activity in old age (Mendelson & Bergmann, 1999). The circadian control of the sleep-wake cycle appears to be weaker in old age. A decrease in the amplitude of the circadian fluctuations of SWS and wakefulness has been observed in old rats (Rosenberg, Zepelin, & Rechtschaffen, 1979; Van Gool & Mirmiran, 1986). When older mice were compared to young mice, they spent more time asleep during the normal active period, whereas they spent more time awake during the normal sleep period (Welsh, Richardson, & Dement, 1986). Similarly, in elderly adults, nocturnal sleep becomes highly fragmented, and daytime naps become more frequent. This phenomenon is particularly prevalent in cognitively impaired older adults. Sleep disruption, nocturnal wanderings, restlessness, and daytime sleepiness constitute a major reason for institutionalization (Sanford, 1975).

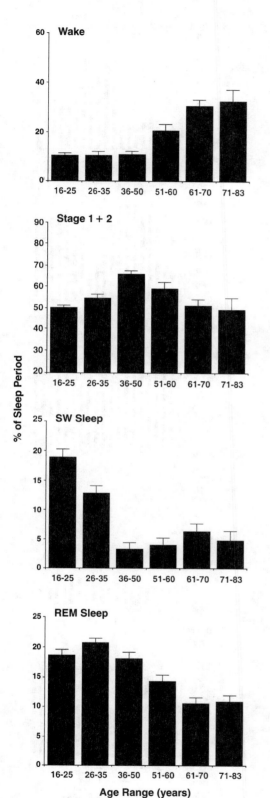

Figure 13.4 Percentages of the sleep period spent in wake, Stages 1 and 2, SWS, and REM sleep as a function of age in 149 healthy nonobese men ages 16–83 years. Means (+SEM [standard error of measurement]) for each age group are shown for each age bracket in each panel. From Van Cauter et al., 2000, *Journal of the American Medical Association 284* (pp. 861–868). Copyrighted 2000, American Medical Association.

BEHAVIORAL AND PHYSIOLOGICAL PROCESSES MODULATED BY CIRCADIAN RHYTHMICITY AND SLEEP-WAKE HOMEOSTASIS

As stated earlier in this chapter, the temporal organization of behavioral and physiological variables across the 24-hour cycle reflects primarily the interaction of endogenous circadian rhythmicity and sleep-wake homeostasis. There are two features of the interaction between these two time-keeping systems that appear to be fairly unique to the human species (Van Cauter & Turek, 2001). First, human sleep is generally consolidated in a single 6- to 9-hour period, whereas fragmentation of the sleeping period is the rule in other mammals. Possibly as a result of this consolidation of the sleep period, the wake-sleep and sleep-wake transitions in humans are associated with physiological changes that are usually more marked than those observed in the animals. Second, humans are also unique in their capacity to ignore circadian signals and to maintain wakefulness for prolonged periods of time despite an increased pressure to go to sleep.

Depending on the parameter under consideration, variability across the 24-hour day may also reflect—in addition to circadian and homeostatic regulation—effects of food intake, postural changes, changes in intensity of physical activity, light-dark transitions, and other stimuli. Therefore, to facilitate the detection of circadian and homeostatic inputs, many investigators have used so-called constant routine conditions, a regimen of 24 hours or more of continuous quiet wakefulness at bed rest in dim indoor light, with constant caloric intake under the form of hourly snacks, intravenous glucose infusion at a constant rate, or constant enteral nutrition. Constant routine conditions attempt to minimize the effects of external stimuli that could alter the expression of endogenous circadian rhythmicity and sleep-wake homeostasis.

To tease apart homeostatic effects from circadian inputs, other studies have taken advantage of the fact that the circadian pacemaker takes several days to adjust to a large abrupt shift of sleep-wake and light-dark cycles. The protocols used in these *shift* studies allow for the effects of sleep to be observed at an abnormal circadian time and for the effects of circadian modulation to be observed in the absence of sleep. Constant routine conditions are generally applied during scheduled wakefulness periods. A third type of protocol used in studies designed to delineate the relative contributions of the circadian clock and the sleep homeostat in the temporal organization of behavioral and physiological variables are so-called forced desynchrony protocols in which the sleep-wake cycles of the research subjects are scheduled to be either too long (typically 28 hours) or too short (typically 20 hours) to entrain the endogenous circadian oscillator.

Under such conditions, the circadian system free-runs with a period of approximately 24.2 hours, and the effects of sleeping and waking can be observed at all circadian phases (Dijk & Czeisler, 1995).

Alertness and Cognitive Performance

A number of studies under constant routine conditions have delineated the temporal variations of subjective alertness (or its antonym, subjective sleepiness) and cognitive performance (i.e., objective alertness or vigilance) on a wide variety of paper-and-pencil as well as computerized cognitive performance tasks across 24 to 40 hours of extended wakefulness (Carrier & Monk, 2000; M. P. Johnson et al., 1992; Leproult, Van Reeth, Byrne, Sturis, & Van Cauter, 1997; Monk et al., 1997; Wright, Badia, Myers, Plenzler, & Hakel, 1997). The results have been remarkably consistent and have indicated that subjective and objective alertness vary in parallel; detectable decreases start around the usual bedtime, when the circulating levels of melatonin, a hormone with sedative properties (Cajochen, Krauchi, & Wirz-Justice, 1997; Sack, Hughes, Edgar, & Lewy, 1997), are increasing. The decrease in subjective and objective alertness continues until a minimum is attained in the early morning hours—that is, between 5:00 and 8:00 a.m. in the majority of adults (Dijk, Duffy, & Czeisler, 1992; Gillberg, Kecklund, & Akerstedt, 1994; Leproult, Van Reeth, et al., 1997; Monk et al., 1997). Both subjective and objective alertness then improve—despite continued wakefulness—suggesting the existence of a waking signal originating from the circadian pacemaker. The two upper panels of Figure 13.5 provide a good illustration of this typical temporal pattern in normal young men who were studied under constant routine conditions for 40 hours (Van Cauter & Turek, 2001). Subjective sleepiness was assessed hourly using a standardized 7-point scale, the Stanford Sleepiness Scale, wherein 1 is "feeling active and vital, alert, wide awake" and 7 corresponds to "almost in reverie, sleep onset soon, lost struggle to remain awake." Objective alertness was also estimated hourly using a computerized simple attention-dependent vigilance task. The throughput was calculated as the number of correct responses per unit of time. Maximum sleepiness coincided with minimum throughput in the early morning. Both sleepiness and performance had markedly improved by midday. Studies using forced desynchrony protocols confirmed that the temporal variations of both subjective and objective alertness during extended wakefulness are under the dual control of the homeostatic process and of a circadian rhythm promoting alertness across the usual waking period (Dijk & Edgar, 1999; Dijk & Czeisler, 1994, 1995; Dijk et al., 1992; Monk, Buysse, Reynolds, Jarrett, & Kupfer, 1992; Monk, Moline, Fookson, & Peetz, 1989).

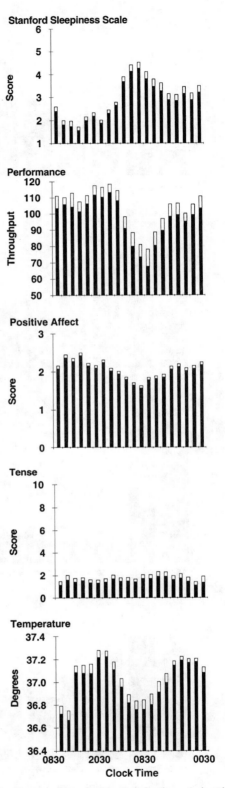

Figure 13.5 Mean profiles of subjective sleepiness (using the Stanford Sleepiness Scale), performance on a vigilance task, positive affect (using the Positive And Negative Affect Schedule), self-perceived stress (on a 10-cm visual analog scale) and body temperature in normal young men studied during 40 consecutive hours of continuous wakefulness under constant routine conditions. Data are represented as mean (black bar) and *SEM* (open bar) for each 2-hour interval.

Mood

Studies performed under constant routine conditions showed that a marked mood impairment occurs in the early morning hours when wakefulness is extended across the night (Monk et al., 1997). The lowest mood scores coincide with maximum subjective sleepiness. Similar to cognitive performance, mood then improves during the daytime hours despite continued sleep deprivation, and effects of sleep loss may no longer be detectable. The improvement in mood parallels the improvement in cognitive performance and the decrease in subjective sleepiness, as illustrated in Figure 13.5, in which the third and fourth panels from the top show the temporal variation of scores of positive affect on the Positive Affect and Negative Affect Schedule (PANAS; Clark, Watson, & Leeka, 1989) and of scores of self-perceived stress on a 10-cm visual analog scale for *tense*. It is apparent that the decrease in positive affect in the early morning hours following a sleepless night is not related to an increase in subjective stress.

The relative contributions of effects of time of day (i.e., circadian) as compared to effects of duration of time awake (i.e., homeostatic) were examined in healthy adults who were studied on a forced desynchrony protocol involving a 28- or 30-hour sleep-wake schedule preventing entrainment of circadian rhythmicity (Boivin et al., 1997). Mood varied primarily with circadian phase rather than with duration of prior wakefulness. However, there was a significant interaction between time of day and duration of prior wakefulness such that the impact of sleep loss on mood can be positive, nil, or negative, depending on circadian phase. In addition, the time during which the circadian variation in mood is at its nadir is prolonged with increased durations of prior wakefulness, implying that subjects who are more sleep-deprived will have greater difficulties shaking the blues of the early morning hours. These observations may be relevant to the high prevalence of mood disorders in shift workers.

Cardiovascular Function

There is a robust diurnal variation in blood pressure and heart rate across a normal 24-hour cycle when subjects are awake and active during the day and asleep at night. Figure 13.6 shows the mean 24-hour profiles of systolic and diastolic blood pressure and of heart rate measured at 10-min intervals in 31 young men who were studied in a standard social and physical environment but slept in the laboratory (Degaute, van de Borne, Linkowski, & Van Cauter, 1991). Blood pressure decreased by 10–15 mm Hg (mercury) during the sleep period, and heart rate decreased by up to 20 beats per

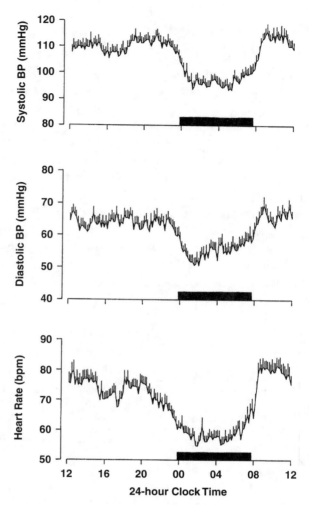

Figure 13.6 Mean 24-hour profiles of systolic and diastolic blood pressure and of heart rate measured at 10-min intervals in 31 healthy young men. The vertical line at each time point represents the *SEM*. The black bars illustrate the bedtime period. From Degaute et al., 1991.

min. Studies performed under constant routine conditions (Kerkhof, Van Dongen, & Bobbert, 1998; Van Dongen, Maislin, & Kerkhof, 2001) have revealed that there is no significant endogenous circadian variation in blood pressure. The nocturnal decline in blood pressure appears related to postural changes and sleep, with the lowest blood pressure being recorded during the deeper stages of NREM sleep. In contrast, a robust circadian variation of heart rate persists under constant routine conditions. The amplitude of the nocturnal decrease in heart rate in subjects who remain awake at bed rest across the night is approximately half of the amplitude observed when the effects of postural changes and sleep are not eliminated. So far, there is no evidence for a contribution of duration of prior wakefulness in the temporal variation of cardiovascular parameters, but few studies have rigorously addressed this issue.

Endocrine and Metabolic Regulation

A prominent feature of the endocrine system is its high degree of temporal organization. Indeed, hormonal concentrations in the peripheral circulation undergo pronounced temporal oscillations over the 24-hour cycle. The characteristics of the 24-hour patterns of hormonal secretions vary from one hormone to the other and exhibit a high degree of day-to-day reproducibility; thus, while one endocrine gland may be actively secreting in a complex, pulsatile pattern, another may be in a quiescent state, and this intricate temporal program of the endocrine system is likely to be of functional significance.

As for neurobehavioral and cardiovascular parameters, the 24-hour secretory profiles of many hormones and metabolic parameters are controlled by the interaction of circadian rhythmicity and sleep-wake homeostasis. The overall wave-shape of the profile may also reflect—to varying degrees—modulatory effects from rhythmic and nonrhythmic factors, such as periodic food intake, postural changes, levels of physical activity, and—within the sleep state—the alternation between NREM and REM stages.

The four upper panels of Figure 13.7 illustrate mean profiles of the plasma levels of hormones secreted by the pituitary or under direct pituitary control—cortisol, thyrotropin (TSH), prolactin (PRL), and growth hormone (GH)—observed in normal subjects who were studied before and during an abrupt 12-hour shift of the sleep-wake and dark-light cycle. The study period extended over a 53-hour span and included an 8-hour period of nocturnal sleep starting at 11:00 p.m., a 28-hour period of continuous wakefulness, and a daytime period of recovery sleep starting 12 hours

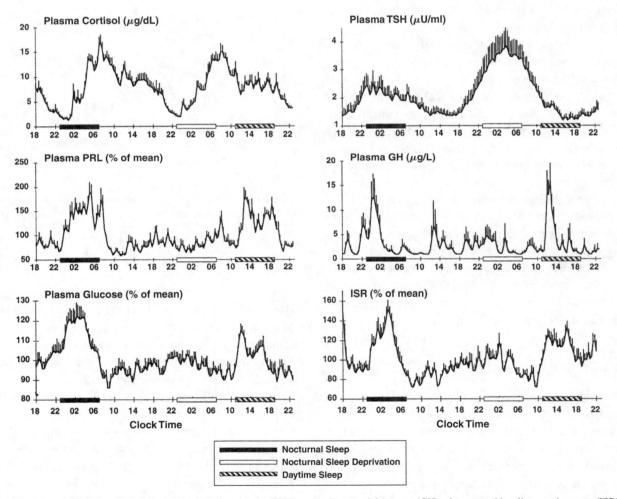

Figure 13.7 Mean (+*SEM*) profiles of plasma cortisol, thyrotropin (TSH), prolactin, growth hormone (GH), glucose, and insulin secretion rates (ISR) in normal young men who were studied over a 53-hour period including 8 hours of nocturnal sleep (black bars), 28 hours of continuous wakefulness, and 8 hours of daytime recovery sleep (stippled bars). Caloric intake was exclusively in the form of an intravenous glucose infusion at a constant rate. This experimental protocol allowed for the effects of time of day (i.e., circadian) to be observed in the absence of sleep and for the effects of sleep to be observed at an abnormal circadian time (i.e., 12 hours out of phase with habitual bedtime). Adapted from Van Cauter et al., 1991 and from Van Cauter and Turek, 2001.

out of phase with the usual bedtime—that is, at 11:00 a.m. (Van Cauter et al., 1991). Constant routine conditions were enforced during scheduled waking periods. To allow for the observation of circadian variations in glucose tolerance in the absence of the effects of feeding and fasting, caloric intake was exclusively in the form of an intravenous glucose infusion at a constant rate. The two lower panels of Figure 13.7 illustrate the temporal profiles of blood glucose and insulin secretion rates (ISR).

The upper panel of Figure 13.7 show that the 12-hour shift of the sleep-wake schedule had relatively little effect on the waveshape of the cortisol profile—consistent with numerous studies indicating that the temporal organization of the hypothalamic-pituitary axis is primarily dependent on circadian timing. Nevertheless, modest modulatory effects of wake-sleep and sleep-wake transitions on corticotropic activity have been clearly demonstrated. Sleep onset is reliably associated with a short-term inhibition of cortisol secretion (Born, Muth, & Fehm, 1988; Van Cauter et al., 1991; Weitzman, Zimmerman, Czeisler, & Ronda, 1983), although this effect may not be detectable when sleep is initiated at the time of the daily maximum of corticotropic activity—that is, in the morning (Weibel, Follenius, Spiegel, Ehrhart, & Brandenberger, 1995). Under conditions of normal nocturnal bedtimes, because cortisol secretion is already quiescent in the late evening, this inhibitory effect simply prolongs the quiescent period of cortisol secretion. This inhibition of hypothalamic-pituitary-adrenal (HPA) activity during sleep occurs during SWS (Follenius, Brandenberger, Bardasept, Libert, & Ehrhart, 1992). Conversely, awakening at the end of the sleep period is consistently followed by a pulse of cortisol secretion. Several studies have shown that awakenings interrupting the sleep period consistently trigger pulses of cortisol secretion (Van Cauter, Copinschi, & Turek, 2001). Thus, sleep fragmentation—as it occurs in normal aging and in persons with insomnia—is associated with increased nocturnal corticotropic activity (Vgontzas et al., 2001).

The contribution of both circadian inputs and sleep-dependent modulation can easily be recognized in the temporal profiles of TSH concentrations. Low and relatively stable daytime TSH levels are followed by a rapid elevation starting in the early evening and peaking around the time of habitual sleep onset (second panel from the top in Figure 13.7). The timing of the nocturnal TSH elevation appears to accurately reflect circadian timing and shifts with the rhythms of body temperature and melatonin (Allan & Czeisler, 1994; Van Cauter et al., 1994). The normal sleep period is associated with a progressive decline in TSH levels, which is related to a consistent decrease of TSH levels during SWS. Daytime basal values resume shortly after morning awakening. The inhibitory effect of sleep on TSH secretion becomes clearly apparent when nocturnal levels are observed during acute sleep deprivation—then TSH secretion is increased by as much as 200% over the levels observed during nocturnal sleep. When sleep occurs during daytime hours, TSH secretion is not suppressed significantly below normal daytime levels.

Contrasting with the strong circadian modulation of activity in the corticotropic and thyrotropic axes, the temporal organization of the release of prolactin and GH is primarily driven by sleep-wake homeostasis (Van Cauter, Plat, & Copinschi, 1998). As can be seen from Figure 13.7, a large portion of the daily output of both hormones occurs during sleep, and the secretory pattern shifts immediately following the shift of the sleep-wake cycle. In both men and women, prolactin levels during sleep correspond to an average increase of more than 200% above daytime levels. Increases in prolactin secretion during sleep are consistently associated with SWS. A modest circadian component in the temporal organization of prolactin secretion can sometimes be detected—particularly in women (Waldstreicher et al., 1996)—but sleep onset, regardless of time of day, is invariably associated with prolactin release. Decreased dopaminergic inhibition of prolactin is the most likely mechanism underlying the sleep-related prolactin elevation. Nocturnal prolactin release is decreased in older adults, consistent with the decrease in sleep intensity and consolidation.

For GH, there is a consistent temporal association between increased pulsatile release and periods of SWS, particularly during the first NREM-REM cycle (Van Cauter et al., 1998). In men, 60–70% of the daily GH secretion occurs during the first hours of sleep. In women, daytime GH pulses are more frequent. Sleep onset will elicit a pulse in GH secretion whether sleep is advanced, delayed, or interrupted and re-initiated. Whereas sleep-wake homeostasis is clearly the major factor controlling the temporal organization of GH release, the inhibitory control of GH secretion by somatostatin appears to be influenced by circadian rhythmicity, with lower nocturnal somatostatinergic tone facilitating growth hormone releasing hormone (GHRH)-dependent release of GH during sleep. Sleep fragmentation and reduced amounts of SWS will generally decrease nocturnal GH secretion. In healthy older adults, the total amount of GH secreted over the 24-hour span is often less than one third of the daily output of young men; the amount of SWS is similarly reduced (Van Cauter et al., 2000; van Coevorden et al., 1991). There is a remarkable parallelism between chronological alterations of GH levels and SWS across adulthood, and correlative evidence suggests that age-related alterations in the somatotropic axis are partly caused by reduced sleep quality.

As seen in the two lower panels of Figure 13.7—despite the fact that glucose was infused at a constant rate throughout the study period—there were robust changes in plasma glucose levels and insulin secretion rates. Under these experimental conditions, hepatic glucose production is markedly suppressed; therefore, changes in plasma glucose levels reflect primarily changes in glucose utilization (Van Cauter, Polonsky, & Scheen, 1997). Glucose levels increase from morning to evening, indicating a decrease in glucose tolerance as the day progresses, reach a maximum around midsleep, and then decrease toward morning values. The pattern of insulin secretion parallels the changes in glucose levels. The nocturnal glucose and insulin elevations readily shift with the shift of sleep-wake schedule, indicating a major effect of the sleep state regardless of time of day (Van Cauter et al., 1991). Nevertheless, in the absence of sleep, an elevation of glucose and insulin secretion from morning until the early part of the usual sleep period can be clearly seen (Figure 13.7). Detailed studies have indicated that when sleep occurs at the normal circadian time, decreased glucose tolerance during the first part of the night is due to decreased glucose utilization in both peripheral tissues—a result of muscle relaxation, anti-insulin-like effects of sleep-onset GH secretion, and reduced cerebral glucose uptake during SWS (Van Cauter et al., 1997). During the second part of the night, these effects subside as sleep becomes shallow, movements and awakenings increase, REM sleep is predominant, and GH secretion is minimal. Thus, complex interactions of circadian and sleep effects—partly mediated by cortisol and GH—result in a consistent pattern of changes of set-point of glucose regulation over the 24-hour period.

CONDITIONS OF ABNORMAL SLEEP AND CIRCADIAN REGULATION

Behavioral Alterations

Acute Sleep Deprivation and Chronic Sleep Curtailment

Immediate effects of acute total sleep deprivation on a variety of neurobehavioral and physiological parameters are well recognized. The adverse effects on subjective alertness, cognitive performance, and mood have been described in previous sections of this chapter. In the absence of sleep, the nocturnal declines in body temperature and heart rate are considerably dampened, and blood pressure does not dip. As illustrated in Figure 13.7, the secretions of GH and prolactin normally associated with sleep onset are largely suppressed.

Until recently, the only well-documented effects of sleep loss on human physiological function were the absence of immediate responses to sleep-wake transitions in conditions of total sleep deprivation and changes in markers of immune function that become evident after prolonged sleep deprivation (Dinges, Douglas, Hamarman, Zaugg, & Kapoor, 1995). Because recovery sleep on the subsequent night is associated with normal temperature and cardiovascular changes and because rebound secretions of hormones normally released during sleep are usually observed, it has often been implicitly assumed that there is no net effect of sleep loss on human physiological function and endocrine status. Nevertheless, acute sleep deprivation—whether total or partial—is associated with an alteration in hypothalamic-pituitary-adrenal (HPA) function on the following day, consisting of an elevation of evening cortisol concentrations (Leproult, Copinschi, Buxton, & Van Cauter, 1997). Because deleterious central as well as metabolic effects of HPA hyperactivity are more pronounced at the time of the usual trough of the rhythm (i.e., in the evening) than at the time of the peak (i.e., in the morning), modest elevations in evening cortisol levels could facilitate the development of central as well as peripheral disturbances associated with glucocorticoid excess, such as memory deficits and insulin resistance (Dallman et al., 1993; McEwen & Sapolsky, 1995). Morning oral glucose tolerance is decreased after a sleepless night as compared to a normal night (VanHelder, Symons, & Radomski, 1993).

Although there have been numerous studies of the effects of acute total sleep deprivation, the much more common real-life condition of chronic partial sleep curtailment has received much less attention. Voluntary sleep restriction is, however, an increasingly common behavior in industrialized societies. Due to socioeconomic and cultural pressures, many individuals tend to curtail sleep to the shortest amount tolerable (Bliwise, 1996; Bonnet & Arand, 1995; Wehr et al., 1993). Sleep duration in America decreased from 9.1 hours in 1910 to less than 7 hours in 2000. In support of sleep curtailment as both harmless and efficient, it has been proposed that a so-called normal (approximately 8-hour) night of sleep is composed of *core sleep,* a 4- to 5-hour period including most of deep NREM sleep, and *optional sleep,* which could—with adequate amounts of motivation—be progressively removed without producing increased daytime sleepiness, mood changes, or detectable decrements in cognitive function (Horne, 1988). More recent studies have disproved this concept and demonstrated that 7–8 consecutive days of sleep curtailment by as little as 2–3 hours per night results in marked decrements in mood and performance (Dinges et al., 1997). Although the consequences of endemic sleep loss for human performance and safety have recently received public attention, it is generally thought that physiological function and health are affected little or not at all.

A recent study from our laboratory examined metabolic and hormonal parameters in healthy young adults studied after 1 week of bedtimes restricted to 4 hours per night and then after 1 week of bedtimes extended to 12 hours per night (Spiegel, Leproult, & Van Cauter, 1999). The upper panels of Figure 13.8 compare the glucose and insulin responses to an intravenous glucose tolerance test performed at 9:00 a.m. on the 5th day of sleep restriction and the 5th day of sleep extension. The parameters of glucose tolerance in the state of sleep debt were consistent with the clinical condition of impaired glucose tolerance. Insulin secretion during the first phase of the response was markedly dampened, as occurs in the early stages of diabetes. The lower panels of Figure 13.8 compares the profiles of sympatho-vagal balance, evening cortisol levels, and nocturnal GH secretion for the two bedtime conditions. In the state of sleep debt (compared to the fully rested condition), sympathetic nervous activity was elevated, evening cortisol levels were higher, and nocturnal GH secretion was prolonged (Spiegel et al., 2000). All three alterations are likely to have contributed to the decrease in glucose tolerance. Decreased brain glucose utilization, which has been documented in sleep-deprived subjects by PET (positron-emission tomography) studies (Thomas et al., 2000), probably contributed also to this metabolic alteration. These results indicate that partial sleep loss under chronic conditions could have long-term adverse health effects and accelerate the development or increase the severity of age-related diseases such as diabetes and hypertension.

Profound alterations of neurobehavioral function were also observed after 1 week of sleep restriction. Ratings of subjective sleepiness and reaction times on tests of cognitive performance were markedly increased, whereas mood scores were significantly lower. These alterations were more severe in the morning than they were later in the day, and a robust diurnal variation of mood and vigilance similar to that seen in depressed subjects was apparent. Remarkably, many of the endocrine, neurobehavioral, and metabolic alterations observed in these healthy young adults after 1 week of severe sleep curtailment were similar to well-documented markers of aging.

Shift Work

Although shift work has been part of modern life for several decades and is voluntarily accepted by millions of workers, it is a major health hazard involving an increased risk of cardiovascular illness, gastrointestinal disorders, insomnia, mood disorders, and infertility (Knutsson, Akerstedt, Jonsson, & Orth-Gomer, 1986). The consequences of shift work are associated with the chronic misalignment of physiological circadian rhythms, the activity-rest cycle, and the unavoidable sleep loss that results. Shift work creates conditions in which some zeitgebers (e.g., an artificial LD cycle) and additional phase-setting factors such as the rest-activity cycle, are shifted while others remain unaltered—for example, the natural LD cycle and the routines of family and social life. Nearly all shift work schedules involve days off every few days, and the worker then usually attempts to revert to daytime activity and nighttime sleep. Thus, shift workers live in an unstable situation of conflicting zeitgebers that almost never allow a complete alignment of endogenous circadian rhythmicity with the sleep-wake/rest-activity cycle and is characterized by a chronic internal desynchrony (Weibel, Spiegel, Follenius, Ehrhart, & Brandenberger, 1996). Components of overt rhythms that are controlled primarily by sleep-wake homeostasis (such as sleep-related GH and prolactin secretion) adapt to the shifted schedule, whereas components reflecting circadian timing (such as the diurnal variation of cortisol secretion) showed little (if any) adaptation. Recent polls have indicated that shift workers are also among the most sleep-deprived segment of the population, with mean sleep duration averaging only 6.5 hours in 2000 (E. O. Johnson, 2000). Thus, in addition to circadian misalignment, shift work is also a condition of chronic sleep debt. Not surprisingly, night work is associated with deficits in performance and vigilance, diminished productivity, and increased accident rates.

The need for strategies to cope with shift work is obvious, particularly in view of the fact that the chronic use of hypnotics in shift work has deleterious rather than beneficial effects. Scheduled exposure to bright light during night work and complete darkness during daytime sleep can accelerate circadian adjustment to a night schedule and improve nighttime alertness and performance (Czeisler et al., 1990; Dawson & Campbell, 1991; Eastman, Stewart, Mahoney, Liu, & Fogg, 1994). This strategy is of limited use for the majority of shift workers, who rarely stay long enough on a given schedule to benefit from this type of intervention. Another experimental approach for improving adaptation to night work is the use of melatonin (Folkard, Arendt, & Clark, 1993). This treatment theoretically combines the phase-shifting effects of the drug with the facilitation of daytime sleep. However, the few controlled trials performed have given mixed results; moreover, optimization of timing of administration, dosage, and formulation need to be evaluated further (Arendt, Skene, Middleton, Lockley, & Deacon, 1997).

Transmeridian Flights and Jet Lag

Upon arrival of a transmeridian flight, the travelers are confronted with a desynchronization between their internal

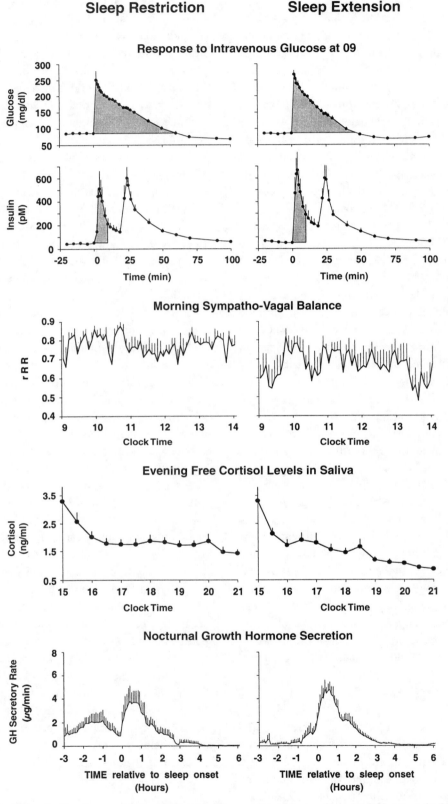

Figure 13.8 *Upper panels:* Glucose and insulin responses to an intravenous glucose tolerance test performed at 9:00 a.m. on the 5th day of sleep restriction to 4 hours per night and the 5th day of sleep extension to 12 hours per night in 11 healthy young men. Adapted from Spiegel et al., 1999. *Lower panels:* Profiles of sympatho-vagal balance (derived from measures of heart rate variability), evening cortisol levels, and nocturnal GH secretion for the two bedtime conditions. Adapted from Spiegel et al., 1999.

circadian rhythms and the periodicity of the new external environment. The lack of synchronization is associated with symptoms of fatigue, impaired mental and psychomotor performance, subjective discomfort, sleep disturbances, and gastrointestinal disorders. Phase-shifts of human circadian rhythms have been studied after actual jet lag as well as after abrupt displacements of the LD cycle, the sleep-wake cycle, or both, designed to reproduce in the laboratory the desynchrony that occurs in jet lag. After an abrupt shift caused by real or simulated jet lag, adaptation is not immediate and requires several days. The rate at which reentrainment occurs differs among variables, and in general it is slower for overt rhythms that are strongly dependent on the circadian system (such as those of cortisol and melatonin secretions) than it is for those that are markedly modulated by sleep-wake homeostasis (such as prolactin and GH secretions).

As a result of differences in the rate of adaptation for different physiological subsystems, abnormal phase relationships between overt rhythms occur during the period of adaptation. Therefore, jet lag involves not only desynchronization between internal and external rhythms, but also a perturbation of internal temporal organization of physiological functions. The overall rate of adaptation depends on the strength of the zeitgebers, and it can be as low as half an hour per day or as high as 3 hours per day. Moreover, the rate of adaptation is not constant: Adaptation occurs at a faster pace during the first few days and progresses at a slower rate thereafter (Aschoff, Hoffmann, Pohl, & Wever, 1975). The rate of adaptation is also dependent on the direction of the shift: Adaptation usually occurs faster after a delay shift (traveling westward) than after an advance shift (traveling eastward; Aschoff et al., 1975). This difference is generally believed to be due to the fact that the endogenous circadian period of humans is longer than 24 hours; therefore, adjustment by delays is more easily achieved than is adjustment by advances. There is strong evidence to suggest that reentrainment after a transmeridian flight is facilitated by exposure to bright light at appropriate circadian phases (Hirschfeld et al., 1996; Wever, 1986). The major difficulty is the timing of light exposure on successive days after the shift. As circadian phase dynamically changes, it is practically impossible (given our current state of knowledge) to predict the optimal timings of light exposure beyond the first day after the shift. It is widely believed that adherence to the local social and meal schedule upon arrival will accelerate the adaptation to jet lag, but this has not been rigorously demonstrated. Laboratory studies suggest that physical exercise scheduled during the period corresponding to the nighttime prior to travel is capable of phase-delaying human rhythms and therefore facilitates adaptation to a delay (i.e., westward) shift (Buxton et al., 1997; Van

Reeth et al., 1994). Appropriately timed use of benzodiazepine hypnotics can also facilitate adaptation to jet lag (Buxton, Copinschi, Van Onderbergen, Karrison, & Van Cauter, 2000).

Pathological Alterations

Insomnia

Insomnia is the experience or complaint of poor quality or quantity of sleep. Three categories of insomnia can be distinguished: *onset insomnia* (difficulty falling asleep), *maintenance insomnia* (waking up frequently during the night), and *termination insomnia* (waking up too early and not being able to fall asleep again). Insomnia is one of the most common complaints encountered by physicians working in primary care settings. In Western industrial countries, approximately one third of the adult population reports at least occasional difficulties sleeping (Ancoli-Israel & Roth, 1999). The prevalence of chronic insomnia is approximately 10% (Hajak, 2000; E. O. Johnson, 2000; Stepanski, Zorick, Roehrs, & Roth, 2000) and increases with age: Approximately one third of subjects older than 65 years are estimated to suffer from chronic insomnia. Insomnia occurs about 1.5 times more often in women than in men; this is especially true for perimenopausal and postmenopausal women (Hublin, Kaprio, Partinen, & Koskenvuo, 2001).

Untreated insomnia may have severe consequences for the health and well-being of the patient. Insomnia is frequently associated with sleepiness, fatigue, impairments in daytime functioning, inability to concentrate, lack of alertness, memory troubles, and mood disorders (*DSM-IV*, 1994). Individuals with chronic insomnia report elevated levels of stress, depression, anxiety, muscle aches, and medical illnesses (Aldrich, 2000). In addition, those with chronic insomnia reported 2.5 times more fatigue-related car accidents than did good sleepers. A recent study has demonstrated that the HPA axis is hyperactive in persons with insomnia (Vgontzas et al., 2001). As in studies of experimental sleep deprivation or sleep restriction, cortisol levels are higher in the evening and during the night. This endocrine alteration could play a role in the mood and memory disturbances that are frequently associated with insomnia, as well as promote the development of insulin resistance.

Obstructive Sleep Apnea

Obstructive sleep apnea syndrome (OSAS) is characterized by episodes of complete or partial pharyngeal obstruction during sleep accompanied by excessive daytime sleepiness. The main symptoms of OSAS are loud and irregular snoring, restless and nonrefreshing sleep, and daytime fatigue. A characteristic pattern of apneic episodes is brief gasps or loud snoring that alternate with episodes of silence typically lasting 20–30 s. Breathing is impaired because there is a reduction in muscle tone at sleep onset and a change in the central control of respiration during sleep (Roth & Roehrs, 2000). These two events result in an abnormality in the anatomy of the upper airway—specifically, the narrowing of the pharynx. The prevalence of the syndrome is between 2% and 5% of the population, but it may be as much as 8% in men 40–59 years of age (Hublin et al., 2001). The strongest risk factors for OSAS are obesity and age of more than 65 years; male gender has also been shown to be a risk factor. Sleep apnea is a major risk factor for hypertension, heart attacks, and stroke. The severe daytime sleepiness that is often associated with OSAS results in a major safety risk for the patient and his or her environment.

The established treatment for moderate to severe OSAS is continuous positive airway pressure (CPAP) therapy via nasal masks. OSAS causes sleep fragmentation and is usually associated with suppression of SWS sleep, REM sleep, or both. Successful treatment of OSAS (as with CPAP) produces a more consolidated sleep pattern with huge rebounds of SWS or REM sleep and prompt relief of daytime sleepiness (Carskadon & Dement, 2000). In addition, treatment with CPAP resulted in a clear increase in the amount of GH secreted during the first few hours of sleep (Cooper, White, Ashworth, Alberti, & Gibson, 1995; Saini et al., 1993).

Delayed and Advanced Sleep Phase Syndrome

Delayed sleep phase syndrome is considered a circadian rhythm sleep disorder. It is characterized by a chronic inability to fall asleep at a normal bedtime and to awake in the morning (Weitzman et al., 1981). It has been proposed that the basis of this disorder is an inability to advance the timing of the circadian sleep-wake cycle after it has been delayed to an abnormal phase by late bedtimes during a weekend or after transmeridian travel. Nonpharmacological chronotherapy involving repeated scheduled exposure to bright light is the treatment of choice for this disorder (Rosenthal et al., 1990).

In contrast, in the advanced sleep phase syndrome, the timing of the major sleep episode is advanced in relation to normal bedtime, resulting in symptoms of extreme evening sleepiness and early morning awakening. The complaint of waking up earlier than desired is common in older adults, but extreme cases of advance sleep phase are very rare. Two recent studies (Jones et al., 1999; Reid et al., 2001) have described families with the advanced sleep phase syndrome; both have concluded that the trait segregates with an autoso-

mal dominant mode. At least one form of familial advanced sleep phase syndrome appears related to an abnormally short endogenous circadian period (Jones et al., 1999) apparently caused by a mutation altering the function of a circadian clock gene, *hPer2* (Toh et al., 2001).

CONCLUSIONS

The present review has attempted to summarize the evidence indicating that every facet of our neurobiology and psychology undergoes consistent temporal variations on a 24-hour time scale. These temporal variations are largely determined by the interaction of two central nervous systems that keep track of time—circadian rhythmicity and sleep homeostasis. The impact of these two time-keeping systems is ubiquitous across all aspects of human function and—for some systems—the combined effects of circadian rhythmicity and sleep regulation may result in modulatory effects that are as large as those associated with the transition from normal to pathological function. The advent of artificial light and the emergence of a 24-hour society in industrialized countries have resulted in major disruptions of the natural control of the temporal organization of human activities, with major consequences for mental and physical well-being, safety, and productivity. During recent years, there has been a rapid increase in the understanding of the neuroanatomical and molecular mechanisms underlying the generation and transmission of the circadian signal and the initiation, duration, and quality of sleep. These advances offer the hope that strategies that improve sleep quality—particularly in older adults and in those suffering from chronic sleep loss—will have benefits for mental and physical health. The rapid progress in basic circadian biology holds the promise that conditions of circadian misalignment such as those that occur in jet lag and shift work will become treatable in a not-so-distant future.

REFERENCES

Aldrich, M. (2000). Cardinal manifestations of sleep disorders. In M. Kryger, T. Roth, & W. Dement (Eds.), *Principles and practices of sleep medicine* (3rd ed., pp. 526–534). Philadelphia: W. B. Saunders.

Allan, J. S., & Czeisler, C. A. (1994). Persistence of the circadian thyrotropin rhythm under constant conditions and after light-induced shifts of circadian phase. *Journal of Clinical Endocrinology and Metabolism, 79,* 508–512.

Ancoli-Israel, S., Kripke, D. F., Jones, D. W., Parker, L., & Hanger, M. A. (1991). 24-hour sleep and light rhythms in nursing home patients. *Sleep Research, 20A,* 410.

Ancoli-Israel, S., & Roth, T. (1999). Characteristics of insomnia in the United States: I. Results of the 1991 National Sleep Foundation Survey. *Sleep, 22*(Suppl. 2), S347–S353.

Arendt, J., Skene, D. J., Middleton, B., Lockley, S. W., & Deacon, S. (1997). Efficacy of melatonin treatment in jet lag, shift work, and blindness. *Journal of Biological Rhythms, 12*(6), 604–617.

Aschoff, J., Hoffmann, K., Pohl, H., & Wever, R. (1975). Reentrainment of circadian rhythms after phase-shifts of the Zeitgeber. *Chronobiologia, 2*(1), 23–78.

Aston-Jones, G., Chen, S., Zhu, Y., & Oshinsky, M. L. (2001). A neural circuit for circadian regulation of arousal. *Nature Neuroscience, 4*(7), 732–738.

Benca, R. M., Obermeyer, W. H., Thisted, R. A., & Gillin, J. C. (1992). Sleep and psychiatric disorders. *Archives of General Psychiatry, 49,* 651–668.

Bliwise, D. L. (1994). Normal aging. In M. H. Kryger, T. Roth, & W. C. Dement (Eds.), *Principles and practices of sleep medicine* (pp. 26–39). Philadelphia: W. B. Saunders.

Bliwise, D. L. (1996). Historical change in the report of daytime fatigue. *Sleep, 19,* 462–464.

Boivin, D. B., Czeisler, C. A., Dijk, D. J., Duffy, J. F., Folkard, S., Minors, D. S., Totterdell, P., & Waterhouse, J. M. (1997). Complex interaction of the sleep-wake cycle and circadian phase modulates mood in healthy subjects. *Archives of General Psychiatry, 54,* 145–152.

Bonnet, M., & Arand, D. (1995). We are chronically sleep deprived. *Sleep, 18,* 908–911.

Borbély, A. A. (1998). Processes underlying sleep regulation. *Hormone Research, 49,* 114–117.

Born, J., Muth, S., & Fehm, H. L. (1988). The significance of sleep onset and slow wave sleep for nocturnal release of growth hormone (GH) and cortisol. *Psychoneuroendocrinology, 13,* 233–243.

Brock, M. A. (1991). Chronobiology and aging. *Journal of American Geriatric Society, 39,* 74–91.

Buxton, O. M., Copinschi, G., Van Onderbergen, A., Karrison, T. G., & Van Cauter, E. (2000). A benzodiazepine hypnotic facilitates adaptation of circadian rhythms and sleep-wake homeostasis to an eight hour delay shift simulating westward jet lag. *Sleep, 23*(7), 915–927.

Buxton, O. M., Frank, S. A., L'Hermite-Balériaux, M., Leproult, R., Turek, F. W., & Van Cauter, E. (1997). Roles of intensity and duration of nocturnal exercise in causing phase-shifts of human circadian rhythms. *American Journal of Physiology (Endocrinology and Metabolism), 273,* E536–E542.

Cajochen, C., Krauchi, K., & Wirz-Justice, A. (1997). The acute soporific action of daytime melatonin administration: Effects on the EEG during wakefulness and subjective alertness. *Journal of Biological Rhythms, 12,* 636–643.

Campbell, S. S., Dawson, D., & Anderson, M. W. (1993). Alleviation of sleep maintenance insomnia with timed exposure to bright light. *Journal of American Geriatric Society, 41,* 829–836.

Campbell, S. S., Kripke, D. F., Gillin, J. C., & Hrubovcak, J. C. (1988). Exposure to light in healthy elderly subjects and Alzheimer's patients. *Physiology and Behavior, 42,* 141–144.

Carrier, J., & Monk, T. H. (2000). Circadian rhythms of performance: New trends. *Chronobiology International, 17,* 719–732.

Carrier, J., Monk, T. H., Buysse, D. J., & Kupfer, D. J. (1996). Amplitude reduction of the circadian temperature and sleep rhythms in the elderly. *Chronobiology International, 13*(5), 373–386.

Carskadon, M. A., & Dement, W. C. (1987). Sleepiness in the normal adolescent. In C. Guilleminault (Ed.), *Sleep and its disorders in children* (pp. 53–66). New York: Raven Press.

Carskadon, M., & Dement, W. C. (2000). Normal human sleep: An overview. In M. Kryger, T. Roth, & W. C. Dement (Eds.), *Principles and practices of sleep medicine* (3rd ed., pp. 15–25). Philadelphia: W. B. Saunders.

Clark, L. A., Watson, D., & Leeka, J. (1989). Diurnal variation in the positive affects. *Motivation and Emotion, 13,* 205–234.

Cooper, B. G., White, J. E., Ashworth, L. A., Alberti, K. G., & Gibson, G. J. (1995). Hormonal and metabolic profiles in subjects with obstructive sleep apnea syndrome and the acute effects of nasal continuous positive airway pressure (CPAP) treatment. *Sleep, 18*(3), 172–179.

Copinschi, G., Leproult, R., & Van Cauter, E. (2001). Sleep and hormonal rhythms in humans. In P. R. Hof & C. V. Mobbs (Eds.), *Functional neurobiology of aging* (pp. 855–868). San Diego, CA: Academic Press.

Czeisler, C. A., Chiasera, A. J., & Duffy, J. F. (1991). Research on sleep, circadian rhythms and aging: Applications to manned spaceflight. *Experimental Gerontology, 26,* 217–232.

Czeisler, C. A., Duffy, J. F., Shanahan, T. L., Brown, E. N., Mitchell, J. F., Rimmer, D. W., Ronda, J. M., Silva, E. J., Allan, J. S., Emens, J. S., Dijk, D.-J., & Kronauer, R. E. (1999). Stability, precision, and near-24-hour period of the human circadian pacemaker. *Science, 284,* 2177–2181.

Czeisler, C. A., Johnson, M. P., Duffy, J. F., Brown, E. N., Ronda, J. M., & Kronauer, R. E. (1990). Exposure to bright light and darkness to treat physiologic maladaptation to night work. *New England Journal of Medicine, 322*(18), 1253–1259.

Dallman, M. F., Strack, A. L., Akana, S. F., Bradbury, M. J., Hanson, E. S., Scribner, K. A., & Smith, M. (1993). Feast and famine: Critical role of glucocorticoids with insulin in daily energy flow. *Frontiers in Neuroendocrinology, 14,* 303–347.

Davis, F. C., Frank, M. G., & Heller, C. H. (1999). Ontogeny of sleep and circadian rhythms. In F. W. Turek & P. C. Zee (Eds.), *Regulation of sleep and circadian rhythms* (pp. 19–62). New York: Marcel Dekker.

Dawson, D., & Campbell, S. S. (1991). Timed exposure to bright light improves sleep and alertness during simulated night shifts. *Sleep, 14,* 511–516.

Degaute, J. P., van de Borne, P., Linkowski, P., & Van Cauter, E. (1991). Quantitative analysis of the 24-hour blood pressure and heart rate patterns in young men. *Hypertension, 18,* 199–210.

Dijk, D.-J., & Czeisler, C. A. (1994). Paradoxical timing of the circadian rhythm of sleep propensity serves to consolidate sleep and wakefulness in humans. *Neuroscience Letters, 166,* 63–68.

Dijk, D.-J., & Czeisler, C. A. (1995). Contribution of the circadian pacemaker and the sleep homeostat to sleep propensity, sleep structure, electroencephalographic slow waves, and sleep spindle activity in humans. *Journal of Neuroscience, 15,* 3526–3538.

Dijk, D.-J., Duffy, J. F., & Czeisler, C. A. (1992). Circadian and sleep/wake dependent aspects of subjective alertness and cognitive performance. *Journal of Sleep Research, 1,* 112–117.

Dijk, D.-J., Duffy, J. F., & Czeisler, C. A. (2001). Age-related increase in awakenings: impaired consolidation of nonREM sleep at all circadian phases. *Sleep, 24*(5), 565–577.

Dijk, D.-J., & Edgar, D. M. (1999). Circadian and homeostatic control of wakefulness and sleep. In P. C. Zee & F. W. Turek (Eds.), *Regulation of sleep and circadian rhythms* (pp. 111–147). New York: Marcel Dekker.

Dinges, D. F., Douglas, S. D., Hamarman, S., Zaugg, L., & Kapoor, S. (1995). Sleep deprivation and human immune function. *Advances in Neuroimmunology, 5,* 97–110.

Dinges, D. F., Pack, F., Williams, K., Gillen, K., Powell, J., Ott, G., Aptowicz, C., & Pack, A. (1997). Cumulative sleepiness, mood disturbance, and psychomotor vigilance performance decrements during a week of sleep restricted to 4–5 hours per night. *Sleep, 20,* 267–277.

Dunlap, J. C. (2000). A new slice on an old problem. *Nature Neuroscience, 3*(4), 305–306.

Eastman, C. I., Stewart, K. T., Mahoney, M. P., Liu, L., & Fogg, L. F. (1994). Dark goggles and bright light improve circadian rhythm adaptation to night-shift work. *Sleep, 17*(6), 535–543.

Ehlers, C. L., Frank, E., & Kupfer, D. J. (1988). Social zeitgebers and biological rhythms. *Archives of General Psychiatry, 45,* 948–952.

Ehlers, C. L., & Kupfer, D. J. (1989). Effects of age on delta and REM sleep parameters. *Electroencephalography and Clinical Neurophysiology, 72,* 118–125.

Feinberg, I. (1976). Functional implications of changes in sleep physiology with age. In R. D. Terry & S. Gershon (Eds.), *Neurobiology of aging* (pp. 23–41). New York: Raven Press.

Feinberg, I., Koresko, R. L., & Heller, N. (1967). EEG sleep patterns as a function of normal and pathological aging in man. *Psychiatry Research, 5,* 107–144.

Folkard, S., Arendt, J., & Clark, M. (1993). Can melatonin improve shift workers' tolerance of the night shift? Some preliminary findings. *Chronobiology International, 10,* 315–320.

Follenius, M., Brandenberger, G., Bardasept, J., Libert, J., & Ehrhart, J. (1992). Nocturnal cortisol release in relation to sleep structure. *Sleep, 15,* 21–27.

Gallopin, T., Fort, P., Eggermann, E., Cauli, B., Luppi, P. H., Rossier, J., Audinat, E., Mühlethaler, M., & Serafin, M. (2000). Identification of sleep-promoting neurons in vitro. *Nature, 404,* 992–995.

Gillberg, M., Kecklund, G., & Akerstedt, T. (1994). Relations between performance and subjective ratings of sleepiness during a night awake. *Sleep, 17,* 236–241.

Hajak, G. (2000). Insomnia in primary care. *Sleep, 23*(Suppl. 3), S54–S63.

Hirschfeld, U., Moreno-Reyes, R., Akseki, E., L'Hermite-Balériaux, M., Leproult, R., Copinschi, G., & Van Cauter, E. (1996). Progressive elevation of plasma thyrotropin during adaptation to simulated jet lag: Effects of treatment with bright light or zolpidem. *Journal of Clinical Endocrinology and Metabolism, 81,* 3270–3277.

Hobson, J. A. (1995). *Sleep.* New York: Scientific American Library.

Horne, J. (1988). *Why we sleep.* Oxford, UK: Oxford University Press.

Hublin, C., Kaprio, J., Partinen, M., & Koskenvuo, M. (2001). Insufficient sleep: a population-based study in adults. *Sleep, 24*(4), 392–400.

Johnson, E. O. (2000). *Sleep in America: 2000.* Washington, DC: National Sleep Foundation.

Johnson, M. P., Duffy, J. F., Dijk, D. J., Ronda, J. M., Dyal, C. M., & Czeisler, C. A. (1992). Short-term memory, alertness and performance: A reappraisal of their relationship to body temperature. *Journal of Sleep Research, 1,* 24–29.

Jones, C. R., Campbell, S. S., Zone, S. E., Cooper, F., DeSano, A., Murphy, P. J., Jones, B., Czajkowski, L., & Ptacek, L. J. (1999). Familial advanced sleep-phase syndrome: A short-period circadian rhythm variant in humans. *Nature Medicine, 5*(9), 1062–1065.

Kerkhof, G. A., Van Dongen, H. P., & Bobbert, A. C. (1998). Absence of endogenous circadian rhythmicity in blood pressure? *American Journal of Hypertension, 11,* 373–377.

King, D. P., & Takahashi, J. S. (2000). Molecular genetics of circadian rhythms in mammals. *Annual Review of Neuroscience, 23,* 713–742.

Knutsson, A., Akerstedt, T., Jonsson, B. G., & Orth-Gomer, K. (1986). Increased risk of ischaemic heart disease in shift workers. *Lancet, 2*(8498), 89–92.

Kolker, D. E., & Turek, F. W. (2001). Circadian rhythms and sleep in aging rodents. In P. R. Hof & C. V. Mobbs (Eds.), *Functional neurobiology of aging* (pp. 869–882). San Diego, CA: Academic Press.

Landolt, H. P., Dijk, D. J., Achermann, P., & Borbely, A. A. (1996). Effects of age on the sleep EEG: Slow-wave activity and spindle frequency in young and middle-aged men. *Brain Research, 738,* 205–212.

Leproult, R., Copinschi, G., Buxton, O., & Van Cauter, E. (1997). Sleep loss results in an elevation of cortisol levels the next evening. *Sleep, 20*(10), 865–870.

Leproult, R., Van Reeth, O., Byrne, M. M., Sturis, J., & Van Cauter, E. (1997). Sleepiness, performance and neuroendocrine function during sleep deprivation: Effects of exposure to bright light or exercise. *Journal of Biological Rhythms, 12,* 245–258.

Lowrey, P. L., Shimomura, K., Antoch, M. P., Yamazaki, S., Zemenides, P. D., Ralph, M. R., Menaker, M., & Takahashi, J. S. (2000). Positional syntenic cloning and functional characterization of the mammalian circadian mutation tau. *Science, 288*(5465), 483–492.

McEwen, B. S., & Sapolsky, R. M. (1995). Stress and cognitive function. *Current Opinions in Neurobiology, 5,* 205–216.

McGinty, D., & Stern, N. (1988). Circadian and sleep-related modulation of hormone levels: Changes with aging. In J. R. Sowers & J. V. Felicetta (Eds.), *Endocrinology of aging* (pp. 75–111). New York: Raven Press.

Mendelson, W. B., & Bergmann, B. M. (1999). EEG delta power during sleep in young and old rats. *Neurobiology of Aging, 20*(6), 669–673.

Monk, T. H., Buysse, D. J., Reynolds, C. F., Berga, S. L., Jarrett, D. B., Begley, A. E., & Kupfer, D. J. (1997). Circadian rhythms in human performance and mood under constant conditions. *Journal of Sleep Research, 6,* 9–18.

Monk, T. H., Buysse, D. J., Reynolds, C. F., Jarrett, D. B., & Kupfer, D. J. (1992). Rhythmic vs. homeostatic influences on mood, activation, and performance in young and old men. *Journal of Gerontology: Psychological Sciences, 47,* 221–227.

Monk, T. H., Moline, M. L., Fookson, J. E., & Peetz, S. M. (1989). Circadian determinants of subjective alertness. *Journal of Biological Rhythms, 4,* 393–404.

Moore, R. Y. (1991). Development of the suprachiasmatic nucleus. In D. C. Klein, R. Y. Moore, & S. M. Reppert (Eds.), *Suprachiasmatic nucleus: The mind's clock* (pp. 391–404). New York: Oxford University Press.

Mrosovsky, N. (1996). Locomotor activity and non-photic influences on the circadian clock. *Biological Reviews, 71,* 343–372.

Naylor, E., Penev, P., Orbeta, L., Janssen, I., Ortiz, R., Colecchia, E. F., Keng, M., Finkel, S., & Zee, P. C. (2000). Daily social and physical activity increases slow-wave sleep and daytime neurophychological performance in the elderly. *Sleep, 23*(1), 87–95.

Penev, P., Zee, P. C., Wallen, E. P., & Turek, F. W. (1995). Aging alters the phase-resetting properties of a serotonin agonist on hamster circadian rhythmicity. *American Journal of Physiology, 268,* R293–R298.

Porkka-Heiskanen, T., Strecker, R. E., Thakkar, M., Bjorkum, A. A., Greene, R. W., & McCarley, R. W. (1997). Adenosine: A mediator of the sleep-inducing effects of prolonged wakefulness. *Science, 276,* 1255–1258.

Prinz, P. N. (1995). Sleep and sleep disorders in older adults. *The Journal of Clinical Neurophysiology, 12,* 139–146.

Prinz, P. N., Peskind, E. R., Vitaliano, P. P., Raskind, M. A., Eisdorfer, C., Zemcuznikov, N., & Gerber, C. J. (1982). Changes in the sleep and waking EEGs of nondemented and demented elderly subjects. *Journal of American Geriatric Society, 30,* 86–93.

Ralph, M., Foster, R. G., Davis, F. C., & Menaker, M. (1990). Transplanted suprachiasmatic nucleus determines circadian period. *Science, 247,* 975–978.

Rechtschaffen, A., & Kales, A. (1968). *A manual of standardized terminology, techniques and scoring system for sleep stages of human subjects.* Los Angeles, CA: UCLA Brain Information Service/Brain Research Institute.

Rechtschaffen, A., & Siegel, J. (2000). Sleep and dreaming. In E. R. Kandel, J. H. Schwartz, & T. M. Jessell (Eds.), *Principles of neural science* (4th ed., pp. 936–947). New York: McGraw-Hill.

Reid, K. J., Chang, A. M., Dubocovich, M. L., Turek, F. W., Takahashi, J. S., & Zee, P. C. (2001). Familial advanced sleep phase syndrome. *Archives of Neurology, 58*(7), 1089–1094.

Reppert, S. M., & Weaver, D. R. (1991). A biological clock is oscillating in the fetal suprachiasmatic nuclei. In D. C. Klein, R. Y. Moore, & S. M. Reppert (Eds.), *Suprachiasmatic nucleus: The mind's clock* (pp. 405–418). New York: Oxford University Press.

Rosenberg, R. S., Zepelin, H., & Rechtschaffen, A. (1979). Sleep in young and old rats. *Journal of Gerontology, 34*(4), 525–532.

Rosenthal, N. E., Joseph-Vanderpool, J. R., Levendosky, A. A., Johnston, S. H., Allen, R., Kelly, K. A., Souetre, E., Schultz, P. M., & Starz, K. E. (1990). Phase-shifting effects of bright morning light as treatment for delayed sleep phase syndrome. *Sleep, 13*(4), 354–361.

Roth, T., & Roehrs, T. (2000). Sleep organization and regulation. *Neurology, 54*(5), S2–S7.

Sack, R. L., Hughes, R. J., Edgar, D. M., & Lewy, A. J. (1997). Sleep-promoting effects of melatonin: At what dose, in whom, under what conditions and by what mechanisms? *Sleep, 20,* 908–915.

Saini, J., Krieger, J., Brandenberger, G., Wittersheim, G., Simon, C., & Follenius, M. (1993). Continuous positive airway pressure treatment: Effects on growth hormone, insulin and glucose profiles in obstructive sleep apnea patients. *Hormone and Metabolic Research, 25*(7), 375–381.

Sancar, A. (2000). Cryptochrome: the second photoactive pigment in the eye and its role in circadian photoreception. *Annual Review of Biochemistry, 69,* 31–67.

Sanford, J. R. (1975). Tolerance of debility in elderly dependents by supporters at home: its significance for hospital practice. *British Medical Journal, 3,* 471–473.

Satinoff, E., Li, H., Tcheng, T. K., Liu, C., McArthur, A. J., Medanic, M., & Gillette, M. U. (1993). Do the suprachiasmatic nuclei oscillate in old rats as they do in young ones? *American Journal of Physiology, 265,* R1216–R1222.

Sherin, J. E., Shiromani, P. J., McCarley, R. W., & Saper, C. B. (1996). Activation of ventrolateral preoptic neurons during sleep. *Science, 271,* 216–219.

Siegel, J. M. (1995). Phylogeny and the function of REM sleep. *Behavioural Brain Research, 69*(9), 29–34.

Siegel, J. M. (1999). The evolution of REM sleep. In R. Lydic & B. Baghdoyan (Eds.), *Handbook of behavioral state control* (pp. 87–100). Boca Raton, FL: CRC Press.

Spiegel, K., Leproult, R., Colecchia, E., L'Hermite-Balériaux, M., Zhiqun, N., Copinschi, G., & Van Cauter, E. (2000). Adaptation of the 24-hour growth hormone profile to a state of sleep debt. *American Journal of Physiology (Endocrinology and Metabolism), 279*(3), R874–R883.

Spiegel, K., Leproult, R., & Van Cauter, E. (1999). Impact of sleep debt on metabolic and endocrine function. *Lancet, 354,* 1435–1439.

Stepanski, E., Zorick, F., Roehrs, T., & Roth, T. (2000). Effects of sleep deprivation on daytime sleepiness in primary insomnia. *Sleep, 23*(2), 215–219.

Thomas, M., Sing, H., Belenky, G., Holcomb, H., Mayberg, H., Dannals, R., Wagner, H., Thorne, D., Popp, K., Rowland, L., Welsh, A., Balwinski, S., & Redmond, D. (2000). Neural basis of alertness and cognitive performance impairments during sleepiness: I. Effects of 24 h of sleep deprivation on waking human regional brain activity. *Journal of Sleep Research, 9*(4), 335–352.

Tobler, I. (2000). Phylogeny of sleep regulation. In M. H. Kryger, T. Roth, & W. C. Dement (Eds.), *Principles and practices of sleep medicine* (pp. 72–81). Philadelphia: W. B. Saunders.

Toh, K. L., Jones, C. R., He, Y., Eide, E. J., Hinz, W. A., Virshup, D. M., Ptacek, L. J., & Fu, Y. H. (2001). An hPer2 phosphorylation site mutation in familial advanced sleep phase syndrome. *Science, 291*(5506), 1040–1043.

Turek, F. W. (1998). Circadian rhythms. *Hormone Research, 49,* 103–113.

Turek, F. W., & Van Reeth, O. (1996). Circadian Rhythms. In M. J. Fregly & C. M. Blatteis (Eds.), *Handbook of physiology: Environmental physiology* (pp. 1329–1360). Oxford, UK: Oxford University Press.

Van Cauter, E., Blackman, J. D., Roland, D., Spire, J. P., Refetoff, S., & Polonsky, K. S. (1991). Modulation of glucose regulation and insulin secretion by circadian rhythmicity and sleep. *The Journal of Clinical Investigation, 88,* 934–942.

Van Cauter, E., Copinschi, G., & Turek, F. W. (2001). Endocrine and other biologic rhythms. In K. L. Becker (Ed.), *Endocrinology* (4th ed., pp. 235–256). Philadelphia: W. B. Saunders.

Van Cauter, E., Leproult, R., & Plat, L. (2000). Age-related changes in slow-wave sleep and REM sleep and relationship with growth hormone and cortisol levels in healthy men. *The Journal of the American Medical Association, 284,* 861–868.

Van Cauter, E., Plat, L., & Copinschi, G. (1998). Interrelations between sleep and the somatotropic axis. *Sleep, 21,* 553–566.

Van Cauter, E., Polonsky, K. S., & Scheen, A. J. (1997). Roles of circadian rhythmicity and sleep in human glucose regulation. *Endocrine Reviews, 18*(5), 716–738.

Van Cauter, E., Sturis, J., Byrne, M. M., Blackman, J. D., Leproult, R., Ofek, G., L'Hermite-Balériaux, M., Refetoff, S., Turek, F. W., & Van Reeth, O. (1994). Demonstration of rapid light-induced advances and delays of the human circadian clock using hormonal phase markers. *American Journal of Physiology, 266,* E953–E963.

Van Cauter, E., & Turek, F. W. (1995). Endocrine and other biological rhythms. In L. J. DeGroot (Ed.), *Endocrinology* (pp. 2487–2548). Philadelphia: W. B. Saunders.

Van Cauter, E., & Turek, F. W. (2001). Roles of sleep-wake and dark-light cycles in the control of endocrine, metabolic, cardiovascular and cognitive function. In B. S. McEwen (Ed.), *Handbook of physiology: Vol. 4. Coping with the environment: Neural and endocrine mechanisms* (pp. 313–330). New York: Oxford University Press.

van Coevorden, A., Mockel, J., Laurent, E., Kerkhofs, M., L'Hermite-Balériaux, M., Decoster, C., Nève, P., & Van Cauter, E. (1991). Neuroendocrine rhythms and sleep in aging men. *American Journal of Physiology, 260,* E651–E661.

Van Dongen, H. P., Maislin, G., & Kerkhof, G. A. (2001). Repeated assessment of the endogenous 24-hour profile of blood pressure under constant routine. *Chronobiology International, 18*(1), 85–98.

Van Gool, W. A., & Mirmiran, M. (1986). Aging and circadian rhythms. In D. F. Swaab, E. Fliers, M. Mirmiran, W. A. Van Gool, & F. Van Haaren (Eds.), *Aging of the brain and Alzheimer's disease* (Vol. 70, pp. 255–278). Amsterdam: Elsevier.

VanHelder, T., Symons, J. D., & Radomski, M. W. (1993). Effects of sleep deprivation and exercise on glucose tolerance. *Aviation, Space and Environmental Medicine, 64*(6), 487–492.

Van Reeth, O., Sturis, J., Byrne, M. M., Blackman, J. D., L'Hermite-Balériaux, M., Leproult, R., Oliner, C., Refetoff, S., Turek, F. W., & Van Cauter, E. (1994). Nocturnal exercise phase delays circadian rhythms of melatonin and thyrotropin in normal men. *American Journal of Physiology (Endocrinology and Metabolism), 266,* E964–E974.

Van Reeth, O., Zhang, Y., Reddy, A., Zee, P. C., & Turek, F. W. (1993). Aging alters the entraining effects of an activity-inducing stimulus on the circadian clock. *Brain Research, 607,* 286–292.

Van Reeth, O., Zhang, Y., Zee, P. C., & Turel, F. W. (1992). Aging alters feedback effects of the activity-rest cycle in the circadian clock. *American Journal of Physiology, 263,* R981–R986.

Vgontzas, A. N., Bixler, E. O., Lin, H. M., Prolo, P., Mastorakos, G., Vela-Bueno, A., Kales, A., & Chrousos, G. P. (2001). Chronic insomnia is associated with nyctohemeral activation of the hypothalamic-pituitary-adrenal axis: Clinical implications. *Journal of Clinical Endocrinology and Metabolism, 86*(8), 3787–3794.

Waldstreicher, J., Duffy, J. F., Brown, E. N., Rogacz, S., Allan, J. S., & Czeisler, C. A. (1996). Gender differences in the temporal organization of prolactin (PRL) secretion: Evidence for a sleep-independent circadian rhythm of circulating PRL levels. A Clinical Research Center study. *Journal of Clinical Endocrinology and Metabolism, 81,* 1483–1487.

Wehr, T., Moul, D., Barbato, G., Giesen, H., Seidel, J., Barker, C., & Bender, C. (1993). Conservation of photoperiod-responsive mechanisms in humans. *American Journal of Physiology, 265,* R846–R857.

Weibel, L., Follenius, M., Spiegel, K., Ehrhart, J., & Brandenberger, G. (1995). Comparative effect of night and daytime sleep on the 24-hour cortisol secretory profile. *Sleep, 18,* 549–556.

Weibel, L., Spiegel, K., Follenius, M., Ehrhart, J., & Brandenberger, G. (1996). Internal dissociation of the circadian markers of the cortisol rhythm in night workers. *American Journal of Physiology, 270*(4, Pt. 1), E608–E613.

Weitzman, E. D., Czeisler, C. A., Coleman, R. M., Spielman, A. J., Zimmerman, J. C., Dement, W., Richardson, G., & Pollak, C. P. (1981). Delayed sleep phase syndrome: A chronobiological disorder with sleep-onset insomnia. *Archives of General Psychiatry, 38*(7), 737–746.

Weitzman, E. D., Zimmerman, J. C., Czeisler, C. A., & Ronda, J. M. (1983). Cortisol secretion is inhibited during sleep in normal man. *Journal of Clinical Endocrinology and Metabolism, 56,* 352–358.

Welsh, D. K., Richardson, G. S., & Dement, W. C. (1986). Effect of age on the circadian pattern of sleep and wakefulness in the mouse. *Journal of Gerontology, 41,* 579–586.

Wever, R. A. (1986). Use of bright light to treat jet lag: Differential effects of normal and bright artificial light on human circadian rhythms. *Annals of the New York Academy of Sciences, 453,* 282–304.

Wise, P. M., Cohen, I. R., Weiland, N. G., & London, D. E. (1988). Aging alters the circadian rhythm of glucose utilization in the suprachiasmatic nucleus. *Proceedings of the National Academy of Sciences, USA, 85,* 5305–5309.

Wright, K. P. J., Badia, P., Myers, B. L., Plenzler, S. C., & Hakel, M. (1997). Caffeine and light effects on nighttime melatonin and temperature levels in sleep-deprived humans. *Brain Research, 747,* 78–84.

Zepelin, H. (2000). Mammalian sleep. In M. H. Kryger, T. Roth, & W. C. Dement (Eds.), *Principles and practices of sleep medicine* (pp. 82–92). Philadelphia: W. B. Saunders.

CHAPTER 14

Motivational Systems

KRISTA McFARLAND AND PETER W. KALIVAS

One of the cardinal features of behavior is that it is goal-directed. Animals seek food or water; they avoid predators and explore novel environments. Humans work overtime to buy a new home, get up early to go to the gym, or put their health and happiness in jeopardy to get drugs. The study of motivation attempts to explain *why* such behaviors occur. From early in the twentieth century when the term *motivation* was first popularized, scholars have consistently described both *activation* and *direction* as the key components of motivated states (e.g., Bindra, 1969; Lashley, 1938; Woodworth, 1918). This notion suggests that in order to understand the antecedent conditions that elicit behavior, one must be able to explain how behavior is stimulated or initiated (i.e., activation) and the reason behavior takes one particular form over another (i.e., direction).

The difficulty inherent in the study of such questions is obvious: Hunger and craving are internal states and thus are not directly observable or measurable. Early in the twentieth century, when psychology was struggling to gain acceptance as a science, J. B. Watson (Watson, 1913, 1919) and later B. F.

Skinner (Skinner, 1950) convincingly argued that psychology must restrict itself to the study of observable, quantifiable phenomena in order to survive. For psychology this subject matter was behavior. Skinner suggested that the science of behavior would exclude "anything of an observed fact which appeals to events taking place somewhere else, at some other level of observation, described in different terms, and measured, if at all, in different dimensions" (1950, p. 193). In other words, he argued that anything falling within the mental or neurobiological realms—and therefore unobservable—should not be studied within psychology.

This argument had a profound effect on the study of motivation. As motivation is essentially an unobservable phenomenon, many in the field eschewed its study in favor of more observable and describable processes. Instead, research focused on reward and reinforcement. As illustrated in Figure 14.1, motivation is an *antecedent* condition that instigates behavior. In contrast, reinforcement is a *consequence* of interaction with the goal object that presumably affects learning and subsequent motivation. In short, reinforcement

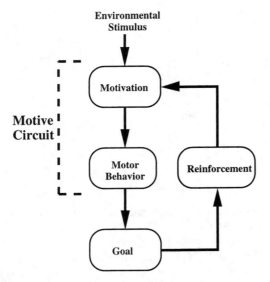

Figure 14.1 Schematic of the relationship between motivation, goal-directed motor behavior, and reinforcement. This chapter focuses on the motive circuit involved in translating motivationally relevant environmental stimuli into goal-directed action.

affects learning, whereas motivation affects the performance of learned behaviors. Unfortunately, inquiry into the neural mechanisms involved in the production of goal-directed behavior has predominantly ignored this distinction; the primary reason was that reinforcement can be operationally defined and measured. Thus, amount of reinforcement (e.g., number of food pellets) and consequent changes in behavior (e.g., number of lever presses or time required to traverse an alley) can be quantified. For this reason, Skinner (and those who followed in his tradition) argued that motivationally significant stimuli should be treated strictly as behavioral reinforcers (Skinner, 1959).

The goal of the present chapter is to review the behavioral, anatomical, and neurobiological evidence regarding the neural substrates of motivated behavior. This involves examination of a motive circuit within the basal forebrain. The motive circuit consists of two parallel circuits that play important roles in the production of motivation and goal-directed behavior—one predominantly associated with motor function and the other primarily associated with limbic functions (see Figure 14.2, Panel A). It is hypothesized that the motor circuit is critical for

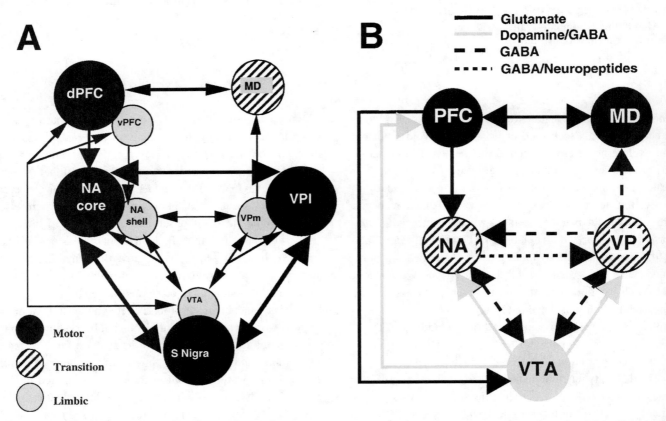

Figure 14.2 Motivational circuitry illustrating the limbic and motor subcircuits (Panel A) and the primary neurotransmitters (Panel B) utilized by the circuit. MD: mediodorsal nucleus of the thalamus; NA: nucleus accumbens; PFC: prefrontal cortex; PFC$_d$: dorsal prefrontal cortex; PFC$_V$: ventral prefrontal cortex; S Nigra: substantia nigra; VP: ventral pallidum; VP$_l$: dorsolateral ventral pallidum; VP$_m$: ventromedial ventral pallidum; VTA: ventral tegmental area.

the production of well-learned behavioral responses, whereas the limbic circuit is important for processing environmental stimuli and transmitting this information to portions of the motor circuit, thus instigating novel and practiced adaptive motor responses. Within this circuit, dopamine, glutamate, gamma-aminobutyric acid (GABA), and neuropeptides are neurotransmitters (see Figure 14.2, Panel B), each conveying potentially distinct information affecting motivation. The present review is organized around the neruotransmitters in this circuit and in reference to the following hypotheses.

1. Glutamate stimulates behavior and the anatomical origin of the activated glutamatergic afferents provides motor memory to provoke the appropriate behavioral response. In addition, under the appropriate conditions glutamate transmission promotes neuroplasticity permitting learning and behavioral adaptations to occur.

2. Dopamine supports plasticity and learning by engaging the appropriate cellular machinery to modify neuronal communication, especially excitatory trasmission.

3. GABA regulates overall circuit tone and thereby serves to bind or sustain an animal's motivational state until the goal object can be achieved.

4. Neuropeptides contribute to subjective valence.

Thus, the neuroanatomical and neurochemical organization of the motive circuit provides the neural basis of motivation and reinforcement and functions to elicit adaptive motor responses in the presence of motivationally significant stimuli.

ANATOMY OF THE MOTIVE CIRCUIT

Historical Perspectives

Early biological studies of motivated behavior focused on the importance of a few individual nuclei in the production of adaptive motor responses. In this respect, the amygdala garnered early attention—beginning with demonstration that bilateral ablation of temporal lobe, including the amygdala, resulted in dramatic changes in emotionality. Formerly aggressive monkeys became tame and willing to approach normally fear-inducing objects (Klüver & Bucy, 1939). Subsequently, animals with amygdala lesions were shown to have impaired avoidance responding to stimuli that signaled shock (Weiskrantz, 1956) as well as impaired visual discrimination for food reward (B. Jones & Mishkin, 1972). Thus, amygdaloid lesions seemed to produce a deficit in the ability to identify and respond appropriately to biologically significant stimuli. These studies, when combined with anatomical

studies demonstrating the amygdala's connectivity with sensory, autonomic, and motor structures (e.g., Aggleton, Burton, & Passingham, 1980; Herzog & Van Hoesen, 1976; Nauta, 1961) suggested a critical modulatory function in regulating motivated behavior.

The other brain region most frequently implicated in the control of motivated behavior was the nucleus accumbens (NA). In 1954, Olds and Milner discovered that animals would work for electrical simulation of the medial forebrain bundle (Olds & Milner, 1954). Later demonstrations that this effect was largely due to stimulation of dopaminergic afferents to the NA (e.g., Corbett & Wise, 1980; Fibiger & Phillips, 1986)—coupled with emerging evidence that the neurochemical mode of action of many drugs of abuse depended on the accumbens (e.g., Kornetsky & Espositio, 1979; Wise, 1982)—indicated a central role in goal-directed behavior. Behavioral evidence, considered in conjunction with the connectivity of the NA with limbic and cortical structures, suggested a probable role in behavior elicited by at least positive motivational stimuli.

Whereas research on the functions of the amygdala arose from a tradition interested in examining its emotional and motivational properties, research on the NA arose from a tradition primarily interested in identifying the neural substrates of reinforcement and reward, an endeavor that has only recently begun to implicate the amygdala. Thus, one perspective valued motivation as a concept, whereas the other was more Skinnerian in orientation. In the now-classic formulation, Mogenson, Jones, and Yim (1980) moved beyond both the separate ideologies and the single nucleus approach in order to suggest that the amygdala and NA form part of a circuit that functions to integrate limbic information and elicit appropriate behavioral responses. This circuit—termed herein the *motive circuit*—was presumed to integrate signals from limbic structures about motivationally important stimuli and recruit motor structures to elicit adaptive behavioral output (i.e., translate motivation into action). More recently, Heimer, Alheid, and Zahm (1993) formalized the anatomical interrelationships between the amygdala and NA in motivation as the extended amygdala. This interconnected series of nuclei—including the central nucleus of the amygdala, bed nucleus of the stria terminalis, medial ventral pallidum (VP), and ventromedial NA—is hypothesized to be a prime contributor of emotional context.

Subcortical Circuitry

Figure 14.2 shows a schematic picture of the circuitry that has been implicated in translating motivational stimuli into the production of goal-directed behavior. A central component of the motive circuit is a trio of interconnected nuclei that display tight topographical organization such that they form two parallel loops through the ventral mesencephalon, ventral striatum, and ventral pallidum (see Figure 14.2, Panel A). The mesoaccumbens system consists of a well-documented dopaminergic projection from the ventral tegmental area (VTA) to the nucleus accumbens in the ventral striatum (Beckstead, Domesick, & Nauta, 1979; Fallon & Moore, 1978), although up to 20% of the pathway contains GABA (Carr & Sesack, 2000a). This projection is reciprocal and topographically organized such that the VTA innervates and receives innervation from ventromedial portions of the nucleus accumbens, termed the *shell* (NA$_s$; Heimer, Zahm, Churchill, Kalivas, & Wohltmann, 1991; Swanson, 1982). Accumbal projections to the VTA contain GABA, dynorphin, and substance P (Churchill, Dilts, & Kalivas, 1990; Napier, Mitrovic, Churchill, Klitenick, & Kalivas, 1995). While the VTA also innervates the medial portions of the accumbens, termed the *core* (NA$_c$; Heimer et al., 1991), reciprocal projections with the NA$_c$ arise from the substantia nigra (SN), which is classically considered a component of the extrapyramidal motor system (Heimer et al., 1991).

The topography of the loop is maintained in the efferents from the NA to the VP. Thus, the NA$_s$ projects to ventromedial portions of the VP (VP$_m$), while the NA$_c$ projects primarily to the dorsolateral, subcomissural VP (VP$_l$; Zahm & Heimer, 1990). The striatopallidal projections have been shown to contain GABA, enkephalin, substance P, and neurotensin (NT; Churchill et al., 1990; Napier et al., 1995), whereas reciprocal projections seem to be primarily GABAergic (Churchill & Kalivas, 1994). Like the NA, the VP exhibits medioloateral topography in its innervation of the mesencephalon, with the VP$_m$ providing GABAergic innervation of the VTA and the VP$_l$ innervating the SN (Kalivas, Churchill, & Klitenick, 1993b; Zahm & Heimer, 1990). However, reciprocal innervation of the VP is not as discrete. The VTA projects to both the VP$_m$ and the VP$_l$, while the SN shows little if any innervation of the VP (Klitenick, Deutch, Churchill, & Kalivas, 1992).

Prefrontal Cortical Input

Afferent innervation of the subcortical circuit arises from a number of sources. Primary among these is the medial prefrontal cortex (PFC) because it maintains topographic connectivity with both the VTA and the NA, and thus forms an extension of the parallel subcortical circuitry. Both the dorsal (PFC$_d$) and ventral (PFC$_v$) prefrontal cortices receive mesocortical dopamine projections from the VTA (Füxe, Hökfelt, Johannson, Lidbrink, & Ljungdahl, 1974), which—like the mesoaccumbens system—has a significant (up to 40%)

GABAergic component (Carr & Sesack, 2000a). Additionally, both the PFC$_d$ and the PFC$_v$ send reciprocal projections back to the VTA, and the PFC$_d$ also sends a projection to SN (Sesack, Deutch, Roth, & Bunney, 1989). Whereas the PFC$_v$ and PFC$_d$ show some degree of mediolateral topography in corticofugal innervation of the ventral mesencephalon, the PFC displays very discrete target specificity in its innervation of the NA. The dorsal PFC$_d$ projects selectively to the NA$_c$, and the PFC$_v$ projects to the NA$_s$ (Berendse, Galis-de Graaf, & Groenewegen, 1992; Sesack et al., 1989). The main transmitter of the efferent PFC projections is glutamate (e.g., Christie, Summers, Stephenson, Cook, & Beart, 1987; Fonnum, Storm-Mathiasen, & Divac, 1981).

Allocortical Afferents

In addition to excitatory afferents arising from the PFC are allocortical glutamatergic inputs, including those from the basolateral amygdala (BLA) and the hippocampus (Figure 14.3). The BLA sends excitatory glutamatergic projections to many nuclei within the motive circuit, including the NA (Wright, Beijer, & Groenewegen, 1996), medial prefrontal cortex (mPFC; Bacon, Headlam, Gabbott, & Smith, 1996; McDonald, 1996), VTA (Otake & Nakamura, 2000), VP (Grove, 1988) and mediodorsal thalamus (MD; Reardon & Mitrofanis, 2000). In turn, the BLA receives a reciprocal dopaminergic projection from the VTA (Brinley-Reed & McDonald, 1999), as well as afferents from the mPFC (Groenewegen, Berendse, Wolters, & Lohman, 1990; McDonald, Mascagni, & Guo, 1996) and VP (Groenewegen, Berendse, & Haber, 1993). Notably, the BLA is also densely innervated by thalamus and sensory cortex (Groenewegen et al., 1990), suggesting that it integrates sensory information about reinforcing stimuli and can then relay this information to the motive circuit.

In addition to the BLA, it is also important to consider the innervation of the VTA and substantia nigra from the central nucleus of the amygdala (Haber & Fudge, 2000). This is thought to be a primary source of enkephalin and neurotensin innervation to the VTA. Likewise, the VTA has a substantive dopaminergic and GABAergic projection to the central nucleus. As part of the extended amygdala (discussed later in this chapter), the central nucleus also provides innervation to the VP$_m$ and NA$_s$ (Heimer et al., 1993). Precisely how the BLA and central nucleus integrate motivationally relevant stimuli and promote learning is a subject of much recent experimental scrutiny; the reader is referred to excellent articles on this topic (Hatfield, Han, Gallagher, & Holland, 1996; Hitchcott & Phillips, 1998; Parkinson, Robbins, & Everitt, 2000). However, it is noteworthy for purposes of this review

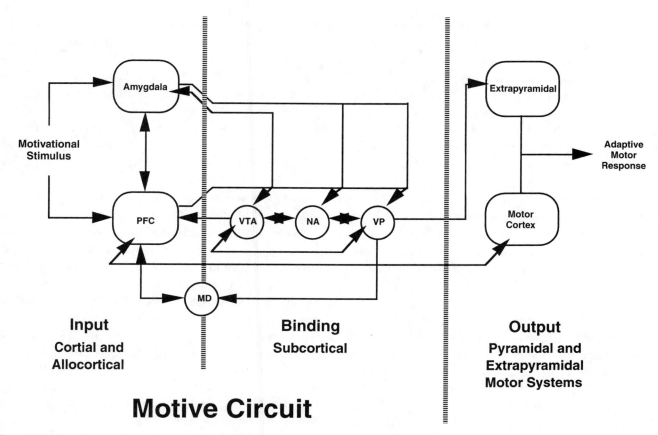

Motive Circuit

Figure 14.3   Overall view of the motive circuit highlighting the translation of motivational stimuli into adaptive behavioral responses. The stimuli are processed in cortical and allocortical regions and transmitted to the subcortical nuclei, which then communicate to the motor systems. The mediodorsal thalamus is illustrated between cortical and subcortical structures due to its role as a conduit of information back to the cortex from subcortical circuitry.

that the central nucleus receives dense excitatory input from the BLA and not only acts as a conduit for providing peptidergic modulation of some nuclei in the motive circuit, but also provides adaptive modulation of autonomic responses to motivationally relevant stimuli.

The hippocampus—primarily via the ventral subiculum—sends glutamatergic efferents to the NA (Groenewegen, Vermeulen-Van der Zee, Te Kortschot, & Witter, 1987; Kelley & Domesick, 1982) and PFC (Carr & Sesack, 1996), but not to the VP (Yang & Mogenson, 1985). It receives a dopaminergic projection from the VTA (Gasbarri, Verney, Innocenzi, Campana, & Pacitti, 1994).

Motor and Limbic Subcircuits

An inspection of Figure 14.2 (A) and the preceding description reveals that there are two subcircuits that comprise the larger motive circuit—one composed of predominantly limbic structures and one of primarily of motor structures. Thus, the VTA, NA_s, and VP_m are associated with limbic structures like the PFC_v, BLA, hippocampus, and bed nucleus of the stria terminalis (BNST). In fact, recent conceptualizations of

the ventral forebrain suggest that the centromedial amygdala, sublenticular VP, BNST, and NA_s form a continuous network termed the *extended amygdala* (Kalivas, Churchill, & Klitenick, 1993a). Conversely, the PFC_d, NA_c, VP_l form contacts with motor structures like the SN, motor cortex, pedunculopontine nucleus (PPN) and subthalamic nucleus. Thus, there are two relatively closed loop systems that can integrate motor and limbic information separately (see Kalivas et al., 1993a, for more details).

Of course, for an individual to effectively integrate incoming motivational stimuli and emit appropriate behavioral responses, there must be interplay between the motor and limbic systems. There are two major pathways that permit such interaction. The first is via the VTA that forms reciprocal connections with both the PFC_d and the PFC_v, as well as both the NA_c and NA_s. Additionally, although it receives a projection only from the VP_m, it sends projections to both the VP_m and VP_l. Thus the permissive topography of VTA efferent projections within the motive circuit positions it to influence the activity of both the motor and limbic subcircuits. The second means of interaction between these two systems is the MD. The VP sends a prominent GABAergic efferent to the MD, with the primary contribution coming from the VP_m and only minor involvement of the VP_l (Mogenson, Ciriello, Garland, & Wu, 1987; Zahm, Williams, & Wohltman, 1996). The MD does not send a reciprocal projection to the VP, but there is reciprocal glutamatergic innervation of the PFC_d (Groenewegen, 1988; Kuroda, Murakami, Shinkai, Ojima, & Kishi, 1995). Thus, the MD receives information from the limbic circuit via the VP_m but sends a projection to the motor associated PFC_d, consequently forming a bridge between limbic and motor circuitry.

It is noteworthy that communication between the limbic and motor subcircuits is rectified to permit more direct information flow from limbic to motor, whereas flow in the reverse direction requires multisynaptic communication. Three rectified projections service this preferential flow from limbic to motor subcircuits, including (a) the dopaminergic and GABAergic innervation by the VTA of the NA_c and VP_m, (b) the GABAergic projection from the VP_m to the MD, and (c) the glutamatergic projection from the PFC to the NA. The location of rectified information flow is strategic for the movement of information from limbic to motor subcircuit, and it has been suggested that information may spiral outwards from the more medial limbic nuclei to the more lateral and dorsal motor nuclei in the motive circuit (Haber & Fudge, 1997; Zahm & Brog, 1992).

Motivationally relevant information can exit the motive circuit to the motor system via a number of different pathways. Hence, the VP_l projects to the PPN, subthalamic nucleus, SN, and subsequently to all parts of the extrapyramidal motor system (Haber, Groenewegen, Grove, & Nauta, 1985). There is also a projection to motor cortex that arises from the PFC_d (Zahm & Brog, 1992). Finally, the SN receives a projection directly from the NA_c. Thus, the motive circuit has several conduits by which it can influence motor behavior following presentation of motivationally relevant stimuli.

DOPAMINERGIC EFFECTS ON MOTIVATED BEHAVIOR

There is abundant evidence that midbrain dopamine systems play an important role in motivated behavior (for reviews, see Ettenberg, 1989; Koob, 1992; Wise, 1982). Thus, administration of dopamine receptor antagonist drugs has been shown to disrupt responding for a variety of reinforcers, including food and water (e.g., Ettenberg & Horvitz, 1990; Gerber, Sing, & Wise, 1981), electrical brain stimulation (e.g., Fouiezos, Hansson, & Wise, 1978; Stellar, Kelley, & Corbett, 1983), and drugs of abuse (e.g., Bozarth & Wise, 1981; de Wit & Wise, 1977; Yokel & Wise, 1976). Despite the well-documented role

of dopamine (DA) in regulating goal-directed behavior, the specific function that DA serves is emerging, but remains uncertain. Theories suggest a role for DA in everything from reward (e.g., Schultz, 1998; Wise & Rompre, 1989) to response initiation or selection (Beninger, 1983; Salamone, Kurth, McCullough, Sokolowski, & Cousins, 1993) to motivation-wanting (Robinson & Berridge, 1993). The following is an attempt to integrate what is known about dopaminergic function in order to frame its role in the production of motivated behavior.

Many postulates suggest that midbrain DA neurons function in reward, indicating that they govern behavior directed toward appetitive (rather than aversive) stimuli. Such suggestions seem at best incomplete because DA neurons have been shown to respond to presentation of aversive as well as appetitive stimuli (e.g., Doherty & Gratton, 1992; Louilot, Le Moal, & Simon, 1986). Additionally, DA receptor antagonism has been shown to disrupt learning about aversive stimuli (Salamone, 1994). Furthermore, DA neurons do not fire in a temporal pattern consistent with a role in pleasure or hedonics. Thus, after reward is expected, DA neurons have been shown to respond not to presentation of the reward itself but instead to presentation of a stimulus that is most predictive of the reward—even before it is presented (Schultz, Apicella, & Ljungberg, 1993). For these reasons, theories of DA function that depend on notions of hedonics and reward have largely been dismissed. However, the notion that DA serves to increase the frequency of future behavior directed toward a stimulus suggests in essence that DA functions in appetitive learning situations is a topic to which we return later in this chapter.

Dopamine Mediates the Learning of Motivational Responding but Not the Emission of Motivated Behavior

Purported roles for DA in wanting or craving, as well as in response initiation or response selection, are versions of motivational theories of DAergic function and are very influential in contemporary thinking about motivated behavior. They suggest that DA is involved in the energizing or directing of behavior toward the appropriate goal. However, behavioral evidence suggests that DA receptor antagonism leaves motivational processes very much intact. For example, animals can be trained to run a straight alley when presented with an olfactory cue (S+) predictive of either food or drug reinforcement in the goal box. Following DA receptor antagonist treatment, such animals still traverse the alley normally when presented with the reinforcement-predictive cue (McFarland & Ettenberg, 1995, 1998). Furthermore, in subjects having undergone training to run an alley for heroin reinforcement and a subsequent period of extinction (with no cues or reinforcement available), haloperidol does not block the ability of the S+ to reinstate drug-seeking behavior (McFarland & Ettenberg, 1997). Additionally, the ability of an S+ conditioned in this fashion to elicit conditioned locomotor activation and a conditioned place preference remain intact during dopamine receptor antagonist treatment (McFarland & Ettenberg, 1999). Together these data strongly suggest that the motivational capacity of the S+ stimulus (i.e., its ability to activate and direct behavior) remains intact despite DA receptor blockade.

Studies examining the role of conditioned stimuli in behavioral activation have produced comparable results. Horvitz and Ettenberg (1991) showed that administration of pimozide did not reduce locomotor activity in the presence of a stimulus previously paired with food delivery. This suggests that the motivational properties of food-paired stimuli are left intact. Such data are also consistent with demonstrations that environments or stimuli previously paired with amphetamine reinforcement retained their conditioned behavior-activating effects under dopamine receptor antagonist challenge (Beninger & Hahn, 1983; Beninger & Herz, 1986). Additionally, preferential responding on a lever associated with conditioned reinforcement is preserved following dopaminergic denervation of the ventral striatum (Everitt & Robbins, 1992; Robbins, Cador, Taylor, & Everitt, 1989). Thus it seems that the motivating capacity of reinforcement-associated cues remains intact following disruption of DA function.

When subjects are actively engaged in operant responding, administration of a DA receptor antagonist produces one of two behavioral patterns. Low doses produce increases in responding similar to those seen when the reinforcer is diminished (e.g., Ettenberg, Pettit, Bloom, & Koob, 1982; Schneider, Davis, Watson, & Smith, 1990). High doses produce within-session declines in operant behavior, similar to extinction curves that result from removal of the reinforcer (e.g., Gallistel, Boytim, Gomita, & Klebanoff, 1982; Gerber, Sing, & Wise, 1981; Wise, 1978). The fact that in both situations, animals will initiate responding and do so with normal (or near-normal) response latencies suggests that the motivation of these subjects to engage in goal-oriented behavior is very much intact.

Franklin and McCoy (1979) trained animals to press a lever in order to receive electrical brain stimulation. They demonstrated that when pretreated with pimozide, animals showed an extinction-like pattern of responding. However, presentation of a conditioned stimulus (CS) that was previously paired with brain stimulation reward successfully reinstated operant responding. Thus, subjects maintained motivational responding to a reward-paired stimulus despite the reinforcement decrement that presumably led to the progressive decline in responding through the initial course of the session. Similarly, Gallistel et al. (1982) showed that although dopamine antagonists elevated brain reward thresholds for intracranial stimulation in a runway paradigm, they did not prevent the motivational effects of priming stimulation that incited animals to run the alley in the first place. Taken together, these data suggest that DA receptor antagonism—although it is capable of blocking the ability of reinforcing stimuli to maintain responding—does not alter the motivation to seek reinforcement.

Further evidence that motivational processes remain intact during DA receptor antagonism comes from choice experiments. In such experiments, subjects are allowed to choose between two alternative responses: one that leads to reinforcer delivery and one that does not. Doses of dopamine receptor antagonist drugs that are sufficient to disrupt operant response rates have little effect on response choices in lever-press (Bowers, Hamilton, Zacharo, & Anisman, 1985; Evenden & Robbins, 1983) or T-maze (Tombaugh, Szostack, & Mills, 1983) tasks. Rats still prefer to make a response that has previously led to reinforcement over one that has not, even following challenge with DA receptor antagonists. Taken together, the data described suggest that the fundamental aspects of motivation remain intact despite disruption of DA transmission.

Although the midbrain DA system does not seem to signal either reward or motivation, it is clear that intact DAergic function is important for both the *acquisition* and *maintenance* of operant responding (for reviews, see Beninger, 1983; di Chiara, Acquas, Tanda, & Cadoni, 1993; Kiyatkin, 1995). Thus, DA must serve a function related to the learning and maintenance of motivated responding, while the emission of previously learned behavior progresses independent of dopamine receptor activation.

Dopamine-Stimulated Plasticity Within Motivational Circuitry

An examination of the firing pattern of DA neurons reveals that most DA neurons display phasic activation after novel stimuli and after delivery of primary reinforcers (e.g., food). Additionally, when a biologically significant stimulus is predicted by an environmental cue, with experience DA neurons come to respond to the predictive cue rather than to the reinforcer itself. Such changes in firing rate produce a pattern of responding whereby DA neurons increase firing to better-than-expected outcomes, remain unaffected by predictable outcomes, and decrease firing in response to worse-than-expected outcomes (for a review, see Schultz, 1998). Thus,

DA neurons respond to the difference between actual reward and expected reward, not the presence of reward itself. This suggests that the function of DA within the production of goal-directed behavior is to signal the need to create an adaptive behavioral response—that is, to promote neuronal plasticity.

Such a suggestion is consistent with evidence regarding the anatomical location of DA synapses. As described earlier, the primary dopaminergic projections within the motive circuit are the mesolimbic and mesocortical systems (Beckstead et al., 1979; Fallon & Moore, 1978; Füxe et al., 1974). Thus, dopamine synapses form on medium spiny neurons of the NA (both core and shell) as well as pyramidal neurons of PFC (both dorsal and ventral). Additionally, the BLA receives dopaminergic innervation. Anatomical studies indicate that DA afferents are well situated to modulate or gate the probability of cells being activated (O'Donnell & Grace, 1995). Thus, DA synapses in both the PFC and NA tend to be located proximal to excitatory contact (Sesack & Pickel, 1990; Yang, Seamans, & Gorelova, 1999)—for example, in the NA, excitatory inputs form on the head of the spine and dopamine terminals synapse on the neck (Carr, O'Donnell, Card, & Sesack, 1999; Smiley & Goldman-Rakic, 1993). Thus, from a purely anatomical perspective, DA synapses seem to be poised to modulate incoming excitatory information.

Ample electrophysiological data also suggest that DA is capable of modulating the efficiency of neuronal responses to other inputs—particularly to glutamate—either supporting or diminishing neuronal activity, depending on the quality of excitatory inputs received by target cells (O'Donnell & Grace, 1995). Both pyramidal cells in the mPFC and spiny cells of the accumbens have been shown to exist in a bistable state (Bazhenov, Timofeev, Steriade, & Sejnowski, 1998; O'Donnell & Grace, 1995; Timofeev, Grenier, & Steriade, 1998; Yim & Mogenson, 1988). Thus, cells fluctuate between a down state in which membrane potential is relatively hyperpolarized and an up state in which membrane potential is relatively depolarized. Dopamine tends to inhibit cells in the down state but tends to excite cells in the up state (Hernandez-Lopez, Bargas, Surmeier, Reyes, & Galarraga, 1997; Kiyatkin & Rebec, 1999, O'Donnell, Greene, Pabello, Lewis, & Grace, 1999; Yang & Seamans, 1996). Thus, if there is more depolarizing (i.e., glutamatergic) input to a cell, DA D_1 receptor activation increases the duration of depolarization via increasing a calcium conductance (Hernandez-Lopez et al., 1997). In the absence of depolarizing input, DA will support the inactive state via D_2 receptor activation of potassium conductances (O'Donnell & Grace, 1996).

Dopamine appears to serve a similar role within the BLA, where there are two types of neurons—inhibitory interneurons and pyramidal-like projection neurons. Stimulation of DA receptors in the BLA increases the firing rate of interneurons, thereby decreasing the firing rate of projection neurons. Furthermore, DA attenuates activation of pyramidal cells in the BLA that is elicited by electrical stimulation of the PFC and MD while potentiating the responses evoked by electrical stimulation of sensory association cortex (Rosenkrantz & Grace, 1999). This organization is suggested to produce a global filtration of inputs such that—upon presentation of an affective stimulus—there is a potentiation of the strongest sensory input and a concomitant dampening of cortical inhibition, thereby augmenting the response to affective stimuli. When considered as a whole, DA seems to increase the signal-to-noise ratio and consequently gate the flow of information within the motive circuit (Le Moal & Simon, 1991; Rosenkrantz & Grace, 1999).

The pattern of DA innervation of its target structures is also consistent with a general filtration and modulatory function. Dopaminergic projections to target structures are very divergent, with each axon being highly ramified (Anden, Füxe, Hamberger, & Hökfelt, 1996; Percheron, Francois, Yelnik, & Fenelon, 1989). Nearly every striatal neuron and many cortical neurons receive dopaminergic innervation. Additionally, these neurons display homogeneous and synchronous responsivity following presentation of motivationally significant stimuli that activate DA cells. Thus, DA neurons broadcast a global wave of activity to the NA and PFC, rather than a stimulus- or response-specific signal (Schultz, 1998). Such a pattern of responding is suited to simultaneous modulation of ongoing activity in these forebrain and allocortical structures.

A Role for Dopamine-Induced Plasticity in the Acquisition of Adaptive Behavior

The data previously outlined suggest that behavioral responding to motivationally relevant stimuli proceeds in at least two phases: the acquisition of a response and the maintenance of a response. During the acquisition phase, synaptic DA is increased by presentation of primary reinforcers or novel stimuli. This DA signal can specifically strengthen those synapses receiving simultaneous excitatory glutamatergic input (e.g., corticostriatal or amygdalostriatal). In this fashion, DA would serve to facilitate the learning of adaptive behavioral responses, as well as increase access of limbic and cortical structures to the motor system. With repeated presentations of motivationally relevant stimuli (either primary or conditioned), these same excitatory inputs would be recruited and strengthened such that they no longer require DAergic influence to elicit motor output. Thus, the primary function of

DA is to facilitate synaptic (and behavioral) plasticity, rather than to directly elicitat motor responses. This helps to explain why behavioral data show that animals do not acquire behavioral responses when DA transmission is disrupted and nevertheless exhibit previously learned behaviors (discussed previously). This explanation is also consistent with the observation that the activity of DA neurons fails to discriminate among different salient stimuli—regardless of valence—or among different sensory modalities. Thus, DA facilitates the learning of goal-directed responses in general, rather than specific motor responses to specific stimuli.

The involvement of DA in both the acquisition and maintenance of operant responding has been difficult to explain with a single theory of DA function. Theories emphasizing the modulatory effects of DA in learning can explain acquisition effects; however, they typically fail to explain effects on maintenance. Thus, if the inhibition of DA neurotransmission blocks plasticity, it should cause a kind of behavioral and neuronal inflexibility that leads to a decrease in responding for reinforcers and a perseverance in previously learned behavioral patterns. However, if one remembers that both increases and decreases in firing rates of DAergic neurons have functional implications, then a possible explanation presents itself. As discussed earlier, increases in DA firing rates seem able to support behavioral and neuronal plasticity leading to the learning of new adaptive responses. Similarly, depressed DA transmission (like that resulting from DA receptor antagonism) provides a signal indicating a less-than-expected outcome. From a functional perspective, such an error signal could lead to compensatory adaptations that would weaken the strength and persistence of the preceding behavior. Thus, it seems possible that both an augmentation and a diminution in DA cell firing rates would elicit behavioral plasticity resulting in a change in behavioral output.

GLUTAMATE AND MOTIVATED BEHAVIOR

Evidence regarding the role of glutamate in the production of motivated behavior has been slower to emerge; this is largely due to the ubiquitous distribution of glutamate within the brain and the relative difficulty in interpreting neurochemical changes in glutamate transmission (McGeer, Eccles, & McGeer, 1987; Timmerman & Westerink, 1997). The presence of glutamate in so many regions has made systemic administration of glutamatergic drugs difficult to characterize in terms of site of action. For this reason, many of the behavioral data helping to elucidate the role of glutamate in goal-directed behavior are indirect. Some information comes from the memory literature, in which food reinforcement is used to encourage subjects to engage in memory-related tasks, and glutamate plays a critical function in long-term potentiation (LTP), which serves as a cellular model of learning and memory (Bliss & Collingridge, 1993; Fonnum, Myhrer, Paulsen, Wangen, & Oksengard, 1995). Thus, glutamate activity is required for the cellular changes that are presumed to underlie learning and memory. Additionally, alterations in glutamate function have been shown to produce concomitant changes in goal-directed behavioral indexes of memory function. Glutamate receptor antagonists have been shown to impair LTP and the establishment of spatial memory in mice (Morris, Anderson, Lynch, & Baudry, 1986), whereas drugs that increase glutamate transmission have been shown to improve memory performance in both mice and individuals with schizophrenia (Firth et al., 1995; Nishikawa, Takasima, & Toru, 1983). Glutamate receptor agonists have been shown to increase speed of performance in a radial-arm maze task and to improve retention of spatial information (Davis et al., 1997). Thus, it seems that increased glutamate transmission facilitates—whereas decreased glutamate transmission impairs—a subject's ability to earn reinforcement in a memory task.

Modulating Glutamate Transmission in the Motive Circuit

The majority of evidence that glutamate acts in motivational circuitry to modulate motivated behavior comes from studies of motor activity. Glutamate receptors are both metabotropic (mGluR) and ionotropic (iGluR), and both classes of receptor have been implicated in the production of locomotor activation. Infusion of the iGluR agonists AMPA (alpha-amino-3-hydroxy-5-methyl-4-isoxazolepropionate) and NMDA (N-methyl-D-aspartate) directly into the NA results in locomotor activation that is DA dependent (e.g., Boldry, Willins, Wallace, & Uretsky, 1991; Donzanti & Uretsky, 1983). Stimulation of iGluRs in the VTA also elicits motor activation, and this effect arises primarily via activating dopamine neurons (Kalivas, Duffy, & Barrow, 1989). Additionally, AMPA and NMDA both stimulate motor activity when infused into the VP (Churchill & Kalivas, 1999; Shreve & Uretsky, 1989). This motor stimulation is blocked by inactivation of the midbrain extrapyramidal area, but not by inactivation of the MD (Churchill & Kalivas, 1999), suggesting that glutamate receptor activation within the VP directly activates motor output to the extrapyramidal motor system. Whereas activation of the NA, VTA, or VP with iGluR agonists elicit locomotor behavior, the infusion of AMPA and NMDA receptor antagonists into the NA or VP decreases the hypermotility elicited by psychomotor stimulant drugs (Willins, Wallace, Miller, & Uretsky, 1992). Furthermore, either pharmacological or electrical stimulation of the ventral subiculum results in hypermotility that is reversed by blockade of ionotropic receptors in the NA (Mogenson & Nielson, 1984; Pornnarin, Floresco, & Phillips, 2000), suggesting that activation of the NA via stimulating glutamatergic afferents also elicits locomotor activation.

Akin to iGluR stimulation, the ability of mGluR agonists to elicit motor activation can be demonstrated in studies showing that intra-accumbens infusion produces increased locomotion when infused bilaterally (Attarian & Almaric, 1997; Kim & Vezina, 1997) and contralateral rotation when infused unilaterally (Kaatz & Albin, 1995; Sacaan, Bymaster, & Schoepp, 1992). Similarly, mGluR activation in the VTA is capable of inducing dopamine-dependent motor activity (Sacaan et al., 1992; Vezina & Kim, 1999), whereas blocking mGluRs in the VTA produced no change in ongoing motor activity (Kim & Vezina, 1998). Together, these studies demonstrate that activating glutamate transmission can elicit motor-activating effects in all subcortical nuclei of the motive circuit, including the VTA, nucleus accumbens, and VP.

Although the behavioral studies directly examining the role of glutamate in the production of goal-directed behavior are sparse relative to those investigating dopamine, recent data suggest it plays a crucial role. Thus, in animals trained to self-administer cocaine, stimulation of ionotropic glutamate receptors within the NA elicits a reinstatement of drug-seeking behavior following a period of abstinence (Cornish, Duffy, & Kalivas, 1999). Furthermore, AMPA—but not DA—receptor antagonism within the NA blocks the reinstatement of drug-seeking elicited by cocaine injection (Cornish & Kalivas, 2000). Moreover, blockade of NMDA receptors—but not D_2—receptors disrupts the guidance of instrumental behavior in a reaction time task. Thus, in well-trained animals, stimuli predicting larger or more favorable reinforcement elicit faster responding than do stimuli predicting smaller or less preferred reinforcement. Administration of APV (2-amino-5-phosphonoraleric acid, an NMDA receptor antagonist)—but not haloperidol—into the NA blocked this shortening of reaction times, suggesting that glutamate receptor activation was critically involved in eliciting such fast responding (Hauber, Bohn, & Giertler, 2000). Additionally, it has been demonstrated that blockade of AMPA-kainate receptors within the NA_s—but not the NA_c—elicits feeding behavior even in satiated rats (Maldonado-Irizarry, Swanson, & Kelley, 1995), an effect that has been attributed to disruption of a tonic excitatory input to the shell, thereby inhibiting the firing rate of a population of neurons within the NA. Taken together, these behavioral data suggest

that glutamate input to the NA plays a critical role in eliciting of goal-directed behaviors, including feeding and drug seeking.

Organization of Glutamatergic Projections Within the Motive Circuit

Some of the best evidence implicating glutamate in the control of motivated behavior is anatomical. Glutamate provides the major excitatory input to the ventral striatum, arising from the PFC, BLA, and hippocampus (for a review, see Parent & Hazrati, 1995). Additionally, neurons within each of these regions respond to presentation of motivationally relevant stimuli. Some BLA neurons have been shown to respond generally to presentation of both positive and negative reinforcers, as well as unfamiliar stimuli, whereas others respond more specifically only to a single reinforcing stimulus. Notably, stimulus-specific neurons show reversible firing rates when the affective value of the stimulus is diminished (e.g., salting a piece of watermelon). Furthermore, activity of neurons within the amygdala does not relate directly to motor output; thus, firing seems to signal ongoing recognition of the affective significance of complex stimuli (for a review, see Ono, Nishijo, & Nishino, 2000).

Firing of pyramidal neurons within the PFC (or orbital prefrontal cortex in primates) has been correlated with presentation of a reinforcer and a stimulus predictive of reinforcer delivery (i.e., reward expectancy; Gray, Maldonado, Wilson, & McNaughton, 1995; Watanabe, 1996). The firing rates of these neurons have been shown to be sensitive to reward preference, stressing the importance of motivational value for responsiveness (Tremblay & Schultz, 1999). Similar to those in the amygdala, neurons in the PFC showed rapid response modifications that were partially reversible following reinforcer devaluation (Rolls, Critchlet, Mason, & Wakeman, 1996).

Processing and anticipation of reward have also been shown to affect firing patterns of hippocampal neurons (Tamura, Ono, Fukuda, & Nishijo, 1992); this has particular relevance for our understanding of motivated behavior because hippocampal—but not cortical, amygdaloid or thalamic—glutamatergic afferents to the nucleus accumbens have the ability to regulate the transition of medium spiny neurons into the up state (O'Donnell & Grace, 1995). Thus, stimulation of the fornix induced bistable cells to switch to the depolarized (active) state, and following transection of the fornix, no bistable cells were observed. More recently, stimulation of BLA afferents has been shown to result in a (comparatively brief) transition to the up state in accumbal neurons (Grace, 2000). Thus, it seems that the glutamatergic afferents to the NA are all sensitive to aspects of motivationally significant stimuli and send excitatory inputs to the NA that are integrated in the production of goal-directed behavior. Consistent with this notion are data demonstrating that glutamate release is responsible for the excitation of medium spiny neurons that occur in response to somatosensory stimuli and during behavior (Calabresi, Pisani, Centonze, & Bernardi, 1997; Wilson & Kawaguchi, 1996).

When considered as a whole, the electrophysiological and behavioral data suggest that activation of glutamatergic afferents to the accumbens produces a state of behavioral activation. Thus, activation of locomotor and goal-directed behavior seems to depend upon glutamatergic input to the NA. Within this context, it seems that the function of glutamate is to activate the production of motivated behavior. Remember that activating or energizing behavior was one of the principal features of motivation. Presumably, the direction is coded in the source of the glutamatergic input that is activated by the eliciting stimulus. Because the PFC, BLA, and hippocampus have been associated with different functional inputs (Kalivas et al., 1993a; Mogenson, Brudzynski, Wu, Yang, & Yim, 1993), it seems likely that these inputs code the memory and motor patterns activated by motivationally significant stimuli.

Glutamate and Plasticity

Although a primary function of glutamate within the motive circuit is activation of preexisting goal-directed behavior, glutamate has a clear and well-characterized role in synaptic and behavioral plasticity. Tetanic stimulation produces both long-term depression or potentiation in various nuclei in motive circuitry, and most studies reveal that these events are blocked by antagonizing excitatory amino acid transmission (Calabresi, Centonze, Gubellini, Marfia, & Benardi, 1999; Geiger et al., 1995). It is significant that recent studies have demonstrated modulation of excitatory transmission-based synaptic plasticity by mesocorticolimbic dopamine transmission (Bonci & Malenka, 1999; Thomas, Malenka, & Bonci, 2000), especially with regard to corticostriatal glutamatergic afferents (Calabresi, de Murtas, & Bernardi, 1997). Consistent with a role for glutamate in behavioral plasticity are data demonstrating that the initiation of long-term behavioral changes associated with chronic drug exposure for cocaine, amphetamine, and opioids is dependent upon glutamate receptor stimulation (Cornish & Kalivas, 2000; Wolf, 1998). Most consistently, glutamatergic neuroplasticity involves NMDA receptor stimulation, although an increasing role for mGluRs—perhaps in concert with iGluR activation—is being recognized (Anwyl, 1999).

GABA AND MOTIVATED BEHAVIOR

Behavioral studies, although they are not numerous, suggest an important role for GABA in the control of goal-directed behavior. Like glutamate, GABA is widely distributed throughout the brain and in vivo neurochemical evaluation of GABA transmission is difficult, making interpretations problematic. It is the most abundant inhibitory neurotransmitter and hyperpolarizes both projection and interneurons (Calabresi, Mercuri, de Murtas, & Bernardi, 1990; M. W. Jones, Kilpatrick, & Phillipson, 1988; Napier, Simson, & Givens, 1991). Consistent with the role of GABA as an inhibitory transmitter, stimulation of GABA receptors in the NA results in a decrease in firing frequency of neurons throughout the motive circuit. In some instances, biphasic effects are observed in projection cells, which results from relatively greater efficacy of GABA agonists or GABA receptor subtypes on GABAergic inhibitory interneurons (Grace & Bunney, 1985). Thus, low levels of GABAergic tone serve to stimulate projection neurons via inhibiting GABAergic interneurons, whereas greater levels of GABAergic tone directly hyperpolarize the projection cells.

Modulating GABA Transmission in the Motive Circuit

Consistent with the role of GABA as an inhibitory transmitter, electrical or pharmacological stimulation of the NA activates GABAergic projection cells, resulting in the suppression of firing in pallidal neurons that is reversed by application of GABA antagonists (D. L. Jones & Mogenson, 1980; Lamour, Dutar, Rascol, & Jobert, 1986). Similarly, stimulation of the VTA inhibits the firing of PFC neurons in a GABA- (and DA-) dependent fashion (Schilstrom et al., 2000). Stimulation of neurons in the NA that project to the VTA produces a more complicated effect on neurons in the VTA, where both excitation of dopamine cells by disinhibition and direct inhibition of secondary (GABAergic) cells is observed (Kalivas, 1993).

The most well-developed pharmacological literature regarding the effects of GABA on motivational circuitry is based on the role of GABA in regulating locomotor activity. In general, stimulating either $GABA_A$ or $GABA_B$ receptor subtypes produces a decrease in motor activity in most nuclei in the motive circuit. Thus, stimulating $GABA_B$ receptors in the VTA inhibits motor activity, whereas stimulation of $GABA_A$ receptors in the NA or VP inhibits activity (Kalivas, 1993). A notable exception to these observations is the effect of $GABA_B$ receptor activation in the MD, where a potent locomotor stimulation is observed (Churchill, Zahm, Duffy, & Kalivas, 1996). Thus, inhibition of the glutamatergic projection from the MD to the PFC promotes locomotor activity, an effect mediated in part by increasing mesoaccumbens dopamine transmission (Chuchill et al., 1996; M. W. Jones et al., 1988).

Direct infusion of either the GABA$_A$ agonist muscimol or the GABA$_B$ agonist baclofen into the NA$_S$ elicits a feeding behavior in satiated rats (Stratford & Kelley, 1997). These effects are probably due to presynaptic inhibition of excitatory glutamatergic drive because baclofen has been shown to inhibit glutamate release in the NA (Uchimura & North, 1991). It has also been demonstrated in striatal spiny neurons that baclofen administration inhibits stimulation-induced excitatory postsynaptic potentials without affecting resting membrane potential, again indicating a presynaptic GABA$_B$-mediated effect on glutamate release (Nisenbaum, Berger, & Grace, 1993). These data suggest that either direct postsynaptic inhibition of NA neurons (GABA$_A$) or presynaptic inhibition of glutamate release (GABA$_B$) can elicit feeding behavior, indicative of a modulatory role for GABA in maintaining tone within the accumbens on the production of behavior. Consistent with this explanation, blockade of GABA$_A$ receptors in the VP$_m$ (which would be functionally equivalent to inhibition of GABA projection neurons within the NA$_s$) has also been shown to elicit feeding behavior (Stratford, Kelley, & Simansky, 1999).

GABA receptor activation also appears to have a role in modulating drug self-administration. Thus, baclofen administration into the NA has been shown to inhibit heroin self-administration (Xi & Stein, 1999), whereas administration of muscimol into the VTA blocks ethanol self-administration (Hodge, Hraguchi, Chappelle, & Samson, 1996). Similarly, the systemic administration of baclofen inhibits cocaine self-administration (Brebner, Phelan, & Roberts, 2000; Roberts & Andrews, 1997).

Considering the pharmacological data previously outlined, it can be concluded that GABA has a modulatory role in the production of goal-directed behavior. Moreover, in general increasing GABA transmission appears to diminish motivated behavior, a notable exception being in the MD or GABA-mediated disinhibition of dopamine cell firing.

GABA and the Binding of Motivational Information

One necessary function of any circuit designed to integrate information and guide behavior is to provide a means to bind information over time. The binding of information in motivational circuitry permits an organism to persevere in goal-directed behavior in the presence of changes in external and internal stimuli. Similar binding of information has been characterized in visual circuitry in which topographically organized feedback loops are proposed to sustain information

over time and facilitate the integration of previous visual stimuli with immediate stimuli, thereby permitting a coherent flow of information over time (Herrnstein, 1971; Yeomans, 1990). It has been proposed that such a topographically organized reciprocal feedback loop in motivational circuitry is formed by part of the limbic subcircuit consisting of the VTA, NA$_s$, and VP$_m$ (see Figure 14.2, Panel A; Kalivas et al., 1993a). As described previously, tone within this subcircuit is maintained by reciprocal GABAergic interconections between these nuclei, and motivated behaviors can be disrupted or promoted by pharmacologically manipulating GABA transmission in any of these nuclei.

GABAergic Interconnection Between the Nucleus Accumbens and Ventral Pallidum

A difficulty arises in interpreting the effects of GABA on behavior when considering the effects of GABAergic tone in the NA and VP. Thus, one would expect inhibition of NA neurons to decrease activity in the GABAergic projection to the VP, thereby increasing activity within the VP via disinhibition (Mogenson et al., 1993). However, inhibition of the VP generally causes the same decrease in behavioral responding seen following inhibition of the NA. Thus, drug administration that results in opposite effects on neuronal activity in the VP produces very similar effects on responding.

This paradox is most apparent when examining the effects of GABA function on locomotor activity. Thus, treatments in the NA that increase motor activity are generally known to be excitatory on spiny cells projecting to the VP, including glutamate receptor agonists, nicotinic agonists, GABA antagonists, and D$_1$ agonists (Austin & Kalivas, 1988; Clarke & White, 1987; Willins, Narayanan, Wallace, & Uretsky, 1993). However, other treatments known to hyperpolarize spiny cells such as D$_2$ and mu opioid agonists also elicit motor activation when microinjected into the NA (Clarke & White, 1987; Hakan & Eyl, 1995). It is noteworthy, however, that the increase in motor activity by D$_2$ agonists in the NA is state-dependent and is only observed in animals with an initial high level of activity (Brudzynski, Wu, & Mogenson, 1993). Also, the motor stimulant response elicited by mu opioid receptor activation is delayed and generally manifested 20–30 min after focal microinjection into the NA (Vezina, Kalivas, & Stewart, 1987). Thus, in contrast to the drugs that electrophysiologically activate spiny cell firing and produce rapid activation of motor activity, those drugs that acutely inhibit cell firing have a state-dependent or modulatory role that may not be indicative of the acute pharmacological inhibition.

Regardless of the ultimate effect the drugs have on the firing frequency of spiny cells, in every instance examined, stimulating GABA$_A$ receptors in the VP prevents the stimulation of motor activity by simultaneous drug administration into the NA. Moreover, the infusion of muscimol into the VP by itself has been shown to produce a decrease (Austin & Kalivas, 1990), no effect (Shreve & Uretsky, 1990), or an increase (Baud, Mayo, le Moal, & Simon, 1989) in locomotor activity—depending on the dose administered. These data seem to indicate that whether motor behavior is induced depends more on the fact that a drug changes ongoing GABAergic tone in the NA to VP projection, regardless of whether the change is an increase or decrease in tone.

Thus, the regulation of behavior by the GABAergic projection from the NA to VP can be excitatory or inhibitory, depending upon the situation. This speaks to a modulatory role for GABA in which either an increase or decrease in background tone can have effects on behavioral responsivity. The state-dependent effects of GABA transmission may be in part due to the fact that spiny cells colocalize GABA with a number of different neuropeptides. Thus, divergent behavioral outcomes could potentially be due to differential activity of various peptides.

GABA-Neuropeptide Colocalization and Valence

There are a variety of neuropeptides within the motive circuit that colocalize with the more traditional transmitters already discussed. Because of their topographical distribution and interaction with these transmitter systems, investigators have examined a role for neuropeptides in the production of goal-directed behavior. The most well-described neuropeptide projections arise from the striatum (including the NA). About 90–95% of striatal neurons are GABAergic projection neurons. These projections neurons can be divided into two subtypes depending upon their projection targets, expression of DA receptors and peptide content. One subtype projects to the SN (striatonigral neurons), whereas the other projects to the VP (striatopallidal neurons; Gerfen, 1993; Kawaguchi, Wilson, & Emson, 1990). These have been termed the *direct* and *indirect* pathways, respectively (Albin, Young, & Penny, 1989).

These two classes of neurons are differentially affected by dopamine based on the classes of DA receptor subtypes that they express. Striatonigral neurons mainly express D$_1$ receptors that are positively coupled to adenylate cyclase, whereas striatopallidal neurons express D$_2$ receptors that are negatively coupled to adenylate cyclase activity (Hersch et al., 1995; Le Moine & Bloch, 1995). Discretion in peptide localization is also observed in the striatonigral neurons that express dynorphin and substance P, whereas striatopallidal neurons express enkephalin and neurotensin (Beckstead & Kersey, 1985; Fallon & Leslie, 1986). It is notable that in the more ventral

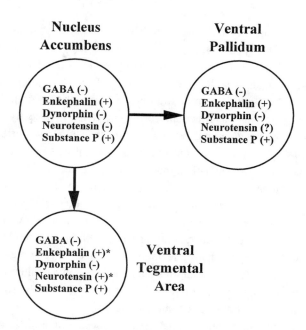

Figure 14.4 Pattern of peptidergic projections from the NA to the VP and VTA. These peptides are colocalized with GABA and can have presynaptic actions to regulate GABA release, as well as postsynaptic effects. Microinjection of peptide agonists into these nuclei can promote (+) or inhibit (−) motor activity (Kalivas, Churchill, & Klitenick, 1993).   *Although they are found in the VTA, these neuropeptides are not colocalized in the GABAergic projection from the NA.

part of the striatum—especially in the shell of the NA—the projection to the VP is more promiscuous with respect to peptide content. Thus the NA to VP projection contains D$_1$ receptors, substance P, and dynorphin, as well as enkephalin, neurotensin, and D$_2$ receptors (Lu, Ghasemzadeh, & Kalivas, 1998). In contrast, the neurons projecting from the NAs to the VTA do not contain D$_2$ receptors or enkephalin. Figure 14.4 illustrates this projection and also indicates whether stimulation of various peptidergic receptors activates (+) or inhibits (−) motor activity in the NA, VTA, or VP.

It seems plausible that the differential distribution of neuropeptides within the spiny cells of the NA reflects a functional difference in the regulation of goal-directed behavior. Consistent with this notion are data showing that the level of DA expression affects the level of peptide expression. For example, 6-hydroxydopamine depletion leads to a decrease in substance P and dynorphin expression in nigrostriatal neurons but results in increased levels of enkephalin expression in striatopallidal neurons (Gerfen et al., 1990; Engber, Boldry, Kuo, & Chase, 1992). Additionally, transgenic animals lacking D$_1$ receptors show decreased expression of substance P and dynorphin, with minimal or no effect on enkephalin expression (Drago, 1994; Drago, Gerfen, Westphal, & Steiner, 1996; Xu et al., 1994). On the other hand, mice that lack D$_2$ receptors show mostly increased enpkephalin expression (Baik et al., 1995). Thus, neuropeptide levels in the striatum are dynamically and differentially regulated by the amount of DA receptor activation.

Not only can DA function affect peptides, but peptide activity can also regulate the function of striatal projection neurons. Dynorphin receptor stimulation in the striatum inhibits the expression of immediate early genes (IEGs) typically induced by cocaine or D_1 receptor agonists (Steiner & Gerfen, 1998). These results indicate that dynorphin acts as a negative feedback mechanism that regulates the activity of striatonigral neurons. In contrast, enkephalin receptor stimulation inhibits the expression of IEGs normally elicited by D_2 receptor blockade, indicating that enkephalin acts as a negative feedback mechanism regulating striatopallidal neurons. We find it interesting that these adaptive changes in gene regulation are induced by situations that are also known to alter motivated behavior—chronic drug use (dynorphin) and chronic loss of D_2 receptor function (enkephalin).

From the previous discussion, it seems that different classes of peptides can have opposing neuronal effects. This opposition seems to hold true for their electrophysiological effects as well. Iontophoretic application of morphine (a mu opioid receptor agonist) or enkephalin (a delta opioid receptor agonist) into the VTA increased the firing rate of mesolimbic DA neurons (Gysling & Wang, 1983). In contrast, kappa opioid receptor agonists decrease neuronal firing rates (Walker, Thompson, Frascella, & Friederich, 1987). These data suggest that mu and kappa opiates have opposing effects on dopaminergic activity, in addition to being differentially regulated be DA receptor activity.

Opioid peptides also have opposite roles in the regulation of certain types of behavioral learning that depend on affective valence. When a novel environment is repeatedly paired with a positive outcome, animals form a preference for that location and choose to spend time in it over an environment paired with a neutral outcome. Similarly, if an environment is paired with an aversive outcome, subjects avoid it when given a choice between that environment and a neutral one. Research has demonstrated that mu receptor agonists elicit place preferences, whereas kappa agonists elicit place aversions. Similarly, animals form a preference for tastes associated mu agonists and an aversion to tastes paired with kappa agonists (Mucha & Herz, 1985). These data indicate that mu activation produces a positive affective state, whereas kappa activation produces a negative one. This suggestion is consistent with reports from human subjects in which dynorphin (and other kappa agonists) has been shown to elicit dysphoria (Pfeiffer, Brandt, & Herz, 1986).

Neuropeptides have similarly been shown to regulate the production of goal-directed behaviors like cocaine seeking. Thus, with repeated exposure to cocaine, animals show an augmented responsivity to its behavioral activating effects. Enkephalin facilitates this phenomenon (Sala et al., 1995), whereas it is attenuated by kappa agonists (Heidbreder, Bobovic-Vuksanovic, Shoaib, & Shippenberg, 1995; Heidbreder, Goldberg, & Shippenberg, 1993). Furthermore, enkephalin and cocaine produce cross-sensitization when infused into the VTA (DuMars, Rodger, & Kalivas, 1988). In fact, repeated administration of enkephalin produced behavioral sensitization (Kalivas, Taylor, & Miller, 1985). Alternatively, the kappa agonist, U69593, blocks the reinstatement of coaine-seeking behavior following a period of drug abstinence (Schenk, Partridge, & Shippenberg, 2000).

Infusion of substance P, the enkephalin analog D-Ala(2)-methionine(2)-enkephalinamide, or mu or delta opioid receptor agonists into the VTA produces locomotor activity (Joyce & Iversen, 1979; Joyce, Koob, Strecker, Iversen, & Bloom, 1981; Kalivas, Widerlov, Stanley, Breese, & Prange, Jr., 1983). Additionally, enkephalin infusion into the NA or SN facilitates spontaneous motor activity (Kalivas, 1985). However kappa opioid agonists attenuate the locomotor activation produced by morphine (Pearl & Glick, 1996), once again suggesting an opposite modulation of behavioral output by neuropeptides.

When considered as a whole, neuropeptides within the motive circuit clearly play a role in regulating behavioral output. Furthermore, whereas mu or delta opioid receptor activation seems to play a generally facilitory role, kappa opioid receptor activation seems to be primarily inhibitory. Thus, at least with the opioid peptides it is plausible that an important function of these peptides within the motive circuit is to provide valence. However, the neurobiological underpinnings to evaluate this hypothesis are largely missing. For example, it is not clear under what electrophysiological or behavioral conditions are the cotransmitted peptides released with or in lieu of GABA. Moreover, in certain instances, notably mu opioid receptor stimulation in the VP, the neuropeptide has both a pre- and postsynaptic action producing opposite effects on projection cells (Napier & Mitrovic, 1999; Olive, Anton, Micevych, Evans, & Maidment, 1997), and it is unclear under what circumstances one or the other receptor population is preferentially activated.

SUMMARY

This review has endeavored to outline the basic circuitry most consistently identified as being important in regulating motivation. It is notable that the circuit contains two overlapping orientations: (a) cortical and subcortical circuitry and (b) limbic and motor circuitry. Moreover, at the outset we hypothesized distinct roles for the major neurotransmitters within the circuit, including dopamine, glutamate, GABA, and various neuropeptides. In this summary we briefly revisit the literature according to these organizing principles.

Cortical and Subcortical Circuitry

Figure 14.2 shows that there exists an interconnected circuit between subcortical nuclei such as the VTA, NA, VP, and MD, and cortical or allocortical structures such as the PFC, amygdala, and hippocampus. To some extent the relationship between the cortical and subcortical nuclei is rectified in that the flow of information is more direct from the cortex to subcortical nuclei than from the subcortical nuclei back to the cortex (the notable exception being the VTA, which projects to all cortical regions). Based upon this anatomy and the contributions that all three cortical regions provide in terms of cognition and memory, it can be proposed that the cortical regions imbue the motivational state with memories linked to the environmental stimulus, ranging from conditioned behavioral responses to salient stimuli provided by the amygdala to incorporating recent information stored as working memory by the prefrontal cortex. The information transmitted by these glutamatergic cortical afferents is integrated in the subcortical nuclei and directed into motor circuitry to facilitate adaptive behavioral responding. Of course, memories are most relevant in guiding behavioral responding to familiar stimuli—and the more novel a stimulus, the less valuable previous experiences will be in generating appropriate behavioral responses. In situations of high novelty, behavior appears to be guided more by subcortical regions of motivational circuitry. Thus, exploratory behavior in response to a novel environment is disrupted most effectively by pharmacological interventions in the VTA, NA, or VP (Hooks & Kalivas, 1995). It is notable that numerous data support a role for dopamine neurons in the VTA in organizing or signaling behavioral responses to novel stimuli (Schultz, 1998).

Motor Versus Limbic Circuitry

The fact that there are two separate, but interactive subcircuits within the motive circuit suggests that they have separable functions in the production of goal-directed behaviors. Limbic structures, like the VTA, BLA, and hippocampus are more intimately connected with the PFC_v, NA_s, and VP_m, whereas motor structures like primary motor cortex, SN, and the PPN are more intimately connected with the PFC_d, NA_c, and VP_l. This leads to the suggestion that the motor loop is more directly involved in sending information about the well-learned responses to motor systems (i.e., procedural memory), whereas the limbic loop is more directly involved in learning about motivationally relevant stimuli and subsequently integrating incoming information about such stimuli when they are presented. This role for the limbic loop is consistent with information showing that animals will learn to self-administer a variety of drugs directly into the NA_s but not the NA_c (for a review, see McBride, Murphy, & Ikemoto, 1999), suggesting that the learning necessary for animals to form an association between their behavior and intracranial drug delivery requires the involvement of limbic processing.

A potential role for the motor loop in the performance of procedural memory is consistent with recent evidence from our laboratory showing that cocaine-induced reinstatement of drug-seeking behavior is mediated by a series circuit from the PFC_d through the NA_c and then out to the motor system via the VP_l (McFarland & Kalivas, 2001). Thus, well-learned behaviors are relatively automatic and can be elicited independent of limbic input. However, reinstatement elicited by drug-predictive cues has been shown to critically depend upon the BLA, a limbic structure (Meil & See, 1997; Grimm & See, 2000), indicating that multiple structures can be involved in the production of behavior. The limbic structure(s) most critical would depend upon the type of sensory and memory processing required for production of the goal-directed behavior. Thus, a stimulus with motivational significance triggers behavior within the limbic subcircuit to the motor subcircuit to initiate the behavioral output.

Within this framework, the PFC_d plays a particularly important role in the initiation of well-learned responses. The PFC_d is a primary projection target of the MD, which forms a rectified bridge between the limbic and motor loops, presumably allowing processing to move from limbic to motor subcircuits. Consistent with an important role by the PFC_d are data demonstrating that damage to the PFC results in deficits in response inhibition (e.g., Bussey, Muir, Everitt, & Robbins, 1997; Roberts & Wallis, 2000; Seamans, Floresco, & Phillips, 1998). Electrophysiological studies examining neuronal activation patterns within the PFC have found that some neurons consistently exhibit altered firing rates immediately preceding the emission of lever-press behavior resulting in delivery of cocaine or heroin (Chang, Zhang, Janak, & Woodward, 1997; Chang, Janak, & Woodward, 2000). It is interesting that many of these neurons show correlated activity with NA neurons. These data are consistent with the notion that the PFC plays an important role in response initiation. Furthermore, in human subjects, regional activation studies have shown that the prefrontal cortex is associated with preparation of motor responses and inhibition of inappropriate responses (Chang et al., 2000; de Zubicaray, Zelaya, Andrew, Williams, & Bullmore, 2000).

Functions for Neurotransmitters in the Motive Circuit

Various hypotheses were proposed at the outset of this review regarding the role of each transmitter. The following summary evaluates the veracity of each hypotheses based upon the key findings previously described.

- *Glutamate stimulates behavior, and the anatomical origin of the activated glutamatergic afferents provides motor memory to provoke the appropriate behavioral response. In addition, under the appropriate conditions glutamate transmission promotes neuroplasticity permitting learning and behavioral adaptations to occur.* This hypothesis is directly supported by the anatomical organization of glutamate projections in the motive circuit in that all glutamate derives from cortical and allocortical structures or within thalamic projections to the cortex. Thus, glutamate is involved primarily in driving and maintaining learned behavioral responses to familiar motivationally relevant stimuli. Indeed, at a cellular level, learned behaviors are thought to great extent to be encoded in changes in excitatory transmission, indicating that neuroadaptations in glutamate transmission contribute to cellular memory. However, in addition to mediating established behaviors, substantial data indicate that glutamate is critical for initial neuroplastic events associated with establishing adaptive behavioral responses. Thus, many changes in gene expression elicited by novel motivational stimuli depend on glutamate transmission, and glutamate receptor antagonists prevent the enduring establishment of adaptive behavioral responses.

- *Dopamine supports plasticity and learning by engaging the appropriate cellular machinery to modify neuronal communication, especially excitatory trasmission.* Dopamine is the most widely studied neurotransmitter in regulating motivation and at various times has been assigned a primary role in most aspects of motivation. Considering the data outlined previously, it can be argued that the primary role for dopamine is in the acquisition of adaptive behavioral responses to motivationally relevant behaviors, with a lesser role in the maintenance of behavioral responding. Thus, dopamine neurons are activated in response to novel, motivationally relevant stimuli and by stimuli that signal an impending reward. In contrast, dopamine has little role in carrying out a well-established adaptive behavioral response.

- *GABA regulates overall circuit tone and thereby serves to bind or sustain an animal's motivational state until the goal object can be achieved.* The most striking anatomical characteristic of GABA neurons within the circuit is the triad of subcortical nuclei that are interconnected by GABAergic projections, including the VTA, NA, and VP. As described previously, this subcortical triad is not involved in the long-term storage of information required for eliciting established adaptive responses. However, it is critical for the execution of both new and established behavioral responses to motivationally relevant stimuli. GABA transmission within each nucleus is responsible for maintaining these behaviors over time. Given the topographic connectivity of the GABA projections, this triad has the potential to provide background tone or state-dependence of responding to motivationally relevant stimuli. Thus, under conditions of high GABA tone, less vigorous behavioral responses would be expected and vice versa. A gradual shifting in GABAergic tone depending on the changing temporal quality of a stimulus would act as an information buffer to maintain continuity of the motivational state over time.

- *Neuropeptides contribute to subjective valence.* The study of neuropeptides has been the least informative to a unified hypothesis of how they may function in the motive circuit. The colocalization of neuropeptides in GABAergic neurons in the NA has been the most carefully studied. At least with regards to the behavioral effects of enkephalin and dynorphin in the NA, the data support a role for the neuropeptides in providing valence to a given stimulus. However, the overall dearth of knowledge regarding the cellular and behavioral regulation of peptide release makes an overarching hypothesis of neuropeptide function impossible to evaluate. Indeed, given the wide variety of neuropeptides within the motive circuit, it seems unlikely that any overarching hypothesis encompassing all of the peptides will be validated.

Conclusions

Although we have now achieved a state of knowledge permitting some general characteristics to be assigned to motivational circuitry, emerging subtleties in how the circuit functions will profoundly impact the generalizations outlined previously. Significant sources of information currently emerging are in at least two arenas:

- In vivo electrophysiological studies that permit the evaluation of ensembles of neurons within a single nucleus or between multiple nuclei will provide direct testing of the postulated roles assigned to the nuclei and transmitters within the circuit. However, the data to date reveal substantial heterogeneity in neuronal responses to various motivationally relevant stimuli, indicating that a large amount of data will be required to accurately describe the patterns of interactions within the circuit.

• Establishing behavioral responses to motivationally relevant stimuli requires both short-term and long-term neuroplasticity. The neurosciences are currently engaged in a revolution affecting our understanding of how changes in gene expression and protein trafficking mediate synaptic plasticity. As this process becomes better understood, it will be applied to behavioral plasticity and the neurosciences will likely experience a large leap forward in comprehending the role of motive circuitry in the acquisition of behavioral responding for motivationally relevant stimuli.

REFERENCES

Aggleton, J. P., Burton, M. J., & Passingham, R. E. (1980). Cortical and subcortical afferents to the amygdala in the rhesus monkey (*Macaca mulatta*). *Brain Research, 190,* 347–368.

Albin, R. L., Young, A. B., & Penny, J. B. (1989). The functional anatomy of basal ganglia disorders. *Trends in Neuroscience, 12,* 366–375.

Anden, N. E., Fuxe, K., Hamberger, B., & Hokfelt, T. (1996). A quantitative study on the nigro-neostriatal dopamine neurons. *Acta Physiologica Scandinavica, 67,* 306–312.

Anwyl, R. (1999). Metabotropic glutamate receptors: Electrophysiological properties and role in plasticity. *Brain Research Reviews, 29,* 83–120.

Attarian, S., & Amalric, M. (1997). Microinfusion of the metabotropic glutamate receptor agonist 1S,3R-1-aminocyclopentane-1,3-dicarboxylic acid into the nucleus accumbens induces dopamine-dependent locomotor activation in the rat. *European Journal of Neuroscience, 9,* 809–816.

Austin, M. C., & Kalivas, P. W. (1988). The effect of cholinergic stimulation in the nucleus accumbens on locomotor behaivor. *Brain Research, 441,* 209–214.

Austin, M. C., & Kalivas, P. W. (1990). Enkephalinergic and GABAergic modulation of motor activity in the ventral pallidum. *Journal of Pharmacology and Experimental Therapeutics, 252,* 1370–1377.

Bacon, S. J., Headlam, A. J., Gabbott, P. L., & Smith, A. D. (1996). Amygdala input to medial prefrontal cortex (mPFC) in the rat: A light and electron microscope study. *Brain Research, 720,* 211–219.

Baik, J.-H., Picetti, R., Saiardi, A., Thiriet, G., Dierich, A., Depaulis, A., et al. (1995). Parkonsonian-like motor impairment in mice lacking dopamine D_2 receptors. *Nature, 377,* 424–428.

Baud, P., Mayo, W., le Moal, M., & Simon, H. (1989). Locomotor hyperactivity in the rat after infusion of muscimol and [D-Ala^2]Met-enkephalin into the nucleus basalis magnocellularis: Possible interaction with cortical cholinergic projections. *Brain Research, 452,* 203–211.

Bazhenov, M., Timofeev, I., Steriade, M., & Sejnowski, T. J. (1998). Cellular and network models for intrathalamic augmenting responses during 10-Hz stimulation. *Journal of Neurophysiology, 79,* 2730–2748.

Beckstead, R. M., Domesick, V. B., & Nauta, W. J. H. (1979). Efferent connections of the substantia nigra and ventral tegmental area in the rat. *Brain Research, 175,* 191–217.

Beckstead, R. M., & Kersey, K. S. (1985). Immunohistochemical demonstration of differential substance P-, Met-enkephalin, and glutamic acid decarboxylase-containing cell and axon distributions in the corpus striatum of the cat. *The Journal of Comparative Neurology, 232,* 481–498.

Beninger, R. J. (1983). The role of dopamine in locomtor activity and learning. *Brain Research Reviews, 6,* 173–196.

Beninger, R. J., & Hahn, B. L. (1983). Pimozide blocks establishment but not expression of amphetamine-produced environment-specific conditioning. *Science, 220,* 1300–1304.

Beninger, R. J., & Herz, R. S. (1986). Pimozide blocks establishment but not expression of cocaine-produced environment-specific conditioning. *Life Sciences, 38,* 1425–1430.

Berendse, H. K., Galis-de Graaf, Y., & Groenewegen, H. J. (1992). Topographical organization and relationship with ventral striatal compartments of prefrontal corticostriatal projections on the rat. *The Journal of Comparative Neurology, 316,* 314–347.

Bindra, D. (Ed.). (1969). *The interrelated mechanisms of reinforcement and motivation, and the nature of their influence on response.* Lincoln: University of Nebraska Press.

Bliss, T. V. P., & Collingridge, G. L. (1993). A synaptic model of memory: Long-term potentiation in the hippocampus. *Nature, 361,* 31–39.

Boldry, R., Willins, D., Wallace, L., & Uretsky, N. (1991). The role of endogenous dopamine in the hypermotility response to intra-accumbens AMPA. *Brain Research, 559,* 100–108.

Bonci, A., & Malenka, R. C. (1999). Properties and plasticity of excitatory synapses on dopaminergic and GABAergic cells in the ventral tegmental area. *Neuroscience, 19,* 3723–3730.

Bowers, W., Hamilton, M., Zacharo, R. M., & Anisman, H. (1985). Differential effects of pimozide on response-rate and choice accuracy in a self-stimulation paradigm in mice. *Pharmacology, Biochemistry, and Behavior, 22,* 512–526.

Bozarth, M. A., & Wise, R. A. (1981). Heroin reward is dependent on a dopaminergic substrate. *Life Sciences, 29,* 1881–1886.

Brebner, K., Phelan, R., & Roberts, D. (2000). Effect of baclofen on cocaine self-administration in rats reinforced under fixed-ratio 1 and progressive-ratio schedules. *Psychopharmacology, 148*(3), 314–321.

Brinley-Reed, M., & McDonald, A. J. (1999). Evidence that dopaminergic axons provide a dense innervation of specific neuronal subpopulations in the rat basolateral amygdala. *Brain Research, 850,* 127–135.

Brudzynski, S. M., Wu, M., & Mogenson, G. J. (1993). Decreases in rat locomotor activity as a result of changes in synaptic transmission to neurons within the mesencephalic locomotor region. *Canadian Journal of Physiological Pharmacology, 71,* 394–406.

Bussey, T. J., Muir, J. L., Everitt, B. J., & Robbins, T. W. (1997). Triple dissociation of anterior cingulate, posterior cingulate, and medial frontal cortices on visual discrimination tasks using a touchscreen testing procedure for the rat. *Behavioral Neuroscience, 111*, 920–936.

Calabresi, P., Centonze, D., Gubellini, P., Marfia, G., & Bernardi, G. (1999). Glutamate-triggered events inducing corticostriatal long-term depression. *The Journal of Neuroscience, 19*, 6102–6110.

Calabresi, P., De Murtas, M., & Bernardi, G. (1997). The neostriatum beyond the motor function: Experimental and clinical evidence. *Neuroscience, 78*, 39–60.

Calabresi, P., Mercuri, N. B., de Murtas, M., & Bernardi, G. (1990). Endogenous GABA mediates presynaptic inhibition of spontaneous and evoked excitatory synaptic potentials in the rat neostriatum. *Neuroscience Letters, 118*, 99–102.

Calabresi, P., Pisani, A., Centonze, D., & Bernardi, G. (1997). Synaptic plasticity and physiological interactions between dopamine and glutamate in the striatum. *Neuroscience and Behavioral Reviews, 21*, 519–523.

Carr, D. B., O'Donnell, P., Card, J., & Sesack, S. (1999). Dopamine terminals in the rat prefrontal cortex synapse on pyramidal cells that project to the nucleus accumbens. *The Journal of Neuroscience, 19*, 11049–11060.

Carr, D. B., & Sesack, S. R. (1996). Hippocampal afferents to the rat prefrontal cortex: Synaptic targets and relation to dopamine terminals. *The Journal of Comparative Neurology, 369*(1), 1–15.

Carr, D. B., & Sesack, S. R. (2000a). GABA-containing neurons in the rat ventral tegmental area project to the prefrontal cortex. *Synapse, 38*(2), 114–123.

Carr, D. B., & Sesack, S. R. (2000b). Projections from the rat prefrontal cortex to the ventral tegmental area: Target specificity in the synaptic associations with mesoaccumbens and mesocortical neurons. *The Journal of Neuroscience, 20*, 3864–3873.

Chang, J. Y., Janak, P. H., & Woodward, D. J. (2000). Neuronal and behavioral correlations in the medial prefrontal cortex and nucleus accumbens during cocaine self-administration by rats. *Neuroscience, 99*, 433–443.

Chang, J. Y., Zhang, L., Janak, P. H., & Woodward, D. J. (1997). Neuronal responses in prefrontal cortex and nucleus accumbens during heroin self-administration in freely moving rats. *Brain Research, 754*, 12–20.

Christie, M. J., Summers, R. J., Stephenson, J. A., Cook, C. J., & Beart, P. M. (1987). Excitatory amino acid projections to the nucleus accumbens septi in the rat: A retrograde transport study utilizing D[3H]aspartate and [3H]GABA. *Neuroscience, 22*, 425–439.

Churchill, L., Dilts, R., & Kalivas, P. (1990). Changes in y-aminobutyric acid,u-opioid and neurotensin receptors in the accumbens-pallidal projection after discrete quinolinic acid lesions in the nucleus accumbens. *Brain Research, 511*, 41–54.

Churchill, L., & Kalivas, P. W. (1994). A topographically organized GABAergic projection from the ventral pallidum to the nucleus accumbens in the rat. *The Journal of Comparative Neurology, 345*, 579–595.

Churchill, L., & Kalivas, P. W. (1999). The involvement of the mediodorsal nucleus of the thalamus and the midbrain extrapyramidal area in locomotion elicited from the ventral pallidum. *Behavioural Brain Research, 104*, 63–71.

Churchill, L., Zahm, D. S., Duffy, T., & Kalivas, P. W. (1996). The mediodorsal nucleus of the thalamus: II. Behavioral and neurochemical effects of GABA agonists. *Neuroscience, 70*, 103–112.

Clarke, D., & White, F. (1987). Review: D_1 dopamine receptor—the search for a function: A critical evaluation of the D_1/D_2 dopamine receptor classification and its functional implications. *Synapse, 1*, 347–360.

Corbett, D., & Wise, R. A. (1980). Intracranial self-stimulation in relation to the ascending dopminergic systems of the midbrain: A moveable microelectrode study. *Brain Research, 185*, 1–15.

Cornish, J. L., Duffy, P., & Kalivas, P. W. (1999). A role of nucleus accumbens glutamate transmission in the relapse to cocaine-seeking behavior. *Neuroscience, 93*, 1359–1368.

Cornish, J. L., & Kalivas, P. W. (2000). Glutamate transmission in the nucleus accumbens mediates relapse in cocaine addiction. *The Journal of Neuroscience, 20*, 1–5.

Davis, C. M., Moskovitz, B., Nguyen, M. A., Tran, B. B., Arai, A., Lynch, G., et al. (1997). A profile of the behavioral changes produced by facilitation of AMPA-type glutamate receptors. *Psychopharmacology, 133*, 161–167.

de Wit, H., & Wise, R. A. (1977). Blockade of cocaine reinforcement in rats with the dopamine receptor blocker pimozide, but not with the noradrenergic blockers phenolamine or phenoxybenzamine. *Canadian Journal of Psychology, 31*, 195–203.

de Zubicaray, G. I., Zelaya, F. O., Andrew, C., Williams, S. C., & Bullmore, E. T. (2000). Cerebral regions associated with verbal response initiation, suppression and strategy use. *Neuropsychologia, 38*, 1292–1304.

di Chiara, G., Acquas, E., Tanda, G., & Cadoni, E. (1993). Drugs of abuse: Biochemical surrogates of specific aspects of natural reward? *Biochemical Society Symposium, 59*, 6581.

Doherty, M. D., & Gratton, A. (1992). High speed chronoamperometric measurements of mesolimbic and nigrostriatal dopamine relelase associated with repeated daily stress. *Brain Research, 586*, 295–302.

Donzanti, B. A., & Uretsky, N. J. (1983). Effects of excitatory amino acids in locomotor activity after bilateral microinjection into the rat nucleus accumbens: Possible dependence on dopaminergic mechanisms. *Neuropharmacology, 22*, 971–970.

Drago, J. (1994). Altered striatal function in a mutant mouse lacking D_1A dopamine receptors. *Neurobiology, 91*, 12564–12568.

Drago, J., Gerfen, C. R., Westphal, H., & Steiner, H. (1996). D_1 dopamine deficient mouse: Cocaine induced regulation of immediate early gene and substance P expression in the striatum. *Neuroscience, 74,* 813–823.

DuMars, L. A., Rodger, L. D., & Kalivas, P. W. (1988). Behavioral cross-sensitization between cocaine and enkephalin in the A10 dopamine region. *Behavioural Brain Research, 27,* 87–91.

Engber, T. M., Boldry, R. C., Kuo, S., & Chase, T. N. (1992). Dopaminergic modulation of striatal neuropeptides: Differential effects of D_1 and D_2 receptor stimulation on somatostatin, neuropeptide Y, neurotensin, dynorphin, enkephalin. *Brain Research, 581,* 261–268.

Ettenberg, A. (1989). Dopamine, neuroleptics and reinforced behavior. *Neuroscience and Behavioral Reviews, 13,* 105–111.

Ettenberg, A., & Horvitz, J. C. (1990). Pimozide prevents the response reinstating effects of water reinforcement in rats. *Pharmacology, Biochemistry, and Behavior, 31,* 861–865.

Ettenberg, A., Pettit, H. O., Bloom, F. E., & Koob, G. F. (1982). Heroin and cocaine intravenous self-administration in rats: Mediation by separate neural systems. *Psychopharmacology, 78,* 204–209.

Evenden, J. L., & Robbins, T. W. (1983). Dissociable effects of d-amphetamine, chlordiazepoxide, and alpha-fluphenthixol on choice and rate measures of reinforcement in the rat. *Psychopharmacology, 79,* 180–186.

Everitt, B. J., & Robbins, T. W. (1992). Amygdala-ventral striatal interactions and reward-related processes. In J. P. Aggleton (Ed.), *The amygdala: Neurobiological aspects of emotion, memory and mental dysfunction* (pp. 401–429). New York: Wiley-Liss.

Fallon, J. H., & Leslie, F. M. (1986). Distribution of dynorphin and enkephalin peptides in the rat brain. *The Journal of Comparative Neurology, 249,* 293–336.

Fallon, J. H., & Moore, R. Y. (1978). Catecholamine innervation of basal forebrain: IV. Topography of the dopamine projection to the basal forebrain and striatum. *The Journal of Comparative Neurology, 180,* 545–580.

Fibiger, H. C., & Phillips, A. G. (1986). Reward, motivation, cognition: Psychobiology of mesotelencephalic dopamine systems. *Handbook of Physiology I, 4,* 647–675.

Firth, C. D., Friston, K. J., Herold, S., Silbersweg, D., Fletcher, P., Cahill, C., et al. (1995). Regional brain activity in chronic schizophrenic patients during the preformance of a verbal fluency task. *British Journal of Psychiatry, 167,* 343–349.

Fonnum, F., Myhrer, T., Paulsen, R. E., Wangen, K., & Oksengard, A. R. (1995). Role of glutamate receptors in memory function and Alzheimer's disease. *Annals of the New York Academy of Sciences, 757,* 475–486.

Fonnum, F., Storm-Mathiasen, J., & Divac, I. (1981). Bichemical evidence for glutamate as neurotransmitter in the cortico-striatal and cortico-thalamic fibres in rat brain. *Neuroscience, 6,* 863–875.

Fouriezos, G., Hansson, P., & Wise, R. A. (1978). Neuroleptic-induced attenuation of brain stimulation reward. *Journal of Comparative Physiological Psychology, 92,* 659–669.

Franklin, K. B. J., & McCoy, S. N. (1979). Pimozide-induced extinction in rats: Stimulus control of responding rules out motor deficit. *Pharmacology, Biochemistry, and Behavior, 11,* 71–76.

Füxe, K., Hökfelt, T., Johansson, O., Lidbrink, P., & Ljungdahl, A. (1974). The origin of the dopamine nerve terminals in limbic and prontal cortex: Evidence for meso-cortico dopamine neurons. *Brain Research, 82,* 349–355.

Gallistel, C. R., Boytim, M., Gomita, Y., & Klebanoff, L. (1982). Does pimozide block the reinforcing effect of brain stimulation? *Pharmacology, Biochemistry, and Behavior, 17,* 769–781.

Gasbarri, A., Verney, C., Innocenzi, R., Campana, E., & Pacitti, C. (1994). Mesolimbic dopaminergic neurons innervating the hippocampal formation in the rat: A combined retrograde tracing and immunohistochemical study. *Brain Research, 668,* 71–79.

Geiger, J. R. P., Melcher, T., Koh, D.-S., Satmann, B., Seeburg, P. H., Jonas, P., et al. (1995). Relative abundance of subunit mRNAs determines gating and Ca^{2+} permeability of AMPA receptors in principal neurons and interneurons in rat CNS. *Neuron, 15,* 193–204.

Gerber, G. J., Sing, J., & Wise, R. A. (1981). Pimozide attenuates lever pressing for water in rats. *Pharmacology, Biochemistry, and Behavior, 14,* 201–205.

Gerfen, C. R. (1993). The neostriatal mosaic: Multiple levels of compartmental organization in the basal ganglia. *Annual Review of Neuroscience, 15,* 285–320.

Gerfen, C. R., Engbar, T. M., Mahan, L. C., Susel, Z., Chase, T. N., Monsma, F. J., Jr., et al. (1990). D_1 and D_2 dopamine receptor-regulated gene expression of striatonigral and striatopallidal neurons. *Science, 250,* 1429–1432.

Grace, A. A. (2000). Gating of information flow within the limbic system and the pathophysiology of schizophrenia. *Brain Research Reviews, 31,* 330–341.

Grace, A. A., & Bunney, B. S. (1985). Opposing effects of striatonigral feedback pathways on midbrain dopamine cell activity. *Brain Research, 333,* 271–284.

Gray, C. M., Maldonado, P. E., Wilson, M., & McNaughton, B. (1995). Tetrodes markedly improve the reliability and yield of single-unit isolation and multi-unit recording in cat striate cortex. *Journal of Neuroscience Methods, 63,* 43–54.

Grimm, J., & See, R. (2000). Dissociation of primary and secondary reward-relevant limbic nuclei in an animal model of relapse. *Neuropsychopharmacolgy, 22,* 473–479.

Groenewegen, H. J. (1988). Organization of afferent connections of the mediodorsal thalamic nucleus in the rat, related to mediodorsal-prefrontal topography. *Neuroscience, 24,* 379–431.

Groenewegen, H. J., Berendse, H. W., & Haber, S. N. (1993). Organization of the output of the ventral striatopallidal system in the rat: Ventral pallidal efferents. *Neuroscience, 57,* 113–142.

Groenewegen, H. J., Berendse, H. W., Wolters, J. G., & Lohman, A. H. (1990). The anatomical relationship of the prefrontal cortex with the striatopallidal system, the thalamus and the amygdala: Evidence for a parallel organization. *Progress in Brain Research, 85,* 95–116.

Groenewegen, H. J., Vermeulen-Van der Zee, A., Te Kortschot, A., & Witter, M. P. (1987). Organization of the projections from the subiculum to the ventral striatum in the rat: A study using anterograde transport of Phaseolus vulgaris-leucoagglutinin. *Neuroscience, 23,* 103–112.

Grove, E. A. (1988). Neural associations of the substantia innominata in the rat: Afferent connections. *The Journal of Comparative Neurology, 277,* 315–346.

Gysling, K., & Wang, R. Y. (1983). Morphine-induced activation of A10 dopamine neurons in the rat brain. *Brain Research, 277,* 119–127.

Haber, S., & Fudge, J. (1997). The primate substantia nigra and VTA: Integrative circuitry and function. *Critical Reviews in Neurobiology, 11,* 323–342.

Haber, S., & Fudge, J. (2000). The central nucleus of the amygdala projection to dopamine subpopulations in primates. *Neuroscience, 97,* 479–494.

Haber, S. N., Groenewegen, H. J., Grove, E. A., & Nauta, W. J. H. (1985). Efferent connections of the ventral pallidum: Evidence of a dual striatopallidofugal pathway. *The Journal of Comparative Neurology, 235,* 322–335.

Hakan, R. L., & Eyl, C. (1995). Neuropharmacology of the nucleus accumbens: Iontophoretic applications of morphine and nicotine have contrasting effects on single-unit responses evoked by ventral pallidal and fimbria stimulations. *Synapse, 20,* 175–184.

Hatfield, T., Han, J., M. C., Gallagher, M., & Holland, P. (1996). Neurotoxic lesions of basolateral, but not central amygdala interfere with Pavlovian second-order conditioning and reinforcer devaluation effects. *The Journal of Neuroscience, 16,* 5256–5265.

Hauber, W., Bohn, I., & Giertler, C. (2000). NMDA, but not dopamine D$_2$, receptors in the rat nucleus accumbens are involved in guidance of instrumental behavior by stimuli predicitng reward magnitude. *The Journal of Neuroscience, 20,* 6282–6288.

Heidbreder, C. A., Bobovic-Vuksanovic, D., Shoaib, M., & Shippenberg, T. S. (1995). Development of behavioral sensitization to cocaine: Influence of kappa opioid receptor agonists. *Journal of Pharmacology and Experimental Therapeutics, 275,* 150–163.

Heidbreder, C. A., Goldberg, S. R., & Shippenberg, T. S. (1993). The kappa-opioid receptor agonist U-69593 attenuates cocaine-induced behavioral sensitization in the rat. *Brain Research, 616,* 335–338.

Heimer, L., Alheid, G. F., & Zahm, D. S. (1993). Basal forebrain organization: An anatomical framework for motor aspects of drive and motivation. In P. W. Kalivas & C. D. Barnes (Eds.), *Limbic motor circuits and neuropsychiatry* (pp. 1–32). Boca Raton, FL: CRC Press.

Heimer, L., Zahm, D. S., Churchill, L., Kalivas, P. W., & Wohltmann, C. (1991). Specificity in the projection patterns of accumbal core and shell in the rat. *Neuroscience, 41,* 89–125.

Hernandez-Lopez, S., Bargas, J., Surmeier, D. J., Reyes, A., & Galarraga, E. (1997). D$_1$ receptor activation enhances evoked discharge in neostriatal medium spiny neurons by modulating an L-type Ca2+ conductance. *The Journal of Neuroscience, 17,* 3334–3342.

Herrnstein, R. J. (1971). Qunatitative hedonism. *Journal of Psychiatric Research, 8,* 399.

Hersch, S. M., Ciliax, B. J., Gutekunst, C.-A., Rees, H. D., Heilman, C. J., Yung, K. K. L., et al. (1995). Electron microscopic analysis of D$_1$ and D$_2$ dopamine receptor proteins in the dorsal striatum and their synaptic relationships with motor corticostriatal afferents. *The Journal of Neuroscience, 15,* 5222–5237.

Herzog, A. G., & Van Hoesen, G. W. (1976). Temporal neocortical afferent connections to the amygdala in the rhesus monkey. *Brain Research, 115,* 57–69.

Hitchcott, P., & Phillips, G. (1998). Double dissociation of the behavioral effects of R(+) 7-OH-DPAT infusions in the central and basolateral amygdala nuclei upon Pavlovian and instrumental conditioned appetitive behaviors. *Psychopharmacology, 140,* 458–469.

Hodge, C., Hraguchi, M., Chappelle, A., & Samson, H. (1996). Effects of ventral tegmental micrinjections of the GABA-A agonist muscimol on self-administration of ethanol and sucrose. *Pharmacology, Biochemistry, and Behavior, 53,* 971–977.

Hooks, M. S., & Kalivas, P. W. (1995). The role of mesoaccumbens-pallidal circuitry in novelty-induced behavioral activation. *Neuroscience, 64,* 587–597.

Horvitz, J. C., & Ettenberg, A. (1991). Conditioned incentive properties of a food-paired conditioned stimulus remain intact during dopamine receptor blockade. *Behavioral Neuroscience, 105,* 536–541.

Jones, B., & Mishkin, M. (1972). Limbic lesions and the problem of stimulus-reinforcement associations. *Experimental Neurology, 36,* 362–377.

Jones, D. L., & Mogenson, G. J. (1980). Nucleus accumbens to globus pallidus GABA projection: Electrophysiological and ionotophoretic investigations. *Brain Research, 188,* 93–105.

Jones, M. W., Kilpatrick, I. C., & Phillipson, O. T. (1988). Dopamine function in the prefrontal cortex of the rat is sensitive to reduction of tonic GABA-mediated inhibition in the thalamic mediodorsal nucleus. *Experimental Brain Research, 69,* 623–634.

Joyce, E. M., & Iversen, S. D. (1979). The effect of morphine applied locally to mesencephalic dopamine cell bodies on spontaneous motor activity in the rat. *Neuroscience Letters, 14,* 207–212.

Joyce, E. M., Koob, G. F., Strecker, R., Iversen, S. D., & Bloom, F. (1981). The behavioral effects of enkephalin analogues injected into the ventral tegmental area and globus pallidus. *Brain Research, 221,* 359–370.

Kaatz, K. W., & Albin, R. L. (1995). Intrastriatal and intrasubthalamic stimulation of metabotropic glutamate receptors: A behavioral and FOS immunohistochemical study. *Neuroscience, 66,* 55–65.

Kalivas, P. W. (1985). Interactions between neuropeptides and dopamine neurons in the ventromedial mesencephalon. *Neuroscience and Behavioral Reviews, 9,* 573–587.

Kalivas, P. W. (1993). Neurotransmitter regulation of dopamine neurons in the ventral tegmental area. *Brain Research Reviews, 18,* 75–113.

Kalivas, P. W., Churchill, L., & Klitenick, M. A. (1993a). The circuitry mediating the translation of motivational stimuli into adaptive motor responses. In P. W. Kalivas & C. D. Barnes (Eds.), *Limbic motor circuits and neuropsychiatry* (pp. 237–287). Boca Raton, FL: CRC Press.

Kalivas, P. W., Churchill, L., & Klitenick, M. A. (1993b). GABA and enkephalin projection from the nucleus accumbens and ventral pallidum to VTA. *Neuroscience, 57,* 1047–1060.

Kalivas, P. W., Duffy, P., & Barrow, J. (1989). Regulation of the mesocorticolimbic dopamine system by glutamic acid receptor subtypes. *Journal of Pharmacology and Experimental Therapeutics, 251,* 378–387.

Kalivas, P. W., Taylor, S., & Miller, J. S. (1985). Sensitization to repeated enkephalin administration into the ventral tegmental area of the rat: I. Behavioral characterization. *Journal of Pharmacology and Experimental Therapeutics, 235,* 537–543.

Kalivas, P. W., Widerlov, E., Stanley, D., Breese, G. R., & Prange, A. J., Jr. (1983). Enkephalin action on the mesolimbic dopamine system: A dopamine-dependent and a dopamine-independent increase in locomotor activity. *Journal of Pharmacology and Experimental Therapeutics, 227,* 229–237.

Kawaguchi, Y., Wilson, C. J., & Emson, P. C. (1990). Projection subtypes of the rat neostriatal matrix cells revealed by intracellular injection of biocytin. *The Journal of Neuroscience, 10,* 3421–3438.

Kelley, A. E., & Domesick, V. B. (1982). The distribution of the projection from the hippocampal formation to the nucleus accumbens in the rat: An anterograde and retrograde horseradish peroxidase study. *Neuroscience, 7,* 2321–2335.

Kim, J. H., & Vezina, P. (1997). Activation of metabotropic glutamate receptors in the rat nucleus accumbens increases locomotor activity in a dopamine-dependent manner. *Journal of Pharmacology and Experimental Therapeutics, 283,* 962–968.

Kim, J. H., & Vezina, P. (1998). Metabotropic glutamate receptors are necessary for sensitization by amphetamine. *NeuroReport, 9,* 403–406.

Kiyatkin, E. A. (1995). Functional significance of mesolimbic dopamine. *Neuroscience and Behavioral Reviews, 19,* 573–598.

Kiyatkin, E. A., & Rebec, G. V. (1999). Striatal neuronal activity and responsiveness to dopamine and glutamate after selective blockade of D_1 and D_2 dopamine receptors in freely moving rats. *The Journal of Neuroscience, 19,* 3594–3609.

Klitenick, M. A., Deutch, A. Y., Churchill, L., & Kalivas, P. W. (1992). Topography and functional role of dopaminergic projections from the ventral mesencephalic tegmentum to the ventral pallidum. *Neuroscience, 50,* 371–386.

Klüver, H., & Bucy, P. C. (1939). Preliminary analysis of the functions of the temporal lobe in monkeys. *Archives of Neurological Psychiatry, 42,* 979–1000.

Koob, G. F. (1992). Neuronal mechanisms of drug reinforcement. *Annals of the New York Academy of Sciences, 654,* 171–191.

Kornetsky, C., & Espositio, R. U. (1979). Euphoriogenic drugs: Effects on reward pathways of the brain. *Federation Proceedings, 38,* 2473.

Kuroda, M., Murakami, K., Shinkai, M., Ojima, H., & Kishi, K. (1995). Electron microscopic evidence that axon terminals from the mediodorsal thalamic nucleus make direct synaptic contacts with callosal cells in the prelimbic cortex of the rat. *Brain Research, 677,* 348–353.

Lamour, Y., Dutar, P., Rascol, O., & Jobert, A. (1986). Basal forebrain neurons projecting to the rat frontoparietal cortex: Electrophysiological and pharmacological properties. *Brain Research, 362,* 122.

Lashley, K. S. (1938). Experimental analysis of instinctive behavior. *Psychological Reviews, 45,* 445–471.

Le Moal, M., & Simon, H. (1991). Mesocorticolimbic dopaminergic network: Functional and regulatory roles. *Physiological Review, 71,* 155–234.

Le Moine, C., & Bloch, B. (1995). D_1 and D_2 dopamine receptor gene expression in the rat striatum: Sensitive cRNA probes demonstrate prominent segregation of D_1 and D_2 mRNAs in the distinct neuronal population of dorsal and ventral striatum. *The Journal of Comparative Neurology, 355,* 418–426.

Louilot, A., Le Moal, M., & Simon, H. (1986). Differential reactivity of dopaminergic neurons in the nucleus accumbens in response to different behavioral situations: An in vivo voltammetric study in freely moving rats. *Brain Research, 397,* 395–400.

Lu, X.-Y., Ghasemzadeh, M. B., & Kalivas, P. W. (1998). Expression of D_1 receptor, D_2 receptor, substance P and enkephalin messenger RNAs in the neurons projecting from the nucleus accumbens. *Neuroscience, 82,* 767–780.

Maldonado-Irizarry, C. S., Swanson, C. J., & Kelley, A. E. (1995). Glutamate receptors in the nucleus accumbens shell control feeding behavior via the lateral hypothalamus. *The Journal of Neuroscience, 15,* 6779–6788.

McBride, W. J., Murphy, J. M., & Ikemoto, S. (1999). Localization of brain reinforcement mechanisms: Intracranial self-administration and intra-cranial place-conditioning studies. *Behavioural Brain Research, 101,* 129–152.

McDonald, A. J. (1996). Glutamate and aspartate immunoreactive neurons of the rat basolateral amygdala: Colocalization of excitory amino acids and projections to the limbic circuit. *The Journal of Comparative Neurology, 365,* 367–379.

McDonald, A. J., Mascagni, F., & Guo, L. (1996). Projections of the medial and lateral prefrontal cortices to the amygdala: A *Phaseolus vulgaris* leucoagglutinin study in the rat. *Neuroscience, 71,* 55–76.

McFarland, K., & Ettenberg, A. (1995). Haloperidol differentially affects reinstatement and motivational processes in rats running an alley for intravenous heroin. *Psychopharmacology, 122,* 346–350.

McFarland, K., & Ettenberg, A. (1997). Reinstatement of drug-seeking behavior produced by heroin-predictive environmental stimuli. *Psychopharmacology, 131,* 86–92.

McFarland, K., & Ettenberg, A. (1998). Haloperidol does not affect motivational processes in an operant runway model of food-seeking behavior. *Behavioral Neuroscience, 112,* 630–635.

McFarland, K., & Ettenberg, A. (1999). Haloperidol does not attenuate conditioned place preferences or locomotor activation produced by heroin- or food-predictive discriminative stimuli. *Pharmacology, Biochemistry, and Behavior.*

McFarland, K., & Kalivas, P. W. (2001). Circuitry mediating cocaine-induced reinstatement. *The Journal of Neuroscience.*

McGeer, P. L., Eccles, J. C., & McGeer, E. G. (1987). *Molecular neurobiology of the mammalian brain.* New York: Plenum Press.

Meil, W. M., & See, R. E. (1997). Lesions of the basolateral amygdala abolish the ability of drug associated cues to reinstate responding during withdrawal from self-administered cocaine. *Behavioural Brain Research, 87,* 139–148.

Mogenson, G. J., Brudzynski, S. M., Wu, M., Yang, C. R., & Yim, C. C. Y. (1993). From motivation to action: A review of dopaminergic regulation of limbic-nucleus accumbens-pedunculopontine nucleus circuitries involved in limbic-motor integration. In P. W. Kalivas & C. D. Barnes (Eds.), *Limbic motor circuits and neuropsychiatry* (pp. 193–236). Boca Raton, FL: CRC Press.

Mogenson, G. J., Ciriello, J., Garland, J., & Wu, M. (1987). Ventral pallidum projections to mediodorsal nucleus of the thalamus: An anatomical and electrophysiological investigation. *Brain Research, 404,* 221–230.

Mogenson, G. J., Jones, D. J., & Yim, C. Y. (1980). From motivation to action: Functional interface between the limbic system and the motor system. *Progress in Neurobiology, 14,* 69–97.

Mogenson, G. J., & Nielson, M. (1984). A study of the contribution of hippocampal-accumbens-pallidal projections to locomotor activity. *Behavioral and Neural Biology, 42,* 38–51.

Morris, R. G. M., Anderson, E., Lynch, G. S., & Baudry, M. (1986). Selective impariment of learning and blockade of long-term potentiation by an N-methyl-D-aspartate receptor antagonist, AP5. *Nature, 319,* 774–776.

Mucha, R. F., & Herz, A. (1985). Motivational properties of kappa and mu opioid receptor agonists studied with place and taste preference conditioning. *Psychopharmacology, 86,* 274–280.

Napier, T. C., & Mitrovic, I. (1999). Opioid modulation of ventral pallidal inputs. *Annals of the New York Academy of Sciences, 877,* 176–201.

Napier, T. C., Mitrovic, I., Churchill, L., Klitenick, M. A., & Kalivas, P. W. (1995). Substance P projection from the nucleus accumbens to the ventral pallidum: Anatomy, electrophysiology and behavior. *Neuroscience, 69,* 59–70.

Napier, T. C., Simson, P. E., & Givens, B. S. (1991). Dopamine electrophysiology of ventral pallidal/substantia innominata neurons: Comparison with the dorsal globus pallidus. *Journal of Pharmacology and Experimental Therapeutics, 258,* 249–257.

Nauta, W. J. H. (1961). Fiber degeneration following lesions of the amygdaloid complex in the monkey. *Journal of Anatomy, 95,* 515–531.

Nisenbaum, E. S., Berger, T. W., & Grace, A. A. (1993). Depression of glutamatergic and GABAergic synaptic responses in striatal spiny neurons by stimulation of presynaptic GABAB receptors. *Synapse, 14,* 221–242.

Nishikawa, T., Takasima, M., & Toru, M. (1983). Increased [3H]kainic acid-binding in the prefrontal cortex in schizophrenia. *Neuroscience Letters, 40,* 245–250.

O'Donnell, P., & Grace, A. A. (1995). Synaptic interactions among excitatory afferents to nucleus accumbens neurons: Hippocampal gating of prefrontal cortical input. *The Journal of Neuroscience, 15,* 3622–3639.

O'Donnell, P., & Grace, A. A. (1996). Dopaminergic reduction of excitability in nucleus accumbens neurons recorded in vitro. *Neuropsychopharmacology, 15,* 87–97.

O'Donnell, P., Greene, J., Pabello, N., Lewis, B. L., & Grace, A. A. (1999). Modulation of cell firing in the nucleus accumbens. *Annals of the New York Academy of Sciences, 877,* 157–175.

Olds, J., & Milner, P. (1954). Positive reinforcement produced by electrical stimulation of septal area and other regions of rat brain. *The Journal of Comparative and Physiological Psychology, 47,* 419–427.

Olive, M. F., Anton, B., Micevych, P., Evans, C. J., & Maidment, N. T. (1997). Presynaptic versus postsynaptic localization of mu and delta opioid receptors in dorsal and ventral striatalpallidal pathways. *The Journal of Neuroscience, 17,* 7471–7479.

Ono, T., Nishijo, H., & Nishino, H. (2000). Functional role of the limbic system and basal ganglia in motivated behavior. *Journal of Neurology, 247*(Suppl. 5), 23–32.

Otake, K., & Nakamura, Y. (2000). Possible pathways through which neurons of the shell of the nucleus accumbens influence the outflow of the core of the nucleus accumbens. *Brain Development, 22*(Suppl. 1), 17–26.

Parent, A., & Hazrati, L.-N. (1995). Functional anatomy of the basal ganglia: I. The cortico-basal ganglia-thalamo-cortical loop. *Brain Research Reviews, 20,* 91–128.

Parkinson, J., Robbins, T., & Everitt, B. (2000). Dissociable roles of the central and basolateral amygdala in appetitive emotional learning. *European Journal of Neuroscience, 12,* 405–413.

Pearl, S. M., & Glick, S. D. (1996). Prolonged antagonism of morphine-induced locomotor stimulation by kappa opioid agonists: Enhancement by prior morphine exposure. *Neuroscience Letters, 212,* 5–8.

Percheron, G., Francois, C., Yelnik, J., & Fenelon, G. (Eds.). (1989). *The primate nigro-striatal-pallido-nigral system: Not a mere loop.* London: John Libbey.

Pfeiffer, A., Brandt, V., & Herz, A. (1986). Psychotomimesis mediated by kappa opiate receptors. *Science, 233,* 774–776.

Pornnarin, T., Floresco, S. B., & Phillips, A. G. (2000). Hyperlocomotion and increased dopamine efflux in the rat nucleus accumbens evoked by electrical stimulation of the ventral subiculum: Role of ionotropic glutamate and dopamine D_1 receptors. *Psychopharmacology, 151,* 242–251.

Reardon, F., & Mitrofanis, J. (2000). Organisation of the amygdalothalamic pathways in rats. *Anatomy and Embryology, 201,* 75–84.

Robbins, T. W., Cador, M., Taylor, J. R., & Everitt, B. J. (1989). Limbic-striatal interactions in reward-related processes. *Biobehavioral Reviews, 13,* 155–162.

Roberts, A. C., & Wallis, J. D. (2000). Inhibitory control and affective processing in the prefrontal cortex: Neurophysiological studies in the common marmoset. *Cerebral Cortex, 10,* 252–262.

Roberts, D. C. S., & Andrews, M. M. (1997). Baclofen suppression of cocaine self-administration: Demonstration using a discrete trials procedure. *Psychopharmacology, 131,* 271–278.

Robinson, T., & Berridge, K. (1993). The neural basis of drug craving: An incentive-sensitization theory of addiction. *Research Reviews, 18,* 247–291.

Rolls, E. T., Critchlet, H. D., Mason, R., & Wakeman, E. A. (1996). Orbitofrontal cortex neurons: Role in olfactory and visual association learning. *Journal of Neurophysiology, 75,* 1970–1981.

Rosenkranz, J. A., & Grace, A. A. (1999). Modulation of basolateral amygdala neuronal firing and afferent drive by dopamine receptor activation in vivo. *Neuroscience, 19,* 11027–11039.

Sacaan, A. I., Bymaster, F. P., & Schoepp, D. D. (1992). Metabotropic glutamate receptor activation produced extrapyramidal motor system activation that is mediated by striatal dopamine. *Journal of Neurochemistry, 59,* 245–251.

Sala, M., Braida, D., Colombo, M., Groppetti, A., Sacco, S., Gori, E., et al. (1995). Behavioral and biochemical evidence of opioidergic involvement in cocaine sensitization. *Journal of Pharmacology and Experimental Therapeutics, 274,* 450–457.

Salamone, J., Kurth, P., McCullough, L., Sokolowski, J., & Cousins, M. (1993). The role of brain dopamine in response initiation: Effects of haloperidol and regionally specific dopamine depletions on the local rate of instrumental responding. *Brain Research, 628,* 218–226.

Salamone, J. D. (1994). The involvement of nucleus accumbens dopamine in appetitive and aversive motivation. *Behavioural Brain Research, 61,* 117–133.

Schenk, S., Partridge, V., & Shippenberg, T. (2000). Reinstatement of exinguished drug-taking behavior in rats: Effect of the kappa-opioid receptor agonist, U69593. *Psychopharmacology, 151*(1), 85–90.

Schilstrom, B., Fagerquist, M., Zhang, X., Hertel, P., Panagis, G., Nomikos, G., et al. (2000). Putative role of presynaptic α7* nicotinic receptors in nicotine stimulated increases of extracellular levels of glutamate and aspartate in the ventral tegmental area. *Synapse, 38,* 413–420.

Schneider, L. H., Davis, J. D., Watson, C. A., & Smith, G. P. (1990). Similar effects of raclopride and reduced sucrose concentration on the microstructure of sucrose sham feeding. *European Journal of Pharmacology, 186,* 61–70.

Schultz, W. (1998). Predictive reward signal of dopamine neurons. *American Journal of Physiology, 80,* 1–27.

Schultz, W., Apicella, P., & Ljungberg, T. (1993). Responses of monkey dopamine neurons to reward and conditioned stimuli during successive steps of learning a delayed response task. *The Journal of Neuroscience, 13,* 900–913.

Seamans, J. K., Floresco, S. B., & Phillips, A. G. (1998). D_1 receptor modulation of hippocampal-prefrontal cortical circuits integrating spatial memory with executive functions in the rat. *The Journal of Neuroscience, 18,* 1613–1621.

Sesack, S. R., Deutch, A. Y., Roth, R. H., & Bunney, B. S. (1989). Topographical organization of the efferent projections of the medial prefrontal cortex in rat: An anterograde tract-tracing study with *Phaseolus vulgais* leucoagglutinin. *The Journal of Comparative Neurology, 290,* 213–242.

Sesack, S. R., & Pickel, V. M. (1990). In the rat medial nucleus accumbens, hippocampal and catecholaminergic terminals converge on spiny neurons and are in apposition to each other. *Brain Research, 527,* 266–272.

Shreve, P. E., & Uretsky, N. J. (1989). AMPA, kalinic acid and N-methyl-D-aspartic acid stimulate locomotor activity after injection into the substantia innominata/lateral preoptic area. *Pharmacology, Biochemistry, and Behavior, 34,* 101–106.

Shreve, P. E., & Uretsky, N. J. (1990). GABA and glutamate interact in the substantia innominata/lateral preoptic area to modulate locomotor activity. *Pharmacology, Biochemistry, and Behavior, 38,* 385–388.

Skinner, B. F. (1950). Are learning theories necessary? *Psychological Reviews, 57,* 193–216.

Skinner, B. F. (Ed.). (1959). *Animal research in the pharmacotherapy of mental disease.* Washington, DC: National Academy of Sciences.

Smiley, J. F., & Goldman-Rakic, P. S. (1993). Heterogeneous targets of dopamine synapses in monkey prefrontal cortex demonstrated by serial section electron microscopy: A laminar analysis using the silver-enhanced diaminobenzidine sulfide (SEDS) immunolabeling technique. *Cerebral Cortex, 3*(3), 223–238.

Steiner, H., & Gerfen, C. R. (1998). Role of dynorphin and enkephalin in the regulation of striatal output pathways and behavior. *Experimental Brain Research, 123,* 60–76.

Stellar, J. R., Kelley, A. E., & Corbett, D. (1983). Effects of peripheral and central dopamine blockade on lateral hypthalamic self-stimulation: Evidence for both reward and motor deficits. *Pharmacology, Biochemistry, and Behavior, 18,* 433–442.

Stratford, T. R., & Kelley, A. E. (1997). GABA in the nucleus accumbens shell participates in the central regulation of feeding behavior. *The Journal of Neuroscience, 17,* 4434–4440.

Stratford, T. R., Kelley, A. E., & Simansky, K. J. (1999). Blockade of GABA$_A$ receptors in the medial ventral pallidum elicits feeding in satiated rats. *Brain Research, 825,* 199–203.

Swanson, L. W. (1982). The projections of the ventral tegmental area and adjacent regions: A combined fluorescent retrograde tracer and immunofluorescence study in the rat. *Brain Research Bulletin, 9,* 321–353.

Tamura, R., Ono, T., Fukuda, M., & Nishijo, H. (1992). Monkey hippocampal neuron responses to complex sensory stimulation during object discrimination. *Hippocampus, 2,* 287–306.

Thomas, M., Malenka, R., & Bonci, A. (2000). Modulation of long-term depression by dopamine in the mesolimbic system. *The Journal of Neuroscience, 20,* 5581–5586.

Timmerman, W., & Westerink, B. H. (1997). Brain microdialysis of GABA and glutamate: What does it signify? *Synapse, 27,* 242–261.

Timofeev, I., Grenier, F., & Steriade, M. (1998). Spike-wave complexes and fast components of cortically generated seizures: IV. Paroxysmal fast runs in cortical and thalamic neurons. *Journal of Neurophysiology, 80,* 1495–1513.

Tombaugh, T. N., Szostak, C., & Mills, P. (1983). Failure of pimozide to disrupt acquisition of light-dark and spatial discrimination problems. *Psychopharmacology, 79,* 161–168.

Tremblay, L., & Schultz, W. (1999). Relative reward preference in primate orbitofrontal cortex. *Nature, 382,* 629–632.

Uchimura, N., & North, R. A. (1991). Baclofen and adenosine inhibit synaptic potentials mediated by gamma-aminobutyric acid and glutamate release in the nucleus accumbens. *Journal of Pharmacology and Experimental Therapeutics, 258,* 663–668.

Vezina, P., Kalivas, P. W., & Stewart, J. (1987). Sensitization occurs to the locomotor effects of morphine and the specific mu opioid receptor agonist, DAGO, administered repeatedly to the VTA but not to the nucleus accumbens. *Brain Research, 417,* 51–58.

Vezina, P., & Kim, J. H. (1999). Metabotropic glutamate receptors and the generation of locomotor activity: Interactions with midbrain dopamine. *Neuroscience and Biobehavioral Reviews, 23,* 577–589.

Walker, J. M., Thompson, L. A., Frascella, J., & Friederich, M. W. (1987). Opposite effects of mu and kappa opiates on the firing-rate of dopamine cells in the substantia nigra of the rat. *European Journal of Pharmacology, 134,* 53–59.

Watanabe, M. (1996). Reward expectancy in primate prefrontal neurons. *Nature, 382,* 629–632.

Watson, J. B. (1913). Psychology as the behaviorist views it. *Psychological Reviews, 20,* 158–177.

Watson, J. B. (1919). *Psychology from the standpoint of a behaviorist.* Philedelphia: J. B. Lippincott.

Weiskrantz, L. (1956). Behavioral changes associated with the ablation of the amygdaloid complex in monkeys. *The Journal of Comparative and Physiological Psychology, 49,* 381–391.

Willins, D. L., Narayanan, S., Wallace, L. J., & Uretsky, N. J. (1993). The role of dopamine and AMPA/kainate receptors in the nucleus accumbens in the hypermotility response to MK801. *Pharmacology, Biochemistry, and Behavior, 46,* 881–887.

Willins, D. L., Wallace, L. J., Miller, D. D., & Uretsky, N. J. (1992). A-Amino-3-hydroxy-5-methylisoxazole-4-propionate/kainate receptor antagonists in the nucleus accumbens and ventral pallidum decrease the hypermotility response to psychostimulant drugs. *Journal of Pharmacology and Experimental Therapeutics, 260,* 1145– 1151.

Wilson, C. J., & Kawaguchi, Y. (1996). The origins of two-state spontaneous membrane potential fluctuations of neostriatal spiny neurons. *The Journal of Neuroscience, 16,* 2397–2410.

Wise, R. A. (1978). Neuroleptic attenuation of intracranial self-stimulation: Reward or performance deficits? *Life Science, 22,* 535–542.

Wise, R. A. (1982). Neuroleptics and operant behavior: The anhedonia hypothesis. *Behavioral Brain Sciences, 5,* 39–88.

Wise, R. A., & Rompre, P. P. (1989). Brain dopamine and reward. *Annual Review of Psychology, 40,* 191–215.

Wolf, M. E. (1998). The role of excitatory amino acids in behavioral sensitization to psychomotor stimulants. *Progress in Neuorobiology, 54,* 679–720.

Woodworth, R. S. (1918). *Dynamic psychology.* New York: Columbia University Press.

Wright, C. I., Beijer, V. J., & Groenewegen, H. J. (1996). Basal amygadaloid complex afferents to the rat nucleus accumbens are compartmentally organized. *The Journal of Neuroscience, 16,* 1877–1893.

Xi, Z.-X., & Stein, E. (1999). Baclofen inhibits heroin self-administration behavior and mesolimbic dopamine release. *Journal of Pharmacology and Experimental Therapeutics, 290,* 1369–1374.

Xu, M., Moratalla, R., Gold, L. H., Hiroi, N., Koob, G. F., Graybiel, A. M., et al. (1994). Dopamine D$_1$ receptor mutant mice are deficient in striatal expression of dynorphin and and in dopamine-mediated behavioral responses. *Cell, 79,* 729–742.

Yang, C. R., & Mogenson, G. J. (1985). An electrophysiological study of the neural projections from the hippocampus to the ventral pallidum and the subpallidal areas by way of the nucleus accumbens. *Neuroscience, 15,* 1015–1025.

Yang, C. R., & Seamans, J. K. (1996). Dopamine D$_1$ receptor actions in layers V-VI rat prefrontal cortex neurons in vitro: Modulation of dendritic-somatic signal integration. *The Journal of Neuroscience, 16,* 1922–1935.

Yang, C. R., Seamans, J. K., & Gorelova, N. (1999). Developing a neuronal model for the pathophysiology of schizophrenia based on the nature of electrophysiological actions of dopamine in the prefrontal cortex. *Neuropsychopharmacology, 21,* 161–194.

Yeomans, J. S. (1990). *Principles of brain stimulation.* New York: Oxford University Press.

Yim, C. Y., & Mogenson, G. J. (1988). Neuromodulatory action of dopamine in the nucleus accumbens: An in vivo intracellular study. *Neuroscience, 26,* 403–411.

Yokel, R. A., & Wise, R. A. (1976). Attenuation of intravenous amphetamine reinforcement by central dopamine blockade in rats. *Psychopharmacology, 48,* 311–318.

Zahm, D. S., & Brog, J. S. (1992). On the significance of subterritories in the "accumbens" part of the rat ventral striatum. *Neuroscience, 50,* 751–767.

Zahm, D. S., & Heimer, L. (1990). Two transpallidal pathways originating in the rat nucleus accumbens. *The Journal of Comparative Neurology, 302,* 437–446.

Zahm, D. S., Williams, E., & Wohltmann, C. (1996). Ventral striatopallidothalamic projection: IV. Relative involvements of neurochemically distinct subterritories in the ventral pallidum and adjacent parts of the rostroventral forebrain. *The Journal of Comparative Neurology, 364,* 340–362.

CHAPTER 15

Emotion

MICHAEL DAVIS AND PETER J. LANG

Fundamental concepts are often the hardest to define. Emotion seems to be one of these concepts. Most people's first try at a definition is to say, "Emotion is what I feel when I see or think about something, the way I react." It's also something hard to control. We get carried away in emotional experience. The sight of a snake frightens us; the smell of a rose pleases us. We all agree that words like love, adore, cherish, hate, and abhor describe our experiences of things we see or imagine. We know what it is to be joyful, happy, anxious, and depressed, and we agree that these mental states can fundamentally change our well-being. When we think further about emotion, we also realize that it is more than mental experience. It is something biological that humans certainly have but machines do not. And emotion is something we feel also going on in other people: We have no trouble inferring that a

baby who coos and smiles is happy, even though the baby does not tell us so verbally—although we may be less certain looking at an animal that can never speak to us.

It seems that everyone knows instinctively what emotion is, yet among scholars the concept of emotion has been the subject of huge debate. Few agree on the proper taxonomy. Are there two fundamental emotions or four or six or many more? Do animals have emotions like people do? Can we have emotion without consciousness? Are emotions innate, or are they all learned? All of these questions have consumed theorists over the years, and a rich literature explores the issues.

It is not the aim of this discourse to resolve these many knotty problems. Rather, it is our purpose to present an organizational framework that will help understanding of the biological foundations of emotion. Considering the data of emotion to be threefold (Lang, 1985, 1994)—affective language, behavior, and physiology—our emphasis here is on the latter two sources. We start with the view that emotions are products of evolution and that their expression in action and physiology is determined in significant part by brain structures and circuits that we share with other species.

This work was supported in part by National Institute of Mental Health Grants MH 47840, MH 57250, MH 58922, and MH 59906 and the Woodruff Foundation to M. D., NSF Contract No. IBN987675 to Emory University, and P50 MH52384, MH 37757, and MH43975 to P. J. L.

Although we cannot know whether animals experience emotion in the same way that humans do, it is clear that the expression of emotion can be very similar across the mammalian phyla. When a rat is confronted with a predatory cat, the animal's behavioral and physiological reactions are highly similar to those displayed, for example, by a human confronted with an intruder in the night. Members of both species freeze, and both show a change in heart rate and in breathing. Both release similar chemicals into their blood streams. In each case these events prepare the organism to attend to the potential threat and to ready the body for quick action. Furthermore, if animal and human escape the danger, both organisms will learn to be aroused and wary if cues related to that context should again be presented. These are patterns of behavior that have been carefully preserved in evolution because they are successful in promoting survival. Thus, much can be learned about the subject of this chapter, the biological basis of emotion, by studying the responses that commonly occur (and their determining neural circuitry) when humans and lower animals confront appetitive or aversive events.

A WORKING DEFINITION OF EMOTION

For the purpose of scientific study, emotion is best defined not as a single reaction, but as a process: Emotion involves multiple responses, organized according to temporal and spatial parameters. Thus, events that are positive-appetitive or aversive-threatening engage attention. They prompt information gathering, and do so more than other less motivationally relevant stimuli. Motive cues also occasion metabolic arousal, anticipatory responses that are oriented towards the engaging event, and this mobilization of the organism can lead to some action. Human beings report emotional experience, often the same emotion (e.g., fear, joy), while the multiple—and very different—components of the process unfold.

Imagine that you are sitting on a park bench reading the newspaper, and you hear voices in the distance. You immediately stop reading the paper, turn your head to the source of the voices, and try to figure out who is approaching. You soon realize it is a group of school children, talking amiably with each other as they approach. You go back to reading the paper and feel little reaction as they pass by.

Now imagine that you hear voices again. You stop reading the paper, turn your head in the direction of the voices, and listen and watch intently. You see a group of teenaged and even older men. They all have studded leather jackets, shaven heads, and heavily tattooed arms. It is clear that they have been drinking, and they are loud and lewd, and two of them are carrying something you cannot quite identify. As they come closer you see the two are carrying baseball bats, and one of them, who seems to be their leader, is staring directly at you. As they get closer and closer you begin to feel more and more apprehensive—you break out in a cold sweat and your breathing deepens. Suddenly you pick up your paper and quickly cross the street, trying not to look back to make it appear as if you intended to cross the street at that moment anyway. One of them shouts something that makes you pick up your pace even more in order to get around the corner out of sight.

In the third scenario you are back on the park bench, and you hear voices once again. You stop reading the paper, turn your head to the voices, and listen and watch intently. Again you hear the voices of a group of young adults, laughing and talking. As they get closer you notice they are your old high school friends, to whom you once were very close. Suddenly you recognize one of your very best friends in high school, whom you have not seen in many years. As he approaches you put down your paper and run to him and give him a big hug.

Emotional processing can be compressed into fractions of a second or can be considerably extended in time. The longer scenarios described here were chosen to highlight emotion's separate components. The sound of distant voices captured attention. This resulted in a cessation of what you were doing (reading the paper) and an active change in your behavior to allow you to take in information about the source of sound. You turned your head and listened and looked intently. Once you had stopped doing what you were doing and oriented to the voices, your brain began processing the input, automatically resolving its motivational relevance. Is the situation innocuous, positive, and potentially pleasant, or negative and threatening? As the various groups came closer, more information was available, and different behaviors resulted. Thus, attention was soon disengaged from the school children, and you continued reading. However, as evidence increased for either a happy encounter or a dangerous confrontation, motivation intensified. That is, the brain was more and more active, orchestrating a variety of changes in your body, initially in facilitating sensory acuity and attention, and then, more and more, to mobilize for action. These preparatory changes were physiologically widespread, involving cardiovascular and other autonomic responses, hormonal release into the blood stream, and a decrease and then a progressive increase in muscle tension. It is interesting to note that the two patterns of change—as you began anticipating a happy reunion or feared facing the dangerous-looking men—were in some ways similar (e.g., in initial sensory system response), and in other ways quite different (e.g., in hormonal biochemistry, and clearly in the final action). In this chapter we try to show that these two general reactions are mediated by overlapping brain circuits, connecting some unique and some common neural structures. That is, emotions are associated with two different but interdependent neural networks, activated either by appetitive or by aversive events.

Before leaving these examples it must also be noted that in many instances of emotional arousal the completing actions do not occur. The dangerous-looking men may change their direction, and you need not flee; when the anticipated friend gets closer, you realize that he is actually a stranger, and you return to your reading. More often, action is simply inhibited: If you run, the chase is on. Perhaps it is best to sit here quietly and wait for the danger to go away. Humans find many reasons to report states of affective arousal that are *not* followed by an action outcome. Indeed, much of emotional life occurs when cues mobilize us for approach or defense, but—for better or for worse—we do not act.

In this chapter we try to explicate what is special about emotional information processing in the brain. We propose that neural networks underlying emotion include direct connections to the brain's primary motivational systems: appetitive and defensive. These neural circuits were laid down early in our evolutionary history, in primitive cortex, subcortex, and midbrain, to mediate behaviors basic to the survival of individuals and species. Unconditioned and conditioned appetitive and aversive stimuli activate these motivational circuits. They determine the general mobilization of the organism, the deployment of reflexive attentional, approach, and defensive behaviors, and mediate the formation of conditioned associations originally based on primary reinforcement.

AFFECTIVE VALENCE, AROUSAL, AND THE PSYCHOPHYSIOLOGY OF EMOTION

The words *emotion* and *motivation* are both derived from the Latin word for *move: movere*. In fact, the behavior of a simple organism such as a flatworm can be characterized almost entirely by two survival movements: direct approach to appetitive stimuli and withdrawal from aversive stimuli (see Schneirla, 1959). This modest motivational repertoire would not, however, implement the many subgoals of more complex beings, nor effectively cope with a richly perceived sensory environment. Chained instrumental acts, behavioral delay, and response inhibition have all evolved, greatly elaborating the simple bidirectional paths of goal-related behavior. Thus danger cues, for example, can prompt an array of coping behaviors—freezing, defensive displays, and fight as well as flight.

Motivated behavior in humans is more adaptive, creative, and less predictable than is that in less evolved species.

Its most singularly human feature is the use of complex language—to communicate, to manipulate symbols in problem solving, and to label and catalog experiences of the world. Furthermore, as already noted, language is one of the major mediums through which we can know the emotional feelings of others. Indeed, for many psychologists and laypeople alike, understanding reported feelings is the cornerstone of emotion studies. Thus, despite our focus on the biological foundations of emotion, it will be useful to consider first how, in general, the self-evaluative language of emotion relates to the sensory system adjustments and autonomic and somatic responses that occur when humans confront emotionally arousing cues.

Feelings are often described as if they were actions. We say we were moved by a story we read or a play we enjoyed. It is not difficult to see in words such as love, adore, and cherish a common desire to approach some object or to think about a pleasant event. Words like hate, abhor, and detest all suggest a desire to avoid some object or thought. Indeed, the view that affects—subjective reports of emotion—might be organized by overarching motivational factors has been a common theoretical view at least since Wundt's (1896) *mental chemistry*. Contemporary studies of natural language categories (Ortony, Clore, & Collins, 1988; Shaver, Schwartz, Kirson, & O'Connor, 1987) suggest that emotional knowledge is hierarchically organized and that the superordinate division is between positivity (pleasant states: love, joy) and negativity (unpleasant states: anger, sadness, fear). Using the semantic differential, Osgood and his associates (e.g., Osgood, Suci, & Tannenbaum, 1957) showed that emotional descriptors were primarily distributed along a bipolar dimension of affective valence—ranging from attraction and pleasure to aversion and displeasure. A dimension of activation—from calm to aroused—also accounted for substantial variance. Similar conclusions have been drawn by other investigators using factor analysis of verbal reports (e.g., Mehrabian & Russell, 1974; Tellegen, 1985) as well as facial expressions (Schlosberg, 1952).

Emotional language appears highly differentiated and subtle; nevertheless, researchers concur that a single dominant factor accounts for a very considerable proportion of the variance in evaluative reports: Feelings are either pleasant or unpleasant. We either want more or less of an affect-arousing stimulus. Indeed, we may want *very much more* of a pleasant stimulus—or *very much less* of one that is unpleasant. Incentives can be scaled as more or less intense, and both pleasant and unpleasant stimulation can lead to different levels of arousal or activation. In the analysis of evaluative language, affective valence is primary, followed by affective arousal. No other factors have ever approached the generality and significance of these two simple variables.

We should not be too surprised, perhaps, to learn that affective valence and arousal find a parallel in motivational theories based on behavioral research with animals. For example, Konorski (1967) founded a motivational typology of unconditioned reflexes, keyed to the reflex's survival role. Exteroceptive reflexes were either *preservative* (e.g., ingestion, copulation, nurture of progeny) or *protective* (e.g., withdrawal from or rejection of noxious agents). He further suggested that affective states were consistent with this biphasic typology: *Preservative* emotions include such affects as sexual passion, joy, and nurturance; fear and anger are *protective* affects. Dickinson and Dearing (1979) developed Konorski's dichotomy into a theory of two opponent motivational systems, *aversive* and *attractive,* each activated by a different but equally wide range of unconditioned stimuli that determine perceptual-motor patterns and the course of learning. In this general view, affective valence is determined by the dominant motive system: the appetitive system (preservative-attractive) prompts positive affect; the defense system (protective-aversive) is the source of negative affect. Affective arousal reflects motivational mobilization, appetitive or defensive, modulated by changes in survival need or in the probability of nociception or appetitive consummation.

Attention and Emotion

As our opening scenarios suggested, emotion begins when attention is captured by a provocative stimulus. Following Pavlov (1927), attention begins with reflexive orienting of the activated sense receptors. Sokolov (1963) later developed a cortical model of this orienting reflex, suggesting that the brain held a template of the current sensory environment. He proposed that the reflex was evoked whenever a change in the perceptual field occurred (a pattern modification that did not match the template). Sokolov also described a second sensory reaction that had a protective function—the defense reflex—evoked when stimuli were intense, approaching the threshold of pain. These concepts of orienting and defense have proved useful even though the underlying phenomena are more complex than was at first appreciated.

Orienting is not, of course, a single reflex arc. Rather, this initial reaction to stimulation involves many subreflexes. In reacting to visual input, for example, there is a muscular aiming of the eye and pupillary dilation, coincident with a general inhibition of the gross somatic muscle activity, with accompanying vascular and cardiac changes. As a stimulus is conceptually resolved, the reflex pattern changes. On the one hand, if input has no motivational relevance, the initial attentional response soon habituates. Cues of appetite or aversion, on the other hand, lead to more sustained, singular patterns of attentional

processing. For example, an animal (reptile or mammal) orienting to a distant predator or other danger cue shows a profound deceleration in heart rate—*fear bradycardia*—not found in response to other events (Campbell, Wood, & McBride, 1997). This heart rate change is accompanied by *freezing*—a statue-like arresting of movement—and a general increase in sensitivity of all the sense receptors. If the predator approaches (shows stalking behavior), there is a increase in systemic activation that culminates in defensive action.

Attentional changes that are similar to the previous—in autonomic and somatic reflexes—occur when humans process affectively engaging stimuli. Furthermore, we respond reflexively even if the stimuli are not actual events, but media representations. Stories, pictures, and films all prompt patterns of bodily change that vary systematically with the reported affective valence (pleasant or unpleasant) and arousal (intensity) of the evoked reactions.

Valence and Arousal

In recent years the psychophysiology of emotional perception has been systematically studied by researchers using a set of standard photographic picture stimuli calibrated for affective response. There are currently over 700 pictures in the International Affective Picture System (IAPS; Lang, Bradley, & Cuthbert, 1998), and each picture is rated for experienced pleasure and arousal by a large normative subject sample. A representative group of IAPS pictures is presented in Figure 15.1 (Bradley, 2000) located in a Cartesian space formed by independent dimensions of rated pleasure and arousal. The distribution of these picture stimuli has an overall boomerang shape. Its two arms extend from a common calm, nonaffective base to either the high-arousal pleasant or high-arousal unpleasant quadrant. This distribution is curiously suggestive of an underlying two-system motivational structure: That is, affective pictures appear to be organized around two vectors—one that reflects a parameter of increasing appetitive motivation (higher self-ratings of arousal with increasing pleasantness) and a mirror image of increasing motivation for defense (higher arousal with ratings of increasing unpleasantness). The slopes of these vectors recall Neal Miller's (1959) description of approach and avoidance gradients, representing response strength over distance, from a remote site to the place of reward or punishment. In Miller's behavioral research, animals showed a precipitous increase in avoidance motivation with greater proximity to a site of punishment; the gradient of approach to a reward was significantly less steep. Similarly, for the picture distribution, the slope of the pleasant (appetitive input) vector is less steep than that of the unpleasant (aversive input) vector, consistent with the view that

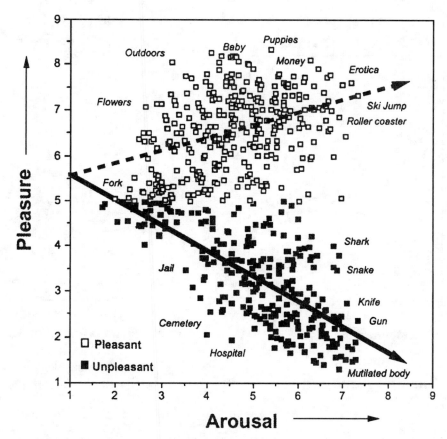

Figure 15.1   Pictures from the International Affective Picture System (Lang, Bradley, & Cuthbert, 1998) are plotted in a two-dimensional (Cartesian) space. Picture location is defined by mean ratings of judged pleasure and emotional arousal as reported by a normative sample. The vectors in the upper and lower portions of the affective space describe hypothesized increasing activation levels in appetitive and defensive motivation that covary with reported arousal.

defense motivation may increment more rapidly with increases in the incentive value of stimuli. Despite considerable effort to fill gaps in the affective picture space (e.g., in the unpleasant–low arousal quadrant) with a wider range of images, this vector pattern has remained stable over repeated studies. Similar distributions have also been obtained for collections of acoustic stimuli (International Affective Digitized Sounds, or IADS; Bradley, Cuthbert, & Lang, 1998) as well as verbal materials (Affective Norms for English Words, or ANEW; Bradley, Lang, & Cuthbert, 1998).

The Psychophysiology of Picture Perception

Studies of IAPS picture stimuli have uncovered highly reliable patterns of physiological and behavioral responses that vary systematically with experienced emotion (see Figure 15.2; Bradley et al., 2001; Greenwald, Bradley, Cuthbert, & Lang, 1998; Greenwald, Cook, & Lang, 1989). Thus, when affective valence ratings are ranked by picture from the most to the least pleasant image, facial muscle activity for each subject during picture viewing shows a strong monotonic relationship with level of affective valence: Corrugator (frown)

muscle action increases linearly as pictures are rated more unpleasant; conversely, zygomatic (smile) muscle activity increases with judged pleasantness. Heart rate is also responsive to differences in affective valence: Unpleasant pictures generally prompt marked deceleration during viewing (recalling the fear bradycardia seen in animals), less than is seen when subjects view pleasant pictures.

Other physiological responses vary with changes in rated emotional arousal, rather than affective valence. Skin conductance—a good general index of autonomic activation—increments monotonically with increases in rated arousal, regardless of picture valence. Electroencephalographic (EEG) measurement shows a distinct, voltage-positive cortical response, evoked directly by the picture stimuli, that is also positively correlated with stimulus arousal (i.e., it is similarly enhanced for both pleasant and unpleasant arousing pictures; Cuthbert, Schupp, Bradley, Birbaumer, & Lang, 1998). These measures appear to index the intensity or activation level of the current motivational state, but they are silent about motivational direction (i.e., appetitive or defensive).

Behaviors elicited in the context of emotional picture perception also covary with motivational parameters. When

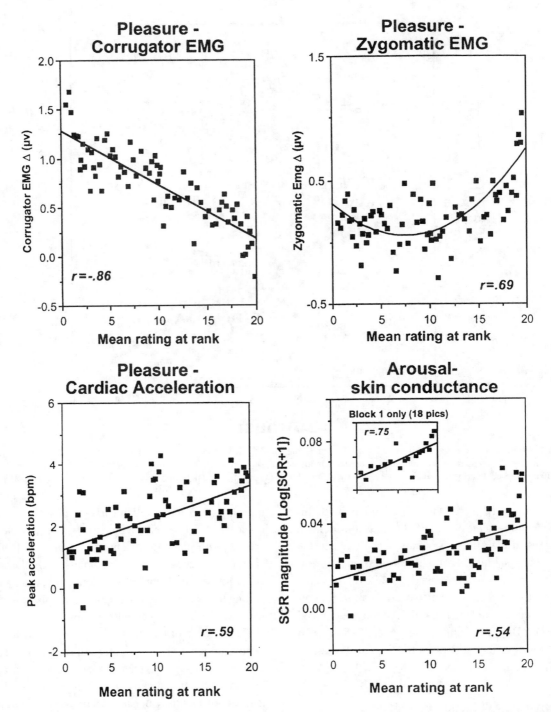

Figure 15.2   Covariation of physiological and self-reported emotional responses when pictures are rank ordered by pleasure or emotional arousal ratings for each subject, and these judgments are averaged over ranks. The mean change in corrugator EMG (top left) and zygomatic EMG (top right) is plotted as a function of the mean pleasure rating when pictures are ranked by pleasantness ratings for each individual. Peak heart rate (HR) change (bottom left) and the mean change in skin conductance (bottom right) are plotted as a function of the mean emotional arousal rating when pictures are ranked by arousal ratings for each individual. In each case, the correlations are significant.

people are first exposed to a new picture, reaction time responses to probes are significantly slower for emotionally arousing than for affectively calm pictures (Bradley, Greenwald, Petry, & Lang, 1992). These data suggest that new activating images may require more attentional resources

at encoding. The amount of time that observers choose to view different pictures also covaries with arousal. When normal subjects are placed in a free-viewing context, arousing unpleasant pictures are viewed as long as arousing pleasant pictures, and both are viewed for a longer duration than are unarousing pictures. As might be inferred from the popularity of slasher movies or from the habitual slowing of traffic at roadside accidents, normal subjects allocate more processing time to arousing, intense images, regardless of affective valence. This relationship does not persist if pictures evoke very high levels of distress: When individuals with phobias view pictures specific to their fears, viewing time is dramatically reduced (see Hamm, Cuthbert, Globisch, & Vaitl, 1997). They also show heart rate acceleration (rather than deceleration), consistent with a precipitous increase in defense motivation and mobilization for active escape.

As the phobia data imply, relationships between specific measures can vary widely for individuals, and to some extent between particular groups. Gender effects are clear. For example, pleasantness ratings covary more closely with facial muscle activity in females than in males; on the other hand, skin conductance changes are more closely correlated with arousal ratings in males than in females (Lang, Greenwald, Bradley, & Hamm, 1993). Overall, however, motivational variables of affective valence and arousal predominate in organizing the picture perception data.

The results of factor analyses of self-report, physiological, and behavioral measures of affect are presented in Table 15.1. The data were obtained from large groups of young, healthy participants. The obtained two-factor solution is clearly very strong: Pleasantness ratings, heart rate, and facial muscles load on a first *affective valence factor;* arousal and interest ratings, viewing time, skin conductance, and cortical EEG load on a second *affective arousal factor.* The cross-loadings for all measures are very low. The data are consistent with the view that reported affective experience is determined in significant part by the individual's motivational state. That is, negative affective valence (unpleasant feelings) is associated with activation of the defense system; positive valence (pleasant feelings) is associated with activation of the appetitive system. Reports of arousal are associated with both states, reflecting an increase in incentive strength and organismic mobilization. The motivational states elicited by these affective cues (and the somatic, cortical, and autonomic substrates of their perception) appear to be fundamentally similar to those occurring when other complex animals stop, look, and listen, sifting through the environmental buzz for cues of danger, social meaning, or incentives to appetite.

NEURAL SUBSTRATES OF AFFECT: ATTENTION, ACTION, AND THE ROLE OF THE AMYGDALA

Humans and animals show great similarity in behavioral and physiological response patterns to appetitive and defensive cues. Furthermore, the reports of affect that only humans provide seem to covary systematically with these shared motivational reactions and hence must involve homologous neural pathways. Thus, it is pertinent to ask, What can the neurophysiological study of animals tell us about human emotion? How are the autonomic and somatic reflex reactions in emotion—the signatures of feeling and affect—determined in the brain?

Much recent research has shown that a brain area called the amygdala is a crucial nodal point in a neural network that mediates motivated attention and preparation for action (i.e., what we have called emotional processing). In man, the amygdala lies deep in the brain's temporal lobe (Figure 15.3). Although this small, almond-shaped structure is made up of several different nuclei, it is popularly imagined as a single unit. Recent research suggests, however, that individual nuclei play very different functional roles. The basolateral amygdala is of particular significance. It projects to several target areas (other amygdala nuclei and nuclei elsewhere in the brain), forming a broad neural network that serves a variety of specialized functions (Figure 15.4). The network is activated by information that comes to the basolateral nucleus (either directly or via the amygdala's lateral nucleus) from the thalamus, hippocampus, and cerebral cortex (for a highly comprehensive review in rats, monkeys, and cats, see McDonald, 1998). The basolateral nucleus then projects to several brain areas, mediating memory and an array of reflex responses that are the basic stuff of emotional processing.

TABLE 15.1   Factor Analyses of Measures of Emotional Picture Processing Sorted Loadings of Dependents Measures on Principal Components

Measure	Factor 1 (Valence)	Factor 2 (Arousal)
From Lang Greenwald, Bradley, & Hamm (1993)		
Valence ratings	.86	−.00
Corrugator muscle*	−.85	.19
Heart rate	.79	−.14
Zygomatic muscle*	.58	.29
Arousal ratings	.15	.83
Interest ratings	.45	.77
Viewing time	−.27	.76
Skin conductance	−.37	.74
From Cuthbert, Schupp, Bradley, Birbaumer, & Lang (1998)		
Valence ratings	.89	.07
Corrugator muscle*	−.83	−.10
Heart rate	.73	−.02
Arousal ratings	−.11	.89
Cortical slow wave	−.06	−.79
Skin conductance	.19	.77

*Bioelectrical potentials from muscles that mediate facial expression.

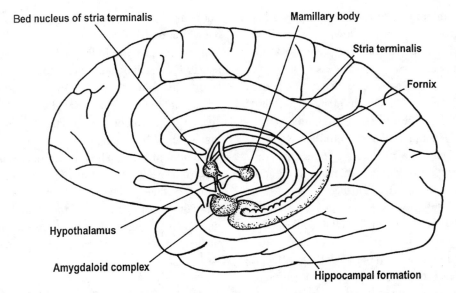

Figure 15.3 Schematic diagram of the amygdaloid complex in the human brain. (From Davis, 2000, with permission, Oxford University Press.)

The Anatomy of Emotion: Projections from the Amygdala's Central Nucleus and the Extended Amygdala

We are now ready to consider more specifically how this emotion network, activated when an animal is under threat or stress, mediates the reflex responses of defense—responses that we often see also in humans when they report unpleasant affect. As noted in Figure 15.4, the projection from the basolateral nucleus to the central nucleus of the amygdala provides a path to target areas that mediate many of the autonomic and somatic changes found in fear and anxiety. A nearby structure, the bed nucleus of the stria terminalis (BNST; sometimes called part of the extended amygdala) has similar projections. Figure 15.5 is a schematic diagram of outputs from the central nucleus (CeA) and the BNST. These nuclei project to specific hypothalamic and brain-stem target areas that mediate most of the visceral and striate muscle events that index emotional processing.

Autonomic and Hormonal Measures of Fear

The amygdala's central nucleus, as well as the BNST, sends prominent projections to the lateral hypothalamus—a key center activating the sympathetic branch of the autonomic nervous system in emotion (LeDoux, Iwata, Cicchetti, & Reis, 1988). In addition, direct projections from the lateral extended amygdala go to the dorsal motor nucleus of the vagus, the nucleus of the solitary tract, and the ventrolateral medulla. These brain-stem nuclei are known to regulate heart rate and blood pressure (Schwaber, Kapp, Higgins, & Rapp, 1982) and may thus modulate cardiovascular responses in emotion. Projections to the parabrachial nucleus are likely to be involved in emotion's respiratory changes (with additional effects, perhaps indirect, on the cardiovascular system), as electrical stimulation and lesions of this nucleus alter breathing patterns. Finally, indirect projections from the amygdala's central nucleus to the paraventricular nucleus (via the BNST and preoptic area) may mediate the slower

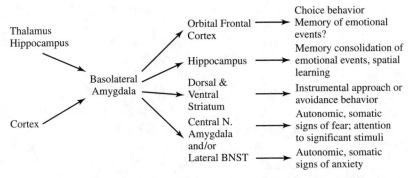

Figure 15.4 Schematic diagram of the outputs of the basolateral nucleus of the amygdala to various target structures and possible functions of these connections.

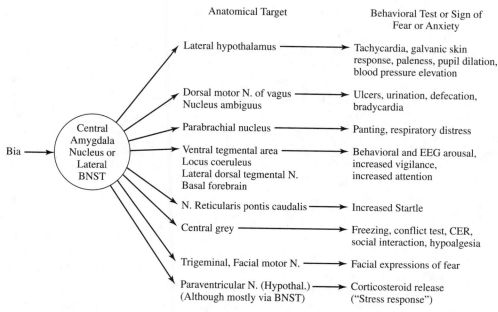

Figure 15.5 Output pathways from the amygdala complex

neuroendocrine responses that are particularly prominent when emotional stimuli are sustained.

Attention, Vigilance, and Conditioned Fear

During emotional stimulation, projections from the central nucleus or BNST to the ventral tegmental area appear to mediate increases in dopamine metabolites in the prefrontal cortex (Goldstein, Rasmusson, Bunney, & Roth, 1996). Cells in the locus coeruleus are also activated, perhaps mediated by projections to its dendritic field or indirectly via projections to the paragigantocellularis nucleus (Aston-Jones, Rajkowski, Kubiak, Valentino, & Shipley, 1996; Redmond, 1977). Furthermore, there are direct projections to the lateral dorsal tegmental nucleus and parabrachial nuclei. These latter nuclei have cholinergic neurons that project to the thalamus and could mediate increased synaptic transmission of its sensory relay neurons. The sensory thalamus is, of course, a primary processor of environmental input. Thus, this sequence of projections, by augmenting cholinergic activation and facilitating thalamic transmission, may contribute to the increased vigilance and superior signal detection found in the attentional phase of emotional processing.

As already noted, most animals and reptiles react to the appearance of a predator in the distance with immobility and sensory orientation toward the threat. This behavioral pattern is accompanied by a profound decrease in heart rate, referred to as fear bradycardia (Campbell et al., 1997). A similar change in heart rate is associated with increased attention in humans (Graham & Clifton, 1966); furthermore, a greater deceleration is generally found in response to stimuli judged to be unpleasant (Bradley, 2000; Lang et al., 1993). Several lines of research suggest that this cardiac response can be mediated by the central nucleus of the amygdala. During Pavlovian aversive conditioning in rabbits, one sees a rapid development of conditioned bradycardia. Pascoe and Kapp (1985) found a high correlation (.71) between the firing frequency of a population of individual neurons in the amygdala's central nucleus and the degree to which heart rate decelerated in response to the conditioned stimulus. Furthermore, as emphasized by Kapp and colleagues (Kapp, Whalen, Supple, & Pascoe, 1992), the central nucleus of the amygdala also has the potential for indirect but widespread effects on cortical activity—mediated by projections to cholinergic neurons that in turn project to the cortex. This is a probable path, prompting the low-voltage, fast-EEG activity that readies the cortex for sensory information processing. These changes in the EEG waveform are acquired during Pavlovian aversive conditioning at the same rate as conditioned bradycardia.

Changes in Motor Behavior

Emotional processing involves both attentional engagement and behaviors preparatory to, or part of, motivated action. Emotion's attentional phase is characterized by immobility. Research by many investigators has implicated projections from the central nucleus of the amygdala to the ventral periaqueductal gray in the freezing response of the rat, whereas projections to the dorsal periaqueductal gray appear to mediate active fight-flight responses. The latter, defensive actions must often be engaged quickly, and both norepinephrine and serotonin facilitate excitation of motor neurons (McCall & Aghajanian, 1979; White & Neuman, 1980). This enhanced motor performance in emotion could be mediated by the lateral extended amygdala's activation of norepinephrine release in the locus coeruleus, or via its projections to serotonin containing raphe neurons.

Experimental Elicitation of Emotional Responses: Amygdala Stimulation

Electrical and Chemical Stimulation

Electrical stimulation of the amygdala (or abnormal electrical activation via temporal lobe seizures) can produce a complex pattern of behavioral and autonomic changes that, taken together, resemble a state of heightened emotion. This effect is probably attributable to amygdala outputs that simultaneously activate the many target areas seen in Figure 15.4. In humans the most common emotional experience reported after electrical stimulation of the amygdala is one of fear or apprehension, accompanied by autonomic reactions (Chapman et al., 1954; Gloor, Olivier, & Quesney, 1981). In animals, electrical or chemical stimulation of the amygdala produces prominent cardiovascular effects that depend on the species, site of stimulation, and state of the animal. Persistent stimulation can also produce gastric ulceration, increases in blood levels of cortisol and epinephrine, and sustained changes in respiration.

Studies in several species indicate that electrical stimulation of the amygdala's central nucleus increases processes associated with attention. Thus, stimulation of the same sites in the central nucleus can produce both bradycardia (Kapp, Wilson, Pascoe, Supple, & Whalen, 1990) and low-voltage, fast-EEG activity in rabbits (Kapp, Supple, & Whalen, 1994) and in rats (Dringenberg & Vanderwolf, 1996). Furthermore, depending on the state of sleep, electrical stimulation of the amygdala in some species activates cholinergic cells that are involved in arousal-like effects. Overall, the orienting reflex has been described as the most common response elicited by electrical stimulation of the amygdala (Applegate, Kapp, Underwood, & McNall, 1983; Ursin & Kaada, 1960).

In many species, electrical or chemical stimulation of the amygdala produces a palpable cessation of ongoing behavior. This immobility facilitates sensory orienting and is a critical attentional component of emotion. In rats, the response is measured by freezing, or by the cessation of operant bar pressing. Electrical stimulation of the amygdala also activates facial motoneurons, eliciting jaw movements, and may be the pathway mediating the facial expressions that characterize emotional states. In fact, amygdala stimulation appears to have very broad effects on the motor system, including the modulation brain-stem reflexes, such as the massenteric, baroreceptor nictitating membrane, eye-blink, and startle reflexes.

In summary, the stimulation data show that the amygdala projects to a variety of target areas, each of which is critical for a different aspect of emotional processing. Moreover, it must be assumed that these connections are already formed in an adult organism, as electrical and chemical stimulation produce these effects in the absence of explicit prior learning. This suggests that a significant part of the behavioral pattern evoked by emotional stimuli may have been hardwired during evolution. Thus, it is only necessary that an initially neutral stimulus activate the amygdala—in association, for example, with an aversive event—for this formerly neutral cue then to produce the full constellation of emotional effects. The complex patterns of behavioral changes seen during emotional processing—the modulation of afferent and efferent systems—are produced by virtue of the innate connections between the amygdala and the implementing brain target sites.

Effects of Amygdala Lesions and Drug Infusion on the Emotion Circuit

Attention to Motivational Cues

If the emotion circuit that we have described is truly a unique, hardwired set of connections, then destruction of the amygdala can be expected to disrupt or eliminate emotion's sensory processing and motor output. Various investigators have provided data in support of this hypothesis, showing, for example, that lesions of the amygdala block attentional responses to stimuli paired with food (cf. Gallagher, Graham, & Holland, 1990). In general, rats with these lesions fail to benefit from procedures that normally facilitate attention to stimuli conditioned to primary reinforcers (Holland & Gallagher, 1993a, 1993b).

As already noted, however, the amygdala is a complex structure in which the different nuclei play different roles. Thus, lesions of the central nucleus and the basolateral nucleus each have unique effects on the phenomenon known as taste-potentiated odor aversion learning. In this test, which requires processing information in two sensory modalities, rats develop aversions to a novel odor paired with illness only when the odor is presented in compound with a distinctive gustatory stimulus. Electrolytic (Bermudez-Rattoni, Grijalva, Kiefer, & Garcia, 1986) or chemical lesions

(Hatfield, Graham, & Gallagher, 1992) of the basolateral but not the central nucleus blocked taste-potentiated odor aversion learning even though they had no effect on taste aversion learning itself. Local infusion of N-methyl-D-aspartate (NMDA) antagonists into the basolateral nucleus also blocked the acquisition but not the expression of taste-potentiated odor aversion, but again had no effect on taste aversion learning (Hatfield & Gallagher, 1995). Based on these and other data, Hatfield, Han, Conley, Gallagher, and Holland (1996) suggested that the amygdala's central nucleus "regulates attentional processing of cues during associative conditioning" (p. 5265), whereas the basolateral nuclei are critically involved in "associative learning processes that give conditioned stimuli access to the motivation value of their associated unconditioned stimuli" (p. 5264). Thus, the different amygdalar nuclei work in concert, orchestrating the components of emotional learning that determine the motivational significance of input and act to maintain the relevant cue as a focus of attention.

Conditioned Emotional States

One of the most widely studied examples of emotion in animals is conditioned fear. Fear is here defined by the pattern of behavior evoked by stimuli previously paired with an aversive event (e.g., electric shock). A large literature indicates that lesions of the amygdala block many measures used to assess conditioned and unconditioned fear (cf. Davis, 2000). These include autonomic measures such as changes in heart rate, blood pressure, ulcers, respiration, and secretion of adrenocorticotropic hormone (ACTH), or corticosteroids into the blood or release of dopamine, norepinephrine, or serotonin in certain brain areas. They include behavioral measures such as freezing, fear-potentiated startle and vocalization, and several operant measures (operant conflict test, conditioned emotional response, avoidance of a electrified shock probe). Furthermore, lesions of the amygdala cause a general taming effect in many species (Goddard, 1964), perhaps analogous to the increase in trust found in humans following surgical amygdala lesions (Adolphs, Tranel, & Damasio, 1998).

Effects of Local Infusion of Drugs

Fear levels vary depending on many circumstances, and they can be mild or extremely intense. It is not surprising, therefore, that the intensity of fear is determined by the interplay of a variety of chemicals in the brain, many of which act directly in the amygdala. Local infusion of compounds that inhibit neuronal activity in the amygdala by acting through gamma-aminobutyric acid (GABA), a major inhibitory neuro-

transmitter in the brain, reduce fear. These include GABA itself, GABA agonists, and benzodiazepines, such as valium, which increase GABA transmission. Drugs that decrease excitatory transmission in the amygdala, such as glutamate antagonists, have similar actions. Neurotransmitters that modulate glutamate excitation or GABA inhibition in the amygdala, such as norepinephrine, dopamine and serotonin, and peptides such as corticotropin-releasing hormone (CRH), cholecystokinin (CCK), neuropeptide Y, vasopressin, thyroid-releasing hormone (TRH), and opiates also are important.

Table 15.2 gives selected examples of some of these studies in which local infusion of various compounds reduces measures of fear. These include GABA or GABA agonists, benzodiazepines, CRH antagonists, opiate agonists, neuropeptide Y, dopamine antagonists, and glutamate antagonists. Table 15.3 gives selected examples of studies in which local infusion of various compounds increase measures of fear. These include GABA antagonists, CRH or CRH analogues, vasopressin, TRH, opiate antagonists, CCK, and CCK analogues. More extensive tables can be found in Davis (2000).

The Role of the Central Nucleus of the Amygdala in Appetitive and Approach Behavior

In a systematic and comprehensive series of experiments, Barry Everitt, Trevor Robbins, and colleagues (cf. Everitt, Cardinal, Hall, Parkinson, & Robbins, 2000) provided a new and very important theory about the role of the amygdala in appetitive conditioning. These studies emphasize the projection from the central nucleus of the amygdala to dopamine neurons in the ventral tegmental area that project to the ventral striatum (nucleus accumbens), a region of the brain that is important for approach behavior when Pavlovian conditioning is measured in appetitive situations.

In one series of experiments using the phenomenon of autoshaping, a light (CS+) is presented followed by delivery of food in a different location, regardless of what the rat is doing. Another stimulus (CS−) is also presented but never followed by food. Under these conditions, rats learn to approach the CS+ light before going to the food hopper to retrieve the food. Bilateral lesions of the central nucleus of the amygdala, but not lesions of the basolateral nucleus of the amygdala (Bla), markedly disrupted this approach behavior (Parkinson, Robbins, & Everitt, 2000). The importance of the central nucleus in this form of approach behavior seems to be mediated by its projection to dopamine-containing neurons in the ventral tegmental area and the consequent release of dopamine in the nucleus accumbens because depletion of dopamine in the nucleus accumbens core eliminates the

TABLE 15.2 Effects of Local Infusion Into the Amygdala of Various Neurotransmitter Agonists on Selected Measures of Fear and Anxiety

Substance	S	Site	Effect of Substance Infused	Reference
GABA or chlordiazepoxide	R	Ce	Decrease stress-induced gastric ulcers	(Sullivan, Henke, Ray, Hebert, & Trimper, 1989)
GABA or Benzodiazepines	R	Bla	Increase punished responding in operant conflict test (Anticonflict effect)	(Green & Vale, 1992; Hodges, Green, & Glenn, 1987; Petersen, Braestrup, & Scheel-Kruger, 1985; Scheel-Kruger & Petersen, 1982; Thomas, Lewise, & Iversen, 1985)
Benzodiazepines	R	Ce	Increase punished responding in operant conflict test (Anticonflict effect)	(Shibata, Kataoka, Yamashita, & Ueki, 1986; Takao, Nagatani, Kasahara, & Hashimoto, 1992)
Midazolam	R	Bla	More time on open arms in plus-maze, no effect on shock probe avoidance	(Pesold & Treit, 1995)
Diazepam	R	Ce or Bla	Decrease freezing to footshock	(Helmstetter, 1993; Young, Helmstetter, Rabchenuk, & Leaton, 1991)
Diazepam	Mice	AC	More time in light side in light-dark box test (Anxiolytic effect)	(Costall, Kelly, Naylor, Onaivi, & Tyers, 1989)
Muscimol	R	Bla	Anxiolytic effect in the social interaction test. No effect in Ce	(Sanders & Shekhar, 1995)
Muscimol	R	Bla	Increase punished responding in operant conflict test (Anticonflict effect). No effect in Ce	(Scheel-Kruger & Petersen, 1982)
a-CRH	R	Ce	Block noise-elicited increase in tryptophan hydroxylase in cortex	(Boadle-Biber, Singh, Corley, Phan, & Dilts, 1993)
a-CRH	R	Ce	Anxiolytic effect (plus maze) in socially defeated rat	(Heinrichs, Pich, Miczek, Britton, & Koob, 1992)
a-CRH	R	Ce	Anxiolytic effect in plus maze during ethanol withdrawal in ethanol dependent rats. No effect in plus maze in non-dependent rats	(Rassnick, Heinrichs, Britton, & Koob, 1993)
a-CRH	R	Ce	Decrease behavioral effects of opiate withdrawal	(Heinrichs, Menzaghi, Schulteis, Koob, & Stinus, 1995)
CRH receptor antisense	R	Ce	Anxiolytic effect in the plus maze in rats that previously experienced defeat stress	(Liebsch et al., 1995)
a-CRH	R	Ce	Decrease duration of freezing to an initial shock treatment or to re-exposure to shock box 24 hrs later	(Swiergiel, Takahashi, & Kalin, 1993)
a-CRH	R	Ce	No effect on grooming and exploration activity under stress-free conditions	(Wiersma, Baauw, Bohus, & Koolhaas, 1995)
Enkephalin analog	R	Ce	Decrease stress-induced gastric ulcers, prevented by 6-OHDA or clozapine	(Ray & Henke, 1990; Ray & Henke, 1991; Ray, Sullivan, & Henke, 1988)
Opiate agonists	Rb	Ce	Block acquisition of conditioned bradycardia	(Gallagher, Kapp, McNall, & Pascoe, 1981; Gallagher, Kapp, & Pascoe, 1982)
Morphine	R	Ce	Anxiolytic effect in social interaction test	(File & Rodgers, 1979)
Neuropeptide Y	R	Bla, Not Ce	Anxiolytic effect in social interaction test, blocked by Y-1 antagonist	(Sajdyk, Vandergriff, & Gehlert, 1999)
Neuropeptide Y1 agonist	R	Ce	Anxiolytic effects in conflict test. NPY-Y2 agonist much less potent	(Heilig et al., 1993)
Oxytocin	R	Ce	Decrease stress-induced bradycardia and immobility responses	(Roozendaal, Wiersma, Driscoll, Koolhaas, & Bohus, 1992)
SCH 23390	R	AC	Decrease expression of fear-potentiated startle	(Lamont & Kokkinidis, 1998)
SCH 23390	R	AC	Decrease acquisition and expression of freezing to tone or context. Not due to state dependent learning	(Guarraci, Frohardt, & Kapp, 1999)
CNQX	R	Bla	Blocks expression of fear-potentiated startle (visual or auditory CS)	(Kim, Campeau, Falls, & Davis, 1993)
NBQX	R	Bla or Ce	Blocks expression of fear-potentiated startle (visual CS)	(Walker & Davis, 1997)
AP 5	R	Bla	Block facilitation of eyeblink conditioning by prior stress when given prior to stressor session	(Shors & Mathew, 1998)
AP5 or CNQX	R	Bla	Anxiolytic effect in social interaction test	(Sajdyk & Shekhar, 1997b)
CNQX	R	Ce	Decrease naloxone precipitated withdrawal signs in morphine dependant rats	(Taylor, Punch, & Elsworth, 1998)

TABLE 15.3   Effects of Local Infusion Into the Amygdala of Various Neurotransmitter Antagonists on Selected Measures of Fear and Anxiety

Substance	S	Site	Effect of Substance Infused	Reference
Bicuculline, picrotoxin	R	Bla	Anxiogenic effects in the social interaction test. Repeated infusion led to sensitization	(Sanders & Shekhar, 1995)
Bicuculline	R	Bla	Anxiogenic effects in social interaction, blocked by either NMDA or non-NMDA antagonists into the amygdala	(Sajdyk & Shekhar, 1997a)
Bic (un)	R	Bla Not Ce	Increases in blood pressure heart rate and locomotor activity. Bigger effect with repeated infusions	(Sanders & Shekhar, 1991; Sanders & Shekhar, 1995)
Bic (un)	R	Bla	Increases in blood pressure, heart rate. Blocked by infusion of either NMDA or non-NMDA antagonists into the amygdala	(Sajdyk & Shekhar, 1997a)
Bic, NMDA, AMPA (un)	R	Bla	Increases in blood pressure, heart rate blocked by either NMDA or non-NMDA antagonists infused into Bla or the dorsomedial hypothalamus	(Soltis, Cook, Stratton, & Flickinger, 1998; Soltis, Cook, Gregg, & Sanders, 1997)
CRH	R	Ce	Increase heart rate. Effect blocked by a-CRH into Ce	(Wiersma, Bohus, & Koolhaas, 1993)
CRH, TRH or CGRP	R	Ce	Increase in blood pressure, heart rate and plasma catecholamines	(Brown & Gray, 1988)
Urocortin or CRH	R	Bla	After repeated subthreshold doses get increase in blood pressure to systemic lactate	(Sajdyk, Schober, Gehlert, & Shekhar, 1999)
CRH	R	Ce, not Bla	Increased grooming and exploration in animals tested under stress-free conditions (i.e., in the home cage)	(Wiersma et al., 1995; Wiersma, Tuinstra, & Koolhaas, 1997)
CRH	R	Ce	Increase defensive burying	(Wiersma, Bohus, & Koolhaas, 1977)
CRH or Urocortin	R	Bla	Anxiogenic effect in plus maze, sensitization with repeated subthreshold doses. Now get behavioral and cardiovascular effects to systemic lactate	(Sajdyk et al., 1999a)
Vasopressin	R	Ce	Increased stress-induced bradycardia and immobility responses in rats bred for low rates of avoidance behavior but not the more aggressive rats that show high avoidance rates	(Roozendaal et al., 1992)
Vasopressin	R	Ce	Bradycardia (low doses) or tachycardia and release of corticosterone (high dose). Tachycardia blocked by oxytocin antagonist	(Roozendaal, Schoorlemmer, Koolhaas, & Bohus, 1993)
Vasopressin	R	Ce	Immobility, seizures second infusion	(Willcox, Poulin, Veale, & Pittman, 1992)
Vasopressin	R	Ce	Immobility in rats bred for low rates of avoidance but not bred for high avoidance rates	(Roozendaal et al., 1992)
TRH	R	Ce	Increase stress-induced gastric ulcers	(Ray & Henke, 1991; Ray et al., 1988)
TRH or physostigmine	R	Ce	Increase stress-induced gastric ulcers, blocked by muscarinic or benzodiazepine agonists	(Ray, Henke, & Sullivan, 1990)
TRH analogue	R	Ce	Increase gastric contractility, blocked by vagotomy	(Morrow, Hodgson, & Garrick, 1996)
TRH	R	Ce	Produce gastric lesions and stimulated acid secretion	(Hernandez, Salaiz, Morin, & Moreira, 1990)
TRH analogue	R	AC	No effect on gastric secretion, whereas large effect after infusion into dorsal vagal complex or nucleus ambiguus	(Ishikawa, Yang, & Tache, 1988)
Naloxone	R	Ce	Increase stress-induced gastric ulcers	(Ray & Henke, 1991; Ray et al., 1988)
Naloxone	R	AC	Elicit certain signs of withdraw (depending on site) in morphine dependant rats (unilateral)	(Calvino, Lagowska, & Ben-Ari, 1979)
Methyl-naloxonium	R	AC	Place aversion to context where injections given to morphine dependant rats	(Stinus, LeMoal, & Koob, 1990)
Methyl-naloxonium	R	AC	Weak withdrawal signs in morphine dependant rats	(Maldonado, Stinus, Gold, & Koob, 1992)
Yohimbine	R	Ce	Facilitation of the startle reflex	(Fendt, Koch, & Schnitzler, 1994)
CCK analogues	R	AC	Anxiogenic effect in plus maze but not clear because significant decrease in overall activity	(Belcheva, Belcheva, Petkov, & Petkov, 1994)
Pentagastrin	R	AC	Increase acoustic startle, blocked by CCK B antagonist that also blocked effect of pentagastrin (icv)	(Frankland, Josselyn, Bradwejn, Vaccarino, & Yeomans, 1997)

acquisition of autoshaping (Parkinson et al., 1998). In contrast, the approach behavior itself seems to be mediated by the anterior cingulate cortex (Bussey, Everitt, & Robbins, 1997) via projections to the nucleus accumbens core (Parkinson, Willoughby, Robbins, & Everitt, 2000).

In another series of experiments, rats were first trained to associate an auditory CS with delivery of food. In a second phase these rats were trained to press a lever to obtain food. In the test phase, presentation of the auditory CS led to an increase in lever pressing for food. Lesions of the central nucleus of the amygdala, but not the Bla, reduced this facilitatory effect (Everitt et al., 2000). These authors speculate that this is mediated by projections from the central nucleus to the mesolimbic dopamine system.

On the other hand, just the opposite effects have been reported when a CS previously paired with food increases the actual consumption of food (Gallagher, 2000). In this case, projections from the posterior division of the basolateral amygdala to the hypothalamus are thought to be involved.

The Basolateral Nucleus Projects Beyond the Amygdala and the Extended Amygdala

It is clear that connections between the amygdala's central nucleus and the BNST are critically involved in many of the autonomic and motor responses seen in emotion. As described earlier, projections from the central nucleus to the mesolimbic dopamine system are involved in modulating certain types of approach behavior, as well as the invigorating effects of a stimulus previously paired with reward on instrumental behavior. However, it is also the case that there are direct connections between the basolateral nucleus and other target areas in the brain. These latter targets are also important mediators of emotional behaviors (see Figure 15.4).

The Ventral Striatum Pathway: Secondary Reinforcement

The Bla projects directly to the nucleus accumbens in the ventral striatum (McDonald, 1991), in close apposition to dopamine terminals of A10 cell bodies in the ventral tegmental area (cf. Everitt & Robbins, 1992). Morgenson and colleagues suggested that the ventral striatum was the site where affective processes in the limbic forebrain gained access to subcortical elements of the motor system that resulted in appetitive actions (cf. Morgenson, 1987).

Projections from the Bla to the nucleus accumbens are critically involved in secondary reinforcement. In this paradigm, a light is paired with food. Animals are then presented with two levers. Pressing one lever turns on the light, whereas pressing the other one does not. Normal rats press

the lever that turns on the light much more often than they press the other lever. Hence, the light serves to reinforce new behavior via its prior association with food and is called a secondary reinforcer. Rats with lesions of the Bla fail to learn this discrimination, whereas rats with lesions of the CeA do (Burns, Robbins, & Everitt, 1993; Cador, Robbins, & Everitt, 1989). Connections between the Bla and the ventral striatum also are involved in conditioned place preference (Everitt, Morris, O'Brien, & Robbins, 1991).

However, the central nucleus of the amygdala also has an important modulatory role on instrumental behavior in these secondary reinforcement paradigms. Drugs that release dopamine (e.g., amphetamine) increase the rate of bar pressing for a light previously paired with food. These facilitative effects also occur after local infusion of amphetamine into the nucleus accumbens (Taylor & Robbins, 1984) and are blocked by local depletion of dopamine in this area via 6-hydroxydopamine (6-OHDA; Taylor & Robbins, 1986). However, 6-OHDA did not block the expression of conditioned reinforcement itself, consistent with the idea that the reinforcement signal comes from some other brain area, such as the Bla, that projects to the nucleus accumbens. These results suggest that two relatively independent processes operate during conditioned reinforcement. First, information from the amygdala concerning the CS-US association is sent to the nucleus accumbens to control instrumental behavior as a conditioned reinforcer. Second, dopamine in the nucleus accumbens modulates this instrumental behavior. The central nucleus of the amygdala, via its projections to the mesolimbic dopamine system, seems to be critical for this invigorating or arousing effect of dopamine. Thus, lesions of the central nucleus block the increase in bar pressing normally produced by infusion of amphetamine into the nucleus accumbens (Robledo, Robbins, & Everitt, 1996), probably by preventing dopamine in the nucleus accumbens shell (Everitt et al., 2000).

The Dorsal Striatum Pathway

As emphasized by McGaugh, Packard, and others, the amygdala modulates memory in a variety of tasks such as inhibitory avoidance and motor or spatial learning (Cahill & McGaugh, 1998; McGaugh et al., 1993; McGaugh, Introini-Collison, Cahill, Kim, & Liang, 1992; Packard, Cahill, & McGaugh, 1994; Packard & Teather, 1998). For example, posttraining intracaudate injections of amphetamine enhanced memory in a visible platform water maze task but had no effect in the spatially guided hidden-platform task (Packard et al., 1994; Packard & Teather, 1998). Conversely, posttraining intrahippocampal infusion of amphetamine enhanced memory in the hidden-platform water-maze task but not in the visible-platform task. However, posttraining intra-amygdala injections of amphetamine enhanced memory in both water-maze tasks (Packard et al., 1994; Packard & Teather, 1998). These findings indicate that the amygdala exerts a modulatory influence on both the hippocampal and caudate-putamen memory systems. Indeed, more recent brain imaging studies in humans show correlations between memory recall of emotional stories and blood flow in the amygdala (Cahill, 2000).

Perhaps similarly, lesions of the central nucleus block freezing but not escape to a tone previously paired with shock, whereas lesions of the basal nucleus of the basolateral complex have just the opposite effect (Amorapanth, LeDoux, & Nader, 2000). However, lesions of the lateral nucleus, which receive sensory information required by both measures, block both freezing and escape. Lesions of the Bla, but not the CeA, also block avoidance of a bar associated with shock (Killcross, Robbins, & Everitt, 1997). Thus basolateral outputs to the dorsal or the ventral striatum may mediate escape or avoidance behavior, given the importance of the striatum in several measures of escape or avoidance learning.

Projections to the Cortex

Research with primates has shown that the basal nucleus of the amygdala projects to several areas in the inferior temporal cortex, continuing into prestriate and striate areas of the occipital lobe (Amaral & Price, 1984; Iwai & Yukie, 1987). Furthermore, the lateral nucleus of the amygdala gets input from an adjacent site in the visual system, which in turn receives hierarchical projections from the several nuclei along the ventral visual stream, extending to the retinal mapping area of the calcarine fissure. These projections could potentially close the loop with the visual system (Amaral, Price, Pitkanen, & Carmichael, 1992), representing an amygdala feedback circuit that may be significant for the sustained perceptual evaluation seen in the early stages of emotional processing.

Following Pavlovian conditioning, presentation of a conditioned stimulus appears to elicit some neural representation of the unconditioned stimulus (US) with which it was paired. In the family cat, for example, the sound of an electric can opener or of a refrigerator door opening may elicit a neural representation of food. This representation prompts predigestive responses and leads the cat to come into the kitchen in expectation of dinner. Based on a procedure called *US devaluation,* several studies suggest that the basolateral amygdala—perhaps via connections with cortical areas such as the perirhinal cortex (cf. Gewirtz & Davis, 1998)—is critical for

retaining these US representations (e.g., Hatfield et al., 1996). Second-order conditioning also depends on a US representation elicited by a conditioned stimulus. Again, lesions of the Bla, but not the central nucleus, block second-order conditioning (Everitt, Cador, & Robbins, 1989; Everitt et al., 1991; Hatfield et al., 1996). This same effect occurs with local infusions of NMDA antagonists into the basolateral nucleus of the amygdala (Gewirtz & Davis, 1997).

Converging evidence also now suggests that the connection between the basolateral nucleus and the prefrontal cortex is critically involved in the way in which a representation of an unconditioned stimulus (e.g., very good, pretty good, very bad, pretty bad) guides approach or avoidance behavior. Analogous to the animal data, patients with late- or early-onset lesions of the orbital regions of the prefrontal cortex frequently ignore important information that could usefully guide their actions and decision making (S. W. Anderson, Bechara, Damasio, Tranel, & Damasio, 1999; Bechara, Damasio, Tranel, & Damasio, 1997; Damasio, 1994). For example, on a gambling task the patients chose high, immediate reward associated with long-term loss rather than low reward associated with positive long-term gains. Clinically, they are reported to have a severe deficit in social skills, to fail to anticipate future consequences, and to make poor life decisions.

Studies using single-unit recording techniques in rats indicate that cells in both the Bla and the orbitofrontal cortex fire differentially to an odor, depending on whether the odor predicts a positive (e.g., sucrose) or negative (e.g., quinine) US. These differential responses emerge before the development of consistent approach or avoidance behavior elicited by that odor (Schoenbaum, Chiba, & Gallagher, 1998). Many cells in the Bla reverse their firing patterns during reversal training (i.e., the cue that used to predict sucrose now predicts quinine and vice versa; Schoenbaum, Chiba, & Gallagher, 1999), although this has not always been observed (e.g., Sanghera, Rolls, & Roper-Hall, 1979). In contrast, many fewer cells in the orbitofrontal cortex showed selectivity before the behavioral criterion was reached, and many fewer reversed their selectivity during reversal training (Schoenbaum et al., 1999). These investigators suggest that cells in the Bla encode the associative significance of cues, whereas cells in the orbitofrontal cortex are active when that information, relayed from the basolateral nucleus, is required to guide motivated choice behavior, presumably via both the motor cortex and the dorsal striatum.

Taken together, these data suggest that the connection between the basolateral complex and the frontal cortex could determine how an expected US is represented in memory, and thus play an important role in guiding motivated behavior and determining the choices that animals make. The effect may depend, however, on direct communication between an amygdala (right or left side) and the adjacent frontal cortex. Thus, when rhesus monkeys had amygdala lesions on one side of the brain and lesions of the frontal cortex on the other side, the degree of unconditioned stimulus devaluation was decreased (Baxter, Parker, Lindner, Izquierdo, & Murray, 2000). That is, lesioned monkeys continued to approach objects signalling a food on which they had recently been satiated (whereas control monkeys consistently chose objects not associated with satiated food).

STUDIES OF THE AMYGDALA IN HUMANS

Neurological Disorders

Clinical studies of neurological patients have shown that some aspects of emotional behavior, particularly the perception of fear, may depend on an intact amygdala. Thus, removal of the amygdala (e.g., in the context of surgery for epilepsy) has been associated both with impairment of emotional face recognition, and with misinterpretation of another's gaze angle (Broks et al., 1998; Calder et al., 1996; A. W. Young et al., 1995). In a very rare case involving a confined, bilateral calcification of the amygdala (Urbach-Wiethe disease), the patient (SM046) could not identify the emotion of fear in pictures of human faces. Moreover, she could not draw a fearful face, even though other emotional faces—happy, sad, angry, and disgusted—were identified and more successfully rendered (Adolphs, Tranel, Damasio, & Damasio, 1994, 1995). Curiously, this patient had no deficit in judging the emotional quality of music (Adolphs & Tranel, 1999). Another patient (SP) with extensive bilateral amygdala damage showed a deficit in her ability to rate levels of fear in human faces. Nevertheless, she had not lost the ability to evaluate vocal expressions of fear correctly (A. K. Anderson & Phelps, 1998), and she appeared perfectly normal in generating a fearful facial expression (A. K. Anderson & Phelps, 2000).

Bilateral amygdalotomy has recently been employed as a treatment for intractable aggression: It is reported that individuals who have undergone this surgery show both a reduction in autonomic arousal levels in response to stressful stimuli and a reduction in the number of aggressive outbursts. The behavior pattern is not, however, wholly suppressed, as these patients continue to have difficulty controlling aggression (G. P. Lee et al., 1998). Patients with unilateral (LeBar, LeDoux, Spencer, & Phelps, 1995) or bilateral (Bechara et al., 1995) lesions of the amygdala are reported to have deficits in classical aversive conditioning of the skin conductance response. In another patient with resection of the right temporal lobe (including the amygdala), M. Morris,

Bradley, Bowers, Lange, and Heilman (1991) found both reduced skin conductance responses and low arousal ratings to unpleasant emotional pictures.

Overall, the effects of amygdala lesions in neurological patients suggest the presence of an emotional deficit. However, the pattern of results is less consistent and specific than that found in experimentally lesioned animals. There is agreement that loss of an amygdala may compromise a patient's ability to interpret facial expression (notably the fear face). However, patients with this difficulty—which could relate to more general visual discrimination problems or difficulty discriminating among facial expressions—do not have problems interpreting emotional cues that come through other sensory systems (e.g., the auditory system). Furthermore, they usually show no deficit in overt expression emotion. The skin conductance data are suggestive. However, given the great variance in skin conductance responding in the normal population (which also includes many nonresponders), they are difficult to evaluate. Finally, although radical amygdalotomy appears to alter some features of aggression, the loss did not have a persistent effect on emotion regulation.

There are of course many reasons why the neurological data may be less robust and less clear in their implications than are the results of animal experimentation. It is important to consider that the primary lesions in patients are random and that the secondary surgical lesions can rarely be wholly precise in terms of the anatomical structure ablated. Furthermore, clinical considerations must always rule over experimental control. Drug intake, the general health status of patients, and the time since the lesion and its evaluation can all be highly variable. Surgery (as in epilepsy) is usually reserved for patients intractable to other treatments. In these cases, the brain disorder has persisted for a considerable time, with unknown effects on brain structure and organization. Thus, defining a comparison group and replicating a result exactly are often not feasible. Finally, it should also be considered that the brain changes with development and often has redundant neural circuits. Although the amygdala may be necessary—in humans as it is in animals—in much basic emotional learning, its functional role in emotional expression could be less critical in the mature human adult.

Brain Imaging

The emergence of neuroimaging technologies has opened a new window into the human brain. Positron-emission tomography (PET) and functional magnetic resonance imaging (fMRI) are two technologies that make possible functional analysis of the amygdala and other brain structures in intact, normal human beings. It is significant that neither method directly assesses neural activation. Rather, fMRI and PET measure regional blood flow in the capillaries of the cerebral parenchyma associated with stimulus presentation. This BOLD (blood oxygen level–dependent) effect has been shown to be systematically correlated with neural firing. Thus, it is possible to assess indirectly the activation of brain structures that mediate the language, the reflexes (autonomic and somatic), and the behavioral acts that are emotion's output.

For technical reasons, the functioning of cortical motor and sensory systems are the easiest to image, and considerable progress has been made in, for example, mapping visual functioning in the human brain (Schneider, Noll, & Cohen, 1993). As already noted, appetitive and threatening stimuli capture attention and appear to accentuate processing in primary sensory areas. Primate research indicates, furthermore, that the amygdala projects to occipital and ventral temporal processing areas of the visual system (Amaral et al., 1992). To evaluate emotional processing in the visual system, Lang, Bradley, Fitzsimmons, et al. (1998) presented evocative picture stimuli (from the IAPS) to normal subjects, recording blood flow

changes in the caudal cortex. Compared to affectively neutral pictures, participants showed dramatically larger areas of activation for picture stimuli rated pleasant or unpleasant. These fMRI findings were particularly strong in areas 18 and 19 of the occipital cortex, as well as in the fusiform cortex. More recent research by this group (Sabatinelli, Bradley, Cuthbert, & Lang, 1996) examined different categories of picture stimuli, confirming previous results and indicating clearly that activation increases monotonically with emotional arousal (see Figure 15.6). Thus, the greatest activity was found for pictures of attack (animal or human) made toward the viewer, for erotic pictures, and for pictures of mutilated bodies. Pictures rated less affectively arousing—household objects, neutral and angry faces, or mildly pleasant family groups showed— significantly less activation. Consistent with these results, PET studies have shown greater activation in the occipital visual system with individuals with phobias viewing pictures of relevant phobic objects (Fredrikson, Wik, Annas, Ericson, & Stone-Elander, 1995; Fredrikson et al., 1993), as well as increased activation, relative to neutral stimulation, in normal subjects viewing a range of unpleasant pictures (Lane et al., 1997).

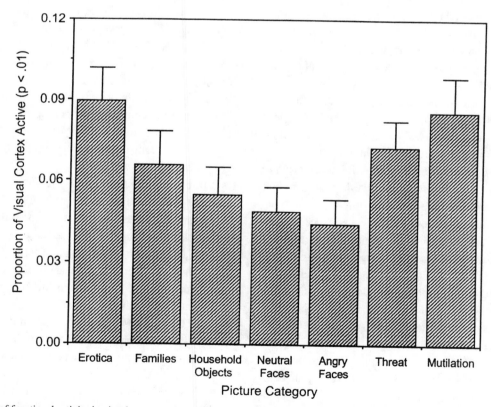

Figure 15.6 Extent of functional activity in visual cortex varies with the rated arousal of picture stimuli. Thus, the most activation (and presumably the most extensive sensory processing) was found for positive erotic pictures and for negative pictures of threatening animals and humans and of human mutilation. This graph represents the proportion of cortical activation across all sampled areas (at a probability threshold of $p < .01$) during picture viewing compared to fixation in a sample of 18 males. In each participant, seven 5-mm coronal slices were acquired, originating 1 cm anterior to the occipital pole and terminating, in most subjects, at the splenium. This proscription covers primary, secondary, and tertiary visual processing areas in occipital, occipitoparietal, and ventral temporal cortex (Bradley, Codispoti, Sabatinelli, Cuthbert, & Lang, 2001).

Structures more anterior in the cortex, and ventrally near the midline where the amygdala is found, generally show smaller, less reliable BOLD effects in fMRI. Nevertheless, human neuroimaging studies generally support a role for the amygdala that may be particular to the processing of emotional stimuli. Irwin et al. (1996) reported that fMRI signal intensity is greater when subjects view graphic photographs of negative material (e.g., mutilated human bodies) compared to when they view neutral pictures. PET images suggest that metabolic activity increases during film clips (Reiman et al., 1997) or IAPS picture stimuli (Lane et al., 1997) that are unpleasant in content, and some data suggest that the amount of amygdala activity during affect-arousing film clips predicts later recall (Cahill et al., 1996). Furthermore, following Pavlovian fear conditioning, the formerly neutral, conditioned stimuli prompt increased fMRI signal intensities from the amygdala (cf. Davis & Whalen, 2001).

There are several studies (e.g., Whalen, 1998) suggesting that pictures of emotional faces engage the amygdala. These are interesting data, as face stimuli generally do not arouse strong emotion as defined by peripheral physiology, activation of the cortical visual system, or verbal report. One hypothesis is that the amygdala serves as a first-stage stimulus discriminator that screens stimuli of potential motivational significance. The finding that fearful faces are sometimes more effective (than other expressions) in activating the amygdala may reflect the inherent ambiguity of the fear face, rather than the exact content of the emotion itself as first suggested by Whalen (1998). Thus, angry faces might be less effective, paradoxically, because they provide more complete information. That is, they suggest a threat *presence* and also define the *source* of that threat. Fearful faces provide information about threat presence but give less information about the source, and thus require further amygdalar analysis. For similar reasons, amygdala activation might be expected to be greatest early in training, when reinforcement schedules are variable, or when stimulus contingencies change—all examples of ambiguity. In fact, in both nonhuman and human subjects, several amygdala-mediated responses (Applegate et al., 1983; Whalen & Kapp, 1991) reach their peak during early conditioning trials and subside thereafter (Masur, Dienst, & O'Neal, 1974; Schneiderman, 1972; Weisz & McInerney, 1990; see also Kapp et al., 1990). Moreover, when stimulus contingencies change (e.g., when a CS is suddenly not followed by shock at the beginning of extinction), there is a reemergence of single-unit activity in the lateral amygdala nucleus in rats (Quirk, Repa, & LeDoux, 1995). In analogous conditions, humans show a resurgence of amygdalar blood flow (LeBar, Gatenby, Gore, LeDoux, & Phelps, 1998).

The imaging results are exciting. However, a more detailed explication of these issues may well require a more refined analysis than imaging technology can currently deliver. As the animal model informs us, the amygdala is not a single structure, but a collection of many nuclei with different functions. Based on imaging and neurological findings, we might speculate that emotional face recognition requires, in particular, activation of the basolateral nuclei of the amygdala. Furthermore, we might conclude that such activation occurs without a coincident transmission to the central nucleus (i.e., the structure that has consequences for the autonomic and somatic reflexes and the experience of emotion). Unfortunately, the gross spatial resolution provided by PET permits us to say only that activation is in the region of the amygdala, and even fMRI cannot yet discriminate individual nuclei.

Emotional Arousal and Emotional Memory

From the perspective of the animal model presented here, input to the amygdala's basolateral nucleus begins the sequence of neural events that underlay emotion, namely, orienting and attention, approach, and defensive behaviors such as avoidance. Basolateral outputs to the central nucleus and the extended amygdala appear to be critical in the increased processing of emotionally significant stimuli, whether pleasant or aversive. Outputs from the central nucleus and BNST in turn mediate many of the autonomic and somatic components of overt action. Direct output to the dorsal striatum, or indirect output via the orbital frontal cortex, appears to be involved in the actual avoidance response. Furthermore, output from the central nucleus and the BNST to the ventral striatum, as well as the orbitofrontal cortex, is also a likely contributor to the execution of approach and choice behavior.

The circuitry just described constitutes a motivational system that is finely tuned to the probability that events will require survival action (e.g., that a remote threat will become an imminent danger or that a sexual provocation will likely to lead to pleasant consummation). In animals, increasing imminence prompts a more general mobilization of the organism, mediated by various neurotransmitters such as acetylcholine, dopamine, norepinephrine, and many peptides such as CRH. These substances act either within the amygdala or at various central target areas to facilitate neural transmission, and they are associated with increasing intensity of appetitive or defensive motivation (and are also roughly correlated with reports of increasing arousal in humans).

This of course is not a new idea. There is a large literature on the role of neurotransmitters and neuromodulators in activating the organism, especially as they pertain to the sleep-wakefulness continuum. However, it is activation specific to emotional arousal that is under consideration, as well as how the strength of this activation might vary with different provocations. For example, what differentiates our remembrance of a walk in the park from our recall of an erotic encounter? What is different about looking at a picture of a garbage can and looking at a picture of a mutilated body? Most of us would say immediately that for each comparison, the latter experience (the erotic encounter or the mutilated body) is more emotionally arousing. What is the physiology of this experience? How does looking at a picture lead to a release of acetylcholine, dopamine, norepinephrine, or CRH?

From the perspective of animal research, we know that the central nucleus of the amygdala and the BNST have direct connections to the neurons in the brain stem that release acetylcholine, dopamine, and norepinephrine and to neurons in the basal forebrain that release ACH. Electrical stimulation of the amygdala has been shown to increase cell firing in many of these neuronal groups. In addition, cells in the lateral division of the amygdala's central nucleus sends CRH-containing terminals to the BNST (Sakanaka, Shibasaki, & Lederis, 1986), where many of the actions of CRH may actually be mediated (Y. Lee & Davis, 1996). Thus, more arousing images and thoughts could activate more cells in amygdala that automatically lead to a release of these neurochemicals.

However, it seems more difficult to account for why one image is considered emotionally upsetting to almost everyone whereas another is not (e.g., a picture of a dental chair vs. a picture of a rocking chair)—or why representation connotes more excitement than another picture (e.g., a picture of a chair on a roller coaster vs. a picture of a rocking chair). In addition, it seems more difficult to account for why one image is especially frightening in one situation but not in another. A picture of a chainsaw in a hospital operating room might well generate a stronger emotional reaction than a picture of the same chainsaw in a hardware store. In addition, it is not obvious why, neurophysiologically, one picture is especially frightening to one individual but less so to another. That is, a picture of a chainsaw in a hospital operating room produces considerably more emotion to the patient facing an amputation than the same picture does to a surgeon who has carried out this operation many times before. The intensity of an emotion generated by a picture depends not only on the particular item (e.g., chainsaw) but also on the content of the picture (hospital operating room vs. hardware store), as well as on the history of the person viewing the picture (future amputee vs. doctor). How then does this translate into levels of transmitter release, producing the many outputs of emotion, with varying affective intensity, almost instantly?

Cognitive Networks

These considerations raise fundamental questions about how information is processed and memories are stored in the human brain. Cognitive psychologists (e.g., J. R. Anderson & Bower, 1974; Kintsch, 1974) suggest that knowledge about events is represented in networks of representations linked by laws of association. They are instantiated by stimuli that match elements in the network. Lang (1994) suggested that emotional memories may be considered networks of this type. These networks include associated information about emotional episodes, coding stimulus events and context, behavior, and interpretive elaborations. When cues match units in the network (e.g., chainsaw, surgical operating room), network processing is initiated: Activity in one unit is transmitted to adjacent units, and depending on the strength of activation, the entire structure may be engaged. The probability of network processing is likely to be increased with the number of units initially stimulated. A hypothesized fear memory network for a snake-phobic individual is presented in Figure 15.7. It can be thought of as a net of linked representations (which, in turn, might be individual neural subnetworks). Only a fraction of its representational units may have higher level language representation, and thus—passing through awareness—be the formative stuff of affective reports.

How do emotional networks differ from other knowledge structures in the brain? It is proposed that emotion networks are singular because they include associative connections to the primary motivational systems in the brain that are the focus of this discourse. In brief, reciprocal projections from cortex to the amygdalar circuit engage the somatic and autonomic reflexes that evolved to ensure the survival of individuals and species.

Levels of Activation

It may be that differences in level of arousal occur because networks activate different numbers of cells in the amygdala depending on the associative history of those stimuli. In fact, most stimuli or situations that produce an emotional reaction do so by virtue of prior conditioning. Monkeys reared in the lab, where serpents are not normally encountered, are generally not afraid of snakes compared with monkeys raised in the wild (Mineka, Davidson, Cook, & Keir, 1984). A baby with his or her finger in a light socket does not feel afraid when the light switch is turned on, whereas a child who was once shocked in a similar situation certainly does. After this association is formed, putting a finger in a socket may be presumed to engage many cells in the amygdala, leading to a large release of neurochemicals and strong activation of the defense motivation system.

Similar amygdala activations can be assumed to occur when we think about an unpleasant experience or look at emotional pictures. The site of a chainsaw in an operating room would activate a neural representation of pain or blood

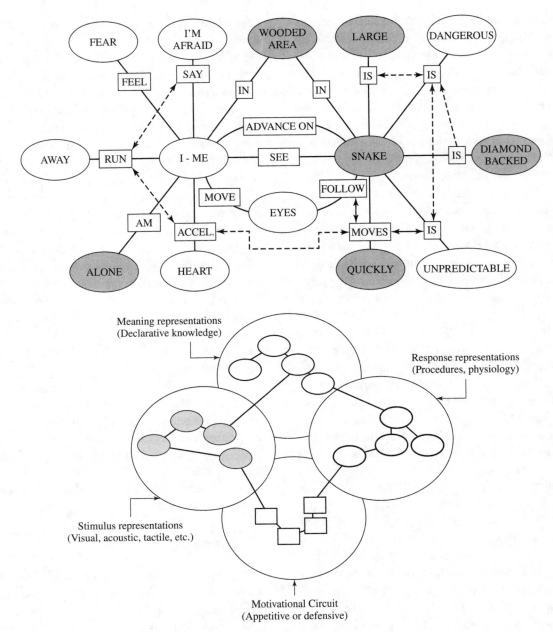

Figure 15.7 Top panel: The cognitive elements of a fear network (Lang, 1985), showing response representations (ovals outlined in heavy black), stimulus representations (gray ovals), and meaning representations (clear ovals). Information units are linked associatively and coded in long-term memory. Thus, through spreading activation, the entire network is activated when stimuli are perceived that match some of its representations. The fear network is here rendered in natural language, with propositional notation. However, it is fundamentally a cortical neural network, with reciprocal connections to primary motivational circuits (appetitive and defensive) in deep cortex, subcortex, and brain stem. Bottom panel: A general schematic of an emotional memory network. Emotional networks differ from other memory networks in the brain in that they include strong associative connections to the motivational circuits that mediate reflexive survival behaviors in most animals. The diagram highlights the interface between the higher order cognitive representations (stimulus, response, and meaning units) that define context and action procedures—and the motivational reflex circuit that is explicated neurophysiologically in the animal model.

and mutilation, which would activate the amygdala by virtue of prior association. The site of a chainsaw in a hardware store would activate a network of cutting wood, which would probably not include strongly associated representations— pain, blood, and mutilation—that may be unconditioned instigators of amygdala activation.

In summary, emotional arousal occurs when a stimulus activates a matching representation in an emotional network. The immediacy and intensity of the affective reaction depends on the general associative strength of the network, and specifically on the associative strength of connections to the amygdala circuit. In humans, this net is broadly cast. Affects can be instantiated vicariously, by language representation and other media or, indeed, by cues not discriminated linguistically (and therefore outside awareness). Thus, many different stimuli, varying across individuals, can prompt an amygdala-dependent release of neurochemicals, with a potentially widespread modulation of sensory and motor systems.

MEASURING EMOTIONAL AROUSAL IN RATS AND HUMANS: THE STARTLE REFLEX AND THE MOTIVATIONAL PRIMING HYPOTHESIS

From an evolutionary perspective, human emotions such as fear or anger are usefully considered as dispositions to action. That is, they may have evolved from preparatory states evoked by threat cues, in which survival depended on delay or inhibition of overt behavior. In this sense, they derive from the first stage of defense that is associated with vigilance and immobility, when the organism is primed to respond, but not yet active.

In most mammals, any abrupt sensory event will prompt a startle response, a chained series of rapid extensor-flexor movements that cascade throughout the body (Landis & Hunt, 1939). This reaction is a defensive reflex, facilitating escape in simpler organisms, and perhaps still serving a protective function in more complex animals (i.e., in avoiding organ injury as in the eye blink or in retraction of the head and torso in the full body startle reflex to avoid attack from above; Li & Yeomans, 1999). Abruptness is the key to startle elicitation: To be effective, the rise time of the eliciting stimulus should be perceptually instantaneous. In human subjects, sudden closure of the eyelids is one of the first, fastest (occurring within 25 ms to 40 ms after startle stimulus onset), and most stable elements in the reflex sequence. It is the preferred measure of startle in humans. In rats, whole body startle is measured in specially designed cages.

When under threat (of pain or predation), animals show an exaggerated startle reflex. As first described by Brown, Kalish, and Farber (1951), the amplitude of the acoustically elicited startle reflex in rats is increased when elicited in the presence of a light previously paired with foot shock. This effect is considered an animal model of fear or anxiety because drugs that reduce fear or anxiety in humans, such as diazepam or buspirone, block the increase in startle in the presence of the conditioned light stimulus but do not affect the basic startle reflex itself (see Davis, Falls, Campeau, & Kim, 1993, for a review). In contrast, during an appetitive state, the startle reflex appears to be partially inhibited; that is, startle amplitude is reduced when elicited in the presence of a light previously paired with food (Schmid, Koch, & Schnitzler,

1995) or rewarding electrical brain stimulation (Yeomans, Steidle, & Li, 2000).

These effects are very like what cognitive psychologists call *priming* in research on human associative behavior. Cognitive priming occurs when a prior stimulus raises the activation level of an associated S-R event. For example, the prime "bread" prompts a faster reaction time response to the word "butter." States of the organism may also prime particular behavior. Thus, clinically depressed individuals respond to nearly all cues with associations that are affectively negative. The potentiated startle observed in animal conditioning can be understood as an instance of motivational state priming. That is, the induced defensive state of the organism primes (increments) an independently instigated reflex that is connected to the defense system (i.e., the startle response).

According to the motivational priming hypothesis (Lang, Bradley, & Cuthbert, 1990, 1997), the defensive startle reflex will be of significantly greater amplitude (and faster) when a prior stimulus has induced a consonant, defensive motivational state. Alternatively, if the appetitive system has been activated, as in states of pleasure, the defensive startle reflex should undergo a reciprocal attenuation. Assuming our postulate that emotions are driven by underlying motive systems, any instance of emotional perception should prompt startle reflex modulation—increasing with unpleasant percepts and decreasing with pleasant percepts. Thus, the startle reflex can serve as a remarkably simple, objective measure of affective valence. It is also a powerful tool for assessing the role of the amygdala circuit in emotion, as well as the premier method that solidly links animal neuroscience research and human psychophysiology.

Startle Modulation in Humans

Like rats, human subjects also show elevated startle amplitude in the presence of cues previously paired with shock (Grillon & Davis, 1997; Hamm, Greenwald, Bradley, & Lang, 1993; Lipp, Sheridan, & Siddle, 1994) or simply when they are told they might receive a shock (Grillon, Ameli, Woods, Merikangas, & Davis, 1991; Grillon, Ameli, Merikangas, Woods, & Davis, 1993). Lang et al. (1990) further theorized that startle modulation was a more general phenomenon and that this reflex could be used to probe the full range of affective responses. That is, to the extent that any perceptual event evoked a state of unpleasant arousal, the probe startle response would be increased in magnitude; to the extent that a foreground stimulus is pleasantly arousing, the startle probe response would be diminished.

When startle probes are administered while subjects view pictures that vary systematically in emotional arousal, results have consistently conformed to the motivational priming hypothesis. As Figure 15.8 illustrates, there is a startle inhibition during pleasant stimuli and potentiation when pictures were judged to be unpleasant: The largest startle blink responses occurred during unpleasant content, and the smallest during pleasant pictures (e.g, Lang, 1995; Lang et al., 1990; Vrana, Spence, & Lang, 1988; and see Bradley, 2000, for a recent review). These emotion-perceptual effects have also been reported in 5-month-old infants viewing smiling, neutral, and angry faces (Balaban, 1995).

Affective modulation of startle is observed for picture stimuli regardless of whether the startle probe is visual, acoustic, or tactile (e.g, Bradley, Lang, & Cuthbert, 1990; Hawk & Cook, 1997), suggesting that modality-specific processes are not primary in these modulatory effects. Furthermore, affective modulation is not confined to visual percepts: When the foreground stimuli consist of short, 6-s sound clips of various affective events (e.g., sounds of love making, babies crying, or bombs bursting) and the startle probe is a visual light flash, the same affect-reflex effect is obtained (Bradley, Zack, & Lang, 1994). Other researchers have found startle potentiation in subjects smelling unpleasant odors (Ehrlichman, Brown, Zhu, & Warrenburg, 1995; Miltner, Matjak, Braun, & Diekmann, 1994), supporting the view that affective reflex modulation is broadly motivational and thus consistent across affective foregrounds of different stimulus modalities.

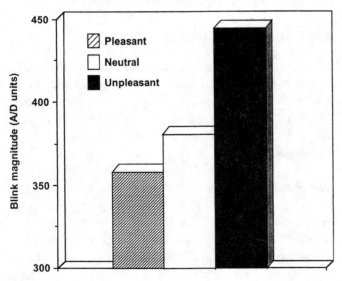

Affective modulation of the startle reflex

Figure 15.8 Startle reflexes are potentiated when viewing unpleasant pictures and inhibited when viewing pleasant pictures, compared with neutral images. This affective modulation of the startle reflex permits an assessment of emotional state in the context of a perceptual task.

Emotional Arousal

Consistent with the motivational priming hypothesis, modulatory effects on the startle reflex appear to increase with greater activation in each motive system. Probe startle potentiation is largest for unpleasant pictures that are rated most arousing; conversely, the most arousing pleasant pictures prompt the greatest probe startle inhibition (Cuthbert, Bradley, & Lang, 1996). Thus, individuals with specific phobias who look at pictures of the phobic object (e.g., snakes or spiders) show startle potentiation well beyond that routinely seen in normal subjects (Hamm et al., 1997). The potentiation is, however, clearly selective: Individuals with phobias show normal reflex inhibition to startle probes when looking at arousing pleasant stimuli (Sabatinelli et al., 1996).

Probe reflex inhibition reflects attentional engagement (Graham, 1992), as well as an appetitive motive state. Consistent with this view, probes presented during less arousing, unpleasant stimuli—pictures of sad events, pollution, ill people—tend to prompt some reflex inhibition. Startle magnitude then increases progressively with reported arousal, and the strongest potentiation occurs during viewing of the most arousing unpleasant stimuli (Cuthbert et al., 1996). In contrast, the most pleasantly arousing percepts show the largest probe startle inhibition.

Emotional Perception

Startle probes have been used to examine the time course of emotional perception (Bradley et al., 2001), beginning with the first apprehension of a cue meaning, milliseconds after an image first appears, and continuing until the percept is fully resolved (Figure 15.9). In this paradigm, startle probes are presented at various times in the stimulus presentation interval on different trials. For early probes, picture onset constitutes a prepulse, clearly drawing attentional resources away from the startle stimulus, resulting in a partial probe startle inhibition for all image contents, whether emotional or not. This diminished reflex in the first few hundred milliseconds of picture exposure is nevertheless significantly more profound for emotionally arousing than for neutral stimuli. That is, compared to neutral pictures, the pleasant and unpleasant stimuli appear already to receive more processing, even though their motivational type, appetitive or defensive, has not yet been determined. This early discrimination of motivationally relevant stimuli has been confirmed by EEG studies. Evoked potential analyses of dipole sources show a distinct difference in bioelectric activity, relative to neutral input, for pictures described as more emotionally arousing—in occipital and parietal cortex—between 150 ms

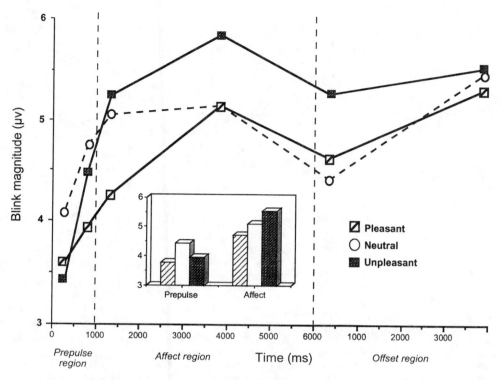

Figure 15.9 Blink reflexes to startle probes presented during viewing of pleasant, neutral, or unpleasant pictures at each of six different times after slide onset. Inset: Probe reflex magnitude averaged over the first two probes (300 ms and 800 ms, postonset: "Early") and the last two probes (i.e., 1300 ms and 3,800 ms: "Late"). In the temporally early prepulse region, greater orienting prompts probe inhibition during emotional picture viewing, regardless of affective valence. In the affect region, the startle probe is potentiated uniquely during unpleasant pictures.

and 250 ms after picture onset (Junghoefer, Bradley, Elbert, & Lang, 2001).

As can be seen in Figure 15.9, when startle is elicited after longer picture exposure and the picture has been resolved as to exact content, the decrease in startle amplitudes continues for pleasurable stimuli; however, unpleasant, arousing stimuli now prompt startle potentiation. In a more than symbolic way, this progression from attentive evaluation of potentially motivationally relevant stimuli to clear emotional content discrimination—with potentiated startle (a motor action) consequent on a resolved unpleasant cue—seems like a microcosm of the defense motivational sequence (attention to action) discussed previously. That is, this rapid change in processing parallels events in a slower time frame, for example, as a friend or possible foe approaches us in the park.

The Role of the Amygdala in Startle Modulation in Rats

Conditioned Fear

Figure 15.10 is a diagrammatic sketch of the pathways that we believe mediate fear-potentiated startle in rats using visual conditioned stimuli. Visual information from the retina projects to both the dorsal lateral geniculate nucleus and lateral posterior nucleus of the thalamus. The dorsal lateral geniculate nucleus projects to the visual cortex, whereas the lateral posterior nucleus projects directly to the basolateral nucleus of the amygdala as well as the perirhinal cortex (Shi & Davis, 1996), which then projects to the lateral or basolateral nuclei of the amygdala. The basolateral nucleus then projects to the central nucleus, which in turn has neural projections to the startle pathway. Electrolytic or chemical lesions of visual thalamus (Shi & Davis, 1996), perirhinal cortex (Campeau & Davis, 1995a; Rosen et al., 1992), or basolateral amygdala (Campeau & Davis, 1995b; Sananes & Davis, 1992) completely block the expression of fear-potentiated startle using a visual CS. None of these lesions affect startle amplitude itself. Lesions (Campeau & Davis, 1995b; Hitchcock & Davis, 1986) and local infusion of glutamate antagonists into the amygdala's central nucleus (Kim, Campeau, Falls, & Davis, 1993; Walker & Davis, 1997) also block fear potentiated startle.

Both conditioned fear and sensitization of startle by foot shocks appear to modulate startle at the level of the nucleus reticularis pontis caudalis (Berg & Davis, 1985; Boulis & Davis, 1989; Krase, Koch, & Schnitzler, 1994). The central nucleus of the amygdala projects directly to the nucleus reticularis pontis caudalis (Rosen, Hitchcock, Sananes,

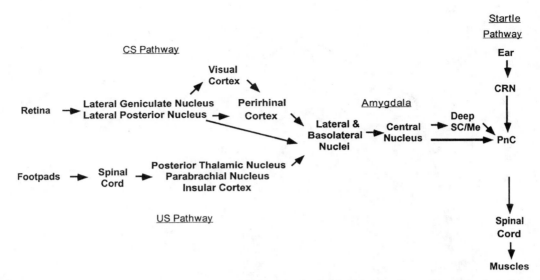

Figure 15.10   Schematic diagram of pathways believed to be involved in the fear-potentiated startle effect in rats using a visual conditioned stimulus. Visual information goes from the retina through the lateral posterior nucleus of the thalamus either directly to the basolateral amygdala or indirectly through the perirhinal cortex to the amygdala. Visual information also goes from the retina to the dorsal lateral geniculate nucleus to the visual cortex and then through the perirhinal cortex to the amygdala. Shock information goes through a series of parallel pathways to reach eventually the basolateral amygdala. The basolateral nucleus of the amygdala projects to the central nucleus, which then projects directly to the startle pathway at the level of the nucleus reticularis pontis caudalis (PnC), as well as indirectly via a synapse in the deep layers of the superior colliculus and mesencephalic reticular formation (Deep SC/Me). The startle reflex itself is mediated by a pathway in the brain stem and spinal cord. Afferents from the cochlea synapse onto a small group of neurons embedding the auditory nerve called cochlear root neurons (CRN), which send heavy projections to the PnC. Axons from cells in the PnC form part of the reticulospinal tract and make both monosynaptic and polysynaptic connections in the spinal cord onto motoneurons.

Miserendino, & Davis, 1991), and electrolytic lesions along this pathway block the expression of fear-potentiated startle (Hitchcock & Davis, 1991). However, an obligatory synapse appears to exist in this pathway because fiber-sparing chemical lesions in the deep layers of superior colliculus or periaqueductal gray also block fear-potentiated startle (Fendt, Koch, & Schnitzler, 1996; Frankland & Yeomans, 1995), as does local infusion of muscimol into the same general area (Meloni & Davis, 1999).

Pleasure-Attenuated Startle

As mentioned earlier, startle amplitude is decreased when elicited in the presence of a cue previously paired with food (Schmid et al., 1995). Moreover, the nucleus accumbens is important for this pleasure-attenuated startle effect because pretraining local infusion of the neurotoxin 6-OHDA into the nucleus accumbens blocks pleasure-attenuated startle (Koch, Schmid, & Schnitzler, 1996). It is possible that the connection between the basolateral nuclei and the ventral striatum may be involved in pleasure-attenuated startle. Unilateral lesions of the basolateral nuclei on one side of the brain, and the nucleus accumbens ablation on the other, would test this hypothesis.

Emotion and the Amygdala in Humans

There are still only a few studies with human subjects that have attempted to relate the startle response directly to amygdala function. Bower et al. (1997) studied a group of 18 epilepsy patients who had undergone anterior temporal resections, involving the amygdala, and who were subsequently evaluated for acoustic startle reactivity (binaurally presented white noise bursts). Volumetric measures of the amygdala were obtained before and after surgery. These investigators reported a significant relationship between a reduction in base startle magnitude and the extent of amygdala loss—a relationship that was particularly strong for the right amygdala. Funayama, Grillon, Davis, and Phelps (2001) reported that epilepsy patients, treated by resection of the right temporal lobe, failed to show an increase in startle amplitude when they viewed highly unpleasant, arousing pictures. Nevertheless, they did show potentiated startle when presented with a light cue that they were told signaled possible electric shock. In dramatic contrast, patients with resection of the left temporal lobe showed normal startle potentiation when viewing highly unpleasant, arousing pictures, but not when exposed to the light-shock paradigm. Thus, the results indicated a double dissociation in affective modulation of startle eye blink, mediated separately by the two amygdalae. In humans, the amygdala's role in startle potentiation appeared to depend on both laterality and type of task. These ablation data are consistent with a recent fMRI study showing preferential activation of the left amygdala when subjects see a cue that they are told may predict shock (Phelps et al., 2001), a procedure that consistently increases the startle reflex (Grillon et al., 1991).

Phelps et al. (2000) used the startle response as an implicit measure of good-bad evaluative judgments, hypothesizing that one race might view other races negatively. While in a MRI scanner, White American participants viewed pictures of Black and White male faces. The pictures were presented again to the same subjects one week later, and during this viewing, startle was elicited by brief bursts of white noise. Focusing on the two amygdalae, the strength of activation to Black versus White faces was correlated with startle potentiation to these same stimuli. The highest correlation with startle potentiation was found for the left-superior amygdala and two small regions in the right insular cortex. An interesting result was that this relationship was not found in a second control experiment in which the Black and White faces were of famous, positively evaluated people.

These data encourage the general hypothesis that startle potentiation in humans is associated with amygdala activation. The laterality effects are provocative but currently hard to interpret. Lateralization of the brain varies widely across species, suggesting that research with mammals other than humans will offer limited guidance. Nevertheless, other investigators have reported differences between the amygdalae in human emotional perception. For example, using PET, J. S. Morris, Frith, Perrett, and Rowland (1996) found more activation (regional cerebral blood flow, or rCBF) in the left amygdala when subjects viewed fearful as opposed to happy facial expressions. In contrast, Cahill et al. (1996) found no increase in either amygdala while their subjects watched unpleasant, arousing films (compared to neutral documentaries). During a subsequent film-recall session, however, these same subjects showed significant relative activation uniquely in the left amygdala when they were cued to retrieve memories of the unpleasant films. J. S. Morris, Ohman, and Dolan (1998) also reported lateralized activation that, curiously, depended on whether previously conditioned pictures of faces (electric shock used as an unconditioned stimulus) were presented masked, and presumably subliminal (right amygdala), or unmasked and supraliminal (left amygdala). Given these provocative but highly various results, laterality will surely continue to be a focus in research, and these efforts should in future yield a better understanding of the phenomenon.

EMOTIONAL PROCESSING: FROM ATTENTION TO ACTION (WITH STOPS ALONG THE WAY)

When a wild rat sees a human at some distance away, the rat freezes in a highly alert, attentive posture. As the human gradually approaches, the rat suddenly darts away if escape is possible. If escape is not possible and the human gets very close, the rat will attack (Blanchard, Flannelly, & Blanchard, 1986). These observations lead Caroline and Robert Blanchard to note that defensive behaviors increase systematically with a reduction in distance from predators and other dangerous or potentially painful stimuli (Blanchard & Blanchard, 1988). Let us recall the scenarios that we discussed at the outset of this chapter—the feelings one might have as the dangerous-looking men approached. Given an available escape route, proximity is associated with an increased probability of active flight. In the absence of an escape option, the best defense may be attack. When the threat stimulus is distant, not clearly discriminable, an animal such as the rat "freezes while oriented toward the predator" (p. S5). The Blanchards noted further that increases in "the amplitude of the startle response to sudden stimuli accompany decreasing defensive distance" (p. S5).

Using the concepts introduced by Timberlake (1993; Timberlake & Lucas, 1989), Fanselow (1991, 1994) has made a parallel analysis of fear behavior, describing three behavioral stages, increasingly proximal to a predator: preencounter defense, preemptive behavior that occurs in a foraging area where predators were previously encountered; postencounter defense, responses prompted by the detection of a distant predator; circa-strike defense, behaviors such as defensive attack that occur in the region of physical contact or its close imminence. Behaviorally, there is a shift from nonspecific threat vigilance at preencounter, to postencounter freezing and orienting to a specific predator or predator cue, to the circa-strike stage when the organism is beyond vigilance and engaged in vigorous defensive action.

During mild electrical stimulation of the amygdala the first reaction is an arrest of ongoing behavior (freezing), bradycardia, and EEG activation. As stimulation increases, the animal suddenly becomes very active and at high levels of stimulation vigorously attempts to escape from the source of stimulation. One may thus conjecture that the site of a predator at some distance leads to a mild activation of the amygdala that produces an increase in attention. As the predator comes closer, activation of the amygdala increases to the point where it now leads to active defensive behavior, including escape. As suggested by Fanselow (1991, 1994) this switch from an attentional mode to an active defense mode may involve a switch from activation of the ventral to the dorsal periaqueductal gray. Work by

Bandler and many others (cf. Bandler & Shipley, 1994) has shown that the ventral periaqueductal gray projects to cardiovascular centers that mediate bradycardia as well as motor systems that mediate freezing. In contrast, the dorsal periaqueductal gray projects to cardiovascular systems that mediate tachycardia and active escape behavior. If one assumes that the ventral periaqueductal gray has a lower threshold for amygdala activation, this would explain why we initially go into an attentional mode as the amygdala is activated by a novel stimulus and sends signals to the periaqueductal gray. As the level of amygdala activation increases as a potential predator approaches, suddenly the higher threshold of activation of the dorsal periaqueductal gray is exceeded, leading to an abrupt switch from a high level of attention to action (e.g., quickly crossing the street to avoid the dangerous-looking men).

Lang et al. (1997) recently proposed an adaptation of the predator stage model for explicating human psychophysiological reactions to unpleasant and threatening stimuli. They suggest that the human laboratory participant, responding to stimuli presented by the experimenter, is functioning at a response stage analogous to postencounter responses; that is, like the freezing rat, he is immobile and vigilant, with easy escape blocked (in this case by instructions and social compliance). For the animal subject, increasing proximity to an aversive stimulus (greater nociceptive imminence) prompts an increase in general activation or arousal. It is proposed that this same effect is generated in the human psychophysiological laboratory because social compliance constrains participants to be passive and stimuli are presented that are less or more threatening or aversive. As illustrated in Figure 15.11, the increased vigilance in the postencounter period is characterized by a progressive augmentation of physiological indexes of attention—greater skin conductance, increased heart rate deceleration, and inhibition of the probe startle reflex when arousal is still relatively low.

The arousal abscissa of Figure 15.11 also constitutes a dimension of greater probability of motor action that modulates the startle response. Thus, as a close encounter becomes more imminent, the direction of the probe response reverses. In place of motor inhibition, the startle reflex now shows a potentiation that progressively increases in magnitude as probes occur more proximal to actual, overt defensive action. Startle potentiation begins in the context of freezing and vigilance and could be viewed as a premature triggering of defensive action. With a further increment in threat the heart rate response also reverses the direction of change from orienting to defense (Graham, 1979; Sokolov, 1963)—from a vigilance-related fear bradycardia to action mobilization and cardiac acceleration.

The biological model of emotion presented here suggests that, depending on level of stimulus aversion (threat, appre-

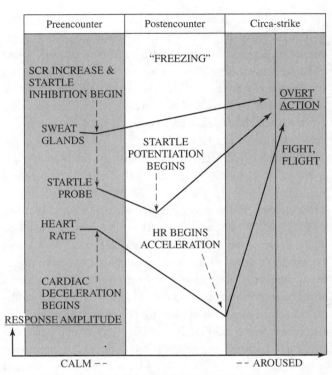

Figure 15.11 A schematic presentation of the defense response cascade generated by increasingly arousing aversive stimuli. The arousal dimension (monotonically covarying with SCR increase) is viewed here as analogous to the distance dimension of predator imminence, as described in studies of animal fear. Stimuli presented in the postencounter period occasion an initial, partial inhibition of startle probe reflexes, freezing, immobility, fear bradycardia, and a focused attentive set. The probability of an overt defensive action increases with imminence of threat (or aversive stimulus arousal). This motor disposition is reflected by an increase in potentiated startle to probe stimuli. Heart rate acceleration and a general sympathetic dominance of the autonomic system are characteristic of the circa-strike period, just prior to overt fight or flight (from Lang et al., 1997).

hension), patterns of physiological change (and in humans, reports of experienced emotional arousal) will systematically vary with the level of defense system activation. Furthermore, the overt behaviors that may result with increasing imminence (circa-strike region) could look fearful, angry, or—given overwhelming stress and no available coping behavior—autonomic and somatic collapse, hopelessness, and depression.

The model's assumed predator is, of course, engaged in parallel dance—first observing quietly the distant prey, stalking forward slowly, increasingly mobilized for what becomes, at circa-strike, a final charge. Overall, it is a parallel progression from attention to action, with a staged increment in appetitive arousal. Although there is currently little data on the predator's anticipatory pleasures—joy of the hunt, satisfaction in its consumption—the neurophysiology of the process is likely to be, in part, similar to what is observed in defense. In general, we have focused in this chapter on the defensive emotions at the expense of positive, pleasant states. As the allusion to predatory pleasures implies, this is mainly attributable to the larger, more programmatic literature on negative emotion. It is fondly to be wished that neuroscientists, cognitive scientists, and other researchers will in future have more time for consideration of the appetitive-positive affects.

EMOTION AND THE BRAIN: CONCLUDING THOUGHTS

We have proposed here that basic emotions are founded on brain circuitry in which the amygdala is a central component. We conceive emotion not as a single reaction, but as a process: In addition to reports of affective experience, emotions engage sequenced somatic and autonomic responses, organized by brain circuits that developed over evolutionary history to ensure the survival of individuals and species. Thus, events that are positive-appetitive or aversive-threatening have an initial advantage in capturing attention. As their affective valence is resolved, these events prompt further information gathering—more according to their degree of motivational significance. Motive cues also occasion the release of neurochemicals, metabolic arousal, anticipatory responses that are oriented toward the engaging event, and a mobilization of the organism that can lead to some action. Sometimes these motivational sequences play out in humans, in the same stimulus-driven way that they occur in less complex organisms. More often, given an elaborate brain that is equipped with language, an interactive memory storage, and a vast behavioral repertoire, motivational reflexes are only being engaged in part, and action is inhibited, delayed, or complexly adapted to the context. Nevertheless, it is this reflex bedrock that generally prompts humans to say that they are emotionally aroused. We may feel joyful, angry, fearful, anxious, or sad and hopeless. Regardless of how the state is labeled, true to emotion's reflex automaticity, we often feel less in control, as if something is happening to us, rather than that emotion is something we are doing—carried along in pleasure and in pain by the very human experience of emotion.

REFERENCES

Adolphs, R., & Tranel, D. (1999). Intact recognition of emotional prosody following amygdala damage. *Neuropsychologia, 37,* 1285–1292.

Adolphs, R., Tranel, D., & Damasio, A. R. (1998). The human amygdala in social judgment. *Nature, 393,* 470–474.

Adolphs, R., Tranel, D., Damasio, H., & Damasio, A. R. (1994). Impaired recognition of emotion in facial expressions following bilateral damage to the human amygdala. *Nature, 372,* 669–672.

Adolphs, R., Tranel, D., Damasio, H., & Damasio, A. R. (1995). Fear and the human amygdala. *Journal of Neuroscience, 15*(9), 5879–5891.

Amaral, D. G., & Price, J. L. (1984). Amygdalo-cortical projections in the monkey (*macaca fascicularis*). *Journal of Comparative Neurology, 230,* 465–496.

Amaral, D. G., Price, J. L., Pitkanen, A., & Carmichael, S. T. (1992). Anatomical organization of the primate amygdaloid complex. In J. Aggleton (Ed.), *The amygdala: Neurobiological aspects of emotion, memory, and mental dysfunction* (pp. 1–66). New York: Wiley.

Amorapanth, P., LeDoux, J. E., & Nader, K. (2000). Different lateral amygdala outputs mediate reactions and actions elicited by a fear-arousing stimulus. *Nature Neuroscience, 3,* 74–79.

Anderson, A. K., & Phelps, E. A. (1998). Intact recognition of vocal expressions of fear following bilateral lesions of the human amygdala. *Neuroreport, 9*(16), 3607–3613.

Anderson, A. K., & Phelps, E. A. (2000). Expression without recognition: Contributions of the human amygdala to emotional communication. *Psychological Science, 11,* 106–111.

Anderson, J. R., & Bower, G. H. (1974). A propositional theory of recognition memory. *Memory and Cognition, 2,* 406–412.

Anderson, S. W., Bechara, A., Damasio, H., Tranel, D., & Damasio, A. R. (1999). Impairment of social and moral behavior related to early damage in human prefrontal cortex. *Nature Neuroscience, 2,* 1032–1037.

Applegate, C. D., Kapp, B. S., Underwood, M. D., & McNall, C. L. (1983). Autonomic and somatomotor effects of amygdala central n. stimulation in awake rabbits. *Physiology and Behavior, 31,* 353–360.

Aston-Jones, G., Rajkowski, J., Kubiak, P., Valentino, R. J., & Shipley, M. T. (1996). Role of the locus coeruleus in emotional activation. *Progress in Brain Research, 107,* 379–402.

Balaban, M. (1995). Affective influences on startle in five-month-old infants: Reactions to facial expressions of emotion. *Child Development, 66,* 23–36.

Bandler, R., & Shipley, M. T. (1994). Columnar organization in the midbrain periaqueductal gray: Modules for emotional expression? *Trends in Neuroscience, 17,* 379–389.

Baxter, M. G., Parker, A., Lindner, C. C. C., Izquierdo, A. D., & Murray, E. A. (2000). Control of response selection by reinforcer value requires interaction of amygdala and orbital prefrontal cortex. *Journal of Neuroscience, 20,* 4311–4319.

Bechara, A., Damasio, H., Tranel, D., & Damasio, A. R. (1997). Deciding advantageously before knowing the advantageous strategy. *Science, 275,* 1293–1294.

Bechara, A., Tranel, D., Damasio, H., Adolphs, R., Rockland, C., & Damasio, A. R. (1995). Double dissociation of conditioning and declarative knowledge relative to the amygdala and hippocampus in humans. *Science, 269*, 1115–1118.

Belcheva, I., Belcheva, S., Petkov, V. V., & Petkov, V. D. (1994). Asymmetry in behavioral responses to cholecystokinin microinjected into rat nucleus accumbens and amygdala. *Neuropharmacology, 33*(8), 995–1002.

Berg, W. K., & Davis, M. (1985). Associative learning modifies startle reflexes at the lateral lemniscus. *Behavioral Neuroscience, 99*, 191–199.

Bermudez-Rattoni, F., Grijalva, C. V., Kiefer, S. W., & Garcia, J. (1986). Flavor-illness aversion: The role of the amygdala in acquisition of taste-potentiated odor aversions. *Physiology and Behavior, 38*, 503–508.

Blanchard, D. C., & Blanchard, R. J. (1988). Ethoexperimental approaches to the biology of emotion. *Annual Review of Psychology, 39*, 43–68.

Blanchard, R. J., Flannelly, K. J., & Blanchard, D. C. (1986). Defensive behavior of laboratory and wild Rattus norvegicus. *Journal of Comparative Psychology, 100*, 101–107.

Boadle-Biber, M. C., Singh, V. B., Corley, K. C., Phan, T. H., & Dilts, R. P. (1993). Evidence that corticotropin-releasing factor within the extended amygdala mediates the activation of tryptophan hydroxylase produced by sound stress in the rat. *Brain Research, 628*, 105–114.

Boulis, N., & Davis, M. (1989). Footshock-induced sensitization of electrically elicited startle reflexes. *Behavioral Neuroscience, 103*, 504–508.

Bower, D., Eckert, M., Gilmore, R., Leonard, C. M., Bauer, R., Roper, S., Bradley, M., Lang, P., & Barta, P. (1997). Startle eyeblink magnitude in humans depends on extent of right amygdala removal. *Society for Neuroscience Abstracts, 23*, 570.

Bradley, M. M. (2000). Emotion and motivation. In J. T. Cacioppo, L. G. Tassinary, & G. Bernston (Eds.), *Handbook of psychophysiology* (pp. 602–642). New York: Cambridge University Press.

Bradley, M. M., Codispoti, M., Sabatinelli, D., Cuthbert, B. N., & Lang, P. J. (2001). *Emotion and picture perception: Affective arousal, semantic content, and sex differences.* Manuscript submitted for publication.

Bradley, M. M., Cuthbert, B. N., & Lang, P. J. (1998). *International affective digitized sounds (IADS).* Gainesville, FL: The Center for Research in Psychophysiology, University of Florida.

Bradley, M. M., Greenwald, M. K., Petry, M., & Lang, P. J. (1992). Remembering pictures: Pleasure and arousal in memory. *Journal of Experimental Psychology: Learning, Memory, and Cognition, 18*, 379–390.

Bradley, M. M., Lang, P. J., & Cuthbert, B. N. (1990). Startle reflex modification: Emotion or attention. *Psychophysiology, 27*, 513–523.

Bradley, M. M., Lang, P. J., & Cuthbert, B. N. (1998). *Affective norms for English words (ANEW). Technical manual and affective ratings.* Gainesville, FL: The Center for the Study of Emotion and Attention, University of Florida.

Bradley, M. M., Lang, P. J., Sabatinelli, D., King, W., Fitzsimmons, J. R., & Desai, P. (2001). *Activation of the visual cortex in emotional perception.* Manuscript submitted for publication.

Bradley, M. M., Zack, J., & Lang, P. J. (1994). Cries, screams, and shouts of joy: Affective responses to environmental sounds. *Psychophysiology, 31*(Suppl. 29).

Broks, P., Young, A. W., Maratos, E. J., Coffey, P. L., Calder, A. J., Isaac, C., Mayes, A. R., Hodges, J. R., Montaldi, D., Cezayirli, E., Roberts, N., & Hadley, D. (1998). Face processing impairments after encephalitis: Amygdala damage and recognition of fear. *Neuropsychologia, 36*, 59–70.

Brown, J. S., Kalish, H. I., & Farber, I. E. (1951). Conditional fear as revealed by magnitude of startle response to an auditory stimulus. *Journal of Experimental Psychology, 41*, 317–328.

Brown, M. R., & Gray, T. S. (1988). Peptide injections into the amygdala of conscious rats: Effects on blood pressure, heart rate and plasma catecholamines. *Regulatory Peptides, 21*, 95–106.

Burns, L. H., Robbins, T. W., & Everitt, B. J. (1993). Differential effects of excitotoxic lesions of the basolateral amygdala, ventral subiculum and medial prefrontal cortex on responding with conditioned reinforcement and locomotor activity potentiated by intra-accumbens infusions of D-amphetamine. *Behavioural Brain Research, 55*, 167–183.

Bussey, T. J., Everitt, B. J., & Robbins, T. W. (1997). Dissociable effects of cingulate and medial frontal cortex lesions on stimulus-reward learning using a novel Pavlovian autoshaping procedure in rats: Implications for the neurobiology of emotion. *Behavioral Neuroscience, 111*, 908–919.

Cador, M., Robbins, T. W., & Everitt, B. J. (1989). Involvement of the amygdala in stimulus-reward associations: Interaction with the ventral striatum. *Neuroscience, 30*(1), 77–86.

Cahill, L. (2000). Modulation of long-term memory storage in humans by emotional arousal: Adrenergic activation and the amygdala. In J. P. Aggleton (Ed.), *The amygdala* (Vol. 2, pp. 425–445). Oxford, UK: Oxford University Press.

Cahill, L., Haier, R. J., Fallon, J., Alkire, M. T., Tang, C., Keator, D., Wu, J., & McGaugh, J. L. (1996). Amygdala activity at encoding correlated with long-term, free recall of emotional information. *Proceedings of the National Academy of Sciences, USA, 93*, 8016–8021.

Cahill, L., & McGaugh, J. L. (1998). Mechanisms of emotional arousal and lasting declarative memory. *Trends in Neuroscience, 21*, 294–299.

Calder, A. J., Young, A. W., Rowland, D., Perrett, D. I., Hodges, J. R., & Etcoff, N. L. (1996). Facial emotion recognition after bilateral amygdala damage: Differentially severe impairment of fear. *Cognitive Neuropsychology, 13*, 699–745.

Calvino, B., Lagowska, J., & Ben-Ari, Y. (1979). Morphine withdrawal syndrome: Differential participation of structures located within the amygdaloid complex and striatum of the rat. *Brain Research, 177,* 19–34.

Campbell, B. A., Wood, G., & McBride, T. (1997). Origins of orienting and defense responses: An evolutionary perspective. In P. J. Lang, R. F. Simmons, & M. T. Balaban (Eds.), *Attention and orienting: Sensory and motivational processes* (pp. 41–67). Hillsdale, NJ: Erlbaum.

Campeau, S., & Davis, M. (1995a). Involvement of subcortical and cortical afferents to the lateral nucleus of the amygdala in fear conditioning measured with fear-potentiated startle in rats trained concurrently with auditory and visual conditioned stimuli. *Journal of Neuroscience, 15,* 2312–2327.

Campeau, S., & Davis, M. (1995b). Involvement of the central nucleus and basolateral complex of the amygdala in fear conditioning measured with fear-potentiated startle in rats trained concurrently with auditory and visual conditioned stimuli. *Journal of Neuroscience, 15,* 2301–2311.

Chapman, W. P., Schroeder, H. R., Guyer, G., Brazier, M. A. B., Fager, C., Poppen, J. L., Solomon, H. C., & Yakolev, P. I. (1954). Physiological evidence concerning the importance of the amygdaloid nuclear region in the integration of circulating function and emotion in man. *Science, 129,* 949–950.

Costall, B., Kelly, M. E., Naylor, R. J., Onaivi, E. S., & Tyers, M. B. (1989). Neuroanatomical sites of action of 5-HT$_3$ receptor agonist and antagonists for alteration of aversive behaviour in the mouse. *British Journal of Pharmacology, 96,* 325–332.

Cuthbert, B. N., Bradley, M. M., & Lang, P. J. (1996). Probing picture perception: Activation and emotion. *Psychophysiology, 33,* 103–111.

Cuthbert, B. N., Schupp, H. T., Bradley, M. M., Birbaumer, N., & Lang, P. J. (1998). *We like to watch: Cortical potentials in emotional perception.* Manuscript submitted for publication.

Damasio, A. R. (1994). *Descartes' error.* New York: Grosset/Putnam.

Davis, M. (2000). The role of the amygdala in conditioned and unconditioned fear and anxiety. In J. P. Aggleton (Ed.), *The amygdala* (Vol. 2, pp. 213–287). Oxford, UK: Oxford University Press.

Davis, M., Falls, W. A., Campeau, S., & Kim, M. (1993). Fear-potentiated startle: A neural and pharmacological analysis. *Behavioral Brain Research, 58,* 175–198.

Davis, M., & Whalen, P. (2001). The amygdala: Vigilance and emotion. *Molecular Psychiatry, 6,* 13–34.

Dickinson, A., & Dearing, M. F. (1979). Appetitive-aversive interactions and inhibitory processes. In A. B. Dickinson & R. A. Boakes (Eds.), *Mechanisms of learning and motivation* (pp. 203–231). Hillsdale, NJ: Erlbaum.

Dringenberg, H. C., & Vanderwolf, C. H. (1996). Cholinergic activation of the electrocorticogram: A8n amygdaloid activating system. *Experimental Brain Research, 108,* 285–296.

Ehrlichman, H., Brown, S., Zhu, J., & Warrenburg, S. (1995). Startle reflex modulation during exposure to pleasant and unpleasant odors. *Psychophysiology, 32,* 150–154.

Everitt, B. J., Cador, M., & Robbins, T. W. (1989). Interactions between the amygdala and ventral striatum in stimulus-reward associations: Studies using a second-order schedule of sexual reinforcement. *Neuroscience, 30,* 63–75.

Everitt, B. J., Cardinal, R. N., Hall, J., Parkinson, J. A., & Robbins, T. W. (2000). Differential involvement of amygdala subsytems in apetitive conditioning and drug addiction. In J. P. Aggleton (Ed.), *The amygdala* (Vol. 2, pp. 353–390). Oxford, UK: Oxford University Press.

Everitt, B. J., Morris, K. A., O'Brien, A., & Robbins, T. W. (1991). The basolateral amygdala-ventral striatal system and conditioned place preference: Further evidence of limbic-striatal interactions underlying reward-related processes. *Neuroscience, 42*(1), 1–18.

Everitt, B. J., & Robbins, T. V. (1992). Amygdala-ventral striatal interactions and reward related processes. In J. P. Aggleton (Ed.), *The amygdala: Neurobiological aspects of emotion, memory, and mental dysfunction* (pp. 401–429). New York: Wiley-Liss.

Fanselow, M. S. (1991). The midbrain periaqueductal gray as a coordinator of action in response to fear and anxiety. In A. Depaulis & R. Bandler (Eds.), *The midbrain periaqueductal gray matter: Functional, anatomical and neurochemical organization* (pp. 151–173). New York: Plenum.

Fanselow, M. S. (1994). Neural organization of the defensive behavior system responsible for fear. *Psychonomic Bulletin and Review, 1,* 429–438.

Fendt, M., Koch, M., & Schnitzler, H.-U. (1996). Lesions of the central gray block conditioned fear as measured with the potentiated startle paradigm. *Behavioural Brain Research, 74,* 127–134.

File, S. E., & Rodgers, R. J. (1979). Partial anxiolytic actions of morphine sulphate following microinjection into the central nucleus of the amygdala in rats. *Pharmacology, Biochemistry, and Behavior, 11,* 313–318.

Frankland, P. W., Josselyn, S. A., Bradwejn, J., Vaccarino, F. J., & Yeomans, J. S. (1997). Activation of amygdala cholecystokininB receptors potentiates the acoustic startle response in the rat. *Journal of Neuroscience, 17,* 1838–1847.

Frankland, P. W., & Yeomans, J. S. (1995). Fear-potentiated startle and electrically evoked startle mediated by synapses in rostrolateral midbrain. *Behavioral Neuroscience, 109,* 669–680.

Fredrikson, M., Wik, G., Annas, P., Ericson, K. A. J., & Stone-Elander, S. (1995). Functional neuroanatomy of visually elicited simple phobic fear: Additional data and theoretical analysis. *Psychophysiology, 32,* 43–48.

Fredrikson, M., Wik, G., Greitz, T., Stone-Elander, S., Ericson, K. A. J., & Sedvall, G. (1993). Regional cerebral blood flow during experimental phobic fear. *Psychophysiology, 30,* 126–130.

Funayama, E. S., Grillon, C. G., Davis, M., & Phelps, E. A. (2001). A double dissociation in the affective modulation of startle in humans: Effects of unilateral temporal lobectomy. *Journal of Cognitive Neuroscience, 13,* 721–729.

Gallagher, M. (2000). The amygdala and associative learning. In J. P. Aggleton (Ed.), *The amygdala* (Vol. 2). Oxford, UK: Oxford University Press.

Gallagher, M., Graham, P. W., & Holland, P. C. (1990). The amygdala central nucleus and appetitive pavlovian conditioning: Lesions impair one class of conditioned behavior. *Journal of Neuroscience, 10,* 1906–1911.

Gallagher, M., Kapp, B. S., McNall, C. L., & Pascoe, J. P. (1981). Opiate effects in the amygdala central nucleus on heart rate conditioning in rabbits. *Pharmacology, Biochemistry, and Behavior, 14,* 497–505.

Gallagher, M., Kapp, B. S., & Pascoe, J. P. (1982). Enkephalin analogue effects in the amygdala central nucleus on conditioned heart rate. *Pharmacology, Biochemistry, and Behavior, 17,* 217–222.

Gewirtz, J., & Davis, M. (1997). Second order fear conditioning prevented by blocking NMDA receptors in the amygdala. *Nature, 388,* 471–474.

Gewirtz, J. C., & Davis, M. (1998). Application of Pavlovian higher-order conditioning to the analysis of the neural substrates of learning and memory. *Neuropharmacology, 37,* 453–460.

Gloor, P., Olivier, A., & Quesney, L. F. (1981). The role of the amygdala in the expression of psychic phenomena in temporal lobe seizures. In Y. Ben-Ari (Ed.), *The amygdaloid complex* (pp. 489–507). New York: Elsevier/North Holland.

Goddard, G. V. (1964). Functions of the amygdala. *Psychological Bulletin, 62,* 89–109.

Goldstein, L. E., Rasmusson, A. M., Bunney, B. S., & Roth, R. H. (1996). Role of the amygdala in the coordination of behavioral, neuroendocrine, and prefrontal cortical monoamine responses to psychological stress in the rat. *Journal of Neuroscience, 16*(15), 4787–4798.

Graham, F. K. (1979). Distinguishing among orienting, defense, and startle reflexes. In H. D. Kimmel, H. van Olst, & F. Orelebeke (Eds.), *The orienting reflex in humans: An international conference sponsored by the Scientific Affairs Division of the North Atlantic Treaty Organization* (pp. 137–167). Hillsdale, NJ: Erlbaum.

Graham, F. K. (1992). Attention: The heartbeat, the blink, and the brain. In B. A. Campbell, H. Hayne, & R. Richardson (Eds.), *Attention and information processing in infants and adults* (pp. 3–29). Hillsdale, NJ: Erlbaum.

Graham, F. K., & Clifton, R. K. (1966). Heart rate change as a component of the orienting response. *Psychological Bulletin, 65,* 305–320.

Green, S., & Vale, A. L. (1992). Role of amygdaloid nuclei in the anxiolytic effects of benzodiazepines in rats. *Behavioural Pharmacology, 3,* 261–264.

Greenwald, M. K., Bradley, M. M., Cuthbert, B. N., & Lang, P. J. (1998). Sensitization of the startle reflex in humans following aversive electric shock exposure. *Behavioral Neuroscience, 112,* 1069–1079.

Greenwald, M. K., Cook, E. W. I., & Lang, P. J. (1989). Affective judgement and psychophysiological response: Dimensional covariation in the evaluation of pictorial stimuli. *Journal of Psychophysiology, 3,* 51–64.

Grillon, C., Ameli, R., Merikangas, K., Woods, S. W., & Davis, M. (1993). Measuring the time course of anticipatory anxiety using the fear-potentiated startle reflex. *Psychophysiology, 30,* 340–346.

Grillon, C., Ameli, R., Woods, S. W., Merikangas, K., & Davis, M. (1991). Fear-potentiated startle in humans: Effects of anticipatory anxiety on the acoustic blink reflex. *Psychophysiology, 28,* 588–595.

Grillon, C., & Davis, M. (1997). Fear-potentiated startle conditioning in humans: Effects of explicit and contextual cue conditioning following paired vs. unpaired training. *Psychophysiology, 34,* 451–458.

Guarraci, F. A., Frohardt, R. J., & Kapp, B. S. (1999). Amygdaloid D1 dopamine receptor involvement in Pavlovian fear conditioning. *Brain Research, 827,* 28–40.

Hamm, A. O., Cuthbert, B. N., Globisch, J., & Vaitl, D. (1997). Fear and startle reflex: Blink modulation and autonomic response patterns in animal mutilation fearful subjects. *Psychophysiology, 34,* 97–107.

Hamm, A. O., Greenwald, M. K., Bradley, M. M., & Lang, P. J. (1993). Emotional learning, hedonic changes, and the startle prove. *Journal of Abnormal Psychology, 102,* 453–465.

Hatfield, T., & Gallagher, M. (1995). Taste-potentiated odor conditioning: Impairment produced by infusion of an N-methyl-D-aspartate antagonist into basolateral amygdala. *Behavioral Neuroscience, 109*(4), 663–668.

Hatfield, T., Graham, P. W., & Gallagher, M. (1992). Taste-potentiated odor aversion: Role of the amygdaloid basolateral complex and central nucleus. *Behavioral Neuroscience, 106,* 286–293.

Hatfield, T., Han, J.-S., Conley, M., Gallagher, M., & Holland, P. (1996). Neurotoxic lesions of basolateral, but not central, amygdala interfere with Pavlovian second-order conditioning and reinforcer devaluation effects. *Journal of Neuroscience, 16,* 5256–5265.

Hawk, L. W., & Cook, E. W. (1997). Affective modulation of tactile startle. *Psychophysiology, 34,* 23–31.

Hebb, D. O. (1949). *The organization of behavior.* New York: Wiley.

Heilig, M., McLeod, S., Brot, M., Henrichs, S. C., Menzaghi, F., Koob, G. F., & Britton, K. T. (1993). Anxiolytic-like action of neuropeptide Y: Mediation by Y1 receptors in amygdala, and dissociation from food intake effects. *Neuropsychopharmacology, 8,* 357–363.

Heinrichs, S. C., Menzaghi, F., Schulteis, G., Koob, G. F., & Stinus, L. (1995). Suppression of corticotropin-releasing factor in the amygdala attenuates aversive consequences of morphine withdrawal. *Behavioural Pharmacology, 6,* 74–80.

Heinrichs, S. C., Pich, E. M., Miczek, K. A., Britton, K. T., & Koob, G. F. (1992). Corticotropin-releasing factor antagonist reduces emotionality in socially defeated rats via direct neurotropic action. *Brain Research, 581,* 190–197.

Helmstetter, F. J. (1993). Stress-induced hypoalgesia and defensive freezing are attenuated by application of diazepam to the amygdala. *Pharmacology, Biochemistry, and Behavior, 44,* 433–438.

Hernandez, D. E., Salaiz, A. B., Morin, P., & Moreira, M. A. (1990). Administration of thyrotropin-releasing hormone into the central nucleus of the amygdala induces gastric lesions in rats. *Brain Research Bulletin, 24,* 697–699.

Hitchcock, J. M., & Davis, M. (1986). Lesions of the amygdala, but not of the cerebellum or red nucleus, block conditioned fear as measured with the potentiated startle paradigm. *Behavioral Neuroscience, 100,* 11–22.

Hitchcock, J. M., & Davis, M. (1991). The efferent pathway of the amygdala involved in conditioned fear as measured with the fear-potentiated startle paradigm. *Behavioral Neuroscience, 105,* 826–842.

Hodges, H., Green, S., & Glenn, B. (1987). Evidence that the amygdala is involved in benzodiazepine and serotonergic effects on punished responding but not on discrimination. *Psychopharmacology, 92,* 491–504.

Holland, P. C., & Gallagher, M. (1993a). The effects of amygdala central nucleus lesions on blocking and unblocking. *Behavioral Neuroscience, 107,* 235–245.

Holland, P. C., & Gallagher, M. (1993b). Amygdala central nucleus lesions disrupt increments, but not decrement, in conditioned stimulus processing. *Behavioral Neuroscience, 107,* 246–253.

Irwin, W., Davidson, R. J., Lowe, M. J., Mock, B. J., Sorenson, J. A., & Turski, P. A. (1996). Human amygdala activation detected with echo-planar functional magnetic resonance imaging. *NeuroReport, 7,* 1765–1769.

Ishikawa, T., Yang, H., & Tache, Y. (1988). Medullary sites of action of the TRH analogue, RX 77368, for stimulation of gastric acid secretion in the rat. *Gastroenterology, 95,* 1470–1476.

Iwai, E., & Yukie, M. (1987). Amygdalofugal and amygdalepetal connetions with modality-specific visual cortical areas in Macaques (*Macaca fuscata, M. mulatta,* and *M. fascicularis*). *Journal of Comparative Neurology, 261,* 362–387.

Junghoefer, M., Bradley, M. M., Elbert, T. R., & Lang, P. J. (2001). Pictures in a rapid stream: Early detection of emotion. *Psychophysiology, 38,* 175–178.

Kapp, B. S., Supple, W. F., & Whalen, P. J. (1994). Effects of electrical stimulation of the amygdaloid central nucleus on neocortical arousal in the rabbit. *Behavioral Neuroscience, 108,* 81–93.

Kapp, B. S., Whalen, P. J., Supple, W. F., & Pascoe, J. P. (1992). Amygdaloid contributions to conditioned arousal and sensory information processing. In J. P. Aggleton (Ed.), *The amygdala: Neurobiological aspects of emotion, memory, and mental dysfunction* (pp. 229–254). New York: Wiley-Liss.

Kapp, B. S., Wilson, A., Pascoe, J. P., Supple, W. F., & Whalen, P. J. (1990). A neuroanatomical systems analysis of conditioned bradycardia in the rabbit. In M. Gabriel & J. Moore (Eds.), *Neurocomputation and learning: Foundations of adaptive networks* (pp. 55–90). New York: Bradford Books.

Killcross, S., Robbins, T. W., & Everitt, B. J. (1997). Different types of fear-conditioned behaviour mediated by separate nuclei within amygdala. *Nature, 388,* 377–380.

Kim, M., Campeau, S., Falls, W. A., & Davis, M. (1993). Infusion of the non-NMDA receptor antagonist CNQX into the amygdala blocks the expression of fear-potentiated startle. *Behavioral and Neural Biology, 59,* 5–8.

Kintsch, W. (1974). *The representation of meaning in memory.* Hillsdale, NJ: Erlbaum.

Koch, M., Schmid, A., & Schnitzler, H.-U. (1996). Pleasure-attenuation of startle is disrupted by lesions of the nucleus accumbens. *NeuroReport, 7,* 1442–1446.

Konorski, J. (1967). *Integrative activity of the brain: An interdisciplinary approach.* Chicago: University of Chicago Press.

Krase, W., Koch, M., & Schnitzler, H. U. (1994). Substance P is involved in the sensitization of the acoustic startle response by footshock in rats. *Behavioral Brain Research, 63,* 81–88.

Lamont, E. W., & Kokkinidis, L. (1998). Infusion of the dopamine D1 receptor antagonist SCH 23390 into the amygdala blocks fear expression in a potentiated startle paradigm. *Brain Research, 795,* 128–136.

Landis, C., & Hunt, W. (1939). *The startle paradigm.* New York: Farrar and Rinehart.

Lane, R. D., Reiman, E. M., Bradley, M. M., Lang, P. J., Ahern, G. L., Davidson, R. J., & Schwartz, G. E. (1997). Neuroanatomical correlates of pleasant and unpleasant emotion. *Neuropsychologia, 35,* 1437–1444.

Lang, P. J. (1985). The cognitive psychophysiology of emotion: Fear and anxiety. In A. H. Tuma & J. D. Maser (Eds.), *Anxiety and the anxiety disorders* (Vol. 3, pp. 131–170). Hillsdale, NJ: Erlbaum.

Lang, P. J. (1994). The motivational organization of emotion: Affect-reflex connections. In S. VanGoozen, N. E. Van De Poll, & J. A. Sargeant (Eds.), *Emotions: Essays on emotion theory* (pp. 61–93). Hillsdale, NJ: Erlbaum.

Lang, P. J. (1995). The emotion probe. *American Psychologist, 50,* 372–385.

Lang, P. J., Bradley, M. M., & Cuthbert, B. N. (1990). Emotion, attention, and the startle reflex. *Psychology Reviews, 97,* 377–395.

Lang, P. J., Bradley, M. M., & Cuthbert, B. N. (1997). Motivated attention: Affect, activation and action. In P. J. Lang, R. F. Simons, & M. F. Balaban (Eds.), *Attention and orienting: Sensory and motivational processes* (pp. 97–135). Hillsdale, NJ: Erlbaum.

Lang, P. J., Bradley, M. M., & Cuthbert, B. N. (1998). *International affective picture system (IAPS).* Gainesville, FL: The Center for Research in Psychophysiology, University of Florida.

Lang, P. J., Bradley, M. M., Fitzsimmons, J. R., Cuthbert, B. N., Scott, J. D., Moulder, B., & Nangia, V. (1998). Emotional arousal and activation of the visual cortex: An fMRI analysis. *Psychophysiology, 35,* 1–13.

Lang, P. J., Greenwald, M. K., Bradley, M. M., & Hamm, A. O. (1993). Looking at Pictures: Affective, facial, visceral and behavioral reactions. *Psychophysiology, 30,* 261–273.

LeBar, K. S., Gatenby, J. C., Gore, J. C., LeDoux, J. E., & Phelps, E. A. (1998). Human amygdala activation during conditioned fear acquisition and extinction: A mixed-trial fMRI study. *Neuron, 20,* 937–945.

LeBar, K. S., LeDoux, J. E., Spencer, D. D., & Phelps, E. A. (1995). Impaired fear conditioning following unilateral temporal lobectomy in humans. *Journal of Neuroscience, 15,* 6846–6855.

LeDoux, J. E., Iwata, J., Cicchetti, P., & Reis, D. J. (1988). Different projections of the central amygdaloid nucleus mediate autonomic and behavioral correlates of conditioned fear. *Journal of Neuroscience, 8,* 2517–2529.

Lee, G. P., Bechara, A., Adolphs, R., Arena, J., Meador, K. J., Loring, D. W., & Smith, J. R. (1998). Clinical and physiological effects of stereotaxic bilateral amygdalotomy for intractable aggression. *Journal of Neuropsychiatry and Clinical Neurosciences, 10,* 413–420.

Lee, Y., & Davis, M. (1996). The role of bed nucleus of the stria terminalis in CRH-enhanced startle: An animal model of anxiety. *Society for Neuroscience Abstracts, 22,* 465.

Li, L., & Yeomans, J. S. (1999). Summation between acoustic and trigeminal stimuli evoking startle. *Neuroscience, 90,* 139–152.

Liebsch, G., Landgraf, R., Gerstberger, R., Probst, J. C., Wotjak, C. T., Engelmann, M., Holsboer, F., & Montkowski, A. (1995). Chronic infusion of a CRH$_1$ receptor antisense oligodeoxynucleotide into the central nucleus of the amygdala reduced anxiety-related behavior in socially defeated rats. *Regulatory Peptides, 59,* 229–239.

Lipp, O. V., Sheridan, J., & Siddle, D. A. (1994). Human blink startle during aversive and nonaversive Pavlovian conditioning. *Journal of Experimental Psychology: Animal Behavioral Processes, 20,* 380–389.

Maldonado, R., Stinus, L., Gold, L. H., & Koob, G. F. (1992). Role of different brain structures in the expression of the physical morphine withdrawal syndrome. *Journal of Pharmacology and Experimental Therapeutics, 261*(2), 669–677.

Masur, J. D., Dienst, F. T., & O'Neal, E. C. (1974). The acquisition of a Pavlovian conditioned response in septally damaged rabbits: Role of a competing response. *Physiological Psychology, 2,* 133–136.

McCall, R. B., & Aghajanian, G. K. (1979). Serotonergic facilitation of facial motoneuron excitation. *Brain Research, 169,* 11–27.

McDonald, A. J. (1991). Topographic organization of amygdaloid projections to the caudatoputamen, nucleus accumbens, and related striateal-like areas of the rat brain. *Neuroscience, 44*(1), 15–33.

McDonald, A. J. (1998). Cortical pathways to the mammalian amygdala. *Progress in Neurobiology, 55,* 257–332.

McGaugh, J. L., Introini-Collison, I. B., Cahill, L., Castellano, C., Dalmaz, C., Parent, M. B., & Williams, C. L. (1993). Neuromodulatory systems and memory storage: Role of the amygdala. *Behavioural Brain Research, 58,* 81–90.

McGaugh, J. L., Introini-Collison, I. B., Cahill, L., Kim, M., & Liang, K. C. (1992). Involvement of the amygdala in neuromodulatory influences on memory storage. In J. P. Aggleton (Ed.), *The amygdala: Neurobiological aspects of emotion, memory, and mental dysfunction* (pp. 431–451). New York: Wiley-Liss.

Mehrabian, A., & Russell, J. A. (1974). *An approach to environmental psychology.* Cambridge, MA: MIT Press.

Meloni, E. G., & Davis, M. (1999). Muscimol in the deep layers of the superior colliculus/mesencephalic reticular formation blocks expression but not acquisition of fear-potentiated startle in rats. *Behavioral Neuroscience, 113,* 1152–1160.

Miller, N. E. (1959). Liberalization of basic S-R concepts: Extensions to conflict behavior, motivation and social learning. In S. Koch (Ed.), *Psychology: A study of a science* (Vol. 2, pp. 196–292). New York: McGraw-Hill.

Miltner, W., Matjak, M., Braun, C., & Diekmann, H. (1994). Emotional qualities of odors and their influence on the startle reflex in humans. *Psychophysiology, 31,* 107–110.

Mineka, S., Davidson, M., Cook, M., & Keir, R. (1984). Observational conditioning of snake fear in rhesus monkeys. *Journal of Abnormal Psychology, 93,* 355–372.

Morgenson, G. M. (1987). Limbic-motor intergration. In A. Epstein & A. R. Morrison (Eds.), *Progress in psychobiology and physiological psychology* (pp. 117–170). New York: Academic Press.

Morris, J. S., Frith, C. D., Perrett, D. I., & Rowland, D. (1996). A differential neural response in the human amygdala to fearful and happy facial expression. *Nature, 383,* 812–815.

Morris, J. S., Ohman, A., & Dolan, R. J. (1998). Conscious and unconscious emotional learning in the human amygdala. *Nature, 393,* 467–470.

Morris, M., Bradley, M., Bowers, D., Lang, P., & Heilman, K. (1991). Valence-specific hypoarousal following right temporal lobectomy. *Journal of Clinical and Experimental Neuropsychology, 13,* 42.

Morrow, N. S., Hodgson, D. M., & Garrick, T. (1996). Microinjection of thyrotropin-releasing hormone analogue into the central nucleus of the amygdala stimulates gastric contractility in rats. *Brain Research, 735,* 141–148.

Ortony, A., Clore, G. L., & Collins, A. (1988). *The cognitive structure of emotions.* Cambridge, UK: Cambridge University Press.

Osgood, C., Suci, G., & Tannenbaum, P. (1957). *The measurement of meaning.* Urbana: University of Illinois.

Packard, M. G., Cahill, L., & McGaugh, J. L. (1994). Amygdala modulation of hippocampal-dependent and caudate nucleus-dependent memory processes. *Proceedings of the National Academy of Sciences, USA, 91*, 8477–8481.

Packard, M. G., & Teather, L. A. (1998). Amygdala modulation of multiple memory systems: Hippocampus and caudate-putamen. *Neurobiology of Learning and Memory, 69*, 163–203.

Parkinson, J. A., Dally, J. W., Bamford, A., Fehrent, B., Robbins, T. W., & Everitt, B. J. (1998). Effects of 6-OHDA lesions of the rat nucleus accumbens on appetitive Pavlovian conditioning. *Journal of Psychopharmacology, 12*, A8.

Parkinson, J. A., Robbins, T. W., & Everitt, B. J. (2000). Dissociable roles of the central and basolateral amygdala in appetitive emotional learning. *European Journal of Neuroscience, 12*, 405–413.

Parkinson, J. A., Willoughby, P. J., Robbins, T. W., & Everitt, B. J. (2000). Disconnection of the anterior cingulater cortex and nucleus accumbens core impairs Pavlovian approach behavior: Further evidence for limbic cortico-ventral striatopallidal systems. *Behavioral Neuroscience, 114*, 42–63.

Pascoe, J. P., & Kapp, B. S. (1985). Electrophysiological characteristics of amygdaloid central nucleus neurons during Pavlovian fear conditioning in the rabbit. *Behavioral Brain Research, 16*, 117–133.

Pavlov, I. P. (1927). *Conditioned reflexes.* Oxford, UK: Oxford University Press.

Pesold, C., & Treit, D. (1995). The central and basolateral amygdala differentially mediate the anxiolytic effects of benzodiazepines. *Brain Research, 671*, 213–221.

Petersen, E. N., Braestrup, C., & Scheel-Kruger, J. (1985). Evidence that the anticonflict effect of midazolam in amygdala is mediated by the specific benzodiazepine receptor. *Neuroscience Letters, 53*, 285–288.

Phelps, E. A., O'Connor, K. J., Cunningham, W. A., Funayama, E. S., Gatenby, J. C., Gore, J. C., & Banaji, M. R. (2000). Performance on indirect measures of race evaluation predicts amygdala activation. *Journal of Cognitive Neuroscience, 12*, 729–738.

Phelps, E. A., O'Connor, K. J., Gatenby, J. C., Gore, J. C., Grillon, C., & Davis, M. (2001). Activation of the left amygdala to a cognitive representation of fear. *Nature Neuroscience, 4*, 437–441.

Quirk, G. J., Repa, J. C., & LeDoux, J. E. (1995). Fear conditioning enhances short-latency auditory responses of lateral amygdala neurons: Parallel recordings in the freely behaving rat. *Neuron, 15*, 1029–1039.

Rassnick, S., Heinrichs, S. C., Britton, K. T., & Koob, G. F. (1993). Microinjection of a corticotroin-releasing factor antagonist into the central nucleus of the amygdala reverses anxiogenic-like effects of ethanol withdrawal. *Brain Research, 605*, 25–32.

Ray, A., & Henke, P. G. (1990). Enkephalin-dopamine interactions in the central amygdalar nucleus during gastric stress ulcer formation in rats. *Behavioural Brain Research, 36*, 179–183.

Ray, A., & Henke, P. G. (1991). TRH-enkephalin interactions in the amygdaloid complex during gastric stress ulcer formation in rats. *Regulatory Peptides, 35*, 11–17.

Ray, A., Henke, P. G., & Sullivan, R. M. (1990). Effects of intra-amygdalar thyrotropin releasing hormone (TRH) and its antagonism by atropine and benzodiazepines during stress ulcer formation in rats. *Pharmacology, Biochemistry, and Behavior, 36*, 597–601.

Ray, A., Sullivan, R. M., & Henke, P. G. (1988). Interactions of thyrotropin-releasing hormone (TRH) with neurotensin and dopamine in the central nucleus of the amygdala during stress ulcer formation in rats. *Neuroscience Letters, 91*, 95–100.

Redmond, D. E., Jr. (1977). Alteration in the function of the nucleus locus: A possible model for studies on anxiety. In I. E. Hanin & E. Usdin (Eds.), *Animal models in psychiatry and neurology* (pp. 292–304). Oxford, UK: Pergamon Press.

Reiman, E. M., Lane, R. D., Ahern, G. L., Schwartz, G. E., Davidson, R. J., Friston, K. J., Yun, L., & Chen, K. (1997). Neuroanatomical correlates of externally and internally generated human emotion. *American Journal of Psychiatry, 54*, 918–925.

Robledo, P., Robbins, T. W., & Everitt, B. J. (1996). Effects of excitotoxic lesions of the central amygdaloid nucleus on the potentiation of reward-related stimuli by intra-accumbens amphetamine. *Behavioral Neuroscience, 110*, 981–990.

Roozendaal, B., Schoorlemmer, G. H., Koolhaas, J. M., & Bohus, B. (1993). Cardiac, neuroendocrine, and behavioral effects of central amygdaloid vasopressinergic and oxytocinergic mechanisms under stress-free conditions in rats. *Brain Research Bulletin, 32*, 573–579.

Roozendaal, B., Wiersma, A., Driscoll, P., Koolhaas, J. M., & Bohus, B. (1992). Vasopressinergic modulation of stress responses in the central amygdala of the Roman high-avoidance and low-avoidance rat. *Brain Research, 596*, 35–40.

Rosen, J. B., Hitchcock, J. M., Miserendino, M. J. D., Falls, W. A., Campeau, S., & Davis, M. (1992). Lesions of the perirhinal cortex but not of the frontal, medial prefrontal, visual, or insular cortex block fear-potentiated startle using a visual conditioned stimulus. *Journal of Neuroscience, 12*, 4624–4633.

Rosen, J. B., Hitchcock, J. M., Sananes, C. B., Miserendino, M. J. D., & Davis, M. (1991). A direct projection from the central nucleus of the amygdala to the acoustic startle pathway: Anterograde and retrograde tracing studies. *Behavioral Neuroscience, 105*, 817–825.

Sabatinelli, D., Bradley, M. M., Cuthbert, B. N., & Lang, P. J. (1996). Wait and see: Aversion and activation in anticipation and perception. *Psychophysiology, 33*, S72.

Sajdyk, T. J., Schober, D. A., Gehlert, D. R., & Shekhar, A. (1999). Role of corticotropin-releasing factor and urocortin within the basolateral amygdala of rats in anxiety and panic responses. *Behavioural Brain Research, 100*, 207–215.

Sajdyk, T. J., & Shekhar, A. (1997a). Excitatory amino acid receptor antagonists block the cardiovascular and anxiety responses elicited by y-aminobutyric acid—a receptor blockade in the basolateral amygdala of rats. *Journal of Pharmacology and Experimental Therapeutics, 283*, 969–977.

Sajdyk, T. J., & Shekhar, A. (1997b). Excitatory amino acid receptors in the bsolateral amygdala regulate anxiety responses in the social interaction test. *Brain Research, 764,* 262–264.

Sajdyk, T. J., Vandergriff, M. G., & Gehlert, D. R. (1999). Amygdalar neuropeptide Y Y-1 receptors mediate the anxiolytic-like actions of neuropeptide Y in the social interaction test. *European Journal of Pharmacology, 368,* 143–147.

Sakanaka, M., Shibasaki, T., & Lederis, K. (1986). Distribution and efferent projections of corticotropin-releasing factor-like immunoreactivity in the rat amygdaloid complex. *Brain Research, 382,* 213–238.

Sananes, C. B., & Davis, M. (1992). N-Methyl-D-Aspartate lesions of the lateral and basolateral nuclei of the amygdala block fear-potentiated startle and shock sensitization of startle. *Behavioral Neuroscience, 106,* 72–80.

Sanders, S. K., & Shekhar, A. (1991). Blockade of GABA$_A$ receptors in the region of the anterior basolateral amygdala of rats elicits increases in heart rate and blood pressure. *Brain Research, 576,* 101–110.

Sanders, S. K., & Shekhar, A. (1995). Regulation of anxiety by GABA$_A$ receptors in the rat amygdala. *Pharmacology, Biochemistry, and Behavior, 52*(4), 701–706.

Sanghera, M. K., Rolls, E. T., & Roper-Hall, A. (1979). Visual responses of neurons in the dorsolateral amygdala of the alert monkey. *Experimental Neurology, 63,* 610–626.

Scheel-Kruger, J., & Petersen, E. N. (1982). Anticonflict effect of the benzodiazepines mediated by a GABAergic mechanism in the amygdala. *European Journal of Pharmacology, 82,* 115–116.

Schlosberg, J. (1952). The description of facial expression in terms of two dimensions. *Journal of Experimental Psychology, 44,* 229–237.

Schmid, A., Koch, M., & Schnitzler, H.-U. (1995). Conditioned pleasure attenuates the startle response in rats. *Neurobiology of Learning and Memory, 64,* 1–3.

Schneider, W., Noll, D., & Cohen, J. (1993). Functional topographic mapping of the cortical ribbon in human vision with conventional MRI scanners. *Nature, 365,* 150–153.

Schneiderman, N. (1972). Response system divergencies in aversive classical conditioning. In A. H. Black & W. F. Prokasy (Eds.), *Classical conditioning: Vol. 3. Current research and theory* (pp. 341–376). New York: Appleton-Century-Crofts.

Schneirla, T. (1959). An evolutionary and developmental theory of biphasic processes underlying approach and withdrawal. In M. Jones (Ed.), *Nebraska symposium on motivation* (pp. 1–42). Lincoln: University of Nebraska Press.

Schoenbaum, G., Chiba, A. A., & Gallagher, M. (1998). Orbitofrontal cortex and basolateral amygdala encode expected outcomes during learning. *Nature Neuroscience, 1,* 155–159.

Schoenbaum, G., Chiba, A. A., & Gallagher, M. (1999). Neural encoding in orbitofrontal cortex and basolateral amygdala during olfactory discrimination learning. *Journal of Neuroscience, 19,* 1876–1884.

Schwaber, J. S., Kapp, B. S., Higgins, G. A., & Rapp, P. R. (1982). Amygdaloid basal forebrain direct connections with the nucleus of the solitary tract and the dorsal motor nucleus. *Journal of Neuroscience, 2,* 1424–1438.

Shaver, P., Schwartz, J., Kirson, D., & O'Connor, C. (1987). Emotion knowledge: Further exploration of a prototype approach. *Journal of Personality and Social Psychology, 52,* 1061–1086.

Shi, C., & Davis, M. (1996). Anatomical tracing and lesion studies of visual pathways involved in fear conditioning measured with fear potentiated startle. *Society for Neuroscience Abstracts, 22,* 1115.

Shibata, K., Kataoka, Y., Yamashita, K., & Ueki, S. (1986). An important role of the central amygdaloid nucleus and mammillary body in the mediation of conflict behavior in rats. *Brain Research, 372,* 159–162.

Shors, T. J., & Mathew, P. R. (1998). NMDA receptor antagonism in the lateral/basolateral but not central nucleus of the amygdala prevents the induction of facilitated learning in response to stress. *Learning and Memory, 5,* 220–230.

Sokolov, E. N. (1963). *Perception and the conditioned reflex.* Oxford, UK: Pergamon Press.

Soltis, R. P., Cook, J. C., Gregg, A. E., Stratton, J. M., & Flickinger, K. A. (1998). EAA receptors in the dorsomedial hypothalamic area mediate the cardiovascular response to activation of the amygdala. *American Journal of Physiology, 275*(2, Pt. 2), R624–R631.

Soltis, R. P., Cook, J. C., Gregg, A. E., & Sanders, B. J. (1997). Interaction of GABA and excitatory amino acids in the basolateral amygdala: Role in cardiovascular regulation. *Journal of Neuroscience, 17,* 9367–9374.

Stinus, L., LeMoal, M., & Koob, G. F. (1990). Nucleus accumbens and amygdala are possible substrates for the aversive stimulus effects of opiate withdrawal. *Neuroscience, 37*(3), 767–773.

Sullivan, R. M., Henke, P. G., Ray, A., Hebert, M. A., & Trimper, J. M. (1989). The GABA/benzodiazepine receptor complex in the central amygdalar nucleus and stress ulcers in rats. *Behavioral and Neural Biology, 51,* 262–269.

Swiergiel, A. H., Takahashi, L. K., & Kalin, N. H. (1993). Attenuation of stress-induced behavior by antagonism of corticotropin-releasing factor in the central amygdala of the rat. *Brain Research, 623,* 229–234.

Takao, K., Nagatani, T., Kasahara, K.-I., & Hashimoto, S. (1992). Role of the central serotonergic system in the anticonflict effect of *d*-AP159. *Pharmacology, Biochemistry, and Behavior, 43,* 503–508.

Taylor, J. R., Punch, L. J., & Elsworth, J. D. (1998). A comparison of the effects of clonidine and CNQX infusion into the locus coeruleus and the amygdala on naloxone-precipitated opiate withdrawal in the rat. *Psychopharmacology, 138,* 133–142.

Taylor, J. R., & Robbins, T. W. (1984). Enhanced behavioral control by conditioned reinforcers following microinjections of d-amphetamine into the nucleus accumbens. *Psychopharmacology, 84,* 405–412.

Taylor, J. R., & Robbins, T. W. (1986). 6-hydroxydopamine lesions of the nucleus accumbens, but not the caudate nucleus, attenuate enhanced responding with reward-related stimuli produced by intra-accumbens d-amphetamine. *Psychopharmacology, 90,* 390–397.

Tellegen, A. (1985). Structures of mood and personality and their relevance to assessing anxiety, with an emphasis on self-report. In A. H. Tuma & J. D. Maser (Eds.), *Anxiety and the anxiety disorders* (pp. 681–706). Hillsdale, NJ: Erlbaum.

Thomas, S. R., Lewis, M. E., & Iversen, S. D. (1985). Correlation of [3H]diazepam binding density with anxiolytic locus in the amygdaloid complex of the rat. *Brain Research, 342,* 85–90.

Timberlake, W. (1993). Behavior systems and reinforcement: An intergrative approach. *Journal of Experimental Analysis of Behavior, 60,* 105–128.

Timberlake, W., & Lucas, G. A. (1989). Behavior systems and learning: From misbehavior to general principles. In S. B. Klein & R. R. Mowrer (Eds.), *Instrumental conditioning theory and the impact of biological constraints on learning* (pp. 237–275). Hillsdale, NJ: Erlbaum.

Ursin, H., & Kaada, B. R. (1960). Functional localization within the amygdaloid complex in the cat. *Electroencephalography and Clinical Neurophysiology, 12,* 109–122.

Vrana, S. R., Spence, E. L., & Lang, P. J. (1988). The startle probe response: A new measure of emotion? *Journal of Abnormal Psychology, 97,* 487–491.

Walker, D. L., & Davis, M. (1997). Double dissociation between the involvement of the bed nucleus of the stria terminalis and the central nucleus of the amygdala in light-enhanced versus fear-potentiated startle. *Journal of Neuroscience, 17,* 9375–9383.

Weisz, D. J., & McInerney, J. (1990). An associative process maintains reflex facilitation of the unconditioned nictitating membrane response during the early stages of training. *Behavioral Neuroscience, 104,* 21–27.

Whalen, P. J. (1998). Fear, vigilance, and ambiguity: Initial neuroimaging studies of the human amygdala. *Current Directions in Psychological Science, 7,* 177–188.

Whalen, P. J., & Kapp, B. S. (1991). Contributions of the amygdaloid central nucleus to the modulation of the nictitating membrane reflex in the rabbit. *Behavioral Neuroscience, 105,* 141–153.

White, S. R., & Neuman, R. S. (1980). Facilitation of spinal motoneuron excitability by 5-hydroxytryptamine and noradrenaline. *Brain Research, 185,* 1–9.

Wiersma, A., Baauw, A. D., Bohus, B., & Koolhaas, J. M. (1995). Behavioural activation produced by CRH but not α-helical CRH (CRH-receptor antagonist) when microinfused into the central nucleus of the amygdala under stress-free conditions. *Psychoneuroendocrinology, 20*(4), 423–432.

Wiersma, A., Bohus, B., & Koolhaas, J. M. (1993). Corticotropin-releasing hormone microinfusion in the central amygdala diminishes a cardiac parasympathetic outflow under stress-free conditions. *Brain Research, 625,* 219–227.

Wiersma, A., Bohus, B., & Koolhaas, J. M. (1997). Corticotropin-releasing hormone microinfusion in the central amygdala enhances active behaviour responses in the conditioned burying paradigm. *Stress, 1,* 113–122.

Wiersma, A., Tuinstra, T., & Koolhaas, J. M. (1997). *Corticotropin-releasing hormone microinfusion into the basolateral nucleus of the amygdala does not induce any changes in cardiovascular, neuroendocrine or behavioural output in a stress-free condition.* Unpublished doctoral dissertation, University of Groningen, The Netherlands.

Willcox, B. J., Poulin, P., Veale, W. L., & Pittman, Q. J. (1992). Vasopressin-induced motor effects: Localization of a sensitive site in the amygdala. *Brain Research, 596,* 58–64.

Wundt, W. (1896). *Grundriss der Psychologie* (Outlines of psychology). Leipzig, Germany: Entgelman.

Yeomans, J. S., Steidle, S., & Li, L. (2000). Conditioned brain-stimulation reward attenuates the acoustic startle reflex in rats. *Society for Neuroscience Abstracts, 30,* 1252.

Young, A. W., Aggleton, J. P., Hellawell, D. J., Johnson, M., Broks, P., & Hanley, J. R. (1995). Face processing impairments after amygdalotomy. *Brain, 118,* 15–24.

Young, B. J., Helmstetter, F. J., Rabchenuk, S. A., & Leaton, R. N. (1991). Effects of systemic and intra-amygdaloid diazepam on long-term habituation of acoustic startle in rats. *Pharmacology, Biochemistry, and Behavior, 39,* 903–909.

CHAPTER 16

Stress, Coping, and Immune Function

ANGELA LIEGEY DOUGALL AND ANDREW BAUM

The term *stress* has been criticized for being too general or nonspecific. For some it is a stimulus, whereas for others it is a response or a combination of stimulus and response. For some it is an inherently psychological process mediated solely by the nervous system and affecting mental health, whereas for others it is a physical syndrome due primarily to exercise or physical insult and mediated by damage or injury to bodily tissue. Over the past 10–20 years, however, depictions of stress and discussions of how it operates and affects us have become more integrated and have been increasingly used as an exemplar or illustration of important *mind-body connections* or pathways linking environments, behaviors, and biological changes to health and well-being. These characterizations describe stress as a relatively non-specific series of biological and psychological changes that support coping and adaptation to threat, harm, danger, or demand posed by the environment. The evolution of conceptions of stress and the increasing focus on stress-related changes in the immune system are the principal topics of this chapter.

Stress is derived from an inherently adaptive process. People live in a constantly changing world in which physical and social conditions require continuous adjustment and adaptation. Many of these changes are small and some are imperceptible, involving little effort in adjusting to them. When people drive their cars, they must make more-or-less continuous, small adjustments with the steering wheel; they are often unaware of these adjustments. However, the sudden appearances of major barriers or obstacles (turns, other vehicles,

potholes) ordinarily require bigger adjustments that demand more effort and awareness. These are similar to more substantial environmental changes that call for more effort for successful adaptation. Mental and physical resources must be marshaled to support this effort, and this mobilization includes many cognitive and bodily changes associated with stress. Some changes are disruptive and are perceived as aversive either because they produce harm or loss or because they pose a threat for future harm or loss (e.g., Lazarus & Folkman, 1984). In response to such appraisals, psychological, behavioral, and physiological responses are activated that enable people to engage in coping strategies that promote adaptation to or accommodation to the situation.

The general readying responses and nonspecific activation associated with coping constitute what most theorists call stress; it helps people achieve adaptation. Stress becomes detrimental when coping strategies are ineffective, demands exceed ability to cope, or activation of psychological, behavioral, and physiological response systems is sustained or unusually intense. Among the systems affected is the immune system, a key component of overall survival because of its critical role in protection from disease. Although all stress response systems work in concert, the immune system has received considerable attention because of its role in infection and disease. The relationships among stress, coping, and immunity are explored after separate discussions of major conceptual models of stress, the strategies people use to cope with stress, and the growing literature on stress-related immune changes.

THE STRESS CONSTRUCT

Although the concept of stress is widely acknowledged, there is little scientific consensus about its definition. Most theorists agree that stress can be adaptive, that it is precipitated by demand or by threatening or harmful events, and that it is often associated with negative moods. Because both biological and psychological response systems are activated, some theorists argue that stress is an emotion. Others maintain that stress is best described as a general state of arousal that prompts and supports action directed toward dealing with the stimulus (e.g., Baum, 1990; Mason, 1971). Operational definitions of stress also vary and can include measures of precipitating events (such as the number of major life changes a person experiences in a given time frame); psychological, physiological, or behavioral responses common in stress; or both the event and the responses. Regardless of how it has been measured, stress appears to be a fundamental component of adjustment and adaptation to environmental change. Theories of stress have evolved over the past 100 years to describe the variety of response patterns to threat, harm, or loss that occur, and work by Cannon, Selye, and Mason in particular has set the stage for modern depictions of stress.

Cannon (1914) was one of the first scientists to study stress. He agreed with major theorists of his time that the body needed to maintain a state of equilibrium. Anything that disturbed or threatened this equilibrium prompted the organism to respond in ways that would restore homeostasis. Some stressful events elicited negative emotions such as anger and fear, and these emotions were associated with activation of the sympathetic nervous system (SNS) and the release of hormones that stimulated other areas in the body. These neurohormonal changes prepared the organism to engage in one of two adaptive behavioral responses: fight or flight. The organism was readied either to stand its ground and fight off the stressor or to flee the situation. Much of this work was based on crude bioassay techniques and an incomplete knowledge of sympathetic physiology, but much of what Cannon proposed has been verified by more recent research. For example, we now know that catecholamines (i.e., epinephrine and norepinephrine) are released during stress or arousal and accomplish many of the actions proposed by Cannon.

Selye (1956/1984) developed a different model of stress, the *general adaptation syndrome* (GAS), based on activity in the hypothalamic-pituitary-adrenocortical (HPA) axis. Beginning his work in the 1930s, Selye characterized stress as a triad of physiological responses to noxious events that included ulceration of the digestive system, enlargement of the adrenal gland, and involution of lymphoid tissues (Selye, 1936). He argued that these responses were driven by activation of the HPA axis and were seen regardless of the type of stressor presented. During initial stages of alarm, large increases in corticosteroids were seen immediately following presentation of the stressor, signifying resource mobilization. After mobilization was accomplished, responding shifted to the second stage, during which the organism resisted or acted to overcome the stressor. Corticosteroids in the adrenal cortex were replenished and adaptation was usually achieved. If adaptation was precluded—as in cases of extreme or persistent stress exposure—exhaustion was reached. This final stage was characterized by a depletion of resources and could result in chronic debilitating disease or death.

Mason (1971) expanded on these models by examining stress responding in a variety of physiological systems. Building on Cannon's work and investigating other bodily systems not directly related to arousal of the SNS or HPA axis, he showed that predictable changes occurred in many systems. Different kinds of stressors elicited different kinds of changes, but emotional responses to stressors such as anger and fear were not specific to the stressor. This meant that the emotional arousal that characterized different stressors made them feel the same across different situations. He concluded that stress was a unified catabolic response serving to maintain the high levels of circulating glucose needed by the body in order to sustain prolonged resistance.

Cannon (1914) and Selye (1956/1984) accurately identified the SNS and the HPA axis as principal drivers of stress responding. Activation of these systems continues to be the focus of studies examining physiological pathways by which stress is induced. Mason's (1971) work integrated these two systems and expanded prevailing views of stress to include general activation across a multitude of biological systems. Other response pathways such as psychological and behavioral responses received less attention in these earlier models. Cannon and Mason incorporated emotional responses such as fear and anger into their theories, considering negative emotions as mechanisms through which threatening stimuli evoked physiological responses. Mason went further in integrating these levels of response, but the conceptions of stress that grew in the fields of biology and medicine were fundamentally different from those developing simultaneously in psychology and psychiatry.

Psychological theories of stress developed independently of these biological models and focused on individual variability in stress responding. Lazarus (1966) argued that stress was the product of the interaction between the person and his or her environment. It was not enough for a stimulus to occur; people had to appraise the event as stressful and—through processes of secondary appraisals—decide on what available coping strategies could be used to deal with the situation and whether the problem should be attacked or accommodated.

These appraisal processes then elicited appropriate psychological, physiological, and behavioral responses.

Central to this model were the processes of cognitive appraisals and coping, both of which were important psychological variables that moderated the relationship between stressful events and bodily reactions. Lazarus (1966) regarded stress as a transactional process in which an individual was constantly acquiring new information and reappraising the situation. Lazarus and Folkman (1984) later expanded on this model and defined stress as the "particular relationship between the person and the environment that is appraised by the person as taxing or exceeding his or her resources and endangering his or her well-being" (p. 19).

This model of stress (Lazarus, 1966; Lazarus & Folkman, 1984) has been the foundation for much of the stress research conducted in the past 40 years. However, it has not been without critics; moreover, as new information has been discovered about the myriad of cognitive processes involved and of bodily responses and health-related outcomes associated with stress, researchers have modified and expanded on this model. Hobfoll (1989) and Hobfoll and Lily (1993) have defined stress in the context of resource loss and conservation. Individuals actively sought to gain and maintain resources; stress was the result of the loss, the threat of loss, or the lack of gain of these resources. In response to stress, individuals acted to minimize the amount of loss experienced. Rahe and Arthur (1978) based their model of stress on the occurrence of major life changes as precipitating events and defined coping as the conscious efforts people used to try to reduce these responses. In contrast, psychological defenses such as denial and repression were unconscious efforts that helped to deflect the initial perception of the significance of the events. Although long-term use of these psychological defenses could result in pathology, short-term use was beneficial in reducing initial psychophysiological responses. Sustained psychophysiological responding not alleviated by coping or defensive efforts lead to illness symptoms, behavior, and disease.

More recently, McEwen (1998; McEwen & Stellar, 1993) proposed a model of allostasis and allostatic load to explain the relationship between stress and disease. Like the earlier biological models of stress proposed by Selye (1936) and Cannon (1914), *allostatic load theory* focused on physiological response pathways—in particular, those regulatory systems that were highly reactive to external stimuli (e.g., the SNS and the HPA axis). Adaptation to challenges was achieved through changes in these allostatic systems, and this process was termed *allostasis*. Allostasis corresponded to Cannon's notion that organisms respond in ways to restore homeostasis when equilibrium was threatened or disturbed; it also corresponds to Selye's conceptualization of the phases of alarm and resistance. Also similar to these earlier theories,

allostasis models assumed that prolonged activation of a physiological system could promote disease. Prolonged activation may have been caused by episodic or repeated acute activation, lack of adaptation, or the failure of the system to shut off or turn on properly. It caused wear and tear on the body, termed *allostatic load*. Allostatic load represented the cumulative effects of stressful life challenges as well as biological, lifestyle, and environmental risk factors for disease such as genetics, health behaviors (smoking, diet, drinking), and disruptions in the sleep-wake cycle. Although the general concept of allostatic load was appealing because it offered a broad framework for studying risk factors for disease, it was difficult to operationalize and study.

All of the aforementioned theories characterize the processes through which stress unfolds differently, but they all assume that stress has an adaptive function involving arousal of bodily response systems that prompt changes that reestablish homeostasis. When stress is unusually intense or sustained, it can cause pathology. Integrative depictions of stress define it as "a negative emotional experience accompanied by predictable biochemical, physiological, and behavioral changes that are directed toward adaptation either by manipulating the situation to alter the stressor or by accommodating its effects" (Baum, 1990, p. 653). After an appraisal of a situation as threatening or harmful, activation of both specific and nonspecific responses continues until the source of stress is eliminated or its effects have been accommodated. This catabolic fight-or-flight reaction is beneficial in the short term but can result in negative physical and mental health effects if these emergency responses are extreme or prolonged. Variability in the stress process occurs through environmental and personal factors that alter stress appraisals and choice of coping efforts.

COPING

Coping is central to most modern conceptions of stress. Stress motivates people to adapt and reduce the aversive effects of a stressor or one's reactions to it; the biological changes that occur support these efforts to manipulate or accommodate these aversive conditions. There are many ways in which people cope, and these methods have been divided into two broad categories based on whether the action is directed at manipulating-altering the situation or at palliating negative emotions (Lazarus & Folkman, 1984; Steptoe, 1989). The first of these actions is *problem-focused coping,* which includes using overt or covert behavioral or cognitive strategies designed to alter the situation or people's relationship to the situation. Behavioral strategies are usually purposeful efforts to eliminate or change the stressor or its proximity; such strategies include running away, avoiding the location of the stressor, and using aggressive behaviors such as fighting an attacker. Manipulations of the event or attempts to terminate the stressor are also used. Cognitive strategies often focus on plans of action or on redefining the situation in a less threatening manner. Specific strategies include seeking information about the problem, selectively attending to certain aspects of the situation, or using cognitive reappraisal and reframing. Problem-focused strategies are more likely to be chosen than are more emotion-focused options and appear to be the most effective when people have some control over the situation (DeGroot, Boeke, Bonke, & Passchier, 1997; Folkman & Lazarus, 1980). For example, breast cancer patients who viewed their disease as controllable and used problem-focused coping reported fewer symptoms of depression and anxiety soon after their diagnosis (Osowiecki & Compas, 1999). In another study, breast cancer patients reported better adjustment to their disease if they engaged in planning or positive reinterpretation (Ben-Zur, Gilbar, & Lev, 2001).

Attempts to decrease emotional responses to an aversive event without altering the situation are termed *emotion-focused coping*. These are generally accommodative in nature and are designed to alter reactions to a stressor rather than the stressor itself. If problem-focused coping can be thought of as danger control or attempts to change the source of a threat, emotion-focused coping would be distress control or action taken to minimize upset or unhappiness (Leventhal, 1980). People may increase their alcohol consumption, cigarette smoking, eating, and use of other substances during stress (e.g., Alexander & Walker, 1994; Greeno & Wing, 1994). Engaging in these appetitive behaviors allows for a temporary respite from dealing with the stressful situation; these behaviors do nothing to change or improve the situation, however, and some are independently associated with health risks. People may also use cognitive emotion-focused strategies such as denial, wishful thinking, and rationalization.

If effective, emotion-focused coping should decrease psychophysiological responding. The term *repressive-defensive coping* has been used to describe people who report low levels of anxiety (i.e., negative emotion) but who exhibit high physiological arousal at the same time. Repressors are also identified by their reports of low anxiety but high defensiveness or social desirability (e.g., King, Taylor, Albright, & Haskell, 1990). This emotion-focused coping style is associated with greater resting cardiovascular arousal as well as with greater increases in cardiovascular reactivity and greater immunosuppression in response to a stressful task (e.g., Jammer & Leigh, 1999; King et al., 1990).

In hindsight, some emotion-focused strategies appear to be maladaptive. While people are engaging in these strategies, little or nothing is done to improve the situation, which has

remained the same or has worsened because no counteractions have been taken (Brenner, Melamed, & Panush, 1994; Redeker, 1992). Consistent with this idea is that emotion-focused coping is often associated with worsening of stress symptoms and disease outcomes. For example, use of avoidance and self-blame has been positively associated with blood pressure reactivity to acute tasks, use of denial has been positively associated with progression to AIDS in patients with HIV infection, and use of wishful thinking coping prospectively predicted symptoms of posttraumatic stress disorder in victims of motor vehicle accidents (Dolan, Sherwood, & Light, 1992; Dougall, Ursano, Posluszny, Fullerton, & Baum, 2001; Kohlman, Weidner, & Messina, 1996; Leserman et al., 2000). Prolonged use of these strategies may preclude the use of more effective strategies, especially if something could have been done to control the situation (Lazarus, 1993). However, in situations in which stressors are short-lived, dissipate on their own (without any problem-focused coping), or both, emotionally focused strategies that insulate people from threat and make distress less likely may be very adaptive (DeGroot et al., 1997). Similarly, in situations characterized by little or no control, these strategies are often preferred and can be adaptive (DeGroot et al., 1997; Folkman & Lazarus, 1980). For example, use of avoidance was associated with less perceived stress in people donating blood, and patients with terminal illnesses who perceived that they had little control over their illness used more emotion-focused coping and less problem-focused coping than did patients who had nonterminal diseases (Kaloupek & Stoupakis, 1985; Kausar & Akram, 1998). When stressors or responses are extreme or prolonged, emotion-focused coping may help to diffuse psychophysiological arousal enough so that the person can conserve energy, reappraise the situation, and decide on more appropriate strategies (cf. Pilette, 1983; Rahe & Arthur, 1978).

Problem-focused and emotion-focused coping are not mutually exclusive and are typically used together or sequentially to alleviate stress. Although many specific types of these strategies have been identified, no single strategy has been found to be universally effective or ineffective. Coping is a dynamic process that constantly changes as the person discovers new information and tries new techniques for dealing with the situation (Aldwin & Brustrom, 1997). Rather than consistency in use of coping, flexibility in the types of strategies used and the relative use of problem-focused and emotion-focused coping appears to be more adaptive (Cantor & Norem, 1989; Lester, Smart, & Baum, 1994; Vitaliano, Maiuro, Russo, & Becker, 1987). Choice of coping can be influenced by the person's perceived control over the situation (as mentioned previously) and by a myriad of other event and person characteristics such as perceived self-efficacy, social support, and personality (e.g., Fleishman, 1984; Gerin, Litt, Deich, & Pickering, 1995; Thoits, 1986). This variability in coping helps to explain the variability seen in psychological, behavioral, and physiological responses to stress.

RESPONSES TO STRESS

As suggested earlier, stress is driven by biological changes that affect a number of bodily systems and prepare organisms to act quickly and decisively. Recently, there has been a burgeoning interest in the possible consequences of stress on immune outcomes. The relatively new interdisciplinary field of *psychoneuroimmunology* examines the bidirectional interactions among the immune system and other psychological and physiological response patterns. The immune system works in concert with other stress systems as a sensory and regulatory system (see Figure 16.1) and is the body's primary defense against infection and disease. Before immune changes in response to stress are described, changes in other psychological, behavioral, and physiological systems are reviewed.

Psychological and Behavioral Responses and Stress

Stressors or appraisals of them as posing threat or excess demand elicit a broad array of responses, including disturbances in mood and behavior. Increases in negative emotions such as anxiety, depression, fear, or anger are often reported during stressor exposure and can persist in some cases long after exposure has ceased (e.g., Delahanty, Dougall, et al., 2000; Dew & Bromet, 1993; Ursano, Fullerton, Kao, & Bhartiya, 1995). During periods of stress, people also experience increases in negative cognitions such as unwanted or uncontrollable thoughts and memories of the stressor (e.g., Dougall, Craig, & Baum, 1999). These cognitions can help people process and cope with the event (Creamer, Burgess, &

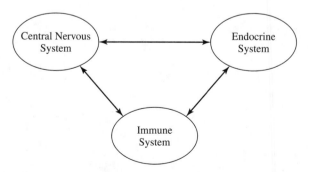

Figure 16.1 The central nervous system, endocrine system (primarily sympathetic hormones and the hypothalamic-pituitary-adrenocortical axis), and the immune system interact through direct innervation, endocrine activity, and release of cytokines and other messengers from immune cells.

Pattison, 1992; Greenberg, 1995; Horowitz, 1986). However, some of these thoughts are unwanted, unbidden, and uncontrollable; they may become acute stressors in their own rights, helping to perpetuate chronic stress (Baum, Cohen, & Hall, 1993; Craig, Heisler, & Baum, 1996). For example, the occurrence of event-related intrusive thoughts predicted long-term distress and physiological responding in victims who were injured in motor vehicle accidents, who were recovery workers at an airplane crash site, and who experienced personal loss as a result of a hurricane (Dougall et al., 1999). Stress associated with these intrusive thoughts may also interfere with decision-making processes, problem solving, or judgments, contributing to new sources of stress and impairing overall efficiency.

Consistent with this prediction, some research has found that stress can be manifested as disruption of behavior and performance. Because attention is typically focused on dealing with stressors when they are present, people who are experiencing stress often report trouble concentrating and poor performance on mundane tasks such as balancing a checking account, monitoring computer screens, or assembling a product (for reviews, see Baba, Jamal, & Tourigny, 1998; Cooper, 1988; Kompier & DiMartino, 1995; Krueger, 1989; McNally, 1997). These effects are likely to be minor but can be detrimental if they are work- or safety-related (e.g., writing a report or driving an automobile). Even transient performance decrements induced by laboratory challenges can persist well after physiological and emotional responding has habituated (Glass & Singer, 1972). Additionally, some people cope with stress by increasing their use of drugs such as alcohol and nicotine, eating diets with less nutritional value, and decreasing physical exercise (Alexander & Walker, 1994; Rosenbloom & Whittington, 1993; Willis, Thomas, Garry, & Goodwin, 1987). Other behavioral changes include increases in aggressive behaviors and deterioration of sleep quality and quantity (e.g., Conway, Vickers, Weid, & Rahe, 1981; Ganley, 1989; Grunberg & Baum, 1985; Mellman, 1997; Sadeh, 1996; Spaccarelli, Bowden, Coatsworth, & Kim, 1997). Prolonged changes in these behaviors may have negative health effects and may potentiate other stress-related responses such as alterations in immunity and other neuroendocrine systems.

Neuroendocrine Responses and Stress

The seminal work of Selye (1956/1984) and Cannon (1914) introduced the now accepted effects of stress on the SNS and the HPA axis. Both of these systems are mobilized when an individual encounters a stressor. Increases in heart rate and blood pressure as well as increases in the release of catecholamines—particularly norepinephrine and epinephrine—are hallmark indicators of SNS arousal. Activation of the HPA axis results in the release of glucocorticoids (e.g., cortisol in humans) from the adrenal cortex. More recent research has demonstrated that these two systems do not function independently; they communicate with one other. For example, catecholamines affect the release of ACTH (adrenocorticotropic hormone) from the pituitary, and corticosteroids enhance the cardiovascular effects of epinephrine and norepinephrine (e.g., Axelrod & Reisine, 1984; Davies & Lefkowitz, 1984; Szafarczyck, Malaval, Laurent, Gibaud, & Assenmacher, 1987). Likewise, the SNS and the HPA axis connect with other bodily systems, including (but not limited to) the gastrointestinal system, the hypothalamic-pituitary-gonadal axis and the immune system (de la Torre, 1994; Weiner, 1992). The generalized activation that results from stimulation of one or the other system is considered to be adaptive in that it serves to mobilize physiological resources enabling the person to cope more effectively. Other neurohormones and peptides that are altered during stress include growth hormone, prolactin, vasopressin, endogenous opioids, thyrotropin-releasing hormone, thyroid-stimulating hormone, somatostatin, insulin, glucagon, glucose, testosterone, follicle stimulating hormone, and luteinizing hormone (for reviews, see de la Torre, 1994; Lundberg, 1984; Weiner, 1992). These psychological, behavioral, and physiological response systems work in concert to help the individual adapt to stress, and many are directly tied to changes in immune status.

Immune Responses and Stress

The immune system is constantly surveying the body—fending off foreign pathogens such as viruses and bacteria and clearing away bodily cells that have died or have mutated or been altered, as in the case of viral host cells or cancer cells. The continuum of health and disease is maintained in part by the immune system's ability to detect and eliminate these infectious and noninfectious agents and to provide mechanisms through which healing can occur. These immune activities have been broken down into two types of immunity—*innate* and *acquired*—based on how the cells, structures, and factors in each of these processes counter incursions of pathogens. Innate or natural immunity represents the body's first line of defense against a pathogen. As the name implies, innate immunity does not require prior exposure to a particular pathogen, nor is it specific to the type of pathogen encountered. A similar cascade of events occurs after each foreign substance is encountered. In contrast, an acquired immune response is specific to the pathogen and usually requires other cells to present the pathogen to the agents of acquired immunity. Acquired immunity also has the ability to remember a pathogen after the immune system has encountered it, resulting in faster and stronger defensive responses upon subsequent exposures. Acquired responses are generally stronger and more effective than innate defenses after exposure has created memory for a particular pathogen, and these aspects of immunity are the basis for vaccination and inoculation.

A variety of cells and structures comprise the immune system. Most research in psychoneuroimmunology focuses on the number and function of lymphocytes, the specialized white blood cells that recognize antigens and are key components of acquired immunity. There are three major types of lymphocytes: natural killer cells, B lymphocytes, and T lymphocytes (see Figure 16.2). Natural killer (NK) cells are large, granular lymphocytes that do not require prior exposure to a

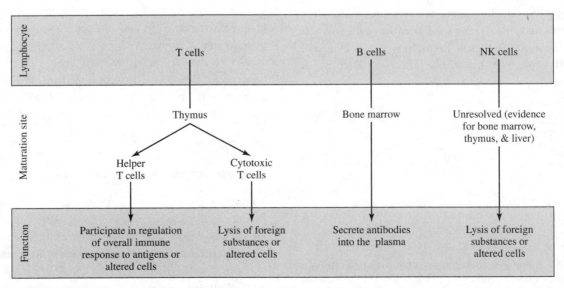

Figure 16.2   Major components of the immune system. T and B cells require prior sensitization by contact with a particular antigen, but NK cells do not. Other cells, including scavenger monocytes and macrophages or neutrophils, are also important; all secrete cytokines that facilitate interaction among cells and with the immune system.

pathogen or altered cell; they function as agents of innate immunity by recognizing and killing virally infected cells and tumor cells spontaneously. They have become popular targets for research in psychoneuroimmunology because of their great sensitivity to stress or psychological variables and because of their apparent relevance to several important disease processes.

The B and T lymphocytes are agents of acquired immunity. Both originate in the bone marrow, but T cells migrate to the thymus (hence the name *T lymphocyte*), where they mature into either helper T cells or cytotoxic T cells. Along with different maturational sites, T and B cells have different mechanisms of action. Upon activation and recognition of an antigen, B cells secrete antibodies (or immunoglobulins) that bind to antigens and trigger a cascade of immune events that lead to the elimination of the antigen. This form of immunity is referred to as *humoral* because the antibodies are free in body fluids (humors). In contrast, T lymphocytes are the major components of cellular immunity and have both regulatory and killer functions. Regulatory T lymphocytes are called *helper T cells* and recognize nonself pathogens through their presentation by the major histocompatibility complex (MHC). Helper T cells then secrete cytokines that serve to activate B cells and other T cells preferentially. Killer T lymphocytes (cytotoxic T cells) lyse and kill cells that exhibit markers of a specific antigen complex.

Effects of stress on immune system activity vary in a number of different ways depending on the type of immune marker measured, the timing of the assessment, and the type of stressful situation encountered. Considerable research has examined immune reactivity to brief laboratory tasks that are thought to be stressful or challenging. These acute stressors are brief, typically 5–30 min long (e.g., Breznitz et al., 1998; Delahanty, Dougall, Browning, Hyman, & Baum, 1998). Immune changes observed during or immediately after acute stress generally include increases in the numbers of some circulating lymphocytes in the peripheral blood, especially NK cells and cytotoxic T cells (e.g., Breznitz et al., 1998; Herbert et al., 1994; Naliboff et al., 1991). Increases in cell numbers are due in part to migration of lymphocytes into the blood stream from lymphoid organs such as the spleen and lymph nodes (Benschop, Rodriguez-Feuuerhahn, & Schedlowski, 1996). One possible reason for these increases is that lymphocytes travel through the blood during periods of acute stress to reach areas of the body such as the gastrointestinal system and the skin, where they act to ward off infection and to promote healing (Dhabhar, 1998).

Despite these increases in numbers, the functional ability of T and B lymphocytes in the peripheral blood is impaired as evidenced by the decreased proliferative response of lymphocytes to mitogen presentation in vitro (e.g., Herbert et al.,

1994; Manuck, Cohen, Rabin, Muldoon, & Bachen, 1991; Zakowski, Cohen, Hall, Wollman, & Baum, 1994). At any given time an individual typically has only a handful of T and B cells with memory for a specific antigen. However, thousands or millions of cells are often needed to mount an effective defense when the antigen is encountered. To accomplish this, immune cells in circulation proliferate when they encounter specific antigens or very strong mitogens, and the ability to proliferate has been used as a measure of immunocompetence. During or after stress, these lymphocytes appear to be inhibited in some way, possibly by concomitant stress-related increases in hormones such as epinephrine and cortisol that bind to immune cell membrane receptors and are associated with changes in cell migration and decreased proliferation (e.g., Crary, Borysenko, et al., 1983; Crary, Hauser, et al., 1983; Daynes, Araneo, Hennebold, Enioutina, & Mu, 1995; Kappel, Poulsen, Galbo, & Pedersen, 1998; Sondergaard, Ullum, Skinhoj, & Pedersen, 1999). In contrast, the cytotoxic activity of NK cells appears to incrementally change in proportion to the number of NK cells in the blood. Like stress-induced changes in NK cell numbers, NK cell cytotoxicity increases during exposure to an acute stressor and then rebounds to below baseline levels after stressor termination (Breznitz et al., 1998; Delahanty, Wang, Maravich, Forlenza, & Baum, 2000; Schedlowski et al., 1993). This change in overall activity appears to be due to changes in cell number—that is, overall cytotoxicity increases if there are more cells available to kill pathogens and cytotoxicity decreases if there are fewer cells available to kill pathogens (Delahanty, Wang, et al., 2000). In sum, acute stressors elicit mobilization of lymphocytes and transitory increases in some agents of innate immunity. In contrast, episodic or chronic stressors such as bereavement, academic stress, and caregiving for ill family members are associated with general immunosuppression.

Chronic stress is generally associated with lower numbers of peripheral blood lymphocytes—in particular, NK cells and cytotoxic T cells—as well as lower levels of NK cell cytotoxicity and lymphocyte proliferation (e.g., Esterling, Kiecolt-Glaser, Bodnar, & Glaser, 1994; Herbert & Cohen, 1993; Kiecolt-Glaser et al., 1987). In addition, chronic stress appears to affect immune responses during acute stressors—in particular, decreasing rather than increasing numbers of T cells and blunting the increases in NK cell numbers and overall cytotoxicity following acute stressor exposure (e.g., Brosschot et al., 1994; Pike et al., 1997). Evidence for chronic stress-related immunosuppression has also been found using indirect measures of immune functioning. Chronic stress has been associated with impairments in the ability of wounds to heal, declines in seroconversion as evidenced by antibody titers 6 months after vaccination, and reactivation and recurrence of latent viruses such as herpes simplex and Epstein-Barr virus (e.g., Glaser, Sheridan, Malarkey, MacCallum, & Kiecolt-Glaser, 2000; Jenkins & Baum, 1995; Kiecolt-Glaser et al., 1987; Kiecolt-Glaser et al., 1988; Kiecolt-Glaser, Marucha, Malarkey, Mercado, & Glaser, 1995; Marucha, Kiecolt-Glaser, & Favagehi, 1998).

Relationships Between Immune Responses and Other Response Systems

The immune system has bidirectional relationships with other stress response systems; many of these relationships appear to be mechanisms through which stress-related immune changes occur. For example, SNS activation is associated with increases in cell mobilization and decreases in cell proliferation during and shortly after acute stress and with decreases in cell mobilization and decreases in lymphocyte activity as a function of chronic stress (Delahanty, Wang, et al., 2000; Manuck et al., 1991; McKinnon, Weisse, Reynolds, Bowles, & Baum, 1989). Similarly, alterations in other physiological systems such as the HPA axis and the hypothalamic-gonadal axis have direct effects on immunity and may be important mechanisms in stress-related immune responding (Daynes et al., 1995; Paavonen, 1994; Schuurs & Verheul, 1990). Negative mood and recurrent negative thoughts about the stressor (e.g., Delahanty, Dougall, Craig, Jenkins, & Baum, 1997; Solomon, Segerstrom, Grohr, Kemeny, & Fahey, 1997) and stress-related changes in behaviors such as decreases in sleep quality and quantity, decreases in exercise, and increases in the intake of recreational drugs may also contribute to immunosuppression (e.g., Eisenstein, & Hilburger, 1998; Galloway & Jokl, 2000; Ironson et al., 1997; Klein, Friedman, & Specter, 1998; McAllister-Sistilli et al., 1998; Watson, Eskelson, & Hartmann, 1984). Not surprisingly, coping styles and resources such as a pessimistic disposition and less available social support have also been associated with immune alterations (e.g., Byrnes et al., 1998; Sieber et al., 1992; Uchino, Cacioppo, & Kiecolt-Glaser, 1996). Clearly, there are multiple pathways through which stress may alter immunity. This cocktail of causal agents contributes to the variability in the relationship between stress and disease processes and suggests several appropriate areas for intervention.

Immune Responses and Health Outcomes

As noted previously, acute exposures to stress appear to mobilize immune cells and to increase some aspects of innate immunity. These changes may be beneficial in warding off opportunistic infections or in guarding against an incursion of pathogens during or shortly after a challenge. In contrast, chronic stress and associated changes in immunity have largely negative effects on resistance to disease processes. If the immune system is not functioning at its optimal level, pathogens and mutated self-cells may escape detection, elimination, or both, and recovery from injuries may be impeded. In fact, people who are experiencing ongoing stress are more susceptible to infectious diseases such as colds, flu, and HIV disease (e.g., Cohen et al., 1998; Stone et al., 1992; for reviews, see Dorian & Garfinkel, 1987; O'Leary, 1990). Additionally, stress has been linked to tumor growth and cancer progression as well as impairments in wound healing (e.g., Ben-Eliyahu, Yirmiya, Liebeskind, Taylor, & Gale, 1991; Bohus, Koolhaas, de Ruiter, & Heijnen, 1992; Kiecolt-Glaser et al., 1995; Marucha et al., 1998; Stefanski & Ben-Eliyahu, 1996). Given these relationships among stress, immunity, and disease, there has been increasing interest in designing and implementing interventions aimed at preventing or minimizing stress-related immune changes.

STRESS MANAGEMENT INTERVENTIONS

Interventions that decrease potentially toxic elements of stress (e.g., anxiety, depression, elevations in blood pressure) should also prevent or reduce stress-related immunosuppression. Probably the most effective way to reduce stress responding is to remove the stimulus. If your car breaks down and you are without transportation, you can either fix it or buy a new one. However, many situations are not easily changed—especially in cases of sudden, acute stressors like assault. A traumatic event like rape can never be undone. Given that direct action is not always feasible or likely to be successful, secondary intervention programs are often used to reduce ongoing stress. These stress management techniques capitalize on the relationships among appraisals, coping, and stress responses. By altering characteristics of the situation or of the person such as felt arousal, perceived control, social support, self-efficacy, and cognitive processes, people learn to reappraise the situation and to deal with a stressor more effectively. As a consequence, reductions in psychological, behavioral, and physiological stress responding are seen.

Research examining changes in immunological indexes after stress management interventions have used cognitive and somatic stress reduction techniques. Cognitive techniques are designed to alter appraisals of the situation and the choice of coping strategies in order to reduce or eliminate perceptions of stress (harm, loss, threat, or challenge) or to help people match their coping efforts to the situation at hand (Fava, 2000). These techniques often enhance perceptions of control, predictability, and social support—all important buffers of stress and its associated consequences. Somatic techniques target physiological arousal and use behavioral strategies such as relaxation training, meditation, biofeedback, and exercise to decrease arousal and facilitate appropriate emotional and behavioral responses (e.g., Carrington et al., 1980; Kiecolt-Glaser et al., 1985; LaPerriere et al., 1990; Murphy, 1984).

A number of recent studies have demonstrated that stress management interventions can be effective in buffering immune changes that occur with stress. Fawzy (1994) conducted a group intervention for patients with malignant melanoma and found that 6 months after the intervention, patients displayed increases in numbers of NK cells and large granular lymphocytes, increases in NK cell cytotoxicity, and decreases in numbers of helper T cells. Increases in large granular lymphocytes and NK cell cytotoxicity were associated with decreases in depression and anxiety, and increases in NK cell cytotoxicity predicted lower rates of cancer recurrence. Similarly, Kiecolt-Glaser et al. (1985) found increases in NK cell cytotoxicity and decreases in distress and antibody titers to herpes simplex virus following 1 month of relaxation training. Elderly residents of the same independent-living facilities who were randomly assigned to a social contact group or to a control group exhibited no changes in these stress measures.

Research conducted by Antoni and colleagues (e.g., Antoni et al., 2000; Cruess et al., 2000) has demonstrated that cognitive-behavioral stress management intervention techniques are effective in buffering stress-related immune changes in patients with HIV disease. They found decreases in negative mood, norepinephrine levels, and cortisol to dehydroepiandrosterone sulfate (DHEA-S) ratio levels as well as decreases in antibody titers to herpes simplex virus Type 2 in HIV-positive patients following completion of their multimodal intervention (Antoni et al., 2000; Cruess et al., 2000). In addition to showing these short-term immune changes, patients in the intervention group had greater numbers of cytotoxic T cells than did the waiting-list control patients 6–12 months after the intervention ended (Antoni et al., 2000). Other research groups have found increases in numbers of helper T cells (the cells that are infected by HIV) in HIV-positive patients who participated in stress management interventions (e.g., Eller, 1995; Taylor, 1995). Stress reduction techniques have also been used to prevent stress-related immune changes associated with notification of HIV serostatus. Asymptomatic, healthy gay men who completed an aerobic exercise training program did not experience the increases in negative affect and decreases in NK cell numbers that were observed in the seropositive control group after notification of HIV serological status (LaPerriere et al., 1990).

Although they are promising, these findings need to be interpreted with caution. Many studies have not found changes in immunity following psychological interventions (e.g., Coates, McKusick, Kuno, & Sites, 1989), and a recent meta-analysis found that stress reduction interventions do not reliably alter immunity (Miller & Cohen, 2001). The effectiveness of stress management interventions in buffering immune responses could be determined by a number of variables. One factor is the extent of stress responding preceding the intervention. In order to reduce stress, the people participating in the intervention need to be experiencing stress. When Miller and Cohen (2001) reexamined the studies they included in their meta-analysis of immune changes following psychological interventions, they found that the few studies that targeted stressed populations demonstrated reliable changes following a stress management intervention. The effectiveness of an intervention also depends on whether immune changes are attributable to stress. Some of the immunosuppression experienced may be a product of chronic disease processes or medical treatment regimens that independently alter immunity, as in the case of cancer or HIV disease. Additionally, stress management interventions are most effective if the participants practice the techniques they learn. In HIV-positive patients, increases in cytotoxic T cells found 6–12 months after a cognitive-behavioral stress management intervention were predicted by greater frequency of use of relaxation techniques at home (Antoni et al., 2000). Likewise, greater practice of relaxation techniques was associated with increases in the percentage of helper T cells during examination stress in medical students (Kiecolt-Glaser et al., 1986). Therefore, depending on the situation, a number of factors may interact to determine the efficacy of a stress management intervention in preventing or counteracting stress-related immunosuppression.

CONCLUSIONS

Stress is a fundamental process characterizing people's interactions with their environments and responses to challenge. Appraisals of threatening or harmful challenges motivate people to take action to either eliminate these stressors (i.e., problem-focused coping) or protect themselves from the stressor's negative impact (i.e., emotion-focused coping). These appraisals and coping efforts elicit a series of specific and nonspecific cognitive, behavioral, and physiological responses. Stress responses in turn promote adaptation by mobilizing catabolic energies that support coping efforts. In most cases, people are able to effectively deal with all types of stressors—from minor irritations such as misplacing one's car keys to extreme stressors such as assault or disaster. People learn from these experiences and move on to encounter new challenges, giving credence to the belief that stress is an inherently adaptive process. Stress becomes detrimental to mental and physical functioning when stressor demands exceed the person's abilities to cope and responding is prolonged or unusually intense.

One response system that has received considerable attention is the immune system because of its role in the detection and elimination of pathogenic agents. Repeated or protracted exposures to stress appear to suppress immune system functioning and may contribute to increased vulnerability to infection and disease. Alterations in other stress response pathways have important effects on immunity as well and appear to be mechanisms through which many of these stress-related immune changes occur. By decreasing cognitive, behavioral, and physiological responding, stress reduction interventions are used to facilitate adaptation and have important implications for decreasing vulnerability to disease processes.

FUTURE DIRECTIONS

Although we have learned a great deal about how the immune system responds during and after stress and how it interacts with other bodily systems, many questions still need further inquiry. Some basic questions about the reciprocal nature of brain-immune system interactions, about mediators between emotional processes or other psychological phenomena and immune system change, and about basic stress-related immunomodulation of disease vulnerability remain to be studied. Gray areas in existing data suggest future directions for both theory and research—not only in psychoneuroimmunology, but also in related disciplines. For example, one question that has plagued chronic stress researchers is how and when acute stress becomes chronic. We know that stress can be an adaptive process, especially in the short-term; moreover, some immune changes during acute stress seem consistent with a mobilization of cells and innate immunity and may provide enhanced protection against opportunistic infections. However, chronic stress responding is associated with a broader, longer-term immunosuppression in which some of the conditions for a reduction in host defense are met. When and how does this transition take place? Research has identified event and person variables such as the duration and nature of the stressor and duration of the perceived threat as determinants of chronic stress responding (Baum et al., 1993; Baum, O'Keeffe, & Davidson, 1990). However, these risk factors do not explain all of the variability seen in stress responding. For example, traumatic events that begin and end within minutes, such as powerful storms or tornados, can elicit long-term stress responding in some victims while the majority of victims recover rapidly. These seemingly inconsistent findings are the impetus for research on identifying both situation and person variables that either promote or inhibit chronic stress responding. The coping skills, strategies, and resources people use to deal with a situation have been a prime target of these investigations. Coping has the added advantage of being modifiable, and teaching people appropriate coping strategies is a basic component of many stress management and mental health interventions. Future research designs need to incorporate more frequent longitudinal assessments and examine multimodal assessments of stress responding (i.e., psychological, behavioral, neuroendocrine, and immunological responses) as well as moderating variables such as coping strategies and resources in order to better characterize the time course of stress responding.

Unfortunately, longitudinal psychoneuroimmunological investigations can become very costly and burdensome to study participants. Researchers need to carefully select outcome variables to minimize cost and burden and to maximize relevance, especially with regard to immune indexes. A substantial challenge is that the interaction between the immune system and stress or other psychological and psychobiological processes is still relatively unexplored when compared with stress and other bodily systems such as the cardiovascular system. Investigation of consistent relationships among stress-sensitive systems such as common regulatory features and processes (e.g., sympathetic innervation, endocrine responsivity, distribution of endocrine and neuropeptide receptors, and HPA axis activity) and shared outcomes may yield additional important information about mechanisms underlying immune system changes and about general markers for organismic vulnerability to disease.

Translational research is also integral to psychoneuroimmunology. Investigations of the complex interactions among psychological, neuroendocrine, and immune systems bear directly on basic research on how immune cells react to antigens and interact with each other. However, these basic investigations have undeniable applied or clinical implications and concurrent and derivative translational research that begins to view real-world infectious phenomena in broader terms represents a critical outcome of this research enterprise. For example, research on periodic exacerbations of autoimmune disorders or reactivation of latent viruses provides important basic data about clinical phenomena and their physiological bases; such research suggests important predictive and ameliorative strategies (e.g., Ackerman, Heyman, Rabin, & Baum, 2000; Jenkins & Baum, 1995; Kiecolt-Glaser & Glaser, 1987). Additionally, as advancements in immunoassays and assessment techniques occur, psychoneuroimmunology research can better focus on the most appropriate components of immunity for each hypothesis being tested.

Interventions designed to reduce overall stress responding can be effective in minimizing stress-related changes in immunity. However, as we have discussed, these effects on the immune system are dependent on several factors (i.e., the population has to be experiencing stress, the immune changes have to be associated with stress, and the population has to actively participate and practice the intervention techniques). Future research needs to thoroughly assess whether stress management interventions are first likely to affect immunity and then to identify barriers to participation within the target population. For example, some populations may be more willing to exercise for an hour than to attend a group session and talk about private issues. Barriers related to ethnic, cultural, and socioeconomic factors also need to be considered. Additionally, it may be prudent to reevaluate the outcome measures used and the timing of the assessments. In some instances, such as a preventive intervention in which people are not likely to experience a great deal of stress, immediate measures of stress responding, including immunity, should be unaffected. However, days or weeks later when they next encounter a major stressor, *if* they use what they learned in the intervention, immune changes should be attenuated. Researchers need to develop longitudinal designs that incorporate these types of issues related to the timing of the intervention in relation to the stressor of interest.

Related to this concern is the fact that the majority of research examining immune changes following psychological interventions have considered populations that are enduring chronic illnesses, such as cancer and HIV disease. Although such research is appropriate and worthwhile, more of this work needs to be done with other chronically stressed populations—including physically healthy people dealing with a stressor—so that immune processes independent of disease processes can be better understood. Research by Cohen and his colleagues (e.g., Cohen, Doyle, & Skoner, 1999; Cohen et al., 1998) on stress-related vulnerability to experimentally applied viruses has begun to address this concern, as have studies of chronically stressed caregivers or of marital conflict (e.g., Esterling et al., 1994; Kiecolt-Glaser et al., 1987; Kiecolt-Glaser et al., 1988). Studies of psychological trauma and stress-related immune system change as well as trauma-related health outcomes are also important in this regard (e.g., Inslicht, Hyman, Larkin, Jenkins, & Baum, 2001; Ironson et al., 1997; McKinnon et al., 1989; Segerstrom, Solomon, Kemeny, & Fahey, 1998).

As research continues to explain the complex interactions among stress response pathways and how these responses are altered by appraisal and coping, our understanding of the stress process and its effects on health and disease will increase. Continued characterization of the beneficial as well as harmful effects of stress will improve our ability to identify modifiable risk factors (e.g., lifestyle, appraisal, coping, and social resources) and will advance the design and implementation of interventions to reduce the negative consequences of stress and promote adaptation.

REFERENCES

Ackerman, K. D., Heyman, R., Rabin, B. S., & Baum, A. (2000). Stress and its relationship to disease activity in multiple sclerosis. *International Journal of Multiple Sclerosis, 7*, 20–29.

Aldwin, C. M., & Brustrom, J. (1997). Theories of coping with chronic stress: Illustrations from the health psychology and aging literatures. In B. H. Gottlieb (Ed.), *Coping with chronic stress* (pp. 75–103). New York: Plenum Press.

Alexander, D. A., & Walker, L. G. (1994). A study of methods used by Scottish police officers to cope with work-induced stress. *Stress Medicine, 10*, 131–138.

Antoni, M. H., Cruess, D. G., Cruess, S., Lutgendorf, S., Kumar, M., Ironson, G., Klimas, N., Fletcher, M. A., & Schneiderman, N. (2000). Cognitive-behavioral stress management intervention effects on anxiety, 24-hr urinary norepinephrine output, and T-cytotoxic/suppressor cells over time among symptomatic HIV-infected gay men. *Journal of Consulting and Clinical Psychology, 68*, 31–45.

Axelrod, J., & Reisine, T. D. (1984). Stress hormones. *Science, 224*, 452–459.

Baba, V. V., Jamal, M., & Tourigny, L. (1998). Work and mental health: A decade in Canadian research. *Canadian Psychology, 39*, 94–107.

Baum, A. (1990). Stress, intrusive imagery, and chronic distress. *Health Psychology, 9*(6), 653–675.

Baum, A., Cohen, L., & Hall, M. (1993). Control and intrusive memories as possible determinants of chronic stress. *Psychosomatic Medicine, 55*, 274–286.

Baum, A., O'Keeffe, M. K., & Davidson, L. M. (1990). Acute stressors and chronic response: The case of traumatic stress. *Journal of Applied Social Psychology, 20*, 1643–1654.

Ben-Eliyahu, S., Yirmiya, R., Liebeskind, J., Taylor, A., & Gale, R. (1991). Stress increases metastatic spread of a mammary tumor in rats: Evidence for mediation by the immune system. *Brain, Behavior, and Immunity, 5*, 193–205.

Ben-Zur, H., Gilbar, O., & Lev, S. (2001). Coping with breast cancer: Patient, spouse, and dyad models. *Psychosomatic Medicine, 63*, 32–39.

Benschop, R. J., Rodriguez-Feuuerhahn, M., & Schedlowski, M. (1996). Catecholamine-induced leukocytosis: Early observations, current research, and future directions. *Brain, Behavior, and Immunity, 10*, 77–91.

Bohus, B., Koolhaas, J. M., de Ruiter, A. J. H., & Heijnen, C. J. (1992). Psycho-social stress: Differential alterations in immune system functions and tumor growth. In R. Kvetnansky, R. McCarty, & J. Axelrod (Eds.), *Stress: Neuroendocrine and molecular approaches* (Vols. 1 & 2, pp. 607–621). Philadelphia: Gordon and Breach Science.

Brenner, G. F., Melamed, B. G., & Panush, R. S. (1994). Optimism and coping as determinants of psychosocial adjustments to rheumatoid arthritis. *Journal of Clinical Psychology in Medical Settings, 1*, 115–134.

Breznitz, S., Ben-Zur, H., Berzon, Y., Weiss, D. W., Levitan, G., Tarcic, N., Lischinsky, S., Greenberg, A., Levi, N., & Zinder, O. (1998). Experimental induction and termination of acute psychological stress in human volunteers: Effects on immunological, neuroendocrine, cardiovascular, and psychological parameters. *Brain, Behavior, and Immunity, 12*, 34–52.

Brosschot, J. F., Benschop, R. J., Godaert, G. L. R., Olff, M., De Smet, M., Heijnen, C. J., & Ballieux, R. E. (1994). Influence of life stress on immunological reactivity to mild psychological stress. *Psychosomatic Medicine, 56*, 216–224.

Byrnes, D. M., Antoni, M. H., Goodkin, K., Efantis-Potter, J., Asthana, D., Simon, T., Munajj, J., Ironson, G., & Fletcher, M. A. (1998). Stressful events, pessimism, natural killer cell cytotoxicity, and cytotoxic/suppressor T cells in HIV+ Black women at risk for cervical cancer. *Psychosomatic Medicine, 60*, 714–722.

Cannon, W. B. (1914). The interrelations of emotions as suggested by recent physiological researches. *American Journal of Physiology, 25*, 256–282.

Cantor, N., & Norem, J. K. (1989). Defensive pessimism and stress and coping. *Social Cognition, 7*, 92–112.

Carrington, P., Collings, G. H., Jr., Benson, H., Robinson, H., Wood, L. W., Lehrer, P. M., Woolfolk, R. L., & Cole, J. W. (1980). The use of meditation-relaxation techniques for the management of stress in a working population. *Journal of Occupational Medicine, 22*, 221–231.

Coates, T. J., McKusick, L., Kuno, R., & Sites, D. P. (1989). Stress reduction training changed number of sexual partners but not immune function in men with HIV. *American Journal of Public Health, 79*, 885–887.

Cohen, S., Doyle W. J., & Skoner, D. P. (1999). Psychological stress, cytokine production, and severity of upper respiratory illness. *Psychosomatic Medicine, 61*, 175–180.

Cohen, S., Frank, E., Doyle, W. J., Skoner, D. P., Rabin, B. S., & Gawltney, J. M., Jr. (1998). Types of stressors that increase susceptibility to the common cold in healthy adults. *Health Psychology, 17*, 214–223.

Conway, T. L., Vickers, R. R., Weid, H. W., & Rahe, R. (1981). Occupational stress and variation in cigarette, coffee, and alcohol consumption. *Journal of Health and Social Behavior, 22*, 155–165.

Cooper, C. (1988). Predicting susceptibility to short-term stress with the defence mechanism test. *Work and Stress, 2*, 49–58.

Craig, K. J., Heisler, J. A., & Baum, A. (1996). Intrusive thoughts and the maintenance of chronic stress. In I. G. Sarason, G. R. Pierce, & B. R. Sarason (Eds.), *Cognitive interference: Theories, methods, and findings. The LEA series in personality and clinical psychology* (pp. 397–413). Mahwah, NJ: Erlbaum.

Crary, B., Borysenko, D. C., Sutherland, D. C., Kutz, I., Borysenko, J. Z., & Benson, H. (1983). Decrease in mitogen responsiveness of mononuclear cells from peripheral blood after epinephrine administration in humans. *Journal of Immunology, 130*, 694–697.

Crary, B., Hauser, S. L., Borysenko, M., Kutz, I., Hoban, C., Ault, K. A., Weiner, H. L., & Benson, H. (1983). Epinephrine-induced changes in the distribution of lymphocyte subsets in peripheral blood of humans. *Journal of Immunology, 131*, 1178–1181.

Creamer, M., Burgess, P., & Pattison, P. (1992). Reaction to trauma: A cognitive processing model. *Journal of Abnormal Psychology, 101*, 452–459.

Cruess, S., Antoni, M., Cruess, D., Fletcher, M. A., Ironson, G., Kumar, M., Lutgendorf, S., Hayes, A., Klimas, N., & Schneiderman, N. (2000). Reductions in herpes simplex virus type 2 antibody titers after cognitive behavioral stress management and relationships with neuroendocrine function, relaxation skills, and social support in HIV-positive men. *Psychosomatic Medicine, 62*, 828–837.

Davies, A. O., & Lefkowitz, R. J. (1984). Regulation of beta-adrenergic receptors by steroid hormones. *Annual Review of Physiology, 46*, 119–130.

Daynes, R. A., Araneo, B. A., Hennebold, J., Enioutina, E., & Mu, H. H. (1995). Steroids as regulators of the mammalian immune response. *Journal of Investigative Dermatology, 105*(1 Suppl.), 14S–19S.

de la Torre, B. (1994). Psychoendocrinologic mechanisms of life stress. *Stress Medicine, 10*, 107–114.

DeGroot, K. I., Boeke, S., Bonke, B., & Passchier, J. (1997). A revaluation of the adaptiveness of avoidant and vigilant coping with surgery. *Psychology and Health, 12*, 711–717.

Delahanty, D. L., Dougall, A. L., Browning, L. J., Hyman, K. B., & Baum, A. (1998). Duration of stressor and natural killer cell activity. *Psychology and Health, 13*, 1121–1134.

Delahanty, D. L., Dougall, A. L., Craig, K. J., Jenkins, F. J., & Baum, A. (1997). Chronic stress and natural killer cell activity after exposure to traumatic death. *Psychosomatic Medicine, 59*, 467–476.

Delahanty, D. L., Dougall, A. L., Hayward, M., Forlenza, M., Hawk, L., & Baum, A. (2000). Gender differences in cardiovascular and natural killer cell reactivity to acute stress following a hassling task. *International Journal of Behavioral Medicine, 7*, 19–27.

Delahanty, D. L., Wang, T., Maravich, C., Forlenza, M., & Baum, A. (2000). Time-of-day effects on response of natural killer cells to acute stress in men and women. *Health Psychology, 19*, 39–45.

Dew, M. A., & Bromet, E. J. (1993). Predictors of temporal patterns of psychiatric distress during 10 years following the nuclear accident at Three Mile Island. *Social Psychiatry and Psychiatric Epidemiology, 28,* 49–55.

Dhabhar, F. S. (1998). Stress-induced enhancement of cell-mediated immunity. *Annals of the New York Academy of Sciences, 840,* 359–372.

Dolan, C. A., Sherwood, A., & Light, K. C. (1992). Cognitive coping strategies and blood pressure responses to real-life stress in healthy young men. *Health Psychology, 11,* 233–240.

Dorian, B., & Garfinkel, P. E. (1987). Stress, immunity, and illness: A review. *Psychological Medicine, 17,* 393–407.

Dougall, A. L., Craig, K. J., & Baum, A. (1999). Assessment of characteristics of intrusive thoughts and their impact on distress among victims of traumatic events. *Psychosomatic Medicine, 61,* 38–48.

Dougall, A. L., Ursano, R. J., Posluszny, D. M., Fullerton, C. S., & Baum, A. (2001). Predictors of posttraumatic stress among victims of motor vehicle accidents. *Psychosomatic Medicine, 63,* 402–411.

Eisenstein, T. K., & Hilburger, M. E. (1998). Opioid modulation of immune responses: Effects on phagocytes and lymphoid cell populations. *Journal of Neuroimmunology, 83,* 36–44.

Eller, L. S. (1995). Effects of two cognitive-behavioral interventions on immunity and symptoms in persons with HIV. *Annals of Behavioral Medicine, 17,* 339–348.

Esterling, B. A., Kiecolt-Glaser, J. K., Bodnar, J. C., & Glaser, R. (1994). Chronic stress, social support, and persistent alterations in the natural killer cell response to cytokines in older adults. *Health Psychology, 13,* 291–298.

Fava, G. A. (2000). Cognitive behavioral therapy. In G. Fink (Ed.), *Encyclopedia of stress* (Vol. 1, pp. 484–487). San Diego, CA: Academic Press.

Fawzy, F. I. (1994). Immune effects of a short-term intervention for cancer patients. *Advances, 10,* 32–33.

Fleishman, J. A. (1984). Personality characteristics and coping patterns. *Journal of Health and Social Behavior, 25,* 229–244.

Folkman, S., & Lazarus, R. S. (1980). An analysis of coping in a middle-aged community sample. *Journal of Health and Social Behavior, 21,* 219–239.

Galloway, M. T., & Jokl, P. (2000). Aging successfully: The importance of physical activity in maintaining health and function. *Journal of the American Academy of Orthopaedic Surgeons, 8,* 37–44.

Ganley, R. M. (1989). Emotion and eating in obesity: A review of the literature. *International Journal of Eating Disorders, 8,* 343–361.

Gerin, W., Litt, M. D., Deich, J., & Pickering, T. G. (1995). Self-efficacy as a moderator of perceived control effects on cardiovascular reactivity: Is enhanced control always beneficial? *Psychosomatic Medicine, 57,* 390–397.

Glaser, R., Sheridan, J., Malarkey, W. B., MacCallum, R. C., & Kiecolt-Glaser, J. K. (2000). Chronic stress modulates the immune response to a pneumococcal pneumonia vaccine. *Psychosomatic Medicine, 62,* 804–807.

Glass, D. C., & Singer, J. E. (1972). *Urban stress: Experiments on noise and social stressors.* New York: Academic Press.

Greenberg, M. A. (1995). Cognitive processing of traumas: The role of intrusive thoughts and reappraisals. *Journal of Applied Social Psychology, 25,* 1262–1296.

Greeno, C. G., & Wing, R. R. (1994). Stress-induced eating. *Psychological Bulletin, 115,* 444–464.

Grunberg, N. E., & Baum, A. (1985). Biological commonalities of stress and substance abuse. In S. Shiffman & T. A. Wills (Eds.), *Coping and substance use* (pp. 25–62). Orlando, FL: Academic Press.

Herbert, T. B., & Cohen, S. (1993). Stress and immunity in humans: A meta-analytic review. *Psychosomatic Medicine, 55,* 364–379.

Herbert, T. B., Cohen, S., Marsland, A. L., Bachen, E. A., Rabin, B. S., Muldoon, M. F., & Manuck, S. B. (1994). Cardiovascular reactivity and the course of immune response to an acute psychological stressor. *Psychosomatic Medicine, 56,* 337–344.

Hobfoll, S. E. (1989). Conservation of resources. *American Psychologist, 44,* 513–524.

Hobfoll, S. E., & Lily, R. (1993). Resource as a strategy for community psychology. *Journal of Community Psychology, 21,* 128–148.

Horowitz, M. J. (1986). *Stress response syndromes* (2nd ed.). New York: Jason Aronson.

Inslicht, S. S., Hyman, K. B., Larkin, G. L., Jenkins, F., & Baum, A. (2001). Domestic violence and health risk: Chronic stress, latent virus antibodies, and health behavior [Abstract]. *Psychosomatic Medicine, 63,* 116.

Ironson, G., Wynings, C., Schneiderman, N., Baum, A., Rodriguez, M., Greenwood, D., Benight, C. C., Antoni, M., LaPerriere, A., Huang, H., Klimas, N., & Fletcher, M. A. (1997). Post traumatic stress symptoms, intrusive thoughts, loss and immune function after Hurricane Andrew. *Psychosomatic Medicine, 59,* 128–141.

Jammer, L. D., & Leigh, H. (1999). Repressive/defensive coping, endogenous opioids and health: How a life so perfect can make you sick. *Psychiatry Research, 85,* 17–31.

Jenkins, F. J., & Baum, A. (1995). Stress and reactivation of latent herpes simplex virus: A fusion of behavioral medicine and molecular biology. *Annals of Behavioral Medicine, 17,* 116–123.

Kaloupek, D. G., & Stoupakis, T. (1985). Coping with a stressful medical procedure: Further investigation with volunteer blood donors. *Journal of Behavioral Medicine, 8,* 131–148.

Kappel, M., Poulsen, T. D., Galbo, H., & Pedersen, B. K. (1998). Effects of elevated plasma noradrenaline concentration on the immune system in humans. *European Journal of Applied Physiology and Occupational Physiology, 79,* 93–98.

Kausar, R., & Akram, M. (1998). Cognitive appraisal and coping of patients with terminal versus nonterminal diseases. *Journal of Behavioural Sciences, 9,* 13–28.

Kiecolt-Glaser, J. K., Fisher, L. D., Ogrocki, P., Stout, J. C., Speicher, C. E., & Glaser, R. (1987). Marital quality, marital disruption, and immune function. *Psychosomatic Medicine, 49*(1), 13–34.

Kiecolt-Glaser, J. K., & Glaser, R. (1987). Psychosocial influences on herpesvirus latency. In E. Kurstak, Z. J. Lipowski, & P. V. Morozov (Eds.), *Viruses, immunity, and mental disorders* (pp. 403–411). New York: Plenum Press.

Kiecolt-Glaser, J. K., Glaser, R., Strain, E. C., Stout, J. C., Tarr, K. L., Holliday, J. E., & Speicher, C. E. (1986). Modulation of cellular immunity in medical students. *Journal of Behavioral Medicine, 9,* 5–21.

Kiecolt-Glaser, J. K., Glaser, R., Williger, D., Stout, J., Messick, G., Sheppard, S., Ricker, D., Romisher, S. C., Briner, W., Bonnell, G., & Donnerberg, R. (1985). Psychosocial enhancement of immunocompetence in a geriatric population. *Health Psychology, 4,* 25–41.

Kiecolt-Glaser, J. K., Kennedy, S., Malkoff, S., Fisher, L., Speicher, C. E., & Glaser, R. (1988). Marital discord and immunity in males. *Psychosomatic Medicine, 50,* 213–229.

Kiecolt-Glaser, J. K., Marucha, P. T., Malarkey, W. B., Mercado, A. M., & Glaser, R. (1995). Slowing of wound healing by psychological stress. *Lancet, 346,* 1194–1196.

King, A. C., Taylor, C. B., Albright, C. A., & Haskell, W. L. (1990). The relationship between repressive and defensive coping styles and blood pressure responses in healthy, middle-aged men and women. *Journal of Psychosomatic Research, 34,* 461–471.

Klein, T. W., Friedman, H., & Specter, S. (1998). Marijuana, immunity and infection. *Journal of Neuroimmunology, 83,* 102–115.

Kohlman, C. W., Weidner, G., & Messina, C. R. (1996). Avoidant coping style and verbal-cardiovascular response dissociation. *Psychology and Health, 11,* 371–384.

Kompier, M. A., & DiMartino, V. (1995). Review of bus drivers' occupational stress and stress prevention. *Stress Medicine, 11,* 253–262.

Krueger, G. P. (1989). Sustained work, fatigue, sleep loss and performance: A review of the issues. *Work and Stress, 3,* 129–141.

LaPerriere, A., Antoni, M. H., Schneiderman, N., Ironson, G., Klimas, N., Caralis, P., & Fletcher, M. A. (1990). Exercise intervention attenuates emotional distress and natural killer cell decrements following notification of positive serologic status for HIV-1. *Biofeedback and Self-regulation, 15,* 229–242.

Lazarus, R. S. (1966). *Psychological stress and the coping process.* New York: McGraw-Hill.

Lazarus, R. S. (1993). Coping theory and research: Past, present, and future. *Psychosomatic Medicine, 55,* 234–247.

Lazarus, R. S., & Folkman, S. (1984). *Stress, appraisal, and coping.* New York: Springer.

Leserman, J., Pettito, J. M., Golden, R. N., Gaynes, B. N., Gu, H., Perkins, D. O., Silva, S. G., Folds, J. D., & Evans, D. L. (2000). Impact of stressful life events, depression, social support, coping, and cortisol on progression to AIDS. *American Journal of Psychiatry, 157,* 1221–1228.

Lester, N., Smart, L., & Baum, A. (1994). Measuring coping flexibility. *Psychology and Health, 9,* 409–424.

Leventhal, H. (1980). Toward a comprehensive theory of emotion. *Advances in Experimental Social Psychology, 13,* 139–207.

Lundberg, U. (1984). Human psychobiology in Scandinavia: II. Psychoneuroendocrinology: Human stress and coping processes. *Scandinavian Journal of Psychology, 25*(3), 214–226.

Manuck, S. B., Cohen, S., Rabin, B. S., Muldoon, M. F., & Bachen, E. A. (1991). Individual differences in cellular immune response to stress. *Psychological Science, 2*(2), 111–115.

Marucha, P. T., Kiecolt-Glaser, J. K., & Favagehi, M. (1998). Mucosal wound healing is impaired by examination stress. *Psychosomatic Medicine, 60,* 362–365.

Mason, J. W. (1971). A re-evaluation of the concept of "non-specificity" in stress theory. *Journal of Psychiatric Research, 8,* 323–333.

McAllister-Sistilli, C. G., Cagiula, A. R., Knopf, S., Rose, C. A., Miller, A. L., & Donny, E. C. (1998). The effects of nicotine on the immune system. *Psychoneuroendocrinology, 23,* 175–187.

McEwen, B. S. (1998). Seminars in medicine of the Beth Israel Deaconess Medical Center: Protective and damaging effects of stress mediators. *New England Journal of Medicine, 338,* 171–179.

McEwen, B. S., & Stellar, E. (1993). Stress and the individual: Mechanisms leading to disease. *Archives of Internal Medicine, 153,* 2093–2101.

McKinnon, W., Weisse, C. S., Reynolds, C. P., Bowles, C. A., & Baum, A. (1989). Chronic stress, leukocyte subpopulations, and humoral response to latent viruses. *Health Psychology, 8*(4), 389–402.

McNally, R. J. (1997). Implicit and explicit memory for trauma-related information in PTSD. In R. Yehuda & A. C. McFarlane (Eds.), *Annals of the New York Academy of Science: Psychobiology of posttraumatic stress disorder* (Vol. 821, pp. 219–224). New York: New York Academy of Sciences.

Mellman, T. A. (1997). Psychobiology of sleep disturbances in posttraumatic stress disorder. In R. Yehuda & A. C. McFarlane (Eds.), *Annals of the New York Academy of Sciences: Psychobiology of posttraumatic stress disorder* (Vol. 821, pp. 142–149). New York: New York Academy of Sciences.

Miller, G. E., & Cohen, S. (2001). Psychological interventions and the immune system: A meta-analytic review and critique. *Health Psychology, 20,* 47–63.

Murphy, L. R. (1984). Stress management in highway maintenance workers. *Journal of Occupational Environmental Medicine, 26,* 436–442.

Naliboff, B. D., Benton, D., Solomon, G. F., Morley, J. E., Fahey, J. L., Bloom, E. T., Makinodan, T., & Gilmore, S. L. (1991). Immunological changes in young and old adults during brief laboratory stress. *Psychosomatic Medicine, 53,* 121–132.

O'Leary, A. (1990). Stress, emotion, and human immune function. *Psychological Bulletin, 108,* 363–382.

Osowiecki, D. M., & Compas, B. E. (1999). A prospective study of coping, perceived control, and psychological adaptation to breast cancer. *Cognitive Therapy and Research, 23,* 169–180.

Paavonen, T. (1994). Hormonal regulation of immune responses. *Annals of Medicine, 26,* 255–258.

Pike, J. L., Smith, T. L., Hauger, R. L., Nicassio, P. M., Patterson, T. L., McClintick, J., Costlow, C., & Irwin, M. R. (1997). Chronic life stress alters sympathetic, neuroendocrine, and immune responsivity to an acute psychological stressor in humans. *Psychosomatic Medicine, 59,* 447–457.

Pilette, W. L. (1983). Magical thinking by inpatient staff members. *Psychiatric Quarterly, 55,* 272–274.

Rahe, R. H., & Arthur, R. J. (1978). Life change and illness studies: Past history and future directions. *Journal of Human Stress, 4,* 3–15.

Redeker, N. S. (1992). The relationship between uncertainty and coping after coronary bypass surgery. *Western Journal of Nursing Research, 14,* 48–68.

Rosenbloom, C. A., & Whittington, F. J. (1993). The effects of bereavement on eating behaviors and nutrient intakes in elderly widowed persons. *Journal of Gerontology, 48,* S223–S229.

Sadeh, A. (1996). Stress, trauma, and sleep in children. *Child and Adolescent Psychiatric Clinics of North America, 5,* 685–700.

Schedlowski, M., Jacobs, R., Stratmann, G., Richter, S., Hädicke, A., Tewes, U., Wagner, T. O. F., & Schmidt, R. E. (1993). Changes of natural killer cells during acute psychological stress. *Journal of Clinical Immunology, 13*(2), 119–126.

Schuurs, A. H. W. M., & Verheul, H. A. M. (1990). Effects of gender and sex steroids on the immune response. *Journal of Steroid Biochemistry, 35,* 157–172.

Segerstrom, S. C., Solomon, G. F., Kemeny, M. E., & Fahey, J. L. (1998). Relationship of worry to immune sequelae of the Northridge earthquake. *Journal of Behavioral Medicine, 21,* 433–450.

Selye, H. (1936). A syndrome produced by diverse nocuous agents. *Nature, 148,* 84–85.

Selye, H. (1984). *The stress of life* (Rev. ed.). New York: McGraw-Hill. (Original work published 1956)

Sieber, W. J., Rodin, J., Larson, L., Ortega, S., Cummings, N., Levy, S., Whiteside, T., & Herberman, R. (1992). Modulation of human natural killer cell activity by exposure to uncontrollable stress. *Brain, Behavior, and Immunity, 6,* 141–156.

Solomon, G. F., Segerstrom, S. C., Grohr, P., Kemeny, M., & Fahey, J. (1997). Shaking up immunity: Psychological and immunological changes after a natural disaster. *Psychosomatic Medicine, 59,* 114–127.

Sondergaard, S. R., Ullum, H., Skinhoj, P., & Pedersen, B. K. (1999). Epinephrine-induced mobilization of natural killer (NK) cells and NK-like T cells in HIV-infected patients. *Cellular Immunology, 197,* 91–98.

Spaccarelli, S., Bowden, B., Coatsworth, J. D., & Kim, S. (1997). Psychosocial correlates of male sexual aggression in a chronic delinquent sample. *Criminal Justice and Behavior, 24,* 71–95.

Stefanski, V., & Ben-Eliyahu, S. (1996). Social confrontation and tumor metastasis in rats: Defeat and beta-adrenergic mechanisms. *Physiology and Behavior, 60,* 277–282.

Steptoe, A. (1989). Coping and psychophysiological reactions. *Advances in Behaviour Research and Therapy, 11,* 259–270.

Stone, A. A., Bovbjerg, D. H., Neale, J. M., Napoli, A., Valdimarsdottir, H., Cox, D., Hayden, F. G., & Gawltney, J. M. (1992). Development of common cold symptoms following experimental rhinovirus infection is related to prior stressful life events. *Behavioral Medicine, 18,* 115–120.

Szafarczyck, A., Malaval, F., Laurent, Á., Gibaud, R., & Assenmacher, I. (1987). Further evidence for a central stimulatory action of catecholamines on ACTH release in the rat. *Endocrinology, 121,* 883–892.

Taylor, D. N. (1995). Effects of a behavioral stress-management program on anxiety, mood, self-esteem, and T-cell count in HIV-positive men. *Psychological Report, 76,* 451–457.

Thoits, P. A. (1986). Social support as coping assistance. *Journal of Consulting and Clinical Psychology, 54,* 416–423.

Uchino, B. N., Cacioppo, J. T., & Kiecolt-Glaser, J. K. (1996). The relationship between social support and physiological processes: A review with emphasis on underlying mechanisms and implications for health. *Psychological Bulletin, 119,* 488–531.

Ursano, R. J., Fullerton, C. S., Kao, T., & Bhartiya, V. R. (1995). Longitudinal assessment of posttraumatic stress disorder and depression after exposure to traumatic death. *Journal of Nervous and Mental Disease, 183,* 36–42.

Vitaliano, P. P., Maiuro, R. D., Russo, J., & Becker, J. (1987). Raw versus relative scores in the assessment of coping strategies. *Journal of Behavioral Medicine, 10,* 1–18.

Watson, R. R., Eskelson, C., & Hartmann, B. R. (1984). Severe alcohol abuse and cellular immune functions. *Arizona Medicine, 41,* 665–668.

Weiner, H. (1992). *Perturbing the organism: The biology of stressful experience.* Chicago: University of Chicago Press.

Willis, L., Thomas, P., Garry, P. J., & Goodwin, J. S. (1987). A prospective study of response to stressful life events in initially healthy elders. *Journal of Gerontology, 42,* 627–630.

Zakowski, S. G., Cohen, L., Hall, M. H., Wollman, K., & Baum, A. (1994). Differential effects of active and passive laboratory stressors on immune function in healthy men. *International Journal of Behavioral Medicine, 1*(2), 163–184.

CHAPTER 17

The Psychology and Ethology of Learning

PETER C. HOLLAND AND GREGORY F. BALL

The study of learning in animals most frequently concerns the adaptation of an individual to its environment through experience (Thorpe, 1963). It has been variously described as *experimental epistemology* (Hilgard & Bower, 1975), that is, the study of the acquisition of knowledge, as the "strengthening . . . or setting up of receptor-effector connections" (C. L. Hull, 1943, p. 69), and as "what happens between the perception of information by our sense organs and the ultimate storage of some part of that information in our brains" (Gould, 1982, p. 260). Regardless of how it was described, it is fair to say that the study of learning in animals was a cornerstone of experimental psychology for many decades, beginning in the early part of the last century. Although it no longer commands as dominant a role in the field of experimental psychology as a whole, its legacy remains in cognitive psychology through its contributions to connectionist modeling of cognitive processes. Furthermore, the study of brain mechanisms of learning and memory remains a major part of biological psychology. In the field of neuroscience, the study of the neural mechanisms of learning has attracted a wide range of investigators from molecular biologists focusing on changes in gene expression in isolated synapses in vitro, to neurophysiologists studying plasticity in brain slices, to cog-

nitive neuroscientists using neuroimaging methods to identify brain areas involved in human learning processes. It is clear that the study of learning will continue to be a major research topic for investigators interested in behavior or neuroscience in the twenty-first century.

There are two major traditions in the study of learning in animals, one within experimental psychology, and one within zoology, especially ethology. Although for several decades the orientations and work of these two traditions seemed antithetical, more recently the study of animal learning has profited from a greater synthesis of these approaches. In this chapter we first develop a few key ideas within each of the separate traditions and then provide three case studies that show how a more synthetic approach, combined with an interest in the neural organization of learning, can provide important insights into the nature of learning. Because this is a handbook of psychology, we emphasize the tradition of experimental psychology.

ETHOLOGICAL APPROACHES TO LEARNING

Ethology has made a key contribution to the study of animal learning. At the same time, the investigation of learning has played an important role in the development of ethological theory. The many exchanges that occurred between ethologists and experimental psychologists just after World War II were especially important in sharpening the research approaches that were adopted by ethologists for the study of learning

This chapter evolved from the authors' lectures for the Cold Spring Harbor Laboratories summer course, "The Biology of Learning and Memory: From Molecules to Behavior." The authors thank the students and faculty of that course over the years for their questions and stimulation.

(e.g., Lehrman, 1953; Schneirla, 1956). In this section we consider generally the ethological approach to the study of behavior and more specifically how this approach manifested itself in studies of animal learning conducted by ethologists. We address these issues by first asking, "What is ethology?" and then discussing the ethological view of learning and its application to the study of learning.

What Is Ethology?

Perhaps the briefest definition of ethology to be commonly adopted is that it is "the biological study of animal behavior" (e.g., Immelman & Beer, 1989; Tinbergen, 1963). This definition fails to capture important nuances that distinguish ethology from other fields in the behavioral and neural sciences that also consider nonhuman animals as subjects. The qualifier that ethology represents a zoological approach to the study of behavior provides a useful additional insight (Beer, 1963; Thorpe, 1979). Zoologists are intrinsically interested in the study of animals for their own sake and on their own terms, rather than as a model system to understand some basic biological process that will be broadly applicable to many life forms including humans. In other words, viewing behavior in zoological terms means that ethologists take an animal-centered view of the study of behavior.

Ethologists therefore first and foremost are interested in understanding how an animal behaves under natural conditions. Thorpe (1979) has observed that ethology along with ecology can be viewed as the scientific legacy of a fascination with natural history in Western culture that can be traced back at least to the 12th century and Francis of Assisi. It is this natural-history orientation toward behavior that all authorities agree is one of the central features of ethology (e.g., Hinde, 1982).

How is a natural-history orientation manifested in the scientific study of behavior? Combining a thorough description of behavior under natural conditions with an understanding of the sensory abilities (and limitations) that an animal possesses is an essential first step in any detailed study of behavior. Such descriptive data are usually collected under field conditions where one can appreciate the challenges that an animal faces. One's appreciation for the possible behavioral capabilities an animal possesses increases markedly when one actually experiences the challenges that an animal normally faces. Adopting a natural-history orientation does not mean that one eschews experimentation. On the contrary, ethologists have often performed experiments and manipulations of various sorts. But an ethologist will always be concerned about the relevance of such manipulations to the natural situation. Just because one can reliably observe an

animal engage in certain behaviors under certain environmental conditions does not mean that one has learned anything of value of the causes of behavior. A good ethologist is always concerned about artifactual responses that might be observed under artificial conditions that can fool one about the actual capabilities that an animal possesses. Finally, the natural-history orientation adopted by ethologists means that they are interested in not only the causes and development of behavior (sometimes called *proximate causes*), as are many other behavioral scientists, but also the adaptive significance and evolution of behavior (sometimes called *ultimate causes of behavior*).

Many ethologists have stressed that this interest in multiple levels of analysis is a key aspect of core ethology (e.g., Hinde 1982; Lorenz, 1981; Tinbergen, 1963). Lorenz (1981) phrased this notion in a way that clearly illustrates the link between ethology and Darwin. He contended that ethology applies to behavior "all those questions asked and those methodologies used as a matter of course in all the other branches of biology since Charles Darwin's time" (p. 1). This interest in the evolution of behavior has framed the ethological approach to the study of learning and has also set the stage for some of the conflicts that occurred between ethologists and experimental psychologists.

To understand ethological approaches to the study of learning we should be familiar with some basic ethological concepts about how behavior is organized. One important notion is that behavior is often packaged into highly stereotyped patterns known as *fixed action patterns* (Lorenz, 1950; Tinbergen, 1951). As observed by Lorenz (1950) and others, the patterning of these fixed action patterns is generally species-specific and can therefore be used as a trait along with morphological and genetic characters to build a taxonomy. Fixed action patterns are often preceded by more variable behavioral responses, known as *appetitive responses,* that put the animal in the situation to express a fixed action pattern (Craig, 1918; Hinde, 1970; Marler & Hamilton, 1966). The fundamental idea is that some stereotyped behaviors result in a functional outcome that is associated with a reduction in motivation whereas other more variable behaviors allow an individual to converge on this functional outcome (Timberlake & Silva, 1995). Although dichotomizing behavior in this way is problematic in some cases (Hinde, 1953), the distinction has been useful to both ethologists and experimental psychologists for the elucidation of the mechanisms mediating many motivated behaviors such as food-seeking and ingestive behavior (Timberlake & Silva, 1995). Furthermore, the study of these species-typical motor behaviors has provided us with insight into how motor systems are organized by the central nervous system to implement complex patterns of behavior (Hinde, 1953; Tinbergen, 1951).

An idea closely related to the fixed action pattern, which was also articulated early in the history of ethology, is that such species-typical behaviors are elicited by environmental stimuli in a highly selective manner. A famous example concerns the territorial responses of male robins. Lack (1939) presented male robins on their territories with a stuffed juvenile robin that had drab brown plumage, with a stuffed male robin with a red breast, or with just a bunch of red feathers. The territorial male robin responded aggressively to the model of the breeding male and ignored the model of a juvenile robin. However, his response to the bunch of red feathers was nearly equal to his response to the male model. This led Lack to conclude that the red breast was the key stimulus out of the myriad of stimuli that might be relevant that the male robin used to guide his aggressive responses. Stimuli like these are known as *sign stimuli*. Many other examples of these sorts of highly selective responses to stimuli in the environment have been reported since they were first described in detail by von Uexkull, a teacher of Lorenz, in the 1920s and 1930s (see Schiller, 1957). A sign stimulus is currently defined as "a single simple feature or a compound of a few simple features that provide only a small fraction of the total sensory input from a situation to an animal, but to which the animal's specific reaction pattern is tuned, so that the stimulus selectively elicits this pattern" (Immelman & Beer, 1989, p. 270). The mechanistic basis of this selective stimulation has been studied to some extent. The simplest examples involve limitations in the relevant sensory receptors or in the tuning of sensory fibers so that the animal can detect only a very restricted part of the sensory world (Marler, 1961). In the case of the male robin, it is clear that the male is able to perceive colors besides red. One can therefore reject the obvious explanation that there is some sort of limitation of sensory receptors responsible for such selective responding. The neural basis of selective responding to stimuli can involve many different mechanisms besides just biases in sensory receptors, including learning processes such as sensitization or habituation.

What is apparent is that complex interpretations of sensory information are being made by the central nervous system to mediate many of these selective responses. Originally, it was thought that these sign stimuli worked via an "innate releasing mechanism" to release action-specific energy that would "fuel" behavioral production (e.g., Lorenz, 1950). This energy model of motivation has been criticized and is no longer held as valid by most ethologists (e.g., Hinde, 1970). However, there are certainly endogenous processes involved in the motivation of fixed action patterns. Most neuroethologists now avoid the terms *motivation* and *drive* and instead try to explain these endogenous processes in physiological terms.

The Ethological View of Learning

Many behavioral and neural scientists continue to think about variation among animals in hierarchical terms. Although the problems with this sort of reasoning have been discussed for many years, going back to Lovejoy's classic monograph (1936; see also Hodos & Campbell, 1969), it is still not unusual to hear about different species being compared on the basis of being "higher" or "lower" vertebrates. Higher and lower in this context refers to the *scale of nature* in which mammals are high on the scale (with primates at the top) and birds reptiles, amphibians, and fish are lower on the scale (Hodos & Campbell, 1969). Invertebrates are of course lower still. There is also an implicit assumption associated with the embrace of hierarchical thinking that the ability to learn a particular behavior is somehow superior or more sophisticated than engaging in a similar behavior when it is unlearned to a large degree. Learning is thought to be associated with more complex nervous systems (such as those possessed by humans), so studying learning in any form will be valuable in understanding human behavior, and one might expect "higher" vertebrates to exhibit more learning and more complex learning than "lower" vertebrates.

With this reasoning in mind it is understandable how many experimental psychologists started to focus on the study of learning in a few convenient species of higher vertebrates so that generalizable principles of learning could be discerned. Even neurobiologists who adopted a reductionist approach to the study of learning and focused on invertebrate species such as the mollusks *Aplysia* (Hawkins & Kandel, 1984; Kandel, 1976) and *Hermissenda* (Alkon, 1983) argued that by studying the cellular and molecular bases of learning in these species, one could gain insight into fundamental processes of brain plasticity that would be widely applicable to many species, including humans. Again in this literature there is an implicit and in some cases explicit assumption that neuroplasticity is an advantageous trait and that the amount of plasticity that a nervous system is capable of is some gauge of the level of sophistication or complexity of that nervous system. At times it seems that in the scientific community the idea that learning and the associated neural plasticity must be a good trait is accepted as being as obvious as the notion that motherhood is a valuable trait as perceived by the community at large.

Ethology adopted a very different view of learning. If one views these issues from the perspective that the function of behavior is to maximize individual reproductive success, then the widespread occurrence of learning is potentially very dangerous. Animals in a given population, in a given habitat, have evolved a particular repertoire of morphological adaptations that make successful reproduction possible. Similarly, as previously discussed, ethologists have argued that species-typical behaviors are also adaptations that have evolved to complement these morphological adaptations to promote individual reproductive success. Learning is a way to bring about behavioral change based on experience. Behavioral change can potentially disrupt adaptive complexes of behavior and have disastrous consequences for the functional outcomes of behavior (i.e., reproductive success). Learning may indeed be advantageous or necessary for certain aspects of the behavior, but it should be highly controlled and limited so that the right sort of learning occurs at the right stage in the life history of the animal. It seems unlikely that open programs of neuroplasticity that facilitate unguided learning would be advantageous in many cases, and therefore they are unlikely to evolve very often.

The ethological argument concerning learning was perhaps most forcefully articulated by Konrad Lorenz, who pointed out that the "more complicated an adapted process, the less chance there is that a random change will improve its adaptiveness" (1965, p. 12). He goes on to point out that there are "no life processes more complicated than those which take place in the central nervous system and control behavior. Random change must, with an overpowering probability, result in their disintegration" (p. 12). These statements succinctly summarize the notion that learning should not necessarily be viewed as a useful trait. The related idea is that when learning does occur, it should be directed. With a rather high degree of invective, Lorenz states, "To anyone tolerably versed in biological thought, it is a matter of course that learning, like any function of comparably high differentiation and survival value, must necessarily be performed by a very species-specific mechanism built into the organic system in the course of its evolution" (p. 12).

The Ethological Approach to the Study of Learning: The Case of Imprinting

The ethological view of learning was perhaps best illustrated by the study of imprinting, first by Konrad Lorenz and then by a variety of other investigators (Bateson, 1966; Hess, 1973). *Imprinting* involves the formation of an attachment by progeny early in life for their mother and then later in life for a mating partner. Imprinting on a mother figure is known as

filial imprinting, whereas an attachment for a mating partner is known as sexual imprinting. Imprinting has been studied in the most detail among bird species with precocial young, such as members of the galliform order (e.g., chickens, turkeys, or quail) as well as members of the anseriform order (e.g., ducks and geese). Imprinting clearly can be considered an example of a learning process because the object that a young animal becomes attached to and will follow around is based on the objects it experiences just after hatching or birth. Lorenz was famous for illustrating how he was able to get young goslings to form attachments to him. Many textbooks of psychology and biology include a picture of Lorenz leading a group of young goslings. This behavior resulted from the fact that the mother was removed so that at hatching the first moving object the goslings encountered was Lorenz, and they did indeed form an attachment with him. Similarly, he demonstrated how these goslings would later court him when they reached sexual maturity.

Filial imprinting can be measured in a variety of ways. The first way involves following the object of attachment. It can also be assessed by behaviors exhibited in the presence of the object (usually indicative of contentment) and behaviors exhibited toward other salient objects in the environment that it is not attached to (usually avoidance behaviors or even fear and panic). Sexual imprinting is measured later in life as a behavioral preference for a mating partner that resembles the object of filial imprinting to some degree.

When Lorenz investigated imprinting in the 1930s, he stressed the aspects of imprinting that made it different from general learning processes. He observed that the learning occurred with a minimal amount of experience (a single exposure for a limited amount of time is sufficient), that the ability to learn was optimal during a restricted period of time early in life (the so-called critical period), that this learning was irreversible (a new stimulus could not replace the original imprinting stimulus), and that it has effects on certain behaviors (sexual behaviors) that are not—indeed cannot be—produced at the time the learning occurs. However, modern results from a series of elegant experiments, carried out primarily by ethologists but also by experimental psychologists, indicate that the differences between imprinting and other examples of learning about single events may not be qualitative, but rather a matter of degree. Variables that influence the imprinting process also influence learning about single events in general. These variables include the quantity and quality of the stimulation, the duration of the stimulation, the animal's state (age and past experience), and events that occur between when the animal has an experience and when it is tested (see Bolhuis, 1991, and Shettleworth, 1998, for reviews). The imprinting saga illustrates how the natural-history approach advocated by ethologists can lead to a rigorous experimental analysis of the variables influencing a learned behavior.

GENERAL PROCESS APPROACHES TO LEARNING

In contrast to the ethologists of the time, early experimental psychologists celebrated the role of individual adaptation to a changing world. Although they seldom articulated these attitudes, it is probably fair to say that for them, evolution provided only the raw materials, the bits and pieces of behavior, and that *experience* provided the opportunity for organized, adaptive behavior. Far from being a potential threat to survival, learning was the key to behavioral adaptation.

Indeed, as late as the middle of the twentieth century, many psychologists were optimistic that a full understanding of behavior, mind, and brain could be derived from a few basic and universal principles of learning. Thus, this orientation to the study of learning was sometimes termed *general process theory*. For example, Clark Hull wrote his classic *Principles of Behavior* (1943) "on the assumption that all behavior, individual and social, moral and immoral, normal and psychopathic, is generated from the same primary laws; that the differences in the objective behavioral manifestations are due to the differing conditions under which habits are set up and function" (p. v). Moreover, these "primary laws" were derivable from study of extremely simplified "model systems," such as rats pressing levers and dogs salivating in anticipation of food. Early study of learning focused on animals not because of any intrinsic interest in animal behavior per se but because animal models provided a much greater degree of experimental control over past and present experience. Thus, in contrast to the animal-centered view of ethologists, experimental psychologists largely ignored their subjects' natural histories and may be said to have adopted an experimenter-centered approach to the study of behavior.

The Reflex Tradition

These optimistic views were based in part on the successes of nineteenth-century physiological reflex theory (e.g., Sechenov, 1863/1965; Sherrington, 1906). In the extreme, the belief was that the activity of the brain (or mind) could be reduced to the translation of stimulus input into particular behavioral responses. Thus, the primary goal of psychology was to specify the relation between explicit stimulus inputs and response outputs. In this section we first consider the traditional models

for the study of these input-output relations and then consider in depth some key ideas that have guided recent study of simple learning processes in animals within this tradition.

Classical and Operant Conditioning

The study of learning in experimental psychology has been dominated by two models, that of classical (or Pavlovian) and operant (or instrumental) conditioning. In classical conditioning a relation or contingency is arranged between two events over which the subject has no control. For example, in Pavlov's laboratory (Pavlov, 1927), the sound of a metronome, the *conditioned stimulus* (CS), was repeatedly followed by the delivery of a food, the *unconditioned stimulus* (US), to a hungry dog. Eventually, the sound of the metronome alone came to elicit components of behavior previously controlled by the food (e.g., secretions of the stomach and salivary glands). In operant conditioning a relation is arranged between the animal's behavior and the occurrence of some event (e.g., food is delivered to a hungry rat each time it presses a lever). In both cases, the arrangement of the appropriate contingencies results in the development of a conditioned reflex, habit, or association such that some stimulus comes to provoke a particular behavioral response automatically. Furthermore, the products of learning were characterizable in a single dimension, the strength of that habit, reflex, or association.

Although proponents of each model often attempted to describe the other model as a special case of their own (e.g., C. L. Hull, 1943; Sheffield, 1965), some key differences are worth noting. Within the Pavlovian model, classical conditioning involved a process whereby the control of existing behavior is transferred from one stimulus to another. In the example described earlier, the metronome may be said to come to substitute for the food in controlling behavior (e.g., Mackintosh, 1974). Although it was widely recognized (C. L. Hull, 1943) that the conditioned (learned) response (CR) to the CS and the original, unconditioned response (UR) to the US need not be identical, the nature of learned behavior was nevertheless determined by the choice of US.

By contrast, within the operant model the learned response was assumed to be unconstrained by the reinforcer, limited only by the subject's behavioral repertoire and the experimenter's skill in extracting the desired behavior from that repertoire. The important feature of events that served as USs or reinforcers was not that they themselves unconditionally controlled behavior, but rather that they "stamped in" associations between stimuli (e.g., the sight of the lever) and responses (pressing the lever) on which they were made contingent, according to a *law of effect* (Thorndike, 1898). By this law, stimuli and responses are associated when they are followed by a "pleasurable event" (p. 103). More generally, behavior is governed by its consequences—its frequency depending on whether it has in the past produced reinforcing events. From the perspective of early learning theorists, it is this ability of animals' behavior to be influenced by its consequences that formed the basis of adaptive behavior in individuals.

Both models emphasized experimental control over the animal's experience and behavior. By isolating the animal from its natural environment in laboratories and still further in relatively small and sterile experimental chambers, influences on behavior other than those of immediate interest to the experiment at hand were thought to be minimized. These extraneous influences included not only distractions such as sights, sounds, or the presence of conspecifics, but also the opportunity to engage in other species-typical behaviors.

Learning, Motivation, and Emotion

Early study of conditioning was intertwined with the study of motivation. It was apparent that the effect of a stimulus on behavior was often modulated by various "states" of the animal, for example, those corresponding to food or water deprivation. The construct of motivation, both championed (Lorenz, 1950) and rejected (Hinde, 1960) in ethology as a device for explaining the generation and organization of behavior, served critical, but fairly proscribed, roles in experimental psychologists' accounts for learning and action. First, motivation was often thought to act as a performance variable energizing behavior at the time of action. Issues that attracted investigation included the specificity of motivational states in modulating behavior (e.g., do motivational states irrelevant to the task solution influence behavior?; Kendler, 1946), whether motivational states would energize behavior in the absence of explicit eliciting cues for that behavior (Sheffield & Campbell, 1954), and whether the energizing properties of motivational states could come to be controlled by external stimuli as a result of conditioning (Seligman, Bravman, & Radford, 1970). Although often framed in very different ways, these questions remain with us (Holland, 1991; Swithers & Hall, 1994).

Second, the establishment of associations was often thought to require the operation of some motivationally based reinforcement process to serve as a catalyst for, or to stamp in, stimulus-response (S-R) associations. The nature of this reinforcement process was the subject of great theoretical debate and spanned a range of possibilities including both the reduction (C. L. Hull, 1943) and the induction (Sheffield & Roby, 1950) of drive states (e.g., hunger, thirst, pain, fear, frustration), as well as the occurrence of consummatory behaviors. The 1950s saw the performance of a variety of experiments designed to test the reinforcement powers of events that, for example, reduced drives but failed to elicit consummatory behaviors (e.g., the delivery of food directly to the stomach or blood stream) or vice versa (e.g., the use of tasty but noncaloric foods, or sham feeding). The issue persists, albeit with altered terminology and purpose; for example, Myers and Hall (2000) found that the sensory and postingestive properties of sucrose can serve different roles in reinforcing Pavlovian conditioning in rats.

By the 1960s, emphasis shifted to concern for the interplay of learning and emotional processes. According to two-process theorists (e.g., Mowrer, 1947; Rescorla & Solomon, 1967), a major role of Pavlovian conditioning was the conditioning of emotional responses (CERs). These CERs were manifested not only in characteristic motor and autonomic responses, but also in the modulation of other, ongoing behavior, including learned operant behavior and unlearned consummatory behavior. *Fear conditioning*—in which, for example, tone-shock pairings endow the tone with the ability to elicit freezing or crouching responses and heart rate changes, to suppress lever pressing for food reward and drinking for its own sake, and to enhance responding to avoid shocks (see Mackintosh, 1974, for examples)—remains one of the more popular preparations for the study of conditioning and its neurobiological bases.

Learning and Temporal Contiguity

Early theories of learning agreed that the formation of associations was critically influenced by time, especially the temporal arrangement of the CS (or an operant response) and the US. Early work with eye-blink conditioning and other preparations suggested that conditioning occurred only when the CS/response occurred slightly before the US, on the order of a few seconds at most. The optimal CS-US interval was described as approximately half a second, with a rapid drop in the rate or amount of conditioning obtained with shorter or longer intervals. However, by the 1960s the most popular laboratory for Pavlovian conditioning procedures (see Mackintosh, 1974, for examples) routinely used CS-US intervals that were one or two orders of magnitude greater (10–100 s). Indeed, the greatest blow to the claim that strict temporal contiguity of CS and US was critical to conditioning was struck by Garcia, Erving, and Koelling (1966), who showed that flavor aversion learning, whereby animals learn to reject flavors that are paired with the induction of illness, occurs readily over intervals measured in hours.

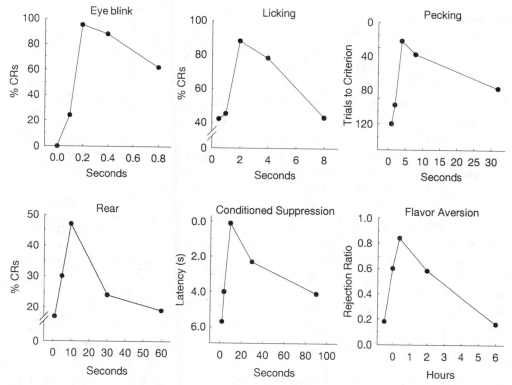

Figure 17.1 Pavlovian conditioning as a function of CS-US interval in six preparations. Each preparation shows an interval function with similar bitonic form, in which there is less conditioning if the interval is too long or too short, but the abscissa time scales differ greatly. Eyelid data, with shock US, are taken from Smith, Coleman, and Gormezano (1969). Licking data, with water US, from Boice and Denny (1965). Pecking data, with food US, from Gibbon et al. (1977). Rear data, with food US, from Holland (1980a). Conditioned suppression data, with shock US, from Yeo (1974). Conditioned flavor aversion data from Barker and Smith (1974). See text for discussion. With permission, from the *Annual Review of Neuroscience,* Volume 11 © 1988 by Annual Reviews www.AnnualReviews.org.

Figure 17.1 shows a set of graphs in which some performance measure is plotted as a function of the CS-US interval in a variety of conditioning preparations. Clearly, there is no best interval for conditioning; rather, different conditioning preparations reveal different parameter spaces. This observation is consistent with Lorenz's claim that characteristics of learning must be highly species specific and task specific. Nevertheless, it is notable that despite the substantial variation in the absolute time intervals over which those functions apply, the functions are remarkably similar in form across a range of preparations. Each is bitonic, with conditioning best at intermediate values, declining rapidly with shorter intervals and declining more slowly with longer intervals.

Another important early finding about the effects of time on conditioning was that the interval between conditioning episodes (the intertrial interval, or ITI) is important as well. Generally, conditioning is facilitated by longer ITIs (Gormezano & Moore, 1969); indeed, the aphorism that spaced practice is better than massed practice survives as a principle in education.

Recent research has indicated a more complex relation between the ITI and the CS-US interval. In many conditioning preparations the CS-US interval function is modulated by the ITI such that the effectiveness of any given CS-US interval in producing conditioning depends on the ITI (Gibbon, Baldock, Locurto, Gold, & Terrace, 1977). Specifically, the ratio between the CS-US interval and the ITI is often a better predictor of conditioning than is either interval alone (for illustrations, see Gallistel & Gibbon, 2000; Holland, 2000; Rescorla, 1988a).

Cognitive Reformulations of Conditioning

Modern thinking about associative learning has taken a different track, following the lead of classical association theory rather than of reflexology. Most contemporary theorists describe conditioning as "the learning of relations among events so as to allow the organism to represent its environment" (Rescorla, 1988b, p. 157). Within this perspective, operant and classical conditioning are models of animals' learning of relations between their own behavior and environmental events, and among environmental events out of their control, respectively. In Tolman and Brunswik's (1935) terms, they model processes whereby animals become sensitive to the "causal texture" of their environment (p. 43).

This description differs in two important ways from earlier ones. First, it stresses a more abstract view of learning, dispensing with the primacy of transfer of control of reflexes or stamping in of habits. Learning a relation between a metronome and food *might* permit transfer of a salivary reflex controlled initially by the food, but it might also produce a range of other behavioral changes. Quantitative models within this perspective seldom relate learning directly to the performance or probability of a response, but instead are couched in terms of constructs like associative strength, signal value, and expectancy. Although these models assume that these constructs are related in some lawful manner to animals' behaviors, they typically voice little concern for the nature or function of the behavioral consequents of association. Behavior is often reduced to a necessary but occasionally inconvenient assay of underlying associative learning.

Second, these more cognitive descriptions of learning emphasize the construction of internal representations of events and their relations, which may then guide behavior. Instead of learning to perform particular behaviors *because of* an arrangement between various events, the animal is assumed to learn *about* the events and their relations. The consequent representational structure then may be used to guide behavior in a more flexible fashion than is accorded by the simple transfer of a reflex from one stimulus to another, or the attachment of a new response to a discriminative stimulus. As a result, more emphasis has been placed on the nature and richness of representational processes, in addition to the rules by which associations are formed.

For the most part, both of these trends have been salutary. The reformulation of the problems of associative learning not only has broadened the domain of inquiry and application of simple learning principles but also has brought learning and behavior theory into more fruitful contact with other branches of psychology. On the other hand, this reformulation has often been construed as leaving behavior itself out of the picture, further separating psychological and ethological approaches. Nevertheless, by freeing associative learning from the confines of the reflex tradition, cognitive reformulations opened the door for considering the behavioral products of learning from ethological perspectives. In a later section we describe several examples in which cognitive perspectives have been combined with interests in behavior and its functions.

Beyond Temporal Contiguity: Information and Contingency

As shown in Figure 17.1, strict temporal contiguity is not *necessary* for associative learning. Likewise, it is now clear that

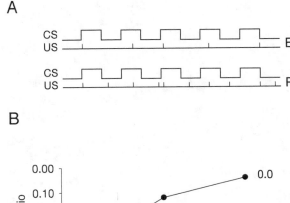

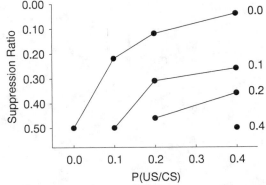

Figure 17.2 A. Schematic representation of a training segment from Rescorla's (1968) contingency experiment, including five CS presentations. In the sequence labeled E the probability of receiving the US during a CS presentation is 1.0, and the probability of receiving the US in the absence of the US is 0. These probabilities produce excitatory conditioning. In the sequence labeled R the probability of receiving the US is 1.0 both during the CS and during equivalent periods in the absence of the CS. This procedure typically produces little or no conditioning asymptotically, despite the same number of CS-US pairings as in the E procedure. B. Fear conditioning as a function of the probability of receiving the US in the presence of the CS (abscissa) and in its absence (parameter). Fear is expressed as the suppression of lever-press responding for a food reward; a suppression ratio of 0 indicates strong conditioning, and a ratio of 0 indicates little or no conditioning. From Rescorla (1968). See text for discussion. With permission, from the *Annual Review of Neuroscience*, Volume 11 © 1988 by Annual Reviews www.AnnualReviews.org.

mere contiguity of two events is also not *sufficient* for associative learning; rather, in some sense one stimulus must provide information about the occurrence of the other. We illustrate this point with two important phenomena, Rescorla's (1968) *contingency effect* and Kamin's (1968) *blocking effect*.

Rescorla (1967, 1968, 1969a) found that the associative learning that developed from repeated pairings of a CS and a US depended on the probability of US presentation in the absence of the CS, in the ITI. Figure 17.2, panel A, shows a cartoon of two conditions in this experiment. In both conditions rats received the same number of US presentations during the CS. Those procedures differed, however, in the probability of US presentation in the ITI. In Group E the US was less probable in the ITI than during the CS, and in Group R the US was equiprobable in the presence and absence of the CS. Despite the identical numbers of CS-US pairings, only rats in

Group E acquired a CR. Indeed, parametric studies showed that the asymptotic level of conditioning attained was a regular function of the probabilities of US delivery during the presence and absence of the CS (Figure 17.2, panel B), as would be expected if animals were calculating the correlation, or contingency, of CS and US.

The Kamin (1968) blocking effect may be the most widely studied example of the insufficiency of temporal contiguity for associative learning. In a basic blocking study two groups of animals each receive pairings of a compound stimulus with a US (e.g., tone + light → food). Prior to this compound training, animals in the Blocking treatment received pairings of one of the stimulus elements (e.g., the light) with the same US, whereas the animals in a Control condition did not. Prior conditioning of the light blocks conditioning to the tone: A test of responding to the tone alone at the end of the experiment showed considerably more responding after the Control treatment than after the Blocking treatment, despite identical conditioning experience with the tone.

In both the contingency and blocking effects, conditioning appears to depend not just on CS-US contiguity alone, but also on the amount of information the target CS provides about the occurrence of the US. When the US is equiprobable in the presence and absence of the CS or when the US is already perfectly predicted by another CS, the target CS fails to acquire conditioning. The development of quantitative learning theories to deal with phenomena like these has led to important advances in the understanding of associative learning. Interestingly, most of these theories have embraced these phenomena by reformulating the idea of contiguity so that it applies to mental events instigated by CSs and USs, rather than the events themselves. One class of theories emphasizes the role of past learning in modulating the effectiveness of reinforcers (USs), whereas another class focuses on changes in the ability of CSs to participate in associative learning.

Variations in the Effectiveness of Reinforcers: The Rescorla-Wagner Model

The Rescorla-Wagner (1972) model has been the most influential modern learning theory. Not only did it provide simple accounts for contingency, blocking, and other puzzling phenomena, but also it led to predictions of a large number of new phenomena, many of which were counter to the intuitions derived from previous conceptualizations of conditioning. Within this model the amount of learning that occurs on a conditioning trial is a simple function of the discrepancy between the expected and actual values of the reinforcer presented on that trial. More formally, $\Delta V_A = \alpha_A \beta_1 (\lambda_1 - V_{\Sigma A..Z})$, where ΔV_A refers to the change in the associative strength (V) of the CS "A" on a given trial, α_A and β_1 are constants that describe the rate of learning about the CS "A" and the US "1," respectively, λ_1 is the maximum amount of associative strength supportable by the US "1," and $V_{\Sigma A..Z}$ refers to the aggregate (total) strength of all CSs (A through Z) present on that trial. The aggregate strength is obtained by a simple summation rule by which the strength of a compound of several elemental CSs is the sum of the strengths of those constituent elements, for example, $V_{AB} = V_A + V_B$.

The key to the Rescorla-Wagner model is that the efficacy of a US in establishing learning on a given conditioning trials depends not just on its intrinsic reinforcing value (λ) but also on the extent to which that value is already anticipated as a consequence of CSs that signal it ($V_{\Sigma A..Z}$). Thus, the effectiveness of a US as a reinforcer is modulated by prior learning. Consider first the course of simple acquisition of conditioning to a CS, A. Because the strength of CS_A is initially zero and there are no other CSs present, the amount of learning about CS_A on the first conditioning trial is large. As associative strength accrues to CS_A, the discrepancy between the actual value of the US (λ) and its expected value ($V_{\Sigma A..Z}$), and hence the increments in learning about CS_A, become proportionally smaller on each successive trial. Thus, this model anticipates the frequently observed, negatively accelerated growth function, or law of diminishing returns. The reinforcer is maximally effective when it is unexpected and gradually becomes ineffective as it becomes better predicted by the CS.

The observation of blocking follows just as simply. In the first phase of a blocking experiment the associative strength of CS_A, V_A, will approach λ. Thus, when the novel CS_B is compounded with CS_A in Phase 2, the US will already be well anticipated on the basis of CS_A; that is, the expression ($\lambda - V_{AB}$) will be small. As a result, the US will be ineffective as a reinforcer, and CS_B will acquire little or no associative strength despite repeated CS_{AB}-US pairings. Likewise, CS_A will acquire little additional associative strength.

By contrast, the rats trained with the Control procedure enter Phase 2 with no conditioning to either CS_A or CS_B. Consequently, for these rats the US *is* an effective reinforcer at the beginning of Phase 2, allowing both CS_A and CS_B to acquire associative strength on each trial until the US is well-predicted by the CS_{AB} compound, that is, when $V_{AB} = \lambda$. The amount that each element (A and B) acquires is a function of its intrinsic rate parameter, α. If $\alpha_A = \alpha_B$, then each will acquire conditioning at the same rate, and the asymptotic strengths of CS_A and CS_B will be equal, $V_A = V_B = 0.5\lambda$. Recall that learning will cease when the US is perfectly anticipated, that is, when $\lambda - (V_A + V_B) = 0$. Thus, the Control rats acquire considerably more strength to the added CS_B

than do the Blocking rats, an outcome that defines the occurrence of blocking.

At the same time, note that asymptotically the strength of CS_A is *lower* in the Control rats ($V_A = 0.5\lambda$), which received initial conditioning of CS_A in compound with CS_B, than in the Blocking rats ($V_A = \lambda$), which received initial conditioning of CS_A alone. This observation of greater conditioning to a CS when it is separately paired with a US than when it is presented in compound with other cues defines another common phenomenon of compound conditioning, *overshadowing*. Within the Rescorla-Wagner model this phenomenon occurs because the US is rendered ineffective as a reinforcer before each individual element can reach λ.

In each of the previous examples, the discrepancy or error term $(\lambda_1 - V_{\Sigma A..Z})$ ranged from 0, which supported no additional learning, to λ, which permitted maximum increments in associative strength. If, however, the aggregate prediction $(V_{\Sigma A..Z})$ is greater than λ, this error term will have a negative value, and ΔV_A will be negative. Within the Rescorla-Wagner model, this loss of associative strength is equated with the acquisition of an opposing tendency: conditioned inhibition. If V_A is driven below zero, CS_A is said to be a conditioned inhibitor. Notably, the conditions under which conditioned inhibition develops—overexpectation of the reinforcer (the aggregate prediction is greater than λ)—are complementary to those that are necessary for the establishment of excitation (the underexpectation of the reinforcer, when the aggregate prediction is less than λ).

Unfortunately, when presented by itself, a stimulus with negative associative strength may not control behavior, and thus may be indistinguishable from a cue with no strength. As a result, a number of indirect tests of inhibitory conditioning have been used. The most common are summation and retardation tests (Rescorla, 1969b). In a summation test, a suspected inhibitor (CS_A) is presented in compound with a known exciter. By the Rescorla-Wagner summation rule $(V_{AB} = V_A + V_B)$, if $V_A < 0$, then V_{AB} will be less than V_B, so CS_A will suppress responding to CS_B. In a retardation test, the suspected inhibitor is paired directly with a US, and the course of excitatory learning is examined. If the stimulus initially possessed inhibitory strength, then it would need to first regain zero strength before showing acquisition of positive associative strength. Thus, relative to controls, acquisition of new excitatory learning would appear slower.

The integration of excitation and inhibition within a common, symmetrical framework permits the model to make some of its most counterintuitive predictions. For example, consider an experiment in which CS_A and CS_B are each first separately paired with a US. As a result V_A and V_B each will approach λ. Next, CS_A and CS_B are combined, and the CS_{AB}

compound is again paired with the US. By the Rescorla-Wagner model, the aggregate prediction provided by CS_{AB} is now 2λ, whereas the US supports only λ. Consequently, pairing of the AB compound with the US results in *losses* of associative strength of CS_A and CS_B (Kremer, 1978; Rescorla, 1970). More surprisingly, if a novel CS_C is added to the compound along with CS_A and CS_B, losses in the strengths of all three stimuli will occur, again proportional to the αs associated with those cues. Because CS_C was novel, loss in its associative strength would lead to its acquiring net conditioned inhibition. Thus, the same physical US may produce new excitatory learning when it is underexpected, no learning when it is perfectly predicted, and inhibitory learning when it is overexpected.

With an additional assumption, the Rescorla-Wagner model was also able to deal with the contingency data described earlier. That assumption was that the experimental context (e.g., the experimental chamber) itself could serve as a CS, like any other event, and hence could potentially modulate conditioning to explicit CSs. Rescorla and Wagner suggested that simple conditioning procedures could then be described as involving various discriminations between a compound of CS + Context and the Context alone. If the US is equiprobable in the presence of the explicit CS (CS + Context) and in its absence (Context), then a situation very much like blocking obtains, in which both a compound stimulus and one element of that compound are reinforced. According to the Rescorla-Wagner model, the explicit CS, like the added CS_B in blocking, should display little evidence of conditioning asymptotically. Not only did the model do an excellent job of predicting the asymptotic levels of conditioning to an explicit CS obtained with different reinforcement probabilities in the presence and absence of the CS (Figure 17.2, panel B), but it also described the trial-by-trial dynamics of acquisition (Rescorla, 1973b). Furthermore, the model correctly predicted that the CS should become inhibitory if the probability of the US was greater during the absence of the CS than in its presence. In that case, because the context alone acquires associative strength, presenting the CS + Context compound with no US (which cannot support conditioning and thus would have a λ of 0) would produce an overexpectation of the US, eventually driving the strength of the explicit CS below zero.

In summary, Rescorla and Wagner (1972) described a simple model that both accounted for an array of otherwise puzzling data and provided a simple trial-by-trial mechanism for their occurrence. Perhaps most important, within this model the conditions for the development of excitation and inhibition are not the occurrence and nonoccurrence of physical events, as in earlier theories, but rather the under- and overexpectation of those events as a result of past learning.

The general notion of error-correction routines, by which the aggregate strength is adjusted to match that supportable by the reinforcer, has had a broad impact on behavior theory. For example, Wagner (1978) presented substantial evidence that the variations in processing of events depending on how well they are predicted on the basis of past learning goes beyond the reinforcement power of stimuli and includes their persistence in memory and their ability to elicit responses. Thus, a surprising event not only is a more effective reinforcer than is an expected event, but, ceteris paribus, also generates larger CRs and is more persistent in memory.

Problems With the Rescorla-Wagner Model

The Rescorla-Wagner model is not perfect. Miller, Barnett, and Grahame (1995) provided an overview of the strengths and weaknesses of this model; we mention four weaknesses. First, although the model gained considerable power by providing symmetrical conditions for the establishment and definition of excitatory and inhibitory learning and by placing excitatory and inhibitory associative strength along the same scale, there is considerable evidence against such symmetry. For example, within the model, presentation of a conditioned inhibitor (a CS with net negative associative strength) by itself should extinguish that inhibition, as the discrepancy between the expected negative value is followed by nothing, an event with a zero λ. But under most circumstances this procedure does not reduce the ability of the conditioned inhibitor to act in summation and retardation tests (e.g., Zimmer-Hart & Rescorla, 1974). Likewise, much data support the claim that the loss of conditioned responding when a previously trained CS_A is no longer followed by the US (extinction) involves not just the reduction in V_A as claimed in the model, but rather the acquisition of a parallel inhibitory structure, maintaining much of the original excitatory learning (Rescorla, 1993). Second, although the Rescorla-Wagner model attributes blocking, overshadowing, and related phenomena to variations in the acquisition of associations, some evidence suggests that they may instead be related to failures in the retrieval of associations (e.g., Miller, McKinzie, Kraebel, & Spear, 1996; but see Holland, 1999). Third, there is ample evidence that the summation assumptions of the Rescorla-Wagner model are unrealistic. Recent data (e.g., Rescorla, 2000) show that apportionment of changes in associative strength among the elements of compounds depends on the training history of those elements, not just on their saliences (αs). Furthermore, it is often simplistic to treat a compound stimulus as no more than the sum of its elements; we discuss some aspects of this notion of configuration later. Finally, although in the interests of simplicity Rescorla and Wagner

(1972) assumed α—the rate parameter for learning about a CS—to be constant, there is compelling evidence that α can vary as a function of experience (e.g., Dickinson & Mackintosh, 1978; Rescorla & Holland, 1982). Indeed, as noted in the next section, many theorists attempted to account for phenomena like blocking by positing learned variations in processing of the CSs, rather than of the US.

Variations in Processing of Conditioned Stimuli

Another class of conditioning theories attributes variations in conditioning in blocking, overshadowing, and related procedures to variations in processing of the CSs, rather than of the US. These models are often termed *attentional models* because the learned alterations in CS processing can be described as learning to direct attention toward or away from particular stimuli, so that certain stimuli are "selected" for controlling action or acquiring learning in blocking-like tasks.

The earliest attentional models relied on the notion of a limited attentional resource to account for stimulus selection effects. For example, Sutherland and Mackintosh (1971) assumed that the acquisition of a CS-US association is accompanied by increased attention to that CS. To the extent that attention is directed to that stimulus, less attention is available for learning about other CSs. As a result, in a blocking experiment an animal fails to learn about the added B stimulus because all of its CS processing resources are consumed by A, leaving no opportunity for B to be associated with the reinforcer. Thus, within this approach, blocking occurs because the added CS is not effectively processed in contiguity with the US.

Subsequent attentional models explored other origins for alterations in effective processing of CSs. For example, Mackintosh (1975) suggested that animals evaluate the ability of each individual CS to predict the US on each conditioning trial, increasing attention (α) to the more predictive cues and decreasing attention to the less predictive cues. In a blocking experiment, prior training of CS_A makes it an excellent predictor of the US. Because the added CS_B is a relatively poor predictor of the US, the animal rapidly learns to ignore it (i.e., reduces its α), so little is learned about it.

Perhaps the most successful approach to variations in processing of CSs is that described by Pearce and Hall (1980). They posited that attention to CSs is a function of how surprising the US is: α is directly related to the absolute value of the Rescorla-Wagner error term, $|\lambda - V_{\Sigma A, Z}|$. Thus, the presentation of a surprising US maintains or enhances the ability of CSs to enter into new associations (α), whereas α is driven low when the US is well predicted. Within this theory, the addition of CS_B when the US is already well predicted in a blocking experiment results in the loss of αCS_B so that little CS_B-US learning can occur. Likewise, if the US is changed (such that $\lambda_2 \neq \lambda_1$) when CS_B is introduced, then αCS_B will remain high, allowing CS_B to be associated with the US. Notably, consistent with much data (e.g., Pearce & Hall, 1980), either increases or decreases in λ will maintain αCS_B within this model. By contrast, within the Rescorla-Wagner model, although increases in λ would permit additional learning about CS_B, decreases in λ would result in inhibitory learning about CS_B. Thus, the observation of this "unblocking" phenomenon when the US is replaced by one with a lower λ has frequently been cited as evidence for enhancements of CS processing. In a later section we show how a combination of behavioral and neurobiological investigations has provided evidence for key portions of these claims.

Representation of CSs: Elemental and Configural Views

Psychologists have taken a number of approaches to how compound CSs are represented. At one extreme, models like the Rescorla-Wagner model describe compound CSs as simply the sum of their elements. This elemental description worked well in characterizing early conditioning data. Nevertheless, there is ample evidence that animals frequently treat compound stimuli as very different from their elements. A commonly cited example is that negative patterning (sometimes called exclusive-or) discriminations are often learned very readily. In these discriminations, CS_A and CS_B are each reinforced when presented alone, but nonreinforced when presented in compound (CS_{AB}). Clearly, no simple summation rule can predict that the strength of a compound of two cues will be less than that of either one alone.

At the other extreme, Pearce (1987) suggested that all stimuli are unitary or configural and cannot be decomposed into separable elements. Thus, training a negative patterning discrimination is in principle no different from training any other discrimination. At the same time, this approach recognizes that a compound may generalize considerably to stimuli that might otherwise be described as its elements, than to other stimuli. This approach has fared remarkably well in predicting the outcomes of a variety of compound conditioning experiments (Pearce, Aydin, & Redhead, 1997), although other data clearly favor more elemental views (Rescorla, 1997).

Other descriptions of compound stimulus processing borrow from both extremes. For example, Rescorla suggested a "unique stimulus" account, in which an AB compound stimulus is described as embracing both the explicit A and B elements and also a perceptually generated configural cue unique to the compound. Within this view, the unique cue

acts like any other stimulus and thus is conceived of as just one more stimulus element within a compound. Rescorla (1972, 1973a) showed how the addition of a unique cue to the Rescorla-Wagner model permitted that elemental model to account for a number of compound conditioning phenomena normally thought to be outside its purview, including negative patterning discriminations.

In response to results from investigations of brain function, a number of theorists have suggested that the elemental and configural aspects of stimulus compounds are processed by different brain systems, and hence may follow different rules. For example, Rudy and Sutherland (1995) suggested that animals acquire both simple elemental associations and configural associations, but that under normal conditions the output of the configural association system suppresses that of the elemental system. In a more elaborate manner, Schmajuk and DiCarlo (1991) formulated a detailed quantitative neural network model in which stimulus elements form both simple associations with output units (the US) and associations with configural, hidden units, which are themselves associated with other stimulus elements and the output units. It is important that although in this model the simple and configural units compete for association in much the same way as specified by Rescorla, they are assumed to be anatomically and functionally distinct, and hence may follow somewhat different rules.

Representation of the Reinforcer

Within the dominant view of associative learning of the 1950s and 1960s, the reinforcer served primarily as a catalyst for the formation of S-R associations between the CS and a response (Figure 17.3, panel A), which Dickinson (1980) termed *procedural learning*. By contrast, most recent learning theories assume that animals learn *about* the events they associate, not just *because of* them.

From this modern perspective, classical CS-US pairings result in the formation of S-S associations between internal representations of the CS and US (Figure 17.3, panel A), which Dickinson (1980) described as *declarative learning*. By this view, the elicitation of CRs by a CS is mediated by its activation of a representation of the US, which in turn evokes those CRs. Evidence for this assertion comes primarily from reinforcer revaluation experiments, in which posttraining changes in the value of the US are spontaneously reflected in later CRs. For example, using rats, Colwill and Motzkin (1994) first paired an auditory CS with food pellets and a visual CS with liquid sucrose. Then, one of the reinforcers was devalued by pairing it with the toxin LiCl in the absence of either of the CSs. Finally, responding to the CSs was

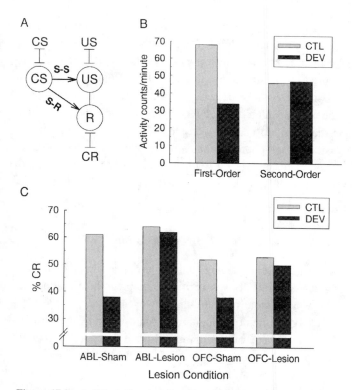

Figure 17.3 A. Schematic representation of stimulus-stimulus (S-S) and stimulus-response (S-R) associations (arrows). The circles indicate hypothetical internal representations of the conditioned stimulus (CS), unconditioned stimulus (US), and a response generator (R). Conditioned responding (CR) is mediated by the US representation when S-S associations are learned but not when S-R associations are learned. B. Test responding elicited by first-order and second-order CSs in a reinforcer revaluation experiment (Holland & Rescorla, 1975). Prior to the test, the food US was devalued by pairing it with rotation-induced illness in rats labeled DEV; illness was induced in the absence of food in the CTL rats. The data indicate that first-order, but not second-order, CRs were mediated by a representation of the food US. C. Test responding in reinforcer revaluation experiments conducted with normal (sham) rats and rats with excitotoxic lesions of the basolateral amygdala (ABL) or the orbitofrontal cortex (OFC). DEV signifies rats for which the food US was devalued by pairings with the toxin lithium chloride; CTL rats received the food and toxin on separate days. The data show that CRs of the sham rats were sensitive to posttraining changes in the value of the US, but CRs of lesioned rats were not. See text for discussion (from Hatfield et al., 1996; Gallagher, McMahan, & Schoenbaum, 1999).

reassessed in the absence of either of the reinforcers. Rats showed a spontaneous loss in responding to the CS that had been paired with the devalued US, relative to responding to the other CS. Comparable results are observed when one of the reinforcers is revalued by a motivational manipulation, for example, selective satiation of the subjects on one food (Holland, 1988; Malkova, Gaffan, & Murray, 1997) or selective enhancement of the value of one of the reinforcers by inducing a specific motivational state (Coldwell & Tordoff, 1993; Rescorla & Freberg, 1978).

Analogous findings suggest that operant responding is also often mediated by activation of an internal representation of

the reinforcer. For example, Colwill and Rescorla (1985) trained rats to perform one response for food pellets and another for liquid sucrose. Devaluation of the food pellets by pairing with toxin produced a spontaneous reduction in the frequency of the first but not the second operant response. Studies like these imply that animals can learn *about* the consequences of their actions (i.e., response-reinforcer associations), not just *because* of the rewarding consequences of those actions (i.e., S-R associations stamped in by the food reinforcer).

The results of other studies suggest that associatively activated representations of events may substitute for their referents in a variety of learning functions (see G. Hall, 1996, for a review). For example, Holland (1981a, 1990a) showed that rats could acquire an aversion to a food flavor if they were made ill in the presence of an auditory CS previously paired with that food. Likewise, presentation of an auditory signal for a particular food could substitute for the food itself in the extinction of a previously established aversion to that food (Holland & Forbes, 1982b) and in the overshadowing of learning of an aversion to another food flavor (Holland, 1983b). Furthermore, in many circumstances learned expectancies of particular events can control ongoing behavior (Holland & Forbes, 1982a; Trapold, 1970).

Representation of CS-US Relations: Occasion Setting

Holland (1983a) suggested that under some circumstances a CS acquires the ability to modulate the action of an association between another CS and the US. This modulatory power, often termed *occasion setting,* is typically studied with conditional discrimination procedures, in which the relation of one CS with the US depends on the presence or absence of another CS. For example, in a serial feature positive (FP) discrimination, a target CS is paired with food only when it is preceded by another feature CS (feature → target → food, target-alone → nothing). If the feature-target interval is sufficiently long, rats solve this discrimination by using the feature to set the occasion for conditioned responding based on target-US associations. By contrast, if the feature and target are delivered simultaneously on food-reinforced trials, rats instead form associations between the feature and the US, as anticipated by theories like the Rescorla-Wagner model.

Several kinds of evidence support a distinction between simple association and occasion setting (see Holland, 1992, and Swartzentruber, 1995, for reviews). Perhaps most convincing is the observation that the ability of a stimulus to act as an occasion setter is independent of any simple associations it may have with the US. For example, after serial FP training, repeated nonreinforced presentations of the feature alone typically have little lasting effect on its ability to modulate responding to the target cue, despite eliminating any CRs due to simple feature-US associations. A more dramatic example is found after feature negative (FN) discrimination training, in which the target is reinforced when presented alone but not reinforced when presented in compound with the feature CS. Analogous to FP discriminations, simultaneous FN discriminations establish inhibitory feature-US associations, whereas serial FN discriminations endow the feature with the ability to inhibit the action of the target-US association. After simultaneous FN training, direct feature-US pairings destroy the feature's inhibitory powers, as measured by summation and retardation tests (Holland, 1984a). By contrast, after serial FN training, direct counterconditioning of the feature in this way often leaves intact (or even enhances) the feature's ability to inhibit responding to the target (Holland, 1984a; Holland, Thornton, & Ciali, 2000; Rescorla, 1991). Thus, a negative occasion setter may at the same time elicit a strong CR and inhibit the ability of other CSs to elicit that CR.

Occasion-setting phenomena have been found in a variety of conditioning preparations, including, for example, autoshaped key pecking in pigeons, conditioned suppression of lever pressing in rats, rabbit eyelid conditioning, and drug discrimination training in rats (see Schmajuk & Holland, 1998, for examples). Not surprisingly, the conditions under which these phenomena are established, as well as the details of the phenomena themselves, vary from preparation to preparation. Nevertheless, the evidence suggests that modulatory functions of CSs are pervasive and substantial. Many investigators have suggested that experimental contexts, which may include spatial, geometric, and other features of the conditioning chamber, time of day, and so forth, are especially likely to play modulatory roles in conditioning (G. Hall & Mondragon, 1998; Holland & Bouton, 1999). Likewise, several researchers (e.g., Davidson, 1993; Holland, 1991; D. M. Skinner, Goddard, & Holland, 1998) have suggested that internal states, like hunger or thirst, may often act by modulating the effectiveness of other cues in eliciting learned or unlearned behaviors.

Researchers have proposed a variety of theoretical accounts of what is learned in occasion setting (see Holland, 1992; Schmajuk, Lamoureux, & Holland, 1998; Swartzentruber, 1995, for reviews). Holland (1983a) and Bonardi (1998) suggested that occasion setters involve hierarchical representation of specific event relations such that the occasion setter is associated with or modulates the activity of a particular CS-US association. Rescorla (1985) suggested that occasion setters act more broadly by modifying a threshold for activation of the US representation by eliciting CSs. A number of accounts

for occasion setting relate it to configural learning more generally (e.g., Brandon & Wagner, 1998; Pearce, 1987, 1994). Within this approach, occasion setters and their targets are configured into a single unit that is distinct from the individual event representations. Each of these approaches captures a portion of the available data, but none is supported unequivocally. Perhaps the most comprehensive and detailed account for occasion-setting phenomena is a neural network model offered by Schmajuk et al. (1998), which expands on the Schmajuk and DiCarlo (1991) model mentioned earlier by combining the modulatory and configural approaches.

The Representation of Temporal Relations

As noted earlier, within most theories of learning, the interval between CS and US was a critical variable in determining the rate or asymptote of learning. However, temporal intervals themselves were not thought to be represented by the animal: The only effect of arranging different temporal relations among events was the establishment of different associative strengths. These differences in associative strength were not distinguishable from those resulting from manipulation of any other variable, such as the amount of training or CS salience.

Contemporary research has shown that CSs also provide information about the time of US delivery. That is, animals learn not only *because of* the arrangement of temporal relations among events, but also *about* those relations (Gallistel & Gibbon, 2000; Gibbon & Church, 1990; Miller & Barnet, 1993; Savastano & Miller, 1998). The most obvious evidence for this assertion comes from studies of response timing. In many conditioning preparations, both operant and classical, the magnitude of conditioned responding increases systematically, exhibiting a peak near the time of US delivery (Figure 17.4, panel A). This temporal distribution of responding within the CS-US interval often displays what is known as the *scalar property* (Gibbon, 1977): Its variance is proportional to its mean. When normalized proportionally to the CS-US interval, the resultant distributions are identical, regardless of CS-US interval (Figure 17.4, panel B). There is currently a great deal of interest in the psychological mechanisms of timing in these circumstances (see Higa, 1998, for a review).

Evidence for timing of US delivery exists even in conditioning situations in which there is no clear-cut temporal gradient of responding. For example, Miller and his colleagues have found that a variety of conditioning phenomena that involve the addition of new stimuli to previously trained CSs in a serial fashion, such as blocking and second-order conditioning, depend on the contiguity of the added stimulus

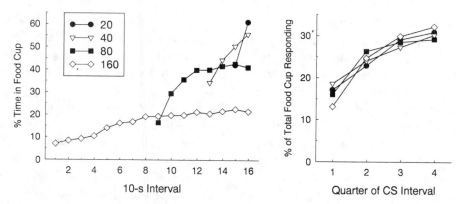

Figure 17.4   A. Temporal distribution of conditioned responding (CRs) over the course of conditioned stimuli (CSs), 20 s, 40 s, 80 s and 160 s. B. Temporal distribution of CRs shown in A, normalized over successive quarters of the CS interval. The functions show superpositioning. See text for discussion (from Holland, 2000).

and the expected time of the US provided by the trained cue, rather than on the temporal relation between the CSs themselves (e.g., Savastano & Miller, 1998).

SYNTHETIC APPROACHES TO THE STUDY OF LEARNING IN ANIMALS

Although modern associationism's emphasis on signal value, associative strength, and so forth seems a far cry from ethological concerns with the functions and origins of behavior, much current research in learning within each of these traditions borrows liberally from the other. This research combines experimenter-centered methods and theoretical constructs from experimental psychology with more animal-centered concerns with natural function and evolution from ethology. Furthermore, the infusion of the methods, interests, and orientations of neuroscience into both arenas has provided additional common ground.

Many synthetic trends can be identified. Researchers from the ethological tradition have been quick to adopt the procedures and analytic tools of experimental psychology to their purposes. More significantly, many of the interests, theoretical constructs, and terminology of experimental psychology have been imported into ethologically oriented research endeavors. For example, the face of behavioral ecology has gradually changed such that a great deal of research, in the field and in the laboratory, has concerned evolutionary and adaptive aspects of memory, representation, and cognition (see Shettleworth, 1998, for extensive treatment of these issues). The study of optimal foraging illustrates this trend. Field observations about food selection have given way to complex models of behavior that have converged to a large degree with related work being conducted by experimental psychologists (e.g., Kacelnik & Bateson, 1997; Kacelnik & Krebs, 1997).

Likewise, experimental psychology has been changed by the more animal-centered approach of ethology. In their study of what they construe as basic psychological processes, experimental psychologists increasingly have selected more ecologically valid tasks and have been more open to questions about the adaptive significance of the behavioral systems that they study. For example, researchers interested in memory processing in rats are abandoning standard auditory-visual tasks in Skinner boxes for spatial learning, odor-guided food selection, and even social learning tasks, which are more characteristic of problems that rats face in nature. Of course, the downside of this ecumenicalism is that we abandon well-controlled (and well-studied) preparations in favor of those that we know little about and that give us less control. But a reasonable response to that problem is simply to take the time to uncover the basic characteristics of these new tasks and to refine them in ways that make greater experimental control possible.

Today, psychologists are more likely to recognize that behaviors sampled in conditioning experiments may be embedded in more extensive behavioral systems, which have been shaped by the demands of the niches in which they evolved. Often, the determinants and characteristics of learning may be better predicted from those perspectives than from any other. Consider two examples. Earlier we mentioned that the optimal CS-US interval differed dramatically across conditioning preparations, a few hundred milliseconds for eyeblink conditioning, several seconds for aversive cardiac conditioning, and tens of minutes for flavor aversion learning. What psychological principles account for these differences? Although there have been attempts to deal with these differences without reference to questions of function (Krane & Wagner, 1975), functional considerations have provided greater insight, or at least simpler rules of thumb. A shock to the eye provokes an eyelid response, but also a number of autonomic responses that may be related to behavioral flight systems. An eye blink is a useful response to a signal that the eye will be insulted within a few hundred milliseconds, but not to a signal that damage may occur in a few seconds. By contrast, heart rate changes in preparation for flight are useful with a warning of a few seconds, but not a few hundred milliseconds. Likewise, a flavor aversion learning mechanism that spans only seconds is unlikely to evolve in animals challenged by slow-acting food toxins. Thus, the particular effective range of interval values may vary on a species- or system-specific basis. At the same time, as noted earlier, the form of interval functions seems conserved more generally.

Another example of the value of considering laboratory tasks from an adaptive perspective is the classic case of *cue-to-consequence selectivity* in the aversive conditioning of rats. Garcia and Koelling (1966; see also Domjan & Wilson, 1972) found that rats readily associated flavors and toxin-induced illness, as well as auditory-visual stimuli and shock-induced pain, but were poor learners of the other combinations, flavor-pain and auditory-visual-illness. Although no simple psychological process predicts this selectivity, it is obvious from a consideration of problems faced by rats in nature. Rats normally select foods (which might make them ill, but are unlikely to cause peripheral pain) primarily by flavor but are unlikely to taste things that are about to cause them pain. Comparative studies, using animals that select food on different bases, support the simple view that animals are better able to solve tasks that are more like the ones they face in nature (e.g., Garcia, Lasiter, Bermudez-Rattoni, & Deems, 1985). Although many psychologists' first reactions to these kinds of findings could be characterized as either defiant or apocalyptic, others were quick to recognize that the ease of associating any two items in conditioning might depend on existing, intrinsic relations between those stimuli (see Rescorla & Holland, 1976). This recognition spilled over into exclusively psychological realms; stimuli related by Gestalt grouping principles such as similarity (Rescorla & Furrow, 1977), spatial proximity (Testa, 1975), and part-whole relations (Rescorla, 1980) all are more readily associated in conditioning studies than are stimuli not sharing those relations.

At the same time, analysis of apparently unique, specialized examples of learning often reveal contributions of more general learning processes. For example, as noted earlier, current research suggests that imprinting shares many features with other examples of single event learning. Furthermore, Hoffman and Ratner (1973) suggested that imprinting may be profitably analyzed in the context of Pavlovian conditioning, in which associations are formed between initially neutral aspects of the imprinting stimulus

and stimulus features that are critical to the initial following responses, as in Pavlovian conditioning. These associations allow the initially neutral aspects of the imprinting stimulus to elicit following responses and to serve as conditioned reinforcers. It is important to recognize that this learning brings the birds in frequent contact with these stimuli, rendering them less likely to elicit fear-withdrawal responses that are typically generated by novel stimuli. As a result, later filial approach behavior is controlled by a variety of perceptual aspects of the imprinting stimulus, but fear-withdrawal responses, which compete with filial behavior, are controlled by stimuli other than the imprinting stimulus. In support of these claims, Hoffman and his colleagues demonstrated the acquisition of these associative functions by neutral stimuli in imprinting situations. Furthermore, they found that adult filial behavior may even be induced to nonimprinted stimuli if the competing fear-withdrawal responses are habituated extensively by forced exposure to those stimuli later in life. They argued that in typical studies of filial imprinting the bird flees from nonimprinted test stimuli and so is never given the opportunity to learn about them. Thus, they interpreted some cases of the apparent time sensitivity and irreversible nature of imprinting as the result of general features of associative learning and habituation, which may be general to a number of species, including primates. Although it is unlikely that Hoffman and Ratner's (1973) account provides anything near a complete account of imprinting, it provides a valuable perspective: Even examples of learning that show apparently unique properties may share more general characteristics.

Given the nature of this volume, it is only fitting to note that the study of biological mechanisms of behavior has also been a powerful trend bringing experimental psychology and ethology together. Indeed, the dividing line between neuroethology and behavioral neuroscience may be fainter still (see Moss & Shettleworth, 1996, for examples). Neuroscience has provided shared methods as well as a general reductionist approach that is less put off by perceived differences in the nature of the hypothetical constructs of the two fields. Furthermore, in some cases, common mechanisms of plasticity seem to underlie examples of learning that seem radically different on the surface. For example, developmental plasticity in the cortex associated with visual experience and adult plasticity in the hippocampus resulting from the induction of long-term potentiation both involve excitatory glutamate, especially the N-methyl-D-aspartate (NMDA) receptor. Indeed, the NMDA receptor is widely involved in many forms of learning and plasticity in a wide variety of species (e.g., Bliss & Collingridge, 1993; Brown, Kairiss, & Keenan, 1990; Constantine-Paton, Cline, & Debskie, 1990).

We do not mean to claim that there is a single synthetic approach to the study of learning, but rather a range of approaches, some drawing more from ethology and others more from experimental psychology. In the remainder of this section we present three case studies that exemplify some of this range. Each analysis has profited from appreciation of both ethological and general process perspectives, as well as an interest in neurobiological mechanism. The first, a study of learning and memory processes in bird song, comes primarily from the ethological end of the continuum; the second, a study of rats' learning to anticipate food, is from the opposite end; and the third, a study of sexual conditioning in quail, falls toward the center. We do not offer them as the best available examples; rather, they reflect our own interests and research. Recent research on the foraging (e.g., Kacelnik & Krebs, 1997) and food caching (e.g., N. S. Clayton & Soha, 1999; Shettleworth & Hampton, 1998; Suzuki & Clayton, 2000) of birds and rodents provide other particularly compelling examples.

Learning and Memory Processes in Bird Song

Dialects and the Early Study of Song Learning

As early as the seventeenth and eighteenth centuries, aviculturists in both Asia and Europe realized that vocal behavior in songbirds is remarkably labile and could be manipulated by experience in ways that the vocalizations of other avian species could not (see Konishi, 1985; Thorpe, 1961; Welty & Baptista, 1988, for discussions of these early ideas). Although bird vocalizations can be influenced by experience, B. F. Skinner (1957) observed that the vocal behavior of nonhuman animals could not be easily manipulated by operant and classical conditioning procedures that are so powerful in modifying other motor patterns. Only recently have such experimental procedures proven to be at all effective in modifying the learning of conspecific vocalizations in birds (e.g., Adret, 1993; Manabe & Dooling, 1997). This limitation suggested that the processes involved in vocal learning could be distinct in many ways from those mediating at least some other learned responses.

The manner in which song is learned was first investigated experimentally by ethologists who were interested, in part, in understanding the origins of intraspecific variation in bird song. The song of all songbirds possesses species-typical attributes that allow one to distinguish one species from another based purely on the song (Ball & Hulse, 1998; Catchpole & Slater, 1995; Searcy & Andersson, 1986). The fact that vocalizations are species typical is true for probably all bird species and indeed for most species that

produce complex vocalizations, including various insect and other vertebrate groups such as anurans (Ball & Hulse, 1998; Searcy & Andersson, 1986). However, unlike most of the species in these other groups, in several songbird species, systematic geographic variation was found within this species-typical pattern. Thus, by listening closely to a song one could identify both the species singing and the place of its origin. Studies of two oscine species, the chaffinch (*Fringilla coelebs*) in England and the white-crowned sparrow (*Zonotrichia leucophyrs*) in the United States, were especially important in establishing the fundamental principles governing the development of bird song. Both chaffinches (Marler, 1952) and white-crowned sparrows (Marler & Tamura, 1964) exhibit such marked geographic variation in their songs that the suggestion arose that these species possess something akin to human dialects. Marler and Tamura (1964) observed that white-crowned sparrows in Marin County, California, could be distinguished from those living around Berkeley, which in turn could be distinguished from those living around Sunset Beach, based on variation in the end phrasing of the song. Although all these birds produced a song that is clearly recognizable to a trained listener as white-crowned sparrow song, the birds also exhibited systematic variation within this song that allowed trained listeners to identify their geographic origin.

Such within-specific variation in song behavior raised questions concerning the origins of song. Does this variation represent genetic variation as had been observed for many morphological traits that vary geographically within a species (Mayr, 1963), or does it result from differences in learning? Thorpe (1958), working with chaffinches, and later Marler (1970), working with white-crowned sparrows, employed methods referred to by the early ethologists as the *Kaspar Hauser approach*. That is, birds were raised in isolation, especially acoustic isolation. These studies demonstrated unequivocally that song is learned. Birds raised in acoustic isolation produce abnormal songs never heard in nature, and these never improve with age. Birds that heard tape-recorded song early in life later developed songs that were species-typical in their structures. This discovery suggested that something akin to cultural transmission occurs in birds.

Of the over 9,000 living bird species that are divided into some 23 orders, vocal learning has been demonstrated in 3 of the orders: the songbird order just described (passeriformes), the order psittaciformes (parrots and related species), and the order trochiliformes (i.e., hummingbirds; Baptista 1996; Baptista & Schuchmann, 1990; Farabaugh & Dooling, 1996). Most experimental work has been conducted on songbirds, and that is our focus here. The songbird order can be divided into two suborders, the oscines (suborder passeres) and the more primitive suboscines. In addition to the morphological differences between oscines and suboscines that the taxonomists have identified, there appear to be qualitative differences in vocal development between these two taxa. Suboscine vocalizations are not learned (Kroodsma, 1988; Kroodsma & Konishi, 1991), and suboscines do not require access to auditory feedback to develop normal vocal behavior. Although this generalization must be considered with some caution, given that few representatives of suboscine families have been studied, these data do suggest that an important qualitative shift in the mechanisms mediating the development of vocal behavior occurred when the oscine passerines evolved as an independent taxonomic group. To conclude, there is no evidence that suboscine species learn their song, but oscine species clearly do.

The Process of Song Acquisition

Since the pioneering work on white-crowned sparrows and chaffinches, studies of many species of oscine songbirds have all found that song is learned (e.g., Kroodsma, 1982; Kroodsma & Baylis, 1982; Marler, 1991; Thorpe, 1958). There are many species-specific and intraspecific variations in song learning among oscines (e.g., Baptista, 1996; Kroodsma, 1996; Marler, 1987, 1991; Marler & Nelson, 1993; Slater, 1989; West & King, 1996; West, King, & Duff, 1990). A variety of approaches have been taken to the study of song learning; in some cases laboratory studies are conducted with the obvious advantage of experimental control, and in other cases field studies are conducted with the obvious advantage of sensitivity to the many environmental factors that impinge on the developmental process. In most cases the focus is on male birds. It is impossible in this brief review to discuss fully the diversity in developmental processes that has been identified. However, some useful generalizations have emerged. Our goal is to highlight important findings that reflect both the laboratory and the field approach. Many important concepts have emerged from studies of bird song that are relevant to a consideration of animal learning as well as human language learning and production such as the idea that many birds are critical- (or sensitive-) period learners and that songbirds have innate predispositions to learn their own species song (suggesting that they possess something akin to the *language acquisition device* described by Chomsky, 1965), and that learned songs may be overproduced and then selected for enduring production in adulthood based on the consequences of social interactions (Marler, 1997).

In some species, called age-independent learners, the ability to learn and modify song may be retained throughout life, whereas in other species this propensity may be age limited (Marler, 1987; Slater, Jones, & Ten Cate, 1993). Among age-limited learners, the learning process can be usefully divided into a *sensory phase* and a *sensorimotor phase* (Marler, 1987). In the sensory phase nestlings hear conspecific vocalizations either from their fathers or from nearby males and form an auditory memory (or sensory template) of some sort that represents these songs. Conspecific songs heard relatively early in development tend to be remembered better than songs heard later, indicating that there is a critical or sensitive period during which auditory memories that guide subsequent song production are most effectively formed (Nelson, 1997). This phenomenon is reminiscent of the postulated critical period learning associated with imprinting or language acquisition; it has been claimed that the ability to easily learn new languages closes off at the onset of adolescence in humans (Lenneberg, 1967; Newport, 1990). In a similar vein, in a variety of songbirds males can acquire songs from remarkably little exposure to song early in life (Nelson, 1997). For example, just 10 to 20 presentations are sufficient for normal song learning in nightingales (*Luscinia megarhynchos;* Hultsch & Todt, 1989) and 30 repetitions on a single day in song sparrows (Peters, Marler, & Nowicki, 1992). Thus, songbirds have superb abilities when it comes to memorizing, and later retrieving from memory, songs they have heard early in life.

During the sensorimotor phase birds reaching puberty (usually during the first spring after they are hatched) first start producing very soft unstructured vocalizations that are referred to as *subsong*. These sounds have often been compared to the babbling of prelinguistic infants. These birds then shift to louder, more stereotyped vocalizations in which rehearsal of previously learned song begins, containing many elements that can be recognized as adult song. This is called *plastic* song. Finally, they develop an adult *crystallized* song that matches the auditory memory formed earlier (Marler & Peters, 1982a). The process is schematized in Figure 17.5.

This entire process is very dependent on auditory feedback. If a bird is deafened after the occurrence of the sensory phase but before the sensorimotor phase, normal song will not develop (Konishi, 1965, 1985). This indicates that auditory feedback is necessary for the final crystallized song to be properly matched to the song previously memorized during the sensory phase. In some species, such as the zebra finch, it was long thought that once song has crystallized into its adult form, auditory feedback was no longer necessary for song maintenance—as if a motor tape of some sort were in place after crystallization that could maintain the song independent of feedback. However, a study of deafened adult male zebra finches (*Taeniopygia guttata*) revealed deficits in the song

Phases of Song Learning

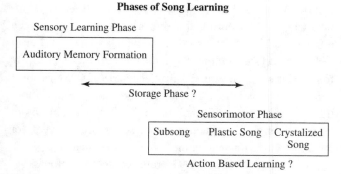

Sensory Learning Phase

Auditory Memory Formation

Storage Phase ?

Sensorimotor Phase

| Subsong | Plastic Song | Crystalized Song |

Action Based Learning ?

Figure 17.5 A diagrammatic representation of the song-learning process. There are two clearly recognized phases: the sensory learning phase, when a young bird hears adult song and stores it in memory, and the sensorimotor phase, when the bird produces song itself and matches the song it is producing to the memory of song it formed during the sensory phase. This matching process is gradual; juvenile birds typically experience three distinct stages of song development at this time: subsong (very soft vocalizations that have little resemblance to adult song), plastic song (loud variable song that has elements similar to adult song), and crystallized song (full adult song, often sung very loudly). In many species more song types are produced during the plastic song phase than are later crystallized. There is evidence that songs are selected for crystallization based on how well they match existing song types being produced where a male may settle. Behavioral interactions between males seem to shape this selection process. This process has been termed action-based learning and bears some resemblance to instrumental learning processes. The sensory learning phase usually occurs early in ontogeny, often close to the time that the nestling bird will fledge. It can then last for several weeks, although this varies greatly among species and can be influenced by experience. Learning during the sensory phase has been termed memory-based learning. This phase may or may not be temporally separated from the sensorimotor phase of song learning, depending on how quickly the young bird matures. A storage phase occurs when there is a clear temporal separation between the sensory phase and the sensorimotor phase.

of deaf males, suggesting that auditory feedback is required throughout life for the maintenance of this stereotyped behavior (Nordeen & Nordeen, 1992).

Depending on the species, the sensory phase and the sensorimotor phase may overlap with one another or may be separated by several months, during which the song memory from the sensory stage is stored and retained without any evidence of overt practice. Recent evidence suggests that in species in which there is a substantial interval between the sensory phase and the sensorimotor phase, significant processing of song information occurs in that interval. Male white-crowned sparrows usually have a hiatus of approximately 5 months between the two phases of song learning, but if they are treated with testosterone they can be induced to sing crystallized song months before they would normally exhibit this behavior (Whaling, Nelson, & Marler, 1995). Nevertheless, the song produced by these birds is abnormal, resembling songs produced by sparrows kept in acoustic isolation (Whaling et al., 1995). This finding suggests that the storage phase is not one of passive retention, but that it contains processes that play

a significant role in song learning (Whaling et al., 1995). However, it is also possible that the vocal production apparatus had not fully matured by 5 months and that this is why the premature song sounds abnormal.

The Auditory Memory That Guides Song Learning

What characterizes the auditory memory that is formed during the sensory phase, and is its formation constrained in any way? At least two important ideas relevant to the study of human language and other areas of cognitive psychology have emerged from studies of this memory for song. One concerns the concept that the process of memory formation involves selective or guided learning in that species-typical vocalizations appear to be privileged: They are learned preferentially. A more controversial idea concerns the degree to which memory encodes species-typical patterns of vocal behavior that exist before a bird even hears the song of its own species. The experimental basis of both of these ideas is well illustrated by studies of song sparrows (*Melospiza melodia*) and swamp sparrows (*Melospiza georgiana*) conducted by Marler and colleagues (see Marler, 1987, for review). These two species are age-limited learners that look alike, and they are members of the same genus and therefore are closely related taxonomically. However, their songs are easily distinguished. Although these species are often raised within earshot of one another, they tend to form memories only for their own species song. This has been verified by laboratory studies, suggesting that the formation of auditory memories is somehow directed such that conspecific songs are preferentially memorized (Marler, 1987). This phenomenon is also suggestive of certain processes that occur during language learning associated with the closure of the critical period for language acquisition in humans. For example the closure of the critical period is thought to involve, among other processes, a loss of the sensitivity to phonetic contrasts from nonnative languages (reviewed in Jusczyk, 1997). In other words, by the time we reach adulthood, humans have a perceptual selectivity not only for human language but also for their own native language.

When raised in acoustic isolation, the abnormal song that is produced retains species-typical attributes such as the number of notes per song and the number of trilled syllables per song (Marler & Sherman, 1985). Even though this isolate song is clearly abnormal, one can still tell apart the isolate song of the two species based on the song's acoustic structure. These are among the data that have led Marler and Nelson (1992) to postulate the somewhat radical hypothesis that the vast majority of information about song may be pre-encoded in innately specified brain circuitry. They argued that auditory experience primarily selects what is to be preserved and later produced as crystallized song from what is to be discarded and never produced later in life. According to this view, then, the postulated auditory memory that guides later song development may be largely specified at birth. This idea remains controversial, but the argument parallels in many ways discussions among cognitive scientists concerning the nature of innate representations that specify the predisposition to learn language in humans (see Chomsky, 1980; Elman et al., 1996; Fodor, 1983; Pinker, 1994).

Recent experiments with white-crowned sparrows support the notion that at least certain aspects of song structure are pre-encoded in the auditory memory guiding song learning (Soha & Marler, 2001). Sparrows were presented with a variety of phrase models that lacked species-typical structure (or syntax). Even though this was not present in the stimulus presented to the sparrows to be copied, the birds successfully copied the model phrases and assembled them into a species-typical structure.

Social Effects on Song Learning

It is important to note that both the sensory and sensorimotor phases of song learning are labile to a certain degree and can be influenced by various types of social and auditory experience. It has been known for some time that the social milieu in which a bird develops can influence the type of song that is eventually crystallized and produced in adulthood. Behavioral interactions of various sorts have been described that influence both the sensory phase and the sensorimotor phase of song learning. For example laboratory studies demonstrated in white-crowned sparrows that the presence of a live bird that tutors a developing juvenile can apparently extend the sensitive period during which auditory memories are formed (Baptista & Petrinovich, 1984), and the number of songs learned by juvenile European starlings (Sturnus vulgaris) is significantly greater when they listened to nearby conspecific male tutors as compared with tape-recorded songs (Chaiken, Böhner, & Marler, 1993). This evidence suggests that either the nature of the auditory memory that is formed is influenced by the social milieu that the bird grows up in or that a particular set of social interactions tends to select songs already in memory that will be produced later in life (see Baptista & Gaunt, 1997, and Nelson, 1997, for contrasting views).

There are data supporting the view that behavioral interactions during the sensorimotor phase influence what songs already in memory will be crystallized and produced by adults. In several species it has been demonstrated that males learn (or have in their memories) more songs during the sensory phase than they will later crystallize and produce as adults (Marler & Peters, 1982b). In field sparrows (Spizella pusilla) interactions even during the sensorimotor period between a male and his neighbors influence which songs will be selected for crystallization and inclusion into the final repertoire (Marler & Nelson, 1993; Nelson, 1992). Songs most similar to the neighbor's songs are retained, whereas those that are different are rejected. It is as if a process akin to operant conditioning influences what songs are selected for later crystallization among those in auditory memory.

Marler and Nelson (1993) referred to this process as action-based learning to contrast it with memory-based learning, which refers to cases where crystallized songs are produced in reference to previously formed memories independently of social interactions during the sensorimotor period. This process of the adult vocal milieu influencing vocal development parallels observations made about babbling in infants. Infants are thought to tune their babbling based on the adult language environment they experience (Boysson-Bardies & Vihman, 1991). Thus the adult vocal environment shapes vocal development in humans as well as in songbirds. In any case, in many species the selection of songs overproduced seems to be highly influenced by the fact that some songs match those being produced locally and others do not. This result indicates that reinforcing aspects of the social interaction lead to the selection of certain behaviors, a notion very reminiscent of Thorndike's concept of selective learning processes in instrumental conditioning. The details of this process remain to be worked out (e.g., how much matching is required for a song to be selected). But again, as we saw with imprinting, at least certain aspects of song learning include processes in common with more general learning processes.

In summary, it is clear from this cursory review that social interactions can influence both the sensory and the sensorimotor phases of song learning. Much remains to be learned about the structure of the auditory memory possessed by developing birds and the degree to which it is formed or modified by experience. Under certain circumstances early experience can have radical effects on the nature of the auditory memory (Baptista, 1996). How these social experiences are able to override the natural limitations on song learning is unknown.

The Neurobiology of Bird Song

One of the most appealing aspects of the study of bird song learning is that a neural circuit has been described in the songbird brain that represents a neural specialization that has evolved in association with the ability to learn, produce, and perceive complex vocalizations (Brenowitz, Margoliash, & Nordeen, 1997; Nottebohm, Stokes, & Leonard, 1976). Thus it is possible to investigate in detail the neural basis of the vocal learning process. For this reason, the neural and endocrine basis of the production, learning, and perception of bird song has emerged as an active area of research in the last 25 years. It is impossible to review in detail the many discoveries that have been made about the relationship between brain and behavior as it relates to song. We describe the basics of the neural system that mediates song behavior and highlight a few findings that demonstrate how the study of bird song learning has influenced studies of the neurobiology of song.

When he began his studies on the neural control of song, Nottebohm noted that the fact that vocal learning requires that motor output be guided by auditory input has important implications for how the neural circuit controlling of song and song learning would be organized (Nottebohm, 1980; Nottebohm et al., 1976). He hypothesized that there should be close connections between the motor system controlling song and the auditory system. This reasoning generated a series of lesion and tract-tracing studies in canaries that resulted in the discovery of the *song system* (Nottebohm, 1996). Subsequently, comparative studies of the song control circuit with other birds clearly indicate that there are several neural features associated with vocal learning and production that are unique to songbirds (Ball, 1994; Brenowitz, 1997; Kroodsma & Konishi, 1991). In particular, studies of canaries (*Serinus canaria*) and zebra finches have revealed a well-defined vocal control circuit that includes a group of interconnected, distinct nuclei that differ in form and structure in the telencephalon, mesencephalon, and brain stem (Bottjer, Meisner, & Arnold, 1984; Nottebohm, Kelley, & Paton, 1982; Nottebohm et al., 1976; Wild, 1997). The telencephalic portion of this circuit appears to be a neural specialization that occurs only in the oscine brain (Brenowitz, 1997; Kroodsma & Konishi, 1991). The song control circuit includes motor nuclei that are involved in song production and nuclei that also exhibit auditory characteristics that appear to be involved in the auditory feedback necessary for vocal learning (for reviews see Brainard & Doupe, 2000; Konishi, 1989; Margoliash, 1997; Nottebohm, 1993; Nottebohm et al., 1990). The motor pathway that is necessary for the production of song in adult birds consists of a series of nuclei that control the neural output to the vocal production organ, the syrinx (Nottebohm, 1993; Nottebohm et al., 1976). This motor pathway is illustrated in Figure 17.6. Three key nuclei in this pathway are the high vocal center (HVc), the robust nucleus of the archistriatum (RA) and a portion of the motor nucleus of the XIIth cranial nerve (nXIIts). These three nuclei form a serial projection (HVc to RA to nXIIts). Efferent projections from motor neurons in nXIIts innervate the syrinx. Song is produced when the muscles associated with the two separate sides of the syrinx are activated, leading to a

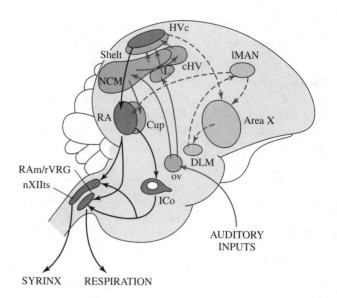

Figure 17.6 Schematic representation of a sagittal view of the song control system of songbirds. It consists of at least two basic pathways. One pathway, essential for song production, involves a projection from nucleus HVc (initially misnamed the hyperstriatum ventrale, pars caudale and therefore sometimes referred to as the high vocal center) to the nucleus robustus archistriatalis (RA) that in turn projects to both the nucleus intercollicularis (ICo) and the tracheosyringeal division of the nucleus of the XIIth cranial nerve (nXIIts). Efferent projections from motor neurons in this brainstem nucleus innervate the vocal production organ, the syrinx. ICo and RA also innervate medullary structures that coordinate song production with respiration. HVc also connects with RA through a more circuitous route (Bottjer et al., 1989). This anterior forebrain pathway consists of a projection from HVc to area X of the lobus parolfactorius (LPO) that in turn projects to the medial portion of the dorsolateral nucleus of the anterior thalamus (DLM). DLM projects to the lateral portion of the nucleus magnocellularis of the anterior neostriatum (lMAN) that in turn projects to RA. In contrast to the more posterior pathway that is needed for song production, the anterior forebrain pathway is involved in song learning, maintenance, and various forms of sensory feedback on song production. Some of the auditory inputs to the song system are also illustrated. Nucleus ovoidalis of the thalamus (Ov) projects to telencephalic auditory areas such as field L (L) and the caudal and medial neostriatum (NCM). These in turn project to other auditory areas adjacent to and connected to the song system such as the caudal ventral hyperstriatum and the shelf near HVc and the RA cup. See text for further details.

change in the configuration of the membranes of the syrinx (Nowicki & Marler, 1988; Suthers, 1997). Projections from RA also innervate brainstem structures that coordinate song production with respiration (Wild, 1997). Lesions to nuclei in this motor pathway have profound effects on song production (e.g., Nottebohm et al., 1976). In particular, lesions to HVc cause deficits in vocal production reminiscent of Broca's aphasia in humans. Electrophysiological studies of neurons in HVc, RA, and nXIIts reveal that their activity is synchronized with singing behavior (McCasland, 1987; Vu, Mazurek, & Kuo, 1994) and that these nuclei are hierarchically organized (Yu & Margoliash, 1996). Nuclei RA and nXIIts are myotopically organized (i.e., organized in relation to syringeal musculature; Vicario, 1991; Vicario & Nottebohm,

1988); however, HVc is not (Fortune & Margoliash, 1995; Yu & Margoliash, 1996). This motor pathway of the song control system thus appears to coordinate temporal and phonological aspects of song.

As illustrated in Figure 17.6, neural impulses from HVc also reach RA through a more circuitous route than the motor pathway (Bottjer, Halsema, Brown, & Miesner, 1989; Okuhata & Saito, 1987). This anterior forebrain pathway consists of a projection from HVc to area X of the lobus parolfactorius (LPO), which in turn projects to the medial portion of the dorsolateral nucleus of the anterior thalamus (DLM). DLM projects to the lateral portion of the nucleus magnocellularis of the anterior neostriatum (lMAN), which in turn projects to RA (Figure 17.6). In adult zebra finches all of the song control nuclei in this anterior forebrain pathway contain cells that are tuned to respond to the presentation of species-specific song (Margoliash, 1997; Solis & Doupe 1997). Auditory information is conveyed to the song system via connections between the telencephalic auditory area, Field L to areas adjacent to HVc and RA (Fortune & Margoliash, 1995; Kelley & Nottebohm, 1979; Vates, Broome, Mello, & Nottebohm, 1996; see Figure 17.6). Related areas for auditory processing include the caudomedial neostriatum (NCM) and the caudal ventral hyperstriatum (cHV; see Figure 17.6). These areas are also connected to HVc and RA (Vates et al., 1996) and have been shown to contain cells that express immediate early genes specifically in response to conspecific song (D. F. Clayton, 1997; Mello, Vicario, & Clayton, 1992), and they have electrophysiological properties that are similarly somewhat selective to conspecific song (Stripling, Volman, & Clayton, 1997). Therefore, these auditory areas may be the part of the neural circuit that is specialized to process conspecific vocalizations.

The anterior forebrain pathway has been implicated in many feedback effects on song production and in the process of song learning. For example, lesions of nuclei in the forebrain pathway of zebra finches (especially area X and the lMAN) before species song is crystallized result in song abnormalities, such as lack of note stereotypy and abnormal song length (e.g., Bottjer et al., 1984; Scharff & Nottebohm, 1991). Similar lesions made after the development of stereotyped song have no effect on song production in adult male zebra finches, although there are effects of such lesions on the maintenance of song in adult white-crowned sparrows (Benton, Nelson, Marler, & DeVoogd, 1998). The neural mechanisms mediating the feedback effects between song production and the stored auditory memory are still not well understood, but many properties of the anterior forebrain pathway provide intriguing hints about how this might work. Song selective neurons, present throughout the anterior

forebrain pathway, respond more strongly to the bird's own song and sometimes to the tutor song (see Brainard & Doupe, 2000, for a review). These cells are clear candidates for at least part of the neural system mediating the comparison between the stored memory and auditory output (Brainard & Doupe, 2000). Interestingly, these responses are strongly gated by the behavioral state of the animal. They are absent or much weaker in anesthetized or sleeping birds (Dave, Yu, & Margoliash, 1998; Schmidt & Konishi, 1998). The significance of this gating remains to be clarified. Brainard and Doupe (2000) speculated that the motor act of singing itself may open the gate so that the feedback effects can be exerted. What is clear is that there are neural specializations in the songbird brain that can be directly related to the auditory-motor interface required for song learning to occur.

Neural changes in the song circuit responsible for the closing of the sensitive period for song learning have yet to be definitively identified (Nordeen & Nordeen, 1997; Nottebohm, 1993). However, developmental changes in the connections between the anterior forebrain pathway and the efferent motor pathway (i.e., the lMAN to RA projection) have been the focus of attention in this regard. What is known (reviewed in Nordeen & Nordeen, 1997) is that there is a dramatic decline in the density of NMDA receptors in male zebra finches in lMAN coincident with both the memory acquisition and sensorimotor phase of song learning. Furthermore, the pharmacological blockade of these receptors does impair song learning, and therefore the NMDA mechanisms that have been implicated in many forms of learning and developmental plasticity are important in the song learning process as well. However, these developmental changes in the NMDA receptors do not close the sensitive period. Manipulations of the timing of the sensitive period either by social isolation or hormone treatment do not change the timing of the decline in NMDA receptors.

The neural basis of sensorimotor learning is very poorly understood. However, as mentioned previously, in many species this learning process involves a selection of song based on social interactions. One intriguing idea is that ascending catecholamine projections to the song system (Appeltants, Absil, Balthazart, & Ball, 2000) are activated by these social interactions and contribute to these selectivity. Immediate early gene induction in the anterior forebrain pathway is profoundly influenced by the social context of song production in male zebra finches (Jarvis, Scharff, Grossman, Ramos, & Nottebohm, 1998). It has been hypothesized that these social context effects on gene expression are regulated by catecholamine projections to the song system (Jarvis et al., 1998). If this is the case, it is also reasonable to postulate that the consequences of song matching on the selection of songs during the sensorimotor phase of song learning could also be regulated by these pathways.

Food-Related Appetitive Learning in Laboratory Rats

As with many animals, a major part of the activity of rats is the procurement and consumption of food. As noted earlier, since Wallace Craig's (1918) work both ethologists and experimental psychologists have distinguished between these appetitive behaviors and the more stereotyped, consummatory aspects of feeding. Although Craig's view was that appetitive behavior was more easily modified by experience, it is clear that both components are subject to modification by learning. Casually speaking, it is advantageous to learn when and where food is available, what kind of food it is, and how much of it there is. Learned signals for food can aid procurement by orienting the animal to the proper location at the right time. But they also can provide the animal with useful information about the ingestive (e.g., flavor) and postingestive (e.g., nutrient absorption) consequences of the expected foodstuffs.

A Behavior Systems Approach to the Anticipation of Food

In traditional approaches to conditioning, the form of Pavlovian CRs is thought to be determined by the choice of the US, which provides the reflexes that can be transferred to the CS. A behavioral systems approach to food-based learning goes beyond this observation by adding the ethological perspective that, besides the simple reflexes elicited by delivery of the particular food US, the animal's learned behavior potentially includes a range of more complex, preorganized behavior systems that are normally involved in the procurement and consumption of food. Both the dynamics of learning itself and the expression of learning in behavior will depend on how the learning task contacts these systems. These points of contact include not only the nature of the US but also the signals (CSs) used, the structure of the local environment (context), and more global conditions including the animal's deprivation and housing conditions.

The power of a behavioral systems approach to understanding food-related associative learning in rats is perhaps best illustrated by the work of Timberlake and his colleagues (e.g., Timberlake & Silva, 1995; see Fanselow, 1994, and Fanselow & Lester, 1985, for comparable discussions of defensive behavior). Timberlake proposed that a variety of individual action patterns related to the procurement and consumption of food is hierarchically arranged within a variety of modules, modes, and subsystems, each of which has its own characteristic elicitors and terminators, as well as timing and sequential properties. For example, Timberlake described a set of actions such as pouncing, grabbing, biting, and gnawing that are organized within a capture module, which in turn is part of a focal search mode within predation. Most important, learning may occur at many points and levels within the system. Within-module learning may result in changes in the stimulus control, frequency, or timing of particular actions, whereas learning that occurs at the supermodular level may alter the relation between whole sets of behaviors organized within each of those modules or modes. Thus, the behaviors displayed in conditioning experiments will vary depending on which of these units are accessed and altered as a function of the events and relations involved in those studies. Within this approach most conditioned behavior may be viewed as the result of the modulation of existing behavioral patterns by associative learning, much as two-process theorists thought CSs modulated ongoing instrumental behavior.

Consider the effects of using as CSs events that are unusual from an experimenter-centered view but obvious from an animal-centered perspective. Timberlake, Wahl, and King (1982) examined the effects of signaling food delivery with a ball bearing that rolled across the chamber floor about 5 s in advance of the food. The rats acquired a sequence of behaviors including chasing the bearing, seizing it, and handling and gnawing it as if it were a food item. These behaviors were not acquired if the rolling ball bearing was unrelated to food delivery, and thus they were the consequence of associative learning. Timberlake described this learned behavior as reflecting the incorporation of existing predatory modules (wild rats chase and consume moving insects) and food-handling modules into a sequence of behaviors culminating in food consumption. It is interesting that similar experiments with a range of rodent species that show varying degrees of insect predation revealed a correlation between their natural predation and the likelihood of ball-bearing chasing and mouthing. Likewise, the form of the conditioned behavior varied with the CS-US interval in a predictable manner. With moderate intervals, the rats engaged in the complete sequence described earlier, reflecting focal search and related modes, but with shorter intervals the food-handling module dominated, and the rats often deposited the bearing in the food cup and gnawed on both the food and the bearing (Silva & Timberlake, 1998). Furthermore, Holland (1984b) found that when a CS is presented after the US (backward conditioning), it often acquires normal postconsummatory behavior such as grooming (see also Silva & Timberlake, 2000).

Timberlake and his colleagues also examined rats' learning within social modules. In one study (Timberlake & Grant, 1975) food delivery was signaled by the arrival of either a restrained live rat or a rat-sized block of wood. Although subject rats oriented to both signals, when the signal was a rat-sized block, their conditioned behavior was dominated by approach and gnawing on the block; but when the signal was another rat, they displayed a variety of social approach and contact behaviors characteristic of normal food-sharing and solicitation activities. Critically, these behaviors were far more frequent when the signaling rat was paired with food delivery than when it was explicitly unpaired with food. Thus, the enhanced social behavior was a consequence of associative learning. Furthermore, the nature of this behavior was consistent with normal patterns of adaptive behavior. For example, Timberlake (1983, 1994) reported that only adult signals of food supported these conditioned behaviors, consistent with observations that adult rats use the food preferences and consummatory behaviors of other adult rats, but not of juveniles, to guide their food selection. Likewise, when water rather than food was used as the US, these behaviors did not appear, consistent with observations that rats' food selection involves social modules, but water consumption does not. Finally, comparative studies with a variety of rodent species found correlations between the extent of food sharing and the conditioning of these kinds of social behaviors.

Although this approach is unquestionably rich in potential, there has been relatively little study of neural and behavioral mechanisms involved in these examples. A more simplistic experimenter-centered approach, in which significant US events like food, water, or electric shock are signaled by various simple visual or auditory CSs, has been profitable in addressing these issues. In line with reflexological expectations, the form of conditioned behavior is dependent on the choice of US: Rats freeze during these CSs when they signal shock, and they approach and contact the delivery cup when they signal food or water deliveries, often gnawing or licking the cup as appropriate (e.g., Holland, 1979). However, as in Timberlake's studies, it is clear that the choice of CS is also important in determining CR form. For example, diffuse auditory cues paired with food typically elicit a quick jump or startle response, followed by agitated head movements, often directed toward the site of food delivery. By contrast, localizable, overhead visual cues (illumination of lamps) paired with food usually first causes the rat to rear on its hind legs, often orienting toward the light source, followed by a more passive contact with the food delivery cup (Holland, 1977). Furthermore, consistent with Timberlake's scheme, if the light source extends significantly into the experimental chamber, the rat is likely to contact it with its paws and mouth as well (Holland, 1980b), integrating more of the normal feeding sequence into the learned behavior.

As in Timberlake's studies, temporal variables are important determinants of response form in this conditioning situation. Not surprisingly, the influence of CS characteristics on CR form is greatest close to CS onset, and the effects of US features are most obvious closest to the normal time of US delivery (Holland, 1979, 1980a, 1980b). Observations that the form of CRs is influenced by the CS-US interval have important implications for the study of the role of time in conditioning. Holland (1980a) found distinct CS-US interval functions for each of the several CRs observed when visual and auditory CSs are paired with food. Depending on the choice of CR measured, the optimal CS-US interval for learning the same tone-food or light-food relation could be identified as 1 s, 5 s, 10 s, or 30 s. Furthermore, although some of those CRs were exquisitely timed to occur maximally near the time of US delivery and exhibited the scalar property, others, like rearing, were mostly confined to the few seconds near CS onset, and still others occurred maximally near the middle of the ISI. As Timberlake pointed out, signals with different temporal relations with the US are likely to contact different modules of food-related behavior. Thus, the experimenter's choice of a behavioral measure of association could lead to vastly different conclusions about the relation of time and association. In fact, data like those of Holland and Timberlake suggest a multiplicity of timing functions, each tuned to a behavioral system, rather than the more popular view of a single estimate of the time of US delivery (Meck & Church, 1982).

All of these results are consistent with a simple view that conditioning produces behavioral adaptation to the altered significance of the CS as well as to the upcoming US. Learning-dependent changes in processing of the CS may be of many sorts. Holland (1977) suggested that the simplest of these may be the conditioning-dependent potentiation of orienting behaviors controlled by the CSs prior to conditioning. Some of the CS-specific behaviors described earlier are also elicited by the CSs prior to their pairing with the US, but they rapidly habituate if the CSs are not paired with food. The potentiation of these initially unconditioned orienting behaviors enhances the likelihood that the rats' behaviors will be guided by the best signals for important events.

Considerable evidence indicates that these CS-dependent products of associative learning are separable from those appropriate to the upcoming US. As noted earlier, the temporal determinants and characteristics of CS- and US-dependent behaviors are often reciprocally related. Furthermore, several experimental manipulations have different effects on the two classes of behaviors (Holland, 1990b).

Finally, a neural systems analysis also supports this distinction. Brain pathways involved in the potentiation of orienting behavior to CSs paired with food are not critical to the acquisition and display of US-dependent behaviors. Gallagher and her colleagues (Gallagher, Graham, & Holland, 1990; Han, McMahan, Holland, & Gallagher, 1997) found that the conditioned potentiation of orienting behavior depends on the integrity of connections between the central nucleus of the amygdala and dorsal striatal regions. Although rats with interruptions in this circuitry were unaffected in their acquisition of US-appropriate food-related behaviors, and in their unconditioned orienting to the CS prior to conditioning, they failed to acquire conditioned orienting with CS-US pairings. Thus, this amygdalar circuitry seems to be critical for the potentiation of existing orienting responses (ORs) to events that have acquired significance through associative learning. Similar neural systems analysis might also be profitably applied to other module-level aspects of conditioned responding, such as those described by Timberlake and his colleagues, to understand better the roles of associative learning in the organization of behavior.

An important question in this kind of research is the extent to which the various CRs that occur under different circumstances indicate independent learning at the module level, for example, within separate neural pathways, and to which they all draw on common learning at some higher level. Despite the independence of brain systems for the learning of CS-specific ORs and food-related CRs, considerable evidence indicates that CSs that elicit differently formed CRs when paired with food nevertheless have a common associative basis at some level. For example, compound conditioning phenomena like blocking, unblocking, and second-order conditioning with simple lights and tones occur largely without regard to the specific CRs controlled by the CSs, suggesting that various CSs have access to properties of the US that determine these effects (Holland, 1977). Answers to these kinds of questions will lead us to better understanding of the organization of behavior through learning.

A Biobehavioral Analysis of Alterations in CS Processing

As noted earlier, there is considerable evidence that experience with a CS can affect its associability, that is, its ability to participate in new learning. Pearce and Hall (1980) proposed that CS associability was adjusted depending on how well predicted its consequences were. Expected outcomes reduce CS associability, whereas surprising events (unpredicted by the stimuli present on that trial) maintain or enhance it. Thus, CSs that consistently predict their outcomes will be less associable than will those that are relatively poor predictors of their consequences. This claim is reasonable from an adaptational perspective: It is more critical to be able to *learn* about

cues whose significance has heretofore been unknown than about cues whose significance is already well established. From that same perspective, however, it is important that *behavior* be controlled by cues whose consequences are well known. Within the Pearce-Hall model, a CS's associability (α) appears only in equations that specify new learning about that CS, and not in those that describe its control of behavior, which is a function only of its associative strength (V_{CS}) and its intrinsic salience (s_{CS}). Thus, the Pearce-Hall model distinguishes between controlled attention for new learning and automatic attention for action. Recent studies of brain pathways involved in appetitive conditioning support these claims and provide some novel insights into the nature of the behavioral processes involved in the modulation of CS associability and learning.

Early behavioral studies that tested the Pearce-Hall model were designed to evaluate contrasting predictions of that model from those of its major alternative, the Rescorla-Wagner model. Consider first the widely described case of unblocking. As noted earlier, learning about one element of a compound CS paired with a US is blocked by prior training of another element of that compound with the same US. Within the Rescorla-Wagner model, that blocking occurs because the US is already well predicted by the first CS when the second element is introduced, and hence is ineffective as a reinforcer. By contrast, within the Pearce-Hall model, blocking occurs because the presentation of a well-predicted US causes the associability of the added CS to be adjusted rapidly downward, minimizing learning about that cue.

In an unblocking procedure the value of the US is changed when the target stimulus is added. If this new value is greater than the original value, both theories predict conditioning of the added cue (unblocking). Within the Rescorla-Wagner model the positive discrepancy between actual and expected US values supports further excitatory learning, and within the Pearce-Hall model that discrepancy maintains the associability of the added CS long enough for it to acquire associative strength as a result of its pairings with the new US. However, if the US value is reduced when the new CS is added, the two models make opposite predictions. Because the discrepancy between actual and anticipated events is negative, it should establish negative (inhibitory) associative strength to the added cue according to the Rescorla-Wagner model. But within the Pearce-Hall model both positive and negative discrepancies enhance or maintain CS associability. Thus, the added CS will acquire excitatory associations with the new (smaller) US. Although the determinants of learned behavior in the case of such downshifts in US value are complex, excitatory learning, as predicted by Pearce and Hall, is often observed (Holland, 1988).

Holland and Gallagher (1993b) and Bucci, Holland, and Gallagher (1998) found that disruption of a brain system, including amygdala CN and the substantia innominata/nucleus basalis and its projections to the posterior parietal cortex prevented unblocking with downshifts in the US value. Other experiments showed that these brain system manipulations also interfered with several other phenomena attributed by Pearce and Hall to surprise-induced associability increases (Han, Holland, & Gallagher, 1999; Holland, Chik, & Zhang, 2001; Holland & Gallagher, 1993a; Holland et al., 2000). At the same time, those manipulations had no effect on simple conditioning, on other measures of sensitivity to the change in US value, on unblocking observed with upshifts in US value, on blocking itself, or on a number of phenomena usually attributed to decreases in CS associability. From the results of a series of selective lesion experiments, Holland and Gallagher (1999) concluded that surprise engages this system, which selectively enhances attentional processing of CSs in a manner consistent with the Pearce-Hall model.

Parallel studies indicated that disruption of a cholinergic septal-hippocampal circuit had complementary effects on decreases in CS associability. These manipulations (hippocampal lesions or cholinergic deafferentiation of hippocampus by immunotoxic lesions of the medial septal area and the vertical limb of the diagonal band) had little effect on phenomena attributed to enhancement of associability but interfered with a variety of phenomena indicative of losses of associability (Baxter, Holland, & Gallagher, 1997; Han, Gallagher, & Holland, 1995).

Holland and Gallagher (1999) concluded that increases and decreases in CS associability, as specified by the Pearce-Hall model, are modulated by two distinct brain systems. Furthermore, some evidence suggests that these systems act independently and additively; most effects of combined destruction of both systems are predictable from the effects of separate lesions (Baxter, Bucci, Holland, & Gallagher, 1999). Moreover, neither system seems critical to the occurrence of phenomena that are easily described without reference to changes in CS processing, including simple conditioning and phenomena attributed to changes in US processing as claimed by the Rescorla-Wagner model (Holland & Gallagher, 1993a, 1993b).

We have taken advantage of this relative independence to parcel out the contributions of attentional and other processes to a variety of behavioral phenomena that may have multiple determinants. For example, Baxter, Gallagher, and Holland (1999) examined the effects of medial septal lesions, which interfere with associability decreases, on blocking. If blocking is the result of losses in associability of the added CS, as specified by the Pearce-Hall model and other attentional theories, then this lesion should reduce blocking. In a test of

responding to the added cue, Baxter, Gallagher, et al. (1999) found no effect of the lesion. However, subsequent learning tests showed the associability of that cue to be greater in the lesioned rats, as would be expected if the lesion interfered with losses in associability in the blocking procedure. Baxter, Gallagher, et al. (1999) concluded that in intact rats, although the blocking procedure did produce reductions in CS associability, those losses were not responsible for the blocking effect, which instead was the result of processes specified by the Rescorla-Wagner model. If a predicted US is ineffective as a reinforcer from the very beginning of the blocking phase, then variations in CS processing that occur over the course of that phase are irrelevant to conditioning at that time.

Likewise, we exploited the CN lesion to help us understand a puzzling discrimination finding reported previously. Rescorla (1991) found that pigeons learned a serial negative patterning (NP) discrimination of the form feature CS → food, target CS → food, feature → target → no food more rapidly than a serial FN discrimination, feature → food, feature → target → no food. Although the latter discrimination can be solved simply by the acquisition of excitation to A and inhibition to X, solution of the patterned discrimination should be more difficult from a variety of perspectives. However, the relative ease of learning of the patterned discrimination might be anticipated within the Pearce-Hall model. In the NP discrimination, X's associability should be enhanced because X is a relatively poor predictor of both A and the US. By contrast, in the FN discrimination, X is a reliable predictor of the occurrence of A and the absence of the US, and thus X's associability should decline. By this view, elimination of surprise-induced enhancements of X's associability by the CN lesion should eliminate the superiority of the NP discrimination learning. Holland et al. (2000) found just this outcome. Furthermore, the CN lesion did not affect learning in variations of the patterning procedure in which there was less opportunity for surprise-induced associability enhancements in normal rats.

In both cases, reduced preparations (Teitelbaum & Pellis, 1992) were used to understand better the nature of learning in the intact preparation. Thus, the study of biological bases of learning can contribute importantly to study at more purely behavioral or psychological levels. Holland and Gallagher (1999) described the use of similar strategies for informing other aspects of behavioral study as well.

Associative Learning and Motivational State

A key to the behavioral systems approach is the idea that associative learning alters behavior by modulating the activity of behavioral systems, which themselves may be organized within larger scale systems. As noted earlier, it has long been presumed that CSs can control a range of behaviors indirectly by modulating motivational systems or states. Thus, a CS paired with food may acquire the ability to influence a broad range of food-motivated behavior. For example, light-food pairings appear to endow the light with food's reinforcing power. In Pavlovian second-order conditioning, subsequent tone-light pairings in the absence of food establish CRs to the tone (Hatfield, Han, Conley, Gallagher, & Holland, 1996; Holland & Rescorla, 1975), and in operant secondary reinforcement procedures, rats learn to press levers that result only in the presentation of that light (Everitt & Robbins, 1992). Likewise, a light paired with food can modulate the frequency of operant lever pressing for that food (Pavlovian-to-instrumental transfer), perhaps by enhancing some motivational state that energizes appetitive behavior involved in food procurement (Dickinson, Smith, & Mirenowicz, 2000). Finally, that same CS can enhance consummatory behavior as well: Food-satiated rats eat more food in the presence of a CS for food than in its absence (Holland, Hatfield, & Gallagher, 2001; Weingarten, 1983; Zamble, 1973).

Although learning theorists have often suggested that these indirectly measured consequences of associative learning are most important because they modulate other kinds of learned behavior and emotional states (e.g., Mowrer, 1947; Rescorla & Solomon, 1967), for the most part they have been treated as just another index of abstract association formation. By contrast, within a behavioral systems approach, they may be quite independent, and hence interesting in their own right. Recent studies of brain systems suggest that these consequences of conditioning operations may be separately organized. For example, second-order conditioning, secondary reinforcement, and CS-potentiated feeding are all disrupted by lesions of the basolateral, but not central, amygdala (Everitt & Robbins, 1992; Gallagher & Holland, 1992; Hatfield et al., 1996; Holland, Hatfield, et al., 2001), whereas the opposite is true of Pavlovian-to-instrumental transfer (J. Hall, Parkinson, Connor, Dickinson, & Everitt, 2001). Moreover, neither lesion affects conditioned approach to the source of the food US (Everitt & Robbins, 1992; Hatfield et al., 1996). Recent evidence suggests that the amygdala's role in these various phenomena involves the modulation of the activity of other brain regions that each organize different behavior systems (e.g., Petrovich, Setlow, Holland, & Gallagher, 2001; Setlow, Holland, & Gallagher, 2002).

Associative Learning and Representation of the Reinforcer

Earlier we noted that Pavlovian CRs often appear to be mediated by a representation of the US because posttraining devaluation of a US can spontaneously (and selectively) reduce responding to CSs paired with that US. It is interesting to note that response systems can be differentially sensitive to these devaluations. For example, Holland and Straub (1979) found a double dissociation between the effects of two ways of devaluing food and various classes of CRs. When food was devalued by toxin-induced illness, ORs to CS onset were unaffected, approach responses were moderately reduced, and responses related to food handling were substantially reduced. In contrast, when food was devalued by motion-induced illness, ORs were most affected, with much smaller effects on later-chain behaviors. Furthermore, food devaluation by satiation (Holland, 1981b) produced across-the-board (but selective) decreases. These data show that different behavioral systems make different use of information made available through learning.

Finally, it is worth noting that sensitivity of CRs to posttraining changes in the value of the reinforcer seems to depend on brain circuitry that includes the orbital frontal cortex and the basolateral amygdala (Baxter, Parker, Lindner, Izquierdo, & Murray, 2000; Hatfield et al., 1996; Malkova et al., 1997; Schoenbaum, Chiba, & Gallagher, 1998). Given the role of basolateral amygdala in many aspects of a CS's acquisition of motivational significance (described in the previous section), it is interesting to speculate that information about sensory properties of the reinforcer, affected in devaluation procedures, and processing of motivational value, may converge in this region.

Sexual Approach Conditioning in Japanese Quail

A Behavior Systems Approach to Sexual Conditioning

As part of a long-term research program devoted to explicating the role of learning in the control of sexual behavior, Domjan and his colleagues (Crawford, Holloway, & Domjan, 1993; Domjan, 1994; Domjan, Akins, & Vandergriff, 1992; Domjan & Hollis, 1988) have developed a variety of behavioral procedures that are appropriate for the investigation of appetitive sexual behavior in quail. These methods include the application of Pavlovian conditioning procedures in which a neutral stimulus such as the illumination of a light or the presentation of a gray foam block serves as the CS that is temporally paired with access to a female that serves as the US. Male quail will quickly come to approach a CS when it is paired with the US in this way. This conditioned approach behavior shows common conditioning phenomena like blocking (Koksal, Domjan, & Weisman, 1994), conditioned inhibition (Crawford & Domjan, 1996), second-order conditioning (Crawford & Domjan, 1995), US devaluation effects (Hilliard & Domjan, 1995; Holloway & Domjan, 1993), context conditioning and context-specificity effects (Crawford, Akins, & Domjan, 1994; Domjan, Greene, & North, 1989), and potentiation of unconditioned sexual behavior (Domjan, Lyons, North, & Bruell, 1986).

As in Timberlake's (1994) and Holland's (1984b) studies, the nature of the conditioned sexual response depends heavily on the nature of the CS. Although quail will learn to approach just about any localizable CS, copulatory responses themselves are not acquired unless the CS includes plumage and other features of a female quail (Cusato & Domjan, 2000; Domjan, O'Nary, & Greene, 1988; Koksal et al., 1994). At the same time, however, CSs that support only approach behavior also have a profound facilitatory effect on copulation if they are presented along with a female quail, shortening the latency of initiation of copulatory behavior and enhancing sperm release (Domjan, Blesbois, & Williams, 1998). Furthermore, the topography of the approach and other CRs depends on the CS-US interval (Akins, Domjan, & Guitierrez, 1994), as in Silva and Timberlake's (1998) and Holland's (1980a) studies of rat feeding CRs.

During the course of these studies, Domjan and his colleagues discovered another phenomenon, which they referred to as a learned social proximity response. This response is a form of associative learning that is acquired by males after they have been allowed to copulate with females (Domjan & Hall, 1986a, 1986b; Domjan et al., 1986). In this procedure, a male is allowed to copulate with a female after the male has observed the female through a window in the test arena. The response involves a remarkable change in a male's behavior: After a single copulation, males will spend the majority of their time (literally for days at a time) standing in front of the window and looking through it at the female (Domjan & Hall, 1986a, 1986b). The response is clearly associative in origin and depends on copulatory rather than visual experience with the female, because it will only be acquired by the male if he actually copulates with the female after seeing her (Balthazart, Reid, Absil, Foidart, & Ball, 1995; Nash, Domjan, & Askins, 1989). Domjan et al. (1992) argued that the learned social proximity response should be viewed as a type of associative learning in which stimuli from a female become directly associated with sexual reinforcement.

Although this social proximity response of male quail can be acquired to a variety of CSs, learning with a female quail CS is clearly privileged. For example, it is more prevalent with a live female quail CS than with various partial models, and stronger with a female quail CS than with a male quail CS (Nash & Domjan, 1991). Furthermore, Domjan et al. (1992) reported that this learned proximity response was acquired even when they introduced delays of 2 to 3 hr between the closing of the window providing a view of a female and the access to the female for copulation. Likewise, Koksal et al. (1994) found that model CSs that more closely resembled female quail visually were less susceptible to blocking by previously trained arbitrary CSs.

Domjan (1994) described the social proximity response as reflecting focal search within more extensive behavior systems in sexual conditioning. When isolated in a large arena, male quail will first pursue a general search for females, and then when a female is localized to a particular place, they exhibit a more focal search. Such variable searching behavior is characteristic of an appetitive behavioral response. As a good example of focal sexual search, the learned social proximity response in male quail thereby provides a useful measure of appetitive sexual behavior that one can contrast with the stereotyped sequence of the neck grab, mounting, and cloacal contact movements characteristic of the consummatory sexual response.

A Neuroendocrine Analysis of Sexual Conditioning

The social proximity response conditioning procedure has provided a very useful way to study the neuroendocrine mechanisms regulating different aspects of male sexual behavior, and in turn, the study of the hormonal and neural mechanisms has told us something about how naturally reinforcing stimuli exert their effects on learned responses. Social proximity response learning is relatively easy to obtain under laboratory conditions, but at the same time it involves aspects of the learning process that occur in male quail when they engage in sexual behavior in a natural context. Furthermore, it appears to provide a good indicator of *appetitive* sexual behavior, in that the male seems clearly to be engaging in this behavior in anticipation of copulatory behavior itself, but this learned behavior does not resemble *consummatory* copulatory behavior. Initial studies demonstrated that the presence of testosterone is required for the development and maintenance of this social proximity response and that this response is acquired only by males, not by females (Domjan, 1987; Domjan & Hall, 1986a, 1986b).

The studies described in this section used a modification of Domjan and Hall's (1986a, 1986b) procedure to assess the neuroendocrine mechanisms mediating appetitive sexual behavior in quail to compare the mechanisms involved in the control of this aspect of sexual behavior with the relatively well characterized mechanisms mediating consummatory sexual behavior. In this modified procedure, quail are tested for relatively brief periods of time (25 min) so that a large number of subjects can be examined each day (Balthazart et al., 1995). All behavioral observations are carried out in an arena containing two compartments. The experimental male is tested by introducing him into the larger compartment that is separated by a sliding door from an adjacent smaller cage where the stimulus female is located. A small window is located in the middle of the sliding door and provides the male with limited visual access to the female. If the door between the female and male is opened and the male is allowed to copulate with the female, there is a radical change in his behavior. As in Domjan's studies, males start to spend an inordinate amount of time (up to 95% of the 5-min period) in the area in front of the window. However, this learned social proximity response only develops if the male is permitted to copulate with the female. If the door between the two compartments is not opened, the response is never acquired. Similarly, if a given male fails to copulate during the first few tests, the acquisition of the proximity response is delayed until the first test when copulation will take place. These observations clearly indicate the reinforcing role of consummatory sexual behavior in the learning of the proximity response (Balthazart et al., 1995). This modification of the original procedure described by Domjan illustrates how a behavioral phenomenon can be modified to suit a more detailed mechanistic investigation while capturing the key features of the natural situation.

Domjan (1987) first demonstrated that the display of appetitive sexual behavior as measured by the learned social proximity response is dependent on the presence of high circulating levels of testosterone: If males are placed on short days that induce testicular regression and suppress testosterone secretion, they do not acquire this response. The steroid-dependence of appetitive sexual behavior was confirmed by a strategy of surgical castration that was combined in some subjects with a testosterone replacement therapy. Castrated subjects never learned the proximity response, but it was acquired by testosterone-treated castrates as well as by sexually mature adult males (Balthazart et al., 1995). The fact that this learned behavior is so dependent of the presence of gonadal steroids provides one with a good opportunity to study the neural mechanisms regulating the behavior. In males in many species including quail, testosterone is locally metabolized in the brain to either an androgen or an estrogen before it exerts its effects on male sexual behavior (Balthazart, 1989; Meisel & Sachs, 1994). By localizing in the brain both the relevant enzymes that metabolize testosterone to androgens or estrogens and the relevant receptors to which these hormones will then bind to exert their effects, one can gain valuable insights into the neural circuit regulating this behavior (Balthazart & Ball, 1998).

Therefore, more detailed studies of the neuroendocrine mechanism regulating this acquired response followed (Balthazart & Ball, 1998). Previous work in quail and in a variety of birds and mammals had demonstrated that the activation of copulatory behavior by testosterone requires its conversion via the enzyme aromatase into the estrogen 17β-estradiol (for a review, see Balthazart, 1989). It was therefore hypothesized that appetitive sexual behavior would similarly be dependent on estrogenic metabolites of testosterone. This was found to be the case based on three independent experimental approaches.

First, the learned proximity response could be acquired by castrated birds if they were systemically treated with either the endogenous estrogen 17β-estradiol, or a synthetic estrogen, diethylstilbestrol (DES). These compounds were found to mimic the behavioral effects of testosterone (Balthazart et al., 1995). This idea was further supported by a second experiment that demonstrated that once the proximity response had been acquired, its expression could be blocked by daily injections of the antiestrogen tamoxifen. Although the inhibition of the appetitive proximity response was paralleled by a marked decrease in copulatory behavior as well, several aspects of the experimental protocol led to the conclusion that the disappearance of the proximity response was not mediated by the decreased copulatory behavior. One might argue, for example, that presentation of a female while copulation was inhibited might serve as a punisher for the proximity response. In this study appetitive sexual behavior was first measured in a series of behavioral tests during which the door separating the male and the female was never opened. In this situation, although males had no access to behavioral feedback of any sort that could indicate that their copulatory behavior was inhibited, they nevertheless exhibited a decline in appetitive behavior. Normally, the proximity response is maintained for long periods of time (over 20 tests during a 5-week period) when birds are tested in this extinction condition (door never opened and reinforcement no longer available). Therefore, the decline in appetitive behavior of the tamoxifen-treated males cannot be attributed to either simple extinction or punishment contingencies (Balthazart et al., 1995). It can therefore be concluded that maintenance of appetitive sexual behavior in quail requires the presence of estrogens.

The final confirmation of this conclusion was obtained in an experiment that assessed the effects of an aromatase inhibitor on the social proximity response that had been acquired by castrated birds treated with testosterone. The response was first learned by one group of castrated birds that received testosterone implants (CX + T groups). A second group of castrates received empty Silastic implants as a control manipulation (CX group); as expected, these birds did not learn the response. CX + T birds were then assigned to one of two subgroups that were matched based on the proximity response they had shown during the last two training tests. Beginning 4 days later, birds in one of the CX + T groups were injected twice a day with an aromatase inhibitor, and the other two groups received control injections. During the period when these injections were administered, appetitive sexual behavior tests were performed. In each series, the first four tests were performed under conditions of extinction (i.e., the door was not opened, so there was no access to the female), but free access to the female (door open) was provided during every fifth test. A specific and significant inhibition of the learned social proximity response was observed in these conditions, and this inhibition appeared to be independent of the accessibility or nonaccessibility of the female. This inhibition developed progressively during the period that the aromatase inhibitor was injected, and the inhibition was maximal during the last behavioral tests. Mean behavioral scores collected during the last three tests (when looking through the window was quantified in addition of the time spent in the test area) are illustrated in Figure 17.7. As can be observed, both responses indicative of appetitive sexual behavior were nearly completely blocked by the aromatase inhibitor.

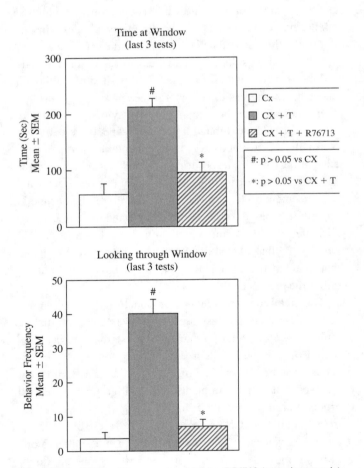

Figure 17.7   Effects of the aromatase inhibitor R76713 (racemic vorozole) on appetitive sexual behavior of castrated male quails that were systemically treated with testosterone (CX + T). One group of castrated birds (CX) received empty Silastic implants as a control. Behavioral scores shown in the figure are the means observed during the last three behavioral tests. Based on two different behavioral measures, the learned social proximity response is significantly inhibited when the metabolic conversion of androgens to estrogens is blocked.

In conclusion, these experiments demonstrate that appetitive aspects of male sexual behavior in quail are activated, as is the case for consummatory sexual behavior, by testosterone acting through its estrogenic metabolites. The endocrine specificity is therefore similar, if not identical, for the activation of both aspects of sexual behavior.

The learned social proximity response is not observed in female quail, even if they are treated with testosterone as adults. This finding suggests that the sex difference in the exhibition of the learned social proximity response is regulated similarly to the sex difference in consummatory sexual behavior (i.e., copulatory behavior) in quail, which is known to be organizational in nature. The term *organizational* means that the sex difference results from the exposure of female embryos to elevated levels of estrogens that causes the demasculinization of the neural substrate mediating the activation of sexual behavior (Balthazart & Ball, 1995). Males do not experience such high estrogen levels as embryos and develop a male-typical neural substrate mediating this behavior. Blocking aromatase activity by treating females on day 9 of incubation with an aromatase inhibitor prevents the demasculinizing effects of endogenous estrogen. This results in the females engaging in male-typical copulatory behavior in response to adult testosterone treatment (Balthazart & Ball, 1995; Balthazart, De Clerck, & Foidart, 1992; Foidart & Balthazart, 1995).

The role of embryonic estrogens in the sexual differentiation of learned social proximity response was tested by blocking estrogen synthesis in ovo. Control males and testosterone-treated females deprived of estrogens during embryonic life learned the social proximity response, but control females did not, despite the presence of high concentrations of testosterone in the plasma. The neural substrate mediating the learned social proximity response is therefore demasculinized by the action of embryonic estrogens during ontogeny, as is consummatory behavior.

Studies of the neural basis of this behavior have also been completed. The preoptic area in quail is known to express the enzyme aromatase as well as androgen and estrogen receptors, so it was an important candidate brain region as being part of the circuit regulating male-typical sexual behavior (Panzica, Viglietti-Panzica, & Balthazart, 1996). Previous lesion and hormone implant studies have implicated a sexually dimorphic nucleus in the preoptic region, the POM, as being necessary and sufficient for the activation of male-typical copulatory behavior (Balthazart & Surlemont, 1990; Balthazart, Surlemont, & Harada, 1992; Panzica et al., 1996). An analysis of the lesion sites within POM in relation to their effectiveness in knocking out different measures of appetitive and consummatory male sexual behaviors indicated that damage to the subdivision of the POM just rostral to the anterior commissure was the most effective in blocking copulatory behavior

(Balthazart, Absil, Gérard, Appeltants, & Ball, 1998). Lesions to the POM inhibited the learned social proximity response (Balthazart et al., 1998). These marked effects of POM lesions on this measure of appetitive sexual behavior are somewhat surprising given suggestions in rodent species that the preoptic region is preferentially involved in the activation of copulatory performance and plays little or not role in anticipatory, motivational, or arousal aspects of male sexual behavior (Everitt, 1995; Liu, Salamone, & Sachs, 1997). Although the completeness of this dissociation between the preoptic region and the regulation of appetitive sexual behavior is probably an oversimplification (Baum, 1995; E. M. Hull, 1995; E. M. Hull, Du, Lorrain, & Matuszewich, 1997), these data do suggest that the involvement of the preoptic regions in both appetitive sexual behavior and consummatory sexual behavior may represent a significant difference in the regulation of male reproductive behavior in quail as compared to rodents and other mammalian species.

However, there is clear evidence of a dissociation in the brain areas regulating these two aspects of male behavior. In the case of the present study we have obtained the best evidence for a dissociation by investigating the significance of different subregions within the POM. Cells within the second and third rostro-caudal subdivisions of the POM seem to be particularly important for the control of appetitive aspects of male sexual behavior. At present, there is no obvious reason why this cell group would be preferentially important in the control of appetitive sexual behavior in male quail. Chemical neuroanatomical studies have not revealed any markers associated with neurotransmitter function that are enriched (or present at low levels) in this region as compared to adjacent parts of the POM (Panzica et al., 1996). Studies of cell activation involving the induction of immediate early genes or the measurement of 2-DG incorporation have not revealed precise subdivisions of the POM that correspond to the areas identified based on these lesions (Meddle et al., 1997). However, *fos* induction was higher in the caudal portion of the POM as compared to rostral portion in association with the occurrence of consummatory sexual behavior. Tract-tracing studies completed to date have not identified specificity in the connectivity of subregions of the POM, but these studies have not been designed to address this question properly. Future studies of variation in the hodological properties of these subregions of the POM are an obvious candidate for further investigation.

CONCLUDING COMMENTS

Overall, the study of animal learning is a much healthier enterprise due to the interactions among ethologists, psychologists, and neurobiologists. It is true that psychologists have often seemed to conceive of learning as a general process or mechanism that evolved early and that has been conserved throughout subsequent evolutionary adaptation. By contrast, ethologists have generally favored the stance that learning reflects niche-specific adaptation to a multitude of problems of survival. Animals did not evolve a single, stand-alone learning process, but rather domain- and task-specific learning embedded within individual adaptive behavioral systems, so there should be a multiplicity of learning rules, each tailored to a particular task or problem.

There is no single resolution of these conflicting views. In some sense both are nearly self-evident. After all, most animals are faced with the same basic problems of space and time, and most possess the same cellular and molecular machinery that make plasticity possible, so some basic laws of association might be quite general (e.g., Anokhin, 1974). Despite early claims for the demise of the idea of general learning processes (Seligman, 1970), it is fair to say that many basic learning phenomena are observed across a wide range of behavioral systems, both in the laboratory and in the field, often applying even in cases of relatively specialized learning. Likewise, at some level, learned behavior reflects the action of behavioral systems that evolved because they served an important function in the natural history of the species. Appreciation for the constraints on those systems in the animal's natural environment is indispensable for understanding learning in more contrived, but often more tractable, laboratory situations.

Despite the central role played by evolution in ethology, we have said very little about questions of the evolution of learning and behavior. A comprehensive theory about the evolution of learning remains elusive. Valuable contributions to an evolutionary theory of learning have been made in recent decades (e.g., Alexander, 1990; Tierney, 1986). However, one of the major challenges that remains a roadblock to a comprehensive theory is that we still do not understand well the costs and benefits of learning in terms of reproductive fitness (Johnston, 1981, 1982). What is clear, as discussed earlier, is that one cannot assume that organizing the development or maintenance of a behavioral trait based on learning will always be beneficial. Mistakes can be made in any system requiring learning, which can have potentially disastrous consequences. What is more difficult to measure is the possibility that learning systems require a more complex and therefore costly brain or genome (Johnston, 1982). Speculations of this sort have been around for years, but there is still no rigorous metric by which to ascertain these potential costs.

Although a true synthesis of the approaches of experimental psychology and ethology may still elude us, the two fields have had mutually beneficial influences on one another. The importance of ecological validity is now generally recognized by experimental psychologists investigating learning processes in animals. Similarly, the value of a detailed experimental analysis of a learning process in a relatively artificial situation is now clearly appreciated by ethologists and behavioral ecologists. Finally, the shared methods, questions, and orientations of neuroscience increasingly pervade the study of both ethology and experimental psychology. This multidisciplinary synergy bodes well for the future of the study of animal learning.

REFERENCES

Adret, P. (1993). Vocal learning induced with operant techniques: An overview. *Netherlands Journal of Zoology, 43,* 125–142.

Akins, C. K., Domjan, M., & Gutierrez, G. (1994). Topography of sexually conditioned behavior in male Japanese-quail (*coturnix-japonica*) depends on the CS-US interval. *Journal of Experimental Psychology: Animal Behavior Processes, 20,* 199–209.

Alexander, R. D. (1990). Epigenetic rules and Darwinian algorithms: The adaptive study of learning and development. *Ethology and Sociobiology, 11,* 241–303.

Alkon, D. L. (1983). Learning in a marine snail. *Scientific American, 249,* 64–74.

Anokhin, P. K. (1974). *Biology and neurophysiology of the conditional reflex and its role in adaptive behavior.* New York: Pergamon Press.

Appeltants, D., Absil, P., Balthazart, J., & Ball, G. F. (2000). Identification of the origin of catecholaminergic inputs to HVc in canaries by retrograde tract tracing combined with tyrosine hydroxylase immunocytochemistry. *Journal of Chemical Neurochemistry, 18,* 117–133.

Ball, G. F. (1994). Neurochemical specializations associated with vocal learning and production in songbirds and budgerigars. *Brain, Behavior, and Evolution, 44,* 234–246.

Ball, G. F., & Hulse, S. H. (1998). Bird song. *American Psychologist, 53,* 37–58.

Balthazart, J. (1989). Steroid metabolism and the activation of social behavior. In J. Balthazart (Ed.), *Advances in comparative and environmental physiology* (Vol. 3, pp. 105–159). Berlin: Springer-Verlag.

Balthazart, J., Absil, P., Gérard, M., Appeltants, D., & Ball, G. F. (1998). Appetitive and consummatory male sexual behavior in Japanese quail are differentially regulated by subregions of the preoptic medial nucleus. *Journal of Neuroscience, 18,* 6512–6527.

Balthazart, J., & Ball, G. F. (1995). Sexual differentiation of brain and behavior in birds. *Trends in Endocrinology and Metabolism, 6,* 21–29.

Balthazart, J., & Ball, G. F. (1998). The Japanese quail as a model system for the investigation of steroid-catecholamine interactions

mediating appetitive and consummatory aspects of male sexual behavior. *Annual Review of Sex Research, 9,* 96–176.

Balthazart, J., De Clerck, A., & Foidart, A. (1992). Behavioral demasculinization of female quail is induced by estrogens: Studies with the new aromatase inhibitor, R76713. *Hormones and Behavior, 26,* 179–203.

Balthazart, J., Reid, J., Absil, P., Foidart, A., & Ball, G. F. (1995). Appetitive as well as consummatory aspects of male sexual behavior in quail are activated by androgens and estrogens. *Behavioral Neuroscience, 109,* 485–501.

Balthazart, J., & Surlemont, C. (1990). Androgen and estrogen action in the preoptic area and activation of copulatory behavior in quail. *Physiology and Behavior, 48,* 599–609.

Balthazart, J., Surlemont, C., & Harada, N. (1992). Aromatase as a cellular marker of testosterone action in the preoptic area. *Physiology and Behavior, 51,* 395–409.

Baptista, L. F. (1996). Nature and nurturing in avian vocal development. In D. E. Kroodsma & E. H. Miller (Eds.), *Ecology and evolution of acoustic communication in birds* (pp. 39–60). Ithaca, NY: Cornell University Press.

Baptista, L. F., & Gaunt, S. L. L. (1997). Social interactions and vocal development in birds. In C. T. Snowdon & M. Hausberger (Eds.), *Social influences on vocal development* (pp. 23–40). Cambridge, UK: Cambridge University Press.

Baptista, L. F., & Petrinovich, L. (1984). Social interactions, sensitive phases and the song template hypothesis in the white-crowned sparrow. *Animal Behaviour, 32,* 172–181.

Baptista, L. F., & Schuchmann, K. L. (1990). Song learning in the anna hummingbird. *Ethology, 84,* 15–26.

Barker, L. M., & Smith, J. C. (1974). A comparison of taste aversions induced by radiation and lithium chloride in CS-US and US-CS paradigms. *Journal of Comparative and Physiological Psychology, 87,* 644–654.

Bateson, P. P. G. (1966). The characteristics and context of imprinting. *Biological Reviews, 41,* 177–220.

Baum, M. J. (1995). Reassessing the role of medial preoptic area/anterior hypothalamic neurons in appetitive aspects of masculine sexual behavior. In J. Bancroft (Ed.), *The pharmacology of sexual function and dysfunction* (pp. 133–139). Amsterdam: Elsevier Science.

Baxter, M. G., Bucci, D. J., Holland, P. C., & Gallagher, M. (1999). Impairments in conditioned stimulus processing after combined selective removal of hippocampal and cortical cholinergic input. *Behavioral Neuroscience, 113,* 486–495.

Baxter, M. G., Gallagher, M., & Holland, P. C. (1999). Blocking can occur without losses in attention in rats with selective removal of hippocampal cholinergic input. *Behavioral Neuroscience, 113,* 881–890.

Baxter, M. G., Holland, P. C., & Gallagher, M. (1997). Disruption of attentional processing by selective removal of hippocampal cholinergic input. *Journal of Neuroscience, 17,* 5230–5236.

Baxter, M. G., Parker, A., Lindner, C. C. C., Izquierdo, A. D., & Murray, E. A. (2000). Control of response selection by reinforcer value requires interaction of amygdala and orbital prefrontal cortex. *Journal of Neuroscience, 20,* 4311–4319.

Beer, C. G. (1963). Ethology: The zoologists' approach to behavior. *Tuatara, 11,* 170–177.

Beer, C. G. (1975). Was professor Lehrman an ethologist? *Animal Behaviour, 23,* 957–964.

Benton, S., Nelson, D. A., Marler, P., & DeVoogd, T. J. (1998). Anterior forebrain pathway is needed for stable song expression in adult male white-crowned sparrows (*Zonotrichia leucophrys*). *Behavioral Brain Research, 96,* 135–150.

Bliss, T. V. P., & Collingridge, G. L. (1993). A synaptic model of memory: Long-term potentation in the hippocampus. *Nature, 361,* 31–39.

Boice, R., & Denny, M. R. (1965). The conditioned licking response in rats as a function of the CS-UCS interval. *Psychonomic Science, 3,* 93–94.

Bolhuis, J. J. (1991). Mechanisms of avian imprinting: A review. *Biological Reviews of the Cambridge Philosophical Society, 66,* 303–345.

Bonardi, C. (1998). Conditional learning: An associative analysis. In N. A. Schmajuk & P. C. Holland (Eds.), *Occasion setting: Associative learning and cognition in animals* (pp. 37–67). Washington, DC: American Psychological Association.

Bottjer, S. W., Halsema, K. A., Brown, S. A., & Miesner, E. A. (1989). Axonal connections of a forebrain nucleus involved with vocal learning in zebra finches. *Journal of Comparative Neurology, 279,* 312–326.

Bottjer, S. W., Miesner, E. A., & Arnold, A. P. (1984). Forebrain lesions disrupt development but not maintenance of song in passerine birds. *Science, 224,* 901–903.

Boysson-Bardies, B. D., & Vihman, M. M. (1991). Adaptation to language: Evidence from babbling and first words in four languages. *Language, 67,* 297–319.

Brainard, M. S., & Doupe, A. J. (2000). Auditory feedback in learning and maintenance of vocal behaviour. *Nature Reviews Neuroscience, 1,* 31–40.

Brandon, S. E., & Wagner, A. R. (1998). Occasion setting: Influences of conditional emotional responses and configural cues. In N. A. Schmajuk & P. C. Holland (Eds.), *Occasion setting: Associative learning and cognition in animals* (pp. 343–382). Washington, DC: American Psychological Association.

Brenowitz, E. A. (1997). Comparative approaches to the avian song system. *Journal of Neurobiology, 33,* 517–531.

Brenowitz, E. A., Margoliash, D., & Nordeen, K. W. (1997). An introduction to birdsong and the avian song system. *Journal of Neurobiology, 33,* 495–500.

Brown, T. H., Kairiss, E. W., & Keenan, C. L. (1990). Hebbian synapses: Biophysical mechanisms and algorithms. *Annual Review of Neuroscience, 13,* 475–511.

Bucci, D. J., Holland, P. C., & Gallagher, P. C. (1998). Removal of cholinergic input to rat posterior parietal cortex disrupts incremental processing of conditioned stimuli. *Journal of Neuroscience, 18,* 8038–8046.

Catchpole, C. K., & Slater, P. J. B. (1995). *Bird song: Biological themes and variations.* New York: Cambridge University Press.

Chaiken, M., Böhner, J., & Marler, P. (1993). Song acquisition in European starlings, *Sturnus vulgaris:* A comparison of the songs of live-tutored, tape-tutored, untutored, and wild-caught males. *Animal Behaviour, 46,* 1079–1090.

Chomsky, N. (1965). *Aspects of a theory of syntax.* Cambridge, MA: MIT Press.

Chomsky, N. (1980). *Rules and representations.* New York: Columbia University Press.

Clayton, D. F. (1997). Role of gene regulation in song circuit development and song learning. *Journal of Neurobiology, 33,* 549–571.

Clayton, N. S., & Soha, J. A. (1999). Memory in avian food caching and song learning: A general mechanism or different processes. *Advances in the Study of Behavior, 28,* 115–173.

Coldwell, S. E., & Tordoff, M. G. (1993). Learned preferences for the flavor of salted food. *Physiology and Behavior, 54,* 999–1004.

Colwill, R. M., & Motzkin, D. K. (1994). Encoding of the unconditioned stimulus in Pavlovian conditioning. *Animal Learning and Behavior, 22,* 384–394.

Colwill, R. M., & Rescorla, R. A. (1985). Post-conditioning devaluation of a reinforcer affects instrumental responding. *Journal of Experimental Psychology: Animal Behavior Processes, 11,* 120–132.

Constantine-Paton, M., Cline, H. T., & Debskie, E. (1990). Patterned activity, synaptic convergence and the NMDA receptor in developing visual pathways. *Annual Review of Neuroscience, 13,* 129–154.

Craig, W. (1918). Appetites and aversions as constituents of instincts. *Biological Bulletin, 34,* 91–107.

Crawford, L. L., Akins, C. K., & Domjan, M. (1994). Stimulus control of copulatory behavior in sexually naive male Japanese quail (*coturnix japonica*): Effects of test context and stimulus movement. *Journal of Comparative Psychology, 108,* 252–261.

Crawford, L. L., & Domjan, M. (1995). 2nd-order sexual conditioning in male Japanese quail (*coturnix japonica*). *Animal Learning and Behavior, 23,* 327–334.

Crawford, L. L., & Domjan, M. (1996). Conditioned inhibition of social approach in male Japanese quail (*Coturnix japonica*) using visual exposure to a female. *Behavioural Processes, 36,* 163–169.

Crawford, L. L., Holloway, K. S., & Domjan, M. (1993). The nature of sexual reinforcement. *Journal of the Experimental Analysis of Behavior, 60,* 55–66.

Cusato, B., & Domjan, M. (2000). Facilitation of appetitive conditioning with naturalistic conditioned stimuli: CS and US factors. *Animal Learning and Behavior, 28,* 247–256.

Dave, A. S., Yu, A. C., & Margoliash, D. (1998). Behavioral state modulation of auditory activity in a vocal motor system. *Science, 282,* 2250–2254.

Davidson, T. L. (1993). The nature and function of interoceptive signals to feed: Toward an integration of physiological and learning perspectives. *Psychological Review, 100,* 640–657.

Dickinson, A. (1980). *Contemporary animal learning theory.* London: Cambridge University Press.

Dickinson, A., & Mackintosh, N. J. (1978). Classical conditioning in animals. *Annual Review of Psychology, 29,* 587–612.

Dickinson, A., Smith, J., & Mirenowicz, J. (2000). Dissociation of Pavlovian and instrumental incentive learning under dopamine antagonists. *Behavioral Neuroscience, 114,* 468–483.

Domjan, M. (1987). Photoperiodic and endocrine control of social proximity behavior in male Japanese quail (*Coturnix coturnix japonica*). *Behavioral Neuroscience, 101,* 385–392.

Domjan, M. (1994). Formulation of a behavior system for sexual conditioning. *Psychonomic Bulletin and Review, 4,* 421–428.

Domjan, M., Akins, C., & Vandergriff, D. H. (1992). Increased responding to female stimuli as a result of sexual experience: Tests of mechanisms of learning. *Quarterly Journal of Experimental Psychology, 45B,* 139–157.

Domjan, M., Blesbois, E., & Williams, J. (1998). The adaptive significance of sexual conditioning: Pavlovian control of sperm release. *Psychological Science, 9*(5), 411–415.

Domjan, M., Greene, P., & North, N. C. (1989). Contextual conditioning and the control of copulatory behavior by species-specific stimuli in male Japanese quail. *Journal of Experimental Psychology: Animal Behavior Processes, 15,* 147–153.

Domjan, M., & Hall, S. (1986a). Determinants of social proximity in Japanese quail (*Coturnix coturnix japonica*): Male behavior. *Journal of Comparative Psychology, 100,* 59–67.

Domjan, M., & Hall, S. (1986b). Sexual dimorphism in the social proximity behavior of Japanese quail (*Coturnix coturnix japonica*). *Journal of Comparative Psychology, 100,* 68–71.

Domjan, M., & Hollis, K. L. (1988). Reproductive behavior: A potential model system for adaptive specializations in learning. In R. C. Bolles & M. D. beecher (Eds.), *Evolution and learning* (pp. 213–237). Hillsdale, NJ: Erlbaum.

Domjan, M., Lyons, R., North, N. C., & Bruell, J. (1986). Sexual Pavlovian conditioned approach behavior in male Japanese quail (*Coturnix coturnix japonica*). *Journal of Comparative Psychology, 100,* 413–421.

Domjan, M., O'Nary, D., & Greene, P. (1988). Conditioning of appetitive and consummatory sexual behavior in male Japanese quail. *Journal of the Experimental Analysis of Behavior, 50,* 505–519.

Domjan, M., & Wilson, N. E. (1972). Specificity of cue to consequence in aversion learning in the rat. *Psychonomic Science, 26,* 143–145.

Elman, J. L., Bates, E. A., Johnson, M. H., Karmiloff-Smith, A., Parisi, D., & Plunkett, K. (1996). *Rethinking innateness.* Cambridge, MA: MIT Press.

Everitt, B. J. (1995). Neuroendocrine mechanisms underlying appetitive and consummatory elements of masculine sexual behavior. In J. Bancroft (Ed.), *The pharmacology of sexual function and dysfunction* (pp. 15–31). Amsterdam: Elsevier.

Everitt, B. J., & Robbins, T. W. (1992). Amygdala-ventral striatal interactions and reward-related processes. In J. Aggleton (Ed.), *The Amygdala: Neurological aspects of emotion, memory, and mental dysfunction* (pp. 401–429). Chichester, UK: Wiley.

Fanselow, M. S. (1994). Neural organization of the defensive behavior system responsible for fear. *Psychonomic Bulletin and Review, 4,* 429–438.

Fanselow, M. S., & Lester, L. S. (1985). A functional behavioristic approach to aversively motivated behavior: Predatory imminence as a determinant of the topography of defensive behavior. In R. C. Bolles & M. D. Beecher (Eds.), *Evolution and learning* (pp. 185–212). Hillsdale, NJ: Erlbaum.

Farabaugh, S. M., & Dooling, R. J. (1996). Acoustic communication in parrots: Laboratory and field studies of budgerigars, *Melopsittacus undulatus.* In D. E. Kroodsma & E. H. Miller (Eds.), *Ecology and evolution of acoustic communication in birds* (pp. 97–118). Ithaca, NY: Cornell University Press.

Fodor, J. (1983). *The modularity of mind.* Cambridge, MA: MIT Press.

Foidart, A., & Balthazart, J. (1995). Sexual differentiation of brain and behavior in quail and zebra finches: Studies with a new aromatase inhibitor, R76713. *Journal of Steroid and Biochemical Molecular Biology, 53,* 267–275.

Fortune, E. S., & Margoliash, D. (1995). Parallel pathways and convergence onto HVc and adjacent neostriatum of adult zebra finches (*Taeniopygia guttata*). *Journal of Comparative Neurology, 360,* 413–441.

Gallagher, M., Graham, P. W., & Holland, P. C. (1990). The amygdala central nucleus and appetitive Pavlovian conditioning: Lesions impair one class of conditioned performance. *Journal of Neuroscience, 10,* 1906–1911.

Gallagher, M., & Holland, P. (1992). Understanding the function of the central nucleus: Is simple conditioning enough? In J. P. Aggleton (Ed.), *The amygdala: Neurobiological aspects of emotion, memory, and mental dysfunction* (pp. 307–321). New York: Wiley-Liss.

Gallagher, M., McMahan, R. W., & Schoenbaum, G. (1999). Orbitofrontal cortex and representation of incentive value in associative learning. *Journal of Neuroscience, 19,* 6610–6614.

Gallistel, C. R., & Gibbon, J. (2000). Time, rate, and conditioning. *Psychological Review, 107,* 289–344.

Garcia, J., Ervin, F. R., & Koelling, R. A. (1966). Learning with prolonged delay of reinforcement. *Psychonomic Science, 5,* 121–122.

Garcia, J., & Koelling, R. A. (1966). Relation of cue to consequence in avoidance learning. *Psychonomic Science, 4,* 123–124.

Garcia, J., Lasiter, P. S., Bermudez-Rattoni, F., & Deems, D. A. (1985). A general theory of aversion learning. *Annals of the New York Academy of Sciences, 443,* 8–21.

Gibbon, J. (1977). Scalar expectancy theory and Weber's law in animal timing. *Psychological Review, 84,* 279–325.

Gibbon, J., Baldock, M. D., Locurto, C. M., Gold, L., & Terrace, H. S. (1977). Trial and intertrial durations in autoshaping. *Journal of Experimental Psychology: Animal Behavior Processes, 3,* 264–284.

Gibbon, J., & Church, R. M. (1990). Representation of time. *Cognition, 37,* 23–54.

Gormezano, I., & Moore, J. W. (1969). Classical conditioning. In M. H. Marx (Ed.), *Learning: Processes* (pp. 121–203). London: MacMillan.

Gould, J. L. (1982). *Ethology: The mechanisms and evolution of behavior.* New York: W. W. Norton.

Hall, G. (1996). Learning about associatively-activated stimulus representations: Implications for acquired equivalence and perceptual learning. *Animal Learning and Behavior, 24,* 233–255.

Hall, G., & Mondragon, E. (1998). Contextual control as occasion setting. In N. A. Schmajuk & P. C. Holland (Eds.), *Occasion setting: Associative learning and cognition in animals* (pp. 199–222). Washington, DC: American Psychological Association.

Hall, J., Parkinson, J. A., Connor, T. M., Dickinson, A., & Everitt, B. J. (2001). Involvement of the central nucleus of the amygdala and nucleus accumbens core in mediating Pavlovian influences on instrumental behavior. *European Journal of Neuroscience, 13,* 1984–1992.

Han, J.-S., Gallagher, M., & Holland, P. C. (1995). Hippocampal lesions disrupt decrements but not increments in conditioned stimulus processing. *Journal of Neuroscience, 11,* 7323–7329.

Han, J.-S., Holland, P. C., & Gallagher, M. (1999). Disconnection of amygdala central nucleus and substantia innominata/nucleus basalis disrupts increments in conditioned stimulus processing. *Behavioral Neuroscience, 113,* 143–151.

Han, J.-S., McMahan, R. W., Holland, P. C., & Gallagher, M. (1997). The role of an amygdalo-nigrostriatal pathway in associative learning. *Journal of Neuroscience, 17,* 3913–3919.

Hatfield, T., Han, J.-S., Conley, M., Gallagher, M., & Holland, P. (1996). Neurotoxic lesions of the basolateral, but not central, amygdala interfere with Pavlovian second-order conditioning and reinforcer-devaluation effects. *Journal of Neuroscience, 16,* 5256–5265.

Hawkins, R. D., & Kandel, E. R. (1984). Is there a cell-biological alphabet for simple forms of learning? *Psychological Review, 91,* 375–391.

Hess, E. H. (1973). *Imprinting.* New York: Van Nostrand.

Higa, J. J. (1998). Interval timing: Is there a clock? *Behavioural Processes, 44,* 87–88.

Hilgard, E. R., & Bower, G. H. (1975). *Theories of learning* (4th ed.). Englewood Cliffs, NJ: Prentice Hall.

Hilliard, S., & Domjan, M. (1995). Effects on sexual conditioning of devaluing the US through satiation. *Quarterly Journal of Experimental Psychology, 48B,* 84–92.

Hinde, R. A. (1953). Appetitive behaviour, consummatory act, and the hierarchical organization of behaviour—with special reference to the great tit (*Parus major*). *Behaviour, 5,* 189–224.

Hinde, R. A. (1960). Energy models of motivation. *Symposia of the Society of Experimental Biology, 14,* 199–213.

Hinde, R. A. (1970). *Animal behaviour* (2nd ed.). New York: McGraw-Hill.

Hinde, R. A. (1982). *Ethology: Its nature and relations with other sciences.* New York: Oxford University Press.

Hodos, W., & Campbell, C. B. G. (1969). Scala Naturae: Why there is no theory in comparative psychology. *Psychological Review, 76,* 337–350.

Hoffman, H. S., & Ratner, A. M. (1973). A reinforcement model of imprinting: Implications for socialization in monkeys and men. *Psychological Review, 80,* 527–544.

Holland, P. C. (1977). Conditioned stimulus as a determinant of the form of the Pavlovian conditioned response. *Journal of Experimental Psychology: Animal Behavior Processes, 3,* 77–104.

Holland, P. C. (1979). The effects of qualitative and quantitative variation in the US on individual components of Pavlovian appetitive conditioned behavior in rats. *Animal Learning and Behavior, 7,* 424–432.

Holland, P. C. (1980a). CS-US interval as a determinant of the form of Pavlovian appetitive conditioned responses. *Journal of Experimental Psychology: Animal Behavior Processes, 6,* 155–174.

Holland, P. C. (1980b). Influence of visual conditioned stimulus characteristics on the form of Pavlovian appetitive conditioned responding in rats. *Journal of Experimental Psychology: Animal Behavior Processes, 6,* 81–97.

Holland, P. C. (1981a). Acquisition of representation-mediated conditioned food aversions. *Learning and Motivation, 12,* 1–18.

Holland, P. C. (1981b). The effects of satiation after first- and second-order appetitive conditioning. *Pavlovian Journal of Biological Science, 16,* 18–24.

Holland, P. C. (1983a). Occasion-setting in Pavlovian feature positive discriminations. In M. L. Commons, R. J. Herrnstein, & A. R. Wagner (Eds.), *Quantitative analyses of behavior: Discrimination processes* (Vol. 4, pp. 183–206). New York: Ballinger.

Holland, P. C. (1983b). Representation-mediated overshadowing and potentiation of conditioned aversions. *Journal of Experimental Psychology: Animal Behavior Processes, 9,* 1–13.

Holland, P. C. (1984a). Differential effects of reinforcement of an inhibitory feature after serial and simultaneous feature negative discrimination training. *Journal of Experimental Psychology: Animal Behavior Processes, 10,* 461–475.

Holland, P. C. (1984b). The origins of Pavlovian conditioned behavior. In G. Bower (Ed.), *The psychology of learning and motivation* (Vol. 18, pp. 129–173). Englewood Cliffs, NJ: Prentice Hall.

Holland, P. C. (1985). Element pretraining influences the content of appetitive serial compound conditioning in rats. *Journal of Experimental Psychology: Animal Behavior Processes, 11,* 367–387.

Holland, P. C. (1988). Excitation and inhibition in unblocking. *Journal of Experimental Psychology: Animal Behavior Processes, 14,* 261–279.

Holland, P. C. (1990a). Event representation in Pavlovian conditioning: Image and action. *Cognition, 37,* 105–131.

Holland, P. C. (1990b). Forms of memory in Pavlovian conditioning. In J. L. McGaugh, N. M. Weinberger, & G. Lynch, (Eds.), *Brain organization and memory: Cells, systems, and circuits* (pp. 78–105). New York: Oxford University Press.

Holland, P. C. (1991). Learning, thirst, and drinking. In D. A. Booth & D. J. Ramsay (Eds.), *Thirst: Physiological and psychological aspects* (pp. 278–294). Berlin: Springer-Verlag.

Holland, P. C. (1992). Occasion setting in Pavlovian conditioning. In D. Medin (Ed.), *The psychology of learning and motivation* (Vol. 28, pp. 69–125). San Diego, CA: Academic Press.

Holland, P. C. (1999). Overshadowing and blocking as acquisition deficits: No recovery after extinction of overshadowing or blocking cues. *Quarterly Journal of Experimental Psychology, 52B,* 307–333.

Holland, P. C. (2000). Trial and intertrial durations in appetitive conditioning in rats. *Animal Learning and Behavior, 28,* 121–135.

Holland, P. C., & Block, H. (1983). Evidence for a unique cue in positive patterning. *Bulletin of the Psychonomic Society, 21,* 297–300.

Holland, P. C., & Bouton, M. E. (1999). Hippocampus and context in classical conditioning. *Current Opinion in Neurobiology, 9,* 195–202.

Holland, P. C., Chik, Y., & Zhang, Q. (2001). Inhibitory learning tests of conditioned stimulus associability in rats with lesions of the amygdala central nucleus. *Behavioral Neuroscience, 115,* 1154–1158.

Holland, P. C., & Forbes, D. T. (1982a). Control of conditional discrimination performance by CS-evoked event representations. *Animal Learning and Behavior, 10,* 249–256.

Holland, P. C., & Forbes, D. T. (1982b). Representation-mediated extinction of flavor aversions. *Learning and Motivation, 13,* 454–471.

Holland, P. C., & Gallagher, M. (1993a). Amygdala central nucleus lesions disrupt increments, but not decrements, in CS processing. *Behavioral Neuroscience, 107,* 246–253.

Holland, P. C., & Gallagher, M. (1993b). Effects of amygdala central nucleus lesions on blocking and unblocking. *Behavioral Neuroscience, 107,* 235–245.

Holland, P. C., & Gallagher, M. (1999). Amygdala circuitry in attentional and representational processes. *Trends in Cognitive Sciences, 3,* 65–73.

Holland, P. C., Hatfield, T., & Gallagher, M. (2001). Rats with lesions of basolateral amygdala show normal increases in conditioned stimulus processing but reduced conditioned potentiation of eating. *Behavioral Neuroscience, 115,* 945–950.

Holland, P. C., & Rescorla, R. A. (1975). The effect of two ways of devaluing the unconditioned stimulus after first- and second-order appetitive conditioning. *Journal of Experimental Psychology: Animal Behavior Processes, 1,* 355–363.

Holland, P. C., & Ross, R. T. (1981). Within-compound associations in serial compound conditioning. *Journal of Experimental Psychology: Animal Behavior Processes, 7,* 228–241.

Holland, P. C., & Straub, J. J. (1979). Differential effects of two ways of devaluing the unconditioned stimulus after Pavlovian appetitive conditioning. *Journal of Experimental Psychology: Animal Behavior Processes, 5,* 65–78.

Holland, P. C., Thornton, J. A., & Ciali, L. (2000). The influence of associability changes in negative patterning and other discriminations. *Journal of Experimental Psychology: Animal Behavior Processes, 26,* 462–476.

Holloway, K. S., & Domjan, M. (1993). Sexual approach conditioning: Tests of unconditioned stimulus devaluation using hormone manipulations. *Journal of Experimental Psychology: Animal Behavior Processes, 19,* 47–55.

Hull, C. L. (1943). *Principles of behavior.* New York: Appleton-Century-Crofts.

Hull, E. M. (1995). Dopaminergic influences on male rat sexual behavior. In P. E. Micevych & R. P. J. Hammer (Eds.), *Neurobiological effects of sex steroid hormones* (pp. 234–253). Cambridge, UK: Cambridge University Press.

Hull, E. M., Du, J. F., Lorrain, D. S., & Matuszewich, L. (1997). Testosterone, preoptic dopamine, and copulation in male rats. *Brain Research Bulletin, 44,* 327–333.

Hultsch, H., & Todt, D. (1989). Memorization and reproduction of songs in nightingales (*Luscinia megarynchos*): Evidence for package formation. *Journal of Comparative Physiology, 165A,* 197–203.

Immelmann, K., & Beer, C. G. (1989). *A dictionary of ethology.* Cambridge, MA: Harvard University Press.

Jarvis, E. D., Scharff, C., Grossman, M. R., Ramos, J. A., & Nottebohm, F. (1998). For whom the bird sings: context-dependent gene expression. *Neuron, 21,* 775–788.

Johnston, T. D. (1981). Contrasting approaches to a theory of learning. *Behavioral and Brain Sciences, 4,* 125–138.

Johnston, T. D. (1982). Selective costs and benefits in the evolution of learning. *Advances in the Study of Behavior, 12,* 65–106.

Jusczyk, P. W. (1997). *The discovery of spoken language.* Cambridge, MA: MIT Press.

Kacelnik, A., & Bateson, M. (1997). Risk sensitivity: Cross-roads for theories of decision making. *Trends in Cognitive Sciences, 1,* 304–309.

Kacelink, A., & Krebs, J. R. (1997). Yanomamo dreams and starling payloads: The logic of optimality. In L. Betzig (Ed.), *Human nature* (pp. 21–35). New York: Oxford University Press.

Kamin, L. J. (1968). Attention-like processes in classical conditioning. In M. R. Jones (Ed.), *Miami Symposium on the Prediction of Behavior: Aversive Stimulation* (pp. 9–32). Coral Gables, FL: University of Miami Press.

Kandel, E. R. (1976). *Cellular basis of behavior.* San Francisco: W. H. Freeman.

Kelley, D. B., & Nottebohm, F. (1979). Projections of a telencephalic auditory nucleus-field L-in the canary. *Journal of Comparative Neurology, 183,* 455–470.

Kendler, H. (1946). The influence of simultaneous hunger and thirst drives upon the learning of two opposed spatial responses of the white rat. *Journal of Experimental Psychology, 36,* 212–220.

Koksal, F., Domjan, M., & Weisman, G. (1994). Blocking of the sexual conditioning of differentially effective conditioned stimulus objects. *Animal Learning and Behavior, 22,* 103–111.

Konishi, M. (1965). The role of auditory feedback in the control of vocalization in the white-crowned sparrow. *Zeitschrift für Tierpsychologie, 22,* 770–783.

Konishi, M. (1985). Birdsong: From behavior to neuron. *Annual Review of Neuroscience, 8,* 125–170.

Konishi, M. (1989). Birdsong for neurobiologists. *Neuron, 3,* 541–549.

Krane, R. V., & Wagner, A. R. (1975). Taste aversion learning with a delayed shock US: Implications for the "generality of the laws of learning." *Journal of Comparative Physiological Psychology, 88,* 882–889.

Kremer, E. (1978). The Rescorla-Wagner model: Losses in associative strength in compound conditioned stimuli. *Journal of Experimental Psychology: Animal Behavior Processes, 4,* 22–36.

Kroodsma, D. E. (1982). Learning and the ontogeny of sound signals in birds. In D. E. Kroodsma & E. H. Miller (Eds.), *Acoustic communication in birds* (Vol. 2, pp. 1–23). New York: Academic Press.

Kroodsma, D. E. (1988). Contrasting styles of song development and their consequences among passerine birds. In R. C. Bolles & M. D. Beecher (Eds.), *Evolution and learning* (pp. 157–184). Hillsdale, NJ: Erlbaum.

Kroodsma, D. E. (1996). Ecology of passerine song development. In D. E. Kroodsma & E. H. Miller (Eds.), *Ecology and evolution of acoustic communication in birds* (pp. 3–19). Ithaca, NY: Cornell University Press.

Kroodsma, D. E., & Baylis, J. R. (1982). Appendix: A world survey of evidence for vocal learning in birds. In D. E. Kroodsma & E. H. Miller (Eds.), *Acoustic communication in birds* (Vol. 2, pp. 311–337). New York: Academic Press.

Kroodsma, D., & Konishi, M. (1991). A suboscine bird (Eastern phoebe, Sayornis phoebe) develops normal song without auditory feedback. *Animal Behaviour, 42,* 477–487.

Lack, D. (1939). The behaviour of the robin: Pts. 1 and 2. *Proceedings of the Zoological Society of London, 109,* 169–178.

Lehrman, D. S. (1953). A critique of Konrad Lorenz's theory of instinctive behavior. *Quarterly Review of Biology, 28,* 337–363.

Lenneberg, E. (1967). *Biological foundations of language.* New York: Wiley.

Liu, Y. C., Salamone, J. D., & Sachs, B. D. (1997). Lesions in medial preoptic area and bed nucleus of stria terminalis: Differential effects on copulatory behavior and noncontact erection in male rats. *Journal of Neuroscience, 17,* 5245–5253.

Lorenz, K. (1950). The comparative method in studying innate behavior patterns. *Symposia of the Society for Experimental Biology, 4,* 221–268.

Lorenz, K. (1965). *Evolution and modification of behavior.* Chicago: University of Chicago Press.

Lorenz, K. (1981). *The foundations of ethology.* New York: Simon and Schuster.

Lovejoy, A. O. (1936). *The great chain of being.* Cambridge, MA: Harvard University Press.

Mackintosh, N. J. (1974). *The psychology of animal learning.* New York: Academic Press.

Mackintosh, N. J. (1975). A theory of attention: Variations in the associability of stimuli with reinforcement. *Psychological Review, 82,* 276–298.

Malkova, L., Gaffan, D., & Murray, E. A. (1997). Excitotoxic lesions of the amygdala fail to produce impairment in visual learning for auditory secondary reinforcement but interfere with reinforcer devaluation effects in rhesus monkeys. *Journal of Neuroscience, 17,* 6011–6020.

Manabe, K., & Dooling, R. J. (1997). Control of vocal production in budgerigars (*Melopsittacus undulatus*): Selective reinforcement, call differentiation, and stimulus control. *Behavioural Processes, 41,* 117–132.

Margoliash, D. (1997). Functional organization of forebrain pathways for song production and perception. *Journal of Neurobiology, 33,* 671–693.

Marler, P. R. (1952). Variations in the song of the chaffinch (*Fingilla coelebs*). *Ibis, 94,* 458–472.

Marler, P. R. (1961). The filtering of external stimuli during instinctive behavior. In W. H. Thorpe & O. L. Zangwill (Eds.), *Current problems in animal behavior* (pp. 150–166). Cambridge, UK: Cambridge University Press.

Marler, P. R. (1970). A comparative approach to vocal learning: Song development in white-crowned sparrows. *Journal of Comparative and Physiological Psychology, 71*(Suppl.), 1–25.

Marler, P. R. (1987). Sensitive periods and the roles of specific and general sensory stimulation in birdsong learning. In J. P. Rauschecker & P. Marler (Eds.), *Imprinting and cortical plasticity* (pp. 99–135). New York: Wiley.

Marler, P. R. (1991). Song-learning: The interface with neuroethology. *Trends in Neuroscience, 14,* 199–206.

Marler, P. R. (1997). Three models of song learning: Evidence from behavior. *Journal of Neurobiology, 33,* 501–516.

Marler, P. R., & Hamilton, W. J. I. (1966). *Mechanisms of animal behavior.* New York: Wiley.

Marler, P. R., & Nelson, D. A. (1992). Neuroselection and song learning in birds: Species universals in a culturally transmitted behavior. *Seminars in the Neurosciences, 4,* 415–423.

Marler, P. R., & Nelson, D. A. (1993). Action-based learning: A new form of developmental plasticity in bird song. *Netherlands Journal of Zoology, 43,* 91–103.

Marler, P. R., & Peters, S. (1982a). Developmental overproduction and selective attrition: New processes in the epigenesis of birdsong. *Developmental Psychobiology, 15,* 269–378.

Marler, P. R., & Peters, S. (1982b). Subsong and plastic song: Their role in the vocal learning process. In D. E. Kroodsma & E. H. Miller (Eds.), *Acoustic communication in birds* (Vol. 2, pp. 25–50). New York: Academic Press.

Marler, P. R., & Sherman, V. (1985). Innate differences in singing behavior of sparrows reared in isolation from adult conspecific song. *Animal Behaviour, 33,* 57–71.

Marler, P. R., & Tamura, M. (1964). Song "dialects" in three populations of white-crowned sparrows. *Science, 146,* 1483–1486.

Mayr, E. (1963). *Animal species and evolution.* Cambridge, MA: Belknap Press.

McCasland, J. S. (1987). Neuronal control of bird song production. *Journal of Neuroscience, 7,* 23–39.

Meck, W. H., & Church, R. M. (1982). Abstraction of temporal attributes. *Journal of Experimental Psychology: Animal Behavior Processes, 8,* 226–243.

Meddle, S. L., King, V. M., Follett, B. K., Wingfield, J. C., Ramenofsky, M., Foidart, A., & Balthazart, J. (1997). Copulation activates Fos-like immunoreactivity in the male quail forebrain. *Behavioral Brain Research, 85,* 143–159.

Meisel, R. L., & Sachs, B. D. (1994). The physiology of male sexual behavior. In E. Knobil & J. D. Neill (Eds.), *The physiology of reproduction* (2nd ed., Vol. 2, pp. 3–105). New York: Raven Press.

Mello, C., Vicario, D. S., & Clayton, D. F. (1992). Song presentation induces gene expression in the songbird forebrain. *Proceedings of the National Academy of Sciences, USA, 89,* 6818–6822.

Miller, R. R., & Barnet, R. C. (1993). The role of time in elementary associations. *Current Directions in Psychological Science, 2,* 106–111.

Miller, R. R., Barnet, R. C., & Grahame, N. J. (1995). Assessment of the Rescorla-Wagner Model. *Psychological Bulletin, 117,* 363–386.

Miller, R. R., McKinzie, D. L., Kraebel, K. S., & Spear, N. E. (1996). Changes in the expression of stimulus selection: Blocking represents selective memory retrieval rather than selective associations. *Learning and Motivation, 27,* 307–316.

Moss, C. F., & Shettleworth, S. J. (1996). *Neuroethological studies of cognitive and perceptual processes.* Boulder, CO: Westview Press.

Mowrer, O. H. (1947). On the dual nature of learning—a reinterpretation of conditioning and problem solving. *Harvard Educational Review, 17,* 102–148.

Myers, K. P., & Hall, W. G. (2000). Conditioned changes in appetitive and consummatory responses to flavors paired with oral or nutrient reinforcers among adult rats. *Physiology and Behavior, 68,* 603–610.

Nash, S., & Domjan, M. (1991). Learning to discriminate the sex of conspecifics in male japanese quail (*Coturnix coturnix japonica*): Tests of "biological constraints." *Journal of Experimental Psychology: Animal Behavior Processes, 17,* 342–353.

Nash, S., Domjan, M., & Askins, M. (1989). Sexual-discrimination learning in male Japanese quail (*Coturnix coturnix japonica*). *Journal of Comparative Psychology, 103,* 347–358.

Nelson, D. A. (1992). Song overproduction and selective attrition lead to song sharing in the field sparrow (*Spizella pusilla*). *Behavioral Ecology and Sociobiology, 30,* 415–424.

Nelson, D. A. (1997). Social interactions and sensitive phases for song learning: A critical review. In C. T. Snowdon & M. Hausberger (Eds.), *Social influences on vocal development* (pp. 7–22). Cambridge, UK: Cambridge University Press.

Newport, E. (1990). Maturational constraints on language learning. *Cognitive Science, 14,* 11–28.

Nordeen, K. W., & Nordeen, E. J. (1992). Auditory feedback is necessary for the maintenance of stereotyped song in adult zebra finches. *Behavioral and Neural Biology, 57,* 58–66.

Nordeen, K. W., & Nordeen, E. J. (1997). Anatomical and synaptic substrates for avian song learning. *Journal of Neurobiology, 33,* 532–548.

Nottebohm, F. (1980). Brain pathways for vocal learning in birds: A review of the first 10 years. In J. M. Sprague & A. N. Epstein (Eds.), *Progress in psychobiology and physiological psychology* (Vol. 9, pp. 85–214). New York: Academic Press.

Nottebohm, F. (1993). The search for neural mechanisms that define the sensitive period for song learning in birds. *Netherlands Journal of Zoology, 43,* 193–234.

Nottebohm, F. (1996). The King Solomon lectures in neuroethology: A white canary on Mount Acropolis. *Journal of Comparative Physiology, 179A,* 149–156.

Nottebohm, F., Alvarez-Buylla, A., Cynx, J., Kirn, J., Ling, C. Y., Nottebohm, M., Suter, R., Tolles, A., & Williams, H. (1990). Song learning in birds: The relation between perception and production. *Philosophical Transactions of the Royal Society of London, 329B,* 115–124.

Nottebohm, F., Kelley, D. B., & Paton, J. A. (1982). Connections of vocal control nuclei in the canary telencephalon. *Journal of Comparative Neurology, 207,* 344–357.

Nottebohm, F., Stokes, T. M., & Leonard, C. M. (1976). Central control of song in the canary, *Serinus canarius. Journal of Comparative Neurology, 165,* 457–486.

Nowicki, S., & Marler, P. R. (1988). How do birds sing? *Music Perception, 5,* 391–426.

Okuhata, S., & Saito, N. (1987). Synaptic connections of thalamo-cerebral vocal control nuclei of the canary. *Brain Research Bulletin, 18,* 35–44.

Panzica, G. C., Viglietti-Panzica, C., & Balthazart, J. (1996). The sexually dimorphic medial preoptic nucleus of quail: A key brain area mediating steroid action on male sexual behavior. *Frontiers in Neuroendocrinology, 17,* 51–125.

Pavlov, I. P. (1927). *Conditioned reflexes: An investigation of the physiological activity of the cerebral cortex* (G. V. Anrep, Trans.). London: Oxford University Press.

Pearce, J. M. (1987). A model for stimulus generalization in Pavlovian conditioning. *Psychological Review, 94*, 61–73.

Pearce, J. M. (1994). Similarity and discrimination: A selective review and a connectionist model. *Psychological Review, 101*, 587–607.

Pearce, J. M., Aydin, A., & Redhead, F. S. (1997). Configural analysis of summation in autoshaping. *Journal of Experimental Psychology: Animal Behavior Processes, 23*, 84–94.

Pearce, J. M., & Hall, G. (1980). A model for Pavlovian learning: Variations in the effectiveness of conditioned but not of unconditioned stimuli. *Psychological Review, 106*, 532–552.

Peters, S., Marler, P., & Nowicki, S. (1992). Song sparrows learn from limited exposure to song models. *Condor, 94*, 1016–1019.

Petrovich, G. D., Setlow, B., Holland, P. C., & Gallagher, M. (2001). Amygdalo-hypothalamic circuit is necessary for CS potentiation of feeding. *Society for Neuroscience Abstract, 422*, 14.

Pinker, S. (1994). *The language instinct*. New York: William Morrow.

Rescorla, R. A. (1967). Pavlovian conditioning and its proper control procedures. *Psychological Review, 74*, 71–80.

Rescorla, R. A. (1968). Probability of shock in the presence and absence of CS in fear conditioning. *Journal of Comparative and Physiological Psychology, 66*, 1–5.

Rescorla, R. A. (1969a). Conditioned inhibition of fear resulting from negative CS-US contingencies. *Journal of Comparative and Physiological Psychology, 67*, 504–509.

Rescorla, R. A. (1969b). Pavlovian conditioned inhibition. *Psychological Bulletin, 72*, 77–94.

Rescorla, R. A. (1970). Reduction in effectiveness of reinforcement after prior excitatory conditioning. *Learning and Motivation, 1*, 372–381.

Rescorla, R. A. (1972). "Configural" conditioning in discrete-trial bar pressing. *Journal of Comparative and Physiological Psychology, 79*, 307–317.

Rescorla, R. A. (1973a). Evidence for a "unique stimulus" account of configural conditioning. *Journal of Comparative and Physiological Psychology, 85*, 331–338.

Rescorla, R. A. (1973b). Informational variables in Pavlovian conditioning. In G. Bower (Ed.), *The psychology of learning and motivation* (Vol. 6, pp. 1–46). New York: Academic Press.

Rescorla, R. A. (1980). *Pavlovian second-order conditioning: Studies in associative learning*. Hillsdale, NJ: Erlbaum.

Rescorla, R. A. (1985). Conditioned inhibition and facilitation. In R. R. Miller & N. E. Spear (Eds.) *Information processing in animals: Conditioned inhibition* (pp. 299–326). Hillsdale, NJ: Erlbaum.

Rescorla, R. A. (1988a). Behavioral studies of Pavlovian conditioning. *Annual Review of Neuroscience, 11*, 329–352.

Rescorla, R. A. (1988b). Pavlovian conditioning: It's not what you think it is. *American Psychologist, 43*(3), 151–160.

Rescorla, R. A. (1991). Separate reinforcement can enhance the effectiveness of modulators. *Journal of Experimental Psychology: Animal Behavior Processes, 17*, 259–269.

Rescorla, R. A. (1993). Preservation of response-outcome associations through extinction. *Animal Learning and Behavior, 21*, 238–245.

Rescorla, R. A. (1997). Summation: Test of a configural theory. *Animal Learning and Behavior, 25*, 200–209.

Rescorla, R. A. (2000). Associative changes in excitors and inhibitors differ when they are conditioned in compound. *Journal of Experimental Psychology: Animal Behavior Processes, 26*, 428–438.

Rescorla, R. A., & Freberg, L. (1978). The extinction of within-compound flavor associations. *Learning and Motivation, 9*, 411–427.

Rescorla, R. A., & Furrow, D. R. (1977). Stimulus similarity as a determinant of Pavlovian conditioning. *Journal of Experimental Psychology: Animal Behavior Processes, 3*, 203–215.

Rescorla, R. A., & Holland, P. C. (1976). Some behavioral approaches to the study of learning. In E. Bennett & M. R. Rozensweig (Eds.), *Neural mechanisms of learning and memory* (pp. 165–192). Cambridge, MA: MIT Press.

Rescorla, R. A., & Holland, P. C. (1982). Behavioral studies of associative learning in animals. *Annual Review of Psychology, 33*, 265–308.

Rescorla, R. A., & Solomon, R. L. (1967). Two process learning theory: Relationships between classical conditioning and instrumental learning. *Psychological Review, 74*, 151–182.

Rescorla, R. A., & Wagner, A. R. (1972). A theory of Pavlovian conditioning: Variations in the effectiveness of reinforcement and nonreinforcement. In A. H. Black & W. F. Prokasy (Eds.), *Classical conditioning* (Vol. 2, pp. 64–99). New York: Appleton-Century-Crofts.

Rudy, J. W., & Sutherland, R. J. (1995). Configural association theory and the hippocampal formation: An appraisal and reconfiguration. *Hippocampus, 5*, 375–389.

Savastano, H. I., & Miller, R. R. (1998). Time as content in Pavlovian conditioning. *Behavioural Processes, 44*, 147–162.

Scharff, C., & Nottebohm, F. (1991). A comparative study of the behavioral deficits following lesions of various parts of the zebra finch song system: Implications for vocal learning. *Journal of Neuroscience, 11*, 2896–2913.

Schiller, C. H. (1957). *Instinctive behavior*. New York: International Universities Press.

Schmajuk, N. A., & DiCarlo, J. J. (1991). A neural network approach to hippocampal function in classical conditioning. *Behavioral Neuroscience, 105*, 82–110.

Schmajuk, N. A., & Holland, P. C. (1998). *Occasion setting: Associative learning and cognition in animals*. Washington, DC: American Psychological Association.

Schmajuk, N. A., Lamoureux, J. A., & Holland, P. C. (1998). Occasion setting: A neural network approach. *Psychological Review, 105,* 3–32.

Schmidt, M. F., & Konishi, M. (1998). Gating of auditory responses in the vocal control system of awake songbirds. *Nature Neuroscience, 1,* 513–518.

Schneirla, T. C. (1956). Interrelationships of the "innate" and the "acquired" in instinctive behavior. In P. Grasse (Ed.), *L'Instinct dans le compartement des animaux et de l'homme* (pp. 387–452). Paris: Masson.

Schoenbaum, G., Chiba, A. A., & Gallagher, M. (1998). Orbitofrontal cortex and basolateral amygdala encode expected outcomes during learning. *Nature Neuroscience, 1,* 155–159.

Searcy, W. A., & Andersson, M. (1986). Sexual selection and the evolution of song. *Annual Review of Ecology Systems, 17,* 507–533.

Sechenov, I. M. (1965). *Reflexes of the brain* (S. Belsky, Trans.). Cambridge, MA: MIT Press. (Original work published 1863).

Seligman, M. E. P. (1970). On the generality of the laws of learning. *Psychological Review, 77,* 406–418.

Seligman, M. E. P., Bravman, S., & Radford, R. (1970). Drinking: Discriminative conditioning in the rat. *Psychonomic Science, 20,* 63–64.

Setlow, B., Holland, P. C., & Gallagher, M. (2002). Disconnection of the basolateral amygdala complex and nucleus accumbens impairs appetitive second-order conditioned responses. *Behavioral Neuroscience, 116,* 267–275.

Sheffield, F. D. (1965). Relation between classical conditioning and instrumental learning. In W. F. Prokasy (Ed.), *Classical conditioning* (pp. 302–322). New York: Appleton-Century-Crofts.

Sheffield, F. D., & Campbell, B. A. (1954). The role of experience in the "spontaneous" activity of hungry rats. *Journal of Comparative and Physiological Psychology, 47,* 97–100.

Sheffield, F. D., & Roby, T. B. (1950). Reward value of a nonnutritive sweet taste. *Journal of Comparative and Physiological Psychology, 43,* 471–481.

Sherrington, C. S. (1906). *The integrative action of the nervous system.* London: A. Constable.

Shettleworth, S. J. (1998). *Cognition, evolution, and behavior.* New York: Oxford University Press.

Shettleworth, S. J., & Hampton, R. H. (1998). Adaptive specialization in food storing birds? Approaches to testing a comparative hypothesis. In I. Pepperberg, R. Balda, & A. Kamil (Eds.), *Animal cognition in nature* (pp. 65–98). San Diego, CA: Academic Press.

Silva, K. M., & Timberlake, W. (1998). The organization and temporal properties of appetitive behavior in rats. *Animal Learning and Behavior, 26,* 182–195.

Silva, K. M., & Timberlake, W. (2000). A clarification of the nature of backward excitatory conditioning. *Learning and Motivation, 31,* 67–80.

Skinner, B. F. (1957). *Verbal behavior.* New York: Appleton-Century-Crofts.

Skinner, D. M., Goddard, M. J., & Holland, P. C. (1998). What can nontraditional features tell us about conditioning and occasion setting? In N. A. Schmajuk & P. C. Holland (Eds.), *Occasion setting: Associative learning and cognition in animals* (pp. 113–144). Washington, DC: American Psychological Association.

Slater, P. J. B. (1989). Bird song learning: Causes and consequences. *Ethology, Ecology, and Evolution, 1,* 19–46.

Slater, P. J. B., Jones, A., & Ten Cate, C. (1993). Can lack of experience delay the end of the sensitive period for song learning? *Netherlands Journal of Zoology, 43,* 80–90.

Smith, M. C., Coleman, S. R., & Gormezano, I. (1969). Classical conditioning of the rabbit's nictitating membrane response at backward, simultaneous, and forward CS-US intervals. *Journal of Comparative and Physiological Psychology, 66,* 679–687.

Soha, J. A., & Marler, P. (2001). Vocal syntax development in the white-crowned sparrow (*Zonotrichia leucophrys*). *Journal of Comparative Psychology, 115,* 172–180.

Solis, M. M., & Doupe, A. J. (1997). Anterior forebrain neurons develop selectivity by an intermediate stage of birdsong learning. *Journal of Neuroscience, 17,* 6447–6462.

Stripling, R., Volman, S. F., & Clayton, D. F. (1997). Response modulation in the zebra finch neostriatum: Relationship to nuclear gene regulation. *Journal of Neuroscience, 17,* 3883–3893.

Sutherland, N. S., & Mackintosh, N. J. (1971). *Mechanisms of animal discrimination learning.* New York: Academic Press.

Suthers, R. A. (1997). Peripheral control and lateralization of birdsong. *Journal of Neurobiology, 33,* 632–652.

Suzuki, W. A., & Clayton, N. S. (2000). The hippocampus and memory: A comparative and ethological perspective. *Current Opinion in Neurobiology, 10,* 768–773.

Swartzentruber, D. (1995). Modulatory mechanisms in Pavlovian conditioning. *Animal Learning and Behavior, 23,* 123–143.

Swithers, S. E., & Hall, W. G. (1994). Does oral experience terminate ingestion? *Appetite, 23,* 113–138.

Teitelbaum, P., & Pellis, P. M. (1992). Toward a synthetic physiological psychology. *Psychological Science, 3,* 4–20.

Testa, T. J. (1975). Effects of similarity of location and temporal intensity pattern of conditioned suppression in rats. *Journal of Experimental Psychology: Animal Behavior Processes, 1,* 114–121.

Thorndike, E. L. (1898). Animal intelligence: An experimental study of the associative processes in animals. *Psychological Monographs, 2*(4, Whole No. 8).

Thorpe, W. H. (1958). The learning of song patterns by birds, with especial reference to the song of the chaffinch, *Fingilla coelebs. Ibis, 100,* 535–570.

Thorpe, W. H. (1961). *Bird-song.* Cambridge, UK: Cambridge University Press.

Thorpe, W. H. (1963). *Learning and instinct in animals.* London: Methuen.

Thorpe, W. H. (1979). *The origins and rise of ethology.* New York: Praeger.

Tierney, A. J. (1986). The evolution of learned and innate behavior: Contributions from genetics and neurobiology to a theory of behavioral evolution. *Animal Learning and Behavior, 14*(4), 339–348.

Timberlake, W. (1983). The functional organization of appetitive behavior: Behavior systems and learning. In M. D. Zeiler & P. Harzem (Eds.), *Advances in the analysis of behavior: Vol. 3. Biological factors in learning* (pp. 177–221). Chichester, UK: Wiley.

Timberlake, W. (1994). Behavior systems, associationism, and Pavlovian conditioning. *Psychonomic Bulletin and Review, 1,* 405–420.

Timberlake, W., & Grant, D. L. (1975). Autoshaping in rats to the presentation of another rat predicting food. *Science, 190,* 690–692.

Timberlake, W., & Silva, K. M. (1995). Appetitive behavior in ethology, psychology, and behavior systems. In N. S. Thompson (Ed.), *Perspectives in ethology: Vol. 11. Behavioral design* (pp. 211–253). New York: Plenum Press.

Timberlake, W., Wahl, G., & King, D. (1982). Stimulus and response contingencies in the misbehavior of rats. *Journal of Experimental Psychology: Animal Behavior Processes, 8,* 62–85.

Tinbergen, N. (1951). *The study of instinct.* Oxford, UK: Clarendon Press.

Tinbergen, N. (1963). On aims and methods of ethology. *Zeitschrift für Tierpsychologie, 20,* 410–433.

Tolman, E. C., & Brunswik, E. (1935). The organism and the causal texture of the environment. *Psychological Review, 42,* 43–77.

Trapold, M. A. (1970). Are expectancies based upon different positive reinforcing events discriminably different? *Learning and Motivation, 1,* 129–140.

Vates, G. E., Broome, B. M., Mello, C. V., & Nottebohm, F. (1996). Auditory pathways of caudal telencephalon and their relation to the song system of adult male zebra finches (*Taenopygia guttata*). *Journal of Comparative Neurology, 366,* 613–642.

Vicario, D. S. (1991). Organization of the zebra finch song control system: Pt. 2. Functional organization of outputs from nucleus *Robustus archistriatalis. Journal of Comparative Neurology, 309,* 486–494.

Vicario, D. S., & Nottebohm, F. (1988). Organization of the zebra finch song control system: Representation of syringeal muscles in the hypoglossal nucleus. *Journal of Comparative Neurology, 271,* 346–354.

Vu, E. T., Mazurek, M. E., & Kuo, Y.-C. (1994). Identification of a forebrain motor programming network for the learned song of zebra finches. *Journal of Neuroscience, 14,* 6924–6934.

Wagner, A. R. (1978). Expectancies and the priming of STM. In S. H. Hulse, H. Fowler, & W. K. Honig (Eds.), *Cognitive processes in animal behavior* (pp. 177–209). Hillsdale, NJ: Erlbaum.

Weingarten, H. P. (1983). Conditioned cues elicit feeding in sated rats: A role for learning in meal initiation. *Science, 220,* 431–433.

Welty, J. C., & Baptista, L. (1988). *The life of birds.* New York: Saunders College.

West, M. J., & King, A. P. (1996). Eco-gen-actics: A systems approach to ontogeny of avian communication. In D. E. Kroodsma & E. H. Miller (Eds.), *Ecology and evolution of acoustic communication in birds* (pp. 20–38). Ithaca, NY: Cornell University Press.

West, M. J., King, A. P., & Duff, M. A. (1990). Communicating about communicating: When innate is not enough. *Developmental Psychobiology, 23,* 585–595.

Whaling, C. S., Nelson, D. A., & Marler, P. R. (1995). Testosterone-induced shortening of the storage phase of song development in birds interferes with vocal learning. *Developmental Psychobiology, 28,* 367–376.

Wild, J. M. (1997). Neural pathways for the control of birdsong production. *Journal of Neurobiology, 33,* 653–670.

Yeo, A. G. (1974). The acquisition of conditioned suppression as a function of interstimulus interval duration. *Quarterly Journal of Experimental Psychology, 26,* 405–416.

Yu, A. C., & Margoliash, D. (1996). Temporal hierarchical control of singing in birds. *Science, 273,* 1871–1875.

Zamble, E. (1973). Augmentation of eating following a signal for feeding in rats. *Learning and Motivation, 4,* 138–147.

Zimmer-Hart, C. L., & Rescorla, R. A. (1974). Extinction of Pavlovian conditioned inhibition. *Journal of Comparative and Physiological Psychology, 86,* 837–845.

CHAPTER 18

Biological Models of Associative Learning

JOSEPH E. STEINMETZ, JEANSOK KIM, AND RICHARD F. THOMPSON

Over the course of the past century extraordinary progress has been made in our understanding of the behavioral properties of basic associative learning and memory and the manner in which the nervous system codes, stores, and retrieves these memories.

Current views recognize a number of different forms or aspects of learning and memory involving different neural systems (Figure 18.1; Squire & Knowlton, 1994). Many workers distinguish between *declarative* and *nondeclarative* or *procedural* memory. Declarative memory generally refers to explicit memories of "what," that is, one's own previous experiences, recognition of similar scenes and objects, and so on. That is clearly slanted toward human verbal memory; some workers have even equated it with the information one can be aware of. However, recognition memory clearly occurs in all mammals studied and even in some invertebrate preparations.

Here we focus on nondeclarative, implicit, or procedural memory: memory of "how." The vast majority of memory processes in infrahuman animals, and many aspects of memory in humans, is of this sort. Consider all your likes and dislikes, all the skilled movements you perform (tennis, golf, swimming, bicycle riding, not to mention walking and talking), and so on. *Procedural* is really a grab-bag category; it even includes some aspects of recognition memory, as in visual priming memory.

The categories of memory shown in Figure 18.1 are of course somewhat arbitrary and by no means mutually exclusive. When an organism learns something important, several of these memory systems can become engaged. At a more general level, all aspects of learning share a common thrust. As Rescorla (1988) stressed, basic associative learning is the way organisms, including humans, learn about causal relationships in the world. It results from exposure to relations among events in the world. For both modern Pavlovian and cognitive views of learning and memory, the individual learns a representation of the causal structure of the world and adjusts this representation through experience to bring it in tune with the real causal structure of the world, striving to reduce any discrepancies or errors between its internal representation and external reality (see also Dudai, 1989; Rescorla & Wagner, 1972; Wagner & Rescorla, 1972).

Nonassociative learning involves the effect of a single event on response probability. The three examples of nonassociative learning that have received the most attention are habituation, dishabituation, and sensitization. Habituation is defined as a reduction in responding to a repeatedly delivered stimulus where adaptation and fatigue do not contribute to the decremented response (see R. F. Thompson & Spencer, 1966). Dishabituation refers to the restoration or recovery of a habituated response by the presentation of another, typically strong stimulus to the animal. Sensitization is an enhancement or augmentation of a response produced by the presentation of a strong stimulus. In vertebrate systems, at least, dishabituation appears to be an instance of sensitization (Groves & Thompson, 1970).

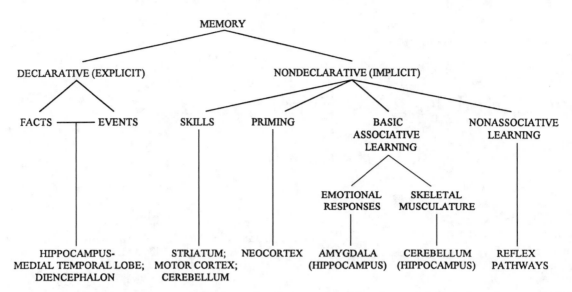

Figure 18.1 Multiple memory systems and their associated brain structures. Memory systems in the brain can be categorized into two major types: declarative and nondeclarative. The nondeclarative system is also referred to as implicit or procedural. Each system is supported by distinct anatomical regions of the brain. Modified from Squire and Knowlton (1994).

Associative learning is a very broad category that includes much of the learning we do, from learning to be afraid to learning to talk to learning a foreign language to learning to play the piano. In essence, associative learning involves the formation of associations among stimuli and responses. It is generally subdivided into classical versus instrumental conditioning or learning. *Classical or Pavlovian* conditioning refers to the procedure in which a neutral stimulus, termed a conditioned stimulus (CS), is paired with a stimulus that elicits a response, termed an unconditioned stimulus (US), for example, food that elicits salivation or a shock to the foot that elicits limb withdrawal. *Instrumental* learning or operant conditioning describes a situation in which the animal or person must perform some response in order to obtain a reward or avoid punishment. That is, the subject can control the occurrence of the US.

Classical or Pavlovian conditioning according to the traditional view is a procedure that refers to the operation of pairing one stimulus, the CS, with a second stimulus, the US, as just noted. The US reliably elicits a response prior to pairing with the CS, termed the unconditioned response (UR). Repeated pairings of the CS and US result in the CS eliciting a response defined as the conditioned response (CR). Critically important variables are order (the CS proceeds the US), timing (the interval between CS and US is critical for most examples of conditioning), and contiguity (the pairing or contiguity of the CS and US is necessary for conditioning). Conditioning procedures in which the CS and US overlap in time are called *delay* conditioning, whereas *trace* conditioning

consists of a procedure in which a time interval of no stimulation exists between the CS and US. It is often, but not always, the case that CR is similar to the UR (i.e., in Pavlov's experiment both are salivation).

A more general and contemporary view of Pavlovian conditioning emphasizes the *relationship* between the CS and US. That is, the information that the CS provides about the occurrence of the US is the critical feature for learning. This perspective on Pavlovian conditioning is consistent with current cognitive views of learning and memory, as noted earlier. Thus, the generation of a new response to the CS that has properties similar to the US is viewed as less important. Indeed, in some situations the CR is quite different from the UR: foot shock causes an increase in activity (UR) in the rat; fear learned to a tone paired with this same foot shock is expressed as freezing (CR). But note that both responses are adaptive. Instead, as noted earlier, conditioning involves learning about the relations between events in the organism's environment. In this view, the key process is the contingencies among events in the organism's environment. Consider the following experiment. A group of rats is given a series of paired-tone CS–foot-shock US trials and learns very well to freeze (the CR) when the CS occurs. Another group of rats is given the same number of paired CS-US trials but is also given a number of US-alone presentations as well. Animals in this group do not learn to freeze to the CS at all. Both groups had the same number of contiguous pairings of CS and US, but the contingency—the probability that CS would be followed by US—was very much lower in the group given US-alone trials as well (see Rescorla, 1988).

Our focus in this chapter is on classical conditioning, but we also consider examples of instrumental learning, particularly processes of instrumental avoidance that relate closely to the phenomena of classical conditioning with an aversive US. Analysis of possible mechanisms underlying processes of learning and memory has been greatly facilitated by the use of *model* systems—simplified preparations in animals in which cellular and molecular mechanisms underlying behavioral plasticity can be analyzed. A number of invertebrate preparations have been used as model systems; spinal reflexes have served as a vertebrate model system. We review this literature briefly here; the major focus of this chapter is brain substrates of learning and memory in behaving mammals.

INVERTEBRATE PREPARATIONS

Certain invertebrate nervous systems have several advantages for analysis of mechanisms of plasticity: They may contain from hundreds to thousands of neurons in contrast to the billions of neurons in vertebrate nervous systems. Many of the neurons are large and can be identified as unique. Circuits can be identified that exhibit plasticity and have only a small number of neurons. As J. M. Beggs et al. (1999) noted,

> For many years, the general belief was that the small number of neurons found in most invertebrates limits their behavioral capabilities to only the simplest forms of behavioral modifications such as habituation and sensitization. However, it has become clear that even invertebrates exhibit more complex behavioral modifications such as classical conditioning, operant conditioning, and higher-order forms of classical conditioning (p. 1415).

In the chapter on basic mechanisms and systems of learning and memory in the recent text on *Fundamental Neuroscience* (Zigmond, Bloom, Landis, Roberts, & Squire, 1999), J. M. Beggs et al. (1999) provided a very helpful summary of invertebrate preparations that have proved useful for providing insights into possible mechanisms underlying learning. We present their summary, unchanged by any editorial comments we might make (J. M. Beggs et al., 1999, Box 55.1, pp. 1416–1417). They treat *Aplysia* and *Hermissenda* separately, as do we. The focus of their summary is on laboratory studies, where analysis of mechanisms can to some degree be done, as opposed to the often-rich behavioral phenomena exhibited by some invertebrate species in the natural or "ethological" state, as in the dance of the honeybee.

Gastropod Mollusks

Pleurobranchaea

The opisthobranch *Pleurobranchaea* is a voracious marine carnivore. When exposed to food, the animal exhibits a characteristic bite-strike response. After pairing a food stimulus (CS) with a strong electric shock to the oral veil (US), the CS, instead of eliciting a bite strike response, elicits a withdrawal and suppression of feeding responses (conditioned response, CR). The task is acquired within a few trials and is retained for up to 4 weeks. Neural correlates of associative learning have been analyzed by examining responses of various identified neurons in the circuit to chemosensory inputs in animals that have been conditioned. One correlate is an enhanced inhibition of command neurons for feeding (London and Gillette, 1986).

Tritonia

The opisthobranch *Tritonia diomedea* undergoes a stereotypic rhythmic swimming behavior in an attempt to escape a noxious stimulus. This response exhibits both habituation and sensitization and involves changes in multiple components of swim behavior in each case (Frost et al., 1996). The neural circuit consists of sensory neurons, pre-central pattern generating (CPG) neurons, CPG neurons and motor neurons. Habituation appears to involve plasticity at multiple loci, including decrement at the first afferent synapse. Sensitization appears to involve an enhanced excitability and synaptic strength of one of the CPG interneurons.

Pond Snail (Lymnaea stagnalis)

The pulmonate *Lymnaea stagnalis* exhibits fairly rapid non-aversive conditioning of feeding behavior. A neutral chemical or mechanical stimulus (CS) to the lips is paired with a strong stimulant of feeding such as sucrose (US) (Kemenes and Benjamin, 1994). Greater levels of rasping, a component of the feeding behavior, can be produced by a single trial, and this response can persist for at least 19 days. The circuit consists of a network of three types of CPG neurons, ten types of motor neurons and a variety of modulatory interneurons. An analogue of the learning occurs in the isolated central nervous system. The enhancement of the feeding motor program appears to be due to an increased activation of the CPG cells by mechanosensory inputs from the lips.

Land Snail (Helix)

Food-avoidance conditioning procedures similar to those used with *Pleurobranchaea* have been adopted for use in the land snail. A food stimulus such as a piece of carrot (CS) is paired with an electric shock to the dorsal surface of the snail (US). After 5–15 pairings, the carrot, instead of eliciting a feeding response, elicits a withdrawal and suppression of feeding responses. The transmitter serotonin appears to have a critical role in learning. Animals injected with a toxin that destroys serotonergic neurons exhibit normal responses to the food and the shocks alone, but are incapable of learning. *Helix* also exhibit habituation and sensitization of avoidance responses elicited by tactile stimuli (Balaban, 1993).

Limax

The pulmonate *Limax* is an herbivore that locomotes toward desirable food odors making it well suited for food-avoidance conditioning. The slug's normal attraction to a preferred food odor (CS) is significantly reduced when the preferred odor is paired with a bitter taste (US). In addition to this example of classical conditioning, food-avoidance in *Limax* exhibits higher-order features of classical conditioning such as blocking and second-order conditioning. An analogue of taste-aversion learning has been shown to occur in the isolated central nervous system, which will facilitate subsequent cellular analyses of learning in *Limax*. The procerebral (PC) lobe in the cerebral ganglion processes olfactory information and is a likely site for the plasticity (Gelperin, 1994).

Arthropods

Cockroach (Periplaneta americana) and Locust (Schistocerca gregaria)

Learned modifications of leg positioning in the cockroach and locust may serve as a valuable preparation for the cellular analysis of operant conditioning. In this preparation, the animal is suspended over a dish containing a fluid. Initially, the insect makes many movements, including those that cause the leg to come in contact with the liquid surface. If contact with the fluid is paired with an electric shock, it learns rapidly to hold its foot away from the fluid. Neural correlates of the conditioning have been observed in somata of the leg motor neurons. These correlates include changes in intrinsic firing rate and membrane conductance.

Crayfish (Procambarus clarkii)

The crayfish tailflip response exhibits habituation and sensitization. A key component of the circuit is a pair of large neurons called the Lateral Giants (LGs), which run the length of

the animal's nerve cord. The LGs are the decision and command cells for the tailflip. Learning is related to changes in the strength of synaptic input driving the LGs.

Honeybee (Apis mellifera)

Honeybees, like other insects, are superb at learning. For example, sensitization of the antenna reflex of *Apis mellifera* is produced as a result of presenting gustatory stimuli to the antennae. Classical conditioning of feeding behavior can be produced by pairing visual or olfactory CSs with sugar solutions (US) to the antennae. The small size of bee neurons is an obstacle in pursuing detailed cellular analyses of these behavioral modifications. Nevertheless, regions of the brain necessary for associative learning have been identified, and some neural correlates have been described. In particular, intracellular recordings have revealed that one identified cell, the ventral unpaired median (VUM) neuron, is sufficient to mediate the reinforcing effects of the US (Hammer and Menzel, 1995).

Drosophila

Since the neural circuitry in the fruit fly is both complex and inaccessible, the fly might seem to be an unpromising subject for studying the neural basis of learning. However, the ease with which genetic studies are performed compensates for the difficulty to perform electrophysiological studies (DeZazzo and Tully, 1995). A frequently used paradigm is a two-stage differential odor-shock avoidance procedure, which is performed on large groups of animals simultaneously rather than on individual animals. Animals learn to avoid odors paired (CS+) with shock but not one explicitly unpaired (CS−). This learning is typically retained for 4–6 hours, but 24 hours to 1-week retention can be produced by a spaced training procedure. Several mutants deficient in learning have been identified. Many of these mutants affect elements of the cAMP-signaling pathway. Recent experiments using inducible genes demonstrate a role for cAMP-responsive transcription factors in the induction of long-term memory. These transcription factors are also important for long-term memory in *Aplysia,* and in vertebrates.

Annelids

Leech

Defensive reflexes in the leech (*Hirudo medicinalis*) exhibit habituation, dishabituation, sensitization and classical conditioning. For example, the shortening response is enhanced following pairing of a light touch to the head (CS) with electric shock to the tail (US). The identified S cells appear critical for sensitization, as their ablation disrupts sensitization. Interestingly, ablation of the S cells only partly disrupts dishabituation, indicating that separate processes contribute to dishabituation and sensitization (Sahley, 1995). Separate processes also contribute to dishabituation and sensitization in *Aplysia*. The transmitter serotonin (5-HT) appears to mediate at least part of the reinforcing effects of sensitizing stimuli and the US. Serotonin appears to play similar roles in *Aplysia*, *Helix*, *Hermissenda* and *Tritonia*.

Nematoda

Caenorhabditis elegans

Although analyses in *C. elegans* are just beginning, this animal promises to be a valuable preparation for the cellular and molecular studies of learning. Its principal advantages are threefold. First, its nervous system is extremely simple. It has a total of 302 neurons, all of which have been described in terms of their locations and synaptic connections. Second, the developmental lineage of each neuron is completely specified. Third, it is amenable to genetic and molecular manipulations. Recently, the animal has been shown to exhibit several forms of learning. When a vibratory stimulus is applied to the medium upon which they locomote, adult *C. elegans* will swim backward. This reaction, known as the tap withdrawal reflex, exhibits habituation, dishabituation, sensitization, long-term (24-hr) retention of habituation training, and context conditioning. Although the neurons are small and difficult to record, aspects of the neural circuit have been described. The particular role of individual neurons is being elucidated using laser ablation to remove specific neurons from the circuit (Wicks and Rankin, 1995).

Aplysia

The marine mollusk *Aplysia* has a relatively simple nervous system with large, identifiable neurons that are accessible for detailed anatomical, biophysical, and biochemical studies. Neurons and neural circuits that mediate many behaviors in *Aplysia* have been identified in heroic studies by Eric Kandel and his many associates (Kandel, 1976). In several cases, these behaviors have been shown to be modified by experience.

Two preparations have been particularly useful: the siphon-gill withdrawal reflex and the tail-siphon withdrawal reflex (Figure 18.2). In the siphon-gill reflex, tactile or electrical stimulation of the siphon causes withdrawal of the siphon and gill, a simple defensive reflex. Stimulation of the tail of the animal elicits a set of defensive responses, including withdrawal of the tail and siphon. Relatively simple neuronal circuits

mediate these reflexes. Indeed, the neural circuits subserving these reflexes can be isolated, with siphon-gill and tail connected, or can be completely isolated from body tissues and studied as neural networks. The key feature of these circuits is that the sensory neurons have monosynaptic connections to the motor neurons.

These circuits exhibit habituation, sensitization, and classical conditioning (see Byrne & Kandel, 1996). Most of the analytic work on classical conditioning has actually been done with sensitization. Short-term sensitization is induced by a single brief train of shock to the body wall (or appropriate nerves) that cause release of modulatory neurotransmitters (e.g., serotonin) from interneurons onto the sensory neurons to enhance transmitter release. The mechanism involves activation of adenylyl cyclase, which leads to increased cAMP in the sensory neurons. This results in protein phosphorylation, which alters membrane channels in the neurons, resulting in membrane depolarization, enhanced excitability, and an increase in the duration of the action potential (Figure 18.3). Other synergistic processes also occur. The net result is that stimulation of the sensory neurons results in increased probability of transmitter release at their terminals and a larger postsynaptic response in the motor neurons. Note that the plasticity here is a presynaptic phenomenon.

Long-term sensitization, unlike short-term sensitization, requires protein synthesis. The repeated sensitizing stimulus leads to more prolonged phosphorylation and activation of nuclear regulatory proteins by protein kinase A (PKA). The key step involves translocation of the catalytic subunit of PKA into the nucleus of sensory neurons where it appears to activate CREB (*c*AMP *r*esponsive *e*lement *b*inding protein) that results in long-term sensitization (Figure 18.3). Following this discovery of the key role of CREB by Dash, Hochner, and Kandel in 1990, much work has been done on the role of CREB in memory processes in mammalian models (see Silva, Kogan, Frankland, & Kida, 1998). One of the newly synthesized proteins initiates internalization and degradation of neuronal cell adhesion molecules (NCAMs), allowing restructuring of the axon terminal arbors. Other synergistic biochemical processes also occur. Eric Kandel received the Nobel prize in physiology and medicine in 2000 in part for his elucidation of these biochemical processes underlying behavioral plasticity in *Aplysia*.

Hermissenda

Another invertebrate model that has proved amenable to cellular and molecular analysis of mechanisms of behavioral plasticity is the Pacific nudibranch *Hermissenda crassicornis*,

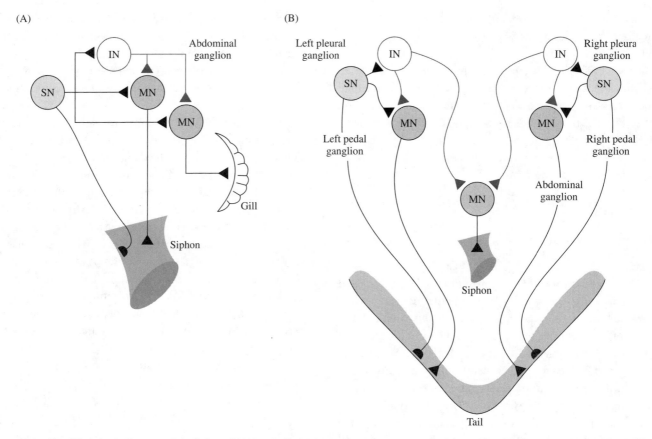

Figure 18.2 Simplified circuit diagrams of the siphon-gill (A) and tail-siphon (B) withdrawal reflexes. Stimuli activate the afferent terminals of the mechano-receptor sensory neurons (SN), whose somata are located in central ganglia. The sensory neurons make excitatory synaptic connections (triangles) with interneurons (IN) and motor neurons (MN). The excitatory interneurons provide a parallel pathway for excitation of the motor neurons. Action potentials elicited in the motor neurons, triggered by the combined input from the SNs and INs, propagate out peripheral nerves to activate muscle cells and produce the subsequent reflex withdrawal of the organs. Modulatory neurons (not shown here), such as those containing serotonin (5-HT), regulate the properties of the circuit elements and, consequently, the strength of the behavioral responses. From J. M. Beggs et al. (1999).

studied in detail by Daniel Alcon and his many associates. The behavioral CR studied involves pairing a light CS with high-speed rotation (stimulating hair cell gravity receptors) as a US. Conditioning results in a CS-elicited suppression of the normal positive phototaxic response and a foot shortening (the normal response to a light is foot lengthening), lasting for days (Figure 18.4). Because the sensory systems activated by the CS and US are central, the conditioning process can be studied in the isolated nervous system (see Alkon, 1989; Crow, 1988). The eyes of *Hermissenda* are very simple, no-image-forming photoreceptors labeled Type A (two) and Type B (three).

Cellular correlates of the CR involve a significant increase in CS-elicited spike frequency and enhanced excitability in the Type B photoreceptor and similar changes in the Type A photoreceptor. Note that, like sensitization in *Aplysia,* these are changes in sensory neurons. Several mechanisms have been discovered to cause this increased excitability in the photoreceptor neurons, most particularly two potassium currents that are reduced as a result of conditioning. Because outward potassium currents reduce cell excitability, reduction in the currents would increase cell excitability, as seen in *Hermissenda* conditioning. Note that these charges are intrinsic to the neurons and not necessarily due to any synaptic processes.

It appears that the phosphoinositide system is responsible for the reduction in K+ currents in *Hermissenda* conditioning. Activation of protein kinase C (PKC) may be initiated by actions of an agonist released by stimulation of the US pathway (Figure 18.5). Serotonergic neurons may provide polysynaptic input to the visual system, acting synergistically (see Alkon, 1989; Crow, 1988; Matzel, Ledehendler, & Alkon, 1990).

It is important to note that a similar decrease in a calcium-dependent slow after-hyperpolarization, mediated by a voltage-gated potassium conductance, results in a learning-induced increase in excitability of pyramidal neurons in the hippocampus of rabbits as a result of eye-blink conditioning

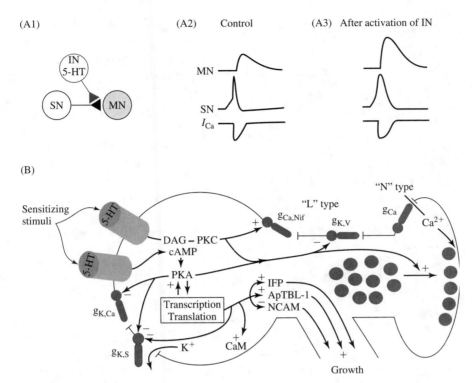

Figure 18.3 Model of heterosynaptic facilitation of the sensorimotor connection that contributes to short- and long-term sensitization of *Aplysia*. (A1) Sensitizing stimuli activate facilitatory interneurons (IN) that release modulatory transmitters, one of which is 5-HT. The modulator leads to an alteration of the properties of the sensory neuron (SN). (A2, A3) An action potential in SN after the sensitizing stimulus results in greater transmitter release and hence a larger postsynaptic potential in the motor neuron (MN) than an action potential before the sensitizing stimulus. For short-term sensitization, the enhancement of transmitter release is due, at least in part, to broadening of the action potential and an enhanced flow of CA^{2+} (I_{Ca}) into the sensory neuron. (B) Molecular events in the sensory neuron. 5-HT released from the facilitatory neuron (A1) binds to at least two distinct classes of receptors on the outer surface of the membrane of the sensory neuron, which leads to the transient activation o two intracellular second messengers, DAG and cAMP. The second messengers, acting through their respective protein kinases, affect multiple cellular processes, the combined effects of which lead to enhanced transmitter release when a subsequent action potential is fired in the sensory neuron. Long-term alterations are achieved through regulation of protein synthesis and growth. Positive (+) and negative (−) signs indicate enhancement and suppression of cellular processes, respectively. From J. M. Beggs et al. (1999).

(de Jonge, Black, Deyo, & Disterhoft, 1990; Disterhoft, Coulter, & Alkon, 1986; and see later discussion).

Comment

Advances in our understanding of the cellular and molecular mechanisms underlying various forms and aspects of behavioral plasticity and memory in at least some of the invertebrate models, particularly *Aplysia* and *Hermissenda,* have been spectacular. There would appear to be clear points of contact with putative mechanisms of memory formation in mammals (e.g., CREB and potassium channel–mediated afterhyperpolarization. Study of these systems in their own right is exciting and eminently worthwhile. However, as egocentric mammals we must ask to what extent these systems and mechanisms apply to mammals. Note that the key processes in both *Aplysia* and *Hermissenda* systems are in the sensory neurons; hence the changes are presynaptic. To date, no such changes have been reported for sensory neurons in mammals. A major

putative mechanism in mammalian learning, long-term potentiation (LTP), appears to be postsynaptic, at least in CA1. We note that studies by Glanzman and associates (Lin & Glanzman, 1994) have shown that postsynaptic changes in the motor neurons may occur in the monosynaptic *Aplysia* circuit. Most of the *Aplysia* results on classical conditioning have actually been obtained for sensitization. In mammalian systems great effort is expanded to rule out sensitization in classical conditioning studies. Indeed, sensitization appears to play no role in mammalian classical conditioning studies.

There are more general issues as well. To what extent do processes of long-term sensitization and classical conditioning play roles in the natural environment in *Aplysia* or in light rotation in *Hermissenda*? That is, are the laboratory studies imposing plasticity that may not normally occur? More generally, are the control procedures used in these invertebrate studies, which are taken from the mammalian literature, entirely appropriate? In some instances the learning procedure itself may have problems. For example, in fruit fly learning,

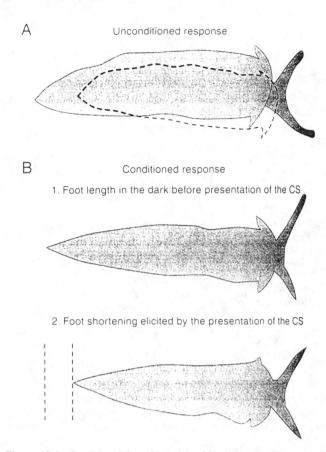

A   Unconditioned response

B   Conditioned response

1. Foot length in the dark before presentation of the CS

2. Foot shortening elicited by the presentation of the CS

Figure 18.4   Conditioned foot shortening of *Hermissenda*. The unconditioned response (UR) is shown in (A) as the outline of the foot represented by the dashed line in response to rotation of the animal, the unconditioned stimulus (US). Comparison of the length of the foot after Pavlovian conditioning in the dark (B1) and in response to the presentation of the conditioned stimulus (CS) in (B2). The area indicated by the dashed lines represents the foot-shortening conditioned response (CR). Pseudorandom and random presentations of the CS and US do not result in the development of phototactic suppression or foot shortening. From Beggs et al. (1999).

individual animals are not trained; the data are single numbers for groups of animals.

The degrees of convergence between mechanisms of memory in invertebrates and mammals will become clearer as we learn more about mechanisms in the mammalian brain. There is much to be done.

SPINAL CONDITIONING

The early history of spinal conditioning—the possibility that classical or instrumental training procedures could induce associative learning-like phenomena in the vertebrate spinal cord—was somewhat controversial. Pavlov's dictum to the effect that associative learning required the cerebral cortex did not help matters.

Shurrager, working in Culler's laboratory (where so many pioneering studies of brain substrates of learning and memory were carried out), published the first modern studies of classical conditioning of spinal reflexes (Shurrager & Culler, 1940, 1941). In brief, they used acute spinal dogs, measured the twitch response of a partially dissected flexor muscle, and gave paw shock as a US and weak stimulation of the tail as CS. They obtained robust acquisition in about half of the animals and demonstrated CS-alone extinction and successively more rapid reacquisition in repeated training and extinction sessions. Unfortunately, adequate controls for sensitization and pseudoconditioning were not run in these studies.

A few years later Kellogg and associates reported negative results in attempts at spinal conditioning (e.g., Deese & Kellogg, 1949; Kellogg, 1947; Kellogg, Deese, & Pronko, 1946). They used chronic spinal dogs and the flexor response of the whole leg. The US was shock to the paw of that leg, and the CS was shock to the opposite hind paw. Kellogg's choice of CS locus was unfortunate. Paw shock elicits a crossed extension reflex that would work against the development of a conditioned flexion response. Pinto and Bromily (1950) completed an extensive spinal conditioning study with long-term acute spinal animals and found only inconclusive evidence because of passive hindquarter movements caused by anterior limb movements.

Patterson, Cegavske, and Thompson (1973) completed a detailed and extensive study of spinal conditioning, using a number of control procedures and conditions, that yielded clear positive results. Animals were anesthetized, spinalized at the twelfth thoracic vertebrae (T-12), given local anesthetics, then paralyzed with flaxedil and given artificial respiration (Figure 18.6). The superficial and deep peroneal motor nerves were dissected out and placed on stimulating ($CS - S_{1n}$ in Figure 18.6) and recording (UR, $CR - R_n$ in Figure 18.6) electrodes. The CS was a weak shock to the superficial peroneal nerve of intensity yielding a motor nerve response to the first pulse. The US was a series of pulses to skin of the left ankle (b in Figure 18.6), yielding a UR (response of deep peroneal nerve). The conditioning group received 75 acquisition trials, 250 ms forward interstimulus interval (ISI), and 50 CS-alone extinction trials. Control groups received explicitly unpaired CS and US trials (75 each). In one series a CS-alone trials group was also included. Two separate experiments were completed; both showed clear evidence of associative learning.

These experiments clearly ruled out sensitization as a process responsible for the increase in CS response in the paired group. The fact that the animals were paralyzed ruled out movement artifacts. Acquisition was rapid, as was extinction,

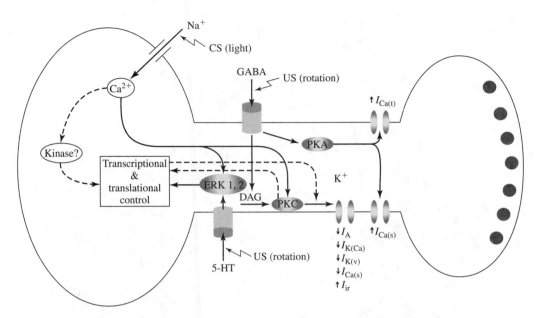

Figure 18.5 Cellular model for the mechanism of Pavlovian conditioning of *Hermissenda*. A modulatory transmitter released by stimulation of the US pathway binds to 5-HT and/or gamma-aminobutyric acid (GABA) receptors. The receptor-activated signal is transmitted through a G protein to the enzyme phospholipase C (not shown). A precursor lipid, PIP_2 (phosphatidylinositol 4,5-biphosphate), is cleaved to yield inositol trisphosphate and diacylglycerol (DAG). The DAG and Ca^{2+} released by inositol trisphosphate from internal stores activate protein kinase C (PKC), which may reduce K^+ currents and enhance cellular excitability. The CS results in increased levels of intracellular Ca^{2+} produced by the depolarizing generator potential and light-induced release of Ca^{2+} from intracellular stores. Pairing specificity may result from synergistic action of Ca^{2+} and PKC-dependent phosphorylation by stimulation of the US pathway or activation of extracellular signal-regulated protein kinases (ERK1,2). Time-dependent activation of second messengers and ionic events have been proposed to account for the reduction of K^+ currents and synaptic enhancement and enhanced excitability. This activation may also be responsible for protein synthesis and gene expression necessary for long-term memory. From Beggs et al. (1999).

just as in the original Shurrager and Culler studies. These results were replicated in careful studies by Durkovic (1975). In a recent and most interesting study, Durkovic and Prokowich (1998) infused intrathecally artificial cerebral spinal fluid (CSF; controls) or artificial CSF with the *N*-methyl-D-aspartate (NMDA) blocker DL-2-amino-5-phosphonovaleric acid (APV) during the conditioning period in acute spinal cats, using procedures described earlier. Both groups showed normal acquisition of the spinal CR. However, the APV group exhibited no retention of the increased response in the 2.5-hr retention period, in contrast to the CSF-alone group. The results suggest that NMDA receptor activation plays a critical role in the establishment of long-term associative plasticity in the spinal cord.

A key issue is the extent to which this form of spinal Pavlovian conditioning resembles Pavlovian conditioning of discrete responses in the intact animal. Patterson and associates completed a heroic series of parametric studies to address this issue, using the same general procedures as Patterson et al. (1973). In brief, spinal conditioning exhibits differential conditioning (A. L. Beggs, Steinmetz, & Patterson, 1985) forward but not backward conditioning (Patterson, 1975), retention of the CR over a period of hours (A. L. Beggs et al.,

1983), increasingly effective conditioning with increasing US strength (Polenchar, Romano, Steinmetz, & Patterson, 1984), and best learning with a 250 onset forward ISI. (See Patterson, 1976, for a detailed review of all studies to that time on spinal conditioning.) All these properties resemble the properties of classical conditioning of discrete responses in intact mammals.

In an interesting recent series of studies Grau and associates paired shock to a hind leg as a CS with intense tail shock as a US in the spinal rat and then examined effect of CS presentations on antinociception on the tail-flick test (Joynes & Grau, 1996). This paradigm is complex in that the CR is a variation on the US. Intense tail shock would seem to induce massive sensitization. Grau interpreted the results, incidentally, as protection from habituation.

The spinal conditioning results just reviewed resemble classical conditioning of discrete responses in intact animals in many properties; nonetheless, they appear to differ from intact animal learning in several ways. First, acquisition is very rapid; most increases in response to the CS occur in the first few trials. Second, and perhaps more important, the onset latency of the CR does not appear to move forward in time over the course of learning. Finally, and seemingly most

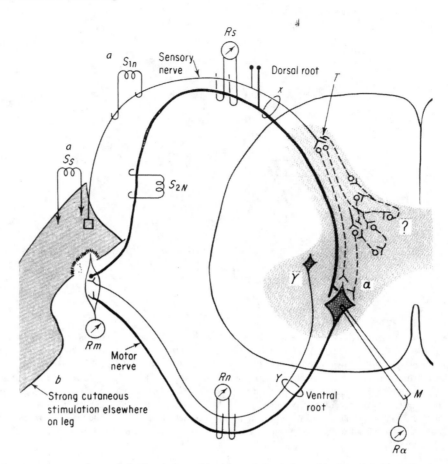

Figure 18.6   Experimental arrangements used to study habituation, sensitization, and classical conditioning of the hind-limb flexion reflex in the acute spinal animal. Electrical stimuli can be delivered to skin (a, S_s; b) or to afferent nerves (S_{1n}, cutaneous nerve; S_{2N}, muscle nerve; x, dorsal root). Responses can be recorded from the muscle (Rm), the motor nerve (Rn), the motor neurons (Rα with microelectrode M), or the ventral root (γ). From Thompson (1967).

important, spinal conditioning involves an alpha response. In most studies the CS elicits the UR-CR before training. As a result of training there is an associatively produced increase in the amplitude of the response to the CS. The fact that spinal conditioning may be alpha conditioning perhaps accounts for the lack of forward shift of the CR onset with training.

The idea that alpha conditioning differs from normal conditions may be somewhat arbitrary. In one experiment in Patterson et al. (1973), two branches of the deep peroneal nerve were recorded during conditioning. One branch showed responses to the CS (superficial peroneal nerve stimulus) prior to training, but the other branch did not. However, by Trial 10 the nonresponsive branch did show a response to the CS. Is it the case that one branch of the nerve showed alpha conditioning, whereas the other branch did not exhibit alpha conditioning but rather showed only normal conditioning?

In unpublished pilot studies Patterson, Thompson, and associates completed some initial analytic studies in an attempt to localize the sites of synaptic plasticity that underlie spinal conditioning. The preparation itself, involving paralysis,

cutaneous nerve stimulation as the CS, strong cutaneous stimulation of the paw as a US, and the recording of motor nerve responses, ruled out changes in sensory receptors or properties of the muscles. Using a monosynaptic test pathway (Rα in Figure 18.6), they ruled out changes in motor neurons. Similarly, changes in the excitability of the cutaneous afferent fibers were ruled out by stimulation of the terminals (T in Figure 18.6) with antidromic recording (Rs in Figure 18.6). Consequently, the mechanisms of synaptic plasticity must reside within the interneuron circuits (? in Figure 18.6) in the spinal gray (see R. F. Thompson, 2001).

What happens in the spinal cord when the limb flexion response is conditioned in the intact animal? In the otherwise intact animal, lesions in the cerebellar nuclei or rubrospinal tract produce complete and specific abolition of the conditioned limb flexion response (see Thompson & Krupa, 1994; Voneida, 1999; see also the later discussion). In fact, normal animals that undergo leg flexion training prior to spinal transection show no retention or savings of CRs in spinal reflexes following transection (J. Steinmetz, personal communication to R. F. Thompson, January, 1984). The isolated spinal cord is thus capable of mediating a kind of associative neuronal plasticity but does not subserve classical conditioning of the limb flexion response in the intact animal. Spinal conditioning is a useful model for studying basic associative plasticity in a simplified neuronal network, but it does not tell us where or how such memories are formed in the intact animal.

FEAR CONDITIONING

Fear as a scientific term describes a brain state in which a set of adaptive (or defensive) responses is activated in the presence of danger (LeDoux, 1996). Although humans and other animals have genetic predispositions to fear certain stimuli, it is also beneficial for animals to have the capacity to learn about new dangers in their environments. For instance, although newborn infants innately exhibit fear to certain stimuli (e.g., loud noises), they do not show inherent fear to flame or heights (two stimuli that most children learn and adults remember to avoid; Fischer & Lazerson, 1984). Accordingly, fear behaviors to many stimuli and events in the environment appear to be acquired.

Classical or Pavlovian fear conditioning has been widely employed for studying the mechanisms by which fear is acquired. Fear conditioning occurs when initially neutral CSs are *contingently* paired with aversive USs that reflexively activate unconditioned fear responses (URs; Rescorla, 1967; Watson & Rayner, 1920). Through CS-US association formation, the CS comes to elicit various CRs that share similar characteristics to innate fear responses (R. J. Blanchard & Blanchard, 1969, 1971; Bolles, 1970; Fanselow, 1984; Kim, Rison, & Fanselow, 1993; LeDoux, Iwata, Pearl, & Reis, 1986). Perhaps the best-known example of fear conditioning is the Little Albert experiment by Watson and Rayner (1920). Little Albert was an 11-month-old infant who initially exhibited curiosity (and no fear) to a white rat by touching and playing with it. As Albert's hand touched the rat, the experimenters banged a steel bar with a hammer behind his head (US), causing him to startle, fall forward, and cry (UR). Afterwards, when the rat (CS) was placed near Little Albert's hand, he withdrew his hand and began to cry (CR). This exhibition of fear toward the rat was allegedly generalized to other white, furry animals and objects (e.g., rabbits, dogs, fur muffs).

Modern investigations of fear conditioning typically employ small mammals (e.g., rats, mice, and rabbits) as subjects and use a tone (or a light or a distinctive environmental setting) as a CS and a mild electric shock (e.g., a foot shock) as a US. Under these circumstances a small number of CS-US pairings produce robust fear learning as evidenced by a variety of fear responses exhibited upon subsequent presentations of the CS. In rats typical fear CR measures include freezing (or movement arrest; D. C. Blanchard & Blanchard, 1972; R. J. Blanchard & Blanchard, 1969; Bolles 1970, Fanselow, 1984; LeDoux, Iwata, Pearl, & Reis, 1986), enhancement of musculature reflexes (e.g., startle; Brown, Kalish, & Farber, 1951; Choi, Lindquist, & Brown, 2001; Davis, 1997; Leaton & Borszcz, 1985), analgesia (Fanselow, 1986; Helmstetter, 1992), 22-kHz ultrasonic vocalization (a distress signal; R. J. Blanchard, Blanchard, Agullana, & Weiss, 1991; Lee, Choi, Brown, & Kim, 2001), and alterations in autonomic nervous system activities (e.g., increased heart rate, increased blood pressure, rapid respiration; Iwata, Chida, & LeDoux, 1987; Iwata, LeDoux, & Reis, 1986; Kapp, Frysinger, Gallagher, & Haselton, 1979; Stiedl & Spiess, 1997). Because fear conditioning occurs rapidly and with lasting effect, it has become a popular behavioral tool for investigating the neurobiological mechanisms of learning and memory (see Davis, 1997; Lavond, Kim, & Thompson, 1993; LeDoux, 1996; Maren & Fanselow, 1996).

Fear can also be rapidly acquired through instrumental or operant conditioning in which the presentation of an aversive stimulus is contingent on the behavior of the animal. A widely employed procedure with rodents is the passive (or inhibitory) avoidance task (Grossman, Grossman, & Walsh, 1975; McGaugh, 1989; Nagel & Kemble, 1976), in which the animal's response (e.g., entering a dark compartment of a box when placed in an adjacent lighted compartment, or stepping down from a platform onto a grid floor) is paired with an aversive experience (e.g., a foot shock). As a function of this response-stimulus pairing, the animal learns to avoid making the response that was followed by the aversive experience.

Amygdala as the Locus of Fear Conditioning

An accumulating body of evidence from lesion, pharmacology, and neural correlates of behavior studies point to the amygdala—an almond-shaped group of nuclei buried deep within the temporal lobes—as the key neural system underlying fear conditioning (see Davis, 1997; Fendt & Fanselow, 1999; Lavond et al., 1993; LeDoux, 1996; Maren & Fanselow, 1996). The amygdala, one of the principal structures of the limbic system (Isaacson, 1974), has long been implicated as a crucial emotive brain center in monkey studies (e.g., Klüver & Bucy, 1937; MacLean & Delgado, 1953; Weiskrantz, 1956). Anatomically, the amygdala is positioned to receive sensory inputs from diverse areas of the brain (e.g., thalamus, hypothalamus, neocortex, olfactory cortex, hippocampus) and to send projections to various autonomic and somatomotor structures that mediate specific fear

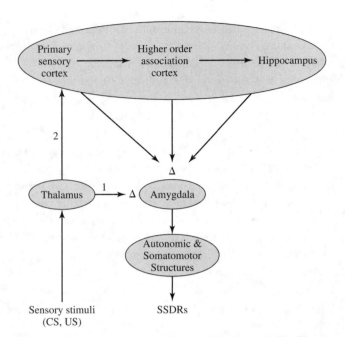

Figure 18.7 A simplified putative fear conditioning model. The CS (e.g., tone) information is processed via two separate pathways to the amygdala. One pathway is through (1) the direct thalamo-amygdalar projection; the second pathway is through (2) the indirect thalamo-cortico-amygdalar projection. The foot-shock US information seems to be conveyed to the amygdala via a diffuse somatosensory pathway. The CS-US association formation is hypothesized to occur in the lateral nucleus of the amygdala. Δ denotes modifiable connections. Adapted from LeDoux (1996).

responses (e.g., bed nucleus of stria terminalis for activating stress hormones, periaqueductal gray matter for defensive behavior, lateral hypothalamus for sympathetic activation; LeDoux, 1996). It is generally accepted that various sensory information enters the amygdala through its basal and lateral nuclei (Aggleton, 2000; LeDoux, 1996), where CS-US association formation is believed to take place (Figure 18.7). These nuclei are reciprocally interconnected with the central nucleus, which appears to be the main amygdaloid output structure that sends projections to various autonomic and somatomotor centers involved in mediating specific fear responses. In this section we examine various types of experimental evidence indicating that the amygdala is the essential site of fear conditioning.

Evidence From Lesion Studies

Permanent and reversible lesions of the amygdala, particularly in the central nucleus (ACe), effectively attenuate or abolish a variety of conditioned fear responses in several mammalian species. In rats, amygdalar lesions impair both acquisition (learning) and expression (performance) of conditioned increase in blood pressure (Iwata et al., 1986), potentiated startle (Hitchcock & Davis, 1986, 1987) and enhanced eye-blink

reflexes (Choi et al., 2001), analgesia (reduction in pain sensitivity; Helmstetter, 1992), 22-kHz ultrasonic vocalization (Antoniadis & McDonald, 2000; Goldstein, Rasmusson, Bunney, & Roth, 1996), and freezing (D. C. Blanchard & Blanchard, 1972; Cousens & Otto, 1998; Iwata et al., 1986; Kim et al., 1993). Similarly, reversible inactivation of neurons (prior to fear conditioning) in the basolateral amygdala complex (BLA), via microinfusing the gamma-aminobutyric acid (GABA) agonist muscimol, blocks the acquisition of conditioned fear; whereas intra-amygdalar muscimol infusions (prior to retention testing) in previously fear-conditioned rats impair the expression of conditioned fear (Helmstetter & Bellgowan, 1994; Muller, Corodimas, Fridel, & LeDoux, 1997). In rabbits, amygdalar lesions have been found to impede conditioned bradycardia (deceleration in heart rate; Kapp et al., 1979; Gentile, Jarrell, Teich, McCabe, & Schneiderman, 1986); whereas in cats, reversible cryogenic (cooling) inactivation of the ACe reduces conditioned blood pressure and respiratory responses (Zhang, Harper, & Ni, 1986).

Besides affecting fear CRs, amygdalar lesions also influence the performance of innate unconditioned fear responses (URs). For instance, amygdalectomized rats fail to display normal defensive freezing behavior in the presence of a cat predator (D. C. Blanchard & Blanchard, 1972). Amygdalar lesions have also been reported to reduce reactivity to the foot-shock US and to block shock-induced sensitization of startle (Hitchcock, Sananes, & Davis, 1989). The fact that lesions to the amygdala interfere with both fear CRs and URs indicates that the amygdala receives both CS and US information (Figure 18.7).

Lesions restricted to particular structures afferent to the amygdala can impede fear conditioning to specific CSs. For example, lesions to the medial geniculate nucleus (MGN) of the thalamus, which relays auditory information to the amygdala (LeDoux, Farb, & Ruggiero, 1990), block the formation of the tone–foot shock association, but not light–foot shock association (Campeau & Davis, 1995; LeDoux et al., 1986). Similarly, in rabbits, Schneiderman and colleagues made partial lesions in the MGN (limited to the medial border) and found that the lesioned animals did not demonstrate differential bradycardia CRs to CS+ and CS− tones, even though the magnitude of the bradycardia response was not affected (Jarrell, Gentile, McCabe, & Schneiderman, 1986). Amygdalar lesions, by contrast, abolished the retention of differential fear conditioning of bradycardia in rabbits (Gentile et al., 1986). These results suggest that the MGN relays auditory CS to the amygdala, where fear conditioning is likely to take place. It has been shown that the MGN sends auditory information to the amygdala both directly (via the thalamo-amygdala pathway) and indirectly (via the thalamo-cortico-amygdala pathway; Figure 18.7), both of which sufficiently support auditory fear conditioning (Romanski & LeDoux, 1992). On the efferent side, the amygdala sends projections to particular hypothalamic and brainstem areas that mediate specific conditioned fear responses (Francis, Hernandez, & Powell, 1981; Hitchcock et al., 1989; Iwata et al., 1986; Kim et al., 1993). For instance, LeDoux and colleagues showed that lesions to the lateral hypothalamus impair conditioned blood pressure response, whereas lesions to the ventrolateral portion of the periaqueductal gray (PAG) matter abolish conditioned freezing response; the lateral hypothalamus lesions do not affect freezing, and the PAG lesions do not alter blood pressure (LeDoux, Iwata, Cicchetti, & Reis, 1988). Lesions to the ventrolateral PAG also do not affect the expression of the conditioned bradycardia response in rabbits (Wilson & Kapp, 1994).

These examples of double dissociations of CSs and CRs, as a result of damaging afferent and efferent structures to the amygdala, are consistent with the view that the amygdala is a critical mediator of fear conditioning. It is interesting to note that recent lesion studies suggest that different amygdalar nuclei (e.g., the central nucleus vs. the basal nucleus of the amygdala) mediate independent fear-learning systems (e.g., the ACe controls the classical fear responses, whereas the BLA controls the instrumental fear responses; Killcross, Robbins, & Everitt, 1997; Nader & LeDoux, 1997; Amorapanth, LeDoux, & Nader, 2000). The possible existence of multiple fear-learning systems is perhaps not unexpected given the evolutionary importance of fear conditioning in survival.

Evidence From Stimulation and Recording Studies

Electrical and chemical stimulation of specific regions in the amygdala can evoke conditioned fear-like responses. In rats, amygdala stimulation produces freezing behavior (Weingarten & White, 1978), cardiovascular changes (Iwata et al., 1987), and acoustically enhanced startle responses (Rosen & Davis, 1988). In rabbits, stimulation of the ACe induces bradycardia, pupillodilation, arrest of ongoing behavior (e.g., movement of the mouth and tongue), and enhanced amplitude of the nictitating membrane reflex (Applegate, Kapp, Underwood, & McNall, 1983; Whalen & Kapp, 1991). Stimulation of the lateral hypothalamus, an efferent target structure of the amygdala, elicits cardiovascular responses in anesthetized rabbits (M. D. Gellman, Schneiderman, Wallach, & LeBlanc, 1981). In dogs that previously underwent alimentary (or salivary) conditioning, electrical and chemical stimulations of the basolateral area of the amygdala have been found to inhibit conditioned secretory reflexes (Danilova, 1986; Shefer, 1988). These data indicate that the amygdala can directly activate various fear responses and also inhibit competing responses (that are incompatible with fear responses). In some cases, however, stimulation of the amygdala can interfere with aversive learning. For example, immediate posttraining stimulation of the amygdala produces amnesia that impairs the formation of fear memory (Gold, Hankins, Edwards, Chester, & McGaugh, 1975; McDonough & Kesner, 1971).

Unit recording studies reveal that neurons in the ACe respond to both CS and US (Pascoe & Kapp, 1985) and undergo learning-related changes during fear conditioning (Applegate, Frysinger, Kapp, & Gallagher, 1982). Using a differential conditioning paradigm, Pascoe and Kapp (1985) reported that ACe neurons exhibited selective increases in single unit activity to a tone (CS+) that signaled the US, but not to a different tone (CS−) that did not signal the US. The conditioned bradycardia response paralleled the neuronal response; it was observed preferentially during the reinforced tone presentation. In addition, the magnitude of the amygdalar unit activity correlated with the magnitude of the conditioned bradycardia response. It appears that during fear conditioning some forms of neurophysiological changes strengthen the CS-amygdala pathway such that the CS becomes capable of eliciting conditioned fear responses.

Long-term potentiation, which is commonly suggested as a candidate synaptic mnemonic mechanism (Collingridge, Kehl, & McLennan, 1983; R. G. Morris, Davis, & Butcher, 1990; Teyler & DiScenna, 1987), has been demonstrated in the amygdala, for example, the external capsule-lateral nucleus of the amygdala (LA) pathway in vitro (Chapman & Bellavance, 1992; Chapman, Kairiss, Keenan, & Brown, 1990), the internal capsule-LA pathway in vitro (Huang & Kandel, 1998), the auditory thalamus-LA pathway in vivo (Clugnet & LeDoux, 1990), and the subiculum-BLA pathway *in vivo* (Maren & Fanselow, 1995). The auditory inputs from the MGN to the LA—a pathway involved in tone fear conditioning (LeDoux, 2000)—demonstrate an enhancement in auditory-evoked potentials (or LTP-like changes) after tone fear conditioning (Rogan & LeDoux, 1995; Rogan, Staubli, & LeDoux, 1997). Similarly, amygdalar slices prepared from fear-conditioned rats demonstrate enhanced synaptic transmission in the MGN-amygdala pathway (McKernan & Shinnick-Gallagher, 1997). Thus, it has been postulated that LTP or LTP-like changes in the amygdala are involved in fear conditioning (Clugnet & LeDoux, 1990; Davis, 1997; Fanselow & Kim, 1994; Maren & Fanselow, 1996; LeDoux, 2000; Miserendino, Sananes, Melia, & Davis, 1990).

Evidence From Pharmacological Studies

Immediate posttraining drug manipulations in the amygdala can impair or enhance aversive memories. In 1978 Gallagher and Kapp first demonstrated that intra-amygdalar infusions of the opioid receptor antagonist naloxone enhance fear conditioning. In contrast, infusions of the opioid agonist levorphanol reduced fear conditioning (Gallagher, Kapp, McNall, & Pascoe, 1981). Subsequent studies indicated that the memory-enhancing effect of opiate antagonists is induced partly by blocking the endogenously released opioids from inhibiting the release of norepinephrine in the amygdala (McGaugh, 1989). For instance, intra-amygdalar infusions of the noradrenergic receptor antagonist propranol impair the retention of an inhibitory avoidance memory (Gallagher et al., 1981) and block the memory-enhancing effect of naloxone (McGaugh, Introini-Collison, & Nagahara, 1988). In contrast to propranol, posttraining intra-amygdalar infusions of norepinephrine enhance the retention of inhibitory avoidance memory (Liang, Juler, & McGaugh, 1986). Based on these and other pharmacological studies, McGaugh and colleagues proposed that interactions of opioid, GABA, noradrenergic, and cholinergic neurochemical systems in the amygdala modulate aversive learning (McGaugh, 2000; McGaugh, Cahill, & Roozendaal, 1996). Recently, pretraining intra-amygdalar infusions of the dopamine (D2) receptor antagonist eticlopride have been shown markedly to attenuate conditioned freezing, indicating that amygdaloid dopamine transmission also contributes to the formation of fear memories (Guarraci, Frohardt, Falls, & Kapp, 2000). Finally, drugs (e.g., diazepam) that decrease fear or anxiety in humans, when infused directly into the amygdala, have been shown to attenuate conditioned fear in rats (Helmstetter, 1993).

Several studies suggest that the NMDA subtype of the glutamate receptor in the amygdala might be involved in the synaptic plasticity process (e.g., LTP) underlying fear conditioning. Because NMDA receptors have been demonstrated to be critical for the induction (but not expression) of LTP in the hippocampus, a similar type of synaptic plasticity in the amygdala has been proposed as a possible cellular mechanism subserving fear conditioning. Consistent with this notion, intra-amygdalar administrations of APV—a competitive NMDA receptor antagonist—have been found to block the acquisition of conditioned fear effectively, as measured by fear-potentiated startle response (Miserendino et al., 1990) and freezing (Fanselow & Kim, 1994). Other studies, however, also found that APV infusions into the amygdala significantly impair the expression of conditioned fear (in previously fear-conditioned rats), as measured by a variety of fear responses including freezing, 22-kHz ultrasonic vocalization, analgesia, and potentiated startle (Fendt, 2001; Lee, Choi, Brown, & Kim, 2001; Lee & Kim, 1998; Maren, Aharonov, Stote, & Fanselow, 1996). It is evident that amygdalar NMDA receptors participate in normal synaptic transmission and, therefore, in the overall functioning of the amygdala.

Several recent studies indicate that the acquisition of fear conditioning in rats requires RNA and protein synthesis in the amygdala. For example, pretraining intra-BLA infusions of the RNA synthesis inhibitor actinomycin-D significantly attenuate fear conditioning (to tone and context CSs) and RNA synthesis in the amygdala (Bailey, Kim, Sun, Thompson, & Helmstetter, 1999). Similarly, immediate posttraining infusions of anisomycin (a protein synthesis inhibitor) and Rp-cAMPS (an inhibitor of PKA) into the LA impair fear conditioning (Schafe & LeDoux, 2000). Once fear conditioning has been established (or consolidated), intra-amygdalar infusions of actinomycin-D, anisomycin and Rp-cAMPS do not affect conditioned fear memories (Bailey et al., 1999; Schafe & LeDoux, 2000). It is interesting that previously consolidated fear memories, when reactivated during retrieval (i.e., during a conditioned tone test), appear to return to a labile state that again requires protein synthesis in the amygdala for reconsolidation (Nader, Schafe, & LeDoux, 2000).

Evidence From Human Studies

Recent findings from human neuropsychological and brain imaging studies are also consistent with findings from animal studies. For example, patients with damage to the amygdala display a selective impairment in the recognition of facial expressions of fear (Adolphs, Tranel, Damasio, & Damasio, 1994) and also exhibit deficits in fear conditioning (LaBar, LeDoux, Spencer, & Phelps, 1995) in contrast to normal subjects. Patients with amygdalar damage are also impaired in recalling emotionally influenced memory (Cahill, Babinsky, Markowitsch, & McGaugh, 1995). Correspondingly, imaging studies show that there is a significantly increased blood flow to the amygdala (as measured by functional magnetic resonance imaging, or fMRI) when normal subjects are presented with pictures of fearful faces (J. S. Morris et al., 1996) or are undergoing fear conditioning (Knight, Smith, Stein, & Helmstetter, 1999; LaBar, Gatenby, Gore, LeDoux, & Phelps, 1998). Functional activation of the amygdala has also been observed (via positron-emission tomography, or PET) during free recall of emotional information (Cahill et al., 1996). These sources of evidence further support the view that the amygdala is crucially involved in fear conditioning or in processing emotional information.

Other Brain Areas

Most of the evidence presented so far indicates that the amygdala is the essential neuronal substrate underlying fear conditioning. It is not clear, however, whether the amygdala is the permanent storage site for long-term fear memory. The site of learning is not necessarily the site of memory storage. For example, fear retention is abolished if the amygdala is lesioned (electrolytically) or reversibly inactivated (via infusions of a local anesthetic agent lidocaine) shortly (1 day) but not long (21 days) after inhibitory avoidance training (Liang et al., 1982), suggesting that long-term fear memory is not stored in the amygdala. In contrast to inhibitory avoidance, however, amygdalar lesions made either shortly (1 day) or long (7 or 28 days) after training effectively abolish conditioned freezing response (Maren, Aharonov, & Fanselow, 1996).

The insular cortex that receives and relays sensory (e.g., visual) information to the amygdala (Turner & Zimmer, 1984) may have some role in the storage of fear memory. Lesions to the most caudal aspect of the insular cortex impair retention of conditioned light-potentiated startle (Rosen et al., 1992). Similarly, reversible inactivation of the insular cortex by a Na^+-channel blocker tetrodotoxin impairs retention of inhibitory avoidance memory (Bermudez-Rattoni, Introini-Collison, & McGaugh, 1991).

The hippocampus seems to be involved in certain types of conditioned fear memory. In rats, conditioned fear to a diffuse contextual cue, but not to a discrete tone cue, is abolished when the hippocampus is lesioned shortly (1 day) after conditioning (Anagnostaras, Maren, & Fanselow 1999; Kim & Fanselow, 1992; Maren, Aharonov, & Fanselow, 1997). However, animals retain a considerable amount of contextual fear when a long delay (28 days) is imposed between the time of conditioning and the time of hippocampectomy. Thus, it appears that the hippocampus is transiently involved in storing contextual fear memory. Similarly, pretraining hippocampal lesions selectively block the acquisition of context fear memory, but not tone fear memory (Phillips & LeDoux, 1992). It is interesting to note that lesions to the nucleus accumbens (a target of hippocampal efferents) also selectively impair contextual fear conditioning without affecting auditory fear conditioning (Riedel, Harrington, Hall, & Macphail, 1997). Hippocampal lesions also impair trace (but not delay) fear conditioning to an auditory CS in rats (as measured by freezing; McEchron, Bouwmeester, Tseng, Weiss, & Disterhoft, 1998) and rabbits (as measured by heart rate; McEchron, Tseng, & Disterhoft, 2000). The notion that the hippocampus is involved in contextual fear memory and trace fear conditioning is also supported by various knockout-transgenic mice studies. In brief, mutant mice with deficient LTP in the hippocampus also exhibit impairments in contextual (but not tone) fear conditioning and trace fear conditioning (e.g., Abeliovich et al., 1993; Bourtchuladze et al., 1994; Huerta, Sun, Wilson, & Tonegawa, 2000).

The perirhinal cortex, which is reciprocally connected to the hippocampus (both directly and indirectly via the entorhinal cortex), also seems to be involved in consolidation and storage of hippocampal-dependent contextual memory.

Neurotoxic lesions of the perirhinal cortex made 1 day (but not 28 days) after training produce marked deficits in contextual fear memory (Bucci, Phillips, & Burwell, 2000).

Finally, lesions of the cerebellar vermis in rats have been found to abolish the conditioned autonomic response (heart rate) without affecting the unconditioned autonomic response (Supple & Leaton, 1990). The vermal lesioned rats also exhibit less freezing to a cat predator and fewer signs of fear in an open field (Supple, Leaton, & Fanselow, 1987). In rabbits, during fear conditioning, single unit recordings of Purkinje cells in the vermis demonstrate selective increases in activity to a tone (CS+) that signaled the US, but not to a different tone (CS−) that did not signal the US. The differential unit activities of the Purkinje cells correlated with the behavioral conditioned autonomic response (Supple, Sebastiani, & Kapp, 1993). These results indicate that the cerebellar vermis is an important part of the autonomic fear conditioning circuit that modulates fear-related behaviors.

Some Unresolved and Critical Issues

Although much is known about the neuroanatomy and neural mechanisms underlying fear conditioning, several unresolved and conflicting issues in the field warrant discussion. This section highlights three major critical issues in fear conditioning.

First, whereas the CS pathway (specifically the auditory projection) to the amygdala is relatively well defined, the foot-shock (US) pathway to the amygdala has not been adequately delineated. A recent study reported that combined lesions of the posterior extension of the intralaminar complex (PINT) and caudal insular cortex (INS) block acquisition of fear-potentiated startle and proposed that PINT-INS projections to the amygdala constitute the essential US pathways involved in fear conditioning (Shi & Davis, 1999). However, another study (Brunzell & Kim, 2001) reported that fear conditioning (as assessed by freezing) was unaffected by either pretraining or posttraining PINT-INS lesions. Specifically, Brunzell and Kim found that pretraining lesions in naive animals do not block the acquisition of fear conditioning, and posttraining lesions in previously fear conditioned animals do not lead to extinction of the CR with continued CS-US training (as would be predicted if the US information does not indeed reach the site of learning). Thus, it appears that the foot-shock (US) pathway is comprised of diffuse, multiple somatosensory pathways to the amygdala (Brunzell, & Kim, 2001). Additional research is required to understand the specific role of the US information—as relayed via tactile versus nociception pathways—in fear conditioning.

Second, as previously mentioned, LTP in the amygdala (demonstrated both in vivo and in vitro) is commonly suggested as a putative synaptic mechanism through which acquired fear is encoded in the amygdala. However, the receptor mechanisms responsible for the induction and expression of amygdalar LTP remain ambiguous and may depend on the particular synapses and input pathway (Chapman et al., 1990; LeDoux, 2000; Weisskopf & LeDoux, 1999), as demonstrated in the hippocampus (Grover & Teyler, 1990; Harris & Cotman, 1986; Johnston, Williams, Jaffe, & Gray, 1992; Zalutsky & Nicoll, 1990). One study (Chapman & Bellavance, 1992) found that APV (an NMDA receptor antagonist) blocks LTP induction in the BLA, but only in such high concentrations that the drug markedly impairs normal synaptic transmission (but see Huang & Kandel, 1998). Similarly, single-unit recordings indicate that normal auditory-evoked responses in the amygdala are considerably attenuated by APV, suggesting that NMDA receptors are involved in normal synaptic transmission of the auditory pathway to the LA that mediates auditory fear conditioning (Li, Phillips, & LeDoux, 1995). Davis and colleagues initially reported that APV infusions into the amygdala selectively block acquisition, but not expression, of conditioned fear, as measured by fear-potentiated startle (Campeau, Miserendino, & Davis, 1992; Miserendino et al., 1990). Their finding is remarkably similar to the effects of APV on hippocampal LTP, that is, blocking induction without affecting expression of the Schaffer collateral/commissural-CA1 LTP (Collingridge et al., 1983). However, recent studies found that intra-amygdalar infusions of APV dramatically interfere with the expression of multiple measures of conditioned fear, such as freezing (Lee & Kim, 1998; Maren et al., 1996), 22-kHz ultrasonic vocalization, analgesia, defecation (Lee et al., 2001), and fear-potentiated startle (Fendt, 2001). These results indicate that amygdalar NMDA receptors participate in normal synaptic transmission and thus the overall functioning of the amygdala. Clearly, additional studies are necessary to understand the receptor mechanisms of synaptic plasticity underlying fear conditioning in the amygdala.

Finally, if the notion that the amygdala is the locus of fear learning is correct, then amygdalar damage should completely and permanently block fear conditioning. However, evidence from conditioned fear studies and inhibitory (or passive) avoidance studies provides conflicting results. Recall that Pavlovian fear conditioning and inhibitory avoidance are considered to be two procedurally different *fear* tasks. McGaugh and colleagues found that although amygdalar lesions affect inhibitory avoidance learning, animals can still learn and retain fear when they are overtrained, which indicates that the amygdala is not necessary for fear learning (Parent, Tomaz, & McGaugh, 1992). Rats that received more training prior to lesions also exhibited far greater retention of inhibitory

avoidance memory. Similarly, amygdalectomized rats learned inhibitory avoidance task when trained extensively. Furthermore, retention of inhibitory avoidance memory is abolished if amygdalar lesions are made shortly after training, but not several days after training (Liang et al., 1982). In contrast to inhibitory avoidance results, the retention of conditioned fear (as measured by freezing) is completely abolished whether amygdalar lesions are made shortly or long after training (Maren et al., 1996), which indicates that the amygdala is necessary in Pavlovian fear conditioning. Recently, it has been reported that amygdalar lesioned rats, exhibiting impairments in conditioned freezing, are capable of demonstrating inhibitory avoidance behavior when both responses are simultaneously assessed in a Y-maze task (Vazdarjanova & McGaugh, 1998). Based on the observation that amygdalar lesions abolish both conditioned and unconditioned freezing but not avoidance behavior, Cahill, Weinberger, Roozendaal, and McGaugh (1999) suggested that the amygdala is critical for the expression (or performance) of reflexive fear reactions rather than the actual learning and storage of fear memory. Instead, based on a series of inhibitory avoidance and immediate posttraining drug injection studies, McGaugh and colleagues proposed that the amygdala critically modulates the consolidation of memory occurring in extra-amygdalar structures (McGaugh, 2000; McGaugh et al., 1996). It appears then that studies employing classical fear conditioning and inhibitory (passive) avoidance provide different insight into the neuronal substrates underlying fear learning and memory. If a common neural mechanism mediates both conditioned fear and inhibitory avoidance, then pharmacological manipulations influencing inhibitory avoidance learning should affect fear conditioning in a similar manner. However, several studies employing rats and mice found that conditioned fear is *not* susceptible to memory modulation by various drugs when conducted in the manner described in inhibitory avoidance tasks (Lee, Berger, Stiedl, Spiess, & Kim, 2001; Wilensky, Schafe, & LeDoux, 1999). Given the discrepancy of these findings from conditioned fear and inhibitory avoidance studies, it is clear that further studies are necessary for understanding the precise role of the amygdala in fear conditioning.

CLASSICAL AND INSTRUMENTAL CONDITIONING OF DISCRETE RESPONSES

Overview

Over the years, the study of the neurobiology of learning and memory has been significantly advanced when standard brain research techniques have been used together with classical or instrumental conditioning of discrete responses such as eye blinks, limb flexions, and jaw movements. For example, classical eye-blink conditioning, used in conjunction with brain recording, lesion, stimulation, and neuropharmacological techniques, has advanced our understanding of the brain systems and processes involved in simple associative learning more than any other behavioral procedure.

There are several reasons for the relatively high degree of success that has been obtained when classical conditioning of discrete responses has been used as a behavioral tool for understanding brain function. First, the stimuli used in classical conditioning are discrete, well defined, and simpler than other more complicated behavioral procedures. Second, the responses measured (e.g., eye blinks, limb flexions, and jaw movements) are relatively simple and discrete. This enables the experimenter to measure easily and accurately the various properties of the response including variables related to response amplitude and timing. Third, in classical conditioning experiments the experimenter controls when stimuli are delivered and thus when responses are expected. This has made lesion, stimulation, and recording experiments relatively easy to interpret. Finally, due to a wide variety of studies conducted by Gormezano and his colleagues as well as other researchers, a huge behavioral database exists concerning the classical conditioning of discrete responses, especially classical eye-blink conditioning (see Gormezano, Kehoe, & Marshall, 1983, for review). This behavioral database has proven useful for designing experiments and interpreting data collected from studies that have been conducted to delineate the neural bases of associative learning. In this section we review the rather large literature that has been generated concerning the neural bases of the classical and instrumental conditioning of discrete responses.

Classical Eye-Blink Conditioning

By far, the most popular paradigm for studying associative learning has been classical conditioning of the eye-blink response. For purposes of this chapter, the eye-blink response refers to a constellation of responses that include movement of the nictitating membrane (in species with this third eyelid) and movement of the external eyelid. In classical eye-blink conditioning, a neutral stimulus called the CS is presented shortly before a second stimulus, called the US. The US reliably elicits a reflexive eye-blink response called the UR. Typically, a tone or a light is used as a CS while a periorbital shock or corneal air puff is used as a US. After 100 or so pairings of the CS and the US, the organism begins blinking to the CS (i.e., the organism has learned that the CS reliably precedes the US and thus can be used as an anticipatory cue). The learned

anticipatory eye blink is called the CR. Over the years, a number of parametric features of the conditioning process have been delineated. For example, (a) the rate of acquisition of the CR generally increases as the intensity of the CS or the US increases; (b) the rate of acquisition is affected by the length of the interstimulus interval (ISI) between the onsets of the CS and the US; (c) conditioning of discrete responses occurs only when ISIs between about 80 and 3,000 ms are used; (d) CS-alone presentations after acquisition training result in extinction of the CR; and (e) unpaired presentations of the CS and the US do not result in CR acquisition.

For several reasons, the rabbit has been the favorite subject for classical eye-blink conditioning. The rabbit is docile and adapts well to mild restraint, and this has facilitated the collection of behavioral and neural data. Also, it is relatively easy to measure accurately movements of the rabbit nictitating membrane or external eyelids. Eye-blink conditioning studies involving other species have also been successfully undertaken. For example, Patterson, Olah, and Clement (1977) developed a nictitating membrane conditioning procedure for the cat. Also, Hesslow and colleagues have published a series of studies concerning the involvement of the cerebellum and brain stem in classical eye-blink conditioning using ferrets as behavioral subjects (e.g., Hesslow & Ivarsson, 1994, 1996). Recently, several investigators have developed rat eye-blink conditioning preparations (e.g., Green, Rogers, Goodlett, & Steinmetz, 2000; Schmajuk & Christiansen, 1990; Skelton, 1988; Stanton, Freeman, & Skelton, 1992), and there has been a renewed interest in human eye-blink conditioning (e.g., see Woodruff-Pak & Steinmetz, 2000, for review).

Early Studies of the Brain Correlates of Classical Eye-Blink Conditioning

Among the earliest studies concerning the neural substrates of classical eye-blink conditioning were those by Oakley and Russell (1972, 1974, 1976, 1977), who examined the possibility that the cerebral cortex was involved in the storage of eye-blink CRs. They showed that rather extensive lesions of cerebral neocortex did not abolish eye-blink CRs that have been established in rabbits trained before the lesions. The cortical lesions had no effect on the acquisition of new CRs when training was delivered to naive rabbits. More recently, Mauk and R. F. Thompson (1987) used decerebration to separate neocortex from lower brain areas. They showed that the decerebrate rabbits retained eye-blink CRs. Together, the decortication and decerebration studies provide solid evidence that the cerebral cortex was not critically involved in acquisition and storage of classical eye-blink CRs.

There is evidence that under some circumstances classically conditioned-related plasticity does occur in neocortex. In an extensive series of studies, Woody and colleagues studied the involvement of portions of neocortex in eye-blink conditioning in cats. In their behavioral paradigm, an auditory CS was paired with a blink-producing glabellar tap US. After several trials, the tone CS produced an eye-blink CR. Cats given unpaired CS and US presentations did not show eye blinks to the CS. Using extracellular and intracellular recording techniques, Woody and colleagues showed that learning-related patterns of CS-evoked unit activity could be found in cortical motor areas and that persistent differences in neuronal excitability could be found in these regions after conditioning (e.g., Woody & Black-Cleworth, 1973; Woody & Engel, 1972). These data suggest that the excitability of neurons in motor neocortical areas may change during this type of eye-blink conditioning. There are several differences between the cat and rabbit preparations, however. For example, the cat conditioned eye-blink response was of very short latency (i.e., less than 20 ms), whereas the rabbit CR is typically longer in latency. Also, many more trials are needed to produce conditioning in the cat preparation. The cerebellum is not critical for the acquisition and performance of the short-latency CR in cats, whereas (as detailed later) the cerebellum is essential for acquisition and performance of the longer latency CR in rabbits (and other mammalian species, for that matter). In addition, extensive lesions of motor cortex in the rabbit do not affect acquisition or performance of classical eye-blink CRs (Ivkovich & Thompson, 1997). Nevertheless, the data from Woody and colleagues demonstrate that under some conditions classical conditioning-related plasticity can occur in regions of neocortex.

In other early studies investigators used brain stimulation techniques to study stimulus pathways in the brain that could potentially be involved in eye-blink conditioning. For example, in a pair of studies, Patterson (1970, 1971) implanted stimulating electrodes into the inferior colliculus and substituted microstimulation of the inferior colliculus for the peripheral tone CS. He observed robust conditioning when the collicular stimulation was paired with a US. These early data suggested that the inferior colliculus might be a portion of the auditory pathway that normally conveyed acoustic CSs used in conditioning. Kettner and Thompson (1982) used signal detection methods in a neural recording study to examine further the involvement of the inferior colliculus in eye-blink conditioning. They showed that while the inferior colliculus effectively encoded a tone CS, patterns of activation did not differ on CR versus non-CR trials, thus indicating that the inferior colliculus was not likely a brain region where CRs were critically encoded. This was contrasted with recording from the hippocampus and cerebellum where CR-related responding could be isolated (as we describe later).

Early studies also examined the motor components of the basic eye-blink conditioning circuitry, in essence defining the essential cranial nerve nuclei and relay nuclei involved in generating the unconditioned and conditioned eye-blink responses (e.g., Cegavske, Patterson, & Thompson, 1979; Cegavske, Thompson, Patterson, & Gormezano, 1976; Young, Cegavske, & Thompson, 1976). In brief, these studies showed that for the rabbit, activation of motoneurons in the abducens and accessory abducens nuclei produced nictitating membrane movement through activation of the retractor bulbi muscle, which caused eyeball retraction and passive movement of the nictitating membrane. The oculomotor and trochlear nerves were found also to be involved to some extent in the eye-blink response along with the facial nerve, which controlled external eyelid closure via activation of the orbicularis oculi muscles (Figure 18.8). Although species like the rabbit and cat have functional nictitating membranes,

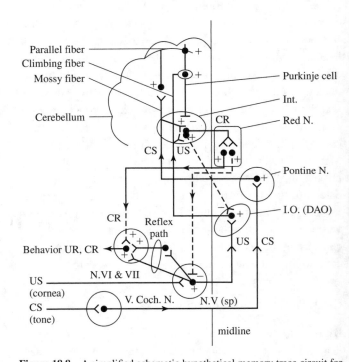

Figure 18.8 A simplified schematic hypothetical memory trace circuit for discrete behavioral responses learned as adaptations to aversive events. The US (corneal air puff) pathway seems to consist of somatosensory projections to the dorsal accessory portion of the inferior olive (DAO) and its climbing fiber projections to the cerebellum. The tone CS pathway seems to consist of auditory projections to pontine nuclei (Pontine N) and mossy fiber projections to the cerebellum. The efferent (eyelid closure) CR pathway projections from the interpositus nucleus (Int) of the cerebellum to the red nucleus (Red N) and via the descending rubral pathway to act ultimately on motor neurons. The interpositus nucleus sends a direct GABAergic inhibitory projection to the inferior olive so that when a CR occurs (eyelid closes), the interpositus directly inhibits the inferior olive. Evidence is most consistent with storage of the memory traces in localized regions of cerebellar cortex and interpositus nucleus. Pluses indicate excitatory, and minuses indicate inhibitory synaptic action. Additional abbreviations: NV(sp), spinal fifth cranial nucleus; N VI, sixth cranial nucleus; N VII, seventh cranial nucleus; V Coch N, ventral cochlear nucleus. Modified from Thompson (1986).

other species like the human and rat do not. Nevertheless, control of the reflexive eye-blink involves similar collections of brain stem nuclei across species. Further, McCormick, Lavond, and Thompson (1982) showed that the occurrences of conditioned nictitating membrane movements and conditioned external eyelid movements were highly correlated, a part of a constellation of responses that are produced by the CS-US pairings.

A variety of data demonstrate that the periorbital shock and air puff USs used in classical conditioning activate the reflexive UR rather directly at the level of the brain stem (Figure 18.8). For example, an air puff US activates neurons in the trigeminal complex, which projects to nuclei involved in generating eye blinks both directly and indirectly (Hiroaka & Shimamura, 1977). Neural recordings taken from the motor nuclei (e.g., the abducens nucleus) revealed that the nuclei were activated when either a UR or a CR occurred and the amplitude-time course of the unit activity was very highly correlated with the CR or the UR that was executed (Cegavske et al., 1979; Cegavske et al., 1976). Lesions of the various motor nuclei abolished portions of the CR and UR, but only those features of the eye-blink response activated by the nuclei that were removed by the lesion (Disterhoft, Quinn, Weiss, & Shipley, 1985; Steinmetz, Lavond, Ivkovich, Logan, & Thompson, 1992). For example, lesions of the abducens nucleus abolished nictitating membrane response while preserving external eyelid responses. Lesions of the facial nucleus produced the opposite effect.

Studies of the Hippocampus and Limbic System

In the 1960s and 1970s a rapidly growing body of literature suggested that the hippocampus and related limbic systems structures were involved in a variety of learning and memory processes. During this time, Thompson and his colleagues recognized the power of using the classical eye-blink conditioning paradigm to study hippocampal function during learning and memory. Specifically, Berger, Thompson, and their colleagues recorded multiple- and single-unit activity from the hippocampus and other limbic system structures during conditioning (Berger, Alger, & Thompson, 1976; Berger, Rinaldi, Weisz, & Thompson, 1983; Berger & Thompson, 1978a, 1978b). They showed that even before behavioral CRs emerged, pyramidal neurons in the hippocampus were activated. At first, pyramidal cell activation was seen during the trial period that was coincident with US presentation. Over time, as additional paired CS-US trials were delivered, the hippocampal activity could be seen during the CS-US interval. Eventually, the pattern of hippocampal activity formed an amplitude-time course model of the CR. Other limbic system structures were also found to be

involved in the eye-blink conditioning process. For example, recordings from the medial septum, which sends cholinergic projections to the hippocampus, revealed stimulus-evoked responses to the CS and the US that declined with training (Berger & Thompson, 1978a). Patterns of action potentials recorded from the lateral septum were similar to the patterns seen in the hippocampus. Many studies have supported the idea that cholinergic activity in the septohippocampal system may play a very important role in eye-blink conditioning. Solomon, Solomon, Van der Schaaf, and Perry (1983), for example, showed that systemic administration of scopolamine, an anticholinergic drugs that alters hippocampal activity, severely impairs delay eye-blink conditioning (and, in fact, is more disruptive than hippocampal abalation). Salvatierra and Berry (1989) later showed that systemic scopolamine suppressed neuronal responses in the hippocampus and lateral septum while slowing the rate of delay eye-blink conditioning. Kaneko and Thompson (1997) more recently showed that central cholinergic blockade essentially blocked trace eye-blink conditioning while slowing the rate of delay conditioning. These studies suggest that the brain's cholinergic system is centrally involved in the modulation of eye-blink conditioning, an idea that is compatible with a large body of research that suggests an important role for the cholinergic system in learning and memory.

Interestingly, an earlier study by Schmaltz and Theios (1972) had shown that rabbits could learn and retain the classically conditioned eye-blink response after the hippocampus was removed. Together with the recording data, these lesion results suggest that while the hippocampus was not critically involved in CR acquisition, it likely plays an important modulatory role in classical eye-blink conditioning. Research conducted after the early lesion and recording studies has concentrated mainly on trying to delineate what role the hippocampus plays in simple associative learning. For example, trace conditioning, a variation of the basic classical eye-blink conditioning procedure, has been used to study the possibility that the hippocampus is involved in memory processing associated with learning. In trace conditioning, the CS is turned on and then turned off; a time period is allowed to elapse; and then the US is presented. Unlike delay conditioning, there is no overlap of the CS and the US during individual trials. In essence, the subject must form a memory of the CS that bridges the trace interval before the US is presented. It has been established that the hippocampus is necessary for this variation of training. For example, lesions of the hippocampus have been shown to abolish or significantly impair trace conditioning without affecting basic delay conditioning (Moyer, Deyo, & Disterhoft, 1990; Port, Romano, Steinmetz, Mikhail, & Patterson, 1986; Solomon, Van der Schaaf, Thompson, & Weisz, 1986). Similar to the recording studies of Berger, Thompson, and colleagues, pyramidal cells in the hippocampus become active during trace conditioning in a CR-related fashion (see Disterhoft & McEchron, 2000, for review). Also, at a more cellular level of analysis, Disterhoft and colleagues have shown that calcium-dependent after-hyperpolarization potentials recorded from hippocampal pyramidal cells are significantly reduced after trace conditioning training (Coulter, Lo Turco, Kubota, Disterhoft, Moore, & Alkon, 1989; Disterhoft, Golden, Read, Coulter, & Alkon, 1988).

A large part of the interest in exploring the involvement of the hippocampus in simple associative learning tasks such as classical eye-blink conditioning was generated by the observation that individuals with amnesia and hippocampal damage, such as the well-known H.M., demonstrated rather severe anterograde amnesia and time-limited retrograde amnesia. Kim, Clark, and Thompson (1995) demonstrated similar amnesia effects for classical eye-blink conditioning. Rabbits were trained using a trace conditioning procedure then given hippocampal lesions either immediately or 1 month after training. Whereas lesions delivered immediately after training effectively abolished CRs, lesions given one month after training had no effect. If the rabbits were trained with a delay procedure and then immediately lesioned, no decrement in responding was seen. However, if these rabbits were then switched to trace conditioning, CR extinction occurred. Together with the Disterhoft data, these data suggested that the hippocampus is involved in memory processing of eye-blink conditioning when stimulus memory demands on the system are relatively high (e.g., during trace conditioning). During simple delay conditioning, however, the CS and the US overlap, and there appears to be no need to hold the CS in memory in anticipation of the US. Although the recording studies show that the hippocampus is engaged during the simpler delay task, apparently the structure is not necessary for learning (and memory) to take place. This implies that critical plasticity for eye-blink conditioning lies in lower brain areas.

Over the last several years, the conceptualization of memory systems in the brain has been dominated by the view that distinct brain systems exist for processing declarative and nondeclarative memories (e.g., Clark & Squire, 2000; Squire, 1992). In the human literature, declarative memories are those memories of one's own experience, as is exemplified by one's memories for events and facts. Nondeclarative memories are essentially all other memories, including memories for skills, habits, procedures, and simple conditioning. Because hippocampal lesions appear to cause amnesia for declarative memories, the hippocampus has therefore been regarded as critically important for the storage of declarative but not nondeclarative memories.

Because hippocampal lesions affect classical eye-blink conditioning in a manner that is very similar to the effects of hippocampal lesions on other memory tasks (i.e., severe anterograde effects with mild, short-term retrograde effects), eye-blink conditioning has provided an excellent model system for exploring the distinction in memory systems (as is evidenced by the data cited above). In addition to the nonhuman animal studies, several human eye-blink conditioning studies have recently been conducted to explore further the multiple memory system idea. For example, McGlinchey-Berroth, Carrillo, Gabrieli, Brawn, and Disterhoft (1997) demonstrated deficits in long-trace eye-blink conditioning in individuals with hippocampal amnesia. Participants given short-trace or delay eye-blink conditioning have not shown the learning and memory deficits. More recently, Squire and colleagues suggested that whether the hippocampus is critically engaged in the learning and memory process may depend for the most part on whether the subjects are aware of the memories they are forming (see Clark & Squire, 2000, for review). In one study they trained participants with amnesia and participants without amnesia on both a delay-differential conditioning procedure and a long (1,000 ms) trace-differential conditioning procedure (Clark & Squire, 1998). Subjects in both groups learned the delay procedure normally although those with amnesia could not recall the experience when questioned about it later. The control subjects could easily learn the long-trace procedure, but the subjects with amnesia could not. These results are compatible with previous literature concerning hippocampal involvement in declarative (trace) versus nondeclarative (delay) memory procedures. Using data from the control subjects in this study, Clark and Squire (1999) also demonstrated that awareness was important for the learning. The control subjects showed a great deal of variability in learning the trace procedure. In examining the individual data, Clark and Squire noted that the subjects who learned the procedure could verbalize the stimulus contingencies whereas the subjects who did not learn the procedure could not (i.e., the subjects who learned trace conditioning were aware of the stimulus contingencies).

In another study, Clark and Squire (1999) directly manipulated awareness and studied conditioning in normal, older adults. This study involved four groups of subjects: Two were given a secondary, attention-demanding task designed to reduce awareness of the conditioning contingencies; a third group was given an explicit explanation of the conditioning contingencies; and a fourth group was given the explicit explanation and the attention-demanding task. Clark and Squire showed that those subjects given trace conditioning and the distraction task did not acquire differential CRs, whereas those given the delay procedure with distraction did acquire differential CRs. The group given knowledge of the CS-US contingency and trace conditioning learned the differential CR, but subjects given knowledge together with the distraction task did not. These data indicate that awareness of the contingency affects trace conditioning although the individuals apparently must have access to the knowledge during the conditioning session to produce CRs.

At the very least, these data provide a wonderful demonstration of the power of analysis afforded by the use of eye-blink conditioning for the study of basic learning and memory phenomena. Future studies will undoubtedly continue to use this paradigm to explore the hippocampus and other brain systems involved in declarative memory.

Studies of the Involvement of Other Higher Brain Areas in Eye-Blink Conditioning

Over the years a number of studies have examined the involvement of other higher brain areas, such as the cerebral cortex, thalamus, amygdala, and neostriatum, in classical eye-blink conditioning. Even though there is ample evidence that higher brain areas are not necessary for conditioning, many studies have provided evidence that these brain areas are recruited during conditioning.

Although Oakley and Steele (e.g., 1972) showed that eye-blink conditioning could be achieved without cerebral neocortex, some studies have demonstrated that neocortex is engaged in eye-blink conditioning and may be encoding the learning process. For example, Fox, Eichenbaum, and Butter (1982) showed that lesions of frontal cortex in rabbits decreased the latencies of conditioned eye-blink responses and retarded extinction of the CRs. Through systematic lesions of brain stem nuclei that interact with frontal cortex, they provided evidence that the frontal cortex may normally provide inhibitory effects on conditioned behavior indirectly through brain stem nuclei that make contact with motor neurons responsible for CR formation.

Given the central nature of the thalamus in distributing information to higher brain areas, several studies have explored whether this structure is involved in eye-blink conditioning. Buchanan and Powell (1988) showed that knife cuts that severed afferent and efferent connections between the prefrontal cortex and the mediodorsal nucleus of the thalamus retarded the rate of conditioning established with a tone CS and periorbital shock US. These lesions abolished the late-occurring tachycardiac component of the conditioned heart rate response that was measured concomitantly. Similar results were obtained when ibotenic acid lesions of the mediodorsal thalamic nuclei were used (Buchanan & Thompson, 1990). These data suggested that the mediodorsal thalamic–prefrontal

circuitry was involved in the sympathetic control associated with somatomotor learning. Other thalamic regions have also been studied. For example, Sears, Logue, and Steinmetz (1996) recorded neuronal activity from the ventrolateral thalamus, which receives input from the cerebellum, among other areas of the brain. Learning-related neuronal activity was recorded from the ventrolateral thalamus, and this activity was abolished after cerebellar lesions. These data suggest that the ventrolateral thalamus receives an efferent copy of learning-related activity that is generated in the cerebellum—an efferent copy that is perhaps used to integrate the learned movement into the ongoing motor activity of the organism.

In agreement with other data suggesting a role for the brain's dopaminergic system in sensorimotor learning and integration, there is evidence that the dopamine system is activated during eye-blink conditioning. Kao and Powell (1988) bilaterally infused 6-hydroxydopamine into the substantia nigra and observed a retardation of both eye-blink conditioning and heart-rate conditioning. The lesions produced significant norepinephrine depletion in the nucleus accumbens, frontal cortex, and hypothalamus and also produced dopamine depletion in the caudate nucleus. Furthermore, the rate of conditioning was highly correlated with the level of dopamine found in the caudate. In another study, White et al. (1994) recorded unit activity from the neostriatum during eye-blink conditioning (see also Richardson & Thompson, 1985). Neostriatal neurons were responsive to the tones and air puffs used as CSs and USs, respectively, and some neurons showed a CR-related pattern of discharge with an onset that preceded the behavioral response. Haloperidol, a dopamine antagonist, caused a disruption of behavioral and neural responding that appeared to be related to CS intensity. This observation was consistent with an earlier study that suggested a role for dopamine in CS processing (Sears & Steinmetz, 1990). These data suggest that the neostriatum may be activated during eye-blink conditioning; consistent with other studies (e.g., Schneider, 1987), the data support the idea that the neostriatum may be modulating the access of sensory inputs to motor output.

Finally, there has been a great deal of recent interest in the role of the amygdala in learning and memory, especially in processing emotional aspects (as discussed earlier). Given that eye-blink conditioning is an aversive conditioning procedure, it was reasonable to assume that the amygdala might be activated during this type of learning. This appears to be the case. Whalen and Kapp (1991) showed that stimulation of the central nucleus of the amygdala increased the amplitude of an eye-blink UR that was subsequently elicited by an air puff US. Further, Weisz, Harden, and Xiang (1992) showed that large electrolytic lesions of the amygdala disrupted the maintenance of reflex facilitation of the eye-blink UR and retarded the acquisition of the eye-blink CR. These data suggest that the amygdala may be involved in US processing, perhaps in processing information concerning the aversiveness of the US (see Richardson & Thompson, 1984). This would be compatible with other studies suggesting a role for the amygdala in emotional processing (e.g., Hitchcock & Davis, 1991; LeDoux, 1995). Consistent with this view, Wagner and associates have developed a theoretical model (AESOP; Wagner & Brandon, 1989) that incorporates both emotive and sensory aspects of classical conditioning and have presented considerable empirical evidence to support the model (Brandon & Wagner, 1991).

In related work, Shors and associates have explored effects of behavioral stress on processes of learning and memory (Shors, 1998). In general, severe stress can markedly impair performance in learning tasks that might be categorized as declarative in rodents (Overmier & Seligman, 1967; see Figure 18.1). This is perhaps consistent with the fact that behavioral stress markedly impairs the subsequent induction of LTP in the hippocampus (rat, CA1 slice; Foy, Foy, Levine, & Thompson, 1990; Foy, Stanton, Levine, & Stanton, 1987; Shors, Levine, & Thompson, 1990; Shors, Seib, Levine, & Thompson, 1989). Indeed, these observations support the view that LTP is a mechanism of declarative memory storage in the hippocampus (Bliss & Collingridge, 1993). Shors, Weiss, and Thompson (1992) discovered that stress actually facilitates classical eye-blink conditioning in rats. It is interesting that a much earlier literature reported a similar effect in humans: High anxious subjects learn eye-blink conditioning better than do low anxious subjects (Taylor, 1951). Shors subsequently showed that this stress facilitation of conditioning is sexually dimorphic, facilitating learning in males but impairing learning in females. The facilitation in males involves the amygdala, whereas the impairment in females is dependent on activational influences of estrogen (Shors, Beylin, Wood, & Gould, 2000; Shors, Lewczyk, Pacynski, Mathew, & Pickett, 1998; Wood & Shors, 1998).

The Critical Involvement of the Cerebellum in Eye-Blink Conditioning

The results of lesion studies involving the cerebral neocortex and limbic system strongly suggested that the learning and memory of classical eye-blink CRs was not critically dependent on higher brain areas but more likely critically involved lower brain stem areas. With this in mind, Thompson and colleagues used a variety of techniques, including systematic lesion and recording methods, in an attempt to find regions of the lower brain that were essential for the acquisition and performance of eye-blink CRs. These experiments suggested a

critical role for the cerebellum in eye-blink conditioning and launched 20 years of research that has strongly supported these early results.

In early studies large aspirations of the cerebellum that included cortex and the deep cerebellar nuclei were found to abolish eye-blink CRs in rabbits trained before the lesion and prevent acquisition of eye-blink CRs in rabbits trained after the lesion (Lincoln, McCormick, & Thompson, 1982; McCormick et al., 1981). Subsequent studies showed that small electrolytic lesions (McCormick & Thompson, 1984a; Steinmetz, Lavond, et al., 1992) as well as kainic acid lesions (Lavond, Hembree, & Thompson, 1985) delivered to a dorsolateral region of the anterior interpositus nucleus on the side ipsilateral to the training permanently abolished the learned responses (Figure 18.8). There appears to be no recovery from the cerebellar lesion (Steinmetz, Logue, & Steinmetz, 1992). Lesions delivered to cerebellar cortex have produced mixed results. Some investigators have reported that lesions delivered to cerebellar cortex abolished CRs (Yeo & Hardiman, 1992; Yeo, Hardiman, & Glickstein, 1985); others have reported little or no effect of the lesion (Woodruff-Pak, Lavond, Logan, Steinmetz, & Thompson, 1993); and others have reported effects on the rate of acquisition and CR amplitude (Lavond & Steinmetz, 1989) and CR timing (Perrett, Ruiz, & Mauk, 1993). These lesion studies established that both the interpositus nucleus and cerebellar cortex were critically involved in eye-blink conditioning.

More recent studies using temporary inactivation techniques such as muscimol infusion (Krupa, Thompson, & Thompson, 1993) or cold probe cooling (Clark, Zhang, & Lavond, 1992) have provided compelling evidence that the cerebellum is necessary for eye-blink conditioning (Figure 18.9). In these studies, the region of the interpositus nucleus was temporarily inactivated by either infusing muscimol (which hyperpolarizes affected neurons) or by cooling with a cold probe (which shuts down neural function). Inactivation of the cerebellum after training abolished conditioned responding for the duration of infusion or cooling. It is even more interesting that when the cerebellum was inactivated during training trials delivered to naive rabbits, the animals showed no signs that paired training had been delivered. That is, after several days of training while the cerebellum was inactivated, no savings in acquisition were seen during subsequent training when the inactivation was removed. One would expect to see savings if essential neuronal plasticity processes were active at other brain sites during training. Because no savings were seen, these studies provided very strong evidence that the basic cellular processes important for plasticity that underlie classical eye-blink conditioning resided in the region of the cerebellum that was inactivated

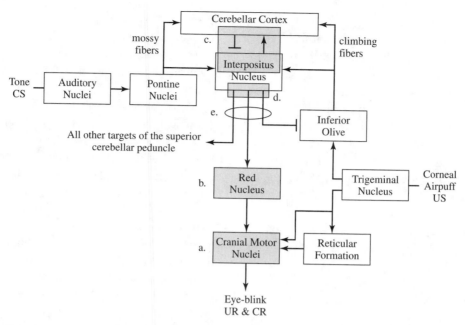

Figure 18.9 Simplified schematic of the essential brain circuitry involved in eye-blink conditioning. Shadowed boxes represents areas that have been reversibly inactivated during training (see text for details). (a) Inactivation of the motor nuclei including facial (seventh) and accessory sixth. (b) Inactivation of magnocellular red nucleus. (c) Inactivation of dorsal aspects of the interpositus nucleus and overlying cerebellar cortex. (d) Inactivation of ventral interpositus and of white matter ventral to the interpositus. (e) Inactivation of the superior cerebellar peduncle (scp) after it exits the cerebellar nuclei. From Thompson and Krupa (1994). Reprinted with permission from the *Annual Review of Neuroscience,* Volume 17 © 1994 by Annual Reviews www.AnnualReviews.org.

by the muscimol infusion or cold-probe cooling. These data provide some of the most compelling evidence to date that plasticity in the cerebellum is essential for classical eye-blink conditioning.

Neural recording studies have also provided evidence for the involvement of the cerebellum in encoding classical eye-blink conditioning. Multiple- and single-unit recordings made in the dorsolateral anterior interpositus nucleus have shown patterns of neuronal spiking that correlated well with the behavioral CR (Berthier & Moore, 1990; Gould & Steinmetz, 1996; McCormick & Thompson, 1984b). Neurons that respond to the CS or the US have been found along with neurons that discharge in a pattern that, when summed, formed amplitude-time course models of the behavioral response. Moreover, the onset of interpositus nucleus spiking typically preceded the behavioral response by 30 ms to 60 ms, a time interval that can be accounted for by synaptic and neural processing delays between the cerebellum and the motor nuclei responsible for producing the CR. Recordings of Purkinje cell activity in cerebellar cortex have also revealed learning-related patterns of unit discharges (Berthier & Moore, 1986; Gould & Steinmetz, 1996; Katz & Steinmetz, 1997). Some cells show CS- or US-related activation patterns, whereas other cells seem to fire in relation to the behavioral response. Purkinje cells have been isolated that increase their firing rate during the CS-US interval while other Purkinje cells

that have been isolated show decreases in their firing rate (see King, Krupa, Foy, & Thompson, 2001; Thompson, 1986). These recording studies provide additional supportive evidence for the involvement of both cerebellar cortex and the interpositus nucleus in eye-blink conditioning. Specifically, the patterns of action potentials recorded in both the nucleus and the cortex appear to be encoding the delivery of the CS and US used during training as well as the learned response that is executed.

The essential stimulus pathways used in projecting the CS and US used in eye-blink conditioning from the periphery to the cerebellum have been delineated. On the CS side, it appears that CSs are projected to the basilar pontine nuclei, which send mossy fiber projections to the interpositus nucleus as well as to the cerebellar cortex (Figure 18.8). The basic CS pathway was established by stimulation, lesion, and recording studies. For example, CS-related responses were evoked in discrete regions of the pontine nuclei, and lesions delivered to these regions abolished conditioned responding (Steinmetz et al., 1987). Microstimulation delivered to these same regions could be substituted for the peripherally administered CS, and robust conditioning was produced (e.g., Steinmetz, 1990; Steinmetz, Rosen, Chapman, Lavond, & Thompson, 1986; Tracy, Thompson, Krupa, & Thompson, 1998). The essential US appears to involve a projection from the region of the eye where the US is delivered to the trigeminal nucleus, which sends projections to a discrete region of the dorsal accessory inferior olive (R. Gellman, Houk, & Gibson, 1983). The inferior olive, in turn, sends climbing fiber projections to the cerebellar cortex and the deep cerebellar nuclei (Figure 18.9). Again, recording, stimulation, and lesion studies were used to establish the connectivity in the US system. Neurons in the dorsal accessory inferior olive were found to be responsive to stimulation of the face, including to presentations of a corneal air puff (Sears & Steinmetz, 1991). Lesions of the inferior olive caused extinction (McCormick, Steinmetz, & Thompson, 1985; Voneida, Christie, Bogdanski, & Chopko, 1990; see also later) or abolition (Yeo, Hardiman, & Glickstein, 1986) of conditioned responding, whereas stimulation of the inferior olive, which produced a variety of discrete responses including eye blinks (depending on precise location of the stimulation), could be substituted for peripheral US to produce robust conditioning (Mauk, Steinmetz, & Thompson, 1986).

The most popular models concerning the cerebellar basis of classical eye-blink conditioning hypothesize that plasticity that is crucial for acquisition and performance of the eye-blink CRs occurs in the cerebellar cortex, the deep cerebellar nuclei, or both regions where a convergence of CS and US input occurs (e.g., Steinmetz, Lavond, & Thompson, 1989; R. F. Thompson, 1986). There is ample electrophysiological and anatomical evidence for convergence of the CS and US in the cortex and deep nuclei of the cerebellum (e.g., Gould, Sears, & Steinmetz, 1993; Steinmetz & Sengelaub, 1992). At this point, it is assumed that paired CS-US presentations somehow produce changes in the firing rate of interpositus neurons, either independently or with critical input from cerebellar cortex, which in turn affects nuclei downstream. In essence, current models assume that before conditioning the CS is not capable of activating cerebellar neurons in a manner that would drive brain stem motor nuclei responsible for the CR. After paired training, however, the firing rates of cerebellar neurons are thought to change such that the CS is now capable of activating brain stem motoneurons involved in conditioned blinking.

The critical CR pathway between the cerebellum and the peripheral eye-blinking musculature has been worked out. Axons from the principle cells of the interpositus nucleus cross the midline and innervate the neurons in the magnocellular region of the red nucleus via the superior cerebellar peduncle (Figure 18.9). Lesions of the peduncle completely abolish the eye-blink (and limb flexion) CRs (McCormick, Guyer, & Thompson, 1982; Voneida, 2000). Similarly, lesions of the red nucleus have been shown to result in eye-blink CR abolition (e.g., Haley, Thompson, & Madden, 1988), and learning-related neuronal activity has been recorded from the red nucleus (Chapman, Steinmetz, Sears, & Thompson, 1990;

Desmond & Moore, 1991). Red nucleus output cells then project axons back across midline and make synaptic contact on neurons in the variety of cranial nerve nuclei (Figure 18.9) involved in generating the eye-blink CR (and UR, for that matter).

Wagner and Donegan (1989), incidentally, showed how a theoretical model of classical conditioning, the sometimes-opponent-process (SOP) model, maps very closely onto the empirical model of the cerebellar circuitry essential for classical conditioning of discrete responses developed by Thompson and associates shown in Figures 18.8 and 18.9.

Interestingly, there is good evidence that in addition to projecting information to the red nucleus, output from the interpositus nucleus also feeds back on the CS and US pathways. Inhibitory projections from the deep nuclei to the dorsal accessory olive have been found (e.g., Andersson, Garwicz, & Hesslow, 1988), and it is known that when CR-related interpositus activity occurs, the inferior olive is inhibited such that US-related activity is not passed to the cerebellum (Sears & Steinmetz, 1991). On the CS side, there are known projections from the interpositus nucleus to the basilar pontine nuclei (likely excitatory), and that CR-related activation of the interpositus may, for some as of yet undetermined reason, project a copy of the CR to the CS input pathway during conditioning (Bao, Chen, & Thompson, 2000; Clark, Gohl, & Lavond, 1997). It is likely that the projections from the interpositus nucleus to the CS and US input pathways to the cerebellum are important for response timing and response topography and also may be responsible for some higher order variations of eye-blink conditioning, such as blocking (see Kim, Krupa, & Thompson, 1998).

Most studies conducted over the last five years or so have been designed to test various aspects of the general model of cerebellar involvement in eye-blink conditioning that were just presented. These studies have examined relationships between cerebellar cortical and nuclear involvement in the acquisition and performance of eye-blink conditioning and have begun the process of delineating neuronal processes that may be involved in establishing and maintaining plasticity that is associated with learning.

Many researchers have suggested that long-term depression (LTD) may play an important role in the acquisition and performance of classically conditioned eye-blink responses (e.g., R. F. Thompson, 1986). Long-term depression is a relatively long-term suppression of cerebellar Purkinje-cell excitability that is produced when climbing fibers and parallel fibers (which receive input from mossy fibers) are conjointly activated (e.g., Ekerot & Kano, 1985; Ito, 1989). Evidence suggests that LTD occurs through the desensitization of quisqualate receptors on Purkinje cells that receive synaptic contact from parallel fiber inputs (e.g., Hemart, Daniel, Jaillard, & Crepel, 1994). It has been proposed that the mossy-fiber CS and climbing-fiber US used in classical eye-blink conditioning converge on Purkinje cells in cerebellar cortex and that LTD results from their coactivation (R. F. Thompson, 1986). Because Purkinje cells inhibit deep nuclear cells to which they send axons, the net effect of the Purkinje cell suppression would be an increase in excitability in the deep nuclei that could allow for the expression of eye-blink CRs through activation of lower motor nuclei. Indirect evidence for a role for LTD in eye-blink conditioning exists. First, convergence of CS and US from mossy-fiber and climbing-fiber sources, respectively, has been anatomically and electrophysiologically established in regions of cerebellar cortex (Gould et al., 1993; Steinmetz & Sengelaub, 1992). Second, recordings from Purkinje cells have shown that some of the neurons demonstrate a conditioning-related decrease in firing rate, as would be expected if LTD occurred as a result of conditioning (Berthier & Moore, 1986; Gould & Steinmetz, 1996).

Schreurs and colleagues intracellularly recorded from rabbit cerebellar slices to study directly the relationship between LTD and conditioning. In an initial study they showed a conditioning-specific increase in the excitability of Purkinje-cell dendrites in slices taken from cerebellar cortical lobule HVI without significant changes in dendritic membrane potential or input resistance (Schreurs, Sanchez-Andres, & Alkon, 1991). Although this initial result supported the idea that learning-specific plasticity took place in Purkinje cells, a decrease in excitability was not seen, as would be expected if LTD occurred. The increase in excitability did, however, explain earlier studies that showed a large number of learning-related excitatory responses recorded extracellularly from Purkinje cells of awake rabbits. Other studies showed that the increase in dendritic excitability of Purkinje cells was a result of alternations in a specific potassium channel (Schreurs, Gusev, Tomsic, Alkon, & Shi, 1998; Schreurs, Tomsic, Gusev, & Alkon, 1997).

Using direct stimulation of parallel fibers and climbing fibers, Schreurs and colleagues have produced an LTD effect in the cerebellar slice preparation (Schreurs & Alkon, 1993). In the presence of the GABA antagonist bicuculline, LTD was produced when climbing fibers were stimulated before parallel fibers, but no response depression was seen when the parallel-fiber stimulation preceded the climbing-fiber stimulation (as is hypothesized to occur during eye-blink conditioning). Depression could be obtained in the absence of bicuculline, however, when parallel fibers were stimulated in the presence of a depolarizing current that induced local, calcium-dependent dendritic spikes. Schreurs, Oh, and Alkon (1996) did produce a form of long-term reduction in Purkinje

cell excitatory postsynaptic potentials (EPSPs) when parallel fibers were stimulated before climbing fibers were. The authors presented trains of stimulation for durations that mimicked conditioning in the intact rabbit. In fact, the trains were presented in nonoverlapping fashion. Consistent depression of EPSP peak amplitude was seen in the slice recordings when parallel fiber stimulation preceded climbing fiber stimulation but not when unpaired stimulations were delivered. In total, these data demonstrate that depending on the order and parameters of stimulation, both increases and decreases in excitability can be seen in Purkinje cells as a result of conjoint activation of parallel (mossy) fibers and climbing fibers. These results provide some direct evidence that cerebellar neurons are capable of showing associative plasticity that could at least in part account for eye-blink conditioning.

Other studies have demonstrated a role for glutamate receptors in plasticity processes associated with eye-blink conditioning. Hauge, Tracy, Baudry, and Thompson (1998) used quantitative autoradiography to examine changes in the ligand binding properties of alpha-amino-3-hydroxy-5-methyl-4-isoxazoleproprionic acid (AMPA) receptors following eye-blink conditioning that was established by pairing a pontine stimulation CS with and an air puff US. Preincubation at 35 °C produced significant decreases in AMPA binding, whereas unpaired CS-US presentations produced no significant effect. These data indicated that eye-blink conditioning is associated with a modification of AMPA-receptor properties in the cerebellum, modification in a direction that is compatible with the hypothesis that LTD is involved in the conditioning process. This hypothesis was further supported by Attwell, Rahman, Ivarsson, and Yeo (1999), who used 6-cyano-7-nitroquinoxaline-2,3-dione (CNQX) infusions into cerebellar cortical lobule HVI to reversibly block AMPA-kainate receptors. Conditioned responses were reversibly blocked by the infusion, thus suggesting that cortical AMPA receptors were important for the expression of eye-blink CRs.

Other studies have examined the role of NMDA receptors in the interpositus nucleus in eye-blink conditioning. A number of studies had demonstrated that systemic injections of the noncompetitive NMDA antagonist MK-801 or PCP and the competitive NMDA antagonist CGP-39551 impaired the acquisition of classical eye-blink conditioning in rabbits and rats but did not affect the performance of the learned response (e.g., Robinson, 1993; Servatius & Shors, 1996; L. T. Thompson & Disterhoft, 1997). Chen and Steinmetz (2000a) further demonstrated that direct infusions of AP5, an NMDA receptor antagonist, in the region of the interpositus nucleus retarded the rate of conditioning but had little, if any, effect on the number of CRs emitted when infused after learning had taken place (although there was an indication that response timing in some rabbits was affected by the AP5 infusions). These studies suggest that NMDA receptors may play a role in the acquisition of classically conditioned eye-blink responses, a result that is compatible with a variety of literature suggesting a rather ubiquitous role for NMDA receptors in plasticity processes.

There is also evidence that protein synthesis in the cerebellum is involved in eye-blink conditioning. Bracha et al. (1998) showed that microinjections of anisomycin, a general protein synthesis inhibitor, into the intermediate cerebellum near the interpositus nucleus impaired the acquisition of conditioning. The anisomycin had no effect on the expression of CRs when infused after asymptotic response levels had been reached. Gomi et al. (1999) further showed that infusion of the transcription inhibitor actinomycin D into the interpositus nucleus of rabbits reversibly blocked the learning but not the performance of eye-blink CRs. In this study, using differential-display polymerase chain reaction (PCR) analysis of interpositus RNAs from trained and control rabbits, they also demonstrated the existence of a 207-base-pair (bp) band that was induced by the conditioning and revealed that training had increased expression of KKIAMRE, a cdc2-related kinase, in interpositus neurons. This result was in agreement with a recent report by Chen and Steinmetz (2000b) that provided evidence that direct infusions of H7, a general protein kinase inhibitor, impaired the acquisition but not the retention of eye-blink CRs. Together, these data provide strong support for the idea that protein synthesis and, more specifically, protein kinase activity in the interpositus nucleus are involved in the acquisition of CRs.

New behavioral and molecular genetics techniques have proven useful for advancing our understanding of cellular processes that might underlie classical eye-blink conditioning. Chen, Bao, Lockard, Kim, and Thompson (1996) showed that partial learning could be seen in Purkinje cell-degeneration (pcd) mutant mice that were given classical eye-blink conditioning trials. Lesions of the interpositus nuclei of the pcd mice, however, produced complete response abolition, thus demonstrating that some residual learning appears to take place in the interpositus nucleus (Chen, Bao, & Thompson, 1999). Qiao et al. (1998) showed a severe deficit in the acquisition of classical eye-blink conditioning in the spontaneous ataxic mutant mouse *stargazer* that have a selective reduction of brain-derived neurotrophic factor (BDNF) mRNA expression in the cerebellum. Impaired eye-blink conditioning was also observed in the *waggler* mutant, which also has a selective deficit in BDNF expression involving cerebellar granule cells (Bao, Chen, Qiao, Knusel, & Thompson, 1998). These data suggest that BDNF may play a role in plasticity processes that underlie eye-blink conditioning.

The data concerning cellular processes involved with eye-blink conditioning seem to suggest that important plasticity processes associated with the learning of this simple, discrete response involve neurons in both cerebellar cortex and the deep cerebellar nuclei. Indeed, it is likely that interactions between cortical and nuclear areas, along with conditioning-related feedback from the cerebellum onto the essential CS and US pathways that project information to the cerebellum, are involved in generating CRs. Some studies designed to examine these interactions are underway, and it is likely that many more will be undertaken in the next several years.

Using Classical Eye-Blink Conditioning to Study Other Behavioral and Neural Phenomena

Many investigators have recognized the usefulness of classical eye-blink conditioning for studying other behavioral and neurological phenomena such as development, aging, neurological impairment, and behavioral and psychological pathologies. Given the well-delineated behavioral bases of this simple form of learning as well as the emerging details concerning the neural substrates that underlie the behavioral plasticity, there has been a growing interest in using eye-blink conditioning to explore a host of basic science issues related to learning and memory as well as a number of clinical and applied phenomena.

Stanton and his colleagues have used eye-blink conditioning to describe the development of associative learning in rats (see Stanton & Freeman, 2000, for review). Using techniques developed by Skelton (1988) for classically conditioning the eye-blink response of freely moving rats, Stanton and his colleagues have conducted a series of studies that have explored the ontogeny of associative learning in the developing rat. For example, they have shown that the development of conditioning parallels the development of the cerebellum: postnatal day (PND) 17 rats do not show evidence of conditioning; PND 20 rats show moderate amounts of learning; and PND 24 rats demonstrate rather robust learning.

At the other end of the life cycle, eye-blink conditioning has been effectively used to study aging in humans and in animal models. Studies have shown that in both humans and non-human animals, age-related changes in conditioning can be seen when either the delay or trace conditioning procedure is used (e.g., Woodruff-Pak, Lavond, Logan, & Thompson, 1987; Woodruff-Pak & Thompson, 1988). Further, age-related deficits in conditioning seem to parallel age-associated changes in brain structures that are critical for eye-blink conditioning, such as the cerebellum and hippocampus (see Woodruff-Pak & Lemieux, 2001, for review). In addition, research by Woodruff-Pak and her colleagues has shown that classical eye-blink conditioning is a very sensitive indicator and predictor of Alzheimer's disease, a degenerative brain disorder that is known to affect brain regions that are important for eye-blink conditioning (see Woodruff-Pak, 2000, for review).

Classical eye-blink conditioning has proven useful for the study of neurological and psychological impairments. For example, Daum and colleagues have shown that persons with cerebellar damage show impaired eye-blink conditioning (Daum et al., 1993) but not persons with other neurological impairments, including temporal lobe lesions (Daum, Channon, & Gray, 1992), Parkinson's disease, and Huntington's disease (see Schugens, Topka, & Daum, 2000, for review). At least some persons with autism are thought to have cerebellar cortical pathologies; and as predicted, deficits in classical eye-blink conditioning have been reported in some persons with autism (Sears, Finn, & Steinmetz, 1994). Specifically, persons with autism show greatly facilitated rates of conditioning and mistimed CRs, which may be due to the pathology in cerebellar cortex and the hippocampus that has been reported. A similar pattern of responding has been reported for individuals with schizophrenia who have been given eye-blink conditioning trials (Sears, Andreasen, & O'Leary, 2000). Finally, eye-blink conditioning has been used to test the basic idea that persons with obsessive-compulsive disorder (OCD) generally acquire aversively motivated CRs more rapidly than do other persons. Tracy, Ghose, Stetcher, McFall, and Steinmetz (1999) showed that under some contextual situations persons with OCD show an extremely rapid acquisition of eye-blink CRs, which supports the idea that these individuals may be sensitive to aversive CRs.

All of these examples demonstrate the great utility of eye-blink conditioning in testing hypotheses concerning behavioral and neural function, a utility that is due to the impressive database that has been assembled concerning behavioral and neural correlates of this simple form of associative learning.

Classical Conditioning of Other Discrete Responses

Although classical eye-blink conditioning has certainly been the most popular paradigm for studying the conditioning of discrete somatic responses, over the years classical conditioning of other response systems has been attempted.

In an early attempt to evaluate the potential role of the inferior colliculus in classical conditioning, Halas and Beardsley (1970) classically conditioned the hind-limb flexion responses of four cats while recording neural activity from the inferior colliculus. Training consisted of paired presentations of a tone CS with a mild electrical shock to the hind paw as a US. In the same cats they also delivered some instrumental conditioning trials where a leg flexion resulted in avoidance of the shock US. Halas and Beardsley reported largely negative results: For three cats the CS produced an inhibition of collicular activity that was not modified by training. For one cat CR-related activity was observed during instrumental but not classical conditioning trials.

Several researchers have studied forelimb flexion conditioning in the cat. Tsukahara and associated conducted a series of studies aimed at delineating the involvement of corticorubrospinal system in classical conditioning of forelimb flexion in cats (e.g., Tsukahara, Oda, & Notsu, 1981). In their studies the CS was electrical stimulation that was delivered to the cerebral peduncle, and the US was an electric shock delivered to the skin of the forelimb. Tsukahara and his colleagues used this preparation to study possible conditioning-related plasticity in the corticorubral system.

Voneida and colleagues have also classically conditioned the limb-flexion response in cats by pairing a tone CS and a mild electric shock to the forelimb as a US (Voneida et al., 1990). They have explored the involvement of the olivocerebellar system in encoding classical forelimb conditioning by delivering lesions to various regions of the inferior olivary complex. Rostromedial olivary lesions, which included spino-olivary and cortico-olivary forelimb projection zones and the olivocerebellar projection area, produced extinction and severe deficits in conditioned responding. This result parallels nicely the results of olivary lesion studies during eye-blink conditioning in the rabbit (McCormick et al., 1985; Yeo, Hardiman, & Glickstein, 1986).

Finally, Marchetti-Gauthier, Meziane, Devigne, and Soumireu-Mourat (1990) examined the effects of bilateral lesions of the cerebellar interpositus nucleus on forelimb flexion conditioning in mice. They used lights and tones as CSs and an electric shock delivered to the forelimb as a US. The mice were restrained in Plexiglas restraint boxes, and forelimb flexion responses were measured using EMG methods. These researchers showed that bilateral lesions of the interpositus nucleus prevented conditioning. However, unlike previous rabbit studies (e.g., Steinmetz, Lavond, et al., 1992), in which bilateral lesions of the interpositus nucleus were delivered after training, no effects of the lesions could be detected in their paradigm. They concluded that in the mouse the interpositus nucleus was necessary for acquisition, but not retention, of classically conditioned forelimb flexion, a most puzzling result and conclusion.

Classical Jaw-Movement Conditioning

In the 1960s Gormezano and colleagues developed a rabbit-appetitive classical conditioning procedure that involves recording a relatively discrete jaw-movement response (e.g., Coleman, Patterson, & Gormezano, 1966; Sheafor & Gormezano, 1972; Smith, DiLollo, & Gormezano, 1966). In this procedure a light or tone CS is paired with a rewarding intraoral water (or saccharin) US. The water US causes a rhythmic jaw movement that is related to consumption. After repeated pairings with the appetitive US, the CS eventually becomes capable of eliciting the jaw-movement response in the absence of the US. In behavioral studies this procedure has proven useful for studying motivational factors that are associated with conditioning. For example, water deprivation prior to conditioning can produce a different motivational state for jaw-movement conditioning and hence alter the rate of acquisition (e.g., Mitchell & Gormezano, 1970). More important for our discussion here, classical jaw-movement conditioning has been effectively used to study the neural bases of simple appetitive learning (for reviews, see Berry, Seager, Asaka, & Borgnis, 2000; Berry, Seager, Asaka, & Griffin, 2001).

Critical CS and US pathways for jaw-movement conditioning have not been delineated. Although the motor pathways for jaw-movement conditioning have not been worked out in as much detail as those for eye-blink conditioning, it is assumed that the trigeminal nucleus, which controls the muscles of mastication (Donga, Dubuc, Kolta, & Lund, 1992), is chiefly involved in generating the UR and CR for this type of learning. The trigeminal is thought to be heavily influence by neocortical and other higher input in the generation of the jaw-movement response, perhaps accounting for the relatively complex rhythmic response pattern that is seen (Dellow & Lund, 1971). Thus, important differences between jaw-movement conditioning and eye-blink conditioning are already apparent—the jaw-movement response is relatively more complex and appears not to involve the cerebellum. This was demonstrated in a study published by Gibbs (1992), who showed that lesions of the interpositus nucleus completely abolished eye-blink CRs but had no affect on jaw-movement CRs recorded from the same rabbits.

Berry and colleagues have conducted an extensive series of studies on the involvement of the hippocampus in this type of appetitive learning. In multiple- and single-unit recording studies they have shown that pyramidal cells in the CA1 area of the hippocampus increased their firing rates over training (e.g., Oliver, Swain, & Berry, 1993; Seager, Borgnis, & Berry, 1997). Berry and colleagues compared hippocampal firing patterns recorded on eye-blink conditioning and jaw-movement conditioning trials by using a discrimination procedure that employed two tones to differentiate air-puff US and water US trials (see Berry et al., 2000). Although excitatory patterns of responding are generally seen, the patterns of spiking during jaw-movement conditioning (i.e., the

magnitude, duration, frequency, and rhythmicity of spiking) were somewhat different than that seen during eye-blink conditioning.

Berry and associates have also successfully used the jaw-movement conditioning procedure to study aging effects as well as cholinergic brain function. Consistent with data from eye-blink conditioning experiments (Woodruff-Pak et al., 1987), they observed that 40- to 49-month-old rabbits were slower to acquire the conditioned jaw-movement response than were 3- to 7-month-old rabbits (Seager et al., 1997). Deficits in hippocampal unit activity were also seen in the aged rabbits. Early in training, young rabbits showed significantly great hippocampal activity just prior to US onset, and the magnitude of this activity was highly correlated with the rate of learning. The rhythmic CRs recorded in the aging rabbits were found to be of a significantly lower frequency than younger rabbits, but no difference in UR rhythmicity was observed. This suggested that the effect of aging was on a neural system that somehow modulated the central pattern generator during CRs, but not URs.

Given previous data indicating an involvement of disruptions of cholinergic systems in aging effects, Berry and colleagues have also studied the effects of cholinergic impairment on jaw-movement conditioning. They found many parallels between aging effects and cholinergic impairment. For example, subcutaneous injections of cholinergic blockers (e.g., scopolamine hydrobromide) resulted in longer acquisition times and also the suppression of conditioning-related hippocampal activity (Salvatierra & Berry, 1989). Further, the cholinergic blocker selectively decreased the frequency of CR rhythmicity similar to the level seen in aged rabbits.

The hippocampal recording, aging, and pharmacological studies described here illustrate the potential usefulness of the classical jaw-movement conditioning procedure for studying the neural bases of the associative learning of discrete responses. It is clear that among other things, the major use of this procedure may be in delineating similarities and differences between appetitive and aversive conditioning processes.

Neural Substrates of the Instrumental Conditioning of Discrete Responses

Instrumental conditioning procedures have also been used to advance our understanding of the neural bases of simple associative learning. While formally similar to classical conditioning procedures (e.g., discrete stimuli are typically used and discrete responses are recorded), instrumental conditioning differs from classical conditioning in one important respect—the response made by the organism affects the delivery of the stimuli used in training. Avoidance conditioning best illustrates the difference between classical and instrumental conditioning. In classical eye-blink conditioning, a US is presented after the CS regardless of whether the subject generates a CR. This task can easily turn into an instrumental task by introducing a contingency between the subject's response and the presentation of the US. For example, in instrumental eye-blink conditioning the US is withheld if the subject executes a CR prior to when the US would normally occur.

Gabriel and colleagues have used an instrumental conditioning procedure to explore extensively the involvement of the forebrain and other structures in simple associative learning (see Gabriel & Talk, 2001, for review). Their procedure, known as *discriminative instrumental avoidance learning,* is an adaptation of a procedure first described by Brogden and Culler (1936). Rabbits are placed in a large rotating wheel apparatus. Two CSs (typically tones of two different frequencies) are presented. One tone frequency (the CS+) is initially followed by a foot-shock US, whereas the second tone frequency (the CS−) is presented alone. If the rabbit steps forward (thus turning the wheel) after tone onset but before shock onset, the shock is not delivered (i.e., the rabbit has successfully avoided the shock). Over several trials, the rabbit learns to respond to the CS+ and ignore the CS−. More recently, Gabriel and colleagues developed an appetitive procedure that parallels the aversive task. In this task the rabbits can receive a reward by approaching and making oral contact with a drinking spout that is presented for a period of time after CS+ presentation. The reward is not delivered if spout contact is made after CS− presentation. In an elegant series of studies, Gabriel and colleagues have recorded brain activity from a variety of brain regions during these forms of learning and have thus described to a large extent the neural systems involved in this learning.

Gabriel and colleagues have described the neural system involved in discriminative instrumental avoidance (and approach) learning as functional modules (Freeman, Cuppernell, Flannery, & Gabriel, 1996; Gabriel & Talk, 2001). Unlike eye-blink conditioning, in which relatively few critical sites for CS-US convergence appear to exist (and most seem to be in the cerebellum), Gabriel and colleagues have proposed that there are many CS-US convergence sites for discriminative instrumental learning, each of which has a rather unique and necessary function for learning to take place. Other CS-US convergence sites are thought to have important modulatory functions. These various sites are referred to as modules, and each module is assumed to receive CS and US input during learning as well as input from other modules.

In an extensive and comprehensive series of studies conducted over the last 25 years or so, Gabriel and colleagues have used mainly lesion and neural recording methods to define and study the modules involved in this type of instrumental learning. An in-depth review of the impressive data set is beyond the scope of this chapter, but a few generalities concerning their findings can be raised. First, the cingulate cortex and associated thalamic nuclei play a very important role in this learning (e.g., Freeman & Gabriel, 1999; Gabriel, 1990; Gabriel, Sparenborg, & Kubota, 1989). These areas seem to comprise a module that is specialized for processing associative attention and also retrieval of information in response to the presentation of task-relevant cues. The involvement of the hippocampus in this type of instrumental learning has also been evaluated (e.g., Kang & Gabriel, 1998). Lesion and recording studies seem to suggest that the hippocampus is a module that is involved in context-based retrieval (i.e., processing the context in which the simple associative cue-based learning occurs). A third major module that has been defined involves the amygdala, which Gabriel and colleagues have identified as important for initiating learning-relevant plasticity in other areas of the brain (e.g., Poremba & Gabriel, 1999). This idea is compatible with the view championed by McGaugh and his colleagues that amygdala efferents are involved mainly in the establishment of memory in a host of nonamygdalar brain areas (e.g., McGaugh & Cahill, 1997).

There appears to be little, if any, overlap in the neural circuitry that encodes classical eye-blink conditioning and discriminative avoidance learning. In two collaborative studies Gabriel and colleagues and Steinmetz and colleagues evaluated the effects of cerebellar lesions (Steinmetz, Sears, Gabriel, Kubota, & Poremba, 1991) and limbic thalamus lesions (Gabriel et al., 1996) on the two procedures. A complete dissociation of lesion effects was observed: Lesions of the interpositus nucleus completely abolished classical eye-blink CRs but had no effect on the discriminative avoidance learning, whereas lesions of the limbic thalamus severely impaired discriminative avoidance learning but had no effect on classical eye-blink conditioning. Differences in the two learning tasks most likely account for the observed dissociation. The avoidance task involves a relatively complex, goal-directed movement in a discriminative context. The classical conditioning task involves a relatively discrete movement in a nondiscriminative context. Also, the interstimulus intervals for the two tasks are widely different—the CS-US interval for the instrumental learning task is usually greater than 5 s, whereas the CS-US interval for the classical conditioning task is never more than 2 se(and more often in the range of 250–500 ms).

Steinmetz and colleagues have recently developed an instrumental bar-press conditioning procedure in rats that has been successfully used to study behavioral, neural, and pharmacological phenomena (Steinmetz et al., 1993). In the aversive version of this task, a tone CS is presented for a period of time, and rats are required to press a response bar during the tone presentation to avoid a mild foot-shock US. A bar press made during the shock presentation terminates the shock, thus allowing an escape response. In the appetitive version of this task, a tone CS is presented for a period of time, and rats receive a food pellet reinforcement if they press the response bar while the tone is on. This preparation has been used in within-subject design experiments. The same rat is trained in both the aversive and appetitive versions of the task using the same tone CS, the same training context, and the same response requirements (i.e., in essence, the only difference between the appetitive and aversive training is the consequences of the bar press). Variations of the task have also been used such as training using a discriminative stimulus to signal appetitive and aversive trials, training on partial or delay reinforcement schedules, and training in conjunction with autonomic recording.

In an initial study Steinmetz et al. (1993) demonstrated that bilateral lesions of the cerebellar interpositus nuclei prevented learning of the aversively motivated bar-press learning when relatively short tone presentation intervals were used. The same rats could acquire the appetitive task normally, thus demonstrating that the lesion-induced deficit was not sensory or motor in nature. This within-subject instrumental learning procedure has also been used successfully to study basic approach and avoidance learning in rats that were bred specifically for alcohol preference (e.g., Blankenship, Finn, & Steinmetz, 1998, 2000) as well as in studies by Garraghty and colleagues designed to assess cognitive impairments associated with the administration of antiepileptic compounds (Banks, Mohr, Besheer, Steinmetz & Garraghty, 1999).

CONCLUSION

Study of the brain substrates of learning and memory is at a most exciting stage. We are rapidly gaining an appreciation of the neural circuits and pathways that form the essential substrates for different forms of learning and memory. On the other hand, analyses of the basic mechanisms of synaptic plasticity, LTP, and LTD are proceeding rapidly. At present, these mechanisms are viewed by many as the most likely candidates for memory storage in the brain (Baudry, Davis, & Thompson, 2000; Bliss & Collingridge, 1993; but see Shors & Matzel, 1997). However, these two approaches have yet to meet. At present, LTP and LTD are mechanisms in search of phenomena, and the various forms of learning and memory

are phenomena in search of mechanisms. It is our fervent hope that the two will meet. The fundamental problem, posed by Karl Lashley in 1929, remains that in order to analyze mechanisms of memory storage, it is first necessary to localize the sites of storage in the brain. This is now close to being accomplished for simpler forms of learning in mammals: classical conditioning of fear (amygdala) and discrete behavioral responses (cerebellum). Only when this has been done can we build a tight causal chain from, for example, LTP in the amygdala or LTD in the cerebellum to the behavioral expression of memory. The problem is more severe in the hippocampus, a structure that prominently displays LTP and LTD and is clearly necessary for declarative-experiential storage (and retrieval) in humans and seemingly in other mammals as well. Virtually nothing is known about the readout, the neural circuitry, from hippocampus to behavioral expression of memory.

To return to molecular biology, the bases of LTP, LTD, and other aspects of synaptic plasticity are likely to be understood in detail at the biochemical, structural, and genetic levels in the next decade or so. Assume for the moment that LTP and LTD are the mechanisms of memory storage in the mammalian brain. Having established this, will we understand memory storage in the brain? The answer is clearly no. All LTP and LTD do is to increase or decrease transmission of information at the synapses where they occur. The nature of the memories so coded is determined entirely by particular complex neural circuits in the brain that form the memories. Molecular-genetic analysis can someday tell us the nature of the *mechanisms* of memory storage and perhaps even the loci of storage, but it can never tell us *what* the memories are. Only a detailed characterization of the neural circuitries that code, store, and retrieve memories, the focus of this chapter, can do this.

REFERENCES

Abeliovich, A., Paylor, R., Chen, C., Kim, J. J., Wehner, J. M., & Tonegawa, S. (1993). PKC gamma mutant mice exhibit mild deficits in spatial and contextual learning. *Cell, 75,* 1263–1271.

Adolphs, R., Tranel, D., Damasio, H., & Damasio, A. (1994). Impaired recognition of emotion in facial expressions following bilateral damage to the human amygdala. *Nature, 372,* 669–672.

Aggleton, J. P. (2000). *The amygdala* (2nd ed.). Oxford, England: Oxford University Press.

Alkon, D. L. (1989). Memory storage and neural systems. *Scientific America, 261,* 42–50.

Amorapanth, P., LeDoux, J. E., & Nader, K. (2000). Different lateral amygdala outputs mediate reactions and actions elicited by a fear-arousing stimulus. *Nature Neuroscience, 3,* 74–79.

Anagnostaras, S. G., Maren, S., & Fanselow, M. S. (1999). Temporally graded retrograde amnesia of contextual fear after hippocampal damage in rats: Within-subjects examination. *Journal of Neuroscience, 19,* 1106–1114.

Andersson, G., Garwicz, M., & Hesslow, G. (1988). Evidence for a GABA-mediated cerebellar inhibition of the inferior olive in the cat. *Experimental Brain Research, 72,* 450–456.

Antoniadis, E. A., & McDonald, R. J. (2000). Amygdala, hippocampus and discriminative fear conditioning to context. *Behavioural Brain Research, 108,* 1–19.

Applegate, C. D., Frysinger, R. C., Kapp, B. S., & Gallagher, M. (1982). Multiple unit activity recorded from the amygdala central nucleus during Pavlovian heart rate conditioning in the rabbit. *Brain Research, 238,* 457–462.

Applegate, C. D., Kapp, B. S., Underwood, M. D., & McNall, C. L. (1983). Autonomic and somatomotor effects of amygdala central nucleus stimulation in awake rabbits. *Physiology and Behavior, 31,* 353–360.

Attwell, P. J. E., Rahman, S., Ivarsson, M., & Yeo, C. H. (1999). Cerebellar cortical-AMPA-kainate receptor blockage prevents performance of classically conditioned nictitating membrane responses. *Journal of Neuroscience, 19,* 41–46.

Bailey, D. J., Kim, J. J., Sun, W., Thompson, R. F., & Helmstetter, F. J. (1999). Acquisition of fear conditioning in rats requires the synthesis of mRNA in the amygdala. *Behavioral Neuroscience, 113,* 276–282.

Balaban, P. (1993). Behavioral neurobiology of learning in terrestrial snails. *Progress in Neurobiology, 41,* 1–19.

Banks, M. K., Mohr, N. L., Besheer, J., Steinmetz, J. E., & Garraghty, P. E. (1999). The effects of phenytoin on instrumental appetitive-to-aversive transfer in rats. *Pharmacology Biochemistry and Behavior, 63,* 465–472.

Bao, S., Chen, L., Qiao, X., Knusel, B., & Thompson, R. F. (1998). Impaired eye-blink conditioning in *waggler,* a mutant mouse with cerebellar BDNF deficiency. *Learning and Memory, 5,* 355–364.

Bao, S., Chen, L., & Thompson, R. F. (2000). Learning- and cerebellum-dependent neuronal activity in the lateral pontine nucleus. *Behavioral Neuroscience, 114,* 254–261.

Baudry, M., Davis, J. L., & Thompson, R. F. (2000). *Advances in synaptic plasticity.* Cambridge, MA: MIT Press.

Beggs, A. L., Steinmetz, J. E., & Patterson, M. M. (1985). Classical conditioning of a flexor nerve response in spinal cats: Effects of tibial nerve CS and a differential conditioning paradigm. *Behavioral Neuroscience, 99,* 496–508.

Beggs, A. L., Steinmetz, J. E., Romano, A. G., & Patterson, M. M. (1983). Extinction and retention of a classically conditioned flexor nerve response in acute spinal cat. *Behavioral Neuroscience, 97,* 530–540.

Beggs, J. M., Brown, T. H., Byrne, J. H., Crow, T., LeDoux, J. E., LeBar, K., & Thompson, R. F. (1999). Learning and memory: Basic mechanisms. In M. J. Zigmond, F. E. Bloom, S. C. Landis,

J. L. Roberts, & L. R. Squire (Eds.), *Fundamental neuroscience* (pp. 1411–1454). New York: Academic Press.

Berger, T. W., Alger, B., & Thompson, R. F. (1976). Neuronal substrate of classical conditioning in the hippocampus. *Science, 192,* 483–485.

Berger, T. W., Rinaldi, P. C., Weisz, D. J., & Thompson, R. F. (1983). Single-unit analysis of different hippocampal cell types during classical conditioning of rabbit nictitating membrane response. *Journal of Neurophysiology, 50,* 1197–1219.

Berger, T. W., & Thompson, R. F. (1978a). Neuronal plasticity in the limbic system during classical conditioning of the rabbit nictitating membrane response: I. The hippocampus. *Brain Research, 145,* 323–346.

Berger, T. W., & Thompson, R. F. (1978b). Neuronal plasticity in the limbic system during classical conditioning of the rabbit nictitating membrane response: II. Septum and mammillary bodies. *Brain Research, 156,* 293–314.

Bermudez-Rattoni, F., Intronini-Collison, I. B., & McGaugh, J. L. (1991). Reversible inactivation of the insular cortex by tetrodotoxin produces retrograde and anterograde amnesia for inhibitory avoidance and spatial learning. *Proceedings of the National Academy of Sciences USA, 88,* 5379–5382.

Berry, S. D., Seager, M. A., Asaka, Y., & Borgnis, R. L. (2000). Motivational issues in aversive and appetitive conditioning paradigms. In D. S. Woodruff-Pak & J. E. Steinmetz (Eds.), *Eyeblink classical conditioning: Vol. 2. Animal models* (pp. 287–312). Boston: Kluwer.

Berry, S. D., Seager, M. A., Asaka, Y., & Griffin, A. L. (2001). The septo-hippocampal system and classical conditioning. In J. E. Steinmetz, M. A. Gluck, & P. R. Solomon (Eds.), *Model systems and the neurobiology of associative learning* (pp. 79–110). Mahwah, NJ: Erlbaum.

Berthier, N. E., & Moore, J. W. (1986). Cerebellar Purkinje cell activity related to the classically conditioned nictitating membrane response. *Experimental Brain Research, 63,* 341–350.

Berthier, N. E., & Moore, J. W. (1990). Activity of deep cerebellar nuclear cells during classical conditioning of nictitating membrane extension in rabbits. *Experimental Brain Research, 83,* 44–54.

Blanchard, D. C., & Blanchard, R. J. (1972). Innate and conditioned reactions to threat in rats with amygdaloid lesions. *Journal of Comparative and Physiological Psychology, 81,* 281–290.

Blanchard, R. J., & Blanchard, D. C. (1969). Crouching as an index of fear. *Journal of Comparative and Physiological Psychology, 67,* 370–375.

Blanchard, R. J., & Blanchard, D. C. (1971). Defensive reactions in the albino rat. *Learning and Motivation, 2,* 351–362.

Blanchard, R. J., Blanchard, D. C., Agullana, R., & Weiss, S. M. (1991). Twenty-two kHz alarm cries to presentation of a predator, by laboratory rats living in visible burrow systems. *Physiology and Behavior, 50,* 967–972.

Blankenship, M. R., Finn, P. R., & Steinmetz, J. E. (1998). A characterization of approach and avoidance learning in alcohol preferring (P) and non-preferring (NP) rats. *Alcoholism: Clinical and Experimental Research, 22,* 1227–1233.

Blankenship, M. R., Finn, P. R., & Steinmetz, J. E. (2000). A characterization of approach and avoidance learning in high alcohol drinking (HAD) and low alcohol drinking (LAD) rats. *Alcoholism: Clinical and Experimental Research, 24,* 1778–1784.

Bliss, T. V. P., & Collingridge, G. L. (1993). A synaptic model of memory: Long term potentiation in the hippocampus. *Nature, 361,* 31–39.

Bolles, R. C. (1970). Species-specific defensive reactions and avoidance learning. *Psychological Review, 71,* 32–48.

Bourtchuladze, R., Frenguelli, B., Blendy, J., Cioffi, D., Schutz, G., & Silva, A. J. (1994). Deficient long-term memory in mice with a targeted mutation of the cAMP-responsive element-binding protein. *Cell, 79,* 59–68.

Bracha, V., Irwin, K. B., Webster, M. L., Wunderlich, D. A., Stachowiak, M. K., & Bloedel, J. R. (1998). Microinjections of anisomycin into the intermediate cerebellum during learning affect the acquisition of classically conditioned responses in the rabbit. *Brain Research, 788,* 169–178.

Brandon, S. E., & Wagner, A. R. (1991). Modulation of a Pavlovian conditioned reflex by a putative emotive conditioned stimulus. *Journal of Experimental Psychology: Animal Behavior Processes, 17,* 299–311.

Brogden, W. J., & Culler, E. (1936). Device for motor conditioning of small animals. *Science, 83,* 269–270.

Brown, J. S., Kalish, H. I., & Farber, I. E. (1951). Conditioned fear as revealed by magnitude of startle response to an auditory stimulus. *Journal of Experimental Psychology, 41,* 317–328.

Brunzell, D. H., & Kim, J. J. (2001). Fear conditioning to tone but not context is attenuated by lesions of insular cortex and posterior extension of intralaminar complex. *Behavioral Neuroscience, 115,* 365–375.

Bucci, D. J., Phillips, R. G., & Burwell, R. B. (2000). Contributions of postrhinal and perirhinal cortices to contextual information processing. *Behavioral Neuroscience, 114,* 882–894.

Buchanan, S. L., & Powell, D. A. (1988). Parasagittal thalamic knife cuts retard Pavlovian eyeblink conditioning and abolish the tachycardiac component of the heart rate conditioned response. *Brain Research Bulletin, 21,* 723–729.

Buchanan, S. L., & Thompson, R. H. (1990). Mediodorsal thalamic lesions and Pavlovian conditioning of heart rate and eyeblink responses in the rabbit. *Behavioral Neuroscience, 104,* 912–918.

Byrne, J. H., & Kandel, E. R. (1996). Presynaptic facilitation revisited: State- and time-dependence. *Journal of Neuroscience, 16,* 425–435.

Cahill, L., Babinsky, R., Markowitsch, H., & McGaugh, J. L. (1995). The amygdala and emotional memory. *Nature, 377,* 295–296.

Cahill, L., Haier, R., Fallon, J., Alkire, M., Tang, C., Keator, D., Wu, J., & McGaugh, J. L. (1996). Amygdala activity at encoding correlated with long-term, free recall of emotional information. *Proceedings of the National Academy of Sciences USA, 93,* 8016–8021.

Cahill, L., Weinberger, N. M., Roozendaal, B., & McGaugh, J. L. (1999). Is the amygdala a locus of "conditioned fear"? Some questions and caveats. *Neuron, 23,* 227–228.

Campeau, S., & Davis, M. (1995). Involvement of subcortical and cortical afferents to the lateral nucleus of the amygdala in fear conditioning measured with fear-potentiated startle in rats trained concurrently with auditory and visual conditioned stimuli. *Journal of Neuroscience, 15,* 2312–2327.

Campeau, S., Miserendino, M. J. D., & Davis, M. (1992). Intra-amydaloid infusion of the N-methyl-D-aspartate receptor antagonist AP5 blocks acquisition but not expression of fear-potentiated startle to an auditory conditioned stimulus. *Behavioral Neuroscience, 106,* 569–574.

Cegavske, C. F., Patterson, M. M., & Thompson, R. F. (1979). Neuronal unit activity in the abducens nucleus during classical conditioning of the nictitating membrane response in the rabbit (oryctolagus cuniculus). *Journal of Comparative Physiological Psychology, 93,* 595–609.

Cegavske, C. F., Thompson, R. F., Patterson, M. M., & Gormezano, I. (1976). Mechanisms of efferent neuronal control of the reflex nictitating membrane response in rabbit (oryctolagus cuniculus). *Journal of Comparative and Physiological Psychology, 90,* 411–423.

Chapman, P. F., & Bellavance, L. L. (1992). Induction of long-term potentiation in the basolateral amygdala does not depend on NMDA receptor activation. *Synapse, 11,* 310–318.

Chapman, P. F., Kairiss, E. W., Keenan, C. L., & Brown, T. H. (1990). Long-term synaptic potentiation in the amygdla. *Synapse, 6,* 271–278.

Chapman, P. F., Steinmetz, J. E., Sears, L. L., & Thompson, R. F. (1990). Effects of lidocaine injection in the interpositus nucleus and red nucleus on conditioned behavioral and neuronal responses. *Brain Research, 537,* 149–156.

Chen, G., & Steinmetz, J. E. (2000a). Intra-cerebellar infusion of NMDA receptor antagonist AP5 disrupts classical eyeblink conditioning in rabbits. *Brain Research, 887,* 144–156.

Chen, G., & Steinmetz, J. E. (2000b). Microinfusion of protein kinase inhibitor H7 in the cerebellum impairs the acquisition but not retention of classical eyeblink conditioning in rabbits. *Brain Research, 856,* 193–201.

Chen, L., Bao, S., Lockard, J. M., Kim, J. J., & Thompson, R. F. (1996). Impaired classical eyeblink conditioning in cerebellar-lesioned and Purkinje cell degeneration (pcd) mutant mice. *Journal of Neuroscience, 16,* 2829–2838.

Chen, L., Bao, S., & Thompson, R. F. (1999). Bilateral lesions of the interpositus nucleus completely prevent eyeblink conditioning in Purkinje cell-degenerated mutant mice. *Behavioral Neuroscience, 113,* 204–210.

Choi, J.-S., Lindquist, D. H., & Brown, T. H. (2001). Amygdala lesions block conditioned enhancement of the early component of the rat eyeblink reflex. *Behavioral Neuroscience, 115,* 764–775.

Clark, R. E., Gohl, E. B., & Lavond, D. G. (1997). The learning-related activity that develops in the pontine nuclei during classical eyeblink conditioning is dependent on the interpositus nucleus. *Learning and Memory, 3,* 532–544.

Clark, R. E., & Squire, L. R. (1998). Classical conditioning and brain systems: The role of awareness. *Science, 280,* 77–81.

Clark, R. E., & Squire, L. R. (1999). Human eyeblink classical eyeblink conditioning: Effects of manipulating awareness of the stimulus contingencies. *Psychological Science, 10,* 14–18.

Clark, R. E., & Squire, L. R. (2000). Awareness and the conditioned eyeblink response. In D. S. Woodruff-Pak & J. E. Steinmetz (Eds.), *Eyeblink classical conditioning: Vol. 1. Applications in humans* (pp. 229–251). Boston: Kluwer.

Clark, R. E., Zhang, A. A., & Lavond, D. G. (1992). Reversible lesions of the cerebellar interpositus nucleus during acquisition and retention of a classically conditioned behavior. *Behavioral Neuroscience, 106,* 879–888.

Clugnet, M.-C., & LeDoux, J. E. (1990). Synaptic plasticity in fear conditioning circuits: Induction of LTP in the lateral nucleus of the amygdala by stimulation of the medial geniculate body. *Journal of Neuroscience, 10,* 2818–2824.

Coleman, S. R., Patterson, M. M., & Gormezano, I. (1966). Conditioned jaw movement in the rabbit: Deprivation procedure and saccharin concentration. *Psychonomic Science, 6,* 39–40.

Collingridge, G. L., Kehl, S. J., & McLennan, H. (1983). Excitatory amino acids in synaptic transmission in the Schaffer collateral-commissural pathway of the rat hippocampus. *Journal of Physiology, 334,* 33–46.

Coulter, D. A., Lo Turco, J. J., Kubota, M., Disterhoft, J. F., Moore, J. W., & Alkon, D. L. (1989). Classical conditioning reduces amplitude and duration of calcium-dependent afterhyperpolarization in rabbit hippocampal pyramidal cells. *Journal of Neurophysiology, 61,* 971–981.

Cousens, G., & Otto, T. (1998). Both pre- and posttraining excitotoxic lesions of the basolateral amygdala abolish the expression of olfactory and contextual fear conditioning. *Behavioral Neuroscience, 112,* 1092–1103.

Crow, T. (1988). Cellular and molecular anyalysis of associative learning and memory in *Hermissenda. Trends in Neuroscience, 11,* 136–142.

Danilova, L. K. (1986). Inhibitory effect of the amygdala on alimentary-conditioned reflexes in the dog. *Zhunal Vysshei Nervnoi Deiatelnosi Imeni I. P. Pavlova, 36,* 319–325.

Dash, P. K., Hochner, B., & Kandel, E. R. (1990). Injection of the cAMP-responsive element into the nucleus of *Aplysia* sensory neurons blocks long-term facilitation. *Nature, 345,* 718–721.

Daum, I., Channon, S., & Gray, J. A. (1992). Classical conditioning after temporal lobe lesions in man: Sparing of simple discrimination and extinction. *Behavioral Brain Research, 52,* 159–165.

Daum, I., Schugens, M. M., Ackermann, H., Lutzenberger, W., Dichgans, J., & Birbaumer, N. (1993). Classical conditioning after cerebellar lesions in humans. *Behavioral Neuroscience, 107,* 748–756.

Davis, M. (1997). Neurobiology of fear responses: The role of the amygdala. *Journal of Neuropsychiatry and Clinical Neurosciences, 9,* 382–402.

Deese, J. E., & Kellogg, W. N. (1949). Some new data on "spinal conditioning." *Journal of Comparative Physiological Psychology, 42,* 157–160.

de Jonge, M. C., Black, J., Deyo, R. A., & Disterhoft, J. F. (1990). Learning-induced afterhyperpolarization reductions in hippocampus are specific for cell type and potassium conductance. *Experimental Brain Research, 80,* 456–462.

Dellow, P. G., & Lund, J. P. (1971). Evidence for central timing of rhythmical mastication. *Journal of Physiology, 215,* 1–13.

Desmond, J. E., & Moore, J. W. (1991). Single-unit activity in red nucleus during the classically conditioned rabbit nictitating membrane response. *Neuroscience Research, 10,* 260–279.

DeZazzo, J., & Tully, T. (1995). Dissection of memory formation: From behavioral pharmacology to molecular genetics. *Trends in Neuroscience, 18,* 212–218.

Disterhoft, J. F., Coulter, D. A., & Alkon, D. L. (1986). Conditioning-specific membrane changes of rabbit hippocampal neurons measured in vitro. *Proceedings of the National Academy of Sciences USA, 83,* 2733–2737.

Disterhoft, J. F., Golden, D. T., Read, H. L., Coulter, D. A., & Alkon, D. L. (1988). AHP reduction in rabbit hippocampal neurons during conditioning correlate with acquisition of the learned response. *Brain Research, 462,* 118–125.

Disterhoft, J. F., & McEchron, M. D. (2000). Cellular alterations in hippocampus during acquisition and consolidation of hippocampus-dependent trace eyeblink conditioning. In D. S. Woodruff-Pak & J. E. Steinmetz (Eds.), *Eyeblink classical conditioning: Vol. 2. Animal models* (pp. 313–334). Boston: Kluwer.

Disterhoft, J. F., Quinn, K. J., Weiss, C., & Shipley, M. T. (1985). Accessory abducens nucleus and conditioned eye retraction nictitating membrane extension in rabbit. *Journal of Neuroscience, 5,* 941–950.

Donga, R., Dubuc, R., Kolta, A., & Lund, J. P. (1992). Evidence that the masticatory muscles receive a direct innervation from cell group k in the rabbit. *Neuroscience, 49,* 951–961.

Dudai, Y. (1989). *The neurobiology of memory.* New York: Oxford University Press.

Durkovic, R. G. (1975). Classical conditioning, sensitization, and habituation of the flexion reflex of the spinal cat. *Physiological Behavior, 14,* 297–304.

Durkovic, R. G., & Prokowich, L. J. (1998). D-2-Amino-5-phosphonovalerate, an NMDA receptor antagonist, blocks induction of associative long-term potentiation of the flexion reflex in spinal cat. *Neuroscience Letters, 257,* 162–164.

Ekerot, C. F., & Kano, M. (1985). Long-term depression of parallel fibre synapses following stimulation of climbing fibres. *Brain Research, 342,* 357–360.

Fanselow, M. S. (1984). What is conditioned fear? *Trends in Neurosciences, 7,* 460–462.

Fanselow, M. S. (1986). Conditioned fear-induced opiate analgesia: A competing motivational state theory of stress-analgesia. *Annals of the New York Academy of Sciences, 467,* 40–54.

Fanselow, M. S., & Kim, J. J. (1994). Acquisition of contextual Pavlovian fear conditioning is blocked by application of an NMDA receptor antagonist D,L-2-amino-5-phosphonovaleric acid to the basolateral amygdala. *Behavioral Neuroscience, 108,* 210–212.

Fendt, M. (2001). Injections of the NMDA receptor antagonist aminophosphonopentanoic acid into the lateral nucleus of the amygdala block the expression of fear-potentiated startle and freezing. *Journal of Neuroscience, 21,* 4111–4115.

Fendt, M., & Fanselow, M. S. (1999). The neuroanatomical and neurochemical basis of conditioned fear. *Neuroscience and Biobehavioral Reviews, 23,* 743–760.

Fischer, K. W., & Lazerson, A. (1984). *Human development.* New York: W. H. Freeman.

Fox, P. C., Eichenbaum, H., & Butter, C. M. (1982). The role of frontal cortex-reticular interactions in performance and extinction of the classically conditioned nictitating membrane response in the rabbit. *Behavioral Brain Research, 5,* 143–156.

Foy, M. R., Foy, J. G., Levine, S., & Thompson, R. F. (1990). Manipulation of pituitary-adrenal activity affects neural plasticity in rodent hippocampus. *Psychological Science, 1,* 201–204.

Foy, M. R., Stanton, M. E., Levine, S., & Thompson, R. F. (1987). Behavioral stress impairs long-term potentiation in rodent hippocampus. *Behavioral and Neural Biology, 48,* 138–149.

Francis, J., Hernandez, L. L., & Powell, D. A. (1981). Lateral hypothalamic lesions: Effects on Pavlovian cardiac and eyeblink conditioning in the rabbit. *Brain Research Bulletin, 6,* 155–163.

Freeman, J. H., Jr., Cuppernell, C., Flannery, K., & Gabriel, M. (1996). Context-specific multi-site cingulate cortical, limbic thalamic, and hippocampal neuronal activity during concurrent discriminative approach and avoidance training in rabbits. *Journal of Neuroscience, 16,* 1538–1549.

Freeman, J. H., Jr., & Gabriel, M. (1999). Changes of cingulothalamic topographic excitation patterns and avoidance response incubation over time following initial discriminative conditioning in rabbits. *Neurobiology of Learning and Memory, 72,* 259–272.

Frost, W. N., Brown, G. D., & Getting, P. A. (1996). Parametric features of habituation of swim cycle number in the marine mollusk *Tritonia diomedea. Neurobiology of Learning and Memory, 65,* 125–134.

Gabriel, M. (1990). Functions of anterior and posterior cingulate cortex during avoidance learning in rabbits. *Progress in Brain Research, 85,* 467–483.

Gabriel, M., Kang, E., Poremba, A., Kubota, Y., Allen, M. T., Miller, D. P., & Steinmetz, J. E. (1996). Neural substrates of discriminative avoidance learning and classical eyeblink conditioning in rabbits: A double dissociation. *Behavioural Brain Research, 82,* 23–30.

Gabriel, M., Sparenborg, S., & Kubota, Y. (1989). Anterior and medial thalamic lesions, discriminative avoidance learning, and cingulate cortical neuronal activity in rabbits. *Experimental Brain Research, 76,* 441–457.

Gabriel, M., & Talk, A. C. (2001). A tale of two paradigms: Lessons learned from parallel studies of discriminative instrumental learning and classical eyeblink conditioning. In J. E. Steinmetz, M. A. Gluck, & P. R. Solomon (Eds.), *Model systems and the neurobiology of associative learning* (pp. 149–186). Mahwah, NJ: Erlbaum.

Gallagher, M., & Kapp, B. S. (1978). Manipulation of opiate activity in the amygdala alters memory processes. *Life Sciences, 23,* 1973–1978.

Gallagher, M., Kapp, B. S., McNall, C. L., & Pascoe, J. P. (1981). Opiate effects in the amygdala central nucleus alters rabbit heart rate conditioning. *Pharmacology, Biochemistry, and Behavior, 14,* 497–505.

Gellman, M. D., Schneiderman, N., Wallach, J. H., & LeBlanc, W. (1981). Cardiovascular responses elicited by hypothalamic stimulation in rabbits reveal a mediolateral organization. *Journal of the Autonomic Nervous System, 4,* 301–317.

Gellman, R., Houk, J. C., & Gibson, A. R. (1983). Somatosensory properties of the inferior olive of the cat. *Journal of Comparative Neurology, 215,* 228–243.

Gelperin, A. (1994). Nitric oxide, odor processing and plasticity. *Netherlands Journal of Zoology, 44,* 159–169.

Gentile, C. G., Jarrell, T. W., Teich, A., McCabe, P. M., & Schneiderman, N. (1986). The role of amygdaloid central nucleus in the retention of differential Pavlovian conditioning of bradycardia in rabbits. *Behavioural Brain Research, 20,* 263–273.

Gibbs, C. M. (1992). Divergent effects on deep cerebellar lesions on two different conditioned somatomotor responses in rabbits. *Brain Research, 585,* 395–399.

Gold, P. E., Hankins, L., Edwards, R. M., Chester, J., & McGaugh, J. L. (1975). Memory interference and facilitation with posttrial amygdala stimulation: Effect on memory varies with footshock level. *Brain Research, 86,* 509–513.

Goldstein, L. E., Rasmusson, A. M., Bunney, B. S., & Roth, R. H. (1996). Role of the amygdala in the coordination of behavioral, neuroendocrine, and prefrontal cortical monoamine responses to psychological stress in the rat. *Journal of Neuroscience, 16,* 4787–4798.

Gomi, H., Sun, W., Finch, C. E., Itohara, S., Yoshimi, K., & Thompson, R. F. (1999). Learning induces a CDC2-related protein kinase, KKIAMRE. *Journal of Neuroscience, 19,* 9530–9537.

Gormezano, I., Kehoe, E. J., & Marshall, B. S. (1983). Twenty years of classical conditioning with the rabbit. *Progress in Psychobiology and Physiological Psychology, 10,* 197–275.

Gould, T. J., Sears, L. L., & Steinmetz, J. E. (1993). Possible CS and US pathways for rabbit classical eyelid conditioning: Electrophysiological evidence for projections from the pontine nuclei and inferior olive to cerebellar cortex and nuclei. *Behavioral and Neural Biology, 60,* 172–185.

Gould, T. J., & Steinmetz, J. E. (1996). Changes in rabbit cerebellar cortical and interpositus nucleus activity during acquisition, extinction and backward classical conditioning. *Neurobiology of Learning and Memory, 65,* 17–34.

Green, J. T., Rogers, R. F., Goodlett, C. R., & Steinmetz, J. E. (2000). Impairment in eyeblink classical conditioning in adult rats exposed to ethanol as neonates. *Alcoholism: Clinical and Experimental Research, 24,* 438–447.

Grossman, S. P., Grossman, L., & Walsh, L. (1975). Functional organization of the rat amygdala with respect to avoidance behavior. *Journal of Comparative and Physiological Psychology, 88,* 829–850.

Grover, L. M., & Teyler, T. J. (1990). Two components of long-term potentiation induced by different patterns of afferent activation. *Nature, 347,* 477–479.

Groves, P. M., & Thompson, R. F. (1970). Habituation: A dual-process theory. *Psychological Reviews, 77,* 419–450.

Guarraci, F. A., Frohardt, R. J., Falls, W. A., & Kapp, B. S. (2000). The effects of intra-amygdaloid infusions of a D2 dopamine receptor antagonist on Pavlovian fear conditioning. *Behavioral Neuroscience, 114,* 647–651.

Halas, E. S., & Beardsley, J. V. (1970). A comparison of conditioned and unconditioned neuronal responses in the inferior colliculus of cats. *Psychonomic Science, 18,* 29–30.

Haley, D. A., Thompson, R. F., & Madden, J. (1988). Pharmacological analysis of the magnocellular red nucleus during classical conditioning of the rabbit nictitating membrane response. *Brain Research, 454,* 131–139.

Hammer, M., & Menzel, R. (1995). Learning and memory in the honeybee. *Journal of Neuroscience, 15,* 1617–1630.

Harris, E. W., & Cotman, C. W. (1986). Long-term potentiation of guinea pig mossy fiber responses is not blocked by N-methyl-D-aspartate antagonists. *Neuroscience Letters, 70,* 132–137.

Hauge, S. A., Tracy, J. A., Baudry, M., & Thompson, R. F. (1998). Selective changes in AMPA receptors in rabbit cerebellum following classical conditioning of the eyelid-nictitating membrane response. *Brain Research, 803,* 9–18.

Helmstetter, F. J. (1992). The amygdala is essential for the expression of conditional hypoalgesia. *Behavioral Neuroscience, 106,* 518–528.

Helmstetter, F. J. (1993). Stress-induced hypoalgesia and defensive freezing are attenuated by application of diazepam to the amygdala. *Pharmacology, Biochemistry, and Behavior, 44,* 433–438.

Helmstetter, F. J., & Bellgowan, P. S. (1994). Effects of muscimol applied to the basolateral amygdala on acquisition and expression of contextual fear conditioning in rats. *Behavioral Neuroscience, 108,* 1005–1009.

Hemart, N., Daniel, H., Jaillard, D., & Crepel, F. (1994). Properties of glutamate receptors are modified during long-term depression in rat cerebellar Purkinje cells. *Neuroscience Research, 19,* 213–221.

Hesslow, G., & Ivarsson, M. (1994). Suppression of cerebellar Purkinje cells during conditioned responses in ferrets. *NeuroReport, 5,* 649–652.

Hesslow, G., & Ivarsson, M. (1996). Inhibition of the inferior olive during conditioned responses in the decerebrate ferret. *Experimental Brain Research, 110,* 36–46.

Hiroaka, M., & Shimamura, M. (1977). Neural mechanisms of the corneal blinking reflex in cats. *Brain Research, 125,* 265–275.

Hitchcock, J. M., & Davis, M. (1986). Lesions of the amygdala, but not of the cerebellum or red nucleus, block conditioned fear as measured with the potentiated startle paradigm. *Behavioral Neuroscience, 100,* 11–22.

Hitchcock, J. M., & Davis, M. (1987). Fear-potentiated startle using an auditory conditioned stimulus: Effect of lesions of the amygdala. *Physiology and Behavior, 39,* 403–408.

Hitchcock, J. M., & Davis, M. (1991). Efferent pathway of the amygdala involved in conditioned fear as measured with the fear-potentiated startle paradigm. *Behavioral Neuroscience, 105,* 826–842.

Hitchcock, J. M., Sananes, C. B., & Davis, M. (1989). Sensitization of the startle reflex by footshock: Blockade by lesions of the central nucleus of the amygdala or its efferent pathway to the brainstem. *Behavioral Neuroscience, 103,* 509–518.

Huang, Y. Y., & Kandel, E. R. (1998). Postsynaptic induction and PKA-dependent expression of LTP in the lateral amygdala. *Neuron, 21,* 169–178.

Huerta, P. T., Sun, L. D., Wilson, M. A., & Tonegawa, S. (2000). Formation of temporal memory requires NMDA receptors within CA1 pyramidal neurons. *Neuron, 25,* 473–480.

Isaacson, R. L. (1974). *The limbic system* (3rd ed.). New York: Plenum.

Ito, M. (1989). Long-term depression. *Annual Review of Neuroscience, 12,* 85–102.

Ivkovich, D., & Thompson, R. F. (1997). Motor cortex lesions do not affect learning or performance of the eyelid response in rabbits. *Behavioral Neuroscience, 111,* 727–738.

Iwata, J., Chida, K., & LeDoux, J. E. (1987). Cardiovascular responses elicited by stimulation of neurons in the central amygdaloid nucleus in awake but not anesthetized rats resemble conditioned emotional responses. *Brain Research, 418,* 183–188.

Iwata, J., LeDoux, J. E., & Reis, D. J. (1986). Destruction of intrinsic neurons in the lateral hypothalamus disrupts the classical conditioning of autonomic but not behavioral emotional responses in the rat. *Brain Research, 368,* 161–166.

Jarrell, T. W., Gentile, C. G., McCabe, P. M., & Schneiderman, N. (1986). The role of the medial geniculate region in differential Pavlovian conditioning of bradycardia in rabbits. *Brain Research, 374*, 126–136.

Johnston, D., Williams, S., Jaffe, D., & Gray, R. (1992). NMDA-receptor independent long-term potentiation. *Annual Review of Physiology, 54*, 489–505.

Joynes, R. L., & Grau, J. W. (1996). Mechanisms of Pavlovian conditioning: Role of protection from habituation in spinal conditioning. *Behavioral Neuroscience, 110*, 1375–1387.

Kandel, E. R. (1976). *Cellular basis of behavior: An introduction to behavioral neurobiology.* San Francisco: W. H. Freeman.

Kaneko, T., & Thompson, R. F. (1997). Disruption of trace conditioning of the nictitating membrane response in rabbits by central cholinergic blockade. *Psychopharmacology, 131*, 161–166.

Kang, E., & Gabriel, M. (1998). Hippocampal modulation of cingulo-thalamic neuronal activity and discriminative avoidance learning in rabbits. *Hippocampus, 8*, 491–510.

Kao, K.-T., & Powell, D. A. (1988). Lesions of the substantia nigra retard Pavlovian eye-blink but not heart rate conditioning in the rabbit. *Behavioral Neuroscience, 102*, 515–525.

Kapp, B. S., Frysinger, R., Gallagher, M., & Haselton, J. (1979). Amygdala central nucleus lesions: Effects on heart rate conditioning in the rabbit. *Physiology and Behavior, 23*, 1109–1117.

Katz, D. B., & Steinmetz, J. E. (1997). Single-unit evidence for eyeblink conditioning in cerebellar cortex is altered, but not eliminated, by interpositus nucleus lesions. *Learning and Memory, 4*, 88–104.

Kellogg, W. N. (1947). Is "spinal conditioning" conditioning? *Journal of Experimental Psychology, 37*, 263–265.

Kellogg, W. N., Deese, J., & Pronko, N. H. (1946). On the behavior of the lumbospinal dog. *Journal of Experimental Psychology, 36*, 503–511.

Kemenes, G., & Benjamin, P. R. (1994). Training in a novel environment improves the appetitive learning performance of the snail, *Lymnaea stagnalis. Behavioral and Neural Biology, 61*, 139–149.

Kettner, R. E., & Thompson, R. F. (1982). Auditory signal detection and decision processes in the nervous system. *Journal of Comparative and Physiological Psychology, 96*, 328–331.

Killcross, S., Robbins, T. W., & Everitt, B. J. (1997). Different types of fear-conditioned behaviour mediated by separate nuclei within amygdala. *Nature, 388*, 377–380.

Kim, J. J., Clark, R. E., & Thompson, R. F. (1995). Hippocampectomy impairs the memory of recently, but not remotely, acquired trace eyeblink conditioned responses. *Behavioral Neuroscience, 109*, 195–203.

Kim, J. J., & Fanselow, M. S. (1992). Modality-specific retrograde amnesia of fear. *Science, 256*, 675–677.

Kim, J. J., Krupa, D. J., & Thompson, R. F. (1998). Inhibitory cerebello-olivary projections and blocking effect in classical conditioning. *Science, 279*, 570–573.

Kim, J. J., Rison, R. A., & Fanselow, M. S. (1993). Effects of amygdala, hippocampus, and periaqueductal gray lesions on short- and long-term contextual fear. *Behavioral Neuroscience, 107*, 1093–1098.

King, D. A. T., Krupa, D. J., Foy, M. R., & Thompson, R. F. (2001). Mechanisms of neuronal conditioning. *International Review of Neurobiology, 45*, 313–337.

Klüver, H., & Bucy, P. C. (1937). "Psychic blindness" and other symptoms following bilateral temporal lobectomy in rhesus monkeys. *American Journal of Physiology, 119*, 352–353.

Knight, D. C., Smith, C. N., Stein, E. A., & Helmstetter, F. J. (1999). Functional MRI of human Pavlovian fear conditioning: Patterns of activation as a function of learning. *NeuroReport, 10*, 3665–3670.

Krupa, D. J., Thompson, J. K., & Thompson, R. F. (1993). Localization of a memory trace in the mammalian brain. *Science, 260*, 989–991.

LaBar, K. S., Gatenby, C., Gore, J. C., LeDoux, J. E., & Phelps, E. A. (1998). Amygdalo-cortical activation during conditioned fear acquisition and extinction: A mixed trial fMRI study. *Neuron, 20*, 937–945.

LaBar, K. S., LeDoux, J. E., Spencer, D. D., & Phelps, E. A. (1995). Impaired fear conditioning following unilateral temporal lobectomy in humans. *Journal of Neuroscience, 15*, 6846–6855.

Lavond, D. G., Hembree, T. L., & Thompson, R. F. (1985). Effect of kainic acid lesions of the cerebellar interpositus nucleus on eyelid conditioning in the rabbit. *Brain Research, 326*, 179–182.

Lavond, D. G., Kim, J. J., & Thompson, R. F. (1993). Mammalian brain substrates of aversive classical conditioning. *Annual Review of Psychology, 44*, 317–342.

Lavond, D. G., & Steinmetz, J. E. (1989). Acquisition of classical conditioning without cerebellar cortex. *Behavioural Brain Research, 33*, 113–164.

Leaton, R. N., & Borszcz, G. S. (1985). Potentiated startle: Its relation to freezing and shock intensity in rats. *Journal of Experimental Psychology: Animal Behavioral Processes, 2*, 248–259.

LeDoux, J. E. (1995). Emotion: Clues from the brain. *Annual Review of Psychology, 46*, 209–235.

LeDoux, J. E. (1996). *The emotional brain.* New York: Simon & Schuster.

LeDoux, J. E. (2000). Emotion circuits in the brain. *Annual Review of Neuroscience, 23*, 155–184.

LeDoux, J. E., Farb, C., & Ruggiero, D. A. (1990). Topographic organization of neurons in the acoustic thalamus that project to the amygdala. *Journal of Neuroscience, 10*, 1043–1054.

LeDoux, J. E., Iwata, J., Cicchetti, P., & Reis, D. J. (1988). Different projections of the central amygdaloid nucleus mediate autonomic and behavioral correlates of conditioned fear. *Journal of Neuroscience, 8*, 2517–2529.

LeDoux, J. E., Iwata, J., Pearl, D., & Reis, D. J. (1986). Disruption of auditory but not visual learning by destruction of intrinsic neurons in the rat medial geniculate body. *Brain Research, 371,* 395–399.

Lee, H. J., Berger, S. Y., Stiedl, O., Spiess, J., & Kim, J. J. (2001). Post-training injections of catecholaminergic drugs do not modulate fear conditioning in rats and mice. *Neuroscience Letters, 303,* 123–126.

Lee, H. J., Choi, J.-S., Brown, T. H., & Kim, J. J. (2001). Amygdalar N-methyl-D-aspartate (NMDA) receptors are critical for the expression of multiple conditioned fear responses. *Journal of Neuroscience, 21,* 4116–4124.

Lee, H. J., & Kim, J. J. (1998). Amygdalar NMDA receptors are critical for new fear learning in previously fear-conditioned rats. *Journal of Neuroscience, 18,* 8444–8454.

Li, X., Phillips, R. G., & LeDoux, J. E. (1995). NMDA and non-NMDA receptors contribute to synaptic transmission between the medial geniculate body and the lateral nucleus of the amygdala. *Experimental Brain Research, 105,* 87–100.

Liang, K. C., Juler, R., & McGaugh, J. L. (1986). Modulating effects of posttraining epinephrine on memory: Involvement of the amygdala noradrenergic system. *Brain Research, 68,* 125–133.

Liang, K. C., McGaugh, J. L., Martinez, J. L., Jensen, R. A., Vasquez, B. J., & Messing, R. B. (1982). Post-training amygdaloid lesions impair retention of an inhibitory avoidance response. *Behavioral Brain Research, 4,* 237–249.

Lin, X. Y., & Glanzman, D. L. (1994). Hebbian induction of long-term potentiation of *Aplysia* sensorimotor synapses: Partial requirement for activation of an NMDA-related receptor. *Proceedings of the Royal Society of London, B 255,* 215–221.

Lincoln, J. S., McCormick, D. A., & Thompson, R. F. (1982). Ipsilateral cerebellar lesions prevent learning of the classically conditioned nictitating membrane/eyelid response. *Brain Research, 242,* 190–193.

London, J. A., & Gillette, R. (1986). Mechanism for food avoidance learning in the central pattern generator of feeding behavior of *Pleurobranchaea californica*. *Proceedings of the National Academy of Sciences USA, 83,* 4058–4062.

MacLean, P. D., & Delgado, J. M. R. (1953). Electrical and chemical stimulation of frontotemporal portion of limbic system in the waking animal. *EEG Clinical Neurophysiology, 5,* 91–100.

Marchetti-Gauthier, E., Meziane, H., Devigne, D., & Soumireu-Mourat, B. (1990). Effects of bilateral lesions of the cerebellar interpositus nuclei on the conditioned forelimb flexion reflex in mice. *Neuroscience Letters, 120,* 34–37.

Maren, S., Aharonov, G., & Fanselow, M. S. (1996). Retrograde abolition of conditional fear after excitotoxic lesions in the basolateral amygdala of rats: Absence of a temporal gradient. *Behavioral Neuroscience, 110,* 708–717.

Maren, S., Aharonov, G., & Fanselow, M. S. (1997). Neurotoxic lesions of the dorsal hippocampus and Pavlovian fear conditioning in rats. *Behavioral Brain Research, 88,* 261–274.

Maren, S., Aharonov, G., Stote, D. L., & Fanselow, M. S. (1996). N-methyl-D-aspartate receptors in the basolateral amygdala are required for both acquisition and expression of conditioned fear in rats. *Behavioral Neuroscience, 110,* 1365–1374.

Maren, S., & Fanselow, M. S. (1995). Synaptic plasticity in the basolateral amygdala induced by hippocampal formation stimulation in vivo. *Journal of Neuroscience, 15,* 7548–7564.

Maren, S., & Fanselow, M. S. (1996). The amygdala and fear conditioning: Has the nut been cracked? *Neuron, 16,* 237–240.

Matzel, L. D., Ledehendler, I. I., & Alkon, D. L. (1990). Relation of short-term associative memory by calcium-dependent protein kinase. *Journal of Neuroscience, 7,* 1198–1206.

Mauk, M. D., Steinmetz, J. E., & Thompson, R. F. (1986). Classical conditioning using stimulation of the inferior olive as the unconditioned stimulus. *Proceedings of the National Academy of Sciences USA, 83,* 5349–5353.

Mauk, M. D., & Thompson, R. F. (1987). Retention of classically conditioned eyelid responses following acute decerebration. *Brain Research, 403,* 89–95.

McCormick, D. A., Guyer, P. E., & Thompson, R. F. (1982). Superior cerebellar peduncle lesions selectively abolish the ipsilateral classically conditioned nictitating membrane/eyelid response of the rabbit. *Brain Research, 244,* 347–350.

McCormick, D. A., Lavond, D. G., Clark, G. A., Kettner, R. R., Rising, C. E., & Thompson, R. F. (1981). The engram found? Role of the cerebellum in classical conditioning of nictitating membrane and eyelid responses. *Bulletin of the Psychonomic Society, 18,* 103–105.

McCormick, D. A., Lavond, D. G., & Thompson, R. F. (1982). Concomitant classical conditioning of the rabbit nictitating membrane and eyelid responses: Correlations and implications. *Physiology and Behavior, 28,* 769–775.

McCormick, D. A., Steinmetz, J. E., & Thompson, R. F. (1985). Lesions of the inferior olivary complex cause extinction of the classically conditioned eyelid response. *Brain Research, 359,* 120–130.

McCormick, D. A., & Thompson, R. F. (1984a). Cerebellum essential involvement in the classically conditioned eyelid response. *Science, 223,* 296–299.

McCormick, D. A., & Thompson, R. F. (1984b). Neuronal responses of the rabbit cerebellum during acquisition and performance of a classically conditioned nictitating membrane-eyelid responses. *The Journal of Neuroscience, 4,* 2811–2822.

McDonough, J. H., & Kesner, R. P. (1971). Amnesia produced by brief electrical stimulation of amygdala or dorsal hippocampus in cats. *Journal of Comparative and Physiological Psychology, 77,* 171–178.

McEchron, M. D., Bouwmeester, H., Tseng, W., Weiss, C., & Disterhoft, J. F. (1998). Hippocampectomy disrupts auditory trace fear conditioning and contextual fear conditioning in the rat. *Hippocampus, 8,* 638–646.

McEchron, M. D., Tseng, W., & Disterhoft, J. F. (2000). Neurotoxic lesions of the dorsal hippocampus disrupt auditory-cued trace heart rate (fear) conditioning in rabbits. *Hippocampus, 10,* 739–751.

McGaugh, J. L. (1989). Involvement of hormonal and neuromodulatory systems in the regulation of memory storage. *Annual Review of Neurosciences, 12,* 255–287.

McGaugh, J. L. (2000). Memory: A century of consolidation. *Science, 287,* 248–251.

McGaugh, J. L., & Cahill, L. (1997). Interaction of neuromodulatory systems in modulating memory storage. *Behavioural Brain Research, 83,* 31–38.

McGaugh J. L., Cahill, L., Roozendaal, B. (1996). Involvement of the amygdala in memory storage: Interaction with other brain systems. *Proceedings of National Academy of Sciences, 93,* 13508–13514.

McGaugh, J. L., Introini-Collison, I. B., & Nagahara, A. H. (1988). Memory-enhancing effects of posttraining naloxone: Involvement of beta-noradrenergic influences in the amygdaloid complex. *Brain Research, 446,* 37–49.

McGlinchey-Berroth, R., Carrillo, M. C., Gabrieli, J. D. E., Brawn, C. M., & Disterhoft, J. F. (1997). Impaired trace eyeblink conditioning in bilateral medial temporal lobe amnesia. *Behavioral Neuroscience, 111,* 873–882.

McKernan, M. G., & Shinnick-Gallagher, P. (1997). Fear conditioning induces a lasting potentiation of synaptic currents in vitro. *Nature, 390,* 607–611.

Miserendino, M. J. D., Sananes, C. B., Melia, K. R., & Davis, M. (1990). Blocking of acquisition but not expression of conditioned fear-potentiated startle by NMDA antagonists in the amygdala. *Nature, 345,* 716–718.

Mitchell, D. S., & Gormezano, I. (1970). Effects of water deprivation on classical appetitive conditioning of the rabbit's jaw movement response. *Learning and Motivation, 1,* 199–206.

Morris, J. S., Frith, C. D., Perrett, D. I., Rowland, D., Young, A. W., Calder, A. J., & Dolan, R. J. (1996). A differential neural response in the human amygdala to fearful and happy facial expressions. *Nature, 383,* 812–815.

Morris, R. G., Davis, S., & Butcher, S. P. (1990). Hippocampal synaptic plasticity and NMDA receptors: A role in information storage? *Philosophical Transactions of the Royal Society of London, 329B,* 187–204.

Moyer, J. R., Deyo, R. A., & Disterhoft, J. F. (1990). Hippocampectomy disrupts trace eye-blink conditioning in rabbits. *Behavioral Neuroscience, 104,* 243–252.

Muller, J., Corodimas, K. P., Fridel, Z., & LeDoux, J. E. (1997). Functional inactivation of the lateral and basal nuclei of the amygdala by muscimol infusion prevents fear conditioning to an explicit conditioned stimulus and to contextual stimuli. *Behavioral Neuroscience, 111,* 683–691.

Nader, K., & LeDoux, J. E. (1997). Is it time to invoke multiple fear learning systems in the amygdala? *Trends in Cognitive Sciences, 7,* 241–246.

Nader, K., Schafe, G. E., & LeDoux, J. E. (2000). Fear memories require protein synthesis in the amygdala for reconsolidation after retrieval. *Nature, 406,* 722–726.

Nagel, J. A., & Kemble, E. D. (1976). Effects of amygdaloid lesions on the performance of rats in four passive avoidance tasks. *Physiology and Behavior, 17(2),* 245–250.

Oakley, D. A., & Russell, I. S. (1972). Neocortical lesions and Pavlovian conditioning. *Physiology and Behavior, 8,* 915–926.

Oakley, D. A., & Russell, I. S. (1974). Differential and reversal conditioning in partially neodecorticate rabbits. *Physiology and Behavior, 13,* 221–230.

Oakley, D. A., & Russell, I. S. (1976). Subcortical nature of Pavlovian differentiation in the rabbit. *Physiology and Behavior, 17,* 947–954.

Oakley, D. A., & Russell, I. S. (1977). Subcortical storage of Pavlovian conditioning in the rabbit. *Physiology and Behavior, 18,* 931–937.

Oliver, C. G., Swain, R. A., & Berry, S. D. (1993). Hippocampal plasticity during jaw movement conditioning in the rabbit. *Brain Research, 608,* 150–154.

Overmier, J. B., & Seligman, M. E. P. (1967). Effects of inescapable shock on subsequent escape and avoidance learning. *Journal of Comparative and Physiological Psychology, 63,* 23–33.

Parent, M. B., Tomaz, C., & McGaugh, J. L. (1992). Increased training in an aversively motivated task attenuates the memory impairing effects of posttraining NMDA-induced amygdala lesions. *Behavioral Neuroscience, 106,* 791–799.

Pascoe, J. P., & Kapp, B. S. (1985). Electrophysiological characteristics of amygdaloid central nucleus neurons during Pavlovian fear conditioning in the rabbit. *Behavioral Brain Research, 16,* 117–133.

Patterson, M. M. (1970). Classical conditioning of the rabbit's (oryctolagus cuniculus) nictitating membrane response with fluctuating ISI and intracranial CS1. *Journal of Comparative Physiological Psychology, 72,* 193–202.

Patterson, M. M. (1971). Inferior colliculus CS intensity effect on rabbit nictitating membrane conditioning. *Physiology and Behavior, 6,* 273–278.

Patterson, M. M. (1975). Effects of forward and backward classical conditioning procedures on a spinal cat hind-limb flexor nerve response. *Physiological Psychology, 3,* 86–91.

Patterson, M. M. (1976). Mechanisms of classical conditioning and fixation in spinal mammals. In A. H. Riesen & R. F. Thompson (Eds.), *Advances in psychobiology* (Vol. 3, pp. 381–434). New York: Wiley.

Patterson, M. M., Cegavske, C. F., & Thompson, R. F. (1973). Effects of classical conditioning paradigm on hindlimb flexor nerve response in immobilized spinal cat. *Journal of Comparative and Physiological Psychology, 84,* 88–97.

Patterson, M. M., Olah, J., & Clement, J. (1977). Classical nictitating membrane conditioning in the awake, normal, restrained cat. *Science, 196,* 1124–1126.

Perrett, S. P., Ruiz, B. P., & Mauk, M. D. (1993). Cerebellar cortex lesions disrupt learning-dependent timing of conditioned eyelid responses. *Journal of Neuroscience, 13,* 1708–1718.

Phillips, R. G., & LeDoux, J. E. (1992). Differential contribution of amygdala and hippocampus to cued and contextual fear conditioning. *Behavioral Neuroscience, 106,* 274–285.

Pinto, R., & Bromily, R. B. (1950). A search for "spinal conditioning" and for evidence that it can become a reflex. *Journal of Experimental Psychology, 40,* 121–130.

Polenchar, B. E., Romano, A. G., Steinmetz, J. E., & Patterson, M. M. (1984). Effects of US parameters on classical conditioning of cat hindlimb flexion. *Animal Learning and Behavior, 12,* 69–72.

Poremba, A., & Gabriel, M. (1999). Amygdala neurons mediate acquisition but not maintenance of instrumental avoidance behavior in rabbits. *Journal of Neuroscience, 19,* 9635–9641.

Port, R. L., Romano, A. G., Steinmetz, J. E., Mikhail, A. A., & Patterson, M. M. (1986). Retention and acquisition of classical trace conditioned responses by rabbits with hippocampal lesions. *Behavioral Neuroscience, 100,* 745–752.

Qiao, X., Chen, L., Gao, H., Bao, S., Hefti, F., Thompson, R. F., & Knusel, B. (1998). Cerebellar brain-derived neurotrophic factor-TrkB defect associated with impairment of eyeblink conditioning in *stargazer* mutant mice. *Journal of Neuroscience, 19,* 6990–6999.

Rescorla, R. A. (1967). Inhibition of delay in Pavlovian fear conditioning. *Journal of Comparative and Physiological Psychology, 64,* 114–120.

Rescorla, R. A. (1988). Behavioral studies of Pavlovian conditioning. *Annual Reviews of Neuroscience, 11,* 329–352.

Rescorla, R. A., & Wagner, A. R. (1972). A theory of Pavlovian conditioning: Variations in the effectiveness of reinforcement and nonreinforcement. In A. H. Black & W. F. Prokasy (Eds.), *Classical conditioning: Vol. 2. Current theory and memory research* (pp. 64–99). New York: Appleton-Century-Crofts.

Richardson, R. T., & Thompson, R. F. (1984). Amygdaloid unit activity during classical conditioning of the nictitating membrane response in the rabbit. *Physiology and Behavior, 32,* 527–539.

Richardson, R. T., & Thompson, R. F. (1985). Unit activity recorded from the globus pallidus during classical conditioning of the rabbit nictitating response. *Brain Research, 332,* 219–229.

Riedel, G., Harrington, N. R., Hall, G., & Macphail, E. M. (1997). Nucleus accumbens lesions impair context, but not cue, conditioning in rats. *NeuroReport, 8,* 2477–2481.

Robinson, G. B. (1993). MK801 retards acquisition of a classically conditioned response without affecting conditioning-related alterations in perforant path-granule cell synaptic transmission. *Psychobiology, 21,* 253–264.

Rogan, M. T., & LeDoux, J. E. (1995). LTP is accompanied by commensurate enhancement of auditory-evoked responses in a fear conditioning circuit. *Neuron, 15,* 127–136.

Rogan, M. T., Staubli, U. V., & LeDoux, J. E. (1997). Fear conditioning induces associative long-term potentiation in the amygdala. *Nature, 390,* 604–607.

Romanski, L. M., & LeDoux, J. E. (1992). Equipotentiality of thalamo-amygdala and thalamo-cortico-amygdala circuits in auditory fear conditioning. *Journal of Neuroscience, 12,* 4501–4509.

Rosen, J. B., & Davis, M. (1988). Enhancement of acoustic startle by electrical stimulation of the amygdala. *Physiology and Behavior, 48,* 343–349.

Rosen, J. B., Hitchcock, J. M., Miserendino, M. J., Falls, W. A., Campeau, S., & Davis, M. (1992). Lesions of the perirhinal cortex but not of the frontal, medial prefrontal, visual, or insular cortex block fear-potentiated startle using a visual conditioned stimulus. *Journal of Neuroscience, 12,* 4624–4633.

Sahley, C. L. (1995). What we have learned from the study of learning in the leech. *Journal of Neurobiology, 27,* 434–445.

Salvatierra, A. T., & Berry, S. D. (1989). Scopolamine disruption of septo-hippocampal activity and classical conditioning. *Behavioral Neuroscience, 103,* 715–721.

Schafe, G. E., & LeDoux, J. E. (2000). Memory consolidation of auditory Pavlovian fear conditioning requires protein synthesis and protein kinase A in the amygdala. *Journal of Neuroscience, 20,* RC96.

Schmajuk, N. A., & Christiansen, B. A. (1990). Eyeblink conditioning in rats. *Physiology and Behavior, 48,* 755–758.

Schmaltz, L. W., & Theios, J. (1972). Acquisition and extinction of a classically conditioned response in hippocampectomized rabbit (*oryctolagus cuniculus*). *Journal of Comparative Physiological Psychology, 79,* 328–333.

Schneider, J. S. (1987). Basal ganglia-motor influences: Role of sensory gating. In J. S. Schneider & T. I. Lidsky (Eds.), *Basal ganglia and behavior: Sensory aspects of motor functioning* (pp. 103–121). Toronto, Canada: Huber.

Schreurs, B. G., & Alkon, D. L. (1993). Rabbit cerebellar slice analysis of long-term depression and its role in classical conditioning. *Brain Research, 631,* 235–240.

Schreurs, B. G., Gusev, P. A., Tomsic, D., Alkon, D. L., & Shi, T. (1998). Intracellular correlates of acquisition and long-term memory of classical conditioning in Purkinje cell dendrites in slices of rabbit cerebellar lobule HVI. *Journal of Neuroscience, 18,* 5498–5507.

Schreurs, B. G., Oh, M. M., & Alkon, D. L. (1996). Pairing-specific long-term depression of Purkinje cell excitatory postsynaptic potentials results from a classical conditioning procedure in the rabbit cerebellar slice. *Journal of Neurophysiology, 75,* 1051–1060.

Schreurs, B. G., Sanchez-Andres, J. V., & Alkon, D. L. (1991). Learning-specific differences in Purkinje-cell dendrites of lobule HVI (lobulus simples): Intracellular recording in a rabbit cerebellar slice. *Brain Research, 548,* 18–22.

Schreurs, B. G., Tomsic, D., Gusev, P. A., & Alkon, D. L. (1997). Dendritic excitability microzones and occluded long-term depression after classical conditioning of the rabbit's nictitating membrane response. *Journal of Neurophysiology, 77,* 86–92.

Schugens, M. M., Topka, H. R., & Daum, I. (2000). Eyeblink conditioning in neurological patients with motor impairments.

In D. S. Woodruff-Pak & J. E. Steinmetz (Eds.) *Eyeblink classical conditioning: Vol. 1. Applications in humans* (pp. 191–204). Boston: Kluwer.

Seager, M. A., Borgnis, R. L., & Berry, S. D. (1997). Delayed acquisition of behavioral and hippocampal responses during jaw movement conditioning in aging rabbits. *Neurobiology of Aging, 18,* 631–639.

Sears, L. L., Andreasen, N. C., & O'Leary, D. S. (2000). Cerebellar functional abnormalities in schizophrenia are suggested by classical eyeblink conditioning. *Biological Psychiatry, 48,* 204–209.

Sears, L. L., Finn, P. R., & Steinmetz, J. E. (1994). Abnormal classical eyeblink conditioning in autism. *Journal of Autism and Developmental Disorders, 24,* 737–751.

Sears, L. L., Logue, S. F., & Steinmetz, J. E. (1996). Involvement of the ventrolateral thalamus in rabbit classical eyeblink conditioning. *Behavioural Brain Research, 74,* 105–117.

Sears, L. L., & Steinmetz, J. E. (1990). Haloperidol impairs classically conditioned nictitating membrane responses and conditioning-related cerebellar interpositus nucleus activity in rabbits. *Pharmacology Biochemistry and Behavior, 36,* 821–830.

Sears, L. L., & Steinmetz, J. E. (1991). Dorsal accessory inferior olive activity diminishes during acquisition of the rabbit classically conditioned eyelid response. *Brain Research, 545,* 114–122.

Servatius, R. J., & Shors, T. J. (1996). Early acquisition, but not retention, of the classical conditioned eyeblink response is N-Methyl-D-Aspartate (NMDA) receptor dependent. *Behavioral Neuroscience, 110,* 1040–1048.

Sheafor, P. J., & Gormezano, I. (1972). Conditioning of the rabbit's (*Oryctolagus cuninulus*) jaw movement response: US magnitude effects on URs, CRs and pseudo-CRs. *Journal of Comparative and Physiological Psychology, 81,* 449–456.

Shefer, S. I. (1988). Food conditioned reflexes in dogs during activation and blockade of the cholinoreactive system of the amygdala. *Zhurnal Vysshi Nervnoi Deiatelnosti Imeni I. P. Pavlova, 38,* 1010–1016.

Shi, C., & Davis, M. (1999). Pain pathways involved in fear conditioning measured with fear-potentiated startle: Lesion studies. *Journal of Neuroscience, 19,* 420–430.

Shors, T. J. (1998). Stress and sex effects on associative learning: For better or for worse. *Neuroscientist, 4,* 353–364.

Shors, T. J., Beylin, A. V., Wood, G. E., & Gould, E. (2000). The modulation of Pavlovian memory. *Behavioural Brain Research, 110,* 39–52.

Shors, T. J., Levine, S., & Thompson, R. F. (1990). Effect of adrenalectomy and demedullaton the stress-induced impairment of long-term potentiation (LTP). *Neuroendocrinology, 51,* 70–75.

Shors, T. J., Lewczyk, C., Pacynski, M., Mathew, P. R., & Pickett, J. (1998). Stages of estrous mediate the stress-induced impairment of associative learning in the female rat. *NeuroReport, 9,* 419–423.

Shors, T. J., & Matzel, L. D. (1997). Long-term potentiation (LTP): What's learning got to do with it? *Behavioral Brain Science, 20,* 597–613.

Shors, T. J., Seib, T. B., Levine, S., & Thompson, R. F. (1989). Inescapable versus escapable shock modulates long-term potentiation in the rat hippocampus. *Science, 244,* 224–226.

Shors, T. J., Weiss, C., & Thompson, R. F. (1992). Stress-induced facilitation of classical conditioning. *Science, 257,* 537–539.

Shurrager, P. S., & Culler, E. (1940). Conditioning in the spinal dog. *Journal of Experimental Psychology, 26,* 133–159.

Shurrager, P. S., & Culler, E. (1941). Conditioned extinction of a reflex in a spinal dog. *Journal of Experimental Psychology, 28,* 287–303.

Silva, A. J., Kogan, J. H., Frankland, P. W., & Kida, S. (1998). Creb and memory. *Annual Reviews of Neuroscience, 21,* 127–148.

Skelton, R. W. (1988). Bilateral cerebellar lesions disrupt conditioned eyelid responses in unrestrained rats. *Behavioral Neuroscience, 102,* 586–590.

Smith, M. C., DiLollo, V., & Gormezano, I. (1966). Conditioned jaw movement in the rabbit. *Journal of Comparative and Physiological Psychology, 62,* 479–483.

Solomon, P. R., Solomon, S. D., Van der Schaaf, E. V., & Perry, H. E. (1983). Altered activity in the hippocampus is more detrimental to classical conditioning than removing the structure. *Science, 220,* 329–331.

Solomon, P. R., Van der Schaaf, E. V., Thompson, R. F., & Weisz, D. J. (1986). Hippocampus and trace conditioning of the rabbit's classically conditioned nictitating membrane response. *Behavioral Neuroscience, 100,* 729–744.

Squire, L. R. (1992). Declarative and nondeclarative memory: Multiple brain systems supporting learning and memory. *Journal of Cognitive Neuroscience, 4,* 232–243.

Squire, L. R., & Knowlton, B. J. (1994). Memory, hippocampus and brain systems. In M. S. Gazzaniga (Ed.), *The cognitive neurosciences* (pp. 825–873). Cambridge, MA: MIT Press.

Stanton, M. E., & Freeman, J. H., Jr. (2000). Developmental studies of eyeblink conditioning in the rat. In D. S. Woodruff-Pak & J. E. Steinmetz (Eds.), *Eyeblink classical conditioning: Vol. 2. Animal models* (pp. 105–134). Boston: Kluwer.

Stanton, M. E., Freeman, J. H., Jr., & Skelton, R. W. (1992). Eyeblink conditioning in the developing rat. *Behavioral Neuroscience, 106,* 657–665.

Steinmetz, J. E. (1990). Neuronal activity in the cerebellar interpositus nucleus during classical NM conditioning with a pontine stimulation CS. *Psychological Science, 1,* 378–382.

Steinmetz, J. E., Lavond, D. G., Ivkovich, D., Logan, C. G., & Thompson, R. F. (1992). Disruption of classical eyelid conditioning after cerebellar lesions: Damage to a memory trace system or a simple performance deficit? *Journal of Neuroscience, 12,* 4403–4426.

Steinmetz, J. E., Lavond, D. G., & Thompson, R. F. (1989). Classical conditioning in rabbits using pontine nucleus stimulation as a conditioned stimulus and inferior olive stimulation as an unconditioned stimulus. *Synapse, 3,* 225–233.

Steinmetz, J. E., Logan, C. G., Rosen, D. J., Thompson, J. K., Lavond, D. G., & Thompson, R. F. (1987). Initial localization of the acoustic conditioned stimulus projection system to the cerebellum during classical eyelid conditioning. *Proceedings of the National Academy of Sciences USA, 84,* 3531–3535.

Steinmetz, J. E., Logue, S. F., & Miller, D. P. (1993). Using signalled bar-pressing tasks to study the neural substrates of appetitive and aversive learning in rats: Behavioral manipulations and cerebellar lesions. *Behavioral Neuroscience, 107,* 941–954.

Steinmetz, J. E., Logue, S. F., & Steinmetz, S. S. (1992). Rabbit classically conditioned eyelid responses do not reappear after interpositus nucleus lesion and extensive post-lesion training. *Behavioural Brain Research, 51,* 103–114.

Steinmetz, J. E., Rosen, D. J., Chapman, P. F., Lavond, D. G., & Thompson, R. F. (1986). Classical conditioning of the rabbit eyelid response with a mossy fiber stimulation CS: I. Pontine nuclei and middle cerebellar peduncle stimulation. *Behavioral Neuroscience, 100,* 871–880.

Steinmetz, J. E., Sears, L. L., Gabriel, M., Kubota, Y., & Poremba, A. (1991). Cerebellar interpositus nucleus lesions disrupt classical nictitating membrane conditioning but not discriminative avoidance learning in rabbits. *Behavioural Brain Research, 45,* 71–80.

Steinmetz, J. E., & Sengelaub, D. R. (1992). Possible CS pathway for classical eyelid conditioning in rabbits: I. Anatomical evidence for direct projections from the pontine nuclei to the cerebellar interpositus nucleus. *Behavioral and Neural Biology, 57,* 103–115.

Stiedl, O., & Spiess, J. (1997). Effect of tone-dependent fear conditioning on heart rate and behavior of C57BL/6N mice. *Behavioral Neuroscience, 111,* 703–711.

Supple, W. F., & Kapp, B. S. (1993). The anterior cerebellar vermis: Essential involvement in classically conditioned bradycardia in the rabbit. *Journal of Neuroscience, 13,* 3705–3711.

Supple, W. F., & Leaton, R. N. (1990). Cerebellar vermis: Essential for classically conditioned bradycardia in the rat. *Brain Research, 509,* 17–23.

Supple, W. F., Leaton, R. N., & Fanselow, M. S. (1987). Effects of cerebellar vermal lesions on species-specific responses, neophobia, and taste-aversion learning in rats. *Physiology and Behavior, 39,* 579–586.

Supple, W. F., Sebastiani, L., & Kapp, B. S. (1993). Purkinje cell responses in the anterior cerebellar vermis during Pavlovian fear conditioning in the rabbit. *NeuroReport, 4,* 975–978.

Taylor, J. A. (1951). The relationship of anxiety to the conditioned eyelid response. *Journal of Experimental Psychology, 44,* 61–64.

Teyler, T. J., & DiScenna, P. (1987). Long-term potentiation. *Annual Review of Neurosciences, 10,* 131–161.

Teyler, T. J., Roemer, R. A., Thompson, R. F., Thompson, J. K., & Voss, J. F. (1976). The role of sensory feedback in EMG response. In D. I. Mostofsky (Ed.), *Behavior control and modification of physiological activity* (pp. 253–267). New York: Prentice-Hall.

Thompson, L. T., & Disterhoft, J. F. (1997). N-methyl-D-aspartate receptors in associative eyeblink conditioning: Both MK-801 and phencyclidine produce task- and dose-dependent impairments. *Journal of Pharmacology and Experimental Therapeutics, 281,* 928–940.

Thompson, R. F. (1967). *Foundations of physiological psychology.* New York: Harper & Row.

Thompson, R. F. (1986). The neurobiology of learning and memory. *Science, 233,* 941–947.

Thompson, R. F. (2001). Spinal plasticity. In M. Patterson & J. Grau (Eds.), *The handbook of spinal cord plasticity* (pp. 1–19). Norwell, MA: Kluwer Press.

Thompson, R. F., & Krupa, D. J. (1994). Organization of memory traces in the mammalian brain. *Annual Review of Neuroscience, 17,* 519–549.

Thompson, R. F., & Spencer, W. A. (1966). Habituation: A model phenomenon for the study of neuronal substrates of behavior. *Psychological Review, 173,* 16–43.

Tracy, J. A., Ghose, S. S., Stetcher, T., McFall, R. M., & Steinmetz, J. E. (1999). Classical conditioning in a nonclinical obsessive-compulsive population. *Psychological Science, 10,* 9–13.

Tracy, J. A., Thompson, J. K., Krupa, D. J., & Thompson, R. F. (1998). Evidence of plasticity in the pontocerebellar conditioned stimulus pathway during classical conditioning of the eyeblink response in the rabbit. *Behavioral Neuroscience, 112,* 267–285.

Tsukahara, N., Oda, Y., & Notsu, T. (1981). Classical conditioning mediated by the red nucleus in the cat. *Journal of Neuroscience, 1,* 72–79.

Turner, B. H., & Zimmer, J. (1984). The architecture and some of the interconnections of the rat's amygdala and lateral periallocortex. *Journal of Comparative Neurology, 227,* 540–557.

Vazdarjanova, A., & McGaugh, J. L. (1998). Basolateral amygdala is not critical for cognitive memory of contextual fear conditioning. *Proceedings of the National Academy of Sciences USA, 95,* 15003–15007.

Voneida, T. J. (1999). The effect of rubrospinal tractotomy on a conditioned limb response in the cat. *Behavioural Brain Research, 105,* 151–162.

Voneida, T. J. (2000). The effect of brachium conjunctivum transection on a conditioned limb response in the cat. *Behavioural Brain Research, 109,* 167–175.

Voneida, T. J., Christie, D., Bogdanski, R., & Chopko, B. (1990). Changes in instrumentally and classically conditioned limb-flexion responses following inferior olivary lesions and olivo-cerebellar tractotomy in the cat. *Journal of Neuroscience, 10,* 3583–3593.

Wagner, A. R., & Brandon, S. E. (1989). Evolution of a structured connectionist model of Pavlovian conditioning (ÆSOP). In S. B. Klein & R. R. Mowrer (Eds.), *Contemporary learning theories: Pavlovian conditioning and the status of traditional learning theories* (pp. 149–189). Hillsdale, NJ: Erlbaum.

Wagner, A. R., & Donegan, N. (1989). Some relationships between a computational model (SOP) and an essential neural circuit for Pavlovian (rabbit eyeblink) conditioning. In R. D. Hawkins & G. H. Bower (Eds.), *Computational models of learning in simple neural systems: Vol. 23. The psychology of learning and motivation* (pp. 157–203). New York: Academic Press.

Wagner, A. R., & Rescorla, R. A. (1972). Inhibition in Pavlovian conditioning: Application of a theory. In R. A. Boakes & M. S. Halliday (Eds.), *Inhibition and learning* (pp. 301–336). London: Academic Press.

Watson, J. B., & Rayner, R. (1920). Conditioned emotional reactions. *Journal of Experimental Psychology, 3,* 1–14.

Weingarten, H., & White, N. (1978). Exploration evoked by electrical stimulation of the amygdala in rats. *Physiological Psychology, 6,* 229–235.

Weiskrantz, L. (1956). Behavioral changes associated with ablation of the amygdaloid complex in monkeys. *Journal of Comparative and Physiological Psychology, 49,* 381–391.

Weisskopf, M. G., & LeDoux, J. E. (1999). Distinct populations of NMDA receptors at subcortical and cortical inputs to principal cells of the lateral amygdala. *Journal of Neurophysiology, 81,* 930–934.

Weisz, D. J., Harden, D. G., & Xiang, Z. (1992). Effects of amygdala lesions on reflex facilitation and conditioned response acquisition during nictitating membrane response conditioning in rabbit. *Behavioral Neuroscience, 106,* 262–273.

Whalen, P. J., & Kapp, B. S. (1991). Contributions of the amygdaloid central nucleus to the modulation of the nictitating membrane reflex in the rabbit. *Behavioral Neuroscience, 105,* 141–153.

White, I. M., Miller, D. P., White, W., Dike, G. L., Rebec, G. V., & Steinmetz, J. E. (1994). Neuronal activity in rabbit neostriatum during classical eyelid conditioning. *Experimental Brain Research, 99,* 179–190.

Wicks, S. R., & Rankin, C. H. (1995). Integration of mechanosensory stimuli in *Caenorhabditis elegans. Journal of Neuroscience, 15,* 2434–2444.

Wilensky, A. E., Schafe, G. E., & LeDoux, J. E. (1999). Functional inactivation of the amygdala before but not after auditory fear conditioning prevents memory formation. *Journal of Neuroscience, 19(24),* RC48.

Wilensky, A. E., Schafe, G. E., & LeDoux, J. E. (2000). The amygdala modulates memory consolidation of fear-motivated inhibitory avoidance learning but not classical fear conditioning. *Journal of Neuroscience, 20,* 7059–7066.

Wilson, A., & Kapp, B. S. (1994). Effect of lesions of the ventrolateral periaqueductal gray on the Pavlovian conditioned heart rate response in the rabbit. *Behavioral and Neural Biology, 62,* 73–76.

Wood, G. E., & Shors, T. J. (1998). Stress facilitates classical conditioning in males, but impairs classical conditioning in females through activational effects of ovarian hormones. *Proceedings of the National Academy of Science USA, 95,* 4066–4071.

Woodruff-Pak, D. S. (2000). Human eyeblink conditioning in normal aging and Alzheimer's disease. In D. S. Woodruff-Pak & J. E. Steinmetz (Eds.), *Eyeblink classical conditioning: Vol. 1. Applications in humans* (pp. 163–189). Boston: Kluwer.

Woodruff-Pak, D. S., Lavond, D. G., Logan, C. G., Steinmetz, J. E., & Thompson, R. F. (1993). Cerebellar cortical lesions and reacquisition in classical conditioning of the nictitating membrane response in rabbits. *Brain Research, 608,* 67–77.

Woodruff-Pak, D. S., Lavond, D. G., Logan, C. G., & Thompson, R. F. (1987). Classical conditioning in 3-, 30- and 45-month old rabbits: Behavioral learning and hippocampal unit acitivity. *Neurobiology of Aging, 8,* 101–108.

Woodruff-Pak, D. S., & Lemieux, S. K. (2001). The cerebellum and associative learning: Parallels and contrasts in rabbits and humans. In J. E. Steinmetz, M. A. Gluck, & P. R. Solomon (Eds.), *Model systems and the neurobiology of associative learning* (pp. 271–294). Mahwah, NJ: Erlbaum.

Woodruff-Pak, D. S., & Steinmetz, J. E. (Eds.). (2000). *Eyeblink classical conditioning: Vol. 1. Human applications.* Boston: Kluwer.

Woodruff-Pak, D. S., & Thompson, R. F. (1988). Classical conditioning of the eyelid response in the delay paradigm in adults aged 18–83 years. *Psychology and Aging, 3,* 219–229.

Woody, C. D., & Black-Cleworth, P. (1973). Differences in excitability of cortical neurons as a function of motor projection in conditioned cats. *Journal of Neurophysiology, 36,* 1004–1116.

Woody, C. D., & Engel, J., Jr. (1972). Changes in unit activity and thresholds to electrical microstimulation at coronal-precurciate cortex of cat with classical conditioning of different facial movements. *Journal of Neurophysiology, 31,* 851–864.

Yeo, C. H., & Hardiman, M. J. (1992). Cerebellar cortex and eyeblink conditioning: A reexamination. *Experimental Brain Research, 88,* 623–638.

Yeo, C. H., Hardiman, M. J., & Glickstein, M. (1985). Classical conditioning of the nictitating membrane response of the rabbit: II. Lesions of the cerebellar cortex. *Experimental Brain Research, 60,* 99–113.

Yeo, C. H., Hardiman, M. J., & Glickstein, M. (1986). Classical conditioning of the nictitating membrane response of the rabbit: IV. Lesions of the inferior olive. *Experimental Brain Research, 63,* 81–92.

Young, R. A., Cegavske, C. F., & Thompson, R. F. (1976). Tone-induced changes in excitability of abducens motoneurons and of the reflex path of nictitating membrane response in rabbit (*oryctolagus cuniculus*). *Journal of Comparative and Physiological Psychology, 90,* 424–434.

Zalutsky, R. A., & Nicoll, R. A. (1990). Comparison of two forms of long-term potentiation in single hippocampal neurons. *Science, 248,* 1619–1624.

Zhang, J. X., Harper, R. M., & Ni, H. (1986). Cryogenic blockade of the central nucleus of the amygdala attenuates aversively

conditioned blood pressure and respiratory responses. *Brain Research, 386,* 136–145.

Zigmond, M. J., Bloom, F. E., Landis, S. C., Roberts, J. L., & Squire, L. R. (Eds.). (1999). *Fundamental neuroscience.* San Diego, CA: American Press.

CHAPTER 19

Memory Systems

HOWARD EICHENBAUM

EARLY VIEWS ON MULTIPLE MEMORY SYSTEMS

The notion that there is more than one kind of memory is an old one, richly woven into the history of theorizing and research in philosophy, psychology, and neuroscience. In 1804 the French philosopher Maine de Biran proposed what may be the first formal theory of multiple memory systems. He viewed all cognition and memory as based on a fundamental mechanism of *habit,* a concept similar to the current term *association.* In his proposal, habits were simple and automatic mechanisms, but they had a broad applicability. Habits were viewed as mediating acquired behaviors that operate independently of conscious control and conscious recollection. In addition, the habit mechanism was also viewed as the basis for more complex, consciously mediated aspects of memory. Main de Biran elaborated his scheme into three distinct forms of memory, each based on the fundamental habit mechanism but also distinct in its contents and properties. One form was called *representative memory,* characterized as expressed in the conscious recollection of a "well-circumscribed idea." The second, designated *mechanical memory,* refers to situations in which the habit mechanism does not generate a recalled idea, but instead only a facilitation of the repetition of a movement. Finally, *sensitive memory* refers to when the habit mechanism generates a feeling—or fantastic, albeit vague or obscure image—without recalling the ideas behind it. Thus, mechanical memory was seen as expressing habits in the form of coordinated actions, and sensitive memory as a habit expressed in the form of an affective component. These two kinds of memory had in common that

they could operate without conscious recall and could be the source of the most inflexible and obstinate behaviors.

Maine de Biran developed his formulation without experiments or consideration of the anatomy or functions of brain systems. And there is no record that Maine de Biran's theory had significant influence over successive developments in memory research. Yet, as it turns out, he was prescient in describing a division of memory systems that is—as you will see—strongly supported by modern cognitive neuroscience.

There has been much progress—and many detours—in both psychological and biological studies on the brain and memory systems before Maine De Biran's scheme was rediscovered. The history of this area has largely preserved the notion of an elemental habit mechanism bolstered by the early discoveries about the existence of reflexes and their conditionability, and many theories have preserved a distinction between simple habits and conscious memory, albeit sometimes in the form of debates in which habits and recollection were polarized as alternatives.

A century after Maine de Biran, the notion of habit as a fundamental mechanism and memory as a more complex phenomenon associated with consciousness was widely held. William James (1890/1918) wrote of them in separate chapters in his treatise *Principles of Psychology.* James considered habit a very primitive mechanism that is common among biological systems and due to plasticity of the organic materials. Within the nervous system, habits were viewed as nothing more than the ready discharge of a well-worn reflex path. But James also attributed to habit great importance in the development of more complicated behavioral repertoires. He suggested that well-practiced behaviors and skills—including walking, writing, fencing, and singing—are mediated by concatenated reflex paths, organized to generate the serial production of movements and unconscious sensations leading to other movements and sensations. He thought of habits as eliminating the need for conscious supervision after a behavior becomes routine; moreover, he recommended early and frequent reinforcement of good habits as a key exercise in ethical and cognitive development.

James distinguished *memory* as something altogether different from habit, albeit based on that mechanism, a very complicated phenomenon with many facets. James is perhaps best known for having originated the distinction between *primary memory* and *secondary memory*. Primary memory is what we today call short-term or working memory. It is a short-lived state in which new information has achieved consciousness and belongs to our stream of thought. James viewed primary memory as the gateway by which material would enter secondary memory or what we now call long-term memory. James defined secondary memory as "the knowledge of an event, or fact, of which meantime we have not been thinking, with the additional consciousness that we have thought or experienced it before" (p. 648). In addition to its personal and temporal aspects, the full characterization of memory was framed in terms of two other properties—its structure as an elaborate network of associations and its basis in habit mechanisms. Thus, James theorized a mechanistic basis for how habits could be elaborated for the formation of multiple and linked associations to support the richness of memory. Thus, the underlying foundation of recall was a complex yet systematic set of associations between any particular item and anything co-occurring in one's previous experiences with the item. He argued that when we search for a memory, we navigate through the elaborate network of the associations—and if successful, locate the sought memory among them. The goodness of memory, he believed, was as much dependent on the number of associations in the network as on the strength of those associations.

THE EXPERIMENTAL ERA: DEBATES ON THE FUNDAMENTAL BASIS OF MEMORY

At the outset of experimental approaches to memory, reductionism reigned. The goal was to identifying basic mechanism of habit as an explanation of memory, eliminating the need for allusions to consciousness. This approach was known as behaviorism, and its origins began separately in the United States and Russia (see Eichenbaum & Cohen, 2001, for review). At the turn of the twentieth century, Thorndike had invented his puzzle box, with which he observed cats learning to manipulate a door latch to allow escape from a holding chamber. Around the same time, Small introduced the maze to studies of animal learning, inspired by the famous garden maze at Hampton Court in London. By 1907 Watson had published his accounts on maze learning by rats, and by 1913 he had written his behaviorist manifesto, formalizing it the next year in his systematic exposition—claiming we need never return to terms such as *consciousness.*

Independently in the early 1900s, Pavlov and Bechterev (physiologists in Russia) had been experimenting on autonomic nervous system reflexes in dogs. Pavlov was studying the physiology of digestion and observed that dogs would secrete saliva not only when given food, but also when presented with an arbitrary stimulus following repeated pairings of the arbitrary stimulus and food delivery. He called this phenomenon the *conditioned reflex.* Bechterev studied the respiratory motor reflex by which cold applied to the skin produces a reflexive catching of the breath, and he discovered that an arbitrary stimulus applied repeatedly at the same time as the cold would eventually set off the same reflex by itself. The neurology of the conditioned reflex—especially as elaborated by Sherrington—gave biological validity to what behaviorists saw as the elemental mechanism of learned behavior.

There were debates about the distinctions between the fundamental association in Pavlovian conditioning versus that in Thorndike's instrumental learning—specifically, whether the critical association was between the stimulus and the response or the stimulus and the reinforcer. Despite this difference, the two viewpoints came to be referred to collectively as stimulus-response or *S-R learning,* and we should consider them as offering a physiological instantiation of the habit mechanism. To the theorists of this time, having a full accounting of S-R learning would solve the problem of memory.

Yet there were detractors from this prominent theme. Early challenges to behaviorism came from the psychologists such as Yerkes and Kohler, whose observations on great apes led them to conclude that animals did not learn complex problems by a combination of random trial and error and eventual reinforcement of a correct solution; rather, at least the higher animals had insights into relationships between means and ends. Tolman (1932) was perhaps the most successful in challenging behaviorism because he developed operational definitions for mentalistic processes including purposive behavior and expectancy. Tolman's goal was to get behind the behavior—not by specifying particular elements of habits or their linkage, but by identifying the complex cognitive mechanisms, purposes, expectations, and insights that guided behavior. Tolman's basic premises were that learning generally involved the acquisition of *knowledge* about the world—in particular, about relationships between and among stimuli and their consequences—and that this knowledge led to expectancies when the animal was put in testing situations. He argued that learning involved the creation of what he called a cognitive map that organized the relations among stimuli and consequences based on interconnections between groups of stimuli. Moreover, he rigorously tested these ideas using the same species (rats) and maze-learning paradigms that were a major focus of the prominent S-R theorists. In a series of studies he showed that rats were capable of solving maze problems by taking novel detours or shortcuts, and they exhibited a capacity for latent learning, in which they acquired problem solutions in the absence of reinforcement. Collectively, in each of these studies rats showed they were capable of learned behaviors that were not previously reinforced and therefore could not be mediated by S-R representations.

A parallel debate emerged from studies on human verbal memory. On the side of reductionism was Herman Ebbinghaus (1885), who had admired the mathematical analyses that had been brought to the psychophysics of perception and sought to develop similarly precise and quantitative methods for the study of memory. Ebbinghaus had rejected the use of introspection as capable of providing evidence on memory. He developed objective assessments of memory in *savings* scores that measured retention in terms of the reduction in trials required to relearn material, and he used statistical analyses to test the reliability of his findings. Furthermore, to create learning materials that were both simple and homogeneous in content, Ebbinghaus invented the nonsense syllable, a meaningless letter string composed of two consonants with a vowel between. With this invention he avoided the confounding influences of interest, beauty, and other features that he felt might affect the memorability of real words, and he simultaneously equalized the length and meaningfulness of the items—that is, by minimizing the former and eliminating the latter. Ebbinghaus was and is still hailed as a pioneer of systematic scientific methodology in the study of human verbal memory. His studies and those that followed provided a detailed characterization of the acquisition and retention of arbitrary associations, as well as examined many phenomena of verbal memory.

This approach also had its detractors. Most prominent among these, perhaps, was the British psychologist Fredric Bartlett (1932), whose work stands in stark contrast to the rigorous methods introduced by Ebbinghaus. Bartlett differed in two major ways. First, his interest was in the mental processes used to recover memories—that is, in *remembering* more so than in *learning*. He was not so interested in the probability of recall, as dominated Ebbinghaus's approach, but in what he called "effort after meaning"—the mental processing taken to search out and ultimately reconstruct memories. Second, Bartlett shuddered at the notion of using nonsense syllables as learning materials. By avoiding meaningful items, he argued, the resulting memories would necessarily lack the rich background of knowledge into which new information is stored. Indeed, the subtitle of Bartlett's book *Remembering* is indeed *A Study in Experimental and Social Psychology*, thus highlighting his view that real memory is embedded in the full fabric of a lifetime of experience, prominently including one's culture.

Barlett's main strategy was called the *method of repeated reproduction*. His most famous material was a short folk tale titled "The War of the Ghosts," which was adapted from the original translation by the explorer Franz Boaz. He selected this story for several reasons: The syntax and prose were derived from a culture quite different from that of his British experimental subjects, the story contents lacked explicit connections between some of the events described, and the tale contained dramatic and supernatural events that would evoke vivid visual imagery on the part of his participants. These qualities were, of course, exactly the sort of thing Ebbinghaus worked so hard to avoid with his nonsense syllables. But Bartlett focused on these features because he was primarily interested in the content and structure of the memory obtained and less interested in the probability of recall of specific items.

Barlett made three general observations on this and other reproductions of the story: First, the story was considerably shortened, mainly by omissions. Second, the syntax became more modern and taken from the participant's culture. Third, the story became more coherent and consequential. From these observations Bartlett concluded that remembering was not simply a process of recovery or forgetting of items, but that memory seemed to evolve over time. Items were not lost or recovered at random; rather, material that was more foreign to the subject, lacked sequence, or was stated in unfamiliar terms was more likely to be lost or changed substantially in both syntax and meaning, becoming more consistent with the subject's common experiences.

To account for these observations, Bartlett developed an account of remembering known as *schema theory*. In his view, the simplest schemas were habit-like traces of items in sequential order of experience. But he elaborated this low-level mechanism, arguing that our experience of particular sequences builds up en masse; particular past events are more or less dated or placed in relation to other associated particular events in a dynamic organization from which one can construct or infer both specific contents of memories and their logical order. Bartlett proposed that remembering is therefore a *reconstructive* process and not one of mere *reproduction,* as Ebbinghaus preferred and as would guide low-level rote memory.

RECONCILIATION: MULTIPLE MEMORY SYSTEMS

The evidence provided by Tolman, Barlett, and others did not resolve the debate, but in general led to more complex constructs of S-R models. The issue has now, however, been largely resolved by the introduction of cognitive neuroscience, and evidence that both habit-like and recollective memory exist and are mediated by distinct neural systems. I describe here two particularly compelling lines of evidence that support this reconciliation, one from the literature on maze learning in rats and the other a classic study in the field of human neuropsychology.

The debate on learning in animals became focused on the central issue of whether rats acquire maze problems by learning specific turning responses or by developing an expectancy of the place of reward. The issue was addressed using a simple T-maze apparatus wherein response versus place strategies could be directly compared by operational definitions (Figure 19.1). The basic task involves the rat beginning each trial at the base of the *T* and being rewarded at the end of only one arm (e.g., the one reached by a right turn). The accountings of what was learned in this situation differ strongly by the two

theoretical approaches. In this situation, then—according to S-R theory—learning involves acquisition of the reinforced left-turn response. By contrast, according to Tolman's account, learning involves the acquisition of a cognitive map of the environment and the expectancy that food was to be found at a particular location in the test room. The critical test involved effectively rotating the *T* by exactly 180° so that the choice arms still ended at the same two loci (albeit which arms reach those loci are now exchanged), and the start point would now be at the opposite end of the room. The S-R theorist would predict that a rat would continue to make the previously reinforced right-turn response at the choice point, leading it to a goal location different from that where the food was provided during training. By contrast, the prediction of Tolman's account was that the rat would switch to a left-turn response in order to arrive at the expected location of food in the same place in the room where it was originally rewarded.

Tolman provided initial evidence in favor of his prediction, but subsequent efforts to replicate this result were mixed. A decade of these experiments indicated that place learning was more often favored, but that there were conditions under which response learning was preferred. His analysis indicated that the nature of the available cues was the primary determining factor for the differences in the results. In general, whenever there were salient extramaze visual cues that differentiated one goal location from the other, a place representation predominated. Conversely, when differential extramaze cues were not prominent, the response strategy would predominate. Such a pattern of results did not, of course, declare a winner in the place versus response debate. Instead these results suggested that both types of representation are available to the rat and that the rat might use either one under conditions of different salient cues or response demands.

This story does not end there. A most elegant explanation of how rats could use both strategies was recently provided by Packard and McGaugh (1996). In this experiment, rats were trained for a week on the T-maze task, then given the rotated-maze probe trial. Then they were trained for another week with the maze in its original orientation and finally presented with an additional probe trial. Packard and McGaugh found that normal rats initially adopted a place representation as reflected in their strong preference for the place of the previous goal during the first probe trial. However, after the additional week of overtraining, normal rats switched, now adopting a response strategy on the final probe test. Therefore, under these training circumstances, rats developed both strategies successively. Their initial acquisition was guided by the development of a cognitive map, but subsequent overtraining led to development of the response habit.

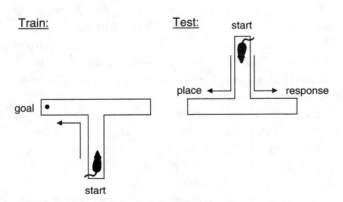

Figure 19.1 Schematic diagram of the T-maze task. The rat is initially trained to turn left in order to obtain rewards at the indicated goal locus. In subsequent testing, the maze is rotated 180° so that the locus of the goal site within the room is identical to that during training, and the rat starts from the opposite end of the room. The rat might continue to turn left, indicating use of the left-turn response strategy; or it might turn right and go to the same locus or reward, indicating use of the place strategy.

But Packard and McGaugh's experiment went beyond merely confirming that the same rats can use both learning strategies. In addition to the pure behavioral testing, Packard and McGaugh also examined whether different brain systems supported these different types of representation. Prior to training, all animals had been implanted with indwelling needles that allowed injection on the probe tests of a local anesthetic or saline placebo directly and locally into one of two brain structures—the hippocampus or the striatum. The results on normal animals previously described were from those subjects that were injected with placebo on both probe tests. However, the effects of the anesthetic were striking. On the first probe trial, animals that were injected with anesthetic into the striatum behaved just as control subjects had—they were predominantly place learners, indicating that the place representation did not depend on the striatum. But the animals that had been injected with anesthetic into the hippocampus showed no preference at all, indicating that they relied on their hippocampus for the place representation and that this was the only representation normally available at that stage of learning. On the second probe test, a different pattern emerged. Whereas control subjects had by that time acquired the response strategy, animals given an anesthetic in the striatum lost the turning response and instead showed a striking opposite preference for the place strategy. Animals given an injection of anesthetic into the hippocampus maintained their response strategy.

Combining these data, a clear picture of the evolution of multiple memory representations emerges. Animals normally develop an initial place representation that is mediated by the hippocampus, and no turning-response representation develops in this initial period. With overtraining, a response representation that is mediated by the striatum is acquired and indeed, it predominates over the hippocampal place representation. The latter is not, however, lost—it can be uncovered, so to speak, by inactivating the striatum and suppressing the turning response strategy. These findings offer compelling evidence that elements of both the S-R and the cognitive map views were right: There are distinct types of memory for place and response, which are distinguished by their performance characteristics as well is by the brain pathways that support such characteristics. It is notable that the Packard and McGaugh experiment was preceded by many other studies demonstrating a specific role for the hippocampus in memory, as well as by a few studies showing specificity in the involvement of the striatum in the acquisition of habits. But this particular study is most striking both in the elegance of the dissociation and in its contact with the history of views on habit and cognitive memory.

In the field of human memory research, the discovery of multiple memory systems came from two major breakthroughs in the study of patients with pervasive, global amnesia. The first of these breakthroughs came with the report by Scoville and Milner (1957) of what has become probably the most famous neurological patient in the literature—the man known by his initials H. M. This patient had the medial temporal lobe area removed to alleviate his severe epileptic attacks. H. M. consequently suffered what appeared to be a nearly complete loss of the ability to form new long-term memories: His impairment—tested over the last 40 or so years—has been shown to extend to verbal and nonverbal memory, spatial and nonspatial memory; indeed, it seems to cut across all categories of learning materials. Yet a second line of discovery about global amnesia revealed a spared domain of learning capacity. Even from the outset, a few exceptions to the otherwise pervasive deficit were apparent. H. M. was able to learn new motor skills, and he showed a facilitation of perceptual identification resulting from prior exposure to objects or words (an effect that later came to be understood as reflective of a preserved priming).

The second breakthrough came in 1980 when Cohen and Squire proposed that these exceptions to amnesia were indicative of a large domain of preserved learning capacities in amnesia. Their conclusion was based on the observation of complete preservation of the acquisition and retention of a perceptual skill (reading mirror-reversed words) in patients with amnesia. These patients showed fully intact skilled performance, yet were markedly impaired both in recognizing the particular words on which they trained and in recollecting their training experiences. These investigators were struck by the dissociation between the ability to benefit or otherwise have performance shaped by a series of training experiences—an ability that appeared fully normal in the amnesic patients—and the capacity to explicitly remember or consciously recollect those training experiences or their contents, which was markedly impaired in the patients. Cohen and Squire attributed the observed dissociation—together with the earlier findings of spared memory in amnesia—to the operation of distinct forms of memory, which they called *procedural memory* and *declarative memory,* respectively. These forms of memory were seen as functionally distinct memory systems—one dedicated to the tuning and modification of networks that support skilled performance, and the other to the encoding, storage, and retrieval on demand of memories for specific facts and events. These functionally distinct memory systems were tied to separate brain systems, with declarative memory seen as critically dependent on the medial temporal-lobe and midline diencephalic structures damaged in various amnesias. Procedural memory was seen as mediated by various brain systems specialized for particular types of skilled performance.

THREE MAJOR MEMORY SYSTEMS IN THE BRAIN

A general, anatomically based framework for some of the major memory systems has emerged from many experiments (like those just described) that provide dissociations among the role of specific brain structures in different forms of memory, combined with the known anatomical pathways of the key structures. In this section I provide an anatomical framework and a preliminary overview of the functional distinctions among these pathways. Subsequent sections elaborate on the functional distinctions in greater detail.

A sketch of some of the most prominent memory pathways currently under investigation is provided in Figure 19.2 (for a

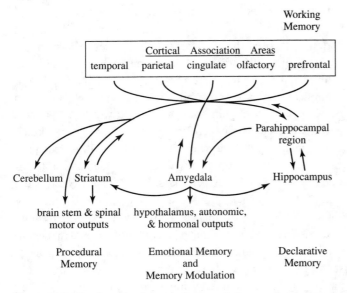

Figure 19.2 A schematic diagram of some of the prominent memory systems of the brain. The origins of major inputs to each of these systems involves widespread areas of the neocortex, and in particular the so-called association areas. This network of cortical areas mediates working memory. Outputs of these cortical areas project in parallel via three main routes. One route is through the parahippocampal region and into the hippocampus. The main outputs of hippocampal and parahippocampal processing are back to the same cortical areas that provided the main inputs. These pathways mediate declarative memory. Another route involves projections into two main subsystems via the striatum and cerebellum that mediate different aspects of motor memory. These pathways involve both projections back to the cortex and outputs to brain stem motor nuclei. The third main route from the cortex is to the amygdala. Outputs of the amygdala project in several directions to hormonal and autonomic outputs. This system mediates the expression of emotional memories. Amygdala outputs also return to the cortex and to the other memory systems to modulate the consolidation of other types of memory processing.

similar outline, see Suzuki, 1996). In this scheme, the origin of each of the memory systems is the vast expanse of the cerebral cortex, focusing in particular on the highest stages of the several distinct sensory and motor processing hierarchies—the cortical association areas. The cerebral cortex thus provides major inputs to each of three main pathways of processing related to distinct memory functions. One pathway is to the hippocampus via the parahippocampal region. As introduced previously, this pathway supports the cognitive form of memory, Tolman's cognitive maps, and declarative memory in humans. The main output of hippocampal and parahippocampal processing is back to the same cortical areas that provided inputs to the hippocampus and are viewed as the long-term repository of declarative memories.

The other two main pathways highlighted here involve cortical inputs to specific subcortical targets as critical nodal points in processing leading to direct output effectors. One of these systems involves the amygdala as a nodal stage in the association of exteroceptive sensory inputs to emotional outputs effected via the hypothalamic-pituitary axis and autonomic nervous system, as well as emotional influences over widespread brain areas. The putative involvement of this pathway in such processing functions has led many to consider this system as specialized for emotional memory.

The other system involves the striatum as a nodal stage in the association of sensory and motor cortical information with voluntary responses via the brain stem motor system. The putative involvement of this pathway in associating cortical representations to specific behavioral responses has led many to consider this system as specialized for habit or skill learning, two forms of procedural memory. An additional, parallel pathway that mediates different aspects of sensorimotor adaptations involves sensory and motor systems pathways through the cerebellum.

The distinct roles of these systems have been compellingly demonstrated in many multiple-dissociation experiments, three of which are summarized here. The first study involves a triple dissociation of memory functions in rats that showed three different patterns of sparing and impairment of memory following damage to the hippocampus, amygdala, and striatum. The other two studies involve double dissociations of memory functions in humans with specific types of brain damage. Taken together, the findings suggest a similar set of memory functions supported by homologous brain areas in animals and humans.

One of the most striking dissociations among memory functions supported by separate brain structures comes from a study by McDonald and White (1993). This study involved multiple experiments in which separate groups of rats were trained on three different versions of the spatial radial maze

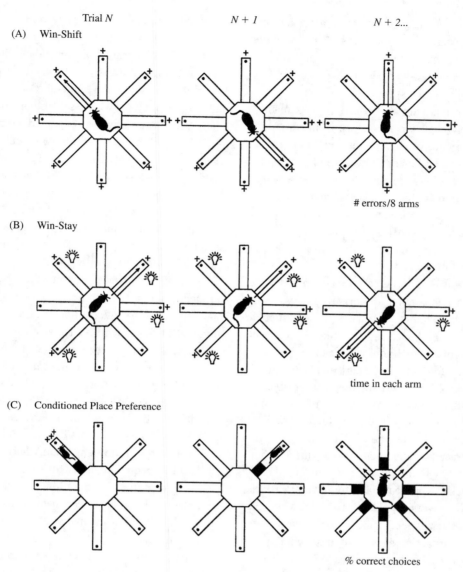

Figure 19.3 Illustrations of example trials in different variants of the radial arm maze task. For each, the measure of performance is indicated below the *N* + 2 trial. See text for description of each variant of the task (+ = rewarded arm).

task (Figure 19.3). Each version of the task used the same maze, the same general spatial cues and approach responses, and the same food rewards. But the stimulus and reward contingencies of each task differed, each focusing on a different kind of memory processing demand. For each task, performance was compared across three separate groups of rats operated to disrupt hippocampal pathways, or the amygdala, or the striatum. In addition, different methods of brain damage were compared. Hippocampal system disruption was accomplished by a fornix transection or by a neurotoxic lesion of the hippocampus. Damage to the amygdala and the striatum was accomplished by electrolytic or neurotoxic lesions of the lateral nucleus of the amygdala or dorsal part of the neostriatum, where cortical sensory input arrive in these structures.

One test was the conventional spatial working memory version of the radial maze task (Figure 19.3). In this version of the task, an eight-arm maze was placed in the midst of a variety of extramaze stimuli in the testing room, providing animals with the opportunity to encode the spatial relations among these stimuli as spatial cues. On every daily trial, a food reward was placed at the end of each of the eight maze arms, and the animal was released from the center and was allowed to retrieve the rewards. Optimal performance would entail entering each arm only once and subsequently avoiding already visited arms in favor of the remaining unvisited arms. The central memory demand of this task was characterized as a *win-shift rule;* such a rule emphasizes memory for each particular daily episode with specific maze arms. Also, the task requires flexible use of memory by using the approach into previously rewarded locations to guide the selection of other new arms to visit. Based on these characteristics of the memory demands, it was expected that performance on this task would require the hippocampal system.

They found that normal animals learned the task readily, improving from nearly chance performance (four errors out of their first eight arm choices) on the initial training trial to an average of fewer than half an error by the end of training. Consistent with expectations, damage to the hippocampal system resulted in an impairment on this version of the radial maze task. Compared to normal animals, rats with fornix transections made more errors by entering previously visited maze arms. By contrast, amygdala and striatum lesions had no effect on task performance.

The second test involved a variant of the same radial maze task (Figure 19.3). In this version, the maze was again surrounded by a curtain, and lamps were used to cue particular maze arms. On the first trial of each daily training session, four arbitrarily selected arms were illuminated and baited with food, whereas the other four arms were dark and had no food. After the first occasion a lit arm was entered, that arm was re-baited so that the animal could return to the arm for a second reward. Subsequently, that lamp in that particular arm was turned off and no more food was provided at that arm. Thus, here the task was characterized by a *win-stay rule* in which animals could approach any lit arm at any time and could even reexecute the approach to a particular arm for reward one time in each daily trial. This version of the task minimized the availability of spatial cues; indeed, it associated rewards with different sets of locations across days. Also, it did not require memory for recent episodes or flexible expression of memory. Thus, performance was not expected to rely upon the hippocampal system. Instead, this task would seem to require memory processes associated with learning consistent with stimulus-response contingencies or simple response habits and so was expected to rely on the striatal system.

Results showed that normal control subjects learned the appropriate behavioral responses to the lit arms gradually over several training sessions. In the first few sessions, they selected lit arms on only 50% of the trials, but by the end of training, they performed at about 80% correct. Consistent with expectations, animals with striatal damage were impaired, barely exceeding chance performance even with extended training. By contrast, animals with fornix transections succeeded in learning and even outperformed the control subjects in learning rate. Animals with amygdala lesions were unimpaired, learning the task at a normal rate.

The third test involved yet another variant of the radial maze task in which animals were separately conditioned to be attracted to one maze arm and habituated to another arm, without performing specific approach movements to either of the arms (Figure 19.3). In this version, the maze was surrounded by a curtain to diminish the salience of spatial cues. Six of the maze arms were blocked off to make them inaccessible, and one of the remaining two arms was illuminated by proximal lamps, whereas the other was only dimly illuminated. After a preliminary session in which rats could explore both available arms, conditioning proceeded with daily exposures to one of the two arms. For each rat, either the lit or the dark arm was associated with food by confining the animal in that arm for 30 min with a large amount of food on four separate trials. On another four trials, the same animal was confined for the same period of time to the other arm, but with no food. Thus, in half of the rats, the lit arm was associated with food availability and the dark arm was not; for the other half of the rats, the opposite association was conditioned. In a final test session, no food was placed on the maze and the access to both the lit and dark arms was allowed. The amount of time spent in each arm for a 20-min session was recorded to measure the preference for each of the two arms. This version of the radial maze task emphasized the strong and separate associations between food reward or absence of reward with a particular maze arm defined by a salient nonspatial cue. This task minimized the availability of spatial relations among stimuli. Also, because the same lit and dark arms used during training were re-presented in testing, the task did not require memory for specific episodes and flexible expression of memory, nor did it require reproduction of specific habitual approach responses. Thus, it was not expected that either the hippocampal system or the striatum would be critical to learning. Instead, learning would seem to depend on memory processes associated with emotional conditioning, and it so was expected to depend upon the amygdala.

They found that normal animals showed a strong preference for the arm associated with food, typically spending 50–100% more time in the maze arm in which they had been fed compared to the arm where no food was previously provided. Consistent with expectations, rats with amygdala damage showed no conditioned preference for the cue arm associated with food. By contrast, rats with fornix transections or striatal lesions showed robust conditioned cue preferences.

A very similar pattern of observations has emerged from analyses of human amnesia. In both studies, the learning and memory capacities of amnesic patients with damage to the medial temporal lobe was compared with that of nonamnesic patients—that is, humans with brain pathologies not producing the classic amnesic syndrome. The two studies differ in their focus on comparing classic amnesia with more specific disorders of learning and memory resulting from damage to the amygdala or striatum, respectively.

In one study, Bechara et al. (1995) examined three patients with selective damage to the hippocampus or amygdala. One patient suffered from Urbach-Wiethe disease, a disorder resulting in selective bilateral calcification of the tissue of the amygdala and sparing the adjacent hippocampus. Another patient experienced multiple cardiac arrests and associated transient hypoxia and ischemia that resulted in selective bilateral hippocampal atrophy, sparing the neighboring amygdala. The third patient suffered herpes simplex encephalitis, resulting in bilateral damage to both the amygdala and hippocampus.

This study focused on a form of autonomic conditioning involving an association between a neutral stimulus and a loud sound. The conditioning stimulus (CS+) was either a monochrome color slide or a pure tone. Participants were initially habituated to the CS+ as well as to several like stimuli (different colors or tones) that would be presented as CS-stimuli. Subsequently, during conditioning the CSs were presented in random order for 2 s each. Each presentation of the CS+ was terminated with the unconditioned stimulus (US), a loud boat horn that was sounded briefly. Autonomic responses to these stimuli were measured as skin conductance changes through electrodermal recordings.

Normal controls showed skin conductance changes to the US and robust conditioning to the CS+, with smaller responses to the CS- stimuli. The patient with selective amygdala damage showed normal unconditioned responses to the US, but failed to develop conditioned responses to the CS+ stimuli. By contrast, the patient with selective hippocampal damage showed robust skin conductance changes to the US and normal conditioning to the CS+ stimuli. This patient also showed responsiveness to the CS- stimuli, but clearly differentiated these from the CS+s. The patient with combined amygdala and hippocampal damage failed to condition, even though he responded to the US.

After the conditioning sessions, the subjects were debriefed with several questions about the stimuli and their relationships. Control subjects and the patient with selective amygdala damage answered most of these questions correctly, but both patients with hippocampal damage were severely impaired in recollecting the task events. These findings demonstrate a clear double dissociation, with a form of emotional conditioning disrupted by amygdala damage and declarative memory for the learning situation impaired by hippocampal damage. The finding that these different forms of memory for the identical stimuli and associations are differentially affected by localized brain damage further supports the notion of multiple memory systems.

In another study, Knowlton, Mangels, and Squire (1996) examined patients in the early stages of Parkinson's disease—associated with degeneration of neurons in the substantia nigra resulting in a major loss of input to the neostriatum—and amnesic patients with damage to the medial temporal lobe or to associated regions of the diencephalon.

Subjects were trained in a probabilistic classification learning task formatted as a weather prediction game. The task involved predicting the one of two outcomes (rain or shine) based on cues from a set of cards. On each trial, one to three cards from a deck of four was presented. Each card was associated with the sunshine outcome only probabilistically—either 75%, 57%, 43%, or 25% of the time—and the outcome with multiple cards was associated with the conjoint probabilities of the cards presented in any of 14 configurations. After presentation of the cards for each trial, the subject was forced to choose between rain and shine, and was then given feedback as to the outcome. The probabilistic nature of the task made it somewhat counterproductive for participants to attempt to recall specific previous trials because repetition of any particular configuration of the cues could lead to different outcomes. Instead the most useful information to be learned concerned the probability associated with particular cues and combinations of cues—acquired gradually across trials, much as habits or skills are acquired.

Over a block of 50 trials, normal subjects gradually improved from pure guessing (50% correct) to about 70% correct, a level consistent with the optimal probability of accuracy in this task. However, the patients with Parkinson's disease failed to show significant learning, and the failure was particularly evident in those patients with more severe Parkinsonian symptoms. By contrast, amnesic patients were successful in learning the task, achieving levels of accuracy not different from that of controls by the end of the 50-trial block.

Subsequent to training on the weather prediction task, these subjects were debriefed with a set of multiple-choice questions about the types of stimulus materials and nature of the task. Normal subjects and those with Parkinson's disease performed very well in recalling the task events. But the amnesic subjects were severely impaired, performing near the chance level of 25% correct. These findings demonstrate a clear double dissociation, with habit or skill learning disrupted by neostriatal damage and declarative memory for the learning events impaired by hippocampal or diencephalic damage, providing further evidence for the view that different forms of memory are represented for the identical learning materials within parallel brain systems.

ELABORATING THE ROLE OF THE THREE MAJOR MEMORY SYSTEMS

This analysis so far has offered only a preliminary view into the distinct functions of the hippocampal, striatum, and amygdala as components of separate memory systems. The remainder of this chapter extends these characterizations, offering greater detail on the full anatomy of the pathways involved in these systems and on their different functional roles. The evidence for these characterizations comes mainly from anatomical neuropsychological studies of the effects of selective damage within these systems. I limit the discussion of a few particularly strong examples of experiments that reveal the scope and nature of their role in memory. For a more comprehensive treatment of each of these and other memory systems, the reader is referred to Eichenbaum and Cohen (2001).

The Declarative Memory System

Ideally, to the extent that the early analyses of cognitive memory are correct, this system should have all the properties of recollective memory outlined by Maine de Biran, James, Tolman, and Bartlett. Indeed, it appears that their characterizations fit the modern description of hippocampal-dependent memory functions quite well. Recall that the common theme in all those theoretical frameworks is that cognitive memory is a network of associations built up from linking the records of many experiences and the ability to search the network via the recollective process for memories; this network employs those memories to solve a myriad of problems.

Beginning in the 1970s several hypotheses about the function of the hippocampus were proposed; each captured some of these aspects of the earlier views on cognitive memory. The two most prominent early views are summarized here. In 1978, O'Keefe and Nadel assigned Tolman's cognitive mapping system to the hippocampus. Their account was based on an interpretation of the accumulated voluminous literature on the behavioral effects of hippocampal damage in animals, showing a preponderance of observed impairments in spatial learning versus inconsistent deficits in nonspatial learning following hippocampal damage; it was also based on O'Keefe's discovery of place cells, hippocampal neurons that fire associated with a rat's location in its environment. O'Keefe and Nadel's analysis went well beyond making a simple distinction between spatial and nonspatial learning modalities. Their proposal about spatial learning involved the acquisition of cognitive maps that corresponded roughly, if not topographically, to the salient features of physical environment. They referred to the domain of memory supported by the hippocampus as a *locale* system that maintains a molar model of spatial relations among objects in the environment—driven by curiosity rather than reinforcement of specific behaviors capable of very rapid learning. By contrast, hippocampal-independent learning was viewed as supported by a *taxon* system that mediates dispositions of specific stimuli into

categories, is driven by reinforcement of approach and avoidance behaviors, and that involves slow and incremental behavioral adaptations.

The other most prominent theory that emerged in this period was Olton, Becker, and Handlemann's (1979) distinction between working memory and reference memory. Notably, Olton's use of the term *working memory* differs in meaning from the same term used in today's characterizations of a form of short term memory in humans and animals. The memory process Olton conceived would today be viewed as more similar to *episodic memory*—memory for a particular experience involving one's own actions—than our current conception of working memory as the contents of current consciousness. To investigate this distinction, Olton invented the radial maze, a maze composed of a central start platform with multiple arms radiating in all directions like the spokes of a wheel. In his classic studies, a bait was placed at the end of each of the arms and then allowed the rat to forage for the food. After several such trials, rats learn to forage efficiently, running down each arm only once without repetition. Good performance requires the animal remember each arm visited in that session and then before the next trial erasing those memories. Olton distinguished working memory from reference memory operationally, using a maze in which many of the arms were never baited. Thus, to be maximally efficient in foraging, animals had to simultaneously demonstrate their capacity for working memory, by visiting each of the baited arms only once, and for reference memory, by consistently avoiding the never-baited arms.

For a comprehensive review of the experimental tests of these theories, as well as other theories, the reader is referred to Cohen and Eichenbaum (1993). For our purposes here, suffice it to say that the each of these theories was supported by specific experimental findings—thus indicating that each captured a critical aspect of hippocampal system function. However, none of these theories could account for all of the findings, including those that formed the major support for the alternative theories. A formulation that seeks to incorporate the central elements of all of these views within the framework of the earlier conceptualizations of cognitive memory is the account espoused by the present author and his colleagues (see Eichenbaum, 2000; Eichenbaum & Cohen, 2001). According to this view, the hippocampal systems plays a critical role both in episodic memory, as proposed by Olton, and in the development of large-scale organized representations, similar to the proposal of O'Keefe and Nadel (but not limited to physical space).

According to this account, the hippocampal memory system is composed of three major components: cerebral cortical areas, the parahippocampal region, and the hippocampus itself (Burwell, Witter, & Amaral, 1995; Suzuki, 1996), and the major pathways of the system are very similar in rats and monkeys (Figure 19.1). The cerebral cortical areas comprise diverse and widespread association regions that are both the source of information to the hippocampal region and the targets of hippocampal output. They project in different ways to the parahippocampal region, a set of interconnected cortical areas immediately surrounding the hippocampus that in turn project into the hippocampus itself. The main outputs of the hippocampus return to the parahippocampal region, which sends back projections broadly to the same cortical association areas that provided the inputs to the parahippocampal region. This pattern of anatomical organization complements the findings from studies of amnesia, leading to the working hypothesis that the parahippocampal region and hippocampus make their contributions to memory by altering the nature, persistence, and organization of memory representations within the cerebral cortex.

There is emerging evidence that neocortical association areas—the parahippocampal region and the hippocampus—play distinct and complementary roles in this memory system. The roles of these areas may be best contrasted in the results of studies on a simple recognition memory task—called *delayed nonmatch to sample* (DNMS)—in which subjects must remember single stimulus across a variable memory delay (see Eichenbaum, Alvarez, & Ramus, 2001). For example, in rats performing an odor-guided version of the DNMS task damage to the orbitofrontal cortex resulted in a deficit in the acquisition of the task when the memory delay was minimal, suggesting an important role in perceptual processing or in learning the nonmatching rule (Otto & Eichenbaum, 1992; Ramus & Eichenbaum, 2000). By contrast, rats with damage to the parahippocampal region acquired the DNMS task at the normal rate and performed well at brief memory delays. However, their memories declined abnormally rapidly as the memory delay was extended beyond a few seconds—indicating a selective role in maintaining a persistent memory of the sample stimulus (see also Young, Otto, Fox, & Eichenbaum, 1997). Little if any deficit in nonspatial DNMS is observed following damage to the hippocampus or its connections via the fornix, indicating the parahippocampal region itself mediates the persistence of memories for single items required to perform DNMS.

Parallel results have been obtained in monkeys performing visually guided versions of the DNMS task. Similar to rats, monkeys with damage to the parahippocampal region perform well when the memory delay is brief. When the memory demand is increased by extending the delay period, however, severe deficits in DNMS are observed (Meunier,

Bachevalier, Mishkin, & Murray, 1993; Zola-Morgan, Squire, Amaral, & Suzuki, 1989), and these impairments are much more severe than those following damage to the hippocampus (Murray & Mishkin, 1998) or its connections via the fornix (Gaffan, 1994a). Examination of performance on the DNMS task with very brief delays has been difficult because the standard protocol used for monkeys is manual. However, using another recognition task that allowed testing at very brief delays, it has recently been demonstrated that inferotemporal area of the cortex is critical for visual recognition even for a 1-s delay—suggesting a role in perceptual processing as opposed to memory—whereas the parahippocampal region is critical for memory in the same task only when recognition was delayed (Buffalo et al., 1999). The parahippocampal region may also play a role at the intersection of perception and memory, in situations in which perceptual processes depend on learned associations among complex stimulus elements (Eichenbaum & Bunsey, 1995; Murray & Bussey, 1999).

It is notable that memory mediated by the hippocampus itself contributes very little to performance in standard DNMS tasks, in that the deficits observed are modest at most compared to the effects of damage to the cortex or parahippocampal region. However, the hippocampus may play an essential role in other types of simple recognition memory tests (Rampon et al., 2000; Zola et al., 2000; see below) and in recognition memory for configurations of items within scenes or places (Cassaday & Rawlins, 1995; Gaffan, 1994b; Wan, Aggleton, & Malcolm, 1999).

Instead, the findings from studies using animal models point to a critical role for the hippocampus itself in central aspects of declarative memory. To understand this role it is important to consider the fundamental properties of declarative memory, as introduced by Cohen and Squire (1980) and subsequently elaborated by many investigators. We acquire our declarative memories through everyday personal experiences; the ability to retain and recall these episodic memories is highly dependent on the hippocampus in humans (Vargha-Khadem et al., 1997). In addition, recent studies have developed animal models of that capture the temporal specificity of events in episodic memory, and have demonstrated critical involvement of the hippocampus itself (Fortin et al., 2002; Kesner et al., 2002; Steele & Morris, 1999). In one study, rats were presented with unique sequences of odors, and probed for their memory of the order in which the items had been presented. Animals with selective hippocampal lesions were severely impaired in remembering the order of events in each episode, even though they could recognize the items as demonstrated in a separate recognition test (Fortin et al., 2002).

The full scope of hippocampal involvement also extends to *semantic memory*, the body of general knowledge about the world that is accrued from linking multiple experiences that share some of the same information (Squire & Zola, 1998). For example, one can learn about one's relatives via personal episodes of meeting and talking about family members and then weave together this information into a body of knowledge constituting one's family tree. Similarly, one can learn about the geographies of one's neighborhood and hometown by taking trips through various areas and eventually interconnecting them into cognitive maps.

In addition, declarative memory for both the episodic and semantic information is special in that the contents of these memories are accessible through various routes. In humans, declarative memory is most commonly expressed through conscious, effortful recollection. This means that one can access and express declarative memories to solve novel problems by making inferences from memory. Thus, even without ever explicitly studying your family tree and its history, you can infer indirect relationships—or the sequence of central events in the family history—from the set of episodic memories about your family. Similarly, without ever studying the map of your neighborhood, you can make navigational inferences from the synthesis of many episodic memories of previous routes taken. Family trees and city layouts are but two examples of the kind of memory space proposed to be mediated by the hippocampal system (Eichenbaum, Dudchenko, Wood, Shapiro, & Tanila, 1999). Within this view, a broad range of such networks can be created, with their central organizing principle the linkage of episodic memories by their common events and places—and a consequent capacity to move among related memories within the network.

These properties of declarative memory depend on the functions of the hippocampus itself. Several experiments have shown that the hippocampus is required in situations in which multiple and distinct but overlapping experiences must be combined into a larger memory representation that mediates flexible, inferential memory expression. For example, in one experiment rats initially learned a series of distinct but overlapping associations between odor stimuli (Bunsey & Eichenbaum, 1996). On each trial, one of two odors was initially presented, followed by a choice between two odors, one of which was baited as the assigned associate for a particular initial odor (A goes with B, not Y; X goes with Y, not B). Following training on two sets of overlapping odor-odor associations (A-B and X-Y, then B-C and Y-Z), subsequent probe tests were used to characterize the extent to which learned representations could be linked to support inferential memory expression. Control rats learned paired associates rapidly

and hippocampal damage did not affect acquisition rate on either of the two training sets. Intact rats also showed that they could link the information from overlapping experiences and employ this information to make inferential judgments in two ways. First, normal rats showed strong *transitivity* across odor pairings that contained a shared item. For example, having learned that odor A goes with odor B and that B goes with C, they could infer that A goes with C. Second, control rats could infer symmetry in paired associate learning. For example, having learned that B goes with C, they could infer that C goes with B. By contrast, rats with selective hippocampal lesions were severely impaired, showing no evidence of transitivity or symmetry.

A similar characterization accounts for the common observation of deficits in spatial learning and memory following hippocampal damage. For example, in the Morris water maze test, rats or mice learn to escape from submersion in a pool by swimming towards a platform located just underneath the surface. It is important to note that training in the conventional version of the task involves an intermixing of four different kinds of trial episodes that differ in the starting point of the swim. Under this condition, animals with hippocampal damage typically fail to acquire the task (Morris, Garrud, Rawlins, & O'Keefe, 1982). However, if the demand for synthesizing a solution from four different types of episodes is eliminated by allowing the animal to repeatedly start from the same start position, animals with hippocampal damage acquire the task almost as readily as do normal rats and use the same distant spatial cues in identifying the escape site (Eichenbaum, Stewart, & Morris, 1990). Nevertheless, even when rats with hippocampal damage are successful in learning to locate the escape platform from a single start position, they are unable to use this information for flexible, inferential memory expression. Thus, after they were trained to find the platform from a single start position, normal rats readily locate the platform from any of a set of novel start positions. Under these same conditions, however, rats with hippocampal damage fail to readily locate the platform, often swimming endlessly and unsuccessfully in a highly familiar environment.

The view that has emerged from these and many other studies is that the hippocampus plays a central role in the creation of a broad range of memory networks, with their central organizing principle the linkage of episodic memories by their common events and places—and a consequent capacity to move among related memories within the network. The scope of such network reaches to various domains relevant to the lives of animals—from knowledge about spatial relations among stimuli in an environment, to categorizations of foods, to learned organizations of odor or visual stimuli or social relationships. Progress is being made in investigating a variety of these domains.

Procedural Memory Systems

Among the most prevalent kinds of memory we use every day is *procedural memory,* the habits, skills, and sensorimotor adaptations that go on constantly in the background of all of our intentional and planned behavior. Because this kind of memory generally falls outside of consciousness, we take it for granted. Yet without it we would be forced to think our way through virtually every step we take and every motion we make in our daily tasks. Fortunately there is a motor memory system or systems, a circuitry involving structures of the motor systems of the brain whose plasticity accomplishes the myriad of unconscious learned behaviors we engage almost every waking moment.

Motor memory is generally separated into two general subtypes (Figure 19.2). One type involves the acquisition of habits and skills—the capacity for a very broad variety of stereotyped and unconscious behavioral repertoires. These can involve a simple refinement of particular repeated motor patterns and extend to the learning of long action sequences in response to highly complex stimuli. These abilities reflect both the acquisition of general skills (writing, piano playing, etc.) and the unique elements of personal style and tempo in the expression of these behaviors. A key structure in this subsystem is the striatum. The striatum receives its cortical inputs from the entire cerebral cortex, and these projections are capable of activity-dependent changes in responsiveness. These projections are topographically organized into divergent and convergent projections into modules within the striatum that could sort and associate somatosensory and motor representations. The striatum projects mainly to other components of the basal ganglia and to the thalamus, which project back to both the premotor and motor cortex as well as the prefrontal association cortex (Figure 19.2). It is notable that there are minimal projections of this circuit to the brain stem motor nuclei and none to the spinal motor apparatus.

The other type of procedural memory involves specific sensory-to-motor adaptations—that is, adjustments of reflexes, such as changing the force exerted to compensate for a new load or acquisition of conditioned reflexes that involve novel motor responses to a new sensory contingency, as characterize many instances of Pavlovian conditioning described earlier. A key structure of this subsystem is the cerebellum. The cerebellum receives cortical input from a cortical area much more restricted than the striatum, including only the strictly sensory and motor areas projecting via

brain stem nuclei into the lateral part of the cerebellar cortex. Like the striatal subsystem, the cerebellum has a thalamic output route to the cerebral cortex, although the cortical target is also more restricted than that of the striatum—limited to motor and premotor cortex. In addition, the cerebellum receives somatic sensory inputs directly from the spinal cord and has major bidirectional connections with brain stem nuclei associated with spinal cord functions. The functional roles of these two subsystems are discussed in turn.

The Striatal Subsystem

The striatal habit system was introduced via experiments that dissociated this system from the hippocampal and amygdala memory systems. Those experiments provided evidence indicating that a role for the striatum in the acquisition of specific stimulus-response associations, as contrasted with declarative memory and emotional memory functions of the hippocampal and amygdala systems, respectively.

The scope of striatal involvement is not limited to a particular sensory or motivational modality or to a particular type of response output. One study by Viaud, White, and Norman (1989) illustrates some of the range of memory mediated by this system and shows a particularly striking dissociation of regions within the striatum in their effects on inhibition of approach behavior conditioned by different cues. In this study, thirsty rats with lesions of the posterior-ventral or ventrolateral regions of the striatum were trained to approach a water spout over several days. Subsequently, they were given foot shocks in the same chamber in the presence of a conditioning cue, which was either a light or an odor. The animals were tested later for their latency to approach the water spout when the conditioning cue was present versus when it was absent. Animals with lesions of the posterior-ventral striatum failed to show discriminative avoidance of the light cue but showed good avoidance of the olfactory cue. Conversely, animals with ventrolateral striatal lesions failed to show discriminative avoidance of the olfactory cue but showed good avoidance of the light cue.

Previously the selective role of the striatum in learning specific turning, T-maze, and approach responses in radial maze were shown. Similar dissociations showing striatal function in stimulus-approach learning have extended this role to aversively motivated learning in the water maze (Packard & McGaugh, 1992). In addition, there is further evidence from maze-learning studies that restrict the nature of response learning by this system. In one of these studies, rats were trained on two tasks on different radial mazes (Cook & Kesner, 1988). In a place-learning (allocentric) task, only one arm of an eight-arm maze was consistently baited, and the rat began each trial from any of the remaining arms chosen at random. In a right-left discrimination (egocentric) task, the animal began each trial in the central area of the maze and two randomly chosen adjacent arms were indicated for a choice. The rat had to choose only the left (or for other rats, the right) of the two arms regardless of its absolute location. Here, too, rats with striatal lesions performed well on the place-learning task but did not learn the right-left discrimination task, indicating a selective role in egocentric response learning.

Taken together the literature from studies of damage to the striatum suggests that the deficit following striatal damage is—or includes—an impairment in generating behavioral responses toward important environmental stimuli. The deficit extends to both approach and avoidance responses and to both egocentric spatial and nonspatial stimuli across many modalities. Even this characterization is not sufficiently comprehensive to explain the full range of impairments in animals and humans (see Eichenbaum & Cohen, 2001). Thus, it is likely that the deficits in egocentric localization and S-R learning in animals with striatal damage may reflect only a subset of the forms of behavioral sequence acquisition mediated by the striatum.

The Cerebellar Subsystem

The anatomy and functions of the cerebellum have long been associated with aspects of motor learning, and most studies have focused on its highly organized circuitry and emphasized its mechanisms for reflex adaptations (for review, see Ebner, Flament, & Shanbhag, 1996). Considerable recent attention has focused on Pavlovian eye-blink conditioning as a model learning paradigm in which to study the role of the cerebellum. In this paradigm, rabbits are placed in restraining chambers where they can be presented with a well-controlled tone or light as the conditioning stimulus (the CS), and a photoelectric device records eye-blinks. In classic delay conditioning, this stimulus lasts 250–1,000 ms and coterminates with an air puff or mild electrical shock to the eyelid (the unconditioned stimulus or US) that produces the reflexive, unconditioned eye blink (the UR). After several pairings of the CS and US, the rabbit begins to produced the eye blink after onset of the CS and prior to presentation of the US. With more training, this conditioned response (CR) occurs somewhat earlier, and its timing becomes optimized so as to be maximal at the US onset, showing that not only is a CR acquired, but also a timing of the CR is established.

The role of the cerebellum and associated areas has been studied extensively by Thompson and his colleagues (for a review, see Thompson & Kim, 1996). In their studies they found that permanent lesions or reversible inactivation of one particular cerebellar nucleus—the interpositus nucleus—result in impairments in the acquisition and retention of classically conditioned eye-blink reflexes, without affecting reflexive eye blinks (URs). Additional compelling data indicating a selective role for the interpositus in this kind of procedural memory come from studies using reversible inactivations of particular areas during training. These studies showed that drug inactivation of the motor nuclei that are essential for production of the CR and UR prevented the elicitation of behavior during training. However, in trials immediately following removal of the inactivation, CRs appeared in full form, showing that the neural circuit that supports UR production is not critical for learning per se. A similar pattern of results was obtained with inactivation of the axons leaving the interpositus or their target in the red nucleus, showing that the final pathway for CR production is also not required to establish the memory trace. By contrast, inactivation of the anterior interpositus nucleus and overlying cortex by drugs (muscimol, lidocaine) or temporary cooling did not affect reflexive blinking, yet resulted in failure of CR development during inactivation and the absence of savings in learning after removal of the inactivation. These results point to a small area of the anterior interpositus nucleus and overlying cerebellar cortex as the essential locus of plasticity in this form of motor learning.

The Emotional Memory System

Perhaps the best studied example of emotional memory involves the brain system that mediates Pavlovian fear conditioning as studied by Joseph LeDoux (1992) and by Michael Davis and their colleagues. This research has focused on the specific elements of the pathways through the amygdala that support the learning of fearful responses to a simple auditory stimulus (Figure 19.1). The critical elements of the relevant amygdala pathways include auditory sensory inputs via the brain stem to circuits through the thalamus. Some of these sensory thalamic areas then project directly to the lateral amygdaloid nucleus. Other thalamic projections follow a route to the primary sensory cortex, then to secondary areas and the perirhinal cortex. Each of these secondary cortical areas are the source of cortical inputs to the amygdala, particularly the lateral and basolateral nuclei of this structure. Those areas of the amygdala project into the central nucleus, which is the source of outputs to subcortical areas controlling a broad range of fear-related behaviors, including autonomic and motor responses.

In this chapter, I provide an overview of the work of LeDoux and his colleagues. LeDoux's studies have examined the neuropsychology and neurophysiology of these structures in animals during the course of a simple tone-cued fear conditioning task. Rats are initially habituated to an operant chamber, then presented with multiple pairings of a 10-s pure tone terminating with a brief electric shock through the floor of the cage. Subsequently conditioned fear was assessed by measuring the autonomic response as reflected in changes to the tone only in arterial pressure and motor responses as reflected in a stereotypical crouching or freezing behavior when the tone is presented, as well as suppression of drinking sweetened water. Unconditioned responses to the tone were evaluated by presenting other animals with unpaired tones and shocks.

Their initial experiments were aimed at identifying the critical auditory input pathway to the amygdala. Animals with selective lesions in the lateral amygdala show dramatically reduced conditioned responses to the tone in the measures of both autonomic and motor responses. Unconditioned responses (consequent to unpaired presentations) were not affected by this damage. Also, animals with damage to the adjacent striatum performed normally, showing anatomical specificity and that the striatal system is not involved in emotional learning.

Subsequent efforts focused on identifying which of the two prominent auditory input pathways to the lateral amygdala was critical. Broad destruction of all auditory areas of the thalamus eliminated conditioned responses. However, selective ablation of either of the two prominent direct inputs to the lateral amygdala were individually ineffective. Thus, lesions of the medial division of the medial geniculate (including all three nuclei that project directly to the lateral amygdala)—or of the entire auditory cortex that projects to the amygdala—did not reduce either the autonomic or freezing response. However, elimination of both of these inputs produced the full effect seen after lateral amygdala lesions. Thus, for this simple type of conditioning—either the direct thalamic input, which offers a crude identification of a sound, or the thalamocortical input pathway, which provides a sophisticated identification of auditory signal—is sufficient to mediate conditioning.

Additional experiments were aimed at an another component of fear conditioning observed in these studies. After conditioning, when rats are replaced in the conditioning chamber they begin to freeze even before the tone is presented. Thus, rats appear to condition both to the tone and to the environmental context in which tones and shock have previously been paired. This contextual fear conditioning is selective to the environment in which conditioning occurs. Furthermore, contextual fear conditioning can be dissociated from conditioning to the tone by presenting conditioned tones in a different environment. Trained animals do not freeze prior to tone presentation in the different environment, but do freeze when the tone is presented.

Moreover, contextual fear conditioning is mediated by a pathway different from that of tone-cued fear conditioning; to demonstrate this, the animals were trained on the standard version of the task, then assessed freezing both immediately after the rats were placed in the conditioning chamber and then subsequently in response to the tone. Amygdala lesions blocked conditioned freezing to both the context and the tone. By contrast, damage to the hippocampus selectively blocked contextual fear conditioning, sparing the conditioned response to the tone.

The amygdala is also critical to the acquisition of positive affective biases, as demonstrated by the McDonald and White (1993) experiment showing a critical role for the amygdala in conditioned place preferences mediated by food rewards. In addition, many other studies have also indicated a selective role for the amygdala in the acquisition of both positive and negative biases for both primary and secondary reinforcers. Furthermore, these studies indicate that the same brain system that mediates the perception and appreciation of emotional stimuli as well as emotional expression is also the system that is critical to the acquisition, consolidation, and expression of emotional memories.

SUMMING UP

The preceding overview is not intended to be a comprehensive review of any of the memory systems outlined previously (see Eichenbaum & Cohen, 2001). Nor does it cover all of the brain's memory systems. In particular, the present review does not consider the prefrontal-posterior cortical network that mediates working memory (see Miller, 2000). In addition, this review did not consider simple forms of sensory adaptation and biasing mediated within the cerebral cortex, such as those that mediate priming (Tulving & Schacter, 1990). And this review did not consider the important role of the amygdala as a key part of a memory modulation system that controls the extent of consolidation of memory in all the systems described previously (see McGaugh, Cahill, & Roozendaal, 1996).

However, the present review does offer an overview of the three major brain systems that mediate the storage and expression of distinct types of long term memory. The hippocampal memory system mediates declarative memory—our capacity to recollect everyday facts and events. The striatal and cerebellar systems mediate forms of procedural memory that allow unconscious acquisition and expression of habits, skills, and sensorimotor adaptations. The amygdala system mediates emotional memory, the unconscious acquisition and expression of biases towards or away from otherwise arbitrary stimuli.

A few closing remarks are in order. Note that the hippocampal system is special in its role in memory per se. The motor and emotional memory systems involve precisely the same brain circuitry as that required for the expression of motor and emotional behavior, respectively. Thus, the forms of unconscious memory these systems mediate can be viewed as tuning and adjustments of the brain's motor and emotional performance systems. The role of the hippocampus seems special in this regard. It is not clear that the hippocampus has a performance function outside of its role in memory.

Finally, it is noteworthy that in a general sort of way, we have come full circle to the same conclusion about multiple forms of memory reached by Main de Biran 200 years ago. It was he who in 1804 proposed that there were three main kinds of memory, characterized as representative, mechanical, and sensitive memory. Now we call these declarative, motor, and emotional memory, respectively, and rely more or less on the same distinctions in properties of memory to define them. However, we do know much more about the neurobiology of these systems. Modern cognitive neuroscience has shown that the differences between these systems come about because they are mediated by different brain pathways, and their distinctive properties are consequences of the special anatomies and operational characteristics of those systems.

REFERENCES

Bartlett, F. C. (1932). *Remembering.* Cambridge, UK: Cambridge University Press.

Bechera, A., Tranel, D., Hanna, D., Adolphs, R., Rockland, C., & Damasio, A. R. (1995). Double dissociation of conditioning and declarative knowledge relative to the amygdala and hippocampus in humans. *Science, 269,* 1115–1118.

Buffalo, E. A., Ramus, S. J., Clark, R. E., Teng, E., Squire, L. R., & Zola, S. M. (1999). *Learning and Memory, 6,* 572–599.

Bunsey, M., & Eichenbaum, H. (1996). Conservation of hippocampal memory function in rats and humans. *Nature, 379,* 255–257.

Burwell, R. D., Witter, M. P., & Amaral, D. G. (1995). Perirhinal and postrhinal cortices in the rat: A review of the neuroanatomical literature and comparison with findings from the monkey brain. *Hippocampus, 5,* 390–408.

Cassaday, H. J., & Rawlins, J. N. P. (1995). Fornix-fimbria section and working memory deficits in rats: Stimulus complexity and stimulus size. *Behavioral Neuroscience, 109,* 594–606.

Cohen, N. J., & Eichenbaum, H. (1993). *Memory, amnesia, and the hippocampal system.* Cambridge, MA: MIT Press.

Cohen, N. J., & Squire, L. R. (1980). Preserved learning and retention of a pattern-analyzing skill in amnesia: Dissociation of knowing how and knowing that. *Science, 210,* 207–210.

Cook, D., & Kesner, R. P. (1988). Caudate nucleus and memory for egocentric localization. *Behavioral and Neural Biology, 49,* 332–343.

Ebbinghaus, H. (1913). *Memory: A contribution to experimental psychology.* New York: Dover. (Original work published 1885)

Ebner, T. J., Flament, D., & Shanbhag, S. (1996). The cerebellum's role in voluntary motor learning: clinical, electrophysiological, and imaging studies. In J. R. Bloedel, T. J. Ebner, & S. P. Wise (Eds.), *The acquisition of motor behavior in vertebrates* (pp. 223–234). Cambridge, MA: MIT Press.

Eichenbaum, H. (2000). A cortical-hippocampal system for declarative memory. *Nature Reviews Neuroscience, 1,* 41–50.

Eichenbaum, H., Alvarez, P., & Ramus, S. (2001). Animal models of amnesia. In L. Cermak (Ed.), *Handbook of neuropsychology: Vol. 4* (2nd ed., pp. 1–24). Amsterdam: Elsevier Sciences.

Eichenbaum, H., & Bunsey, M. (1995). On the binding of associations in memory: Clues from studies on the role of the hippocampal region in paired-associate learning. *Current Directions in Psychological Science, 4,* 19–23.

Eichenbaum, H., & Cohen, N. J. (2001). *From conditioning to conscious recollection: Memory systems of the brain.* Oxford, UK: Oxford University Press.

Eichenbaum, H., Dudchenko, P., Wood, E., Shapiro, M., & Tanila, H. (1999). The hippocampus, memory, and place cells: Is it spatial memory or memory space? *Neuron, 23,* 1–20.

Eichenbaum, H., Stewart, C., & Morris, R. G. M. (1990). Hippocampal representation in spatial learning. *Journal of Neuroscience, 10,* 331–339.

Fortin, N. J., Agster, K. L., & Eichenbaum, H. (2002). Critical role of the hippocampus in memory for sequences of events. *Nature Neuroscience, 5,* 458–462.

Gaffan, D. (1994a). Dissociated effects of perirhinal cortex ablation, fornix transection and amygdalectomy: Evidence for multiple memory systems in the primate temporal lobe. *Experimental Brain Research, 99,* 411–422.

Gaffan, D. (1994b). Scene-specific memory for objects: A model of episodic memory impairment in monkeys with fornix transection. *Journal of Cognitive Neuroscience, 6,* 305–320.

James, W. (1918). *The principles of psychology.* New York: Holt. (Original work published 1890)

Kesner, R. P., Gilbert, P. E., & Barua, L. A. (2002). The role of the hippocampus in memory for the temporal order of a sequence of odors. *Behavioral Neuroscience, 116,* 286–290.

Knowlton, B. J., Mangels, J. A., & Squire, L. R. (1996). A neostriatal habit learning system in humans. *Science, 273,* 1399–1401.

LeDoux, J. E. (1992). Brain mechanisms of emotion and emotional learning. *Current Opinion in Neurobiology, 2,* 191–197.

Maine de Biran. (1929). *The influence of habit on the faculty of thinking.* Baltimore: Williams & Wilkins. (Original work published 1804)

McDonald, R. J., & White, N. M. (1993). A triple dissociation of memory systems: Hippocampus, amygdala, and dorsal striatum. *Behavioral Neuroscience, 107,* 3–22.

McGaugh, J. L., Cahill, L., & Roozendaal, B. (1996). Involvement of the amygdala in memory storage: Interactions with other brain systems. *Proceedings of the National Academy of Sciences, 93,* 13508–13514.

Meunier, M., Bachevalier, J., Mishkin, M., & Murray, E. A. (1993). Effects on visual recognition of combined and separate ablations of the entorhinal and perirhinal cortex in rhesus monkeys. *Journal of Neruoscience, 13,* 5418–5432.

Miller, E. K. (2000). The prefrontal cortex and cognitive control. *Nature Reviews Neuroscience, 1,* 59–65.

Morris, R. G. M., Garrud, P., Rawlins, J. P., & O'Keefe, J. (1982). Place navigation impaired in rats with hippocampal lesions. *Nature, 297,* 681–683.

Murray, E. A., & Bussey, T. J. (1999). Perceptual-mnemonic functions of the perirhinal cortex. *Trends in Cognitive Sciences, 3,* 142–151.

Murray, E .A., & Mishkin, M. (1998). Object recognition and location memory in monkeys with excitotoxic lesions of the amygdala and hippocampus. *Journal of Neuroscience 18*(16), 6568–6582.

O'Keefe, J. A., & Nadel, L. (1978). *The hippocampus as a cognitive map.* Oxford, UK: Oxford University Press.

Olton, D. S., Becker, J. T., & Handlemann, G. E. (1979). Hippocampus, space, and memory. *Brain and Behavioral Sciences, 2,* 313–365.

Otto, T., & Eichenbaum, H. (1992). Complementary roles of orbital prefrontal cortex and the perirhinal-entorhinal cortices in an odor-guided delayed non-matching to sample task. *Behavioral Neuroscience, 106,* 763–776.

Packard, M. G., & McGaugh, J. L. (1992). Double dissociation of fornix and caudate nucleus lesions on acquistion of two water maze tasks: Further evidence for multiple memory systems. *Behavioral Neuroscience, 106,* 439–446.

Packard, M. G., & McGaugh, J. L. (1996). Inactivation of hippocampus or caudate nucleus with lidocaine differentially affects expression of place and response learning. *Neurobiology of Learning and Memory, 65,* 65–72.

Rampon, C., Tang, Y.-P., Goodhouse, J., Shimizu, E., Kyin, M., & Tsien, J. (2000). Enrichment induces structural changes and recovery from non-spatial memory deficits in CA1 NMDAR1-knockout mice. *Nature Neuroscience, 3,* 238–244.

Ramus, S. J., & Eichenbaum, H. (2000). Neural correlates of olfactory recognition memory in the rat orbitofrontal cortex. *Journal of Neuroscience, 20,* 8199–8208.

Scoville, W. B., & Milner, B. (1957). Loss of recent memory after bilateral hippocampal lesions. *Journal of Neurology, Neurosurgery, and Psychiatry, 20,* 11–21.

Squire, L. R., & Zola, S. M. (1998). Episodic memory, semantic memory and amnesia *Hippocampus, 8,* 205–211.

Steele, R. J., & Morris, R. G. M. (1999). Delay dependent impairment in matching-to-place task with chronic and intrahippocampal infusion of the NMDA-antagonist D-AP5. *Hippocampus, 9,* 118–136.

Suzuki, W. A. (1996). Neuroanatomy of the monkey entorhinal, perirhinal, and parahippocampal cortices: Organization of cortical inputs and interconnections with amygdala and striatum. *Seminars in the Neurosciences, 8,* 3–12.

Thompson, R. F., & Kim, J. J. (1996). Memory systems in the brain and localization of a memory. *Proceedings of the National Academy of Sciences, 93,* 13438–13444.

Tolman, E. C. (1951). *Purposive behavior in animals and men.* Berkeley: University of California Press. (Original work published 1932)

Tulving, E., & Schacter, D. L. (1990). Priming and human memory systems. *Science, 247,* 301–306.

Vargha-Khadem, F., Gadin, D. G., Watkins, K. E., Connelly, A., Van Paesschen, W., & Mishkin, M. (1997). Differential effects of early hippocampal pathology on episodic and semantic memory. *Science, 277,* 376–380.

Viaud, M., White, D., & Norman, M. (1989). Dissociation of visual and olfactory conditioning in the neostriatum of rats. *Behavioural Brain Research, 32,* 31–42.

Wan, H., Aggleton, J. P., & Malcolm, W. B. (1999). Different contributions of the hippocampus and perirhinal cortex to recognition memory. *Journal of Neuroscience, 19,* 1142–1148.

Young, B. J., Otto, T., Fox, G. D., & Eichenbaum, H. (1997). Memory representation within the parahippocampal region. *Journal of Neuroscience, 17,* 5183–5195.

Zola, S. M., Squire, L. R., Teng, E., Stefanacci, L., Buffalo, E. A., & Clark, R. E. (2000). Impaired recognition memory in monkeys after damage limited to the hippocampal region. *Journal of Neuroscience, 20,* 451–463.

Zola-Morgan, S., Squire, L. R., Amaral, D. G., & Suzuki, W. (1989). Lesions of perirhinal and parahippocampal cortex that spare the amygdala and the hippocampal formation produce severe memory impairment. *Journal of Neuroscience, 9,* 4355–4370.

CHAPTER 20

Primate Cognition

MARC D. HAUSER

In *The Wizard of Oz*, Dorothy and Toto pick up three some-what lost characters, each in search of an extra bit of anatomy. The Tin Man wants a heart, the Lion wants circuitry for courage, and the Scarecrow wants a brain. Given modern technology, the Tin Man is in business; heart transplants are a piece of cake. The Lion probably just needs a testosterone patch, thereby restoring his machismo. The Scarecrow, how-ever, is currently out of luck—although perhaps not for long. We already have the ability to transplant parts of one species' brain into another and have the different parts work together in functional harmony. For example, the neuroscientist Evan Balaban (1997) has demonstrated through a fetal transplant technique that one can create a chimeric bird brain whose head bobs like a quail and crows like a chicken. By thinking about neural chimeras and species-typical behaviors, we can learn a great deal about how the brain evolved and how the neural circuitry underlying thought evolved as well; how-ever, we do not have to go to such extremes. We can adopt the scientific tool that ultimately led to Darwin's dangerous idea: the comparative method. As Darwin and subsequent students of evolution have so elegantly argued, to understand the evolution of mind and brain we can tap into the diversity of living species, using observations and experiments to under-stand the extent to which different species converge or di-verge with respect to the contents of their thoughts, as well as the processes by which they come to understand the world in which they live (Hauser, 2000; Heyes & Huber, 2000). This essay represents an attempt to flesh out this research pro-gram, building on the conceptual and empirical foundations that currently exist (Hauser, 2000; Heyes & Huber, 2000;

Shettleworth, 1998). I first consider a sample of problems that require careful attention before the fruits of the compar-ative approach can be tasted. Next, I review two case studies that I believe illustrate the power of the comparative approach. This review and the case studies selected are bi-ased in two ways: Most of the work focuses on primates (be-cause this is what the editors asked me to do, and it happens to be the taxonomic group on which I work!), and the case studies represent conceptual problems that I have explored. To alleviate the criticism that I am a primate chauvinist, let me state at the outset that for many of the examples I discuss, primates are unlikely to be unique in the capacities exposed and are often not the best group for working out the mecha-nistic details. They are, however, an important group for understanding problems relating to human evolution and the potential sources of our own intellectual heritage; I elaborate on this issue in the first section of this chapter. Although I focus on problems that I have worked on in some detail, such focus in no way implies that these areas are more important than others. My primary reason for focusing on the cases described in the second section is that I believe they make deep connections with studies of brain function and infant cognitive development—two disciplines that should be better connected to studies of primate cognition.

Phylogenetic Considerations About Homology and Homoplasy

A central problem in comparative biology is determining the evolutionary mechanisms underlying similarity between species. As evolutionary theorists point out, however, there are two coarse-grained categories of similarity, and each provides insights into phylogenetic patterns and the history of selection pressures. One category concerns *homologies,* identified as characteristics that are shared between two species because of evolution by descent from a common ancestor that also expressed the same characteristic. The second category concerns *homoplasies,* characteristics that independently evolved in different taxonomic groups due quite often to the process of convergence.

To illustrate the importance of this distinction, consider an example from outside of the Primate order: brood parasitism in birds (Sherry, 1997, 2000). In a wide variety of birds, breeding individuals dump their eggs into a host nest rather than rear the young on their own. The benefit to the parasites, of course, is that they only pay the cost of producing the egg, leaving the costs of rearing to the host. In one of the more carefully studied species—the brown-headed cowbird—females lay approximately 40 eggs per year and use the nests of more than 200 different host species; the large number of hosts is critical to their success because from an evolutionary perspective, such variation reduces the opportunity to develop a discriminating recognition system. Before dumping their eggs, cowbirds must scout the area, find suitable hosts, remember where they are, and then drop them off at a suitable time with respect to the host's reproductive cycle; dumping an egg before the nest is complete or after all of the host's eggs have been laid can lead to abandonment. Because egg dumping is the female's responsibility, one might expect to find sex differences in memory, with females showing greater abilities than males. And if such sex differences exist, then there must be a neural mechanism underlying this behavioral difference. Analyses by Sherry, Forbes, Khurgel, and Ivy (1993) have revealed that female cowbirds have a larger hippocampus than do male cowbirds, although there are no differences in overall brain size. These results show that selection can operate on neural specializations, leading to adaptations that are well suited to particular ecological problems. One must, however, move cautiously with such interpretations because it is possible that sex differences in the hippocampus are simply present in all blackbirds (i.e., the subfamily to which cowbirds belong). If all blackbirds show a sex difference in hippocampal size, then we have an example of a homology, and claims for a selective adaptation within the brown-headed cowbird are unwarranted. To show that this sex difference represents an adaptation—one designed to meet the challenges of specific ecological pressures—comparative data are crucial.

In studies of red-winged blackbirds and common grackles—two blackbird species that raise their own young—it has been shown that there are no sex differences in hippocampal size (Reboreda, Clayton, & Kacelnik, 1996; Sherry et al., 1993). Furthermore, in the shiny cowbird, whose females parasitize over 150 host species, there is a significant size difference in the hippocampus in favor of females, whereas in the screaming cowbird in which both male and female search for a host, there is no difference in hippocampal size. These data add considerable strength to the claim that sex differences in hippocampal size are the result of selection for adaptations to current ecological conditions and that such conditions are only present in some blackbird species.

Primatologists have often aimed their comparative efforts at humans, and this is particularly the case in the study of cognition. When human and nonhuman primates show the same phenotypic patterns or characters, it is often assumed that such similarities represent cases of homology. It is possible, however, that the similarity represents a case of homoplasy. Many cases of putative homologies within the primates (e.g., face recognition; Kanwisher, Downing, Epstein, & Kourtzi, in press; Kanwisher, McDermott, & Chun, 1997; Perrett et al., 1988; Perrett et al., 1984) have been defended on the basis of plausibility—specifically, that it is unlikely for the character to have evolved twice, once in each lineage. Although this is a reasonable argument to make for primates as a group, each case must be considered on its own. It is certainly possible that some traits shared in common between two species evolved after the divergence point. Moreover, in cases in which the putatively homologous character is a behavioral trait, it is possible that the underlying mechanisms differ between species. Conversely, cases of apparent homoplasy at the behavioral or anatomical level may actually represent cases of homoplasy at the genetic level, as the revolutionary studies of hox-home-obox genes have revealed (Carroll, Weatherbee, & Langeland, 1995; Gerhart & Kirschner, 1997).

Although there are historical reasons for drawing comparisons between human and nonhuman primate cognition, there are two potential problems with this kind of focus. First, when neuroscientists look to animals for comparative data, they tend to draw classificatory boundaries with respect to higher order taxa such as *animal, vertebrate,* or *monkey.* Consequently, there are numerous books and articles on the neurobiology of spatial memory, visual attention, decision making, and categorization that speak of comparisons between humans and "animals" or "monkeys and birds." For example, in a recent review article on the neurobiology of face perception, Haxby, Hoffman, and Gobbini (2000) state that in *"the monkey* [italics added], neurons that respond selectively to faces are found in patches of cortex in the superior temporal sulcus and in the inferior temporal gyrus" (p. 225). In a different article on the same topic, Tarr and Gauthier (2000) state that support "for feature maps comes from *monkey* [italics added] neurophysiology suggesting a topography of features in inferior temporal cortex (IT) and from human fMRI [functional magnetic resonance imaging] studies indicating that across a single task, different stimuli selectively activate different regions of the ventral temporal cortex" (p. 764). In each of these quotes, *the monkey* is the rhesus monkey. Although this particular species has been the model animal for studies focusing on the neurobiology of vision, we should be careful in assuming that rhesus are representative of primates, including both closely and distantly related species. For example, because some primates have a limited suite of facial musculature (Huber, 1931), they rarely produce facial expressions, and when they do, they have a small repertoire. Furthermore, although some primates such as rhesus exhibit the characteristic inversion effect shown in humans (i.e., faster and more accurate recognition of upright faces than of inverted faces), not all species do, even though faces clearly play an important role in their social behavior (Weiss, Ghazanfar, Miller, & Hauser, 2002). As I document in the following discussion, there are often important differences between species—even within the same genus—and such differences are informative with respect to the selective pressures on brain organization. Although one might reasonably ask whether *any* animal is capable of a cognitive computation that is characteristically human, a far richer evolutionary account would not only explore whether nonhuman animals can carry out the computation, but which species and why. Thus, in cases in which we share with other animals a particular computational ability, is this because of phylogenetic inertia, because of similar social and ecological pressures, or both? By thinking about socioecological pressures we are more likely to pinpoint appropriate species for our comparative analysis. Second, studies of cognitive evolution should also focus on similarities and differences between nonhuman primates—independently of the patterns obtained for humans. This is important because it allows us to map patterns of primate mind-brain evolution onto existing phylogenies that have used molecular, anatomical, behavioral, and ecological characters (Allman, 1999; Deacon, 1997; Deaner, Nunn, & van Schaik, 2000; Di Fiore & Rendall, 1994).

In the literature reviewed in the following discussion, it should become apparent to the reader that our understanding of many cognitive traits is restricted to only a handful of species. For example, although we know a great deal about asymmetries in hand use—and in coarse-grained anatomy for a number of primate species—our knowledge of behavioral and neurophysiological asymmetries associated with the perception and production of communicative signals is largely restricted to two macaque species (*Macaca mulatta, Macaca fuscata*) and chimpanzees (*Pan troglodytes;* Weiss et al., 2002). As a result, our ability to draw inferences about the patterns of evolution is minimal. An important goal of this essay, therefore, is to draw attention to what we know about the few species that have been studied; I also hope to inspire others to collect the relevant data on other species.

Comparative Methods for Comparative Cognition

A problem facing students of human infant and nonhuman animal cognition is that we cannot use language to ask about the thoughts and emotions underlying their behavior. In response to this problem, researchers have developed clever methodologies. Often, however, the methods used are designed for one species or a specific age group, and thus either cannot or have not been applied to other species or age groups. Additionally, in cases in which the same method has been applied to different species or age groups, a question arises as to the appropriateness of the method in asking questions about similarities or differences in cognitive abilities or competences. If we are to understand how the minds of different species evolved, then we must not only acknowledge these methodological problems, but also systematically confront them in our studies. Macphail (1987a, 1987b) sounded this warning almost 15 years ago, and the problems are still with us today.

On an extremely general level, there have been two methodological approaches to the study of animal cognition. On the one hand are studies typically run in a laboratory environment that involve some kind of training to shape an animal's initial behavior. After being trained to make a certain kind of response, subjects are often tested on generalization conditions designed to reveal what they have learned or can learn beyond the initial training period. On the other hand are studies run both in the laboratory and in the wild that tap spontaneous cognitive capacities. Here, the goal has been to understand how animals use species-typical behavior to solve problems. Both approaches are associated with benefits and costs. Independently of such methodological economics, however, it is clear that if we are to understand what neurocognitive processes mediate a particular behavior and whether such processes are similar or different across species, then we need tools that can be applied to different species with little or no change. This point has been made before but requires repeating because of the potential pitfalls associated with making assessments of differences and similarities in performance on a task. There are two critical questions or problems. First, does species or age-group A perform worse than does species or age-group B because A lacks a particular ability or because the task fails to engage a species-typical or age-appropriate motor response? For example, A might fail not because it lacks the conceptual resources to solve the task but because A lacks the requisite motor competences. Second, when species or age-group A performs as well or in the same way as species or age-group B, is this because members of A and B are solving the problem in the same or a different way? It has often been assumed that similarities in performance are guided by similarities in the underlying mechanism, but this need not be the case.

An elegant example of the second problem comes from the study of animal cultures or traditions. In a variety of species, one finds that members of one population perform a behavior not seen in other populations of the same species. In such cases, if differences in ecology or genetics can be ruled out as causes of interpopulation differences, then it seems reasonable to conclude that such differences arise due to learning. Of interest to those studying such traditions is how they were invented, passed on to others, and then maintained over time (Byrne & Russon, 1998; Galef, 1992; Heyes & Galef, 1996; Tomasello, Kruger, & Ratner, 1993; Whiten & Ham, 1992). Studies of wild chimpanzees highlight the extraordinary variation in tool use technology seen among populations that lack significant genetic or ecological differences, but studies of chickadees highlight the importance of conducting carefully controlled experiments to determine how homogeneity in the expression of a behavior emerged within the population. Sherry and Galef (1984, 1990) explored the famous studies of Fisher and Hinde (1949) on milk bottle opening in blue tits by running experiments with black-capped chickadees in captivity. The goal of these experiments was to assess whether the homogeneity among blue tits emerged because of imitation as opposed to some other transmission mechanism. One set of naive individuals watched as a demonstrator removed foil from a milk bottle and then skimmed the cream. These individuals were then placed alone in a cage with a foil-capped milk bottle. A second group of naive individuals was first placed alone in a cage with an uncapped milk bottle; the foil was placed next to the bottle. In the next session, these individuals were placed alone in a cage with a foil-capped milk bottle. When Sherry and Galef compared the speed with which individuals in these two groups learned to remove the foil from the milk bottle, they found no statistically significant differences. These studies show that what may appear to be an example of imitation (e.g., all the blue tits learned by copying from one genius tit to remove the foil) or some other form of social learning may in fact not be social at all. In the chickadee case, one group clearly learned from a demonstrator, but the second group learned by deduction—by seeing the foil next to the bottle and skimming the milk, such individuals solved the problem by playing the equivalent of Jeopardy: The answer is *Drinking milk with foil next to the bottle.* The question is *How do you drink milk from a foil-capped bottle?*

I emphasize these two problems throughout the rest of this chapter. In addition, I focus on methods that involve little to no training and that can be used across a variety of primate species with little to no change; in many cases, these techniques are likely to be effective with nonprimate animals as well, thereby broadening the depth of our comparative analysis. Most important is that because the methods described have been used with human infants and can readily be used in neurophysiological preparations with animals, we are in an excellent position to forge a link between ethologists, cognitive developmentalists, and neuroscientists.

Domain-Specific Systems of Knowledge

Some might claim that evolutionary psychologists have an obsession with modularity—or with massive modularity, as Jerry Fodor (2000) has recently put it. In fact, Fodor's recent treatment of modularity and his explicit criticisms of evolutionary psychology might come as a surprise given that the man has long been a champion of modular views of the mind anchored by a strong nativist perspective (Fodor, 1983). What is at stake in this debate, as well as a parallel one with those who think that the mind is merely a collection of general learning mechanisms, is how nature has carved the mind into specialized mechanisms that come equipped with knowledge of the world. As Fodor correctly points out, some evolutionary psychologists have mistakenly assumed that a commitment to domain specificity and modularity is a commitment to innateness. These are orthogonal issues. Of concern here—and a mediating force in the selection of empirical cases in the following discussion—is the hypothesis of category or domain specificity. To say that the mind consists of domain-specific systems is to claim that different domains of knowledge are guided by specific learning mechanisms or computations, often associated with dedicated neural circuitry. As I have argued elsewhere (Hauser, 2000), building on the views of Fodor (1983, 2000), Pinker (1994, 1997), and others (Caramazza, Hillis, Leek, & Miozzo, 1994; Carey & Spelke, 1994; Dehaene, 1997; Hirschfeld & Gelman, 1994), the domain-specificity perspective is not only a powerful theoretical argument, but is also a highly effective research strategy because it forces one to explore how particular features and principles guide and constrain the organization and acquisition of knowledge. It is simply an empirical question whether it is domain-specific systems all the way down or some combination of domain-specific and domain-general mechanisms and whether domain-specific or -general mechanisms are equipped with innate knowledge, and if so, what this knowledge is and how it permits learning of a certain kind. The domain-specificity perspective has already played a critical role in studies of patients with brain damage (e.g., cases of category-specific deficits for fruits, vegetables, faces; Caramazza & Shelton, 1998), in neuroimaging experiments of normal human adults (Kanwisher et al., in press), and in understanding conceptual development in infancy and early childhood (Carey & Spelke, 1994; Keil, 1994). It is high time that more students of animal behavior reap the benefits of this perspective; some already have (Cheney & Seyfarth, 1985; Gallistel, 1990; Hauser, 1997; Santos, Hauser, & Spelke, 2001).

To illustrate, consider the domain of spatial knowledge. We know from hundreds of studies of insects, fish, birds, and mammals that animals are equipped with two basic mechanisms for navigating in the world: dead reckoning, whereby the speed and distance traveled are automatically updated and used to find the most direct route to a target location; and piloting, whereby distinctive landmarks are used to find specific targets within a highly familiar area (Gallistel, 1990; Healy, 1998; Shettleworth, 1998). When animals use landmarks, certain features are more reliable than others are. Thus, for example, if home is located next to a white birch tree, what is relevant about the birch is its specific shape and consistent location but not its color or orientation. After all, if the birch falls over or undergoes a color change due to a shift in the seasons, it is still a reliable landmark. To explore whether animals are able to conjoin information from two different properties of a spatial environment, Cheng (1986) set up an experiment with rats. In the first condition, subjects were first placed in a rectangular room with four white walls and then shown a baited corner. Next, they were spun around with their eyes closed in order to disorient them. When they were released, subjects searched for the food in either the correct (i.e., baited) or geometrically opposite corner. These data suggest that rats can use the geometry of the room to find a target location. In the second condition, the rectangular room consisted of three white walls and one black wall. Although the task was the same, subjects were provided with a potentially salient, nongeometric feature (i.e., a colored wall) that could serve as a landmark. Under these circumstances, however, rats searched exactly as they did in Condition 1, looking in either the correct or geometrically opposite corner. What these results show is that rats are unable to conjoin geometric with nongeometric features in the context of spatial disorientation, leading Cheng to conclude that rats are equipped with a geometric

module—one that is highly encapsulated with respect to information coming in from other domains. It is unlikely that this kind of question and experimental design would have been set up outside a domain-specificity perspective.

An interesting twist on Cheng's results—one emphasizing the importance of comparative work—comes from studies of human toddlers and adults, as well as studies of chickens and rhesus monkeys. Specifically, Hermer and Spelke (1994, 1996; Hermer-Vazquez, Spelke, & Katsnelson, 1999) showed that when toddlers are run on Cheng's disorientation task, they perform exactly like rats—searching in the correct or geometrically opposite corner even when there are highly salient landmarks (e.g., a tree in one corner and a large plastic gnome in the other). However, when adults are run on this task, they perform like rats and toddlers in the all-white room, but search primarily in the correct corner when given a landmark. What Hermer and Spelke have argued is that in order to conjoin geometric and nongeometric features following disorientation, language is necessary. Specifically, adults solve the disorientation problem by saying something like *The baited location is to the right of the black wall.* When adults are prevented from using language by imposing a verbal shadowing task, they go back to looking like toddlers and rats. If language is necessary for conjoining geometric with nongeometric features, then clearly no animal should solve this task. Although Cheng's results would seem to support this claim, studies of chickens (Vallortigara, Zanforlin, & Pasti, 1990) and rhesus monkeys (Gouteux, Thinus-Blanc, & Vauclair, 2001) do not. Specifically, both of these species solve the disorientation task when landmarks are provided, although training was involved in both studies. Critically, then, these studies show that although language might be used by humans to conjoin geometric and nongeometric features, it is certainly not necessary. Whether there is a geometric module in the Fodorian sense depends on the species, as well as on the task, thereby emphasizing both the importance of cross-species comparisons and the application of different methods.

HOW TO STUDY COGNITIVE EVOLUTION: TWO TEST CASES

The Construction of a Number Sense

Children have the capacity to acquire the number system. They can learn to count and somehow know that it is possible to continue to add one indefinitely. They can also readily acquire the technique of arithmetical calculation. If a child did not already know that it is possible to add one indefinitely, it could never learn this fact. Rather, taught the numerals 1, 2, 3, etc., up to some number *n,* it would assume that that is the end of the story" (Chomsky, 1988, p. 167).

If there is anything that is distinctively human, it is our capacity to represent quantities with symbols, to use such symbols with abstract functions or operators, and to put these elements together to create the language of mathematics. Granted, not all cultures have the kind of formal mathematics that some of us learned in school. However, all cultures have a system of symbolic quantification, including number words and grammatical mechanisms for distinguishing (minimally) one object from many (Butterworth, 1999; Dehaene, 1997). Furthermore, all cultures care about quantification because— by our nature as humans—we have a sense of fairness (Ridley, 1996; J. Q. Wilson, 1987) that mediates exchange and sharing, whether it is over mongongo nuts and bush meat or high-tech stocks. Moreover, when one explores some of the ancient systems for representing numbers, one uncovers an extraordinarily nonrandom pattern: All cultures have distinctive and rationally assigned symbols for the numbers one, two, and three (sometimes four), but then change to a different notational system for numbers greater than three or four. Thus, for example, the Romans developed the systematically transparent system that mapped one to I, two to II, and three to III, but then modified the system at four with the introduction of a new symbol (*V*)—and thus the introduction of a new rule—to create a new pattern (IV). Similarly, in English we use the words *first, second* and *third,* but then shift to using *fourth, fifth, sixth,* and so on, or *-th* all the way up. Why shouldn't we write the Roman numeral for four as IIII, or use the word *fourd* or *fourst?* What privileges the numbers one to three or four? Such consistency across cultures suggests that humans are endowed with a number sense, a domain-specific system that is universally present and forms the foundation of our mathematical talents. It also suggests something special about the numbers one through four as opposed to numbers greater than four. Of concern here, then, is what this representational mechanism is like, how early in life it can be detected, how it mediates the child's path to numerical competence, and whether this capacity is uniquely human or shared with other animals? If we share with other animals a number sense, then what have the millions of years of biological and cultural evolution added that enable us to carry out computations that no other animal can and to develop elegant and often esoteric mathematics that can only be enjoyed by those rare human beings with a passion and gift for higher mathematics? To address these questions, I first provide a brief review of some of the relevant work on human infants, focusing on some of the earliest evidence for spontaneous numerical representations; I focus on infants in particular because this age group provides

the best opportunity to explore the hypothesis that biology has provided us with a numerical foundation that is then elaborated and enriched as a function of language as well as of other cognitive resources and experiences. Next I look at the evidence for numerical computations in nonhuman animals, contrasting studies that involve training with those that do not. I conclude with a brief discussion of what is currently known about the neural basis of number representation in human and nonhuman animals; then I review how work in this area forces a reconsideration of the theory that has been developed to explain nonlinguistic numerical representations.

Number Representation in Human Infants

If in fact some aspects of our number sense are universal, then we ought to pick up traces of this capacity in human infants. According to one view, championed by such cognitive scientists as Fodor (1975) and Pinker (1994, 1997), not only should infants have some of the core principles underlying our number sense, but such principles should also be continuous with the capacity observed in adults. This is the *continuity thesis* of human cognitive development. According to a second view articulated most recently by Carey and Spelke (in press), we are born with a core set of principles that put into play our capacity to acquire mathematics, but over development we acquire new representational resources that literally transform the earlier representations; this is the *discontinuity thesis.* According to either view, it is essential to establish what the infant is handed by biology—with respect to its capacity to compute numerosities—and how such mechanisms mediate subsequent learning.

During the 1980s, several developmental psychologists asked whether human infants could discriminate stimuli based on their numerical differences (Antell & Keating, 1983; Starkey & Cooper, 1980; Starkey, Spelke, & Gelman, 1990; Strauss & Curtis, 1981). In the classic design, an experimenter presented an infant with stimuli of a constant number, but with variability introduced in terms of either the kind of objects presented or the spatial arrangement of items such as dots on a monitor. Thus, for example, an infant would be habituated to slides consisting of two dots randomly arrayed within the frame and then would be tested with slides consisting of either three dots or two dots presented in a new spatial arrangement. Results from these experiments suggested that young infants were sensitive to different numerosities and were capable of discriminating one from two, two from three, and in some experiments, three from four. Moreover, work by Spelke and colleagues (Spelke, 1979; Spelke, Born, & Chu, 1983) indicated that the infant's representation of number appeared abstract and amodal as evidenced by the fact that they classified two dots and two beeps as the *same,* but two dots and three beeps as *different.*

In 1992, Wynn published an important paper suggesting that infants could not only discriminate numerosities, but could also operate over them, carrying out simple additions and subtractions. Taking advantage of the expectancy violation procedure developed to explore visual perception, Wynn first familiarized 4- to 5-month-old infants with an empty stage and with a stage showing either one, two, or three Mickey Mouse dolls. Next she ran infants on one of three versions of a test trial involving the addition of one object to another. In the expected or possible test, the infant watched as one Mickey was placed on the stage, an occluder raised to hide Mickey, a second Mickey introduced behind the occluder, and then the occluder removed to reveal two Mickeys (i.e., 1 + 1 = 2). This is an expected or possible outcome if the infant sees the first Mickey on the stage, maintains a representation of one Mickey behind the occluder, updates this representation to two Mickeys when the second is introduced, and then maintains this representation until the occluder is removed revealing precisely two Mickeys. In the two unexpected or impossible test trials, the presentation was identical to the expected version except that when the occluder was removed, the infant saw either one or three Mickeys (i.e., 1 + 1 = 1 or 3). If—as sketched for the expected test trial—infants store a representation of two Mickeys when the occluder is in place, then when the experimenter removes the occluder and reveals either one less or one more Mickey, they should look longer than they do when the outcome is precisely two Mickeys; this is exactly what Wynn observed in her studies. She also observed a similar difference in looking time in a subtraction event, contrasting a 2 − 1 = 1 outcome with a 2 − 1 = 2 outcome (Wynn, 1992). Wynn concluded that infants have an innate capacity to compute simple additions and subtractions.

Since Wynn's publication, there has been a flurry of activity by infancy researchers interested in the development of numerical representations. Several issues are at stake. First, to what extent can the infant's representation be considered numerical? Second, given differences in methodological procedures across studies, are experimenters testing the same thing? Third, what ontogenetic changes arise with respect to the representation of number? What is the role of innate constraints on learning and what kinds of experience are either necessary or sufficient with respect to developing the core principles of a number system (e.g., one-to-one correspondence, abstract, ordinal relationships, cardinality; Gelman & Gallistel, 1986)? Finally, how—from a computational perspective—do infants compute numerosities, and are there differences between small and large numbers, as well as between approximate and exact calculations?

Although the level of activity in this area has been high, it is difficult to provide a concise and unambiguous summary at this point due to differences between studies in experimental design, behavioral assays, and stimuli presented. Thus, some studies have used a looking time technique, whereas others use a reaching procedure; some use computer generated displays, whereas others use real objects; some require the use of working memory, and others do not; and so forth. To illustrate, consider a set of studies that have used the looking time technique. Following up on Wynn's original work, Simon, Hespos, and Rochat (1995) provided a replication, but also an interesting twist. By the age of approximately 5 months, although infants appear sensitive to the number of objects placed behind an occluder, they do not appear sensitive to the properties or kinds of object. Thus, if infants see two identical Ernie dolls (from *Sesame Street*) placed behind an occluder, they look equally long at an outcome of two Ernie dolls as they do at an outcome of one Ernie and one Bert or two Berts. These results fit in nicely with recent work by Xu and Carey (1996, 2000; Xu, Carey, & Welch, 1999) suggesting that it is not until the age of approximately 12 months that infants discriminate objects based on their properties or kinds (for an opposing position, see Needham and Baillargeon, 2000). Koechlin, Dehaene, and Mehler (1997) then showed that when infants detect a violation in number, they do so even when the spatial arrangement of the objects changes. Thus, if objects are rotated on a disc (a lazy Susan), infants look longer at outcomes with different numbers of objects but not different spatial arrangements of the same number of objects. Uller, Carey, Huntley-Fenner, and Klatt (1999) also provided a replication of Wynn's original design but showed that the outcome depends on whether the infant first sees one object on the stage followed by occlusion or starts by seeing an empty stage followed by the introduction of two objects behind the occluder. Specifically, although 5-month-old infants looked longer in the unexpected test trials of an *object-first* 1 + 1 condition (i.e., outcomes of 1 and 3; Wynn's original design), they did not discriminate between these outcomes until the age of 8 months when tested on a *screen-first* design. These results suggest that independently of the content of the infant's representation, working memory plays a crucial role; the object-first design demands only a single update in memory, whereas the screen-first design requires two.

All of the work reviewed thus far suggests that infants can discriminate small numerosities on the order of three to four. When we consider all of these studies together, however, we are left with a problem. Whereas the earlier experiments on number involved presentations that did not recruit working memory (i.e., the stimuli to be discriminated were always in view), the more recent experiments using expectancy violation do. Although it might be the case that the same mechanism underlies all of the findings to date, it is possible that there are different mechanisms and that some of the findings can be better explained by a system that is not strictly numerical, but rather tied more generally to what infants know about objects, especially under occlusion (Leslie, Xu, Tremoulet, & Scholl, 1998; Simon, 1997; Simon et al., 1995). Some of the most recent work in this area speaks directly to this problem.

In the early work on number representation in infants, the experimental stimuli were poorly controlled with respect to factors that might covary with number, and thus enable the infant to discriminate on the basis of features other than numerosity. Thus, in the original work by Starkey and colleagues, although infants appeared to discriminate between stimuli consisting of two versus three dots, they might have also discriminated between these stimuli on the basis of spatial extent, contour, or density. In a study by Mix, Levine, and Huttenlocher (1997) that provided more stringent controls for these factors, there was no evidence that infants were discriminating on the basis of number; rather, findings suggested that infants discriminated based on contour dimensions. However, in another study with even more careful controls, Xu and Spelke (2000) showed that infants could discriminate 8 from 16 dots but not 8 from 12 dots. In this study, number was the only relevant dimension. Xu and Spelke argued that in this particular task, infants were discriminating on the basis of ratios, and thus that they were capable of computing 2:1 but not 3:2. If correct, this suggests that on some tasks at least, infants can discriminate large numbers but are subject to the constraints associated with Weber's law—that is, when infants discriminate stimuli on the basis of large numerosities, they are subject to the effects of distance (numbers that are further apart on the number line are more readily discriminated) and magnitude (holding the difference between two numbers constant, larger numbers (e.g., 125 and 126) are more difficult to discriminate than are small numbers (e.g., five and six; Moyer & Landauer, 1967). Along similar lines, a study by Wynn and Chiang (1999) has shown that whereas infants succeed (look longer at the unexpected condition) on a 1 + 1 = 2 versus 1 task, they fail at a 5 + 5 = 5 versus 10 task.

Complicating matters further are three additional studies with human infants using three completely different techniques. Feigenson, Carey, and Hauser (2001) attempted a replication of Wynn's original findings with Mickey Mouse dolls, but used LEGO blocks that could be built in such a way as to explicitly control for area or volume. Under these more stringent conditions, results showed that infants looked longer when the outcome violated the expected volume or area, but not when it violated the number of objects. Thus, although infants might be sensitive to number, under the conditions tested, they are more sensitive to changes in volume and area. In a study by Wynn (1996) designed to explore whether the infants' representation of number was restricted to discrete visual or auditory objects, infants were habituated to a puppet that jumped in bouts of two or three hops. Thus, for example, one group of infants watched as a puppet jumped in a cycle of two up and down hops, paused, two more up and down hops, then paused, and so on. After they reached a criterion level of habituation, they were presented with the same puppet, who now hopped in a cycle of either two or three hops. Only when the number of hops changed did the infants dishabituate; this pattern was obtained in the face of controls for overall duration of the hops as well as interhop intervals. These results suggest that infants can discriminate two from three both for discrete objects and for events. In a third and final test variant, Feigenson et al. (2002) presented infants with a two-choice box task, originally developed by Hauser, Carey, and Hauser (2000) for rhesus monkeys (discussed later in this chapter). In general, infants watched as an experimenter sequentially placed different numbers of crackers into each of the two opaque boxes and then allowed the infant to search and retrieve the crackers in one box; for example, the infant might see the experimenter place one cracker into one box and then two crackers into the second box. Thus, if infants prefer more crackers over fewer crackers, they should selectively search in the box with more. Results showed that infants selectively preferred the box with two crackers over one and three over two, but showed no systematic preference for four versus three as well as for six versus three. Moreover, when number was systematically tested against surface area (e.g., one cracker vs. two crackers equal in surface area to one), infants selected the box associated with the larger surface area. Thus, in parallel with the work by Mix and colleagues, infants at this early age and in these particular tasks appear to weight volume and surface area over number.

These more recent results raise several important points. First, the work by Feigenson et al. reinforces the point made earlier that in order to claim that infants or any other nonlinguistic creature discriminates stimuli on the basis of their numerical differences, one must eliminate all other possible factors such as volume, contour, density and so forth. Second, Wynn's results suggest that if infants do in fact have a number sense, that it may—under some circumstances—be quite abstract (i.e., capable of computing over discrete objects and events). Third, several of the results reported in the preceding discussion suggest that when infants discriminate stimuli on the basis of number, they can do so precisely if the numbers involved are less than about four. If, as implicated by the work of Xu and Spelke, infants' numerical abilities were simply subject to Weber's law, they should have no problem with six versus three (Feigenson et al., 2002) as this reduces to a ratio of 2:1, which they pass when the number of cookies is one versus two.

These data raise one of two possible interpretations. Either these tasks are tapping different mechanisms, or there is one mechanism that is differentially effected by each of the tasks. As I discuss more completely later in this chapter, it is possible that there is one system involved in precisely computing small numerosities, a second system for approximately computing large numerosities, and a third system for precisely computing large numerosities. Rather than explicate these possibilities here, I turn next to work on animals. This work is not only critical to our understanding of number representation in humans—both infants and adults—but is also important because much of the theory derives from this work.

Number Representation in Animals: Why Might Selection Favor Numerical Computation?

There are two ways to motivate work on numerical representation in animals. On the one hand, we can ask whether there are socioecologically significant situations in which animals might profit from or require numerical computations. If so, then given sufficient variation between individuals and the coupling between computational capacity and reproductive success or fitness, selection might favor such capacities. On the other hand, we can ask whether—independent of selection for such capacities in nature—animals are capable of learning numerical discriminations and operations. Here I discuss the first approach, briefly reviewing the kinds of conditions that might select for a capacity to compute number or quantity. In the next section I turn to the second approach and show how training experiments have revealed an underlying capacity for number quantification. Subsequently, I show how we can unite both approaches to conduct experiments that tap spontaneous abilities for number representation.

There are at least three coarse-grained contexts in which one might expect to find evidence of a capacity for number representation: care of young, feeding competition, and intra- or intergroup aggression. We know, for example, that in species that produce multiple young per litter or clutch, the allocation of parental care or investment depends critically on the number of young—both presently available and to be produced in the future (Clutton-Brock, 1992; Trivers, 1972). However, based on studies with birds, and especially brood parasites (Davies, 2000; Kilner, Noble, & Davies, 1999), it appears that parents do not adjust the amount of care allocated

as a function of the exact number of young present. Rather, the allocation of parental care seems to be an approximate affair. In a similar vein, although a wide variety of avian species cache their food, often concealing and then retrieving thousands of seeds in thousands of different locations, there is no evidence that such individuals recall the precise numbers; rather, they recall an approximate number of seeds from an approximate number of locations (Balda, Kamil, & Bednekoff, 1997; Vander Wall, 1990). To push further, although studies of optimal foraging (Stephens & Krebs, 1986) clearly show that animals are highly sensitive to the energetic returns from different food patches, they do not appear to be calculating the precise number of food items in a patch, but rather the relative rates of return in one area as opposed to another (Ydenberg, 1998). Finally, although a coalition of two animals typically outcompetes an animal on its own and large groups outcompete smaller groups, there is no evidence that the precise number of individuals in one coalition or one group is used to assess competitive advantage; again, it is the relative number of individuals that seems to count (Harcourt & de Waal, 1992). These data suggest that if animals naturally have a system for numerical representation, then it is one that computes numbers approximately and not precisely.

In contrast to the work discussed thus far, recent experimental work on lions and chimpanzees suggests that under conditions of intergroup competition, individuals might assess the number of competitors prior to deciding whether to attack or flee. McComb, Packer, and Pusey (1994) presented lion prides with playbacks of roars from a single individual or three individuals. The extent to which the listening pride approached the speaker or roared back was contingent upon the number of individuals roaring, with the most aggressive response elicited by the simulation of three intruders. Moreover, the response to one versus three intruders was mediated by the number of lions in the pride, with stronger responses coming from larger prides. Like lions, chimpanzees are also confronted with threats from neighboring communities. Based on over 40 years of field research from sites all over East and West Africa, observations suggest that when chimpanzees from one community encounter chimpanzees from a foreign community, they will attack and kill the intruder if the ratio of adult males is 3:1 in favor of the attacking party. To test this observation, M. L. Wilson, Hauser, and Wrangham (2001) ran a series of playback experiments. Specifically, chimpanzee parties from the Kanyawara community in Kibale National Park, Uganda were presented with playbacks of a pant-hoot from a foreign adult male. When the party consisted of adult females and their offspring but no adult males, subjects stayed still or moved in the opposite direction from the speaker, and they remained completely silent (Figure 20.1). When parties

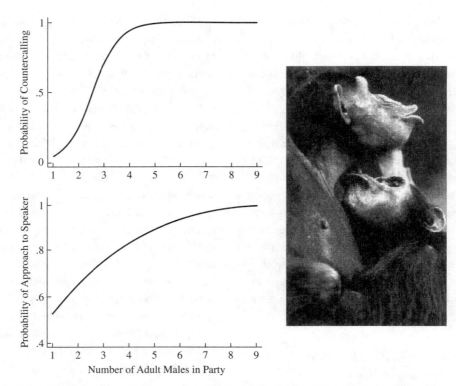

Figure 20.1 Response of chimpanzees to playbacks of a foreign male's pant-hoot vocalizations. Results from a logistic regression fitted to the probability of countercalling (upper panel) and approaching the speaker (lower panel) as a function of the number of adult males in the party. Only the number of adults males in the party had a statistically significant effect on countercalling and approach.

consisted of at least one to two adult males, individuals approached the speaker about 50% of the time but did so silently. In striking contrast, when the party consisted of three or more adult males, individuals always approached the speaker and did so while calling loudly.

These results suggest that like lions, chimpanzees in large parties have a competitive advantage. When the number of adult males exceeds two, there are significant benefits (or possibly low costs) associated with launching an aggressive attack on a foreigner. Given the limits of the behavioral assay (i.e., approaching the speaker, calling back to the playback), it appears that chimpanzees have the capacity to discriminate between no adult males, one to two adult males, and three or more adult males. Whether they can make more fine-grained discriminations (e.g., between one and two adult males or between three and four) remains to be explored, and may require different testing procedures.

In sum, there is ample evidence that animals can spontaneously compute the quantity of objects in the environment, be they animate or inanimate. What these studies fail to illuminate is the extent to which the capacity to compute quantities is based on precise numerical calculations, approximate numerical calculations, or rough estimates of quantity that have little to do with the more formal and abstract properties

of a number system. The following two sections shed some light on this problem.

Number Representation in Animals: Extracting the Substrate Through Training

There is a rich literature on number in animals based on classic operant techniques. This work, which started over 40 years ago, was intimately tied to research on timing (Church & Boradbent, 1990; Gallistel, 1990; Gibbon, 1977; Staddon & Higa, 1999). In the work on timing, results from common laboratory animals (rats and pigeons) demonstrated that subjects could represent temporal intervals and use such representations to compute complex operations that are isomorphic with division and subtraction. Moreover, work at the neurobiological level (reviewed in Gibbon, Malapani, Dale, & Gallistel, 1997) revealed a tight coupling in such animals between behavioral measures of timing and activation of basal ganglia and cerebellum. For example, lesioning of the nigrostriatal dopaminergic system of the basal ganglia greatly reduced the accuracy of interval timing in rats, whereas administration of dopamine can reinstate such accuracy following the lesion; it is interesting that recent work on patients with Parkinson's disease reveals deficits in timing and corresponding (correlated) imbalances in dopamine.

Given that animals can operate on temporal intervals, it is clear that they have the capacity for mathematical operations. The question of interest here is whether they can generate distinct representations of number and use these to control behavior. As Gallistel (1990) has pointed out in his review of this literature, a minimum criterion for representing number is the capacity to form a one-to-one mapping between numerosity (events or objects) and brain circuitry responsible for controlling behavior. Since this work started, there has been little debate concerning the ability of animals to discriminate on the basis of numerical differences between stimuli but considerable debate concerning how number is represented—in particular, whether it is digital and precise (one-to-one correspondence between object or event and a symbol) or analog and approximate. In the classic studies on rats (Mechner, 1958; Platt & Johnson, 1971), experimenters presented subjects with two response levers, A and B. Subjects had to learn that on some proportion of trials, pressing Lever A N number of times followed by pressing Lever B once delivered food. On the remaining trials, pressing Lever A $N + 1$ times delivered food. Results showed that as the number of target responses increased, so did the degree of error—that is, although the median number of presses by the subject corresponded quite well to the target number, as the target number's value increased, so did the variance. These studies, together with dozens more, have shown that subjects can discriminate (a) large numbers approximately; (b) stimuli based on number, time, or both simultaneously; and (c) the number of motor responses (lever presses or key pecks) or audio-visual stimuli (tones or light flashes). Moreover, these studies have shown that the subject's capacity to discriminate on the basis of number of responses or stimuli is not affected by motivational state, the mechanics of depressing a lever (i.e., how long it takes, how hard it is to move it), or the combination of stimuli from two different modalities (e.g., summing the number of sound bursts and light flashes).

Using the same classic techniques, studies of nonhuman primates have generally revealed comparable abilities (Olthof, Iden, & Roberts, 1997; Rumbaugh & Washburn, 1993; Thomas, Fowlkes, & Vickery, 1980; Washburn & Rumbaugh, 1991). A recent study by Brannon and Terrace (1998, 2000), however, stands out because of the degree to which the experimenters controlled for potentially confounding variables and the extent to which subjects spontaneously generalized from a small set of numerosities to a larger set, providing evidence that they can represent the numerosities one through nine on an ordinal scale. In the training phase, three rhesus monkeys were reinforced for responding to the numerosities one, two, three, and four in ascending, descending, or nonmonotonic numerical order (i.e., 3- > 1- > 4- > 2). The stimuli—clip art images positioned within a frame—were presented on a touch-sensitive screen. Each of the four different frames appeared in a different relative position on the screen across trials, and in no trial could the subject respond in the correct order unless it had extracted the correct numbers and their ordinal relations. Thus, for example, on some trials the area of the frame covered by one object was less than two, which was less than three, which was less than four; on other trials, however, the frame with one object was larger than the frame with four objects; under these circumstances, only the number of items within the frame can be used to pick out the correct response sequence.

Subjects trained on the ascending or descending pattern were readily able to order novel pairs of the numerosities 1- > 4; the subject trained on the nonmonotonic pattern never learned the task. For subjects trained on the ascending but not the descending order, there was clear evidence of generalization to novel pairings of the numerosities 5- > 9. Based on the accuracy of their responses as well as reaction time, the rhesus monkey's performance is consistent with Weber's law as evidenced by the fact that subjects showed distance and magnitude effects. Thus, for small numbers and large differences between pairs, accuracy was high and reaction time was low; for large numbers and small differences between pairs, accuracy was low and reaction time was high. These results—together with earlier work on rats and pigeons—suggest that animals represent number on an ordinal scale but that their representation is in the form of an analog magnitude with scalar variability.

A completely different training approach to the problem of number representation in animals comes from work involving apes that have been reared by humans and taught the meaning of Arabic numerals. In the standard setup—exemplified by the work of Matsuzawa (1985) and Boysen (Boysen & Bernston, 1989)—subjects are trained to make a one-to-one association between an Arabic numeral and the corresponding quantity of a particular object, usually food. Early in training, only a few numerals are presented, and gradually, new objects of the appropriate quantities are introduced so that the subject learns to generalize across objects; this is critical, of course, because subjects must learn that number is an abstract concept independent of the type of object or objects to be enumerated. A characteristic of all of these studies, including Pepperberg's (1994, 2000) work on an african gray parrot, is that each subject requires an immense amount of training before it can master the correspondence between symbol and quantity; even when subjects have mastered a subset of the integer count list, they never generalize with respect to new symbols. Thus, for example, Matsuzawa's star chimpanzee Ai required as long to learn the first half of the integer count list as the second half, and when she learned the quantity associated with one symbol, the relationship appeared approximate rather than precise. Thus, when she had learned the Arabic numerals *1, 2, 3,* and *4,* her understanding of *4* was *four or more* rather than *precisely four.*

These criticisms of the work on number in apes should in no way take away from the extraordinary capacities that have been demonstrated (Boysen, 1997). Thus, for example, these chimpanzees can order the numbers within the count list, understand cardinality, add either the number of objects or Arabic numerals in one box with those in another to come up with the precise sum, and determine the equivalencies of fractions (e.g., half an apple and half a glass of water). In a recent experiment by Kawai and Matsuzawa (2000), one subject was first trained to press between three to five numerals in their ordinal sequence. In the next phase, as soon as the first numeral was pressed, the others were occluded by a white square, thereby requiring the subject to recall the numerals, their ordinal relations, and their spatial positions. With the actual numbers no longer in view, this subject pressed the squares corresponding to the correct numbers. These remarkable studies show that chimpanzees can learn the integer count list, and that when they operate over these symbols, their performance looks exactly like our own under the same conditions. The problem is that the nature of their underlying representation is at some level very different from our own—that is, when young children learn the integer count list, they appear to learn it first as a meaningless list, with only the most primitive understanding of what each number word means. Thus, they start by understanding that *one* means one, but that *two, three, four,* and so on mean more than one. Gradually, they build an understanding of two, three, and four, and then the system explodes, with all of the remaining symbols or number words falling into place. What these children have learned is the successor function, the fact that one can count to infinity by simply adding one on to the previous number word. Chimpanzees never get this "aha" experience, at least under the training conditions tested.

In sum, nonhuman primates tested under a variety of training conditions are capable of learning many of the key properties of the number system, including one-to-one correspondence, ordinality, and cardinality. When primates represent number, they appear to do so on the basis of mental magnitudes, a system that represents number approximately as a quantity—one that can be operated upon with functions that are isomorphic with addition, subtraction, division, and multiplication. I turn next to a discussion of whether animals—in particular, nonhuman primates—represent number spontaneously in the absence of training,

and if so, whether this representation is similar to or different from the representations revealed through training.

Number Representation in Animals: Extracting the Spontaneously Available Substrate

The work previously reviewed suggests that under a variety of training regimes, animals have the capacity to acquire some of the core principles underlying numerical computation and representation. Because one goal of comparative research is to understand how and why humans and animals diverged and converged with respect to certain cognitive capacities, it is important to assess what capacities come naturally and spontaneously to animals in the absence of training, for it is precisely such spontaneous abilities that seem so extraordinary in our own species.

Hauser, MacNeilage, and Ware (1996) were the first to use the expectancy violation procedure on animals to explore spontaneous numerical representation. Given the uncertainty of using this procedure with animals—especially semi-free-ranging rhesus monkeys living on the island of Cayo Santiago, Puerto Rico—a simplified version of Wynn's (1992) original design was implemented. Specifically, the goal was to capture the logic of this technique (i.e., no training, looking as a measure, differences captured by contrasting consistent and inconsistent physical events), but to simplify the overall procedure. Thus, we used a between-subject design, ran each subject on only a single trial, and used a purple eggplant rather than a Mickey Mouse doll in order to increase the salience of the object. After we located an adult sitting alone and visually isolated from all other group members, we set up a stage. Subjects in Group 1 (possible: $0 + 1 = 1$) watched as an experimenter set down an empty stage, introduced an occluder in front of the stage, presented a single eggplant, lowered it behind the occluder, removed the occluder to reveal one eggplant, and then filmed the subject's response for 10 s. Subjects in Group 2 (possible: $0 + 1 + 1 = 2$) watched as an experimenter set down an empty stage, introduced an occluder in front of the stage, presented a single eggplant and lowered it behind the occluder, presented a second eggplant and lowered it behind the occluder, removed the occluder to reveal two eggplants, and then filmed the subject's response for 10 s. Subjects in Group 3 (impossible: $0 + 1 + 1 = 1$) watched as an experimenter set down an empty stage, introduced an occluder in front of the stage, presented a single eggplant and lowered it behind the occluder, presented a second eggplant and lowered it behind the occluder, removed the occluder to reveal one eggplant, and then filmed the subject's response for 10 s. In parallel with Wynn's results, subjects looked longer in the impossible outcome than they did in either of the possible outcomes.

Having had success with this simplified version of Wynn's design, we ran a more comparable design involving two familiarization trials followed by either a possible or impossible outcome. The results were identical to those in the first condition, with a highly significant increase in response (both over the prior familiarization and when contrasted with the other tests) in the *impossible* test trial, but no change in the two *possible* test trial outcomes. The same pattern of response was also obtained in a 2 − 1 = 1 versus 2 test.

These first results using the expectancy violation technique showed that at least one nonhuman animal could be tested in the same way as human infants and with highly interpretable and comparable patterns. Four problems remained. First, because rhesus had not yet been tested on a 1 + 1 = 2 versus 3 condition, it was not yet clear whether they expected precisely two objects following a 1 + 1 operation or whether they expected something like two or more objects. Second, although these results suggest that rhesus can spontaneously compute additions and subtractions of small numbers, it is possible that the differences in looking time are due to differences in surface area or volume, as appears to be the case in comparable experiments on human infants. Third—in contrast to the work on human infants and on nonhuman animals trained in an operant task—it is unclear from these studies whether the rhesus monkey's capacity to compute over a small number of objects generalizes to larger numbers, and if so, whether their capacity to discriminate larger numbers is precise or approximate. Fourth, although the looking time technique is powerful and of considerable use in comparative studies, it fails to reveal whether the subject can act on the knowledge that is revealed by differential looking at possible and impossible events.

Over the past 5 years, our lab has systematically addressed these issues in two nonhuman primate species—rhesus macaques and cotton-top tamarins. First, basing our conclusions on a series of looking time experiments, we have shown that adults of these two species can compute addition and subtraction operations on small numbers of objects. Specifically, when rhesus macaques see a 1 + 1 operation, they expect precisely two objects, as evidenced by the fact that they look longer at outcomes of one and three; tamarins show the same pattern of response when tested in captivity (Hauser & Carey, 1998, in review; Uller, 1997; Uller, Hauser, & Carey, 2001). Further, rhesus monkeys look longer at the unexpected or impossible outcome in the following conditions: 2 + 1 = 2 versus 3, 1 + 1 = 2 versus 1 big one (equal in volume to the two smaller objects), and 3 − 1 = 2 versus 3. They fail, however, on 1 + 1 + 1 = 2 versus 3, and 2 + 1 + 1 = 3 versus 4 versus 5. These failures, with multiple updates and numbers larger than three parallel the findings reported previously for infants; I will return to the theoretical implications of these patterns later in this chapter.

Second, we developed a new technique to explore spontaneous number representation in animals, a procedure that taps into our subjects' natural tendencies to forage and maximize returns. In the first condition (Hauser et al., 2000), we presented semi-free-ranging rhesus monkeys with two empty boxes, placed them on the ground approximately 5 m away from the subject, and then—in sequence—put one piece of apple into one box and a rock into the other. After the experimenter finished loading the boxes, he or she walked away and allowed the subject to approach. Consistently, subjects approached and selected the box with apple. In subsequent conditions, we systematically contrasted different quantities of apple, counterbalancing for the side first loaded and the side with the larger number of apple pieces; for each condition, we ran a total of 15 subjects, and each individual was only tested once. Under these test conditions, subjects selected the box with the larger number of apple slices for two versus one, three versus two, four versus three, and five versus three but showed no preference for five versus four, six versus five, eight versus four, and even eight versus three (Figure 20.2). These results suggest that adult rhesus track the number of objects placed into each box, recall what has been placed in each box, and contrast the quantities before approaching and selecting one box over the other. Given the pattern of results, the capacity to discriminate appears limited to quantities less than four, with no detectable ratio effects. In other words, if our search task tapped a magnitude system that was subject to Weber's law, then given success on two versus one, subjects should have been successful on eight versus four. Thus, rhesus monkeys appear to be capable of spontaneous and precise small number quantification.

In our search task, the number of apple pieces placed into each box is confounded by time, as well as by volume or

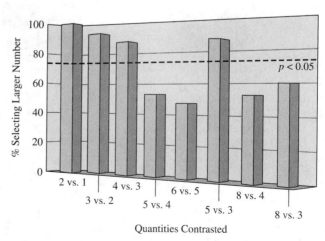

Figure 20.2 Proportion of adult rhesus monkeys selecting the larger number of apple slices over the smaller for eight different conditions. A statistically significant ($0.05 < p < 0.01$) proportion of subjects picked the larger quantity for 2 versus 1, 3 versus 2, 4 versus 3, and 5 versus 3.

surface area. Thus, for example, subjects could pick the box with more apple slices not because they were tracking the number of pieces, but because they were timing the duration of apple-placing events; similarly, they could use the overall volume or surface area to assess which box has more apple-stuff. To control for time, we ran a second experiment in which we held constant the number of objects going into each box but manipulated the kind of objects going in. Specifically, we placed N apple slices into Box 1 versus $N-1$ apple slices and a rock into Box 2. Although the time required to place objects into each of the two boxes was the same, subjects consistently picked the box with more apple slices, following the same patterns as in the first experiment. As an initial attempt to control for volume, we also ran a condition contrasting half an apple with three pieces of apple equal in volume to the half piece. Here, subjects picked three pieces over one, suggesting that number rather than volume is primary.

To determine whether the capacity to compute simple additions translates to other mathematical operations, we ran a comparable set of experiments with subtraction (Sulkowski & Hauser, 2001). The only difference in our protocol was that we first presented different quantities of objects (plums) on two physically separated stages, occluded the objects with freestanding occluders, reached behind the occluders, and then removed or added objects. Results showed that rhesus monkeys correctly computed the outcome of subtraction events involving three or fewer objects on each stage, even when the identity of the objects was different. Specifically, when presented with two food quantities, rhesus selected the larger quantity following subtractions of one piece of food from two or three; this preference was maintained when subjects were required to distinguish food from nonfood subtractions and when food was subtracted from either one or both initial quantities (Figure 20.3, top). Furthermore, rhesus monkeys were able to represent zero as well as equality (Figure 20.3, bottom) when two identical quantities were contrasted. We have yet to determine—using the search technique—whether rhesus

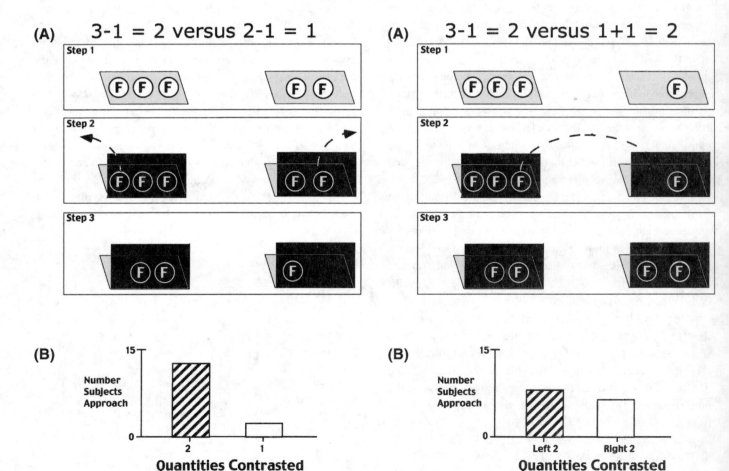

Figure 20.3   Results of a search task involving subtraction of objects from an occluded stage. On the left side of the figure, (A) subjects watched as one plum was removed from a stage with three initial plums, and one plum was removed from the other stage with an initial two plums. (B) Subjects consistently picked the stage with two plums over one plum. On the right side of the figure, (A) subjects watched as one plum was transferred from one stage to the other, resulting in two occluded plums on each side. (B) Here, rhesus fail to show a systematic bias to approach one stage over the other.

monkeys can subtract larger quantities of objects and whether they are attending to number or volume as demonstrated in the addition experiments.

In summary, we have demonstrated, using two different methods (looking time and search) on two nonhuman primate species (cotton-top tamarins and rhesus monkeys) under two testing conditions (laboratory-housed, semi-free-ranging), that at least some nonhuman primates spontaneously represent number. All of the results suggest that there is a limit on spontaneous number discrimination on the order of three to four. These data suggest, in parallel with comparable tests of human infants, that in the absence of training, pre- and nonlinguistic animals have a precise, small number system. Under different testing conditions, such as those evidenced by Xu and Spelke's (2000) work on infants and Brannon and Terrace's (1998) work on rhesus, subjects tap an approximate, large number system. In the next section, I return to the distinction between small and large numbers and examine the ontogenetic path from these two systems to a precise large number system—one that is liberated from the constraints of Weber's law.

Different Number Systems? Insights From Evolutionary Biology, Developmental Psychology, and Cognitive Neuroscience

My goal thus far has been to review what is known about number representation in nonlinguistic creatures—especially nonhuman and human primates. Studies of human infants less than a year of age provide evidence that under certain testing conditions, subjects readily and precisely discriminate small numbers of objects, usually in the range of three to four, and according to at least one study are capable of discriminating two actions (puppet jumps) from three; in some of these studies, infants appear to be paying greater attention to continuous variables such as volume, surface area, or contour, than to the number of discrete objects. In those studies showing sensitivity to small numbers, results suggest that it is in fact discrete number rather than ratios given that they discriminate between one and two but not between 3 and 6 or 5 and 10. However, these data stand in contrast to results showing that when all possible confounding factors are carefully controlled, infants readily discriminate 8 from 16 but not 8 from 12. Thus, at least under some circumstances, infants can discriminate large numbers approximately, and their discrimination appears to be based on Weber's law.

Studies of nonhuman primates—together with experiments on rats and pigeons—suggest that nonlinguistic animals can be trained to discriminate large numbers approximately, can spontaneously represent small numbers precisely, and with training on Arabic numerals can learn the integer count list from 0–10. Due to the small number of nonhuman primate

species tested and the wide range of methodological techniques employed, we are not yet in the position to say whether some species are more proficient on tasks of number discrimination than others. Nonetheless, the patterns emerging from nonhuman primates fit nicely with those emerging from human infants. When spontaneous methods are used, both species show evidence of precise small number discrimination and large approximate number discrimination. It is interesting that in both cases in which large approximate discrimination has been demonstrated (Brannon & Terrace, 1998, 2000; Xu & Spelke, 2000), the task involves visual stimuli that can be directly perceived, and with no memory load. In contrast, in cases in which precise small number discrimination has been demonstrated (Feigenson et al., 2002; Hauser et al., 2000; Hauser et al., 1996), the quantities to be contrasted disappear out of sight and must be evaluated as a set of stored representations. How can we account for the patterns of variation, and in what sense is it reasonable to claim that the abilities of nonlinguistic creatures—both human and nonhuman primates—represent the biological foundations of our culturally elaborated number sense?

At present, two models dominate the literature on number representation (Carey, in press; Dehaene, 1997; Dehaene, 2000; Gallistel, 1990; Gallistel & Gelman, 2000). Some argue that one model is necessary and sufficient, whereas others argue that both are necessary and sufficient. The first model can be traced to the early literature on number discrimination in laboratory animals, which—as has been pointed out here—was closely coupled with studies of timing. Specifically, Meck and Church (1983) suggested that animals represent number as mental magnitudes with scalar variability; recall the pattern of results from Mechner (1958) and Platt and Johnson (1971) in which subjects showed that as the target number of presses increased, so did the mean and variance of the subject's actual presses. To account for these patterns and the representations presumed to underlie them, Meck and Church proposed an accumulator mechanism whereby each object or event is enumerated or represented as an impulse of activation from the nervous system. To extract number (or time), the accumulator stores each impulse until the end of counting (or timing), and then transfers this information into memory, where it outputs one value for the impulses counted. This process or system can be schematically represented as a growing number line:

$1 = \_$

$2 = \_\_$

$3 = \_\_\_$

$4 = \_\_\_\_$

$\cdots$

$8 = _____$

Because of variability or noise in the remembered magnitude, the output from the accumulator is an approximation of number, with variability increasing in proportion to magnitude, or what is referred to as scalar variability (Church & Boradbent, 1990; Gibbon, 1977; Gibbon et al., 1997; Roberts, 2000; Whalen, Gallistel, & Gelman, 1999). As Gallistel and Gelman (2000) have recently articulated, under the accumulator model "numerosity is never represented exactly in the nonverbal or preverbal mind, with the possible exception of the first three or four numerosities" (p. 60). Nonetheless, there are at least two advantages of the accumulator model as a mechanism of nonlinguistic number representation. First, it generates a representational format—mental magnitudes with scalar variability—that can be operated over by such arithmetic operations as addition, subtraction, multiplication, and division. Second, it takes as input signals from any sensory modality, and as such, is abstract as demanded by mathematics (e.g., a counting system should be able to enumerate bursts of sound, discrete objects, or actions).

The second model (Carey & Spelke, in press; Hauser & Carey, 1998; Hauser et al., 2000; Simon, 1997) is based on the idea that number—especially small numbers less than about four—may be represented by a system that is used by adults for object-based attention and tracking (Kahneman, 1992; Scholl & Pylyshyn, 1999; Trick, 1994). The basic idea is as follows: When we see an object, we pick it out from the background, using metaphorical fingers of attention to track its movements. For each object, a file is opened and tagged. Based on psychophysical studies of humans, the number of objects (files) that can be simultaneously tracked (opened) is small, on the order of three to five. Thus, for example, in the looking time study involving $1 + 1 = 2$, rhesus monkeys watched as one eggplant was placed on stage, occluded, and then a second eggplant was added behind the screen before the outcome was revealed. In this case, one object file is opened for the first eggplant, followed by an updating of this representation and the opening of a second object file when the second eggplant is added. Next, when the occluder is removed, the number of eggplants revealed either matches or mismatches the number of eggplants that were concealed or the number of object files that were opened. In the original model, the system that opens a file does not register what the object is or what features are associated with it. It simply provides a mechanism for object tracking. More recently, however, experiments by Blaser, Pylyshyn, and Holcombe (2000) indicate that humans can track the changing features of an object that is static in one place; as such, humans can track the object as it moves through a feature space. This shows in theory that the object file mechanism is sensitive to both locational and featural cues.

Under the object file model, although there is no explicit representation of number, there is a mechanism capable of providing at least four criteria for constructing numerical representations (Carey & Spelke, in press). First, by using spatiotemporal information, object files are opened based on principles of individuation and numerical identity. Specifically, only entities with clearly articulated object properties (e.g., bounded, moves in a continuous spatiotemporal path) can be enumerated, and each one of these entities is uniquely specified by a set of spatiotemporal coordinates. Second, if one or more object files are opened, opening a new one provides a mechanism for adding one item to an array of items—an operation that is likely to be important for the successor function that is crucial to the integer count list. Third, object files are based on one-to-one correspondence (one file opened for each object, up to a limit of approximately four) and thus may contribute to the establishment of numerical equivalence. Fourth, although the number of object files that can be simultaneously opened is limited, it is precise and not subject to Weber's law (distance and magnitude effects).

The advantages of each of the models are at least partially offset by disadvantages—both in explaining the existing patterns of results on human and nonhuman animals and in accounting for how human children (at least) acquire a mapping from these initial representational formats (mental magnitudes or object files) to what ultimately becomes a sophisticated understanding of mathematics. One way to reconcile the pattern of results observed, as well as current debates in the literature that pit one model against the other, is to defend a two-model approach—one that views the biological foundations of our number system as depending upon a precise small number mechanism and an approximate large number mechanism. This is precisely the tact that Carey and Spelke (in press) have recently adopted.

Consider once again the work on nonhuman primates and human infants. If number is strictly represented as a mental magnitude, then it is not possible to account for the fact that human infants successfully discriminate two from three dots, but fail to discriminate four from six and 8 from 12 dots (Starkey & Cooper, 1980; Starkey et al., 1990; Xu & Spelke, 2000); the same holds for the observation that rhesus monkeys selectively choose three pieces of apple over two but not eight over four (Hauser et al., 2000). If human infants and rhesus monkeys *only* tapped a magnitude representation of number, in which Weber's law holds (i.e., the discriminability of two perceived magnitudes is determined by the ratio of objective magnitudes), then these values should be discriminable because they differ by the same ratio. On the other hand, a magnitude system can account for the fact that human infants are able to discriminate 8 from 16 dots, and rhesus monkeys can discriminate numbers between one and nine, but with a significant decrease in performance as a function of the distance and magnitude of the specific numerical pairings (i.e., one vs. two is easier than seven vs. eight but harder than one vs. four). These results—and the numerical values on which they are based—well exceed the presumed limits of an object file representation. Putting these findings together leads to the suggestion that there might be two relevant systems, one (the object file mechanism) handling small numbers with precision and the other (the accumulator mechanism) handling large numbers approximately.

At present, the two-mechanisms account provides the best explanation for what has been observed in studies of number discrimination among human and nonhuman primates. However, I do not believe that either mechanism—alone or combined—satisfactorily handles the current patterns of variation. To clarify, consider the object file model for precise, small-number discrimination. This model was originally formulated to account for visual object tracking and yet is currently being used to account for an abstract concept such as number, which—by definition—must be able to handle any format of input. As some of the studies previously reviewed suggest, there is evidence for numerical discrimination of sounds and actions. Consequently, in order for the object file mechanism to work in the case of number, one would have to broaden its scope, allowing files to be opened independently of input. This is possible, of course, but we can no longer be confident that the kinds of constraints that have been documented for visual object tracking hold for sounds, actions, or some combination of input formats (see Cowan, 2001, for a possible solution); it is also possible that the object file mechanism works for visual objects and that some other mechanism is recruited for other modalities. Further, although Carey and Spelke (in press) are correct in stating that an object file mechanism sets up critical criteria for number representation, it is not at all clear how such criteria can ultimately service or map onto a fully mature system of mathematics and the representations required. For example, although the opening of files is at some level similar to the successor function, it is clearly not *the* function because by definition, functions are not constrained or limited to a finite set; they are open-ended. A final limitation of the object file mechanism is that it cannot account for the pattern observed in the two-choice box test run on rhesus monkeys. In this task, the total number of objects tracked well exceeds the presumed limits of this mechanism—that is, rhesus monkeys successfully discriminated four pieces of apple in one box from three in the other, for a total of seven pieces of apple. Moreover, the object file model was not developed to handle operations within each file—a move that is required to handle the sequential

updating of objects placed within each box. These problems do not necessarily invalidate the general notion of an object file mechanism for small number discrimination, but they do suggest that the details of the model must be changed, and checked by both behavioral and neurobiological investigations; I turn to these shortly.

Although the accumulator model solves many of the problems associated with the object file mechanism (e.g., no difficulties with varied inputs, multiple accumulators, large numbers, and abstract mathematical functions), it cannot account for precise number discrimination within the range explored, and has difficulty explaining how the developing child generates the appropriate mapping between an approximate number system and a precise one. Some, such as Gallistel and Gelman (2000), have argued that the evidence for small number discrimination in human infants and nonhuman primates is actually not numerical at all. Rather, what appears to be a numerical discrimination is actually just the by-product of the object tracking system. Their main argument here is that this system simply fails to generate the kind of representational format that can be operated over in terms of the basic operations of arithmetic. Although this debate has yet to be resolved, at least some evidence from rhesus monkeys suggests that they are capable of operations that appear isomorphic with addition and subtraction of small numbers (Hauser et al., 2000; Sulkowski & Hauser, 2001). The second point is that if humans come equipped with a mental magnitude system, then the mapping between magnitudes and integers should be relatively straightforward. And yet, work on the child's acquisition of a count system suggest that it is anything but straightforward. Studies by Wynn (1998) have shown that children under the age of 3 years have acquired the number words but have little understanding of their meaning. Thus, they may count "one, two, three, four. . ." but not know that two means precisely two things, and that after counting the number of cookies on a plate, the last number in the count list represents the total number or the cardinal value. In fact, it is not until the age of approximately 3.5 years that the child grasps the integer count list, with a full appreciation of the successor function and a precise understanding of the meaning of small and large numbers.

The difficulties articulated with each of the models must not be underestimated. At present, however, there are no easy solutions. There are, nonetheless, some interesting directions for future work in this area, involving both additional studies at the behavioral level as well as new studies at the neural level. To conclude, I briefly discuss two such exciting directions. Carey and Spelke (in press) have argued that a key to understanding how an organism develops or evolves from the biological primitives of our number system—small precise and large approximate—to the full-blown, mature system is to explore how language adds on a new and crucial cognitive resource that permits the mapping between systems. Thus, the strong form of Carey and Spelke's claim is that in the absence of language, the organism will never develop a precise, large number system and consequently will never acquire what all humans with language acquire in the absence of formal schooling. Evidence in favor of this position comes from looking at human-reared chimpanzees who have been taught the Arabic numerals. Although their abilities are impressive, none of these animals have ever generalized beyond the original training set, and their capacity for discrimination appears tied to a mental magnitude representation. There are, however, two critical tests that have yet to be conducted with such animals. First, if Carey and Spelke are correct, the only way to get a proper mapping between the biologically primitive system and the fully developed human adult system is to acquire an arbitrary list of tokens, as appears to occur in all human children. Thus, before human children understand the count list (one-to-one correspondence, ordinality, cardinality), they spout the words in the count list. With this list in place, they can then tap into the biologically primitive system; how this connection is actually forged is still unclear. One would therefore predict that if chimpanzees are first taught the arbitrary count list and then taught the mapping between Arabic numerals and quantities, they should be able to generalize to larger numbers spontaneously, as do human children. A second possible test of this hypothesis involves apes that have had some level of language training. None of the chimpanzees tested thus far on number representation have had any formal training in a natural language. If one grants some level of linguistic ability to these animals (see next section), one can ask whether such additional resources help in acquiring the kind of number representation that we have.

A second approach to understanding both the similarities and differences in number representation across species and age groups comes from recent studies of the underlying neural mechanisms (Butterworth, 1999; Dehaene, 1997, 2000). Neuropsychological studies of patients suggests that deficits in number processing are dissociated from deficits in language processing, and that the deficit is abstract (i.e., computational problems arise for both visually and auditorily presented numbers). For example, some patients can tell you which letter falls between *B* and *D* but cannot tell you which number falls between two and four; others have problems reading number words but not nonnumber words. Combined with recent neuroimaging studies, it has been suggested that the intraparietal cortex is selectively involved in approximate number computations, whereas the prefrontal cortex (especially the left hemisphere) is selectively involved in exact number computation. This work stands in contrast to studies of rats indicating that the most likely locus for approximate number (and timing) computation is in the basal ganglia and cerebellum. In order to make headway on the neural basis of number representation, there are several obvious studies. First, if nonhuman animals lack a precise large number system, then during computations of large numbers, there should be no activation of prefrontal cortices and dominant activation of intraparietal cortex. Second, for subjects with explicit training on Arabic numerals as well as language, one might expect to see some activation of prefrontal regions. Third, given the abundant evidence that timing mechanisms are guided by circuits in the basal ganglia and cerebellum, it is essential that future studies of number in animals and humans focus in on these areas. For example, although Parkinson's patients show impairments on timing discriminations, we do not know whether they show comparable deficits for number or whether administration of dopamine-based medication would alter such deficits. Furthermore, given the capacity to carry out fMRI and positron-emission tomography (PET) studies with nonhuman animals (Logothetis & Sheinberg, 1996; Rolls, 2000), it is possible to explore how a nonlinguistic brain represents number and whether this neural machinery is the same as in humans, both young and old. Such studies of anatomical localization will enable us to determine whether the observed similarities between nonhuman primates and human infants are instances of homology or homoplasy.

Language and the Speech Is Special Debate

"Seen our way, speech perception takes place in a specialized phonetic mode, different from the generally auditory mode and served, accordingly, by a different neurobiology." (Liberman & Mattingly, 1988, p. 775)

Introduction to the Debate

In a recent lecture at MIT (Massachusetts Institute of Technology) entitled "Language and the Brain," Noam Chomsky spent a substantial proportion of time discussing why the comparative approach to the study of human language (Hauser, 1996)—especially the use of evolutionary theory (Pinker & Bloom, 1990)—has yet to inform our understanding of language, including why it has its own particular design features, is present in all humans, exhibits a characteristic pattern of development, and is grounded by a suite of formal parameters or constraints. This critical position is not a dismissal of the comparative method or of evolutionary theory. Rather, it represents a challenge to evolutionarily oriented scientists to find evidence—one way or the other—that will help us understand the design of language. In one sense, this challenge is no different from any other in the study of comparative biology, including such superb examples as the evolution of the vertebrate eye, avian wing, and primate hand. In this section, I take on Chomsky's challenge by discussing a research program that I believe has great promise—perhaps more so than do other approaches to the problem of language evolution. In particular, the approach I advocate here represents a return to the classic speech-is-special debate—especially an exploration of the mechanisms that mediate the acquisition of spoken language (for an extensive review, see Trout, 2000). This approach is, in a nutshell, as follows: To establish the unique design features of human language, one must first describe the landscape of mechanisms—both necessary and sufficient—for an organism to acquire language. Next, one must assess how such mechanisms constrain the form of learnable languages. If one establishes that some of these mechanisms are shared with other organisms, then it cannot be the case that such mechanisms evolved *for* language; rather, they must have evolved for other computational problems and then, during human evolution, were co-opted for language processing. Although there are problems associated with this approach (see the following discussion), by systematically examining a suite of mechanisms employed by humans (both young and old) to acquire language and checking to see which ones are absent among nonhuman animals, we will be in a strong position to specify those mechanisms that evolved specifically *for* language and that are part of our unique endowment, or what Chomsky has referred to as the faculty of language.

As a brief illustration of this approach, its logic, and its potential pitfalls, consider our system of speech production. Although on a coarse-grained level we share with other mammals a comparable vocal tract, no other mammal produces speech—either the content or the actual sounds—and none of our nearest living relatives (apes and monkeys) have the capacity to imitate sounds. This comparative claim is either trivially true or of considerable interest. To show how it is trivially true, consider the following parallel comment: No other animal except bats and dolphins produces biosonar sounds. To turn this into an interesting comparative claim, one must show how the target mechanism mediates the particular function, and how in the absence of such a mechanism there can be no system with a comparable func-

tion. Returning to speech production, if you accept the motor theory (Liberman & Mattingly, 1985)—that the phonetic mode entails the perception of gestures, not sounds—then animals should not have a phonetic mode because surely they do not perceive human gestures. They could, however, perceive the species-typical gestures for making their own species-typical sounds, but because their vocal tract is in fact different (Fitch, 2000), the percept should be fundamentally different as well. So, either this is true (it could be true even if the motor theory is wrong) or it is false (that is, animals perceive speech in a way that is similar to that of humans, in which case the motor theory must be wrong). If it is false, then the perceptual system has undergone little evolutionary change. Going one step further, if we find differences in perception among species, then we need to ask why there are specific perceptual mechanisms that we have that animals lack, and vice versa. Is it because the production system dragged our perceptual system along, or did the perception system open up a new range of possible sounds? Is it because we experienced a perceptual problem in our past that required a new mechanism, but the evolutionary pressure is not one linked to speech? These are all possibilities, and a comparative approach to language evolution must address them.

Before turning to some of the relevant empirical work, let me briefly mention three other comparative approaches to the study of language evolution that I believe have met with mixed success, at least with respect to current reception by linguists and psycholinguists. The first, pioneered by Lieberman (1968, 1984; Lieberman, Klatt, & Wilson, 1969) over 30 years ago, involves exploration into the mechanisms of speech production. In contrast to all other animals, the position of the larynx is substantially lower in modern humans. This anatomical difference, together with the accompanying changes in the supralaryngeal vocal tract (e.g., two-plus tube, bent at a 90° angle, permitting resonances in both the nasal and oropharyngeal cavities) and neural circuitry for motor control, have led to the capacity to generate a far richer array of formant frequencies. This enhanced frequency range is relevant to the evolution of language, so the argument goes, because there would have been strong selection on humans to evolve an efficient acoustic vehicle for conveying information about complex ideas. Although current work on this topic—especially by Fitch (2000)—shows that many of the adaptations for vocal production seen in humans are not unique, it is clear that work on vocal production has not yet illuminated those problems that are of deepest concern to linguists. In exploring the literature, it appears that only a small circle of linguists—mostly those working on phonology

(MacNeilage, 1998; Studdert-Kennedy, 1998)—have been at all influenced by the comparative data.

The second approach—also started over 30 years ago—focuses on whether nonhuman animals have the potential to acquire a human language (Gardner & Gardner, 1969; Herman & Uyeyama, 1999; Pepperberg, 2000; Premack, 1986; Savage-Rumbaugh, 1986; Savage-Rumbaugh et al., 1993). More than any other approach, this work has certainly captured the attention of linguists (for a critical review, see Wallman, 1992), although the level of impact has been mixed and highly variable over the years. In general, there have been two areas of concern or debate: One, what does it mean to show that an ape's brain has the potential to acquire some aspects of human language, although such characteristics are not employed in their own communicative systems? Two, to what extent is the proclaimed capacity of some animals to signal symbolically and to combine symbols into new expressions truly like the human capacity to use words and to form sentences? At present, I do not think that there is a satisfactory answer to the first question. Even if we accept only a limited capacity for symbolic signaling and syntactic constructions in human-trained animals (Deacon, 1997), it is not at all clear why an animal with such potential would not employ its capacities when communicating with others of its kind. As is pointed out later in this chapter, the natural repertoires of animals fail to show anything like the capacity of human-reared individuals to produce or comprehend referential signals that can be recombined into new expressions; even more surprising, the best evidence for a symbolic system in the natural repertoires of animals has come from studies of monkeys, not apes! As for the second question, the jury is still out, but new data coming in from Savage-Rumbaugh's lab in particular will have to be treated critically but fairly by linguists; if there is to be a science that includes language-trained animals, then linguists must work with comparative psychologists so that reasonable standards can be set and explored.

A third approach stems from classical ethology and focuses on the natural communication of animals. These studies, conducted primarily in the wild, have asked whether animals can produce signals that refer to objects and events in the external environment, and whether they can combine these signals to create utterances with a potentially infinite range of possible meanings. Since the pioneering work on vervet monkey alarm calls (Marler, 1978; Seyfarth, Cheney, & Marler, 1980a, 1980b; Struhsaker, 1967), which implied a relatively primitive system of referential signals, there have been several other studies showing that this capacity is present in other species (several old-world monkeys and domestic chickens) and can be extended to other contexts outside of predator-prey

interactions (Cheney & Seyfarth, 1988, 1990; Dittus, 1984; Evans & Marler, 1995; Fischer, 1998; Gouzoules, Gouzoules, & Marler, 1984; Hauser, 1998; Marler, Dufty, & Pickert, 1986; Zuberbuhler, Cheney, & Seyfarth, 1999; Zuberbuhler, Noe, & Seyfarth, 1997). Furthermore, some studies have suggested that animals can recombine discrete elements of their repertoire to produce new signals (Cleveland & Snowdon, 1981; Hailman & Ficken, 1987; Robinson, 1979, 1982). Although some linguists have discussed this work (Bickerton, 1990; Pinker, 1994), it has generally made no impact on how linguists think about the problem of reference or syntax (for a recent review, see Jackendoff, 1999). I believe there is a simple reason for this. In terms of reference, the apparent capacity in animals is so fundamentally different from that in humans that it is not at all clear whether one should think about the calls of some birds and primates as precursors to our words or as something completely different and disconnected from the evolutionary path to human referential signals. For example, although vervet and diana monkey alarm calls may in fact stand for a particular predator and thus function like a label in our natural languages, the underlying capacity for generating referential signals is highly impoverished relative to even a 1-year-old child. The signals of animals are restricted to the present (i.e., they do not provide information about past events or future encounters) and can be entirely predicted by current context (i.e., if you know what the animal has recently experienced, you can predict what vocalization it will produce, if it produces one at all). Moreover, the system appears closed, with no evidence that animals can create new utterances designed to meet new situations; this stands in contrast to the evidence that animals—especially chimpanzees—have the capacity to solve novel ecological and social problems in new ways, inventing new tools or new strategies for overthrowing a competitor (Hauser, 2000; Whiten et al., 1999). Similarly, of the studies exploring the possibility of syntactic constructions, there is no evidence that combination signals have anything like new meaning; rather, when animals appear to combine discrete signals into new strings, the only detectable change appears to be associated with the caller's affective state; in the case of songbirds, in which the evidence for rule-guided changes in structure is most apparent, syllable arrangement plays no role in meaning or function; rather, it conveys information about species, sex, and individual identity—and in some cases, reproductive potential.

The Speech Is Special Debate: Some History

In the 1960s, Liberman and his colleagues at the Haskins lab (Liberman, Cooper, Shankweiler, & Studdert-Kennedy, 1967; Liberman, Delattre, & Cooper, 1958; Liberman, Harris,

Hoffman, & Griffith, 1957) began to explore in detail the mechanisms underlying human speech perception. What is interesting about the claims emerging from Haskins at this time is that they were intellectually allied with Chomsky's (1957, 1965, 1966) position concerning the special nature of human language. In particular, it is clear that Chomsky thought of the language organ as uniquely human and that its capacity for generating syntactical structure evolved for reasons that had nothing to do with communication (Chomsky, 1988). Although one can certainly challenge this claim, what is important for biologists about Chomsky's position is that it sets up a testable hypothesis about the nature of the comparative database (Hauser, 1996). Specifically, if humans are truly unique with respect to the language organ, then we should see little to no evidence of precursor mechanisms in other animals. This brings us back to Liberman and the Haskins lab. In particular, much of the early work on speech perception was aimed at identifying particular signatures of an underlying, specialized mechanism. Perhaps one of the most important and early entries into this problem was Liberman's discovery of the phenomenon of categorical perception; note that for Chomsky, data on perceptual mechanisms are only of interest in so far as they interface with and constrain core computational mechanisms that are central to the faculty of language.

Categorical Perception of Speech and Species-Typical Vocalizations

When we perceive speech, we clearly create categories. Using an artificially created acoustic continuum running from /ba/ to /pa/, human adults show excellent discrimination of between-category exemplars and poor discrimination of within-category exemplars. To determine whether the mechanism underlying categorical perception is specialized for speech, uniquely human, and fine-tuned by the linguistic environment, new methods were required, as were subjects other than human adults. In response to this demand, the phenomenon of categorical perception was soon explored in (a) adult humans using nonspeech acoustic signals as well as visual signals, (b) human infants using a habituation procedure with the presentation of speech stimuli, and (c) animals using operant techniques and the precise speech stimuli used to first demonstrate the phenomenon in adult humans (Harnad, 1987). Results showed that categorical perception could be demonstrated for nonspeech stimuli in adults (Bornstein, 1987; Remez, Rubin, Pisoni, & Carrell, 1981) and for speech stimuli in both human infants (Eimas, Siqueland, Jusczyk, & Vigorito, 1971) and nonhuman animals (Kuhl & Miller, 1975; Kuhl & Padden, 1982, 1983). Although the earliest

work on animals was restricted to mammals (i.e., chinchillas, macaques), more recent studies have provided comparable evidence in birds (Dent, Brittan-Powell, Dooling, & Pierce, 1997; Kluender, Diehl, & Killeen, 1987); this suggests that the mechanism underlying categorical perception in humans may be shared with other animals and may have evolved at least as far back as the divergence point with birds.

The parallel results on humans and animals raise at least two important points. First, although this finding does not rule out the importance of categorical perception in speech processing, it does suggest that the underlying mechanism is unlikely to have evolved *for* speech. In other words, the capacity to treat an acoustic continuum as comprised of discrete acoustic categories is a general auditory mechanism that evolved before humans were producing the sounds of speech. Second, although the behavior associated with classifying exemplars into discrete categories is similar to what has been observed in humans, we must move cautiously in assuming that the underlying mechanism is precisely the same. Specifically, studies of categorical perception in animals and humans employ different techniques. Animals are trained to respond to particular categories and then are tested for spontaneous generalization. In contrast, tests of humans involve spontaneous classification and are also explicitly influenced by instructions. Thus, for example, in the elegant experiments on sine wave speech by Remez, human listeners show patterns of classification if they are informed that they will be listening to speech stimuli different from patterns they show if they are not told about the nature of the stimuli. Thus, although animals clearly classify an acoustic continuum into discrete categories and show the same kinds of boundary effects as do humans, they may in fact be using quite different mechanisms in processing such stimuli.

Emphasizing the point that categorical perception—at least the behavioral phenomenon—most likely evolved prior to the evolution of speech are experiments involving the presentation of species-typical vocalizations, as opposed to speech (reviewed in Hauser, 1996; Kuhl, 1989; Wyttenbach & Hoy, 1999). And here, the breadth of species tested is extraordinary, including field crickets (Wyttenbach, May, & Hoy, 1996), swamp sparrows (Nelson & Marler, 1989), mice (Ehret & Haack, 1981), pygmy marmosets (Snowdon, 1987), and Japanese macaques (May, Moody, & Stebbins, 1989). One of the best examples—based on methodological elegance as well as functional and ecological considerations—comes from Wyttenbach and Hoy's work on the field cricket. In this species, individuals produce a contact call of 4–5 kHz. When conspecifics hear this call, they often approach. In contrast, predatory bats produce ultrasonic signals in the 25–80 kHz range, and when crickets hear such sounds, they move away. The perceptual task therefore involves a discrimination between two ecologically meaningful acoustic signals—one that elicits approach and a second that elicits avoidance. Laboratory experiments had already indicated a transition between approach and avoidance in the 10–20 kHz range. In the labeling task, crickets were presented with signals that varied from 2.5–40 kHz. Results showed an abrupt transition from approach to avoid between 13–16 kHz, providing strong evidence of a categorical boundary. In the discrimination task, crickets were habituated to 20 kHz pulses (i.e., a signal that elicits escape), and a photocell was used to measure the movement of the subject's hind leg. After subjects habituated (i.e., showed little to no escape response), they then received one test stimulus from a different frequency and one 20 kHz stimulus. Of the frequencies tested, only stimuli falling below 16 kHz caused dishabituation; no stimuli falling in the ultrasound range caused dishabituation, providing strong evidence of between-category discrimination.

Beyond Categorical Perception

The history of work on categorical perception provides an elegant example of the comparative method. If you want to know whether a mechanism has evolved specifically for a particular function in a particular species, then the only way to address this question is by running experiments on a broad array of species. With respect to categorical perception, at least, it appears that the underlying mechanism did not evolve for processing speech. To repeat, because of differences in methods, and the lack of neurophysiological work, we can not be absolutely confident that the underlying mechanisms are exactly the same across species even though the classificatory results are the same. Nonetheless, a question arises from such work: What, if anything, is special about speech, especially with respect to processing mechanisms? Until the early 1990s, scientists studying animals pursued this problem, focusing on different phonemic contrasts as well as formant perception (Lotto, Kluender, & Holt, 1998; Sinnott, 1989; Sinnott & Brown, 1997; Sinnott, Petersen, & Hopp, 1985; Sommers, Moody, Prosen, & Stebbins, 1992); most of this work suggested common mechanisms shared by humans and nonhuman primates. In the early 1990s, however, Patricia (Kuhl 1991; Kuhl, Williams, Lacerda, Stevens, & Lindblom, 1992) published two papers showing that human adults and infants but not rhesus monkeys perceive a distinction between so-called *good* and *bad* exemplars of a phonemic class. The good exemplars, or *prototypes,* functioned like perceptual magnets, anchoring the category and making it more difficult to distinguish the prototype from sounds that are acoustically similar;

nonprototypes function in a different way and are readily distinguished from more prototypical exemplars. In the same way that robins and sparrows but not penguins or storks are prototypical birds because they carry the most common or salient visual features (e.g., feathers, beak, wings) within the category bird, prototypical phonemes consist of the most common or salient acoustical features. Although there is controversy in the literature concerning the validity of this work in thinking about the perceptual organization and development of speech (Kluender, Lotto, Holt, & Bloedel, 1998; Lotto et al., 1998), my concern here is with the comparative claim. Because Kuhl failed to find evidence that rhesus monkeys distinguish prototypical from nonprototypical instances of a phonetic category, she argued that the perceptual magnet effect represents a uniquely human mechanism specialized for processing speech. Moreover, because prototypes are formed on the basis of experience with the language environment, Kuhl further argued that each linguistic community will have prototypical exemplars tuned to the particular morphology of their natural language (Kuhl, 2000).

To address the comparative claim, Kluender and colleagues (1998) attempted a replication of Kuhl's original findings, using European starlings and the English vowels /i/ and /I/, as well as the Swedish vowels /y/ and /u/; these represent the stimuli used in Kuhl's original work on the prototype effect. Based on a mel scale of the first and second formants, these vowels have distinctive prototypes that are acoustically nonoverlapping. After starlings were trained to respond to exemplars from these vowel categories, they readily generalized to novel exemplars. More important was that the extent to which they classified a novel exemplar as a member of one vowel category or another was almost completely predicted by the first and second for meant frequencies, as well as by the exemplar's distance from the prototype or centroid of the vowel sound. Because the starlings' responses were graded and matched human adult listeners' ratings of *goodness* for a particular vowel class, Kluender and colleagues conclude—contra Kuhl—that the perceptual magnet effect is not uniquely human and can be better explained by general auditory mechanisms.

In contrast to the extensive comparative work on categorical perception, we have only two studies of the perceptual magnet effect in animals. One study of macaques claims that animals lack such capacities, whereas a second study of starlings claims that animals have such capacities. If starlings perceive vowel prototypes but macaques do not, then this provides evidence of a homoplasy—a character that is similar between species because of convergent evolution. Future work on this problem must focus on whether the failure with macaques is due to methodological issues (e.g., would a different testing procedure provide different results?) or to an absence of a capacity. If macaques lack this capacity and starlings have it, then our evolutionary account must reject the claim concerning uniqueness but attempt to explain why the capacity evolved at least twice—once in the group leading to songbirds and once in the group leading to modern humans; of course, we must also leave open the possibility of a difference in the actual mechanism underlying a perceptual magnet effect in starlings and humans.

What Mechanisms Are Spontaneously Available to Animals for Speech Perception and Language Acquisition?

To date, every time a claim has been made that a particular mechanism X is special to speech, animal studies have generally shown that the claim is false, at least at a general level of behavioral responses. Speech scientists might argue, however, that these studies are based on extensive training regimes, and thus fail to show what animals spontaneously perceive—or more appropriately, *how* they actually perceive the stimuli. They might also argue that the range of phenomenon explored is narrow and thus fails to capture the essential design features of language (Trout, 2000). In parallel with our work on number (discussed earlier in this chapter), my students and I have been pushing the development of methodological tools that involve no training and can be used with human infants, thereby providing a more direct route to understanding which mechanisms are spontaneously available to animals for processing speech and which are uniquely human. Next, I describe several recent experiments designed to explore which of the many mechanisms employed by human infants and children during language acquisition are spontaneously available to other animals.

As mentioned earlier in this chapter, a powerful technique for exploring spontaneous perceptual distinctions is the habituation-dishabituation technique (Cheney & Seyfarth, 1988; Eimas et al., 1971; Hauser, 1998). Given the variety of conditions in which our animals live, each situation demands a slightly different use of this technique. The logic underlying our use of the procedure for exploring the mechanisms of speech perception is, however, the same. In general, we habituate a subject to different exemplars from within an acoustic class and then present them with a test stimulus. A response is scored if the subject turns and orients in the direction of the speaker. We consider the subject to be habituated if it fails to orient toward the speaker on at least two consecutive trials; as such, all subjects enter the test trial having failed to respond on the previous two trials. The advantage of this approach is that we can not only score whether they

respond to the test stimulus, but in some cases we can also score the magnitude of their response—that is, we can score the amount of time spent looking in the direction of the speaker. In the case of speech stimuli, duration is not a reliable measure, whereas in the case of conspecific vocalizations it is.

The first habituation-dishabituation playback experiment on speech perception was run by the collaboration of Franck Ramus, Marc Hauser, Cory Miller, Dylan Morris, and Jacques Mehler (2000). Theoretically, we wanted to understand whether the capacity of human infants to both discriminate and subsequently acquire two natural languages is based on a mechanism that is uniquely human or shared with other species. Although animals clearly lack the capacity to produce most of the sounds of our natural languages, their hearing system is such (at least for most primates; Stebbins, 1983) that they may be able to hear some of the critical acoustic features that distinguish one language from another. To explore this problem, we asked whether French-born human neonates and cotton-top tamarin monkeys can discriminate sentences of Dutch from sentences of Japanese and whether the capacity to discriminate these two languages depends on whether they are played in a forward (i.e., normal) or backwards direction; given the fact that adult humans process backwards speech quite differently from forward speech, we expected to find some differences, although not necessarily in both species. Methodologically, we wanted to determine whether tests of speech processing could be run on neonates and captive cotton-top tamarins using the same stimuli and procedure. Specifically, would tamarins attend to sentences from a natural language, and could we implement the habituation-dishabituation technique to ask questions about discrimination? These methodological questions were significant because all prior work on speech perception in animals involved operant training procedures and relatively short segments of speech (i.e., phonemes or syllables) as opposed to naturally produced sentences.

Neonates and adult tamarins were tested in four different conditions involving naturally produced sentences of Dutch and Japanese. In the first language change condition, we habituated subjects to sentences from one language played in the normal-forward direction and then tested them with sentences from the second language played in the normal-forward direction. In the second language change condition, we played all sentences backwards, but with the same shift from one language to the other. In the first speaker change condition—run as a control for the language change condition—we habituated subjects to normal-forward sentences produced by two speakers of one language and then tested them with normal-forward sentences of a language that was the same but spoken by two new speakers. The second speaker change condition was the same but with the sentences played backwards.

There were a few differences in the testing procedures used for neonates and tamarins. The behavioral assay for neonates was a high-amplitude sucking response, whereas for tamarins we used a head-orienting response in the direction of the concealed speaker. For neonates, we played back habituation stimuli until the sucking response attenuated to 25% less than it was the previous minute; then we maintained this level for 2 consecutive minutes. After subjects were habituated, we played a cycle of test stimuli. For tamarins, in contrast, we played back exemplars from the habituation category until the subject failed to orient on two consecutive trials. Following habituation, we played back sentences of the test category. If subjects failed to respond in the test trial, we played a posttest stimulus—specifically, a tamarin alarm call. The logic behind the posttest was to ensure that the tamarins had not habituated to the entire playback setup. Thus, if they failed to respond in the posttest, we assumed that they had habituated to the setup and reran the entire session a few weeks later.

Neonates failed to discriminate the two languages played forward and also failed to discriminate the two speakers. Rather than run the backwards condition with natural speech, we decided to synthesize the sentences and run the experiment again with new subjects. One explanation for the failure with natural speech was that discrimination was impaired by the significant acoustic variability imposed by the different speakers. Consequently, synthetic speech provides a tool for looking at language discrimination while eliminating speaker variability. When synthetic speech was used, neonates dishabituated in the language change condition, but only if the sentences were played forward; in the backward speech condition, subjects failed to dishabituate.

In contrast to the data on neonates tested with natural speech, tamarins showed evidence of discrimination in the forward, language-change condition but failed to show evidence of discrimination in any of the other conditions (Figure 20.4). When the synthetic stimuli were used, the results were generally the same. Only the forward language-change condition elicited a statistically significant level of discrimination, although the backward speaker change was nearly significant; thus, there was a nonsignificant difference between the language- and speaker-change condition. When the data from the natural and synthetic stimuli were combined, tamarins showed a highly significant discrimination of the forward language-change condition but no other condition.

These results allow us to make five points with respect to studying the *speech is special* problem. First, the same

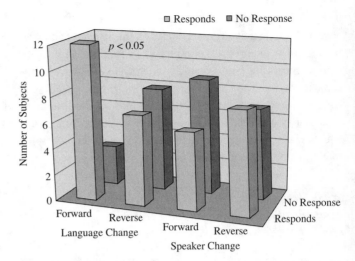

Figure 20.4 Results from experiments on cotton-top tamarins, contrasting their responses to naturally produced sentences of Dutch and Japanese played forward and backwards. The *y*-axis plots the number of subjects dishabituating (i.e., Responding) in the test trial or transferring habituation (i.e., No Response). Two conditions are contrasted: Language Change, in which subjects are habituated to one language and then tested on a different language; and Speaker Change, in which subjects are habituated to two speakers of one language and then tested with two new speakers of the same language.

method can be used with human infants and nonhuman animals. Specifically, the habituation-dishabituation paradigm provides a powerful tool to explore similarities and differences in perceptual mechanisms and avoids the potential problems associated with training. Second, animals such as cotton-top tamarins not only attend to isolated syllables as previously demonstrated in studies of categorical perception, but also attend to strings of continuous speech. Consequently, it is now possible to ask comparative questions about some of the higher order properties of spoken languages, including some of the relevant prosodic or paralinguistic information. Third, given the fact that tamarins discriminate sentences of Dutch from sentences of Japanese in the face of speaker variability, they are clearly able to extract acoustic equivalence classes. This capacity is not present in the human neonate, coming on line a few months after birth (Jusczyk, 1997; Oller, 2000). Fourth, because tamarins fail to discriminate sentences of Dutch from sentences of Japanese when such sentences are played backwards, their capacity to discriminate such sentences when played forward shows that they must be using specific properties of speech as opposed to low-level cues. Fifth, given that the tamarins' capacity to discriminate Dutch from Japanese was weaker in the second test involving synthetic speech, it is possible that newborns and tamarins are responding to somewhat different acoustic cues. In particular, newborns may be more sensitive to prosodic differences (e.g., rhythm), whereas tamarins may be more sensitive to phonetic contrasts. Future research will explore this possibility.

A real-world problem facing the human infant is how to segment the continuous acoustic stream of speech into functional units such as words and phrases. How, more specifically, does the infant know where one word ends and another begins? One might think that such information comes for free, given that there are pauses between words. Such changes in the time-amplitude envelope would provide the relevant cues some of the time but would not provide a reliable mechanism, given that coarticulatory effects create pauses within words as well as continuity in the signal between words. Similarly, although it is clear that adults may help infants pick out words within a sentence, thanks in part to their dramatic emphasis (e.g., Look at the *ball!*), such stress patterns do not help with all or even most words within a sentence (e.g., no stress cues help with *Look, at,* and *the*). A recent attempt to tackle this problem comes from work that follows up on a suggestion from early work in computational linguistics—in particular, the possibility that infants extract words from the acoustic stream by paying attention to the statistical properties of a given language. For example, when we hear the consonant string *st*, there are many phonemes that we might expect to follow (e.g., *ork, ing, ack*) but some that we explicitly would not expect (e.g., *kro, gni, cak*). Saffran, Aslin, and Newport (1996) tested the hypothesis that infants are equipped with mechanisms that enable them to extract the statistical regularities of a particular language. Eight-month-old infants were familiarized for 2 min with a continuous string of synthetically created syllables (e.g., *tibudopabiku-daropigolatupabiku*. . .), with all prosodic and coarticulatory effects removed. Within this continuous acoustic stream, some three-syllable sequences always clustered together (i.e., always had a transitional probability of 1.0 between adjacent syllables—*pabiku*), whereas other syllables were only sometimes followed by another syllable (e.g., when the syllable *pi* occurred, it was followed by *gola* one third of the time, and by *daro* or *tibu* the other times). To determine whether infants would extract such statistics, they were presented with three types of test items following familiarization: *words* consisting of syllables with a transitional probability of 1.0, *part words* in which the first two syllables had a transitional probability of 1.0 and the third syllable had a transitional probability of 0.33, and *nonwords* in which the three syllables were never associated (transitional probability of 0.0) in the familiarization corpus. Based on dozens of comparable studies on human infants, Saffran et al. predicted that if the infants have computed the appropriate statistics and extracted the functional words from this artificial language, then they should show little to no orienting response to familiar words but

should show interest and an orienting response to both the part words and the nonwords. Results provided strong support for this hypothesis. Although some interpreted this finding as providing evidence against a strong nativist position on language acquisition (i.e., the capacity to compute transitional probabilities is domain-general, not domain-specific) while others argued that these capacities simply cannot do the work required for language acquisition, they undoubtedly show an early capacity to compute conditional statistics. And it is precisely these kinds of computations—together with others—that might help put the child on the path to acquiring a language. Regardless of the outcome of this debate, one can also ask whether the capacity to compute such statistics is uniquely human and—equally important—special to language.

Saffran, Newport, and Aslin have attacked the *special to language* problem by showing that—at least for transitional probabilities—the same kinds of results hold for melodies, patterns of light, and motor routines (Saffran, Johnson, Aslin, & Newport, 1999). A different approach comes from testing nonhuman animals.

Several studies of pigeons, capuchin monkeys, and rhesus monkeys demonstrate that under operant conditions, individuals can learn to respond to the serial order of a set of approximately 8–10 visual or auditory items (D'Amato & Colombo, 1990; Orlov, Yakoviev, Hochstein, & Zohary, 2000; Terrace, 1993; Terrace, Chen, & Newman, 1995; Wright & Rivera, 1997). These results show that at least some animals—and especially some primates—have the capacity to attend to strings of items, extract the relevant order or relationship between items, and use their memory of prior responses to guide future responses. In addition to these data, observations and experiments on foraging behavior and vocal communication suggest that nonhuman animals also engage in statistical computations. For example, results from optimal foraging experiments indicate that animals calculate rates of return, sometimes using Bayesian statistics, and some animals produce strings of vocalizations such that the function of the signal is determined by the order of elements (Hailman & Ficken, 1987; Hauser, 2000; Stephens & Krebs, 1986). Recently, studies by Savage-Rumbaugh and colleagues (1993) suggest that at least some human-reared bonobos have some comprehension of speech and specifically attend to the order in which words are put together in a spoken utterance; regardless of whether their capacity is considered to be at the level of human adults, these observations suggest that bonobos have the capacity to extract words from a speech stream and at some level appreciate that the order of words within an utterance plays a role in meaning. Together, these studies suggest that like human adults and infants, nonhuman animals may also be equipped with statistical learning mechanisms.

Based on the previously reported evidence, Hauser, Newport, and Aslin (2001) used the original Saffran et al. (1996) material in order to attempt a replication with cotton-top tamarin monkeys of the statistical learning effects observed with human infants. The procedure was the same as that used with human infants, with two exceptions. Unlike human infants, who were exposed to the familiarization material for 2 minutes and then presented with the test items (in association with a flashing light), the tamarins were exposed in their home room to 21 min of the familiarization material on Day 1; then on Day 2 we presented individuals located in a soundproof chamber with 1 min of the familiarization material followed by a randomly presented set of test items. We divided our colony into two groups. One group received Version A of the language, whereas the second group received Version B; the transitional probabilities were the same for both languages, but the potential test items differed in terms of their syllabic content. On the first test session, we compared the tamarins' responses to words versus nonwords. On the second session, we compared their response to words and part words. Like the tests on the infants, these tests had several possible outcomes. If tamarins simply respond to novelty as opposed to familiarity, then they might show a significantly higher level of response (i.e., orienting to the concealed speaker) in the word versus nonword condition but fail to show a difference between word and part word; in other words, because the first two syllables are familiar in the part-word comparison, while the third is novel, this difference may be insufficient to differentiate the two test items. In contrast, if tamarins compute the transitional probabilities, then nonwords and part words are both novel and should elicit a greater number of responses when contrasted with words. Like human infants, tamarins oriented to playbacks of nonwords and words more often than to words (Figure 20.5). This result is powerful not only because tamarins show the same kind of response as do human infants, but also because the methods and stimuli are largely the same and involve no training.

In terms of comparative inferences, our results on statistical learning should be treated somewhat cautiously because of subtle differences in methods between species, the lack of information on where in the brain such statistics are being computed, and the degree to which such computations can operate over any kind of input (i.e., visual, motoric, melodic). Methodologically, the tamarins received far more experience with the familiarization material than did the infants. We provided the tamarins with more input because we were unsure about the time that they would even listen to such synthetic

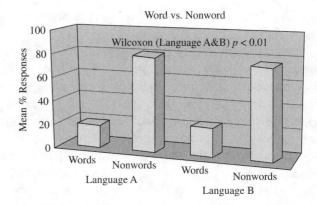

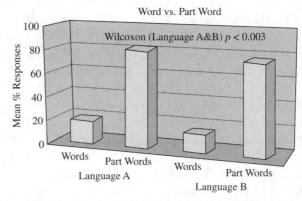

Figure 20.5 Results of a replication with tamarins of Saffran and colleagues' statistical learning experiment. Results show the proportion of subjects orienting toward the speaker in response to playbacks of words versus nonwords (upper panel) and words versus part words (lower panel). Languages A and B were simply two versions of a continuous speech stream with the same transitional probabilities.

speech, no less orient to it. Nonetheless, future work must establish how much experience is necessary in order to derive the appropriate statistics and how the properties of certain statistics are either learnable or unlearnable by both humans and nonhumans. For example, can human infants and nonhuman animals learn about statistical correlations between nonadjacent elements, and if so, over what kinds of distances? Assuming that human infants or toddlers can compute a different class of statistics than can nonhuman animals, which of these statistics are critically and perhaps uniquely involved in the acquisition of language but no other domain?

Implications for Linguistics and the Neurosciences

What can be said about our verbal abilities? Unique or not? If I had to place a wager, I would bet that humans share with other animals the core mechanisms for speech perception. More precisely, we inherited from animals a suite of perceptual mechanisms for listening to speech—ones that are quite general and did not evolve for processing speech. Whether the similarities across species represent cases of homology or homoplasy cannot be answered at present and will require additional neuroanatomical work, tracing circuitry, and establishing functional connectivity. What is perhaps uniquely human, however, is our capacity to take the units that comprise spoken and signed language and recombine them into an infinite variety of meaningful expressions. Although much work remains, my guess is that animals will lack the capacity for recursion, and their capacity for statistical inference will be restricted to items that are in close temporal proximity. With the ability to run animals and human infants on the same tasks with the same material, we will soon be in a strong position to pinpoint when during evolution and ontogeny we acquired our specially designed system for language.

One direction that is likely to be extremely productive—in contributing to our basic understanding of how human infants acquire a language and how the brain's plasticity and representational structure change over time—is to use nonhuman animals as models for exploring the specific effects of experience on acoustic processing. One of the major revolutions within the neurosciences over the last 10 or so years has been the discovery that there is plasticity in the adult brain, dictated in part by experience (Kaas, 2000; Recanzone, 2000). This revolution actually started earlier, driven in part by the magnificent findings on some songbird species—their capacity to learn new songs each season, guided by changes in the volume of key nuclei and the shift in levels of circulating testosterone (Alvarez-Buylla, Kirn, & Nottebohm, 1990; Alvarez-Buylla, Theelen, & Nottebohm, 1988; Doupe, Brainard, & Hessler, 2000). More recent work on mammals (mostly rats and some primates) has shown that when an individual engages in repetitive motor routines or is repeatedly presented with sounds falling within a particular frequency range, the relevant cortical representations are dramatically altered (Jenkins, Merzenich, Ochs, Allard, & Guic-Robles, 1990; Kaas, 2000; Kilgard & Merzenich, 1998; Recanzone, 2000). Similar kinds of effects have been suggested in cases of human infants and language acquisition (Kuhl, 2000), as well as patients reporting phantom limb effects (Ramachandran, 1993; Yang et al., 1994).

Given the evidence for cortical plasticity, we are ideally placed to provide our subjects with specific linguistic experience and then test for reorganization of perceptual sensitivity. For example, consider the results on tamarins showing a capacity to distinguish two different languages from two different rhythmic groups (i.e., Dutch and Japanese). Studies of human infants suggest that whereas natives of one rhythmic group (e.g., French) can discriminate sentences of their own language from sentences of another language within the same rhythmic group (e.g., Spanish), infants exposed to a language that falls outside this rhythmic group cannot discriminate French from Spanish. To test whether this follows from general auditory principles or from a specialized speech mechanism that is uniquely human, we can passively expose our subjects to sentences from one language over a period of weeks or months and then explore whether such experience influences their capacity to discriminate the so-called native language with other languages, as well as the capacity to make fine-grained discriminations within the exposed language. Similarly, it is possible to selectively expose captive primate infants at different stages of development and thereby determine whether there are critical periods for exposure and their consequences. These results can then be used to fuel studies exploring the neurophysiology underlying behavioral or perceptual changes.

COMPARATIVE COGNITION: THE NEXT GENERATION

Comparative studies of animal minds have entered a new era. This shift is due in part to a clearing of earlier conceptual veils—theoretical perspectives that saw animals as mindless, at the base of some intellectual hierarchy, or as mere pawns to be maneuvered for purely biomedical gains. The new era of investigation is based on a marriage between Darwin's theory of evolution and the representational-computational theory of mind that tends to dominate much of current cognitive science. Underlying or supporting this marriage are a set of methodological tools that have been developed by ethologists, animal learning psychologists, cognitive scientists, neuroscientists, and developmentalists. In this essay, I have attempted to highlight some of the empirical offspring from this new marriage by discussing two problems: the capacity to represent numerosities and the mechanisms recruited to process speech. In the case of number, studies show that a wide variety of animals—primates included—have the ability to discriminate small numbers precisely and large numbers approximately. At present, it appears that over the course of human evolution, we acquired a mechanism that allowed only our species to discriminate large numbers precisely; this capacity ultimately led to our unique gift for complex mathematics. Although it is a currently untested hypothesis, one candidate mechanism is language—in particular, the combinatorial and recursive aspects that underlie our capacity to create an infinite number of meaningful verbal and mathematical expressions. With respect to speech-processing mechanisms, I have argued that we share with other animals all of the core perceptual tools for extracting the salient features of the speech stream. At present, there are no clear-cut mechanisms that we have that no other animal has. But this work is only in its infancy, with many more important processes to investigate from a comparative perspective.

What I have emphasized in this essay is that the future of comparative studies of cognition—especially comparisons between human and nonhuman primates—hangs on three factors. First, to understand loci of convergence and divergence in cognitive capacities, we must develop methods that can be used across species, with little to no modification. I have focused primarily on methods that involve no training because I believe that these are most appropriate for comparative studies of animals and human infants. This focus in no way implies that other methods—especially those involving intensive training—are less important. On the contrary, a complete understanding of cognitive abilities in primates will come from the use of different methods that can be brought to bear on the same set of conceptual problems. Second, studies at the behavioral level must be united with studies at the neural level. Methodologically, this is important because we should use behavioral tasks that are sensitive to the problems that each species evolved to solve. Theoretically, this is important as well because we should use our understanding of the neural mechanisms to refine our assessments of whether similarity at the level of behavior is mediated by similarity at the level of the brain. Because similarity at one level may not be matched by similarity at another, we may end up with different kinds of claims with respect to the distinction between homology and homoplasy. Third, studies of primate cognition are increasingly being used to constrain theoretical arguments in the study of human cognition—in particular, infant cognitive development. In the same way that humans with damage to particular regions of the brain can be used to explore the functional architecture of the human mind, studies of nonhuman primates can be used to test which aspects of the mind are possible in the absence of language. Turning one of David Premack's famous quotes around, even though nonhuman primates do not have language, they nonetheless have interesting thoughts.

REFERENCES

Allman, J. (1999). *Evolving brains.* New York: Wiley.

Alvarez-Buylla, A., Kirn, J. R., & Nottebohm, F. (1990). Birth of projection neurons in adult avian brain may be related to perceptual or motor learning. *Science, 249,* 1444–1446.

Alvarez-Buylla, A., Theelen, M., & Nottebohm, F. (1988). Birth of projection neurons in the higher vocal center of the canary forebrain before, during, and after song learning. *Proceedings of the National Academy of Sciences, 85,* 8722–8726.

Antell, S., & Keating, D. P. (1983). Perception of numerical invariance in neonates. *Child Development, 54,* 695–701.

Balaban, E. (1997). Changes in multiple brain regions underlie species differences in a complex, congenital behavior. *Proceedings of the National Academy of Sciences, 94,* 2001–2006.

Balda, R. P., Kamil, A. C., & Bednekoff, P. A. (1997). Predicting cognitive capacities from natural histories: Examples from four Corvid species. *Current Ornithology, 13,* 33–66.

Bickerton, D. (1990). *Species and language.* Chicago: University of Chicago Press.

Blaser, E., Pylyshyn, Z., & Holcombe, A. O. (2000). Tracking an object through feature space. *Nature, 408,* 196–199.

Bornstein, M. H. (1987). Perceptual categories in vision and audition. In S. Harnad (Ed.), *Categorical perception* (pp. 287–300). Cambridge, UK: Cambridge University Press.

Boysen, S. T. (1997). Representation of quantities by apes. *Advances in the Study of Behavior, 26,* 435–462.

Boysen, S. T., & Bernston, G. G. (1989). Numerical competence in a chimpanzee. *Journal of Comparative Psychology, 103,* 23–31.

Brannon, E. M., & Terrace, H. S. (1998). Ordering of the numerosities 1 to 9 by monkeys. *Science, 282,* 746–749.

Brannon, E. M., & Terrace, H. S. (2000). Representation of the numerosities 1–9 by rhesus macaques (*Macaca mulatta*). *Journal of Experimental Psychology: Animal Behavior Processes, 26,* 31–49.

Butterworth, B. (1999). *What counts: How every brain is hardwired for math.* New York: Free Press.

Byrne, R. W., & Russon, A. E. (1998). Learning by imitation: A hierarchical approach. *Behavioral and Brain Sciences, 21,* 667–684.

Caramazza, A., Hillis, A., Leek, E. C., & Miozzo, M. (1994). The organization of lexical knowledge in the brain: Evidence from category and modality-specific deficits. In L. A. Hirschfield & S. A. Gelman (Eds.), *Mapping the mind: Domain specificity in cognition and culture* (pp. 68–84). Cambridge, UK: Cambridge University Press.

Caramazza, A., & Shelton, J. R. (1998). Domain-specific knowledge systems in the brain: The animate-inanimate distinction. *Journal of Cognitive Neuroscience, 10,* 1–34.

Carey, S. (in press). *The origins of concepts.* Cambridge, MA: MIT Press.

Carey, S., & Spelke, E. S. (1994). Domain-specific knowledge and conceptual change. In L. Herschfeld & S. Gelman (Eds.), *Mapping the mind: Domain-specificity in cognition and culture* (pp. 169–201). Cambridge, UK: Cambridge University Press.

Carey, S., & Spelke, E. S. (in press). On conceptual change: counting and number. In J. Mehler & L. Bonati (Eds.), *Developmental cognitive science.* Cambridge, MA: MIT Press.

Carroll, S. B., Weatherbee, S. D., & Langeland, J. A. (1995). Homeotic genes and the regulation and evolution of insect wing number. *Nature, 375,* 58–61.

Cheney, D. L., & Seyfarth, R. M. (1985). Social and non-social knowledge in vervet monkeys. *Philosophical Transactions of the Royal Society of London, 308B,* 187–201.

Cheney, D. L., & Seyfarth, R. M. (1988). Assessment of meaning and the detection of unreliable signals by vervet monkeys. *Animal Behaviour, 36,* 477–486.

Cheney, D. L., & Seyfarth, R. M. (1990). *How monkeys see the world: Inside the mind of another species.* Chicago: University of Chicago Press.

Cheng, K. (1986). A purely geometric module in the rat's spatial representation. *Cognition, 23,* 149–178.

Chomsky, N. (1957). *Syntactic structures.* The Hague, The Netherlands: Mouton.

Chomsky, N. (1965). *Aspects of the theory of syntax.* Cambridge, MA: MIT Press.

Chomsky, N. (1966). *Cartesian linguistics.* New York: Harper and Row.

Chomsky, N. (1988). *Language and problems of knowledge.* Cambridge, MA: MIT Press.

Church, R. M., & Boradbent, H. A. (1990). Alternative representations of time, number, and rate. *Cognition, 37,* 55–81.

Cleveland, J., & Snowdon, C. T. (1981). The complex vocal repertoire of the adult cotton-top tamarin, *Saguinus oedipus oedipus. Zeitschrift fur Tierpsychologie, 58,* 231–270.

Clutton-Brock, T. H. (1992). *The evolution of parental care.* Princeton, NJ: Princeton University Press.

Cowan, N. (2001). The magical number 4 in short-term memory: a reconsideration of mental storage capacity. *Behavioral and Brain Sciences, 24,* 5–43.

D'Amato, M., & Colombo, M. (1990). The symbolic distance effect in monkeys (*Cebus apella*). *Animal learning and behavior, 18,* 133–140.

Davies, N. B. (2000). *Cuckoos, cowbirds and other cheats.* New York: Academic Press.

Deacon, T. W. (1997). *The symbolic species: The co-evolution of language and the brain.* New York: Norton.

Deaner, R. O., Nunn, C. L., & van Schaik, C. P. (2000). Comparative tests of primate cognition: different scaling methods produce different results. *Brain, Behavior and Evolution, 232,* 1–8.

Dehaene, S. (1997). *The number sense.* Oxford, UK: Oxford University Press.

Dehaene, S. (2000). Cerebral bases of number processing and calculation. In M. Gazzaniga (Ed.), *The new cognitive neurosciences.* (2nd ed., pp. 987–998). Cambridge, MA: MIT Press.

Dent, M. L., Brittan-Powell, F., Dooling, R. J., & Pierce, A. (1997). Perception of synthetic /ba/-/wa/ speech continuum by budgerigars (*Melopsittacus undulatus*). *Journal of the Acoustical Society of America, 102,* 1891–1897.

Di Fiore, A., & Rendall, D. (1994). Evolution of social organization: a reappraisal for primates by using phylogenetic methods. *Proceedings of the National Academy of Sciences, 91,* 9941–9945.

Dittus, W. P. G. (1984). Toque macaque food calls: Semantic communication concerning food distribution in the environment. *Animal Behaviour, 32,* 470–477.

Doupe, A. J., Brainard, M. S., & Hessler, N. A. (2000). The song system: neural circuits essential throughout life for vocal behavior and plasticity. In M. Gazzaniga (Ed.), *The new cognitive neurosciences* (pp. 451–468). Cambridge, MA: MIT Press.

Ehret, G., & Haack, B. (1981). Categorical perception of mouse pup ultrasounds by lactating females. *Naturwissenshaften, 68,* 208.

Eimas, P. D., Siqueland, P., Jusczyk, P., & Vigorito, J. (1971). Speech perception in infants. *171,* 303–306.

Evans, C. S., & Marler, P. (1995). Language and animal communication: Parallels and contrasts. In H. Roitblatt (Ed.), *Comparative approaches to cognitive science* (pp. 241–282). Cambridge, MA: MIT Press.

Feigenson, L., Carey, S., & Hauser, M. D. (2002). The representations underlying infants' choice of more: Object files versus analog magnitudes. *Psychological Science, 13,* 150–156.

Feigenson, L., Carey, S., & Spelke, E. S. (2002). Infants' discrimination of number vs. continuous extent. *Cognitive Psychology 44,* 33–66.

Fischer, J. (1998). Barbary macaques categorize shrill barks into two call types. *Animal Behaviour, 55,* 799–807.

Fisher, J., & Hinde, R. A. (1949). The Opening of milk bottles by birds. *British Birds, 42,* 347–357.

Fitch, W. T. (2000). The evolution of speech: a comparative review. *Trends in Cognitive Sciences, 4,* 258–267.

Fodor, J. A. (1975). *The language of thought.* Cambridge, MA: Harvard University Press.

Fodor, J. A. (1983). *The modularity of mind.* Cambridge, MA: MIT Press.

Fodor, J. A. (2000). *The mind doesn't work that way.* Cambridge, MA: MIT Press.

Galef, B. G., Jr. (1992). The question of animal culture. *Human Nature, 3,* 157–178.

Gallistel, C. R. (1990). *The organization of learning.* Cambridge, MA: MIT Press.

Gallistel, C. R., & Gelman, R. (2000). Non-verbal numerical cognition: from reals to integers. *Trends in Cognitive Sciences, 4,* 59–65.

Gardner, R. A., & Gardner, B. T. (1969). Teaching sign language to a chimpanzee. *Science, 165,* 664–672.

Gelman, R., & Gallistel, C. R. (1986). *The child's understanding of number.* Cambridge, MA: Harvard University Press.

Gerhart, J., & Kirschner, M. (1997). *Cells, embryos, and evolution.* Oxford, UK: Blackwell Scientific.

Gibbon, J. (1977). Scalar expectancy theory and Weber's Law in animal timing. *Psychological Review, 84,* 279–335.

Gibbon, J., Malapani, C., Dale, C. L., & Gallistel, C. R. (1997). Toward a neurobiology of temporal cognition: advances and challenges. *Current Opinions in Neurobiology, 7,* 170–184.

Gouteux, S., Thinus-Blanc, C., & Vauclair, J. (2001). Rhesus monkeys use geometric and non-geometric information during a reorientation task. *Journal of Experimental Psychology: General, 130,* 505–519.

Gouzoules, S., Gouzoules, H., & Marler, P. (1984). Rhesus monkey (*Macaca mulatta*) screams: representational signalling in the recruitment of agonistic aid. *Animal Behaviour, 32,* 182–193.

Hailman, J. P., & Ficken, M. S. (1987). Combinatorial animal communication with computable syntax: Chick-a-dee calling qualifies as 'language' by structural linguistics. *Animal Behaviour, 34,* 1899–1901.

Harcourt, A. H., & de Waal, F. B. M. (1992). *Coalitions and alliances in humans and other animals.* Oxford, UK: Oxford University Press.

Harnad, S. (1987). *Categorical perception: The groundwork of cognition.* Cambridge, UK: Cambridge University Press.

Hauser, M. D. (1996). *The evolution of communication.* Cambridge, MA: MIT Press.

Hauser, M. D. (1997). Artifactual kinds and functional design features: What a primate understands without language. *Cognition, 64,* 285–308.

Hauser, M. D. (1998). Functional referents and acoustic similarity: Field playback experiments with rhesus monkeys. *Animal Behaviour, 55,* 1647–1658.

Hauser, M. D. (2000). *Wild minds: What animals really think.* New York: Henry Holt.

Hauser, M. D., & Carey, S. (1998). Building a cognitive creature from a set of primitives: Evolutionary and developmental insights. In D. Cummins & C. Allen (Eds.), *The evolution of mind* (pp. 51–106). Oxford, UK: Oxford University Press.

Hauser, M. D., & Carey, S. (in preparation). *Limits on spontaneous number processing in rhesus monkeys: Evidence from an expectancy violation procedure.* Manuscript in review.

Hauser, M. D., Carey, S., & Hauser, L. B. (2000). Spontaneous number representation in semi-free-ranging rhesus monkeys. *Proceedings of the Royal Society, London, 267,* 829–833.

Hauser, M. D., MacNeilage, P., & Ware, M. (1996). Numerical representations in primates. *Proceedings of the National Academy of Sciences, 93,* 1514–1517.

Hauser, M. D., Newport, E. L., & Aslin, R. N. (2001). Segmenting a continuous acoustic speech stream: Serial learning in cotton-top tamarin monkeys. *Cognition, 78,* B58–B64.

Haxby, J. V., Hoffman, E. A., & Gobbini, M. I. (2000). The distributed human neural system for face perception. *Trends in Cognitive Science, 4,* 223–232.

Healy, S. (1998). *Spatial representation in animals.* Oxford, UK: Oxford University Press.

Herman, L. M., & Uyeyama, R. K. (1999). The dolphin's grammatical competency: Comments on Kako (1999). *Animal Learning and Behavior, 27,* 18–23.

Hermer, L., & Spelke, E. S. (1994). A geometric process for spatial reorientation in young children. *Nature, 370,* 57–59.

Hermer, L., & Spelke, E. S. (1996). Modularity and development: The case of spatial reorientation. *Cognition, 61,* 195–232.

Hermer-Vazquez, L., Spelke, E., & Katsnelson, A. (1999). Sources of flexibility in human cognition: Dual-task studies of space and language. *Cognitive Psychology, 39,* 3–36.

Heyes, C. M., & Galef, B. G. (1996). *Social learning in animals: The roots of culture.* San Diego, CA: Academic Press.

Heyes, C. M., & Huber, L. (2000). *The evolution of cognition.* Cambridge, MA: MIT Press.

Hirschfeld, L. A., & Gelman, S. A. (1994). *Mapping the mind: Domain specificity in cognition and culture.* Cambridge, UK: Cambridge University Press.

Huber, E. (1931). *Evolution of the facial musculature and facial expression.* Baltimore: Johns Hopkins University Press.

Jackendoff, R. (1999). Possible stages in the evolution of the language capacity. *Trends in Cognitive Science, 3,* 272–279.

Jenkins, W. M., Merzenich, M. M., Ochs, M. T., Allard, T., & Guic-Robles, E. (1990). Functional reorganization of primar somatosensory cortex in adult owl monkeys after behaviorally controlled tactile stimulation. *Journal of Neurophysiology, 63,* 82–104.

Jusczyk, P. W. (1997). *The discovery of spoken language.* Cambridge, MA: MIT Press.

Kaas, J. H. (2000). The reorganization of sensory and motor maps after injury in adult mammals. In M. Gazzaniga (Ed.), *The new cognitive neurosciences* (pp. 223–236). Cambridge, MA: MIT Press.

Kahneman, D., Treisman, A., & Gibbs, B. (1992). The reviewing of object files: Object specific integration of information. *Cognitive Psychology, 24,* 175–219.

Kanwisher, N., Downing, P., Epstein, R., & Kourtzi, Z. (in press). Functional neuroimaging of human visual recognition. In Kingstone & Cabeza (Eds.), *The handbook on functional neuroimaging.* Cambridge, MA: MIT Press.

Kanwisher, N., McDermott, J., & Chun, M. M. (1997). The fusiform face area: A module in human extrastriate cortex specialized for face perception. *Journal of Neuroscience, 17,* 4302–4311.

Kawai, N., & Matsuzawa, T. (2000). Numerical memory span in a chimpanzee. *Nature, 403,* 39–40.

Keil, F. C. (1994). The birth and nurturance of concepts by domains: The origins of concepts of living things. In L. A. Hirschfield & S. A. Gelman (Eds.), *Mapping the mind: Domain specificity in cognition and culture* (pp. 234–254). Cambridge, UK: Cambridge University Press.

Kilgard, M. P., & Merzenich, M. M. (1998). Cortical reorganization enabled by nucleus basalis activity. *Science, 278,* 1714–1718.

Kilner, R. M., Noble, D. G., & Davies, N. B. (1999). Signals of need in parent-offspring communication and their exploitation by the common cuckoo. *Nature, 397,* 667–672.

Kluender, K. R., Diehl, R., & Killeen, P. R. (1987). Japanese quail can learn phonetic categories. *Science, 237,* 1195–1197.

Kluender, K. R., Lotto, A. J., Holt, L. L., & Bloedel, S. L. (1998). Role of experience for language-specific functional mappings of vowel sounds. *Journal of the Acoustical Society of America, 104,* 3568–3582.

Koechlin, E., Dehaene, S., & Mehler, J. (1997). Numerical transformations in five-month old human infants. *Mathematical Cognition, 3,* 89–104.

Kuhl, P. K. (1989). On babies, birds, modules, and mechanisms: A comparative approach to the acquisition of vocal communication. In R. J. Dooling & S. H. Hulse (Eds.), *The comparative psychology of audition* (pp. 379–422). Hillsdale, NJ: Erlbaum.

Kuhl, P. K. (1991). Human adults and human infants show a "perceptual magnet effect" for the prototypes of speech categories, monkeys do not. *Perception and Psychophysics, 50,* 93–107.

Kuhl, P. K. (2000). Language, mind, and brain: Experience alters perception. In M. Gazzaniga (Ed.), *The new cognitive neurosciences* (2nd ed., pp. 99–118). Cambridge, MA: MIT Press.

Kuhl, P. K., & Miller, J. D. (1975). Speech perception by the chinchilla: Voiced-voiceless distinction in alveolar plosive consonants. *Science, 190,* 69–72.

Kuhl, P. K., & Padden, D. M. (1982). Enhanced discriminability at the phonetic boundaries for the voicing feature in macaques. *Perception and Psychophysics, 32,* 542–550.

Kuhl, P. K., & Padden, D. M. (1983). Enhanced discriminability at the phonetic boundaries for the place feature in macaques. *Journal of the Acoustical Society of America, 73,* 1003–1010.

Kuhl, P. K., Williams, K. A., Lacerda, F., Stevens, K. N., & Lindblom, B. (1992). Linguistic experience alters phonetic perception in infants by 6 months of age. *Science, 255,* 606–608.

Leslie, A. M., Xu, F., Tremoulet, P. D., & Scholl, B. J. (1998). Indexing and the object concept: Developing 'what' and 'where' systems. *Trends in Cognitive Science, 2,* 10–18.

Liberman, A. M., Cooper, F. S., Shankweiler, D. P., & Studdert-Kennedy, M. (1967). Perception of the speech code. *Psychological Review, 74,* 431–461.

Liberman, A. M., Delattre, P. C., & Cooper, F. S. (1958). Some rules for the distinction between voiced and voiceless stops in initial position. *Language and Speech, 1,* 153–167.

Liberman, A. M., Harris, K. S., Hoffman, H. S., & Griffith, B. C. (1957). The discrimination of speech sounds within and across phoneme boundaries. *Journal of Experimental Psychology, 54,* 358–368.

Liberman, A. M., & Mattingly, I. G. (1985). The motor theory of speech perception revised. *Cognition, 21,* 1–36.

Liberman, A. M., & Mattingly, I. G. (1988). Specialized perceiving systems for speech and other biologically significant sounds. In G. M. Edelman, W. E. Gail, & W. M. Cowan (Eds.), *Auditory function* (pp. 775–793). New York: Wiley.

Lieberman, P. (1968). Primate vocalizations and human linguistic ability. *Journal of the Acoustical Society of America, 44,* 1574–1584.

Lieberman, P. (1984). *The biology and evolution of language.* Cambridge, MA: Harvard University Press.

Lieberman, P., Klatt, D. H., & Wilson, W. H. (1969). Vocal tract limitations on the vowel repertoires of rhesus monkeys and other nonhuman primates. *Science, 164,* 1185–1187.

Logothetis, N. K., & Sheinberg, D. L. (1996). Visual object recognition. *Annual Review of Neuroscience, 19,* 577–621.

Lotto, A. J., Kluender, K. R., & Holt, L. L. (1998). Depolarizing the perceptual magnet effect. *Journal of the Acoustical Society of America, 103,* 3648–3655.

MacNeilage, P. F. (1998). The frame/content theory of evolution of speech production. *Behavioral and Brain Sciences, 21,* 499–546.

Macphail, E. (1987a). The comparative psychology of intelligence. *Behavioral and Brain Sciences, 10,* 645–695.

Macphail, E. (1987b). Intelligence: A comparative approach. In C. Blakemore & S. Greenfield (Eds.), *Mindwaves: Thoughts on intelligence, identity and consciousness* (pp. 177–194). Oxford, UK: Basil Blackwell.

Marler, P. (1978). Primate vocalizations: Affective or symbolic? In G. Bourne (Ed.), *Progress in ape research* (pp. 85–96). New York: Academic Press.

Marler, P., Dufty, A., & Pickert, R. (1986). Vocal communication in the domestic chicken. Pt. 1. Does a sender communicate information about the quality of a food referent to a receiver? *Animal Behaviour, 34,* 188–193.

Matsuzawa, T. (1985). Use of numbers by a chimpanzee. *Nature, 315,* 57–59.

May, B., Moody, D. B., & Stebbins, W. C. (1989). Categorical perception of conspecific communication sounds by Japanese macaques, *Macaca fuscata. Journal of the Acoustical Society of America, 85,* 837–847.

McComb, K., Packer, C., & Pusey, A. (1994). Roaring and numerical assessment in contests between groups of female lions, *Panthera leo. Animal Behaviour, 47,* 379–387.

Mechner, F. (1958). Probability relations within response sequences under ratio reinforcement. *Journal of the Experimental Analysis of Behavior, 1,* 109–122.

Meck, W. H., & Church, R. M. (1983). A mode control model of counting and timing processes. *Journal of Experimental Psychology: Animal Behavior Processes, 9,* 320–334.

Mix, K. S., Levine, S. C., & Huttenlocher, J. (1997). Numerical abstraction in infants: another look. *Developmental Psychology, 33,* 423–428.

Moyer, R. S., & Landauer, T. K. (1967). Time required for judgements of numerical inequality. *Nature, 215,* 1519–1520.

Needham, A., & Baillargeon, R. (2000). Infants' use of featural and experiential information in segregating and individuating objects: A reply to Xu, Carey, and Welch. *Cognition, 74,* 255–284.

Nelson, D. A., & Marler, P. (1989). Categorical perception of a natural stimulus continuum: Birdsong. *Science, 244,* 976–978.

Olthof, A., Iden, C. M., & Roberts, W. A. (1997). Judgement of ordinality and summation of number by squirrel monkeys. *Journal of Experimental Psychology: Animal Behavior Processes, 23,* 325–339.

Orlov, T., Yakoviev, V., Hochstein, S., & Zohary, E. (2000). Macaque monkeys categorize images by their ordinal number. *Nature, 404,* 77–80.

Pepperberg, I. M. (1994). Numerical competence in an African gray parrot (*Psittacus erithacus*). *Journal of Comparative Psychology, 108,* 36–44.

Pepperberg, I. M. (2000). *The Alex studies.* Cambridge, MA: Harvard University Press.

Perrett, D. I., Mistlin, A. J., Chitty, A. J., Smith, P. A., Potter, D. D., Broennimann, R., & Haries, M. (1988). Specialized face processing and hemispheric asymmetry in man and monkey: evidence from single unit and reaction time studies. *Behavioural Brain Research, 29,* 245–258.

Perrett, D. I., Smith, A. J., Potter, D. D., Mistlin, A. J., Head, A. S., Milner, A. D., & Jeeves, M. A. (1984). Neurones responsive to faces in the temporal cortex: Studies of functional organization, sensitivity to identity and relation to perception. *Human Neurobiology, 3,* 197–208.

Pinker, S. (1994). *The language instinct.* New York: William Morrow.

Pinker, S. (1997). *How the mind works.* New York: W. W. Norton.

Pinker, S., & Bloom, P. (1990). Natural language and natural selection. *Behavioral and Brain Sciences, 13,* 707–784.

Platt, J. R., & Johnson, D. M. (1971). Localization of position within a homogeneous behavior chain: Effects of error contingencies. *Learning and Motivation, 2,* 386–414.

Premack, D. (1986). *Gavagai! or the future history of the animal language controversy.* Cambridge, MA: MIT Press.

Ramachandran, V. S. (1993). Behavioral and magnetoencephalographic correlates of plasticity in the adult brain. *Proceedings of the National Academy of Sciences, 90,* 10413–10420.

Ramus, F., Hauser, M. D., Miller, C. T., Morris, D., & Mehler, J. (2000). Language discrimination by human newborns and cotton-top tamarins. *Science, 288,* 349–351.

Reboreda, J. C., Clayton, N. S., & Kacelnik, A. (1996). Species and sex differences in hippocampus size in parasitic and non-parasitic cowbirds. *Neuroreport, 7,* 505–508.

Recanzone, G. H. (2000). Cerebral cortical plasticity: Perception and skill acquisition. In M. Gazzaniga (Ed.), *The new cognitive neurosciences* (pp. 237–247). Cambridge, MA: MIT Press.

Remez, R. E., Rubin, P. E., Pisoni, D. B., & Carrell, T. D. (1981). Speech perception without traditional speech cues. *Science, 212,* 947–950.

Ridley, M. (1996). *The origins of virtue.* New York: Viking Press.

Robinson, J. G. (1979). An analysis of the organization of vocal communication in the titi monkey. *Callicebus moloch. Zeitschrift fur Tierpsychologie, 49,* 381–405.

Robinson, J. G. (1982). Vocal systems regulating within-group spacing. In C. T. Snowdon, C. R. Brown, & M. R. Petersen (Eds.), *Primate communication* (pp. 94–116). Cambridge, UK: Cambridge University Press.

Rolls, E. T. (2000). Functions of the primate temporal lobe cortical visual areas in invariant visual object and face recognition. *Neuron, 27,* 205–218.

Rumbaugh, D. M., & Washburn, D. A. (1993). Counting by chimpanzees and ordinality judgements by macaques in video-formatted tasks. In S. T. Boysen & E. J. Capaldi (Eds.), *The development of numerical competence: Animal and human models* (pp. 87–108). Hillsdale, NJ: Erlbaum.

Saffran, J. R., Aslin, R. N., & Newport, E. L. (1996). Statistical learning by 8-month-old infants. *Science, 274,* 1926–1928.

Saffran, J. R., Johnson, E., Aslin, R. N., & Newport, E. (1999). Statistical learning of tone sequences by human infants and adults. *Cognition, 70,* 27–52.

Santos, L. R., Hauser, M. D., & Spelke, E. S. (2001). Recognition and categorization of biologically significant objects in rhesus monkeys (*Macaca mulatta*): The domain of food. *Cognition, 82,* 127–155.

Savage-Rumbaugh, E. S. (1986). *Ape language: From conditioned response to symbol.* New York: Columbia University Press.

Savage-Rumbaugh, E. S., Murphy, J., Sevcik, R. A., Brakke, K. E., Williams, S. L., & Rumbaugh, D. M. (1993). Language comprehension in ape and child. *Monographs of the Society for Research in Child Development, 58,* 1–221.

Scholl, B. J., & Pylyshyn, Z. W. (1999). Tracking multiple items through occlusion: Clues to visual objecthood. *Cognitive Psychology, 38,* 259–290.

Seyfarth, R. M., Cheney, D. L., & Marler, P. (1980a). Monkey responses to three different alarm calls: Evidence of predator classification and semantic communication. *Science, 210,* 801–803.

Seyfarth, R. M., Cheney, D. L., & Marler, P. (1980b). Vervet monkey alarm calls: semantic communication in a free-ranging primate. *Animal Behaviour, 28,* 1070–1094.

Sherry, D. F. (1997). Cross-species comparisons. In M. Daly (Ed.), *Characterizing human psychological adaptations* (pp. 181–194). New York: Wiley.

Sherry, D. F. (2000). What sex differences in spatial ability tell us about the evolution of cognition. In M. Gazzaniga (Ed.), *The new cognitive neurosciences* (2nd ed., pp. 1209–1217). Cambridge, MA: MIT Press.

Sherry, D. F., Forbes, M. R. L., Khurgel, M., & Ivy, G. O. (1993). Females have a larger hippocampus than males in the brood-parasitic brown-headed cowbird. *Proceedings of the National Academy of Sciences, 90,* 7839–7843.

Sherry, D. F., & Galef, B. G. (1984). Cultural transmission without imitation: Milk bottle opening by birds. *Animal Behaviour, 32,* 937–938.

Sherry, D. F., & Galef, B. G. (1990). Social learning without imitation: More about milk bottle opening by birds. *Animal Behaviour, 40,* 987–989.

Shettleworth, S. (1998). *Cognition, evolution and behavior.* New York: Oxford University Press.

Simon, T. J. (1997). Reconceptualizing the origins of number knowledge: A "non-numerical" account. *Cognitive Development, 12,* 349–372.

Simon, T. J., Hespos, S., & Rochat, P. (1995). Do infants understand simple arithmetic? A replication of Wynn (1992). *Cognitive Development, 10,* 253–269.

Sinnott, J. M. (1989). Detection and discrimination of synthetic English vowels by Old World monkeys (*Cercopithecus, Macaca*) and humans. *Journal of the Acoustical Society of America, 86,* 557–565.

Sinnott, J. M., & Brown, C. H. (1997). Perception of the English liquid/ra-la/ contrast by humans and monkeys. *Journal of the Acoustical Society of America, 102,* 588–602.

Sinnott, J. M., Petersen, M. R., & Hopp, S. L. (1985). Frequency and intensity discrimination in humans and monkeys. *Journal of the Acoustical Society of America, 78,* 1977–1985.

Snowdon, C. T. (1987). A naturalistic view of categorical perception. In S. Harnad (Ed.), *Categorical perception* (pp. 332–354). Cambridge, UK: Cambridge University Press.

Sommers, M. S., Moody, D. B., Prosen, C. A., & Stebbins, W. C. (1992). Formant frequency discrimination by Japanese macaques (*Macaca fuscata*). *Journal of the Acoustical Society of America, 91,* 3499–3510.

Spelke, E. S. (1979). Perceiving bimodally specified events in infancy, *Developmental Psychology, 15,* 626–636.

Spelke, E. S., Born, W. S., & Chu, F. (1983). Perception of moving, sounding objects by 4-month-old infants. *Perception, 12,* 719–732.

Staddon, J. E. R., & Higa, J. J. (1999). Time and memory: Towards a pacemaker-free theory of interval timing. *Journal of the Experimental Analysis of Behavior, 71,* 215–251.

Starkey, P., & Cooper, R. (1980). Perception of numbers by human infants. *Science, 210,* 1033–1035.

Starkey, P., Spelke, E. S., & Gelman, R. (1990). Numerical abstraction by human infants. *Cognition, 36,* 97–127.

Stebbins, W. C. (1983). *The acoustic sense of animals.* Cambridge, UK: Harvard University Press.

Stephens, D., & Krebs, J. R. (1986). *Optimal foraging theory.* Princeton, NJ: Princeton University.

Strauss, M. S., & Curtis, L. E. (1981). Infant perception of numerosity. *Child Development, 52,* 1146–1152.

Struhsaker, T. T. (1967). Auditory communication among vervet monkeys (*Cercopithecus aethiops*). In S. A. Altmann (Ed.), *Social communication among primates* (pp. 281–324). Chicago: Chicago University Press.

Studdert-Kennedy, M. (1998). The particulate origins of language generativity: From syllable to gesture. In J. Hurford, M. Studdert-Kennedy, & C. Knight (Eds.), *Approaches to the evolution of language: Social and cognitive bases* (pp. 202–221). Cambridge, UK: Cambridge University Press.

Sulkowski, G. M., & Hauser, M. D. (2001). Can rhesus monkeys spontaneously subtract? *Cognition, 79,* 239–262.

Tarr, M. J., & Gauthier, I. (2000). FFA: A flexible fusiform area for subordinate-level visual processing automatized by expertise. *Nature Neuroscience, 3,* 764–769.

Terrace, H. (1993). The phylogeny and ontogeny of serial memory: List learning by pigeons and monkeys. *Psychological Science, 4,* 162–169.

Terrace, H., Chen, S., & Newman, A. (1995). Serial learning with a wild card by pigeons: Effect of list length. *Journal of Comparative Psychology, 109,* 162–172.

Thomas, R. K., Fowlkes, D., & Vickery, J. D. (1980). Conceptual numerousness judgments by squirrel monkeys. *American Journal of Psychology, 93,* 247–257.

Tomasello, M., Kruger, A., & Ratner, H. (1993). Cultural learning. *Behavioral and Brain Sciences, 16,* 495–552.

Trivers, R. L. (1972). Parental investment and sexual selection. In B. Campbell (Ed.), *Sexual selection and the descent of man* (pp. 136–179). Chicago: Aldine Press.

Trout, J. D. (2000). The biological basis of speech: what to infer from talking to the animals. *Psychological Review, 143,* 112–146.

Uller, C. (1997). *Origins of numerical concepts: A comparative study of human infants and nonhuman primates.* Unpublished doctoral dissertation, MIT, Cambridge, MA.

Uller, C., Carey, S., Huntley-Fenner, G., & Klatt, L. (1999). What representations might underlie infant numerical knowledge. *Cognitive Development, 14,* 1–36.

Uller, C., Hauser, M. D., & Carey, S. (2001). Spontaneous representation of number in cotton-top tamarins. *Journal of Comparative Psychology, 115,* 248–257.

Vallortigara, G., Zanforlin, M., & Pasti, G. (1990). Geometric modules in animals' spatial representations: A test with chicks (*Gallus gallus domesticus*). *Journal of Comparative Psychology, 104,* 248–254.

Vander Wall, S. B. (1990). *Food hoarding in animals.* Chicago: University of Chicago Press.

Wallman, J. (1992). *Aping language.* New York: Cambridge University Press.

Washburn, D. A., & Rumbaugh, D. M. (1991). Ordinal judgements of numerical symbols by macaques (*Macaca mulatta*). *Psychological Science, 2,* 190–193.

Weiss, D. J., Ghazanfar, A. A., Miller, C. T., & Hauser, M. D. (2002). Specialized processing of primate facial and vocal expressions: Evidence for cerebral asymmetries. In L. Rogers & R. Andrews (Eds.), *Cerebral vertebrate lateralization* (pp. 480–530). New York: Cambridge University Press.

Whalen, J., Gallistel, C. R., & Gelman, R. (1999). Nonverbal counting in humans: The psychophysics of number representation. *Psychological Science, 10,* 130–137.

Whiten, A., Goodall, J., McGrew, W. C., Nishida, T., Reynolds, V., Sugiyama, Y., Tutin, C. E. G., Wrangham, R. W., & Boesch, C. (1999). Cultures in chimpanzees. *Nature, 399,* 682–685.

Whiten, A., & Ham, R. (1992). On the nature and evolution of imitation in the animal kingdom: Reappraisal of a century of research. In P. J. B. Slater, J. S. Rosnblatt, C.Beer, & M. Milinski (Eds.), *Advances in the study of behavior* (pp. 239–283). New York: Academic Press.

Wilson, J. Q. (1987). *The moral sense.* New York: Basic Books.

Wilson, M. L., Hauser, M. D., & Wrangham, R. W. (2001). Does participation in cooperative intergroup conflict depend on numerical assessment, range location or rank for wild chimpanzees? *Animal Behaviour, 61,* 1203–1216.

Wright, A. A., & Rivera, J. J. (1997). Memory of auditory lists by rhesus monkey (*Macaca mulatta*). *Journal of Experimental Psychology: Animal Behavior Processes, 23,* 441–449.

Wynn, K. (1992). Addition and subtraction by human infants. *Nature, 358,* 749–750.

Wynn, K. (1996). Infants' individuation and enumeration of actions. *Psychological Science, 7,* 164–169.

Wynn, K. (1998). Psychological foundations of number: Numerical competence in human infants. *Trends in Cognitive Sciences, 2,* 296–303.

Wyttenbach, R. A., & Hoy, R. R. (1999). Categorical perception of behaviorally relevant stimuli by crickets. In M. D. Hauser & M. Konishi (Eds.), *The design of animal communication* (pp. 559–576). Cambridge, MA: MIT Press.

Wyttenbach, R. A., May, M. L., & Hoy, R. R. (1996). Categorical perception of sound frequencies by crickets. *Science, 273,* 1542–1544.

Xu, F., & Carey, S. (1996). Infants' metaphysics: The case of numerical identity. *Cognitive Psychology, 30,* 111–153.

Xu, F., & Carey, S. (2000). The emergence of kind concepts: A rejoinder to Needham and Baillargeon. *Cognition, 74,* 285–301.

Xu, F., Carey, S., & Welch, J. (1999). Infants' ability to use object kind information for object individuation. *Cognition, 70,* 137–166.

Xu, F., & Spelke, E. S. (2000). Large number discrimination in 6-month old infants. *Cognition, 74,* B1–B11.

Yang, T. T., Gallen, C. C., Ramachandran, V. S., Cobb, S., Schwartz, B. J., & Bloom, F. E. (1994). Noninvasive detection of cerebral plasticity in adult human somatosensory cortex. *NeuroReport, 5,* 701–704.

Ydenberg, R. C. (1998). Behavioral decisions about foraging and predator avoidance. In R. Dukas (Ed.), *Cognitive ecology* (pp. 343–378). Chicago: University of Chicago Press.

Zuberbuhler, K., Cheney, D. L., & Seyfarth, R. M. (1999). Conceptual semantics in a nonhuman primate. *Journal of Comparative Psychology, 113,* 33–42.

Zuberbuhler, K., Noe, R., & Seyfarth, R. M. (1997). Diana monkey long-distance calls: Messages for conspecifics and predators. *Animal Behaviour, 53,* 589–604.

CHAPTER 21

Language

ELEANOR M. SAFFRAN AND MYRNA F. SCHWARTZ

Language is a means of communicating information from one individual to others. It is a code that human societies have developed for the expression of meaning. Across all societies, the code involves words, as well as rules for linking words together (*syntax*). *Words* are arbitrary collections of sounds, produced by articulatory gestures (or manual signing, or writing) that convey particular meanings; a typical speaker acquires a vocabulary of at least 30,000 words in his or her native language. *Sentences* are combinations of words, governed by the syntax of the language, that encode more complex and, in many cases, novel messages. *Comprehension* entails recovery of the meaning intended by the speaker (or signer, or writer); *production* entails translating the message the speaker (or signer, or writer) wishes to convey into a series of words, constrained by the syntax of the language. Most children acquire the spoken words and syntax of their language community within a short period of time, and seemingly effortlessly. Once acquired, language comprehension and production processes appear automatic; people cannot help but understand what they hear in their native language,

and they usually produce coherent sentences with little apparent effort, even when they are engaged in other tasks.

Language is a uniquely human capacity. Although there is evidence of learned responses to specific calls in primates, and of brain asymmetries in chimpanzees that may foreshadow the asymmetrical representation of language in the human brain (Gannon, Holloway, Broadfield, & Braun, 1998), other animals do not exhibit communicative behavior that compares with the richness, structure, and combinatorial capacity of human language. Hence the investigation of language function and of language-brain relationships requires the use of human subjects. In recent years, the development of methods for monitoring brain activity as people engage in cognitive tasks has provided a means of studying language-brain relationships in normal individuals. These techniques complement the study of disruptions to language function caused by brain damage—the *aphasias*—which for some time served as the primary means of investigating the neural substrates of language. The breakdown patterns observed in aphasia will be the focus of much of this chapter. We will also review evidence from studies that examine language activity in the normal brain.

We begin with an overview of relevant brain anatomy, historical treatment of aphasic disorders, and techniques

Preparation of this chapter was supported by grant RO1DC00191-20 from the NIH National Institute on Deafness and Other Communication Disorders (NIDCD).

currently being used to investigate brain-behavior relationships. Following this, we present a more detailed discussion of three specific content areas: semantics (the representation of meaning), spoken language comprehension, and spoken language production.

BRAIN AND LANGUAGE: A BRIEF INTRODUCTION

Brain Anatomy

The human brain is a very complex structure composed of billions of nerve cells (neurons) and their interconnections, which occur at *synapses,* or points of contact between one neuron and another. The vast majority of these synapses are formed between *axons,* which may travel short or long distances between neurons, and processes called *dendrites,* which extend from neuronal cell bodies. Such connections govern the patterns of activation among neurons and, thereby, the physical and mental activity of the organism. While the connectivity patterns are to some extent genetically determined, a major characteristic of the nervous system is the *plasticity* of neural connections. Organisms must learn to modify their behavior as a function of their experience; the child's acquisition of the language s/he hears is an especially relevant example.

Insofar as language capability is concerned, the key structures reside in the *cerebral cortex*—the mantle of cells six layers deep that is the topmost structure of the brain. This tissue has an undulating appearance, composed of hills (*gyri*) and valleys (*fissures* or *sulci*) between them; this pattern reflects the folding of the cortex to fit within the limited space in the skull. In the majority of individuals, whether right- or left-handed, it is the left hemisphere of the cerebral cortex that has primary responsibility for language function.

Each hemisphere is divided into four lobes: the frontal, parietal, occipital, and temporal lobes. The *occipital lobe* has primary responsibility for visual function, which extends into neighboring areas of the temporal and parietal lobes. The *frontal lobe* is concerned with motor programming, including speech, as well as high-level cognitive functions. For example, sequential behavior is the province of prefrontal cortex, situated anterior to the frontal motor and premotor areas, which occupy the more posterior portions of the frontal lobe. Auditory processing is performed by areas of the *temporal lobe,* much of which is also concerned with language. There is evidence that inferior portions of the temporal lobe support semantic functions, whereas structures buried in the medial portions of the temporal lobe (the hippocampus,

the amygdala) are concerned with mechanisms of memory and emotion. The *parietal lobe* is concerned with tactile and other sensory experiences of the body, and has an important role in spatial and attentional functions; it is involved in language, as well.

In the early years of the twentieth century, a neuroanatomist named Brodmann examined cortical tissue under the microscope and assigned numbers to areas that appeared different both with respect to types of neurons and their densities. A map of Brodmann's areas can be found in Figure 21.1. To a large extent, these histological differences are associated with differences in function. The Brodmann numerical scheme is still in use today; for example, functional imaging studies of the human brain employ these numerical designations. Some areas have also been given names. For example, the deep fissure separating the temporal from the frontal and parietal lobes is known as the *lateral* or *Sylvian fissure;* areas bordering this fissure in the left hemisphere are essential to language, and the language zone of the left hemisphere is sometimes referred to as the *perisylvian* area. Another map containing names of regions that are relevant to a discussion of language is presented in Figure 21.2.

Although it has long been known that there are functional differences between the two cerebral hemispheres, it was not until the 1960s that corresponding differences in structure were identified. For example, Geschwind and Levitsky (1968) found that an area called the *planum temporale,* at the juncture of the temporal and parietal lobes, is generally larger in the left hemisphere than the right; this area is involved in language. However, it has recently been shown that chimpanzee brains contain the same asymmetry (Gannon et al., 1998), a finding that undermines what appeared to be a strong relationship between structural enlargement and functional capability. It may be, however, that this asymmetry foreshadows the dedication of this area to language function.

The cortical role in language depends critically on the receipt of information from lower brain centers, including the thalamus. The *thalamus* is an egg-shaped structure at the top of the brain stem, divided into regions called *nuclei.* Thalamic nuclei send projections to areas of the cortex and receive inputs from these areas. For example, auditory input from the medial geniculate nucleus of the thalamus projects to the temporal lobe; fibers from the lateral geniculate nucleus carry visual input to the occipital lobe. An extensive network of white matter, consisting of axons, underlies the six cell layers of the cortex, connecting cortical regions as well as carrying information to and from subcortical regions. The two hemispheres of the cerebral cortex are connected via an extensive network of fibers called the *corpus callosum.* This is the fiber tract that is severed in the procedure known

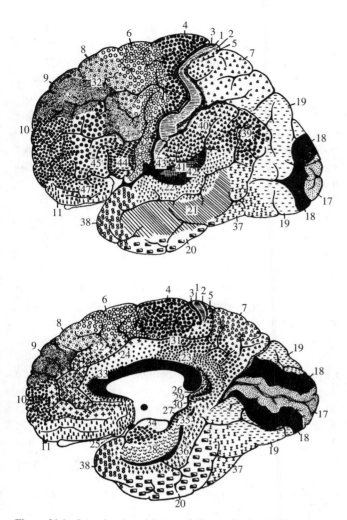

Figure 21.1   Lateral and mesial view of a human brain with the cytoarchitonic areas proposed by Brodmann in 1909. From *Lesion Analysis in Neuropsychology* (p. 11), by H. Damasio and A. R. Damasio, 1989, New York: Oxford University Press. Copyright 1989 by Oxford University Press. Reprinted with permission.

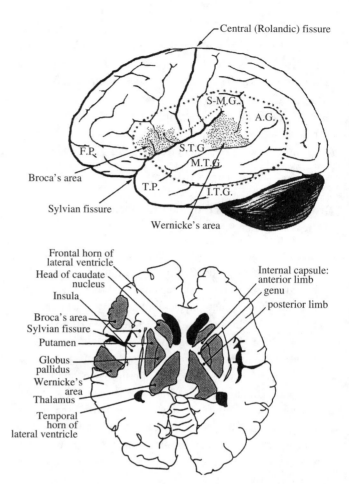

Figure 21.2   Top: Lateral view of the left cerebral hemisphere showing the perisylvian language zone. Bottom: Horizontal section of the brain at the level of Wernicke's and Broca's areas. A.G.: angular gyrus; F.P.: frontal pole; I.T.G.: inferior temporal gyrus; M.T.G.: middle temporal gyrus; O.P.: occipital pole; S.M.G.: supramarginal gyrus; S.T.G.: superior temporal gyrus; T.P.: temporal pole. Reprinted from *Anomia: Neuroanatomical and Cognitive Correlates* (pp. 4–5), by H. Goodglass and A. Wingfield, copyright 1997, by permission of the publisher Academic Press. Reprinted with permission.

as the *split brain operation,* which is performed to relieve the spread of epileptic discharges that fail to respond to pharmacological intervention (e.g., Gazzaniga, 1983). There is evidence that other structures, such as the *basal ganglia,* which are located beneath the cerebral cortex, also contribute to language function (e.g., A. R. Damasio, Damasio, Rizzo, Varney, & Gersch, 1982; Naeser et al., 1982). The basal ganglia project to areas of the frontal cortex and are essential to motor activity. The motor aspects of speech production depend on the integrity of connections from motor areas in the frontal cortex to nuclei in the brain stem, which innervate the articulatory musculature.

The nature of the connection patterns is also important. Both hemispheres receive input from both ears and both eyes. However, in the case of vision, the left hemisphere is sensitive to the right half of space (or visual field), which

projects from the left half of each retina—and vice versa for the visual projection to the right hemisphere. Thus, if the visual area of the left hemisphere is lesioned, vision from the right visual field is interrupted. The receipt of visual information from both eyes (but from the same visual field) is essential for depth vision. Cases where part or all of a hemifield is lost are termed *hemianopias.* If the corpus callosum is severed (or the posterior part of it lesioned), the left hemisphere will receive information from only the right visual field, and the right hemisphere from only the left visual field. The connectivity pattern is different for the auditory system, where fibers cross over at several levels from right to left and vice versa; however, the projection to each hemisphere from the ear on the opposite side dominates, reflecting the larger number of fibers that each receives from the contralateral ear. In the case of sensory and motor function, the left hemisphere receives input and exerts motor control over the right half of the body, and the right hemisphere does the same for the left. Because certain language areas lie in close proximity to left hemisphere motor cortex, some aphasic patients will have motor weakness on the right, particularly affecting the upper limb. Lesions of left temporal cortex, which also result in aphasia, may disrupt fibers carrying information to visual cortex, resulting in defects in the right visual field.

Historical Background to the Classification of the Aphasias

Systematic observation of the relationships between brain damage and language dysfunction began in the middle of the nineteenth century. The first steps in this direction are generally credited to a French physician, Paul Broca, who also had an interest in anthropology. Prior to his work, the strongest claims about mind-brain relationships were made by *phrenologists,* who took bumps on the skull to reflect the development of cortical areas beneath. Phrenologists attempted to localize such functions as spirituality and parental love; they also made claims about language, assigning it to the anterior tips of both frontal lobes, an area that lies just behind the eye. (The basis for this assignment was the acquaintance of phrenology's founder, Gall, with an articulate schoolmate who had protruding eyes!)

Broca was properly skeptical about these pseudoscientific views, believing that functions must be directly related to the convolutions of the cerebral cortex. He observed a patient (Monsieur Leborgne) with a severe speech production impairment, whose output was limited to a single monosyllable ("tan"); in contrast, the gentleman's comprehension of language appeared to be well preserved. Leborgne passed away, and Broca was able to examine his brain. He found an area of damage in the left inferior frontal lobe and later confirmed this observation in another patient with an articulatory impairment. Broca observed several additional patients with similar problems, although he did not always have information about the underlying neuropathology. In 1865, he postulated that the left frontal lobe was the substrate for the "faculty of articulate language." He speculated that this function of the left frontal lobe was related to the left hemisphere's control of the usually dominant right hand (Broca, 1865). Broca also hypothesized that the right hemisphere was responsible for language in left-handers, a conjecture that later proved to be incorrect, although there is evidence that language is less completely lateralized to the left hemisphere in left-handers (e.g., Rasmussen & Milner, 1977).

Several years later, a German physician, Carl Wernicke, observed a different form of language impairment, characterized by a severe comprehension deficit. In contrast to Broca's cases, these patients spoke fluently, although their output was often uninterpretable. They frequently produced *paraphasias* (substituted words or speech segments), sometimes uttered nonwords (*neologisms*), and relied heavily on pronouns or general terms such as "place" and "thing." Wernicke was able to examine the brain of one of the patients, and found a lesion in the superior temporal gyrus on the left. The area of damage was located in what would now be called the *auditory association area,* at the junction of the left temporal and parietal lobes. (Association cortex typically borders primary sensory cortex, which receives input from subcortical nuclei; association areas are involved in the further processing of sensory information.) As auditory comprehension and speech production were both compromised by the lesion, Wernicke (1874) speculated that this region contained "auditory word images" acquired in learning the language. In addition to their role in interpreting speech input, he suggested that these images guided the articulatory functions that were localized in Broca's area. He further speculated that the anatomical connection between Wernicke's and Broca's areas would allow the listener to repeat the speech of others; damage to this pathway, he predicted, should result in a disorder in which production would be error-prone, although comprehension would be preserved. The existence of this disorder (*conduction aphasia*) was subsequently confirmed, although the locus of damage that gives rise to it is still debated (H. Damasio & Damasio, 1989; Dronkers, Redfern, & Knight, 2000).

Wernicke's early theory of brain-language relationships was elaborated by Leopold Lichtheim (1885), whose model is represented in Figure 21.3. Lichtheim added a *concept center,* which would serve as the seat of understanding for the listener (hence its connection to Wernicke's area) as well as the source of the messages ultimately expressed by the speaker (it is also connected to Broca's area). Although he referred to it as a center, he believed that this information was diffusely represented in the brain. Lichtheim's model predicted several disorders not yet observed. Among these were the *transcortical aphasias* (sensory and motor), in which repetition was better preserved than spontaneous production due to the isolation of Broca's or Wernicke's area from the concept center. Transcortical sensory aphasia also involved a comprehension problem, due to the disconnection between Wernicke's area and conceptual information. Lichtheim also predicted a receptive disorder—*word deafness*—resulting from the disconnection of Wernicke's area from auditory input, and a production

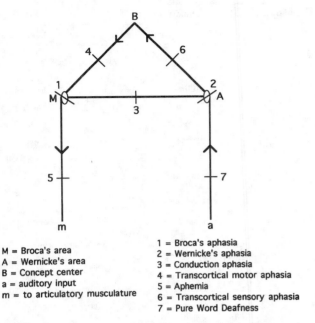

Figure 21.3 Leopold Lichtheim's center-and-tract model of the organization of language in the brain.

disorder—*aphemia*—resulting from damage to the pathway from Broca's area to brain centers concerned with motor implementation of spoken output. All of these patterns were later reported. The Wernicke-Lichtheim approach, which relied heavily on connections among brain centers, came to be known as *connectionism* (not to be confused with current computer models of cognitive function, which use the same term). Table 21.1 shows the taxonomy of aphasia syndromes, which took shape under this approach and is still in use today.

Connectionist aphasiology has always drawn opposition. One of the early critics was Sigmund Freud, who published a monograph on aphasia in 1891. Freud argued that the connectionist view was too simplistic to account for so complex a function as human language. He also showed that it could not explain the symptoms of several cases of aphasia that had been reported in the literature (Freud, 1891/1953). Contemporary language scientists would agree; the connectionist approach focused on word comprehension and production, completely ignoring sentence-level processes. (Famed neurologist Arnold Pick stood apart from this tradition and made outstanding contributions to the study of sentence-level breakdown; see Pick, 1913). Most of those who studied aphasia in the early to mid-twentiethth century adopted a more holistic approach to language-brain relationships (e.g., Head, 1926; Marie, 1906). However, the center-based approach, with emphasis on the importance of connections between areas responsible for particular functions, was revived in the

1960s, largely through the efforts of neurologist Norman Geschwind. He published two celebrated papers that explained a range of cognitive disturbances, in animals and man, in terms of the severing of connections between brain regions (Geschwind, 1965). Insofar as language was concerned, he favored the approach initiated by Wernicke and elaborated by Lichtheim. At about the same time, Schuell and her colleagues at the University of Minnesota conducted large group studies of aphasics, which led them to conclude that the language area of the brain was not differentiated with respect to function—that it operated as a whole (Schuell, Jenkins, & Carroll, 1962). One major difference between these approaches is that Geschwind was looking primarily at cases with restricted lesions, whereas the Minnesota study enrolled patients irrespective of the nature of their lesions and likely included individuals with extensive brain damage.

To a large extent, these polar views—componential or modular versus holistic—continue to characterize the debate among aphasia researchers, and in a somewhat different guise, among language researchers in general. Are language tasks delegated to distinct processing components that operate to a large degree independently of one another (the modular view) or does the system operate with a good deal of interaction? Is there a separate syntactic component, or are syntactic functions subsumed by the lexicon? We will try to address such questions wherever we can. It should be appreciated, however, that in many instances the answers are, at best, provisional. In view of the complexity of language processes, it is not surprising that many issues remain controversial. (To sample contemporary arguments against the modular approach, see Dick et al., 2001, and Van Orden, Pennington, & Stone, 2001.)

Methods Used to Study Brain-Language Relationships

Localizing Brain Lesions

Although encased in the protective skull, the brain is nevertheless susceptible to a wide variety of disorders. The circulatory system is the primary cause of aphasic impairments. Most are caused by disruption of the left middle cerebral artery, which supplies the lateral surface of the left hemisphere, including brain regions concerned with language function. Circulatory disorders include those that block an artery (*ischemia*), hemorrhages involving rupture of a blood vessel, and aneurysms, in which a weak arterial wall ultimately allows blood to leak into brain tissue—a major cause of aphasia in younger individuals. Other disorders include tumors, infections, degenerative diseases (such as Alzheimer's), and

TABLE 21.1   Description of the Major Aphasia Syndromes

	Symptoms Defined by Classical Connectionist Aphasiology		
Syndrome	Speech Fluency	Functional Comprehension	Repetition
Broca's aphasia	Non-fluent; impaired articulation, impaired prosody	Preserved	Impaired
Wernicke's aphasia	Fluent; paraphasic; sometimes excessive	Impaired	Impaired
Conduction aphasia	Fluent, paraphasic	Preserved	Impaired
Transcortical sensory	Fluent, paraphasic	Impaired	Preserved
Transcortical motor	Preserved but sparse	Preserved	Preserved
Anomia	Variable	Preserved	Preserved
Global aphasia	Variable	Impaired	Impaired

	Symptoms Defined by Cognitive Approach		
	Lexical Retrieval	Sentence Comprehension	Sentence Production
Broca's aphasia	Variable; better for nouns than verbs	Often impaired for complex, reversible sentences	Agrammatic; omission and substitution of closed class vocabulary
Wernicke's aphasia	Impaired	Impaired	Structured but paraphasic
Conduction aphasia	Variable	Variable; may be impaired for long and/or complex sentences	Structured but paraphasic
Transcortical sensory	Impaired	Impaired	Structured but paraphasic
Transcortical motor	Variable	Preserved	Variable
Anomia	Impaired	Preserved	Structured but impaired by word-finding difficulty
Global aphasia	Impaired	Impaired	Impaired

traumatic brain injuries produced by falls, bullets, and vehicular accidents.

Until the early 1970s, techniques for imaging the brain in vivo were rudimentary; radiological techniques did not have much sensitivity. To gain precise information about the location of brain damage, it was necessary to examine the brain after the patient had died, or to rely on descriptions of tissue removed at surgery. The development of the *CT scan* (CT is an acronym for computer-assisted tomography) improved matters considerably. This is an X-ray procedure that is enhanced by the use of computers; it is possible to acquire images of successive slices through the brain, and due to differences in the density of neural tissue (denser tissue absorbs more radiation), to localize the damage rather precisely. *Magnetic resonance imaging (MRI),* also developed in the 1970s, led to further advances in brain imaging. One advantage of this technique is that it does not utilize radiation. Instead, a magnetic field is imposed that causes certain atoms (usually hydrogen, a major component of water) to orient in a particular direction; subsequent imposition of a radio frequency signal causes the atoms to spin, giving off radio waves that are registered by a computer. Again, it is possible to examine serial slices of brain tissue. The signal varies with the content of the tissue and yields sharp images that are becoming increasingly refined in their degree of resolution. These techniques have provided a great deal of information on lesion sites, which can then be related to the nature of the language impairment. Computerized methods for compiling lesion data across the brains of patients with similar deficits are proving particularly useful (e.g., Dronkers et al., 2000).

Although aphasia research has yielded much informative data, it must be acknowledged that the evidence is problematic in some respects. The injuries result from disease or trauma, accidents of nature that afford no control over the locus or size of the lesion. Moreover, the damage is often extensive, which makes it difficult to isolate the regions responsible for specific language functions. For example, the lesion that results in chronic Broca's aphasia extends well beyond the area identified by Broca (Mohr et al., 1978), and it has been claimed that the same applies to Wernicke's aphasia (Dronkers et al., 2000). Some cases of Broca's and Wernicke's aphasias have lesions that completely spare the classical Broca's and Wernicke's areas (Dronkers et al.). Furthermore, the delineation of these areas is complicated by the fact that human brains differ in the size and precise localization of particular areas (e.g., Uylings, Malofeeva, Bogolepova, Amunts, & Zilles, 1999).

Some aphasia researchers have tried to interpret aphasic deficits as purely subtractive, taking the residual behavior to represent normalcy minus the damaged component (e.g., Caramazza, 1984). This view is theoretically appealing, but increasingly untenable. Patients with language disorders struggle to communicate. In doing so, they often employ compensatory strategies, which speech pathologists strongly encourage in their attempts to rehabilitate aphasic disorders. This introduces another source of variability: Do different behavior patterns reflect different deficits, or different ways of compensating for the same underlying impairment?

It is also becoming clear that, in some cases at least, regions of the right hemisphere, normally thought to be little involved in basic language functions, provide support for residual language in aphasia. For example, functional imaging studies have shown increased brain activity in areas of the right hemisphere that are homologous to damaged language areas on the left (e.g., Cardebat et al., 1994; Weiller et al., 1995). Other studies have shown that patients whose language has improved subsequent to left hemisphere damage become worse as a result of subsequent right hemisphere lesions (e.g., Basso, Gardelli, Grassi, & Mariotti, 1989). These considerations should be kept in mind as we review the data; where appropriate, we will refer to them explicitly.

There are other reasons to be cautious when drawing inferences about lesion-deficit relations. A functional deficit, even if consistently related to the same locus of injury, may not directly reflect the localization of the impaired function. Much of the brain's activity depends on connections between sets of neurons, and the deficit may reflect disruption of connectivity patterns as opposed to localization of the function at the site of damage per se. This point is supported by metabolic imaging studies of brain-damaged patients (see next subsection), which have shown hypometabolic changes at sites remote from the structural lesion, and, in some cases, changes in regions of brain of that show no evidence of focal brain damage on CT or MRI (e.g., Breedin, Saffran, & Coslett, 1994).

Imaging Brain Metabolism With Positron Emission Tomography

The imaging methods discussed previously provide static images of brain structures. With positron emission tomography (PET), it has become possible to explore the physiological effects of a structural lesion, for example, by measuring regional metabolism of glucose, the major energy source used by the brain. *PET* (and the lesser used *SPECT*) are methods that localize and quantify the radiation arising from positron-emitting isotopes, which are injected into the bloodstream and which accumulate in different brain regions in proportion to the metabolic activity of those regions and the demands of this activity for greater cerebral blood flow (for a readable introduction, see Metter, 1987). The use of PET in studies of functional brain activity is discussed next. PET has also been used productively to measure resting-state activity in brains damaged by stroke or other neurological insult. As noted above, such studies have revealed that the areas of brain that are metabolically altered by a structural brain lesion far exceed the boundaries of the structural lesion. Furthermore, the metabolic maps provide a very different picture of function-lesion correlations in patients with aphasia (Metter; Metter et al., 1990).

Imaging Functional Brain Activity

A major innovation in cognitive neuroscience has been the extension of PET and MRI methods to the measurement of regional activation associated with ongoing cognitive behavior. What follows is a brief overview; for further details, the reader is referred to Friston (1997), Rugg (1999), and references therein.

As implied earlier, there is a close coupling between the changes in activity level of a region of brain and changes in its blood supply, such that increased activity leads to an increase in blood supply. In so-called *cognitive activation* studies with PET, images are acquired while the subject performs two conditions: an experimental condition and a control condition that ideally differs from the experimental condition with respect to only a single cognitive operation. Computerized methods are then used to subtract the activation patterns in the control state from that induced by the experimental state. Regions that achieve above-threshold activation after the subtraction are taken to subserve the cognitive operation(s) of interest.

Functional MRI (fMRI) takes advantage of a hemodynamic effect called *BOLD,* for *blood oxygenation level dependent.* It happens that oxygen flows to activated brain areas in excess of the amount needed, so that the oxygen content of blood is higher when it leaves a highly active area compared with a less active one. Dynamic changes in the ratio of oxygenated to nonoxygenated blood as a cognitive task is performed thus provides an index of the changes of brain activity in areas of interest. Signals obtained from certain MRI measures are sensitive to these changes in blood oxygenation and, by extension, regional brain activity.

FMRI has a number of advantages over PET, not the least of which is that it does not require injection of radioactive compounds. This aspect of PET limits the number of scans that can safely be obtained from a single subject, which generally necessitates the pooling of data across subjects. FMRI, in contrast, can be used with single subjects. Moreover, the images can be acquired over shorter time periods (seconds, as opposed to minutes in the case of PET), and have better spatial resolution. On the other hand, fMRI suffers from artifacts introduced by movements, including small head movements such as occur during speech. This has limited fMRI research on speech production; however methods for correcting such artifacts are continually evolving and we can expect to see more such studies in the future. We can also expect more research on the application of fMRI methods to brain injured populations. As it stands, the hemodynamic models related to BOLD are of questionable validity when applied to patients with cerebrovascular alterations due to stroke or trauma.

Many fMRI experiments employ the same blocked designs and subtraction logic as are used with PET. This approach has been criticized, in that the results are heavily dependent on the choice of the control task. Indeed, it is arguable whether the idealized single-component difference between experimental and control tasks is ever, in reality, achieved (e.g., Friston, 1997). Other methods currently in use include parametric designs, in which the difficulty of a task is systematically varied and regions are identified that show a corresponding increase in activation; and designs in which trials, rather than blocks of trials, constitute the unit of analysis (Zarahn, Aguirre, & D'Esposito, 1997). Some of these newer methods take advantage of fMRI's sensitivity to transient signal change in order to examine the dynamic response to a sensory event, similar to the electrophysiological ERP technique, discussed next.

Electrophysiological Methods

Electrophysiological methods have been used both to record events in the brain, and, by introducing current, to interfere with brain activity. Potentials temporally linked to sensory stimuli and recorded from the scalp—*event-related potentials,* or *ERPs*—have proved extremely useful for mapping the time course of cognitive operations; but as the source of the current is difficult to specify, this approach is less useful for the localization of brain activity (see Kutas, Federeier, & Sereno, 1999, for a more extensive treatment of this topic). More precise localization data have been acquired from electrode grids placed on the cortex prior to surgical intervention, usually in cases of intractable epilepsy (e.g., Nobre, Allison, & McCarthy, 1994). In some cases, electrodes have been used to apply current to brain regions, which disrupts ongoing brain

activity. In the 1950s, such studies were used to map general brain functions (e.g., Penfield & Roberts, 1959); more recently, the technique has been used to identify brain areas associated with specific language functions (e.g., Boatman, Lesser, & Gordon, 1995; Ojemann & Mateer, 1979).

Recently, ERP techniques have been used to investigate aphasic disorders. One advantage of this approach is that it does not require a response on the part of the subject. Overt responses are often delayed or hesitant in patients with aphasia; in some cases, the patient may even say "yes" when he or she means "no," or vice versa. The ERP methodology utilizes standard electrophysiological responses, such as the one generated by *semantic anomaly* (e.g., Kutas & Hillyard, 1980). This signal is called the *N400*—N because it involves a negative change from the baseline of ongoing electrical activity, and 400 because it occurs 400 msec after the anomalous word (e.g., after "socks," given the sentence "He spread his warm bread with socks"). The amplitude of the N400 is related to the difficulty in integrating the word into the sentence context; in the following examples, it is smaller in the case of number 1 than number 2 (Hagoort, Brown, & Osterhout, 1999). There is evidence that the N400 is reduced in aphasics with severe comprehension deficits (Swaab, Brown, & Hagoort, 1997).

1. The girl put the sweet in her *mouth* after the lesson.
2. The girl put the sweet in her *pocket* after the lesson.

Magnetic Stimulation and Recording

Electrical activity in the brain generates magnetic changes that can be recorded from the surface of the skull (*magneto-encepholography,* or *MEG;* see Rugg, 1999, for more details.) With respect to the source of the activity, MEG is more restrictive than ERP, in that the decline in strength of the magnetic field drops off more sharply than that of the electrical field. This technique is now being applied in attempts to localize brain activity related to language function (e.g., Levelt, Praamstra, Meyer, Helenius, & Salmelin, 1998).

The application of a magnetic field to points on the skull, which generates electrical interference, has also been used to disrupt the brain's electrical activity in the cortex below. This technique can be used to help localize brain activity in relation to ongoing tasks (e.g., Coslett & Monsul, 1994).

Inferences From Patterns of Language Breakdown

In addition to the use of patient data to localize language function in the brain, the patterns of language breakdown in aphasia are of interest for their bearing on the functional organization of language. For example, if it could be shown convincingly that syntactic processes are disrupted independently of lexical functions, and vice versa, it would lend support to the theory that these capacities constitute separate components of the language system. Over the past 25 years or so, this has been the enterprise of the field known as *cognitive neuropsychology*. Cognitive neuropsychologists study the fractionation of cognitive functions in cases of brain damage, with the aim of informing models of the functional architecture of human cognition. This work extends well beyond language, to research in perception, memory, attention, action, and so forth, but a good deal of this effort has focused on the language-processing system.

Much of this research involves the detailed study of individual cases. There are several reasons for this. One is that characterization of the deficit involves extensive examination, often with tasks devised specifically for the patient. These studies often take months to complete, and would be difficult to conduct with a large group of subjects. The second has to do with variability. The classical syndrome descriptors (e.g., Broca's aphasia, Wernicke's aphasia) tolerate a wide range of variation. For example, many patients considered to be Broca's aphasics exhibit *agrammatic production* (reduction in syntactic complexity; omission of grammatical morphemes), but not all of them do, at least not to a degree that is clinically apparent. A third reason is that there are some disorders of considerable theoretical interest that are quite rare; examples of those to be discussed include *word deafness* and *semantic dementia*. If not studied as single cases, many of these disorders could not be investigated at all. Of course, it is risky to make generalizations on the basis of a single instance, and in the vast majority of cases the patterns have been replicated in other patients. It is also comforting to note that recent studies of brain activation in normal subjects have confirmed many of the functions assigned to particular areas on the basis of lesion data.

Computational Models and Simulated Lesions

The area of language study known as *psycholinguistics* aims to explain language performance in terms of transformations in the language code such as are affected at particular processing stages. Researchers interested in the cognitive neuroscience of language take as their ultimate to specify how these encoding-decoding operations are related to specific areas of the brain.

Until relatively recently, the models took the form of box-and-arrow diagrams representing how information flowed from one stage of processing to the next. Over the past decade, there has been an increasing interest in computational models that characterize the processing of information in enough detail that they can be implemented on a computer and experiments can be conducted as computer simulations. These models can also be *lesioned*—that is, they can be altered in some way (e.g., by increasing noise levels, weakening connections, etc.) to simulate effects of brain damage. (See Saffran, Dell, & Schwartz, 2000, for discussion of several such models.) Although vastly simplified in relation to the real language system, computational models seek to capture basic principles of neural function, in that the elements that comprise the model receive activation and pass this activation on to other units. Some models employ feedback as well as feed-forward activation, as feedback appears to be a widespread feature of neural systems. There are some that contain inhibitory as well as excitatory connections between units. One important class of models starts out with random connections from the layer receiving the input to the layer of units that generates output; the model is then trained by strengthening connections that produce the correct output. These are termed *parallel distributed processing (PDP)* models (e.g., McClelland & Rumelhart, 1986; see Plaut & Shallice, 1993, for one application to the effects of brain damage). In these models, the information about the relationship between input and output units is distributed across elements in a so-called *hidden layer* (or in some cases, layers) of units, which is intermediate between input and output. For example, consider the fact that there is no consistent relationship between semantics and phonology; cats and dogs share some similarities, but the sounds of the words that denote these entities are completely different. As a result of the inconsistent mapping between semantics and phonology, the relationship between them must be represented in a hidden layer. In other models (called localist models), the modeler specifies the connections among elements.

The attempt to model the effects of brain damage provides another way of testing the adequacy of computational models (in addition to simulating data from psycholinguistic experiments). In other words, it should be possible to take a model capable of generating normal language patterns and damage it so that it produces abnormal patterns that are actually observed following injury to the brain (e.g., Saffran et al., 2000; Haarmann, Just, & Carpenter, 1997). It is also possible that these efforts to simulate effects of lesions will yield insights into the nature of pathological states, and even contribute to approaches to remediating these disorders (Plaut, 1996). We will provide some examples of computer-based lesion studies as we go along.

THE SEMANTIC REPRESENTATION OF OBJECTS

In 1972, psychologist Endel Tulving introduced the term *semantic memory* to denote the compendium of information that represents one's knowledge of the world as derived from both linguistic and nonlinguistic sources. Tulving was interested in distinguishing this store of general knowledge from *episodic* or *autobiographical memory,* which preserves information about an individual's personal experiences. That tigers have stripes, that cars have engines, that Egypt is in Africa—these facts are among the contents of semantic memory, whereas personal remembrances such as the site of one's last vacation or the details of one's most recent restaurant meal are entered in episodic memory. In this section, we consider how the brain represents one particular aspect of semantic memory—the knowledge that allows one to generate and understand words and pictures. Our major source of evidence will be individuals whose store of semantic knowledge is severely compromised by brain damage.

Semantic Disorders

Semantic Dementia

In the syndrome that has come to be known as *semantic dementia,* there is progressive erosion of semantic memory with relative sparing of other cognitive functions (Snowden, Goulding, & Neary, 1989; and for earlier cases that conform to this description, Schwartz, Marin, & Saffran, 1979, and Warrington, 1975). Patients initially complain of inability to remember the names of people, places, and things. Formal testing confirms a word retrieval deficit, often accompanied by impairment in word comprehension. As the disorder progresses, most patients also lose the ability to answer questions about real or depicted objects (e.g., regarding their color, size, or country of origin) or to indicate which two of three pictured objects are more closely related (e.g., horse, cow, bear). In other words, the semantic impairment affects nonverbal as well as verbal concepts. On the other hand, the ability of these patients to handle and use objects in practical tasks is generally far better than what their naming and matching performance would predict. This is presumed to reflect their preserved sensorimotor knowledge or practical problem solving (Hodges, Bozeat, Lambon Ralph, Patterson, & Spatt, 2000; and for critical discussion, Buxbaum, Schwartz, & Carew, 1997).

Semantic dementia is the manifestation of a degenerative brain disease (cause unknown) that targets the temporal lobes, in most cases predominantly the left (Hodges, Patterson, Oxbury, & Funnell, 1992). Radiological investi-

gation with CT or MRI often reveals focal atrophy in the anterior and inferior temporal regions of one (the left) or both hemispheres. A quantitative analysis of gray-matter volumetric changes in 6 cases revealed that the atrophy begins in the temporal pole (Brodmann's area [BA] 38) and spreads anteriorly into the adjacent ventromedial frontal region, and posteriorly into the inferior and medial temporal gyri (Mummery et al., 2000). In support of this, Breedin, Saffran, and colleague (1994) found SPECT abnormalities that were maximal in the anterior inferior temporal lobes in a semantic dementia patient who exhibited no structural brain changes on MRI. Other functional imaging studies with SPECT or PET have described hypometabolism outside the regions of atrophy, most notably in the temporo-occipital-parietal area known to be important for object identification and naming (e.g., Mummery et al., 1999). It is likely that this posterior hypometabolism reflects disruption of connections from the damaged anterior temporal lobes (Mummery et al., 2000).

Remarkably, the neuropathology in semantic dementia spares the classical anterior and posterior language zones (the parts damaged in Wernicke's and Broca's aphasias). As a result, aspects of language processing, including word repetition and grammatical encoding, remain largely intact (Schwartz et al., 1979; Breedin & Saffran, 1999). Also spared is the neural substrate for formation of episodic memories, in the medial temporal lobes and hippocampus. Thus, unlike Alzheimer's disease, in which day-to-day memory loss is often one of the earliest symptoms, semantic dementia leaves recent autobiographical memory well preserved long into the course of the disease (Snowden, Griffiths, & Neary, 1994). Eventually, however, the degenerative process invades other areas and a general dementia sets it, rendering the individual incapable of caring for him- or herself. Autopsy studies of brain tissue reveal a spectrum of non-Alzheimer's pathological changes, including, in many cases, those indicative of Pick's disease (Hodges, Garrard, & Patterson, 1998).

The loss of verbal and nonverbal concepts in semantic dementia happens gradually, in that specific features are lost before more general ones. This can be shown by asking subjects to name objects aloud, match words to pictures, or answer probe questions regarding the physical or other characteristics of objects. Until late in the clinical course, errors are mostly within category, such as naming a fork a "spoon" or a cow a "horse" (e.g., Schwartz et al., 1979). We saw something similar in the drawings of a patient who was formerly an artist. Her early depictions of named objects was generally accurate for category-level information, but not identifying detail (Figure 21.4).

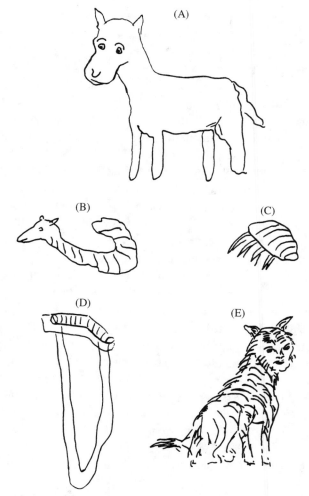

Figure 21.4   Drawings by a patient with degenerative dementia featuring semantic loss. The patient, a former artist, attempted to draw each item as it was named by the examiner. (A) Moose, (B) frog, (C) guitar, (D) telephone, (E) cat. From "Deterioration of Language in Progressive Aphasia: A Case Study," by M. F. Schwartz and J. B. Chawluk, 1990, *Modular Deficits in Alzheimer-Type Dementia*, Cambridge, MA: MIT Press, ed. M. F. Schwartz, p. 264. Copyright 1990 by MIT Press. Reprinted with permission.

When asked to define words, semantic dementia patients provide little information about an object's perceptual characteristics (Lambon Ralph, Graham, & Patterson, 1999). Other than this, most semantic dementia patients demonstrate no striking selectivity in their semantic loss. There are, however, patients whose semantic impairment affects some types of entities more than others. The most impressive instances of selective impairment are the disorders that have been termed *category specific*. We turn to these next.

Disproportionate Impairment for Living Things

This condition was first described in detail by Warrington and Shallice (1984). They studied four patients, three of whom

who were suffering the aftereffects of herpes encephalitis, which generally includes dense amnesia (reflecting damage to medial temporal and inferior frontal lobe structures) along with semantic impairment; the fourth patient had semantic dementia. The disproportionate impact on living things emerged clearly on a definitions test. For example, one patient defined a compass as "tools for telling direction you are going," whereas a snail was, "an insect animal." Another defined submarine as a "ship that goes underneath the sea," but a spider as "person looking for things, he was a spider for a nation or country." Warrington and Shallice's patients were also impaired in their knowledge of foods, a category that includes manufactured items (e.g., bread, pizza) as well as biological entities such as fruits and vegetables. There were also indications of impairment on certain categories of man-made things, such as gemstones, fabrics, and musical instruments.

Warrington and Shallice's study was followed by a number of others demonstrating similar deficits involving living things and foodstuffs in patients with damage to the temporal lobes (see Saffran & Schwartz, 1994, for a review of cases). The claim that these impairments represent the loss of knowledge for certain categories of object did not go unchallenged, however. In some cases, living and non-living categories were not matched for frequency or familiarity, and there are a few patients whose category differences disappeared when these factors were adequately controlled (Funnell & Sheridan, 1992; Stewart, Parkin, & Hunkin, 1992). This can be a particular problem with animals, which tend to be rated as less familiar than artifacts. On the other hand, foods are more familiar, yet they pattern with animals. Other factors that could contribute to the difficulty of living things include visual complexity and similarity in form, which are generally greater for living things than for artifacts (e.g., Gaffan & Heywood, 1993; Humphreys, Lamote, & Lloyd-Jones, 1995). In most cases, however, control of these factors through stimulus selection (e.g., Funnell & De Mornay Davies, 1997) or statistical analyses (e.g., Farah, Meyer, & McMullen, 1996) has not eliminated category-specific deficits for living things. Moreover, the factors that render living things more difficult cannot explain the occurrence of the opposite pattern—greater impairment on man-made objects than living things.

Disproportionate Impairment for Artifacts

This pattern was described in two case studies by Warrington and McCarthy (1983, 1987), and subsequently in patients studied by Behrmann and Leiberthal (1989), Hillis and Caramazza (1991), and Sacchett and Humphreys (1992). The subjects of these reports were aphasics with left hemisphere lesions. Three of the four cases had lesions involving frontoparietal cortex; in the fourth case (the patient reported by Hillis and Caramazza) the lesion involved the left temporal and basal ganglia, which project to the frontal lobe. Because Warrington and McCarthy's patients (VER and YOT) were severely aphasic, they could be tested only on word comprehension. On a word-to-picture matching test, YOT scored 67% correct on artifacts, 86% correct on living things, and 83% on food; VER scored 58% correct on artifacts and 88% on food. YOT also proved to be impaired on body parts, scoring only 22% on this highly familiar category. Tested on picture naming, CW (Sacchett & Humphreys) and JJ (Hillis & Caramazza) scored 35% and 45%, respectively, on artifacts and body parts and 95% and 92%, respectively, on living things. Breedin, Martin, and Saffran (1994) have demonstrated a similar pattern in patients with left frontoparietal lesions using a word-similarity judgment task. One consistent finding is that the decrement on artifacts is associated with impaired performance on body parts.

The Weighted-Features Account of Category-Specific Disorders

How can we account for these category-specific semantic disorders? We have already mentioned the possibility that the brain organizes knowledge according to semantic category: animals in one network, foods in another, tools in a third, and so on. (See Caramazza & Shelton, 1998, for a proposal along these lines.) Warrington and her colleagues (Warrington & Shallice, 1984; Warrington & McCarthy, 1987) have taken a different stance, hypothesizing that category specificity in semantic breakdown reflects the properties that figure most importantly in the representations of objects. Warrington and Shallice pointed out that, unlike most plants and animals, artifacts

> have clearly defined functions. The evolutionary development of tool use has led to finer and finer functional differentiations of artifacts for an increasing range of purposes. Individual inanimate objects have specific functions that are designed for activities appropriate to their function . . . jar, jug and vase are identified in terms of their function, namely, to hold a particular type of object, but the sensory features of each can vary considerably. By contrast, functional attributes contribute minimally to the identification of living things (e.g., lion, tiger and leopard), whereas sensory attributes provide the definitive characteristics (e.g., plain, striped, or spotted). (p. 849)

The idea here is that perceptual properties are more heavily weighted in differentiating representations of living things, whereas functional information figures more importantly in the representations of artifacts. The perceptual properties of living things are, of course, intrinsic to the entities and largely immutable, whereas, in the case of artifacts, many properties are free to vary. The range of objects that currently serve as radios, for example, necessitates that they be defined in terms of their function as opposed to their shape, color, or composition. The differential weighting of perceptual information in the case of living things was confirmed by Farah and McClelland (1991), who asked subjects to count the number of visual and functional descriptors in dictionary definitions of living and non-living entities. Visual properties dominated in both sets, but more so (a ratio of nearly 8:1) in the case of living things compared with artifacts (1.4:1).

The relative-weighting account does not deny that artifacts may have distinctive visual properties. However, it predicts that the loss of perceptual properties should be particularly damaging to the representations of living things, which are largely distinguished from one another by their physical characteristics. In contrast, artifacts are differentiated in terms of function, as well as by the manner in which they are manipulated. Body parts may pattern with artifacts because they, too, are differentiated by their functions, or possibly as a consequence of their roles in the utilization of these objects. In contrast, manufactured foods would be expected to pattern with living things: Foods serve the same basic function and are in large part distinguished by their sensory properties, such as color, shape, and taste.

The differential-weighting account is consistent with a model of semantic memory in which information about an object is distributed across a number of brain subsystems specialized for a particular type of knowledge. Allport (1985) outlined a network model (see Figure 21.5) consisting of subsystems that are specialized for particular types of information (visual, tactile, action-oriented). Information about a particular object (e.g., a telephone) is distributed across these subsystems, which are linked to one another by associations among co-occurring features. As a result, activation of features of an object in one subsystem will automatically activate other features of the object in other subsystems. On the assumption that these subsystems are anatomically distinct, it should be possible to disrupt them independently.

Warrington and McCarthy (1987) speculated that there might even be a finer-grained differentiation within the semantic system, such that some perceptual features (e.g., shape) figure more heavily in the representations of animals, whereas others (e.g., color, taste) are more salient in the distinctions among fruits and vegetables. As the experience of objects rests on their sensory and sensorimotor properties, it is reasonable to assume that these various characteristics are

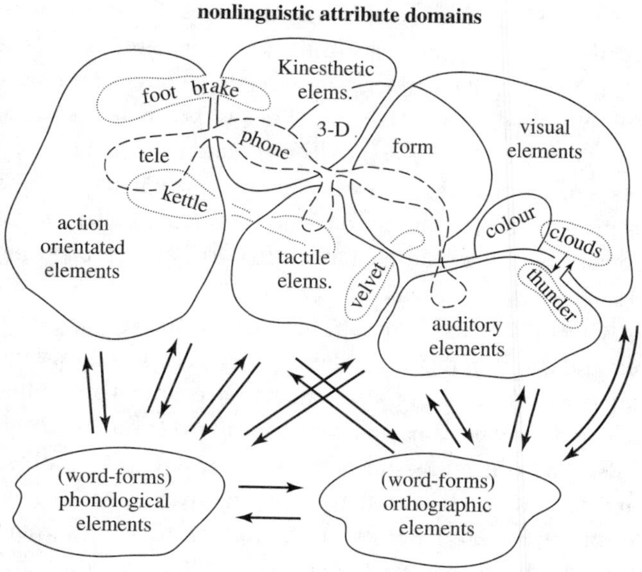

nonlinguistic attribute domains

Figure 21.5 Allport's model has object concepts represented as auto-associated activity patterns (dotted outlines) distributed across many different sensory and motor attribute domains. Spoken and written word forms are similarly represented as auto-associated patterns within their corresponding ("phonological"/"orthographic") attribute domains. Mappings between word forms and word meanings are embodied as distributed matrices of interconnections between attribute domains. From "Distributed Memory, Modular Subsystems, and Dysphasia," by D. A. Allport, in *Current Perspectives in Dysphasia,* 1985, Edinburgh: Churchill Livingstone, ed. S. K. Newman and R. Epstein, p. 53. Copyright 1985 by Churchill Livingstone. Reprinted with permission.

experienced through different modalities and that they are registered in different subsystems. As Shallice (1988) has put it,

> such a developmental process can be viewed as one in which individual units (neurons) within the network come to be most influenced by input from particular input channels, and, in turn, come to have most effect on particular output channels. Complementarily, an individual concept will come to be most strongly represented in the activity of those units that correspond to the pattern of input-output pathways most required in the concept's identification and use. The sets of units that are most critical for a related group of categories would then come to form semi-modules. . . . The capacity to distinguish between members of a particular category would depend on whether there are sufficient neurons preserved in the relevant partially specialised region to allow the network to respond . . . differentially to the different items in the category. (pp. 302–303)

Although this position has sometimes been formulated in terms of distinct visual and verbal semantic systems (e.g., McCarthy & Warrington, 1988), "visual semantic" and "verbal semantic" can be conceptualized as "partially specialized subregions," to use the terminology suggested by Shallice.

It is possible to account for a number of neuropsychological phenomena within the framework of a distributed model. As we said, disproportionate impairment of living things (and foodstuffs) would reflect damage—or lack of access—to perceptual properties, which are heavily weighted in the representations of these entities. Worse performance on artifacts would reflect the loss of functional or perhaps action-based sensorimotor information (see Buxbaum & Saffran, 1998). The model also allows for the selective disruption of linkages between attribute domains, as well as damage to connections between specific domains and input and output systems. The literature contains descriptions of disorders of the latter type. For example, McCarthy and Warrington (1988) studied a patient (TOB) who was impaired on living things when queried verbally, but who was able to describe living things adequately when provided with pictures. Asked to define the word *dolphin,* for example, TOB said "a fish or a bird," but when shown a picture he responded, "lives in water . . . trained to jump up and come out . . . In America during the war years they started to get this particular animal to go through to look into ships." We have recently tested a patient with a similar deficit. She could not, for example, define the meaning of the word *candle,* responding that it had something to do with food (from can, perhaps, or candy), but when shown a picture she said, "You put them on the table at dinner, and they provide light." The same patient performed at normal levels on an associative matching test with pictures but was severely impaired when the same items were presented as words. The model could account for this pattern by disruption of the linkages between lexical representations (word forms in Figure 21.5) and semantic information. Based on Warrington and McCarthy's (1987) suggestion of finer-grained distinctions, one should also see patients with deficits selective to animals or foods. Such patients have been reported; for example, Hart and Gordon (1992) described a patient who was impaired on animals but not fruits and vegetables, and Hart, Berndt, and Caramazza (1985) have reported the opposite pattern.

Does the living-things deficit go along with poor processing of perceptual features, as the weighted-features model would have it? This issue has been investigated in a number of different studies, with mixed results. Some have been favorable to the model (e.g., Breedin, Martin, et al., 1994; De Renzi & Lucchelli, 1994; Farah, Hammond, Mehta, & Ratcliff, 1989; Forde, Francis, Riddoch, Rumiati, & Humphreys, 1997; Gainotti & Silveri, 1996; Moss, Tyler, & Jennings, 1997), while others have found no difference between perceptual and other features (e.g., Barbarotto, Capitani, Spinnler, & Travelli, 1995; Caramazza & Shelton, 1998; Funnell & De Mornay Davies, 1996). Moreover, the positive findings are not as strong as they could be, in that the loss of perceptual information has generally been restricted to living things (Caramazza & Shelton). To explain why this feature deficit does not apply to artifacts as well, proponents of the model have proposed that because the features of man-made things are often closely related to their functions, it may be possible to generate perceptual properties for objects whose functional properties are retained (Moss et al., 1997; see also De Renzi & Lucchelli, 1994).

Despite these mixed findings, the weighted-features account, in our view, still merits serious consideration. For one thing, the anatomical locus of the living-things deficit is consistent with impaired processing of perceptual features. These patients tend to have damage in the inferior temporal cortex bilaterally (Breedin, Saffran, et al., 1994; Gainotti & Silveri, 1996; and note that herpes simplex encephalitis preferentially strikes at inferior and medial temporal cortices). The affected area borders on the region of visual association cortex that is concerned with the recognition of objects; and information from other sensory association areas converges on the anterior inferotemporal cortex on its way to medial structures such as the hippocampus. The model also makes sense from an evolutionary perspective. The need to know about the world in which we live is not unique to humans. Although language vastly expands the means for acquiring information, we, like other animals, learn about the world through visual and other sensory input.

Imaging Semantics in the Normal Brain

Recently, functional imaging techniques have been used in association with semantic tasks to identify brain regions involved in semantic operations. The neurologically intact participant is asked to name objects aloud or subvocally, to generate items from particular categories (e.g., names of animals), or to answer probe questions, at the same time that his or her brain activity is being imaged by PET or fMRI. One question addressed in such studies is whether semantic judgments to pictures and words activate a common substrate. The findings are that they do, and that the substrate is distributed within and around the left temporal lobe, specifically the temporoparietal junction, temporal-occipital junction (fusiform gyrus; BA 37), middle temporal gyrus, and inferior frontal gyrus (BA 11/47; Vandenberghe, Price, Wise, Josephs, & Frackowiak, 1996). This corresponds closely to the lesion sites in semantic dementia, except that anterior temporal lobe is not part of the activated network (see Murtha, Chertkow, Beauregard, & Evans, 1999). This raises questions as to whether anterior temporal atrophy affects semantic storage directly (as suggested by Breedin, Saffran,

et al., 1994, among others) or indirectly, by interrupting connections to components of the semantic network located farther back in the temporal and occipital lobes. A third possibility, argued by H. Damasio, Grabowski, Tranel, Hichwa, and Damasio (1996), is that the left anterior temporal lobe plays a key role in mediating between semantics and the mental lexicon, such that damage to this area disrupts not semantics but lexical-phonological retrieval (for opposing arguments, see Murtha et al., 1999).

Other activation studies have sought to specify the particular functions of regions in this distributed network, by varying properties of the primary and baseline tasks. One finding is that the temporal-occipital area (fusiform gyrus; BA 37) is involved in the processing of semantics (Murtha et al., 1999), and not low-level perceptual processing (Kanwisher, Woods, Iacoboni, & Mazziotta, 1997). Support for this comes from a study by Beauregard and colleagues (1997), who described left fusiform activity during passive viewing of animal names but not abstract words. The suggestion from this study, and from others reporting enhanced fusiform activation during the processing of living entities (Perani et al., 1995), is that the left fusiform area is an important component of the circuitry involved in the processing of animate entities or visual semantic features.

As to the neural circuitry of inanimate entities, a study by A. Martin, Wiggs, Ungerleider, and Haxby (1996) comports well with the lesion evidence and the weighted-features account. These investigators examined silent and oral naming of animals and tools against a baseline task that involved the viewing of nonsense figures. In this study, both types of objects generated activity in the fusiform gyrus bilaterally; however, tools selectively activated left-middle temporal areas and the left premotor area. The premotor area activated in tool naming was also active in a previous study in which subjects imagined grasping objects with the right hand (A. Martin, Haxby, Lalonde, & Ungerleider, 1995). The implication is that sensorimotor circuits involved in grasp programming are activated during the naming of tools, and, hence, that grasp information is part of the semantic representation of tools (see also Grafton, Fadiga, Arbib, & Rizzolatti, 1997). It should be noted that not all neuroimaging studies of tools have described premotor activation. However, there is convergent evidence that whereas the network activated by animals has a bilateral distribution, the network for tools is restricted to the left hemisphere (Cappa, Perani, Schnur, Tettamanti, & Fazio, 1998; Perani et al., 1995; and for lesion evidence, Tranel, Damasio, & Damasio, 1997).

Recent studies have also shed light on why the left prefrontal region (BA 44, 45, 46, 47) is frequently activated in semantic tasks. It appears that these areas are not, as once thought, involved in the storage of semantic information (e.g., Peterson, Fox, Posner, Mintun, & Raichle, 1988). Rather, prefrontal activation in semantic tasks varies as a function of task difficulty and is more likely related to control processes, such as working memory (Murtha et al., 1999) and competitive selection (Thompson-Schill, D'Esposito, Aguirre, & Farah, 1997).

THE COMPREHENSION OF SPOKEN LANGUAGE

The comprehension of spoken input is a complex process, involving (a) analysis of speech sounds via the extraction of spectral and temporal cues from the speech signal; (b) use of the products of this analysis to access entries in the internal lexicon and ultimately the meanings of words; (c) syntactic analysis if the input is sentential; and (d) interpretation of the meaning of the sentence, a process that requires the integration of several different forms of information (lexical, syntactic, and semantic).

Speech Perception and Word Deafness

Spoken speech poses a number of problems for the listener. Much of the information is carried by rapid changes in the speech signal—the cues that differentiate consonants, for example. Also, the information in the speech stream is transient; although readers can reexamine a word (and there is evidence that they do; see, e.g., Altmann, Garnham, & Dennis, 1992), listeners cannot, particularly if the current word is followed (and thereby overwritten) by others. There are additional difficulties, identified in the literature as the segmentation and invariance problems. The segmentation problem refers to the fact that there are often no spaces—no silent gaps—to signal the boundaries between the words of an utterance. There is evidence that consistency in the stress patterns of words may be utilized for this purpose; for example, English generally places stress on the first syllable of nouns, a pattern that infants become familiar with during the first year of life (Jusczyk, Cutler, & Redanz, 1993). The invariance problem refers to the variability of the signals associated with a given phoneme, which reflect the influence of the phonemes that surround it (*coarticulation*). This variation is evident in spectrographic displays of speech stimuli, where it can be seen, for example, that the sound associated with the /b/ in *about* is not the same as that of the /b/ in *table*. Although speech perception has been studied extensively, there is no general agreement on how the human auditory system copes with these complexities (see Miller & Eimas, 1995, for a review).

There is also no consensus on the mechanisms that underlie the ability to identify spoken words. Some investigators claim that words are recognized on the basis of auditory properties alone (e.g., Klatt, 1989); others maintain that word perception is phonetically based, or that it utilizes abstract phonological representations, or relies on the analysis of syllabic units (see Miller & Eimas, 1995, for a summary of these views). Across languages, word recognition may depend on different aspects of auditory input; for example, some languages (Thai, Mandarin Chinese) utilize tonal information, although most do not.

There is experimental evidence that contextual information is influential in the perception of speech. For example, partial phonological information is more likely to be filled in by the perceiver if the absent phoneme (replaced by a cough or noise) is part of a word as opposed to a nonword (Ganong, 1980; Warren, 1970). This suggests that there is feedback from partially activated lexical representations to prelexical stages of analysis of the input signal; some models of speech perception incorporate such effects (e.g., McClelland & Elman, 1986), but others manage to accommodate this result without adopting this assumption (Miller & Eimas, 1995). There is also evidence that contextual information from other words in the sentence facilitates word recognition. Listeners are quicker to recognize a previously identified target word in a sentence context if the syntax is correct and the sentence is semantically coherent (e.g., Marslen-Wilson & Tyler, 1980). On the other hand, it has also been shown that word recognition does not require either full or accurate input; remarkably, the identification of a word is seldom impeded by errors on the part of the speaker or partial masking by noise (e.g., Miller & Eimas). It appears that words are activated in parallel on the basis of partial information (e.g., hearing the sound "sih" will activate city, citizen, silly, simple, etc.) and some words can be recognized before they are completed (the *cohort theory;* Marslen-Wilson & Welsh, 1978) although the presence of activated neighbors can also slow recognition of a given word (Luce, Pisoni, & Goldinger, 1990).

Whatever the nature of the mechanisms for speech perception and lexical access, it is clear that they are supported by portions of the temporal lobe—the left temporal lobe, in particular. A portion of the superior temporal gyrus (Brodmann's area 41, or Heschl's gyrus), which extends medially into the Sylvian fissure, is the location of A1—primary auditory cortex, the brain region that receives input from earlier processing stations in the auditory pathway. Primary auditory cortex is surrounded by auditory association cortex, where the incoming signals undergo additional processing and identification. Evidence from functional imaging studies indicates that the left temporal lobe is more sensitive than the right when responding to auditory stimuli of brief temporal duration, an important characteristic of speech (e.g., Fitch, Miller, & Tallal, 1997). It is sometimes suggested that the left hemisphere's dominant role in language function is an outgrowth of its capacity to process rapid changes in auditory signals (J. Schwartz & Tallal, 1980).

Lesions in the left temporal auditory association area (Wernicke's area), which lies posterior and lateral to A1, give rise to an array of deficits that include impaired comprehension of spoken language as well as disturbances in production (see later discussion of Wernicke's aphasia). More rare are cases in which the impairment is limited to speech perception. This disorder, known as *pure word deafness,* results from smaller lesions in the left temporal lobe, or in some cases from damage to the temporal lobes bilaterally (e.g., Takahashi et al., 1992; Yaqub, Gascon, Al-Nosha, & Whitaker, 1988). Both types of lesion are likely to cut off auditory input to the left temporal lobe; the input pathways include fibers from the thalamus (medial geniculate nucleus) and from the homologous area in the right hemisphere that projects to the left temporal lobe via the corpus callosum. One illustration of the effect of bilateral lesions is the case reported by Praamstra, Hagoort, Maasen, and Crul (1991). This patient initially manifested Wernicke's aphasia as a result of a left temporal lesion; several years later, he suffered a right temporal lesion, which produced word deafness.

Patients with pure word deafness retain the ability to speak, and to understand written language; and while they continue to perceive spoken language as such, they have great difficulty comprehending speech and in repeating what is said to them. As an English-speaking word-deaf patient remarked to one of us, it seemed to him that people were speaking in a foreign language, and that his ears were disconnected from his voice (Saffran, Marin, & Yeni-Komshian, 1976). Word-deaf patients retain the ability to perceive vowels, which are long lasting and constant in form; but they perform poorly on tests of phoneme discrimination and identification that involve consonants. Consonants involve signals that undergo changes in frequency, and some include components that are very brief in duration.

Although word-deaf patients are severely impaired under most conditions, their comprehension of spoken language improves somewhat if they are allowed to read lips, or if other contextual information is provided (e.g., Saffran et al., 1976; Shindo, Kaga, & Tanaka, 1991). These effects suggest that top-down processes (information fed back from word representations) can be used to disambiguate a signal that is noisy or degraded. Some of these patients have no difficulty identifying nonspeech sounds, such as those produced by animals or musical instruments (e.g., Saffran et al.). Failure to recognize nonspeech stimuli is termed *auditory agnosia,* a condition generally associated with right temporal lobe lesions (e.g., Fujii et al., 1990). For a recent review and case summaries, see Simons and Lambon Ralph (1999).

Lexical Comprehension and Wernicke's Aphasia

To comprehend a word, it is necessary for the input signal to contact the appropriate entry in the *mental lexicon.* The lexical entry provides access to the word's meaning and to its grammatical properties (whether it is a noun or a verb; if a verb, whether it is transitive or intransitive, etc.), information that is required for the computation of syntactic structure.

Word comprehension failure is a cardinal feature of the syndrome known as Wernicke's aphasia. These patients typically have large left temporal lobe lesions including not just the classical Wernicke's area (posterior part of superior temporal gyrus) but also the posterior middle temporal gyrus and underlying white matter (Dronkers et al., 2000). Recent evidence suggests that a lesion restricted to Wernicke's area will not produce a chronic Wernicke's aphasia (Basso, Lecours, Moraschini, & Vanier, 1985; Dronkers et al.).

Wernicke's aphasia is far more common than word deafness, and its impact on language functions is more extensive. The comprehension problem is not limited to spoken language; reading comprehension is usually affected as well, although there are cases in which the patient does much better with printed than spoken input (e.g., Ellis, Miller, & Sin, 1983; Heilman, Rothi, Campanella, & Wolfson, 1979; Hillis, Boatman, Hart, & Gordon, 1999). In addition, there are deficits in language production, written as well as spoken. These patients tend to have difficulty finding the right words. Instead, they may substitute words that are related in meaning, or they may rely on pronouns and general terms such as *place* and *thing.* Their production may also be riddled with nonwords (neologisms). In extreme cases, speech is reduced to semantic or neologistic jargon, which is difficult if not impossible to comprehend.

The nature of the word comprehension deficit in Wernicke's aphasia is not well understood. Although it was earlier thought that the deficit reflects impaired phoneme perception (e.g., Luria, 1966), it is now recognized that there is little correlation between phoneme perception deficits and auditory comprehension impairments in aphasics (Blumstein, 1994). For example, Blumstein and her colleagues have demonstrated that patients with preserved phoneme discrimination may nevertheless be impaired in identifying speech sounds (Blumstein, Cooper, Zurif, & Caramazza, 1977; Blumstein, Tartter, Nigro, & Statlender, 1984), implying that comprehension may falter as a consequence of the speech input's failing to contact phonemic representations. The evidence is less than definitive, however, since the phonemic identification task requires matching the spoken input to a printed representation, and it is not clear that all the patients tested in this way have been capable of meeting the task demands.

Another likely locus for impaired word comprehension is in the access to semantic representations. Word comprehension is most often assessed by means of word-picture matching tests. Wernicke's aphasics perform poorly on such tests, and they have particular difficulty when the foils are phonologically similar to the target or belong to the same semantic category. The latter effect implicates semantic processing: If the patient were simply unable to perceive the speech sounds or map them onto a phonemic representation, the semantic similarity of the foils would not matter. That it does matter indicates that the perceived word is not accessing the full set of semantic features that distinguish one category member from another; recall that the same pattern was evident in semantic dementia.

One factor that differentiates at least some aphasics from semantic dementia patients is the aphasics' relatively well preserved performance on tests that utilize pictorial material exclusively. A task of this nature is the Pyramids and Palm Trees test developed by Howard and Patterson (1992), in which the subject is required to match one of two pictures to a third on the basis of conceptual similarity (e.g., a palm or pine tree to a pyramid). The same task can be administered using word stimuli. Patients who do well on the picture version of the test but poorly on comparable word-based assessments clearly have difficulty accessing meaning from words. The neurological basis for such word-only semantic deficits has not been established. However, Hart and Gordon (1990) performed an anatomical study on 3 aphasic patients with unusually pure semantic comprehension deficits, manifested on tests with spoken and written words and with pictures. Lesion overlap was found in the posterior temporal (BA 22, 21) and inferior parietal (BA 39, 40) regions (Hart & Gordon). It is possible that lesions here disrupt pathways between regions concerned with phonemic or lexical aspects of word recognition and those where semantic information is stored.

The fact that Wernicke's patients tend to perform better on picture-word matching tests when the foils are unrelated to the target suggests that they retain some knowledge of the meaning of the word. Other tasks provide additional evidence along these lines. One paradigm used to demonstrate partial preservation of semantic information depends on activation mediated by relationships among words, or *priming*. The subject hears or sees a word (the prime) that bears a relationship to a second word (the target); the task entails a response to the target, such as lexical decision (deciding whether it is a word or not) or pronunciation (if the word is written). Presentation of a semantically related prime normally speeds the response to the target word, in comparison to a prime that bears no relationship to the target. Milberg and Blumstein and their colleagues have shown that Wernicke's aphasics who perform poorly on word comprehension tasks demonstrate semantic priming effects on tasks such as lexical decision (e.g., Milberg & Blumstein, 1981; Milberg, Blumstein, & Dworetzky, 1988).

Phonological and Word Processing: Conclusions

It can be concluded that the left temporal lobe (superior temporal gyrus in particular) has special responsibility for the perception of speech and for contact with stored lexical information (phonemic and semantic). Evidence cited earlier suggests that semantic information is distributed over extensive areas of the brain; however, it seems likely that associations between the phonological specifications for words and their meanings are supported by structures in the left temporal lobe. It is interesting that damage to this region generally does not produce total loss of comprehension ability. What is compromised is the specificity of the comprehension process: Patients are prone to semantic error, and may show less selectivity to phonological information that is off target. These are properties that might be predicted of a degraded lexical network. What cannot be ascertained with any certainty at present is the extent to which these response characteristics reflect the behavior of residual left hemisphere functions, dependence on right hemisphere mechanisms, or both. As noted earlier, there is evidence that recovery from aphasia sometimes depends on right hemisphere structures, as subsequent damage to the right hemisphere returns the patient to prerecovery levels of language performance (e.g., Basso et al., 1989). The recent use of functional imaging has uncovered cases in which the right temporal lobe shows greater activation in subjects with left temporal lesions, compared to normal subjects (e.g., Cardebat et al., 1994; Weiller et al., 1995).

Sentence Comprehension

The lexical representation of a word is presumed also to specify the grammatical information needed to compute sentence-level syntactic structure (e.g., whether the word is a noun or verb, and if a verb, whether it is transitive or intransitive). This information is used to parse the word string into constituent phrases (noun phrase, verb phrase) that are then related to one another in a way that specifies structural information, such as which nouns go with which verbs; what is the subject of the main verb, the direct object of the embedded verb; and so on.

These early operations—sometimes designated the *first-pass parse* (Frazier, 1990)—are in the service of recovering the underlying message. Subsequent operations (the *second-pass parse*) interpret the nouns in relation to the verb, in order to ascertain who did what to whom. These operations are highly complex, in that they entail integration of information recovered from the lexical entry of the verb (e.g., what arguments it assigns) with the structural relations given in the first-pass parse. The importance of the structural information is readily conveyed by the difference between these sentences: *John gave Mary the broccoli* and *Mary gave John the broccoli*. Both sentences contain the same words, but the structural positions occupied by the nouns—and hence the meaning of the two sentences—are different. In the first, John is the subject and hence the agent of the exchange action; in the second, John is the direct object and hence the recipient. It must be appreciated that the mapping between syntactic arguments and thematic roles is different for different verbs; in the case of *receive,* for example, the sentential subject is the recipient, not the agent; in the case of *pass,* the sentential subject can also be the *theme* (what passes; as in *The broccoli passed from John to Mary*).

The ease of recovering thematic role information depends, in part, on constituent structure, and it is made more difficult when there is a delay between the occurrence of a word and the information that specifies its thematic role. For example, in the object relative sentence *The man that Tom's sister Mary gave the broccoli to was named John,* many words intervene between when *the man* appears and when it can be assigned the role of recipient.

There are also instances in which the structure of the sentence is temporarily ambiguous. Consider a sentence containing a reduced relative clause that is not marked by a relative pronoun, for example, *The defendant examined by the lawyer turned out to be guilty,* where defendant might initially be taken as the subject of the verb. This ambiguity can only be resolved by information that comes later in the sentence. An issue much debated in the sentence comprehension literature concerns the degree of independence of syntactic and semantic processing—specifically, whether early syntactic processing is influenced by the meaning of the verb. Some linguists and psycholinguists favor autonomous syntactic processing, at least in the early recovery of constituent structure (e.g., Frazier, 1990), although a good deal of the recent evidence supports interaction (e.g., Trueswell, Tanenhaus, & Garnsey, 1994). The case for interaction is strengthened by recent ERP studies that focus on a component of the ERP waveform (the N400) that is sensitive to semantic processing during sen-

tence (and discourse) comprehension. The fact that this component is present within 200 ms of the first word and increases in amplitude with successive words is taken as evidence that semantic processing operates early and incrementally across a sentence (Brown, Hagoort, & Kutas, 2001).

Sentence Comprehension Disorders

Not surprisingly, patients who are impaired at the single-word level (e.g., Wernicke's aphasics) are also impaired in comprehending sentences. Of greater interest is the performance of patients who do relatively well on single-word comprehension. The group whose sentence processing performance has attracted most interest is that of agrammatic Broca's aphasics. These are patients whose primary deficit is in producing sentences; their output is characterized by simple and fragmented phrase structure and the omission and substitution of closed-class elements. By *closed-class elements* we mean free-standing function words (e.g., *to, the, is*) and bound affixes (e.g., *-ing, -ed*). In contrast to nouns, verbs, and adjectives, this segment of the vocabulary does not expand over the lifetime, hence the designation *closed class.* The nature of agrammatic speech is discussed in detail shortly; for present purposes, the important point is that agrammatic Broca's aphasics typically demonstrate good comprehension of single words, particularly concrete nouns. They also do well with sentence comprehension, but only when the sentences and picture choices are semantically constrained. To understand what is meant by this, compare the following example of a nonreversible sentence, example number 3, with the semantically reversible sentence, example number 4. Whereas the lexical content constrains the meaning of number 3, in that apples cannot eat and boys are unlikely to be red, it does not constrain the meaning of number 4. An individual who was not sensitive to—or failed to utilize—the syntactic structure of number 4 would have difficulty determining which person was kissing the other, and which of the two happened to be tall.

3. The apple that the boy ate was red.

4. The boy that the girl kissed was tall.

In 1976, Caramazza and Zurif demonstrated that agrammatic Broca's aphasics had difficulty understanding semantically reversible sentences such as number 4, although they performed quite well on semantically constrained sentences such as number 3. This finding has been replicated many times since. The comprehension pattern defined by good performance on semantically constrained sentences but poor performance on semantically reversible sentences has come to be known as *receptive agrammatism.*

Receptive agrammatism is most apparent with sentences like number 4, which, in addition to being reversible, also violates standard word order. In English, the agent generally precedes the verb and the recipient or patient follows it. In object relatives such as sentence 4 and passive sentences such as *The boy was kissed by the girl,* the recipient of the action (the boy) does not occupy the postverbal position, as it does in the canonical active (*The girl kissed the boy*). Object relatives and passives pose serious problems for receptive agrammatics.

The combination of agrammatic production and the apparent failure to use syntactic information in sentence comprehension gave rise to the notion of a central syntactic impairment in Broca's aphasia that affected receptive and expressive language processing in similar ways (e.g., Berndt & Caramazza, 1980). It was suggested, for example, that receptive agrammatism reflected an insensitivity to closed-class elements that paralleled the patients' difficulty in retrieving these elements in sentence production (e.g., Bradley, Garrett, & Zurif, 1980; for a more recent version of this hypothesis, see Pulvermuller, 1995). One implication of this view was that some or all aspects of syntactic knowledge was represented in the area of the left frontal lobe that is damaged in Broca's aphasia. However, this hypothesis was soon challenged by other findings.

First, there were reports of patients who exhibited expressive agrammatism without receptive agrammatism (e.g., Miceli, Mazzucchi, Menn, & Goodglass, 1983; Nespoulous et al., 1988). Second, Linebarger, Schwartz, and Saffran (1983; and Linebarger, 1990, 1995) found that some patients with expressive and receptive agrammatism showed preserved sensitivity to a wide range of grammatical violations, including some that involved noncanonical sentence structures (e.g., **John was finally kissed Louise*) and the types of closed-class elements that were absent from their speech (e.g., the passive morphology in the example just given). Testing in other laboratories confirmed these results (e.g., Shankweiler, Crain, Gorrell, & Tuller, 1989; Wulfeck, 1988) and ruled out the possibility that success in the grammaticality judgment task might be achieved without benefit of a syntactic analysis, for example, by simply rejecting unusual prosodic patterns created by the omission or addition of sentence constituents. (For evidence against this interpretation, see Berndt, Salasoo, Mitchum, & Blumstein, 1988.)

Word monitoring is another paradigm that has been used to investigate syntactic processing in aphasics. In this task, the subject hears a word that subsequently recurs in the context of a sentence. The instructions are to press a button when the word reappears. This method is highly sensitive to syntactic and semantic constraints; response latencies are shorter for words that appear in semantically anomalous but syntactically well-formed sentences (as in the following example 6) as compared to scrambled word strings (example 7), and they are shorter still for sentences that are semantically coherent (example 5; Marslen-Wilson & Tyler, 1980). Word monitoring is also sensitive to syntactic violation. For example, subjects take longer to recognize *dog* in example number 8 than in number 9.

5. Normal   The bishop placed the *crown* on the king's head

6. Anomalous   The shelf kept the *crown* on the apartment's church

7. Scrambled   Shelf on the church *crown* the apartment's the kept

(probe is *crown*)

The monitoring task has the virtue of simplicity: All the subject has to do is detect the word target; conscious deliberation as to grammaticality or plausibility is not required. Some agrammatic patients tested on this task have shown normal patterns of sensitivity to grammatical violations (Tyler, 1992; Tyler, Ostrin, Cooke, & Moss, 1995).

8. *He continued to struggle the *dog* but he couldn't break free.

9. He continued to struggle with *dog* but he couldn't break free.

Note the paradox: Agrammatics demonstrate sensitivity to structural constraints in monitoring and grammaticality judgment tasks, yet they fail to use structure information to guide sentence interpretation. To explain this paradox, we and our colleagues have suggested that the patients are impaired in utilizing the products of the first-pass parse to form accurate, verb-specific linkages between syntactic arguments and thematic roles. We termed this the *mapping hypothesis* (e.g., Linebarger, 1995; M. F. Schwartz, Linebarger, & Saffran, 1985; M. F. Schwartz, Linebarger, Saffran, & Pate, 1987). A different but related formulation was proposed by Grodzinsky (1990, 2000). According to Chomsky's (1981) government and binding theory, some sentences are derived by movement of constituents from canonical positions to other positions in the sentence. This movement leaves behind a trace (t), which co-indexes the empty position with the element that was moved. In example 10, the trace (t_1) co-indexes *the boy* with the empty direct object, which establishes its thematic role as the recipient of the kissing action:

10. The boy$_1$ was kissed t_1 by the girl.

Grodzinsky claimed that receptive agrammatism stems from inability to represent or utilize traces. As evidence he cited the fact that patients perform well on sentences that lack traces (e.g., active voice sentences in English) and poorly on those that contain them (e.g., passives and object relatives). While this generalization holds for many patients, there are also many exceptions; Berndt, Mitchum, and Haendiges (1996) found that across a number of studies, approximately one third of the patients performed poorly on actives, and another third performed equally poorly on actives and passives. Moreover, it has been shown that patients retain their sensitivity to traces in grammaticality judgment tasks, where they detect violations that illegally fill a gap that marks the presence of a trace (Linebarger, 1995). Nevertheless, the debate goes on; for the most recent statement of the trace-deletion hypothesis, see Grodzinsky (2000); for opposing arguments, see the discussion that accompanies that article.

The mapping-deficit hypothesis gave rise to efforts to rehabilitate receptive agrammatism by focusing on the relations between structural positions and thematic roles. These efforts have yielded mixed results (see reviews in Fink, 2001; Marshall, 1995) and a renewed appreciation for all that is required for mapping to be accomplished successfully. For one thing, the patient must retain access to the relevant information about verbs—their argument structure and their mapping requirement. This is clearly a problem for some patients (Breedin & Martin, 1996). Moreover, because thematic role assignment is an integrative process, with multiple forms of information contributing, it is demanding of computational resources. Conceivably, then, the deficit in sentence comprehension results from reduced resource capacity.

The resource account has been forcefully argued based on the finding that neurologically intact individuals show similar performance decrements as aphasics (albeit less severe) under experimental conditions that restrict resources (e.g., *rapid serial visual presentation [RSVP]* of sentence materials; Miyake, Carpenter, & Just, 1994). Moreover, the affected resource has been equated with "working memory for comprehension" and invoked also to explain why certain neurologically intact individuals (including healthy older adults) have trouble understanding syntactically complex sentences, such as object relatives (Just & Carpenter, 1992). On the other hand, it has been shown that Alzheimer's patients with marked reduction in this working memory capacity do not show the aphasic comprehension pattern. Comprehension in these patients is systematically related to the number of propositions expressed in the sentence but not to the syntactic complexity, whereas in aphasics it is affected by both factors. Caplan and Waters (1999) argue that the contrasting comprehension patterns in these two populations result from different deficits: The aphasics are deficient in a resource dedicated to the computation of syntactic structure, whereas the problem in the Alzheimer's patients reflects a general working memory limitation. Whether this account will stand up to further testing remains to be seen.

Neuroanatomy of Sentence Comprehension

Aphasia research demonstrates that both the posterior and anterior language areas are involved in language comprehension. To this point, functional imaging studies have corroborated the involvement of these areas, but have done little to elucidate their functions further.

Auditory stimuli activate superior temporal cortex in both cerebral hemispheres (Habib & Demonet, 1996; Demonet et al., 1992). The region activated by words as well as nonwords generally includes BA 22, 41, and 42 bilaterally (e.g., Binder et al., 1997). The left superior temporal lobe is activated by spoken stimuli in a language (Tamil) unfamiliar to the subjects (who were French), indicating that this area may be involved in prelexical processing of speech input (Mazoyer et al., 1993; but see Naatanen et al., 1997, for evidence of a language-specific response in the left temporal lobe).

Studies using electric current to disrupt operations carried out by the stimulated brain area have confirmed the importance of left temporal lobe structures in speech perception and comprehension. Boatman and colleagues (1995) examined such effects in three patients with indwelling subdural electrode arrays, implanted prior to surgery for intractable epilepsy. Three types of tasks were administered, with and without electrical stimulation: phoneme discrimination (e.g., *pa-ta*); phoneme identification (matching a consonant-vowel syllable to an array of four written choices); and word and sentence comprehension. Stimulation sites in the left superior temporal gyrus elicited several different patterns: comprehension impaired, but discrimination and identification spared; comprehension and identification impaired, but discrimination spared; discrimination, identification, and comprehension all impaired. In each patient, the sites where stimulation disrupted all three functions were located more anteriorly than the sites where comprehension alone was impaired.

Sentence comprehension has been examined using functional imaging techniques. Several PET studies have shown greater regional cerebral blood blow (rCBF) in Broca's area as a function of increased syntactic complexity (Caplan, Alpert, & Waters, 1998; Stromswold, Caplan, Alpert, & Rauch, 1996). However, in an fMRI study by Just, Carpenter, Keller, Eddy, and Thulborn (1996), activity increased in both Broca's and Wernicke's areas as syntactic complexity increased, and the same was true (albeit at a lower level) for the right hemisphere homologues of these two areas. A more recent fMRI study describes right perisylvian activation during a grammaticality judgment task that required repair of the anomalous element, but not otherwise (Meyer, Friederici, & von Cramon, 2000). This unexpected evidence for a right hemisphere contribution to sentence processing is sure to be followed up and clarified in the next generation of functional imaging studies.

Another recent fMRI study, this one involving sentence reading, found activation in Broca's and Wernicke's areas, along with a region in the anterior temporal lobe (Bavelier et al., 1997) that was also active in an earlier PET study involving sentence materials (Mazoyer et al., 1993). It has been suggested that this anterior temporal area plays a role in morphosyntactic processing (Dronkers, Wilkins, Van Valin, Redfern, & Jaeger, 1994).

Sentence Comprehension: Conclusions

Despite extensive research, the contributions to sentence comprehension of Wernicke's and Broca's areas remain obscure. The patient studies just reviewed indicate that agrammatic Broca's aphasics, who tend to have large frontoparietal lesions, still manage to perform well on syntactic processing tasks that are not resource demanding (i.e., grammaticality judgment tasks and comprehension of sentences with canonical word order). It may be that these more automatic syntactic tasks are supported by circuitry in and around Wernicke's area, in which case the various resource accounts of comprehension deficit in Broca's patients become increasingly plausible. Certainly, the proximity of Broca's area to the dorsolateral prefrontal structures known to play a role in executive working memory (BA 46, 9) lends credence to idea that the role of Broca's area in syntactic processing is related to temporary information storage or manipulation (Caplan et al., 1998; Miyake et al., 1994). In the domain of visual processing, there is evidence that prefrontal cortex operates in tandem with more posterior brain regions to sustain activation across a delay (e.g., Goldman-Rakic, 1995; Smith et al., 1995). Our suspicion is that Broca's area plays a similar role with respect to the language-processing regions in the temporal lobes.

THE PRODUCTION OF SPOKEN LANGUAGE

Lexical Retrieval

To a first approximation, one can conceptualize the production of a sentence as comprehension in reverse. The speaker's task is to formulate a message that specifies the thematic content of the sentence, select the words and the syntactic form suitable to express this content, order the words in a manner dictated by the syntax, and encode this in a phonetic form for articulation.

It occasionally happens in normal speech that the selection of words from the mental lexicon (i.e., *lexical retrieval*) goes awry, such that the wrong word is uttered (examples 11, 12), or the right word at the wrong time (example 13), or with the wrong pronunciation (14). At other times, lexical retrieval comes up short, leading to the effortful search known as the *tip-of-the-tongue (TOT) state.*

11. It's a far cry from the twenty-five *dollar* days. (cents: semantic error)

12. You look all set for an *exhibition*. (expedition: formal error)

13. I left the *briefcase* in my *cigar*. (word exchange error)

14. *j*epartment (department: sound error)

Close scrutiny of TOTs and speech errors has given rise to an influential theory of production that incorporates two stages of lexical retrieval, each associated with a controlling structure. The controlling structures are often conceptualized as frames with slots that receive the lexical representations (Bock & Levelt, 1994; Dell, 1986; Garrett, 1975; MacKay, 1972; Shattuck-Hufnagel, 1979). The first stage of lexical retrieval ends with selection of an abstract (prephonological) word form that is specified semantically and syntactically (Kempen & Huijbers, 1983). This is known as the *lemma*. Lemma retrieval is controlled by a syntactic frame; selected lemmas are inserted into slots marked for subject noun, main verb, and so on. The second stage of lexical retrieval adds phonological form information. This stage is controlled by frames that specify the phonological structure of a word or phrase; selected segments are inserted into slots marked for syllable onset consonant, medial vowel, and the like.

The two-stage theory explains TOTs as instances in which the lemma is retrieved but phonological retrieval fails. The speaker knows what she wants to say and can supply a definition or synonym. If the language is one that marks nouns for grammatical gender, the speaker in TOT may retain access to this syntactic feature despite being unable to report anything about how the word sounds (Badecker, Miozzo, & Zanuttini, 1995; Vigliocco, Antonini, & Garrett, 1997). However, retrieval of phonology is not always completely blocked. In one third to one half of experimentally elicited TOTs, speakers demonstrate partial access, in that they accurately report the first sound or letter of the sought-after word, its length or stress pattern, or words that sound similar to the target (see Brown, 1991, for review). This indicates that a word's phonology is represented in piecemeal fashion and that second-stage retrieval involves multiple selection acts and a process of assembly. This is consistent with phonological speech errors, wherein individual phonological units, typically phonemes, undergo substitution (see example 14), addition (example 15), or deletion (16), or movement to a new location in the word or phrase (17–19).

15. winn*d*ing (winning: sound addition)

16. *tremenly* (tremendously; deletion)

17. *l*ork *y*ibrary (York library: sound exchange)

18. *l*eading list (reading list: sound anticipation)

19. beef n*ee*dle (beef noodle: sound perseveration)

A question much debated in the speech production literature is whether the two stages of lexical retrieval are informationally encapsulated (i.e., *modular*). They are rightly considered modular if semantic-syntactic information does not influence phonological retrieval and phonological information does not influence lemma retrieval. An influential model of this type is described in Levelt, Roelofs, and Meyer (1999). The alternative to the modular model is one that postulates *interactive activation* (Dell, 1986; Dell & Reich, 1981; Harley, 1984; Houghton, 1990; Stemberger, 1985). The hallmark of interactive activation models is their nonmodularity; because activation spreads continuously and bidirectionally, early stages of processing are influenced by information from later stages, and vice versa (McClelland & Rumelhart, 1981).

Do semantic and phonological information sources interact during word retrieval? There is evidence on both sides. Although most word substitution errors bear either a semantic (example 11) or phonological (12) relation to the target, the frequency of mixed (semantic plus phonological) word substitution errors (e.g., *pelican* for *penguin*) is significantly higher, for both normals and aphasics, than the modular model predicts it should be (Dell & Reich, 1981; Harley, 1984; N. Martin, Weisberg, & Saffran, 1989; N. Martin, Gagnon, Schwartz, Dell, & Saffran, 1996). Whereas the mixed error evidence favors the interactive model, however, experiments on the time course of semantic and phonological retrieval in lexical access show conclusively that the interaction, if it exists at all, must be limited. At the earliest points, processing appears to be exclusively semantic; however, just prior to articulation, the retrieval of phonological information completely dominates that of semantic information (Levelt et al., 1991; Schriefers, Meyer, & Levelt, 1990).

In response to these findings, Dell and colleagues have proposed an interactive activation model of retrieval in which interactivity is combined with a two-step selection process (Dell, Schwartz, Martin, Saffran, & Gagnon, 1997; see also Dell & O'Seaghdha, 1991). In effect, the model represents a compromise between strictly modular accounts and more fully interactive ones.

An Interactive Activation Model of Lexical Retrieval

Like other interactive activation models of lexical processing, the two-step interactive activation model (henceforth, 2-IA) has lexical knowledge represented in a layered network of units or nodes. *Nodes* are not repositories for stored information, but rather simple, neuron-like devices that collect, summate, and transmit activation. An important distinction among connectionist models is whether they use a local or distributed style of representation. In localist models, nodes stand in one-to-one correspondence with psychologically meaningful properties. Such is the case in the 2-IA model, where the top level in the network represents semantic features, the middle level represents known lemmas, and the bottom level represents phonemes (Figure 21.6).

In this model, a *concept* is represented as a collection of semantic features. When these features are turned on (e.g., by a to-be-named picture), activation spreads freely for some period of time. It spreads to lemmas, which send a portion of their activation down to phonemes and up to the semantic features. From the phonemes, activation spreads back up to lemmas. This reciprocal feedback from phonemes to lemmas, occurring prior to lemma selection, is what makes the model interactive; information about the target's phonology (step 2 information) is entering into selection at the first (semantic-syntactic) stage of lexical retrieval. After some time (assumed to vary with speech rate), the most highly activated lemma is selected by the syntactic frame (a single noun frame, in the case of naming). The second step happens when, after another period of activation spread, the most activated onset, vowel, and coda phonemes are selected. This ends the trial. If the model selects *cat* at step 1 and /k/, /æ/ and /t/ at step 2, it has performed correctly. Otherwise it has made an error.

All connections in the 2-IA model are excitatory and bidirectional. At each step in time, a node's activation level is determined by what it was on the prior time step, the rate at which it dissipates activation (the *decay factor*), and how much activation it is receiving from other nodes. The latter is determined by the strength of its connections, as well as random noise that is added to the model to simulate a variety of probabilistic influences. To simplify matters, all connections in the model are assigned the same weights, so that all transmit activation with the same strength. Similarly, all nodes lose activation at the same (decay) rate. The weight and decay parameters are preset; there is no learning in the model.

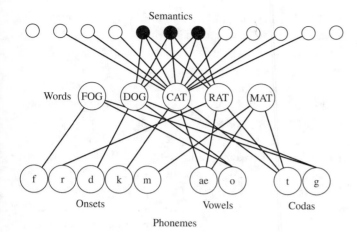

Semantics

Words

FOG   DOG   CAT   RAT   MAT

f   r   d   k   m   ae   o   t   g

Onsets   Vowels   Codas

Phonemes

Figure 21.6 Illustration of a lexical network for the interactive two-step model of naming. Connections are excitatory and bidirectional. The common semantic features of *cat, dog,* and *rat* are shaded in black. From "Lexical Access in Aphasic and Nonphasic Speakers," by G. S. Dell, M. F. Schwartz, N. Martin, E. M. Saffran, and D. A. Gagnon, 1997, *Psychological Review, 104,* pp. 801–838. Copyright 1997 by American Psychological Association, Washington, D.C.

We have seen that the model's feedback connections cause it to behave interactively. What makes the model quasi-modular is what happens at each of the selection steps. First, the selected node is linked to the controlling frame (syntactic at step 1, phonological at step 2) and its activation level is set to zero (postselection inhibition). Next, the selected node is given a strong activation jolt by the controlling frame, to get the next stage of encoding started. On account of these jolts, which operate in top-down fashion, semantic influences predominate early and phonological influence late in a trial, just as the experimental evidence requires (Dell & O'Seaghdha, 1991).

Let us now consider errors. Misselections at step 1 can give rise to semantic, formal, mixed, or unrelated errors. Semantic errors (*dog* for *cat*) are encouraged by the overlap in semantic features (see Figure 21.6). (The model does not specify the content of the features, but the overlap is intended to represent the fact that the concepts *dog* and *cat,* for example, share features such as "animate," "animal," "pet," etc.) The features activated by a picture of a cat will also partially activate the semantic neighbors of *cat,* namely *dog* and *rat.* This sets up a competition among the semantically related lemmas and, because the system is noisy, the target will sometimes lose out, resulting in a semantic error.

Formal errors (*mat* for *cat*) are encouraged by bottom-up feedback to lemmas from the primed phonemes (/a/, /t/). The effect of this feedback is to activate the phonological neighbors of *cat,* thereby setting the stage for a formal error to be generated at step 1.

Neighbors of cat that are related to it semantically and phonologically (i.e., mixed competitors) benefit from both top-down and bottom-up activation. This confers an advantaged for these mixed neighbors over those that are purely semantic or purely phonological. As we noted earlier, it has consistently been found that semantic and formal influences are not independent (i.e., mixed errors are more likely than semantic errors that happen to be phonologically related or phonological errors that happen to be semantically related; e.g., del Viso, Igoa, & Garcia-Albert, 1991; Dell & Reich, 1981; N. Martin et al., 1989). Bottom-up feedback is the model's way of explaining this mixed error effect.

Unrelated competitors benefit from neither top-down nor bottom-up activation. Still, in a noisy system, they will sometimes be selected, thereby creating an unrelated error.

Misselections at step 2 give rise to sound errors. Most of these are neologisms (e.g., *dat* for *cat*), but word errors may also arise at this step, when the substituted phoneme happens by chance to create another word (*rat; mat*).

This simple model can handle a number of facts about speech errors. We have already discussed how it explains the mixed error effect. Now consider formal errors: The speech error literature shows that such errors nearly always respect the syntactic category of the target (Fay & Cutler, 1977). In the model, this results from having formals arise at lemma selection, which is controlled by the syntactic frame. Moreover, the model's interactivity explains why having many phonological neighbors has a protective effect against TOT states, formal errors, and phonological errors (Gordon, 2001; Harley & Bown, 1998; Vitevitch & Sommers, 2001; Vitevitch, 1997, 2001): Bottom-up feedback from the activated neighbors helps the target accumulate activation faster and more effectively than might otherwise be the case.

Finally, it has been shown that when the model is implemented on a computer, it is possible to set the parameters (i.e., connection weight, decay, noise, etc.) so that the model's output closely matches the naming patterns of normal speakers performing the Philadelphia Naming Test (PNT; Roach, Schwartz, Martin, Grewal, & Brecher, 1996). By *naming pattern* we mean the proportion of correct responses and various types of error that are produced. Simulated lesions, created by altering only one or two of the model's parameters away from the normal setting, produce a diverse array of naming patterns closely matching the data of individual aphasic subjects. Moreover, the type of lesion that the model assigned to the patients turns out to be predictive of a number of other aspects of their behavior (Dell et al., 1997; Foygel & Dell, 2000).

We believe that the many accomplishments of the model constitute strong evidence for the correctness of 2-IA architecture for lexical retrieval. Not all agree with this, however. For lively debate and discussion, the reader should consult Ruml and Caramazza (2000) and the rejoinder in Dell and colleagues (2000), as well as Rapp and Goldrick (2000).

Disorders of Lexical Retrieval

Lexical retrieval failures are ubiquitous in aphasia. On picture naming tests, the standard for measuring lexical retrieval, aphasics routinely score below normal. Differences across aphasia subtypes, which are marked in conversational speech, are reduced in picture naming, with semantic and phonological errors occurring in all groups (Howard, Patterson, Franklin, Orchard-Lisle, & Morton, 1984). Severity effects are well documented: Patients who score lower on naming tests tend to produce errors that are more remote, semantically and phonologically, from the targets (Dell et al., 1997; Schuell & Jenkins, 1961; Schwartz & Brecher, 2000). On the other hand, individual patients of comparable severity may exhibit distinctive error patterns, featuring predominant or exclusive occurrence of one type of error or another. In-depth study of such patients has yielded important insights into the nature of lexical retrieval and the adequacy of current models. What follows is a brief and selective review.

Semantic Errors

Semantic impairment such as is evident on lexical comprehension tasks also predisposes to semantic errors in naming and other production tasks (Gainotti, Silveri, Villa, & Miceli, 1984). Patient KE, studied by Hillis, Rapp, Romani, and Carmazza (1990), provides a particularly clear example. Following a left hemisphere stroke, KE evinced significant difficulties in comprehension and production of single words. On a comprehension test involving auditory word-picture match, he chose the semantic foil on 40% of trials. He produced semantic errors at approximately the same rate in picture naming (38%) and on a variety of other lexical tasks (e.g., 32% semantic errors in written naming; 35% in oral reading). This pattern, and the fact that the same items elicited semantic errors in naming and comprehension tasks, indicates a common source for the semantic errors, presumably in the semantic system (see also Allport & Funnell, 1981; Howard & Orchard-Lisle, 1984).

Caramazza and colleagues have reported on other patients who produced high rates of semantic errors in naming, but who had intact lexical comprehension (Caramazza & Hillis, 1990; Rapp, Benzing, & Caramazza, 1997). Like KE, these patients made no formal or phonological errors in naming. The 2-IA model has difficulty explaining this pure semantic error pattern in patients with intact semantics, at least with

the simulated lesions that have thus far been entertained. For example, lesioning the model in a way that restricts the spread of activation from semantics to lemmas promotes formal as well as semantic errors (on account of the feedback from phonemes), and lesioning it in a way that limits the spread of activation from lemmas to phonemes promotes phonological (nonword) errors. (For analysis and discussion, see Foygel & Dell, 2000; Rapp & Goldrick, 2000). The alternative model invoked by Caramazza and Hillis assumes that semantic representations directly activate phonological word forms (*lexemes*), and that they do so to a degree proportional to their shared semantics. For example, the semantic representation of *chair* activates the phonological forms for *table, sofa, couch,* and the like, in addition to that for *chair*. Normally, *chair* will be the most activated, and consequently will be produced. However, the argument goes, brain damage may render particular lexemes resistant to retrieval; and when that happens, another of the activated semantic cohort is likely to be substituted. In this way, the model accounts for the pure semantic naming pattern in patients with intact comprehension. However, the model has no explanation for formal errors, our next topic.

Formal Errors

Throughout much of the history of aphasia studies, formal errors were looked upon as another form of phonological distortion, in the same category as nonword errors. As these errors began to take on importance in psycholinguistic production theories (Fay & Cutler, 1977), they attracted more interest from aphasiologists as well. The close scrutiny paid off with evidence that in certain patients the frequency of formal errors is greater than chance (i.e., greater than the frequency of word errors that happen to be phonologically related to the target or of phonological errors that happen by chance to be words). Moreover, compared to a corpus of words generated from random phoneme sequences, the formal errors gathered from patients are more likely to be nouns and to have a higher frequency of occurrence (Gagnon, Schwartz, Martin, Dell, & Saffran, 1997). This is clear indication that formal errors, at least in some patients, arise at the lexical stage and not from postlexical phonological substitution.

There have been several case studies published of patients who produce formal errors in naming at rates high enough to rule out chance occurrence (Best, 1996; Blanken, 1990, 1998; N. Martin & Saffran, 1992). NC, the patient reported by N. Martin and Saffran, was subsequently the subject of a modelling study in which his naming and repetition patterns were simulated with the computer-implemented 2-IA model (N. Martin, Dell, Saffran, & Schwartz, 1994; N. Martin,

Saffran, & Dell, 1996). This study showed that when the model was lesioned by increasing the rate of activation decay throughout the network, the pattern of errors closely matched the high-formals pattern that NC produced early in his clinical course. Over time, NC's performance improved and the naming pattern shifted in the direction of the normal pattern (more semantic than formal errors). This recovery pattern also was simulated, by shifting the value of the decay parameter closer to the normal setting. The reason a 2-IA decay impairment promotes formal errors is that it allows operations occurring late in the retrieval interval (i.e., activation of phoneme nodes and phoneme-to-word feedback) to exert a more substantial influence on the character of errors than operations occurring earlier. For naming, this entails that formals are favored over semantic errors. This contrasts with a connection strength lesion, which limits the extent to which higher nodes prime lower nodes and additionally limit the feedback from lower to higher nodes. With network-wide lesions of connection strength, the rate of formal errors is lower, relative to semantic errors and nonwords.

Acquired Tip-of-the-Tongue Phenomena

Persons with aphasia frequently profess to knowing the word that names a given picture or that meets a definition, while at the same time being unable to say it. What is it that the patient actually knows in this state? One possibility is that he or she has in mind the preverbal concept that is appropriate to the picture or definition. Another possibility is that the patient has a specific word in mind and thus is in a state akin to TOT. The fact that first-phoneme cueing has a facilitative effect on word retrieval for many aphasic patients strongly supports the latter account.

An early TOT elicitation study, performed with patients from all the major aphasic categories, found that Broca's, conduction, and Wernicke's aphasics reliably succeeded in identifying the first letter of words they were unable to access in naming. The conduction group exhibited such partial knowledge more often than the others, whereas the anomic group did not exceed the chance rate for first-letter identification (Goodglass, Kaplan, Weintraub, & Ackerman, 1976). Case studies have shown that individual anomic patients vary in the type and amount of information that remains accessible to them. A patient reported by Badecker and colleagues (1995), who was a native Italian speaker, was unable to report anything at all about the phonological forms of words he failed to access in naming and sentence completion tasks. On the other hand, this patient was invariably able to report the grammatical gender of the words that eluded him, a clear indication that he had accessed the corresponding lemma. A French-speaking patient, in addition to being able to report grammatical gender, often provided spelling information (e.g., first letter) and, amazingly, the alternative meaning for a name that happened to be a homophone (Henaff Gonon, Bruckert, & Michel, 1989). An example from English would be if a patient failed to name a picture of a pad (tablet) but reported that the elusive word was slang for *apartment*. Anomic patient GM, studied in Lambon Ralph, Sage, and Roberts (2000), correctly reported the number of syllables of unavailable words and whether they were compounds, but he was unable to provide first letter or sound information.

It is apparent, then, that anomic and other patients are frequently in a condition in which they access less than the complete phonological specification of the target word. This is more likely to happen with low frequency words than high. Frequency is known to operate at the level of phonological retrieval (Jescheniak & Levelt, 1994), and it is consistent with this that patients access more phonological information in connection with high-frequency targets than low (Kay & Ellis, 1987).

For some patients, successful retrieval of target phonology is also subject to semantic influences. For example, GM, the anomic patient studied by Lambon Ralph and colleagues (2000), produced more omissions in naming when the picture was preceded by a semantically related word (semantic priming) and when naming trials were blocked by semantic category. Other patients are susceptible to *miscueing,* such that phonological retrieval is suppressed when a name is cued by the first sound of a semantic relative (e.g., picture of a tiger cued with the sound /l/; Howard & Orchard-Lisle, 1984). Miscueing induces some patients to make semantic substitutions (*lion*), which, if their semantics are intact, they promptly reject as the correct answer (Lambon Ralph et al.).

These acquired TOT phenomena strongly support models of lexical access that distinguish lemma retrieval from phonological retrieval and that allow phonological activation to begin even before lemma selection has been finalized (the *cascading activation* assumption; see McClelland, 1979). Without lemmas, it is hard to explain how access to grammatical features can be preserved in the absence of phonology. Without cascading activation, miscuing would be a mystery: Why would hearing /l/ induce the patient to say *lion* unless the phonology of *lion* had already been primed by the picture of the tiger? On a more basic level, these TOT phenomena demonstrate convincingly that one can activate partial information about a word's pronunciation. This point is critical to the understanding of neologisms, our next topic.

Target-Related Neologisms

In an influential paper, Ellis et al., 1983 (also see Miller & Ellis, 1987) showed that the neologisms produced by a Wernicke's aphasic patient (RD) had much in common with TOT phenomena. Relative to the target words, RD's neologisms contained the correct phonemes and the correct number of syllables more often than would be expected by chance. Also, the probability of his being able to produce a word correctly was strongly dependent on frequency of usage; neologisms occurred much more often to low-frequency words. These seminal findings have been replicated in larger studies as well (e.g., Gagnon et al., 1997; Schwartz, Wilshire, Gagnon, & Polansky, 2002).

Our group has analyzed hundreds of neologisms generated by fluent aphasic patients tested on the PNT. These errors turn out to be graded with respect to target overlap: In some cases, error and target share many phonemes; in other cases, they share few. In general, there is a strong effect of severity, such that patients with low correctness scores in naming are likely to make more neologisms—and more remote neologisms—than are those with high correctness scores (Schwartz & Brecher, 2000; Schwartz et al., 2002). In addition, certain patients produce a disproportionate number of such errors. The Wernicke's aphasic patient, RD, is one such case. Most others described in the literature are individuals with conduction aphasia (e.g., Caplan, Vanier, & Baker, 1986; Pate, Saffran, & Martin, 1987).

According to the 2-IA model, neologisms arise when—on the second retrieval step—one or more incorrect phonemes are selected. Such errors are encouraged by weak connections between lemmas and phonemes; very weak connections create a high rate of neologisms, including many that are remote from the target. (In runs of the model, extreme weakness causes phonemes to be selected at random.) Such a locus for neologisms is consistent with the finding that the neologism rate is higher for words that are low in frequency (see previous discussion) and that occupy sparse phonological neighborhoods (Gordon, 2002; Vitevitch, 2002).

Weak phonological connections constitute the model's explanation for TOT states as well as for neologisms. Why do some patients with hypothesized weak connections mostly omit responses and engage in TOT search, whereas others produce errors containing mixtures of correct and incorrect phonemes? A popular explanation centers on monitoring. The notion is that the omitters are capable of monitoring their internal speech for the quality of phonological access and therefore can suppress inaccuracies prior to or during articulation. The neologism producers, in contrast, do not routinely monitor their internal speech or suppress incipient errors. The

spontaneous speech of Wernicke's aphasia often evolves from neologistic to *anomic*—that is, to speech that contains mostly generic words (e.g., *thing, place*) and word-finding gaps (Kertesz & Benson, 1970). Presumably, the underlying retrieval problem persists while the ability to monitor recovers. A recent study of naming recovery described a patient who showed a decline in neologisms over time, in conjunction with a rise in omissions. His rate of self-corrections also increased over time but only for neologisms; there was no change in his ability to self-correct semantic errors (Schwartz & Brecher, 2000). It appears, then, that a complete account of lexical retrieval breakdown will have to include metalinguistic abilities such as self-monitoring and error detection. An important finding in this regard is that monitoring abilities in patients are not predicted by their performance on comprehension tests (Nickels & Howard, 1995), as some accounts would have predicted (e.g., Levelt, 1983).

The evidence reviewed so far supports the view that neologisms arise from faulty access to lexical phonology, when a wholly or partially deficient representation is filled in with substituted material. At one time, the substituted material was attributed to a neologism-producing device (Butterworth, 1979), but a more satisfactory account is that the substituted segments are constituents of the semantic and phonological neighbors activated in the course of lemma selection. This explanation is supported by a number of lines of evidence, including the miscuing phenomenon and the fact that the speed and accuracy of phonological access is influenced by the density of the target's phonological neighborhood (Vitevitch, 2001). Additional evidence on this point is provided in O'Seaghda and Marin (1997) and Peterson and Savoy (1998).

This evidence notwithstanding, there is reason to believe that neologisms sometimes arise *subsequent* to lexical retrieval, at a point at which the retrieved phonemes are inserted into the structural frames that control selection and that specify consonant-vowel structure, syllable boundaries, and stress pattern across units as large as a phonological or syntactic phrase. (For differing versions of this process, see Dell, 1986; Garrett, 1982; Levelt et al., 1999; Shattuck-Hufnagel, 1979; and for arguments supporting a postlexical locus for at least some neologisms, see Buckingham, 1977, 1985, 1987; Butterworth, 1979; Ellis, 1985; Kohn, 1993; Kohn & Smith, 1994, 1995).

A postlexical locus has long been proposed for normal sound errors in order to account for such errors' key properties: (a) the phonotactic regularity of errors, (b) the fact that consonants substitute for consonants and vowels for vowels, (c) syllable structure preservation in errors that move around, and (d) the fact that movement errors typically span a distance corresponding to a phonological or syntactic phrase.

In the aphasia literature, the postlexical account has been invoked primarily to explain why certain patients with conduction aphasia show a striking uniformity in the rate and characteristics of their neologisms across all types of production tasks, and why errors occur also in nonwords, which presumably are not lexically represented (Caplan et al., 1986; Pate et al., 1987).

Production models are now being designed that can account for many of the aforementioned characteristics of errors in terms of the architecture of the lexicon and the processing characteristics of lexical retrieval (e.g., Dell, Juliano, & Govindjee, 1993; Hartley & Houghton, 1996; Levelt et al., 1999; Vousden, Brown, & Harley, 2000). It remains to be seen whether such models will obviate the need for a postlexical phonological encoding stage.

Neuroanatomy of Lexical Retrieval

Indefrey and Levelt (2000) recently reviewed 58 studies that investigated the cerebral localization for word production. The majority of these involved PET or fMRI, but some utilized other techniques, including lesion analysis and event-related electrical and magnetic cortical activity (ERP, MEG). Indefrey and Levelt's meta-analysis began with analysis of the word-production tasks utilized in the various studies: picture naming, verb and noun generation, word reading, word repetition, and others. A primary distinction was drawn between task-specific *lead-in* processes and the *core component* processes of word production. The core components they recognize include all that we have discussed here (e.g., lemma selection, phonological encoding-assembly). It also includes the subsequent processes of phonetic encoding and articulation. For each core component, Indefrey and Levelt identified brain regions that were reliably activated in experimental tasks sharing that component and not reliably activated in tasks that do not share that component. The following is a summary of results of this meta-analysis:

Lemma Selection

Activation of a lemma by semantics is a process shared by picture naming and word generation but not necessarily word reading. The evidence implicates the left middle temporal gyrus—especially the midportion—as a critical locus for the lexical processes up to and including lemma selection.

Lexeme Selection

The term *lexeme* refers to the lexical-phonological specification that some models postulate as the sole lexical level (e.g.,

Caramazza & Miozzo, 1997) and others postulate in addition to the lemma (e.g., Levelt et al., 1999). Indefrey and Levelt (2000), who adopt the latter position, maintain that lexeme selection takes place in picture naming, word generation, and word reading, but not in pseudoword reading. The regional activations that conform to this pattern are those in the left posterior superior and middle temporal gyri (corresponding in all or part to Wernicke's area), as well as the left thalamus.

Phonological Encoding-Assembly

This component is considered present in all production tasks. Although no single region was activated in all the reviewed studies, the regions that came closest to fulfilling the requirement were the left posterior inferior frontal gyrus (Broca's area) and the left middle superior temporal gyrus.

Phonetic Encoding and Articulation

To isolate these peripheral components of word production, the authors looked for areas that were activated in all overt pronunciation tasks that used silent tasks as the control condition, but that were not activated in silent tasks or tasks that controlled for articulation. This pattern was matched by a number of areas known to be involved in motor planning and control: parts of the pre- and postcentral gyri of both hemispheres, right supplementary motor area (SMA), and left and medial cerebellum.

Grammatical Encoding

What processes of mind and brain enable the ordinary speaker to structure words grammatically and in accordance with the intended message? The question is made more compelling—and the answers more elusive—by the fact that these processes operate outside of conscious awareness and beyond the reach of our introspection. In this section, we outline a theory of grammatical encoding that addresses key issues but also has many unresolved details. The theory has its roots in studies of spontaneous speech errors conducted throughout the 1970s and 1980s (e.g., Baars, Motley, & MacKay, 1975; Dell, 1986; Fromkin, 1971; Garrett, 1975, 1980, 1982; MacKay, 1987; Shattuck-Hufnagel, 1979; Stemberger, 1985). It continues to be refined and elaborated though behavioral experiments (see Bock & Levelt, 1994; Levelt, 1989, for reviews), aphasia studies (Berndt, 2001; Garrett, 1982; Saffran, 1982; Schwartz, 1987) and computational modeling (e.g., Dell, 1986; Dell, Chang, & Griffin, 1999; Roelofs, 1992; Stemberger, 1985). Our treatment of the theory follows closely that of Bock and Levelt, 1994.

Readers interested in learning more should consult that reference, as well as Levelt's 1989 book, *Speaking*.

The outlines of the theory are shown in Figures 21.7 and 21.8, which illustrate production of the sentence *She was handing him the broccoli*. The steps to encoding begin with the message, which expresses the intended meaning of the sentence, including the structure of the event (i.e., what the action is, who or what plays the role of agent, theme, etc.; Figure 21.7). Next come the two ordered procedures that together constitute grammatical encoding. The first procedure (*functional processing*) assigns predicate-argument relations; the second procedure (*positional processing*) builds constitute structure (Figure 21.8).

The lexical entities that participate in functional processing are the lemmas of our previous discussion. The predicate-argument structure constitutes the frame that selects lemmas and assigns each to an argument role. In the type of speech error known as the *word exchange* (see Example 13), two lemmas are misassigned the other's role. This interpretation of word exchanges is made clearer by considering the exchange error in Example 20, which involves pronouns.

20. Intended: *She* handed *him* the broccoli.

Uttered: *He* handed *her* the broccoli.

In this error, the lemma for *feminine pronoun singular* and the lemma for *masculine pronoun singular* have been misassigned: The feminine pronoun fills the dative (indirect object) slot, and the masculine pronoun fills the nominative (subject) slot. In English, such misassignments emerge as exchanges of serial position, but this is true only because English uses fixed word order to express syntactic functions. In languages in which word order is freer and syntactic functions are marked by affixes, the exchanged nouns would carry the misassigned case (as the pronouns do in this example) regardless of how they were ordered. This is important because the functional frame is not concerned with serial order.

Assigning serial order is the business of the positional-processing stage, and it happens through the building of constituent structure. The entities that participate in positional processing are phrase fragments such as those shown in Figure 21.9 and the lexically specified arguments that attach to these fragments (Lapointe & Dell, 1989). When everything goes as planned, the nominative argument attaches to the slotted terminal branch of the Subject-NP fragment, the verb to the slotted terminal branch of the VP fragment, and so on. However, sometimes things go awry and the arguments attach to the wrong fragments. This is the presumed mechanism for the type of speech error known as the *stranding exchange:*

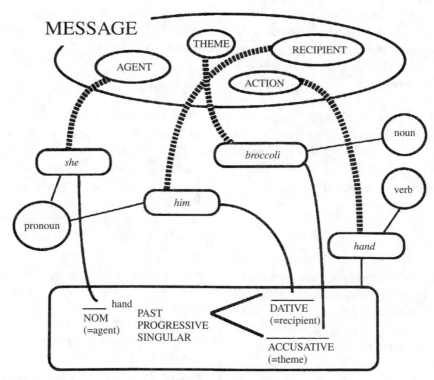

Figure 21.7 The elements of functional processing. From "Language Production: Grammatical Encoding," by J. K. Bock and W. J. M. Levelt, in *Handbook of Psycholinguistics,* 1994, San Diego: Academic Press, ed. M. A. Gernsbacher, p. 968. Copyright 1994 by Harcourt, Inc. Reprinted with permission.

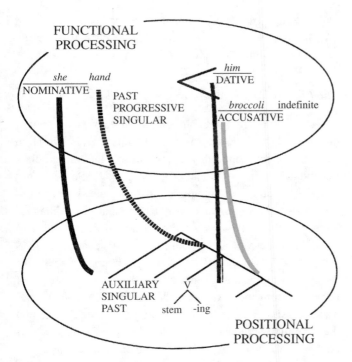

Figure 21.8 An illustration of the two stages of grammatical encoding. From "Language Production: Grammatical Encoding," by J. K. Bock and W. J. M. Levelt, in *Handbook of Psycholinguistics,* 1994, San Diego: Academic Press, ed. M. A. Gernsbacher, p. 977. Copyright 1994 by Harcourt, Inc. Reprinted with permission.

21. Target: I'm not in the *mood* for *read*ing

   Error: I'm not in the *read* for *mood*ing.

The features of stranding exchanges are telling: First, the exchanging entities are not words (as in Example 13) but rather stem morphemes. (In this example, *reading* is morphologically decomposed into the stem, *read,* and affix, -*ing.*) Critically, the affix is stranded in its targeted location. Second, stranding exchanges—unlike word exchanges—do not respect grammatical class (e.g., in Example 21, a noun stem has exchanged with a verb stem), nor are the exchanging elements semantically related. The most important constraint on stranding exchanges is *proximity;* the interacting elements almost always occupy adjacent phrases in the same clause. Yet they can be separated by one or more closed-class words (such as *for* in this example); and closed-class words do not participate in stranding exchanges (i.e., one never sees errors like *I'm not in the mood* read for*ing.* Apparently, closed-class words are invisible to the mechanism that inserts stems in fragments (and that is responsible for stranding exchanges). This is a key point, and we return to it later in this chapter.

The stem morphemes that participate in positional processing are equivalent to the phonologically specified lexemes discussed in the previous section. (This is supported by

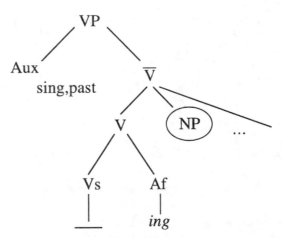

Figure 21.9 Example of a phrase fragment (after Lapointe & Dell, 1989). The circled node indicates the site of attachment of the NP phrase fragment that corresponds to the direct object. The dash indicates the slot that the lexically-specified verb will fill. The bound affix (-ing) is phonologically specified on the fragment; the free-standing function word (Aux) is not.

evidence that the entities that participate in stranding exchanges are often phonologically related; see Garrett, 1975; Lapointe & Dell, 1989.) Selecting a lexeme for insertion into a fragment slot triggers the process of phonological encoding, whereby the segments of the selected lexeme are selected and ordered. Among the types of phonological error that can arise at phonological encoding are so-called movement errors such as those in previous Examples 11 through 13. The existence of such errors indicates that more than one fragment is phonologically encoded at a time; the fact that the errors involve adjacent stems indicates that the span of anticipatory encoding is quite limited.

Disorders of Grammatical Encoding

Classical Agrammatism

Classical agrammatism has historically been considered a defining symptom of Broca's aphasia, along with slow, poorly articulated, and dysprosodic. *Classical agrammatism* refers to the simplification and fragmentation of constituent structure and to the tendency to omit closed-class words. Persons with Broca's aphasia exhibit agrammatism in spontaneous speech, event picture description, and sentence repetition. Table 21.2 reproduces sample picture descriptions we obtained from 10 mild-to-moderate agrammatic patients.

Cognitive Neuroscience of Language

To a first approximation, the fragmentation of sentence structure can be understood as a breakdown in the retrieval and coordination of phrase fragments. But what about the omission

**TABLE 21.2   Attempts at Picture Description by
10 Agrammatic Aphasics**

(Picture shows a young girl handing a bouquet of flowers to her teacher.)

(Pt. 1) "The young . . . the girl . . . the little girl is . . . the flower."

(Pt. 2) "The girl is flower the woman."

(Pt. 3) "Girl is . . . going to flowers."

(Pt. 4) "The girl is . . . is roses. The girl is rosing. The woman and the little girl was rosed."

(Pt. 5) "The girl is giving . . . giving the teacher . . . giving it teacher."

(Pt. 6) "The girl is flowering."

(Pt. 7) "The teacher is . . . the girl . . . giving the girl and the flowers."

(Pt. 8) "Girl is handing flowers to teacher."

(Pt. 9) "The flowers . . . the girl bringing the teacher."

(Pt. 10) "The girl is flowers . . . teachers."

of function words? Earlier we noted that frequently used words are not subject to TOTs and phonological error as often as infrequent words; the same is true for short words, compared to long ones. Since function words are among the shortest and most frequent words in the language, their omission from agrammatic speech is unlikely to be due to failure of lexical-phonological retrieval. In support of this, agrammatics have been reported who produce function words normally in single word production tasks but omit them in the context of phrase- and sentence production (Nespoulous et al., 1988). This suggests that syntactic influences are at play, but beyond this, there is little agreement.

The next section puts forward a view that ascribes closed class omissions to the positional processing stage of grammatical encoding. We must acknowledge at the outset, however, that the evidence to be reviewed is not complete, and the arguments no unassailable. In particular, it is now widely acknowledged that fluent aphasics, as well as nonfluent agrammatics, have problems producing closed class elements in connected speech (e.g., Haarmann & Kolk, 1992; Caplan & Hanna, 1998), and whether this manifests primarily in omissions or in substitutions is affected by the speaker's language (Menn & Obler, 1990) and by the task he or she is given (Hofstede & Kolk, 1994); moreover, the probablility that a given closed class element will be produced correctly is in part a function of its semantic and prosodic salience (Goodglass, 1973; Kean, 1979). Psychologist Herman Kolk argues that the best way to reconcile these diverse findings is to assume that aphasics of all kinds suffer from a reduced capacity for producing sentences and that they adapt to this impairment in various ways, depending on the particular task they are given and on other characteristics of their aphasia. In patients for whom speaking is effortful, i.e., most Broca's aphasics, such adaptation takes the form of omission of the

elements that carry least semantic weight, namely those of the closed-class vocabulary (Kolk & Heeschen, 1992; Kolk & Van Grunsven, 1985; see also Dick et al., 2001).

The Closed-Class Hypothesis

The closed-class hypothesis is a highly influential account of closed-class omissions; this account relates this symptom to the computational distinctiveness of the closed-class vocabulary at the positional processing stage. Several lines of evidence support computation distinctiveness; for example, closed-class elements do not participate in exchanges arising at this level and these elements are not subject to phonological error (but see Dell, 1990; Ellis et al., 1983). As formulated by Garrett (1975; 1980), the hypothesis explains these facts by proposing that closed-class elements are not retrieved from the lexicon in the way that open-class elements are, but instead come phonologically prepackaged on the terminal branches of positional frames. Because exchanges arise when lexically retrieved elements are assigned to the wrong slots, and closed-class words are not among the elements so assigned, they are not subject to exchange errors. Furthermore, because they are phonologically prepackaged, closed-class words are not subject to the substitutions, additions, and so on that happen at phonological assembly. On the other hand, if one assumes that the essential problem in agrammatism is generating positional frames, then their status as essential constituents of such frames would be expected to confer vulnerability on the closed-class elements.

Garrett's hypothesis was subsequently expanded and modified by Lapointe (Lapointe, 1983, 1985), based on evidence that free and bound closed-class elements behave differently in agrammatic speech. Lapointe's analysis of published cases of English- and Italian-speaking agrammatism revealed that the tendency to omit was restricted to freestanding function words; bound affixes, in contrast, were more likely to undergo substitution. Earlier studies had failed to notice the substitutions because English agrammatics tend to overuse bare verb stems—and this tendency lends itself to characterization as omission of the inflectional affix. Lapointe's analysis treats this instead as substitution of the infinitive. Infinitives are among the least marked (i.e., least complex) verb forms in English, in terms of the semantic notions they encode. The markedness hierarchy is central to Lapointe's account of verb-phrase production in agrammatism and provides an explanation for some of the across-language differences that one observes. For example, in Italian, the infinitive meaning is not expressed by the bare stem but rather by an affix. Accordingly, Italian agrammatics do not produce the bare verb stem, but they do substitute the infinitive affix for other, more marked, affixes.

Lapointe proposed that only affixes come fully specified on the terminal branches of phrase fragments. Function words, in contrast, are specified more abstractly and are subject to a separate retrieval process. The retrieval of phrase fragments and function words, according to Lapointe, utilizes a shared resource that is of limited supply in agrammatism. Consequently, the search for phrase fragments often terminates with the least marked fragments being retrieved and exhausts the resource capacity before the function words can be retrieved.

Additional evidence now suggests that function words are not inherent constituents of phrase fragments. The evidence comes from experiments in *structural priming* conducted by Bock and her colleagues with normal speakers. The essential observation behind structural priming is that speakers tend to repeat the structure of a sentence heard or spoken previously—even when the sentences differ in lexical and message-level content (Bock, 1986, 1989; Bock & Loebell, 1990; Bock, Loebell, & Morey, 1992). Analyses suggest that the effect of the prior exposure is to enhance the availability of the prime sentence's constituent structure (e.g., whether it contains a prepositional phrase), making it more likely that the relevant phrase fragments will subsequently be repeated. The key finding (for present purposes) is that strong structural priming can be obtained even when the sentences differ in function word content (e.g., different prepositions). If the function words were an inherent part of the phrase fragments, fragments with different prepositions should prime one another less well than do those with identical prepositions; however, this is not the case (Bock, 1989).

Interestingly, structural priming can also be produced in agrammatic aphasic patients (Hartsuiker & Kolk, 1998; Saffran & Martin, 1997), in whom it yields complex structures of the sort that these patients rarely produce spontaneously (e.g., passives datives). This evidence is consistent with a resource account of agrammatic production. It also shows that constituent structure can be primed independently of any lexical content—including the function words—because priming with a transitive passive, such as in *The boy was hit by a rock,* for example, often produces an NP-V-PP structure (as is appropriate to a passive) that contains the wrong preposition, affix, or both.

Fractional Agrammatism

In certain conditions, omission and substitution of closed-class elements can be observed in patients who speak fluently and without the syntactic fragmentation evident in Table 21.2 (e.g., Haarmann & Kolk, 1992; Miceli et al., 1983, Case 2). The reverse pattern has also been described: A patient's speech is fragmented but rich in closed-class vocabulary

(Berndt, 1987; Saffran, Schwartz, & Marin, 1980a). To reconcile these findings with the original or revised version of the closed-class hypothesis, the syntactic fragmentation must be attributed to a separate resource decrement (Lapointe, 1985) or to a syntactic process that is independent of closed-class retrieval (Saffran et al, 1980a; Schwartz, 1987). The next section spells out the argument for syntactic deficits at the function assignment stage.

Functional Processing Deficits

In 1980 our group demonstrated for the first time that patients with agrammatic Broca's aphasia have difficulty using word order to express the predicate-argument structure of a sentence (Saffran, Schwartz, & Marin, 1980b). Asked to describe simple events (e.g., a boy pushing a girl) or locative states (e.g., a pencil in the sink), our patients not infrequently began with the wrong noun and sometimes produced complete subject-object reversals. We replicated the effect in a sentence anagram task that required no speaking at all.

This word-order deficit, now well established, emerges only with specially designed materials—namely, those that exclude nonsyntactic strategies, such as mentioning the animate or most salient entity first or ordering the entities in accordance with their left-right placement in the picture (Chatterjee, Maher, & Heilman, 1995; Deloche & Seron, 1981; Menn et al., 1998; Saffran et al., 1980b). It has also been reported in a few fluent aphasic patients, whose production of constituent structures and closed-class elements was largely if not entirely intact (Caramazza & Miceli, 1991; R. Martin & Blossom-Stach, 1986). Such cases establish definitively that the word-order deficit is not a consequence of positional processing impairment; rather, it reflects impairment at the prior stage of predicate-argument assignment.

Earlier we noted that the verb plays a central role in predicate-argument assignment. It should not be surprising, then, that the semantic and syntactic properties of verbs (and other predicates, such as prepositions) have been found to influence the word-order problem (Jones, 1984; Saffran et al., 1980b). It has been known for some time that agrammatism is associated with impaired verb access (e.g., Miceli, Silveri, Villa, & Caramazza, 1984; Saffran et al., 1980a; Zingeser & Berndt, 1990) and that the verb-access deficit can arise at multiple levels (e.g., Berndt, Mitchum, Haendiges, & Sandson, 1997). Elucidating the relationship between verb impairments and grammatical encoding deficits remains an active area of research (Breedin & Martin, 1996; Breedin, Saffran & Schwartz, 1998; Gordon & Dell, 2002).

If agrammatics' syntactic fragmentation were to stem from functional processing deficits involving verb use and predicate-argument assignment, it would explain why syntactic fragmentation and closed class omissions do not invariably co-occur. This account of syntactic fragmentation receives support from the speech samples in Table 21.2, where much of the struggle seems to arise in connection with finding the correct verb and conveying the functional roles of the three participants.

Neuroanatomy of Grammatical Encoding

Classical agrammatism is part of the clinical picture of Broca's aphasia; consequently, the search for the anatomical substrate of grammatical encoding has focused on Broca's area. Modern lesion studies have not been encouraging in this regard: They have shown that agrammatic Broca's aphasia does not result from a lesion restricted to Broca's area, but rather requires extension into adjacent frontal and parietal areas overlying the insula (i.e., frontal and parietal operculum) and to the insula itself (Dronkers et al., 2000; Mohr et al., 1978). More problematic still is the evidence that agrammatic Broca's aphasia can be produced by posterior lesions that completely spare Broca's area (Basso et al., 1985; Dronkers et al., 2000; Willmes & Poeck, 1993). A lesion correlation study focused specifically on agrammatism found that the responsible lesions, when localized, were distributed widely around the left perisylvian area (Vanier & Caplan, 1990). On one hand, this is not surprising; given the complexity of grammatical encoding and the evidence that it fractionates at multiple levels, it is unlikely to be localized to a single site. On the other hand, in our review of the functional imaging literature relating to sentence comprehension, Broca's area was consistently found to activate in response to the syntactic load of the sentence. Could it be that this area is critical for syntactic processing in comprehension but not in production? This seems unlikely prima facie, given its location in close proximity to motor cortex. Moreover, in the only functional imaging study to date that utilized a speech production design, the results implicated the left Rolandic operculum, caudally adjacent to Broca's area, as important for grammatical encoding (Indefrey et al., 2001).

At this time there is no simple way to reconcile the discrepant findings from lesion and metabolic imaging studies. However, it is important to remember that structural damage can produce far-reaching metabolic abnormality, so that the fact that a lesion is localized outside Broca's area does not necessarily mean that the neural tissue there is functioning normally (Metter, 1987).

Contemporary neuroscience is increasingly coming to the view that Broca's area is both too big and too small to serve as the neurological substrate for grammatical encoding. It is too big in the sense that it is structurally and functionally decomposable; it is too small in the sense that any one of its functions probably can only be understood in the context of a spatially distributed network of structures. An interesting characterization of the neural network for grammatical encoding has recently been put forward by Ullman and colleagues. Their declarative-procedural model of language maps the lexical-syntactic distinction onto the declarative-procedural memory systems of the brain. The following quote, taken from a recent review, concerns the procedural system as it relates to grammatical encoding (Ullman, 2001; references contained in the quoted passages are omitted here; our additions appear within in brackets).

> [Procedural memory] has been implicated in learning new, and controlling well-established, motor and cognitive skills. Learning and remembering these procedures is largely implicit . . . The [procedural memory] system is rooted in portions of the frontal cortex (including Broca's area and the supplementary motor area), the basal ganglia, parietal cortex and the dentate nucleus of the cerebellum . . . [Procedural memory] is important for learning or processing skills that involve action sequences. The execution of these skills seems to be guided in real time by the posterior parietal cortex, which is densely connected to frontal regions. Inferior parietal regions might serve as a repository for knowledge of skills, including information about stored sequences [phrase fragments?].
>
> . . . Procedural memory subserves the implicit learning and use of a symbol-manipulating grammar across subdomains that include syntax, morphology and possibly phonology (how sounds are combined). The system might be especially important in grammatical-structure building—that is, in the sequential and hierarchical combination of stored forms ('walk' + '-ed') and abstract representations into complex structures . . . One or more circuits between the basal ganglia and particular frontal regions might subserve grammatical processing and perhaps even finer distinctions, such as morphology versus syntax. From this point of view, the frontal cortex and basal ganglia are 'domain general,' in that they subserve non-linguistic and linguistic processes, but contain parallel, 'domain'-specific' circuits. (Ullman, 2001, p. 718)

The declarative/procedural model of language has so far been thoroughly tested only in the domain of past-tense processing (regular past tense formation is thought to involve the procedural system, irregular past tense formation the declarative system). Nevertheless, the model has attracted much attention on account of its admirable attempt to reconcile the theoretical description of language behavior with basic neurobiological principles. We expect to see more of this in the coming years.

CONCLUDING COMMENTS

The history of the biological characterization of language can be divided into phases. The early history was dominated by a simple and elegant neurological theory that reduced language to sensory and motor images. The second phase, which began in the mid 1970s and took linguistic theory as a jumping-off point, evolved techniques of behavioral experimentation to arrive at a richly detailed characterization of how neurologically intact speakers represent and use language, and how localized brain damage affects these psycholinguistic processes. We have now entered a third phase, characterized by the advent of models that simulate psycholinguistic stages and processes via the combined computations of neuron-like elements, and by the growth of functional imaging technology capable of localizing the neural networks that perform such computations. Computational modeling and functional brain imaging are the tools of cognitive neuroscience. As they mature, and as their availability and influence spreads, they are likely to provide new insights into the enduring mysteries surrounding language: What computational specializations did the human brain evolve for language? How did these emerge in phylogenesis? How do these neural specializations shape first-language learning, and how are they shaped by it? And what kind of plasticity is available to the brain that has experienced injury to these specialized mechanisms? When these questions are answered, we will have arrived at a truly comprehensive understanding of the biology of human language.

REFERENCES

Allport, D. A. (1985). Distributed memory, modular subsystems, and dysphasia. In S. K. Newman & R. Epstein (Eds.), *Current perspectives in dysphasia* (pp. 32–60). Edinburgh, Scotland: Churchill Livingstone.

Allport, D. A., & Funnell, E. (1981). Components of the mental lexicon. *Philosophical Transactions of the Royal Society of London, 295B,* 397–410.

Altmann, G. T. M., Garnham, A., & Dennis, Y. (1992). Avoiding the garden path: Eye movements in context. *Journal of Memory and Language, 31,* 685–712.

Baars, B. J., Motley, M. T., & MacKay, D. G. (1975). Output editing for lexical status in artificially elicited slips of the tongue. *Journal of Verbal Learning and Verbal Behavior, 14,* 382–391.

Badecker, W., Miozzo, M., & Zanuttini, R. (1995). The two-stage model of lexical retrieval: Evidence from a case of anomia with selective preservation of grammatical gender. *Cognition, 57,* 193–216.

Barbarotto, R., Capitani, E., Spinnler, H., & Travelli, C. (1995). Slowly progressive semantic impairment with category specificity. *Neurocase, 1,* 107–119.

Basso, A., Gardelli, M., Grassi, M. P., & Mariotti, M. (1989). The role of the right hemisphere in recovery from aphasia: Two case studies. *Cortex, 25,* 555–556.

Basso, A., Lecours, A. R., Moraschini, S., & Vanier, M. (1985). Anatomoclinical correlations of the aphasias as defined through computerized tomography: Exceptions. *Brain and Language, 26,* 201–229.

Bavelier, D., Corin, D., Jezzard, P., Padmanabhan, S., Clark, V. P., & Karni, A. P. (1997). Sentence reading: A functional MRI study at 4 Telsa. *Journal of Cognitive Neuroscience, 9,* 664–686.

Beauregard, M., Chertkow, H., Bub, D., Murtha, S., Dixon, R., & Evans, A. (1997). The neural substrate for concrete, abstract, and emotional word lexica: A positron emission tomography study. *Journal of Cognitive Neuroscience, 9,* 441–461.

Behrmann, M., & Leiberthal, T. (1989). Category-specific treatment of lexical-semantic deficit: A single case study of global aphasia. *British Journal of Disorders of Communication, 24,* 281–299.

Berndt, R. S. (1987). Symptom co-occurrence and dissociation in the interpretation of agrammatism. In M. Coltheart, G. Sartori, & R. Job (Eds.), *The cognitive neuropscyhology of language,* (pp. 221–233). London: Erlbaum.

Berndt, R. S. (2001). More than just words: Sentence production in aphasia. In R. S. Berndt (Ed.), *Handbook of neuropsychology* (2nd ed., Vol. 3, pp. 173–187). Amsterdam: Elsevier.

Berndt, R. S., & Caramazza, A. (1980). A redefinition of the syndrome of Broca's aphasia: Implications for a neuropsychological model of language. *Applied Linguistics, 1,* 225–287.

Berndt, R. S., Mitchum, C., & Haendiges, A. (1996). Comprehension of reversible sentences in "agrammatism": A meta-analysis. *Cognition, 58,* 289–308.

Berndt, R. S., Mitchum, C., Haendiges, A., & Sandson, J. (1997). Verb retrieval in aphasia: 1. Characterizing single word impairments. *Brain and Language, 56,* 68–106.

Berndt, R. S., Salasoo, A., Mitchum, C., & Blumstein, S. E. (1988). The role of intonation cues in aphasic patients' performance of the grammaticality judgment task. *Brain and Language, 34,* 65–97.

Best, W. M. (1996). When racquets are baskets but baskets are biscuits, where do the words come from? A single-case study of formal paraphasia. *Cognitive Neuropsychology, 3,* 369–409.

Binder, J. R., Frost, J. A., Hammeke, T. A., Cox, R. W., Rao, S. M., & Prieto, T. (1997). Human brain language areas identified by functional magnetic resonance imaging. *Journal of Neuroscience, 17,* 353–362.

Blanken, G. (1990). Formal paraphasias: A single case study. *Brain and Language, 38,* 534–554.

Blanken, G. (1998). Lexicalisation in speech production: Evidence from form-related word substitutions in aphasia. *Cognitive Neuropsychology, 15,* 321–360.

Blumstein, S. E. (1994). Impairments of speech production and speech perception in aphasia. *Philosophical Transactions of the Royal Society of London, 346B,* 29–36.

Blumstein, S. E., Cooper, W. E., Zurif, E. B., & Caramazza, A. (1977). The perception and production of voice-onset time in aphasia. *Neuropsychologia, 15,* 371–383.

Blumstein, S. E., Tartter, V. C., Nigro, G., & Statlender, S. (1984). Acoustic cues for the perception of place of articulation in aphasia. *Brain and Language, 22,* 128–149.

Boatman, D., Lesser, R., & Gordon, B. (1995). Auditory speech processing in the left temporal lobe: An electrical interference study. *Brain and Language, 51,* 269–290.

Bock, J. K. (1986). Syntactic persistence in language production. *Cognitive Psychology, 18,* 355–387.

Bock, J. K. (1989). Closed-class immanence in sentence production. *Cognition, 31,* 163–186.

Bock, J. K., & Levelt, W. J. M. (1994). Language production: Grammatical encoding. In M. A. Gernsbacher (Ed.), *Handbook of psycholinguistics* (pp. 945–984). San Diego: Academic Press.

Bock, J. K., & Loebell, H. (1990). Framing sentences. *Cognition, 35,* 1–39.

Bock, J. K., Loebell, H., & Morey, R. (1992). From conceptual roles to structural relations: Bridging the syntactic cleft. *Psychological Review, 99,* 150–171.

Bradley, D. C., Garrett, M. F., & Zurif, E. B. (1980). Syntactic deficits in Broca's aphasia. In D. Caplan (Ed.), *Biological studies of mental processes* (pp. 269–286). Cambridge: MIT Press.

Breedin, S. D., & Martin, R. C. (1996). Patterns of verb impairment in aphasia: Analysis of four cases. *Cognitive Neuropsychology, 13,* 51–91.

Breedin, S. D., Martin, N., & Saffran, E. M. (1994). Category-specific semantic impairments: An infrequent occurrence? *Brain and Language, 47,* 383–386.

Breedin, S. D., & Saffran, E. M. (1999). Sentence processing in the face of semantic loss: A case study. *Journal of Experimental Psychology: General, 128,* 547–565.

Breedin, S. D., Saffran, E. M., & Coslett, H. B. (1994). Reversal of the concreteness effect in a patient with semantic dementia. *Cognitive Neuropsychology, 11,* 617–660.

Breedin, S. D., Saffran, E. M., & Schwartz, M. F. (1998). Semantic factors in verb retrieval: An effect of complexity. *Brain and Language, 63,* 1–31.

Broca, P. (1865). Sur le siege de la faculte de langage articule. *Bulletin d'Anthropologie, 5,* 377–393.

Brown, A. S. (1991). A review of the tip-of-the-tongue experience. *Psychological Bulletin, 109,* 204–223.

Brown, C. M., Hagoort, P., & Kutas, M. (2001). Postlexical integration processes in language comprehension: Evidence from brain imaging research. In M. Gazzaniga (Ed.), *The new cognitive neurosciences* (2nd ed., pp. 881–896). Cambridge: MIT Press.

Buckingham, H. D. (1977). The conduction theory and neologistic jargon. *Language and Speech, 20,* 174–184.

Buckingham, H. D. (1985). *Perseveration in aphasia.* Edinburgh, Scotland: Churchill Livingstone.

Buckingham, H. D. (1987). Phonemic paraphasias and psycholinguistic production models for neologistic jargon. *Aphasiology, 1,* 381–400.

Butterworth, B. (1979). Hesitation and the production of verbal paraphasias and neologisms in jargon aphasia. *Brain and Language, 8,* 133–161.

Buxbaum, L. J., & Saffran, E. M. (1998). Knowing "how" vs. "what for": A new dissociation. *Brain and Language, 65,* 73–86.

Buxbaum, L. J., Schwartz, M. F., & Carew, T. G. (1997). The role of semantic memory in object use. *Cognitive Neuropsychology, 14,* 219–254.

Caplan, D., Alpert, N., & Waters, G. (1998). Effects of syntactic structure and propositional number on patterns of regional cerebral blood flow. *Journal of Cognitive Neuroscience, 10,* 541–552.

Caplan, D., & Hanna, J. E. (1998). Sentence production by aphasic patients in a constrained task. *Brain and Language, 63,* 184–218.

Caplan, D., Vanier, M., & Baker, E. (1986). A case study of reproduction conduction aphasia: 1. Word production. *Cognitive Neuropsychology, 3,* 99–128.

Caplan, D., & Waters, G. S. (1999). Verbal working memory and sentence comprehension. *Behavioral and Brain Sciences, 22,* 77–94.

Cappa, S. F., Perani, D., Schnur, T., Tettamanti, M., & Fazio, F. (1998). The effects of semantic category and knowledge type on lexical-semantic access: A PET study. *Neuroimage, 8,* 350–359.

Caramazza, A. (1984). The logic of neuropsychological research and the problem of patient classification in aphasia. *Brain and Language, 21,* 9–20.

Caramazza, A., & Hillis, A. E. (1990). Where do semantic errors come from? *Cortex, 26*(1), 95–122.

Caramazza, A., & Miceli, G. (1991). Selective impairment of thematic role assignment in sentence processing. *Brain and Language, 41,* 402–436.

Caramazza, A., & Miozzo, M. (1997). The relation between syntactic and phonological knowledge in lexical access: Evidence from the "tip-of-the-tongue" phenomenon. *Cognition, 64,* 309–343.

Caramazza, A., & Shelton, J. R. (1998). Domain-specific knowledge systems in the brain: The animate-inanimate distinction. *Journal of Cognitive Neuroscience, 10,* 1–34.

Caramazza, A., & Zurif, E. G. (1976). Dissociation of algorithmic and heuristic processes in sentence comprehension: Evidence from aphasia. *Brain and Language, 3,* 572–582.

Cardebat, D., Demonet, J.-F., Celsis, P., Puel, M., Viallard, G., & Marc-Vergnes, J.-P. (1994). Right temporal compensatory mechanisms in a deep dysphasic patient: A case report with activation study by PET. *Neuropsychologia, 32,* 97–103.

Chatterjee, A., Maher, L. M., & Heilman, K. M. (1995). Spatial characteristics of thematic role representation. *Neuropsychologia, 33,* 643–648.

Chomsky, N. (1981). *Lectures on government and binding.* Dordrecht, Holland: Foris.

Coslett, H. B., & Monsul, N. (1994). Reading and the right hemisphere: Evidence from transcranial magnetic stimulation. *Brain and Language, 46,* 198–211.

Damasio, A. R., Damasio, H., Rizzo, M., Varney, N., & Gersch, F. (1982). Aphasia with nonhemorrhagic lesions in the basal ganglia and internal capsule. *Archives of Neurology, 39,* 15–20.

Damasio, H., & Damasio, A. R. (1989). *Lesion analysis in neuropsychology.* New York: Oxford University Press.

Damasio, H., Grabowski, T. J., Tranel, D., Hichwa, R. D., & Damasio, A. R. (1996). A neural bases for lexical retrieval. *Nature, 380,* 499–505.

De Renzi, E., & Lucchelli, F. (1994). Are semantic systems separately represented in the brain? The case of living category impairment. *Cortex, 30,* 3–25.

del Viso, S., Igoa, J. M., & Garcia-Albert, J. E. (1991). On the autonomy of phonological encoding: Evidence from slips of the tongue in Spanish. *Journal of Psycholinguistic Research, 20,* 161–185.

Dell, G. S. (1986). A spreading activation theory of retrieval in sentence production. *Psychological Review, 93,* 283–321.

Dell, G. S. (1990). Effects of frequency and vocabulary type of phonological speech errors. *Language and Cognitive Processes, 5,* 313–349.

Dell, G. S., Chang, G., & Griffin, Z. M. (1999). Connectionist models of language production: Lexical access and grammatical encoding. *Cognitive Science, 23,* 517–542.

Dell, G. S., Juliano, C., & Govindjee, A. (1993). Structure and content in language production: A theory of frame constraints in phonological speech errors. *Cognitive Science, 17,* 149–195.

Dell, G. S., & O'Seaghdha, P. (1991). Mediated and convergent lexical priming in language production: A comment on Levelt et al. *Psychological Review, 98,* 604–614.

Dell, G. S., & Reich, P. A. (1981). Stages in sentence production: An analysis of speech error data. *Journal of Verbal Learning and Verbal Behavior, 20,* 611–629.

Dell, G. S., Schwartz, M. F., Martin, N., Saffran, E. M., & Gagnon, D. (1997). Lexical access in aphasic and non-aphasic speakers. *Psychological Review, 104,* 811–838.

Dell, G. S., Schwartz, M. F., Martin, N., Saffran, E. M., & Gagnon, D. (2000). The role of computational models in neuropsychological investigations of language: Reply to Ruml and Caramazza. *Psychological Review, 107,* 635–645.

Deloche, G., & Seron, X. (1981). Sentence understanding and knowledge of the world: Evidence from a sentence-picture matching task performed by aphasic patients. *Brain and Language, 14,* 57–69.

Demonet, J.-F., Chollet, F., Ramsay, S., Cardebat, D., Nespoulous, J.-L., Wise, R. J. S., Rascol, A., & Frackowiak, R. S. J. (1992). The anatomy of phonological and semantic processing in normal subjects. *Brain, 115,* 1753–1768.

Dick, F., Bates, E., Wulfeck, B., Utman, J. A., Dronkers, N., & Gernsbacher, M. A. (2001). Language deficits, localization, and grammar: Evidence for a distributive model of language breakdown in aphasic patients and neurologically intact individuals. *Psychological Review, 108,* 759–788.

Dronkers, N. F., Redfern, B. B., & Knight, R. T. (2000). The neural architecture of language disorders. In M. Gazzaniga (Ed.), *The new cognitive neurosciences* (2nd ed., pp. 949–960). Cambridge: Bradford/MIT Press.

Dronkers, N. F., Wilkins, D. P., Van Valin, R. D. J., Redfern, B. B., & Jaeger, J. J. (1994). A reconsideration of the brain areas involved in the disruption of morphosyntactic comprehension. *Brain and Language, 47,* 461–463.

Ellis, A. W. (1985). The production of spoken words: A cognitive neuropsychological perspective. In A. W. Ellis (Ed.), *Progress in the psychology of language* (pp. 107–145). Hillsdale, NJ: Erlbaum.

Ellis, A. W., Miller, D., & Sin, G. (1983). Wernicke's aphasia and normal language processing: A case study in cognitive neuropsychology. *Cognition, 15,* 111–114.

Farah, M., Hammond, K. H., Mehta, Z., & Ratcliff, G. (1989). Category-specificity and modality-specificity in semantic memory. *Neuropsychologia, 27,* 193–200.

Farah, M., & McClelland, J. (1991). A computational model of semantic memory impairment: Modality specificity and emergent category specificity. *Journal of Experimental Psychology: General, 120,* 339–357.

Farah, M., Meyer, M. M., & McMullen, P. A. (1996). The living/nonliving dissociation is not an artifact: Giving an a priori implausible hypothesis a strong test. *Cognitive Neuropsychology, 13,* 137–154.

Fay, D., & Cutler, A. (1977). Malapropisms and the structure of the mental lexicon. *Linguistics Inquiry, 8*(3), 505–520.

Fitch, R. H., Miller, S., & Tallal, P. (1997). Neurobiology of speech perception. *Annual Review of Neuroscience, 20,* 331–353.

Forde, E. M. E., Francis, D., Riddoch, J. J., Rumiati, R. I., & Humphreys, G. W. (1997). On the links between visual knowledge and naming: A single case study of a patient with a category-specific impairment for living things. *Cognitive Neuropsychology, 14,* 403–458.

Foygel, D., & Dell, G. S. (2000). Models of impaired lexical access in speech production. *Journal of Memory and Language, 43,* 182–216.

Frazier, L. (1990). Exploring the architecture of the language processing system. In G. T. M. Altmann (Ed.), *Cognitive models of speech processing* (pp. 409–433). Cambridge: MIT Press.

Freud, S. (1953). *On aphasia.* New York: International University Press. (Original work published 1891)

Friston, K. J. (1997). Imaging cognitive anatomy. *Trends in Cognitive Sciences, 1,* 21–27.

Fromkin, V. A. (1971). The non-anomalous nature of anomalous utterances. *Language, 47*(1), 26–52.

Fujii, T., Fukatsu, R., Watabe, S., Ohnuma, A., Teramura, K., Kimura, I., Saso, S., & Kogure, K. (1990). Auditory sound agnosia without aphasia following a right temporal lobe lesion. *Cortex, 26,* 263–268.

Funnell, E., & De Mornay Davies, P. (1996). JBR: A reassessment of concept familiarity and a category-specific disorder for living things. *Neurocase, 2,* 461–474.

Funnell, E., & Sheridan, J. (1992). Categories of knowledge? Unfamiliar aspects of living and nonliving things. *Cognitive Neuropsychology, 9,* 135–154.

Gaffan, D., & Heywood, C. A. (1993). A spurious category-specific visual agnosia for living things in normal humans and nonhuman primates. *Journal of Cognitive Neuroscience, 5,* 118–128.

Gagnon, D., Schwartz, M., Martin, N., Dell, G., & Saffran, E. M. (1997). The origins of form-related paraphasias in aphasic naming. *Brain and Language, 59,* 450–472.

Gainotti, G., & Silveri, M. C. (1996). Cognitive and anatomical locus of lesion in a patient with a category-specific semantic impairment for living things. *Cognitive Neuropsychology, 13,* 357–389.

Gainotti, G., Silveri, C., Villa, G., & Miceli, G. (1984). Anomia with and without lexical comprehension disorders. *Brain and Language, 29,* 18–33.

Gannon, P. J., Holloway, R. L., Broadfield, D. C., & Braun, A. R. (1998). Asymmetry of chimpanzee planum temporale: Human-like pattern of Wernicke's brain language area homolog. *Science, 279,* 220–222.

Ganong, W. F. (1980). Phonetic categorization in auditory word perception. *Journal of Experimental Psychology: Human Perception and Performance, 6,* 110–125.

Garrett, M. F. (1975). The analysis of sentence production. In G. H. Bower (Ed.), *The psychology of learning and motivation* (pp. 133–175). London: Academic Press.

Garrett, M. F. (1980). Levels of processing in sentence production. In B. Butterworth (Ed.), *Language production* (Vol. 1, pp. 177–220). London: Academic Press.

Garrett, M. F. (1982). Production of speech: Observations from normal and pathological language. In A. Ellis (Ed.), *Normality and pathology in cognitive functions* (pp. 19–76). London: Academic Press.

Gazzaniga, M. S. (1983). Right hemisphere language following brain bisection: A 20 year perspective. *American Psychologist, 38,* 525–537.

Geschwind, N. (1965). Disconnection syndromes in animals and man. *Brain, 8,* 237–294, 585–644.

Geschwind, N., & Levitsky, W. (1968). Human and brain left-right asymmetries in temporal speech region. *Science, 161,* 186–187.

Goldman-Rakic, P. (1995). Architecture of the prefrontal cortex and the central executive. In J. Grafman, K. J. Holyoak, & F. Boller (Eds.), *Structure and functions of the human prefrontal cortex* (Vol. 769, *Annals of the New York Academy of Sciences,* pp. 71–84). New York: New York Academy of Sciences.

Goodglass, H. (1973). Studies on the grammar of aphasics. In H. Goodglass & S. Blumstein (Eds.), *Psycholinguistics and aphasia.* Baltimore: Johns Hopkins University Press.

Goodglass, H., Kaplan, E., Weintraub, S., & Ackerman, N. (1976). The "tip-of-the-tongue" phenomenon in aphasia. *Cortex, 12,* 145–153.

Gordon, J. K. (2001). Phonological neighborhood effects in aphasic speech errors: Spontaneous and structured contexts. Manuscript submitted for publication.

Gordon, J. K., & Dell, G. S. (2002). Learning to divide the labour between syntax and semantics: A connectionist account of deficits in light and heavy verb production. *Brain and Cognition, 48,* 376–381.

Grafton, S. T., Fadiga, L., Arbib, M. A., & Rizzolatti, G. (1997). Premotor cortex activation during observation and naming of familiar tools. *Neuroimage, 6,* 231–236.

Grodzinsky, Y. (1990). *Theoretical perspectives on language deficits.* Cambridge: MIT Press.

Grodzinsky, Y. (2000). The neurology of syntax: Language use without Broca's area. *Behavioral and Brain Sciences, 23,* 1–21.

Haarmann, H. J., Just, M. A., & Carpenter, P. A. (1997). Aphasic sentence comprehension as a resource deficit: A computational approach. *Brain and Language, 59,* 76–120.

Haarmann, H. J., & Kolk, H. H. J. (1992). The production of grammatical morphology in Broca's and Wernicke's aphasics: Speed and accuracy factors. *Cortex, 28,* 97–102.

Habib, M., & Demonet, J.-F. (1996). Cognitive neuroanatomy of language: The contribution of functional neuroimaging. *Aphasiology, 10,* 217–234.

Hagoort, P., Brown, C. M., & Osterhout, L. (1999). The neurocognition of syntactic processing. In C. M. Brown & P. Hagoort (Eds.), *The neurocognition of language* (pp. 273–305). Oxford: Oxford University Press.

Harley, T. A. (1984). A critique of top-down independent levels models of speech production: Evidence from non-plan-internal speech errors. *Cognitive Science, 8,* 191–219.

Harley, T. A., & Bown, H. E. (1998). What causes a tip-of-the-tongue state? Evidence for lexical neighborhood effects in speech production. *British Journal of Psychology, 89,* 151–174.

Hart, J., Berndt, R. S., & Caramazza, A. (1985). Category-specific naming deficit following cerebral infarction. *Nature, 316,* 439–440.

Hart, J., & Gordon, B. (1990). Delineation of single-word semantic comprehension deficits in aphasia, with anatomical correlation. *Annals of Neurology, 27,* 226–231.

Hart, J., & Gordon, B. (1992). Neural subsystems for object knowledge. *Nature, 359,* 60–64.

Hartley, T., & Houghton, G. (1996). A linguistically constrained model of short-term memory for nonwords. *Journal of Memory and Language, 35,* 1–31.

Hartsuiker, R. J., & Kolk, H. H. J. (1998). Syntactic facilitation in agrammatic sentence production. *Brain and Language, 62,* 221–254.

Head, H. (1926). *Aphasia and kindred disorders of speech.* Cambridge: Cambridge University Press.

Heilman, K. M., Rothi, L., Campanella, D., & Wolfson, S. (1979). Wernicke's and global aphasia without alexia. *Archives of Neurology, 36,* 129–133.

Henaff Gonon, M., Bruckert, R., & Michel, F. (1989). Lexicalization in an anomic patient. *Neuropsychologia, 27,* 391–407.

Hillis, A. E., & Caramazza, A. (1991). Category-specific naming and comprehension impairment: A double dissociation. *Brain, 114,* 2081–2094.

Hillis, A. E., Boatman, D., Hart, J., & Gordon, B. (1999). Making sense out of jargon: A neurolinguistic and computational account of jargon aphasia. *Neurology, 53,* 1813–1824.

Hillis, A. E., Rapp, B., Romani, D., & Carmazza, A. (1990). Selective impairments of semantics in lexical processing. *Cognitive Neuropsychology, 7,* 191–243.

Hodges, J. R., Bozeat, S., Lambon Ralph, M., Patterson, K., & Spatt, J. (2000). The role of conceptual knowledge in object use: Evidence from semantic dementia. *Brain, 123,* 1913–1925.

Hodges, J. R., Garrard, P., & Patterson, K. (1998). Semantic dementia. In A. Kertesz & D. G. Munoz (Eds.), *Pick's disease and Pick complex* (pp. 83–104). New York: Wiley-Liss.

Hodges, J. R., Patterson, K., Oxbury, S., & Funnell, E. (1992). Semantic dementia: Progressive fluent aphasia with temporal lobe atrophy. *Brain, 115,* 1783–1806.

Hofstede, B. T. M., & Kolk, H. H. J. (1994). The effects of task variation on the production of grammatical morphology in Broca's aphasia: A multiple case study. *Brain and Language, 46,* 278–328.

Houghton, G. (1990). The problem serial order: A neural network model of sequence learning and recall. In R. Dale, C. Mellish, & M. Zock (Eds.), *Current research in natural language generation* (pp. 287–319). London: Academic Press.

Howard, D., & Orchard-Lisle, V. (1984). On the origin of semantic errors in naming: Evidence from the case of a global aphasic. *Cognitive Neuropsychology, 1,* 163–190.

Howard, D., & Patterson, K. (1992). *Pyramids and palm trees: A test of semantic access from pictures and words.* Bury St. Edmunds, UK: Thames Valley Test Company.

Howard, D., Patterson, K. E., Franklin, S., Orchard-Lisle, V. M., & Morton, J. (1984). Consistency and variability in picture naming by aphasic patients. In F. C. Rose (Ed.), *Recent advances in aphasiology* (pp. 263–276). New York: Raven.

Humphreys, G. W., Lamote, C., & Lloyd-Jones, T. J. (1995). An interactive activation approach to object processing: Effects of structural similarity, name frequency, and task in normality and pathology. *Memory, 3,* 535–586.

Indefrey, P., Brown, C. M., Hellwig, F., Amunts, K., Herzog, H., Seitz, R., et al. (2001). A neural correlate of syntactic encoding during speech production. *Proceedings of the National Academy of Sciences, 98,* 5933–5936.

Indefrey, P., & Levelt, W. J. M. (2000). The neural correlates of language production. In M. S. Gazzaniga (Ed.), *The new cognitive neurosciences* (2nd ed., pp. 845–866). Cambridge: MIT Press.

Jescheniak, J. D., & Levelt, W. J. M. (1994). Word frequency effects in speech production: Retrieval of syntactic information and of phonological form. *Journal of Experimental Psychology: Learning, Memory, & Cognition, 20,* 824–483.

Jones, E. V. (1984). Word order processing in aphasia: Effect of verb semantics. In F. C. Rose (Ed.), *Advances in neurology* (Vol. 42, pp. 159–181). New York: Raven.

Jusczyk, P. W., Cutler, A., & Redanz, N. (1993). Preference for the predominant stress patterns of English words. *Child Development, 64,* 675–687.

Just, M. A., & Carpenter, P. A. (1992). A capacity theory of comprehension: Individual differences in working memory. *Psychological Review, 99,* 122–149.

Just, M. A., Carpenter, P. A., Keller, T. A., Eddy, W. F., & Thulborn, K. R. (1996). Brain activation modulated by sentence comprehension. *Science, 274,* 114–116.

Kanwisher, N. H., Woods, R. P., Iacoboni, M., & Mazziotta, J. C. (1997). A locus in human extrastriate cortex for visual shape analysis. *Journal of Cognitive Neuroscience, 9,* 133–142.

Kay, J., & Ellis, A. W. (1987). A cognitive neuropsychological case study of anomia: Implications for psychological models of word retrieval. *Brain, 110,* 613–629.

Kean, M.-L. (1979). Agrammatism: A phonological deficit? *Cognition, 7,* 69–73.

Kempen, G., & Huijbers, P. (1983). The lexical process in sentence production and naming: Indirect election of words. *Cognition, 14,* 185–209.

Kertesz, A., & Benson, D. E. (1970). Neologistic jargon: A clinico-pathological study. *Cortex, 6,* 362–387.

Klatt, D. H. (1989). Review of selected models of speech perception. In W. D. Marslen-Wilson (Ed.), *Lexical representation and process* (pp. 169–226). Cambridge: MIT Press.

Kohn, S. E. (1993). Segmental disorders in aphasia. In G. Blanken, J. Dittmann, H. Grimm, J. C. Marshall, & C.-W. Wallesch (Eds.), *Linguistic disorders and pathologies* (pp. 197–209). Berlin: Walter de Gruyter.

Kohn, S. E., & Smith, K. L. (1994). Distinctions between two phonological output deficits. *Applied Psycholinguistics, 15,* 75–95.

Kohn, S. E., & Smith, K. L. (1995). Serial effects of phonemic planning during word production. *Aphasiology, 7,* 209–222.

Kolk, H., & Heeschen, C. (1992). Agrammatism, paragrammatism, and the management of language. *Language and Cognitive Processes, 7,* 89–129.

Kolk, H., & Van Grunsven, M. J. E. (1985). Agrammatism as a variable phenomenon. *Cognitive Neuropsychology, 2,* 347–384.

Kutas, M., Federeier, K. D., & Sereno, M. I. (1999). Current approaches to mapping language in electromagnetic space. In C. Brown & P. Hagoort (Eds.), *The neurocognition of language* (pp. 359–392). Oxford: Oxford University Press.

Kutas, M., & Hillyard, S. A. (1980). Reading senseless sentences: Brain potentials reflect semantic anomaly. *Science, 207,* 203–205.

Lambon Ralph, M. A., Graham, K. S., & Patterson, K. (1999). Is a picture worth a thousand words? Evidence from concept definitions by patients with semantic dementia. *Brain and Language, 70,* 309–335.

Lambon Ralph, M. A., Sage, K., & Roberts, J. (2000). Classical anomia: A neuropsychological perspective on speech production. *Neuropsychologia, 38,* 186–202.

Lapointe, S. (1983). Some issues in the linguistic description of agrammatism. *Cognition, 14,* 1–40.

Lapointe, S. (1985). A theory of verb form use in the speech of agrammatic aphasics. *Brain and Language, 24,* 100–155.

Lapointe, S., & Dell, G. S. (1989). A synthesis of some recent work in sentence production. In G. N. Carlson & M. K. Tanenhaus (Eds.), *Linguistic structure in language processing* (pp. 107–156). Dordrecht: Kluwer Academic Publishers.

Levelt, W. J. M. (1983). Monitoring and self-repair in speech. *Cognition, 14,* 41–104.

Levelt, W. J. M. (1989). *Speaking: From intention to articulation.* Cambridge: MIT Press.

Levelt, W. J. M., Praamstra, P., Meyer, A. S., Helenius, P., & Salmelin, R. (1998). An MEG study of picture naming. *Journal of Cognitive Neuroscience, 10,* 553–567.

Levelt, W. J. M., Roelofs, A., & Meyer, A. S. (1999). A theory of lexical access in speech production. *Behavioral and Brain Sciences, 22,* 1–75.

Levelt, W. J. M., Schriefers, H., Vorberg, D., Meyer, A. S., Pechmann, T., & Havinga, J. (1991). The time course of lexical access in speech production: A study of picture naming. *Psychological Review, 98,* 122–142.

Lichtheim, L. (1885). On aphasia. *Brain, 7,* 433–484.

Linebarger, M. (1990). Neuropsychology of sentence parsing. In A. Caramazza (Ed.), *Cognitive neuropsychology and neurolinguistics: Advances in models of cognitive function and impairment* (pp. 55–122). Hillsdale, NJ: Erlbaum.

Linebarger, M. (1995). Agrammatism as evidence about grammar. *Brain and Language, 50,* 52–91.

Linebarger, M., Schwartz, M. F., & Saffran, E. M. (1983). Sensitivity to grammatical structure in so-called agrammatic aphasics. *Cognition, 13,* 641–662.

Luce, P. A., Pisoni, D. B., & Goldinger, S. D. (1990). Similarity neighborhoods of spoken words. In G. T. M. Altmann (Ed.), *Cognitive models of speech processing* (pp. 122–147). Cambridge: MIT Press.

Luria, A. R. (1966). *Higher cortical functions in man.* New York: Basic Books.

MacKay, D. G. (1972). The structure of words and syllables: Evidence from errors in speech. *Cognitive Psychology, 3,* 210–227.

MacKay, D. G. (1987). *The organization of perception and action: A theory for language and other cognitive skills.* New York: Springer.

Marie, P. (1906). Revision de la question de l'aphasie: La troisieme convolution frontale gauche ne joue aucun role speciale dans la fonction du langage. *Semaine Medicale (Paris), 21,* 241–247.

Marshall, J. (1995). The mapping hypothesis and aphasia therapy. *Aphasiology, 9*(6), 517–539.

Marslen-Wilson, W. D., & Tyler, L. K. (1980). The temporal structure of spoken language understanding. *Cognition, 8,* 1–71.

Marslen-Wilson, W. D., & Welsh, A. (1978). Processing interactions and lexical access during word recognition in continuous speech. *Cognitive Psychology, 10,* 29–63.

Martin, A., Haxby, J. V., Lalonde, C. L., & Ungerleider, L. G. (1995). Discrete cortical regions associated with knowledge of color and knowledge of action. *Science, 270,* 102–105.

Martin, A., Wiggs, C. L., Ungerleider, L. G., & Haxby, J. V. (1996). Neural correlates of category-specific knowledge. *Nature, 379,* 649–652.

Martin, N., Dell, G. S., Saffran, E. M., & Schwartz, M. F. (1994). Origins of paraphasias in deep dysphasia: Testing the consequences of a decay impairment to an interactive spreading activation model of lexical retrieval. *Brain and Language, 47,* 609–660.

Martin, N., Gagnon, D., Schwartz, M. F., Dell, G. S., & Saffran, E. M. (1996). Phonological facilitation of semantic errors in normal and aphasic speakers. *Language and Cognitive Processes, 11,* 257–282.

Martin, N., & Saffran, E. M. (1992). A computational account of deep dysphasia: Evidence from a single case study. *Brain and Language, 43,* 240–274.

Martin, N., Saffran, E. M., & Dell, G. S. (1996). Recovery in deep dysphasia: Evidence for a relationship between auditory-verbal STM capacity and lexical errors in repetition. *Brain and Language, 52,* 83–113.

Martin, N., Weisberg, R. W., & Saffran, E. M. (1989). Variables influencing the occurrence of naming errors: Implications for models of lexical retrieval. *Journal of Memory and Language, 28,* 462–485.

Martin, R., & Blossom-Stach, C. (1986). Evidence of syntactic deficits in a fluent aphasic. *Brain and Language, 28,* 196–234.

Mazoyer, G. M., Tzourio, N., Frak, V. C., Syrota, A., Murayama, N., & Levrier, O. (1993). The cortical representation of speech. *Journal of Cognitive Neuroscience, 5,* 467–479.

McCarthy, R. A., & Warrington, E. K. (1988). Evidence for modality-specific meaning systems in the brain. *Nature, 334,* 428–430.

McClelland, J. L. (1979). On the time relations of mental processes: An examination of systems of processes in cascade. *Psychological Review, 86,* 287–330.

McClelland, J. L., & Elman, J. L. (1986). The TRACE model of speech perception. *Cognitive Neuropsychology, 18,* 1–86.

McClelland, J. L., & Rumelhart, D. E. (1981). An interactive activation model of the effects of context on perception: Part 1. *Psychological Review, 88,* 375–407.

McClelland, J. L., & Rumelhart, D. (1986). *Parallel distributed processing* (Vol. 1). Cambridge: MIT Press.

Menn, L., & Obler, L. K. (1990). Cross-language data and theories of agrammatism. In L. Menn & L. K. Obler (Eds.), *Agrammatic aphasia* (Vol. 2, pp. 1369–1389). Amsterdam: John Benjamin.

Menn, L., Reilly, K. F., Hayashi, M., Kamio, A., Fujita, I., & Sasanuma, S. (1998). The interaction of preserved pragmatics and impaired syntax in Japanese and English aphasic speech. *Brain and Language, 61,* 183–225.

Metter, E. J. (1987). Neuroanatomy and physiology of aphasia: Evidence from positron emission tomography. *Aphasiology, 1,* 3–33.

Metter, E. J., Hanson, W. R., Jackson, C. A., Kempler, D., van Lancker, D., Mazziotta, J. C., & Phelps, M. E. (1990). Temporoparietal cortex in aphasia: Evidence from positron emission tomography. *Archives of Neurology, 47,* 1235–1238.

Meyer, M., Friederici, A. D., & von Cramon, D. Y. (2000). Neurocognition of auditory sentence comprehension: Event related fMRI reveals sensitivity to syntactic violations and task demands. *Cognitive Brain Research, 9,* 19–33.

Miceli, G. A., Mazzucchi, A., Menn, L., & Goodglass, H. (1983). Contrasting cases of Italian agrammatic aphasics without comprehension disorder. *Brain and Language, 19,* 56–97.

Miceli, G. A., Silveri, C., Villa, G., & Caramazza, A. (1984). The basis for the agrammatic's difficulty in producing main verbs. *Cortex, 20,* 207–220.

Milberg, W., & Blumstein, S. E. (1981). Lexical decision and aphasia: Evidence for semantic processing. *Brain and Language, 14,* 371–385.

Milberg, W., Blumstein, S. E., & Dworetzky, B. (1988). Phonological processing and lexical access in aphasia. *Brain and Language, 34,* 279–293.

Miller, D., & Ellis, A. W. (1987). Speech and writing error in "neologistic jargonaphasia": A lexical activation hypothesis. In M. Coltheart, G. Santori, & R. Job (Eds.), *The cognitive neuropsychology of language* (pp. 253–271). London: Erlbaum.

Miller, J. L., & Eimas, P. D. (1995). Speech perception: From signal to word. *Annual Review of Psychology, 46,* 467–492.

Miyake, A., Carpenter, P. A., & Just, M. A. (1994). A capacity approach to syntactic comprehension disorders: Making normal adults perform like aphasic patients. *Cognitive Neuropsychology, 11,* 671–717.

Mohr, J. P., Pessin, M. S., Finkelstein, S., Funkenstein, H. H., Duncan, G. W., & Davis, K. (1978). Broca's aphasia: Pathological and clinical. *Neurology, 28,* 311–324.

Moss, H. E., Tyler, L. K., & Jennings, F. (1997). When leopards lose their spots: Knowledge of visual properties in category-specific deficits for living things. *Cognitive Neuropsychology, 14,* 901–950.

Mummery, C. J., Patterson, K., Price, C., Ashburner, J., Frackowiak, R. S., & Hodges, J. R. (2000). A voxel-based morphometry study of semantic dementia: Relationship between temporal lobe atrophy and semantic memory. *Annals of Neurology, 47,* 36–45.

Mummery, C. J., Patterson, K., Wise, R. J. S., Vandenberghe, R., Price, C. J., & Hodges, J. R. (1999). Disrupted temporal lobe connections in semantic dementia. *Brain, 122,* 61–73.

Murtha, S., Chertkow, H., Beauregard, M., & Evans, A. (1999). The neural substrate of picture naming. *Journal of Cognitive Neuroscience, 11,* 399–423.

Naatanen, R., Lehtokoski, A., Lennes, M., Cheour, M., Huotilainen, M., Iivonen, A., Vainio, M., Alku, P., Ilmoniemi, R. J., Luuk, A., Allik, J., Sinkkonen, J., & Alho, K. (1997). Language-specific phoneme representations revealed by electric and magnetic brain responses. *Nature, 385,* 432–434.

Naeser, M. A., Alexander, M. P., Helm-Estabrooks, N. R. G., Levine, H. L., Laughlin, S. A., & Geschwind, N. (1982). Aphasia with predominantly subcortical lesion sites. *Archives of Neurology, 39,* 2–14.

Nespoulous, J.-L., Dordain, M., Perron, C., Ska, B., Caplan, D., Mehler, J., & Lecours, A. R. (1988). Agrammatism in sentence production without comprehension deficits: Reduced availability of syntactic structures and/or grammatical morphemes: A case study. *Brain and Language, 33,* 273–295.

Nickels, L., & Howard, D. (1995). Phonological errors in aphasic naming: Comprehension, monitoring, and lexicality. *Cortex, 31,* 209–237.

Nobre, A. C., Allison, T., & McCarthy, G. (1994). Word recognition in the human inferior temporal lobe. *Nature, 372,* 260–264.

O'Seaghda, P. G., & Marin, J. W. (1997). Mediated semantic-phonological priming: Calling distant relatives. *Journal of Memory and Language, 36,* 226–252.

Ojemann, G., & Mateer, C. (1979). Human language cortex: Localization of memory, syntax, and sequential motor-phoneme identification systems. *Science, 205,* 1401–1403.

Pate, D. S., Saffran, E. M., & Martin, N. (1987). Specifying the nature of the production impairment in a conduction aphasic: A case study. *Language and Cognitive Processes, 2,* 43–84.

Penfield, W., & Roberts, L. (1959). *Speech and brain mechanisms.* Princeton: Princeton University Press.

Perani, D., Cappa, S. F., Bettinardi, V., Bressi, S., Gorno-Tempini, M., Matarrese, M., & Fazio, F. (1995). Different neural systems for the recognition of animals and man-made tools. *Neuro-Report, 6,* 1637–1641.

Peterson, P. R., & Savoy, P. (1998). Lexical selection and phonological encoding during language production: Evidence for cascaded processing. *Journal of Experimental Psychology: Learning, Memory, & Cognition, 24,* 539–557.

Peterson, S. E., Fox, P. T., Posner, M. I., Mintun, M. A., & Raichle, M. E. (1988). Positron emission tomographic studies of the cortical anatomy of single-word processing. *Nature, 331,* 585–589.

Pick, A. (1913). *Die agrammatischen sprachstorungen.* Berlin: Springer.

Plaut, D. C. (1996). Relearning after damage in connectionist networks: Toward a theory of rehabilitation. *Brain and Language, 52,* 25–82.

Plaut, D. C., & Shallice, T. (1993). Deep dyslexia: A case study of connectionist neuropsychology. *Cognitive Neuropsychology, 10,* 377–500.

Praamstra, P., Hagoort, P., Maasen, B., & Crul, T. (1991). Word deafness and auditory cortical function: A case history and hypothesis. *Brain,* 1197–1225.

Pulvermuller, F. (1995). Agrammatism: Behavioral description and neurobiological explanation. *Journal of Cognitive Neuroscience, 7,* 165–181.

Rapp, B., Benzing, L., & Caramazza, A. (1997). The autonomy of lexical orthography. *Cognitive Neuropsychology, 14,* 71–104.

Rapp, B., & Goldrick, M. (2000). Discreteness and interactivity in spoken word production. *Psychological Review, 107,* 460–499.

Rasmussen, T., & Milner, B. (1977). The role of early left-brain injury in determining lateralization of cerebral speech functions. In S. J. Dimond & D. A. Blizard (Eds.), *Evolution and lateralization of the brain* (Vol. 299 of Annals of the New York Academy of Sciences, pp. 355–369). New York: New York Academy of Sciences.

Roach, A., Schwartz, M. F., Martin, N., Grewal, R. S., & Brecher, A. (1996). The Philadelphia naming test: Scoring and rationale. *Clinical Aphasiology, 24,* 121–133.

Roelofs, A. (1992). A spreading activation theory of lemma retrieval in speaking. *Cognition, 42,* 107–142.

Rugg, M. D. (1999). Functional neuroimaging in cognitive neuroscience. In C. Brown & P. Hagoort (Eds.), *The neurocognition of language* (pp. 15–36). Oxford: Oxford University Press.

Ruml, W., & Caramazza, A. (2000). An evaluation of a computational model of lexical access: Comments on Dell et al. (1977). *Psychological Review, 107,* 609–634.

Sacchett, C., & Humphreys, G. W. (1992). Calling a squirrel a squirrel but a canoe a wigwam: A category-specific deficit for artifactual objects and body parts. *Cognitive Neuropsychology, 9,* 73–86.

Saffran, E. M. (1982). Neuropsychological approaches to the study of language. *British Journal of Psychology, 73,* 317–337.

Saffran, E. M., Dell, G. S., & Schwartz, M. F. (2000). Computational modeling of language disorders. In M. S. Gazzaniga (Ed.), *The new cognitive neurosciences* (pp. 933–948). Cambridge: MIT Press.

Saffran, E. M., Marin, O. S. M., & Yeni-Komshian, G. (1976). An analysis of speech perception in word deafness. *Brain and Language, 3,* 209–228.

Saffran, E. M., & Martin, N. (1997). Effects of structural priming on sentence production in aphasics. *Language and Cognitive Processes, 12,* 877–882.

Saffran, E. M., & Schwartz, M. F. (1994). Of cabbages and things: Semantic memory from a neuropsychological perspective—A tutorial review. In C. Umilta & M. Moscovitch (Eds.), *Attention and performance XV: Conscious and nonconscious information processing* (pp. 507–536). Cambridge, MA: Bradford.

Saffran, E. M., Schwartz, M. F., & Marin, O. S. M. (1980a). Evidence from aphasia: Isolating the components of a production model. In B. Butterworth (Ed.), *Language production* (Vol. 1, pp. 221–241). London: Academic Press.

Saffran, E. M., Schwartz, M. F., & Marin, O. S. M. (1980b). The word order problem in agrammatism: I. Production. *Brain and Language, 10,* 249–262.

Schriefers, H., Meyer, A. S., & Levelt, W. J. M. (1990). Exploring the time-course of lexical access in production: Picture-word interference studies. *Journal of Memory and Language, 29,* 86–102.

Schuell, H., & Jenkins, J. J. (1961). Reduction of vocabulary in aphasia. *Brain, 84,* 243–261.

Schuell, H., Jenkins, J. J., & Carroll, J. M. (1962). Factor analysis of the Minnesota Test for differential diagnosis of aphasia. *Journal of Speech and Hearing Research, 5,* 439–469.

Schwartz, J., & Tallal, P. (1980). Rate of acoustic change may underlie hemispheric specialization for speech perception. *Science, 207,* 1380–1381.

Schwartz, M. F. (1987). Patterns of speech production deficit within and across aphasia syndromes: Application of a psycholinguistic model. In M. Colheart:, R. Job, & G. Sartori (Eds.), *The cognitive neuropsychology of language.* London: Erlbaum.

Schwartz, M. F., & Brecher, A. (2000). A model-driven analysis of severity, response characteristics, and partial recovery in aphasics' picture naming. *Brain and Language, 73,* 62–91.

Schwartz, M. F., Linebarger, M. C., & Saffran, E. M. (1985). The status of the syntactic deficit theory of agrammatism. In M.-L. Kean (Ed.), *Agrammatism.* Orlando, FL: Academic Press.

Schwartz, M. F., Linebarger, M. C., Saffran, E. M., & Pate, D. S. (1987). Syntactic transparency and sentence interpretation in aphasia. *Language and Cognitive Processes, 2,* 85–113.

Schwartz, M. F., Marin, O. S. M., & Saffran, E. M. (1979). Dissociation of language function in dementia: A case study. *Brain and Language, 7,* 277–306.

Schwartz, M. F., Wilshire, C. E., Gagnon, D., & Polansky, M. (2002). *The origins of nonword phonological errors in aphasics' picture naming.* Manuscript in progress.

Shallice, T. (1988). *From neuropsychology to mental structure.* Cambridge: Cambridge University Press.

Shankweiler, D., Crain, S., Gorrell, P., & Tuller, B. (1989). Reception of language in Broca's aphasia. *Language and Cognitive Processes, 4,* 1–33.

Shattuck-Hufnagel, S. (1979). Speech errors as evidence for a serial ordering mechanism in speech production. In W. E. Cooper & E. C. T. Walker (Eds.), *Sentence processing: Psycholinguistic studies presented to Merrill Garrett* (pp. 295–342). Hillsdale, NJ: Erlbaum.

Shindo, M., Kaga, K., & Tanaka, Y. (1991). Speech discrimination and lip reading in patients with word deafness or auditory agnosia. *Brain and Language, 4,* 153–161.

Simons, J. S., & Lambon Ralph, M. A. (1999). The auditory agnosias. *Neurocase, 5,* 379–406.

Smith, E. E., Jonides, J., Koeppe, R. A., Awh, E., Schumache, E. H., & Minoshima, S. (1995). Spatial vs. object working memory: PET investigations. *Journal of Cognitive Neuroscience, 7,* 337–356.

Snowden, J. S., Goulding, P. J., & Neary, D. (1989). Semantic dementia: A form of circumscribed cerebral atrophy. *Behavioural Neurology, 2,* 167–182.

Snowden, J. S., Griffiths, H., & Neary, D. (1994). Semantic dementia: Autobiographical contribution to preservation of meaning. *Cognitive Neuropsychology, 11,* 265–288.

Stemberger, J. P. (1985). An interactive activation model of language production. In A. Ellis (Ed.), *Progress in the psychology of language* (pp. 143–186). London: Erlbaum.

Stewart, F., Parkin, A. J., & Hunkin, N. M. (1992). Naming impairments following recovery from herpes simplex encephalitis: Category specific? *Quarterly Journal of Experimental Psychology, 44A,* 261–284.

Stromswold, K., Caplan, D., Alpert, N., & Rauch, S. (1996). Localization of syntactic comprehension by positron emission tomography. *Brain and Language, 52,* 452–473.

Swaab, T., Brown, C., & Hagoort, P. (1997). Spoken sentence comprehension in aphasia: Event-relate potential evidence for a lexical integration deficit. *Journal of Cognitive Neuroscience, 9,* 39–66.

Takahashi, N., Kawamura, M., Shinotou, H., Hirayama, K., Kaga, K., & Shindo, M. (1992). Pure word deafness due to left hemisphere damage. *Cortex, 28,* 295–303.

Thompson-Schill, S. L., D'Esposito, M., Aguirre, G. K., & Farah, M. J. (1997). Role of left inferior prefrontal cortex in retrieval of semantic knowledge: A reevaluation. *Proceedings of the National Academy of Sciences, 94,* 14792–14797.

Tranel, D., Damasio, H., & Damasio, A. (1997). A neural basis for the retrieval of conceptual knowledge. *Neuropsychologia, 35,* 1319–1327.

Trueswell, J. C., Tanenhaus, M. K., & Garnsey, S. M. (1994). Semantic influences on parsing: Use of thematic role information in syntactic ambiguity resolution. *Journal of Memory and Language, 33,* 285–318.

Tulving, E. (1972). Episodic and semantic memory. In E. Tulving & W. Donaldson (Eds.), *Organization of memory.* New York: Academic Press.

Tyler, L. K. (1992). *Spoken language comprehension: An experimental approach to disordered and normal processing.* Cambridge: MIT Press.

Tyler, L. K., Ostrin, R. K., Cooke, M., & Moss, H. E. (1995). Automatic access of lexical information in Broca's aphasics: Against the automaticity hypothesis. *Brain and Language, 48,* 131–162.

Ullman, M. T. (2001). A neurocognitive perspective on language: The declarative/procedural model. *Nature Reviews/Neuroscience, 2,* 717–726.

Uylings, H. B. M., Malofeeva, L. J., Bogolepova, I. N., Amunts, K., & Zilles, K. (1999). Broca's language area from a neuroanatomical and developmental perspective. In C. Brown & P. Hagoort (Eds.), *The neurocognition of language* (pp. 319–336). Oxford: Oxford University Press.

Van Orden, G. C., Pennington, B. F., & Stone, G. O. (2001). What do double dissociations prove? *Cognitive Science, 25,* 111–172.

Vandenberghe, R., Price, C., Wise, R., Josephs, O., & Frackowiak, R. S. J. (1996). Functional anatomy of a common semantic system for words and pictures. *Nature, 383,* 254–256.

Vanier, M., & Caplan, D. (1990). CT-scan correlates of agrammatism. In L. Menn & L. K. Obler (Eds.), *Agrammatic aphasia: A cross-language narrative source book* (pp. 37–114). Amsterdam: Benjamins.

Vigliocco, G., Antonini, T., & Garrett, M. F. (1997). Grammatical gender is on the tip of Italian tongues. *Psychological Science, 8,* 314–317.

Vitevitch, M. S. (1997). The neighborhood characteristics of malapropisms. *Language and Speech, 40,* 211–228.

Vitevitch, M. S. (2001). *The influence of phonological similarity neighborhoods on speech production.* Manuscript submitted for publication.

Vitevitch, M. S., & Sommers, M. S. (2001). *The role of phonological neighbors in the tip-of-the-tongue state.* Manuscript submitted for publication.

Vousden, J. I., Brown, G. D., & Harley, T. A. (2000). Serial control of phonology in speech production: A hierarchical model. *Cognitive Psychology, 41,* 101–175.

Warren, R. M. (1970). Perceptual restoration of missing speech sounds. *Science, 167,* 392–393.

Warrington, E. K. (1975). The selective impairment of semantic memory. *Quarterly Journal of Experimental Psychology, 27,* 635–657.

Warrington, E. K., & McCarthy, R. A. (1983). Category-specific access dysphasia. *Brain, 106,* 859–878.

Warrington, E. K., & McCarthy, R. A. (1987). Categories of knowledge: Further fractionations and an attempted integration. *Brain, 110,* 1273–1296.

Warrington, E. K., & Shallice, T. (1984). Category-specific semantic impairments. *Brain, 107,* 829–853.

Weiller, C., Isensee, C., Rijntejes, M., Huber, W. I., Muller, S., Bier, D., Dutschka, K., Woods, R. P., North, J., & Diener, H. C. (1995). Recovery from Wernicke's aphasia: A position emission tomographic study. *Annals of Neurology, 37,* 723–732.

Wernicke, C. (1874). *Der aphasische symtomencomplex.* Breslau: Cohn and Weigart.

Willmes, K., & Poeck, K. (1993). To what extent can aphasic syndromes be localized? *Brain, 116,* 1527–1540.

Wulfeck, B. (1998). Grammaticality judgments and sentence comprehension in aphasia. *Journal of Speech, Language, and Hearing Research, 31,* 72–81.

Yaqub, B. A., Gascon, G. G., Al-Nosha, M., & Whitaker, H. (1988). Pure word deafness (acquired verbal auditory agnosia) in an Arabic speaking patient. *Brain, 111,* 457–466.

Zarahn, E., Aguirre, G., & D'Esposito, M. (1997). A trial-based experimental design for fMRI. *Neuroimage, 6,* 122–138.

Zingeser, L. B., & Berndt, R. S. (1990). Retrieval of nouns and verbs by agrammatic and anomic aphasics. *Brain and Language, 39,* 14–32.

CHAPTER 22

Psychological Function in Computational Models of Neural Networks

RANDALL C. O'REILLY AND YUKO MUNAKATA

The overarching goal of cognitive neuroscience is to understand how the brain gives rise to thought. Toward this goal, researchers employ various methods to measure neural variables while people and other animals think. A complementary method—computer models of neural networks—allows unparalleled levels of control and supports the further understanding of the relation between brain and mind. Using these models, one can simulate a network of interacting neurons and measure cognitive function in these networks at the same time. Furthermore, many variables in these networks can be manipulated so that their effects on cognitive processes can be observed.

In this chapter we provide an up-to-date review of some of the core principles and prominent applications of computational models in cognitive neuroscience, based on our recent textbook on this topic (O'Reilly & Munakata, 2000). We begin with a summary of some of the basic questions confronting computational modelers in cognitive neuroscience. We then discuss provisional answers to these questions, showing how they apply to a range of empirical data. Throughout, and in closing, we discuss challenges to neural network models. We will see how some network models can have possibly problematic properties, often driven by constraints from biology or cognition, but the models can nonetheless help to advance the field of cognitive neuroscience.

BASIC MECHANISTIC QUESTIONS FACING COMPUTATIONAL MODELS

As soon as one is faced with the task of constructing a neural network from scratch, several important questions immediately arise:

- How do the neurons talk to each other? We know a lot about the answers to this question from neuroscience, but there are some more specific questions that models raise, including the following:
  - What kind of information do spikes contain—is it just the rate of spiking, or are more detailed signals being conveyed in the timing of individual spikes?
  - How are spike inputs from other neurons integrated together within the neuron—does each input just add into an overall sum, or are different inputs treated differently?
  - Are there basic network-level patterns of interaction between neurons that apply across a wide range of cognitive functions?
- How do networks learn from experience? Networks with even a few tens of neurons can exhibit complex and varied patterns of behavior depending on how the neurons are interconnected. Brain-sized networks with billions of

neurons are thus almost incomprehensibly complex. The brain requires a powerful way of setting all of these patterns of interconnectivity to achieve useful behaviors in the face of all the other random possibilities.

- How does the myriad of complex perceptual inputs get organized into a coherent internal representation of the environment?
- How are memories of previous experience stored, organized, and retrieved?
- How does higher level cognition arise from networks of neurons?

There are many other such questions that one could ask, but we focus on relatively brief treatments of these due to space limitations (see O'Reilly & Munakata, 2000, for a comprehensive treatment of a wide range of cognitive phenomena). In the process of addressing each of these questions, we develop a set of basic mechanisms for computational cognitive neuroscience modeling.

THE NEURAL ACTIVATION FUNCTION

The first two questions we raised ("What kind of information do spikes contain?" and "How are spike inputs from other neurons integrated together within the neuron?") can be addressed by developing what is commonly called an *activation function* for a simulated neuron. This activation function provides a mathematical formalism (i.e., an *algorithm*) for describing how neurons talk to each other. The currency of this neural communication is referred to as activation—neurons communicate by activating each other. Fortunately, neuroscience has developed a relatively advanced understanding the basic operation of a neuron. We summarize the key facts here.

A neuron receives input from other neurons through *synapses* located on branching processes called *dendrites*. These inputs are somehow integrated together as an electrical voltage (referred to as the *membrane potential*) in the *cell body*. If this voltage exceeds a certain value (called the *threshold*), the neuron will trigger a *spike* of electrical activity down its *axon*, which is another branching process that terminates on the synapses of other neurons. This input to other neurons thus continues the propagation of information through the brain.

All of these properties are central to the simulated neurons in neural network models. One can frame these properties in terms of a *detector*. This detector model provides a clear

functional role for the biological properties of the neuron (O'Reilly & Munakata, 2000). Specifically, we can think of a neuron as detecting the existence of some set of conditions and responding with a signal that communicates the extent to which those conditions have been met. Think of a smoke detector, which is constantly sampling the air looking for conditions that indicate the presence of a fire. In the brain, neurons in the early stages of the visual system are constantly sampling the visual input by looking for conditions that indicate the presence of very simple visual features such as bars of light at a given position and orientation in the visual scene. Higher up in the visual system are neurons that detect different sets of objects. One can interpret virtually any neural activation in the brain in the general language of detecting some kind of pattern of activity in the inputs.

The match between the detector model and the biological features of the neuron is shown in Figure 22.1. The dendrites provide detector inputs, which are integrated into an overall signal in the cell body that the neuron can use to determine if what it is detecting is actually there. The firing threshold acts just like a smoke detector threshold: There must be sufficient evidence of a fire before an alarm should be triggered, and similarly the neuron must accumulate a sufficient voltage before it can send information to other neurons.

A critical aspect of simulated neurons (also called *units*) is that they have adjustable parameters called *weights* that determine how much influence the different inputs have on them. In the neuron, these weights correspond to the strength of the individual synapses connecting neurons—some synapses produce more electrical voltage input than others. Thus, some inputs weigh more heavily into the detection decision than do others. These weights provide the critical parameters for specifying what the neuron detects. Essentially, neurons can detect *patterns of activity* over their inputs, and those input patterns that best fit the pattern of weights produce the largest detection response. A perhaps more tangible example of this kind of operation would be obtained by looking

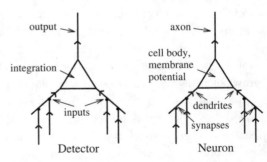

Figure 22.1   The detector model can be used to understand to the function of corresponding neural components.

through a piece of paper with a shape cut out of it (e.g., an L shape). If you look through this mask at a black computer screen with different shapes being displayed on it in a bright color, you see the most light if the displayed shape exactly matches the cutout shape. Similarly, a neuron gets the most activation if its inputs match its pattern of weights.

There is a progression of increasingly more complex ways of simulating the basic activation function of a neuron (Figure 22.2). In the simplest kind of neural model, a unit simply adds up the weighted inputs from other neurons (called the *net input* to a unit) and sends the results directly on to other neurons. This is a *linear unit*. It turns out that linear units, like linear equations, are not very powerful in a computational sense—the effects of layers and layers of linear units can all be summarized by just one such layer. The next most complex kind of unit is a *threshold linear unit,* which is just like a linear unit except that it has a threshold (much like a real neuron) so that if its net input is below the threshold, it does not send any activation to other units. Because neurons can fire only so fast, it also makes sense to think of a *saturation* point in the activation function, above which the activation cannot go. The widely used *sigmoidal unit* (Figure 22.2) provides a more graded function that exhibits both threshold-like and saturating properties.

These simplified models of the neural activation function are at the heart of a controversy surrounding the nature of the neural code. Specifically, in mapping these models onto the brain, the simulated neural activations are real-valued numbers, so we have to assume that they represent something like the *average firing rate* of neurons, not the individual spikes themselves. Thus, a major question is, Does the firing rate

capture the essence of the information that real neurons communicate to each other, or does the precise timing of the spikes contain more information that would be lost with a rate code? The debate over the nature of the information encoded in the neural spike train has inspired a number of empirical studies across a range of different animals, with some demonstrations that detailed spike timing matters in some parts of the brain (e.g., Reike, Warland, van Steveninck, & Bialek, 1996). However, recordings in the cortex of primates, which is the most relevant for understanding human cognition, have been largely consistent with the rate code simplification in neural networks (Tovee, Rolls, Treves, & Bellis, 1993).

Moving beyond these highly simplified model neurons, one can incorporate equations that simulate the electrical behavior of biological neurons. It has long been known that the electrical properties of neurons can be understood in terms of the familiar concepts of resistors and capacitors, the so-called *equivalent circuit* model of the neuron. A key issue that arises here is the extent to which a neuron behaves like a single coherent electrical system, or whether one needs to keep track of electrical potentials at many different locations along the neuron. At the simplest extreme is a *point neuron,* which has the entire geometry of the neuron reduced to a single point in space, such that only one electrical potential needs to be computed. These biologically based units are not much more complex than the units just described, yet they do a better job of capturing the behavior of real neurons. For this reason, we used the point neuron model in O'Reilly and Munakata (2000). Much more complex neural models have also been explored using many different electrical *compartments* (e.g., Koch & Segev, 1998).

The debate over how many compartments to use in a neural model centers on the issue of how real neurons integrate all of their inputs. If neurons are effectively electrically unitary (as in a point neuron), they essentially add their inputs together, just as in the simplified models. If, however, different parts of the neuron have very different electrical potentials, then inputs coming into these different parts can have very different effects, and therefore a simple additive integration would underestimate the real complexity of neurons (e.g., Shepherd & Brayton, 1987). Although it is by no means the final word on these issues, a recent analysis (Jaffe & Carnevale, 1999) supports the idea that the point neuron model captures much of the integration properties of real cortical neurons. Specifically, they found that as long as there was not a long primary dendrite (as in most cortical pyramidal neurons), the impact of inputs at various places on the dendritic tree was roughly the same when measured at the soma.

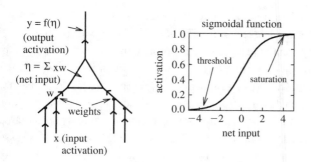

Figure 22.2 Basic equations for simple models of neurons. Input activation from other neurons x is multiplied times the weight value w, and summed together to get the net input ($\eta = \sum xw$). The output activation y is then computed as a function $f(\eta)$ of the net input. In the simplest kind of *linear* model, there is no output function, $y = \eta$. A more complex model has a *threshold*, below which activation does not occur: $y = \eta$ if $h > \theta$; 0 otherwise. A saturation point can also be imposed, so that activation y has a maximal limit. The *sigmoidal* function $f(\eta) = \frac{1}{1+e^{-\eta}}$ produces a graded, continuous-valued function that has both threshold-like and saturating properties.

One important biological constraint that the point neuron captures but the simpler sigmoidal-style units do not is that excitation and inhibition are separated in the brain. Thus, a given neuron will send either an excitatory or an inhibitory output to other neurons. Excitatory outputs result in the excitation of other neurons, whereas inhibitory outputs counteract this excitation and make the receiving neuron less likely to become activated. In the simpler sigmoidal unit, weights are typically allowed to be either positive or negative, which violates this biological constraint.

In summary, one could argue that the point neuron model captures the essential properties of individual neural computations. Although this model undoubtedly commits errors of omission by not capturing many details of real neurons, in some cases the functional relevance of such details may be approximated by the point neuron model (e.g., the functional relevance of a synapse may boil down to its efficacy, which can be approximated by a weight parameter, without capturing all of the biological details of actual synapses). In other cases, such details may not be all that functionally important. At the least, such a simple model does not have obvious errors of commission; that is, it does not attribute any computational powers to the model neurons that are unlikely to be true of real neurons.

NETWORK INTERACTIONS

In this section we move beyond the individual neuron and consider the properties of networks of interconnected neurons with the next of our overarching questions in mind: "Are there basic network-level patterns of interaction between neurons that apply across a wide range of cognitive functions?" By identifying basic network-level interactions, we can develop a vocabulary of mechanistically grounded concepts for understanding how neural networks behave.

Before identifying these network properties, we need to know what the cortical network looks like. The six-layered structure of the cortex varies in different areas of the brain. Based on this information and anatomical studies of connectivity, one can summarize the roles of the six-layered cortical structure in terms of the following as three *functional* layers (Figure 22.3; O'Reilly & Munakata, 2000):

- The *input* layer corresponds to cortical Layer 4, which usually receives the sensory input by way of a subcortical brain area called the *thalamus,* which receives information from the retina and other sense organs.

- The *output* layer corresponds to the *deep* cortical Layers 5 and 6, which send motor commands and other outputs to

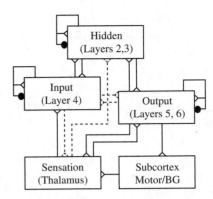

Figure 22.3   A simple, three-layer interpretation of cortical structure that is consistent with general connectivity patterns and provides a useful starting point for modeling. Direct excitatory connectivity is shown by the open triangular connections. Inhibitory interneurons are indicated by the filled circular connections; these operate within each cortical layer and receive the same types of excitatory connections as the excitatory neurons do. Dotted lines indicate connections that may exist but are not consistent with the feedforward flow of information from input to hidden to output (with feedback projections along the same pathways). Limited data make it difficult to determine how prevalent and important these connections are.

a wide range of subcortical areas, including the *basal ganglia.*

- The *hidden* layer (so called because it is not directly visible via either the inputs or outputs) corresponds to the *superficial* (upper) cortical Layers 2 and 3 (cortical Layer 1 is largely just axons). These layers receive inputs locally from the other cortical layers and also from other more distant superficial cortical layers. The superficial layers usually project outputs back to these same more distant cortical areas, and to the deep (output) layers locally.

Thus, at a very coarse level, sensory information flows into the input layer, gets processed in some way by the hidden layer, and the results of this processing give rise to motor outputs in the output layer. This trajectory of information flow is actually spread across many different cortical areas, each of which has the same six-layered structure. However, input areas tend to have a more pronounced Layer 4; output areas have more pronounced Layers 5 and 6; and hidden (association) areas have more pronounced Layers 2 and 3. Figure 22.4 summarizes these layer-level specializations in different brain areas, as they contribute to the big loop of information flow through the brain.

Thus, based on the structure of the cortex, it is reasonable for neural network models to be composed of the three functional layers (input, one or more hidden layers, and an output layer). The biology also tells us that the primary neuron type (the *pyramidal neuron*) that connects between layers and between brain areas is excitatory, whereas there are a

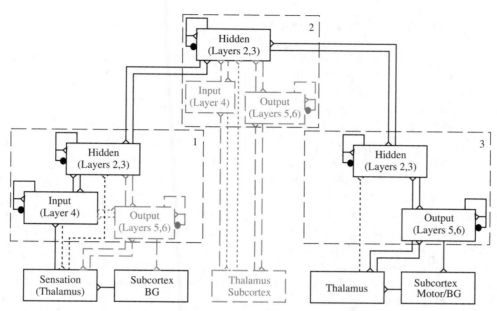

Figure 22.4   Larger scale version of cortical circuitry, showing the three different types of cortical areas: *1* is an *input area,* which has a well-developed Layer 4 receiving sensory input from the thalamus, but not producing motor output directly. *2* is a *hidden area* (often called a higher level association area), which receives input from input areas (or other hidden areas) and sends outputs to output areas (or other hidden areas). It has reduced input and output layers and communicates primarily via Layer 2–3 connectivity. *3* is an *output area* (motor control area) projecting to subcortical brain areas that drive the motor system, which has no real Layer 4 (and a larger Layer 5). Dashed lines indicate layers and connections that are reduced in importance for a given area, and dotted lines again represent connections which may exist but are not consistent with the input-hidden-output model of feed-forward information flow. In all cases, reciprocal backward projections complement the feed-forward projections, enabling bidirectional, interactive processing.

number of inhibitory *interneurons* that have more local patterns of connectivity. The excitatory connectivity is generally *bidirectional,* meaning that excitation flows from input to hidden to output, and at the same time backward from output to hidden to input.

Using these features of the biology, we can frame the basic network-level interactions in terms of three different kinds of neural connectivity between functional layers of neurons (O'Reilly & Munakata, 2000):

- *Unidirectional (feed-forward) excitation:* When one layer of neurons sends activation to another layer, the patterns of activation in the sending layer get *transformed,* by *emphasizing* some distinctions while *collapsing* across others. Each neural detector contributes to the transformation by its own selectivities in what it detects and what it ignores. These transformations are the basic information-processing operations in the brain, creating ever more abstract and powerful *categories* of information over subsequent layers of processing.

- *Bidirectional (feedback) excitation:* When two layers each send activation to the other (also called *interactivity* or *recurrence*), the layers can amplify each other's activations, giving rise to a variety of phenomena including *pattern completion, resonance, mutual support,* and *attractor*

dynamics. This also allows for the feed-forward-style transformations to proceed in both directions.

- *Inhibitory competition:* Feed-forward communication of inhibition across layers and feedback inhibition within a layer combine to produce a competition among neurons within a layer—only those neurons receiving the strongest amount of excitation will remain active in the face of this competition.

The overall picture is this: Sensory information gets processed by a cascade of hidden layers, where each hidden layer extracts some particular kind of information while discarding others. For example, it is well known that different parts of the visual system extract color, motion, object identity, and object location information. Extracting this information requires carefully tuned patterns of weights that emphasize the relevant information while ignoring the irrelevant. For example, where the visual image of an object appears on retina is irrelevant for identifying what the object is, but differences in the shape of the image are critical. Conversely, shape information is irrelevant for locating that object in space, but retinal position (along with eye, head, and body positions) is relevant. Essentially, the brain extracts ever more abstract executive summaries of the environment and then uses this information to formulate plans of action, which are then executed through projections to the output layers.

Superimposed on this input-output flow of information are the complex dynamics that arise from bidirectional connectivity and inhibition. Bidirectional connectivity enables the brain to fill in missing input information using higher level knowledge. For example, a hidden area that encodes words at an abstract level can fill in the missing pieces of a garbled phone message by relying on knowledge of who is speaking, and what they are likely to be saying. In combination with inhibitory competition, bidirectional connectivity also ensures that all the different brain areas focus on the same thing at the same time: Neurons processing information relevant to other brain areas will be reinforced through the bidirectional excitation, and this extra excitation will lead to greater inhibition on other neurons that are not relevant to other brain areas, thereby shutting them off. At a cognitive level, we can think of this interplay of bidirectional excitation and inhibition as giving rise to *attention*. We explore this idea in a subsequent section.

LEARNING MECHANISMS

In many psychological theories, learning assumes a relatively tangential role. People assume that the brain systems that they hypothesize arise through some complex interaction between genetic structures and experience, but the details of exactly how the systems came to be are often too difficult to confront while trying to provide a theory about the mature system. In contrast, learning plays an essential role in most neural network models because generally the best way to get a neural network to do something useful is to have it learn based on its experiences (i.e., to change its weights according to a learning mechanism, based on patterns of activations that get presented to the input layer of the network). To see why, you must first appreciate that a network's behavior is determined by the patterns of weights over its units. Even relatively small networks have three layers (input, hidden, output) of, say, 20 units each, with full connectivity between layers, meaning that there are a minimum of 800 connection weights (400 for input-hidden connections and another 400 for hidden-output connections, and more if you include bidirectional connectivity back from the output to the hidden, and any kind of inhibitory connectivity that might be used). It is virtually impossible to set such a large number of weights by hand, so learning takes center stage. For the same reason, neural networks have proven to be a useful tool for exploring a range of developmental issues (Elman et al., 1996; Munakata & Stedron, 2001).

A considerable amount of research has been conducted on neural mechanisms of synaptic modification, which is the biological equivalent of changing the weights between neural units, as would be required by a learning mechanism. The overall finding from these studies is that connection strengths between neurons (weights) can be made to go either up or down depending on the relationship between the activations of the sending and receiving neurons. When the weight goes up, it is referred to as *long-term potentiation* (LTP), and when it goes down it is called *long-term depression* (LTD).

One well-supported account of what causes LTP versus LTD is based on the concentration of calcium ions in the receiving neuron's dendrite in the vicinity of the synapse (Bear & Malenka, 1994; Lisman, 1989, 1944). Calcium ions can enter the dendrite through various means, but the dominant contributor in cortical neurons is probably the opening of N-methyl-D-aspartate (NMDA) channels located at excitatory synapses. It is interesting that NMDA channels open (to allow calcium ions to enter) only if two things happen: (a) The sending neuron fires and releases neurotransmitter that binds to the NMDA channel, and (b) the receiving neuron's electrical potential increases above a critical level. Thus, calcium ion concentration tends to reflect the extent to which both sending and receiving neurons are active. The calcium ion model further stipulates that LTP (weight increases) will occur when calcium ion concentration is very high, whereas LTD (weight decreases) occur if calcium ion concentration is elevated, but not so high (Figure 22.5). If there is no change in calcium ion concentration, no weight change occurs. Putting this calcium mechanism together with the requirements for opening the NMDA channel, it is clear that weight increases should occur when both the sending and receiving neurons are strongly active together. Conditions where LTD will occur are less clear.

The biological mechanisms just described are remarkably consistent with Hebb's (1949) postulate that groups of neurons that are active together should increase the strength of their interconnectivity—the brain should learn about things that go together. In other words, under the *Hebbian* learning principle, which appears to be supported by biological

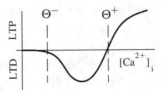

Figure 22.5 Relationship between long-term potentiation (LTP) and long-term depression (LTD), where a moderate amount of increased intracellular calcium ion concentration leads to LTD, but at a larger amount leads to LTP.

synaptic modification mechanisms, the brain encodes *correlated* events. These correlations are meaningful because correlation is a good (though imperfect) clue for causation, and cooccurring items can be more efficiently represented together within a common representational structure (e.g., the concept "college dorm room" evokes a whole slew of cooccurring items such as pizza boxes, posters, boom boxes, etc.).

Many computational models of Hebbian learning have been developed (e.g., Bienenstock, Cooper, & Munro, 1982; Carpenter & Grossberg, 1987; Grossberg, 1976; Kohonen, 1984; Linsker, 1988; Miller, Keller, & Stryker, 1989; Oja, 1982; Rumelhart & Zipser, 1986), with applications to a range of different cognitive and neural phenomena. Despite the successes of these models, Hebbian learning has some significant limitations. Specifically, Hebbian learning cannot learn arbitrary input-output transformations (McClelland & Rumelhart, 1988; O'Reilly & Munakata, 2000). To see why this is an important limitation, we can refer back to the input-hidden-output network structure discussed in the previous section. In general, the organism's learning task can be construed as learning a set of hidden representations based on sensory inputs that produce useful output patterns (behavioral responses). It is important to note that the relationship between sensory inputs and motor outputs can be highly complex and essentially arbitrary.

The limitations of Hebbian learning are most evident when compared with the other major form of neural-network learning mechanism, *error-driven learning*. In error-driven learning, the network's weights are adjusted according to the differences between the output pattern the network actually produced and the output pattern it should have produced (i.e., the error). If the network executes a pulling motion when it gets a push command, it can adjust the connections to specifically correct this error. Error-driven learning mechanisms have been around for a long time in one form or another (Widrow & Hoff, 1960), and they have been applied to a wide range of animal learning phenomena (e.g., Rescorla & Wagner, 1972). However, these earlier versions were limited to learning connections between an input and output layer only; they could not handle the training of intermediate hidden-layer representations. This limitation was seized upon by Minsky and Papert (1969) in their devastating critique showing that these neural networks were very limited in the kinds of input-output mappings they could learn, which had the effect of significantly curtailing research in this field. However, the extension of error-driven learning mechanisms to networks with (multiple) hidden layers via the *error-backpropagation* learning procedure, and the concomitant demonstration that these networks could learn virtually any input-output mapping revived interest some 15 years later

(Rumelhart, Hinton, & Williams, 1986; the idea had also been developed several times before: Bryson & Ho, 1969; Parker, 1985; Werbos, 1974).

Error-driven mechanisms can learn many input-output mapping problems that Hebbian learning simply fails to learn (O'Reilly & Munakata, 2000). The reason is clear: Hebbian learning is designed to encode correlations, not to learn arbitrary input-output mappings. However, instead of arguing for the exclusive superiority of one learning mechanism over the other, one can obtain complementary benefits by using both kinds of learning mechanisms (Hebbian and error-driven). This combination of both types of learning, together with an inhibitory competition mechanisms, is the defining characteristic of the *Leabra* framework (O'Reilly, 1996b, 1998; O'Reilly & Munakata, 2000). In short, error-driven learning provides the ability to learn arbitrary input-output mappings, whereas Hebbian learning provides a useful tendency to encode correlated information. Furthermore, Hebbian learning acts locally at each neuron and is therefore a relatively fast and reliable form of learning, whereas error-driven learning depends on distant error signals that can become weak and unreliable as they propagate through multiple hidden layers.

One potential problem with the Leabra framework and all other network models that rely on error-driven learning is a possible error of commission with respect to the known neurobiology. Indeed, much has been made in the literature about the biological implausibility of the error-backpropagation learning mechanism, which appears to require a type of signal that has never been measured in neurons to propagate in the reverse direction of most neural signals (e.g., Crick, 1989; Zipser & Andersen, 1988).

Furthermore, it has not been clear where the necessary desired outputs for generating error signals could plausibly come from. However, it has recently been shown that bidirectional activation propagation (as discussed in the previous section) can be used to perform essentially the same error-driven learning as backpropagation (O'Reilly, 1996a), using any of a number of readily available teaching signals. The resulting algorithm generalizes the recirculation algorithm of Hinton and McClelland (1988) and is thus called *GeneRec*. GeneRec provides the error-driven component of the Leabra algorithm.

The basic idea behind GeneRec is that instead of propagating an error signal, which is a difference between two terms, one can propagate the two terms separately as activation signals and then take their difference locally at each unit. This works by having two phases of activations for computing the two terms. In the *expectation* phase, the bidirectionally connected network processes an input activation pattern into a state that reflects the expected consequences or correlates of that input pattern. Then, in the *outcome* phase, the network experiences actual consequences or correlates. The difference between outcome and expectation is the error signal, and the bidirectional connectivity propagates this error signal throughout the network via local activation signals.

The GeneRec analysis also showed that Boltzmann machine learning and its deterministic versions (Ackley, Hinton, & Sejnowski, 1985; Hinton, 1989; Movellan, 1990; Peterson & Anderson, 1987) can be seen as variants of this more biologically plausible version of the backpropagation algorithm. This means that all of the existing approaches to error-driven learning using activation-based signals converge on essentially the same basic mechanism, making it more plausible that this is the way the brain does error-driven learning. Furthermore, the form of synaptic modification necessary to implement this algorithm is consistent with (though not directly validated by) the calcium ion–based synaptic modification mechanism described earlier. Finally, there are many sources in the natural environment for the necessary outcome phase signals in the form of actual environmental outcomes that can be compared with internal expectations to provide error signals (McClelland, 1994; O'Reilly, 1996a). Thus, one does not need to have an explicit teacher to perform error-driven learning.

To summarize, learning mechanisms are at once the most important and most controversial aspects of neural network models. In this discussion we have seen that Hebbian learning mechanisms make close contact with biological mechanisms, whereas error-driven mechanisms have been motivated largely from top-down constraints from cognition— they are the only known mechanisms capable of learning the kinds of things that we know people can learn. The two kinds of mechanisms may be combined in a biologically plausible and powerful way.

PERCEPTUAL PROCESSING AND ATTENTION

Having presented some of the most central ideas behind the basic mechanisms used in neural network models, we now turn to applications of these mechanisms for understanding cognitive phenomena. These same mechanisms have been applied to a wide variety of phenomena; we focus here on perception, attention, memory, and higher level cognition. The first question we address was stated in the introduction: "How does the myriad of complex perceptual inputs get organized into a coherent internal representation of the environment?"

We describe two different ways that neural network models have provided insight into this question. The first is by addressing the *representational* problem: What kinds of representations provide an efficient, computationally useful encoding of the perceptual world for a neural network, and do these representations look anything like those actually found in the brain? We will see that the interaction between Hebbian learning mechanisms and inhibitory competition can produce visual representations very much like those found in the brain. The second is by addressing the *attentional* problem: Given the huge overload of perceptual information that impinges on us at every moment (e.g., as you try to read this chapter), how does our brain focus on and select out the most relevant information (hopefully this chapter!) for further processing? We will see that the interaction between inhibitory competition and bidirectional activation flow can produce emergent attentional dynamics that simulate the behavior of both intact individuals and those with brain lesions on a visual attention task.

The Structure of Representations in Primary Visual Cortex

One way of understanding what representations in primary visual cortex (V1) should look like from a computational perspective is simply to present a range of visual images to a model network and allow its learning mechanisms to develop representations that encode these images. This is indeed what a number of modelers have done, using natural visual scenes that were preprocessed in a manner consistent with the contrast-enhancement properties of the retina (e.g., Bell & Sejnowski, 1997; Olshausen & Field, 1996; O'Reilly & Munakata, 2000; van Hateren & van der Schaaff, 1997). The Olshausen and Field model demonstrated that *sparse* representations (with relatively few active neurons) provide a useful basis for encoding real-world (visual) environments, but this model was not based on known biological principles. Subsequent work replicated the same general results using more biologically based principles of Hebbian learning and sparseness constraints in the form of inhibitory competition between neurons (O'Reilly & Munakata, 2000). Furthermore, lateral excitatory connections within this network produced a *topographic organization* of representations, where neighboring units had similar representations.

Figure 22.6 shows the results from the O'Reilly and Munakata (2000) model of 14×14 hidden units (representing V1 neurons) receiving inputs from a 12×12 simulated retina. This figure shows that the simulated neurons have developed *oriented edge detectors;* the neurons are maximally activated by visual inputs that have transitions between dark and light regions separated by edges at various angles. We can understand why the network develops these receptive fields in

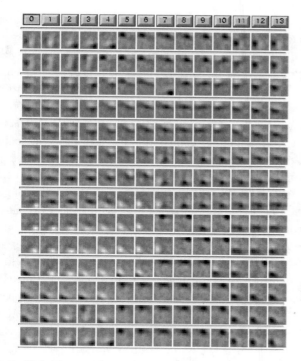

Figure 22.6 The receptive fields of model V1 neurons (from O'Reilly & Munakata, 2000). The broader 14 × 14 grid contains individual unit receptive fields, within which there is a smaller 12 × 12 grid representing weights from a simulated retina. Lighter shades indicate areas of on-center response, and darker shades indicate areas of off-center response to retinal inputs.

terms of the proclivity of Hebbian learning to encode correlational structure. Natural objects tend to have piecewise linear edges so that strong correlations exist among pixels of light along these edges. However, Hebbian learning alone is not enough to produce these receptive field patterns. As emphasized by Olshausen and Field (1996), a constraint of having only a relatively few units active at any time (implemented by inhibitory competition in our model) is also important. This constraint is appropriate because only a relatively small number of oriented edges are present in any given image. Furthermore, in the process of learning, inhibition ensures that units compete and specialize to represent different aspects of the input. At an intuitive level, this learning process is analogous to the effects of competition and natural selection in biological evolution (e.g., Edelman, 1987). Thus, each unit carves out a different niche in the space of all possible reliable correlations in the input images; these niches are oriented edge detectors.

This analysis shows that we can understand the general principles of why computational models develop their representations, and why these are appropriate for a given domain of input patterns. However, do these principles help us understand how the brain works? They can if the representations developed by the model look like those in the brain. It turns out that they do; V1 neurons have long been known to encode oriented edges of light (Hubel & Wiesel, 1962; Marr, 1982).

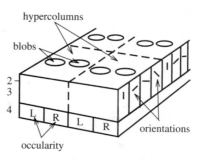

Figure 22.7 Structure of a cortical hypercolumn, that represents a full range of orientations (in Layers 2–3), ocular dominance columns (in Layer 4, one for each eye), and surface features (in the blobs). Each such hypercolumn is focused within one region of retinal space, and neighboring hypercolumns represent neighboring regions.

Furthermore, one can find systematic variations in orientation, size, position, and *polarity* (i.e., going from light-to-dark or dark-to-light, or dark-light-dark and light-dark-light) in both the simulated and real V1 receptive fields. In the brain, the different types of edge detectors (together with other neurons that appear to encode visual surface properties) are packed into the two-dimensional sheet of the visual cortex according to a *topographic* organization. The large-scale organization is a *retinotopic map* that preserves the topography of the retinal image in the cortical sheet. At the smaller scale are *hypercolumns* (Figure 22.7) containing smoothly varying progressions of oriented edge detectors, among other things (Livingstone & Hubel, 1988). The topography shown in Figure 22.6 is consistent with this within-hypercolumn structure. The hypercolumn also contains *ocular dominance columns,* in which V1 neurons respond preferentially to input from one eye or the other (see Miller et al., 1989, for a Hebbian-based model). For reviews of the many computational models of various V1 structures, see Swindale (1996) and Erwin, Obermayer, and Schulten (1995).

To summarize, computational models incorporating the basic mechanisms of Hebbian learning and inhibitory competition can help us understand why V1 has the representations it does.

Spatial Attention and the Effects of Parietal Lobe Damage

The dynamics of activation flow through the network are as important as the weight patterns of the neurons in the network. One of the most widely studied manifestations of these dynamics is attention to different regions of visual space. Spatial attention has classically been operationalized according to the Posner spatial cuing task (Posner, Walker, Friedrich, & Rafal, 1984; Figure 22.8). When attention is drawn or cued to one region of space, participants are then

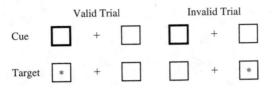

Figure 22.8 The Posner spatial attention task. The cue is a brightening or highlighting of one of the boxes that focuses attention to that region of space. Reaction times to detect the target are faster when this cue is valid (the target appears in that same region) than when it is invalid (the target appears elsewhere).

faster to detect a target in that region (a validly cued trial) than a target elsewhere (an invalidly cued trial). Patients with damage to the parietal lobe have particular difficulty with invalidly cued trials.

The traditional account of the spatial attention data involves a sequence of modular processes that have been associated with different brain areas (Posner et al., 1984; Figure 22.9). Specifically, the parietal brain damage data are accounted for in terms of a disengage module associated with the parietal lobe (Posner et al., 1984). This module typically allows one to disengage from an attended location to attend elsewhere. This process of disengaging takes time, leading to the slower detection of targets in unattended locations. Further, the disengage module is impaired with parietal damage, leading patients to have difficulty disengaging from attention drawn to one side of space.

Biologically based computational models, based on reinforcing excitatory connections and competitive inhibitory connections, provide an alternative explanation for these phenomena (Cohen, Romero, Farah, & Servan-Schreiber,

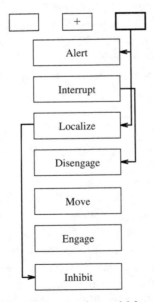

Figure 22.9 The information-processing model for attentional processing according to Posner and colleagues.

1994; O'Reilly & Munakata, 2000). In this framework, the facilitory effects of drawing attention to one region of space result from bidirectional excitatory connections between spatial and other representations of that region. This excitatory support makes it easier to process information in that region because neurons are already receiving supporting excitation. The slowing that comes on the invalid trials results from inhibitory competition between different spatial regions—to activate a different spatial location requires inhibiting the previously active region. Under this model, damage to the parietal lobe simply impairs the ability of the corresponding region in space to have sufficient excitatory support to compete effectively with other regions.

The two models make distinct predictions (Cohen et al., 1994; O'Reilly & Munakata, 2000). For example, following *bilateral* parietal damage, the disengage model predicts disengage deficits on both sides of space, but the competitive inhibition model predicts *reduced* attentional effects (smaller valid and invalid trial effects). Data support the latter model (Coslett & Saffran, 1991; Verfaellie, Rapcsak, & Heilman, 1990), demonstrating the utility of biologically based computational models for alternative theories of cognitive phenomena.

MECHANISMS OF MEMORY

In a computer, there are several different kinds of memory systems, each specialized to optimize some characteristics at the cost of others. For example, the RAM in a system is much faster than hard disk memory, but it also has a much smaller capacity. There are basic tradeoffs between speed and capacity that are resolved by having different systems optimized separately for each. Human memory can also be understood in terms of a set of tradeoffs between different incompatible capacities. These basic tradeoffs are different than those behind the computer components (although one can see some similarities); they are motivated instead by a consideration of conflicting capacities of neural networks. We discuss two different kinds of tradeoffs here, one that can help us understand the complementary roles of the hippocampus and cortex in learning and another that relates to the specializations of the frontal cortex in working memory.

Complementary Hippocampal and Cortical Learning Systems

One important set of tradeoffs involves two basic types of learning that an organism must engage in: learning about

TABLE 22.1 Two Incompatible Goals

	Remember Specifics	Extract Generalities
Example:	Where is car parked?	Best parking strategy?
Need to:	Avoid interference	Accumulate experience
	Solution:	
1.	Separate reps (keep days separate)	Overlapping reps (integrate over days)
2.	Fast learning (encode immediately)	Slow learning (integrate over days)
3.	Learn automatically	Task-driven learning
	These are incompatible, need two different systems:	
System:	Hippocampus	Neocortex

This table shows computational motivation for two complementary learning and memory systems in the brain because there are two incompatible goals that such systems need to solve. One goal is to remember specific information—in this example, where one's car is parked on a specific day. The other goal is to extract generalities across many experiences, for example in developing the best parking strategy over a number of different experiences. The neural solutions to these goals are incompatible: One requires representations to be kept separate, learned quickly, and automatically, whereas the other requires overlapping representations and slow learning to integrate over experiences and is driven by task-specific constraints. Thus, it makes sense to have two separate neural systems separately optimized for each of these goals.

specifics versus learning about generalities (Table 22.1). Because the neural mechanisms for achieving these types of learning are in direct conflict, the brain has evolved two separate brain structures to achieve these types of learning (McClelland, McNaughton, & O'Reilly, 1995; O'Reilly & Rudy, 2000, 2001). The hippocampus appears to be specialized for learning about specifics, while the neocortex is good at extracting generalities.

Specifically, learning about specifics requires keeping representations separated (to avoid interference), whereas learning about generalities requires overlapping representations that encode shared structure across many different experiences. Furthermore, learning about generalities requires a slow learning rate to integrate new information gradually with existing knowledge, while learning about specifics can occur rapidly. This rapid learning is particularly important for *episodic* memory, where the goal is to encode the details of specific events as they unfold.

In the example in Table 22.1, one can encode different kinds of information from experiences related to parking one's car. If one wants to remember the specifics of where the car is parked on a given day, it is important to encode this information using representations (populations of neurons) that are separate from representations for other such events, to minimize the *interference* that leads to forgetting. In a neural network, interference results from weights shared across multiple representations because the different representations

will pull these weights in different directions. Furthermore, one has only a short period of time to encode the parking location (unless you want to sit there and study it for hours), so rapid learning is required.

In contrast, if one wants to learn about the best strategy for parking (e.g., best location for a given time of day), one needs to integrate over many different experiences because any given day's experience does not provide a statistically reliable picture of the average situation. To accumulate information over individual experiences, one needs to ensure that these different experiences affect at least some of the same underlying neural representations—if you want to add things up, you need to put them all in the same place. Furthermore, given that the goal is computing something like an average, each event needs to make a relatively small contribution. In computing an average, you multiply each number by $1/N$, where N is the total number of items (events) to average over. As this becomes larger, each event makes a smaller contribution. In neural terms this means using a small learning rate so that weights change only a small amount for each experience.

Thus, it is clear that these two kinds of learning are in direct conflict, and therefore that it would make sense to have two different neural systems specialized for each of these types of learning. This conclusion coincides nicely with a large body of data concerning the properties of the hippocampus and the cortex. It has been known for some time that damage to the hippocampus in the medial temporal lobe can produce severe memory deficits while also leaving unimpaired certain kinds of learning and memory (Scoville & Milner, 1957; Squire, 1992). Although the precise characterization of the contributions of the hippocampus versus surrounding cortical areas has been a topic of considerable debate, it is possible to reconcile much of the data with the computational principles just described (O'Reilly & Rudy, 2001). Furthermore, detailed biological properties of the hippocampus are ideally suited for maximizing the separation between neural representations of different events, enabling rapid episodic learning with minimal interference (O'Reilly & McClelland, 1994).

In the domain of human memory, the dual mechanisms of neocortex and hippocampus provide a natural fit with dual-process models of recognition memory (Aggleton & Brown, 1999; Aggleton & Shaw, 1996; Curran, 2000; Holdstock et al., 2002; Jacoby, Yonelinas, & Jennings, 1997; O'Reilly, Norman, & McClelland, 1998; Vargha-Khadem et al., 1997). These models hold that recognition can be subserved by two different processes, a *recollection* process and a *familiarity* process. Recollection involves the recall of specific episodic details about the item and thus fits well with the hippocampal principles developed here. Indeed, we have simulated distinctive aspects of recollection using a model based on many of the detailed biological properties of the hippocampus (O'Reilly et al., 1998). Familiarity is a nonspecific sense that the item has been seen recently. We argue that this can be sub-served by the small weight changes produced by slow cortical learning. Current simulation work has shown that a simple cortical model can account for a number of distinctive properties of the familiarity signal (Norman, O'Reilly, & Huber, 2000).

Models implementing the specialized hippocampal and cortical systems have also been shown to account for a wide range of learning and memory findings in rats, including non-linear discrimination, incidental conjunctive encoding, fear conditioning, and transitive inference (O'Reilly & Rudy, 2001). Also, there are a large number of important models of the hippocampus and cortical learning systems in the literature, many of which share important features with those described here (e.g., Alvarez & Squire, 1994; Burgess, Recce, & O'Keefe, 1994; Hasselmo & Wyble, 1997; Levy, 1989; Marr, 1971; Moll & Miikkulainen, 1997; Samsonovich & McNaughton, 1997; Treves & Rolls, 1994).

Complementary Posterior and Prefrontal Cortical Systems

Another important set of tradeoffs involves the extent to which a representation activates related representations, for example, the extent to which a neural representation of smoke activates the associated representation of fire. In some cases, such as when you want to remember that it was actually only smoke that you saw coming from the forest and not fire (e.g., to provide an accurate report about the situation to others), it would be best actively to maintain only smoke without activating fire. In other cases, such as when you want to form inferences based on seeing the smoke (e.g., to evaluate possible courses of action to take, such as bringing water), it would be best for smoke to activate fire. These goals of activating versus not activating related representations are obviously in conflict (and this problem gets much worse when the inferences are less certain than smoke → fire); this tradeoff provides a potential way to understand the specializations between posterior cortex and prefrontal cortex. Specifically, prefrontal cortex may be specialized for active maintenance (a component of working memory) without activating associated representations, whereas posterior cortex may be specialized for inference based on activating associated representations.

The most obvious neural network mechanism for achieving active maintenance is recurrent bidirectional excitatory connectivity, where activation constantly circulates among

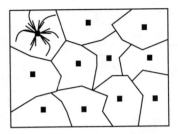

Figure 22.10 Attractor states (small squares) and their basins of attraction (surrounding regions), where nearby activation states are attracted to the central attractor state. Each stable attractor state could be used to maintain information actively over time. Note that the two-dimensional activation space represented here is a considerable simplification of the high-dimensional activation state over all the units in the network.

active units, refreshing and maintaining their activation (Braver, Cohen, & Servan-Schreiber, 1995; Dehaene & Changeux, 1989; Munakata, 1998; Zipser, Kehoe, Littlewort, & Fuster, 1993). One can think of the effects of these recurrent connections in terms of an *attractor*, where the activation pattern of the network is attracted toward a stable state that persists over time (Figure 22.10). An attractor is useful for memory because any perturbation away from that activation state is pulled back into the attractor, allowing in principle for relatively robust active maintenance in the face of noise and interference from ongoing processing.

The area around the attractor where perturbations are pulled back is called the *basin of attraction*. For robust active maintenance, one needs to have attractors with wide basins of attraction so that noise and other sources of interference will not pull the network out of its attractor. When there are many closely related representations linked by distributed connections, the basin of attraction around each representation is relatively narrow (i.e., the network can easily slip from one representation into the next). Thus, densely interconnected distributed representations will tend to conflict with the ability to maintain a specific representation actively over time.

The prefrontal cortex appears to have the relevant specializations for active maintenance. There is considerable physiological evidence that the prefrontal cortex subserves the active maintenance of information over time (i.e., as encoded in the persistent firing of frontal neurons; e.g., Fuster, 1989; Goldman-Rakic, 1987; Miller, Erickson, & Desimone, 1996). Many computational models of this basic active maintenance function have been developed (Braver et al., 1995; Camperi & Wang, 1997; Dehaene & Changeux, 1989; Durstewitz, Seamans, & Sejnowski, 2000; Seung, 1998; Zipser et al., 1993). Further, the prefrontal cortex may have more isolated patterns of connectivity—neurons there appear to be interconnected within self-contained stripe patterns (Levitt, Lewis, Yoshioka, & Lund, 1993), and isocoding microcolumns of neurons have been recorded (Rao, Williams, & Goldman-Rakic,

1999). Computational models have explored the impact of such connectivity and attractor dynamics on active maintenance (O'Reilly, Braver, & Cohen, 1999; O'Reilly, Mozer, Munakata, & Miyake, 1999). Models in which there are features that can participate equally in different distributed representations effectively have no attractors and cannot maintain information over time in the absence of external inputs. The activation instead spreads across the distributed representations, resulting in a loss of the original information. With distributed representations that sustain attractors, active maintenance succeeds, but not in the presence of significant amounts of noise. Wider attractor basins are necessary. With such wider attractor basins, as when units are completely *isolated* from each other, this prevents activation spread and yields very robust active maintenance, but at the loss of the ability to perform inference via activation spread.

Thus, computational models and considerations have helped to understand the specializations of posterior and prefrontal cortex, and how the prefrontal cortex might play a role in subserving working memory.

THE PREFRONTAL CORTEX AND HIGHER LEVEL COGNITION

The prefrontal cortex is also important for a range of complex cognitive functions, such as planning and problem solving, described generally as falling under the umbrella of *higher level cognition*. Many theories summarize the function of frontal cortex in terms of executive control, controlled processing, or a central executive (e.g., Baddeley, 1986; Gathercole, 1994; Shallice, 1982; Shiffrin & Schneider, 1977), without explaining at a mechanistic level how such functionality could be achieved or why the prefrontal cortex would be specialized for such functionality. We saw in the preceding section how a consideration of computational tradeoffs has helped to understand the issue of specialization. In this section we see how computational models have provided an important tool for exploring specific mechanisms that might achieve executive-like functionality.

One proposal along these lines is that the fundamental mechanism of active maintenance enables all the other executive-like functionality ascribed to the frontal cortex (Cohen, Braver, & O'Reilly, 1996; Goldman-Rakic, 1987; Munakata, 1998; O'Reilly, Braver, et al., 1999; O'Reilly & Munakata, 2000; Roberts & Pennington, 1996). As elaborated later, a number of models have demonstrated that active maintenance can account for frontal involvement in a range of different tasks that might otherwise appear to have nothing to do with simply maintaining information over time.

For example, several models have demonstrated that frontal contributions to inhibitory tasks can be explained in terms of active maintenance instead of an explicit inhibitory function. Actively maintained representations can support (via bidirectional excitatory connectivity) correct choices, which will therefore indirectly inhibit incorrect ones via standard lateral inhibition mechanisms within the cortex. A model of the Stroop task provided an early demonstration of this point (Cohen, Dunbar, & McClelland, 1990). In this task, color words (e.g., "red") are presented in different colors, and people are instructed either to read the word or to name the color of ink that the word is written in. In the conflict condition, the ink color and word are different. Because we have so much experience reading, we naturally tend to read the word, even if instructed to name the color, such that responses are slower and more error-prone in the color-naming conflict condition than in the word-reading one. These color-naming problems are selectively magnified with frontal damage. This frontal deficit has typically been interpreted in terms of the frontal cortex's helping to inhibit the dominant word-reading pathway. However, Cohen et al. (1990) showed that they could account for both normal and frontal-damage data by assuming that the frontal cortex instead supports the color-naming pathway, which then collaterally inhibits the word-reading pathway. Similar models have demonstrated that in infants, the ability to inhibit *perseverative* reaching (searching for a hidden toy at a previous hiding location rather than at its current location) can develop simply through increasing abilities to actively maintain a representation of the correct hiding location (Dehaene & Changeux, 1989; Munakata, 1998). Again, such findings challenge the standard interpretation that inhibitory abilities per se must develop for improved performance on this task (Diamond, 1991).

The activation-based processing model of frontal function can also explain why frontal cortex facilitates rapid switching between different categorization rules in the Wisconsin card-sorting task and related tasks. In these tasks, subjects learn to categorize stimuli according to one rule via feedback from the experimenter, after which the rule is switched. With frontal damage, patients tend to perseverate in using the previous rule. A computational model of a related ID/ED categorization task demonstrated that the ability to update active memories rapidly in frontal cortex can account for detailed patterns of data in monkeys with frontal damage (O'Reilly & Munakata, 2000; O'Reilly, Noelle, Braver, & Cohen, 2002).

In short, computational models of frontal function can provide mechanistic explanations that unify the disparate roles of the frontal cortex, from working memory to cognitive control and planning and problem solving. However, a major remaining challenge is to explore whether truly complex, intelligent behavior can be captured using these basic mechanisms.

CHALLENGES

Most researchers agree that if a network model captures in sufficient detail the essential neural processes, it can provide a truly valuable tool for advancing our understanding of the relation between brain and mind. However, there is skepticism regarding whether (a) enough is known about the neurobiology at this time to constrain models sufficiently and (b) current models violate or fail to include important aspects of the known neurobiology.

We contrasted errors of omission (aspects of the biology that are missing or simplified in the models) with errors of commission (aspects of the models that are unlikely to be true given what we already know about the brain). We saw that in many cases network models make errors of omission, but not errors of commission. For example, it is possible to make network models that make no errors of commission at the level of network interactions, in that they follow the general excitatory and inhibitory connectivity patterns of the cortex (e.g., O'Reilly & Munakata, 2000; Somers, Nelson, & Sur, 1995; Lumer, Edelman, & Tononi, 1997; and many others). However, these networks undoubtedly make many errors of omission, given that there is considerable complexity in the wiring structures of the human cortex. As in other cases discussed earlier, it is not yet clear what functional significance (if any) these omissions might have.

In the few cases where there may be errors of commission (e.g., in error-driven learning algorithms), strong top-down constraints from cognition (e.g., the fact that people can learn difficult tasks) drive these possibly problematic properties. Considerable progress has been made in developing error-driven learning algorithms that are more consistent with known biology (while retaining the powerful capabilities), but several assumptions remain untested.

Instead of denying outright the value of any given approach, we argue that science will be advanced through the contest of different theories as they attempt to explain increasing amounts of data, and that computational models provide a valuable source of theorizing that can provide novel insights and approaches to understanding complex phenomena of cognitive neuroscience. This is true even if the models are simplified and even if they contain some aspects that violate what we know about the brain—verbal theories are equally (if not more) likely to contain the same flaws. Often, however, these flaws are hidden by the vagueness of the verbal theories, while computational models have the virtue or vice of exposing all the gory details and assumptions required to implement a working simulation.

In short, we think that a major value of computational modeling is engaging in the *process* of working out explicit, mechanistic theories of how the brain gives rise to cognitive function. This process is iterative, cumulative, and not without controversy. However, its primary advantage is in directly confronting the major questions that need to be answered to understand how the brain does what it does.

GENERAL DISCUSSION

In this article we have touched on most of the central aspects of computational neural network models for psychological modeling. Building from individual neurons to networks thereof, we have shown how these networks incorporate many detailed aspects of the known neurobiology, while still remaining somewhat abstract. We emphasized that there are modeling formalisms that do not make any obvious errors of commission; that is, they do not violate any well known properties of the neural networks of the brain. Nevertheless, it remains to be tested how important the many errors of omission are for the biological fidelity of these models. We then showed how these models can speak to important issues in cognitive neuroscience, including issues in perception, attention, memory, and higher level cognition.

In the domain of perception, we showed how basic learning mechanisms and forms of neural interaction (inhibitory competition) can lead to the development of efficient representations for encoding the visual environment. We further summarized how attentional effects, which are needed to manage the overflow of perceptual input, fall naturally out of the combined neural dynamics of bidirectional connectivity and inhibitory competition. When these neural mechanisms are used to simulate spatial attention tasks widely used in cognitive psychology, they provide novel explanations of both intact and brain-damaged performance, which accord better with the data than do theories based on a more abstract information-processing approach.

In the domain of learning and memory, we showed how an understanding of the capacities of fundamental neural mechanisms can lead to insights into how the brain has divided up the overall function of memory. Specifically, computational tradeoffs—between learning specifics versus learning generalities and between interconnected and isolated representations—suggest that different brain areas should be specialized to perform these different functions. This fits well with a wide range of data. Thus, the computational models help us to understand not only *how* the brain is organized to perform cognitive functions, but also *why* it might be organized this way in the first place.

In the domain of higher level cognition, we showed how models have helped to begin addressing the mechanisms that might underlie complex behaviors, such as those that require moving beyond habitual or prepotent responses. Specifically, active maintenance subserved by prefrontal cortex may support alternative choices, allowing habitual behaviors to be inhibited via lateral inhibitory mechanisms within the cortex. The ability to update activation-based representations in prefrontal cortex rapidly may be a critical component of flexible behavior.

In conclusion, we hope that these examples provide a sufficient basis to understand both the strengths of neural network models and the criticisms surrounding them. Even though there are undoubtedly many missing features of these models, we think that they capture enough of the most important properties to provide satisfying simulations of cognitive phenomena. Furthermore, the very endeavor of creating these models raises a large number of important questions that are only beginning to be answered. Models should thus serve as an important part of the process of scientific progress in understanding human cognition.

REFERENCES

Ackley, D. H., Hinton, G. E., & Sejnowski, T. J. (1985). A learning algorithm for Boltzmann machines. *Cognitive Science, 9,* 147–169.

Aggleton, J. P., & Brown, M. W. (1999). Episodic memory, amnesia, and the hippocampal-anterior thalamic axis. *Behavioral and Brain Sciences, 22,* 425–490.

Aggleton, J. P., & Shaw, C. (1996). Amnesia and recognition memory: A re-analysis of psychometric data. *Neuropsychologia, 34,* 51–62.

Alvarez, P., & Squire, L. R. (1994). Memory consolidation and the medial temporal lobe: A simple network model. *Proceedings of the National Academy of Sciences, USA, 91,* 7041–7045.

Baddeley, A. D. (1986). *Working memory.* New York: Oxford University Press.

Bear, M. F., & Malenka, R. C. (1994). Synaptic plasticity: LTP and LTD. *Current Opinion in Neurobiology, 4,* 389–399.

Bell, A. J., & Sejnowski, T. J. (1997). The independent components of natural images are edge filters. *Vision Research, 37,* 3327–3338.

Bienenstock, E. L., Cooper, L. N., & Munro, P. W. (1982). Theory for the development of neuron selectivity: Orientation specificity and binocular interaction in visual cortex. *Journal of Neuroscience, 2*(2), 32–48.

Braver, T. S., Cohen, J. D., & Servan-Schreiber, D. (1995). A computational model of prefrontal cortex function. In D. S. Touretzky, G. Tesauro, & T. K. Leen (Eds.), *Advances in neural information processing systems* (pp. 141–148). Cambridge, MA: MIT Press.

Bryson, A. E., & Ho, Y. C. (1969). *Applied optimal control.* New York: Blaisdell.

Burgess, N., Recce, M., & O'Keefe, J. (1994). A model of hippocampal function. *Neural Networks, 7,* 1065–1083.

Camperi, M., & Wang, X. J. (1997). Modeling delay-period activity in the prefrontal cortex during working memory tasks. In J. Bower (Ed.), *Computational neuroscience* (pp. 273–279). New York: Plenum Press.

Carpenter, G., & Grossberg, S. (1987). A massively parallel architecture for a self-organizing neural pattern recognition machine. *Computer Vision, Graphics, and Image Processing, 37,* 54–115.

Cohen, J. D., Braver, T. S., & O'Reilly, R. C. (1996). A computational approach to prefrontal cortex, cognitive control, and schizophrenia: Recent developments and current challenges. *Philosophical Transactions of the Royal Society, London, 351B,* 1515–1527.

Cohen, J. D., Dunbar, K., & McClelland, J. L. (1990). On the control of automatic processes: A parallel distributed processing model of the Stroop effect. *Psychological Review, 97*(3), 332–361.

Cohen, J. D., Romero, R. D., Farah, M. J., & Servan-Schreiber, D. (1994). Mechanisms of spatial attention: The relation of macrostructure to microstructure in parietal neglect. *Journal of Cognitive Neuroscience, 6,* 377.

Coslett, H. B., & Saffran, E. (1991). Simultanagnosia: To see but not two see. *Brain, 114,* 1523–1545.

Crick, F. H. C. (1989). The recent excitement about neural networks. *Nature, 337,* 129–132.

Curran, T. (2000). Brain potentials of recollection and familiarity. *Memory and Cognition, 28,* 923.

Dehaene, S., & Changeux, J. P. (1989). A simple model of prefrontal cortex function in delayed-response tasks. *Journal of Cognitive Neuroscience, 1,* 244–261.

Diamond, A. (1991). Neuropsychological insights into the meaning of object concept development. In S. Carey & R. Gelman (Eds.), *The epigenesis of mind* (pp. 67–110). Mahwah, NJ: Erlbaum.

Durstewitz, D., Seamans, J. K., & Sejnowski, T. J. (2000). Dopamine-mediated stabilization of delay-period activity in a network model of prefrontal cortex. *Journal of Neurophysiology, 83,* 1733.

Edelman, G. (1987). *Neural darwinism.* New York: Basic Books.

Elman, J. L., Bates, E. A., Johnson, M. H., Karmiloff-Smith, A., Parisi, D., & Plunkett, K. (1996). *Rethinking innateness: A connectionist perspective on development.* Cambridge, MA: MIT Press.

Erwin, E., Obermayer, K., & Schulten, K. (1995). Models of orientation and ocular dominance columns in the visual cortex: A critical comparison. *Neural Computation, 7,* 425–468.

Fuster, J. M. (1989). *The prefrontal cortex: Anatomy, physiology and neuropsychology of the frontal lobe.* New York: Raven Press.

Gathercole, S. E. (1994). Neuropsychology and working memory: A review. *Neuropsychology, 8*(4), 494–505.

Goldman-Rakic, P. S. (1987). Circuitry of primate prefrontal cortex and regulation of behavior by representational memory. *Handbook of Physiology: The Nervous System, 5,* 373–417.

Grossberg, S. (1976). Adaptive pattern classification and universal recoding: I. Parallel development and coding of neural feature detectors. *Biological Cybernetics, 23,* 121–134.

Hasselmo, M. E., & Wyble, B. (1997). Free recall and recognition in a network model of the hippocampus: Simulating effects of scopolamine on human memory function. *Behavioural Brain Research, 89,* 1–34.

Hebb, D. O. (1949). *The organization of behavior.* New York: Wiley.

Hinton, G. E. (1989). Deterministic Boltzmann learning performs steepest descent in weight-space. *Neural Computation, 1,* 143–150.

Hinton, G. E., & McClelland, J. L. (1988). Learning representations by recirculation. In D. Z. Anderson (Ed.), *Neural information processing systems: 1987* (pp. 358–366). New York: American Institute of Physics.

Holdstock, J. S., Mayes, A. R., Roberts, N., Cezayirli, E., Isaac, C. L., O'Reilly, R. C., et al. (2002). Memory dissociations following human hippocampal damage. *Hippocampus, 12,* 246–257.

Hubel, D., & Wiesel, T. N. (1962). Receptive fields, binocular interaction, and functional architecture in the cat's visual cortex. *Journal of Physiology, 160,* 106–154.

Jacoby, L. L., Yonelinas, A. P., & Jennings, J. M. (1997). The relation between conscious and unconscious (automatic) influences: A declaration of independence. In J. D. Cohen & J. W. Schooler (Eds.), *Scientific approaches to consciousness* (pp. 13–47). Mahwah, NJ: Erlbaum.

Jaffe, D. B., & Carnevale, N. T. (1999). Passive normalization of synaptic integration influenced by dendritic architecture. *Journal of Neurophysiology, 82,* 3268–3285.

Koch, C., & Segev, I. (Eds.). (1998). *Methods in neuronal modeling* (2nd ed.). Cambridge, MA: MIT Press.

Kohonen, T. (1984). *Self-organization and associative memory.* Berlin, Germany: Springer-Verlag.

Levitt, J. B., Lewis, D. A., Yoshioka, T., & Lund, J. S. (1993). Topography of pyramidal neuron intrinsic connections in macaque monkey prefrontal cortex (areas 9 & 46). *Journal of Comparative Neurology, 338,* 360–376.

Levy, W. B. (1989). A computational approach to hippocampal function. In R. D. Hawkins & G. H. Bower (Eds.), *Computational models of learning in simple neural systems* (pp. 243–304). San Diego, CA: Academic Press.

Linsker, R. (1988). Self-organization in a perceptual network. *Computer, 21*(3), 105–117.

Lisman, J. E. (1989). A mechanism for the Hebb and the anti-Hebb processes underlying learning and memory. *Proceedings of the National Academy of Sciences, USA, 86,* 9574–9578.

Lisman, J. E. (1994). The CaM Kinase II hypothesis for the storage of synaptic memory. *Trends in Neurosciences, 17,* 406.

Livingstone, M., & Hubel, D. (1988). Segregation of form, color, movement, and depth: Anatomy, physiology, and perception. *Science, 240,* 740–749.

Lumer, E., Edelman, G., & Tononi, G. (1997). Neural dynamics in a model of the thalamocortical system: I. Layers, loops and the emergence of fast synchronous rhythms. *Cerebral Cortex, 7,* 207–227.

Marr, D. (1971). Simple memory: A theory for archicortex. *Philosophical Transactions of the Royal Society, London, 262B,* 23–81.

Marr, D. (1982). *Vision.* New York: Freeman.

McClelland, J. L. (1994). The interaction of nature and nurture in development: A parallel distributed processing perspective. In P. Bertelson, P. Eelen, & G. D'Ydewalle (Eds.), *Current advances in psychological science: Ongoing research* (pp. 57–88). Hillsdale, NJ: Erlbaum.

McClelland, J. L., McNaughton, B. L., & O'Reilly, R. C. (1995). Why there are complementary learning systems in the hippocampus and neocortex: Insights from the successes and failures of connectionist models of learning and memory. *Psychological Review, 102,* 419–457.

McClelland, J. L., & Rumelhart, D. E. (Eds.). (1988). *Explorations in parallel distributed processing: A handbook of models, programs, and exercises.* Cambridge, MA: MIT Press.

Miller, E. K., Erickson, C. A., & Desimone, R. (1996). Neural mechanisms of visual working memory in prefrontal cortex of the macaque. *Journal of Neuroscience, 16,* 5154.

Miller, K. D., Keller, J. B., & Stryker, M. P. (1989). Ocular dominance column development: Analysis and simulation. *Science, 245,* 605–615.

Minsky, M. L., & Papert, S. A. (1969). *Perceptrons.* Cambridge, MA: MIT Press.

Moll, M., & Miikkulainen, R. (1997). Convergence-zone episodic memory: Analysis and simulations. *Neural Networks, 10,* 1017–1036.

Movellan, J. R. (1990). Contrastive Hebbian learning in the continuous Hopfield model. In D. S. Touretzky, G. E. Hinton, & T. J. Sejnowski (Eds.), *Proceedings of the 1989 connectionist models summer school* (pp. 10–17). San Mateo, CA: Morgan Kaufman.

Munakata, Y. (1998). Infant perseveration and implications for object permanence theories: A PDP model of the AB̄ task. *Developmental Science, 1,* 161–184.

Munakata, Y., & Stedron, J. M. (2001). Neural network models of cognitive development. In C. A. Nelson & M. Luciana (Eds.), *Handbook of developmental cognitive neuroscience* (pp. 159–171). Cambridge, MA: MIT Press.

Norman K. A. & O'Reilly, R. C. (in press). Modeling hippocampal and neocortical contributions to recognition memory: A complementary learning systems approach. *Psychological Review.*

Oja, E. (1982). A simplified neuron model as a principal component analyzer. *Journal of Mathematical Biology, 15,* 267–273.

Olshausen, B. A., & Field, D. J. (1996). Emergence of simple-cell receptive field properties by learning a sparse code for natural images. *Nature, 381,* 607.

O'Reilly, R. C. (1996a). Biologically plausible error-driven learning using local activation differences: The generalized recirculation algorithm. *Neural Computation, 8*(5), 895–938.

O'Reilly, R. C. (1996b). *The Leabra model of neural interactions and learning in the neocortex.* Unpublished doctoral dissertation, Carnegie Mellon University, Pittsburgh, PA.

O'Reilly, R. C. (1998). Six principles for biologically-based computational models of cortical cognition. *Trends in Cognitive Sciences, 2*(11), 455–462.

O'Reilly, R. C., Braver, T. S., & Cohen, J. D. (1999). A biologically based computational model of working memory. In A. Miyake & P. Shah (Eds.), *Models of working memory: Mechanisms of active maintenance and executive control* (pp. 375–411). New York: Cambridge University Press.

O'Reilly, R. C., & McClelland, J. L. (1994). Hippocampal conjunctive encoding, storage, and recall: Avoiding a tradeoff. *Hippocampus, 4*(6), 661–682.

O'Reilly, R. C., Mozer, M., Munakata, Y., & Miyake, A. (1999). Discrete representations in working memory: A hypothesis and computational investigations. *The second international conference on cognitive science* (pp. 183–188). Tokyo: Japanese Cognitive Science Society.

O'Reilly, R. C., & Munakata, Y. (2000). *Computational explorations in cognitive neuroscience: Understanding the mind by simulating the brain.* Cambridge, MA: MIT Press.

O'Reilly, R. C., Noelle, D., Braver, T. S., & Cohen, J. D. (2002). Prefrontal cortex and dynamic categorization tasks: Representational organization and neuromodulatory control. *Cerebral Cortex, 12,* 246–257.

O'Reilly, R. C., Norman, K. A., & McClelland, J. L. (1998). A hippocampal model of recognition memory. In M. I. Jordan, M. J. Kearns, & S. A. Solla (Eds.), *Advances in neural information processing systems 10* (pp. 73–79). Cambridge, MA: MIT Press.

O'Reilly, R. C., & Rudy, J. W. (2000). Computational principles of learning in the neocortex and hippocampus. *Hippocampus, 10,* 389–397.

O'Reilly, R. C., & Rudy, J. W. (2001). Conjunctive representations in learning and memory: Principles of cortical and hippocampal function. *Psychological Review, 108,* 311–345.

Parker, D. B. (1985). *Learning logic* (Tech. Rep. No. TR-47). Cambridge, MA: Massachusetts Institute of Technology, Center for Computational Research in Economics and Management Science.

Peterson, C., & Anderson, J. R. (1987). A mean field theory learning algorithm for neural networks. *Complex Systems, 1,* 995–1019.

Posner, M. I., Walker, J. A., Friedrich, F. J., & Rafal, R. D. (1984). Effects of parietal lobe injury on covert orienting of visual attention. *Journal of Neuroscience, 4,* 1863–1874.

Rao, S. G., Williams, G. V., & Goldman-Rakic, P. S. (1999). Isodirectional tuning of adjacent interneurons and pyramidal cells during working memory: Evidence for microcolumnar organization in PFC. *Journal of Neurophysiology, 81,* 1903.

Reike, F., Warland, D., van Steveninck, R., & Bialek, W. (1996). *Spikes: Exploring the neural code.* Cambridge, MA: MIT Press.

Rescorla, R. A., & Wagner, A. R. (1972). A theory of Pavlovian conditioning: Variation in the effectiveness of reinforcement and non-reinforcement. In A. H. Black & W. F. Prokasy (Eds.), *Classical conditioning II: Theory and research* (pp. 64–99). New York: Appleton-Century-Crofts.

Roberts, R. J., & Pennington, B. F. (1996). In interactive framework for examining prefrontal cognitive processes. *Developmental Neuropsychology, 12*(1), 105–126.

Rumelhart, D. E., Hinton, G. E., & Williams, R. J. (1986). Learning internal representations by error propagation. In D. E. Rumelhart, J. L. McClelland, & PDP Research Group (Eds.), *Parallel distributed processing: Vol. 1. Foundations* (pp. 318–362). Cambridge, MA: MIT Press.

Rumelhart, D. E., & Zipser, D. (1986). Feature discovery by competitive learning. In D. E. Rumelhart, J. L. McClelland, & PDP Research Group (Eds.), *Parallel distributed processing: Vol. 1. Foundations* (pp. 151–193). Cambridge, MA: MIT Press.

Samsonovich, A., & McNaughton, B. L. (1997). Path integration and cognitive mapping in a continuous attractor neural network model. *Journal of Neuroscience, 17,* 5900–5920.

Scoville, W. B., & Milner, B. (1957). Loss of recent memory after bilateral hippocampal lesions. *Journal of Neurology, Neurosurgery, and Psychiatry, 20,* 11–21.

Seung, H. S. (1998). Continuous attractors and oculomotor control. *Neural Networks, 11,* 1253.

Shallice, T. (1982). Specific impairments of planning. *Philosophical Transactions of the Royal Society, London, 298B,* 199–209.

Shepherd, G. M., & Brayton, R. K. (1987). Logic operations are properties of computer-simulated interactions between excitable dendritic spines. *Neuroscience, 21,* 151–166.

Shiffrin, R. M., & Schneider, W. (1977). Controlled and automatic human information processing: II. Perceptual learning, automatic attending, and a general theory. *Psychological Review, 84,* 127–190.

Somers, D., Nelson, S., & Sur, M. (1995). An emergent model of orientation selectivity in cat visual cortical simple cells. *Journal of Neuroscience, 15,* 5448.

Squire, L. R. (1992). Memory and the hippocampus: A synthesis from findings with rats, monkeys, and humans. *Psychological Review, 99,* 195–231.

Swindale, N. V. (1996). The development of topography in the visual cortex: A review of models. *Network: Computation in Neural Systems, 7,* 161–247.

Tovee, M. J., Rolls, E. T., Treves, A., & Bellis, R. P. (1993). Information encoding and the responses of single neurons in the primate temporal visual cortex. *Journal of Neurophysiology, 70,* 640–654.

Treves, A., & Rolls, E. T. (1994). A computational analysis of the role of the hippocampus in memory. *Hippocampus, 4,* 374–392.

van Hateren, J. H., & van der Schaaff, A. (1997). Independent component filters of natural images compared with simple cells in primary visual cortex. *Proceedings of the Royal Society, London, 265B,* 359–366.

Vargha-Khadem, F., Gadian, D. G., Watkins, K. E., Connelly, A., Van Paesschen, W., & Mishkin, M. (1997). Differential effects of early hippocampal pathology on episodic and semantic memory. *Science, 277,* 376–380.

Verfaellie, M., Rapcsak, S. Z., & Heilman, K. M. (1990). Impaired shifting of attention in Balint's syndrome. *Brain and Cognition, 12,* 195–204.

Werbos, P. (1974). *Beyond regression: New tools for prediction and analysis in the behavioral sciences.* Unpublished doctoral dissertation, Harvard University, Boston.

Widrow, B., & Hoff, M. E. (1960). Adaptive switching circuits. *Institute of Radio Engineers, Western Electronic Show and Convention: Convention record, part 4* (pp. 96–104), August 23.

Zipser D., & Andersen, R. A. (1988). A backpropagation programmed network that simulates response properties of a subset of posterior parietal neurons. *Nature, 331,* 679–684.

Zipser, D., Kehoe, B. Littlewort, G., & Fuster, J. (1993). A spiking network model of short-term active memory. *Journal of Neuroscience, 13,* 3406–3420.

CHAPTER 23

Environment and Development of the Nervous System

JAMES E. BLACK

Remodeling of neural circuitry in response to experience occurs in diverse animal species, in numerous components of the brain, and at many points in development through adulthood. Some animal species have evolved special capabilities to extract information from the environment and put it to use in survival, but the abilities vary considerably. Some qualities of information are often quite simple, such as chemotaxis (e.g., moving away from noxious chemicals) or pheromones that initiate reproductive sequences. At first glance it would appear that many invertebrates do not learn much from experience, but the limited learning capacity of the lowly sea slug was the model system leading to one of the recent Nobel prizes in neuroscience (Kandel, 2001). The relative simplicity of that system made it accessible to study, but other invertebrate species have found niches where the ability to assimilate enormous amounts of information quickly has had survival value. Two species are of particular interest as illustrations: The honeybee leaving the hive for the first time incorporates a large amount of information about landmarks and food resources and undergoes substantial remodeling of its small brain (Fahrbach, Moore, Capaldi, Farris, & Robinson, 1998). Clearly there has been an adaptive value in this social species to develop a spe-

cialized brain system to store information rapidly on the very first flight out of the hive in a relatively permanent rewiring of the brain. Although less is known about what happens to the brain of octopuses, they have clearly adapted to a niche where survival is dependent on observation of the environment and incorporation of information about prey patterns. It is of considerable interest not only that octopuses are extremely smart in laboratory settings, but also that they can actually learn by observing one another, a type of learning one associates with higher animals. In other words, in their phylogenetic history, some species have found experience not useful for survival (e.g., jellyfish or lemmings), whereas other species facing challenging niches have evolved the capacity to extract enormous amounts of information. The information serves both to refine the structure of the brain and to incorporate information useful for survival. This evolutionary strategy apparently has developed independently in species as diverse as honeybees, octopuses, some species of birds, and some (but not all) mammals. In this chapter I review some recent neural plasticity research suggesting some general themes of how species use experience in organizing brain development.

One important theme is recognition that the vast majority of brain structure is *not* plastic; indeed, there are long-established mechanisms in place to protect or repair changes caused by the environment. Early development can be characterized by *canalization* (Waddington, 1971): When the developing brain is constructing complex, genetically determined neural systems, these should not be disturbed by minor changes in neuron number, temperature, or nutrients, for example. As noted in

This work was supported by grants from the National Alliance for Research on Schizophrenia and Affective Disorders, Cure Autism Now, and the McDonnell Foundation, and by the generous intellectual help from my colleagues in the NIH Early Experience, Stress, Neurobiology, and Prevention Science Network.

many neural network models of learning, a relatively rigid framework of neural connections laid down in early development helps organize and constrain the effects of experience (e.g., Quartz & Sejnowski, 1997). Although I emphasize the genetic regulation of early brain development, recent neuroscience research has demonstrated the potentially important influence of some environmental factors (e.g., prenatal stress or alcohol exposure) that can influence the organism's later ability to incorporate experience into brain structure.

A second theme is recognition of the specialization of many neural systems to play orchestrated roles in brain development (Black & Greenough, 1986). In many ways the genetically programmed substrates set the stage for the safety of the young organism, the timing of experience, and its quality. For example, early in postnatal development many infant mammals will modify brain structures to help orient themselves to maternal protection and sustenance. Their cerebral cortex, on the other hand, is relatively undeveloped at this stage and will only become capable of structural changes in response to experience much later. Some systems respond to experience only within a narrow developmental window (i.e., a sensitive period), whereas other important systems are open-ended and can incorporate experience through all of adulthood. Aspects of play have their peak at a time when visual motor skills are progressing from rudimentary to refined through a process of nearly constant, safe practice. As discussed later, in may cases the developmentally programmed systems generally overproduce synaptic connections and use experience to prune away the unnecessary ones.

However, as Piaget (1980) pointed out toward the end of his life, there is a third important category: information that provides useful, idiosyncratic survival value to the individual that could not have been predicted in its nature or timing. For a small number of species this type of learning is quite important, and the species appear to have evolved specialized systems that allow storage of salient information whenever needed. Examples of such individualized, idiosyncratic information might be the location of food caches for a squirrel, new tricks for a falcon catching its rodent prey, a college student studying calculus, a person taking up tennis for the first time, or a taxi driver learning the roads in a new city. This lifelong, open-ended neural plasticity is necessarily regulated by neural and hormonal modulation and appears to create new synaptic connections to incorporate experience (Black & Greenough, 1986).

GENE-DRIVEN PROCESSES

It is sometimes easy to overemphasize the genetic contribution to behavior because of the recent explosion of knowledge in this area. We now know much of the molecular biology of cell differentiation, neuron migration, and cell regulation and signaling. These processes are capable of building enormously complex neural structures without any input from the external environment. Indeed, in order to protect brain development, much of the basic organization of most nervous systems is largely impervious to experience. Neural activity that is intrinsically driven, such as that arising from the retina of the cat or monkey in utero, can play a role in these organization processes. The entrenchment (or resistance to environmental influences) during embryonic development was termed *canalization* by Waddington (1971). Clearly, minor perturbations of pH or temperature should not have drastic effects on embryogenesis if a species is to survive. Extending that concept to the postnatal period, it would seem adaptive for many species that brain development not be too sensitive to variations in nutrition or experience. It would be adaptive for brain development to be resilient to fairly major trauma, which it often is through early childhood.

Tens of thousands of genes are uniquely expressed in brain development, helping regulate cell number, neuron migration, the overall pattern of brain organization, the shape and connections of individual cells, and even the microstructure of the molecules surrounding a synapse (Kandel, 2001). For perspective, consider that I received a version of the Human Genome Project's DNA sequence distributed to fit on a single CD-ROM, and presumably the developing embryo is able to use this (relatively) simple information to sculpt and arrange one of the most complex objects in the universe, one that I can hold in my hands. This is not to imply that the process of going from genetic information to neural structure is at all easy, for this area is presently one of the most challenging and exciting areas of science and biotechnology.

I am not advocating a determinist view of brain development, however. Some species have a survival advantage if they can adapt to the environment or incorporate information from it. Indeed, many mammalian species have evolved specialized structures that can incorporate massive amounts of information. Because they have a long evolutionary history, the specialized systems vary across species and occur in multiple brain regions, such that there is not a single place or process for learning and memory. I will argue that some types of neural plasticity have evolved to be incorporated into the developmental schedule of brain development, whereas others have evolved to serve the individual's needs by incorporating information unique to that individual's environment.

Although I resort to metaphors of "schedules" and "scaffolding," I would like to emphasize a more contemporary model of brain development: that derived from the study of dynamic, nonlinear systems. From the dynamic systems perspective, individuals can use the interaction of genetic constraints and environmental information to self-organize highly complex systems (especially brains). Each organism follows a potentially unique and partly self-determined developmental path of brain assembly to the extent that each has unique experiences. The genetically determined restrictions (e.g., the initial cortical architecture) serve as constraints to the system, allowing environmental information interacting with existing neural structures to organize and refine neural connections substantially.

I will not go into further detail here, but I wish to emphasize a balanced view of genotype-driven processes providing much of the basic structure of the brain, which is to an extent resistant to experience. Some of these genetically determined structures have evolved to constrain and organize experiential information, facilitating its storage in the brain in massive quantities. Although much of the remainder of this article focuses on neural plasticity, it is important to remember that such processes have a complex and genetically determined foundation. Deviations in that foundation (e.g., genetic disease or structural lesions) can have a profound impact on how experience shapes the brain, as well as on how therapeutic efforts can help restore it.

EXPERIENCE-EXPECTANT DEVELOPMENT

Although numerous examples of neural plasticity have been found in mammalian species, much of plasticity can be classified into two basic categories. *Experience-expectant development* involves a readiness of the brain to receive specific types of information from the environment. This readiness occurs during critical or sensitive stages in development during which there are central adaptations to information that is reliably present for all members of the species. This information includes major sensory experience, such as patterned visual information, as well as information affecting social, emotional, and cognitive development. One aspect of the brain's readiness to receive this expected information is the overproduction of neural connections, of which a subset is selectively retained on the basis of experience.

A general process observed in many mammalian species is that a surplus of connections is produced, a large portion of which is subsequently eliminated. Evidence for overproduction and partial elimination of synapses during development has been found in many brain regions and species including cat (Cragg, 1975), rodent (Greenough & Chang, 1988), monkey (Boothe, Greenough, Lund, & Wrege, 1979; Bourgeois, Goldman-Rakic, & Rakic, 1994), and humans (Conel, 1939–1967). The overshoot in the number of synapses produced in cortical areas in many animals, including humans, has been estimated to be roughly double the number found in adults (P. R. Huttenlocher & de Courten,

1987; see P. R. Huttenlocher, 1994, for review). In humans, synaptic density and estimates of total synapse numbers in the visual cortex reach a peak at approximately 8 months of age, with synapse numbers declining thereafter (e.g., P. R. Huttenlocher & de Courten, 1987). Another important finding by P. R. Huttenlocher (1979) was that human frontal cortex has its blooming and pruning of synapse substantially delayed, with its peak occurring during childhood. A recent large-scale longitudinal magnetic resonance imaging (MRI) study found that many cortical regions will expand their gray matter volume and then contract during development, with frontal and parietal regions doing this in adolescence and later (Gledd et al., 1999).

The process of overproduction and selective elimination of synapses appears to be a mechanism whereby the brain is made ready to capture critical and highly reliable information from the environment. This possibility is supported by several lines of research, reviewed next, indicating that the pruning into structured patterns of functional neural connections requires appropriate patterns of neural activity that are obtained through experience. These events occur during known critical or sensitive periods. Furthermore, the pruning appears to be driven by competitive interactions between neural connections such that inactive neural connections are lost and connections that are most actively driven by experience are selectively maintained. In many cases it appears that regulation of neural plasticity systems has evolved to take advantage of information that could be expected for all juvenile members (i.e., it has an adaptive value for the whole species, not just for individuals). Many of the experiments described in this section disturb some aspect of the expected experience, often with substantial disruptions of further development.

Visual Deprivation

Studies of the effects of early visual deprivation have provided some of the strongest examples of experience inducing neural structure during development. Together they indicate a direct link between patterns of experience-expectant visual information and patterns of neural connectivity. Experimental visual deprivation falls into two main classes. Binocular deprivation of vision can be complete, depriving animals of all visual stimuli, or partial, depriving animals of patterned visual stimuli. This is achieved, for example, by raising animals in complete darkness or by suturing both eyelids shut, respectively. Partial deprivation reduces or distorts visual experience in some fashion. Complete deprivation of both eyes leads to a loss in complex visuomotor learning and in the precision of neuronal response properties, but it preserves balance in eye dominance and basic perceptual skills (e.g., Zablocka & Zernicki, 1990). In contrast, selective deprivation of one eye during the critical period leads to a drastic reduction in its control over visual cortex neurons and behavior, and the nondeprived eye correspondingly gains in control. The degree of recovery from deprivation depends on the species and the deprivation period's onset and duration.

Binocular Deprivation

Studies of binocular deprivation have shown that appropriate visual stimulation during certain stages of development is critical for the development of normal neural connectivity in the visual system. Dark rearing or bilateral lid closure in developing animals results in behavioral, physiological, and structural abnormalities in visual pathways (e.g., Michalski & Wrobel, 1994; Riesen, 1965; Wiesel & Hubel, 1965). The severity and reversibility of the visual impairments are dependent on the onset and duration of the deprivation, corresponding to defined sensitive periods of a given species (Walk & Gibson, 1961). Even short periods of early visual deprivation can result in impairments in visuomotor skills, such as visually guided placement of the forepaw in cats (Crabtree & Riesen, 1979). The structural effects of dark rearing include smaller neuronal dendritic fields, reduced spine density, and reduced numbers of synapses per neuron within the visual cortex (Coleman & Riesen, 1968; Cragg, 1975; Valverde, 1971). In kittens, for example, developmental binocular deprivation results in a 40% reduction in the number of adult visual cortex synapses (Cragg, 1975).

Selective Deprivation

Selective deprivation experiments have indicated the importance of specific types of visual experience to normal brain development. For example, kittens reared in a strobe-illuminated environment have plentiful visual patterns but are selectively deprived of any experience of movement (i.e., movement in the visual field would appear jerky or disconnected). Specific impairments in motion perception have been found in such kittens (Marchand, Cremieux, & Amblard, 1990). These animals had visual cortical neurons that were insensitive to visual motion (Cynader & Cmerneko, 1976), and they were impaired on visuomotor behavioral tasks that utilize motion (Hein, Held, & Gower, 1970).

Other work has limited visual experience to specific visual patterns, or contours. Hirsch and Spinelli (1970) raised kittens in chambers with one eye exposed to just horizontal stripes and the other eye to just vertical stripes. Physiological recordings of visual cortical neurons of these kittens revealed that they were most responsive to stimuli oriented in the direction of the stripes that they had experienced. Behaviorally,

stripe-reared animals perform best on tests using stimuli in the orientation to which they were exposed during development (Corrigan & Carpenter, 1979; Pettigrew & Freeman, 1973). Unlike dark rearing or bilateral lid closure, stripe rearing does not appear to result in an overall diminishment of neuronal size, but it does alter the orientation of the neuronal dendritic arbors (Coleman, Flood, Whitehead, & Emerson, 1981; Tieman & Hirsch, 1982). Thus, neural function appears to be determined by the pattern, in addition to the overall number, of neural connections.

Monocular Deprivation

A great deal has been learned about experience-expectant processes from one particular deprivation model. In species with stereoscopic vision, including cats and monkeys, binocular regions of the cortex receive information from each eye via projections from the lateral geniculate nucleus in adjacent stripes or columns within cortical layer IV, termed ocular dominance columns. With normal experience early in development, the cortical input associated with each eye initially projects in overlapping terminal fields within layer IV. During development in normal animals, these axonal terminal fields are selectively pruned, resulting in sharply defined borders between ocular dominance columns in adult animals. The neurons of this layer send convergent input to other layers, made up in large majority of binocularly driven neurons (LeVay, Wiesel, & Hubel, 1980).

Early studies of monocular deprivation in stereoscopic animals appeared to show that the formation of the ocular dominance columns is dependent on the visual input from each eye during the critical period, becoming one of the most often cited examples in textbooks of experience shaping brain structure. In monocularly deprived monkeys, the axons projecting from the deprived eye regress, whereas the axons from the experienced eye do not. As a result, the columns corresponding to the deprived eye thin, whereas the columns of the nondeprived eye are enlarged relative to normal animals (Antonini & Stryker, 1993; LeVay et al., 1980). Thus, the axonal terminals from the dominant eye appear to be maintained selectively at the expense of the inactive input of the deprived eye, which has its excessive synapses eliminated. Physiologically, the number and responsiveness of cells activated by the deprived eye are severely decreased (Wiesel & Hubel, 1965). Functionally, monocular deprivation for an extended period during development results in near blindness to visual input in the deprived eye. In contrast, binocular deprivation principally results in a loss of visual acuity. Physiologically, it reduces but does not abolish the response of neurons to visual stimuli (Wiesel & Hubel, 1965).

It also does not prevent the formation of ocular dominance columns, although the segregation of columns is well below normal (LeVay et al., 1980; Mower, Caplan, Christen, & Duffy, 1985; Swindale, 1988). However, it now appears that in many respects the ocular dominance columns are established well before any visual experience and independently of competitive neural activity (Crowley & Katz, 2002). The effects of early experience and the critical period remain quite robust, so a revisionist interpretation is that the columns are established by genetically driven mechanisms and provide scaffolding for the effects of later experience.

The physiological and anatomical effects of monocular deprivation occur fairly rapidly. Antonini and Stryker (1993) found that the shrinkage of geniculocortical arbors corresponding to the deprived eye was profound in cats with only 6 to 7 days of monocular deprivation, similar to that found after 33 days of deprivation. Like binocular deprivation, the recovery from the deprivation is sensitive to the time of onset and the duration of the deprivation. Monocular deprivation corresponding to the sensitive period of a given species results in enduring impairments and physiological nonresponsiveness (e.g., Wiesel & Hubel, 1965), whereas even very extensive deprivation in adult animals has little effect (Blakemore, Garey, & Vital-Durand, 1978). In humans, early monocular deprivation resulting from congenital cataracts can have severe effects on acuity, even after treatment, whereas adults who develop cataracts in one eye show little posttreatment impairment (Bowering, Maurer, Lewis, & Brent, 1993). The sensitive period for monocular deprivation effects can be affected by prior experience. For example, the maximum sensitivity to monocular deprivation effects in kittens is normally during the fourth and fifth weeks after birth (Hubel & Wiesel, 1970; Olson & Freeman, 1978). Cynader and Mitchell (1980) found that kittens dark-reared from birth to several months of age maintained a physiological sensitivity to monocular deprivation at ages that normal kittens are insensitive. Dark-reared animals do not, however, simply show normal visual development at this later age. With binocular deprivation early in life, the ocular dominance columns of layer IV do not segregate in a fully normal pattern and do not maintain a structural sensitivity to monocular deprivation effects (Mower et al., 1985).

Deprivation in Other Sensory Systems

Although much of the research has utilized the visual system, experience-expectant processes can be observed in other sensory systems. Within layer IV of the somatosensory cortex in rodents, each whisker is represented by a distinctly clustered group of neurons arranged in what have been called *barrels* (Woolsey & Van der Loos, 1970). The cell bodies of these neurons form the barrel walls with a cell-sparse region forming the barrel hollow. In adult animals the input from each whisker (via the thalamus) terminates predominantly within the barrel hollows. Positioned to receive this input, most of the dendrites of the neurons lining the barrel wall are also oriented into the barrel hollow. This distinctive pattern of barrel walls surrounding a hollow forms after birth, prior to which neurons in this region appear homogenous. Because there is simultaneous regression of dendrites inside the barrel walls and continued growth of dendrites in the barrel hollows, these overlapping processes mask the expected synapse overproduction and pruning back because the overall pattern is one of dendritic expansion (Greenough & Chang, 1988). If not for the location of information provided by the structure of the barrel, this dendritic regression would be entirely masked.

Many rodents use their vibrissae (highly developed whiskers) to navigate in the dark (along with heightened olfactory perception). One might expect, therefore, that the whisker barrel region, with its overlapping blooming and pruning of synapses, would be sensitive to experience. Indeed, Glazewski and Fox (1996) were able to demonstrate experience-expectant plasticity in the barrel field cortex of young rats by reducing the complement of vibrissae on one side of the muzzle to a single whisker for a period of 7, 20, or 60 days. The vibrissa dominance distribution was shifted significantly toward the spared vibrissa, which gained control of more neurons in barrel cortex while the deprived whiskers lost control. As the deprived whiskers grew back in, they progressively gained back some control of neurons from the spared whisker. Whisker deprivation had the strongest effects in weanling animals, and very little in adult rats.

Humans appear to have something like a critical period for attachment, in that if the expected nurturing behavior does not occur in a timely manner, then subsequent emotional development will be disrupted. Human and primate studies have revealed substantial effects of disrupted attachment on behavior and endocrine function, but little is known about any underlying neural plasticity. The phenomenon known as *imprinting* (e.g., by which newly hatched chicks learn to recognize mothers) involves both the formation of new synapses and elimination of preexisting synapses (Horn, 1986; Patel, Rose, & Stewart, 1988). Imprinting fits our definition of experience-expectant neural plasticity, but it is an example of social rather than perceptual development. It is important to note that various primate species are differentially sensitive to maternal deprivation and it would appear that humans are one of the relatively sensitive species. For example, rhesus monkeys raised in isolation show an enduring and heightened responses to stress; abnormal motor behaviors including stereotyped movements, sexual dysfunction, and eating disorders; and various extreme forms of social and emotional dysfunction (Sackett, 1972). The effects of total social isolation are more severe than the effects of partial isolation, which permits visual and auditory interactions with other animals but no direct contact. Martin, Spicer, Lewis, Gluck, and Cork (1991) found that socially deprived rhesus monkeys showed a marked reduction in the dopaminergic and peptidergic innervation within the caudate-putamen, substantia nigra, and globus pallidus. In addition to evidence of reduced neuronal growth and development, socially deprived monkeys show brain abnormalities more typical of neurological disorders. It is important to note, however, that many of these studies confound social deprivation with experiential deprivation, such that we still know relatively little about structural brain changes related to each social experience.

EXPERIENCE-DEPENDENT DEVELOPMENT

Experience-dependent development involves the brain's adaptation to information that is unique to an individual. This type of adaptation does not occur within strictly defined critical periods as the timing or nature of such experience cannot be reliably anticipated. Therefore, this type of neural plasticity is likely to be active throughout life. It is important to recognize, however, that such systems cannot be constantly "on" and recording information. They need to have some kind of regulatory process that helps filter important information from the extraneous material. Although this type of process does not have fixed windows of plasticity, there may be necessary sequential dependencies on prior development. For example, a child learns algebra before she masters calculus. Sometimes experience-dependent processes will depend on prior experience-expectant ones, as in language development with a universal sensitive period followed by more idiosyncratic expansion of grammar and vocabulary.

Manipulating Environmental Complexity

One important central mechanism for experience-dependent development is the formation of new neural connections, in contrast to the overproduction and pruning back of synapses often associated with experience-expectant processes. This idea was initially supported by experiments in which the overall complexity of an animal's environment is manipulated as well as from experiments using specific learning tasks. Modifying the complexity of an animal's environment can have profound effects on behavior and on brain structure both in late development (e.g., after weaning in rats) and in

adulthood. In experimental manipulations, animals are typically housed in one of three conditions: individual cages (IC), in which the animals are housed alone in standard laboratory cages; social cages (SC), in which animals are housed with another rat in the same type of cage; and complex or enriched environments (EC), in which animals are housed in large groups in cages filled with changing arrangements of toys and other objects. Raising animals in an enriched environment provides ample opportunity for exploration and permits animals to experience complex social interactions, including play behavior, as well as the manipulation and spatial components of complex multidimensional arrangements of objects.

Following a tradition established by the well-known Berkeley group (e.g., Bennett, Diamond, Krech, & Rosenzweig, 1964), the experimental groups are often referred to as enriched and impoverished. It is important to emphasize that these are more accurately described in terms of varying degrees of *deprivation,* relative to the typical environment of feral rats. Barring considerations of stress or nutrition, I would argue that EC rats experience something close to normal brain development and that EC brains would closely resemble those of rats raised in the wild. Although a great deal of useful information can be obtained from laboratory animals, it is important in this chapter to understand that standard animals are generally overfed, understimulated, and physically out of shape.

Animals raised in complex environments are superior on many different types of learning tasks (reviewed in Black & Greenough, 1986). Various studies have suggested that EC animals may use more and different types of cues to solve tasks and may possess enhanced information-processing rates and capacities (Greenough, Volkmar, & Juraska, 1973; Juraska, Henderson, & Muller, 1984; Thinus-Blanc, 1981). Their superiority in complex mazes may rely in part on a greater familiarity with complicated spatial arrangements obtained through their rearing environment. These abilities are generalized across a wide range of other learning tests, however, suggesting that the EC's abilities do not simply lie in specific types of information gathered from the rearing environment. Rather, the brain adaptation to complex environment rearing involves changing how information is processed (i.e., the EC rat appears to have learned to learn better).

Examinations of brain structures of animals reared in complex environments reveal a growth of neurons and synaptic connections in comparison to siblings raised in standard cages. This phenomenon has been most prominently studied in the visual cortex, which shows an overall increase in thickness, volume, and weight (e.g., Bennett et al., 1964); dendritic branching, complexity, and spine density (e.g., Greenough, Volkmar, & Juraska, 1973; Holloway, 1966); synapses per neuron (Turner & Greenough, 1983, 1985); and larger synaptic contacts (Sirevaag & Greenough, 1985) in rats reared in complex environments. The number of synapses in EC rats is elevated by approximately 20% to 25% within superficial layers of the visual cortex (Turner & Greenough, 1985). Comparable anatomical data have been reported in cats given complex experience (Beaulieu & Colonnier, 1987).

The effects of environmental complexity have many different dimensions. The EC effects on brain structure cannot be attributed to general metabolic, hormonal, or stress differences across the different rearing conditions (reviewed in Black, Sirevaag, Wallace, Savin, & Greenough, 1989). Thus, the structural brain changes may be specifically the result of altered neuronal activity and information storage. Young EC rats will add new capillaries to visual cortex, presumably in support of increased metabolic activity (Black, Sirevaag, & Greenough, 1987). Rats reared in a complex environment tend to have slower growth of skeleton and internal organs (Black et al., 1989), as well as altered immune system responsivity (Kingston & Hoffman-Goetz, 1996). Evidence that male and female rats differ in their responses to the complex environment in both the visual cortex and the hippocampus suggest at least a modulatory role for sex hormones in the EC-IC brain effects, at least in early postnatal development (Juraska, 1984). Multiple brain regions can show evidence of structural change in EC animals, including the temporal cortex (Greenough et al., 1973), the striatum (Comery, Shah, & Greenough, 1995), the hippocampus (Juraska, 1984), the superior colliculus (Fuchs, Montemayor, & Greenough, 1990), and cerebellum (Floeter & Greenough, 1979; Pysh & Weiss, 1979). Mice reared in a complex environment will have more neurons in the dentate gyrus (Kempermann, Kuhn, & Gage, 1997). Significant changes in rat cortical thickness and dendritic branching can be detected after just four days of enrichment (Wallace, Kilman, Withers, & Greenough, 1992). These effects are not limited to young animals, as changes in neuronal dendrites and synapses in adult rats placed in the complex environment are substantial, although smaller than those found in rats reared from weaning in EC (e.g., Green, Greenough, & Schlumpf, 1983; Juraska, Greenough, Elliott, Mack, & Berkowitz, 1980).

Structural Effects of Learning

Although many activities occur in an EC environment, clearly one of the most important is learning. If learning in the EC environment results in structural brain changes, then similar changes would be expected in animals in response to a variety of training procedures. Such studies have indeed demonstrated that major brain changes occur during learning. These changes have been found in the specific brain regions apparently involved in the learning. For example, training in complex mazes requiring visuospatial memory has been found to result in increased dendritic arbors of the visual cortex in adult rats (Greenough, Juraska, & Volkmar, 1979). When split-brain procedures were performed and unilateral occluders placed in one eye, dendrites of neurons in the monocular cortex mediating vision in the unoccluded eye showed greater growth in comparison to the ipsilateral cortex (Chang & Greenough, 1982).

Training animals on motor learning tasks has also been found to result in site-specific neuronal changes. Rats extensively trained to use one forelimb to reach through a tube to receive cookies show dendritic growth within the region of the cortex involved in forelimb function (Greenough, Larson, & Withers, 1985) in comparison to controls. When rats were allowed to use only one forelimb for reaching, dendritic arborizations within the cortex opposite the trained forelimb were significantly increased relative to the cortex opposite the untrained forelimb. Furthermore, reach training selectively alters only certain subpopulations of neurons (e.g., layer II/III pyramidal neurons showing forked apical shafts; Withers & Greenough, 1989). Reach training may produce similar results in developing animals as well. Rat pups trained to reach with one forelimb over 9 days beginning at weaning show increased cortical thickness in the hemisphere opposite the trained limb in comparison to the nontrained limb (Díaz, Pinto-Hamuy, & Fernández, 1994).

A critical question is whether these training-induced brain changes are due to special processes of information storage or simply are an effect of increased activity within the affected brain systems. This question has been addressed in a motor learning paradigm in which rats are required to master several new complex motor coordination tasks ("acrobatic" rats). These animals showed increased numbers of synapses per Purkinje neuron within the cerebellum in comparison to inactive controls (Black, Isaacs, Anderson, Alcantara, & Greenough, 1990). Animals exhibiting greater amounts of motor activity in running wheels or treadmills (Black et al., 1990), or yoked-control animals that made an equivalent amount of movement in a simple straight alley (Kleim et al., 1997), did not show significant alterations in synaptic connections in the cerebellum. Thus, learning, and not simply the repetitive use of synapses that may occur during dull physical exercise, led to synaptogenesis in the cerebellum.

It is interesting that the exercising animals did show some structural changes: The density of capillaries in the involved region of cerebellum was significantly increased, corresponding to what would be seen if new blood vessels developed to support increased metabolic demand (Black et al., 1990). This indicates that the brain can independently generate adaptive changes in different cellular components. When metabolic stamina is required, vasculature is added. When motor skills need to be learned or refined, new synapses modify neural organization.

NEURAL PLASTICITY IN HUMANS

Due to ethical and technical limitations, it has been quite difficult to demonstrate that the human brain has neural plasticity processes similar to those for other species just described. If one considers the massive amount of information that humans incorporate (e.g., consider language learning alone) and that this material can be retained for decades without rehearsal, that information seemingly must be stored as lasting structural neural changes. Although present evidence cannot directly describe any changes in synaptic strength or number, human neural plasticity can be described in terms of experience-expectant and experience-dependent processes.

One kind of human experience-expectant process that is sensitive to selective deprivation involves perceptual mismatch from both eyes—for example, when one eye is deviated outward (strabismus) during early development. Similar to the cat and monkey studies described earlier, if the two eyes are sending competing and conflicting signals to the visual cortex during the sensitive period, the brain effectively shuts down or becomes insensitive to the nondominant eye. In humans, the resulting perceptual disorder is termed amblyopia (or lazy eye), and it results in clear perceptual deficits if surgery does not correct this visual misalignment during the critical period. The strabismus-related perceptual deficit was the first and still best established example of human neural plasticity (Crawford, Harwerth, Smith, & von Noorden, 1993). Recent technology, such as positron-emission tomography (PET), has demonstrated that patients with uncorrected strabismus use different areas of cortex for visual processing than do normal controls (e.g., Demer, 1993). Pharmacological manipulations suggest that human visual cortex plasticity is similarly influenced by gamma-aminobutyric acid (GABA), N-methyl-D-aspartate (NMDA), and acetylcholine as demonstrated in animal studies (Boroojerdi, Battaglia, Muellbacher, & Cohen, 2001). Although the timing, regulation, and structural changes of this sensitive period need further study, the early evidence suggests a clear parallel to the studies described earlier of kittens with selective deprivation of vision.

Some preliminary evidence exists that humans can alter brain function with extensive training, corresponding to the experience-dependent processes already described. For example, using functional magnetic resonance imaging (fMRI) to measure regional blood flow in the brain, Karni et al. (1995) demonstrated increased cortical involvement after training subjects in a finger-tapping sequence. Elbert, Pantev, Weinbruch, Rockstroh, and Taub (1995) showed substantial expansion of cortical involvement associated with the amount of training to play the violin. Rehabilitation therapy after brain injury produced similar fMRI changes (Frackowiak, 1996). Motor training also causes changes in cerebellum function (Doyon et al., 2002) that correspond to the anatomical changes observed with acrobatic training of rats. Nobody can yet show directly that humans produce new synapses with this type of learning, but these fMRI changes are what we would expect if synaptogenesis were occurring in an experience-dependent process.

In one of the few studies showing a structural, as opposed to functional, change in response to experience, Maguire et al. (2000) studied London taxi drivers with MRI. The researchers found larger volumes of anterior hippocampi associated with longer training. This finding suggests that there are structural changes in humans in response to the storing of enormous amounts of geographic information learned during two years of training.

Not all experience-related changes in human brain function are positive adaptations. Just as rats can suffer hippocampal damage and memory impairment when exposed to chronic stress, there is emerging evidence that stress can affect humans as well. Initial studies of Vietnam veterans who had experienced combat stress revealed memory impairment in otherwise healthy, middle-aged men (Bremner et al., 1993). Just as in the rat studies, early trauma can have lasting effects on stress regulation. For example, Yehuda et al. (1995) demonstrated endocrine dysregulation persisting for decades following exposure to trauma, in this case with survivors of the Holocaust. Bremner et al. (1995) later confirmed that the memory deficits in Vietnam veterans were associated with atrophy of the hippocampus, reflecting possible neuron damage or cell death. The size of the superior temporal gyrus, a structure involved in language, is also negatively affected by early trauma in children with posttraumatic stress disorder (De Bellis et al., 2002). Patients, both young and old, often describe an indelibility of the trauma memory with lasting effects on affective regulation (sometimes manifested as posttraumatic stress disorder or personality disorders), suggesting that structural changes may typically underlie these symptoms.

CONCLUSION

In conclusion, experience is increasingly important in building a brain as we look up the phylogenetic ladder toward humans. Recent neuroscience research reveals a number of important, interconnected principles of brain development of relevance to psychologists. First, many aspects of brain structure are genetically predetermined and serve as the scaffolding for the encoding of experience during development. Thus, the metaphor of the blank slate is inaccurate. A better metaphor for development is that of formatting the hard drive (genetics) before information may be stored (experience).

Second, I would like to emphasize the dynamic systems perspective, such that early brain pathology or distorted experience may set a maladaptive course for development, but the organism will often make efforts to compensate for it. At one level, different parts of the brain may try to compensate, and beyond that the organism may seek out new experience in areas where it has strength. Plasticity is a central feature of mammalian brains, and one should not consider early brain damage or aberrant experience as determining the organism's fate forever. It is with this second principle of dynamic systems that the hard drive metaphor breaks down. Unlike brains, hard drives do not sculpt or mend themselves.

Third, in describing information storage mechanisms, I have tried to define the similarities and differences between maturation and learning. Maturation consists of experience-expectant processes. Experiences leading to maturation have survival value for the entire species and may be critical to survival. Learning involves experience-dependent processes that may be critical for idiosyncratic information that may in turn be critical to the individual's functioning. In addition, some aspects of experience (e.g., play in juvenile EC-IC rearing) may influence both experience-expectant and experience-dependent processes. In fact, these processes probably cannot be entirely isolated because they have substantial interactive consequences for how the brain processes information and because they share mechanisms at the cellular level.

Fourth, the evidence that different species have different susceptibilities to experience and that brain areas are differentially influenced by experience suggests that information storage mechanisms have not remained stable through evolution. As more complicated sensory, motor, and information-processing schemes evolved, experience was utilized in two ways: (a) to shape common features of the nervous system through experiences common to members of the species and (b) to provide for storage of information about the unique environment of the individual. The underlying mechanisms may have diverged to meet these separate needs, such that system-wide overproduction at a specific maturational stage, followed by selection, subserves storage of common information, whereas local activity-dependent synaptogenesis, again followed by selection, subserves later storage of unique information.

Fifth, I described experience-expectant processes in terms of the species-wide reliability of some types of experience. I suggested that species survival may be facilitated by information-storage processes anticipating an experience with identical timing and features for all juvenile members. A structural correlate of expectation may be a temporary overproduction of synapses during the sensitive period with a subsequent pruning back of inappropriate synapses. This experience-expectant blooming of new synapses is distributed more or less uniformly across the entire population of homologous cells. The neuromodulatory event that triggers this synapse overproduction may be under maturational control or may be activity dependent (as after eye opening), but it is diffuse and pervasive. The expected experience produces patterned activity of neurons, effectively targeting which synapses will be selected, as illustrated for monocular deprivation in binocular species.

Experience-dependent mechanisms, on the other hand, may utilize synapse generation and preservation in different balance for a quite different effect. Because these neural plasticity mechanisms cannot anticipate the timing or specific features of such idiosyncratic experience, the sensitive period is necessarily left wide open. Here synapses are generated locally, upon demand of some modulatory signal. The specific nature of modulation, which could be locally elicited by neural activity or by hormonal signals, remains an open question for future research. The organism's active participation is important in obtaining and stabilizing experience. For example, juvenile play or adult attention may serve both to extract new information (increase contrast) and to help repeat it or stabilize it (increase coherence). This experience-dependent localized shaping of connectivity suggests that very multimodal and diverse experience (as in EC) would produce widespread increases in synaptic frequency, but that relatively specific experience (as in training tasks) would produce more localized increases.

Sixth, animals raised in EC differ from ICs primarily in the complexity of experience available, so that self-initiation of experience (e.g., exploratory activity) is a key determinant of timing and quality of experience. This feature is consistent with the dynamic systems perspective of development (e.g., Thelen & Smith, 1995) in that the connectivity modifications observed in the EC animals appear more related to how neural activity is processed than how much is processed. For example, both EC and IC animals use approximately the same amount of light (average intensity on the retina) quite differently—one with self-initiated activity and its visual consequences, the other with dull routine. Some species (probably including humans) have altered behavior so as to increase the likelihood of obtaining enriched experience. For example, weanling rats are generally quite playful and active in comparison to adults, probably due to the same burst of playful activity we observe in kittens, puppies, and toddlers. The burst of playfulness may be developmentally programmed and generally useful to all members of a species (Haight & Black, 2001; Ikemoto & Panksepp, 1992; Smith, 1982).

Seventh, I argued earlier that brain development can be viewed as an elaborate scaffolding of gene-driven, experience-expectant, and experience-dependent processes. Although it is oversimplifying to use linear terms like scaffolding or schedule, it is important to see that many components are quite dependent on the completion of earlier steps. Thus, the later synaptic blooming and pruning of human frontal cortex compared to visual cortex may reflect a sequential dependency. Neural and cognitive development may require the strictly ordered sequence of the development of sensory modalities (e.g., touch before vision; Gottlieb, 1973; Turkewitz & Kenny, 1982). Multiple sensitive periods may (a) prevent competition between modalities and (b) help integrate information across modalities (e.g., touch coming before vision may help in the development of visuomotor skills). It is interesting to speculate on the specific roles of the protracted overproduction and loss of synapses observed by P. R. Huttenlocher (1994) in human prefrontal cortex. In visual cortex, properties such as stereoscopic depth perception and the orientation tuning of receptive fields develop through experience during the early part of postnatal life. If a particular aspect of experience is missing, then subsequent visual function is disturbed. It might be of value for students of cognitive development to consider, for prefrontal cortex, what constitutes the cognitive equivalent of exposure to expected visual experience.

Another developmental process with innate roots but nonetheless quite dependent on early experience is language acquisition. Although the question of whether language has an innate deep structure is still debated, it is clear that children rapidly acquire an enormous amount of vocabulary, grammar, and related information, and that there is a critical period for language acquisition. One of possibly hundreds of genes involved has been tentatively identified. The specialized cortical adaptation of Broca's area also exists in the great apes, suggesting that it has been present for some

5 million years and is now part of the scaffolding structure on which humans have hung language (Cantalupo & Hopkins, 2001). For middle-class American families, the rate of vocabulary acquisition is directly related to the amount of verbal stimulation the mother provides (e.g., J. Huttenlocher, Haight, Bryk, Seltzer, & Lyons, 1991). There is apparently a sensitive period for acquiring the ability to discriminate speech contrasts. For example, prior to 6 or so months of life, infants from English-speaking homes are able to discriminate speech contrasts from a variety of languages, including Thai, Czech, and Swedish, much the way native adult speakers are able to. However, sometime between 6 and 12 months, this ability is gradually lost, such that after this age infants become more like adults who are most proficient in discriminating the speech contrasts from their native language (Kuhl, 1993). Language is another area where play and child-directed experience are important parts of learning, as is reciprocity between parent and child. Preliminary findings suggestive of experience-dependent neural plasticity in language were from a quantitative neuroanatomy of Jacobs, Schall, and Scheibel (1993), who found a clear relationship between the amount of education up to the university level and the amount of dendritic branching of neurons in Broca's area. Thus, language provides a vertical example that includes influences from genetic and neuroanatomical domains, evidence suggestive of an experience-expectant process, the coconstruction of enriched experience, and the possibility of lifelong or experience-dependent information storage.

Finally, the scaffolding of information from one domain being used to support a new domain of development can be seen in an older but still elegant series of experiments (Hein & Diamond, 1971; Held & Hein, 1963), in which kittens rode in a gondola that allowed vision but restricted movement, wore large collars that allowed free movement but prevented visualization of their paws, or had surgery that prevented their eyes from tracking their paws in space. These kittens had normal overall amounts of visual and proprioceptive information, but the lack of perceptual integration in these modalities caused profound behavioral pathology. Note that all of the types of deprivation described here either interfere with contrast (less information; e.g., monocular deprivation, strobe rearing, or stripe rearing) or coherence (less consistency of input; e.g., strabismus, wearing prisms, or riding in gondolas).

An important direction for future research is the examination of behavioral changes that may lead to synaptic changes in several of the functions known to be subserved by the human prefrontal cortex. For example, it has long been known that the ability to use strategies to solve problems and to engage in hypothetico-deductive reasoning are abilities that are heavily dependent on regions of the prefrontal cortex. Generally, it is not until formal schooling begins that these problem-solving skills are fostered, encouraged, and eventually required. Given the long trajectory of synaptic pruning that goes on in this region of the brain (see P. R. Huttenlocher, 1994, for review), it would stand to reason that these experiences may cultivate the circuits that will lead eventually to more sophisticated forms of thought, such as the cluster of abilities referred to as executive functions and social behavior (Post, 1992).

REFERENCES

Antonini, A., & Stryker, M. P. (1993). Rapid remodeling of axonal arbors in the visual cortex. *Science, 260,* 1819–1821.

Beaulieu, C., & Colonnier, M. (1987). Effect of the richness of the environment on the cat visual cortex. *Journal of Comparative Neurology, 266,* 478–494.

Bennett, E. L., Diamond, M. C., Krech, D., & Rosenzweig, M. R. (1964). Chemical and anatomical plasticity of brain. *Science, 146,* 610–619.

Black, J. E., & Greenough, W. T. (1986). Induction of pattern in neural structure by experience: Implications for cognitive development. In M. E. Lamb, A. L. Brown, & B. Rogoff (Eds.), *Advances in developmental psychology* (Vol. 4, pp. 1–50). Hillsdale, NJ: Erlbaum.

Black, J. E., Isaacs, K. R., Anderson, B. J., Alcantara, A. A., & Greenough, W. T. (1990). Learning causes synaptogenesis, while motor activity causes angiogenesis, in cerebellar cortex of adult rats. *Proceedings of the National Academy of Sciences, 87,* 5568–5572.

Black, J. E., Sirevaag, A. M., & Greenough, W. T. (1987). Complex experience promotes capillary formation in young rat visual cortex. *Neuroscience Letters, 83,* 351–355.

Black, J. E., Sirevaag, A. M., Wallace, C. S., Savin, M. H., & Greenough, W. T. (1989). Effects of complex experience on somatic growth and organ development in rats. *Developmental Psychobiology, 22,* 727–752.

Blakemore, C., Garey, L. J., & Vital-Durand, F. (1978). The physiological effects of monocular deprivation and their reversal in the monkey's visual cortex. *Journal of Physiology (London), 283,* 223–262.

Boothe, R. G., Greenough, W. T., Lund, J. S., & Wrege, K. (1979). A quantitative investigation of spine and dendritic development of neurons in visual cortex (Area 17) of Macaca nemistrina monkeys. *Journal of Comparative Neurology, 186,* 473–490.

Boroojerdi, B., Battaglia, F., Muellbacher, W., & Cohen, L. G. (2001). Mechanisms underlying rapid experience-dependent plasticity in the human visual cortex. *Proceedings of the National Academy of Sciences, 98,* 14698–14701.

Bourgeois, J. P., Goldman-Rakic, P. S., & Rakic, P. (1994). Synaptogenesis in the prefrontal cortex of rhesus monkeys. *Cerebral Cortex, 4,* 78–96.

Bowering, E. R., Maurer, D., Lewis, T. L., & Brent, H. P. (1993). Sensitivity in the nasal and temporal hemifields in children treated for cataract. *Investigatory Ophthalmology and Vision Science, 34,* 3501–3509.

Bremner, J. D., Scott, T. M., Delaney, R. C., Southwick, S. M., Mason, J. W., Johnson, D. R., Innis, R. B., McCarthy, G., & Charney, D. S. (1993). Deficits in short-term memory in post-traumatic stress disorder. *American Journal of Psychiatry, 150,* 1015–1019.

Bremner, J. D., Innis, R. B., Ng, C. K., Staib, L. H., Salomon, R. M., Bronen, R. A., Duncan, J., Southwick, S. M., Krystal, J. H., Rich, D., Zubal, G., Dey, H., Soufer, R., & Charney, D. S. (1993). MRI-based measurement of hippocampal volume in Patients with combat-related posttraumatic stress disorder. *American Journal of Psychiatry, 152,* 973–981.

Cantalupo, C., & Hopkins, W. D. (2001). Broca's area in great apes. *Nature, 414,* 546–550.

Chang, F.-L. F., & Greenough, W. T. (1982). Lateralized effects of monocular training on dendritic branching in adult split-brain rats. *Brain Research, 232,* 283–292.

Coleman, P. D., Flood, D. G., Whitehead, M. C., & Emerson, R. C. (1981). Spatial sampling by dendritic trees in visual cortex. *Brain Research, 214,* 1–21.

Coleman, P. D., & Riesen, A. H. (1968). Environmental effects on cortical dendritic fields: I. Rearing in the dark. *Journal of Anatomy, 102,* 363–374.

Comery, T. A., Shah, R., & Greenough, W. T. (1995). Differential rearing alters spine density on medium-sized spiny neurons in the rat corpus striatum: Evidence for association of morphological plasticity with early response gene expression. *Neurobiology Learning Memory, 63,* 217–219.

Conel, J. L. (1939–1967). *The postnatal development of the human cerebral cortex* (Vols. 1–8). Cambridge, MA: Harvard University Press.

Corrigan, J. G., & Carpenter, D. L. (1979). Early selective visual experience and pattern discrimination in hooded rats. *Developmental Psychobiology, 12,* 67–72.

Crabtree, J. W., & Riesen, A. H. (1979). Effects of the duration of dark rearing on visually guided behavior in the kitten. *Developmental Psychobiology, 12,* 291–303.

Cragg, B. G. (1975). The development of synapses in the visual system of the cat. *Journal of Comparative Neurology, 160,* 147–166.

Crawford, M. L., Harwerth, R. S., Smith, E. L., & von Noorden, G. K. (1993). Keeping an eye on the brain: The role of visual experience in monkeys and children. *Journal of General Psychology, 120,* 7–19.

Crowley, J. C., & Katz, L. C. (2002). Ocular dominance development revisited. *Current Opinion in Neurobiology, 12,* 104–109.

Cynader, M., & Cmerneko, G. (1976). Abolition of direction selectivity in the visual cortex of the cat. *Science, 193,* 504–505.

Cynader, M., & Mitchell, D. E. (1980). Prolonged sensitivity to monocular deprivation in dark-reared cats. *Journal of Neurophysiology, 43,* 1026–1040.

De Bellis, M. D., Keshavan, M. S., Frustaci, K., Shifflett, H., Iyengar, S., Beers, S. R., & Hall, J. (2002). Superior temporal gyrus volumes in maltreated children and adolescents with PTSD. *Biological Psychiatry, 51,* 544–552.

Demer, J. L. (1993). Positron-emission tomographic studies of cortical function in human amblyopia. *Neuroscience and Biobehavioral Review, 17,* 469–476.

Díaz, E., Pinto-Hamuy, T., & Fernández, V. (1994). Interhemispheric structural asymmetry induced by a lateralized reaching task in the rat motor cortex. *European Journal of Neuroscience, 6,* 1235–1238.

Doyon, J., Song, A. W., Karni, A., Lalonde, F., Adams, M. M., & Ungerleider, L. G. (2002). Experience-dependent changes in cerebellar contributions to motor sequence learning. *Proceedings of the National Academy of Sciences USA, 99,* 1017–1022.

Elbert, T., Pantev, C., Wienbruch, C., Rockstroh, B., & Taub, E. (1995). Increased cortical representation of the fingers of the left hand in string players. *Science, 270,* 305–307.

Fahrbach, S. E., Moore, D., Capaldi, E. A., Farris, S. M., & Robinson, G. E. (1998). Experience-expectant plasticity in the mushroom bodies of the honeybee. *Learning and Memory, 5,* 115–123.

Floeter, M. K., & Greenough, W. T. (1979). Cerebellar plasticity: Modification of Purkinje cell structure by differential rearing in monkeys. *Science, 206,* 227–229.

Frackowiak, R. S. J. (1996). Plasticity and the human brain: Insights from functional imaging. *Neuroscientist, 2,* 353–362.

Fuchs, J. L., Montemayor, M., & Greenough, W. T. (1990). Effect of environmental complexity on size of the superior colliculus. *Behavioral and Neural Biology, 54,* 198–203.

Glazewski, S., & Fox, K. (1996). Time course of experience-dependent synaptic potentiation and depression in barrel cortex of adolescent rats. *Journal of Neurophysiology, 75,* 1714–1729.

Gledd, J. N., Blumenthal, J., Jeffries, N. O., Casetellanos, F. X., Liu, H., Zijdenbos, A., Paus, T., Evans, A. C., & Rapaport, J. L. (1999). Brain development during childhood and adolescence: A longitudinal MRI study. *Nature Neuroscience, 2,* 861–863.

Gottlieb, G. (1973). Introduction to behavioral embryology. In G. Gottlieb (Ed.), *Studies on the development of behavior and the nervous system: Vol. 1. Behavioral embryology* (pp. 3–45). New York: Academic Press.

Green, E. J., Greenough, W. T., & Schlumpf, B. E. (1983). Effects of complex or isolated environments on cortical dendrites of middle-aged rats. *Brain Research, 264,* 233–240.

Greenough, W. T., & Chang, F.-L. F. (1988). Dendritic pattern formation involves both oriented regression and oriented growth in the barrels of mouse somatosensory cortex. *Brain Research, 471,* 148–152.

Greenough, W. T., Juraska, J. M., & Volkmar, F. R. (1979). Maze training effects on dendritic branching in occipital cortex of adult rats. *Behavioral and Neural Biology, 26,* 287–297.

Greenough, W. T., Larson, J. R., & Withers, G. S. (1985). Effects of unilateral and bilateral training in a reaching task on dendritic branching of neurons in the rat motor-sensory forelimb cortex. *Behavioral and Neural Biology, 44,* 301–314.

Greenough, W. T., & Volkmar, F. R. (1973). Pattern of dendritic branching in occipital cortex of rats reared in complex environments. *Experimental Neurology, 40,* 491–504.

Greenough, W. T., Volkmar, F. R., & Juraska, J. M. (1973). Effects of rearing complexity on dendritic branching in frontolateral and temporal cortex of the rat. *Experimental Neurology, 41,* 371–378.

Haight, W. L., & Black, J. E. (2001). A comparative approach to play: Cross-species and cross-cultural perspectives of play in development. *Human Development, 44,* 228–234.

Hein, A., & Diamond, R. (1971). Contributions of eye movements to the representation of space. In A. Hein & M. Jeannerod (Eds.), *Spatially oriented behavior* (pp. 119–134). New York: Springer.

Hein, A., Held, R., & Gower, E. C. (1970). Development and segmentation of visually controlled movement by selective exposure during rearing. *Journal of Comparative Physiological Psychology, 73,* 181–187.

Held, R., & Hein, A. (1963). Development and segmentation of visually controlled movement by selective exposure during rearing. *Journal of Comparative and Physiological Psychology, 73,* 181–187.

Hirsch, H. V. B., & Spinelli, D. N. (1970). Visual experience modifies distribution of horizontally and vertically oriented receptive fields in cats. *Science, 168,* 869–871.

Holloway, R. L. (1966). Dendritic branching: Some preliminary results of training and complexity in rat visual cortex. *Brain Research, 2,* 393–396.

Horn, G. (1986). Imprinting, learning, and memory. *Behavioral Neuroscience, 100,* 825–832.

Hubel, D. H., & Wiesel, T. N. (1970). The period of susceptibility to the physiological effects of unilateral eye closure in kittens. *Journal of Physiology (London), 206,* 419–436.

Huttenlocher, J., Haight, W., Bryk, A., Seltzer, M., & Lyons, T. (1991). Early vocabulary growth: Relation to language input and gender. *Developmental Psychology, 27,* 236–248.

Huttenlocher, P. R. (1979). Synaptic density in human frontal cortex: Developmental changes and effects of aging. *Brain Research, 163,* 195–205.

Huttenlocher, P. R. (1994). Synaptogenesis, synapse elimination, and neural plasticity in human cerebral cortex. In C. A. Nelson (Ed.), *Minnesota symposia on child psychology: Vol. 27. Threats to optimal development: Integrating biological, psychological, and social risk factors* (pp. 35–54). Hillsdale, NJ: Erlbaum.

Huttenlocher, P. R., & de Courten, C. (1987). The development of synapses in striate cortex of man. *Human Neurobiology, 6,* 1–9.

Ikemoto, S., & Panksepp, J. (1992). The effects of early social isolation on the motivation for social play in juvenile rats. *Developmental Psychobiology, 25,* 261–274.

Jacobs, B., Schall, M., & Scheibel, A. B. (1993). A quantitative dendritic analysis of Wernicke's area in humans: II. Gender, hemispheric, and environmental factors. *Journal of Comparative Neurology, 327,* 97–111.

Juraska, J. M. (1984). Sex differences in dendritic response to differential experience in the rat visual cortex. *Brain Research, 295,* 27–34.

Juraska, J. M., Greenough, W. T., Elliott, C., Mack, K. J., & Berkowitz, R. (1980). Plasticity in adult rat visual cortex: An examination of several cell populations after differential rearing. *Behavioral and Neural Biology, 29,* 157–167.

Juraska, J. M., Henderson, C., & Muller, J. (1984). Differential rearing experience, gender, and radial maze performance. *Developmental Psychobiology, 17,* 209–215.

Kandel, E. R. (2001). The molecular biology of memory storage: A dialogue between genes and synapses. *Science, 294,* 1030–1038.

Karni, A., Meyer, G., Jezzard, P., Adams, M. M., Turner, R., & Ungerleider, L. G. (1995). Functional MRI evidence for adult motor cortex plasticity during motor skill learning. *Nature, 377,* 155–158.

Kempermann, G., Kuhn, H. G., & Gage, F. H. (1997). More hippocampal neurons in adult mice living in an enriched environment. *Nature, 386,* 483–485.

Kingston, S. G., & Hoffman-Goetz, L. (1996). Effect of environmental enrichment and housing density on immune system reactivity to acute exercise stress. *Physiology and Behavior, 60,* 145–150.

Kleim, J. A., Swain, R. A., Czerlanis, C. M., Kelly, J. L., Pipitone, M. A., & Greenough, W. T. (1997). Learning-dependent dendritic hypertrophy of cerebellar stellate cells: Plasticity of local circuit neurons. *Neurobiology of Learning and Memory, 67,* 29–33.

Kolb, B., & Gibb, R. (1991). Environmental enrichment and cortical injury: Behavioral and anatomical consequences of frontal cortex lesions. *Cerebral Cortex, 1,* 189–198.

Kuhl, P. K. (1993). Innate predispositions and the effects of experience in speech perceptions, the native language magnet theory. In B. de Boysson-Bardies, S. de Schonen, P. Juscyzyk, P. McNeilage, & J. Morton (Eds.), *Developmental neurocognition: Speech and face processing in the first year of life* (pp. 132–151). Dordrecht, The Netherlands: Kluwer Academic.

LeVay, S., Wiesel, T. N., & Hubel, D. H. (1980). The development of ocular dominance columns in normal and visually deprived monkeys. *Journal of Comparative Neurology, 191,* 1–51.

Maguire, E. A., Gadian, D. G., Johnsrude, I. S., Good, C. D., Ashburn, J., Frackowiak, R. S. J., & Frith, C. D. (2000). Navigation-related structural changes in the hippocampi of taxi drivers. *Proceedings of the National Academy of Sciences, 97,* 4398–4403.

Marchand, A. R., Cremieux, J., & Amblard, B. (1990). Early sensory determinants of locomotor speed in adult cats: II. Effects of strobe rearing on vestibular functions. *Behavioral Brain Research, 37,* 227–235.

Martin, L. J., Spicer, D. M., Lewis, M. H., Gluck, J. P., & Cork, L. C. (1991). Social deprivation of infant rhesus monkeys alters the chemoarchitecture of the brain: I. Subcortical regions. *Journal of Neuroscience, 11,* 3344–3358.

Michalski, A., & Wrobel, A. (1994). Correlated activity of lateral geniculate neurones in binocularly deprived cats. *Acta Neurobiologica Experimenta, 54,* 3–10.

Mower, G. D., Caplan, C. J., Christen, W. G., & Duffy, F. H. (1985). Dark rearing prolongs physiological but not anatomical plasticity of the cat visual cortex. *Journal of Comparative Neurology, 235,* 448–466.

Olson, C. R., & Freeman, R. D. (1978). Monocular deprivation and recovery during sensitive period in kittens. *Journal of Neurophysiology, 41,* 65–74.

Patel, S. N., Rose, S. P., & Stewart, M. G. (1988). Training induced dendritic spine density changes are specifically related to memory formation processes in the chick, *Gallus domesticus. Brain Research, 463,* 168–173.

Pettigrew, J. D., & Freeman, R. D. (1973). Visual experience without lines: Effect on developing cortical neurons. *Science, 182,* 599–601.

Piaget, J. (1980). *Adaptation and intelligence: Organic selection and phenocopy* (S. S. Eames, Trans.). Chicago: University of Chicago Press.

Post, R. M. (1992). Transduction of psychosocial stress into the neurobiology of recurrent affective disorder. *American Journal of Psychiatry, 149,* 999–1010.

Pysh, J. J., & Weiss, M. (1979). Exercise during development induces an increase in Purkinje cell dendritic tree size. *Science, 206,* 230–232.

Quartz, S. R., & Sejnowski, T. J. (1997). The neural basis of cognitive development: A constructivist manifesto. *Behavioral and Brain Sciences, 20,* 537–556.

Riesen, A. H. (1965). Effects of visual deprivation on perceptual function and the neural substrate. In J. DeAjuriaguerra (Ed.), *Symposium bel air II: Desafferentation experimentale et clinique* (pp. 47–66). Geneva, Switzerland: George & Cie.

Sackett, G. P. (1972). Prospects for research on schizophrenia: III. Neurophysiology: Isolation-rearing in primates. *Neuroscience Research Program Bulletin, 10,* 388–392.

Sirevaag, A. M., & Greenough, W. T. (1985). Differential rearing effects on rat visual cortex synapses: II. Synaptic morphometry. *Developmental Brain Research, 19,* 215–226.

Smith, P. K. (1982). Does play matter? Functional and evolutionary aspects of animal and human play. *Behavioral and Brain Sciences, 5,* 139–184.

Swindale, N. V. (1988). Role of visual experience in promoting segregation of eye dominance patches in the visual cortex of the cat. *Journal of Comparative Neurology, 267,* 472–488.

Thelen, E., & Smith, A. (1995). *A dynamic systems approach to the development of cognition and action.* Cambridge, MA: MIT Press.

Thinus-Blanc, C. (1981). Volume discrimination learning in golden hamsters: Effects of the structure of complex rearing cages. *Developmental Psychobiology, 14,* 397–403.

Tieman, S. B., & Hirsch, H. V. B. (1982). Exposure to lines of only one orientation modifies dendritic morphology of cells in the visual cortex of the cat. *Journal of Comparative Neurology, 211,* 353–362.

Turkewitz, G., & Kenny, P. A. (1982). Limitations on input as a basis for neural organization and perceptual development: A preliminary theoretical statement. *Developmental Psychobiology, 15,* 357–368.

Turner, A. M., & Greenough, W. T. (1983). Synapses per neuron and synaptic dimensions in occipital cortex of rats reared in complex, social, or isolation housing. *Acta Stereologica, 2*(Suppl. 1), 239–244.

Turner, A. M., & Greenough, W. T. (1985). Differential rearing effects on rat visual cortex synapses: I. Synaptic and neuronal density and synapses per neuron. *Brain Research, 329,* 195–203.

Valverde, F. (1971). Rate and extent of recovery from dark rearing in the mouse. *Brain Research, 33,* 1–11.

Waddington, C. H. (1971). Concepts of development. In E. Tobach, L. R. Aronson, & E. Shaw (Eds.), *The biopsychology of development* (pp. 17–23). New York: Academic Press.

Walk, R. D., & Gibson, E. J. (1961). A comparative and analytical study of visual depth perception. *Psychological Monographs, 75* (No. 15).

Wallace, C. S., Kilman, V. L., Withers, G. S., & Greenough, W. T. (1992). Increases in dendritic length in occipital cortex after four days of differential housing in weanling rats. *Behavioral and Neural Biology, 58,* 64–68.

Wiesel, T. N., & Hubel, D. H. (1965). Comparison of the effects of unilateral and bilateral eye closure on cortical unit responses in kittens. *Journal of Neurophysiology, 28,* 1029–1040.

Withers, G. S., & Greenough, W. T. (1989). Reach training selectively alters dendritic branching in subpopulations of layer II–III pyramids in rat motor-somatosensory forelimb cortex. *Neuropsychologia, 27,* 61–69.

Woolsey, T., & van der Loos, H. (1970). The structural organization of Layer IV (SI) of the mouse cerebral cortex: The description of a cortical field composed of discrete cytoarchitectonic units. *Brain Research, 17,* 205–242.

Yehuda, R., Kahana, B., Binder-Byrnes, K., Southwick, S. M., Mason, J. W., & Giller, E. L. (1995). Low urinary cortisol excretion in Holocaust survivors with posttraumatic stress disorder. *American Journal of Psychiatry, 152,* 982–986.

Zablocka, T., & Zernicki, B. (1990). Partition between stimuli slows down greatly discrimination learning in binocularly deprived cats. *Behavioral Brain Research, 36,* 13–19.

Author Index

Subject Index

THIS BOOK
DISCARD
CIRCULATE